'43
89/
R62

FINANCIAL INSTITUTIONS MANAGEMENT

A Modern Perspective

THE IRWIN/MCGRAW-HILL SERIES IN FINANCE, INSURANCE AND REAL ESTATE

FINANCIAL MANAGEMENT

Benninga and Sarig
Corporate Finance: A Valuation Approach

Block and Hirt
Foundations of Financial Management
Ninth Edition

Brealey and Myers
Principles of Corporate Finance
Sixth Edition

Brealey, Myers and Marcus
Fundamentals of Corporate Finance
Second Edition

Brooks
FinGaine Online 3.0

Bruner
Case Studies in Finance: Managing for Corporate Value Creation
Third Edition

Chew
The New Corporate Finance: Where Theory Meets Practice
Second Edition

Graduate Management Admissions Council, Robert F. Bruner, Kenneth Eades and Robert Harris
Essentials of Finance: With an Accounting Review
Fully interactive CD-ROM derived from Finance Interactive 1997 Pre-MBA Edition Finance Interactive: Pre-MBA Series 2000
Second Edition

Grinblatt and Titman
Financial Markets and Corporate Strategy

Helfert
Techniques of Financial Analysis: A Guide to Value Creation
Tenth Edition

Higgins
Analysis for Financial Management
Fifth Edition

Hite
A Programmed Learning Guide to Finance

Kester, Fruhan, Piper and Ruback
Case Problems in Finance
Eleventh Edition

Nunnally and Plath
Cases in Finance
Second Edition

Ross, Westerfield and Jaffe
Corporate Finance
Fifth Edition

Ross, Westerfield and Jordan
Essentials of Corporate Finance
Second Edition

Ross, Westerfield and Jordan
Fundamentals of Corporate Finance
Fifth Edition

Smith
The Modern Theory of Corporate Finance
Second Edition

White
Financial Analysis with an Electronic Calculator
Fourth Edition

INVESTMENTS

Bodie, Kane and Marcus
Essentials of Investments
Third Edition

Bodie, Kane and Marcus
Investments
Fourth Edition

Cohen, Zinbarg and Zeikel
Investment Analysis and Portfolio Management
Fifth Edition

Corrado and Jordan
Fundamentals of Investments: Valuation and Management

Farrell
Portfolio Management: Theory and Applications
Second Edition

Hirt and Block
Fundamentals of Investment Management
Sixth Edition

Jarrow
Modelling Fixed Income Securities and Interest Rate Options

Morningstar, Inc. and Remaley
U.S. Equities OnFloppy Educational Version
Annual Edition

Shimko
The Innovative Investor
Excel Version

FINANCIAL INSTITUTIONS AND MARKETS

Cornett and Saunders
Fundamentals of Financial Institutions Management

Rose
Commercial Bank Management
Third Edition

Rose
Money and Capital Markets: Financial Institutions and Instruments in a Global Marketplace
Seventh Edition

Rose and Kolari
Financial Institutions: Understanding and Managing Financial Services
Fifth Edition

Santomero and Babbel
Financial Markets, Instruments, and Institutions

Saunders
Financial Institutions Management: A Modern Perspective
Third Edition

INTERNATIONAL FINANCE

Eun and Resnick
International Financial Management

Kester and Leuhriman
Case Problems in International Finance
Second Edition

Levi
International Finance
Third Edition

Levich
International Financial Markets: Prices and Policies

Stonehill and Eiteman
Finance: An International Perspective

REAL ESTATE

Brueggeman and Fisher
Real Estate Finance and Investments
Tenth Edition

Corgel, Smith and Ling
Real Estate Perspectives: An Introduction to Real Estate
Third Edition

Lusht
Real Estate Valuation: Principles and Applications

Sirmans
Real Estate Finance
Second Edition

FINANCIAL PLANNING AND INSURANCE

Allen, Melone, Rosenbloom and VanDerhei
Pension Planning: Pension, Profit-Sharing, and Other Deferred Compensation Plans
Eighth Edition

Crawford
Life and Health Insurance Law
Eighth Edition (LOMA)

Harrington and Niehaus
Risk Management and Insurance

Hirsch
Casualty Claim Practice
Sixth Edition

Kapoor, Dlabay and Hughes
Personal Finance
Fifth Edition

Skipper
International Risk and Insurance: An Environmental-Managerial Approach

Williams, Smith and Young
Risk Management and Insurance
Eighth Edition

THIRD EDITION

FINANCIAL INSTITUTIONS MANAGEMENT

A Modern Perspective

Anthony Saunders

John M. Schiff Professor of Finance
Salomon Center
Stern School of Business
New York University

Boston   Burr Ridge, IL   Dubuque, IA   Madison, WI
New York   San Francisco   St. Louis
Bangkok   Bogotá   Caracas   Lisbon   London   Madrid   Mexico City
Milan   New Delhi   Seoul   Singapore   Sydney   Taipei   Toronto

McGraw-Hill Higher Education

*A Division of The **McGraw-Hill** Companies*

FINANCIAL INSTITUTIONS MANAGEMENT: A MODERN PERSPECTIVE THIRD EDITION

This book is printed on acid-free paper.

domestic   1 2 3 4 5 6 7 8 9 0 QPD/QPD 9 0 9 8 7 6 5 4 3 2 1 0 9

international 1 2 3 4 5 6 7 8 9 0 QPD/QPD 9 0 9 8 7 6 5 4 3 2 1 0 9

ISBN 0-07-303259-X

Vice president/Editor in chief: *Michael W. Junior*
Publisher: *Craig S. Beytien*
Senior sponsoring editor: *Randall Adams*
Developmental editors: *Terry Eynon/Sarah Pearson*
Senior marketing manager: *Katie Rose Matthews*
Project manager: *Christina Thornton-Villagomez*
Production supervisor: *Michael R. McCormick*
Designer: *Jennifer McQueen Hollingsworth*
Cover illustration: *Paul Johnson*
Supplement coordinator: *Matthew Perry*
Compositor: *GAC Indianapolis*
Typeface: *10.5/12 Times Roman*
Printer: *R. R. Donnelley & Sons Inc.*

Library of Congress Cataloging-in-Publication Data

Saunders, Anthony.
    Financial institutions management : a modern perspective / Anthony
Saunders. — 3rd ed.
        p. cm.
    Includes bibliographical references and index.
    ISBN 0-07-303259-X
    1. Financial institutions—United States—Management.   2. Risk
management—United States.   3. Financial services industry—United
States—Management.   I. Title.
HG181.S33   1999
332.1′068—dc21   98-54993

INTERNATIONAL EDITION   ISBN 0-07-116985-7

http://www.mhhe.com

This book is dedicated to Pat, Nicholas, and Emily and to my parents, Meyer and Evelyn.

Anthony Saunders is the John M. Schiff Professor of Finance and Chair of the Department of Finance at the Stern School of Business at New York University. Professor Saunders received his PhD from the London School of Economics and has taught both undergraduate- and graduate-level courses at NYU since 1978. Throughout his academic career, his teaching and research have specialized in financial institutions and international banking. He has served as a visiting professor all over the world, including INSEAD, the Stockholm School of Economics, and the University of Melbourne. He is currently on the Executive Committee of the Salomon Center for the Study of Financial Institutions, NYU.

Professor Saunders holds positions on the Board of Academic Consultants of the Federal Reserve Board of Governors as well as the Council of Research Advisors for the Federal National Mortgage Association. In addition, Dr. Saunders has acted as a visiting scholar at the Comptroller of the Currency and at the Federal Reserve Bank of Philadelphia. He also held a visiting position in the research department of the International Monetary Fund. He is the editor of the *Journal of Banking and Finance* and the *Journal of Financial Markets, Instruments and Institutions,* as well as the associate editor of eight other journals, including *Financial Management* and the *Journal of Money, Credit and Banking.* His research has been published in all the major money and banking and finance journals and in several books. In addition, he has authored or coauthored several professional books, the most recent of which is *Credit Risk Measurement: New Approaches to Value at Risk and Other Paradigms,* John Wiley and Sons, New York, 1999.

PREFACE

The financial services industry continues to undergo dramatic changes. Not only are the boundaries between traditional industry sectors, such as commercial banking and investment banking, breaking down but competition is becoming increasingly global in nature. Indeed, the 1998 merger between Travelers and Citicorp to create the new Citigroup is just one example of the emergence of newly structured global financial intermediaries. Many forces are contributing to this breakdown in interindustry and intercountry barriers, including financial innovation, technology, taxation, and regulation. It is in this context that this book is written.

Although the traditional nature of each sector's product activity is analyzed, a greater emphasis is placed on *new* areas of activities such as asset securitization, off-balance-sheet banking, and international banking.

The third edition of this text takes the same innovative approach taken in the first two editions and focuses on managing return and risk in modern financial institutions (FIs). *Financial Institutions Management's* central theme is that the risks faced by FI managers and the methods and markets through which these risks are managed are becoming increasingly similar whether an institution is chartered as a commercial bank, a savings bank, an investment bank, or an insurance company.

As in any stockholder-owned corporation, the goal of FI managers should always be to maximize the value of the financial intermediary. However, pursuit of value maximization does not mean that risk management can be ignored.

Indeed, modern FIs are in the risk-management business. As we discuss in this book, in a world of perfect and frictionless capital markets, FIs would not exist and individuals would manage their own financial assets and portfolios. But since real-world financial markets are not perfect, FIs provide the positive function of bearing and managing risk on behalf of their customers through the pooling of risks and the sale of their services as risk specialists.

Intended Audience

Financial Institutions Management: A Modern Perspective is aimed at upper-level undergraduate and MBA audiences. Occasionally there are more technical sections that are marked with an asterisk (*). *Sections highlighted with an * may be included or dropped from the chapter reading, depending on the rigor of the course, without harming the continuity of the chapters.*

Main Features

Throughout the text, special features have been integrated to encourage students' interaction with the text and to aid them in absorbing the material. Some of these features include:

- **Chapter-opening outlines,** which offer students a snapshot view of what they can expect to learn from each chapter discussion.
- **Bold key terms and marginal glossary,** which emphasize the main terms and concepts throughout the chapter. They emphasize the most important terms and aid in studying.
- **Concept questions,** which allow students to test themselves on the main concepts within each major chapter section.
- **Professional Perspectives boxes,** which feature financial practitioners and how they apply some of the topics throughout the text.
- **Contemporary Perspectives boxes,** which demonstrate the application of chapter material in real current events.
- **Integrative problem material,** which covers all the main topics within the chapter.

Organization

Since our focus is on return and risk and the sources of that return and risk, this book relates ways in which the managers of modern FIs can expand return with a managed level of risk to achieve the best, or most favorable, return-risk outcome for FI owners.

Chapters 1 to 5 provide an overview describing the key balance sheet and regulatory features of the major sectors of the U.S. financial services industry. We discuss depository institutions in Chapter 1, insurance institutions in Chapter 2, securities firms and investment banks in Chapter 3, mutual funds in Chapter 4, and finance companies in Chapter 5. Chapter 6 takes an analytical look at how financial intermediation benefits today's economy.

In Chapter 7 we start the risk-measurement section with an overview of the risks facing a modern FI. In Chapters 8 and 9 we investigate the net interest margin as a source of profitability and risk, with a focus on the effects of interest rate volatility and the mismatching of asset and liability durations on FI risk exposure. In Chapter 10 we analyze market risk, a risk that results when FIs actively trade bonds, equities, and foreign currencies.

In Chapter 11 we look at the measurement of credit risk on individual loans and bonds and how this risk adversely impacts an FI's profits through losses and provisions against the loan and debt security portfolio. In Chapter 12 we look at the risk of loan (asset) portfolios and the effects of loan concentrations on risk exposure. Modern FIs do more than generate returns and bear risk through traditional maturity mismatching and credit extensions. They also are increasingly engaging in off-balance-sheet activities to generate fee income (Chapter 13), making technological investments to reduce costs (Chapter 14), pursuing foreign exchange activities and overseas financial investments (Chapter 15), and engaging in sovereign lending and securities activities (Chapter 16). Each of these has implications for the size and variability of an FI's profit and/or revenues. In addition, as a by-product of the provision of their interest rate and credit intermediation services, FIs face liquidity risk. We analyze the special nature of this risk in Chapter 17.

In Chapter 18 we begin the risk-management section by looking at ways in which FIs can insulate themselves from liquidity risk. In Chapter 19 we look at the key role deposit insurance and other guaranty schemes play in reducing liquidity risk. At the core of FI risk insulation is the size and adequacy of the owners' capital stake, which is the focus of Chapter 20. Chapters 21 to 23 analyze how and why product diversification and geographic diversification—both domestic and international—can improve an FI's return-risk performance and the impact of regulation on the diversification opportunity set. Chapters 24 through 28 review various new markets and instruments that have been innovated or engineered to allow FIs to better manage three important types of risk: interest rate risk, credit risk, and foreign exchange risk. These markets and instruments and their strategic use by FIs include futures and forwards (Chapter 24); options, caps, floors, and collars (Chapter 25); swaps (Chapter 26); loan sales (Chapter 27); and securitization (Chapter 28).

Changes in This Edition

Each chapter in this edition has been revised thoroughly to reflect the most up-to-date information available. End of chapter questions and problem material have also been revised to provide a more complete selection of testing material.

The following are some of the highlights of this revision.

In Part I, Introduction, we have increased our coverage of nonbank financial institutions to reflect the changing landscape of the financial institutions industry. In keeping with this, three new chapters have been added that focus, respectively, on the securities firm and investment banking industry (Chapter 3), the mutual fund industry (Chapter 4), and finance companies (Chapter 5). In addition, a new appendix to Chapter 1 describes the DuPont analysis or decomposition of an FI's return on equity (ROE).

In Part II, Measuring Risk, a wealth of new information has been added. The market risk chapter (Chapter 10) goes into more details about alternative approaches to measuring market risk, including RiskMetrics, historic (back) simulation, and Monte Carlo simulation.

Chapter 11, Credit Risk: Individual Loan Risk, discusses the revolution in new approaches to measuring credit risk. Importantly, two appendixes have been added. The first is on J. P. Morgan's CreditMetrics; the second is on Credit Suisse Financial Products' (CSFP) new approach called Credit Risk$^+$.

In Chapter 16, Sovereign Risk, the importance of assessing the sovereign risk of a borrowing country is underscored by the recent examples provided by the crisis in Asia and Russia and the effects of this crisis on FIs as diverse as banks, investment banks, and hedge funds—such as Long-Term Capital Management. Clearly, these events are likely to have serious repercussions for fund flows from U.S. to emerging-market countries for a long time.

In Part III, the focus moves from the measurement of risk to the management of risk. In this edition, some chapters have been rearranged to permit a better flow of information and to emphasize the increasing internationalization of U.S. FIs.

Chapter 21, Product Diversification, looks in detail at the recent Travelers–Citicorp merger and the implications this merger has for the growth of universal banking in the United States. The chapter on geographic diversification has been expanded and split to reflect the increased move toward nationwide branching in the United States, the importance of foreign banks in the United States, and the growth of U.S. FI presence overseas—especially in emerging markets. Chapter 22 focuses on domestic diversification, while Chapter 23 focuses on international diversification.

Chapters 24 ("Futures and Forwards"), 25 ("Options, Caps, Flows, and Collars"), and 26 ("Swaps") have been expanded to cover the dramatic growth in credit derivatives. In particular, new instruments such as credit options, credit forwards, and credit swaps are covered and the role they play in hedging credit risk is described.

Ancillaries

To assist in course preparation, the following ancillaries are offered:

- Through a unique arrangement with Dow Jones, the price of the special *WSJ* version of the text includes a 10-week subscription to this business periodical. Please contact your Irwin/McGraw-Hill representative for ordering information.
- The Instructor's Manual/Test Bank, prepared by Ernie Swift, Georgia State University, includes detailed chapter contents, additional examples for use in the classroom, PowerPoint teaching notes, complete solutions to end of chapter questions and problem material, and additional problems for test material.
- The PowerPoint Presentation System was created by Kenneth Stanton of Southern Illinois University. It contains useful and graphically enhanced outlines, summaries, and exhibits from the text. The slides can be edited, printed, or arranged to fit the needs of your course.
- Computest, our computerized version of the test bank, allows the instructor to pick and choose the order and number of questions to include for each test.

Acknowledgments

Finally, I would like to thank innumerable colleagues who assisted with the first, second, and third editions of this book. Of great help were the book reviewers whose painstaking comments and advice guided the third edition through its first and second revisions.

Michael H. Anderson
Suffolk University
M. E. Bond
University of Memphis
Yen Mow Chen
San Francisco State University
Jeffrey A. Clark
Florida State University
S. Steven Cole
University of North Texas
Paul Ellinger
University of Illinois
James H. Gilkeson
University of Central Florida
John H. Hand
Auburn University
Kevin Jacques
Georgetown University and Office of the Comptroller of the Currency

Julapa Jagtiani
Federal Reserve Bank of Chicago
Nelson J. Lacey
University of Massachusetts at Amherst
Robert Lamy
Wake Forest University
Rick LeCompte
Wichita State University
Patricia C. Matthews
Mount Union College
Robert McLeod
University of Alabama
Tara Rice
Boston College
Richard Stolz
California State University—Fullerton
Sonya Williams-Stanton
University of Michigan Ann Arbor

I very much appreciate the contributions of Terry Eynon, Randall Adams, and Sarah Pearson at Irwin/McGraw-Hill and my secretaries and assistants Robyn Vanterpoul, Ingrid Persaud, and Anand Srinivasan.

Anthony Saunders

BRIEF CONTENTS

CONTENTS

LIST OF CONTEMPORARY PERSPECTIVES BOXES

LIST OF PROFESSIONAL PERSPECTIVES BOXES

Efficiency in Banking, Allen N. Berger, *Board of Governors of the Federal Reserve System and Wharton Financial Institutions Center*

Scale and Scope Economies, Loretta J. Mester, *Federal Reserve Bank of Philadelphia*

Small Bank Purchases Big Loans, Lawrence G. Goldberg, *University of Miami,* and Jean LeGrand, *Gulfstream Associates*

The Mortgage Prepayment Option, Prafulla G. Nabar, *Lehman Brothers*

FINANCIAL INSTITUTIONS MANAGEMENT

A Modern Perspective

CHAPTER

1

THE FINANCIAL SERVICES INDUSTRY
Depository Institutions

Introduction

The theme of this book is that the products sold and the risks faced by modern financial institutions (FIs) are becoming increasingly similar, as are the techniques used to measure and manage those risks. To illustrate this, Tables 1–1A and 1–1B contrast the products sold by the financial services industry in 1950 with those sold in 1999. In this chapter we begin by describing three major FI groups—commercial banks, savings institutions, and credit unions—which are also called depository institutions because a significant proportion of their funds comes from customer deposits. In Chapters 2 through 5 other (nondepository) FIs will be described. We focus on three major characteristics of each group: (1) size, structure, and composition of the industry group, (2) balance sheets and recent trends, and (3) regulation.

Table 1–2 lists the largest commercial banks and savings banks in 1998. The ranking is by asset size and reflects the dramatic trend towards consolidation and

TABLE 1–1A   Products Sold by the U.S. Financial Services Industry, 1950

Institution	Payment Services	Savings Products	Fiduciary Services	Lending Business	Lending Consumer	Underwriting Issuance of Equity	Underwriting Issuance of Debt	Insurance and Risk Management Products
Depository institutions	X	X	X	X	X			
Insurance companies		X		*				X
Finance companies				*	X			
Securities firms		X	X			X	X	
Pension funds		X						
Mutual funds		X						

*Minor involvement.

TABLE 1–1B   Products Sold by the U.S. Financial Services Industry, 1999

Institution	Payment Services	Savings Products	Fiduciary Services	Lending Business	Lending Consumer	Underwriting Issuance of Equity	Underwriting Issuance of Debt	Insurance and Risk Management Products
Depository institutions	X	X	X	X	X	†	†	X
Insurance companies	X	X	X	X	X	†	†	X
Finance companies	X	X	X	X	X	†	†	X
Securities firms	X	X	X	X	X	X	X	X
Pension funds		X	X	X				X
Mutual funds	X	X	X					X

†Selective involvement via affiliates.

TABLE 1–2   The Largest Depository Institutions, 1998

Banks and savings institutions ranked by total assets on December 31, 1997, in billions of dollars.

Company	Assets
Citigroup*	$697
BankAmerica*	571
Chase Manhattan	366
J.P. Morgan	262
Banc One*	240
First Union*	206
Norwest-Wells Fargo*†	191
Washington Mutual*	144
Bankers Trust New York‡	140
Fleet Financial	86

*Merger pending
†Through March 1998
‡Since merged with Deutsche Bank
Source: Keefe, Bruyette & Woods and *New York Times,* June 9 1998, p. 102.

FIGURE 1–1

*Breakdown of Loan
Portfolios*

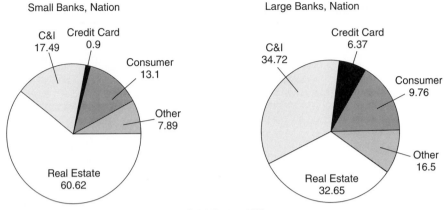

Source: Banking Brief, Federal Reserve Bank of Philadelphia, June 1998.
Note: Small banks are defined as banks with assets less than $1 billion. Large banks are defined as banks with assets of $1 billion or more.

mergers among financial service firms at the end of the 1990s. The largest bank is Citigroup, created from the merger of Citicorp and Travelers Insurance, and the second largest, BankAmerica, was created by the merger of the old BankAmerica and Nationsbank. It might be noted that Washington Mutual is the largest savings bank in the country—reflecting some 22 mergers and acquisitions by the Seattle-based bank since 1990, including HF Ahmanson, then the nation's second largest savings bank.

Commercial Banks

Commercial Bank
A bank that accepts deposits and makes consumer, commercial, and real estate loans.

Commercial banks comprise the largest group of depository institutions in size. They perform functions similar to those of savings institutions and credit unions; that is, they accept deposits (liabilities) and make loans (assets). However, they differ in their composition of assets and liabilities, which are much more varied. Commercial bank liabilities usually include several types of nondeposit sources of funds, while their loans are broader in range, including consumer, commercial, and real estate loans. Commercial banking activity is also regulated separately from the activities of savings institutions and credit unions. Within the banking industry the structure and composition of assets and liabilities also vary significantly across banks of different asset sizes. For example, as shown in Figure 1–1, small banks make proportionately fewer commercial loans (C and I loans) than do big banks.

Size, Structure, and Composition of the Industry

In 1997 the United States had 9,308 commercial banks. Even though this may seem a large number, in fact the number of banks has been shrinking. For example, in 1985 there were 14,416 banks, and in 1989 there were 12,744. In subsequent chapters we explore reasons for the drop in numbers [e.g., technology changes (Chapter 14), regulatory changes (Chapters 21 and 22), and competition[1] (Chapter 22)].

---

[1]In particular, Chapter 22 provides a detailed discussion of the merger wave that swept the commercial banking industry in the 1990s.

TABLE 1–3   Summary Statistics for U.S. Commercial Banks, 1997

Year	$0–$100 million	$100 million– $1 billion	$1 billion– $10 billion	$10 billion+
Number of banks	6,047	2,888	306	67
Percent of U.S. banks	65.0%	31.0%	3.4%	0.6%
Total assets ($ billions)	$273.4	$711	$916	$2,870.8
Percent of U.S. total assets	5.7%	14.9%	19.2%	60.2%

Source: Federal Deposit Insurance Corporation.

Community Bank
A bank that specializes in retail or consumer banking.

Regional or Superregional Bank
A bank that engages in a complete array of wholesale commercial banking activities.

Federal Funds Market
An interbank market for short-term borrowing and lending of bank reserves.

Money Center Bank
A bank that has a heavy reliance on nondeposit or borrowed sources of funds.

Note the size distribution of the commercial banking industry, as shown in Table 1–3. As can be seen, there are many small banks. In fact, 8,935 banks, or 96 percent, accounted for approximately 20.6 percent of the assets of the industry in 1997. These smaller or **community banks**—under $1 billion in asset size—tend to specialize in retail or consumer banking, such as providing residential mortgages and consumer loans and accessing the local deposit base. The majority of banks in the largest two size classes ($1 billion and above) are often either **regional or super-regional banks.** They engage in a more complete array of wholesale commercial banking activities, encompassing consumer and residential lending as well as commercial and industrial lending (so-called C and I loans), both regionally and nationally. In addition, the big banks access markets for purchased funds—such as the interbank or **federal funds market**—to finance their lending and investment activities. However, some of the very biggest banks often have the separate title **money center banks.** For example, in 1998 Salomon Brothers equity research department identified seven banking organizations as comprising their money center bank group: Bank of New York, Bankers Trust, Chase Manhattan, Citigroup, J.P. Morgan, Republic NY Corporation, and Banc One.[2,3] This number has been declining because of megamergers.

It is important to note that asset or lending size does not necessarily make a bank a money center bank. Thus, the new BankAmerica Corporation, with $571 billion in assets in 1998 (the second largest U.S. bank organization, created out of its merger with Nationsbank), is not a money center bank, while Republic NY Corporation (with only $58 billion in assets) is. What makes a bank a money center bank is partly location and partly its heavy reliance on nondeposit or borrowed sources of funds.[4] In fact, because of its extensive retail branch network,[5] Bank of America—the main subsidiary bank of the new BankAmerica Corporation—tends to be a net supplier of funds on the interbank market (federal funds market). By contrast, money center banks such as J.P. Morgan and Bankers Trust have no retail branches and rely almost entirely on wholesale and borrowed funds as sources of assets or liabilities. Money center banks are also major participants in foreign currency markets and are therefore subject to foreign exchange risk (see Chapter 15).

---

[2]Banc One's inclusion results from its acquisition of First Chicago in 1998.

[3]These banking organizations are mostly holding companies that own and control the shares of a bank or banks.

[4]A money center bank normally is headquartered in New York or Chicago. These are the traditional national and regional centers for correspondent banking services offered to smaller community banks.

[5]In 1998 Bank of America had over 1,000 branches.

TABLE 1–4   **ROA and ROE of Different Size Banks, 1990–1997**

Percentage Return on Assets (insured commercial banks by consolidated assets)

Year	All Banks	$0–$100 million	$100 million–$1 billion	$1 billion–$10 billion	$10 billion+
1990	0.49%	0.79%	0.78%	0.76%	0.38%
1991	0.54	0.83	0.83	0.54	0.44
1992	0.95	1.08	1.05	0.95	0.92
1993	1.22	1.16	1.19	1.33	1.24
1994	1.17	1.16	1.22	1.19	1.17
1995	1.17	1.18	1.25	1.28	1.10
1996	1.19	1.23	1.29	1.31	1.10
1997	1.24	1.25	1.39	1.30	1.18

Percentage Return on Equity (insured commercial banks by consolidated assets)

Year	All Banks	$0–$100 million	$100 million–$1 billion	$1 billion–$10 billion	$10 billion+
1990	7.64%	9.02%	9.95%	10.25%	6.68%
1991	8.05	9.40	10.51	7.50	7.35
1992	13.24	11.93	12.60	12.52	13.86
1993	15.67	12.29	13.61	14.02	16.81
1994	14.90	12.01	13.49	14.19	15.73
1995	14.68	11.37	13.48	15.04	15.60
1996	14.40	11.69	13.63	14.82	14.93
1997	14.71	11.57	14.50	14.30	15.32

Source: Federal Deposit Insurance Corporation.

Spread
The difference between lending and deposit rates.

The bigger banks tend to fund themselves in national markets and lend to larger corporations. This means that the **spreads** (i.e., the difference between lending and deposit rates) in the past often were narrower than those of smaller regional banks, which were more sheltered from competition in highly localized markets. However, as the barriers to interstate competition and expansion in banking have fallen in recent years, the largest banks' return on equity (ROE) generally has outperformed that of the smallest banks, especially those with assets under $100 million (see Table 1–4).[6] Appendix 1A, shows how a bank's ROE can be decomposed to examine the different underlying sources of profitability. This decomposition of ROE is often referred to as "DuPont" analysis.

Balance Sheet and Recent Trends

Assets.   Figure 1–2 shows the broad trends over the 1951–97 period in the four principal earning asset areas of commercial banks: business loans (or commercial and industrial loans), securities, mortgages, and consumer loans. Although business loans were the major asset in bank balance sheets between 1965 and 1990, there has been a sudden drop in their importance (as a proportion of the balance sheet) since 1990. This drop has been mirrored by an offsetting rise in holdings of securities and

---

[6]Arguably, the improved performance of larger banks also reflects improvements in the macroeconomy since the end of the 1989–92 recession. That is, the improvement in big banks' profitability may be temporary rather than permanent.

FIGURE 1–2

*Portfolio Shift: U.S.
Commercial Banks'
Financial Assets*

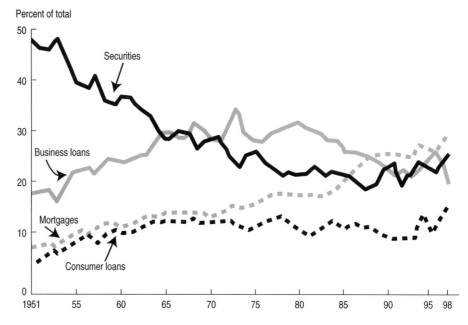

Source: Federal Reserve Bank of San Francisco and *Federal Reserve Bulletin.*

mortgages. These trends reflect a number of long-term and temporary influences. One important long-term influence has been the growth of the commercial paper market, which has become an alternative funding source for major corporations. Another has been the securitization of mortgages—the pooling and packaging of mortgage loans for sale in the form of bonds. A more temporary influence was the so-called credit crunch and decline in the demand for business loans as a result of the economic downturn and recession of the 1989–92 period.

Look at the detailed balance sheet for all U.S. commercial banks as of August 27, 1997 (Table 1–5). Total loans amount to $3,083.4 billion and fall into four broad classes: business or commercial and industrial ($830.4 billion); commercial and residential real estate ($1,197 billion); individual, such as consumer loans for auto purchases and credit card debt ($520.7 billion); and all other loans, such as lesser developed country (LDC) loans ($393.8 billion). In the investment security portfolio of $1,027.7 billion, U.S. government securities, such as Treasury bonds, comprised $721.2 billion, with other securities (in particular, municipal securities and investment grade corporate bonds) making up the rest.[7]

A major inference we can draw from this asset structure is that credit or default exposure is a major risk faced by modern commercial bank managers (see Chapters 11 and 12).

Liabilities.   Commercial banks have two major sources of funds other than the equity provided by owners: deposits and borrowed or other liability funds. A major

---

[7]The footnotes to commercial bank balance sheets also distinguish between securities held by banks for trading purposes, normally for less than one year, and those held for longer-term investment purposes. The large money center banks are often active in the secondary market trading of government securities, reflecting their important role as primary dealers in government securities at the time of Treasury security auctions.

TABLE 1–5   Balance Sheet (all U.S. commercial banks)
As of August 27, 1997 (in billions of dollars)

Assets				
Loans and securities				$4,111.1
Investment securities			$1,027.7	
U.S. government securities		$ 721.2		
Other		306.5		
Total loans			3,083.4	
Interbank loans		198.7		
Loans excluding interbank		2,884.7		
Commercial and industrial	$ 830.4			
Real estate	1,197.0			
Revolving home equity	$ 94.2			
Other	1,102.8			
Individual	520.7			
All other	393.8			
Less: reserve for loan losses	57.2			
Total cash assets				281.6
Other assets				285.6
Total assets				4,678.3
Liabilities				
Total deposits				$3,029.0
Transaction accounts			$ 711.8	
Nontransaction accounts			2,317.2	
Large time deposits		608.8		
Other		1,708.4		
Borrowings				750.4
From banks in United States			276.5	
From nonbanks in United States			473.9	
Other liabilities				487.4
Total liabilities				4,266.8
Residual (assets less liabilities)				411.5

Source: *Federal Reserve Bulletin,* November 1997, p. A15 (seasonally adjusted).

difference between banks and other firms is banks' high leverage. For example, banks had an average ratio of equity to assets of 8.8 percent in 1997; this implies that 91.2 percent of their assets were funded by debt, either deposits or borrowed funds.

Note in Table 1–5, the aggregate balance sheet of U.S. banks, that deposits amounted to $3,029 billion and borrowings and other liabilities were $750.4 and $487.4 billion, respectively. Of the total stock of deposits, transaction accounts comprised 23.5 percent, or $711.8 billion. **Transaction accounts** are checkable deposits that bear no interest (so-called demand deposits) or are interest bearing (most commonly called **NOW** accounts or negotiable order of withdrawal accounts). Since their introduction in 1980, interest-bearing checking accounts—especially NOW accounts—have dominated the transaction accounts of banks. However, since limitations are imposed on the ability of corporations to hold such accounts and since there are minimum balance requirements for NOW accounts, noninterest-bearing demand deposits are still held. The second major segment of deposits is retail or household savings and time deposits, normally individual account holdings of less than $100,000. Important components of bank retail savings accounts are small nontransaction accounts, which include passbook savings accounts and retail

Transaction Accounts
The sum of noninterest-bearing demand deposits and interest-bearing checking accounts.

NOW Account
An interest-bearing checking account.

Money Market Mutual Fund
A specialized (mutual fund) FI that offers depositlike interest-bearing claims to savers.

Negotiable CDs
Fixed-maturity interest-bearing deposits with face values over $100,000 that can be resold in the secondary market.

time deposits. Small nontransaction accounts comprise 56.4 percent of total deposits. However, this disguises an important trend in the supply of these deposits to banks. Specifically, retail savings and time deposits have been falling in recent years, largely as a result of competition from **money market mutual funds**.[8] These funds pay a competitive rate of interest based on wholesale money market rates by pooling and investing funds (see Chapter 4) while requiring relatively small-denomination investments by mutual fund investors.

The third major source of deposit funds consists of large time deposits (over $100,000),[9] which amounted to $608.8 billion, or approximately 20.1 percent of the stock of deposits, in August 1997. These are primarily **negotiable certificates of deposit** (deposit claims with promised interest rates and fixed maturities of at least 14 days) that can be resold to outside investors in an organized secondary market. As such, they are usually distinguished from retail time deposits by their negotiability and secondary market liquidity.

Nondeposit liabilities comprise borrowings and other liabilities that together total 29 percent of all bank liabilities, or $1,237.8 billion. These categories include a broad array of instruments, such as purchases of federal funds (bank reserves) on the interbank market and repurchase agreements (temporary swaps of securities for federal funds) at the short end of the maturity spectrum to the issuance of notes and bonds at the longer end.[10]

Overall, the liability structure of bank balance sheets tends to reflect a shorter maturity structure than does the asset portfolio with relatively more liquid instruments such as deposits and interbank borrowings—used to fund less liquid assets such as loans. Thus, maturity mismatch or interest rate risk and liquidity risk are key exposure concerns for bank managers (see Chapters 8, 9, and 17).

Off-Balance-Sheet Activities.   Looking at the balance sheet alone tends to disguise many fee-related activities conducted by banks off the balance sheet. These activities include issuing various types of guarantees (such as letters of credit) that often have a strong insurance underwriting element and making commitments to lend in the future for a fee. They also involve engaging in futures, forward, option, and swap derivative transactions that are not reflected in the current balance sheet. As we discuss in Chapter 13, off-balance-sheet activities are increasing in importance compared to the on-balance-sheet activities of many of the nation's largest banks. This is due to increased competition from other FIs and financial instruments in traditional areas of activity—commercial lending and deposit taking—as well as to fee, interest rate risk management, and regulatory incentives to move off the balance sheet. As will be discussed, these activities expose banks to new and important credit and other risks.

Regulation

The Regulators.   Unlike countries that have one or sometimes two regulators, U.S. banks may be subject to the supervision and regulations of up to four separate regulators. The key regulators are the Federal Deposit Insurance Corporation

---

[8]See U.S. General Accounting Office, "Mutual Funds: Impact on Bank Deposits and Credit Availability," GAO/GGD (September 1995).

[9]$100,000 is the cap for explicit coverage under bank deposit insurance. We discuss this in more detail in Chapter 19.

[10]These instruments are explained in greater detail in later chapters, especially Chapter 18.

(FDIC), the Office of the Comptroller of the Currency (OCC), the Federal Reserve System (FRS), and state bank regulators. Next, we look at the principal roles played by each regulator. Appendix 1B lists in greater detail the regulators that oversee the various activities of depository institutions.

The FDIC. Established in 1933, the Federal Deposit Insurance Corporation insures the deposits of member banks. In so doing, it levies insurance premiums on member banks, manages the deposit insurance fund, and carries out bank examinations. Further, when an insured bank is closed, the FDIC acts as the receiver and liquidator—although the closure decision itself is technically in the hands of the bank chartering or licensing agency, such as the OCC. Because of the problems in the thrift industry and the insolvency of the savings and loan (S & L) insurance fund (FSLIC) in 1989, the FDIC now manages both the commercial bank insurance fund and the savings and loan insurance fund. The Bank Insurance Fund is called BIF, and the S&L fund is called SAIF (Savings Association Insurance Fund). The number of FDIC-BIF insured banks and the division between nationally chartered and state-chartered banks is shown in Figure 1–3.

Office of the Comptroller of the Currency (OCC). The OCC is the oldest bank regulatory agency; established in 1863, it is a subagency of the U.S. Treasury. Its primary function is to charter so-called national banks as well as to close them. In addition, the OCC examines national banks and has the power to approve or disapprove their merger applications. However, instead of seeking a national charter, banks can be chartered by any of 50 individual state bank regulatory agencies. The choice of being a nationally chartered or state-chartered bank lies at the foundation of the **dual banking system** in the United States. While most large banks, such as BankAmerica, choose national charters, this is not always the case. For example, Morgan Guaranty, the money center bank subsidiary of J.P. Morgan, is chartered as a state bank under New York State law. In September 1997, 2,656 banks were *nationally* chartered and 6,652 were *state* chartered, with approximately 56 percent and 44 percent of total commercial bank assets, respectively.

Dual Banking System
The coexistence of both nationally chartered and state-chartered banks in the United States.

Federal Reserve System. Apart from being concerned with the conduct of monetary policy, as this country's central bank the Federal Reserve also has regulatory power over some banks and, when relevant, their holding company parents. All the nationally chartered banks shown in Figure 1–3 are automatically members of the Federal Reserve system; 992 state-chartered banks also have chosen to become members. Since 1980, all banks have had to meet the same noninterest-bearing reserve requirements whether they are members of the Federal Reserve System (FRS) or not. The primary advantages of FRS membership are direct access to the federal funds wire transfer network for nationwide interbank borrowing and lending of reserves and to the discount window for lender of last resort borrowing of funds. Finally, many banks are often owned and controlled by parent **holding companies;** for example, J.P. Morgan is the parent holding company of Morgan Guaranty (a bank). Because the holding company's management can influence decisions taken by a bank subsidiary and thus influence its risk exposure, the Federal Reserve System regulates and examines bank holding companies as well.[11]

Holding Company
A parent company that owns a controlling interest in a subsidiary bank or other FI.

---

[11]The Securities and Exchange Commission (SEC) has the power to regulate the specialized securities subsidiaries of bank holding companies (so-called Section 20 subsidiaries).

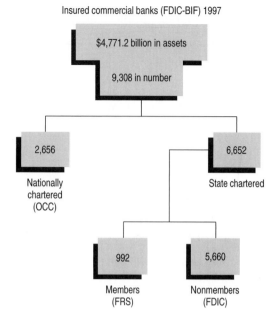

FIGURE 1–3

Bank Regulators

Insured commercial banks (FDIC-BIF) 1997

$4,771.2 billion in assets

9,308 in number

2,656
Nationally
chartered
(OCC)

6,652
State chartered

992
Members
(FRS)

5,660
Nonmembers
(FDIC)

Source: FDIC (internal figures).

Regulations.   Commercial banks are among the most regulated firms in the U.S. economy. Because of the inherent special nature of banking and banking contracts (see Chapter 6), regulators have imposed numerous restrictions on their product and geographic activities. Table 1–6 lists the major laws from the McFadden Act of 1927 to the Riegle-Neal Interstate Banking and Efficiency Act of 1994 and describes the key features of each act briefly.

Even though we will go into greater detail about these regulations in later chapters, we now note the major objectives of each of these laws. The 1927 McFadden Act sought to restrict interstate bank branching, while the 1933 Glass-Steagall Act sought to separate commercial banking from investment banking by limiting the powers of commercial banks to engage in securities activities. Restrictions on the nonbank activities of commercial banks were strengthened by the Bank Holding Company Act of 1956 and its 1970 amendments, which limited the ability of a bank's parent holding company to engage in commercial, insurance, and other nonbank financial service activities. The 1978 International Banking Act extended federal regulation, such as the McFadden and Glass-Steagall Acts, to foreign branches and agencies in the United States for the first time, thereby seeking to level the competitive playing field between domestic and foreign banks. The 1980 DIDMCA and the 1982 DIA are mainly deregulation acts in that they eliminated interest ceilings on deposits and gave banks (and thrifts) new liability and asset powers.[12] As we discuss in the next section on thrifts, this deregulation is blamed in part for the thrift crisis that resulted in widespread failures and the insolvency of the FSLIC in 1989.

---

[12]In particular, Regulation Q ceilings on bank deposit rates were phased out in stages between March 1980 and March 1986.

TABLE 1–6   Major Bank Laws
Major Features

1927 The McFadden Act
1. Made branching of nationally chartered banks subject to the same branching regulations as state-chartered banks.
2. Liberalized national banks' securities underwriting activities, which previously had to be conducted through state-chartered affiliates.

1933 The Banking Acts of 1933
1. The Glass-Steagall Act generally prohibited commercial banks from underwriting securities with four exceptions:
   a. Municipal general obligation bonds.
   b. U.S. government bonds.
   c. Private placements.
   d. Real estate loans.
2. In addition, the Acts established the FDIC to insure bank deposits.

1956 The Bank Holding Company Act
1. Restricted the banking and nonbanking acquisition activities of multibank holding companies.
2. Empowered the Federal Reserve to regulate multibank holding companies by:
   a. Determining permissible activities.
   b. Exercising supervisory authority.
   c. Exercising chartering authority.
   d. Conducting bank examinations.

1970 Amendments to the Bank Holding Company Act of 1956
1. Extended the BHC Act of 1956 to one-bank holding companies.
2. Restricted permissible BHC activities to those "closely related to banking."

1978 International Banking Act
1. Regulated foreign bank branches and agencies in the United States.
2. Subjected foreign banks to the McFadden and Glass-Steagall Acts.
3. Gave foreign banks access to Fedwire, the discount window, and deposit insurance.

1980 Depository Institutions Deregulation and Monetary Control Act (DIDMCA)
1. Set a six-year phaseout for Regulation Q interest rate ceilings on small time and savings deposits.
2. Authorized NOW accounts nationwide.
3. Introduced uniform reserve requirements for state-chartered and nationally chartered banks.
4. Increased the ceiling on deposit insurance coverage from $40,000 to $100,000.
5. Allowed federally chartered thrifts to make consumer and commercial loans (subject to size restrictions).

1982 Garn-St. Germain Depository Institutions Act (DIA)
1. Introduced money market deposit accounts (MMDAs) and super NOW accounts as interest rate-bearing savings accounts with limited check-writing features.
2. Allowed federally chartered thrifts more extensive lending powers and demand deposit-taking powers.
3. Allowed sound commercial banks to acquire failed savings banks.
4. Reaffirmed limitations on bank powers to underwrite and distribute insurance.

1987 Competitive Equality in Banking Act (CEBA)
1. Redefined the definition of a *bank* to limit the growth of nonbank banks.
2. Sought to recapitalize the Federal Savings and Loan Insurance Corporation (FSLIC).

TABLE 1–6   (*continued*)

1989 Financial Institutions Reform Recovery and Enforcement Act (FIRREA)

1. Limited savings banks' investments in nonresidential real estate, required divestiture of junk bond holdings (by 1994), and imposed a restrictive asset test to qualify as a savings bank [the qualified thrift lender test (QTL)].
2. Equalized the capital requirements of thrifts and banks.
3. Replaced FSLIC with FDIC-SAIF.
4. Replaced the Federal Home Loan Bank Board as the charterer of federal savings and loans with the Office of Thrift Supervision (OTS), an agency of the Treasury.
5. Created the Resolution Trust Corporation (RTC) to resolve failed and failing savings banks.

1991 Federal Deposit Insurance Corporation Improvement Act (FDICIA)

1. Introduced prompt corrective action (PCA), requiring mandatory interventions by regulators whenever a bank's capital falls.
2. Introduced risk-based deposit insurance premiums beginning in 1993.
3. Limited the use of "too big to fail" bailouts by federal regulators for large banks.
4. Extended federal regulation over foreign bank branches and agencies in the Foreign Bank Supervision and Enhancement Act (FBSEA).

1994 Riegle-Neal Interstate Banking and Branching Efficiency Act

1. Permits bank holding companies to acquire banks in other states, starting September 1995.
2. Invalidates the laws of states that allow interstate banking only on a regional or reciprocal basis.
3. Beginning in June 1997, bank holding companies were permitted to convert out-of-state subsidiary banks into branches of a single interstate bank.
4. Newly chartered branches will also be permitted interstate if allowed by state law.

Nonbank Bank
A firm that undertakes many of the activities of a commercial bank without meeting the legal definition of a bank.

The Competitive Equality in Banking Act (CEBA) of 1987 sought to impose controls over a growing number of **nonbank banks** that were established to get around interstate banking restrictions and restrictions on nonbank ownership of banks imposed under the 1927 McFadden and the 1956 Bank Holding Company Acts. In 1989 Congress responded to the problems of thrift banks and the collapse of the FSLIC with the passage of FIRREA. In 1991 Congress enacted FDICIA to deal with a large number of bank failures and the threatened insolvency of the FDIC, the insurance fund for commercial banks. Both FIRREA and FDICIA sought to pull back from some of the deregulatory elements of the 1980 DIDMCA and the 1982 DIA. In 1994 the Riegle-Neal Act rolled back many of the restrictions on interstate banking imposed by the 1927 McFadden and the 1956 Bank Holding Company Acts. In particular, since June 1997 bank holding companies have been permitted to convert their bank subsidiaries in various states into branches, thus making nationwide branching possible for the first time in 70 years.

Concept Questions

1. What are the major assets held by commercial banks?
2. What are the major sources of funding for commercial banks?
3. Describe the responsibilities of the three federal regulatory agencies in the United States.
4. What are the major regulations that have affected the operations of U.S. commercial banks?

Savings Institutions

Savings and Loans
Banks that specialize in
residential mortgages
mostly backed by short-
term deposits and other
funds.

Savings institutions comprise two different groups of FIs: **savings and loan associations** (S&Ls) and savings banks (SBs). They usually are grouped together because they not only provide important mortgage and/or lending services to households but also are important recipients of household savings. Historically, S&Ls have concentrated mostly on residential mortgages, while savings banks have been operated as more diversified S&Ls that have a large concentration of residential mortgage assets but hold commercial loans, corporate bonds, and corporate stock as well. In the next section, we review these groups in turn.

Savings and Loans (S&Ls)

Size, Structure, and Composition of the Industry.   The S&L industry prospered throughout most of the 20th century. These specialized institutions made long-term residential mortgages backed by short-term savings deposits. This was made possible largely by the Federal Reserve's policy of smoothing or targeting interest rates (especially in the 1960s and 1970s until October 1979) and the generally upward-sloping shape of the yield curve, or the term structure of interest rates. There were periods, such as the early 1960s, when the yield curve sloped downward. But for most of the post–Second World War period, the upward-sloping yield curve meant that interest rates on 30-year residential mortgage assets exceeded rates on short-term savings and time deposit liabilities. Moreover, significant shocks to interest rates were generally absent due to the Fed's policy of interest rate smoothing.

At the end of the 1970s, slightly fewer than 4,000 S&Ls had assets of approximately $0.6 trillion. Over the period October 1979 to October 1982, however, the Federal Reserve radically changed its monetary policy strategy by targeting bank reserves rather than interest rates in an attempt to lower the underlying rate of inflation (see Chapter 8 for more details). The Fed's restrictive monetary policy action led to a sudden and dramatic surge in interest rates, with rates on T-bills rising as high as 16 percent. This increase in short-term rates and the cost of funds had two effects. First, S&Ls faced negative interest spreads or **net interest margins** (i.e., interest income minus interest expense divided by earning assets) in funding much of their fixed-rate long-term residential mortgage portfolios over this period. Second, they had to pay more competitive interest rates on savings deposits to prevent **disintermediation** and the reinvestment of those funds in money market mutual fund accounts. Their ability to do this was constrained by the Federal Reserve's **Regulation Q ceilings,** which limited the rates S&Ls could pay on traditional passbook savings account and retail time deposits.[13]

Net Interest Margin
Interest income minus in-
terest expense divided by
earning assets.

Disintermediation
Withdrawal of deposits
from S&Ls and other de-
pository institutions and
their reinvestment else-
where.

Regulation Q Ceiling
An interest ceiling im-
posed on small savings
and time deposits at banks
and thrifts until 1986.

In part to overcome the effects of rising rates and disintermediation on the S&L industry, Congress passed the DIDMCA and DIA (see Table 1–6); these acts expanded the deposit-taking and asset-investment powers of S&Ls. On the liability side, S&Ls were allowed to offer NOW accounts and more market rate sensitive liabilities such as money market deposit accounts to limit disintermediation and compete for funds. On the asset side, they were allowed to offer floating or adjustable rate mortgages and to a limited extent expand into consumer and commercial lending. In addition, many state-chartered thrifts—especially in California, Texas, and

---

[13]These Regulation Q ceilings were usually set at rates of 5¼ or 5½ percent.

Florida—received wider investment powers that included real estate development loans often made through special-purpose subsidiaries. Note the structural shifts in S&L balance sheets between 1977 and 1982 in Table 1–7 and the effects on industry profits in Table 1–8.

For many S&Ls, the new powers created safer and more diversified institutions. For a small but significant group whose earnings and shareholders' capital were being eroded in traditional lines of business, however, this created an opportunity to take more risks in an attempt to return to profitability. This risk-taking or moral hazard behavior was accentuated by the policies of the S&L insurer, FSLIC. It chose not to close capital-depleted, economically insolvent S&Ls (a policy of **regulator forbearance**)and to maintain deposit insurance premium assessments independent of the risk of the S&L institution (see Chapter 19).[14] As a result, there was an increasing number of failures in the 1982–89 period aligned with rapid asset growth of the industry. Thus, while S&Ls decreased in number from 4,000 in 1980 to 2,600 in 1989, or by 35 percent, their assets actually doubled from $600 billion to $1.2 trillion over that period.

The large number of S&L failures, especially in 1988 and 1989, depleted the resources of the FSLIC to such an extent that by 1989 it was massively insolvent. The resulting legislation—the FIRREA of 1989—abolished the FSLIC and created a new insurance fund (SAIF) under the management of the FDIC. In addition, the Act

Regulator Forbearance
A policy of not closing economically insolvent FIs but allowing them to continue in operation.

TABLE 1–7   **Balance Sheets of Savings and Loans**
Percent of Total Assets and Liabilities

Item	1977	1982
Liabilities		
Fixed ceiling liabilities	87.3%	22.0%
Passbook and NOW accounts	33.9	15.6
Fixed ceiling time deposits	53.4	6.4
Market ceiling small time deposits	0.0	52.8
Money market certificates	0.0	28.6
Small saver certificates	0.0	19.3
Other small time deposits	0.0	4.9
Discretionary liabilities	8.6	23.2
Large time deposits	2.1	8.1
FHLB advances	4.7	10.3
Other borrowings	1.8	4.6
Other liabilities	4.0	2.0
Assets		
Mortgage assets	86.0	81.1
Fixed rate	86.0	74.9
Adjustable rate	0.0	6.2
Nonmortgage loans	2.3	2.6
Cash and investments	9.2	11.2
Other assets	2.5	5.1

Source: *Federal Reserve Bulletin,* December 1982.

[14]We discuss moral hazard behavior and the empirical evidence regarding such behavior in more detail in Chapter 19.

TABLE 1–8   Net Income at Thrift Institutions
Amounts in Billions of Dollars; Percentages at Annual Rates

Year	FSLIC-Insured Savings and Loan Associations		All Operating Mutual Savings Banks	
	Amount	*As a Percent of Average Assets*	*Amount*	*As a Percent of Average Assets*
1970	.9	.57	.2	.27
1971	1.3	.71	.4	.48
1972	1.7	.77	.6	.60
1973	1.9	.76	.6	.54
1974	1.5	.54	.4	.35
1975	1.4	.47	.4	.38
1976	2.3	.63	.6	.45
1977	3.2	.77	.8	.55
1978	3.9	.82	.9	.58
1979	3.6	.67	.7	.46
1980	.8	.14	−.2	−.12
1981	−4.6	−.73	−1.4	−.83
H1	−1.5	−.49	−.5	−.56
H2	−3.1	−.97	−.9	−1.10
1982–H1	−3.3	−1.01	−.8	−.92

H = half year.
Source: *Federal Reserve Bulletin,* December 1982.

created the Resolution Trust Corporation (RTC) to close the most insolvent S&Ls.[15] Further, FIRREA strengthened the capital requirements of S&Ls and constrained their nonmortgage-related asset-holding powers under a newly imposed qualified thrift lender, or **QTL test.**

QTL Test
Qualified thrift lender test that sets a floor on the mortgage-related assets held by thrifts (currently 65 percent).

As a result of the closing of weak S&Ls and the strengthening of capital requirements, the industry shrunk significantly, both in numbers and in asset size, in the 1990s. Thus, S&Ls decreased in number from 2,600 in 1989 to 1,481 in 1997 (43 percent), and assets shrank from $1.2 trillion to $708 billion (41 percent) over that same period.

Balance Sheet and Recent Trends.   Even in its new shrunken state, concerns have been raised about the future viability of the S&L industry in traditional mortgage lending areas. This is partly due to intense competition for mortgages from other financial institutions, such as commercial banks and specialized mortgage bankers.[16] It is also due to the securitization of mortgages into mortgage-backed security pools by government-sponsored enterprises, which we discuss further in Chapter 28.[17] In addition, long-term mortgage lending exposes an FI to significant credit, interest rate, and liquidity risks.

A 1992 study found that surviving thrifts improved their profit margin (6.93 percent in 1992 compared to 4.51 percent in 1987) and reduced their leverage while

[15]At the time of its dissolution in 1995, the RTC had resolved or closed more than 700 savings banks.
[16]See, for example, W. R. Keeton and A. D. McKibben, "Changes in the Depository Industry in Tenth District States," Kansas City, *Economic Review,* Third Quarter 1997, pp. 55–76.
[17]The major enterprises are GNMA, FNMA, and FHLMC.

maintaining a relatively stable level of asset turnover.[18] Nevertheless, this improved performance was aided by the relatively low interest rate levels in the early 1990s, which helped S&Ls expand their net interest margins (NIMs). The unresolved question is whether S&Ls could survive another period of sharply rising interest rates such as the early 1980s, given their restrained powers of asset diversification and heavy reliance on mortgage assets required by the QTL test for these institutions.[19] Indeed, S&L profitability weakened in 1997 due to higher short-term rates (which impact the interest expenses or cost of funds of S&Ls) and lower long-term rates (which impact their interest income). While the **profit margin** (i.e., net income divided by total operating income) stood at 10.3 percent in 1997, the net interest margins of S&Ls narrowed from 3.48 percent in 1992 to 3.24 percent in 1997.

Profit Margin
Net income divided by total operating income.

Table 1–9, column (2), shows the balance sheet of SAIF-insured S&Ls in 1997. On this balance sheet, mortgages and mortgage-backed securities (securitized pools of mortgages) comprise 80.93 percent of total assets. As noted earlier, the FDICIA uses the qualified thrift lender test to establish a minimum holding of 65 percent in mortgage-related assets for S&Ls. Reflecting the enhanced lending powers

TABLE 1–9   Assets and Liabilities of Savings Banks and S&Ls, June 30, 1997

	(1) BIF-Insured Savings Banks		(2) SAIF-Insured Institutions (S&Ls)*	
	($ Millions)	*(Percent)*	*($ Millions)*	*(Percent)*
Cash and due	$ 5,279	1.64%	$ 16,962	2.40%
U.S. Treasury and federal agency obligations	11,464	3.56	24,726	3.49
Mortgage loans	187,554	58.25	441,875	62.41
MBS (includes CMOs, POs, IOs)	59,490	18.48	131,166	18.52
Bonds, notes, debentures, and other securities	17,526	5.44	16,174	2.28
Corporate stock	5,568	1.73	3,662	0.52
Commercial loans	6,220	1.93	9,092	1.28
Consumer loans	15,652	4.86	31,169	4.40
Other loans and financing leases	768	0.24	1,393	0.20
Less: allowance for loan losses and unearned income	2,515	0.78	4,333	0.61
Other assets	14,985	4.65	36,197	5.11
Total assets	321,991	100.00	708,083	100.00
Total deposits	234,233	72.75	485,806	68.61
Borrowings and mortgages warehousing	40,122	12.46	113,077	15.97
Federal funds, repository, and FHLB advances	16,205	5.03	41,289	5.83
Other liabilities	3,341	1.04	8,184	1.16
Total liabilities	293,901	91.28	648,356	91.57
Net worth†	28,090	8.72	59,727	8.43
Total liabilities and net worth	321,991	100.00	708,083	100.00
Number of banks		371		1,481

*Excludes institutions in RTC conservatorship.

†Includes limited life preferred stock for BIF-insured state chartered savings banks and redeemable preferred stock and minority interest for SAIF-insured institutions and BIF-insured FSBs.

Source: FDIC.

---

[18]Rossi, "The Viability of the Thrift Industry" (OTS, Washington, D.C., December 1992).

[19]The FIRREA required 70 percent of S&L assets to be mortgage related. The FDICIA reduced this to 65 percent.

established under the 1980 DIDMCA and the 1982 DIA, commercial loans and consumer loans amounted to 1.28 and 4.40 percent of assets, respectively. Finally, S&Ls are required to hold cash and investment securities for liquidity purposes and to meet regulator-imposed reserve requirements. In June 1997, cash and U.S. Treasury securities holdings amounted to 5.89 percent of total assets.

On the liability side of the balance sheet, small time and savings deposits are still the predominant source of funds, with total deposits accounting for 68.61 percent of total liabilities and net worth. The second most important source of funds consists of borrowings from the Federal Home Loan Banks (FHLBs), of which there are 12; these banks in turn are owned by the S&Ls themselves. Because of their size and government-sponsored status, FHLBs have access to wholesale money markets and the capital market for notes and bonds and can relend the funds borrowed on these markets to S&Ls at a small markup over wholesale cost. Other borrowed funds include repurchase agreements and direct federal fund borrowings. Finally, net worth is the book value of the equity holders' capital contribution; it amounted to 8.43 percent in 1997.

Regulation.   The two main regulators of S&Ls are the Office of Thrift Supervision (OTS) and the FDIC-SAIF Fund.

The Office of Thrift Supervision.   Established in 1989 under FIRREA, this office charters and examines all federal S&Ls. Further, when S&Ls are held by parent holding companies, it supervises the holding companies as well. State-chartered S&Ls are regulated by state agencies rather than by the Office of Thrift Supervision.

The FDIC-SAIF Fund.   Also established in 1989 under FIRREA and in the wake of FSLIC insolvency, the FDIC oversees and manages the Savings Association Insurance Fund (SAIF). In 1996, as part of a plan to recapitalize the SAIF, commercial banks were required to pay for part of the burden. In return, Congress promised to eventually merge bank and thrift charters (and hence insurance funds) into one. This will require thrifts to operate under the same regulatory structure that applies to commercial banks.

Concept Questions

1. Are S&Ls likely to be more or less exposed to interest rate risk than are banks? Explain your answer.
2. How do adjustable rate mortgages help S&Ls?
3. Why should S&Ls with little or no equity capital seek to take more risk than well-capitalized S&Ls?
4. Why could it be argued that the QTL test makes S&Ls more rather than less risky?

Savings Banks

Size, Structure, and Composition of the Industry.   Traditionally, savings banks were established as **mutual organizations** (in which the depositors are also legally the owners of the bank) in states that permitted such organizations. These states are largely confined to the East Coast—for example, New York, New Jersey, and the New England states. In recent years, many of these institutions—similar to S&Ls—

Mutual Organization
A savings bank in which the depositors are also the legal owners of the bank.

have switched from mutual to stock charters. In addition, some (fewer than 20) have switched to federal charters. In June 1997, 371 state-chartered mutual savings banks had $321 billion in assets; their deposits are insured by the FDIC under the BIF. This distinguishes savings banks from S&Ls, whose deposits are insured under the FDIC-SAIF.

Balance Sheet and Recent Trends.   Notice the major similarities and differences between S&Ls and **savings banks** in Table 1–9, which shows their respective assets and liabilities in June 1997. Savings banks [column (1) of Table 1–9] have a heavy concentration of 76.73 percent in mortgage loans and mortgage-backed securities (MBSs), but this is less than the S&Ls' 80.93 percent in these assets. Over the years, savings banks have been allowed to diversify more into corporate bonds and stocks; their holdings are 7.17 percent compared to 2.8 percent for S&Ls. On the liability side, the major difference is that savings banks are more reliant on deposits than S&Ls are and therefore have fewer borrowings. Finally, the ratio of the book value of net worth to total liabilities and net worth for savings banks stood at 8.72 percent (compared to 8.43 percent for S&Ls) in 1997.

Regulation.   Savings banks may be regulated at both the federal and state levels.

The FDIC-BIF.   Savings banks are insured under the FDIC's BIF and are thus subject to supervision and examination by the FDIC.

Other Regulators.   State-chartered savings banks (the vast majority) are regulated by state agencies. Savings banks that adopt federal charters are subject to the regulations of the OTS (the same as S&Ls).

Concept Questions

1. List four characteristics that differentiate savings banks from S&Ls.
2. How are savings banks regulated?

Credit Unions

Credit unions (CUs) are nonprofit depository institutions owned by members (depositors) with a common bond (e.g., university students and employees, police associations, military bases) whose objective is to satisfy the depository and lending needs of their members. CU member deposits (shares) are used to provide loans to other members in need of funds. Any earnings from these loans are used to pay higher rates on member deposits, charge lower rates on member loans, or attract new members to the CU. Because credit unions do not issue common stock, the members are legally the owners of a CU. Also, because credit unions are nonprofit organizations, their net income is not taxed and they are not subject to the local investment requirements established under the 1977 Community Reinvestment Act. This tax-exempt status allows CUs to offer higher rates on deposits, and charge lower rates on some types of loan, than banks and S&Ls. This is shown in Figure 1–4.

Size, Structure, and Composition of the Industry and Recent Trends

Credit unions are the most numerous of the institutions that comprise the depository institutions segment of the FI industry, totaling 11,328 in 1997. Moreover, they were

Savings Banks
Mostly mutually owned banks that specialize in residential mortgages funded by deposits.

Credit Unions
Nonprofit depository institutions, owned by members with a common bond, specializing in small consumer loans.

Figure 1–4

*Credit Union versus Bank
Interest Rates*

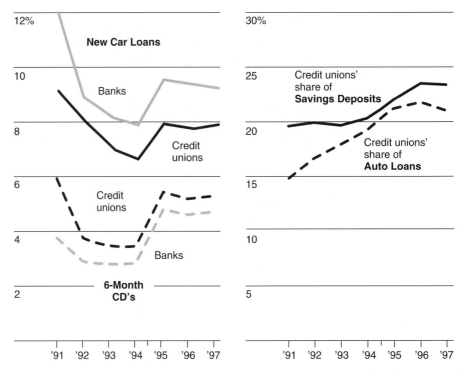

Sources: *Bank Rate Monitor* (interest rates); Federal Reserve and the National Credit Union Administration; and *New York Times,* February 26, 1997, p.D1.

less affected by the crisis that impacted commercial banks and savings institutions in the 1980s [20] because more than 43 percent of their assets are in the form of small consumer loans, often for amounts less than $10,000. In addition, CUs tend to hold large amounts of government securities (almost 30 percent of their assets in 1997) and relatively small amounts of residential mortgages. Their lending activities are funded by savings deposits contributed by 70 million members who share some common thread or bond of association, usually geographic or occupational in nature.

To attract and keep customers, CUs have had to expand their services to compete with those of banks and S&Ls. For example, CUs now offer products and services ranging from mortgages and auto loans (their traditional services) to credit lines and automated teller machines. Some credit unions now offer business and commercial loans to their employer groups. Because of their tax-exempt status, CUs can charge lower rates on these loans, providing CUs with a cost advantage over banks and S&Ls that is very attractive to customers.

As CUs have expanded in number, size, and services, bankers have claimed that CUs are unfairly competing with small banks that have historically been the major lenders in small towns. For example, the American Bankers Association has stated that the tax exemption for CUs gives them the equivalent of a $1 billion a year

[20]Credit unions have been covered by federal deposit insurance guarantees since 1971 (under the National Credit Union Share Insurance Fund). The depositor coverage cap of $100,000 is the same as that which currently exists for both commercial banks and savings banks.

subsidy. The Credit Union National Association's (CUNA) response is that any cost to taxpayers from CUs' tax-exempt status is more than made up in benefits to members and therefore the social good they create. CUNA estimates that the benefits of CU membership can range from $200 to $500 a year per member or, with almost 70 million members, a total benefit of $14 billion to $35 billion per year.

In 1997 the banking industry filed two lawsuits in its push to narrow the widening membership rules governing credit unions that followed a 1982 legal interpretation of the original 1934 Federal Credit Union Act's definition of what comprises a "group having a common bond of occupation or association." The first lawsuit challenged an occupation-based credit union's ability to accept members from companies unrelated to the firm that originally sponsored the CU. In the second lawsuit, the American Bankers Association asked the courts to bar the federal government from letting occupation-based credit unions convert to community-based charters. Bankers argued in both lawsuits that such actions, broadening the membership of credit unions under other than occupation-based guidelines, would further exploit an unfair advantage allowed by the credit unions' tax-exempt status. As discussed in the Contemporary Perspectives box on p. 23, in February 1998 the Supreme Court sided with banks, stating that credit unions could no longer accept members who did not share the common bond of membership.

Table 1–10 shows the assets and liabilities for credit unions in September 30, 1997. In that year more than 12,300 credit unions had assets of $349.2 billion. This compares to $155 billion in assets in 1987, for a growth rate over 10 years of 125 percent. Individually, credit unions tend to be very small, with an average size of $28.3 million in 1997 compared to $465.1 million for banks. The total assets of all credit unions are approximately half the size of those of the largest U.S. banking organization, Citigroup.[21]

Regulation

Like savings banks and S&Ls, credit unions can be federally chartered or state chartered. Approximately two-thirds of credit unions are federally chartered and subject to National Credit Union Administration (NCUA) regulation. In addition, through its insurance fund (NCUIF), NCUA provides deposit insurance guarantees of up to $100,000 for insured credit unions. Currently, NCUIF covers 98 percent of all credit union deposits.

Concept Questions

1. Why have credit unions prospered in recent years compared to S&Ls and savings banks?
2. What is the major asset held by credit unions?

---

[21]While in the United States credit unions account for a relatively small proportion of the financial services industry, in many less-developed countries they play an important role in mobilizing savings at the rural level. One very important credit union–type FI, first developed in Bangladesh and extended to other LDCs, has been the Grameen bank. See, for example, H. K. Hassan and L. Renteria-Guerrero, "The Experience of the Grameen bank of Bangladesh in Community Development," *International Journal of Social Economics* 24, no 12 (1997), pp. 1488–1523.

TABLE 1–10   Assets and Liabilities of Credit Unions, September 30, 1997

	Billions of Dollars	Percent
Assets		
Checkable deposits and currency	$ 7.0	2.0%
Time and savings deposits	16.8	4.8
Federal funds and security RPs	3.8	1.1
Open market paper	0.2	0.1
U.S. government securities	68.3	19.5
Treasury	15.8	4.5
Agency	52.5	15.0
Home mortgages	84.4	24.2
Consumer credit	150.7	43.1
Credit market instruments	303.6	86.9
Mutual fund shares	2.5	0.7
Miscellaneous assets	15.5	4.5
Total assets	349.2	100.0
Liabilities and Equity		
Checkable	36.8	10.5
Small time and savings	258.9	74.2
Large time	13.4	3.8
Shares and deposits	309.1	88.5
Other loans and advances	0.5	0.2
Miscellaneous liabilities	7.0	2.0
Total liabilities	316.6	90.7
Total ownership shares	32.6	9.3

Source: *Federal Reserve Bulletin,* December 1997, p. 74.

Summary

This chapter provided an overview of the major activities of commercial banks, savings institutions, and credit unions. It also described the agencies that regulate these depository institutions. The Federal Reserve System, the FDIC, the OTS, and the Office of the Comptroller of the Currency, in conjunction with state regulators, form the spectrum of agencies that oversee the activities of these institutions. Each of these institutions relies heavily on deposits to fund its activities, although borrowed funds are becoming increasingly important for the largest institutions. Historically, commercial banks have concentrated on commercial or business lending and on investing in securities, while savings institutions have concentrated on mortgage lending and credit unions have concentrated on consumer lending. These differences are being eroded due to competitive forces, regulation, and changing financial and business technology. Specifically, in the late 1990s, the largest group of assets in commercial bank portfolios are mortgage-related, and the largest banking organization, Citigroup, was created out of a merger with an insurance company (Travelers) that owned a major securities firm (Salomon Brothers).

Questions and Problems

1. What is the difference between community banks, regional banks, and money center banks? Contrast the business activities, location, and markets of each of these bank groups.

2. Use the data in Table 1–4 for the banks in the two asset size groups *(a)* $100 million–$1 billion and *(b)* over $10 billion to answer the following questions.

   a. Why have the ratios for ROA and ROE increased consistently for both groups over the seven-year period? Identify and discuss the primary variables which affect ROA and ROE as they relate to these two size groups.

   b. With the exception of one year, why is ROA for the smaller banks consistently larger than ROA for the large banks?

Contemporary Perspectives

CREDIT UNIONS LOSE TO BANKS IN HIGH COURT

Membership Expansion Is Invalidated by Ruling

Linda Greenhouse

The Supreme Court gave the banking industry an important if perhaps temporary victory today in an intensifying battle to stop the expansion of credit unions. It invalidated a Federal regulation that had allowed millions of people to join the alternatives to banks.

The Court's ruling threw into question the status of as many as 20 million customers of credit unions, the organizations that were born out of the hardships of the Great Depression and have grown into pesky bank rivals in recent years with an array of basic, affordable services ranging from mortgages to checking accounts to A.T.M.'s.

"If this decision is allowed to stand, it would be a massive loss for consumers and choice," said Dan A. Mica, president of the Credit Union National Association. "We think we are a counterbalance to banks, and if we were not there the cost of services would go up for all consumers."

Partly because they expected such a ruling, credit union leaders had been gathering support in Congress for a bill that would permit them to expand their membership, effectively overturning the Court's decision. The battle will now shift to that bill, which has 138 co-sponsors from both parties.

But banks have vowed to fight the bill, and it remains unclear how many credit union customers will ultimately be affected when the battle is resolved.

Representatives of the banking industry disavowed any desire to force credit unions to drop members.

"It is not our intent to create credit union widows and orphans," Monique E. Hanis, director of marketing for the Independent Bankers Association, said. The American Bankers Association, the industry's main trade group, also said it would not seek a solution that forced credit unions to give up members. However, Virginia McGuire, a spokeswoman for the American Bankers Association, said it was possible that credit unions might have to give up some groups of members that joined since July 30, 1996, when a lower-court decision set the stage for the Court's ruling today.

The question of how to remedy the regulation's invalidity is now before the Federal District Court here, which has delayed that phase of the case for more than a year while the Supreme Court reviewed the merits of the issue.

By a vote of 5 to 4, the Court invalidated a 1982 Federal regulation that had permitted thousands of credit unions to expand their membership base far beyond the relatively narrow employee and community groups around which credit unions were originally organized.

The American Bankers Association had challenged the 1982 regulation on the ground that it violated a 1934 Federal law requiring credit unions to limit membership to "groups having a common bond of occupation or association." In an opinion by Justice Clarence Thomas, the Supreme Court agreed.

The regulation issued by the National Credit Union Administration interpreted the phrase "common bond" so broadly, Justice Thomas said, that "it would be permissible to grant a charter to a conglomerate credit union whose members would include the employees of every company in the United States."

The majority opinion, which upheld a 1996 ruling by the United States Court of Appeals for the District of Columbia Circuit, was joined by Chief Justice William H. Rehnquist and by Justices Anthony M. Kennedy, Ruth Bader Ginsburg and Antonin Scalia.

The four dissenters—Justices Sandra Day O'Connor, John Paul Stevens, David H. Souter and Stephen G. Breyer—did not address the merits of the case. Rather, they disputed the bankers right to have brought the suit in the first place. Banks did not have standing to challenge the regulation, the dissenters said in an opinion by Justice O'Connor, because banks' competitive stake in the outcome did not place them within the "zone of interests" of the statute at issue, which was aimed at regulating credit unions.

Even though the effects of the Court's decision may be temporary, leaders of the credit union industry continued to warn today that membership for millions of people was still at risk. By coincidence, 4,000 credit union members were in Washington today for the first phase of a lobbying effort in expectation of a Supreme Court defeat. "This is a major, massive survival issue for us and we plan to win," Mr. Mica said.

While the legislative outlook is uncertain, the credit unions appear to have won the initial support of some of the more powerful members of Congress.

On the question of the implications of applying the ruling retroactively. "It is inconceivable to me that Congress will allow millions of Americans to be kicked out of the financial institution of their choice," said Representative Jim Leach, an Iowa Republican and the House Banking Committee chairman. He plans to hold hearings on credit union membership next month.

On Tuesday, the House Speaker, Newt Gingrich, announced his support of the bill that would write the

Contemporary Perspectives

invalidated regulation into law. The sponsors are Representatives Steven C. LaTourette, Republican of Ohio, and Paul E. Kanjorski, Democrat of Pennsylvania. While no corresponding measure has been introduced in the Senate, Senator Alfonse M. D'Amato, the New York Republican who is chairman of the Senate Banking Committee, said today that "Congress should and will enact legislation to restore the basic right of Americans to join credit unions."

Given the lobbying power of both sides of the debate, analysts said they expected a real struggle when legislation was presented before the House Banking Committee.

"We intend to nullify the court's decision," Mr. LaTourette said today. "I would be shocked if the House and Senate didn't get something to the President before we adjourn for the year."

Edward F. Furash, chairman and chief executive of Furash & Company, a Washington-based financial service industry consultancy, said he expected a "big huge fight" on Capitol Hill.

The case today, the National Credit Union Administration v. the First National Bank & Trust Company, No. 96-843, is rooted in the recession of the early 1980's. Faced with the prospect of bailing out the credit unions of small companies that were failing in substantial numbers, the National Credit Union Administration looked for ways to insulate credit unions from the fortunes of single employers.

For nearly 50 years, the agency had interpreted the Depression-era statute that put credit unions under Federal regulation as placing sharp limits on membership. Section 109 of the Federal Credit Union Act of 1934 provides that "Federal credit union membership shall be limited to groups having a common bond of occupation or association, or to groups within a well-defined neighborhood, community, or rural district." For employee-based credit unions, the agency had interpreted this language to require all members of the credit union to be united by a "common bond."

Under its reinterpretation issued in 1982, however, the credit union administration began permitting membership by wholly unrelated employee groups, as long as each group had its own common bond. A rapid expansion of credit unions resulted. Today, 3,600 of the 7,000 federally chartered credit unions have members from multiple occupational groups, including many of the biggest credit unions, with 32 million members and 79 percent of all deposits.

Enabled by Federal tax regulations to offer relatively low rates on loans and services, the credit unions began vigorous head-to-head competition with local banks for home mortgages, car loans and checking accounts. Not surprisingly, the banks fought back with lawsuits.

The target of the case before the Court was the AT&T Family Credit Union, based in Winston-Salem, N.C., and

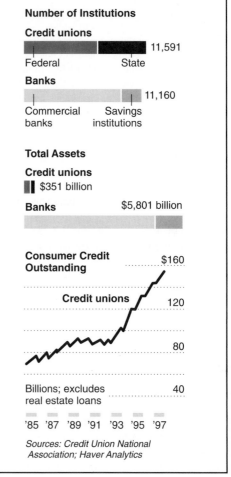

Credit Unions at a Glance

While their cousins, mutual savings banks and S. & L.'s, were evolving away from community self-help origins into ordinary profitmaking businesses, credit unions have stayed closer to their original mission of providing basic banking services and loans inexpensively to their owner-members.

Number of Institutions

Credit unions

11,591

Federal   State

Banks

11,160

Commercial   Savings
banks   institutions

Total Assets

Credit unions

$351 billion

Banks $5,801 billion

Consumer Credit Outstanding $160

Credit unions   120

80

Billions; excludes real estate loans   40

'85 '87 '89 '91 '93 '95 '97

Sources: Credit Union National Association; Haver Analytics

The New York Times

originally created in 1952 to serve employees of the Western Electric Company. It now has 300 employees of a Coca-Cola bottler and the Duke Power Company.

c. Why is the ratio for ROE consistently larger for the large bank group?

d. Using the information on ROE decomposition in Appendix 1A, calculate the ratio of equity to total assets for each of the two bank groups for the period 1990–97. Why has there been such dramatic change in the values over this time period, and why is there a difference in the size of the ratio for the two groups?

3. What factors have caused the decrease in loan volume relative to other assets on the balance sheets of commercial banks? How has each of these factors been related to the change and development of the financial services industry during the 1990s? What strategic changes have banks implemented to deal with changes in the financial services environment?

4. What are the major uses of funds for commercial banks in the United States? What are the primary risks to the bank caused by each use of funds? Which of the risks is most critical to the continuing operation of a bank?

5. What are the major sources of funds for commercial banks in the United States? How is the landscape for these funds changing and why?

6. What are the three major segments of deposit funding? How are these segments changing over time? Why? What strategic impact do these changes have on the profitable operation of a bank?

7. How does the liability maturity structure of a bank's balance sheet compare with the maturity structure of the asset portfolio? What risks are created or intensified by these differences?

8. The following balance sheet accounts have been taken from the annual report for a U.S. bank. Arrange the accounts in balance sheet order and determine the value of total assets. Based on the balance sheet structure, would you classify this bank as a community bank, regional bank, or a money center bank?

Premises	$ 1,078	Net loans	$29,981
Savings deposits	$ 3,292	Short-term borrowing	$ 2,080
Cash	$ 2,660	Other liabilities	$ 778
NOW accounts	$12,816	Equity	$ 3,272
Long-term debt	$ 1,191	Investment securities	$ 5,334
Other assets	$ 1,633	Demand deposits	$ 5,939
Intangible assets	$ 758	Certificates of deposit (under $100,000)	$ 9,853
Other time deposits	$ 2,333	Federal funds sold	$ 110

9. For each of the following banking organizations, identify which regulatory agencies (OCC, FRB, FDIC, or state banking commission) may have some regulatory supervision responsibility:

A state-chartered, nonmember nonholding-company bank.
A state-chartered, nonmember holding-company bank.
A state-chartered member bank.
A nationally chartered nonholding-company bank.
A nationally chartered holding-company bank.

10. Explain, from a balance sheet and financial market standpoint, how a savings and loan (S&L) company could consistently make a profit during the first three decades after World War II. What happened in 1979 to cause the failure of many S&Ls during the early 1980s? What was the effect of this change on the operating statements of S&Ls?

11. How did two pieces of regulatory legislation—DIDMCA in 1980 and DIA in 1982—change the operating profitability of S&Ls in the early 1980s? What impact did these pieces of legislation ultimately have on the risk posture of the S&L industry? How did the FSLIC react to this change in operating performance and risk?

12. How do the asset and liability structures of an S&L compare with the asset and liability structures of a commercial bank? How do these structural differences affect the risks and operating performance of an S&L?

13. How do savings banks differ from savings and loan associations? Differentiate in terms of risk, operating performance, balance sheet structure, and regulatory responsibility.

14. How did the Financial Institutions Reform, Recovery, and Enforcement Act (FIRREA) of 1989 and the Federal Deposit Insurance Corporation Improvement Act of 1991 reverse some of the key features of earlier legislation?

15. What are the main features of the Riegle-Neal Interstate Banking and Branching Efficiency Act of 1994? What major impact on commercial banking activity is expected from this legislation?

16. What is the "common bond" membership qualification under which credit unions have been formed and operated? How does this qualification affect the operational objective of a credit union?

17. What are the operating advantages of credit unions which have caused concern among commercial bankers? What has been the response of the Credit Union National Association to the banks' criticism?

18. How does the asset structure of credit unions compare with the asset structure of commercial banks and savings and loan associations? Refer to Tables 1–5, 1–9, and 1–10 to formulate your answer.

APPENDIX 1A
FINANCIAL STATEMENT ANALYSIS USING A RETURN ON EQUITY (ROE) FRAMEWORK

Between 1992 and 1997 the commercial banking industry experienced a period of record profits. This was quite a change from the late 1980s and early 1990s, when banks were failing in record numbers. Despite record profits, many FIs have areas of weakness and inefficiency which need to be addressed. One way of identifying weaknesses and problem areas is through an analysis of financial statements. In particular, an analysis of selected accounting ratios—so-called ratio analysis—allows FI managers to evaluate the current performance of an FI, the change in an FI's performance over time (*time series analysis* of ratios over a period of time), and the performance of an FI relative to competitor banks (*cross-sectional analysis* of ratios across a group of banks).

Figure 1A–1 provides a summary of the breakdown of the return on equity (ROE) framework. This framework is similar to the DuPont analysis frequently used by managers of nonfi-

nancial institutions. The ROE framework starts with a frequently used measure of profitability—return on equity (ROE)—and then decomposes ROE to identify strengths and weaknesses in an FI's performance.[1] Such a decomposition provides a convenient and systematic method for identifying the strengths and weaknesses of an FI's performance. Identification of strengths and weaknesses and the reasons for them provides a useful tool for FI managers as they look for ways to improve performance. Figure 1A–2 summarizes the role of ROE and the first two levels (from Figure 1A–1) of its decomposition in analyzing an FI's performance.

[1]Many large banks also use a risk-adjusted return on capital (RAROC) measure to evaluate the impact of credit risk on bank performance. ROE does not consider the bank's risk in lending as does RAROC. RAROC is described in Chapter 11.

FIGURE 1A–1

Breakdown of ROE into Various Financial Ratios

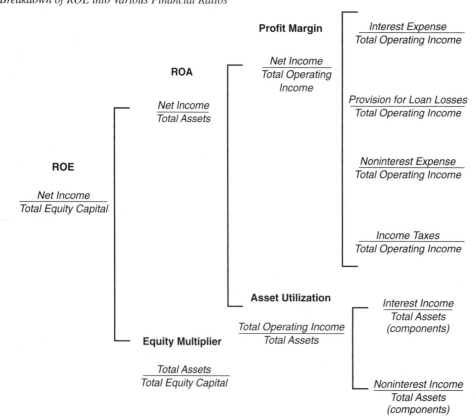

FIGURE 1A–2

Role of ROE, ROA, EM, PM, and AU in Analyzing an FI's Performance

Return on Equity (ROE): measures overall profitability of the FI per dollar of equity.

Return on Assets (ROA): measures profit generated relative to the FI's assets.

Equity Multiplier (EM): measures the extent to which assets of the FI are funded with equity relative to debt.

Profit Margin (PM): measures the ability to pay expenses and generate net income from interest and noninterest income.

Asset Utilization (AU): measures the amount of interest and noninterest income generated per dollar of total assets.

These ratios are related as follows (see Figure 1A–1):

$$ROE = ROA \times EM$$
$$ROA = PM \times AU$$

In turn, the PM and AU ratios can also be broken down and shown to depend on key financial ratios (see Figure 1A–1).

APPENDIX 1B
DEPOSITORY INSTITUTIONS AND THEIR REGULATORS

The matrix provides an overview of primary regulators of depository institutions. It is not intended to cover each area of regulatory responsibility in detail.

A.	National banks	Federal Reserve, FDIC, OCC
B.	State member bank	State authority, Federal Reserve, FDIC
C.	State nonmember banks, insured	State authority, Federal Reserve, FDIC
D.	Noninsured state banks	State authority, Federal Reserve, FTC
E.	Insured savings association, federal*	OTS, Federal Reserve, FDIC
	Insured savings association, state†	State authority, OTS, Federal Reserve, FDIC
F.	Uninsured savings association, state associations	State authority, Federal Reserve, FTC
G.	Credit unions, federal	NCUA, Federal Reserve, state authority
	Credit unions, state	State authority, NCUA, Federal Reserve, FTC
H.	Bank holding companies	Federal Reserve, state authority, FTC
I.	Savings association holding company	OTS, state authority, Federal Reserve, FTC
J.	Foreign branches of U.S. banks, national and state members	Federal Reserve, state authority, OCC
	Foreign branches of U.S. banks, insured state nonmembers	State authority, FDIC
K.	Edge Act corporations	Federal Reserve
	Agreement corporations	State authority, Federal Reserve
L.	U.S. branches and agencies of foreign banks, federal	OCC, Federal Reserve, FDIC, FTC, state authority
	U.S. branches and agencies of foreign banks, state	State authority, Federal Reserve, FDIC, OCC, FTC

Note: FDIC = Federal Deposit Insurance Corporation; FTC = Federal Trade Commission; Federal Reserve: Board of Governors of the Federal Reserve System/Federal Reserve Banks; NCUA = National Credit Union Administration; OCC = Office of the Comptroller of Currency; OTS = Office of Thrift Supervision.

*Federal savings associations include any thrift institution such as federal savings banks, federally chartered under Section 5 of the Home Owners' Act.

†State savings associations include any state-chartered savings bank, savings and loan association, building and loan association, homestead association, or cooperative bank.

Source: Public Information Department Federal Reserve Bank of New York, 33 Liberty Street, New York, NY 10045.

CHAPTER 2

THE FINANCIAL SERVICES INDUSTRY

Insurance Companies

Introduction

The primary function of insurance companies is to protect individuals and corporations (policyholders) from adverse events. By accepting premiums, insurance companies promise policyholders compensation if certain specified events occur. The industry is classified into two major groups: life and property-casualty. Life insurance provides protection against the possibility of untimely death, illnesses, and retirement. Property insurance protects against personal injury and liability such as accidents, theft, and fire. However, as will become clear, insurance companies also sell a variety of investment products in a similar fashion to other financial service firms, such as mutual funds (Chapter 4) and depository institutions (Chapter 1).

As in Chapter 1, where we discussed banks and thrifts, in this chapter we describe the main features of insurance companies by concentrating on (1) the size, structure, and composition of the industry in which they operate, (2) balance sheets and recent trends, and (3) regulations.

Life Insurance Companies

Size, Structure, and Composition of the Industry

In 1997, the United States had 1,563 life insurance companies compared to 1,758 in 1980. The aggregate assets of life insurance companies were $2.3 trillion at the end of 1997 compared to $0.48 trillion in 1980. Although not in the numbers seen in the banking industry, the life insurance industry has seen some major mergers in recent years as competition within the industry and from other FIs has increased. In addition, many of the largest mutually organized insurance companies, such as Prudential, are seeking to convert to stockholder-controlled companies. In so doing, they will gain access to the equity market in order to realize additional capital for future business expansions and to compete with the rapidly consolidating banking industry. Since a mutual company is owned by its policyholders, the existing capital and reserves (equal to accumulated past profits) would have to be distributed to the insurer's policyholders. It is estimated that the current policyholders of Prudential will receive a one-time payout exceeding $12 billion (about $1,100 per policyholder). Table 2–1 lists the top 10 insurers in the United States, while Figure 2–1 describes the process by which a mutual insurer can be converted into a stock insurance company. Figure 2–2 shows the structure of Prudential, this country's largest insurance company.

TABLE 2–1   Biggest Life Insurers

Rank	Insurance Company	Form of Ownership	Assets in billions
1	Prudential of America	Mutual	$178.62
2	Metropolitan Life	Mutual	162.48
3	Teachers Insurance and Annuity	Stock	86.36
4	New York Life	Mutual	62.73
5	Northwestern Mutual Life	Mutual	62.68
6	Connecticut General Life	Stock	62.28
7	Principal Mutual Life	Mutual	56.84
8	Equitable Life Assurance	Stock	54.74
9	John Hancock Mutual Life	Mutual	53.59
10	Massachusetts Mutual Life	Mutual	53.35

Source: Reprinted with permission from *New York Times,* February 13, 1998, p. D3.

FIGURE 2–1

Converting a Mutual Insurer to Stock Ownership

Mutual Insurers

Stock Conversion

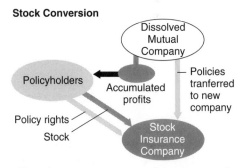

Unlike ordinary companies that sell insurance, mutual insurance companies are co-ops owned by their policyholders. Policyholders have a dual relationship with the company, as customer and as owner. Most of the company's profits are paid out to policyholders as policy dividends; the remainder is retained as a reserve and tends to build up over time.

The main way to convert a mutual company to stock ownership is to liquidate the mutual company. Much of the accumulated profits of the old mutual company and the bulk of the stock of the new company would be distributed to the mutual policyholders. The new stock company would then issue more shares to raise capital, make acquisitions, or reward management, just like any other company, and continue to pay dividends on policies.

Source: Adapted from *New York Times,* Money and Business Section, June 8, 1997, p. 11. Copyright © 1997 by the New York Times. Reprinted by permission.

FIGURE 2–2

*Insurance Colossus:
Prudential*

Figures for 1996, the latest available, except where noted; dollar figures in billions.

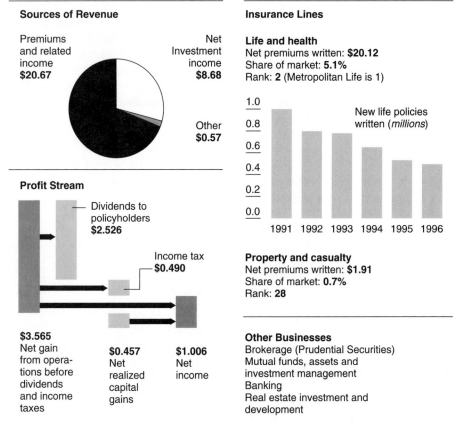

Sources of Revenue

Premiums and related income **$20.67**

Net Investment income **$8.68**

Other **$0.57**

Profit Stream

Dividends to policyholders **$2.526**

Income tax **$0.490**

$3.565 Net gain from operations before dividends and income taxes

$0.457 Net realized capital gains

$1.006 Net income

Insurance Lines

Life and health
Net premiums written: **$20.12**
Share of market: **5.1%**
Rank: **2** (Metropolitan Life is 1)

New life policies written (*millions*)

1991 1992 1993 1994 1995 1996

Property and casualty
Net premiums written: **$1.91**
Share of market: **0.7%**
Rank: **28**

Other Businesses
Brokerage (Prudential Securities)
Mutual funds, assets and investment management
Banking
Real estate investment and development

Source: *New York Times,* February 13, 1998, p. D3, Copyright © by the New York Times. Reprinted by permission.

Life insurance allows individuals and their beneficiaries to protect against losses in income through premature death or retirement. By pooling risks, life insurance transfers income-related uncertainties from the insured individual to a group. While life insurance may be the core activity area, modern life insurance companies also sell annuity contracts, manage pension plans, and provide accident and health insurance (see Figure 2–2). We discuss these different activity lines in the following sections.

Life Insurance. The four basic classes or lines of life insurance are distinguished by the manner in which they are sold or marketed to purchasers. These classes are (1) ordinary life, (2) group life, (3) industrial life, and (4) credit life. Among the life insurance policies in force in the United States in 1990s, ordinary life accounted for approximately 60 percent, group life for less than 40 percent, industrial life for less than 1 percent, and credit life for less than 2 percent of the almost $20 trillion contract value in force. In recent years sales of basic life insurance policies have declined in the face of competition from annuities and mutual funds. For example, in 1982 Americans bought 17.7 million new policies; in 1997 they bought 11.1 million, a drop of more than one-third.

Ordinary Life.   Ordinary life insurance involves policies marketed on an individual basis, usually in units of $1,000, on which policyholders make periodic premium payments. Despite the enormous variety of contractual forms, there are essentially five basic contractual types. The first three are traditional forms of ordinary life insurance, and the last two are newer contracts that originated in the 1970s and 1980s due to increased competition for savings from other segments of the financial services industry. The three traditional contractual forms are term life, whole life, and endowment life. The two newer forms are variable life and universal life. The key features of each of these contractual forms are as follows:

- **Term life.** A term life policy is the closest to pure life insurance, with no savings element attached. Essentially, the individual receives a payout contingent on death during the coverage period. The term of coverage can vary from as little as 1 year to 40 years or more.
- **Whole life.** A whole life policy protects the individual over an entire lifetime. In return for periodic or level premiums, the individual's beneficiaries receive the face value of the life insurance contract on death. Thus, there is certainty that if the policyholder continues to make premium payments, the insurance company will make a payment—unlike term insurance. As a result, whole life has a savings element as well as a pure insurance element.
- **Endowment life.** An endowment life policy combines a pure (term) insurance element with a savings element. It guarantees a payout to the beneficiaries of the policy if death occurs during some endowment period (e.g., prior to reaching retirement age). An insured person who lives to the endowment date receives the face amount of the policy.
- **Variable life.** Unlike traditional policies that promise to pay the insured the fixed or face amount of a policy if a contingency arises, variable life insurance invests fixed premium payments in mutual funds of stocks, bonds, and money market instruments. Usually, policyholders can choose mutual fund investments to reflect their risk preferences. Thus, variable life provides an alternative way to build savings compared to the more traditional policies such as whole life because the value of the policy increases or decreases with the asset returns of the mutual fund in which the premiums are invested.
- **Universal life and variable universal life.** Universal life allows both the premium amounts and the maturity of the life contract to be changed by the insured, unlike traditional policies that maintain premiums at a given level over a fixed contract period. In addition, for some contracts, insurers invest premiums in money, equity, or bond mutual funds—as in variable life insurance—so that the savings or investment component of the contract reflects market returns. In this case, the policy is called variable universal life.

Group Life Insurance.   Group life insurance covers a large number of insured persons under a single policy. Usually issued to corporate employers, these policies may be either contributory or noncontributory for the employees. Cost economies represent the principal advantage of group life over ordinary life policies. Cost economies result from mass administration of plans, lower costs for evaluating individuals through medical screening and other rating systems, and reduced selling and commission costs.

Industrial Life.   Industrial life insurance currently represents a very small area of coverage. Industrial life usually involves weekly payments directly collected by representatives of the companies. To a large extent, the growth of group life insurance has led to the demise of industrial life as a major activity class.

Credit life.   Credit life insurance is sold to protect lenders against a borrower's death prior to the repayment of a debt contract such as a mortgage or car loan. Usually, the face amount of the insurance policy reflects the outstanding principal and interest on the loan.

Other Life Insurer Activities.   Three other major activities of life insurance companies involve the sale of annuities, private pension plans, and accident and health insurance.

Annuities.   Annuities represent the reverse of life insurance activities. While life insurance involved different contractual methods of *building up* a fund, annuities involve different methods of *liquidating* a fund, such as paying out a fund's proceeds. As with life insurance contracts, many different types of annuity contracts have been developed. Specifically, they can be sold to an individual or a group and on a fixed or a variable basis by being linked to the return on some underlying investment portfolio. Individuals can purchase annuities with a single payment or with payments spread over a number of years. Importantly, the annuity builds up a fund whose returns are tax deferred; that is, they are not subject to capital gains taxes on their investments. Payments may be structured to start immediately, or they can be deferred (at which time taxes are paid based on the income tax rate of the annuity receiver). These payments may cease on death or continue to be paid to beneficiaries for a number of years after death. Annuity sales in 1997 were $110 billion ($85 billion of which were variable annuities), topping the $100 billion mark for the second year in a row.[1] However, with the 1997 reduction in the capital gains tax rate from 28 percent to 20 percent, the rate of growth of the annuity market has started to decline[2] as investors have switched to direct investments in mutual funds instead (see Chapter 4).

Private Pension Funds.   Insurance companies offer many alternative pension plans to private employers in an effort to attract this business from other financial service companies, such as commercial banks and security firms. Some of their innovative pension plans are based on guaranteed investment contracts (GICs). This means the insurer guarantees not only the rate of interest credited to a pension plan over a given period—for example, five years—but also the annuity rates on beneficiaries' contracts. Other plans include immediate participation and separate account plans that follow more aggressive investment strategies than traditional life insurance, such as investing premiums in special-purpose equity mutual funds. At the end of 1997, life insurance companies were managing $1.24 trillion in pension fund assets, equal to 35 percent of all private pension plans.

Accident and Health Insurance.   While life insurance protects against mortality risk, accident and health insurance protect against morbidity or ill health risk. Over $100 billion in premiums was written by life and health companies in the

---

[1]As discussed in Chapter 21, life insurers are facing increasingly intense competition from banks in the annuity product market.

[2]See, for example, "Annuity Sales Slip Amid Adverse Factors," *Wall Street Journal,* May 11, 1998, p. C22.

accident–health area in 1997. The major activity line is group insurance, providing health insurance coverage to corporate employees. Other coverages include credit health plans by which individuals have their debt repayments insured against unexpected health contingencies and various types of renewable, nonrenewable, and guaranteed health and accident plans for individuals. In many respects, the loss exposures faced by insurers in accident and health lines are more similar to those faced under property-casualty insurance than to those faced under traditional life insurance (see section on property-casualty insurance, which follows shortly).

Balance Sheet and Recent Trends

Assets.   Because of the long-term nature of their liabilities (as a result of the long-term nature of life insurance policyholders' claims) and the need to generate competitive returns on the savings elements of life insurance products, life insurance companies concentrate their asset investments at the longer end of the maturity spectrum (e.g., bonds, equities, and government securities). Look at Table 2–2, where we show the distribution of life insurance companies' assets.

TABLE 2–2   Life Insurance Companies
Distribution of Assets of U.S. Life Insurance Companies

Year	Total Assets (millions)	Government Securities	Corporate Securities Bonds	Stocks	Mortgages	Real Estate	Policy Loans	Miscellaneous US Assets
1917	$ 5,941	9.6%	33.2%	1.4%	34.0%	3.0%	13.6%	5.2%
1920	7,320	18.4	26.7	1.0	33.4	2.3	11.7	6.5
1925	11,538	11.3	26.2	0.7	41.7	2.3	12.5	5.3
1930	18,880	8.0	26.0	2.8	40.2	2.9	14.9	5.2
1935	23,216	20.4	22.9	2.5	23.1	8.6	15.2	7.3
1940	30,802	27.5	28.1	2.0	19.4	6.7	10.0	6.3
1945	44,797	50.3	22.5	2.2	14.8	1.9	4.4	3.9
1950	64,020	25.2	36.3	3.3	25.1	2.2	3.8	4.1
1955	90,432	13.1	39.7	4.0	32.6	2.9	3.6	4.1
1960	119,576	9.9	39.1	4.2	34.9	3.1	4.4	4.4
1965	158,884	7.5	36.7	5.7	37.8	3.0	4.8	4.5
1970	207,254	5.3	35.3	7.4	35.9	3.0	7.8	5.3
1975	289,304	5.2	36.6	9.7	30.8	3.3	8.5	5.9
1980	479,210	6.9	37.5	9.9	27.4	3.1	8.6	6.6
1985	825,901	15.0	36.0	9.4	20.8	3.5	6.6	8.7
1986	937,551	15.4	36.5	9.7	20.6	3.4	5.8	8.6
1987	1,044,459	14.5	38.8	9.3	20.4	3.3	5.1	8.6
1988	1,166,870	13.7	41.2	8.9	20.0	3.2	4.6*	8.4
1989	1,299,756	13.7	41.4	9.7	19.5	3.1	4.4	8.2
1990	1,408,208	15.0	41.4	9.1	19.2	3.1	4.4	7.8
1991	1,551,201	17.4	40.2	10.6	17.1	3.0	4.3	7.4
1992	1,664,531	19.2	40.3	11.5	14.8	3.1	4.3	6.8
1993	1,839,127	20.9	39.7	13.7	12.5	2.9	4.2	6.1
1994	1,930,500	20.4	41.0	14.6	11.2	2.2	4.4	6.2
1995	2,131,900	18.6	41.4	17.4	9.9	1.9	4.5	6.3
1996	2,271,700	17.0	42.4	21.0	9.0	1.7	4.4	4.5
1997	2,510,400	15.9	41.5	23.8	8.3	1.6	4.2	4.7

Note: Beginning with 1962, these data include the assets of separate accounts.

*Excludes some $600 million of policy loans securitized during 1988.

Source: *Spectator Year Book;* American Council of Life Insurance, *Life Insurance Fact Book,* 1994; *Best's Review,* October 1996; and *Federal Reserve Bulletin,* December 11, 1997.

Policy Loans
Loans made by an insurance company to its policyholders using their policies as collateral.

Policy Reserves
A liability item for insurers that reflects their expected payment commitments on existing policy contracts.

Surrender Value of a Policy
The cash value of a policy received from the insurer if a policyholder surrenders the policy before maturity. The cash surrender value is normally only a portion of the contract's face value.

Separate Account
Annuity programs sponsored by life insurance companies in which the payoff on the policy is linked to the assets in which policy premiums are invested.

McCarran-Ferguson Act of 1945
Legislation confirming the primacy of state over federal regulation of insurance companies.

As you can see, in 1997, 15.9 percent of assets were invested in government securities, 65.3 percent in corporate bonds and stocks, and 8.3 percent in mortgages, with other loans—including **policy loans** (loans made to policyholders using their policies as collateral)—comprising the balance. The major trends have been a long-term increase in the proportion of bonds and equities[3] and a decline in the proportion of mortgages in the balance sheet (see below).

Liabilities.   The aggregate balance sheet for the life insurance industry at the end of 1996 is shown in Table 2–3. Looking at the liability side of the balance sheet, we see that $1,218 trillion, or 52.9 percent, of total liabilities and capital are net **policy reserves** (the expected payment commitment on existing policy contracts). These reserves are based on actuarial assumptions regarding the insurers' expected future liability commitments to pay out on present contracts, including death benefits, matured endowments (lump sum or otherwise), and the cash **surrender values of policies** (the cash value paid to the policyholder if the policy is surrendered before it matures). Even though the actuarial assumptions underlying policy reserves are normally very conservative, unexpected fluctuations in future required payouts can occur; that is, underwriting life insurance is risky. For example, mortality rates—and life insurance payouts—might unexpectedly increase above those defined by historically based mortality tables as a result of a catastrophic epidemic illness such as AIDS. To meet unexpected future losses, the life insurer holds a capital and surplus reserve fund with which to meet such losses. The capital and surplus reserves of life insurers in 1996 were $138 billion, or 6 percent of total assets.[4] **Separate account** business represented 24.7 percent of total assets in 1996. A separate account is a fund established and held separately from the insurance company's other assets. These funds may be invested without regard to the usual diversification restrictions; that is, they may be invested in all stocks, all bonds, and so forth. The payoff on the life insurance policy thus depends on the return on the funds in the separate account. Another important life insurer liability, GICs (9 percent of total assets), are short- and medium-term debt instruments sold by insurance companies to fund their pension plan business (see premium and deposit funds in Table 2–3).

Regulation

The most important legislation affecting the regulation of life insurance companies is the **McCarran-Ferguson Act of 1945,** which confirms the primacy of state over federal regulation of insurance companies. Thus, unlike the depository institutions we discussed in Chapter 1, which can be chartered either at the federal or the state level, chartering of life insurers is done entirely at the state level. In addition to chartering, state insurance commissions supervise and examine insurance companies by using a coordinated examination system developed by the National Association of Insurance Commissioners (NAIC). An example of state insurance regulatory actions is the 1997 case of Prudential Insurance Company. Prudential's policyholders filed and settled a class-action lawsuit claiming that Prudential's sales

---

[3]The bull market of the 1980s and 1990s probably constitutes a major reason for the large percentage of assets invested in equities.

[4]An additional line of defense against unexpected underwriting losses is the insurer's investment income from its asset portfolio plus any new premium income flows.

TABLE 2–3   Life Insurance Industry Balance Sheet as of December 31, 1996
(in thousands of dollars)

Assets

Bonds	$1,197,999,008	52.0%
Preferred stock	10,431,334	0.5
Common stock	54,340,911	2.4
Mortgage loans	204,018,925	8.9
Real estate	37,645,179	1.6
Policy loans	98,254,683	4.3
Cash and deposits	3,490,208	0.1
Short-term investments	38,381,262	1.7
Other invested assets	23,183,948	1.0
Life and annuity premium due	12,869,630	0.6
Accident and health premium due	5,219,878	0.2
Accrued investment income	23,799,912	1.0
Separate account assets	572,368,902	24.8
Other assets	21,010,068	0.9
Total assets	$2,303,013,848	100.0

Liabilities and Capital/Surplus

Net policy reserves		$1,217,958,797	52.9
Policy claims		24,572,051	1.1
Policy dividend accumulations		20,048,648	0.9
Dividend reserve		13,805,878	0.6
Premium and deposit funds		201,701,005	8.7
Commissions, taxes, expenses		16,585,666	0.7
Securities valuation reserve		32,684,136	1.4
Other liabilities		68,479,141	3.0
Separate account business		569,461,870	24.7
Total capital and surplus		137,716,655	6.0
Capital	$ 3,822,710		0.2
Treasury stock	(359,666)		0.0
Paid-in and contributed surplus	55,638,348		2.4
Surplus notes	10,756,976		0.5
Unassigned surplus	55,100,944		2.4
Other surplus	2,034,149		0.1
Other reserves	10,723,194		0.4
Total liabilities and capital/surplus		$2,303,013,848	100.0

Source: Reprinted with permission from *Best's Aggregates & Averages,* Life-Health, 1997, p. 3.

representatives defrauded customers by talking them into using the built-up cash value of older life insurance coverages to buy new, costlier policies. An 18-month deceptive sales practices investigation was undertaken by a task force of state insurance regulators from 45 states. The report resulting from this investigation was instrumental in determining the legal settlement.[5]

Insurance Guaranty Fund
Required contributions from within-state insurance companies to compensate insurance company policyholders if there is a failure.

Other than supervision and examination, states promote life **insurance guaranty funds.** In most cases these are not permanent funds (like the FDIC) but involve required contributions from surviving within-state insurance companies to compensate the policyholders of an insurer after a failure has taken place.

---

[5]See, for example, "Prudential's Policy Sales, off by 27% in the U.S.," *New York Times,* Business Day, March 4, 1998, p. D1.

Concept Questions

1. What is the difference between a life insurance contract and an annuity contract?
2. Describe the different forms of ordinary life insurance.
3. Why do life insurance companies invest in long-term assets?
4. What is the major source of life insurance underwriting risk?
5. Who are the main regulators of the life insurance industry?
6. Why is traditional life insurance in decline?

Property-Casualty Insurance

Size, Structure, and Composition of the Industry

Currently, some 2,300 companies sell property-casualty (PC) insurance, with approximately 700 firms writing PC business in all or most of the United States. The U.S. PC insurance industry is quite concentrated. Collectively, the top 10 firms have a 42 percent share of the overall PC market measured by premiums written.[6] Table 2–4 shows the average two-firm concentration ratios for 18 property-casualty lines

TABLE 2–4   Two-Firm Insurance Seller Premium Concentrations for 18 Property-Casualty Lines, 1986–1996

	Two-Firm (seller)	
	Concentration 1986	Ratio 1996
Fire	13.5%	12.1%
Allied lines	11.6	12.3
Farm owners multiple peril	9.8	12.0
Homeowners multiple peril	27.9	35.1
Commercial multiple peril	14.1	12.4
Ocean marine	20.0	22.7
Inland marine	15.7	17.6
Medical malpractice	24.4	14.3
Workers' compensation	16.8	13.8
Other liability	18.4	25.5
Aircraft	23.0	25.0
Private passenger auto liability	29.9	33.2
Commercial auto liability	11.9	10.9
Private passenger auto physical damage	29.3	34.8
Commercial auto physical damage	7.6	10.4
Fidelity	34.5	32.1
Surety	13.5	14.9
Boiler and machinery	40.0	30.0
Total	13.9	19.2

Source: Reprinted with permission from *Best's Review,* August 1987 and 1997.

[6]*Best's Review,* August, 1997, p. 32.

over the 1986–96 period. In 1986, these concentration ratios varied from a low of 7.6 percent in commercial auto physical damage to a high of 40 percent in boiler and machinery, and the top two PC insurance sellers (State Farm and Allstate) wrote 13.9 percent of all insurance premiums. In 1996, concentration ratios ranged from 10.4 percent in commercial auto physical damage to 35.1 percent in homeowners multiple peril and the top two firms (again, State Farm and Allstate) wrote 19.2 percent of all PC insurance premiums. Thus, the industry leaders appear to be increasing their domination of this financial service sector. In terms of the worldwide volume of PC insurance, U.S. firms wrote some 42 percent of premiums.[7] The total assets of the PC industry in December 1996 were $802 billion, or approximately 35 percent of the life insurance industry's assets.

Property-Casualty Insurance.   Property insurance involves insurance coverages related to the loss of real and personal property. Casualty—or, perhaps more accurately, liability—insurance concerns protection against legal liability exposures. However, the distinctions between the two broad areas of property and liability insurance are increasingly becoming blurred. This is due to the tendency of PC insurers to offer multiple activity line coverages combining features of property and liability insurance into single policy packages, for example, homeowners multiple peril insurance. Below, we describe the key features of the main PC lines. Note, however, that some PC activity lines are marketed as different products to both individuals and commercial firms (e.g., auto insurance) while other lines are marketed to one specific group (e.g., boiler and machinery insurance targeted at commercial purchasers). To understand the importance of each line in terms of premium income, look at Table 2–5. Figure 2–3 shows the changing composition in **net premiums written** (NPW) (the entire amount of premiums on insurance contracts written) for major PC lines over the 1960–96 period. Important PC lines include the following:

Net Premiums Written
The entire amount of premiums on insurance contracts written.

Fire insurance and allied lines. Protects against the perils of fire, lightning, and removal of property damaged in a fire (3.3 percent of all premiums written in 1996; 16.6 percent in 1960).

Homeowners multiple peril (MP) insurance. Protects against multiple perils of damage to a personal dwelling and personal property as well as providing liability coverage against the financial consequences of legal liability due to injury done to others. Thus, it combines features of both property and liability insurance (10 percent of all premiums written in 1996; 5.2 percent in 1960).

Commercial multiple peril insurance. Protects commercial firms against perils similar to homeowners multiple peril insurance (7.7 percent of all premiums written in 1996; 0.4 percent in 1960).

Automobile liability and physical damage (PD) insurance. Provides protection against (1) losses resulting from legal liability due to the ownership or use of the vehicle (auto liability) and (2) theft of or damage to vehicles (auto physical damage) (47.1 percent of all premiums written in 1996; 43 percent in 1960).

Liability insurance (other than auto). Provides either individuals or commercial firms with protection against nonautomobile-related legal liability. For commercial firms, this includes protection against liabilities

---

[7]Ibid., p. 56.

TABLE 2–5   Property and Casualty Insurance
Industry Underwriting by Lines, 1996

	Premiums Written*
Fire	4,881,916
Allied lines	4,116,993
Multiple peril (MP) crop	1,394,777
Farm owners MP	1,392,079
Homeowners MP	27,201,471
Commercial MP—nonliability	11,235,307
Commercial MP—liability	9,611,270
Mortgage guaranty	1,825,333
Ocean marine	1,782,286
Inland marine	6,785,562
Financial guaranty	972,490
Medical malpractice	5,912,266
Earthquake	1,349,542
Group accident and health (A&H)	3,325,366
Other A&H	2,180,999
Workers' compensation	27,098,363
Other liability	22,142,908
Products liability	2,051,763
Private passenger auto liability	69,001,161
Commercial auto liability	13,478,433
Private passenger auto physical damage (PD)	40,155,430
Commercial auto PD	4,804,689
Aircraft	1,164,052
Fidelity	909,606
Surety	2,737,035
Glass	13,902
Burglary and theft	126,976
Boiler and machinery	763,308
Credit	406,139
Other lines	2,103,027
Totals	270,924,449

*In thousands
Source: Reprinted with permission from *Best's Review,* August 1997, p. 32.

relating to their business operations (other than personal injury to employees covered by workers' compensation insurance) and product liability hazards (8.2 percent of all premiums written in 1996; 6.6 percent in 1960).

Balance Sheet and Recent Trends

The Balance Sheet and Underwriting Risk.   The balance sheet of PC firms at the end of 1996 is shown in Table 2–6. Similar to life insurance companies, PC insurers invest the majority of their assets in long-term securities. Bonds ($486.6 billion), preferred stock ($11.5 billion), and common stock ($104.2 billion) comprised 75.1 percent of total assets in 1996. Looking at their liabilities, we can see that major components are the loss reserves set aside to meet expected losses ($301.8 billion) from *underwriting* the PC lines just described and the loss adjustment expense ($63.5 billion) item, which relates to expected administrative and related costs of

FIGURE 2–3

*Industry Net Premiums
Written by Product Lines,
1960–1996*

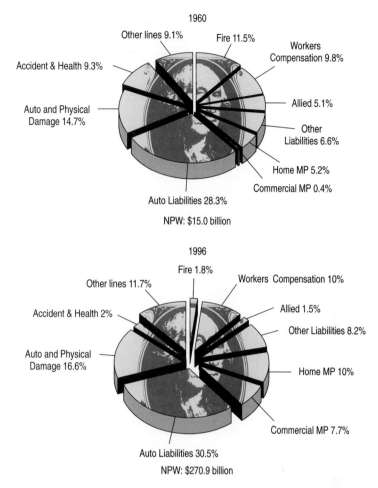

Source: Reprinted with permission from *A. M. Best's Aggregates and Averages,* Property-Casualty, 1994, p. 183; and *Best's Review,* August 1997, p. 32.

Unearned Premiums
Reserve set aside that
contains the portion of a
premium that has been
paid before insurance
coverage has been
provided.

adjusting (settling) these claims. The two items combined comprise 45.5 percent of total liabilities and capital. **Unearned premiums** (a reserve set-aside that contains the portion of a premium that has been paid before insurance coverage has been provided) are also a major liability, representing 13.5 percent of total liabilities and capital.

To understand how and why a loss reserve on the liability side of the balance sheet is established, we need to understand the risks of underwriting PC insurance. In particular, PC underwriting risk results when the premiums generated on a given insurance line are insufficient to cover (1) the claims (losses) incurred insuring against the peril and (2) the administrative expenses of providing that insurance (legal expenses, commissions, taxes, etc.) after taking into account (3) the investment income generated between the time premiums are received and the time claims are paid. Thus, underwriting risk may result from (1) unexpected increases in loss rates, (2) unexpected increases in expenses, and/or (3) unexpected decreases in investment yields or returns. Next, we look more carefully at each of these three areas of PC underwriting risk.

TABLE 2–6   Balance Sheet for the Property-Casualty Industry in December 31, 1996
(in thousands of dollars)

Assets

Unaffiliated investments	$700,806,046	87.3%
Bonds	486,575,994	60.7%
Preferred stocks	11,492,176	1.4
Common stocks	104,215,858	13.0
Mortgage loans	2,312,336	0.3
Real estate investments	1,683,626	0.2
Collateral loans	25,423	0.0
Cash and short-term investments	38,769,653	4.8
Other invested assets	13,220,260	1.7
Investments in affiliates	34,974,473	4.4
Real estate, office	7,536,246	0.9
Premium balance	57,521,904	7.2
Reinsurance funds	4,144,388	0.5
Reinsurance recoverable	10,625,248	1.3
Federal income taxes recoverable	1,393,750	0.2
Electronic data processing equipment	2,147,875	0.3
Accrued interest	8,631,287	1.1
Receivables from affiliates	5,828,213	0.7
Association accounts	2,617,529	0.3
Receivable uninsured accident and health plans	53,422	0.0
Future investment income on loss reserves	217,845	0.0
Other assets	8,320,453	1.1
Total assets	802,307,961	100.0

Liabilities and Capital/Surplus

Losses	301,795,151	37.6
Loss adjustment expenses	63,523,411	7.9
Reinsurance payable on paid losses	2,049,871	0.3
Commissions, taxes, expenses	12,244,889	1.5
Federal income taxes	2,394,884	0.3
Borrowed money	459,801	0.1
Interest on borrowed money	20,514	0.0
Unearned premiums	108,535,560	13.5
Dividends to stockholders	379,113	0.0
Dividends to policyholders	1,693,746	0.2
Reinsurance funds	8,833,614	1.1
Loss portfolio transfer (assumed)	1,024,222	0.1
Loss portfolio transfer (ceded)	(1,638,186)	–0.2
Amounts retained for others	4,745,314	0.6
Foreign exchange rate adjustments	603,855	0.1
Drafts outstanding	5,884,879	0.7
Payable to affiliates	4,147,101	0.5
Payable for securities	1,445,923	0.2
Amounts held for uninsured accident and health plans	15,484	0.0
Discount on loss reserve	(321,720)	–0.0
Other liabilities	19,828,399	2.45
Conditional reserves	9,114,739	1.1
Policyholders' surplus	255,527,396	31.9
Capital paid up	$ 7,626,170	1.0
Guaranty funds	264,404	0.0
Surplus notes	4,065,629	0.5
Assigned funds	115,162,334	14.4
Unassigned funds	128,408,858	16.0
Total liabilities and capital/surplus	$802,307,961	100.0

Source: Reprinted with permission from *A. M. Best's Aggregates and Averages,* Property-Casualty, 1997, p. 2.

Loss Risk. The key feature of claims loss exposure is the actuarial *predictability* of losses relative to premiums earned. This predictability depends on a number of characteristics or features of the perils insured, specifically:

- **Property versus liability.** In general, the maximum levels of losses are more predictable for property lines than for liability lines. For example, the monetary value of the loss of or damage to an auto is relatively easy to calculate, while the upper limit to the losses an insurer might be exposed to in a product liability line—for example, asbestos damage to workers' health under other liability insurance—may be difficult if not impossible to estimate.

- **Severity versus frequency.** In general, loss rates are more predictable on low-severity, high-frequency lines than they are on high-severity, low-frequency lines. For example, losses in fire, auto, and homeowners peril lines tend to involve events expected to occur with a high frequency and to be independently distributed across any pool of the insured. Furthermore, the dollar loss on each event in the insured pool tends to be relatively small. Applying the law of large numbers, the expected loss potential of such lines—the **frequency of loss** times the extent of the damage (**severity of loss**)—may be estimable within quite small probability bounds. Other lines, such as earthquake, hurricane, and financial guaranty insurance, tend to insure very low probability (frequency) events. Here the probabilities are not always stationary, the individual risks in the insured pool are not independent, and the severity of the loss could be enormous. This means that estimating expected loss rates (frequency times severity) is extremely difficult in these coverage areas. This higher uncertainty of losses forces PC firms to invest in more short-term assets and hold a larger percentage of capital and reserves than life insurance firms hold.

- **Long tail versus short tail.** Some liability lines suffer from a long-tail risk exposure phenomenon that makes the estimation of expected losses difficult. This **long-tail loss** arises in policies where the peril occurs during a coverage period but a claim is not made or reported until many years later. Losses incurred but not reported have caused insurers significant problems in lines such as medical malpractice and other liability insurance where product damage suits (e.g., the Dalkon shield case and asbestos cases) have mushroomed many years after the event occurred and the coverage period expired.[8]

- **Product inflation versus social inflation.** Loss rates on all PC property policies are adversely affected by unexpected increases in inflation. Such increases were triggered, for example, by the oil price shocks of 1973 and 1978. However, in addition to a systematic unexpected inflation risk in each line, there may be line-specific inflation risks. The inflation risk of property lines is likely to reflect the approximate underlying inflation risk of the economy. Liability lines may be subject to social inflation, as reflected in juries' willingness to award punitive and other liability damages at rates far above the underlying rate of inflation. Such social inflation has been particularly prevalent in commercial liability and medical malpractice insurance and has been directly attributed by some analysts to faults in the U.S. civil litigation system.

The **loss ratio** measures the actual losses incurred on a line. It measures the ratio of losses incurred to **premium earned** (premiums received and earned on insurance contracts because time has passed with no claim being filed). Thus, a loss

Frequency of Loss
The probability of a loss occurring.

Severity of Loss
The size of the loss.

Long-Tail Loss
A claim that is made some time after a policy was written.

Loss Ratio
Measures the ratio of pure losses incurred to premiums earned.

Premiums Earned
Premiums received and earned on insurance contracts because time has passed with no claim being filed.

---

[8]In some product liability cases, such as those involving asbestos, the nature of the risk being covered was not fully understood at the time many of the policies were written.

ratio less than 100 means that premiums earned were sufficient to cover losses incurred on that line. Aggregate loss ratios for the period 1951–96 are shown in Table 2–7. Notice there has been a steady increase in industry loss ratios over the period, increasing from the 60 percent range in the 1950s to the 70 and 80 percent range in the 1980s and 1990s. For example, in 1996, the aggregate loss ratio on all PC lines was 79.7.

Expense Risk. The two major sources of expense risk to PC insurers are loss adjustment expenses (LAE) and commissions and other expenses. Loss adjustment expenses relate to the costs surrounding the loss settlement process; for example, many PC insurers employ adjusters who determine the liability of the insurer and the size of the adjustment or settlement to be made. The other major area of expense occurs in the commission costs paid to insurance brokers and sales agents and other expenses related to the acquisition of business. Table 2–7 shows the expense ratio for PC insurers over the 1951–96 period.[9] In contrast to the increasing trend in the loss ratio, the expense ratio generally decreased over the period shown. These two sources of expense can account for significant portions of premiums. In 1996, for example, expenses—other than LAE—amounted to 26.2 percent of premiums written. Clearly, sharp rises in insurance broker commissions and other operating costs can rapidly render an insurance line unprofitable. Indeed, one of the reasons for the secular decline in the expense ratio has been the switch in the way PC insurance has been distributed. Specifically, rather than relying on independent brokers to sell policies (the American agency method of distribution), large insurance companies are increasingly selling insurance to the public directly through their own brokers (the direct writer method of distribution). A number of researchers[10] have found that the costs of the American agency distribution system are much higher than those of the direct writer distribution system.

A common measure of the overall underwriting profitability of a line, which includes both loss and expense experience, is the **combined ratio.** Technically, the combined ratio is equal to the loss ratio plus the ratios of LAE to premiums earned, commissions, and other acquisition costs and general expense costs to premiums written, minus any dividends paid to policyholders as a proportion of premiums earned. The combined ratio after dividends adds any dividends paid to policyholders as a proportion of premiums earned to the combined ratio. If the combined ratio is less than 100, premiums alone are sufficient to cover both losses and expenses related to the line.

If premiums are insufficient and the combined ratio exceeds 100, the PC insurer must rely on investment income on premiums for overall profitability. For example, in 1996 the combined ratio before dividend payments was 105.9, indicating that premiums alone were insufficient to cover the costs of both losses and expenses related to writing PC insurance. Table 2–7 presents the combined ratio and its components for the PC industry for the year 1951–96. We see that the trend over this period is toward decreased profitability. The industry's premiums generally covered losses and expenses until the 1980s. Since then premiums have been unable to cover losses and expenses (i.e., combined ratios have been consistently greater than 100).

Combined Ratio
Measures the overall underwriting profitability of a line and is equal to the loss ratio plus the ratios of loss adjustment expenses to premiums earned and commission and other acquisition costs to premiums written minus any dividends paid to policyholders as a proportion of premiums earned.

[9]Note that the loss adjustment expense component of total expenses has been added to losses incurred in Table 2–7 to calculate the loss ratio.

[10]See, for example, N. D. Chidambaran, T. A. Pugel, and A. Saunders, "An Investigation of the Performance of the U.S. Property-Casualty Insurance Industry," *Journal of Risk and Insurance* 64 (June 1997), pp. 371–82; and J. D. Cummins and J. Van Derhei, "A Note on the Relative Efficiency of Property-Liability Insurance Distribution Systems," *Bell Journal of Economics* (Autumn 1979), pp. 709–19.

TABLE 2–7   Industry Underwriting Ratios

Year	Loss Ratio*	Expense Ratio†	Combined Ratio	Dividends to Policyholders‡	Combined Ratio after Dividends
1951	60.3	34.0	94.3	2.6	96.9
1952	59.0	33.2	92.2	2.4	94.6
1953	57.9	32.9	90.9	2.6	93.4
1954	57.5	33.7	91.2	2.7	93.9
1955	58.9	33.9	92.9	2.7	95.6
1956	63.8	34.2	98.0	2.7	100.7
1957	66.1	33.7	99.8	2.4	102.3
1958	64.0	33.3	97.3	2.3	99.6
1959	63.0	32.5	95.5	2.2	97.7
1960	63.8	32.2	96.0	2.2	98.1
1961	64.2	32.3	96.5	2.1	98.6
1962	65.1	32.1	97.2	1.9	99.0
1963	67.7	32.2	99.9	2.1	102.0
1964	69.5	31.5	101.0	2.0	103.0
1965	70.3	30.4	100.7	1.9	102.6
1966	67.5	29.6	97.1	1.9	99.0
1967	68.7	29.5	98.2	2.0	100.2
1968	70.4	29.1	99.5	2.0	101.5
1969	72.2	28.4	100.6	1.9	102.5
1970	70.8	27.6	98.4	1.7	100.1
1971	67.5	27.2	94.7	1.7	96.4
1972	66.6	27.7	94.3	1.9	96.2
1973	69.3	28.0	97.3	1.9	99.2
1974	75.5	28.2	103.7	1.7	105.4
1975	79.3	27.3	106.6	1.3	107.9
1976	75.4	25.9	101.3	1.1	102.4
1977	70.7	25.3	96.0	1.2	97.2
1978	70.1	25.8	95.9	1.6	97.5
1979	73.1	26.0	99.1	1.5	100.6
1980	74.9	26.5	101.4	1.7	103.1
1981	76.8	27.4	104.1	1.9	106.0
1982	79.8	27.9	107.7	1.9	109.6
1983	81.5	28.4	109.9	2.1	112.0
1984	88.2	27.9	116.1	1.8	118.0
1985	88.7	25.9	114.6	1.6	116.3
1986	81.6	25.1	106.7	1.3	108.0
1987	77.9	25.3	103.3	1.3	104.6
1988	78.3	25.7	104.0	1.4	105.4
1989	82.0	26.0	107.9	1.3	109.2
1990	82.3	26.0	108.3	1.2	109.6
1991	81.1	26.4	107.6	1.3	108.8
1992	88.1	26.5	114.6	1.2	115.7
1993	79.5	26.2	105.7	1.1	106.9
1994	81.1	26.0	107.1	1.3	108.4
1995	78.8	26.2	105.0	1.4	106.4
1996	79.7	26.2	105.9	1.1	107.0

*Losses and adjustment expenses incurred to premiums earned.

†Expenses incurred (before federal income taxes) to premiums written.

‡Dividends to policyholders to premiums earned.

Source: Reprinted with permission from *A. M. Best's Aggregates and Averages,* Property-Casualty, 1994, p. 158; and *Best's Review,* May 1997.

Operating Ratio
A measure of the overall profitability of a PC insurer; it equals the combined ratio minus the investment yield.

Investment Yield/Return Risk. As discussed above, when the combined ratio is more than 100, overall profitability can be ensured only by a sufficient investment return on premiums earned. That is, PC firms invest premiums in assets between the time they are received and the time they are paid out to meet claims. For example, in 1996 net investment income to premiums earned (or the PC insurers' investment yield) was 10 percent. As a result, the overall average profitability (or **operating ratio**) of PC insurers was 97. It was equal to the combined ratio after dividends (107) minus the investment yield (10). Since the operating ratio was less than 100, PC insurers were profitable in 1996. However, lower net returns on investments (e.g., 6 percent rather than 10 percent) would have meant that underwriting PC insurance was marginally unprofitable (i.e., the operating ratio of insurers in this case would have been 101.). Thus, the effect of interest rates and default rates on PC insurers' investments is crucial to PC insurers' overall profitability. That is, measuring and managing credit and interest rate risk are key concerns of PC managers.

Consider the following example. Suppose an insurance company's projected loss ratio is 79.8 percent, its expense ratio is 27.9 percent, and it pays 2 percent of its premiums earned to policyholders as dividends. The combined ratio (after dividends) for this insurance company is equal to

$$\underset{79.8}{\text{Loss ratio}} + \underset{27.9}{\text{Expense ratio}} + \underset{2.0}{\text{Dividend ratio}} = \underset{109.7}{\text{Combined ratio after dividends}}$$

Thus, expected losses on all PC lines, expenses, and dividends exceeded premiums earned by 9.7 percent.

If the company's investment portfolio, however, yielded 12 percent, the operating ratio and overall profitability of the PC insurer would be, respectively,

$$
\begin{aligned}
\text{Operating ratio} &= \text{Combined ratio after dividends} - \text{Investment yield} \\
&= \qquad\qquad 109.7 \qquad\qquad\qquad - \qquad 12.0 \\
&= \qquad\qquad 97.7 \text{ percent}
\end{aligned}
$$

and

$$
\begin{aligned}
\text{Overall profitability} &= 100 - \text{Operating ratio} \\
&= 100 - 97.7 \\
&= 2.3 \text{ percent}
\end{aligned}
$$

Given the importance of investment returns to PC insurers' profitability, we can see from the balance sheet in Table 2–6 that bonds—both Treasury and corporate—dominated the asset portfolios of PC insurers. Bonds comprised 60.7 percent of total assets and 69.4 percent of financial assets (so-called unaffiliated investments) in 1996.

Finally, if losses, expenses, and other costs are higher and investment yields are lower than expected so that operating losses are incurred, PC insurers carry a significant amount of surplus reserves (policyholder surplus) to reduce the risk of insolvency. In 1996, the ratio of policyholder surplus to assets was 31.9 percent.

Recent Trends. The period 1987–96 was not very profitable for the PC industry. In particular, the combined ratio (the measure of loss plus expense risk) increased from 104.6 in 1987 to 115.7 in 1992 (see Table 2–7). The major reason for this rise was a succession of catastrophes from Hurricane Hugo in 1989, the San Francisco earthquake in 1991, the Oakland fires of 1991, and the more than $15 billion in losses

Underwriting Cycle
The tendency of profits in the PC industry to follow a cyclical pattern.

incurred in Florida as a result of Hurricane Andrew in 1991. In the terminology of PC insurers, the industry was in the trough of an **underwriting cycle,** or underwriting conditions were hard. As an example of how bad things were in this industry, after 20 years of profits, Lloyd's of London (arguably one of the world's most well known and respected insurers) posted a £510 million loss in 1991.[11]

In 1993 the industry showed signs of improvement, with the combined ratio falling to 106.9. However, in 1994 that ratio rose again to 108.4 partly as a result of the Northridge earthquake with estimated losses of $7 billion to $10 billion. The industry ratio fell back down to 104.8 in 1996. Despite the $7.35 billion in catastrophe costs incurred, 1996 was considered a good year. While catastrophes should be random, the period 1984–96 was characterized by a number of catastrophes of historically high severity. This is shown in Figure 2–4.

The traditional reaction to losses or poor profit results has been the exit from the industry—through failure or acquisition—of less profitable firms and a rapid increase in premiums among the remaining firms. Historically, this has resulted in a fall in the combined ratio as premiums rise and an improvement occurs in the operating ratio and PC industry profitability. In the late 1990s, the PC industry was in a phase of firm exit and consolidation consistent with the initial upward phase of the profitability cycle. As the underwriting profitability cycle approaches its peak, however, new entrants to the industry tend to emerge. These new entrants compete by cutting premiums and lowering underwriting quality standards, thus setting the stage for a downturn in the cycle again. On average, underwriting cycles measured from peak to peak can last anywhere from 6 to 10 years.

Regulation

As with life insurance companies, PC insurers are chartered by states and regulated by state commissions. In addition, state guaranty funds provide some protection to policyholders if an insurance company fails. The National Association of Insurance Commissioners (NAIC) also provides various services to state regulatory commissions. These services include a standardized examination system called IRIS (Insurance Regulatory Information System) to identify insurers with loss, combined, and other ratios outside the normal ranges.

An additional burden that PC insurers face in some activity lines—especially auto insurance and workers' compensation insurance—is rate regulation. That is, given the public utility nature of some insurance lines, state commissioners set ceilings on premiums and premium increases, usually based on specific cost of capital and line risk exposure formulas for the insurance suppliers. This had led to some insurers leaving states such as New Jersey, Florida, and California, which have the most restrictive regulations.[12]

Concept Questions

1. Why do PC insurers hold more capital and reserves than do life insurers?

---

[11]As explained by Lloyd's management, the loss was a result of four years of unprecedented disaster claims. As a result of their losses, a group of Lloyd's investors sued the company for negligence in their business operations (some of these cases are still working their way through the legal system in the late 1990s).

[12]J. A. Fields, C. Ghosh, and L. S. Klein, "From Competition to Regulation: The Six-Year Battle to Regulate California's Insurance Markets," Working Paper, University of Connecticut, March 1996.

FIGURE 2–4

U.S. Catastrophes, 1949–1996, Adjusted for Inflation (I.A.)

Catastrophe	Year	I.A. Amount* U.S. $(millions)
Hurricane Andrew	1992	15,900
Northridge earthquake	1994	7,200
Hurricane Hugo	1989	4,939
Hurricane Betsy	1965	2,346
Hurricane Opal	1995	2,100
Blizzard of 1996	1996	2,000
Hurricane Iniki	1992	1,646
Blizzard of 1993	1993	1,625
Hurricane Fran	1995	1,600
Hurricane Frederic	1979	1,575
Wind, hail, tornadoes	1974	1,395
Freeze	1983	1,280
Oakland fire	1991	1,273
Hurricane Cecelia	1970	1,169
Wind	1950	1,136
California earthquake	1989	1,130
Texas hailstorm	1995	1,100
Hurricane Alicia	1983	983
L.A. riots	1992	797

Mean = $90,929,977
1,163 catastrophes
Average 25.3 catastrophes per year
Average 6.3 catastrophes per quarter

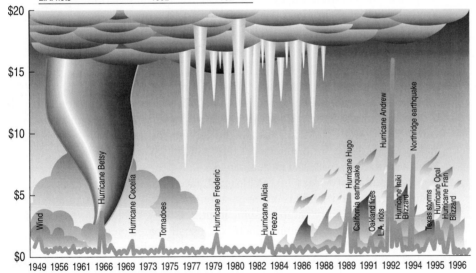

Source: Richard L. Sandor, Centre Financial Products, 1949–1994; author's research, 1995–1996.

2. Why are life insurers' assets, on average, longer in maturity than those of PC insurers?

3. Describe the main lines of insurance offered by PC insurers.

4. What are the components of the combined ratio?

5. How does the operating ratio differ from the combined ratio?

6. Why does the combined ratio tend to behave cyclically?

Summary

This chapter examined the activities and regulation of insurance companies. The first part of the chapter described the various classes of life insurance and recent trends. The second part covered property-casualty companies. The various lines that comprise property-casualty insurance are becoming increasingly blurred as multiple activity line coverages are offered. Both life and property-casualty insurance companies are regulated at the state rather than the federal level. In addition, both are coming under threat from other financial service firms that offer similar or competitive products.

Questions and Problems

1. What is the primary function of an insurance company? How does this function compare with the primary function of a depository institution?

2. Contrast the balance sheet of a life insurance company with the balance sheet of a commercial bank and that of a savings and loan association. Explain the balance sheet differences in terms of the differences in the primary functions of the three organizations.

3. How has the composition of assets of U.S. life insurance companies changed over time?

4. What are the similarities and differences among the four basic lines of life insurance products?

5. How do life insurance companies earn a profit? How does investment in junk bonds increase their returns, and what are the drawbacks?

6. Explain how annuity activities represent the reverse of life insurance activities.

7. Explain how life insurance and annuity products can be used to create a steady stream of cash disbursements and payments to avoid paying or receiving a single lump-sum cash amount.

8. *a.* Calculate the annual cash flows of a $1 million, 20-year fixed-payment annuity earning a guaranteed 10 percent per annum if payments are to begin at the end of the current year.

    b. Calculate the annual cash flows of a $1 million, 20-year fixed-payment annuity earning a guaranteed 10 percent per annum if payments are to begin at the end of year 5.

    c. What is the amount of the annuity purchase required if you wish to receive a fixed payment of $200,000 for 20 years? Assume that the annuity will earn 10 percent per annum.

9. You deposit $10,000 annually into a life insurance fund for the next 10 years, after which time you plan to retire.

    a. If the deposits are made at the beginning of the year and earn an interest rate of 8 percent, what will be the amount of retirement funds at the end of year 10?

    b. Instead of a lump sum, you wish to receive annuities for the next 20 years (years 11 through 30). What is

the constant annual payment you expect to receive at the beginning of each year if you assume an interest rate of 8 percent during the distribution period?

   c. Repeat parts *(a)* and *(b)* above assuming earning rates of 7 percent and 9 percent during the deposit period and earning rates of 7 percent and 9 percent during the distribution period. During which period does the change in the earning rate have the greatest impact?

10. *a.* Suppose a 65-year-old person wants to purchase an annuity from an insurance company that would pay $20,000 per year until the end of that person's life. The insurance company expects this person to live for 15 more years and would be willing to pay 6 percent on the annuity. How much should the insurance company ask this person to pay for the annuity?

    b. A second 65-year-old person wants the same $20,000 annuity, but this person is much healthier and is expected to live for 20 years. If the same 6 percent interest rate applies, how much should this healthier person be charged for the annuity?

    c. In each case, what is the difference in the purchase price of the annuity if the distribution payments are made at the beginning of the year?

11. How would the balance sheet of a life insurance company change if it offered to run a private pension fund for another company?

12. How does the regulation of insurance companies differ from the regulation of depository institutions? What are the major pieces of life insurance regulatory legislation?

13. How have the product lines, which are based on net premiums, changed over time?

14. Contrast the balance sheet of a property-casualty insurance company with the balance sheet of a commercial bank. Explain the balance sheet differences in terms of the differences in the primary functions of the two organizations.

15. What are the two major activity lines of property-casualty insurance firms?

16. What are the three sources of underwriting risk in the property-casualty insurance industry?

17. How do increases in unexpected inflation affect property-casualty insurers?

18. Identify the four characteristics or features of the perils insured against by property-casualty insurance. Rank the features in terms of actuarial predictability and total loss potential.

19. Insurance companies will charge a higher premium for which of the insurance lines listed below? Why?

    a. Low-severity, high-frequency lines versus high-severity, low-frequency lines.

    b. Long-tail lines versus short-tail lines?

20. What does the loss ratio measure? What has been the long-term trend of the loss ratio? Why?

21. What does the expense ratio measure? Identify and explain the two major sources of expense risk to a property-casualty insurer. Why has the long-term trend in this ratio been decreasing?

22. How is the combined ratio defined? What does it measure?

23. What is the investment yield on premiums earned? Why has this ratio become so important to property-casualty insurers?

24. Since 1981, what has been the necessary investment yield for the industry to enable the operating ratio to be less than 100 in each year? How is this requirement related to the interest rate risk and credit risk faced by a property-casualty insurer?

25. An insurance company's projected loss ratio is 77.5 percent, and its loss adjustment expense ratio is 12.9 percent. The company estimates that commission payments and dividends to policyholders will be 16 percent. What must be the minimum yield on investments to achieve a positive operating ratio?

26. *a.* What is the combined ratio for a property insurer who has a simple loss ratio of 73 percent, a loss adjustment expense of 12.5 percent, and a ratio of commissions and other acquisition expenses of 18 percent?

    b. What is the combined ratio adjusted for investment yield if the company earns an investment yield of 8 percent?

27. An insurance company collected $3.6 million in premiums and disbursed $1.96 million in losses. Loss adjustment expenses amounted to 6.6 percent, and dividends paid to policyholders totaled 1.2 percent. The total income generated from the company's investments was $170,000 after all expenses were paid. What is the net profitability in dollars?

CHAPTER 3

THE FINANCIAL SERVICES INDUSTRY

Securities Firms and Investment Banks

Chapter Outline

Introduction

Securities firms and investment banks underwrite securities and engage in related activities such as trading, market making, and advising (e.g., on mergers and acquisitions). While the largest companies in this industry provide multiple services, many firms concentrate their services in only one area, either securities dealing, trading, or securities underwriting. Specifically, securities firms specialize primarily in the purchase, sale, and brokerage of securities (i.e., more on the retail side of the business), while investment banks primarily engage in originating, underwriting, and distributing issues of securities (i.e., more on the wholesale side of the business). They also undertake corporate finance activities such as advising on mergers, acquisitions, and corporate restructuring. Figure 3–1 highlights the booming nature of this line of business. Total volume of domestic mergers and acquisitions grew from under $200 billion in 1990 to $919 billion in 1997 and to $910 billion by the first half of 1998. This merger wave has not been restricted to the United States. For example, in the first six months of 1998 there were over 10,400 merger and acquisition (M and A) deals globally, with Goldman Sachs advising on 160 transactions with a market value of $549 billion. In 1998, important M and A deals included Daimler-Benz's acquisition of Chrysler and SBC Communications' acquistion of Ameritech, indicating a worldwide trend toward consolidation to exploit the benefits of scale and size.

In this chapter we present an overview of (1) the size, structure, and composition of the industry, (2) the balance sheet and recent trends, and (3) the regulation of the industry.

FIGURE 3–1

Attracting Partners

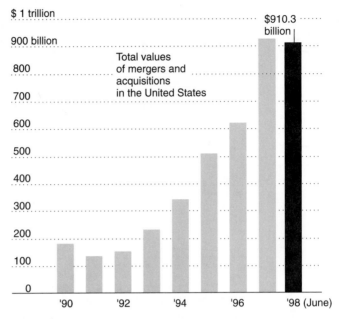

Source: *New York Times,* June 26, 1998, p. D1. Copyright © 1998 by The New York Times. Reprinted by permission.

Size, Structure, and Composition of the Industry

Beginning in 1980 and extending up to the stock market crash of October 19, 1987, the number of firms in the industry expanded dramatically from 5,248 to 9,515. The aftermath of the crash saw a major shakeout, with the number of firms declining to 7,776 by 1996, a decline of 18 percent since 1987. Concentration of business among the largest firms over this period has increased dramatically. The largest investment bank in 1987, Salomon Brothers, held capital of $3.21 billion. By 1997 the largest investment bank, Merrill Lynch, held capital of $33 billion. Some of the significant growth in size has come through M and A by the top-ranked firms. Table 3–1 lists major U.S. securities industry M and A transactions, many of which involve repeated ownership changes of the same company. Notice from this table that six major mergers occurred in 1997 and 1998. Notice too how many recent mergers and acquisitions have been interindustry mergers (i.e., insurance companies and investment banks). Recent regulatory changes (discussed below and described in detail in Chapter 21) are the cause for such mergers.

The firms in the industry can be divided along a number of dimensions. First are the largest firms, the so-called national full-line firms, which service both retail customers (especially in acting as **broker-dealers,** thus assisting in the trading of existing securities) and corporate customers (such as **underwriting,** thus assisting in the issue of new securities). The major (ranked by capital) national full-line firms are Merrill Lynch and Morgan Stanley/Dean Witter Discover. In 1997 Morgan Stanley, ranked sixth in size of capital, and Dean Witter Discover, ranked fifth in capital size, merged to create one of the largest investment banks in the world. Second are the national full-line firms that specialize more in corporate finance and are highly active in trading securities. Examples are Goldman Sachs and Salomon Brothers/Smith Barney, the investment banking arm of Citigroup (created from the merger of Travelers and Citicorp in 1998). Third, the rest of the industry comprises:

Broker-Dealers
Assist in the trading of existing securities.

Underwriting
Assisting in the issue of new securities.

TABLE 3–1   **Major U.S. Securities Industry Merger and Acquisition Transactions**

Rank	Deal	Price in billions*	Year
1.	Citicorp mergers with Travelers (who owns Smith Barney and Salomon)	$83.0	1998
2.	Dean Witter merges with Morgan Stanley	10.2	1997
3.	Travelers acquires Salomon Inc.	9.0	1997
4.	Sears spins off Dean Witter, Discover	5.0	1993
5.	Mellon Bank acquires Dreyfus	1.8	1993
6.	American Express spins off Lehman Bros. Holdings	1.6	1994
7.	Fleet Financial acquires Quick and Reilly	1.6	1997
8.	Primerica acquires Shearson	1.2	1993
9.	NationsBank acquires Montgomery Securities	1.2	1997
10.	Credit Suisse acquires First Boston	1.1	1988
11.	Shearson Lehman acquires E.F. Hutton	1.0	1987
12.	American Express acquires Shearson	0.9	1981
13.	Primerica acquires Smith Barney	0.8	1987
14.	Paine Webber acquires Kidder Peabody	0.7	1994
15.	U.S. Bancorp acquires Piper Jaffray	0.7	1997
16.	ING Group acquires Furman Selz	0.6	1997
17.	Societe Generale acquires Cowen and Co.	0.6	1998
18.	BankBoston acquires Robertson Stephens	0.6	1998

*Value of Dean Witter, Discover shares to be exchanged for Morgan Stanley stock, based on closing price of $40.625 on February 5, 1997.

Source: Securities Data Company and *The Wall Street Journal,* author's figures.

1. Specialized investment bank subsidiaries of commercial bank holding companies (such as J.P. Morgan).[1]

Discount Broker
A stockbroker that conducts trades for customers but does not offer investment advice.

2. Specialized **discount brokers** that effect trades for customers without offering investment advice or tips (such as Charles Schwab).[2]

3. Regional securities firms that are often subdivided into large, medium, and small categories and concentrate on servicing customers in a particular region, such as New York or California.

Next we discuss the seven key activity areas for securities firms.[3]

1. Investing.   Investing involves not only managing pools of assets such as closed- and open-ended mutual funds but also managing pension funds in competition with life insurance companies. Securities firms can manage such funds either as agents for other investors or as principals for themselves. The objective in funds management is to choose asset allocations to beat some return-risk performance benchmark.[4] Since this business generates fees that are based on the size of the pool of assets managed, it tends to produce a more stable flow of income than does either investment banking or trading (discussed next).

---

[1]These so-called Section 20 subsidiaries are discussed in more detail in Chapter 21. Since 1987 bank holding companies have been allowed to establish special investment bank subsidiaries (so-called Section 20 subsidiaries) that can underwrite corporate debt and equity, subject to a number of restrictions. Most importantly, the gross revenue earned from underwriting corporate securities is currently capped at 25 percent of the total gross revenues earned by Section 20 subsidiary.

[2]Discount brokers usually charge lower commissions than do full-service brokers such as Merrill Lynch.

[3]See Ernest Bloch, *Inside Investment Banking,* 2d ed. (Chicago: Irwin, 1989), for a similar list.

[4]Such as the "securities market line" given the fund's "beta."

TABLE 3–2   Top Underwriters of U.S. Debt and Equity

Manager	Full Year 1997		Full Year 1996		
	Amount in Billions	Market Share	Amount in Billions	Rank	Market Share
Merrill Lynch	$ 208.1	16.1%	$155.2	1	16.0%
Salomon Smith Barney	167.0	12.9	126.1	2	13.0
Morgan Stanley Dean Witter	139.5	10.8	91.1	5	9.4
Goldman, Sachs	137.3	10.6	99.1	4	10.2
Lehman Brothers	121.0	9.4	102.3	3	10.6
J.P. Morgan	104.0	8.0	69.0	6	7.1
Credit Suisse First Boston	67.7	5.2	61.3	7	6.3
Bear, Stearns	57.5	4.4	45.7	8	4.7
Donaldson, Lufkin & Jenrette	46.0	3.6	37.3	9	3.9
Chase Manhattan	33.1	2.6	17.7	11	1.8
Top 10	$1,081.3	83.6%	$804.7	—	83.2%
Industry Total	$1,293.0	100.0%	$967.6	—	100.0%

Source: Reprinted with permission of Securities Data Company.

IPO
An initial or first-time public offering of debt or equity by a corporation.

Private Placement
A securities issue placed with one or a few large institutional investors.

2. Investment Banking. Investment banking refers to activities related to underwriting and distributing new issues of debt and equity. New issues can be either primary, the first-time issues of companies (sometimes called **IPOs** (initial public offerings)), or secondary issues (the new issues of seasoned firms whose debt or equity is already trading). Table 3–2 lists the top 10 underwriters of U.S. debt and equity for 1997. The top 10 common underwriters represented 83.6 percent of the industry total, suggesting that the industry is dominated by a handful of "top tier" underwriting firms.

Securities underwritings can be undertaken through either public offerings or private offerings. In a private offering, the investment banker acts as a **private placement** agent for a fee, placing the securities with one or a few large institutional investors such as life insurance companies.[5] In a public offering, the securities may be underwritten on a best-efforts or a firm commitment basis, and the securities may be offered to the public at large. With best-efforts underwriting, investment bankers act as *agents* on a fee basis related to their success in placing the issue. In firm commitment underwriting, the investment banker acts as a *principal,* purchasing the securities from the issuer at one price and seeking to place them with public investors at a slightly higher price. Finally, in addition to investment banking operations in the corporate securities markets, the investment banker may participate as an underwriter (primary dealer) in government, municipal, and asset-backed securities. Table 3–3 shows the top ranked underwriters for 1997 in the different areas of securities underwriting. Table 3–4 shows the rapid growth in all areas of underwriting activity over the 1992–97 period.

3. Market Making. Market making involves creating a secondary market in an asset. Thus, in addition to being primary dealers in government securities and underwriters of corporate bonds and equities, investment bankers make a secondary

[5]See *Federal Reserve Bulletin,* February 1993, for an excellent description of the private placement market. Issuers of privately placed securities do not have to register with the SEC since the placements are made only to large, sophisticated investors.

TABLE 3–3   Who's Number 1 in Each Market

Type	Full Year 1997		Full Year 1996	
	Amount in Billions	*Top-Ranked Manager*	*Amount in Billions*	*Top-Ranked Manager*
U.S. domestic	$1,293.0	Merrill Lynch	$967.6	Merrill Lynch
Straight debt	741.1	Merrill Lynch	544.7	Merrill Lynch
Convertible debt	8.4	Goldman, Sachs	9.3	Merrill Lynch
Junk bonds*	103.5	DLJ	39.4	DLJ
Investment grade debt	460.5	Merrill Lynch	307.5	Merrill Lynch
Mortgage debt	194.6	Salomon S.B.	100.9	Lehman Brothers
Collateralized securities	183.4	Merrill Lynch	151.3	Merrill Lynch
Preferred stock	33.6	Merrill Lynch	37.2	Merrill Lynch
Common stock	117.6	Merrill Lynch	115.2	Goldman, Sachs
IPOs	43.1	Goldman, Sachs	49.8	Goldman, Sachs
International debt	474.9	Merrill Lynch	422.9	Merrill Lynch
International equity	21.3	Merrill Lynch	35.6	Goldman, Sachs
U.S. issuers	1,308.1	Merrill Lynch	951.1	Merrill Lynch
Municipal new issues	214.6	Salomon S.B.	181.7	Goldman, Sachs

*Includes Rule 144a issues; excludes split-rated issues.

Source: Reprinted with permission of Securities Data Company.

TABLE 3–4   Capital Market Activity, 1992–1997
(in billions of dollars)

	1997	1996	1995	1994	1993	1992
U.S. Domestic New Issues						
U.S. MTNs*	284.7	255.3	404.9	282.8	260.3	169.4
Investment grade debt	726.1	518.9	417.3	342.5	389.2	281.1
Collateralized securities	378.0	252.3	154.1	252.5	478.9	428.2
Junk and convertibles	174.8	121.4	30.2	36.4	69.5	53.7
Muncipal debt	214.8	181.7	154.9	161.3	287.8	231.7
Total debt	1,778.4	1,329.6	1,161.4	1,075.5	1,485.7	1,164.1
Preferred stock	59.2	45.6	16.3	15.5	22.4	20.9
Common stock	118.5	115.4	81.7	61.6	101.7	72.4
Total equity	177.7	161.0	98.0	77.1	124.1	93.3
Total domestic	1,956.1	1,490.6	1,259.4	1,152.5	1,609.8	1,257.4
International Issues						
Euro MTNs*	407.2	392.6	251.6	257.2	149.8	96.9
Euro and foreign bonds	635.2	537.4	385.1	485.2	482.7	335.9
International equity	54.8	51.0	32.1	32.4	27.7	17.8
Total international	1,097.2	971.0	743.6	774.8	660.2	450.6
"Worldwide" total	3,053.3	2,471.6	2,003.0	1,927.3	2,270.0	1,708.0
Global Syndicated Bank						
Loans and NIFS†	1,265.8	1,400	1,098	785.6	555.4	403.0

*MTNs = Medium-Term Notes
†NIFS = Note Issuance Facilities.

Source: Roy Smith, New York University.

market in these instruments. Market making can involve either agency or principal transactions. *Agency* transactions are two-way transactions on behalf of *customers,* for example, acting as a *stockbroker* or dealer for a fee or commission. In *principal* transactions, the market maker seeks to profit on the price movements of securities and takes either long or short inventory positions for its own account. (Or an inventory position may be taken to stabilize the market in the securities.[6]) Normally, market making can be a fairly profitable business; however, in periods of market stress or high volatility, these profits can rapidly disappear. For example, on the NYSE market makers, in return for having monopoly power in market making for individual stocks (e.g., IBM), have an "affirmative obligation" to buy stocks from sellers even when the market is crashing. This caused a number of actual and near bankruptcies for NYSE market makers at the time of the October 1987 market crash. On NASDAQ, which has a system of competing market makers, liquidity was significantly impaired at the time of the crash and a number of firms had to withdraw from market making.[7]

4. Trading.   Trading is closely related to the market-making activities just described, where a trader takes an active net position in an underlying instrument or asset. There are at least four types of trading activities:

1. *Position trading* involves purchases of large blocks of securities to facilitate smooth functioning of the secondary markets in such securities.
2. *Pure arbitrage* entails buying an asset in one market at one price and selling it immediately in another market at a higher price.
3. *Risk arbitrage* involves buying blocks of securities in anticipation of some information release, such as a merger or takeover announcement or a Federal Reserve interest rate announcement.[8]
4. *Program trading* is associated with seeking a risk arbitrage between a cash market price (e.g., the Standard & Poor's 500 Stock Market Index) and the *futures* market price of that instrument, often with the aid of high-powered computers.[9]

As with many activities of securities firms, such trading can be conducted on behalf of a customer as an agent or on behalf of the firm as a principal. Many brokers are also starting to offer on-line trading services to their customers. Thus, customers may now conduct trading activities from their homes and offices.

Cash Management Account
Money market mutual fund sold by investment banks that offer check-writing privileges.

5. Cash Management.   Investment banks offer bank deposit–like **cash management accounts** (CMAs) to individual investors. Most of these accounts allow customers to write checks against some type of mutual fund account (e.g., money market mutual fund). These accounts, when issued in association with commercial banks and thrifts, can even be covered by federal deposit insurance from the FDIC. CMAs have been instrumental in the securities industry's efforts to provide commercial banking services.

---

[6]In general, full-service investment banks can become market makers in stocks on NASDAQ, but they have been prevented until recently, from acting as market-making specialists on the NYSE.

[7]See, for example, W. A. Christie and P. H. Schultz, "Dealer Markets under Stress: The Performance of NASDAQ Market Makers during the November 15, 1991, Market Break," *Journal of Financial Services Research* 13 (June 1998), pp. 205–30.

[8]It is termed *risk arbitrage* because if the event does not actually occur—for example, if a merger does not take place or the Federal Reserve does not change interest rates—the trader stands to lose money.

[9]An example would be buying the cash S&P index and selling futures contracts on the S&P index. Since stocks and futures contracts trade in different markets, their prices are not always equal. Moreover, program trading can occur between futures and cash markets in other assets, for example, commodities.

6. Mergers and Acquisitions.   Investment banks are frequently involved in providing advice or assisting in mergers and acquisitions. For example, they will assist in finding merger partners, underwriting new securities to be issued by the merged firms, assessing the value of target firms, recommending terms of the merger agreement, and even helping target firms prevent a merger (for example, poison-pill provisions written into a potential target firm's securities contracts). As noted in the introduction to this chapter, there is currently a global wave of M and A activity that is generating large profits for firms such as Goldman Sachs and Merrill Lynch.[10]

7. Back-Office and Other Service Functions.   These functions include custody and escrow services, clearance and settlement services, and research and other advisory services. In performing these functions, a securities firm normally acts as an agent for a fee.

Concept Questions

1. Describe the difference between brokerage services and underwriting services.
2. What are the key areas of activities for securities firms?
3. Describe the difference between a best-efforts offering and a firm commitment offering.
4. What are the four trading activities performed by securities firms?

Balance Sheet and Recent Trends

A major effect of the 1987 stock market crash was a sharp decline in stock market trading volume and thus in brokerage commissions earned by securities firms over the 1987–91 period. Commission income began to recover only after 1992, with record equity trading volumes being achieved in 1995–99 when the Dow Jones and S&P indexes hit new highs. However, the decline in brokerage commissions actually began over 20 years ago in 1977 and is reflective of an overall long-term fall in the importance of commission income, as a percentage of revenues, for securities firms as a result of the abolition of fixed commissions on securities trades by the Securities and Exchange Commission (SEC) in May 1975 and the fierce competition for wholesale commissions and trades that followed (see Figure 3–2).

Also affecting the profitability of the securities industry was the decline in new equity issues over the 1987–91 period and a decline in bond and equity underwriting in general. This was partly a result of the stock market crash, partly due to a decline in mergers and acquisitions, partly due to a general economic recession, and partly due to investor concerns about junk bonds after the Michael Milken/Ivan Boesky–Drexel Burnham Lambert scandal, which resulted in that firm's failure.

Between 1992 and 1997, however, the securities industry showed a resurgence in profitability.[11] The two principal reasons for this (other than the resurgence of stock market volumes and record M and A activity) were enhanced fixed-income

---

[10]Often, in addition to providing M and A advisory services, an investment banker will be involved in underwriting new securities that help finance an M and A. See L. Allen, J. Jagtiani, and A. Saunders, "The Role of Financial Advisors in Mergers and Acquisitions," unpublished working paper, New York University, 1998.

[11]Pretax return on equity for broker–dealers rose from 2.2 percent in 1990 to 22, 26.7, and 29.1 percent in 1992, 1993, and 1996, respectively.

FIGURE 3–2

*Commission Income as
a Percentage of Total
Revenues*

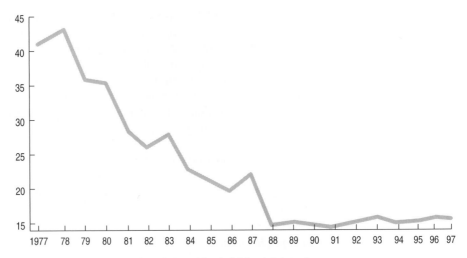

Sources: Securities and Exchange Commission and Standard & Poor's *Industry Surveys.*

trading profits and increased growth in new issue underwritings. Between 1987 and 1997 securities firms in the aggregate nearly tripled their holdings of fixed-income securities (corporate, foreign, mortgage-backed, and Treasury bonds) in a successful strategic move to enhance trading profits. However, a heavy reliance on fixed-income trading can produce losses if interest rates (and other asset prices) move in an unexpected direction. For example, Merrill Lynch, Goldman Sachs and a number of other securities firms announced large trading losses on their Russian bond trading activities in 1998. Thus, interest rate risk and sovereign risk are now focal areas of investment bank risk exposure.

The growth in underwriting activity over the 1992–97 period is evident from the fact that the total dollar value of domestic underwriting activity grew from $1,257 billion in 1992 to $1,956 billion in 1997 (see Table 3–4).

Despite the resurgence in the underwriting business, the 1990s presented a new challenge for traditional underwriters. Specifically, in 1987 the Federal Reserve allowed bank holding companies to expand their activities in securities underwriting (activities that were prohibited since the Glass-Steagall Act was passed in 1933). By 1997, the special investment bank subsidiaries (so-called Section 20 subsidiaries) of commercial banks had captured over 20 percent of the corporate debt underwriting market and two of these subsidiaries, those of J. P. Morgan and Chase, were among the top ten underwriters of domestic equity and debt (see Table 3–2).

Note the current importance of securities trading and underwriting in the consolidated balance sheet of all securities firms in Table 3–5. Looking at the asset portfolio, long positions in securities and commodities accounted for 26.6 percent of assets, while reverse repurchase agreements—securities purchased under agreements to resell (i.e., the broker gives a short-term loan to the repurchase agreement seller)—accounted for 35.8 percent of assets.

With respect to liabilities, repurchase agreements were the major source of funds; these are securities temporarily lent in exchange for cash received. Repurchase agreements—securities sold under agreements to repurchase—amounted to 47.7 percent of total liabilities and equity. The other major sources of funds were securities and commodities sold short for future delivery and broker-call loans from banks. Equity capital amounted to only 3.8 percent of total assets, while total capital

Questions and Problems

1. Explain how securities firms differ from investment banks. In what ways are they financial intermediaries?

2. In what ways have changes in the investment banking industry mirrored changes in the commerical banking industry?

3. How do the operating activities, and thus the balance sheet structures, of securities firms differ from the operating activities of depository institutions such as commercial banks and insurance firms? How are the balance sheet structures of securities firms similar to those of other financial intermediaries?

4. What are the different types of firms in the securities industry, and how does each type differ from the others?

5. What are the seven key activity areas for securities firms? How does each activity area assist in the generation of profits, and what are the major risks for each area?

6. One of the major activity areas of securities firms is trading.
   a. What is the difference between pure arbitrage and risk arbitrage?
   b. What is the difference between position trading and program trading?

7. If an investor observes that the price of a stock trading in one exchange is different from the price in another exchange, what form of arbitrage is applicable, and how can the investor participate in that arbitrage?

8. An investor notices that an ounce of gold is priced at $318 in London and $325 in New York.
   a. What action could the investor take to try to profit from the price discrepancy?
   b. Under which of the four trading activities would this action be classified?
   c. If the investor is correct in identifying the discrepancy, what pattern should the two prices take in the short-term future?
   d. What may be some impediments to the success of this transaction?

9. What is the difference between an IPO and a secondary issue?

10. What is the difference between a private placement and a public offering?

11. What are the risk implications to an investment banker from underwriting on a best-efforts basis versus a firm commitment basis? If you operated a company issuing stock for the first time, which type of underwriting would you prefer? Why? What factors may cause you to choose the alternative?

12. An investment banker agrees to underwrite a $500,000,000, ten-year, 8 percent semiannual bond issue for KDO Corporation on a firm commitment basis. The investment banker pays KDO on Thursday and plans to begin a public sale on Friday. What type of interest rate movement does the investment bank fear while holding these securities? If interest rates rise 0.05 percent, or 5 basis points, overnight, what will be the impact on the profits of the investment banker? What if the market interest rate falls 5 basis points?

13. An investment banker pays $23.50 per share for 4,000,000 shares of JCN Company. It then sells those shares to the public for $25 per share. How much money does JCN receive? What is the profit to the investment banker? What is the stock price of JCN?

14. XYZ, Inc., has issued 10,000,000 new shares. An investment banker agrees to underwrite these shares on a best-efforts basis. The investment banker is able to sell 8,400,000 shares for $27 per share, and it charges XYZ $0.675 per share sold. How much money does XYZ receive? What is the profit to the investment banker? What is the stock price of XYZ?

15. Which type of security accounts for most underwriting in the United States? Which is likely to be more costly to underwrite: corporate debt or equity? Why?

16. How do agency transactions differ from principal transactions for market makers?

17. What three factors are given credit for the steady decline in brokerage commissions as a percentage of total revenues over the period beginning in 1977 and ending in 1991?

18. What factors are given credit for the resurgence of profitability in the securities industry beginning in 1992? Are firms that trade in fixed-income securities more or less likely to have volatile profits? Why?

19. What impact did regulatory change in the commercial banking arena in the middle to late 1980s have on the competitive nature of the securities industry? What benefits could a commercial bank obtain from entrance into the investment banking business?

20. What were the largest single asset and the largest single liability of securities firms in 1996? Are these asset and liability categories related? Exactly how does a repurchase agreement work?

21. How did the National Securities Markets Improvement Act of 1996 (NSMIA) change the regulatory structure of the securities industry?

22. Identify four major regulatory organizations that are involved in the daily operations of the investment securities industry and explain their role in providing smoothly operating markets.

THE FINANCIAL SERVICES INDUSTRY

Mutual Funds

Introduction

Mutual funds are financial intermediaries that pool the financial resources of individuals and companies and invest in diversified portfolios of assets. An open-ended mutual fund (the major type of mutual fund) continuously stands ready to sell new shares to investors and to redeem outstanding shares on demand at their fair market value. Thus, these funds provide opportunities for small investors to invest in financial securities and diversify risk. Mutual funds are also able to generate greater economies of scale by incurring lower transaction costs and commissions than are incurred when individual investors buy securities directly. As a result of the tremendous increase in the market value of financial assets, such as equities, in the 1990s (for example, the S&P 500 index saw a return of over 25 percent in 1997 and 1998) and the relatively low-cost opportunity mutual funds provide to investors (particularly small investors) who want to hold such assets, the mutual fund industry boomed in size and customers in the 1990s. At the end of 1997 more than 5,300 different stock and bond mutual companies held total assets of $3.7 trillion. If we add money market mutual funds, the number of funds rises close to 8,000 and the

1997 value of assets under management rises to $4.5 trillion.[1] In this chapter we provide an overview of the services offered by mutual funds and highlight their rapid growth over the last decade.

Size, Structure, and Composition of the Industry

Historical Trends

The first mutual fund was founded in Boston in 1924. The industry grew very slowly at first; by 1970, 360 funds held about $50 billion in assets. Due to the advent of money market mutual funds in 1972 (as investors looked for ways to earn market rates on short-term funds when bank deposit rates were constrained by regulatory ceilings) and that of tax-exempt money market mutual funds in 1979 and an explosion of special-purpose equity, bond, and derivative funds (as capital market values soared in the 1990s), there has been a dramatic growth in the number of funds and in the asset size of the industry. Table 4–1 documents the tremendous increase from 1940 though 1996 of specialist stock and bond mutual funds. For example, total assets invested in mutual funds (other than money market mutual funds) grew from $0.4 billion in 1940 to $2,637.4 billion in 1996. The majority of this growth occurred during the bull market run in the 1990s (total assets in 1990 were $568.5 billion). As can be seen in Figure 4–1, in terms of asset size, the mutual fund industry is larger than the life insurance industry but smaller than the commercial banking industry. This makes mutual funds the second most important FI group in the United States as measured by asset size.

The tremendous growth in this area of FI services has not gone unnoticed by commercial banks. Banks' share of all mutual fund assets managed was about 14 percent in 1997. Some of this growth has occurred through banks buying mutual fund companies, for example, Mellon buying Dreyfus. However, most of the

TABLE 4–1   Growth of Mutual Funds from 1940 to 1996*

Year	Total Net Assets, billions	Gross Sales, billions	Redemptions, billions	Net Sales, billions	Shareholders, thousands	Number of Companies
1996	$2,637.4	$684.8	$398.7	$286.1	118,752	5,305
1995	2,070.5	477.2	313.6	168.7	101,597	4,764
1994	1,550.5	474.0	329.7	144.2	89,484	4,394
1993	1,510.0	511.6	231.4	280.2	70,049	3,638
1992	1,100.1	364.4	165.5	198.9	53,975	2,985
1991	853.1	236.6	116.3	120.3	45,030	2,606
1990	568.5	149.5	98.3	51.3	39,614	2,362
1980	58.4	10.0	8.2	1.8	7,325	458
1970	47.6	4.6	3.0	1.6	10,690	356
1960	17.0	2.1	0.8	1.3	4,898	161
1950	2.5	0.5	0.3	0.2	939	98
1940	0.4	N/A	N/A	N/A	296	68

*Data pertain to conventional fund members of the Investment Company Institute; money market funds are not included. Institute "gross sales" figures include the proceeds of initial fund underwritings prior to 1970.

Source: *Perspective* 3, no. 1 (March 1997), Investment Company Institute, Washington, D.C.

[1]See The Investment Company Institute, "Mutual Fund Developments in 1997," March 1998.

FIGURE 4–1

Assets of Major Financial Intermediaries, 1990 and 1997 (Third Quarter) (in trillions of dollars)

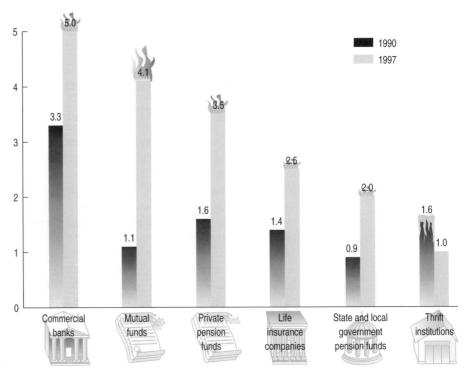

Note: Data for 1990 are year end; data for 1997 are at the end of the third quarter. Commercial banks include U.S.-chartered commercial banks, foreign banking offices in the United States, bank holding companies, and banks in U.S.-affiliated areas.
Source: Federal Reserve Board.

growth has come from the conversion of bank common trust funds into mutual funds.[2] For example, in 1997, $8.6 billion of bank common trust funds was converted into equity mutual funds, and another $4.5 billion into bond funds.

Different Types of Mutual Funds

The mutual fund industry is usually divided into two sectors: short-term funds and long-term funds. Long-term funds comprise **bond and income funds** (comprised of fixed-income securities) and **equity funds** (comprised of common and preferred stock securities). Short-term funds comprise taxable **money market mutual funds** (MMMFs) and tax-exempt money market mutual funds. Figure 4–2 shows how the mix of stock, bond, and money market fund assets changed between 1985, 1990, and 1997. As can be seen, there has been a strong recent trend toward investing in stock mutual funds, although part of the growth of stock funds reflects the rise in share values during the 1990s.

In 1997, 76.4 percent of all mutual fund assets were in long-term funds; the remaining funds, or 23.6 percent, were in money market mutual funds. As you can see in Figure 4–2, the proportion invested in long-term versus short-term funds can vary considerably over time. For example, the share of money market funds was 46.6 percent in 1990 compared to 23.6 percent in 1997. Money market mutual funds

Bond and Income Funds
Funds that contain fixed-income capital market debt securities.

Equity Funds
Funds that contain common and preferred stock securities.

Money Market Mutual Funds
Funds that contain various mixtures of money market securities.

---

[2]The Small Business Job Protection Act of 1996 facilitated these conversions by allowing them to occur without capital gains taxes being levied at the time of a conversion.

FIGURE 4–2

Share of Assets of Stock, Bond, and Money Market Mutual Funds, 1985–1997

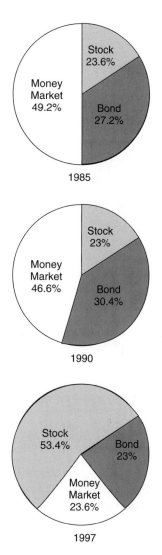

Source: Investment Company Institute; and *New York Times,* February 2, 1997, p. F4, and January 5, 1998, p. C33.

provide an alternative investment to interest-bearing deposits at commercial banks, which may explain the growth in MMMFs in the 1980s, when the spread earned on MMMF investments relative to deposits was mostly positive (see Figure 4–3). Both investments are relatively safe and earn short-term returns. The major difference between the two is that interest-bearing deposits (below $100,000 in size) are fully insured but due to bank regulatory costs (such as reserve requirements, capital requirements, and deposit insurance premiums) generally offer lower returns than do noninsured MMMFs. Thus, the net gain in switching to MMMFs is higher returns in exchange for the loss of deposit insurance coverage. Many investors appeared willing to give up insurance coverage to obtain additional returns in the 1980s. However, the decline in the relative importance of short-term funds and the increase in the relative importance of long-term funds in the 1990s reflects the dramatic rise in equity returns over the 1990–97 period even though MMMF interest spreads over bank deposits were mostly positive.

FIGURE 4–3

*Interest Rate Spread and
Net New Cash Flow to
Retail Money Market
Funds, 1985–1997*

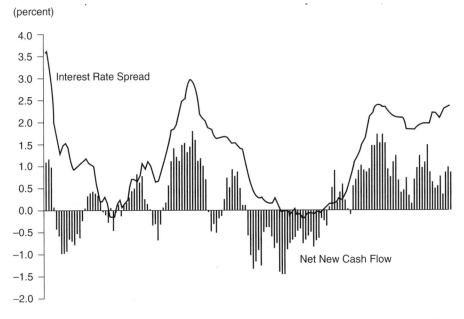

(percent)

Note: Net new cash flow is a percentage of retail money market fund assets and is shown as a six-month moving average. The interest rate spread is the difference between the taxable money market fund yield and the average interest rate on savings deposits; the series is plotted with a six-month lag.

Source: Investment Company Institute, *Perspectives* 3, no. 1 (March 1998), p. 7.

It is estimated that 37 million households (37 percent of all households) owned mutual funds in 1996. Table 4–2 lists some characteristics of household mutual fund owners. Compared to those who made their first purchase in 1990 or earlier, notice that individuals who made their first purchase of mutual fund shares after 1990 are younger (37 years old versus 46 years old), earn less ($50,000 versus $60,000), invest smaller amounts ($7,000 versus $25,000), and are fully aware that there is risk in mutual fund investments (100 percent versus 96 percent). Most household owners are using mutual funds as retirement savings vehicles (77 percent); 27 percent are using these funds as a vehicle for saving for their children's education. Interestingly, more families with less than a college degree are investing in mutual funds (40 percent for first purchasers in or before 1990, versus 45 percent for first purchasers in 1991 or later). The equity bull markets of the 1990s, the reduction in transaction costs, and the diversification benefits achievable through mutual funds are the likely reasons behind these changes.

Mutual Fund Objectives

The aggregate figures for long-term bond and income and equity funds tend to obscure the fact that there are many different funds in these groups. Table 4–3 classifies 18 major categories of investment objectives for mutual funds. These objectives are shown along with the assets allocated to each major category in 1996. A fund objective provides general information about the types of securities a mutual fund will hold as assets. For example, aggressive growth funds hold securities (mainly equities) of the highest-growth and highest-risk firms; growth funds would also

TABLE 4–2   Selected Characteristics of Household Owners of Mutual Funds[1]

	First Purchase in 1990 or Earlier	*First Purchase in 1991 or Later*
Demographic Characteristics		
Median age	46	37
Percent of households		
Married	73	63
Employed full- or part-time	79	88
Minor children[2]	41	48
Four-year college degree or more	60	55
Financial Characteristics		
Median household income	$60,000	$50,000
Median household financial assets[3]	$70,000	$25,000
Percent of households owning		
Individual stocks	57	48
Individual bonds	27	19
Annuities	29	18
IRA	75	60
401 (k)	51	50
Mutual Fund Ownership Characteristics[4]		
Median mutual fund assets	$25,000	$7,000
Medium number of funds owned	3	2
Percent		
Household assets in mutual funds[5]	36	28
Fund types owned		
Equity	75	71
Bond and income	50	38
Money market	54	45
Investment Goal[6]		
Retirement	81	77
Education	24	27
Risk Tolerance Profile[7]		
Willing to take		
Substantial risk with expectation of substantial gain	8	10
Above-average risk with expectation of above-average gain	36	38
Above-average risk with expectation of average gain	41	36
Below-average risk with expectation of below-average gain	10	13
No risk	6	3
Awareness: agreed that investing in stock and bond funds involves risk	96	100
Evaluations: assessed risk of most recent stock or bond fund purchase	67	71
Horizon: assessed mutual fund risk in time frame exceeding five years	65	62

[1]Characteristics of primary financial decision maker in the household.

[2]Percent of married households.

[3]Excludes assets in employer-sponsored retirement plans.

[4]Excludes mutual funds in employer-sponsored retirement plans.

[5]Excludes any mutual fund assets held in employer-sponsored retirement plans.

[6]Multiple responses included.

[7]Responses of households with an investment goal.

Source: *Perspectives* 3, no. 1 (March 1997), Investment Company Institute, Washington, D.C.

TABLE 4–3   **Total Net Asset Value of Equity and Bond and Income Funds by Investment Objective, December 31, 1996**

Type of Fund	Combined Assets, millions of dollars	Percent of Total
Total net assets	$2,637,398.0	100.0%
Aggressive growth	274,802.1	10.4
Growth	482,082.2	18.3
Growth and income	589,104.2	22.3
Precious metals	4,949.1	0.2
International	177,414.4	6.7
Global equity	106,554.1	4.0
Income—equity	116,022.8	4.4
Flexible portfolio	63,360.2	2.4
Balanced	99,202.0	3.8
Income—mixed	88,324.6	3.4
Income—bond	100,889.4	3.8
U.S. government income	79,507.9	3.0
Ginnie Mae	51,331.6	2.0
Global bond	37,458.4	1.4
Corporate bond	35,573.7	1.4
High-yield bond	78,260.3	3.0
National municipal bond—long-term	135,631.4	5.1
State municipal bond—long-term	116,929.6	4.4

Source: *Perspectives* 3, no. 1 (March 1997), Investment Company Institute, Washington D.C.

hold high-growth, high-risk securities, but neither the growth nor the risk in these funds would be as high as it is in the aggressive growth funds. Historically, mutual funds have had to send out lengthy prospectuses describing their objectives and investments. In 1997, the SEC recommended a new, simpler procedure in which investors would be sent a two-page profile of the fund written in "plain" English. The idea is to increase the ability of investors to understand the risks related to the investment objectives or profile of a fund.

Table 4–4 lists the largest (in total assets held) 20 mutual funds available at the end of 1997, including the fund objective, 12-month and 5-year return, and net asset value (discussed below). Fidelity's Magellan Fund was (despite being closed to new investors) the largest fund at year-end. Fidelity and Vanguard offered 11 of the top 20 funds measured by asset size. Many of the top funds list either growth or growth and income as the fund objective, and all of the top 20 funds performed well during the bull market of the 1990s. Five-year returns ran from a low of 95.9 percent for American Fund's European/Pacific to 151.8 percent for Fidelity's Growth and Income Fund. Thus, investors in these funds doubled or more than doubled their money. However, it should be noted that the risk of returns [e.g., the fund's total return risk or even its "beta" (or systematic risk)] is rarely mentioned in prospectuses or advertisements.

Investor Returns from Mutual Fund Ownership

The return an investor gets from investing in mutual fund shares reflects three aspects of the underlying portfolio of mutual fund assets. First, income and dividends are earned on those assets; second, capital gains occur when assets are sold

---

TABLE 4–4   **The Biggest Mutual Funds**

Fund	Objective	Total Assets, millions	Total Return 12 month	Total Return 5 year	NAV
Fidelity Magellan	Growth	$63,035	20.4%	128.3%	91.53
Vanguard Index: 500	Growth/income	48,264	26.0	139.0	86.86
American Funds: InvCoA	Growth/income	39,235	24.4	119.5	27.47
American Funds: WshMut	Growth/income	37,179	27.6	148.9	29.55
Fidelity Invest: Grw/Inc	Growth/income	35,485	24.5	151.8	36.84
Fidelity Invest: Contra	Growth	30,263	17.7	138.1	44.89
Vanguard: WndsII	Growth/income	23,545	25.6	146.7	27.62
Fidelity Invest: Puritan	Balanced	22,377	18.6	108.0	18.98
American Century: Ultra	Growth	22,204	15.2	122.0	26.20
Vanguard: Welltn	Balanced	21,340	19.6	111.0	28.92
Vanguard: Wndsr	Growth/income	20,833	17.3	135.5	16.45
Fidelity Invest: Eq/Inc	Equity/income	20,545	24.8	145.3	50.68
Fidelity Advisor: Grw Opp	Growth	20,408	22.7	146.4	41.08
American Funds: Income	Equity/income	19,708	20.0	99.7	17.50
Janus: Fund	Capital appreciation	19,179	16.5	98.4	28.61
American Funds: Eupac	International	18,733	8.7	95.9	25.47
Putnam Funds A: Grw/Inc	Growth/income	17,044	19.0	129.4	18.95
Fidelity Invest: Equity II	Equity/income	16,651	21.9	127.0	26.11
American Funds: NewPer	Growth/income	16,096	12.7	106.0	18.87
Dean Witter: Div/Grw	Growth/income	15,400	20.3	115.6	52.68

Source: Reprinted with permission from the *Southern Illinoisan,* December 26, 1997.

Marked-to-Market
Adjusting asset and balance sheet values to reflect current market prices.

NAV
The net asset value of a mutual fund is equal to the market value of the assets in the mutual fund portfolio divided by the number of shares outstanding.

by a mutual fund at prices higher than the purchase price; third, capital appreciation in the underlying values of the assets held in a fund's portfolio add to the value of mutual fund shares. With respect to capital appreciation, mutual fund assets are normally **marked-to-market** daily. This means that the managers of the fund calculate the current value of each mutual fund share by computing the daily market value of the fund's total asset portfolio, which is then divided by the number of mutual fund shares outstanding. The resulting value is called the net asset value (**NAV**) of the fund. This is the price the investor gets when selling shares back to the fund that day or buying any new shares in the fund on that day. For example, suppose a mutual fund contains 1,000 shares of Sears, Roebuck currently trading at $56, 2,000 shares of Mobil Oil currently trading at $70.25, and 1,500 shares of Household International currently trading at $120.50. The fund currently has 15,000 shares outstanding held by investors. Thus, today the NAV of the fund is calculated as:

$$\text{NAV} = (1{,}000 \times \$56 + 2{,}000 \times \$70.25 + 1{,}500 \times \$120.50) \div 15{,}000 = \$25.15$$

If next month Sears shares increased to $62, Mobil shares increased to $78, and Household International shares increased to $150, the NAV (assuming the same number of investors) would increase to

$$\text{NAV} = (1{,}000 \times \$62 + 2{,}000 \times \$78 + 1{,}500 \times \$150) \div 15{,}000 = \$29.53$$

Open-End Mutual Fund
The supply of shares in the fund is not fixed but can increase or decrease daily with purchases and redemptions of shares.

Most mutual funds are **open-end** in that the number of shares outstanding fluctuates up and down daily with the amount of share redemptions and new purchases. With open-end mutual funds, investors buy and sell shares from and to the mutual fund company. Thus, the demand for shares determines the number outstanding and the NAV of shares is determined solely by the market value of the underlying securities held in the mutual fund divided by the number of shareholders outstanding. For example, in the case above, suppose that today 1,000 additional investors buy into the mutual fund at the current NAV of $25.15. This means that the fund manager now has $25,150 in additional funds to invest. Suppose the fund manager decides to use these additional funds to buy additional shares in Sears. At today's market price he or she can buy $25,150 ÷ $56 = 449 additional shares of Sears. Thus, the mutual fund's new portfolio of shares would be 1,449 in Sears, 2,000 in Mobil, and 1,500 in Household International. At the end of the month the NAV of the portfolio would be

$$NAV = (1,449 \times \$62 + 2,000 \times \$78 + 1,500 \times \$150) \div 16,000 = \$29.43$$

given the appreciation in value of all three stocks over the month.

Note that the fund's value changed over the month due to both capital appreciation and investment size. In this case, the independent effect on the fund's NAV of the new investors was negative, since the 1,000 additional investors resulted in the fund having a lower NAV at the end of the month than it would have had if the number of investors had remained static (i.e., $29.43 versus $29.53).

> **Closed-End Investment Companies**
> Specialized investment companies that invest in securities and assets of other firms but have a fixed supply of shares outstanding themselves.

> **REIT**
> A real estate investment trust. A closed-end investment company that specializes in investing in mortgages, property, or real estate company shares.

Open-ended mutual funds can be contrasted to most regular corporations traded on stock exchanges and to **closed-end investment companies,** which have fixed quantities of shares outstanding at any given time. For example, real estate investment trusts (**REITs**) are closed-end investment companies that specialize in investment in real estate company shares and/or in buying mortgages.[3] With closed-end funds, investors must buy and sell the investment company's shares on a stock exchange similar to the trading of corporate stock. Since the number of shares available for purchase at any moment in time is fixed, the value of the fund's shares is determined not only by the value of the underlying shares but also by the demand for the investment company's shares themselves. When demand is high, the shares can trade at more than the NAV of the securities held in the fund. In this case, the fund is said to be trading at a premium, that is, at more than the fair market value of the securities held. When the value of the closed-end fund's shares are less than the NAV of its assets, its shares are said to be trading at a discount, that is, at less than the fair market value of the securities held. For example, in March 1998, the 16 largest closed-ended funds specializing in U.S. equities were trading at an average discount of over 7 percent.[4]

Load versus No-Load Funds

> **Load Fund**
> A mutual fund with an up-front sales or commission charge that has to be paid by the investor.

> **No-Load Fund**
> A mutual fund that does not charge up-front fees or commission charges on the sale of mutual fund shares to investors.

An investor who buys a mutual fund share may be subject to a sales charge, sometimes as high as 8.5 percent. In this case, the fund is called a **load fund.** Other funds that directly market shares to investors do not use sales agents working for commissions and have no up-front commission charges; these are called **no-load funds.** In general, these funds retain a small percentage of investable funds

---

[3]Many closed-end funds are specialized funds that invest in shares in countries such as Argentina, Brazil, and Mexico. The shares of these closed-end funds are traded on the NYSE or the over-the-counter market. The total market value of funds invested in closed-end funds was $137.1 billion at the end of the third quarter of 1996. This compares to $3,059.8 billion invested in open-ended funds at that time.

[4]See Closed-End Funds, "Mutual Funds Report," *New York Times,* Money and Business (Part 2), April 5, 1998, p. 35.

12b–1 Fees
Fees relating to the distribution and other operating costs of mutual fund shares.

to meet distribution costs and other operating costs. Such annual fees are known as **12b–1 fees** after the SEC rule covering such charges.[5]

The argument in favor of load funds is that they are more closely managed and therefore better managed. However, the cost of this increased attention may not be worthwhile. For example, Table 4–5 lists the top 10 performing U.S. stock funds over the five-year period September 1992 through September 1997 before and after adjusting returns for any up-front "load" fees. Notice that the ranking of every fund is reduced by at least one position and as much as seven positions when the return is adjusted for these load or sale charges. Indeed, investors are increasingly recognizing that this cost disadvantage outweighs the benefits of greater management attention. In 1985, load funds encompassed almost 70 percent of mutual fund sales, while no-load funds accounted for just over 30 percent. By 1997, however, no-load fund sales led load fund sales by 57 to 43 percent.[6]

Table 4–6 presents mutual fund quotes from *The Wall Street Journal* on Friday, February 27, 1998. The quote for Vanguard Index Funds includes information on each fund's NAV, the change in NAV from the previous day, fund name and objective, year-to-date return, four-week return, one- through five-year return and rating (A through D), and maximum initial (sales) charge. The maximum initial charge is listed as 0.00 for each of the Vanguard Index Funds, meaning that they are all *no-load* funds.

Concept Questions

1. Where do mutual funds rank in terms of asset size among all FI industries?
2. Describe the difference between short-term and long-term mutual funds.
3. What have been the trends in the number of mutual funds since 1980?
4. What are the two biggest mutual fund companies? How have their funds performed in recent years?
5. Describe the difference between open-end and closed-end mutual funds.

TABLE 4–5   Impact of Load Charges on Mutual Fund Returns

Fund	Total Return	Load	Adjusted Return	Rank
AIM Aggressive Growth	31.6%	5.50%	30.1%	2
PBHG Growth	30.7	None	30.7	1
Franklin California Growth I	30.0	4.50	28.8	4
Spectra	29.9	None	29.9	3
FPA Capital	29.3	6.50	27.5	10
Franklin Small Cap Growth I	29.2	4.50	28.0	7
Robertson Stephens Value & Growth A	28.6	None	28.6	5
RSI Retirement Emerging Growth	28.3	None	28.3	6
Vanguard Primecap	27.9	None	27.9	8
Putnam New Opportunities A	27.9	5.75	26.4	17

Source: *Perspectives* 3, no. 1 (March 1997), Investment Company Institute.

---

[5]12b–1 fees are limited to a maximum of 0.25 percent.
[6]See, for example, "Paying for Advice, If Not for Load Funds," *New York Times,* October 26, 1997.

TABLE 4–6   **Mutual Fund Quote**

NAV	Net Chg	Fund Name	Inv* Obj	YTD % ret	4 Wk % ret	Total Return 1 Yr	Total Return 3 Yr-R	Total Return 5 Yr-R	Max Init Chrg
		Vanguard Index Fds:							
97.56	+ 0.55	500	GI	+ 8.3	+ 7.5	+ 32.3 A	+ 31.6 A	+ 21.5 A	0.00
17.11	+ 0.05	Balanced	BL	+ 5.0	+ 4.7	+ 22.9 A	+ 21.4 B	+ 14.8 B	0.00
10.14	+ 0.10	EmerMkt r	EM	+ 1.5	+ 11.9	− 22.9 E	+ 3.1 C	NS ..	0.00
22.54	+ 0.12	Europe	EU	+ 12.0	+ 7.8	+ 36.2 A	+ 26.5 A	+ 21.9 A	0.00
32.61	+ 0.25	Exten	MC	+ 6.0	+ 8.1	+ 30.2 B	+ 26.3 B	+ 18.8 B	0.00
32.61	+ 0.24	Extenist	...	NA	NA	NA ..	NA ..	NA ..	0.00
24.93	+ 0.10	Growth	GR	+ 10.7	+ 7.4	+ 35.8 A	+ 34.2 A	+ 22.4 A	0.00
97.03	+ 0.55	Instldx	GI	+ 8.3	+ 7.5	+ 32.5 A	+ 31.8 A	+ 21.7 A	0.00
97.03	+ 0.54	InstPlus	GI	+ 8.3	+ 7.5	NS ..	NS ..	NS ..	0.00
10.22	− 0.01	ITBond	IG	+ 1.2	+ 0.4	+ 10.3 A	+ 9.7 A	NS ..	0.00
10.76	− 0.03	LTBond	LG	+ 0.8	+ 0.7	+ 15.8 A	NA ..	NS ..	0.00
8.20	+ 0.11	Pacific	PR	+ 6.2	− 1.2	− 16.1 B	− 6.4 C	+ 1.9 B	0.00
25.11	+ 0.17	SmCap	SC	+ 5.7	+ 7.8	+ 30.6 B	+ 25.0 C	+18.4 C	0.00
25.12	+ 0.17	SmCapist	SC	+ 5.8	+ 7.8	NS ..	NS ..	NS ..	0.00
10.02	− 0.01	STBond	SG	+ 1.1	+ 0.2	+ 7.5 A	+ 7.4 A	NS ..	0.00
10.10	− 0.01	TotBd	IG	+ 1.1	+ 0.5	+ 10.1 A	+ 9.3 A	+ 6.9 A	0.00
10.10	− 0.01	TotBdist	IG	+ 1.1	+ 0.5	+ 10.3 A	NS ..	NS ..	0.00
10.76	+ 0.08	TotIntl	IL	+ 9.0	+ 5.6	+ 8.1 D	NS ..	NS ..	0.00
24.40	+ 0.14	TotSt	GR	+ 7.8	+ 7.7	+ 31.7 B	+ 29.6 B	+ 20.3 B	0.00
24.40	+ 0.14	TotStlst	GR	+ 7.8	+ 7.7	NS ..	NS ..	NS ..	0.00
22.08	+0.16	Value	GI	+ 5.9	+ 7.6	+ 28.4 C	+ 28.9 C	+ 20.5 B	0.00

*GI = growth and income fund; BL = balanced fund; EM = emerging-market fund; EU = European region fund; MC = middle-sized company fund; GR = growth fund; IG = intermediate maturity Treasury and government agency bond fund; LG = long-term Treasury and government agency bond fund; PR = Pacific region fund; SC = small company fund.

Source: *The Wall Street Journal*, February 27, 1998, p. C25. Reprinted by permission of The Wall Street Journal © 1998 Dow Jones & Company, Inc. All Rights Reserved Worldwide.

Balance Sheet and Recent Trends

Money Market Funds

Look at the distribution of assets of money market mutual funds from 1991 through September 1997 shown in Table 4–7. As you can see, in the third quarter of 1997, most of their assets were invested in short-term financial securities such as foreign deposits, domestic checkable deposits and currency, time and savings deposits, repurchase agreements (RPs), open market paper (mostly commercial paper), and U.S. government securities. Short-maturity asset holdings are an objective of these funds so that they can retain their depositlike nature. In fact, most money market mutual fund shares have their values fixed at $1. Asset value fluctuations due to interest rate changes and any small default risk and capital gains or losses on assets are adjusted for by increasing or reducing the number of $1 shares owned by the investor.

Long-Term Funds

Note the asset composition of long-term mutual funds shown in Table 4–8. As might be expected, it reflects the popularity of different types of bond or equity funds at that time. Underscoring the attractiveness of equity funds on September 30, 1997,

TABLE 4–7   Distribution of Assets in Money Market Mutual Funds from 1991 through September 30, 1997
(in billions of dollars)

	1991	1992	1993	1994	1995	1996	1997
Total financial assets	535.0	539.5	559.6	602.9	745.3	891.1	1,005.1
Foreign deposits	21.4	20.3	10.0	15.7	19.7	23.1	23.0
Checkable deposits and currency	− 0.2	− 2.7	− 1.2	− 2.5	− 3.5	− 1.1	− 2.2
Time and savings deposits	35.1	34.6	31.9	31.4	52.3	82.7	115.0
Security RPs	67.0	65.9	66.4	68.8	87.8	103.8	124.7
Credit market instruments	403.9	408.6	429.0	459.0	545.5	634.3	678.7
Open market paper	190.6	173.6	164.4	187.2	235.5	273.9	323.6
U.S. government securities	118.9	132.7	147.2	143.3	160.8	192.0	163.5
Treasury	78.3	78.4	79.4	66.1	70.0	90.2	75.0
Agency	40.6	54.3	67.8	77.2	90.8	101.8	88.5
Municipal securities	90.6	96.0	105.6	113.4	127.7	144.5	158.9
Corporate and foreign bonds	3.8	6.3	11.7	15.2	21.5	23.9	32.7
Miscellaneous assets	7.7	12.7	23.7	30.6	43.4	48.3	65.9

Source: *Federal Reserve Bulletin,* December 11, 1997, p. 77.

TABLE 4–8   Distribution of Assets in Bond, Income, and Equity Mutual Funds from 1991 through September 30, 1997
(in billions of dollars)

	1991	1992	1993	1994	1995	1996	1997
Total financial assets	769.5	992.5	1,375.4	1,477.3	1,852.8	2,342.4	2,981.1
Security RPs	12.2	21.9	38.7	43.1	50.2	47.5	60.2
Credit market instruments	440.2	566.4	725.9	718.8	771.3	820.2	891.7
Open market paper	12.2	21.9	38.7	43.1	50.2	47.5	60.2
U.S. government securities	200.6	257.4	306.6	296.2	315.1	330.2	350.5
Treasury	133.5	169.5	200.9	194.1	205.3	214.1	226.1
Agency	67.1	87.9	105.7	102.1	109.9	116.1	124.4
Municipal securities	139.7	168.4	211.3	207.0	210.2	213.3	219.2
Corporate and foreign bonds	87.7	118.7	169.3	172.4	195.7	229.5	261.8
Corporate equities	308.9	401.3	607.4	709.6	1,024.9	1,470.0	2,021.7
Miscellaneous assets	8.2	3.0	3.3	5.9	6.3	4.7	7.5
Total shares outstanding	769.5	992.5	1,375.4	1,477.3	1,852.8	2,342.4	2,981.1

Source: *Federal Reserve Bulletin,* December 11, 1997, p. 77.

was the fact that stocks comprised over 67.8 percent of total long-term mutual fund asset portfolios. U.S. government securities and municipal bonds were the next most popular assets (19.1 percent of the asset portfolio). In contrast, look at the distribution of assets in 1991, when the equity markets were not doing so well. Equities made up only 40.1 percent of the long-term mutual fund portfolios. Government securities and municipals were the largest asset group at 44.2 percent of total assets.

Concept Questions

1. Describe the major assets held by mutual funds in the 1990s.
2. How does the asset distribution differ between money market mutual funds and long-term mutual funds?

Regulation

Because mutual funds accept funds from small investors, this industry is one of the most closely regulated among the nondepository financial institution groups. Regulations are enacted to protect investors against possible abuses by managers of mutual funds. The SEC is the primary regulator of mutual funds. Specifically, the Securities Act of 1933 requires a mutual fund to file a registration statement with the SEC and sets rules and procedures regarding the fund's prospectus sent to investors. In addition, the Securities Exchange Act of 1934 makes the purchase and sale of mutual fund shares subject to various antifraud provisions. This regulation requires that a mutual fund furnish full and accurate information on all financial and corporate matters to prospective fund purchasers. The 1934 act also appointed the National Association of Securities Dealers (NASD) to supervise mutual fund share distributions.

In 1940 Congress passed the Investment Advisers Act and the Investment Company Act. The Investment Advisers Act regulates the activities of mutual fund advisers. The Investment Company Act sets out rules to prevent conflicts of interest, fraud, and excessive fees or charges for fund shares.

In recent years, the passage of the Insider Trading and Securities Fraud Enforcement Act of 1988 has required mutual funds to develop mechanisms and procedures to avoid insider trading abuses. In addition, the ability of mutual funds to conduct their business is affected by the Market Reform Act of 1990, which was passed in the wake of the 1987 stock market crash. This act allows the SEC to introduce circuit breakers to halt trading on exchanges and to restrict program trading when it deems necessary. Finally, the National Securities Markets Improvement Act (NSMIA) of 1996 also applies to mutual fund companies. Specifically, the NSMIA exempts mutual fund sellers from oversight by state securities regulators, thus reducing their regulatory burden.

Concept Questions

1. Who is the primary regulator of mutual fund companies?
2. How did the NSMIA affect mutual funds?

Summary

This chapter provided an overview of the mutual fund industry. Mutual funds pool funds from individuals and corporations and invest in diversified asset portfolios. Given the tremendous growth in the market values of financial assets—such as equities—in the 1990s and the cost-effective way in which mutual funds allow small investors to participate in these markets, mutual funds have grown tremendously in size, number of funds, and number of shareholders. We looked at the two major categories of mutual funds—short-term and long-term open-ended funds—highlighting the differences in their growth rates and the composition of their assets. We also looked at the calculation of the net asset values (NAV) of mutual fund shares. Finally, we contrasted open-ended mutual funds with closed-ended mutual funds.

Questions and Problems

1. What is a mutual fund? In what sense is it a financial intermediary?

2. What are money market mutual funds? In what assets do these funds typically invest? What factors caused the strong growth in this type of fund during the late 1970s and 1980s?

3. What are long-term mutual funds? In what assets do these funds usually invest? What factors caused the strong growth in this type of fund during the 1990s?

4. How do the composition and size of short-term funds differ from the composition and size of long-term funds?

5. How does the risk of short-term funds differ from the risk of long-term funds?

6. What are the economic reasons for the existence of mutual funds; that is, what benefits do mutual funds provide for investors? Why do individuals rather than corporations hold most mutual funds shares?

7. What are the principal demographics of household owners who first purchased mutual funds after 1991 compared to those of household owners who first purchased funds before 1990? What are the primary reasons why household owners invest in mutual funds?

8. What change in regulatory guidelines occurred in 1997 which had the primary purpose of giving investors a better understanding of the risks and objectives of a fund?

9. What are the three possible components reflected in the return an investor receives from a mutual fund?

10. An investor purchases a mutual fund for $50. The fund pays dividends of $1.50, distributes a capital gain of $2, and charges a fee of $2 when the fund is sold one year later for $52.50. What is the net rate of return from this investment?

11. How is the net asset value (NAV) of a mutual fund determined? What is meant by the term *marked-to-market daily?*

12. A mutual fund has 400 shares of Fiat, Inc., currently trading at $7, and 400 shares of Microsoft, Inc., currently trading at $70. The fund has 100 shares outstanding.

    a. What is the net asset value (NAV) of the fund?

    b. If investors expect the price of Fiat shares to increase to $9 and the price of Microsoft shares to decrease to $55 by the end of the year, what is the expected NAV at the end of the year?

    c. Assume that the expected price of the Fiat shares is realized at $9. What is the maximum price decrease that can occur to the Microsoft shares to realize an end-of-year NAV equal to the NAV estimated in (*a*)?

13. What is the difference between open-end and closed-end mutual funds? Which type of fund tends to be more specialized in asset selection? How does a closed-end fund provide another source of return from which an investor may either gain or lose?

14. Open-end Fund A has 100 shares of ATT valued at $100 each and 50 shares of Toro valued at $50 each. Closed-end Fund B has 75 shares of ATT and 100 shares of Toro. Each fund has 100 shares of stock outstanding.

    a. What are the NAVs of both funds using these prices?

    b. Assume that in one month the price of ATT stock has increased to $105 and the price of Toro stock has decreased to $45. How do these changes impact the NAV of both funds? If the funds were purchased at the NAV prices in (*a*) and sold at month end, what would be the realized returns on the investments?

    c. Assume that another 100 shares of ATT are added to Fund A. What is the effect on Fund A's NAV if the stock prices remain unchanged from the original prices?

15. What is the difference between a load fund and a no-load fund? Is the argument that load funds are more closely managed and therefore have higher returns supported by the evidence presented in Table 4–5?

16. Suppose you have a choice between a load fund with no annual 12b–1 fee and a no-load fund with a maximum 12b–1 fee. What is a 12b–1 fee? How would the length of your expected investment horizon, or holding period, influence your choice between these two funds?

17. Why did the proportion of equities in long-term funds increase from 40.1 percent in 1991 to over 62 percent by the third quarter of 1997? How might an investor's preference for a mutual funds objectives change over time?

18. Who are the primary regulators of the mutual fund industry? How do their regulatory goals differ from those of other types of financial institutions?

CHAPTER 5

THE FINANCIAL SERVICES INDUSTRY

Finance Companies

Introduction

The primary function of finance companies is to make loans to both individuals and corporations. The services provided by finance companies include consumer lending, business lending, and mortgage financing. Some of their loans are similar to commercial bank loans, such as consumer and auto loans, but others are more specialized. Finance companies differ from banks in that they do not accept deposits but instead rely on short- and long-term debt as a source of funds. Additionally, finance companies often lend to customers commercial banks find too risky. In this chapter we look at the services provided by this industry and the competitive and financial situation facing these firms.

Size, Structure, and Composition of the Industry

Finance companies originated during the Depression, when General Electric Corp. created General Electric Capital Corp. (GECC) as a means of financing appliance sales to cash-constrained customers who were unable to get installment credit from banks. By the late 1950s banks were more willing to make installment loans, and so finance companies began looking outside their parent companies for business. A look at GECC's loan and lease portfolio today shows leases for over 65,000 railcars and 160 commercial airlines and over $1 billion in leveraged buyout financing and $20 billion in mortgage insurance premiums, along with over $350 million in loans to General Electric customers.

TABLE 5–1   Assets and Liabilities of U.S. Finance Companies on September 30, 1997

	Billions of Dollars		*Percent of Total Assets*
Assets			
Accounts receivable gross		$656.8	73.3
Consumer	$255.0		28.5
Business	313.1		34.9
Real estate	88.7		9.9
Less reserves for unearned income	(58.0)		(6.5)
Less reserves for losses	(13.7)		(1.5)
Accounts receivable net		585.1	65.3
All other		310.5	34.7
Total assets		895.6	100.0
Liabilities and Capital			
Bank loans		19.3	2.2
Commercial paper		190.2	21.2
Debt due to parent		61.7	6.9
Debt not elsewhere classified		348.5	38.9
All other liabilities		177.2	19.8
Capital, surplus, and undivided profits		98.7	11.0
Total liabilities and capital		895.6	100.0

Source: *Federal Reserve Bulletin,* December 1997, p. A33.

Sales Finance Institutions
Institutions that specialize in making loans to the customers of a particular retailer or manufacturer.

Personal Credit Institutions
Institutions that specialize in making installment and other loans to consumers.

Business Credit Institutions
Institutions that specialize in making business loans.

Factoring
The process of purchasing accounts receivable from corporations (often at a discount), usually with no recourse to the seller if the receivables go bad.

Finance companies have been among the fastest growing FI groups in recent years. In the third quarter of 1997 their assets stood at $895.6 billion (see Table 5–1). Comparing this to assets at the end of 1977 (reported in Table 5–2) of $104.3 billion, this industry has experienced growth of over 758 percent in the last 20 years. GMAC Commercial Mortgage Corp. (GMACCM), a subsidiary of General Motors Acceptance Corp. (GMAC), is in fact the largest commercial mortgage lender in the United States, with a mortgage portfolio over $40 billion in place. The company announced in 1997 that it had plans to expand its product mix to create one of the world's leading "one-stop" commercial finance companies.

The three major types of finance companies are (1) sales finance institutions, (2) personal credit institutions, and (3) business credit institutions. **Sales finance institutions** (e.g., Ford Motor Credit and Sears Roebuck Acceptance Corp.) specialize in making loans to the customers of a particular retailer or manufacturer. **Personal credit institutions** (e.g., Household Finance Corp. and American General Finance) specialize in making installment and other loans to consumers. **Business credit institutions** (e.g., CIT Group and Heller Financial) are companies that provide financing to corporations, especially through equipment leasing and **factoring,** in which the finance company purchases accounts receivable from corporate customers. These accounts are purchased at a discount from their face value, and the finance company takes over the responsibility for collecting the accounts receivable. Many finance companies perform more than one of these three services (e.g., GMAC).

The industry is quite concentrated, with the largest 20 firms accounting for more than 80 percent of its assets. In addition, many of the largest finance companies, such as General Motors Acceptance Corporation (GMAC), tend to be wholly owned or captive subsidiaries of major manufacturing companies. A major role of a

**TABLE 5–2   Assets and Liabilities of U.S. Finance Companies
on December 31, 1977**

		Billions of Dollars	Percent of Total Assets
Assets			
Accounts receivable gross		$ 99.2	95.1
Consumer	$44.0		42.2
Business	55.2		52.9
Less reserves for unearned income and losses	(12.7)		(12.2)
Accounts receivable net		86.5	82.9
Cash and bank deposit		2.6	2.5
Securities		0.9	0.9
All others		14.3	13.7
Total assets		104.3	100.0
Liabilities and Capital			
Bank loans		5.9	5.7
Commercial paper		29.6	28.4
Debt			
Short-term		6.2	5.9
Long-term		36.0	34.5
Other		11.5	11.0
Capital, surplus, and undivided profits		15.1	14.5
Total liabilities and capital		104.3	100.0

Source: *Federal Reserve Bulletin,* June 1978, p. A39.

Captive Finance Company
A finance company that is wholly owned by a parent corporation.

captive finance company is to provide financing for the purchase of products manufactured by the parent, such as GM cars. In turn, the parent company is often a major source of debt finance for the captive finance company.

Concept Questions

1. What are the three major types of finance companies? What types of customers do each serve?
2. What is a captive finance company?

Balance Sheet and Recent Trends

As mentioned above, finance companies provide three basic lending services: customer lending, consumer lending, and business lending. In Table 5–1 we show the balance sheet of finance companies in the third quarter of 1997. As you can see, business and consumer loans (called accounts receivable) are the major assets held by finance companies, accounting for 63.4 percent of total assets. Comparing the figures in Table 5–1 to those in Table 5–2 for 1977, we see that 95.1 percent of total assets were consumer and business loans in 1977. Thus, over the last 20 years finance companies have replaced consumer and business loans with increasing amounts of real estate loans and other assets.

Table 5–3 shows the breakdown of the industry's loans from 1994 through August 1997 in these three areas. In recent years, the fastest growing areas of asset business have been in the nonconsumer finance areas, especially leasing and

TABLE 5–3   Finance Company Loans Outstanding from 1994 through August 1997[1]

(in billions of dollars)

	1994	1995	1996	August 1997
Consumer	248.0	285.8	310.6	323.1
Motor vehicle loans	70.2	81.1	86.7	88.4
Motor vehicle leases	67.5	80.8	92.5	98.8
Revolving[2]	25.9	28.5	32.5	33.6
Other[3]	38.4	42.6	33.2	35.4
Securitized assets				
Motor vehicle loans	32.8	34.8	36.8	38.2
Motor vehicle leases	2.2	3.5	8.7	8.9
Revolving	n.a	n.a.	0.0	0.0
Other	11.2	14.7	20.1	19.7
Real estate	66.9	72.4	111.9	123.5
One- to four-family	n.a	n.a.	52.1	58.9
Other	n.a.	n.a.	30.5	30.4
Securitized real estate assets[4]				
One- to four-family	n.a.	n.a.	28.9	33.9
Other	n.a.	n.a.	0.4	0.3
Business	298.6	331.2	347.2	339.3
Motor vehicles	62.0	66.5	67.1	65.2
Retail loans	18.5	21.8	25.1	25.3
Wholesale loans[5]	35.2	36.6	33.0	30.5
Leases	8.3	8.0	9.0	9.4
Equipment	166.7	188.0	194.8	189.0
Loans	48.9	58.6	59.9	51.3
Leases	117.8	129.4	134.9	137.6
Other business receivables[6]	46.2	47.2	47.6	52.5
Securitized assets[4]				
Motor vehicles	14.3	20.6	24.0	19.8
Retail loans	1.5	1.8	2.7	2.3
Wholesale loans	12.8	18.8	21.3	17.5[1]
Leases	n.a.	n.a.	0.0	0.0
Equipment	8.9	8.1	11.3	10.3
Loans	4.7	5.3	4.7	4.1
Leases	4.2	2.8	6.6	6.2
Other business receivables[6]	0.5	0.8	2.4	2.4
Total	613.5	689.5	769.7	785.9

[1]Owned receivables are those carried on the balance sheet of the institution. Managed receivables are outstanding balances of pools upon which securities have been issued; these balances are no longer carried on the balance sheets of the loan originator.

[2]Excludes revolving credit reported as held by depository institutions that are subsidiaries of finance companies.

[3]Includes personal cash loans, mobile home loans, and loans to purchase other types of consumer goods, such as appliances, apparel, boats, and recreation vehicles.

[4]Outstanding balances of pools on which securities have been issued; these balances are no longer carried on the balance sheets of the loan originator.

[5]Credit arising from transactions between manufacturers and dealers, that is, floor plan financing.

[6]Includes loans on commercial accounts receivable, factored commercial accounts, and receivable dealer capital; small loans used primarily for business or farm purposes; and wholesale and lease paper for mobile homes, campers, and travel trailers.

Source: *Federal Reserve Bulletin*, December 1997, p. A33.

TABLE 5–4   Consumer Credit Interest Rates for 1994 through August 1997

Type	1994	1995	1996	August 1997
Commercial bank new car	8.12%	9.57%	9.05%	8.99%
Auto finance company new car	9.79%	11.19%	9.84%	5.93%

Source: *Federal Reserve Bulletin,* November 1997, p. A36.

business lending. In August 1997 consumer loans constituted 41.1 percent of all finance company loans, mortgages represented 15.7 percent, and business loans comprised the largest category of loans at 43.2 percent. The growth in leasing was encouraged by tax incentives provided under the 1981 Economic Recovery Act.

Consumer Loans

Consumer loans consist of motor vehicle loans and leases, other consumer loans, and securitized loans from each category. Motor vehicle loans and leases are traditionally the major type of consumer loan (72.5 percent of the consumer loan portfolio in August 1997). As can be seen from Table 5–4, finance companies generally charge higher rates for automobile loans than do commercial banks. From 1994 to August 1997, auto finance companies charged interest rates 0.79 to 1.67 percent higher than those of commercial banks. The year 1997 proved to be an anomaly in regard to the generally higher rates on new car loans from finance companies relative to commercial banks. Because of economic problems in emerging-market countries (see Chapter 16), new car sales by U.S. firms in 1997 were lower than normal. As an incentive to clear the expanding stock of new cars, auto finance companies owned by the major auto manufacturers slashed interest rates on new car loans (some to as low as 3.9 percent). This type of low rate offered by finance companies, however, is rare.

Subprime Lender
A finance company that lends to high-risk customers.

Loan Sharks
Subprime lenders that charge unfairly exorbitant rates to desperate subprime borrowers.

The different rates generally seen on bank versus finance company consumer loans are due to the fact that finance companies generally attract riskier customers than do commercial banks. In fact, customers who seek individual (or business loans) from finance companies are often those judged too risky to obtain loans from commercial banks or thrifts. It is in fact possible for individuals to get a mortgage from a **subprime lender** finance company even with a bankruptcy on their records. Banks would rarely do this. Most finance companies that offer these mortgages, however, charge rates commensurate with the higher risk, and there are a few **loan shark** companies that prey on desperate consumers, charging exorbitant rates as high as 30 percent or more. The Contemporary Perspectives box on p. 80 points out that such subprime lending by finance companies has landed some industry participants in less than a prime position themselves.

Other consumer loans include personal cash loans, mobile home loans, and loans to purchase other types of consumer goods, such as appliances, apparel, general merchandise, and recreational vehicles. In August 1997 other consumer loans made up 27.5 percent of the consumer loan portfolio of finance companies.

Mortgages

Residential and commercial mortgages have become a major component in finance company portfolios. Referring again to Table 5–2, finance companies did not deal

Securitized Mortgage Assets
Mortgages packaged and used as assets backing secondary market securities.

in mortgages in 1977. Mortgages include all loans secured by liens on any type of real estate. Mortgages can be made either directly or as **securitized mortgage assets** (e.g., mortgages packaged and used as assets backing secondary market securities).[1] The mortgages in the loan portfolio can be first or second mortgages in the form of home equity loans. Home equity loans have become very profitable for finance companies since the Tax Reform Act of 1986 was passed, disallowing the tax deductibility of consumers' interest payments other than those on home mortgages. Also, the bad debt expense and administrative costs on home equity loans are lower than those on other finance company loans. At the end of 1997 home equity debt totaled more than $130 billion, with five finance companies (such as Contifinancial) accounting for over $20 billion in securitized home equity loans.

Business Loans

Business loans comprise the largest portion of the loan portfolio of finance companies. Finance companies have several advantages over commercial banks in offering services to small business customers.[2] First, as mentioned earlier, they are not subject to regulations that restrict the types of products and services they can offer. Second, because finance companies do not accept deposits, they have no bank-type regulators looking directly over their shoulders.[3] Third, being in many cases subsidiaries of holding companies, finance companies often have substantial industry and product expertise. Fourth, as mentioned in regard to consumer loans, finance companies are more willing to accept risky customers than are commercial banks. Fifth, finance companies generally have lower overheads than banks have; for example, they do not need tellers or branches for deposit taking.

The major subcategories of business loans are retail and wholesale motor vehicle loans and leases (19.2 percent of all business loans in August 1997), equipment loans (55.7 percent), other business loans (15.5 percent), and securitized business assets (9.6 percent). Motor vehicle loans consist of retail loans that assist in transactions between the retail seller of the product and the ultimate consumer, for example, passenger car fleets and commercial land vehicles for which licenses are required. Wholesale loans are loan agreements between parties other than the companies' consumers. For example, GMAC provides wholesale financing to GM dealers for inventory floor plans. These activities extend to retail and wholesale leasing of motor vehicles as well. Business lending activities of finance companies also include equipment loans, with the finance company either owning or leasing the equipment directly to its industrial customer or providing the financial backing for a leveraged lease, a working capital loan, or a loan to purchase or remodel the customer's facility. Indeed, equipment loans are currently the major category of business loans for finance companies. Other business loans include loans to businesses to finance accounts receivable, factored commercial accounts, small farm loans, and wholesale and lease paper for mobile homes, campers, and trailers.

To finance asset growth, finance companies have relied primarily on short-term commercial paper and other debt (longer-term notes and bonds). As reported in

---

[1]We discuss the securitization of mortgages in more detail in Chapter 28.

[2]See also M. Carey et al., "Does Corporate Lending by Banks and Finance Companies Differ? Evidence on Specialization in Private Debt Contracting," *Journal of Finance* 53 (June 1998), pp. 845–78.

[3]Finance companies do, of course, have market participants looking over their shoulders and monitoring their activities.

Contemporary Perspectives

A RISKY BUSINESS GETS EVEN RISKIER: BIG LOSSES AND BAD ACCOUNTING LEAVE "SUBPRIME" LENDERS REELING

Barnaby J. Feder

The business of lending money to the millions of Americans with tarnished credit ratings—or none at all—has always been a walk on capitalism's wild side.

"Subprime" lending, as the business is known, is a volatile world of big risks, staggering profit potential and almost no barriers to entry. Its clients vary from swindlers with no intention of paying off their loans to hard-working immigrants and victims of personal tragedies like layoffs or debilitating illness. And the hardball tactics some lenders use to encourage borrowing or to collect on loans breed both lawsuits and criticism from consumer groups. . . .

In a business where the line between exploiting risk and drowning in it is thin, some players have gone "too close to the edge," said William A. Brandt Jr., a corporate turnaround specialist, shortly after he was brought in late last month to stabilize the Mercury Finance Company in the wake of disclosures that its earnings reports had been falsified from 1993 on.

The turmoil is rooted in the relentless growth in the number of Americans with blemishes on their credit records, ranging from repeated late payments to outright bankruptcy, making them a market far too large to ignore. Now with everyone from the biggest banks and giant credit companies like GE Capital to ambitious entrepreneurs piling in, the competitive pressures are exposing the cracks caused by ill-conceived growth strategies, poor management of operations and outright greed.

There had been periodic reminders that not everyone would be successful. In early 1995, Search Capital Group Inc., a rapidly expanding Dallas lender in the used-car market, was forced to put its eight operating units into bankruptcy. And the attempt that year by TFC Enterprise to expand into civilian subprime auto loans from its core business of loans to soldiers generated huge losses through "a mixture of ineptitude and undue optimism," according to David Karsten, the chief financial officer since a new team of managers took over at TFC last year.

But it took the news of the padding of Mercury's books to really stun Wall Street. The company, based in the Chicago suburb of Lake Forest, Ill., is a relative giant in the $70 billion subprime auto loan sector, with some $1.5 billion in loans outstanding and a carefully cultivated reputation for sound, penny-pinching management. . . .

It is not just Mercury's fans who have been surprised. "I never dreamed this would happen," said Matthew Lindenbaum, a principal at Basswood Partners, a Paramus, N.J., money manager that concentrates on financial stocks. Mr. Lindenbaum had been one of the few analysts warning that the kind of explosive growth Mercury and others had been reporting often led to problems that investors detected too late to save themselves.

Table 5–1, in 1997 commercial paper amounted to $190.2 billion (21.2 percent of total assets), while other debt (debt due to parents and debt not elsewhere classified) totaled $410.2 billion (45.8 percent). Total capital comprised $98.7 billion (11 percent of total liabilities and capital), and bank loans totaled $19.3 billion (2.2 percent). Comparing these figures with those for 1977 (in Table 5–2), commercial paper was used more in 1977 (28.4 percent of total liabilities and capital), while other debt (short- and long-term) was less significant as a source of financing (40.4 percent). Finance companies also now rely less heavily on bank loans for financing and hold less capital.[4] In 1977, bank loans accounted for 5.7 percent of total liabilities and capital was 14.5 percent of the total.

As discussed above, unlike banks and thrifts, finance companies cannot issue deposits. Rather, to finance assets, finance companies are now the largest issuers in

---

[4]For more on the relative capital adequacy of finance companies versus banks, see M. L. Kwast and S. W. Passmore, "The Subsidy Provided by the Federal Safety Net: Theory, Measurement and Containment," Federal Reserve Board of Governors Working Paper 1997–58.

Contemporary Perspectives

Any impulse investors had to write off Mercury's woes as an aberration took a severe hit on Thursday. Reports from the industry trenches included a bankruptcy filing by the Jayhawk Acceptance Corporation, which finances car loans to some of the nation's riskiest buyers; the delay until Monday of an earnings report from First Enterprise Financial because of unexpected loan losses, and the downgrading of securities issued by Olympic Financial Ltd.

So far, the bad news has been heavily concentrated in the volatile auto-lending sector, but analysts say that investors are bound to be more cautious about the entire subprime world, at least for a while.

"It's going to have an effect on mortgages and credit cards," said Jewel Bickford, managing director of Rothschild Capital Markets in New York, which helps finance companies assemble packages of auto loans, mortgages, credit card receivables, and other assets that are sold as securities to investors. . . .

The success stories have been even more striking in other subprime markets. Investors in the Green Tree Financial Company of St. Paul, the leading subprime lender in mobile homes, enjoyed a return of 83.2 percent annually from 1991 through 1995, assuming they reinvested dividends—one of the best performances ever on Wall Street.

Borrowing money cheaply and lending it at sky-high rates is not the only way subprime lenders turbo-charge profit margins. Many pay discounted prices for the loans that auto dealers send them, which provides an added cushion against losses. And, in a tactic often criticized by consumer advocates, car buyers are cajoled into buying insurance policies that would appear to pay off the loans in the event of death or disability but are much more expensive and limited in their coverage than many purchasers realize. It is easy to see why Wall Street fell in love with the finance companies. . . .

Lately, though, meeting expectations is becoming tougher as competition forces growth-driven finance companies to make riskier loans and share more of the pie with auto dealers. At the same time, as Olympic's debt downgrade highlighted, many finance companies will have to offer sweeter terms to their creditors to calm nerves after the recent bad news from Mercury and Jayhawk. . . .

"Subprime is an incredible business if you can manage it," said Mr. Mack, who is now chief executive of the Pinnacle Finance Company, a privately held Minneapolis provider of home improvement loans to people with credit problems. . . .

Source: *New York Times,* February 12, 1997, p.1. Copyright © 1997 by The New York Times. Reprinted by permission.

the short-term commercial paper market, with many having direct sale programs in which commercial paper is sold directly to mutual funds and other institutional investors on a continuous day-by-day basis. Most commercial paper issues have maturities of 30 days or less, although they can be issued with maturities of up to 270 days.[5]

The outlook for the industry as a whole is quite bright. Loan demand among lower- and middle-income consumers is strong. Because many of these potential borrowers have very low savings, no slowdown in the demand for finance company services is expected. The largest finance companies—those which lend to less risky individual and business customers as well as subprime borrowers (e.g., Household International, Associates First Capital, and Beneficial)—are experiencing strong profits and loan growth. (The industry's assets as a whole grew at a rate of 15.7 percent in 1997.) As such, the most successful finance companies are becoming

[5]Commercial paper issued with a maturity longer than 270 days has to be registered with the SEC (i.e., it is treated the same as publicly placed bonds).

takeover targets for other financial service firms. For example, in 1998 First Union Bank, the second largest bank home equity lender, acquired Money Store, the second largest nonbank home equity lender, to create the largest home equity lender in the country. This is another example of integration and consolidation among firms in the financial services sector.

Concept Questions

1. How have the major assets held by finance companies changed in the last 20 years?
2. How do subprime lender finance company customers differ from consumer loan customers at banks?
3. What advantages do finance companies offer over commercial banks to small business customers?

Regulation

The Federal Reserve defines a finance company as a firm (other than a depository institution) whose primary assets are loans to individuals and businesses. Finance companies, like depository institutions, then, are financial intermediaries that borrow funds for relending, making a profit on the difference between the interest rate on borrowed funds and the rate charged on the loans. Also like depository institutions, finance companies are subject to any state-imposed usury ceilings on the maximum loan rate assigned to any individual customer. However, because finance companies do not accept deposits, they are not subject to extensive oversight by any specific federal or state regulators—they are much less regulated than are banks and thrifts.[6] The lack of regulatory oversight for these companies enables them to offer a wide scope of "bank-type" services yet avoid the expense of regulatory compliance, such as that imposed on banks and thrifts by the Community Reinvestment Act of 1977, which requires these institutions to keep and file extensive reports showing that they are not discriminating in their lending practices in their local communities (see Chapter 1).

Since finance companies are heavy borrowers in the capital markets, they need to signal their solvency and safety to investors. Signals of solvency and safety are usually sent by holding higher equity or capital-asset ratios—and therefore lower leverage ratios—than banks hold. For example, the third quarter of 1997 aggregate balance sheet (Table 5–1) shows a capital–assets ratio of 11 percent for finance companies. This can be compared to the capital–asset ratio for commercial banks of 8.8 percent in the same period. Also, some captive finance companies use default protection guarantees from their parent companies and/or guarantees such as letters of credit or lines of credit purchased for a fee from high-quality commercial or investment banks as additional protection against default risk and credit losses.

Concept Questions

1. Since finance companies seem to compete in the same lending markets as banks, why aren't they subject to the same regulations as banks?
2. How do finance companies signal solvency and safety to investors?

---

[6]Like any corporation, they are subject to SEC disclosure rules.

Summary

This chapter provided an overview of the finance company industry. This industry competes directly with depository institutions for its high-quality (prime) loan customers by specializing in consumer loans, real estate loans, and business loans. The industry also services subprime borrowers deemed too risky for most depository institutions. However, because firms in this industry do not accept deposits, they are not regulated to the same extent as are depository institutions.

Because they do not have access to deposits for their funding, finance companies rely instead on short- and long-term debt, especially commercial paper. Currently, the industry is generally growing and profitable, although the subprime lending sector of the industry is experiencing some financial problems as consumer default rates on loans and credit cards rise (see Chapter 10).

Questions and Problems

1. What is the primary function of finance companies? How do finance companies differ from commercial banks?

2. What are the three major types of finance companies? To which market segments do these companies provide service?

3. What have been the major changes in the accounts receivable balances of finance companies over the 20-year period 1977–1997?

4. What are the major types of consumer loans? Why are the rates charged by consumer finance companies typically higher than those charged by commercial banks?

5. What are securitized mortgage assets? Why have home equity loans become popular?

6. What advantages do finance companies have over commercial banks in offering services to small business customers? What are the major subcategories of business loans? Which category is the largest?

7. What have been the primary sources of financing for finance companies?

8. How do finance companies make money? What risks does this process entail? How do these risks differ for a finance company versus a commercial bank?

9. Compare Tables 5–1 and 3–5. Which firms have higher ratios of capital to total assets; finance companies or securities firms? What does this comparison indicate about the relative strengths of these two types of firms?

10. How does the amount of equity as a percentage of total assets compare for finance companies and commercial banks? What accounts for this difference?

11. Why do finance companies face less regulation than do commercial banks? How does this advantage translate into performance advantages? What is the major performance disadvantage?

CHAPTER

6

WHY ARE FINANCIAL INTERMEDIARIES SPECIAL?

Chapter Outline

Introduction

Among all private corporations, financial intermediaries (FIs) are singled out for special regulatory attention.[1] To justify such regulation, advocates usually argue that FIs provide special functions or services and that major disturbances to or interfer-

[1]Some public utility suppliers, such as gas, electric, telephone, and water companies, are also singled out for regulation because of the special nature of their services and the costs imposed on society if they fail.

84

FIGURE 6–1

*Flow of Funds in a World
without FIs*

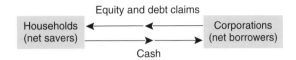

Negative Externality
An action by an economic
agent imposing costs on
other economic agents.

ences with those functions can lead to adverse effects on the rest of the economy—
what economists call **negative externalities.**[2] We first examine this specialness
question in general; that is what are the special functions FIs—both depository institutions and nondepository institutions—provide, and how do those functions benefit the economy? Second, we investigate what makes some FIs more special than
others. Third, we look at how unique and long-lived the special functions of FIs really are.

Financial Intermediaries' Specialness

To understand the important economic function of FIs, imagine a simple world in
which FIs do not exist. In such a world, households generating excess savings by
consuming less than they earn would have the basic choice: They could hold cash
as an asset or invest in the securities issued by corporations. In general, corporations
issue securities to finance their investments in real assets and cover the gap between
their investment plans and their internally generated savings such as retained
earnings.

As shown in Figure 6–1, in such a world savings would flow from households
to corporations; in return, financial claims (equity and debt securities) would flow
from corporations to household savers.

In an economy without FIs, the level of fund flows between household savers
and the corporate sectors is likely to be quite low. There are several reasons for this.
Once they have lent money to a firm by buying its financial claims, households
need to monitor or check the actions of that firm. They must be sure that the firm's
management neither absconds with nor wastes the funds on any projects with low
or negative net present values. Such monitoring actions are extremely costly for any
given household because they require considerable time and expense to collect sufficiently high-quality information relative to the size of the average household
saver's investments. Given this, it is likely that each household would prefer to
leave the monitoring to others; in the end, little or no monitoring would be done.
The resulting lack of monitoring would reduce the attractiveness and increase the
risk of investing in corporate debt and equity.

Covenant
Legal clauses in a bond
contract that require the
issuer of bonds to take or
avoid certain actions.

In the real world, bondholders partially alleviate these problems by requiring
restrictive clauses or **covenants** in bond contracts. Such covenants restrict the risky
nature of projects that a firm's management can undertake. Bondholders also hire a
bond trustee to oversee compliance with these covenants. However, the enforcement and monitoring of covenants are still quite costly, especially if the debt is long
term and is renewed infrequently.

The relatively long-term nature of corporate equity and debt also creates a second disincentive for household investors to hold the direct financial claims issued

---

[2]A good example of a negative externality is the costs faced by small businesses in a one-bank town if the
local bank fails. These businesses could find it difficult to get financing elsewhere, and their customers could
be similarly disadvantaged. As a result, the failure of the bank may have a negative or contagious effect on the
economic prospects of the whole community, resulting in lower sales. production, and employment.

Liquidity
The ease of converting an asset into cash.

Price Risk
The risk that the sale price of an asset will be lower than the purchase price of that asset.

by corporations. Specifically, given the choice between holding cash and holding long-term securities, households may well choose to hold cash for **liquidity** reasons, especially if they plan to use savings to finance consumption expenditures in the near future.

Finally, even though real-world financial markets provide some liquidity services by allowing households to trade corporate debt and equity securities among themselves, investors also face a **price risk** on sale of securities, and the secondary market trading of securities involves various transaction costs. That is, the price at which household investors can sell securities on secondary markets such as the New York Stock Exchange may well differ from the price they initially paid for the securities.

Because of (1) monitoring costs, (2) liquidity costs, and (3) price risk, the average household saver may view direct investment in corporate securities as an unattractive proposition and prefer either not to save or to save in the form of cash.

However, the economy has developed an alternative and indirect way to channel household savings to the corporate sector. This is to channel savings via FIs. Due to the costs of monitoring, liquidity, and price risk, as well as for some other reasons explained later, savers often prefer to hold the financial claims issued by FIs rather than those issued by corporations.

Consider Figure 6–2, which is a closer representation than Figure 6–1 of the world in which we live and the way funds flow in our economy. Notice how financial intermediaries or institutions are standing, or intermediating, between the household and corporate sectors.

These intermediaries fulfill two functions; any given FI might specialize in one or the other or might do both simultaneously. The first function is the brokerage function. When acting as a pure broker, an FI acts as an agent for the saver by providing information and transaction services. For example, full-service securities firms (e.g., Merrill Lynch) carry out investment research and make investment recommendations for their retail (or household) clients as well as conducting the purchase or sale of securities for commission fees. Discount brokers (e.g., Charles Schwab) carry out the purchase or sale of securities at better prices and with greater efficiency than household savers could achieve by trading on their own. Independent insurance brokers identify the best types of insurance policies household savers can buy to fit their savings–retirement plans. In fulfilling a brokerage function, the FI plays an extremely important role by reducing transaction and information costs or imperfections between households and corporations. Thus, the FI encourages a higher rate of savings than would otherwise exist.

Asset Transformer
An FI issues financial claims that are more attractive to household savers than the claims directly issued by corporations.

Primary Securities
Securities issued by corporations and backed by the real assets of those corporations.

Secondary Securities
Securities issued by FIs and backed by primary securities.

The second function is the asset-transformation function. In acting as an **asset transformer,** the FI issues financial claims that are far more attractive to household savers than the claims directly issued by corporations. That is, for many households, the financial claims issued by FIs dominate those issued directly by corporations due to lower monitoring costs, lower liquidity costs, and lower price risk. In acting as asset transformers, FIs purchase the financial claims issued by corporations—equities, bonds, and other debt claims called **primary securities**—and finance these purchases by selling financial claims to household investors and other sectors in the form of deposits, insurance policies, and so on. The financial claims of FIs may be considered **secondary securities** because these assets are backed by the primary securities issued by commercial corporations that in turn invest in real assets.

Simplified balance sheets of a commercial firm and an FI are shown in Table 6–1. Note that in the real world FIs hold a small proportion of their assets in the form of real assets such as bank branch buildings. These simplified balance sheets

FIGURE 6–2

Flow of Funds in a World with FIs

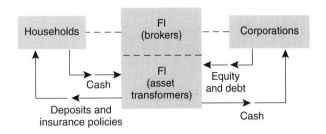

TABLE 6–1   Simplified Balance Sheets for a Commercial Firm and an FI

Commercial Firm		Financial Intermediary	
Assets	*Liabilities*	*Assets*	*Liabilities*
Real assets (plant machinery)	Primary securities (debt, equity)	Primary securities (debt, equity)	Secondary securities (deposits and insurance policies)

reflect a reasonably accurate characterization of the operational differences between commercial firms and FIs.

How can FIs purchase the direct or primary securities issued by corporations and profitably transform them into secondary securities more attractive to household savers? This question strikes at the very heart of what makes FIs special and important to the economy. The answer lies in the ability of FIs to better resolve the three costs facing a saver who chooses to invest directly in corporate securities.

Information Costs

Agency Costs
Costs relating to the risk that the owners and managers of firms that receive savers' funds will take actions with those funds contrary to the best interests of the savers.

One problem faced by an average saver directly investing in a commercial firm's financial claims is the high cost of information collection. Household savers must monitor the actions of firms in a timely and complete fashion after purchasing securities. Failure to monitor exposes investors to **agency costs,** that is, the risk that the firm's owners or managers will take actions with the saver's money contrary to the promises contained in the covenants of its securities contracts. Agency costs arise whenever economic agents enter into contracts in a world of incomplete information and thus costly information collection. The more difficult and costly it is to collect information, the more likely it is that contracts will be broken. In this case the saver (the so-called principal) could be harmed by the actions taken by the borrowing firm (the so-called agent). One solution to this problem is for a large number of small savers to place their funds with a single FI. This FI groups these funds together and invests in the direct or primary financial claims issued by firms. This agglomeration of funds resolves a number of problems. First, the large FI now has a much greater incentive to collect information and monitor actions of the firm because it has far more at stake than does any small individual household. This alleviates the free-rider problem that exists when small household savers leave it to each other to collect information and monitor the actions of firms. In a sense, small savers have appointed the FI as a **delegated monitor** to act on their behalf.[3] Not only does the FI have a greater incentive to collect information, the average cost of

Delegated Monitor
An economic agent appointed to act on behalf of smaller agents in collecting information and/or investing funds on their behalf.

---

[3]For a theoretical modeling of the delegated monitor function, see D. W. Diamond. "Financial Intermediaries and Delegated Monitoring." *Review of Economic Studies* 51 (1984). pp. 393–414; and J. H. Boyd and E. C. Prescott, "Financial Intermediary—Coalitions," *Journal of Economic Theory* 38 (1986), pp. 211–32.

collecting information is lower. For example, the cost to a small investor of buying a $100 broker's report may seem inordinately high for a $10,000 investment. For an FI with $10 million under management, however, the cost seems trivial. Such economies of scale of information production and collection tend to enhance the advantages to savers of using FIs rather than directly investing themselves.

Second, associated with the greater incentive to monitor and the costs involved in failing to monitor appropriately, FIs may develop new secondary securities that enable them to monitor more effectively. Thus, a richer menu of contracts may improve the monitoring abilities of FIs. Perhaps the classic example of this is the bank loan. Bank loans are generally shorter-term debt contracts than bond contracts. This short-term nature allows the FI to exercise more monitoring power and control over the borrower. In particular, the information the FI generates regarding the firm is frequently updated as its loan renewal decisions are made. When bank loan contracts are sufficiently short term, the banker becomes almost like an insider to the firm regarding informational familiarity with its operations and financial conditions. Indeed, this more frequent monitoring often replaces the need for the relatively inflexible and hard-to-enforce covenants found in bond contracts.[4] Moreover, by acting as a partial corporate insider and sending favorable information signals regarding the firm and its performance through bank loan renewals, the holders of outside debt and equity also benefit by acting on this information, as can firms which are then able to issue their securities at a lower cost. Thus, by acting as a delegated monitor and producing better and more timely information, FIs reduce the degree of information imperfection and asymmetry between the ultimate suppliers and users of funds in the economy.

Liquidity and Price Risk

In addition to improving the flow and quality of information, FIs provide financial or secondary claims to household savers. Often, these claims have superior liquidity attributes compared to primary securities such as corporate equity and bonds. For example, banks and thrifts issue transaction account deposit contracts with a fixed principal value (and often a guaranteed interest rate) that can be withdrawn immediately on demand by household savers. Money market mutual funds issue shares to household savers that allow those savers to enjoy almost fixed principal (depositlike) contracts while often earning interest rates higher than those on bank deposits. Even life insurance companies allow policyholders to borrow against their policies held with the company at very short notice. The real puzzle is how FIs such as depository institutions can offer highly liquid and low price-risk contracts to savers on the liability side of their balance sheets while investing in relatively illiquid and higher price-risk securities issued by corporations on the asset side. Furthermore, how can FIs be confident enough to guarantee that they can provide liquidity services to investors and savers when they themselves invest in risky asset portfolios? And why should savers and investors believe FIs' promises regarding the liquidity of their investments?

---

[4]For a further description and discussion of the special or unique nature of bank loans, see E. Fama, "What's Different about Banks?" *Journal of Monetary Economics* 15 (1985). pp. 29–39; C. James, "Some Evidence on the Uniqueness of Bank Loans," *Journal of Financial Economics* 19 (1987), pp. 217–35; M. T. Billett, M. J. Flannery, and J. A. Garfinkel, "The Effect of Lender Identity on a Borrowing Firm's Equity Return," *Journal of Finance* 50 (1995), pp. 699–718: and W. A. Kracaw and M. Zenner, "The Wealth Effects of Bank Financing Announcements in Hightly Leveraged Transactions," *Journal of Finance* 57 (1996), pp. 1931–46.

Diversify
The ability of an economic agent to reduce risk by holding a number of securities in a portfolio.

The answers to these questions lie in the ability of FIs to **diversify** away some but not all of their portfolio risks. The concept of diversification is familiar to all students of finance: Basically, as long as the returns on different investments are not perfectly *positively* correlated, by exploiting the benefits of size FIs diversify away significant amounts of portfolio risk—especially the risk specific to the individual firm issuing any given security. Indeed, experiments in the United States and the United Kingdom have shown that diversifying across just 15 securities can bring significant diversification benefits to FIs and portfolio managers.[5] Further, as the number of securities in an FI's asset portfolio increases, portfolio risk falls, albeit at a diminishing rate. What is really going on here is that FIs exploit the law of large numbers in their investments, whereas due to their small size, many household savers are constrained to holding relatively undiversified portfolios. This risk diversification allows an FI to predict more accurately its expected return on its asset portfolio. A domestically and globally diversified FI may be able to generate an almost risk-free return on its assets. As a result, it can credibly fulfill its promise to households to supply highly liquid claims with little price or capital value risk. A good example of this is the ability of a bank to offer highly liquid demand deposits—with a fixed principal value—as liabilities while at the same time investing in risky loans as assets. As long as an FI is sufficiently large to gain from diversification and monitoring, its financial claims are likely to be viewed as liquid and attractive to small savers compared to direct investments in the capital market. The smaller and the less diversified an FI becomes, the less able it is to credibly promise household savers that its financial claims are highly liquid and of low capital risk. Specifically, the less diversified the FI, the higher the probability that it will default on its liability obligations and the more risky and illiquid its claims.[6] In reality, the majority of financial institution failures involve small FIs that are relatively undiversified productwise and geographically. For example, there were widespread failures of smaller U.S. banks, thrifts, and insurance companies in the Southwest during the slump in oil and gas prices in the 1980s.[7]

Other Special Services

The preceding discussion has concentrated on three general or special services provided by FIs: reducing household savers' monitoring costs, increasing their liquidity, and reducing their price-risk exposure. Next, we discuss two other special services provided by FIs: reduced transaction costs and maturity intermediation or asset transformation.

Reduced Transaction Cost.   Just as FIs provide potential economies of scale in information collection, they also provide potential economies of scale in transaction costs. For example, since May 1, 1975, fixed commissions for equity trades on the NYSE have been abolished. As a result, small retail buyers face higher commission charges or transaction costs than do large wholesale buyers. By grouping their assets in FIs that purchase assets in bulk—such as in mutual funds and pension

[5]For a review of such studies, see E. J. Elton and M. J. Gruber, *Modern Portfolio Theory and Investment Analysis,* 6th ed. (New York: John Wiley & Sons, 1998), chapter 2.

[6]For a theoretical modeling of the link between credible deposit contracts and diversification, see Boyd and Prescott, "Financial Intermediary Coalitions," pp. 211–32.

[7]Nevertheless, in the 1980s, 9 of the 10 biggest banking organizations in Texas also had to be closed, merged, or reorganized, in large part because of their undiversified exposures to the heavily oil- and gas-dependent Texas economy.

funds—household savers can reduce the transaction costs of their asset purchases. In addition, bid-ask (buy-sell) spreads are normally lower for assets bought and sold in large quantities.

Maturity Intermediation.   An additional dimension of FIs' ability to reduce risk by diversification is that they can better bear the risk of mismatching the maturities of their assets and liabilities than can small household savers. Thus, FIs offer maturity intermediation services to the rest of the economy. Specifically, through maturity mismatching, FIs can produce new types of contracts, such as long-term mortgage loans to households, while still raising funds with short-term liability contracts. Further, while such mismatches can subject an FI to interest rate risk (see Chapters 8 and 9), a large FI is better able to manage this risk through its superior access to markets and instruments for hedging such as loan sales and securitization (Chapters 27 and 28); futures (Chapter 24); swaps (Chapter 26); and options, caps, floors, and collars (Chapter 25).

Concept Questions

1. What are the three major risks to household savers from direct security purchases?
2. What are two major differences between brokers (such as security brokers) and depository institutions (such as commercial banks)?
3. What are primary securities and secondary securities?
4. What is the link between asset diversification and the liquidity of deposit contracts?

Other Aspects of Specialness

The theory of the flow of funds points to three principal reasons for believing that FIs are special along with two other associated reasons. In reality, academics, policymakers, and regulators identify other areas of specialness relating to certain specific functions of FIs or groups of FIs. We discuss these next.

The Transmission of Monetary Policy

The highly liquid nature of bank and thrift deposits has resulted in their acceptance by the public as the most widely used medium of exchange in the economy. As you can see from the notes to Table 6–2, at the core of the three most commonly used definitions of the money supply—M1, M2, and M3—lie bank and/or thrift deposit contracts. Because the liabilities of depository institutions are a significant component of the money supply that impacts the rate of inflation, depository institutions and commercial banks play a key role in the *transmission of monetary policy* from the central bank to the rest of the economy. That is, banks are the conduit through which monetary policy actions impact the rest of the financial sector and the economy in general.

Credit Allocation

A further reason why FIs are often viewed as special is that they are the major and sometimes only source of finance for a particular sector of the economy preidentified as being in special need of finance. Policymakers in the United States and a number of other countries, such as the United Kingdom, have identified *residential real estate* as needing special subsidies. This has enhanced the specialness of FIs that most commonly service the needs of that sector. In the United States, S&Ls and savings banks have traditionally served the credit needs of the residential real estate sector.[8] In a similar fashion, farming is an especially important area of the economy in terms of the overall social welfare of the population. The U.S. government has even directly encouraged financial institutions to specialize in financing this area of activity through the creation of Federal Farm Credit Banks.

Intergenerational Wealth Transfers or Time Intermediation

The ability of savers to transfer wealth between youth and old age and across generations is also of great importance to the social well-being of a country. Because of this, life insurance and pension funds are often especially encouraged, via special taxation relief and other subsidy mechanisms to service and accommodate those needs.

Payment Services

Depository institutions such as banks and thrifts are special in that the efficiency with which they provide payment services directly benefits the economy. Two important payment services are check-clearing and wire transfer services. For example, on any given day, approximately $2 trillion of payments are effected through Fedwire and CHIPS, the two large wholesale payment wire networks in the United States. Any breakdowns in these systems probably would produce gridlock in the payment system with resulting harmful effects to the economy.

Denomination Intermediation

Both money market and debt-equity mutual funds are special because they provide services relating to denomination intermediation. Because they are sold in very large denominations, many assets are either out of reach of individual savers or would result in savers holding highly undiversified asset portfolios. For example, the minimum size of a negotiable CD is $100,000 and commercial paper (short-term corporate debt) is often sold in minimum packages of $250,000 or more. Individually, a saver may be unable to purchase such instruments. However, by buying shares in a money market mutual fund along with other small investors, household savers overcome the constraints to buying assets imposed by large minimum denomination sizes. Such indirect access to these markets may allow small savers to generate higher returns on their portfolios as well.

Concept Questions

1. Why does the need for denomination intermediation arise?
2. What are the two major sectors that society has identified as deserving special attention in credit allocation?
3. Why is monetary policy transmitted through the banking system?

---

[8]E. Laderman and W. Passmore, "Is Mortgage Lending by Savings Associations Special?" Finance and Economics Discussion Series, Federal Reserve Board, 1998–25, find, however, that the elimination of specialized savings banks in the United States would not have a major effect on mortgage borrowers.

TABLE 6–2   **Money Stock, Liquid Assets, and Debt Measures**
Billions of Dollars, Averages of Daily Figures, Seasonally Adjusted

Measures	1992 Dec.	1997 Dec.
M1	1,024.8	1,076.0
M2	3,509.0	4,040.2
M3	4,183.0	5,382.6
L	5,057.1	6,626.5
Debt	11,706.1	15,153.5

Notes: Composition of the money stock measures and debt is as follows:

M1: (1) currency outside the U.S. Treasury, Federal Reserve Banks, and the vaults of depository institutions, (2) travelers checks of nonbank issuers, (3) demand deposits at all commercial banks other than those owed to depository institutions, the U.S. government, and foreign banks and official institutions, less cash items in the process of collection and Federal Reserve float, and (4) other checkable deposits (OCDs), consisting of negotiable order of withdrawal (NOW) and automatic transfer service (ATS) accounts at depository institutions, credit union share draft accounts, and demand deposits at thrift institutions. Seasonally adjusted M1 is computed by summing currency, travelers checks, demand deposits, and OCDs, each seasonally adjusted separately.

M2: M1 plus (1) overnight (and continuing contract) repurchase agreements (RPs) issued by all depository institutions and overnight Eurodollars issued to U.S. residents by foreign branches of U.S. banks worldwide, (2) savings (including MMDAs) and small time deposits (time deposits—including retail RPs—in amounts of less than $100,000), and (3) balances in both taxable and tax-exempt general-purpose and broker-dealer money market funds. Excludes individual retirement accounts (IRAs) and Keogh balances at depository institutions and money market funds. Also excludes all balances held by U.S. commercial banks, money market funds (general purpose and broker-dealer), foreign governments and commercial banks, and the U.S. government. Seasonally adjusted M2 is computed by adjusting its non-M1 component as a whole and then adding this result to seasonally adjusted M1.

M3: M2 plus (1) large time deposits and term RP liabilities (in amounts or $100,000 or more) issued by all depository institutions, (2) term Eurodollars held by U.S. residents at foreign branches of U.S. banks worldwide and at all banking offices in the United Kingdom and Canada, and (3) balances in both taxable and tax-exempt, institution-only money market funds. Excludes amounts held by depository institutions, the U.S. government, money market funds, and foreign banks and official institutions. Also excluded is the estimated amount of overnight RPs and Eurodollars held by institution-only money market funds. Seasonally adjusted M3 is computed by adjusting its non-M2 component as a whole and then adding this result to seasonally adjusted M2.

L: M3 plus the nonbank public holdings of U.S. savings bonds, short-term Treasury securities, commercial paper, and bankers acceptances, net of money market fund holdings of these assets. Seasonally adjusted L is computed by summing U.S. savings bonds, short-term Treasury securities, commercial paper, and bankers acceptances, each seasonally adjusted separately, and then adding this result to M3.

Debt: The debt aggregate is the outstanding credit market debt of the domestic nonfinancial sectors—the federal sector (U.S. government, not including government-sponsored enterprises or federally related mortgage pools) and the nonfederal sectors (state and local governments, households and nonprofit organizations, nonfinancial corporate and nonfarm noncorporate businesses, and farms). Nonfederal debt consists of mortgages, tax-exempt and corporate bonds, consumer credit, bank loans, commercial paper, and other loans. The data, which are derived from the Federal Reserve Board's flow of funds accounts, are break-adjusted (that is, discontinuities in the data have been smoothed into the series) and month-averaged (that is, the data have been derived by averaging adjacent month-end levels).

Source: *Federal Reserve Bulletin,* Table A15, various years.

Specialness and Regulation

In the preceding section, FIs were shown to be special because of the various services they provide to sectors of the economy. The general areas of FI specialness include:

- Information services.
- Liquidity services.
- Price-risk reduction services.
- Transaction cost services.
- Maturity intermediation services.

Areas of institution-specific specialness are as follows:

- Money supply transmission (banks).
- Credit allocation (thrifts, farm banks).
- Intergenerational transfers (pensions funds, life insurance companies).
- Payment services (banks, thrifts).
- Denomination intermediation (mutual funds, pension funds).

Failure to provide these services or a breakdown in their efficient provision can be costly to both the ultimate sources (households) and users (firms) of savings. The *negative externalities* affecting firms and households when something goes wrong in the FI sector of the economy make a case for regulation. Thus, bank failures may destroy household savings and at the same time restrict a firm's access to credit. Insurance company failures may leave households totally exposed in old age to catastrophic illnesses and sudden drops in income on retirement. Further, individual FI failures may create doubts in savers' minds regarding the stability and solvency of FIs in general and cause panics and even runs on sound institutions. In addition, racial, sexual, age, or other discrimination—such as mortgage **redlining**—may unfairly exclude some potential financial service consumers from the marketplace. This type of market failure needs to be corrected by regulation. Although regulation may be socially beneficial, it also imposes private costs, or a regulatory burden, on individual FI owners and managers. Consequently, regulation is an attempt to enhance the social welfare benefits and mitigate the social costs of the provision of FI services. The private costs of regulation relative to its private benefits, for the producers of financial services, is called the **net regulatory burden.**[9]

Six types of regulation seek to enhance the net social welfare benefits of financial intermediaries' services: (1) safety and soundness regulation, (2) monetary policy regulation, (3) credit allocation regulation, (4) consumer protection regulation, (5) investor protection regulation, and (6) entry and chartering regulation. Regulation can be imposed at the federal or the state level and occasionally at the international level, as in the case of bank capital requirements (see Chapter 20).

Finally, some of these regulations are functional in nature, covering all FIs that carry out certain functions, such as payment services, while others are institution specific. Because of the historically segmented nature of the U.S. FI system, many regulations in that system are institution specific, for example, consumer protection legislation imposed on bank credit allocation to local communities. Merton[10] and others have argued that because of the rapidly changing nature of institutions in the financial system, regulation ought to be increasingly based on a functional perspective, i.e., all FIs providing a similar function (whether banks, thrifts, or insurance companies) should be similarly regulated in the provision of that service.

Safety and Soundness Regulation

To protect depositors and borrowers against the risk of FI failure due, for example, to a lack of diversification in asset portfolios, regulators have developed layers of protective mechanisms. In the first layer of protection are requirements encouraging FIs to diversify their assets. Thus, banks are required not to make loans exceeding

Redlining
The procedure by which a banker refuses to make loans to residents living inside given geographic boundaries.

Net Regulatory Burden
The difference between the private costs of regulations and the private benefits for the producers of financial services.

---

[9]Other regulated firms such as gas and electric utilities also face a complex set of regulation imposing a net-regulatory burden on their operations.

[10]Robert C. Merton, "A Functional Perspective of Financial Intermediation," *Financial Management* 24 (Summer 1995), pp. 23–41.

more than 15 percent of their own equity capital funds to any one company or borrower. A bank that has 6 percent of its assets funded by its own capital (and therefore 94 percent by deposits) can lend no more than 0.9 percent of its assets to any one party.

The second layer of protection concerns the minimum level of capital or equity funds that the owners of an FI need to contribute to the funding of its operations. For example, bank, thrift, and insurance regulators are concerned with the minimum ratio of capital to (risk) assets. The higher the proportion of capital contributed by owners, the greater the protection against insolvency risk to outside liability claimholders such as depositors and insurance policyholders. This is because losses on the asset portfolio due, for example, to the lack of diversification are legally borne by the equity holder first, and only after equity is totally wiped out by outside liability holders.[11] Consequently, by varying the required degree of equity capital, FI regulators can directly affect the degree of risk exposure faced by nonequity claimholders in FIs. (See Chapter 20 for more discussion on the role of capital in FIs.)

The third layer of protection is the provision of guaranty funds such as the Bank Insurance Fund (BIF) for banks, the Savings Association Insurance Fund (SAIF) for savings and loans, the Security Investors Protection Corporation (SIPC) for securities firms, and the state guaranty funds established (with regulator encouragement) to meet insolvency losses to small claimholders in the life and property-casualty insurance industries. By protecting FI claimholders, when an FI collapses and owners' equity or net worth is wiped out, these funds create a demand for regulation of the insured institutions to protect the funds' resources (see Chapter 19 for more discussion). For example, the FDIC monitors and regulates participants in both BIF and SAIF.

The fourth layer of regulation is monitoring and surveillance itself. Whether banks, securities firms, or insurance companies, regulators subject all FIs to varying degrees of monitoring and surveillance. This involves on-site examination as well as an FI's production of accounting statements and reports on a timely basis for off-site evaluation. Just as savers appoint FIs as delegated monitors to evaluate the behavior and actions of ultimate borrowers, society appoints regulators to monitor the behavior and performance of FIs.

Finally, note that regulation is not without costs for those regulated. For example, society's regulators may require FIs to have more equity capital than private owners believe is in their own best interests. Similarly, producing the information requested by regulators is costly for FIs because it involves the time of managers, lawyers, and accountants. Again, the socially optimal amount of information may differ from an FI's privately optimal amount.[12]

As noted earlier, the differences between the private benefits to an FI from being regulated—such as insurance fund guarantees—and the private costs it faces from adhering to regulation—such as examinations—is called the *net regulatory burden.* The higher the net regulatory burden on FIs, the more inefficiently they produce any given set of financial services from a private (FI) owner's perspective.

---

[11]Thus, equity holders are junior claimants and debt holders are senior claimants to an FI's assets.

[12]Also, a social cost rather than social benefit from regulation is the potential risk-increasing behavior (often called moral hazard) that results if deposit insurance and other guaranty funds provide coverage to FIs and their liability holders at less than the actuarially fair price (see Chapter 19 for further discussion).

Monetary Policy Regulation

Outside Money
The part of the money supply directly produced by the government or central bank, such as notes and coin.

Inside Money
The part of the money supply produced by the private banking system.

Another motivation for regulation concerns the special role banks play in the transmission of monetary policy from the Federal Reserve (the central bank) to the rest of the economy. The problem is that the central bank directly controls only the quantity of notes and coin in the economy—called **outside money**—whereas the bulk of the money supply consists of bank deposits—called **inside money.** In theory, a central bank can vary the quantity of cash or outside money and directly affect a bank's reserve position as well as the amount of loans and deposits it can create without formally regulating the bank's portfolio. In practice, regulators have chosen to impose formal controls.[13] In most countries, regulators commonly impose a minimum level of required cash reserves to be held against deposits. Some argue that imposing such reserve requirements makes the control of the money supply and its transmission more predictable. Such reserves also add to an FI's net regulatory burden if they are more than the institution believes are necessary for its own liquidity purposes. In general, whether banks or insurance companies, all FIs would choose to hold some cash reserves—even noninterest bearing—to meet the liquidity and transaction needs of their customers directly. For well-managed FIs, however, this optimal level is normally low, especially if the central bank (or other regulatory body) does not pay interest on required reserves. As a result, FIs often view required reserves as similar to a tax and as a positive cost of undertaking intermediation.[14]

Credit Allocation Regulation

Credit allocation regulation supports the FI's lending to socially important sectors such as housing and farming. These regulations may require an FI to hold a minimum amount of assets in one particular sector of the economy or, alternatively, to set maximum interest rates, prices, or fees to subsidize certain sectors. Examples of asset restrictions include the qualified thrift lender test (QTL), which requires thrifts to hold 65 percent of their assets in residential mortgage-related assets to retain a thrift charter, and insurance regulations, such as those in New York State that set maximums on the amount of foreign or international assets in which insurance companies can invest. Examples of interest rate restrictions are the usury laws set in many states on the maximum rates that can be charged on mortgages and/or consumer loans and regulations (now abolished) such as the Federal Reserve's Regulation Q maximums on time and savings deposit interest rates.

Such price and quantity restrictions may have justification on social welfare grounds—especially if society has a preference for strong (and subsidized) housing and farming sectors. However, they can also be harmful to FIs that have to bear the

---

[13]In classic central banking theory, the quantity of bank deposits (D) is determined as the product of 1 over the banking system's required (or desired) ratio of cash reserves to deposits (r) times the quantity of bank reserves (R) outstanding, where R is comprised of notes and coin plus bank deposits held on reserve at the central bank. $D = (1/r) \times R$. Thus, by varying R, given a relatively stable reserve ratio (r), the central bank can directly affect D, the quantity of deposits or inside money that, as just noted, is a large component of the money supply. Even if not required to do so by regulation, banks would still tend to hold some cash reserves as a liquidity precaution against the sudden withdrawal of deposits or the sudden arrival of new loan demand.

[14]In the United States, bank reserves held with the central bank (the Federal Reserve or the Fed) are noninterest bearing. In some other countries, interest is paid on bank reserves, thereby lowering the "regulatory tax" effect.

private costs of meeting many of these regulations. To the extent that the net private costs of such restrictions are positive, they add to the costs and reduce the efficiency with which FIs undertake intermediation.

Consumer Protection Regulation

Congress passed the Community Reinvestment Act (CRA) and the Home Mortgage Disclosure Act (HMDA) to prevent discrimination in lending. For example, since 1975, the HMDA has assisted the public in determining whether banks and other mortgage-lending institutions are meeting the needs of their local communities. HMDA is especially concerned about discrimination on the basis of age, race, sex, or income. Since 1990, depository institutions have reported on a standardized form to their chief federal regulator the reasons why credit was granted or denied. To get some idea of the information production cost of regulatory compliance in this area, the Federal Financial Institutions Examination Council (FFIEC) processes information on as many as 6 million mortgage transactions from over 9,300 institutions each quarter. (The council is a federal supervisory body comprising the members of the Federal Reserve, the Federal Deposit Insurance Corporation, and the Office of the Comptroller of the Currency.[15] Many analysts believe that community and consumer protection laws are imposing a considerable net regulatory burden on FIs without providing offsetting social benefits that enhance equal access to mortgage and lending markets. However, as deregulation proceeds and the trend toward consolidation and universal banking (see Chapter 1) continues, it is likely that such laws will be extended beyond banks to other financial service providers, such as insurance companies, which are not currently subject to CRA community lending requirements.

Investor Protection Regulation

A considerable number of laws protect investors who use investment banks directly to purchase securities and/or indirectly to access securities markets through investing in mutual or pension funds. Various laws protect investors against abuses such as insider trading, lack of disclosure, outright malfeasance, and breach of fiduciary responsibilities. Important legislation affecting investment banks and mutual funds includes the Securities Acts of 1933 and 1934 and the Investment Company Act of 1940. As with consumer protection legislation, compliance with these acts can impose a net regulatory burden on FIs.

Entry Regulation

The entry and activities of FIs are also regulated. Increasing or decreasing the cost of entry into a financial sector affects the profitability of firms already competing in that industry. Thus, the industries heavily protected against new entrants by high direct costs (e.g., through capital contribution) and high indirect costs (e.g., by restricting individuals who can establish FIs) of entry produce bigger profits for existing firms than those in which entry is relatively easy. In addition, regulations

---

[15]The FFIEC also publishes aggregate statistics and analysis of CRA and HMDA data. The Federal Reserve and other regulators also rate bank compliance. For example, in 1997 the Federal Reserve judged 19.7 percent of the banks examined to be outstanding in CRA compliance, 78.2 percent as satisfactory, 1.6 percent as needing to improve, and 0.5 percent as being in noncompliance.

define the scope of permitted activities under a given charter. The broader the set of financial service activities permitted under a given charter, the more valuable that charter is likely to be. Thus, barriers to entry and regulations pertaining to the scope of permitted activities affect the *charter value* of an FI and the size of its net regulatory burden.

Concept Questions

1. Why should more regulation be imposed on FIs than on other types of private corporations?
2. Define the concept of net regulatory burden.
3. What six major types of regulation do FIs face?

The Changing Dynamics of Specialness

At any moment in time, each FI supplies a set of financial services (brokerage related, asset transformation related, or both) and is subject to a given net regulatory burden. As the demands for the special features of financial services change due to changing preferences and technology, one or more areas of the financial services industry become less profitable. Similarly, changing regulations can increase or decrease the net regulatory burden faced in supplying financial services in any given area. These demand, cost, and regulatory pressures are reflected in changing market shares in different financial service areas as some contract and others expand. Clearly, an FI seeking to survive and prosper must be flexible enough to move to growing financial service areas and away from those that are contracting. If regulatory activity restrictions inhibit or reduce the flexibility with which FIs can alter their product mix, this will reduce their competitive ability and the efficiency with which financial services are delivered. That is, activity barriers within the financial services industry may reduce the ability to diversify and potentially add to the net regulatory burden faced by FIs.

Trends in the United States

In Table 6–3 we show the changing shares of total assets in the U.S. financial services industry from 1860 to 1997. A number of important trends are clearly evident: Most apparent is the decline in the total share of depository institutions since the Second World War. Specifically, the share of commercial banks declined from 55.9 to 36.1 percent between 1948 and 1997, while the share of thrifts (mutual savings banks, savings and loans, and credit unions) fell from 12.3 to 10.8 percent over the same period.[16] Similarly, life insurance companies also witnessed a secular decline in their share, from 24.3 to 19.3 percent.

The most dramatically increasing trends are the rising shares of pension funds and investment companies. Pension funds (private plus state and local) increased

---

[16]Although bank assets as a percentage of assets in the financial sector may have declined in recent years, this does not necessarily mean that banking activity has fallen. Boyd and Gertler show that banking activity has risen, albeit moderately, when measured against the growth of GDP (see J. H. Boyd and M. Gertler, "Are Banks Dead? Or, Are the Reports Greatly Exaggerated?" Federal Reserve Bank of Minneapolis, Research Department, Working Paper, May 1994). In addition, off-balance-sheet activity has replaced some of the traditional activities of commercial banks (see Chapter 13).

TABLE 6–3   Percentage Shares of Assets of Financial Institutions in the United States, 1860–1997

	1860	1880	1900	1912	1922	1929	1939	1948	1960	1970	1980	1997*
Commercial banks	71.4%	60.6%	62.9%	64.5%	63.3%	53.7%	51.2%	55.9%	38.2%	37.9%	34.8%	36.1%
Thrift institutions	17.8	22.8	18.2	14.8	13.9	14.0	13.6	12.3	19.7	20.4	21.4	10.8
Insurance companies	10.7	13.9	13.8	16.6	16.7	18.6	27.2	24.3	23.8	18.9	16.1	19.3
Investment companies	—	—	—	—	0.0	2.4	1.9	1.3	2.9	3.5	3.6	14.3
Pension funds	—	—	0.0	0.0	0.0	0.7	2.1	3.1	9.7	13.0	17.4	11.6
Finance companies	—	0.0	0.0	0.0	0.0	2.0	2.2	2.0	4.6	4.8	5.1	5.9
Securities brokers and dealers	0.0	0.0	3.8	3.0	5.3	8.1	1.5	1.0	1.1	1.2	1.1	1.5
Mortgage companies	0.0	2.7	1.3	1.2	0.8	0.6	0.3	0.1	†	†	0.4	0.3
Real estate investment trusts	—	—	—	—	—	—	—	—	0.0	0.3	0.1	0.2
Total (percent)	100.0%	100.0%	100.0%	100.0%	100.0%	100.0%	100.0%	100.0%	100.0%	100.0%	100.0%	100.0%
Total (trillion dollars)	.001	.005	.016	.034	.075	.123	.129	.281	.596	1.328	4.025	11.38

Columns may not add to 100% due to rounding.
*As of June 30, 1997.
†Data not available.
Source: Randall Kroszner, "The Evolution of Universal Banking and Its Regulation in Twentieth Century America," chapter 3 in Anthony Saunders and Ingo Walter, eds., *Universal Banking Financial System Design Reconsidered* (Burr Ridge, IL: Irwin, 1996); and *Federal Reserve Bulletin,* Table 1.60.

their asset share from 3.1 to 11.6 percent, while investment companies (mutual funds and money market mutual funds) increased theirs from 1.3 to 14.3 percent.

Pension funds and investment companies differ from banks and insurance companies in that they give savers cheaper access to the direct securities markets. They do so by exploiting the comparative advantages of size and diversification, with the transformation of financial claims, such as maturity transformation, a lesser concern. Thus, open-ended mutual funds buy stocks and bonds directly in financial markets and issue to savers shares whose value is linked in a direct pro rata fashion to the value of the mutual fund's asset portfolio. Similarly, money market mutual funds invest in short-term financial assets such as commercial paper, CDs, and Treasury bills and issue shares linked directly to the value of the underlying portfolio. To the extent that these funds efficiently diversify, they also offer price-risk protection and liquidity services.

The maturity and return characteristics of the financial claims issued by pension and mutual funds closely reflect the maturities of the direct equity and debt securities portfolios in which they invest. In contrast, banks, thrifts, and insurance companies have lower correlations between their asset portfolio maturities and the promised maturity of their liabilities. Thus, banks may partially fund a 10-year commercial loan with demand deposits; a thrift may fund 30-year conventional mortgages with three-month time deposits; and a life insurance company may fund the purchase of 30-year junk bonds with a 7-year fixed-interest guaranteed investment contract (GIC).[17]

---

[17]The close links between the performance of their assets and liabilities has led to mutual funds and pension funds being called "transparent" intermediaries. By contrast, the lower correlation between the performance of the assets and liabilities of banks, thrifts, and insurance companies has led to their being called "opaque" intermediaries. See Steven A. Ross, "Institutional Markets, Financial Marketing and Financial Innovation," *Journal of Finance,* July 1989, pp. 541–56.

To the extent that the financial services market is efficient and these trends reflect the forces of demand and supply, they indicate a current trend: Savers increasingly prefer investments that closely mimic diversified investments in the *direct* securities markets over the transformed financial claims offered by traditional FIs. This trend may also indicate that the net regulatory burden on traditional FIs—such as banks and insurance companies—is higher than that on pension funds and investment companies. As a result, traditional FIs are unable to produce their services as cost efficiently as they could previously.

Future Trends

The growth of mutual and pension funds coupled with investors' recent focus on direct investments in primary securities may be the beginning of a secular trend away from intermediation as the most efficient mechanism for savers to channel funds to borrowers. While this trend may reflect changed investors' preferences toward risk and return, it may also reflect a decline in the relative costs of direct securities investment versus investment via FIs. This decline in costs has led to many FI products being "commoditized" and sold directly in financial markets; for example, many options initially offered over the counter by FIs eventually migrate to the public option markets as trading volume grows and trading terms become standardized. As Merton has noted, financial markets "tend to be efficient institutional alternatives to intermediaries when the products have standardized terms, can serve a large number of customers and are well-enough understood for transactors to be comfortable in assessing their prices . . . intermediaries are better suited for low volume products."[18]

Recent regulatory changes in the United States are partially alleviating the net regulatory burden by allowing FIs to move across traditional product boundaries and lines. For example, banks have been acquiring mutual funds and expanding their asset and pension fund management businesses as well as the range of their security underwriting activities. At the same time banking organizations (such as bank holding companies) are getting bigger via mergers and other forms of consolidation. Larger size accommodates this expansion in service offerings while providing an enhanced potential to diversify risk and lower (average) costs.[19] As a result, bank profitability in the late 1990s has been considerably better than in the early 1990s (see Chapter 1). Nevertheless, the direct financial markets are evolving even faster; due to technological advances, the costs of direct access by savers are ever falling. A good example of this is the private placement market, where securities are directly sold by corporations to investors without underwriters and with a minimum of public disclosure about the issuing firm. Privately placed bonds and equity have traditionally been the most illiquid of securities, with only the very largest FIs or institutional investors being able or willing to hold them in the absence of a secondary market. In April 1990, the Securities and Exchange Commission amended Regulation 144A. This allowed large investors to begin trading these privately placed securities among themselves even though, in general, privately placed securities do not satisfy the stringent disclosure and informational requirements imposed

---

[18]R. Merton, "A Functional Perspective of Financial Intermediation," *Financial Management,* Summer 1995, p. 26.

[19]The number of banks in the United States dropped from 12,230 in 1990 to 9,054 at the end of 1997, a decline of 26 percent. This decline is even more dramatic when it is realized that 885 new bank charters were granted in the 1990–97 period.

<u>**TABLE 6–4**</u>   **U.S. Private Placements**
(in billions of dollars)

	1990	1991	1992	1993	1994	1995	1996	1997
144A placements	3.7	20.9	41.7	91.3	65.8	71.3	132.1	261.8
Total private placements	128.6	110.4	109.5	174.0	133.8	132.6	200.8	353.1

Source: *Investment Dealer's Digest,* various issues.

by the SEC on approved publicly registered issues. While the SEC defined the large investors able to trade privately placed securities as those with assets of $100 million or more—which excludes all but the very wealthiest household savers—it is reasonable to ask how long this size restriction will stay in effect. As they get more sophisticated and the costs of information acquisition fall, savers will increasingly demand access to the private placement market. In such a world, savers would have a choice not only between the secondary securities from FIs and the primary securities publicly offered by corporations but also between publicly offered (registered) securities and privately offered (unregistered) securities.[20] The recent growth of the 144A Private Placement market is shown in Table 6–4.

Concept Questions

1. Is the share of bank and thrift assets growing as a proportion of total FI assets in the United States?
2. What are the fastest growing FIs in the United States?
3. Define privately placed securities.

Summary

This chapter described the various factors and forces impacting financial intermediaries and the specialness of the services they provide. These forces suggest that in the future, FIs that have historically relied on making profits by performing traditional special functions such as asset transformation and the provision of liquidity services will need to expand into selling financial services that interface with direct security market transactions such as asset management, insurance, and underwriting services. This is not to say that specialized or niche FIs cannot survive but rather that only the most efficient FIs will prosper as the competitive value of a specialized FI charter declines.

The major theme of this book is the measurement and management of FI risks. In particular, although we might categorize or group FIs and label them life insurance companies, banks, finance companies, and so on, in fact they face risks that are more common than different. Specifically, all the FIs

described in this and the previous five chapters (1) hold some assets that are potentially subject to default or credit risk and (2) tend to mismatch the maturities of their balance sheets to a greater or lesser extent and are thus exposed to interest rate risk. Moreover, all are exposed to some degree of saver withdrawal or liquidity risk depending on the type of claims sold to liability holders. And most are exposed to some type of underwriting risk, whether through the sale of securities or by issuing various types of credit guarantees on or off the balance sheet. Finally. all are exposed to operating cost risks because the production of financial services requires the use of real resources and back-office support systems.

In the rest of this textbook, we investigate the ways in which managers of FIs are measuring and managing this inventory of risks to produce the best return-risk trade-off for shareholders in an increasingly competitive and contestable market environment.

---

[20]Moreover, in 1999 the Internet gave small savers direct access to IPO's via a number of newly founded "cyber-space" underwriting firms. Until this technological advance, IPO's had been the preserve of mostly institutional buyers.

Questions and Problems

1. Explain how economic transactions between household savers of funds and corporate users of funds would occur in a world without financial intermediaries.

2. Identify and explain three economic disincentives that probably would dampen the flow of funds between household savers of funds and corporate users of funds in an economic world without financial intermediaries.

3. Identify and explain the two functions in which FIs may specialize that enable the smooth flow of funds from household savers to corporate users.

4. In what sense are the financial claims of FIs considered *secondary securities,* while the financial claims of commercial corporations are considered *primary securities?* How does the transformation process, or intermediation, reduce the risk, or economic disincentives, to savers?

5. Explain how financial institutions act as delegated monitors. What secondary benefits often accrue to the entire financial system because of this monitoring process?

6. What are five general areas of FI specialness that are caused by providing various services to sectors of the economy?

7. How do FIs solve the information and related *agency costs* when household savers invest directly in securities issued by corporations? What are agency costs? What is the *free-rider* problem?

8. What often is the benefit to the lenders, borrowers, and financial markets in general of the solution to the information problem provided by large financial institutions?

9. How do FIs alleviate the problem of liquidity risk faced by investors who wish to invest in the securities of corporations?

10. How do financial institutions help individual savers diversify their portfolio risks? Which type of financial institution is best able to achieve this goal?

11. How can financial institutions invest in high-risk assets with funding provided by low-risk liabilities from savers?

12. How can individual savers use financial institutions to reduce the transaction costs of investing in financial assets?

13. What is *maturity intermediation?* What are some of the ways in which the risks of maturity intermediation are managed by financial intermediaries?

14. What are five areas of institution-specific FI specialness, and which types of institutions are most likely to be the service providers?

15. What are the differences between the various definitions of the money supply: M1, M2, and M3. Why is it important to track the level of the money supply?

16. Go to the Web site of the Federal Reserve Board and find the latest figures for MI, M2, and M3. By what percentage have these measures of the money supply grown over the past year? The Web site is http://bog.frb.fed.us/.

17. How do depository institutions such as commercial banks assist in the implementation and transmission of monetary policy?

18. What is meant by credit allocation regulation? What social benefit is this type of regulation intended to provide?

19. Which intermediaries best fulfill the intergenerational wealth transfer function? What is this wealth transfer process?

20. What are two of the most important payment services provided by financial institutions? To what extent do these services efficiently provide benefits to the economy?

21. What is denomination intermediation? How do FIs assist in this process?

22. What is *negative externality?* In what ways do the existence of negative externalities justify the extra regulatory attention received by financial institutions?

23. If financial markets operated perfectly and costlessly, would there be a need for financial intermediaries?

24. Why are FIs among the most regulated sectors in the world? When is the net regulatory burden positive?

25. What forms of protection and regulation do the regulators of FIs impose to ensure their safety and soundness?

26. In the transmission of monetary policy, what is the difference between *inside money* and *outside money?* How does the Federal Reserve Board try to control the amount of inside money? How can this regulatory position create a cost for depository financial institutions?

27. What are some examples of credit allocation regulation? How can this attempt to create social benefits create costs to a private institution?

28. What is the purpose of the Home Mortgage Disclosure Act? What are the social benefits desired from the legislation? How does the implementation of this legislation create a net regulatory burden on financial institutions?

29. What legislation has been passed specifically to protect investors who use investment banks directly or indirectly to purchase securities? Give some examples of the types of abuses for which protection is provided.

30. How do regulations regarding barriers to entry and the scope of permitted activities affect the *charter value* of financial institutions?

31. What reasons have been given for the growth of pension funds and investment companies at the expense of "traditional" banks and insurance companies?

32. What are some of the methods banking organizations have employed to reduce the net regulatory burden? What has been the effect on profitability?

33. What characteristics of financial products are necessary for financial markets to become efficient alternatives to financial intermediaries? Can you give some examples of the commoditization of products which were previously the sole property of financial institutions?

34. In what way has Regulation 144A of the Securities and Exchange Commission provided an incentive to the process of financial insitution disintermediation?

CHAPTER 7

RISKS OF FINANCIAL INTERMEDIATION

Introduction

In this chapter we introduce the fundamental risks faced by modern FIs. Briefly, these include interest rate risk, market risk, credit risk, off-balance-sheet risk, technology and operational risk, foreign exchange risk, country or sovereign risk, liquidity risk, and insolvency risk. Although we discuss these risks separately, they are in many cases interrelated. The effective management of these risks is central to the performance of an FI. In later chapters we analyze these risks more deeply. By the end of this chapter you will have a basic understanding of the variety and complexity of the risks facing managers of modern FIs as well as the need for good risk management tools and systems.

Interest Rate Risk

Chapter 6 discussed asset transformation as a key special function of FIs. Asset transformation involves buying primary securities and issuing secondary securities. The primary securities purchased by FIs often have maturity and liquidity characteristics different from those of the secondary securities FIs sell. In mismatching the maturities of assets and liabilities as part of their asset transformation function, FIs potentially expose themselves to **interest rate risk.**

Interest Rate Risk
The risk incurred by an FI when the maturities of its assets and liabilities are mismatched.

Consider, for example, an FI that issues liabilities of one-year maturity to finance the purchase of assets with a two-year maturity. We show this in the following time lines:

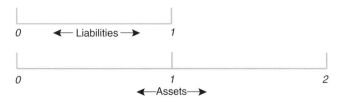

In this time line the FI can be viewed as being "short-funded." That is, the maturity of its liabilities is less than the maturity of its assets.

Suppose the cost of funds (liabilities) for an FI is 9 percent per annum and the interest return on an asset is 10 percent per annum. Over the first year the FI can lock in a profit spread of 1 percent (10 percent − 9 percent) by borrowing short term (for one year) and lending long term (for two years). However, its profits for the second year are uncertain. If the level of interest rates does not change, the FI can *refinance* its liabilities at 9 percent and lock in a 1 percent profit for the second year as well. There is always a risk, however, that interest rates could change between years 1 and 2. If interest rates were to rise and the FI could borrow new one-year liabilities only at 11 percent in the second year, its profit spread in the second year would actually be negative; that is, 10 percent − 11 percent = −1 percent. The positive spread earned in the first year by the FI from holding assets with a longer maturity than its liabilities would be offset by a negative spread in the second year. As a result, whenever an FI holds longer-term assets relative to liabilities, it potentially exposes itself to **refinancing risk.** This is the risk that the cost of rolling over or reborrowing funds could be more than the return earned on asset investments. The classic example of this type of mismatch was demonstrated by U.S. thrifts or savings banks during the 1980s (see Chapter 1).

Refinancing Risk
The risk that the cost of rolling over or reborrowing funds will rise above the returns being earned on asset investments.

An alternative balance sheet structure would have the FI borrowing for a longer term than the assets in which it invests. In the time line below the FI is "long-funded." The maturity of its liabilities is longer than the maturity of its assets. Using a similar example, suppose the FI borrowed funds at 9 percent per annum for two years and invested the funds in an asset that yields 10 percent for one year. This is shown as follows:

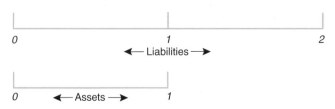

As before, the bank locks in a one-year profit spread of 1 percent, the difference between the 9 percent cost of funds and the 10 percent return on assets in the first year. At the end of the first year, the asset matures and the funds that have been borrowed for two years have to be reinvested. Suppose interest rates fall between the first and second years so that in the second year the return on assets is 8 percent. The FI would face a loss or negative spread in the second year of 1 percent (that is, 8 percent asset return minus 9 percent cost of funds), which would offset the positive 1 percent spread in the first year. Thus, the FI was exposed to **reinvestment risk;** by holding shorter-term assets relative to liabilities, it faced uncertainty about the interest rate at which it could reinvest funds borrowed for a longer period. In recent years, good examples of this exposure have been provided by banks that have borrowed fixed-rate deposits while investing in floating-rate loans; that is, loans whose interest rates are changed or adjusted frequently.

Reinvestment Risk
The risk that the returns on funds to be reinvested will fall below the cost of funds.

In addition to a potential refinancing or reinvestment risk that occurs when interest rates change, an FI faces *market value* risk as well. Remember that the market value of an asset or liability is conceptually equal to the discounted future cash flows from that asset. Therefore, rising interest rates increase the discount rate on those cash flows and reduce the market value of that asset or liability. Conversely, falling interest rates increase the market values of assets and liabilities. Moreover, mismatching maturities by holding longer-term assets than liabilities means that when interest rates rise, the market value of the FI's assets falls by a greater amount than its liabilities. This exposes the FI to the risk of economic loss and insolvency.

If holding assets and liabilities with mismatched maturities exposes FIs to reinvestment (or refinancing) and market value risks, FIs can be approximately hedged or protected against interest rate changes by matching the maturity of their assets and liabilities.[1] This has resulted in the general philosophy that matching maturities is somehow the best policy to hedge interest rate risk for FIs that are averse to risk. Note that matching maturities works against an active asset-transformation function for FIs. That is, FIs cannot be asset transformers and direct balance sheet hedgers at the same time. While reducing exposure to interest rate risk, matching maturities may also reduce the profitability of being FIs because any returns from acting as specialized risk-bearing asset transformers are eliminated. As a result, some FIs emphasize asset–liability maturity mismatching more than others. For example, banks and thrifts traditionally hold longer-term assets than liabilities, whereas life insurance companies tend to match the long-term nature of their liabilities with long-term assets. Finally, matching maturities hedges interest rate risk only in a very approximate rather than complete fashion. The reasons for this are technical, relating to the difference between the average life (or duration) and maturity of an asset or liability and whether the FI partly funds its assets with equity capital as well as debt liabilities. In the preceding simple example, the FI financed its assets completely with borrowed funds. In the real world, FIs use a mix of debt liabilities and stockholders' equity to finance asset purchases. When assets and debt liabilities are not equal, hedging risk (i.e., insulating FI's stockholder's equity values) may be achieved by not exactly matching the maturities (or average lives)

---

[1]This assumes that FIs can directly "control" the maturities of their assets and liabilities. As interest rates fall, many mortgage borrowers seek to "prepay" their existing loans and refinance at a lower rate. This prepayment risk—which is directly related to interest rate movements—can be viewed as a further interest rate related risk. Prepayment risk is discussed in detail in Chapter 28.

of assets and liabilities. We discuss these issues more fully in Chapters 8 and 9 and the methods and instruments to hedge interest rate risk in Chapters 24 through 26.[2]

Concept Questions

1. What is refinancing risk? What type of FI best illustrated this concept in the 1980s?
2. Why does a rise in the level of interest rates adversely affect the market value of both assets and liabilities?
3. Explain the concept of maturity matching.

Market Risk

Market Risk
The risk incurred in the trading of assets and liabilities due to changes in interest rates, exchange rates, and other asset prices.

Market risk arises whenever FIs actively trade assets and liabilities (and derivatives) rather than holding them for longer-term investment, funding, or hedging purposes. As discussed in Chapters 1 to 6, the traditional franchises of commercial and investment banks have declined in recent years. For large commercial banks such as the money center banks, the decline in income from traditional deposit taking and lending activities has been matched by a greater reliance on income from trading. Similarly, the decline in underwriting and brokerage income for the large investment banks has also been met by more active and aggressive trading in securities and other assets. Mutual fund managers, who actively manage their asset portfolios, are also exposed to market risk.

To see the type of risk involved in active trading, consider the case of Barings, the 200-year-old British merchant bank that failed due to trading losses in February 1995. In this case, the bank (or, more specifically, one trader, Nick Leeson) was betting that the Japanese Nikkei Stock Market Index would rise by buying futures on that index (some $8 billion worth). However, for a number of reasons—including the Kobe earthquake—the index actually fell. As a result, over a period of one month, the bank lost over $1.2 billion on its trading positions, rendering the bank insolvent.[3] That is, the losses on its futures positions exceeded the bank's own equity capital resources. Of course, if the Nikkei Index had actually risen, the bank would have made very large profits and might still be in business. Another good example involves the trading losses incurred by commercial banks, investment banks, and mutual funds in Russian assets as a result of the dramatic decline in the value of the Russian ruble from 6 to $1 to 16 to $1 in August and September 1998.

As the above examples illustrate, trading or market risk is present whenever an FI takes an open or unhedged long (buy) or sell (short) position in bonds, equities, commodities, and derivatives and prices change in a direction opposite to that

[2]We assumed in our example that interest payments are paid only at the end of each year and could be changed only then. In reality, many loan and deposit rates adjust frequently or float as market rates change. For example, suppose a bank makes a one-year loan whose interest rate and interest rate payments are adjusted each quarter while fully funding the loan with a one-year CD that pays principal and interest at the end of the year. Even though the maturities of the loan and CD are equal to a year, the FI would not be fully hedged in a cash flow sense against interest rate risk since changes in interest rates over the year affect the cash flows (interest payments) on the loan but not those on deposits.

In particular, if interest rates were to fall, the FI might lose on the loan in terms of net interest income (interest revenue minus interest expense). The reason for this loss is that the average life of the loan in a cash flow sense is less than that of the deposit because cash flows on the loan are received, on average, earlier than are those paid on the deposit.

[3]Barings was eventually acquired by ING, a Dutch bank.

expected. As a result, the more volatile are asset prices, the greater are the market risks faced by FIs that adopt open trading positions. This requires FI management (and regulators) to put in place controls to limit positions taken by traders as well as models to measure the market risk exposure of an FI on a day-to-day basis. These market risk measurement models are discussed in Chapter 10.

Concept Questions

1. What is trading or market risk?
2. What modern conditions have led to an increase in this particular type of risk for FIs?

Credit Risk

Credit Risk
The risk that the promised cash flows from loans and securities held by FIs may not be paid in full.

Credit risk arises because promised cash flows on the primary securities held by FIs may or may not be paid in full. Virtually all types of FIs face this risk. However, in general, FIs that make loans or buy bonds with long maturities are more exposed than are FIs that make loans or buy bonds with short maturities. This means, for example, that banks, thrifts, and life insurance companies are more exposed to credit risk than are money market mutual funds and property-casualty insurance companies. If the principal on all financial claims held by FIs was paid in full on maturity and interest payments were made on the promised dates, FIs would always receive back the original principal lent plus an interest return. That is, they would face no credit risk. If a borrower defaults, both the principal loaned and the interest payments expected to be received are at risk. As a result, many financial claims issued by corporations and held by FIs promise a limited or fixed upside return. This takes the form of interest payments to the investor with a high probability and a large downside risk (loss of loan principal and promised interest) with a much smaller probability. Good examples of financial claims issued with these return-risk trade-offs are fixed-income coupon bonds issued by corporations and bank loans. In both cases, an FI investing in these claims earns the coupon on the bond or the interest promised on the loan if no borrower default occurs. On default, the FI earns zero interest on the asset and may lose all or part of the principal lent, depending on its ability to access some of the borrower's assets through bankruptcy and insolvency proceedings.

Look at the distribution of dollar returns for an FI investing in risky loans or bonds in Figure 7–1. As you see, the spike in the distribution indicates a high probability (but less than 1) of repayment of principal and promised interest in full. Problems with cash flows at the corporate level can result in varying degrees of default risk. These range from partial or complete default on interest payments—the range between principal and principal plus interest in Figure 7–1—and partial or complete default on the principal lent, the range between principal and zero. Given this limited upside return and long-tailed downside risk, it is incumbent on FIs to estimate expected default risk on bonds and loans held as assets and to demand risk premiums on those securities commensurate with that risk exposure.

The return distribution for credit risk suggests that FIs need to both monitor and collect information about firms whose assets are in their portfolios. Thus, managerial efficiency and credit risk management strategy affect the shape of the loan return distribution. Moreover, the credit risk distribution in Figure 7–1 is for an investment in a single asset exposed to default risk. One of the advantages FIs have over individual household investors is the ability to diversify some credit risk away

Figure 7–1

The Return Distribution on Risky Debt (Loans/Bonds)

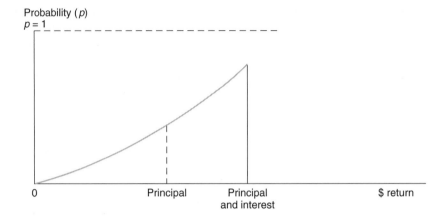

by exploiting the law of large numbers in their asset investment portfolios (see Chapter 6). In the framework of Figure 7–1, diversification across assets exposed to credit risk moderates the long-tailed downside risk of the return distribution.

FIs earn the maximum dollar return when all bonds and loans pay off interest and principal in full. In reality, some loans or bonds default on interest payments, principal payments, or both. Thus, the mean return on the asset portfolio would be less than the maximum possible in a risk-free, no-default case. The effect of risk diversification is to truncate or limit the probabilities of the bad outcomes in the portfolio. In effect, diversification reduces individual **firm-specific credit risk,** such as the risk specific to holding the bonds or loans of General Motors or IBM, while leaving the FI still exposed to **systematic credit risk,** such as factors that increase the default risk of all firms in the economy. We describe methods to measure the default risk of individual corporate claims such as bonds and loans in Chapter 11. In Chapter 12, we investigate methods of measuring the risk in portfolios of such claims. Chapter 27 discusses various methods—for example, loan sales, reschedulings, and a good bank–bad bank structure—to manage and control credit risk exposures better, while Chapters 24 to 26 discuss the role of the newly innovated credit derivative markets in hedging credit risk.

Firm-Specific Credit Risk
The risk of default of the borrowing firm associated with the specific types of project risk taken by that firm.

Systematic Credit Risk
The risk of default associated with general economywide or macro-conditions affecting all borrowers.

Concept Questions

1. Why does credit risk exist for FIs?
2. How does diversification affect an FI's credit risk exposure?

Off-Balance-Sheet Risk

Off-Balance-Sheet Risk
The risk incurred by an FI due to activities related to contingent assets and liabilities.

One of the most striking trends for many modern FIs has been the growth in their off-balance sheet activities and thus their **off-balance-sheet risk.** While all FIs to some extent engage in off-balance-sheet activities, most attention has been drawn to the activities of banks, especially large banks. By contrast, off-balance-sheet activities have been less of a concern to smaller depository institutions and many insurance companies. An off-balance-sheet activity, by definition, does not appear on the current balance sheet because it does not concern holding a *current primary* claim (asset) or the issuance of a *current secondary* claim (liability). Instead, off-balance-sheet activities affect the *future* shape of an FI's balance sheet in that they involve the creation of contingent assets and liabilities. As such, accountants

Letter of Credit
A credit guaranty issued by an FI for a fee on which payment is contingent on some future event occurring.

place them "below the bottom line" when they report an FI's balance sheet. A good example of an off-balance-sheet activity is the issuance of standby **letter of credit** guarantees by insurance companies and banks to back the issuance of municipal bonds. Many state and local governments could not issue such securities without *letter of credit guarantees* promising principal and interest payments to investors by the bank or insurance company should the municipality default on its future obligations. Thus, the letter of credit guarantees payment if a municipal government (e.g., New York State) faces financial problems in paying the promised interest payments and/or the principal on the bonds it issues. If a municipal government's cash flow is sufficiently strong to pay off the principal and interest on the debt it issues, the letter of credit guaranty issued by an FI expires unused. Nothing appears on the FI's balance sheet today or in the future. However, the fee earned for issuing the letter of credit guaranty appears on the FI's income statement.

As a result, the ability to earn fee income while not loading up or expanding the balance sheet has become an important motivation for FIs to pursue off-balance-sheet business. Unfortunately, this activity is not risk free. Suppose the municipal government defaults on its bond interest and principal payments. Then the contingent liability or guaranty the FI issued becomes an actual or real balance sheet liability. That is, the FI has to use its own equity to compensate investors in municipal bonds. Indeed, significant losses in off-balance-sheet activities can cause an FI to fail, just as major losses due to balance sheet default and interest rates risks can cause an FI to fail.

Letters of credit are just one example of off-balance-sheet activities. Others include loan commitments by banks, mortgage servicing contracts by thrifts, and positions in forwards, futures, swaps, and other derivative securities by almost all large FIs. While some of these activities are structured to reduce an FI's exposure to credit, interest rate, and foreign exchange risks, mismanagement or inappropriate use of these instruments can result in major losses to FIs. We detail the specific nature of the risks of off-balance-sheet activities more fully in Chapter 13.

Concept Questions

1. Why are letter of credit guarantees an off-balance-sheet item?
2. Why are FIs motivated to pursue off-balance-sheet business? What are the risks?

Technology and Operational Risk

Technological innovation has been a major concern of FIs in recent years. In the 1980s and 1990s, banks, insurance companies, and investment companies all sought to improve operational efficiency with major investments in internal and external communications, computers, and an expanded technological infrastructure. Good examples are the automated teller machine (ATM) networks developed by banks at the retail level and the automated clearing houses (ACH) and wire transfer payment networks such as the Clearing House Interbank Payments Systems (CHIPS) developed at the wholesale level. Indeed, a global financial services firm such as Citigroup has operations in more than 100 countries connected in real time by a proprietary-owned satellite system. The objective of technological expansion is to lower operating costs, increase profits, and capture new markets for the FI. In current terminology, it is to allow the FI to exploit better potential economies of scale and economies of scope in

Economies of Scale
The degree to which an FI's average unit costs of producing financial services fall as its outputs of services increase.

Economies of Scope
The degree to which an FI can generate cost synergies by producing multiple financial service products.

Technology Risk
The risks incurred by an FI when technological investments do not produce the cost savings anticipated.

Operational Risk
The risk that existing technology or support systems may malfunction or break down.

selling its products. **Economies of scale** imply an FI's ability to lower its average costs of operations by expanding its output of financial services. **Economies of scope** imply an FI's ability to generate cost synergies by producing more than one output with the same inputs. For example, an FI could use the same information on the quality of customers stored in its computers to expand the sale of both loan products and insurance products. That is, the same information (e.g., age, job, size of family, or income) can identify both potential loan and life insurance customers. Indeed, the attempt to better exploit such economies of scope lies behind megamergers such as that of Citicorp with Travelers to create Citigroup, an FI that services over 100 million customers in areas such as banking, securities, and insurance.

Technology risk occurs when technological investments do not produce the anticipated cost savings in economies of scale or scope. Diseconomies of scale, for example, arise because of excess capacity, redundant technology, and/or organizational bureaucratic inefficiencies (red tape) that get worse as an FI grows. Diseconomies of scope arise when an FI fails to generate perceived synergies or cost savings through major new technology investments. We describe the measurement and evidence of economies of scale and scope in FIs in Chapter 14. Technological risk can result in major losses in the competitive efficiency of an FI and ultimately result in its long-term failure. Similarly, gains from technological investments can produce performance superior to rivals' as well as allow an FI to develop new and innovative products, enhancing its long-run survival chances.

Operational risk is partly related to technology risk and can arise whenever existing technology malfunctions or back-office support systems break down. For example, major banks use the federal funds market both to sell and to buy funds from other banks for periods as short as a day. Their payment messages travel along a wire transfer network called Fedwire. Suppose the Bank of New York wished to lend federal funds to a California bank. It would transmit an electronic message instructing the Federal Reserve Bank of New York to deduct reserves from its account and send a message by Fedwire to credit the California borrowing bank's account at its own Federal Reserve Bank. Thus, funds would be credited to the Californian's bank account at the Federal Reserve Bank of San Francisco. Normally, this system functions highly efficiently; occasionally, risk exposures such as that actually faced by the Bank of New York in 1985 can arise. Specifically, the Bank of New York's computer system failed to register incoming payment (funds borrowed) messages on Fedwire but still processed outbound (funds lent) messages. As a result, at the end of the day the bank faced a huge net payment position on funds lent that it had to settle with other banks. The Bank of New York could do this only by arranging emergency loans from the Federal Reserve. Even though such computer glitches are rare, their occurrence can cause major dislocations in the FIs involved and potentially disrupt the financial system in general. A more recent technological risk concern is related to the so-called millennium bug, also known as the "Y2K" problem. This refers to the inability of financial services software to identify the century relating to a transaction, since most "old" computer code identifies only the last two digits of a year, for example, 00 for the year 2000. One implication of this is that 00 will be read as relating to a transaction in the year 1900 rather than the year 2000. Estimates of the worldwide costs of correcting the Y2K problem run into the hundreds of billions of dollars.

Back-office support systems combine labor and technology to provide clearance, settlement, and other services to back the underlying on- and off-balance-sheet transactions of FIs. Prior to 1975, most transactions among securities firms and their customers were paper based. As the market volume of trades rose, severe backlogs in settling and clearing transactions occurred because of the general inefficiency of decentralized paper-based systems. Such problems stimulated the development of centralized depositories as well as computerized trading and settlement in the securities industry.

Concept Questions

1. What is the difference between economies of scale and economies of scope?
2. How is operational risk related to technology risk?
3. How does technological expansion help an FI better exploit economies of scale and economies of scope? When might technology risk interfere with these goals?

Foreign Exchange Risk

Increasingly, FIs have recognized that both direct foreign investment and foreign portfolio investments can extend the operational and financial benefits available from purely domestic investments. Thus, U.S. pension funds that held approximately 5 percent of their assets in foreign securities in the early 1990s now hold close to 10 percent of their assets in foreign securities. Japanese pension funds currently hold more than 30 percent of their assets in foreign securities plus an additional 10 percent in foreign currency deposits. At the same time, many large U.S. banks, investment banks, and mutual funds have become more global in their orientation. To the extent that the returns on domestic and foreign investments are imperfectly correlated, there are potential gains for an FI that expands its asset holdings and liability funding beyond the domestic frontier.

The returns on domestic and foreign direct investing and portfolio investments are not perfectly correlated for two reasons. The first is that the underlying technologies of various economies differ as do the firms in those economies. For example, one economy may be agriculture based while another is industry based. Given different economic infrastructures, one economy could be expanding while another is contracting. The second reason is that exchange rate changes may not be perfectly correlated across countries. This means the dollar–euro exchange rate may be appreciating while the dollar–yen exchange rate may be falling.

One potential benefit from an FI becoming increasingly global in its outlook is the ability to expand abroad directly or to expand a financial asset portfolio to include foreign securities as well as domestic securities. Even so, undiversified foreign expansion—such as establishing operations in only one country or buying the securities of corporations in only one country—exposes an FI to **foreign exchange risk** in addition to interest rate risk and default risk.

To see how foreign exchange risk arises, suppose a U.S. FI makes a loan to a British company in pounds sterling (£). If the British pound depreciates in value relative to the U.S. dollar, the principal and interest payments received by U.S. investors will be devalued in dollar terms. Indeed, were the British pound to fall far enough over the investment period, when cash flows are converted back into dollars, the overall return could be negative. That is, on the conversion of principal and interest payments from sterling into dollars, foreign exchange losses can offset the promised value of local currency interest payments at the original exchange rate at which the investment occurred.

Foreign Exchange Risk
The risk that exchange rate changes can affect the value of an FI's assets and liabilities located abroad.

FIGURE 7–2

The Foreign Asset and Liability Position: A Net Long Asset Position in Pounds

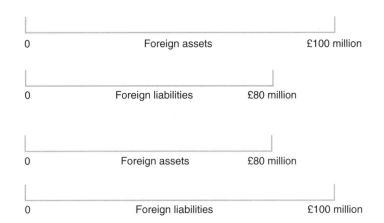

FIGURE 7–3

The Foreign Asset and Liability Position: Net Short Asset Position in Pounds

In general, an FI can hold assets denominated in a foreign currency and/or issue foreign liabilities. Consider an FI that holds British pound loans as assets (£100 million) and funds £80 million of them with British pound certificates of deposit. The difference between the £100 million in pound loans and £80 million in pound CDs is funded by dollar CDs (i.e., £20 million pounds worth of dollar CDs). See Figure 7–2.

In this case, the U.S. FI is *net long* £20 million in British assets; that is, it holds more foreign assets than liabilities. The U.S. FI will suffer losses if the exchange rate for pounds falls or depreciates against the dollar over this period. In dollar terms, the value of the British pound loan assets would fall or decrease in value by more than the British pound CD liabilities. That is, the FI is exposed to the risk that its net foreign assets may have to be liquidated at an exchange rate lower than the one that existed when the FI entered into the foreign asset–liability position.

Instead, the FI could have £20 million more foreign liabilities than assets: then it would be holding a *net short* position in foreign assets, as shown in Figure 7–3.

In this second case, the FI would be exposed to foreign exchange risk if the pound appreciated against the dollar over the investment period. This is the case because the cost of its British pound liabilities in dollar terms would rise faster than the return on its pound assets. Consequently, to be approximately hedged, the FI must match its assets and liabilities in each foreign currency.

Note that the FI is only approximately hedged unless we also assume that foreign assets and liabilities are of exactly the same maturity.[4] Consider what happens if the FI matches the size of its foreign currency book (British pound assets = British pound liabilities = £100 million in that currency) but mismatches the maturities so that the pound sterling assets are of six-month maturity and the liabilities are of three-month maturity. The FI would then be exposed to foreign interest rate risk—the risk that British interest rates would rise when it has to roll over its £100 million British CD liabilities at the end of the third month. Consequently, an FI that matches both the size and maturities of its exposure in assets and liabilities of a given currency is hedged or immunized against foreign currency and foreign interest rate risk. To the extent that FIs mismatch their portfolio and maturity exposures in different currency assets and liabilities, both foreign currency and foreign interest rate risks are present. As already noted, if foreign exchange rate and interest rate

---

[4]Technically speaking, hedging requires matching the durations (average lives of assets and liabilities) rather than simple maturities.

changes are not perfectly correlated across countries, an FI can diversify away part, if not all, of its foreign currency risk. We discuss the measurement and evaluation of an FI's foreign currency risk exposure in depth in Chapter 15.

Concept Questions

1. Explain why the returns on domestic and foreign portfolio investments are not, in general, perfectly correlated.
2. A U.S. bank is net long in European assets. If the euro appreciates against the dollar, will the bank gain or lose?
3. A U.S. bank is net short in European assets. If the euro appreciates against the dollar, will the bank gain or lose?

Country or Sovereign Risk

Country or Sovereign Risk
The risk that repayments from foreign borrowers may be interrupted because of interference from foreign governments.

As we noted in the previous section, a globally oriented FI that mismatches the size and maturities of its foreign assets and liabilities would be exposed to foreign currency and foreign interest rate risks. Even beyond these risks and even when investing in dollars, investing in assets in a foreign country can expose an FI to a third foreign investment risk, **country or sovereign risk.** Country or sovereign risk is a more serious credit risk than faced by an FI that purchases domestic assets such as the bonds and loans of domestic corporations. For example, when a domestic corporation is unable or unwilling to repay a loan, as a claimholder an FI usually has recourse to the bankruptcy courts and eventually may recoup at least a portion of its original investment as the assets of the defaulted firm are liquidated or restructured. By comparison, a foreign corporation may be unable to repay the principal or interest on its issued claims even if it would like to. Most commonly, the government of the country may prohibit payment or limit payments due to foreign currency shortages and political reasons. In the 1980s the governments of Argentina, Peru, and Brazil imposed restrictions with various degrees of stringency on the debt repayments of domestic corporations and agencies in hard currencies such as dollars to overseas investors. More recently, in 1998, the governments of Russia, Korea, Indonesia, and Thailand had great difficulty raising sufficient dollars to repay, or rollover, the foreign debt of the government and local corporations. As a result, "bailouts" had to be arranged with the aid of both the IMF and the World Bank, and much of this debt had its maturity extended. In the event of such restrictions or inability to pay, the FI claimholder has little if any recourse to the local bankruptcy courts or an international civil claims court. The major leverage available to an FI to ensure or increase repayment probabilities is its control over the future supply of loans or funds to the country concerned. However, such leverage may be very weak in the face of a collapsing country and currency. Chapter 16 discusses how country risk is measured and considers possible financial market solutions to the country risk exposure problems of a globally oriented FI.

Concept Questions

1. Can a bank be subject to sovereign risk if it lends only to AAA or the highest quality foreign corporations?
2. What is one major way an FI can discipline a country that threatens not to repay its loans?

Liquidity Risk

Liquidity risk arises whenever an FI's liability holders, such as depositors or insurance policyholders, demand immediate cash for their financial claims. When liability holders demand cash immediacy—that is, put their financial claims back to the FI—the FI must either borrow additional funds or sell off assets to meet the demand for the withdrawal of funds. The most liquid asset of all is cash, and FIs can use this asset to directly meet liability holders' demands to withdraw funds. Although FIs minimize their cash assets because such holdings earn no interest, low holdings are generally not a problem. Day-to-day withdrawals by liability holders are usually predictable, and FIs can normally expect to borrow additional funds to meet any shortfalls of cash on the money and financial markets.

However, there are times when an FI can face a liquidity crisis. Due to either a lack of confidence in the FI or some unexpected need for cash, liability holders may demand *larger* withdrawals than normal. When all or many FIs are facing similar abnormally large cash demands, the cost of additional funds rises and their supply becomes restricted or they become unavailable. As a consequence, FIs may have to sell some of their less liquid assets to meet the withdrawal demands of liability holders. This results in a more serious liquidity risk; some assets with thin markets generate lower prices when the sale is immediate than they would if the FI had more time to negotiate the sale. As a result, the liquidation of some assets at low or "fire-sale" prices could threaten the solvency of an FI. Good examples of such illiquid assets are bank loans to small firms. Such serious liquidity problems may eventually result in a run in which all liability claimholders seek to withdraw their funds simultaneously from the FI. This turns the FI's liquidity problem into a solvency problem and can cause it to fail.

We examine the nature of normal, abnormal, and run-type liquidity risks and their impact on banks, thrifts, insurance companies, and other FIs in more detail in Chapter 17.

Concept Questions

1. Why might an FI face a sudden liquidity crisis?
2. What circumstances might lead an FI to liquidate assets at fire-sale prices?

Insolvency Risk

Insolvency risk is a consequence or outcome of excessive interest rate, market, credit, off-balance-sheet, technological, foreign exchange, sovereign, and liquidity risks. Technically, insolvency occurs whenever the internal capital or equity resources of an FI's owners are inadequate to meet losses incurred due to one or more risks of a nature described in the preceding sections. In general, the more equity capital to borrowed funds an FI has—that is, the lower its leverage—the better able it is to withstand losses, whether due to adverse interest rate changes, unexpected credit losses, or other reasons. Thus, both management and regulators focus on the management of an FI's capital and its capital adequacy as key measures of its ability to remain solvent and grow. The issue of what is an adequate level of capital to manage an FI's risk exposure is discussed in Chapter 20.

Concept Questions

1. When does insolvency risk occur?
2. How is insolvency risk related to the other risks discussed in this chapter?

Other Risks and the Interaction of Risks

In this chapter we have concentrated on nine major risks continuously impacting FI managers' decision-making processes and risk management strategies. Even though the previous discussion has described them independently, in reality these risks are often interdependent. For example, when interest rates rise, corporations find it more difficult to maintain promised payments on their debt. Thus, over some range of interest rate movements, credit and interest rate risks are positively correlated. Similarly, foreign exchange rate changes and interest rate changes are also highly correlated. When the Federal Reserve changes a key interest rate (such as the Fed funds rate) through its monetary policy actions, exchange rates are also likely to change. This means FI managers are faced with making trade-offs among these various risks. Moreover, various other risks, often of a more discrete type, have an impact on an FI's profitability and risk exposure as well. Discrete risks might include a sudden change in taxation such as the Tax Reform Act of 1986, which subjected banks to a minimum corporate tax rate of 20 percent (the alternative minimum tax) and limited their ability to expense the cost of funds used to purchase tax-free municipal bonds. Such changes can affect the attractiveness of some types of assets over others as well as the liquidity of the balance sheet. For example, banks' demand for municipal bonds to hold as assets fell quite dramatically after the 1986 tax law change, and the municipal bond market became quite illiquid for a time.

Other discrete risks—often called event risks—involve sudden and unexpected changes in financial market conditions due to war, revolution, or sudden collapse such as the 1929 and 1987 stock market crashes. These have a major impact on an FI's risk exposure. Other event risks include fraud, theft, malfeasance, and breach of fiduciary trust; all of these can ultimately cause an FI to fail or be severely harmed.[5]

Finally, more general macroeconomic risks, such as increased inflation, inflation volatility, and unemployment, can all feed back and directly and indirectly impact an FI's level of interest rate, credit, and liquidity risk exposure. For example, inflation was very volatile in the 1979–82 period in the United States. Interest rates reflected this volatility. During periods in which an FI faces high and volatile inflation and interest rates, its interest rate risk exposure from mismatching its balance sheet maturities tends to rise. Its credit risk exposure also rises because borrowing firms with fixed-price product contracts often find it difficult to keep up their loan payments when inflation and interest rates rise abruptly.

Concept Questions

1. What is meant by the term *event risk*?
2. What are some examples of event and general macroeconomic risks that impact FIs?

---

[5]Fraud and similar types of risk can also be viewed as part of an FI's operational risk.

Summary

This chapter provided an overview of the nine major risks faced by modern FIs. They face *interest rate risk* when their assets and liabilities are maturity mismatched. They incur *market risk* on their trading assets and liabilities if there are adverse movements in interest rates, exchange rates, or other asset prices. They face *credit risk* or default risk if their clients default on their loans and other obligations. Modern-day FIs also engage in significant off-balance-sheet activities that expose them to *off-balance-sheet risks:* contingent asset and liability risks. The advent of sophisticated technology and automation exposes FIs to both *technological risk* and *operational risk.* If FIs conduct foreign business, they are subject to additional risks, namely *foreign exchange* and *sovereign risks. Liquidity risk* is a result of a serious run on an FI because of excessive withdrawals or problems in refinancing. Finally, *insolvency risk* occurs when an FI's capital is insufficient to withstand a relative decline in the value of assets. The effective management of these risks determines the success or failure of a modern FI. The chapters that follow analyze each of these risks in greater detail, beginning with interest rate risk.

Questions and Problems

1. What is the process of *asset transformation* performed by a financial institution? Why does this process often lead to the creation of *interest rate risk?* What is interest rate risk?

2. What is *refinancing risk?* How is refinancing risk part of interest rate risk? If an FI funds long-term assets with short-term liabilities, what will be the impact on earnings of an increase in the rate of interest? A decrease in the rate of interest?

3. What is *reinvestment risk?* How is reinvestment risk part of interest rate risk? If an FI funds short-term assets with long-term liabilities, what will be the impact on earnings of a decrease in the rate of interest? An increase in the rate of interest?

4. The sales literature of a mutual fund claims that the fund has no risk exposure since it invests exclusively in federal government securities which are free of default risk. Is this claim true? Explain why or why not.

5. What is *economic or market value risk?* In what manner is this risk adversely realized in the economic performance of an FI?

6. A financial institution has the following balance sheet structure:

Assets		Liabilities and Equity	
Cash	$ 1,000	Certificate of deposit	$10,000
Bond	$10,000	Equity	$ 1,000
Total assets	$11,000	Total liabilities and equity	$11,000

The bond has a ten-year maturity and a fixed-rate coupon of 10 percent. The certificate of deposit has a one-year maturity and a 6 percent fixed rate of interest. The FI expects no additional asset growth.

   a. What will be the net interest income at the end of the first year? *Note:* Net interest income equals interest income minus interest expense.

   b. If at the end of year 1 market interest rates have increased 100 basis points (1 percent), what will be the net interest income for the second year? Is this result caused by reinvestment risk or refinancing risk?

   c. Assuming that market interest rates increase 1 percent, the bond will have a value of $9,446 at the end of year 1. What will be the market value of equity for the FI?

   d. If market interest rates had decreased 100 basis points by the end of year 1, would the market value of equity be higher or lower than $1,000? Why?

   e. What factors have caused the change in operating performance and market value for this firm?

7. How does the policy of matching the maturities of assets and liabilities work (*a*) to minimize interest rate risk and (*b*) against the asset-transformation function of FIs?

8. Corporate bonds usually pay interest semiannually. If a company decided to change from semiannual to annual interest payments, how would this affect the bond's interest rate risk?

9. Two ten-year bonds are being considered for an investment that may have to be liquidated before the maturity of the bonds. The first bond is a ten-year premium bond with a coupon rate higher than its required rate of return, and the second bond is a zero-coupon bond that pays only a lump-sum payment after ten years with no interest over its life. Which bond would have more interest rate risk? That is, which bond's price would change by a larger amount for a given change in interest rates? Explain your answer.

10. Consider again the two bonds in problem (9). If the investment goal is to leave the assets untouched until

maturity, such as for a child's education or for one's retirement, which of the two bonds has more interest rate risk? What is the source of this risk?

11. A money market mutual fund bought $1,000,000 of two-year Treasury notes six months ago. During this time, the value of the securities has increased, but for tax reasons the mutual fund wants to postpone any sale for two more months. What type of risk does the mutual fund face for the next two months?

12. A bank invested $50 million in a two-year asset paying 10 percent interest per annum and simultaneously issued a $50 million, one-year liability paying 8 percent interest per annum. What will be the impact on the bank's net interest income if at the end of the first year all interest rates have increased by 1 percent (100 basis points)?

13. What is *market risk?* How do the results of this risk surface in the operating performance of financial institutions? What actions can be taken by an FI's management to minimize the effects of this risk?

14. What is *credit risk?* Which types of FIs are more susceptible to this type of risk? Why?

15. What is the difference between *firm-specific credit risk* and *systematic credit risk?* How can an FI alleviate firm-specific credit risk?

16. Many banks and S&Ls that failed in the 1980s had made loans to oil companies in Louisiana, Texas, and Oklahoma. When oil prices fell, these companies, the regional economy, and the banks and S&Ls all experienced financial problems. What types of risk were inherent in the loans that were made by these banks and S&Ls?

17. What is the nature of an off-balance-sheet activity? How does an FI benefit from such activities? Identify the various risks that these activities generate for an FI and explain how these risks can create varying degrees of financial stress for the FI at a later time.

18. What is *technology risk?* What is the difference between *economies of scale* and *economies of scope?* How can these economies create benefits for an FI? How can these economies prove harmful to an FI?

19. What is the difference between technology risk and *operational risk?* How does internationalizing the payments system among banks increase operational risk?

20. What two factors provide potential benefits to FIs that expand their asset holdings and liability funding sources beyond their domestic economies?

21. What is *foreign exchange risk?* What does it mean for an FI to be *net long* in foreign assets? What does it mean for an FI to be *net short* in foreign assets? In each case, what must happen to the foreign exchange rate to cause the FI to suffer losses?

22. If you expect the French franc to depreciate in the near future, would a U.S.-based FI in Paris prefer to be net long or net short in its asset positions? Discuss.

23. If international capital markets are well integrated and operate efficiently, will banks be exposed to foreign exchange risk? What are the sources of foreign exchange risk for FIs?

24. If an FI has the same amount of foreign assets and foreign liabilities in the same currency, has that FI necessarily reduced to zero the risk involved in these international transactions? Explain.

25. A U.S. insurance company invests $1,000,000 in a private placement of German bonds. Each bond pays DM300 in interest per year for 20 years. If the current exchange rate is DM1.7612/$, what is the nature of the insurance company's exchange rate risk? Specifically, what type of exchange rate movement concerns this insurance company?

26. Assume that a bank has assets located in Germany that are worth DM150 million on which it earns an average of 8 percent per year. The bank has DM100 million in liabilities on which it pays an average of 6 percent per year. The current spot rate is DM1.50/$.

   a. If the exchange rate at the end of the year is DM2.00/$, will the dollar have appreciated or depreciated against the mark?

   b. Given the change in the exchange rate, what is the effect in dollars on the net interest income from the foreign assets and liabilities? *Note:* The net interest income is interest income minus interest expense.

   c. What is the effect of the exchange rate change on the value of assets and liabilities in dollars?

27. Six months ago, Qualitybank, LTD., issued a $100 million, one-year maturity CD denominated in German deutsche marks (Euromark CD). On the same date, $60 million was invested in a DM-denominated loan and $40 million was invested in a U.S. Treasury bill. The exchange rate on this date was DM1.7382/$. Assume no repayment of principal and an exchange rate today of DM1.3905/$.

   a. What is the current value of the Euromark CD principal (in dollars and DM)?

   b. What is the current value of the German loan principal (in dollars and DM)?

   c. What is the current value of the U.S. Treasury bill (in dollars and DM)?

   d. What is Qualitybank's profit/loss from this transaction (in dollars and DM)?

28. Suppose you purchase a 10-year, AAA-rated Swiss bond for par that is paying an annual coupon of 8 percent. The bond has a face value of 1,000 Swiss francs (SF). The

spot rate at the time of purchase is SF1.50/$. At the end of the year, the bond is downgraded to AA and the yield increases to 10 percent. In addition, the SF appreciates to SF1.35/$.

a. What is the loss or gain to a Swiss investor who holds this bond for a year? What portion of this loss or gain is due to foreign exchange risk? What portion is due to interest rate risk?

b. What is the loss or gain to a U.S. investor who holds this bond for a year? What portion of this loss or gain is due to foreign exchange risk? What portion is due to interest rate risk?

29. What is *country or sovereign risk?* What remedy does an FI realistically have in the event of a collapsing country or currency?

30. Characterize the risk exposure(s) of the following FI transactions by choosing one or more of the risk types listed below:

a. Interest rate risk   *d.* Technology risk
b. Credit risk   *e.* Foreign exchange rate risk
c. Off-balance-sheet risk   *f.* Country or sovereign risk

(1) A bank finances a $10 million, six-year fixed-rate commercial loan by selling one-year certificates of deposit.

(2) An insurance company invests its policy premiums in a long-term municipal bond portfolio.

(3) A French bank sells two-year fixed-rate notes to finance a two-year fixed-rate loan to a British entrepreneur.

(4) A Japanese bank acquires an Austrian bank to facilitate clearing operations.

(5) A mutual fund completely hedges its interest rate risk exposure by using forward contingent contracts.

(6) A bond dealer uses his own equity to buy Mexican debt on the less-developed country (LDC) bond market.

(7) A securities firm sells a package of mortgage loans as mortgage backed securities.

31. Consider these four types of risks: credit, foreign exchange, market, and sovereign. These risks can be separated into two pairs of risk types in which each pair consists of two related risk types, with one being a subset of the other. How would you pair off the risk types, and which risk types may be considered a subset of another type?

32. What is *liquidity risk?* What routine operating factors allow FIs to deal with this risk in times of normal economic activity? What market reality can create severe financial difficulty for an FI in times of extreme liquidity crises?

33. Why can *insolvency risk* be classified as a consequence or outcome of any or all of the other types of risks?

34. Discuss the interrelationships among the different sources of bank risk exposure. Why would the construction of a bank risk-management model to measure and manage only one type of risk be incomplete?

PART

II

MEASURING RISK

<table>
<tr><td>

CHAPTER

〰〰

8

〰〰

</td><td>

INTEREST RATE RISK I

</td></tr>
</table>

Introduction

Net Worth
The value of an FI to its owners; this is equal to the difference between the market value of assets and that of liabilities.

In Chapter 7 we established that while performing their asset-transformation functions, FIs often mismatch the maturities of their assets and liabilities. In so doing, they expose themselves to interest rate risk. For example, in the 1980s a large number of thrifts suffered economic insolvency (i.e., the **net worth** or equity of their owners was eradicated) due to major increases in interest rates. All FIs tend to mis-

120

match their balance sheet maturities to some degree. However, measuring interest rate risk exposure by looking only at the size of the maturity mismatch can be misleading. As we shall also see in this chapter, the Federal Reserve's monetary policy is a key determinant of interest rate risk.

The Central Bank and Interest Rate Risk

Underlying the movement of interest rates is the strategy of the central bank, or the Federal Reserve. If the Federal Reserve smooths or targets the level of interest rates, unexpected interest rate shocks and interest rate volatility tend to be small. Accordingly, the risk exposure to an FI from mismatching the maturities of its assets and liabilities also tends to be small. However, to the extent that the Federal Reserve targets the supply of bank reserves and is willing to let interest rates find their own levels, the volatility of interest rates can be very high. Figure 8–1 shows the interest rate on U.S. 91-day T-bills for the 1965–98 period. The first observation is that the degree of volatility appears to have increased over time. The second is that the relative degree of volatility, or interest rate uncertainty, is directly linked to the Federal Reserve's monetary policy strategy. Specifically, between October 1979 and October 1982, the Federal Reserve targeted bank reserves during the so-called nonborrowed reserves target regime.[1] The volatility of interest rates in this period was far greater than it was in the two regimes surrounding this period. Note how the Federal Reserve targeted interest rates during the 1965 to October 1979 period and smoothed interest rates after October 1982 under the so-called borrowed reserves targeting regime. Indeed, the 1979–82 period was the genesis for the interest rate risk problems facing those thrifts that specialized in making long-term conventional mortgage loans funded by short-term deposits such as CDs.[2] It also should be noted that while Federal Reserve actions are targeted mostly at short-term rates (especially the Federal funds rate), changes in short-term rates usually feed through to the whole term structure of interest rates. The linkages between short-term rates and long-term rates and theories of the "term structure of interest rates" are discussed in the appendix to this chapter.

The volatility of interest rates and the risk that the Federal Reserve may return to a more overtly reserve-targeting regime similar to that in 1979–82 puts the measurement and management of interest rate risk at the head of the problems facing modern financial institution managers. In this chapter and Chapter 9 we analyze the different ways in which an FI might measure the exposure it faces in running a mismatched maturity book (or gap) between its assets and its liabilities in a world of interest rate volatility.

In particular, we concentrate on three ways, or models, of measuring the asset-liability gap exposure of an FI:

The repricing (or funding gap) model.

The maturity model.

The duration model.

---

[1]For more details, see A. Saunders and T. Urich, "The Effects of Shifts in Monetary Policy and Reserve Accounting Regimes on Bank Reserve Management Behavior in the Federal Funds Market," *Journal of Banking and Finance* 12 (1988), pp. 523–35.

[2]Certificates of deposit usually are issued with maturities of less than one year.

% Rate of Interest

FIGURE 8–1

Interest Rate on U.S. 91-Day Treasury Bills, 1965–1998.

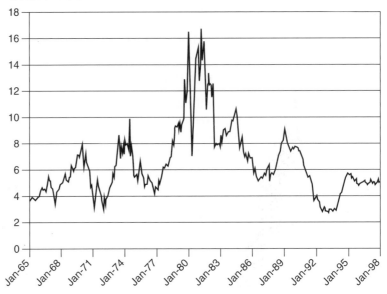

Source: Bloomberg Machine.

Concept Questions

1. How is the Federal Reserve's monetary policy linked to the degree of interest rate uncertainty faced by FIs?
2. How did the Federal Reserve's monetary policy strategy affect FIs over the period October 1979 to October 1982?

The Repricing Model

Repricing Gap
The difference between assets whose interest rates will be repriced or changed over some future period (rate-sensitive assets) and liabilities whose interest rates will be repriced or changed over some future period (rate-sensitive liabilities).

The repricing or funding gap model is essentially a book value accounting cash flow analysis of the **repricing gap** between the interest revenue earned on an FI's assets and the interest paid on its liabilities over a particular period. This contrasts with the market value–based maturity and duration models discussed later in this chapter and Chapter 9.

In recent years, the Federal Reserve has required commercial banks to report quarterly on their call reports the repricing gaps for assets and liabilities with these maturities:

1. One day.
2. More than one day to three months.
3. More than three months to six months.
4. More than 6 months to 12 months.
5. More than one year to five years.
6. Over five years.

Under the repricing gap approach, a bank calculates the gaps in each maturity bucket by looking at the rate sensitivity of each asset (RSA) and the rate sensitivity of each liability (RSL) on its balance sheet. Rate sensitivity here means the time to

TABLE 8–1   Repricing Gap
(in millions of dollars)

	1 Assets	2 Liabilities	3 Gaps	4 Cumulative Gap
1. One day	$ 20	$ 30	$−10	$−10
2. More than one day–three months	30	40	−10	−20
3. More than three months–six months	70	85	−15	−35
4. More than 6 months–12 months	90	70	+20	−15
5. More than one year–five years	40	30	+10	−5
6. Over five years	10	5	+5	0
	$260	$260		

repricing of the asset or liability. More simply, it means how long the FI manager has to wait to change the posted rates on any asset or liability. In many cases this occurs on a date prior to maturity.

Table 8–1 shows how the assets and liabilities of a bank are categorized into each of the six previously defined buckets according to their time to repricing.

While the cumulative gap over the whole balance sheet must by definition be zero [see Table 8–1, column (4)], the advantage of the repricing model lies in its information value and its simplicity in pointing to an FI's *net interest income exposure* (or earnings exposure) to interest rate changes in different maturity buckets.[3]

For example, the one-day gap indicates a negative $10 million difference between assets and liabilities being repriced in one day. Assets and liabilities that are repriced each day are likely to be interbank borrowings on the federal funds or repurchase agreement market (see Chapter 1). Thus, this gap indicates that a rise in the federal funds rate would lower the bank's *net interest income* because the bank has more rate-sensitive liabilities than assets in this bucket. In other words, it has purchased more short-term funds (such as federal funds) than it has lent. Specifically, let

ΔNII_i = Change in net interest income in the ith bucket.

GAP_i = The dollar size of the gap between the book value of assets and liabilities in maturity bucket i.

ΔR_i = The change in the level of interest rates impacting assets and liabilities in the ith bucket; then:

$$\Delta NII_i = (GAP_i)\, \Delta R_i = (RSA_i - RSL_i)\, \Delta R_i$$

In this first bucket, if the gap is negative $10 million and federal fund rates rise 1 percent, the annualized change in the bank's future net interest income is[4]

$$\Delta NII_i = (-\$10 \text{ million}) \times .01 = -\$100,000$$

---

[3]If we include equity capital as a long-term (over five years) liability.

[4]One can also calculate an "average" gap. If it is assumed that assets and liabilities reprice on *average* halfway through the period, the one-year gap measure calculated above will be divided by 2.

This approach is very simple and intuitive. Remember, however, from Chapter 7 and our overview of interest rate risk that capital or market value losses also occur when rates rise. The capital loss effect that is measured by both the maturity and duration models developed later in this chapter and in Chapter 9 is lost here. The reason for this is that in the book value accounting world of the repricing model, assets and liability values are reported at their *historic* values or costs. Thus, interest rate changes affect only current interest income or interest costs—that is, net interest income.[5]

The FI manager can also estimate cumulative gaps *(CGAP)* over various repricing categories or buckets. A common cumulative gap of interest is the one-year repricing gap estimated from Table 8–1 as:

$$CGAP = (-\$10) + (-\$10) + (-\$15) + \$20 = -\$15 \text{ million}$$

If ΔR_i is the average rate change affecting assets and liabilities that can be repriced within a year, the cumulative effect on the bank's net interest income is

$$\Delta NII_i = (CGAP)\, \Delta R_i$$
$$= (-\$15 \text{ million})(.01) = -\$150,000$$

We can now look at how an FI manager would calculate the cumulative one-year gap from a balance sheet. Remember that the manager asks: Will or can this asset or liability have its interest rate changed within the next year? If the answer is yes, it is a rate-sensitive asset or liability; if the answer is no, it is not rate sensitive.

Consider the simplified balance sheet facing the FI manager in Table 8–2. Instead of the original maturities, the maturities are those remaining on different assets and liabilities at the time the repricing gap is estimated.

Rate-Sensitive Assets

Looking down the asset side of the balance sheet, the following four are one-year rate-sensitive assets (RSA):

1. *Short-term consumer loans: $50 million.* These are repriced at end of the year and just make the one-year cutoff.
2. *Three-month T-bills: $30 million.* These are repriced on maturity (rollover) every three months.
3. *Six-month T-notes: $35 million.* These are repriced on maturity (rollover) every six months.
4. *30-year floating-rate mortgages: $40 million.* These are repriced (i.e., the mortgage rate is reset) every nine months. Thus, these long-term assets are rate-sensitive assets in the context of the repricing model with a one-year repricing horizon.

Summing these four items produces one-year rate-sensitive assets (RSA) of $155 million.

---

[5]For example, a 30-year bond purchased 10 years ago when rates were 13 percent would be reported as having the same book (accounting) value as when rates are 7 percent. In a market value world, the gains and losses to asset and liability values would be reflected in the balance sheet as rates changed.

TABLE 8–2   Simple Bank Balance Sheet
(in millions of dollars)

Assets		Liabilities	
1. Short-term consumer loans (one-year maturity)	$ 50	1. Equity capital (fixed)	$ 20
2. Long-term consumer loans (two-year maturity)	25	2. Demand deposits	40
3. Three-month Treasury bills	30	3. Passbook savings	30
4. Six-month Treasury notes	35	4. Three-month CDs	40
5. Three-year Treasury bonds	70	5. Three-month bankers acceptances	20
6. 10-year, fixed-rate mortgages	20	6. Six-month commercial paper	60
7. 30-year, floating-rate mortgages (rate adjusted every nine months)	40	7. One-year time deposits	20
		8. Two-year time deposits	40
	$270		$270

Rate-Sensitive Liabilities

Looking down the liability side of the balance sheet, the following four liability items clearly fit the one-year rate or repricing sensitivity test:

1. *Three-month CDs: $40 million.* These mature in three months and are repriced on rollover.
2. *Three-month bankers acceptances: $20 million.* The same as applies to CDs.
3. *Six-month commercial paper: $60 million.* These mature and are repriced every six months.
4. *One-year time deposits: $20 million.* These get repriced right at the end of the one-year gap horizon.

Summing these four items produces one-year rate-sensitive liabilities (RSL) of $140 million.

Note that demand deposits (or transaction accounts in general) were not included here. We can make strong arguments for and against their inclusion as rate-sensitive liabilities (RSL).

Against Inclusion.   The explicit interest rate on demand deposits is zero by regulation. Further, while the rate on transaction accounts such as NOW accounts is positive, the rates paid by banks are very sticky. Moreover, many demand deposits act as core deposits for banks, meaning they are a long-term source of funds.

For Inclusion.   Even if they pay no explicit interest rates, they do pay implicit interest in the form of the bank not charging fully for checking services through fees. Further, if interest rates rise, individuals draw down (or run off) their demand deposits, forcing the bank to replace them with higher-yielding, interest-bearing, rate-sensitive funds. This is most likely to occur when the interest rates on alternative instruments are high. In such an environment, the opportunity cost of holding funds in demand deposit accounts is likely to be larger than it is in a low-interest-rate environment.

Very similar arguments for and against inclusion can be made for retail pass-book savings accounts. Although Federal Reserve Regulation Q ceilings on the maximum rates for these accounts were abolished in March 1986, banks still adjust these rates only infrequently. However, savers tend to withdraw funds from these accounts when rates rise, forcing banks into more expensive fund substitutions.[6]

The four repriced liabilities of $40 + $20 + $60 + $20 sum to $140 million, and the four repriced assets of $50 + $30 + $35 + $40 sum to $155 million. Given this, the cumulative one-year repricing gap *(CGAP)* for the bank is

$$CGAP = \text{One-year rate-sensitive assets} - \text{one-year rate-sensitive liabilities}$$
$$= RSA - RSL$$
$$= \$155 - \$140 = \$15 \text{ million}$$

This can also be expressed as a percentage of assets (typically called the *gap ratio*):

$$\frac{CGAP}{A} = \frac{\$15 \text{ million}}{\$270 \text{ million}} = .056 = 5.6\%$$

Expressing the repricing gap in this way is useful since it tells us: (1) the direction of the interest rate exposure (positive or negative *CGAP*) and (2) the scale of that exposure as indicated by dividing the gap by the asset size of the institution.

In our example the bank has 5.6 percent more rate-sensitive assets than liabilities as a percentage of assets. If rates rise by +1 percent, the *CGAP* will project the annual change in net interest income *(ΔNII)* of the bank as approximately

$$\Delta NII = CGAP \times \Delta R$$
$$= (\$15 \text{ million}) \times .01$$
$$= \$150,000$$

Look at the one-year percentage gaps of various large regional and money center banks over the 1993–96 period in Table 8–3. Notice that some banks take quite large interest rate gambles relative to their asset sizes. For example, J. P. Morgan had a negative gap ratio of 15.8 percent in 1993.

You can see from the preceding discussion that the rate-sensitivity gap can be a useful tool for managers and regulators in identifying interest rate risk taking or exposure. Nevertheless, the repricing gap model has a number of serious weaknesses.[7]

Concept Questions

1. Why is it useful to express the repricing gap in terms of a percentage of assets? What specific information does this provide?
2. How can banks change the size and the direction of their repricing gap?
3. Summarize the case for and against the inclusion of demand deposits as a rate-sensitive liability.

---

[6]The Federal Reserve's repricing report has traditionally viewed transaction accounts and passbook savings accounts as rate-*in*sensitive liabilities, as we have done in this example.

[7]See E. Brewer, "Bank Gap Management and the Use of Financial Futures," Federal Reserve Bank of Chicago, *Economic Perspectives,* March–April 1985, for an excellent analysis of the repricing model and its strengths and weaknesses.

TABLE 8–3   Rate-Sensitivity Gap as a Percentage of Total Assets

	1993	*1994*	*1995*	*1996*
Bank of America	0.0%	0.8%	−1.0%	0.8%
Bankers Trust Company	2.3	−1.5	−0.4	−3.5
Barnett Banks	9.7	4.9	7.7	3.9
Boatmen's Bancshares	3.6	−5.9	3.3	n.a.
Chemical Bank	−5.0	−5.0	4.0	n.a.
CoreStates Financial	0.5	−0.8	0.4	0.1
Comerica	1.0	−5.0	−1.0	−3.7
First Bank System	7.2	3.2	1.1	0.4
First Interstate Bank, CA	10.0	7.4	3.1	n.a.
Fleet Financial	−4.4	−3.2	2.1	2.4
J.P. Morgan & Company	−15.8	−0.5	−1.3	−2.3
Mellon Bank	0.3	3.8	8.4	3.4
NationsBank	−9.9	−11.6	−16.8	−21.4
National City	−26.0	−3.4	4.0	7.1
Norwest	4.2	−4.4	−4.2	−4.2
PNC Bank	−8.6	−1.5	7.0	4.4
State Street Boston	8.0	−14.0	−3.0	−8.4
U.S. Bancorp	3.8	−10.2	−6.8	0.8
Wachovia	−1.5	−1.0	−4.2	−10.6
Wells Fargo Bank	2.7	1.0	−0.8	−1.3
Average	−0.9	−1.4	0.1	−2.0

Notes: Rate-sensitive assets include all assets repricing or maturing within one year and comprise loans and leases, debt security, and other interest-bearing assets. Rate-sensitive liabilities are all those liabilities scheduled to reprice or mature within one year and include domestic time certificates of deposits of $100,000 or more, all other domestic time deposits, total deposits in foreign offices, money market deposit accounts, Super NOWs, and demand notes issued to the U.S. Treasury.

Source: Annual reports.

Weaknesses of the Repricing Model

The repricing model has three shortcomings: (1) It ignores market value effects, (2) it is overaggregative, and (3) it fails to deal with the problem of runoffs. In this section we discuss each of these weaknesses in more detail.

Market Value Effects

As was discussed in the overview of FI risks (Chapter 7), interest rate changes have a market value effect in addition to an income effect on asset and liability values. The repricing model ignores the market value effect—implicitly assuming a book value accounting approach. As such, the repricing gap is only a *partial* measure of the true interest rate exposure of an FI.

Overaggregation

The problem of defining buckets over a range of maturities ignores information regarding the distribution of assets and liabilities within that bucket. For example, the dollar values of rate-sensitive assets and liabilities within any maturity bucket range may be equal; however, on average, liabilities may be repriced toward the end of the bucket's range, while assets may be repriced toward the beginning.

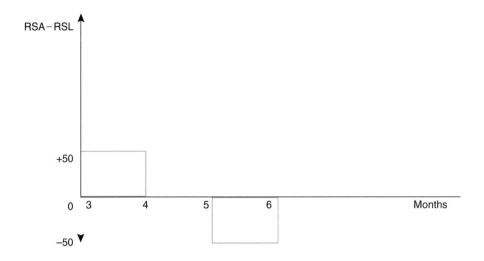

Look at the simple example for the three-month to six-month bucket in Figure 8–2. Note that $50 million more rate-sensitive assets than liabilities are repriced between months 3 and 4, while $50 million more liabilities than assets are repriced between months 5 and 6. The bank in its call report would show a zero repricing gap for the three-month to six-month bucket $(+50 + (-50) = 0)$. But as you can easily see, the bank's assets and liabilities are *mismatched* within the bucket. Clearly, the shorter the range over which bucket gaps are calculated, the smaller this problem is. If an FI manager calculated one-day bucket gaps out into the future, this would give a very good idea of the net interest income exposure to rate changes. Reportedly, many large banks have internal systems that indicate their repricing gaps on any given day in the future (252 days' time, 1,329 days' time, etc.). This suggests that although regulators require the reporting of repricing gaps over only relatively wide maturity bucket ranges, FI managers could set in place internal information systems to report the daily future patterns of such gaps.[8]

The Problem of Runoffs

In the simple repricing model discussed above, we assumed that all consumer loans matured in 1 year or that all conventional mortgages matured in 30 years. In reality, the bank continuously originates and retires consumer and mortgage loans as it creates and retires deposits. For example, today, some 30-year original maturity mortgages may have only 1 year left before they mature; that is, they are in their 29th year. In addition, virtually all long-term mortgages pay at least some principal and interest back to the bank each month. As a result, the bank receives a **runoff** cash flow from its conventional mortgage portfolio that can be reinvested at current

Runoffs
Periodic cash flow of
interest and principal
amortization payments
on long-term assets
such as conventional
mortgages that can be
reinvested at market rates.

---

[8]Another way to deal with the overaggregation problem is by adjusting the buckets for the time to interest rate repricing within the bucket. Let RSA and RSL be rate-sensitive assets and liabilities in a bucket, let R denote initial interest rates on an asset or liability, and let K denote new interest rates after repricing. Let t be the proportion of the bucket period for which the asset's (liability's) old interest rate (R) is in effect, and thus, $1 - t$ is the proportion of the bucket period in which the new interest rate (K) is in operation:

$$\Delta NII = \text{RSA}\,[(1 + R_A)^{tA} \times (1 + K_A)^{1-tA}] - \text{RSL}[(1 + R_L)^{tL} \times (1 + K_L)^{1-tL}]$$

See Brewer, "Bank Gap Management," for more details.

TABLE 8–4   Runoffs of Different Assets and Liabilities
(in millions of dollars)

	Assets			Liabilities		
Item	*$ Amount Runoff in Less Than One Year*	*$ Amount Runoff in More Than One Year*	*Item*	*$ Amount Runoff in Less Than One Year*	*$ Amount Runoff in More Than One Year*
1. Short-term consumer loans	$ 50	—	1. Equity	—	$20
2. Long-term consumer loans	5	$20	2. Demand deposits	$ 30	10
3. Three-month T-bills	30	—	3. Passbook savings	15	15
4. Six-month T-bills	35	—	4. Three-month CDs	40	—
5. Three-year notes	10	60	5. Three-month bankers acceptances	20	—
6. 10-year mortgages	2	18	6. Six-month commercial paper	60	—
7. 30-year floating-rate mortgages	40	—	7. One-year time deposits	20	—
			8. Two-year time deposits	20	20
	$172	$98		$205	$65

market rates; that is, this runoff component is rate sensitive. The bank manager can easily deal with this in the repricing model by identifying for each asset and liability item the proportion that will run off, reprice, or mature within the next year. For example, consider Table 8–4.

Notice in this table that while the original maturity of an asset or liability may be long term, these assets and liabilities still generate some cash flows that can be reinvested at market rates. Table 8–4 is a more sophisticated measure of the one-year repricing gap that takes into account the cash flows received on each asset and liability item during that year. Adjusted for runoffs, the repricing gap (in millions) is

$$GAP = \$172 - \$205 = -\$33$$

Note that the runoffs themselves are not independent of interest rate changes. Specifically, when interest rates rise, many people may delay repaying their mortgages (and the principal on those mortgages), causing the runoff amount of $2 million on 10-year mortgages in Table 8–4 to be overly optimistic. Similarly, when interest rates fall, people may prepay their fixed-rate mortgages to refinance at a lower interest rate. Then runoffs could balloon to a number much greater than $2 million. This sensitivity of runoffs to interest rate changes is a further weakness of the repricing model.[9]

The Maturity Model

Book Value Accounting
The assets and liabilities of the FI are recorded at historic values.

In most countries FIs report their balance sheets by using **book value accounting.** This records the historic values of securities purchased, loans made, and liabilities sold. For example, for U.S. banks, investment assets (i.e., those expected to be held

---

[9]A further criticism of the repricing model is its failure to incorporate income generated from an FI's off-balance-sheet derivatives portfolio. For example, the repricing model might show a gain of $150,000 if rates rise by 1 percent due to the positive on-balance-sheet gap (RSA > RSL). However, this net income gain could be offset by lower projected income from futures, swaps, caps, and so on. Thus, off-balance-sheet items need to be integrated into the repricing gap (as for the duration gap discussed in Chapter 9).

for more than a year) are recorded at book values while those assets expected to be used for trading (held for less than one year) are reported according to market values.[10] The recording of market values means that assets or liabilities are revalued to reflect current market conditions. Thus, if a fixed-coupon bond had been purchased at $100 per $100 of face value in a low–interest rate environment, a rise in current market rates would reduce the present value of the cash flows from the bond to the investor. Such a rise also reduces the price—say, to $97—at which it could be sold in the secondary market today. That is, marking to market, implied by the **market value accounting method,** reflects economic reality or the true values of assets and liabilities if the FI's portfolio were to be liquidated at today's securities prices rather than at the prices when the assets and liabilities were originally purchased or sold. In the maturity and duration model, developed below and in Chapter 9, the effects of interest rate changes on the market values of assets and liabilities are explicitly taken into account. This contrasts with the repricing model, discussed above, where such effects are ignored.

Market Value Accounting
The assets and liabilities of the FI are revalued according to the current level of interest rates.

The Maturity Model: An Example

Consider the value of a bond held by an FI that has one year to maturity, one single annual coupon of 10 percent (C) plus a face value of 100 (F) to be paid on maturity, and a current yield (R) to maturity (reflecting current interest rates) of 10 percent. The price of the one-year bond, P_1^B, is

$$P_1^B = \frac{F + C}{(1 + R)} = \frac{100 + 10}{1.1} = 100$$

Suppose the Federal Reserve tightens monetary policy so that the required yield on the bond rises instantaneously to 11 percent. The market value of the bond falls to

$$P_1^B = \frac{100 + 10}{1.11} = 99.10$$

Thus, the market value of the bond is now only $99.10 per $100 of face value, while its original book value was $100. The FI has suffered a capital loss (ΔP_1) of $0.90 per $100 of face value in holding this bond, or

$$\Delta P_1 = 99.10 - 100 = -0.90\%$$

This example simply demonstrates the fact that

$$\frac{\Delta P}{\Delta R} < 0$$

A rise in the required yield to maturity reduces the price of fixed-income securities held in FI portfolios. Note that if the bond under consideration were issued as a liability by the FI (e.g., a fixed-interest deposit such as a CD) rather than being held as an asset, the effect would be the same—the market value of the FI's deposits would fall. However, the economic interpretation is different. Although rising interest rates that reduce the market value of assets are bad news, the reduction in

---

[10]More accurately, they are reported at the lower of cost or current market value (LOCOM). However, both the SEC and the Financial Accounting Standards Board (FASB) have strongly advocated that FIs switch to full market value accounting in the near future. Currently, *FASB 115* requires FIs to value certain bonds at market prices but not loans.

the market value of liabilities is good news for the FI. The economic intuition is straightforward. Suppose the bank issued a one-year deposit with a promised interest rate of 10 percent and principal or face value of $100.[11] When the current level of interest rates is 10 percent, the market value of the liability is 100:

$$P_1^D = \frac{100 + 10}{(1.1)} = 100$$

If interest rates on new one-year deposits rise instantaneously to 11 percent, the bank has gained by locking in a promised interest payment to depositors of only 10 percent. The market value of the bank's liability to its depositors would fall to $99.10; alternatively, this would be the price the bank would need to pay the depositor if it repurchased the deposit in the secondary market:

$$P_1^D = \frac{100 + 10}{(1.11)} = 99.10$$

That is, the bank gained from paying only 10 percent on its deposits rather than 11 percent if they were newly issued after the rise in interest rates.

As a result, in a market value accounting framework, rising interest rates generally lower the market values of both assets and liabilities on an FI's balance sheet. Clearly, falling interest rates have the reverse effect—they increase the market values of both assets and liabilities.

In the preceding example, both the bond and the deposit were of one-year maturity. We can easily show that if the bond or deposit had a two-year maturity with the same annual coupon rate, the same increase in market interest rates from 10 to 11 percent would have had a more *negative* effect on the market value of the bond's (and deposit's) price. That is, before the rise in required yield:

$$P_2^B = \frac{10}{(1.1)} + \frac{10 + 100}{(1.1)^2} = 100$$

after the rise in market yields from 10 to 11 percent:

$$P_2^B = \frac{10}{(1.11)} + \frac{10 + 100}{(1.11)^2} = 98.29$$

and

$$\Delta P_2 = 98.29 - 100 = -1.71\%$$

This example demonstrates another general rule of portfolio management for FIs: The *longer* the maturity of a fixed income asset or liability, the greater its fall in price and market value for any given increase in the level of market interest rates:

$$\frac{\Delta P_1}{\Delta R} < \frac{\Delta P_2}{\Delta R} < \cdots < \frac{\Delta P_{30}}{\Delta R}$$

Note, however, that while a two-year bond's fall in price is greater than the one-year bond's, the difference between the two price falls, $\Delta P_2 - \Delta P_1$, is $- 1.71\% - (-0.9\%) = - 0.81\%$. The fall in a three-year, 10 percent coupon bond's price when

---

[11]In this example we assume for simplicity that the promised interest rate on the deposit is 10 percent. In reality, for returns to intermediation to prevail, the promised rate on deposits would be less than the promised rate (coupon) on assets.

FIGURE 8–3

The Relationship Between
ΔR, Maturity, and ΔP

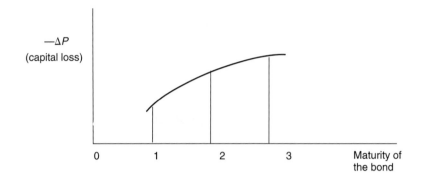

yield increases to 11 percent is − 2.44 percent. Thus, $\Delta P_3 - \Delta P_2 = -2.44\% - (-1.71\%) = -0.73\%$. This establishes an important result: While P_3 falls more than P_2 and P_2 falls more than P_1, the size of the capital loss increases at a diminishing rate as we move into the higher maturity ranges. This effect is graphed in Figure 8–3.

So far we have shown that for an FI's fixed-income assets and liabilities:

1. A rise (fall) in interest rates generally leads to a fall (rise) in the market value of an asset or liability.
2. The longer the maturity of a fixed-income asset or liability, the greater the fall (rise) in market value for any given interest rate increase (decrease).
3. The fall in the value of longer-term securities increases at a diminishing rate for any given increase in interest rates.

The Maturity Model with a Portfolio of Assets and Liabilities

The preceding general rules can be extended beyond an FI holding an individual asset or liability to an FI holding a portfolio of assets and liabilities. Let M_A be the weighted-average maturity of an FI's assets and M_L the weighted-average maturity of an FI's liabilities such that

$$M_i = W_{i1}M_{i1} + W_{i2}M_{i2} + \ldots + W_{in}M_{in}$$

where

M_i = The weighted-average maturity of an FI's assets (liabilities), $i = A\ or\ L$
W_{ij} = The importance of each asset (liability) in the asset (liability) portfolio as measured by the market value of that asset (liability) position relative to the market value of all the assets (liabilities)
M_{ij} = The maturity of the jth asset (or liability), $j = 1 \ldots n$

This equation shows that the maturity of a portfolio of assets or liabilities is a weighted average of the maturities of the assets or liabilities that comprise that portfolio. In a portfolio context, the same three principles prevail as for an individual security:

1. A rise in interest rates generally reduces the market values of an FI's asset and liability portfolios.

2. The longer the maturity of the asset or liability portfolio, the greater the fall in value for any given interest rate increase.

3. The fall in value of the asset or liability portfolio increases with its maturity at a diminishing rate.

Given the preceding, the net effect of rising or falling interest rates on an FI's balance sheet depends on the extent and direction in which the FI mismatches the maturities of its asset and liability portfolios, that is, whether its maturity gap, $M_A - M_L$, is greater than, equal to, or less than zero.

Consider the case where $M_A - M_L > 0$; that is, the maturity of assets is longer than the maturity of liabilities. This is the case of most commercial banks and thrifts. These FIs tend to hold large amounts of relatively longer-term fixed-income assets such as conventional mortgages, consumer loans, commercial loans, and bonds while issuing shorter-term liabilities, such as certificates of deposit with fixed interest payments promised to the depositors.[12]

Look at the simplified portfolio of a representative bank in Table 8–5 and notice that all assets and liabilities are marked to market; that is, we are using a market value accounting framework. Note that in the real world, reported balance sheets differ from Table 8–5 because historic or book value accounting rules are used. In Table 8–5 the difference between the market value of the bank's assets (A) and the market value of its liabilities such as deposits (L) is called the net worth or true equity value (E) of the bank. This is the economic value of the bank owners' stake in the FI. In other words, it is the money the owners would get if they could liquidate the bank's assets and liabilities at today's prices in the financial markets by selling off loans and bonds and repurchasing deposits at the best prices. This is also clear from the balance sheet identity:

$$E = A - L$$

Suppose that initially the bank's balance sheet looks like Table 8–6. As has been demonstrated, when interest rates rise, the market values of both assets and liabilities fall. However, in this example, with more long-term assets than liabilities, the market value of the asset portfolio (A) falls by more than the market value of the liability portfolio (L). The change in the value of the bank's net worth is the difference between the changes in the market value of its assets and liabilities:

TABLE 8–5   The Market Value Balance Sheet of a Bank

Assets	*Liabilities*
Long-term assets (A)	Short-term liabilities (L)
	Net worth (E)

---

[12]These assets generate periodic interest payments such as coupons that are fixed over the assets' life. In Chapter 9 we discuss interest payments fluctuating with market interest rates, such as on an adjustable rate mortgage.

TABLE 8–6   Initial Values of a Bank's Assets and Liabilities
(in millions of dollars)

Assets	Liabilities
$A = 100$ (long term)	$90 = L$ (short term)
	$10 = E$
100	100

TABLE 8–7   A Bank's Market Value Balance Sheet after a Rise in Interest Rates of 1% with Longer-Term Assets

Assets	Liabilities
$A = 97.56$	$L = 89.19$
	$E = 8.37$
97.56	97.56

$$\text{or} \quad \Delta E \quad = \quad \Delta A \quad - \quad \Delta L$$
$$-1.63 \quad = \quad (-2.44) \quad - \quad (-0.81)$$

$$\Delta E \qquad\qquad = \qquad\qquad \Delta A \qquad\qquad - \qquad\qquad \Delta L$$

(change in bank net worth)	(change in market value of assets)	(change in market value of liabilities)

To see the effect on bank net worth of having longer-term assets than liabilities, suppose the bank in Table 8–6 had $100 million invested in three-year, 10 percent coupon bonds and raised $90 million with one-year deposits paying a promised interest rate of 10 percent. We showed earlier that if market interest rates rise 1 percent from 10 to 11 percent, the value of three-year bonds falls 2.44 percent while the value of one-year deposits falls 0.9 percent. In Table 8–7 we depict this fall in asset and liability market values and the associated effects on bank net worth.

Because the bank's assets have a three-year maturity compared to its one-year maturity liabilities, the value of its assets has fallen by more than has the value of its liabilities. The net worth of the bank declines from $10 million to $8.37 million, a loss of $1.63 million, or 16.3 percent! Thus, it is clear that with a *maturity gap* of two years

$$M_A - M_L = 2 \text{ years}$$
$$(3) - (1)$$

a 1 percentage point rise in interest rates can cause the bank's owners or stockholders to take a big hit to their net worth. Indeed, if a 1 percent rise in interest rates leads to a fall of 16.3 percent in the bank's net worth, it is not unreasonable to ask how large an interest rate change would need to occur to render the bank economically insolvent by reducing its owners' equity stake or net worth to zero. That is, what increase in interest rates would make ΔE fall by 10 so that all the owners' net worth would be eliminated, such that after the interest rate rise

$$E \leq 0$$

TABLE 8–8   A Bank Becomes Insolvent after a 7 Percent Rate Increase

Assets	Liabilities
$A = 84.53$	$L = 84.62$
	$E = -0.09$
84.53	84.53

$$or \quad \Delta E = \Delta A - \Delta L$$
$$-10.09 = -15.47 - (-5.38)$$

TABLE 8–9   A Bank with an Extreme Maturity Mismatch (dollars)

Assets	Liabilities
$A = 100$	$L = 90$ (1-year deposits)
(30-year discount bonds)	$E = 10$
100	100

Deep-Discount Bonds
Often called zero-coupon bonds because they do not pay any coupon interest over the life of the bond. Instead, they make a single payment of principal or face value on maturity.

For the answer to this question, look at Table 8–8. If interest rates were to rise a full 7 percent from 10 to 17 percent, the bank's equity (E) would fall by just over 10, rendering the FI economically insolvent.[13]

Suppose the bank had adopted an even more extreme maturity gap by investing all its assets in 30-year **deep-discount bonds** while continuing to raise funds by issuing 1-year deposits with promised interest payments of 10 percent, as shown in Table 8–9. Deep-discount bonds pay $100 face value on maturity and no coupon interest in the intervening period. The price (P_{30}) an investor is willing to pay today for the bond becomes the present value of the $100 face value to be received in 30 years' time. Assuming annual compounding and a current level of interest rates of 10 percent,

$$P_{30} = \frac{\$100}{(1.1)^{30}} = \$5.73$$

Thus, an FI manager would be willing to pay $5.73 per $100 of face value. If interest rates were to rise 1 percent as we have shown, the market value of the bank's one-year deposit liabilities would fall 0.9 percent. However, the fall in the price of the 30-year discount bond asset would be to

$$P_{30} = \frac{\$100}{(1.11)^{30}} = \$4.37$$

Or, as a percentage change $(\Delta P_{30}/P_{30})\% = -23.73\%$

---

[13]Here we are talking about economic insolvency. The legal and regulatory definition may vary, depending on what type of accounting rules are used. In particular, under the Federal Deposit Insurance Corporation Improvement Act (FDICIA) (November 1991), a bank is required to be placed in conservatorship by regulators when the book value of its net worth falls below 2 percent. However, the true or market value of net worth may well be less than this figure at that time.

TABLE 8–10   The Effect of a 1 Percent Rise in Interest Rates on the Net Worth of a Bank with an Extreme Asset and Liability Mismatch

Assets	Liabilities
$A = 76.27$	$L = \quad 89.19$
	$E = -12.92$
76.27	76.27

$$or \quad \Delta E \quad = \quad \Delta A \quad - \quad \Delta L$$
$$-22.92 \quad = (-23.73) \quad - \quad (-0.81)$$

Look at Table 8–10 to see the effect on the market value balance sheet and the bank's net worth after a rise of 1 percent in interest rates. It is clear from Table 8–10 that a mere 1 percent increase in interest rates completely eliminates the bank's 10 in net worth and renders it completely and massively insolvent (net worth is -12.92 after the rise in rates). Given this example, you should not be surprised that savings and loans with 30-year fixed-rate mortgages as assets and one-year and less CDs as liabilities suffered badly during the 1979–82 period, when interest rates rose so dramatically (see Figure 8–1 also).

From the preceding examples, you might infer that the best way for an FI to **immunize** or protect itself from interest rate risk would be for its managers to match the maturities of its assets and liabilities, that is, to construct its balance sheet so that its **maturity gap,** the difference between the weighted-average maturity of its assets and liabilities, is zero:

$$M_A - M_L = 0$$

However, as we discuss next, maturity matching does not always protect an FI against interest rate risk.

Immunize
Immunization occurs when an FI's equity holders are fully protected against interest rate risk.

Maturity Gap
The difference between the weighted-average maturities of an FI's assets and liabilities.

Concept Questions

1. How does book value accounting differ from market value accounting?
2. In a market value accounting framework, what impact do rising interest rates have on the market values of an FI's assets and liabilities?
3. Using the example in Table 8–10, what would be the effect on this FI's net worth if it held one-year discount bonds (with a yield of 10 percent) as assets? Explain your findings.

Maturity Matching and Interest Rate Exposure

Duration
The average life of an asset or liability or, more technically, the weighted-average time to maturity using the relative present values of the asset or liability cash flows as weights.

While a strategy of matching asset and liability maturities moves the bank in the direction of hedging itself against interest rate risk, it is easy to show that this strategy does not always eliminate all interest rate risk for an FI. Indeed, we show in Chapter 9 that immunization against interest rate risk requires the bank to take into account:

1. The **duration** or average life of asset or (liability) cash flows rather than the maturity of assets and liabilities.

FIGURE 8–4

One-Year CD
Cash Flows

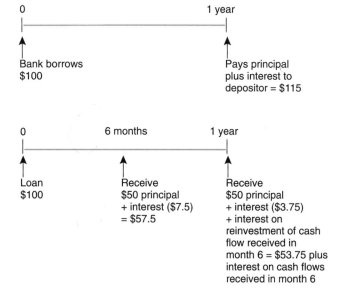

FIGURE 8–5

One-Year Loan
Cash Flow

2. The degree of leverage in the bank's balance sheet, that is, the proportion of assets funded by liabilities (such as deposits) rather than by equity.

We show next, using a simple example, that an FI choosing to directly match the maturities of its assets and liabilities does not necessarily achieve perfect immunization or protection for its equity holders against interest rate risk. Consider the example of a bank that issues a one-year CD to a depositor. This CD has a face value of $100 and an interest rate promised to depositors of 15 percent. Thus, on maturity at the end of the year, the bank has to repay the borrower $100 plus $15 interest, or $115, as shown in Figure 8–4.

Suppose the bank lends $100 for one year to a corporate borrower at a 15 percent annual interest rate. However, contractually the bank requires half of the loan ($50) to be repaid after six months and the last half to be repaid at the end of the year. Note that although the maturity of the loan = maturity of the deposit = 1 year, the cash flow earned on the loan may be greater or less than the $115 required to pay off depositors, depending on what happens to interest rates over the one-year period. You can see this in Figure 8–5.

At the end of the first six months, the bank receives a $50 repayment in loan principal plus $7.5 in interest ($100 \times \frac{1}{2}$ year $\times 15$ percent) for a total midyear cash flow of $57.5. At the end of the year, the bank receives $50 as the final repayment of loan principal plus $3.75 interest ($50 \times \frac{1}{2}$ year $\times 15$ percent) plus the reinvestment income earned from relending the $57.5 received six months earlier. If interest rates do not change over the period, the bank's extra return from its ability to reinvest part of the cash flow for the last six months will be ($57.5 \times \frac{1}{2} \times 15$ percent) = 4.3125. We summarize the total cash flow on the bank's one-year loan in Table 8–11.

As you can see, by the end of the year, the cash paid in on the loan exceeded the cash paid out on the deposit by $0.5625. The reason for this is the ability of the bank to reinvest part of the principal and interest over the second half of the year at 15 percent. Suppose that instead of interest rates staying unchanged at 15 percent throughout the whole one-year period, they had fallen to 12 percent over the last six

TABLE 8–11   Cash Flow on a Loan with a 15 Percent Interest Rate

Cash Flow at 1/2 Year	
Principal	$ 50.00
Interest	7.50
Cash Flow at 1 Year	
Principal	$ 50.00
Interest	3.75
Reinvestment income	4.3125
	$115.5625

TABLE 8–12   Cash Flow on the Loan When the Beginning Rate of 15 Percent Falls to 12 Percent

Cash Flow at 1/2 Year	
Principal	$ 50.00
Interest	7.50
Cash Flow at 1 Year	
Principal	$ 50.00
Interest	3.75
Reinvestment income	3.45
	$114.70

months in the year. This fall in rates would affect neither the promised deposit rate of 15 percent nor the promised loan rate of 15 percent because they are set at time 0 when the deposit and loan were originated and do not change throughout the year. What is affected is the bank's reinvestment income on the $57.5 cash flow received on the loan at the end of six months. It can be relent for the final six months of the year only at the new lower interest rate of 12 percent (see Table 8–12).

The only change to the asset cash flows for the bank comes from the reinvestment of the $57.5 received at the end of six months at the lower interest rate of 12 percent. This produces the smaller reinvestment income of $3.45 ($57.5 × 1/2 × 12 percent) rather than $4.3125 when rates stayed at 15 percent throughout the year. Rather than making a profit of $0.5625 from intermediation, the bank loses $0.3. Note that this loss occurs due to interest rates changing, even when the FI had matched the maturity of its assets and liabilities, $M_A = M_L = 1$ year.

Despite the matching of maturities, the FI is still exposed to interest rate risk because the *timing* of the *cash flows* on the deposit and loan are not perfectly matched. In a sense, the cash flows on the loan are received, on average, earlier than are those on the deposit, where all cash flows occur at the end of the year. In the next chapter we show that only by matching the average lives of assets and liabilities—that is, by taking into account the precise timing of arrival of cash flows—can an FI immunize itself against interest rate risk. In a cash flow sense, the average life, or *duration,* of an asset or liability usually, but not always, differs from its maturity. In particular, we demonstrate in the next chapter that for our simple one-year maturity deposit and one-year maturity loan case, maturity and duration differ. While the maturity of the deposit (M_D) equals the maturity of the loan (M_L), the duration of the loan (D_L) is less than the duration of the deposit (D_D). This duration mismatch exposes an FI to interest rate risk.

Concept Questions

1. Can an FI achieve perfect immunization against interest rate risk by matching the maturities of its assets and liabilities? Explain your answer.
2. Suppose the average maturity of an FI's assets are equal to its liabilities. If interest rates fall, why could an FI's net worth still decline? Explain your answer.

Summary

In this chapter we introduced two methods of measuring the interest rate risk exposure of an FI: the repricing model and the maturity model. The repricing model looks at the difference or gap between an FI's rate-sensitive assets and rate-sensitive liabilities to measure interest rate risk, while the maturity model uses the difference between the average maturity of an FI's assets and that of its liabilities to measure interest rate risk. It was demonstrated that both the repricing model

and the maturity model have difficulty in accurately measuring the interest rate risk of an FI. In particular, the repricing model ignores the market value effects of interest rate changes while the maturity model ignores the timing of the arrival of cash flows on assets and liabilities. More complete and accurate measures of an FI's exposure are duration and the duration gap, which are explained in the next chapter.

Questions and Problems

1. What is the repricing gap? In using this model to evaluate interest rate risk, what is meant by rate sensitivity? On what financial performance variable does the repricing model focus? Explain.
2. What is a maturity bucket in the repricing model? Why is the length of time selected for repricing assets and liabilities important in using the repricing model?
3. Calculate the repricing gap and the impact on net interest income of a 1 percent increase in interest rates for each of the following positions:

   - Rate-sensitive assets = $200 million
     Rate-sensitive liabilities = $100 million
   - Rate-sensitive assets = $100 million
     Rate-sensitive liabilities = $150 million
   - Rate-sensitive assets = $150 million
     Rate-sensitive liabilities = $140 million

   a. Calculate the impact on net interest income of each of the above situations, assuming a 1 percent decrease in interest rates.
   b. What conclusion can you draw about the repricing model from these results?
4. What are the reasons for not including demand deposits as rate-sensitive liabilities in the repricing analysis for a

commercial bank? What is the subtle but potentially strong reason for including demand deposits in the total of rate-sensitive liabilities? Can the same argument be made for passbook savings accounts?
5. What is the gap ratio? What is the value of this ratio to interest rate risk managers and regulators?
6. Which of the following assets or liabilities fit the one-year rate or repricing sensitivity test?

   91-day U.S. Treasury bills
   1-year U.S. Treasury notes
   20-year U.S. Treasury bonds
   20-year floating-rate corporate bonds with annual repricing
   30-year floating-rate mortgages with repricing every two years
   30-year floating-rate mortgages with repricing every six months
   Overnight fed funds
   9-month fixed-rate CDs
   1-year fixed-rate CDs
   5-year floating-rate CDs with annual repricing
   Common stock

7. Consider the following balance sheet for WatchoverU Savings, Inc. (in millions):

Assets		Liabilities and Equity	
Floating-rate mortgages		Demand deposits	
(currently 10% annually)	$50	(currently 6% annually)	$ 70
30-year fixed-rate loans		Time deposits	
(currently 7% annually)	50	(currently 6% annually)	20
		Equity	10
Total assets	$100	Total liabilities and equity	$100

a. What is WatchoverU's expected net interest income at year end?

b. What will be the net interest income at year end if interest rates rise 2 percent?

c. Using the cumulative repricing gap model, what is the expected net interest income for a 2 percent increase in interest rates?

8. What are some of the weaknesses of the repricing model? How have large banks solved the problem of choosing the optimal time period for repricing? What is runoff cash flow, and how does this amount affect the repricing model's analysis?

9. Use the following information about a hypothetical government security dealer named M. P. Jorgan. Market yields are in parentheses, and amounts are in millions.

Assets		Liabilities and Equity	
Cash	$10	Overnight repos	$170
1 month T-bills (7.05%)	75	Subordinated debt	150
3 month T-bills (7.25%)	75	7-year fixed rate (8.55%)	
2 year T-notes (7.50%)	50		
8 year T-notes (8.96%)	100		
5 year munis (floating rate)	25		
(8.20% reset every			
6 months)		Equity	15
Total assets and liabilities	$335	Total liabilities and equity	$335

a. What is the funding or repricing gap if the planning period is 30 days? 91 days? 2 years? Recall that cash is a noninterest-earning asset.

b. What is the impact over the next 30 days on net interest income if all interest rates rise 50 basis points? Decrease 75 basis points?

c. The following one-year runoffs are expected: $10 million for two-year T-notes and $20 million for eight-year T-notes. What is the one-year repricing gap?

d. If runoffs are considered, what is the effect on net interest income at year end if interest rates rise 50 basis points? Decrease 75 basis points?

10. What is the difference between book value accounting and market value accounting? How do interest rate changes affect the value of bank assets and liabilities under the two methods? What is marking to market?

11. Why is it important to use market values as opposed to book values in evaluating the net worth of an FI? What are some of the advantages of using book values as opposed to market values?

12. Consider a $1,000 bond with a fixed-rate 10 percent annual coupon (Cpn %) and a maturity (N) of 10 years. The bond currently is trading to a market yield to maturity (YTM) of 10 percent. Complete the following table.

N	Cpn%	YTM	Price	From Par, $ Change in Price	From Par, % Change in Price
8	10%	9%			
9	10%	9%			
10	10%	9%			
10	10%	10%	$1,000.00		
10	10%	11%			
11	10%	11%			
12	10%	11%			

Use this information to verify the three principles of interest rate–price relationships for fixed-rate financial assets.

13. Consider a 12-year, 12 percent annual coupon bond with a required return of 10 percent. The bond has a face value of $1,000.

a. What is the price of the bond?

b. If interest rates rise to 11 percent, what is the price of the bond?

c. What has been the percentage change in price?

d. Repeat parts (a), (b), and (c) for a 16-year bond.

e. What do the respective changes in bond prices indicate?

14. Consider a five-year, 15 percent annual coupon bond with a face value of $1,000. The bond is trading at a market yield to maturity of 12 percent.

a. What is the price of the bond?

b. If the market yield to maturity increases 1 percent, what will be the bond's new price?

c. Using your answers to parts (a) and (b), what is the percentage change in the bond's price as a result of the 1 percent increase in interest rates?

d. Repeat parts (b) and (c) assuming a 1 percent decrease in interest rates.

e. What do the differences in your answers indicate about the rate-price relationships of fixed-rate assets?

15. What is a maturity gap? How can the maturity model be used to immunize an FI's portfolio? What is the critical requirement that allows maturity matching to have some success in immunizing the balance sheet of an FI?

16. Nearby Bank has the following balance sheet (in millions):

Assets		Liabilities and Equity	
Cash	$ 60	Demand deposits	$140
5-year treasury notes	60	1-year Certificates of deposit	160
30-year mortgages	200	Equity	20
Total assets	$320	Total liabilities and equity	$320

What is the maturity gap for Nearby Bank? Is Nearby Bank more exposed to an increase or a decrease in interest rates? Explain why?

17. County Bank has the following market value balance sheet (in millions, all interest at annual rates):

Assets		Liabilities and Equity	
Cash	$ 20	Demand deposits	$100
15-year commercial loan at 10% interest, balloon payment	160	5-year CDs at 6% interest, balloon payment	210
30-year mortgages at 8% interest, monthly amortizing	300	20-year debentures at 7% interest	120
		Equity	50
Total assets	$480	Total liabilities and equity	$480

a. What is the maturity gap for County Bank?

b. What will be the maturity gap if the interest rates on all assets and liabilities increase 1 percent?

c. What will happen to the market value of the equity?

d. If interest rates increase 2 percent, would the bank be solvent?

18. Given that bank balance sheets typically are accounted in book value terms, why should regulators or anyone else be concerned about how interest rates affect the market values of assets and liabilities?

19. If a bank manager is certain that interest rates are going to increase within the next six months, how should the bank manager adjust the bank's maturity gap to take advantage of this anticipated increase? What if the manager believed rates would fall? Would your suggested adjustments be difficult or easy to achieve?

20. Consumer Bank has $20 million in cash and a $180 million loan portfolio. The assets are funded with demand deposits of $18 million, a $162 million CD, and $20 million in equity. The loan portfolio has a maturity of 2 years, earns interest at an annual rate of 7 percent, and is amortized monthly. The bank pays 7 percent annual interest on the CD, but the interest will not be paid until the CD matures at the end of 2 years.

a. What is the maturity gap for Consumer Bank?

b. Is Consumer Bank immunized or protected against changes in interest rates? Why or why not?

c. Does Consumer Bank face interest rate risk? That is, if market interest rates increase or decrease 1 percent, what happens to the value of the equity?

d. How can a decrease in interest rates create interest rate risk?

21. FI International holds seven-year Acme International bonds and two-year Beta Corporation bonds. The Acme bonds are yielding 12 percent and the Beta bonds are yielding 14 percent under current market conditions.

a. What is the weighted-average maturity of FI's bond portfolio if 40 percent is in Acme bonds and 60 percent is in Beta bonds?

b. What proportion of Acme and Beta bonds should be held to have a weighted-average yield of 13.5 percent?

c. What will be the weighted-average maturity of the bond portfolio if the weighted-average yield is realized?

22. An insurance company has invested in the following fixed-income securities: (*a*) $10,000,000 of five-year Treasury notes paying 5 percent interest and selling at par value, (*b*) $5,800,000 of 10-year bonds paying 7 percent interest with a par value of $6,000,000, and (*c*) $6,200,000 of 20-year subordinated debentures paying 9 percent interest with a par value of $6,000,000.

a. What is the weighted-average maturity of this portfolio of assets?

b. If interest rates change so that the yields on all of the securities decrease 1 percent, how does the weighted-average maturity of the portfolio change?

c. Explain the changes in the maturity values if the yields increase 1 percent.

d. Assume that the insurance company has no other assets. What will be the effect on the market value of the company's equity if the interest rate changes in (*b*) and (*c*) occur?

23. The following is a simplified FI balance sheet:

Assets		Liabilities and Equity	
Loans	$1,000	Deposits	$ 850
		Equity	150
Total assets	$1,000	Total liabilities and equity	$1,000

The average maturity of loans is four years, and the average maturity of deposits is two years. Assume that loan and deposit balances are reported as book value, zero-coupon items.

a. Assume that interest rates on both loans and deposits are 9 percent. What is the market value of equity?

b. What must be the interest rate on deposits to force the market value of equity to be zero? What economic market conditions must exist to make this situation possible?

c. Assume that interest rates on both loans and deposits are 9 percent. What must be the average maturity of deposits for the market value of equity to be zero?

24. Gunnison Insurance has reported the following balance sheet (in thousands):

Assets		Liabilities and Equity	
2-year Treasury note	$175	1-year commercial paper	$135
15-year munis	165	5-year note	160
		Equity	45
Total assets	$340	Total liabilities and equity	$340

All securities are selling at par equal to book value. The two-year notes are yielding 5 percent, and the 15-year munis are yielding 9 percent. The one-year commercial paper pays 4.5 percent, and the five-year notes pay 8 percent. All instruments pay interest annually.

a. What is the weighted-average maturity of the assets for Gunnison?

b. What is the weighted-average maturity of the liabilities for Gunison?

c. What is the maturity gap for Gunnison?

d. What does your answer to part (c) imply about the interest rate exposure of Gunnison Insurance?

e. Calculate the values of all four securities of Gunnison Insurance's balance sheet assuming that all interest rates increase 2 percent. What is the dollar change in the total asset and total liability values? What is the percentage change in these values?

f. What is the dollar impact on the market value of equity for Gunnison? What is the percentage change in the value of the equity?

g. What would be the impact on Gunnison's market value of equity if the liabilities paid interest semiannually instead of annually?

25. Scandia Bank has issued a one-year, $1 million CD paying 5.75 percent to fund a one-year loan paying an interest rate of 6 percent. The principal of the loan will be paid in two installments: $500,000 in 6 months and the balance at the end of the year.

a. What is the maturity gap of Scandia Bank? According to the maturity model, what does this maturity gap imply about the interest rate risk exposure faced by Scandia Bank?

b. What is the expected net interest income at the end of the year?

c. What would be the effect on annual net interest income of a 2 percent interest rate increase that occurred immediately after the loan was made? What would be the effect of a 2 percent decrease in rates?

d. What do these results indicate about the ability of the maturity model to immunize portfolios against interest rate exposure?

26. EDF Bank has a very simple balance sheet. Assets consist of a two-year, $1 million loan which pays an interest rate of LIBOR plus 4 percent annually. The loan is funded with a two-year deposit on which the bank pays LIBOR plus 3.5 percent interest annually. LIBOR currently is at 4 percent, and both the loan and the deposit principal will not be paid until maturity.

a. What is the maturity gap of this balance sheet?

b. What is the expected net interest income in year 1 and year 2?

c. Immediately prior to the beginning of year 2, LIBOR rates increased to 6 percent. What is the expected net interest income in year 2? What would be the effect on net interest income of a 2 percent decrease in LIBOR?

d. How would your results be affected if the interest payments on the loan were received semiannually?

e. What implications do these results have for the effectiveness of the maturity model as an immunization strategy?

The following questions and problems are based on material in the appendix to the chapter.

27. The current one-year Treasury bill rate is 5.2 percent, and the expected one-year rate 12 months from now is 5.8 percent. According to the unbiased expectations theory, what should be the current rate for a two-year Treasury security?

28. A recent edition of *The Wall Street Journal* reported interest rates of 6 percent, 6.35 percent, 6.65 percent, and 6.75 percent for three-year, four-year, five-year, and six-year Treasury notes, respectively. According to the unbiased expectations theory, what are the expected one-year rates for years 4, 5, and 6?

29. How does the liquidity premium theory of the term structure of interest rates differ from the unbiased expectations theory? In a normal economic environment, that is, an upward-sloping yield curve, what is the relationship of liquidity premiums for successive years into the future? Why?

APPENDIX 8A
TERM STRUCTURE OF INTEREST RATES

To explain the process of estimating the impact of an unexpected shock in short-term interest rates on the entire term structure of interest rates, we can use the theory of the term structure of interest rates or the yield curve. The term *structure of interest rates* compares the market yields on securities assuming that all characteristics (default risk, coupon rate, etc.) except maturity are the same. The yield curve for Treasury securities is the most commonly reported and analyzed yield curve. The shape of the yield curve on Treasury securities has taken many forms over the years, but the four most common shapes are shown in Figure 8A–1. In graph (a), yields rise steadily with maturity when the yield curve is upward sloping. This is the most commonly seen yield curve. Graph (b) shows an inverted or downward-sloping yield curve where yields decline as maturity increases. Inverted yield curves were prevalent just before interest rates dropped in early 1992. Graph (c) shows a humped yield curve, one most recently seen in mid-1991 to late 1991. Finally, graph (d) shows a flat yield curve in which the yield to maturity is not affected by the term to maturity. This shape of the yield curve was last seen in fall 1989. Explanations for the shape of the yield curve fall predominantly into three theories: the unbiased expectations theory, the liquidity premium theory, and the market segmentation theory.

Unbiased Expectations Theory

According to the unbiased expectations theory for the term structure of interest rates, at a given point in time the yield curve reflects the market's current expectations of future short-term rates. Thus, an upward-sloping yield curve reflects the market's expectation that short-term rates will rise throughout the relevant time period (e.g., the Federal Reserve is expected to tighten monetary policy in the future). Similarly, a flat yield curve reflects the expectation that short-term rates will remain constant over the relevant time period. The unbiased expectations theory posits that long-term rates are a geometric average of current and expected short-term interest rates. That is, the interest rate that equates the return on a series of short-term security investments with the return on a long-term security with an equivalent maturity reflects the market's forecast of future interest rates. The mathematical equation representing this relationship is

FIGURE 8A–1

Common Shapes for Yield Curves on Treasury Securities

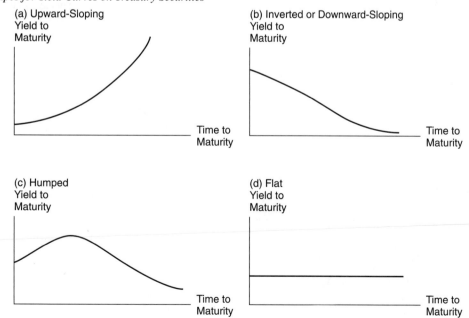

$$\overline{R}_N = [(1 + \overline{R}_1)(1 + E(\tilde{r}_2)) \ldots (1 + E(\tilde{r}_N))]^{1/N} - 1$$

where

$\overline{R}_N$ = actual *N*-period rate
N = term to maturity
$\overline{R}_1$ = current one-year rate
$E(\tilde{r}_i)$ = expected one-year (forward) yield during period I.

For example, suppose one-year Treasury bill rates for the next four years are expected to be as follows:

$$\overline{R}_1 = 6\%,\ E(\tilde{r}_2) = 7\%,\ E(\tilde{r}_3) = 7.5\%,\ E(\tilde{r}_4) = 8.5\%$$

This would be consistent with the market expecting the Federal Reserve to increasingly tighten monetary policy. Using the unbiased expectations theory, current long-term rates for one-, two-, three-, and four-year maturity Treasury securities should be:

$\overline{R}_1 = 6\%$
$\overline{R}_2 = [(1+.06)(1+.07)]^{1/2} - 1 = 6.499\%$
$\overline{R}_3 = [(1+.06)(1+.07)(1+.075)]^{1/3} - 1 = 6.832\%$
$\overline{R}_4 = [(1+.06)(1+.07)(1+.075)(1+.085)]^{1/4} - 1 = 7.246\%$

And the yield curve should look like:

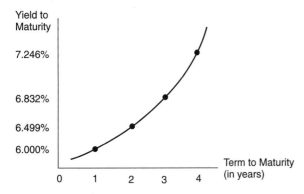

Thus, the current yield curve reflects the market's expectation of consistently rising short-term interest rates in the future.

Liquidity Premium Theory

The unbiased expectations theory has the shortcoming that it neglects to recognize that forward rates are not perfect predictors of future interest rates. If forward rates were perfect predictors of future interest rates, future prices of Treasury securities would be known with certainty. The return over any investment period would be certain and independent of the maturity of the instrument initially purchased and of the time at which the investor needs to liquidate the security. However, with uncertainty about future interest rates (and future monetary policy actions) and hence about future security prices, these instruments become risky in the sense that the return over a future investment period is unknown. In other words,

because of future uncertainty of return, there is a risk in holding long-term securities and that risk increases with the security's maturity.

The liquidity premium theory of the term structure of interest rates allows for this future uncertainty. It is based on the idea that investors will hold long-term maturities if they are offered a premium to compensate for the future uncertainty associated with the long term. In other words, the liquidity premium theory states that long-term rates are the geometric average of current and expected short-term rates plus a "liquidity" or risk premium that increases with the maturity of the security. Thus, according to the liquidity premium theory, an upward-sloping yield curve may reflect the market's expectation that future short-term rates will rise, be flat, or fall, while the liquidity premium increases such that overall the yield to maturity on securities increases with the term to maturity. The liquidity premium theory may be mathematically represented as

$$\overline{R}_N = [(1 + \overline{R}_1)(1 + E(\tilde{r}_2) + L_2) \ldots (1 + E(\tilde{r}_N) + L_N)]^{1/N} - 1$$

where

L_t = liquidity premium for a period t and $L_2 < L_3 < \ldots < L_N$.

Market Segmentation Theory

Market segmentation theory rejects the assumption that risk premiums must rise uniformly with maturity but instead recognizes that investors have specific maturity needs. Accordingly, securities with different maturities are not seen as perfect substitutes under market segmentation theory. Instead, investors have holding periods dictated by the nature of the assets and liabilities they hold. As a result, interest rates are determined by distinct supply and demand conditions within a particular maturity bucket or market segment (e.g., the short end and the long end of the market). Market segmentation theory then assumes that neither investors nor borrowers are willing to shift from one maturity sector to another to take advantage of opportunities arising from changes in yields (e.g., insurance companies generally prefer long-term securities and banks generally prefer short-term securities). Figure 8A–2 demonstrates how changes in the supply curve for short- versus long-term bonds result in changes in the shape of the yield curve. Such a change may occur if the Treasury decides to issue fewer short-term bonds and more long-term bonds (i.e., to lengthen the average maturity of government debt outstanding). Specifically in Figure 8A–2, the higher the yield on securities, the higher the demand for them. Thus, as the supply of securities decreases in the short-term market and increases in the long-term market, the shape of the yield curve becomes steeper. If the supply of short-term securities increased while the supply of long-term securities had decreased, the yield curve would have become flatter (and may even have sloped downward).

FIGURE 8A–2

Market Segmentation and Determination of the Slope of the Yield Curve

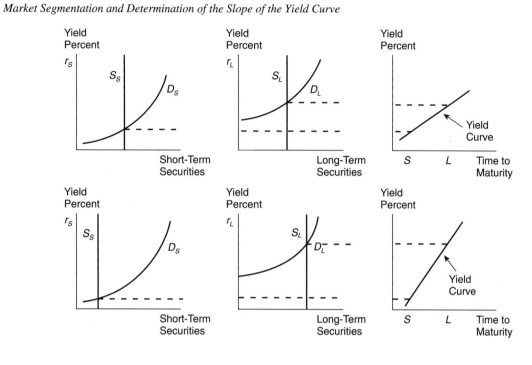

INTEREST RATE RISK II

Introduction

In this second chapter on measuring interest rate risk, we explain the concept of *duration* and see that duration and the duration gap are more accurate measures of an FI's interest rate risk exposure than is the simple maturity model described in Chapter 8. We begin by presenting the basic arithmetic needed to calculate the duration of an asset or liability. Then we analyze the economic meaning of the number we calculate for duration. This number, which measures the average life of an asset or liability, also has *economic* meaning as the interest sensitivity (or interest elasticity) of that asset or liability's value. Next, we show how the duration measure can be used to protect an FI (or immunize its portfolio) against interest rate risk. Finally, in the appendix, we examine some problems in applying the duration measure to real-world FIs' balance-sheets.

Duration

Duration is a more complete measure of an asset or liability's interest rate sensitivity than is maturity because duration takes into account the time of arrival of all cash flows as well as the asset or liability's maturity. Consider the example of the one-year loan at the end of Chapter 8. This loan had a 15 percent interest rate and required repayment of half the $100 in principal at the end of six months and the other half at the end of the year. The promised cash flows *(CF)* received by the bank from the borrower at the end of one-half year and at the end of the year appear in Figure 9–1.

$CF_{1/2}$ is the $50 promised repayment of principal plus the $7.5 promised interest payment at the end of the first half of the year. CF_1 is the promised cash flow at the end of the year and is equal to the second $50 promised principal repayment plus $3.75 promised interest ($50 \times \frac{1}{2} \times 15\%$). To compare the relative sizes of these two cash flows, we should put them in the same dimensions. This is the case because $1 of principal or interest received at the end of a year is worth less to the bank in terms of the time value of money than $1 of principal or interest received at the end of six months. Since interest rates are 15 percent per annum, the present values of the two cash flows are as shown in Figure 9–2.

FIGURE 9–1

Promised Cash Flows on the One-Year Loan

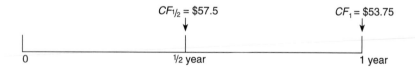

	$CF_{1/2}$ = $57.5	CF_1 = $53.75
0	½ year	1 year

---

*Some of the more difficult technical sections in this and a few other chapters are marked with an asterisk. These can be skipped by students less interested in the more technical sections of these chapters.

Figure 9–2

*PV of the Cash Flows
From the Loan*

$$CF_{1/2} = \$\ 57.5 \qquad PV_{1/2} = \$57.5/(1.075) = \$53.49$$
$$CF_{1/2} = \$\ 53.75 \qquad PV_{1} = \$53.75/(1.075)^2 = \$46.51$$
$$CF_{1/2} + CF_{1} = \$111.25 \qquad PV_{1/2} + PV_{1} = \$100.00$$

Note that since $CF_{1/2}$, the cash flows received at the end of one-half year, are received earlier, they are discounted at $(1 + \frac{1}{2}R)$; this is smaller than the discount rate on the cash flow received at the end of the year $(1 + \frac{1}{2}R)^2$.[1]

In Figure 9–2 we summarize the *PV*s of the cash flows from the loan.

Technically speaking, duration is the *weighted-average* time to maturity using the relative present values of the cash flows as weights. As Figure 9–2 shows, we receive some cash flows at one-half year and some at one year. In duration analysis, we weight the time at which cash flows are received by the relative importance in present value terms of the cash flows arriving at each point in time. In present value terms, the relative importance of the cash flows arriving at time $t = \frac{1}{2}$ year and time $t = 1$ year are as follows:

Time (t)	Weight (x)		
1/2 year	$X_{1/2} = \dfrac{PV_{1/2}}{PV_{1/2} + PV_{1}} =$	$\dfrac{53.49}{100.00}$	$= .5349 = 53.49\%$
1 year	$X_{1} = \dfrac{PV_{1}}{PV_{1/2} + PV_{1}} =$	$\dfrac{46.51}{100.00}$	$= .4651 = 46.51\%$
		1.0	100%

In present value terms, 53.49 percent of cash flows on the loan are received at the end of six months $(t = \frac{1}{2})$ and 46.51 percent are received at the end of the year $(t = 1)$. By definition, the sum of the (present value) cash flow weights must equal 1:

$$X_{1/2} + X_{1} = 1$$
$$.5349 + .4651 = 1$$

We can now calculate the duration *(D)* or the average life of the loan using the present value of its cash flows as weights:

$$D_{1} = X_{1/2}(\tfrac{1}{2}) + X_{1}(1)$$
$$= .5349(\tfrac{1}{2}) + .4651(1) = .7326 \text{ years}$$

Thus, while the maturity of the loan is one year, its duration or average life in a cash flow sense is only .7326 year. The duration is less than the maturity of the loan because in present value terms 53.49 percent of the cash flows are received at the

---

[1]We use here the Treasury formula for calculating the present values of cash flows on a security that pays cash flows semiannually.

FIGURE 9–3

PV of the Cash Flows of the Deposit

end of one-half year. Note that duration is measured in years since we weight the time *(t)* at which cash flows are received by the relative present value importance of cash flows ($X_{1/2}$, X_1, etc.).

To learn why the bank was still exposed to interest rate risk while matching maturities under the maturity model in the example at the end of Chapter 8, we next calculate the duration of the one-year, 15 percent interest certificate of deposit. The bank promises to make all cash payments to depositors at the end of the year; that is, $CF_1 = \$115$, which is the promised principal and interest repayment to the depositor. Since weights are calculated in present value terms:[2]

$$CF_1 = \$115, PV_1 = \$115/1.15 = \$100$$

We show this in Figure 9–3. Because all cash flows are received at the end of the year, $X_1 = PV_1/PV_1 = 1$, the duration of the deposit is

$$D_D = X_1 \times (1)$$

$$D_D = 1 \times (1) = 1 \text{ year}$$

Thus, only when all cash flows are paid or received at the end of the period with no intervening cash flows does duration equal maturity. This example also illustrates that while the maturity gap between the loan and the deposit is zero, the duration gap is negative:

$$M_L - M_D = 1 - 1 = 0$$

$$D_L - D_D = .7326 - 1 = -.2674 \text{ years}$$

As will become clearer, to measure and to hedge interest rate risk, the bank needs to manage its duration gap rather than its maturity gap.

Concept Questions

1. Why is duration considered a more complete measure of an asset or liability's interest rate sensitivity than maturity?
2. When is the duration of an asset equal to its maturity?

A General Formula for Duration

You can calculate the duration for any fixed-income security by using this general formula:[3]

---

[2]Since the CD is like an annual coupon bond, the annual discount rate is $1/1 + R = 1/1.15$.

[3]In the following material a number of useful examples and formulas were suggested by G. Hawawini of INSEAD. For more discussion of the duration model and a number of those examples, see G. Hawawini, "Controlling the Interest Rate Risk of Bonds: An Introduction to Duration Analysis and Immunization Strategies," *Finanzmarket and Portfolio Management* 1 (1986–87), pp. 8–18.

$$D = \frac{\sum\limits_{t=1}^{N} CF_t \times DF_t \times t}{\sum\limits_{t=1}^{N} CF_t \times DF_t} = \frac{\sum\limits_{t=1}^{N} PV_t \times t}{\sum\limits_{t=1}^{N} PV_t}$$

where

D = Duration measured in years

CF_t = Cash flow received on the security at end of period t

N = Last period in which the cash flow is received

DF_t = Discount factor $= 1/(1 + R)^t$, where R is the yield or current level of interest rates in the market

$\sum\limits_{t=1}^{N}$ = Summation sign for addition of all terms from $t = 1$ to $t = N$

PV_t = Present value of the cash flow at the end of the period t, which equals $CF_t \times DF_t$

To help you fully understand this formula, we look at some examples next.

The Duration of a Six-Year Eurobond

Eurobonds pay coupons *annually.* Suppose the annual coupon is 8 percent, the face value of the bond is $1,000, and the current yield to maturity *(R)* is also 8 percent. We show the calculation of its duration in Table 9–1.

TABLE 9–1   **The Duration of a Six-Year Eurobond with 8 Percent Coupon and Yield**

t	CF_t	DF_t	$CF_t \times DF_t$	$CF_t \times DF_t \times t$
1	80	0.9259	74.07	74.07
2	80	0.8573	68.59	137.18
3	80	0.7938	63.51	190.53
4	80	0.7350	58.80	235.20
5	80	0.6806	54.45	272.25
6	1,080	0.6302	680.58	4,083.48
			1,000.00	4,992.71

$$D = \frac{4,992.71}{1,000} = 4.993 \text{ years}$$

The Duration of a Two-Year U.S. Treasury Bond

U.S. Treasury bonds pay coupon interest semiannually. Suppose the annual coupon rate is 8 percent, the face value is $1,000, and the annual yield to maturity R is 12 percent. See Table 9–2 for the calculation of the duration of this bond.[4]

Next, we look at two other types of bonds that are useful in understanding duration.

---

[4]Here we use the Treasury formula for discounting bonds with semiannual coupons: $(1 + 1/2R)^x$ where x is the number of semiannual coupon payments. Thus, at $t = \frac{1}{2}$, the discount rate is (1.06), at $t = 1$ the discount rate is $(1.06)^2$, and so on.

TABLE 9–2   The Duration of a Two-Year U.S. Treasury Bond with 8 Percent Coupon and 12 Percent Yield

t	CF_t	DF_t	$CF_t \times DF_t$	$CF_t \times DF_t \times t$
1/2	40	.9434	37.74	18.87
1	40	.8900	35.60	35.60
1 1/2	40	.8396	33.58	50.37
2	1,040	.7921	823.78	1,647.56
			930.70	1,752.4

$$D = \frac{1,752.4}{930.70} = 1.88 \text{ years}$$

The Duration of a Zero-Coupon Bond

In recent years the U.S. Treasury has created zero-coupon bonds that allow securities firms and other investors to strip individual coupons and the principal from regular Treasury bonds and sell them to investors as separate securities. Elsewhere, such as in the Eurobond markets, corporations have issued discount or zero-coupon bonds directly. U.S. T-bills and commercial paper usually are issued on a discount basis and are further examples of discount bonds. These bonds sell at a discount from face value on issue and pay the face value (e.g., $1,000) on maturity. The current price an investor is willing to pay for such a bond is equal to its present value, or

$$P = \frac{1,000}{(1 + R)^N}$$

where R is the required annually compounded yield to maturity, N is the number of periods to maturity, and P is the price. Because there are no intervening cash flows such as coupons between issue and maturity, the following must be true:

$$D_B = M_B$$

That is, the duration of a discount instrument equals its maturity.

The Duration of a Consol Bond (Perpetuities)

Although consol bonds have yet to be issued in the United States, they are of theoretical interest in exploring the differences between maturity and duration. A consol bond is a bond that pays a fixed coupon each year. The novel feature of this bond is that it *never* matures; that is, it is a perpetuity:

$$M_c = \infty$$

In fact, consol bonds that were issued by the British government in the 1890s to finance the Boer Wars in South Africa are still outstanding. However, while its maturity is theoretically infinity, the formula for the duration of a consol bond is[5]

---

[5]For reasons of space, we do not provide formal proof here. Interested readers might refer to G. Hawawini, "Controlling the Interest Rate Risk."

$$D_c = 1 + \frac{1}{R}$$

where R is the required yield to maturity. If the yield curve implies $R = 5$ percent, then the duration of the consol bond would be

$$D_c = 1 + \frac{1}{.05} = 21$$

Thus, while maturity is infinite, duration is finite. Moreover, as interest rates rise, the duration of the consol bond falls. For example, consider the 1979–82 period, when some yields rose to around 20 percent on long-term government bonds. Then

$$D_c = 1 + \frac{1}{.2} = 6 \text{ years}$$

Concept Questions

1. Calculate the duration of a one-year, 8 percent coupon, 10 percent yield bond that pays coupons quarterly.
2. What is the duration of a zero-coupon bond?

Features of Duration

From the preceding examples, we derive three important features of duration relating to the maturity, yield, and coupon interest of the security being analyzed.

Duration and Maturity

Duration *increases* with the maturity of a fixed-income asset or liability, but at a *decreasing* rate:

$$\frac{\partial D}{\partial M} > 0 \qquad \frac{\partial D^2}{\partial^2 M} < 0$$

To see this, look at Figure 9–4, where we plot duration against maturity for a three-year, a six-year, and a consol bond using the *same yield of 8 percent* for all three and assuming an annual coupon of 8 percent on each bond.

Duration and Yield

Duration decreases as yield increases:

$$\frac{\partial D}{\partial R} < 0$$

To prove this, consider the consol bond: When $R = 8$ percent, as we show in Figure 9–4, $D = 13.5$ years. If R increases to 9 percent, then $D = 12.11$ years. This makes sense intuitively because higher yields discount later cash flows more heavily and the relative importance, or weights, of those later cash flows decline compared to earlier cash flows on an asset or liability.

Duration and Coupon Interest

The higher the coupon or promised interest payment on the security, the lower its duration:

FIGURE 9–4

Duration versus Maturity

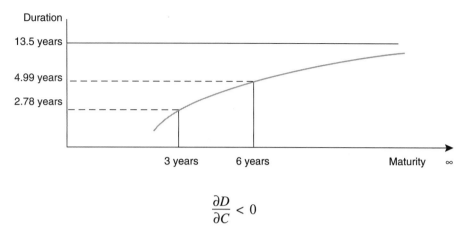

$$\frac{\partial D}{\partial C} < 0$$

This is due to the fact that the larger are the coupons or promised interest payments, the more quickly cash flows are received by investors and the higher are the present value weights of those cash flows in the duration calculation.[6]

Concept Questions

1. Which has the longest duration, a 30-year, 8 percent, zero-coupon or discount bond or an 8 percent infinite maturity consol bond?
2. Do high-coupon bonds have high or low durations?

The Economic Meaning of Duration

So far we have calculated duration for a number of different fixed-income assets and liabilities. Now we are ready to make the direct link between the number measured in years we call duration and the interest rate sensitivity of an asset or liability or of an FI's entire portfolio.

Duration is a *direct* measure of the interest rate sensitivity or elasticity of an asset or liability. In other words, the larger is the numerical value of *D* that is calculated for an asset or liability, the more sensitive the price of that asset or liability is to changes or shocks in interest rates.

Consider the following equation showing that the current price of a bond is equal to the present value of the coupons and principal payment on the bond:

$$P = \frac{C}{(1 + R)} + \frac{C}{(1 + R)^2} + \ldots + \frac{C + F}{(1 + R)^N} \tag{1}$$

where

P = Price on the bond
C = Coupon (annual)
R = Yield to maturity
N = Number of periods to maturity
F = Face value of the bond

---

[6]For example, consider two bonds, each with two years left to maturity. Both have a face value of $100, but the first bond pays a coupon of 6 percent and the second bond pays a higher coupon of 12 percent. As a result, the cash flows from the first bond will be $6 (in year 1) and $106 (in year 2). By comparison, the cash flows on the second bond will be $12 (in year 1) and $112 (in year 2). On average, a dollar of cash flow is received quicker for bond 2 than for bond 1.

We want to find out how the price of the bond (P) changes when yields (R) rise. We know that bond prices fall, but we want to derive a direct measure of the size of this fall (i.e., its degree of price sensitivity).

Taking the derivative of the bond's price (P) with respect to the yield to maturity (R), we get

$$\frac{dP}{dR} = \frac{-C}{(1 + R)^2} + \frac{-2C}{(1 + R)^3} + \ldots + \frac{-N(C + F)}{(1 + R)^{N+1}} \tag{2}$$

By rearranging, we get

$$\frac{dP}{dR} = -\frac{1}{1 + R}\left[\frac{C}{(1 + R)} + \frac{2C}{(1 + R)^2} + \ldots + \frac{N(C + F)}{(1 + R)^N}\right] \tag{3}$$

We have shown that duration (D) is the weighted-average time to maturity using the present value of cash flows as weights; that is, by definition,

$$D = \frac{1 \times \dfrac{C}{(1 + R)} + 2 \times \dfrac{C}{(1 + R)^2} + \ldots + N \times \dfrac{(C + F)}{(1 + R)^N}}{\dfrac{C}{(1 + R)} + \dfrac{C}{(1 + R)^2} + \ldots + \dfrac{(C + F)}{(1 + R)^N}} \tag{4}$$

Since the denominator of the duration equation is simply the price *(P)* of the bond that is equal to the present value of the cash flows on the bond, then

$$D = \frac{1 \times \dfrac{C}{(1 + R)} + 2 \times \dfrac{C}{(1 + R)^2} + \ldots + N \times \dfrac{(C + F)}{(1 + R)^N}}{P} \tag{5}$$

Multiplying both sides of this equation by P, we get

$$P \times D = 1 \times \frac{C}{(1 + R)} + 2 \times \frac{C}{(1 + R)^2} + \ldots + N \times \frac{C + F}{(1 + R)^N} \tag{6}$$

The term on the right side of Equation (6) is the same term as that in square brackets in Equation (3). Substituting Equation (6) into Equation (3), we get

$$\frac{dP}{dR} = -\frac{1}{1 + R}[P \times D] \tag{7}$$

By cross multiplying:

$$\frac{dP}{dR} \times \frac{1 + R}{P} = -D \tag{8}$$

or, alternatively,

$$\frac{\dfrac{dP}{P}}{\dfrac{dR}{(1 + R)}} = -D \tag{9}$$

The economic interpretation of Equations (8) and (9) is that the number D is the *interest elasticity,* or sensitivity, of the security's price to small interest rate changes. That is, it describes the percentage price fall of the bond (dP/P) for any given (present value) increase in required interest rates or yields ($dR/1 + R$).

FIGURE 9–5

The Proportional Relationship between Price Changes and Yield Changes on a Bond Implied by the Duration Model

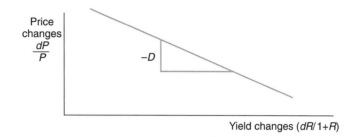

Equations (8) and (9) can be rearranged in another useful way for interpretation regarding interest sensitivity:

$$\frac{dP}{P} = -D\left[\frac{dR}{1+R}\right] \tag{10}$$

Equation (10) and Figure 9–5, its graphic representation, show that for small changes in interest rates, bond prices move *in an inversely proportional* fashion according to the size of D. Next, we use duration to measure the interest sensitivity of an asset or liability.

The Six-Year Eurobond

Consider the example of the six-year Eurobond with an 8 percent coupon and 8 percent yield. We determined in Table 9–1 that its duration was approximately $D = 4.99$ years. Suppose that yields were to rise by one basis point (1/100th of 1 percent) from 8 to 8.01 percent. Then

$$\frac{dP}{P} = -(4.99)\left[\frac{.0001}{1.08}\right]$$
$$= -.000462$$
$$\text{or} -0.0462\%$$

The bond price had been $1,000, which was the present value of a six-year bond with 8 percent coupons and 8 percent yield. However, the duration model predicts that the price of the bond would fall to $999.538 after the increase in yield by one basis point.[7]

The Consol Bond

Consider the consol bond with an 8 percent coupon, an 8 percent yield, and a calculated duration of 13.5 years. Thus:

$$\frac{dP}{P} = -(13.5)\left[\frac{.0001}{1.08}\right]$$
$$= -.00125$$
$$\text{or a } -0.125\% \text{ price fall}$$

---

[7]That is, the price would fall by .0462 percent, or by $0.462. To calculate the dollar change in value, we can rewrite the equation as $dP = (P)(-D)(dR/1 + R) = (\$1,000)(-4.99)(.0001/1.08) = -\$0.462$.

As you can see, for any given change in yields, long-duration securities suffer a greater capital loss or receive a greater capital gain than do short-duration securities.

Semiannual Coupon, Two-Year Maturity, Treasury Bonds

For fixed-income assets or liabilities whose interest payments are received semiannually or more frequently than annually, the formula in Equation (10) has to be modified slightly. For semiannual payments:

$$\frac{dP}{P} = -D\left[\frac{dR}{1 + \frac{1}{2}R}\right] \tag{11}$$

The only difference between Equation (11) and Equation (10) is the introduction of a $\frac{1}{2}$ in the discount rate term $1 + \frac{1}{2}R$ to take into account the semiannual payments of interest.

Recall the two-year T-bond with semiannual coupons whose duration we derived in Table 9–2 as 1.88 years when annual yields were 8 percent. A one-basis-point rise in interest rates would have the following predicted effect on its price:

$$\frac{dP}{P} = -1.88\left[\frac{.0001}{1.04}\right]$$
$$= -.00018$$

or a 0.018 percent price fall.

Concept Questions

1. What is the relationship between the duration of a bond and the interest elasticity of a bond?
2. How would the formula in Equation (11) have to be modified to take into account quarterly coupon payments and monthly coupon payments?

Duration and Immunization

So far you have learned how to calculate duration and understand that the duration measure has economic meaning as it indicates the interest sensitivity or elasticity of an asset or liability's value. For FIs, the major relevance of duration is as a measure for managing interest rate risk exposure. Also important is the role of duration in allowing the FI to immunize its balance sheet or some subset of that balance sheet against interest rate risk. In the following sections we consider two examples of how FIs can use the duration measure for immunization purposes. The first is its use by insurance company and pension fund managers to help meet promised cash flow payments to policyholders or beneficiaries at a particular time in the future. The second is its use to immunize or insulate the whole balance sheet of an FI against interest rate risk.

Duration and Immunizing Future Payments

Frequently, pension fund and life insurance company managers face the problem of structuring their asset investments so they can pay out a given cash amount to policyholders in some future period. The classic example of this is an insurance policy that pays the holder some lump sum on reaching retirement age. The risk to the life insurance company manager is that interest rates on the funds generated from investing the retiree's premiums could fall. Thus, the target or promised amount could not be met from the accumulated returns on the premiums invested. In effect, the insurance company would be forced to draw down its reserves and net worth to meet its payout commitments. (See Chapter 2 for a discussion of this risk.)

Suppose that we are in 2001 and the insurer has to make a guaranteed payment to an investor in five years, 2006. For simplicity, we assume that this target guaranteed payment is $1,469, a lump-sum policy payout on retirement. Of course, realistically this payment would be much larger, but the underlying principles of the example do not change by scaling up or down the payout amount.

To immunize or protect itself against interest rate risk, the insurer needs to determine which investments would produce a cash flow of exactly $1,469 in five years regardless of what happens to interest rates in the immediate future. The FI investing either in a five-year maturity and duration zero-coupon bond or in a coupon bond with a five-year duration would produce a $1,469 cash flow in five years no matter what happened to interest rates in the immediate future. Next, we consider the two strategies: buying five-year maturity (and duration) deep-discount bonds and buying five-year duration coupon bonds.

Buy Five-Year Maturity Discount Bonds.   Given a $1,000 face value and an 8 percent yield and assuming annual compounding, the current price per five-year discount bond would be $680.58 per bond:

$$P = 680.58 = \frac{1,000}{(1.08)^5}$$

If the insurer bought 1,469 of these bonds at a total cost of $1,000 in 2001, these investments would produce exactly $1,469 on maturity in five years ($1,000 $\times (1.08)^5 = \$1,469$). The reason is that the duration of this bond portfolio exactly matches the target horizon for the insurer's future liability to its policyholders. Intuitively, since no intervening cash flows or coupons are paid by the issuer of the zero-coupon discount bonds, future changes in interest rates have no reinvestment income effect. Thus, the return would be unaffected by intervening interest rate changes.

Suppose no five-year discount bonds exist. Then the portfolio manager may seek to invest in appropriate duration coupon bonds to hedge interest rate risk. In this example the appropriate investment would be in five-year duration coupon-bearing bonds.

Buy a Five-Year Duration Coupon Bond.   We demonstrated earlier in Table 9–1 that a six-year maturity Eurobond paying 8 percent coupons with an 8 percent yield to maturity had a duration of 4.99 years, or approximately five years. If we buy this six-year maturity, five-year duration bond in 2001 and hold it for five years until 2006, the term exactly matches the target horizon of the insurer. The cash flows generated at the end of five years will be $1,469 whether interest rates stay at 8 percent or instantaneously (immediately) rise to 9 percent or fall to 7 percent. Thus, buying a coupon bond whose duration exactly matches the time horizon of the insurer also immunizes the insurer against interest rate changes.

Interest Rates Remain at 8 Percent.   The cash flows received by the insurer on the bond if interest rates stay at 8 percent throughout the five years would be

1. Coupons, 5 × $80 $ 400
2. Reinvestment income   69
3. Proceeds from sale of bond at end of the fifth year   __1,000__
                                                                $1,469

This is how to calculate each of the three components of the insurer's income from the bond investment:

1. *Coupons.* The $400 from coupons is simply the annual coupon of $80 received in each of the five years.

2. *Reinvestment income.* Because the coupons are received annually, they can be reinvested at 8 percent as they are received, generating an additional cash flow of $69.[8]

3. *Bond sale proceeds.* The proceeds from the sale are calculated by recognizing that the six-year bond has just one year left to maturity when it is sold by the insurance company at the end of the fifth year. That is:

What fair market price can the insurer expect to get when selling the bond at the end of the fifth year with one year left to maturity? A buyer would be willing to pay the present value of the $1,080—final coupon plus face value—to be received at the end of the one remaining year, or

$$P_5 = \frac{1,080}{1.08} = \$1,000$$

Thus, the insurer would be able to sell the one remaining cash flow of $1,080, to be received in the bond's final year, for $1,000.

Next, we show that since this bond has a duration of five years, exactly matching the insurer's target period, even if interest rates were to instantaneously fall to 7 percent or rise to 9 percent, the expected cash flows from the bond would still exactly sum to $1,469. That is, the coupons + reinvestment income + principal at the end of the fifth year would be immunized. In other words, the cash flows on the

---

[8]Receiving annual coupons of $80 is equivalent to receiving an annuity of $80. There are tables and formulas that help us calculate the value of $1 received each year over a given number of years that can be reinvested at a given interest rate. The appropriate terminal value of receiving $1 a year for five years and reinvesting at 8 percent can be deteremined from the Future Value of an Annuity Factor (FVAF) Tables (see appendix at the end of the book), whose general formula is

$$FVAF_{n,R} = \left[\frac{(1 + R)^n - 1}{R}\right]$$

In our example:

$$FVAF_{5,8\%} = \left[\frac{(1 + .08)^5 - 1}{.08}\right] = 5.867$$

Thus, the reinvestment income for $80 of coupons per year is

Reinvestment income = (80 × 5.867) − 400 = 469 − 400 = 69

Note that we take away $400 since we have already counted the simple coupon income (5 × $80).

bond would be protected against interest rate changes. The following sections provide examples of rates falling from 8 to 7 percent and rising from 8 to 9 percent.

Interest Rates Fall to 7 Percent.   In this example with falling interest rates, the cash flows over the five years would be

1. Coupons, 5 × $80	$ 400
2. Reinvestment income	60
3. Bond sale proceeds	1,009
	$1,469

As you can see, the total proceeds over the five years are unchanged from what they were when interest rates were 8 percent. To see why this occurs, consider what happens to the three parts of the cash flow when rates fall to 7 percent:

1. *Coupons.* Are unchanged since the insurer still gets five annual coupons of $80 = $400.

2. *Reinvestment income.* The coupons can now only be reinvested at the lower rate of 7 percent. Reinvestment income is only $60.[9]

3. *Bond sale proceeds.* When the six-year maturity bond is sold at the end of the fifth year with one cash flow of $1,080 remaining, investors are now willing to pay more:

$$P_5 = \frac{1,080}{1.07} = 1,009$$

That is, the bond can be sold for $9 more than it could have when rates were 8 percent. The reason for this is that investors can get only 7 percent on newly issued bonds, while this older bond was issued with a higher coupon of 8 percent.

By comparing reinvestment income with bond sale proceeds, you can see that the fall in rates has produced a *gain* on the bond sale proceeds of $9. This exactly offsets the loss of reinvestment income of $9 due to reinvesting at a lower interest rate. Thus, total cash flows remain unchanged at $1,469.

Interest Rates Rise to 9 Percent.   In this example with rising interest rates, the proceeds from the bond investment are

1. Coupons, 5 × $80	$ 400
2. Reinvestment income [(5.985 × 80) − 400]	78
3. Bond sale proceeds (1,080/1.09)	991
	$1,469

Notice that the rise in interest rates from 8 percent to 9 percent leaves the final terminal cash flow unaffected at $1,469. The rise in rates has generated $9 extra reinvestment income ($78 − $69), but the price at which the bond can be sold at the end of the fifth year has declined from $1,000 to $991, equal to a capital loss of $9. Thus, the gain in reinvestment income is exactly offset by the capital loss on the sale of the bond.

---

[9] $FVAF_{5,7\%} = \left[\dfrac{(1 + .07)^5 - 1}{.07} \right] = 5.751$

Reinvestment income = (5.751 × 80) − 400 = 60, which is $9 less than it was when rates were 8 percent.

This example demonstrates that matching the duration of a coupon bond—or any fixed interest rate instrument such as a loan or mortgage—to the FI's target or investment horizon *immunizes* the FI against instantaneous shocks to interest rates. The gains or losses on reinvestment income that result from an interest rate change are exactly offset by losses or gains from the bond proceeds on sale.

Immunizing the Whole Balance Sheet of an FI

So far we have looked at the durations of individual instruments and how we can select individual fixed-income securities to protect FIs such as life insurance companies and pensions funds with precommitted liabilities such as future pension plan payouts. The duration model can also evaluate the overall interest rate exposure for an FI, that is, measure the *duration gap* on its balance sheet.

The Duration Gap for a Financial Institution.   To estimate the overall duration gap, we determine first the duration of an FI's asset portfolio and the duration of its liability portfolio. These can be calculated as

$$D_A = X_{1A}D_1^A + X_{2A}D_2^A + \ldots + X_{nA}D_n^A$$

and

$$D_L = X_{1L}D_1^L + X_{2L}D_2^L + \ldots + X_{nL}D_n^L$$

where

$$X_{1j} + X_{2j} + \ldots + X_{nj} = 1 \text{ and } j = A, L$$

The *X*s in the equation are the market value proportions of each asset or liability held in the respective asset and liability portfolios. Thus, if new 30-year Treasury bonds were 1 percent of a life insurer's portfolio and D_1^A (the duration of those bonds) was equal to 9.25 years, then $X_{1A}D_1^A = .01(9.25) = 0.0925$. More simply, the duration of a portfolio of assets or liabilities is a market value weighted average of the individual durations of the assets or liabilities on the FI's balance sheet.[10]

Consider an FI's simplified market value balance sheet:

Assets ($)	Liabilities ($)
A = 100	L = 90
	E = 10
100	100

From the balance sheet:

$$A = L + E$$
$$\text{and } \Delta A = \Delta L + \Delta E$$
$$\text{or } \Delta E = \Delta A - \Delta L$$

---

[10]This derivation of an FI's duration gap closely follows G. Kaufman, "Measuring and Managing Interest Rate Risk: A Primer," Federal Reserve Bank of Chicago, *Economic Perspectives*, 1984, pp. 16–29.

That is, when interest rates change, the change in the FI's net worth is equal to the difference between the change in the market values of assets and liabilities on each side of the balance sheet. This should be familiar from our discussion of the maturity model in Chapter 8. The difference here is that we want to relate the sensitivity of an FI's net worth (ΔE) to its duration mismatch rather than to its maturity mismatch. As we have already shown, duration is a more accurate measure of the interest rate sensitivity of an asset or liability than is maturity.

Since $\Delta E = \Delta A - \Delta L$, we need to determine how ΔA and ΔL—the changes in the market values of assets and liabilities on the balance sheet—are related to duration.[11]

From the duration model:

$$\frac{\Delta A}{A} = -D_A \frac{\Delta R}{(1 + R)} \tag{12}$$

$$\frac{\Delta L}{L} = -D_L \frac{\Delta R}{(1 + R)} \tag{13}$$

Here we have simply substituted $\Delta A/A$ or $\Delta L/L$, the proportional change in the market values of assets or liabilities, for $\Delta P/P$, the change in any single bond's price and D_A or D_L, the duration of the FI's asset or liability portfolio, for D_i, the duration on any given bond, deposit, or loan. The term $\Delta R/(1 + R)$ reflects the shock to interest rates as before. These equations can be rewritten as

$$\Delta A = -D_A \times A \times \frac{\Delta R}{(1 + R)} \tag{14}$$

and

$$\Delta L = -D_L \times L \times \frac{\Delta R}{(1 + R)} \tag{15}$$

Since $\Delta E = \Delta A - \Delta L$, we can substitute these two expressions into this equation:

$$\Delta E = \left[-D_A \times A \times \frac{\Delta R}{(1 + R)}\right] - \left[-D_L \times L \times \frac{\Delta R}{(1 + R)}\right] \tag{16}$$

Assuming that the level of rates and the expected shock to interest rates are the same for both assets and liabilities:[12]

$$\Delta E = [-D_A A + D_L L] \frac{\Delta R}{(1 + R)} \tag{17}$$

or

$$\Delta E = -[D_A A - D_L L] \frac{\Delta R}{(1 + R)} \tag{18}$$

---

[11]In what follows, we use the Δ (change) notation instead of d (derivative notation) to recognize that interest rate changes tend to be discrete rather than infinitesimally small. For example, in real-world financial markets, the smallest observed rate change is usually one basis point, or 1/100th of 1 percent.

[12]This assumption is standard in "Macauley" duration analysis. While restrictive, this assumption can be relaxed. However, if this is done, the duration measure changes, as is discussed later in the appendix to this chapter.

To rearrange the equation in a slightly more intuitive fashion, we multiply and divide both terms $D_A A$ and $D_L L$ by A (assets):

$$\Delta E = -\left[D_A \frac{A}{A} - D_L \frac{L}{A} \right] \times A \times \frac{\Delta R}{(1 + R)} \qquad (19)$$

$$\Delta E = -[D_A - D_L k] \times A \times \frac{\Delta R}{(1 + R)} \qquad (20)$$

where $k = L/A$ is a measure of the FI's leverage, that is, the amount of borrowed funds or liabilities rather than owners' equity used to fund its asset portfolio. The effect of interest rate changes on the market value of an FI's equity or net worth (ΔE) breaks down into three effects:

1. *The leverage adjusted duration gap* $= [D_A - D_L k]$. This gap is measured in years and reflects the degree of duration mismatch in an FI's balance sheet. Specifically, the larger this gap is *in absolute terms,* the more exposed the FI is to interest rate shocks.

2. *The size of the FI.*   The term A measures the size of the FI's assets. The larger the scale of the FI, the larger the dollar size of the potential net worth exposure from any given interest rate shock.

3. *The size of the interest rate shock* $= \Delta R/(1 + R)$.   The larger the shock, the greater the FI's exposure.

Given this, we express the exposure of the net worth of the FI as $\Delta E = -$[Adjusted duration gap] $\times$ Asset size $\times$ Interest rate shock.

While interest rate shocks are largely external to the bank and often result from changes in the Federal Reserve's monetary policy (as discussed in the first section of Chapter 8), the size of the duration gap and the size of the FI are under the control of management.

Using an example, the next section explains how a manager can use information on an FI's duration gap to restructure the balance sheet to immunize stockholders net worth against interest rate risk.

Duration Gap Measurement and Exposure: An Example.   Suppose the FI manager calculates that

$$D_A = 5 \ years$$
$$D_L = 3 \ years$$

Then the manager learns from an economic forecasting unit that rates are expected to rise from 10 to 11 percent in the immediate future; that is,

$$\Delta R = 1\% = .01$$
$$1 + R = 1.10$$

The FI's initial balance sheet is assumed to be:

Assets ($ millions)	*Liabilities ($ millions)*
$A = 100$	$L = \ 90$
	$E = \ 10$
100	100

The FI's manager would calculate the potential loss to equity holders' net worth (E) if the forecast of rising rates proves true as follows:

$$\Delta E = -(D_A - kD_L) \times A \times \frac{\Delta R}{(1 + R)}$$

$$= -(5 - (.9)(3)) \times \$100 \text{ million} \times \frac{.01}{1.1} = -\$2.09 \text{ million}$$

The bank could lose $2.09 million in net worth if rates rose 1 percent. Since the FI started with $10 million, the loss of $2.09 million is almost 21 percent of its initial net worth. The market value balance sheet after the rise in rates by 1 percent would look like this:

Assets ($ millions)	Liabilities ($ millions)
A = 95.45	L = 87.54
	E = 7.91
95.45	95.45

Even though the rise in interest rates would not push the FI into economic insolvency, it reduces the FI's net worth-to-assets ratio from 10 (10/100) to 8.29 percent (7.91/95.45). To counter this effect, the manager might reduce the FI's adjusted duration gap. In an extreme case, the gap might be reduced to zero:

$$\Delta E = -[0] \times A \times \Delta R/(1 + R) = 0$$

To do this, the FI should not directly set $D_A = D_L$, which ignores the fact that the bank's assets (A) do not equal its borrowed liabilities (L) and that k is not equal to 1. To see the importance of factoring in leverage, suppose the manager increased the duration of the FI's liabilities to five years, the same as D_A. Then

$$\Delta E = -[5 - (.9)(5)] \times \$100 \text{ million} \times (.01/1.1) = -\$0.45 \text{ million}$$

The FI would still be exposed to a loss of $0.45 million if rates rose 1 percent. An appropriate strategy would involve changing D_L until

$$D_A = D_L k = 5 \text{ years}$$
$$\Delta E = -[5 - (.9)5.55] \times \$100 \text{ million} \times (.01/1.1) = 0$$

The appropriate strategy would be for the FI manager to set $D_L = 5.55$ years, or slightly longer than $D_A = 5$ years, to compensate for the fact that only 90 percent of assets are funded by borrowed liabilities, with the other 10 percent funded by equity. Note that the FI manager has at least three other ways to reduce the adjusted duration gap to zero:

1. *Reduce D_A.* Reduce D_A from 5 years to 2.7 years [(equal to $D_L k$ or 3(.9)] such that

$$[D_A - kD_L] = [2.7 - (.9)(3)] = 0$$

2. *Reduce D_A and increase D_L.* Shorten the duration of assets and lengthen the duration of liabilities at the same time. One possibility would be to *reduce D_A* to 4 years and to *increase D_L* to 4.44 years such that

$$[D_A - kD_L] = [4 - (.9)(4.44)] = 0$$

3. *Change k and D_L.* Increase k (leverage) from .9 to .95 and increase D_L from 3 years to 5.26 years such that

$$[D_A - kD_L] = [5 - (.95)(5.26)] = 0$$

Concept Questions

1. Referring back to the example of the insurer on page 157, suppose rates fell to 6 percent. Would the FI's portfolio still be immunized? What if rates rose to 10 percent?
2. How is the overall duration gap for an FI calculated?
3. How can a manager use information on an FI's duration gap to restructure, and thereby immunize, the balance sheet against interest rate risk?
4. Suppose $D_A = 3$ years, $D_L = 6$ years, $k = .8$, and $A = \$100$ million. What is the effect on owners' net worth if $\Delta R/(1 + R)$ rises 1 percent?

Immunization and Regulatory Considerations

In the above section we assumed that the FI manager wants to structure the duration of assets and liabilities to immunize the equity or net worth stake (E) of the FI's equity owners from interest rate shocks. However, regulators periodically monitor the solvency or net worth position of FIs. As we discuss in greater detail in Chapter 20 on capital adequacy, regulators set minimum target ratios for a bank's net worth. The simplest is the ratio of bank capital (net worth) to its assets, or

$$\frac{E}{A} = \text{Capital (net worth) ratio}$$

While this target has normally been formulated in book value accounting terms for banks, it is evaluated in a market value context for investment banks. Also, the SEC has long advocated a capital ratio based on market value accounting for U.S. banks.

Suppose the FI manager is close to the minimum regulatory required E/A ratio (e.g., 4 percent for banks) and wants to immunize against any fall in this ratio if interest rates rise.[13] That is, the immunization target is no longer $\Delta E = 0$ when rates change but $\Delta(E/A) = 0$.

Obviously, immunizing ΔE cannot be the same strategy as immunizing $\Delta(E/A)$, the net worth ratio. As a result, the FI manager has a problem. A portfolio constructed to immunize ΔE would have a different duration match from that required to immunize $\Delta(E/A)$. Or, more simply, the manager could satisfy either the FI's stockholders or the regulators *but not both* simultaneously.

More specifically, when the objective is to immunize ΔE, to set $\Delta E = 0$, the FI manager should structure the balance sheet so that

$$D_A = kD_L$$

By comparison, to immunize the net worth ratio, to set $\Delta(E/A), = 0$, the manager needs to set

---

[13]In actuality, banks face three required minimum capital ratios. The 4 percent rule used in this example is for the leverage ratio (see Chapter 20 for more details).

$$D_A = D_L$$

In this scenario, the leverage adjustment effect (k) drops out.[14] If $D_A = 5$, then immunizing the net worth ratio would require setting $D_L = 5$.

Concept Questions

1. What minimum target ratio is typically used by regulators to measure a bank's net worth relative to its assets?
2. Is immunizing a bank's net worth the same as immunizing its net worth–assets ratio? If not, why not?

In the appendix that follows, we analyze some of the practical problems in estimating duration and duration gaps for "real-world" FIs.

Summary

This chapter analyzed the duration model approach to measuring interest rate risk. The duration model is superior to the simple maturity model in that it incorporates the timing of cash flows as well as maturity effects into a simple measure of interest rate risk. The duration measure could be used to immunize a particular liability as well as the whole FI balance sheet. In the appendix to this chapter we identify a number of potential problems in applying the duration model in real-world scenarios. However, the duration model is fairly robust and can deal with a large number of real-world complexities, such as credit risk, convexity, floating interest rates, and uncertain maturities.

Questions and Problems

1. What are the two different general interpretations of the concept of duration, and what is the technical definition of this term? How does duration differ from maturity?

2. Two bonds are available for purchase in the financial markets. The first bond is a two-year, $1,000 bond that pays an annual coupon of 10 percent. The second bond is a two-year, $1,000 zero-coupon bond.

   a. What is the duration of the coupon bond if the current yield to maturity (YTM) is 8 percent? 10 percent? 12 percent? (*Hint:* You may wish to create a spreadsheet program to assist in the calculations.)

   b. How does the change in the current YTM affect the duration of this coupon bond?

   c. Calculate the duration of the zero-coupon bond with a YTM of 8 percent, 10 percent, and 12 percent.

   d. How does the change in the current YTM affect the duration of the zero-coupon bond?

   e. Why does the change in the YTM affect the coupon bond differently than it affects the zero-coupon bond?

3. A 1-year, $100,000 loan carries a market interest rate of 12 percent. The loan requires payment of accrued interest and one-half of the principal at the end of 6 months. The remaining principal and the accrued interest are due at the end of the year.

   a. What is the duration of this loan?

   b. What will be the cash flows at the end of six months and at the end of the year?

   c. What is the present value of each cash flow discounted at the market rate? What is the total present value?

   d. What proportion of the total present value of cash flows occurs at the end of six months? What proportion occurs at the end of the year?

   e. What is the weighted-average life of the cash flows on the loan?

   f. How does this weighted-average life compare to the duration calculated in part (a) above?

4. What is the duration of a five-year, $1,000 Treasury bond with a 10 percent semiannual coupon selling at par? Selling with a YTM of 12 percent? 14 percent? What can you conclude about the relationship between duration and yield to maturity? Plot the relationship. Why does this relationship exist?

---

[14]See Kaufman, "Measuring and Managing Interest Rate Risk: A Primer," for a proof.

5. Consider three Treasury bonds which each have 10 percent semiannual coupons and trade at par.

   a. Calculate the duration for a bond that has a maturity of four years, three years, and two years.

   b. What conclusions can you reach about the relationship between duration and the time to maturity? Plot the relationship.

6. A six-year, $10,000 CD pays 6 percent interest annually. What is the duration of the CD? What would be the duration if interest were paid semiannually? What is the relationship of duration to the relative frequency of interest payments?

7. What is the duration of a consol bond that sells at a YTM of 8 percent? 10 percent? 12 percent? What is a consol bond? Would a consol trading at a YTM of 10 percent have a greater duration than a 20-year zero-coupon bond trading at the same YTM? Why?

8. Maximum Pension Fund is attempting to balance one of the bond portfolios under its management. The fund has identified three bonds which have five-year maturities and trade at a YTM of 9 percent. The bonds differ only in that the coupons are 7 percent, 9 percent, and 11 percent.

   a. What is the duration for each bond?

   b. What is the relationship between duration and the amount of coupon interest that is paid? Plot the relationship.

9. An insurance company is analyzing three bonds and is using duration as the measure of interest rate risk. The three bonds all trade at a YTM of 10 percent and have $10,000 par values. The bonds differ only in the amount of annual coupon interest they pay: 8, 10, or 12 percent.

   a. What is the duration for each five-year bond?

   b. What is the relationship between duration and the amount of coupon interest which is paid?

10. You can obtain a loan for $100,000 at a rate of 10 percent for two years. You have a choice of paying the principal at the end of the second year or amortizing the loan, that is, paying interest and principal in equal payments each year. The loan is priced at par.

    a. What is the duration of the loan under both methods of payment?

    b. Explain the difference in the two results.

11. How is duration related to the interest elasticity of a fixed-income security? What is the relationship between duration and the price of the fixed-income security?

12. You have discovered that the price of a bond rose from $975 to $995 when the YTM fell from 9.75 percent to 9.25 percent. What is the duration of the bond?

13. Calculate the duration of a two-year, $1,000 bond that pays an annual coupon of 10 percent and trades at a yield of 14 percent. What is the expected change in the price of the bond if interest rates decline by 0.50 percent (50 basis points)?

14. The duration of an 11-year, $1,000 Treasury bond paying a 10 percent semiannual coupon and selling at par has been estimated at 6.9 years.

    a. What is the modified duration of the bond (Modified Duration = $D/1 + R$)?

    b. What will be the estimated price change of the bond if market interest rates increase 0.10 percent (10 basis points)? If rates decrease 0.20 percent (20 basis points)?

    c. What would the actual price of the bond be under each rate change situation in part (b) using the traditional present value bond pricing techniques? What is the amount of error in each case?

15. Suppose you purchase a five-year, 13.76 percent bond that is priced to yield 10 percent.

    a. Show that the duration of this annual payment bond is equal to four years.

    b. Show that if interest rates rise to 11 percent within the next year and your investment horizon is four years from today, you will still earn a 10 percent yield on your investment.

    c. Show that a 10 percent yield also will be earned if interest rates fall next year to 9 percent.

16. Consider the case where an investor holds a bond for a period of time longer than the duration of the bond, that is, longer than the original investment horizon.

    a. If market interest rates rise, will the return that is earned exceed or fall short of the original required rate of return? Explain.

    b. What will happen to the realized return if market interest rates decrease? Explain.

    c. Recalculate parts (b) and (c) of problem 15 above, assuming that the bond is held for all five years, to verify your answers to parts (a) and (b) of this problem.

    d. If either calculation in part (c) is greater than the original required rate of return, why would an investor ever try to match the duration of an asset with his or her investment horizon?

17. Two banks are being examined by the regulators to determine the interest rate sensitivity of their balance sheets. Bank A has assets composed solely of a 10-year, 12 percent $1 million loan. The loan is financed with a 10-year, 10 percent $1 million CD. Bank B has assets composed solely of a 7-year, 12 percent zero-coupon bond with a current (market) value of $894,006.2 and a maturity (principal) value of $1,976,362.88. The bond is financed with a 10-year, 8.275 percent coupon $1,000,000 face value CD with a YTM of 10 percent. The loan and the CDs pay interest annually, with principal due at maturity.

    a. If market interest rates increase 1 percent (100 basis points), how do the market values of the assets and liabilities of each bank change? That is, what will be the net effect on the market value of the equity for each bank?

b. What accounts for the differences in the changes in the market value of equity between the two banks?

c. Verify your results above by calculating the duration for the assets and liabilities of each bank and estimate the changes in value for the expected change in interest rates. Summarize your results.

18. If you use duration only to immunize your portfolio, what three factors affect changes in the net worth of a financial institution when interest rates change?

19. Financial Institution XY has assets of $1 million invested in a 30-year, 10 percent semiannual coupon Treasury bond selling at par. The duration of this bond has been estimated at 9.94 years. The assets are financed with equity and a $900,000, two-year 7.25 percent semiannual coupon capital note selling at par.

a. What is the leverage-adjusted duration gap of Financial Institution XY?

b. What is the impact on equity value if the relative change in all market interest rates is a decrease of 20 basis points? *Note:* The relative change in interest rates is $\Delta R/(1 + R/2) = -0.0020$.

c. Using the information you calculated in parts (a) and (b), infer a general statement about the desired duration gap for a financial institution if interest rates are expected to increase or decrease.

d. Verify your inference by calculating the change in market value of equity assuming that the relative change in all market interest rates is an increase of 30 basis points.

e. What would the duration of the assets need to be to immunize the equity from changes in market interest rates?

20. The balance sheet for Gotbucks Bank, Inc. (GBI) is presented below ($ millions).

Assets		Liabilities and Equity	
Cash	$ 30	Core deposits	$ 20
Federal funds	20	Federal funds	50
Loans (floating)	105	Euro CDs	130
Loans (fixed)	65	Equity	20
Total assets	$220	Total liabilities and equity	$220

Notes to the balance sheet: The Fed funds rate is 8.5 percent, the floating loan rate is LIBOR +4 percent, and currently LIBOR is 11 percent. Fixed-rate loans have five-year maturities, are priced at par, and pay 12 percent annual interest. Core deposits are fixed rate for two years at 8 percent paid annually. Euros currently yield 9 percent.

a. What is the duration of the fixed-rate loan portfolio of Gotbucks Bank?

b. If the duration of the floating-rate loans and fed funds is 0.36 years, what is the duration of GBI's assets?

c. What is the duration of the core deposits if they are priced at par?

d. If the duration of the Euro CDs and fed funds liabilities is 0.401 years, what is the duration of GBI's liabilities?

e. What is GBI's duration gap? What is its interest rate risk exposure?

f. What is the impact on the market value of equity if the relative change in all market interest rates is an increase of 1 percent (100 basis points)? Note that the relative change in interest rates is $\Delta R/(1 + R) = 0.01$.

g. What is the impact on the market value of equity if the relative change in all market interest rates is a decrease of 0.5 percent (-50 basis points)?

h. What variables are available to GBI to immunize the bank? How much would each variable need to change to get DGAP to equal 0?

21. Hands Insurance Company issued a $90 million, one-year zero-coupon note at 8 percent add-on annual interest (paying one coupon at the end of the year). The proceeds were used to fund a $100 million, two-year commercial loan at 10 percent annual interest. Immediately after these transactions were simultaneously closed, all market interest rates increased 1.5 percent (150 basis points).

a. What is the true market value of the loan investment and the liability after the change in interest rates?

b. What impact did these changes in market value have on the market value of the FI's equity?

c. What was the duration of the loan investment and the liability at the time of issuance?

d. Use these duration values to calculate the expected change in the value of the loan and the liability for the predicted increase of 1.5 percent in interest rates.

e. What was the duration gap of Hands Insurance Company after the issuance of the asset and note?

f. What was the change in equity value forecast by this duration gap for the predicted increase in interest rates of 1.5 percent?

g. If the interest rate prediction had been available during the time period in which the loan and the liability were being negotiated, what suggestions would you offer to reduce the possible effect on the equity of the company? What are the difficulties in implementing your ideas?

22. The following balance sheet information is available (amounts in $ thousands and duration in years) for a financial institution:

	Amount	Duration
T-bills	$ 90	0.50
T-notes	55	0.90
T-bonds	176	x
Loans	2,724	7.00
Deposits	2,092	1.00
Federal funds	238	0.01
Equity	715	

Treasury bonds are five-year maturities paying 6 percent semiannually and selling at par.

a. What is the duration of the T-bond portfolio?

b. What is the average duration of all the assets?

c. What is the average duration of all the liabilities?

d. What is the leverage-adjusted duration gap? What is the interest rate risk exposure?

e. What is the forecast impact on the market value of equity caused by a relative upward shift in the entire yield curve of 0.5 percent [i.e., $\Delta R/(1+R) = 0.0050$]?

f. If the yield curve shifts downward 0.25 percent [i.e., $\Delta R/(1+R) = -0.0025$], what is the forecasted impact on the market value of equity?

g. What variables are available to the financial institution to immunize the balance sheet? How much would each variable need to change to get DGAP to equal 0?

23. Assume that a goal of the regulatory agencies of financial institutions is to immunize the ratio of equity to total assets, that is, $\Delta(E/A) = 0$. Explain how this goal changes the desired duration gap for the institution. Why does this differ from the duration gap necessary to immunize the total equity? How would your answers to part (*h*) in problem 20 and part (*g*) in problem 22 change if immunizing equity to total assets was the goal?

The following questions and problems are based on material in the appendix to the chapter.

24. Identify and discuss three criticisms of using the duration model to immunize the portfolio of a financial institution.

25. In general, what changes have occurred in the financial markets which allow financial institutions to more rapidly and efficiently restructure their balance sheets to meet desired goals? Why is it critical for an investment manager who has a portfolio immunized to match a desired investment horizon to rebalance the portfolio periodically? Why is convexity a desirable feature to capture in a portfolio of assets? What is convexity?

26. A financial institution has an investment horizon of 2 years, 9.5 months. The institution has converted all assets into a portfolio of 8 percent, $1,000 3-year bonds that are trading at a YTM of 10 percent. The bonds pay interest annually. The portfolio manager believes that the assets are immunized against interest rate changes.

a. Is the portfolio immunized at the time of the bond purchase? What is the duration of the bonds?

b. Will the portfolio be immunized one year later?

c. Assume that one-year, 8 percent zero-coupon bonds are available in one year. What proportion of the original portfolio should be placed in zeros to rebalance the portfolio?

27. MLK Bank has an asset portfolio that consists of $100 million of 30-year, 8 percent coupon $1,000 bonds that sell at par.

a. What will be the bond's new prices if market yields change immediately by +/− 0.10 percent? What will be the new prices if market yields change immediately by +/−2.00 percent?

b. The duration of these bonds is 12.1608 years. What are the predicted bond prices in each of the four cases using the duration rule? What is the amount of error between the duration prediction and the actual market values?

c. Given that convexity is 212.4, what are the bond price predictions in each of the four cases using the duration plus convexity relationship? What is the amount of error in these predictions?

d. Diagram and label clearly the results in parts (*a*), (*b*), and (*c*).

28. Estimate the convexity for each of the following three bonds, which all trade at YTM of 8 percent and have face values of $1,000.

A 7-year, zero-coupon bond

A 7-year, 10 percent annual coupon bond

A 10-year, 10 percent annual coupon bond which has a duration value of 6.994 years (i.e., approximately 7 years).

Rank the bonds in terms of convexity and express the convexity relationship between zeros and coupon bonds in terms of maturity and duration equivalencies.

29. A 10-year, 10 percent annual coupon $1,000 bond trades at a YTM of 8 percent. The bond has a duration of 6.994 years. What is the modified duration of this bond? What is the practical value of calculating modified duration? Does modified duration change the result of using the duration relationship to estimate price sensitivity?

APPENDIX 9A:
DIFFICULTIES IN APPLYING THE DURATION MODEL TO REAL-WORLD FI BALANCE SHEETS*

Critics of the duration model have often claimed that it is difficult to apply in real-world situations. However, as we show in the following sections, duration measures and immunization strategies are useful in most real-world situations. In fact, the model recently proposed by the Bank for International Settlements to monitor bank interest rate risk taking is heavily based on the duration model. Next, we look at the various criticisms of the duration model and discuss ways in which a modern FI manager would deal with them in practice.

Duration Matching Can Be Costly*

Critics charge that although in principle an FI manager can change D_A and D_L to immunize the FI against interest rate risk, restructuring the balance sheet of a large and complex FI can be both time-consuming and costly. While this argument may have been true historically, the growth of purchased funds, asset securitization, and loan sales markets has considerably eased the speed and lowered the transaction costs of major balance sheet restructurings. (See Chapters 27 and 28 for a discussion of these strategies.) Moreover, an FI manager could still manage risk exposure using the duration model by employing techniques other than direct portfolio rebalancing to immunize against interest rate risk. Managers can get many of the same results of direct duration matching by taking hedging positions in the markets for derivative securities, such as futures and forwards (Chapter 24); options, caps, floors, and collars (Chapter 25); and swaps (Chapter 26).[1]

Immunization Is a Dynamic Problem*

Immunization is an aspect of the duration model that is not well understood. Let's go back to the earlier immunization example, where an insurer sought to buy bonds providing an accumulated cash flow of $1,469 in five years no matter what happened to interest rates. We showed that buying a six-year maturity, 8 percent coupon bond with a five-year duration would immunize the insurer against an instantaneous change in interest rates. The word *instantaneous* is very important here. This means a change in interest rates immediately after purchasing the bond. However, interest rates can change at any time over the holding period. Further, the duration of a bond changes as time passes, that is, as it approaches maturity

or the target horizon date. Not only that, but duration changes at a different rate than does real or calendar time.

To see this, consider the initially hedged position where the insurer bought the five-year duration (six-year maturity), 8 percent coupon bond in 2001 to match its cash flow target of $1,469 in 2006. Suppose the FI manager puts the bond in the bottom drawer of a desk and doesn't think about it for a year, believing the insurance company's position is fully hedged. After one year has passed, suppose interest rates (yields) have fallen from 8 percent to 7 percent and the manager opens the drawer of the desk and finds the bond. Knowing the target date is now only four years away, the manager recalculates the duration of the bond. Imagine the manager's shock on finding that the same 8 percent coupon bond with a 7 percent yield and only five years left to maturity has a duration of 4.33 years. This means the insurance company is no longer hedged; the 4.33-year duration of this bond portfolio *exceeds* the investment horizon of four years. As a result, the manager has to restructure the bond portfolio to remain immunized. One way to do this would be to sell some of the five-year bonds (4.33-year duration) and buy some bonds of shorter duration so that the overall duration of the investment portfolio is four years.

For example, suppose the insurer rebalances his portfolio with 50 percent invested in 4.33-year duration bonds and 50 percent in 3.67-year zero coupon bonds. Because duration and maturity are the same for discount bonds, the duration of the asset portfolio would be

$$D_A = [4.33 \times .5] + [3.67 \times .5] = 4 \text{ years}$$

This simple example demonstrates that immunization based on duration is a dynamic strategy. In theory, it requires the portfolio manager to rebalance the portfolio continuously to ensure that the duration of the investment portfolio exactly matches the investment horizon (i.e., the duration of liabilities). Because continuous rebalancing may not be easy to do and involves costly transaction fees, most portfolio managers seek to be only approximately dynamically immunized against interest rate changes by rebalancing at discrete intervals, such as quarterly. That is, there is a trade-off between being perfectly immunized and the transaction costs of maintaining an immunized balance sheet dynamically.

Large Interest Rate Changes and Convexity*

Duration accurately measures the price sensitivity of fixed-income securities for small changes in interest rates of the order of one basis point. But suppose interest rate shocks are much larger, of the order of 2 percent or 200 basis points. Then duration becomes a less accurate predictor of how much

---

[1]In particular, instead of direct immunization of a positive duration gap ($D_A > D_L$), an FI manager could sell futures (forwards), take the fixed-rate side of an interest rate swap, buy put options on bonds, and/or buy an interest rate cap.

FIGURE 9A–1

Duration versus True Relationship

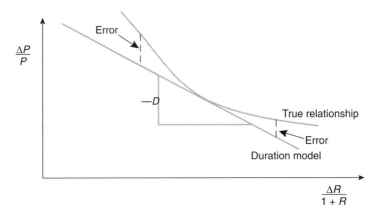

the prices of securities will change and therefore a less accurate measure of interest rate sensitivity. Looking at Figure 9A–1, you can see the reason for this. Note first the change in a bond's price due to yield changes according to the duration model and second the true relationship, as calculated directly, using the exact present value calculation for bond valuation.

The duration model predicts that the relationship between rate shocks and bond price changes will be proportional to D (duration). However, by precisely calculating the true change in bond prices, we would find that for large interest rate increases, duration overpredicts the *fall* in bond prices, while for large interest rate decreases, it underpredicts the *increase* in bond prices. That is, the duration model predicts symmetric effects for rate increases and decreases on bond prices. As Figure 9A–1 shows, in actuality, for rate increases the *capital loss effect* tends to be smaller than the *capital gain effect* is for rate decreases. This is the result of the bond price–yield relationship exhibiting a property called **convexity** rather than *linearity,* as assumed by the basic duration model.

Note that convexity is a desirable feature for an FI manager to capture in a portfolio of assets. Buying a bond or a portfolio of assets that exhibits a lot of convexity or bentness in the price-yield curve relationship is similar to buying partial interest rate risk insurance. Specifically, high convexity means that for equally large changes of interest rates up and down (e.g., plus or minus 2 percent), the capital gain effect of a rate decrease more than offsets the capital loss effect of a rate increase. As we show later, all fixed-income assets or liabilities exhibit some convexity in their price-yield relationships.[2]

To see the importance of accounting for the effects of convexity in assessing the impact of large rate changes on an FI's portfolio, consider the six-year Eurobond with an 8 percent coupon and yield. According to Table 9–1, its duration is 4.99 years and its current price P_0 will be $1,000 at a yield of 8 percent:

$$P_0 = \frac{80}{(1.08)} + \frac{80}{(1.08)^2} + \frac{80}{(1.08)^3} +$$
$$\frac{80}{(1.08)^4} + \frac{80}{(1.08)^5} + \frac{1,080}{(1.08)^6} = \$1,000$$

This is point A on the price–yield curve in Figure 9A–2.

If rates rise from 8 to 10 percent, the duration model predicts that the bond price will fall by 9.2457 percent; that is:

$$\frac{\Delta P}{P} = -4.99\left[\frac{.02}{1.08}\right] = -9.2457\%$$

or, from a price of $1,000 to $907.543 (see point B in Figure 9A–2). However, calculating the exact change in the bond's price after a rise in yield to 10 percent, we find that

$$P_0 = \frac{80}{(1.1)} + \frac{80}{(1.1)^2} + \frac{80}{(1.1)^3} +$$
$$\frac{80}{(1.1)^4} + \frac{80}{(1.1)^5} + \frac{1,080}{(1.1)^6} = \$912.895$$

This is point C in Figure 9A–2. As you can see, the true or actual fall in price is less than the predicted fall by $5.352. This means that there is just over a 0.5 percent error using the duration model. The reason for this is the natural convexity to the price–yield curve as yields rise.

Reversing the experiment reveals that the duration model would predict the bond's price to rise by 9.2457 percent if yields fell from 8 to 6 percent, resulting in a predicted price of $1,092.457 (see point D in Figure 9A–2). By comparison, the true or actual change in price can be computed as $1,098.347 by estimating the present value of the bond's coupons and its face value with a 6 percent yield (see point E in Figure 9A–2). The duration model has underpredicted the bond price increase by $5.89 or by over 0.5 percent of the true price increase.

An important question for the FI manager is whether a 0.5 percent error is big enough to be concerned about. This depends on the size of the interest rate change and the size of the portfolio under management. Clearly, 0.5 percent of a large number will still be a large number!

So far, we have established these three characteristics of convexity:

---

[2]To be more precise, fixed-income securities without special option features such as callable bonds and mortgage-backed securities. A callable bond tends to exhibit negative convexity (or concavity), as do some mortgage-backed securities.

FIGURE 9A–2

*The Price–Yield Curve for
the Six-Year Eurobond*

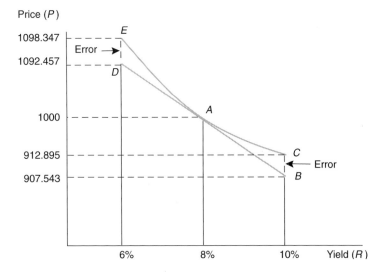

FIGURE 9A–3

*The Natural Convexity
of Bonds*

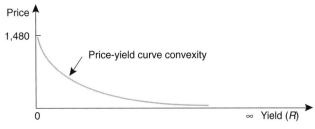

1. *Convexity is desirable.* The greater the convexity of a security or a portfolio of securities, the more insurance or interest rate protection an FI manager has against rate increases and the greater the potential gains after interest rate falls.

2. *Convexity and duration.* The larger the interest rate changes and the more convex a fixed-income security or portfolio, the greater the error the FI manager faces in using just duration (and duration matching) to immunize exposure to interest rate shocks.

3. *All fixed-income securities are convex.*[3] To see this, we can take the six-year, 8 percent coupon, 8 percent yield bond and look at two extreme price-yield scenarios. What is the price on the bond if yields falls to zero, and what is its price if yields rise to some very large number such as infinity?

When $R = 0$:

$$P = \frac{80}{(1+0)} + \ldots + \frac{1{,}080}{(1+0)^6} = \$1{,}480$$

The price is just the simple undiscounted sum of the coupon values and the face value. Since yields can never go below zero, $1,480 is the maximum possible price for the bond.

When $R = \infty$,

$$P = \frac{80}{(1+\infty)} + \ldots + \frac{1{,}080}{(1+\infty)^6} \approx 0$$

As the yield goes to infinity, the bond price falls asymptotically toward zero, but by definition a bond's price can never be negative. Thus, zero must be the minimum bond price (see Figure 9A–3).

Since convexity is a desirable feature for assets, the FI manager might ask: Can we measure convexity? And can we incorporate this measurement in the duration model to adjust for or offset the error in prediction due to its presence? The answer to both questions is yes.

Theoretically speaking, duration is the slope of the price-yield curve, and convexity, or curvature, is the change in the slope of the price-yield curve. Consider the total effect of a change in interest rates on a bond's price as being broken into a number of separate effects. The precise mathematical derivation of these separate effects is based on a Taylor series expansion that you might remember from your math classes. Essentially, the first-order effect (dP/dR) of an interest rate change on the bond's price is the price–yield curve slope effect, which is measured by duration. The second-order effect (dP^2/d^2R) measures the change in the slope of the price-yield curve; this is the curvature or convexity effect. There are also third-, fourth-, and higher-order effects from the Taylor series expansion, but for all practical purposes these effects can be ignored.

We have noted that overlooking the curvature of the price–yield curve may cause errors in predicting the interest sensitivity of our portfolio of assets and liabilities, especially when

[3]This applies to fixed-income securities without special option features such as calls and puts.

FIGURE 9A–4

*Convexity and the
Price-Yield Curve*

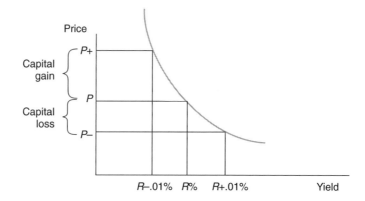

yields change by large amounts. We can adjust for this by explicitly recognizing the second-order effect of yield changes by measuring the change in the slope of the price-yield curve around a given point. Just as D (duration) measures the slope effect *(dP/dR),* we introduce a new parameter *(CX)* to measure the curvature effect (dP^2/d^2R) of the price-yield curve.

The resulting equation, predicting the change in a security's price $(\Delta P/P)$, is

$$\frac{\Delta P}{P} = -D\frac{\Delta R}{(1+R)} + \frac{1}{2}CX(\Delta R)^2 \quad (1)$$

or

$$\frac{\Delta P}{P} = -MD\,\Delta R + \frac{1}{2}CX(\Delta R)^2 \quad (2)$$

The first term in Equation (1) is the simple duration model that over- or under-predicts price changes for large changes in interest rates, and the second term is the second-order effect of interest rate changes, that is, the convexity or curvature adjustment. In Equation (1), the first term D can be divided by $1 + R$ to produce what practitioners call **modified duration** *(MD).* You can see this in Equation (2). This form is more intuitive because we multiply *MD* by the simple change in $R(\Delta R)$ rather than by the discounted change in $R(\Delta R/1 + R)$. In the convexity term, the number ½ and $(\Delta R)^2$ result from the fact that the convexity effect is the second-order effect of interest rate changes while duration is the first-order effect. The parameter *CX* reflects the degree of curvature in the price-yield curve at the current yield level, that is, the degree to which the *capital gain effect* exceeds the *capital loss effect* for an equal change in yields up or down. At best, the FI manager can only approximate the curvature effect by using a parametric measure of *CX.* Even though calculus is based on infinitesimally small changes, in financial markets the smallest change in yields normally observed is one basis point, or a 1/100th of 1 percent change. One possible way to measure *CX* is introduced next.

As just discussed, the convexity effect is the degree to which the capital gain effect more than offsets the capital loss effect for an equal increase and decrease in interest rates at the current interest rate level. In Figure 9A–4 we depict yields changing upward by one basis point $(R + .01\%)$ and down-

ward by one basis point $(R - .01\%)$. Because convexity measures the curvature of the price-yield curve around the rate level R percent, it intuitively measures the degree to which the capital gain effect of a small yield decrease exceeds the capital loss effect of a small yield increase.[4] Definitionally, the *CX* parameter equals

$$CX = \begin{matrix}\text{Scaling}\\\text{factor}\end{matrix}\begin{bmatrix}\text{The capital} & \text{The capital}\\\text{loss from one-} & \text{gain from a}\\\text{basis-point rise} + \text{one-basis-point}\\\text{in yield} & \text{fall in yield}\\\text{(negative effect)} & \text{(positive effect)}\end{bmatrix}$$

The sum of the two terms in the brackets reflect the degree to which the capital gain effect exceeds the capital loss effect for a small one-basis-point interest rate change down and up. The scaling factor normalizes this measure to account for a larger 1 percent change in rates. Remember, when interest rates change by a large amount, the convexity effect is important to measure. A commonly used scaling factor is 10^8 so that[5]

$$CX = 10^8\left[\frac{\Delta P-}{P} + \frac{\Delta P+}{P}\right]$$

Calculation of *CX*.* To calculate the convexity of the 8 percent coupon, 8 percent yield, six-year maturity Eurobond that had a price of $1,000:[6]

---

[4]We are trying to approximate as best we can the change in the slope of the price-yield curve at R percent. In theory, the changes are infinitesimally small (dR), but in reality, the smallest yield change normally observed is one basis point (ΔR).

[5]This is consistent with the effect of a 1 percent (100 basis points) change in rates.

[6]You can easily check that $999.53785 is the price of the six-year bond when rates are 8.01 percent and $1,000.46243 is the price of the bond when rates fall to 7.99 percent. Since we are dealing in small numbers and convexity is sensitive to the number of decimal places assumed, use at least five decimal places in calculating the capital gain or loss. In fact, the more decimal places used, the greater the accuracy of the CX measure.

Table 9A-1   Properties of Convexity

	1. Convexity Increases with Bond Maturity			2. Convexity Varies with Coupon		3. For Same Duration, Zero-Coupon Bonds Are Less Convex than Coupon Bonds	
	Example			Example		Example	
	A	B	C	A	B	A	B
	$N = 6$	$N = 18$	$N = \infty$	$N = 6$	$N = 6$	$N = 6$	$N = 5$
	$R = 8\%$	$R = 8\%$	$R = 8\%$	$R = 8\%$	$R = 8\%$	$R = 8\%$	$R = 8\%$
	$C = 8\%$	$C = 8\%$	$C = 8\%$	$C = 8\%$	$C = 0\%$	$C = 8\%$	$C = 0\%$
	$D = 5$	$D = 10.12$	$D = 13.5$	$D = 5$	$D = 6$	$D = 5$	$D = 5$
	$CX = 28$	$CX = 130$	$CX = 312$	$CX = 28$	$CX = 36$	$CX = 28$	$CX = 25.72$

$$CX = 10^8 \left[\frac{999.53785 - 1{,}000}{1{,}000} + \frac{1{,}000.46243 - 1{,}000}{1{,}000} \right]$$

$$\underbrace{\hspace{3cm}}_{\substack{\text{Capital loss from} \\ \text{a one-basis-point} \\ \text{increase in rates}}} + \underbrace{\hspace{3cm}}_{\substack{\text{Capital gain from} \\ \text{a one-basis-point} \\ \text{decrease in rates}}}$$

$$CX = 10^8[0.0000028]$$
$$CX = 28$$

This value for CX can be inserted into the bond price prediction Equation (2) with the convexity adjustment:

$$\frac{\Delta P}{P} = -MD\ \Delta R + \frac{1}{2}(28)\Delta R^2$$

Assuming a 2 percent increase in R (from 8 to 10 percent),

$$\frac{\Delta P}{P} = -\left[\frac{4.99}{1.08}\right].02 + \frac{1}{2}(28)(.02)^2$$
$$= -.0924 + .0056 = -.0868 \text{ or } -8.68\%$$

The simple duration model (the first term) predicts that a 2 percent rise in interest rates will cause the bond's price to fall 9.24 percent. However, for large changes in yields, the duration model overpredicts the price fall. The duration model with the second-order convexity adjustment predicts a price fall of 8.68 percent; it adds back 0.56 percent due to the convexity effect. This is much closer to the true fall in the six-year, 8 percent coupon bond's price if we calculated this using 10 percent to discount the coupon and face value cash flows on the bond. The true value of the bond price fall is 8.71 percent. That is, using the convexity adjustment reduces the error between predicted value and true value to just a few basis points.[7]

In Table 9A-1 we calculate various properties of convexity, where

N = Time to maturity
R = Yield to maturity
C = Annual coupon
D = Duration
CX = Convexity

Part 1 of Table 9A-1 shows that as the bond's maturity (N) increases, so does its convexity (CX). As a result, long-term bonds have more convexity—which is a desirable property—than do short-term bonds. This property is similar to that possessed by duration.[8]

Part 2 of Table 9A-1 shows that coupon bonds of the same maturity (N) have less convexity than do zero-coupon bonds. However, for coupon bonds and discount or zero-coupon bonds of the same duration, part 3 of the table shows that the coupon bond has more convexity. We depict the convexity of both in Figure 9A-5.

Finally, before leaving convexity, we might look at one important use of the concept by managers of insurance companies, pension funds, and mutual funds. Remembering that convexity is a desirable form of interest rate insurance, FI managers could structure an asset portfolio to maximize its desirable effects. As an example, consider a pension fund manager with a 15-year payout horizon. To immunize the risk of interest rate changes, the manager purchases bonds with a 15-year duration. Consider two alternative strategies to achieve this:

---

[7] It is possible to use the third moment of the Taylor series expansion to reduce this small error (8.71 percent versus 8.68 percent) even further. In practice, few people do this.

[8] Note that the CX measure differs according to the level of interest rates. For example, we are measuring CX in Table 9A-1 when yields are 8 percent. If yields were 12 percent, the CX number would change. This is intuitively reasonable, as the curvature of the price-yield curve differs at each point on the price-yield curve. Note that duration also changes with the level of interest rates.

Strategy 1: Invest 100 percent of resources in a 15-year deep-discount bond with an 8 percent yield.

Strategy 2: Invest 50 percent in the very short-term money market (federal funds) and 50 percent in 30-year deep-discount bonds with an 8 percent yield.

The duration (D) and convexities (CX) of these two asset portfolios are:

Strategy 1: $D = 15$, $CX = 206$

Strategy 2:[9] $D = \frac{1}{2}(0) + \frac{1}{2}(30) = 15$, $CX = \frac{1}{2}(0) + \frac{1}{2}(797) = 398.5$

Strategies 1 and 2 have the same durations, but strategy 2 has a greater convexity. Strategy 2 is often called a barbell portfolio, as shown in Figure 9A–6 by the shaded bars.[10] Strategy 1 is the unshaded bar. To the extent that the

market does not price (or fully price) convexity, the barbell strategy dominates the direct duration matching strategy (number one).[11]

More generally, an FI manager may seek to attain greater convexity in the asset portfolio than in the liability portfolio, as shown in Figure 9A–7. As a result, both positive and negative shocks to interest rates would have beneficial effects on the FI's net worth.

---

[9] The duration and convexity of one-day federal funds are approximately zero.

[10] This is called a barbell because the weights are equally loaded at the extreme ends of the duration range or bar as in weight lifting.

[11] In a world in which convexity is priced, the long-term 30-year bond's price would rise to reflect the competition among buyers to include this more convex bond in their barbell asset portfolios. Thus, buying bond insurance—in the form of the barbell portfolio—would involve an additional cost to the FI manager. In addition, to be hedged in both a duration sense and a convexity sense, the manager should not choose the convexity of the asset portfolio without seeking to match it to the convexity of its liability portfolio. For further discussion of the convexity "trap" that results when an FI mismatches its asset and liability convexities, see J. H. Gilkeson and S. D. Smith, "The Convexity Trap: Pitfalls in Financing Mortgage Portfolios and Related Securities," Federal Reserve Bank of Atlanta, Economic Review, November–December 1992, pp. 17–27.

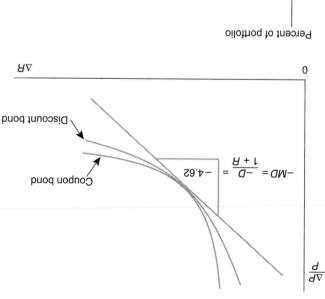

FIGURE 9A–6
Barbell Strategy

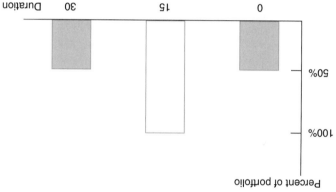

FIGURE 9A–5
Convexity of a Coupon versus a Discount Bond with the Same Duration

Concept Questions

1. Why do critics argue that the duration model is difficult to apply in real-world situations? How can these arguments be countered?
2. What is convexity? Is it a desirable feature for assets?
3. Calculate the convexity of an 8 percent yield zero-coupon bond with a face value of $1,000 and a maturity of 14 years.
4. Calculate the convexity of an 8 percent yield, 8 percent coupon, three-year maturity Eurobond with a face value of $1,000.

The Problem of the Flat Term Structure*

We have been calculating simple or Macaulay duration, which was named after an economist who was among the first to develop the *duration* concept. A key assumption of the simple duration model is that the yield curve or the term structure of interest rates is flat and that when rates change, the yield curve shifts in a parallel fashion. We show this in Figure 9A–8.

In the real world, the yield curve can take many shapes and at best may only approximate a flat yield curve. If the yield curve is not flat, using simple duration could be a potential source of error in predicting asset and liability interest rate sensitivities. Many models can deal with this problem. These models differ according to the shapes and shocks to the yield curve that are assumed.

Suppose the yield curve is not flat but shifts in such a manner that the yields on different maturity discount bonds change in a proportional fashion.[12] Consider calculating the duration of the six-year Eurobond when the yield curve is not flat at 8 percent. Instead, the yield curve looks like the one in Figure 9A–9.

---

[12] We are interested in the yield curve on discount bonds because these yields reflect the time value of money for single payments at different maturity dates. Thus, we can use these yields as discount rates for cash flows on a security to calculate appropriate present values of its cash flows and its duration.

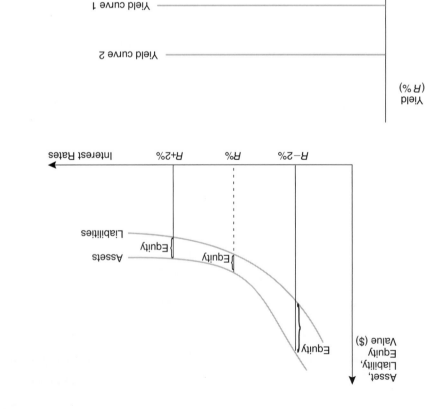

FIGURE 9A–7
Assets are More Convex Than Liabilities

FIGURE 9A–8
Yield Curve Underlying Macaulay Duration

The Problem of Default Risk*

The models and the duration calculations we have looked at assume that the issuer of bonds or the borrower of a loan pays the promised interest and principal with a probability of 1; we assume no default or delay in the payment of cash flows. In the real world, problems with principal and interest payments are common and lead to restructuring and workouts on debt contracts as bankers and bond trustees renegotiate with borrowers; that is, the borrower reschedules or recontracts interest and principal payments rather than defaulting outright. If we view default risk as synonymous with the rescheduling of cash flows to a later date, this is quite easy to deal with in duration models.

Consider the six-year, 8 percent coupon, 8 percent yield Eurobond. Suppose the issuer gets into difficulty and cannot pay the first coupon. Instead, the borrower and the FI agree that the unpaid interest can be paid in year 2. This alleviates part of the cash flow pressure on the borrower while lengthening the duration of the bond from the FI's perspective (see Table 9A-3). The effect of rescheduling the first interest payment is to increase duration from approximately 5 years to 5.08 years.

More generally, an FI manager unsure of the future cash flows because of future default risk might multiply the promised cash flow (CF_t) by the probability of repayment (p_t) in year t to generate expected cash flows in year t—$E(CF_t)$.[15]

$$E(CF_t) = p_t \times CF_t$$

Chapter 11 suggests a number of ways to generate these repayment probabilities. Once the cash flows have been adjusted for default risk, a duration measure can be directly

Suppose the yield on one-year discount bonds rises. Assume also that the discounted changes in longer-maturity discount bonds yields are just proportional to the change in the one-year discount yield:

$$\frac{\Delta R_1}{1+R_1} = \frac{\Delta R_2}{1+R_2} = \cdots = \frac{\Delta R_6}{1+R_6}$$

Given this quite restrictive assumption, we can prove that the appropriate duration measure of the bond—call it D^*— can be derived by discounting the coupons and principal value of the bond by the discount rates or yields on appropriate maturity zero-coupon bonds. Given the discount bond yield curve plotted in Figure 9A-9, D^* is calculated in Table 9A-2.[13] Notice that D^* is 4.92 years, while simple Macauley duration (with an assumed flat 8 percent yield curve) is 4.99 years. D^* and D differ because, by taking into account the upward-sloping yield curve in Figure 9A-9, the later cash flows are discounted at higher rates than they are under the flat yield curve assumption underlying Macauley's measure D.

With respect to the FI manager's problem, choosing to use D^* instead of D does not change the basic problem except for a concern with the gap between the D^* on assets and leverage-weighted liabilities:

$$D_A^* - kD_L^*$$

However, remember that the D^* was calculated under very restrictive assumptions about the yield curve. If we change these assumptions in any way, the measure of D^* changes.[14]

---

[13]For more details, see Hawawini, "Controlling the Interest Rate Risk"; and G. O. Bierwag, G. G. Kaufman, and A. Toevs, "Duration: Its Development and Use in Bond Portfolio Management," *Financial Analysts Journal* 39 (1983), pp. 15–35.

[14]A number of authors have identified other nonstandard measures of duration for more complex yield curve shapes and shifts. See, for example, Bierwag, Kaufman, and Toevs, "Duration: Its Development."

[15]The probability of repayment is between 0 and 1.

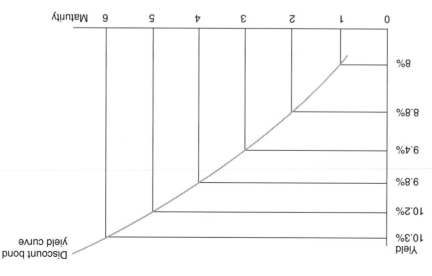

FIGURE 9A-9
Nonflat Yield Curve

TABLE 9A–2   Duration with an Upward-Sloping Yield Curve

t	CF	DF	CF × DF	CF × DF ×t
1	80	$\frac{1}{(1.08)} = 0.9259$	74.07	74.07
2	80	$\frac{1}{(1.088)^2} = 0.8448$	67.58	135.16
3	80	$\frac{1}{(1.094)^3} = 0.7637$	61.10	183.3
4	80	$\frac{1}{(1.098)^4} = 0.6880$	55.04	220.16
5	80	$\frac{1}{(1.102)^5} = 0.6153$	49.22	246.1
6	1,080	$\frac{1}{(1.103)^6} = 0.5553$	599.75	3,598.50
			906.76	4,457.29

$$D^* = \frac{4,457.29}{906.76} = 4.91562$$

TABLE 9A–3   Duration and Rescheduling

t	CF	DF	CF × DF	CF × DF × t
1	0	.9259	0	0
2	160	.8573	137.17	274.34
3	80	.7938	63.51	190.53
4	80	.7350	58.80	235.21
5	80	.6806	54.45	272.25
6	1,080	.6302	680.58	4,083.48
			994.51	5,055.81

$$D = \frac{5,055.81}{994.51} = 5.0837 \text{ years}$$

calculated in the same manner as the Macauley formula (or D^*) except that $E(CF_t)$ replaces CF_t.[16]

Concept Questions

1. When can using simple duration become a potential source of error in predicting asset and liability interest rate sensitivities?
2. What is the effect of an upward-sloping yield curve on the measurment of duration?

3. How might an FI manager incorporate default risk when using the duration model?

Floating-Rate Loans and Bonds*

The duration models we have looked at assume that the interest rates on loans or the coupons on bonds are fixed at issue and remain unchanged until maturity. However, many bonds and loans carry floating interest rates. Examples include loan rates indexed to LIBOR (London Interbank Offered Rate) and adjustable rate mortgages (ARMs) whose rates can be indexed to Treasury or other securities yields. Moreover, in the 1980s, many banks and security firms either issued or underwrote perpetual floating-rate notes (FRNs). These are like consol bonds in that they never mature; unlike consols, their coupons fluctuate with market rates. The FI manager, who wants to analyze overall gap exposure, may ask: What are the durations of

---

[16]Alternatively, the promised cash flow could be discounted by the appropriate discount yield on a risk-free Treasury security plus an appropriate credit-risk spread: that is, $CF_t /(1 + d_t + S_t)^t$, where CF_t is the promised cash flow in year t, d_t is the yield on a t-period zero-coupon Treasury bond, and S_t is a credit-risk premium.

FIGURE 9A-10

Floating-Rate Note

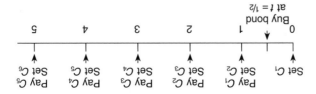

such floating-rate securities? The duration of a floating-rate instrument is generally the time interval between the purchase of the security and the time when the next coupon or interest payment is readjusted to reflect current interest rate conditions. We call this the time to repricing of the instrument.

For example, suppose the investor bought a perpetual floating-rate note. These floating-rate notes never mature. At the beginning of each year, the FI sets the coupon rate, which is paid at the end of that year. Suppose the investor buys the bond in the middle of the first year ($t = \frac{1}{2}$) rather than at the beginning (see Figure 9A-10).

The present value of the bond from time of purchase is[17]

$$P = \frac{C_1}{(1 + 1/2R)} + \frac{C_2}{(1 + 1/2R)(1 + R)} + \frac{C_3}{(1 + 1/2R)(1 + R)^2} + \frac{C_4}{(1 + 1/2R)(1 + R)^3} + \cdots + \frac{C_\infty}{(1 + 1/2R)(1 + R)^{\infty-1}}$$

Note three important aspects of this present value equation. First, the investor has to wait only a half year to get the first coupon payment—hence, the discount rate is $(1 + \frac{1}{2}R)$. Second, the investor knows with certainty only the size of the first coupon C_1, which was preset at the beginning of the first coupon period to reflect interest rates at that time. The FI set the first coupon rate six months before the investor bought the bond. Third, the other coupons on the bond, C_2, C_3, C_4, C_5, ... C_∞ are unknown at the time the bond is purchased because they depend on the level of interest rates at the time they are reset (see Figure 9A-10).

To derive the duration of the bond, rewrite the cash flows at one-half year onward as

$$P = \frac{1}{(1 + 1/2R)} + (1 + 1/2R) \left[\frac{C_2}{(1 + R)} + \frac{C_4}{(1 + R)^2} + \frac{C_3}{(1 + R)^3} + \cdots + \frac{C_\infty}{(1 + R)^{\infty-1}} \right]$$

[17]This formula follows the Eurobond convention that any cash flows received in less than one full coupon period's time are discounted using simple interest. Thus, we use $1 + \frac{1}{2}R$ rather than $(1 + R)^{1/2}$ for the first coupon's cash flow in the example above. Also see R. A. Grobel, "Understanding the Duration of Floating Rate Notes" MIMED (New York: Salomon Brothers, 1986).

where P is the present value of the bond (the bond price) at one-half year, the time of purchase.

The term in brackets is the present value or fair price (P_1) of the bond if it were sold at the end of year 1, the beginning of the second coupon period. As long as the variable coupons exactly match fluctuations in yields or interest rates, the present value of the cash flow in the square brackets is unaffected by interest rate changes. Thus,

$$P = \frac{C_1}{(1 + 1/2R)} + \frac{P_1}{(1 + 1/2R)}$$

Since C_1 is a fixed cash flow preset before the investor bought the bond and P_1 is a fixed cash flow in present value terms, buying this bond is similar to buying two single-payment deep-discount bonds each with a maturity of six months. Because the duration of a deep-discount bond is the same as its maturity, this FRN bond has

$$D = 1/2 \text{ year}$$

As indicated earlier, a half year is exactly the interval between the time when the bond was purchased and the time when it was first repriced.[18]

Concept Questions

1. What types of bonds and loans pay floating interest rates?
2. How do you measure the duration of a security that pays floating interest rates?

[18]Another case might be where an FI manager bought a bond whose coupon floated but repaid fixed principal (many loans are priced like this). Calculating the duration on this bond or loan is straightforward. First, we have to think of it as two bonds: a floating-rate bond that pays a variable coupon (C) every year and a deep-discount bond that pays a fixed amount (F) on maturity. The duration of the first bond is the time between purchase and the first coupon reset date, $D = \frac{1}{2}$ year in the preceding example. While the duration of the deep-discount bond equals its maturity, $D =$ three years for a three-year bond. The duration of the bond as a whole is the weighted average of a half year and three years, where the weights (w_1) and ($1 - w_1$) reflect the present values of, respectively, the coupon cash flows and face value to the present value of the total cash flows (the sum of the two present values). Thus,

$$D = w_1(1/2) + (1 - w_1)(3)$$

Demand Deposits and Passbook Savings*

Many banks and thrifts hold large amounts of checking and passbook savings account liabilities. This is especially true for smaller banks. The problem in assessing the duration of such claims is that their maturities are open-ended and many demand deposit accounts do not turnover very frequently. Although demand deposits allow holders to demand cash immediately—suggesting a very short maturity—many customers tend to retain demand deposit balances for lengthy periods. In the parlance of banking, they behave as if they were a bank's **core deposits.** A problem arises because defining the duration of a security requires defining its maturity. Yet demand deposits have open-ended maturities. One way for an FI manager to get around this problem is to analyze the runoff, or the turnover characteristics, of the FI's demand and passbook savings account deposits. For example, suppose the manager learned that on average each dollar in demand deposit accounts turned over five times a year. This suggests an average turnover or maturity per dollar of around 73 days.[19]

A second method is to consider demand deposits as bonds that can be instantaneously put back to the bank in return for cash. As instantaneously putable bonds, the duration of demand deposits is approximately zero.

A third approach is more directly in line with the idea of duration as a measure of interest rate sensitivity. It looks at the withdrawal sensitivity of demand deposits $(\Delta DD/DD)$ to interest rate changes (ΔR). Because demand deposits and to a lesser extent passbook savings deposits pay either low explicit or **implicit interest**—where implicit interest takes forms such as subsidized checking fees—there tends to be enhanced withdrawals and switching into higher yielding instruments as rates rise. You can use a number of quantitative techniques to test this sensitivity, including linear and nonlinear time series regression analysis.

A fourth approach is to use simulation analysis. This is based on forecasts of future interest rates and the net withdrawals by depositors from their accounts over some future time period. Taking the discounted present values of these cash flows, a duration measure can be calculated.[20]

Concept Questions

1. What are four approaches that could be used in calculating the duration of a demand deposit?

Mortgages and Mortgage-Backed Securities*

Calculating the durations of mortgages and mortgage-backed securities is difficult because of prepayment risk. Essentially, as the level of interest rates falls, mortgage holders have the option to prepay their old mortgages and refinance with a new mortgage at a lower interest rate. In the terminology of finance, fixed-rate mortgages and mortgage-backed securities contain an embedded option. To calculate duration, it is necessary to project the future cash flows on an asset. Consequently, to calculate the duration of mortgages, we need to model the prepayment behavior of mortgage holders. Possible ways to do this are left to Chapter 28 on mortgage asset securitization.

Futures, Options, Swaps, Caps, and Other Contingent Claims*

When interest rates change, so do the values of (off-balance-sheet) derivative instruments such as futures, options, swaps, and caps (see Chapter 13). Market value gains and losses on these instruments can also have an impact on the net worth (E) of an FI. The calculation of the durations of these instruments is left to Chapters 24 to 26. However, it should be noted that a fully fledged duration gap model of an FI should take into account the durations of its derivatives portfolio as well as the duration of its on-balance-sheet assets and liabilities. This is especially so today as more and more FIs take positions in derivative contracts.

[19]That is, 365 days/5 = 73 days.

[20]For a very sophisticated model along these lines, see "The OTS Market Value Model" (Washington, D.C.: OTS, 1994).

10

MARKET RISK

Chapter Outline

Introduction

In recent years, the trading activities of FIs have raised considerable concern among regulators and FI analysts alike. Major FIs such as Merrill Lynch, Salomon Brothers, and J. P. Morgan have taken big hits to their profits from losses in trading.[1] Moreover, in February 1995, Barings, the U.K. merchant bank, was forced into insolvency as a result of losses on its trading in Japanese stock index futures. In

---

*Difficult subsection

[1] For example, one trader cost Merrill Lynch over $370 million in 1987 by taking a position in mortgage-backed security strips.

Contemporary Perspectives

CHASE PLACES BETS IN HIGH-STAKES MARKETS

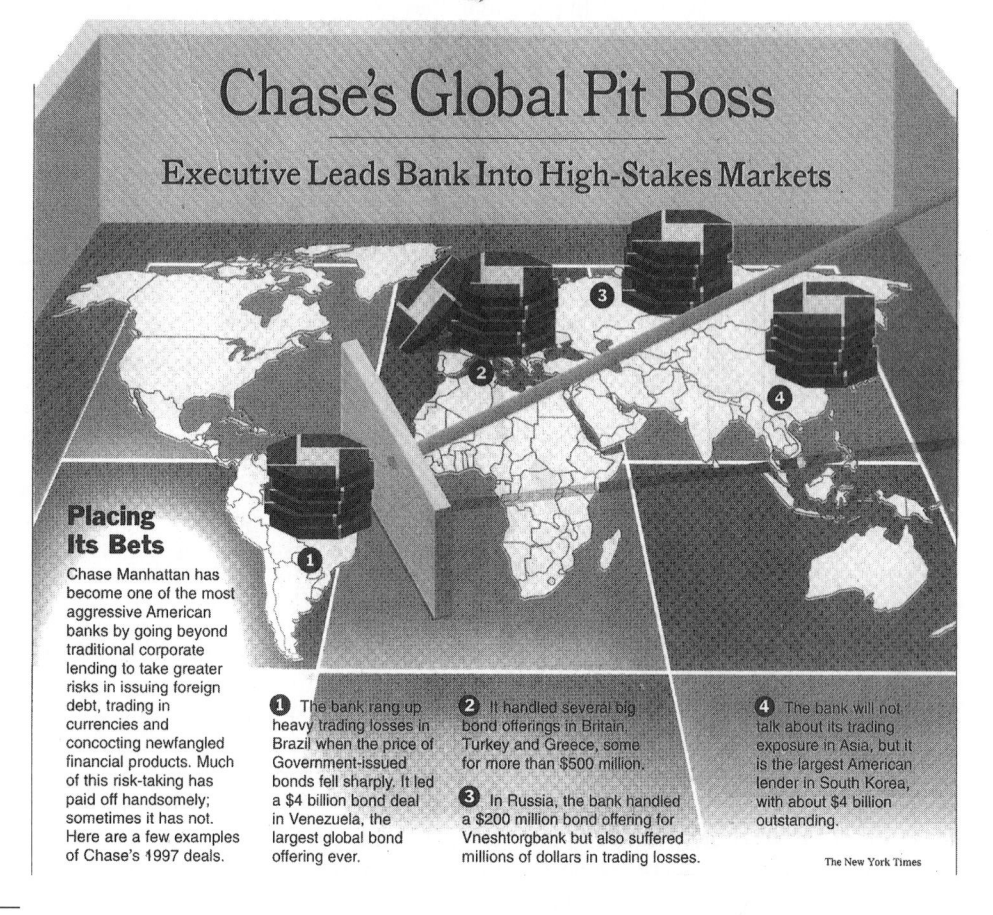

Business Day

The New York Times

Chase's Global Pit Boss

Executive Leads Bank Into High-Stakes Markets

Placing Its Bets

Chase Manhattan has become one of the most aggressive American banks by going beyond traditional corporate lending to take greater risks in issuing foreign debt, trading in currencies and concocting newfangled financial products. Much of this risk-taking has paid off handsomely; sometimes it has not. Here are a few examples of Chase's 1997 deals.

1 The bank rang up heavy trading losses in Brazil when the price of Government-issued bonds fell sharply. It led a $4 billion bond deal in Venezuela, the largest global bond offering ever.

2 It handled several big bond offerings in Britain, Turkey and Greece, some for more than $500 million.

3 In Russia, the bank handled a $200 million bond offering for Vneshtorgbank but also suffered millions of dollars in trading losses.

4 The bank will not talk about its trading exposure in Asia, but it is the largest American lender in South Korea, with about $4 billion outstanding.

The New York Times

September 1995, a similar incident took place at the New York branch of a leading Japanese bank, Daiwa Bank. The Contemporary Perspectives box above shows the various trading exposures and losses of Chase Manhattan during 1997, a relatively turbulent year that featured considerable currency and financial market volatility in Eastern Europe and Asia. This volatility was magnified further throughout 1998 with additional losses on Russian bonds as the ruble fell in value and the prices of Russian bonds collapsed. As traditional commercial and investment banking

franchises shrink and markets become more complex (e.g., emerging country equity and bond markets and new sophisticated derivative contracts), concerns are only likely to increase regarding the threats to FI solvency from trading.

Conceptually, an FI's trading portfolio can be differentiated from its investment portfolio by time horizon and liquidity. The trading portfolio contains assets, liabilities, and derivative contracts that can be quickly bought or sold on organized financial markets. With the increasing securitization of bank loans (e.g., mortgages), more and more assets have become liquid and tradable. Of course, with time, every asset and liability can be sold. While bank regulators have normally viewed tradable assets as those being held for horizons of less than one year, private FIs take an even shorter-term view. In particular, they are concerned about the fluctuation in value—or value at risk (VAR)—of their trading account assets and liabilities for periods as short as one day—especially if such fluctuations pose a threat to their solvency.

Market risk (or value at risk) can be defined as the uncertainty of an FI's earnings resulting from changes in market conditions such as the price of an asset, interest rates, market volatility, and market liquidity.[2] This uncertainty can be measured over periods as short as a day or as long as a year. Moreover, market risk can be defined in absolute terms as a *dollar* exposure amount or as a relative amount against some benchmark. In the sections that follow, we will concentrate on absolute dollar measures of market risk.

Market Risk Measurement

There are at least five reasons why market risk measurement is important:

1. *Management information.* Provides senior management with information on the risk exposure taken by traders. This risk exposure can then be compared to the capital resources of the FI. Such an information system appears to have been lacking in the Barings failure.

2. *Setting limits.* Measures the market risk of traders' portfolios, which will allow the establishment of economically logical position limits per trader in each area of trading.

3. *Resource allocation.* Compares returns to market risks in different areas of trading, which may allow the identification of areas with the greatest potential return per unit of risk into which more capital and resources can be directed.

4. *Performance evaluation.* Relatedly, calculates the return-risk ratio of traders, which may allow a more rational bonus system to be put in place. That is, those traders with the highest returns may simply be the ones who have taken the greatest risks. It is not clear that they should receive higher compensation than traders with lower returns and lower risk exposures.

5. *Regulation.* With the BIS and Federal Reserve currently regulating (since 1998) market risk through capital requirements (discussed later in this chapter), private sector benchmarks are important since in certain cases regulators are allowing banks to use their own models to calculate their capital requirements.[3]

---

[2] J. P. Morgan, *Introduction to RiskMetrics* (New York: October 1994), p. 2.

[3] Since regulators are concerned with the social costs of a failure or insolvency, including contagion effects and other externalities, regulatory models will normally tend to be more conservative than private sector models that are concerned only with the private costs of failure.

TABLE 10-1 JPM's Trading Business

	Fixed Income	Foreign Exchange STIRT*	Commodities	Derivatives	Equities	Emergency Markets	Proprietary	Total
Number of active locations	14	12	5	8	11	7	11	14
Number of independent risk-taking units	30	21	8	16	14	11	19	120
Thousands of transactions per day	<5	>5	<1	<1	>5	<1	<1	>20
Billions of dollars in daily trading volume	>10	>30	1	1	<1	1	8	>50

*Short-term interest rate instruments.

Source: J. P. Morgan, *Introduction to RiskMetrics* (New York: October 1994).

Calculating Market Risk Exposure

Large commercial banks, investment banks, insurance companies, and mutual funds have all developed market risk models. In developing these models—so called internal models—three major approaches have been followed:

- RiskMetrics (or the variance/covariance approach)
- Historic or back simulation
- Monte Carlo simulation

We consider RiskMetrics[4] first and then compare it to other internal model approaches, such as historic or back simulation.

The RiskMetrics Model

The ultimate objective of market risk measurement models can best be seen from the following quote by Dennis Weatherstone, former chairman of J. P. Morgan (JPM): "At close of business each day tell me what the market risks are across all businesses and locations." In a nutshell, the chairman of J. P. Morgan wants a single *dollar* number at 4:15 PM New York time that tells him J. P. Morgan's market risk exposure the next day—especially if that day turns out to be a "bad" day.

This is nontrivial, given the extent of JPM's trading business. As shown in Table 10-1, when JPM developed its RiskMetrics Model it had 14 active trading locations with 120 independent units trading fixed income securities, foreign exchange, commodities, derivatives, emerging-market securities, and proprietary assets, with a total daily volume exceeding $50 billion. This scale and variety of activities is typical of the major money center banks, large overseas banks (e.g., Deutsche Bank, and Barclays), and major investment banks. Here, we will concentrate on measuring the market risk exposure on a daily basis of a major FI using the RiskMetrics approach. As will be discussed later,

[4] J. P. Morgan (JPM) first developed RiskMetrics in 1994. In 1998 the development group formed a separate company, partly owned by JPM.

measuring the risk exposure for periods longer than a day (e.g., five days) is under certain assumptions a simple transformation of the daily risk exposure number. Essentially, the FI is concerned with how much it can potentially lose if market conditions move adversely tomorrow; that is,

Market risk = Estimated potential loss under adverse circumstances

More specifically, the market risk in terms of the FI's daily earnings at risk will have three measurable components:

$$\text{Daily earnings at risk} = \begin{pmatrix}\text{Dollar value} \\ \text{of the position}\end{pmatrix} \times \begin{pmatrix}\text{Price} \\ \text{sensitivity}\end{pmatrix} \times \begin{pmatrix}\text{Potential adverse} \\ \text{move in yield}\end{pmatrix} \quad (1)$$

Since price sensitivity multiplied by adverse yield move measures the degree of price volatility of an asset, we can also write Equation (1) as Equation (2):

$$\text{Daily earnings at risk} = (\text{Dollar value of the position}) \times (\text{Price volatility}) \quad (2)$$

We concentrate on how the RiskMetrics model calculates daily earnings at risk in three trading areas—fixed income, foreign exchange (FX), and equities—and then how it estimates the aggregate risk of the whole trading portfolio to meet Dennis Weatherstone's objective of a single aggregate dollar exposure measure across the whole bank at 4:15 PM each day.[5]

The Market Risk of Fixed-Income Securities

Suppose an FI has a $1 million market value position in zero-coupon bonds of seven years to maturity with a face value of $1,631,483.[6] Today's yield on these bonds is 7.243 percent per annum. These bonds are held as part of the trading portfolio. Thus,

Dollar market value of position = $1 million

The FI manager wants to know the potential exposure faced by the FI if a scenario occurs resulting in an adverse or reasonably bad market move against the FI tomorrow. How much will be lost depends on the price volatility of the bond. From the duration model in Chapter 9 we know that

$$\text{Daily price volatility} = (\text{Price sensitivity to a small change in yield}) \times (\text{Adverse daily yield move})$$
$$= (-MD) \times (\text{Adverse daily yield move})$$

The modified duration (MD) of this bond is[7]

$$MD = \frac{D}{1 + R} = \frac{7}{(1.07243)} = 6.527$$

given that the yield on the bond is $R = 7.243$ percent. To estimate price volatility, the bond's MD needs to be multiplied by the adverse daily yield move. Suppose we want to measure adverse yield changes such that there is only a 5 percent chance

---

[5] It is clear from the above discussion that interest rate risk (see Chapters 8 and 9) is part of market risk. However, in market risk models we are concerned with the interest rate sensitivity of the fixed-income securities held as part of an FI's active trading portfolio. Many fixed-income securities are held as part of an FI's investment portfolio. While the latter are subject to interest rate risk, they will not be included in a market risk calculation.

[6] The face value of the bonds is $1,631,483—that is, $1,631,483/(1.07243)$^7 = $1,000,000 market value.

[7] Assuming annual compounding for simplicity.

FIGURE 10–1

*Adverse Rate Move,
Seven-Year Rates*

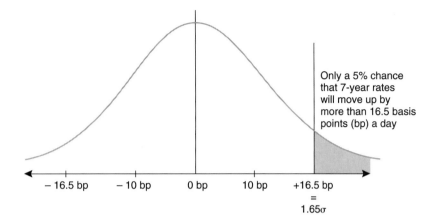

that the yield changes will be greater than this given amount in either direction—or, since we are concerned only with bad outcomes, that there is 1 chance in 20 (or a 5 percent chance) that the next day's yield change (or shock) will exceed this given adverse amount.

If it is assumed that yield changes are normally distributed,[8] we can fit a normal distribution to the histogram of recent past changes in rates to get an estimate of the size of this adverse rate move. From statistics, we know that 90 percent of the area under the normal distribution is to be found within ± 1.65 standard deviations (σ) from the mean—that is, 1.65σ. Suppose over the last year the mean change in daily yields on seven-year zeros was 0 percent[9] while the standard deviation was 10 basis points (or 0.001), so that 1.65σ is 16.5 basis points (bp).[10] This is shown in Figure 10–1.

We can now calculate the potential daily price volatility on seven-year discount bonds as

$$\text{Price volatility} = (-MD) \times (\text{Potential adverse move in yield})$$
$$= (-6.527) \times (.00165)$$
$$= -.01077 \text{ or } -1.077\%$$

Given this price volatility and the initial market value of the seven-year bond portfolio,[11]

$$\text{Daily earnings at risks} = (\text{Dollar value of position}) \times (\text{Price volatility})$$
$$= (\$1,000,000) \times (.01077)$$
$$= \$10,770$$

that is, the potential daily loss on the position is $10,770 if the one bad day in 20 occurs tomorrow. We can extend this analysis to calculate the potential loss over

---

[8]In reality, many asset return distributions—such as exchange rates and interest rates—have "fat tails." Thus, the normal distribution will tend to underestimate extreme outcomes. This is a major criticism of the RiskMetrics modeling approach.

[9]If the mean were nonzero (e.g., -1 basis point), this could be added to the 16.5 bp to project the yield shock.

[10]RiskMetrics weights more recent observations more highly than past observations (this is called *exponential weighting*). This allows more recent news to be more heavily reflected in the calculation of σ. Regular σ calculations put an equal weight on all past observations.

[11]Since we are calculating loss, we drop the minus sign here.

2, 3 . . . N days. If we assume that yield shocks are independent,[12] and that the FI is "locked in" to holding this asset for N number of days, then the N-day market value at risk (*VAR*) is related to daily earnings at risk (*DEAR*) by

$$VAR = DEAR \times \sqrt{N}$$

If N is five days, then

$$VAR = \$10,770 \times \sqrt{5} = \$24,082$$

If N is 10 days, then[13]

$$VAR = \$10,770 \times \sqrt{10} = \$34,057$$

In the above calculations, we estimated price sensitivity using modified duration. However, the RiskMetrics model generally prefers using the present value of cash flow changes as the price sensitivity weights over modified durations. Essentially, each cash flow is discounted by the appropriate zero-coupon rate to generate the daily earnings at risk measure. If we used the direct cash flow calculation in this case, the loss would be $\$10,771.2$.[14] The estimates in this case are very close.

Foreign Exchange

Like other large FIs, JPM actively trades in foreign exchange (FX). Remember that

$$DEAR = (\text{Dollar value of position}) \times (\text{Price volatility})$$

Suppose the bank had a Swf 1.6 million trading position in spot Swiss francs today. We want to calculate the daily earnings at risk from this position.

The first step is to calculate the dollar value of the position:

$$\begin{aligned} \text{Dollar value of position} &= (\text{FX position}) \times (\text{Swf/\$ spot exchange rate}) \\ &= (\text{Swf 1.6 million}) \times (\text{\$ per unit of foreign currency}) \end{aligned}$$

If the exchange rate is Swf 1.60/\$1 or \$0.625/Swf, then

$$\begin{aligned} \text{Dollar value of position} &= (\text{Swf 1.6 million}) \times (\$0.625/\text{Swf}) \\ &= \$1 \text{ million} \end{aligned}$$

Suppose that, looking back at the daily changes in the Swf/\$ exchange rate over the past year, we find that σ of the spot exchange rate was 56.5 bp. However, we are

---

[12]The assumption that there is no autocorrelation in yield shocks is a strong assumption. Much recent literature suggests that shocks are autocorrelated in many asset markets over relatively long horizons. To understand why we take the square-root of N, consider a 5-day holding period. The σ_5^2, or five-day variance, equals the current one-day variance σ_1^2 times 5, or

$$\sigma_5^2 = \sigma_1^2 \times 5$$

The standard deviation of this equation is

$$\sigma_5 = \sigma_1 \times \sqrt{5}$$

or in the terminology of RiskMetrics,

$$VAR = DEAR \times \sqrt{5}.$$

[13]Under the BIS 1998 market risk capital requirements, a 10-day holding period ($N = 10$) is assumed to measure exposure.

[14]The initial market value of the seven-year zero was $\$1,000,000$ or $\$1,631,483/(1.07243)^7$. The (loss) effect on each \$1 (market value) invested in the bond of a rise in rates by 1 bp from 7.243 percent to 7.253 percent is .0006528. However, the adverse rate move is 16.5 bp. Thus

$$DEAR = (\$1 \text{ million}) \times (.0006528) \times (16.5) = \$10,771.2$$

interested in adverse moves—that is, bad moves that will not be exceeded more than 5 percent of the time or 1.65 σ:

$$\text{FX volatility} = 1.65 \times 56.5 \text{ bp} = 93.2 \text{ bp or } 0.932\%$$

Thus:

$$\begin{aligned}
DEAR &= (\text{Dollar value of position}) \times (\text{FX volatility}) \\
&= (\$1 \text{ million}) \times (.00932) \\
&= \$9,320
\end{aligned}$$

This is the potential daily loss exposure to the FI from the Swf 1.6 million spot currency holding in Swiss currency.

Equities

Many large FIs also take positions in equities. As is well known from the Capital Asset Pricing Model (CAPM), there are two types of risk to an equity position in an individual stock i:[15]

$$\text{Total risk} = \text{Systematic risk} + \text{Unsystematic risk}$$
$$\sigma_{it}^2 = \beta_i^2 \sigma_{mt}^2 + \sigma_{eit}^2$$

Systematic risk reflects the comovement of that stock with the market portfolio (reflected by the stock's beta (β_i) and the volatility of the market portfolio (σ_{mt}), while unsystematic risk is specific to the firm itself (σ_{eit}).

In a very well-diversified portfolio, unsystematic risk can be largely diversified away, leaving behind systematic (undiversifiable) market risk. If the FI's trading portfolio holds (replicates) the stock market index portfolio, the β of that portfolio will be 1 since the movement of the FI's portfolio with the market will be 1-to-1.

Suppose the FI holds a $1 million trading position in stocks that reflect a U.S. stock market index (e.g., the Wilshire 5000). Then *DEAR* would be

$$\begin{aligned}
DEAR &= (\text{Dollar value of position}) \times (\text{Stock market return volatility}) \\
&= (\$1,000,000) \times (1.65 \, \sigma_m).
\end{aligned}$$

If, over the last year, the σ_m of the daily changes in returns on the stock market index was 2 percent, then $1.65 \, \sigma_m = 3.3$ percent. In this case

$$\begin{aligned}
DEAR &= (\$1,000,000) \times (0.033) \\
&= \$33,000
\end{aligned}$$

In less well diversified portfolios or portfolios of individual stocks, the effect of unsystematic risk σ_{eit} on the value of the trading position would need to be added. Moreover, if the CAPM does not offer a good explanation of asset pricing compared to, say, multi-index arbitrage pricing theory (APT), a degree of error will be built into the *DEAR* calculation.[16]

Portfolio Aggregation

In the sections above, we analyzed the daily earnings at risk of individual trading positions. In this chapter, we looked at a seven-year, zero-coupon, fixed-income security ($1 million market value), a position in spot Swf ($1 million market value),

---

[15]This assumes that systematic and unsystematic risks are independent of each other.

[16]As noted in the introduction, derivatives are also used for trading purposes. To calculate its *DEAR*, a derivative has to be converted into a position in the underlying asset (e.g., bond, FX, or equity).

TABLE 10–2   Correlations (ρ_{ij}) among Assets

	Seven-Year Zero	Swf/$1	U.S. Stock Index
Seven-year zero	—	−.2	.4
Swf/$1		—	.1
U.S. stock index			—

and a position in the U.S. stock market index ($1 million market value). The individual *DEAR*s were:

1. Seven-year zero = $10,770
2. Swf spot = $9,320
3. U.S. equities = $33,000

However, senior management wants to know the aggregate risk of the whole trading position. To calculate this, we *cannot* simply sum the three *DEAR*s— $10,770 + $9,320 + $33,000 = $53,090—because this would ignore any degree of offsetting covariance or correlation among the fixed-income, FX, and equity trading positions. In particular, some of these asset shocks (adverse moves) may be negatively correlated. As is well known from modern portfolio theory, this will reduce the degree of portfolio risk.

Table 10–2 shows a hypothetical correlation matrix between daily seven-year zero coupon bond yield changes, Swf/$ spot exchange rate changes, and changes in daily returns on a U.S. stock market index (Wilshire 5000).

From Table 10–2, the correlation between the seven-year zero and Swf/$ is negative (−.2), while the seven-year zero's yield changes and U.S. stock returns (.4) and Swf/$ shocks (.1) are positively correlated.

Using this correlation matrix along with the individual asset *DEAR*s, we can calculate the risk of the whole (three-asset) trading portfolio as[17]

$$DEAR \text{ portfolio} = \begin{bmatrix} (DEAR_z)^2 + (DEAR_{Swf})^2 + (DEAR_{U.S.})^2 \\ + (2 \times \rho_{z,Swf} \times DEAR_z \times DEAR_{Swf}) \\ + (2 \times \rho_{z,U.S.} \times DEAR_z \times DEAR_{U.S.}) \\ + (2 \times \rho_{U.S.Swf} \times DEAR_{U.S.} \times DEAR_{Swf}) \end{bmatrix}^{1/2} \quad (3)$$

Substituting into this equation the calculated individual *DEAR*s (in thousands of dollars), we get

$$DEAR \text{ portfolio} = \begin{bmatrix} (10.77)^2 + (9.32)^2 + (33)^2 + 2\,(-.2)\,(10.77)\,(9.32) \\ + 2\,(.4)\,(10.77)\,(33) + 2\,(.1)\,(9.32)\,(33) \end{bmatrix}^{1/2}$$

$$= \$39,969$$

As can be seen, taking into account the risk of each trading position as well as the correlation structure among those positions' returns, we get a lower measure of portfolio trading risk ($39,969) compared to the case where we simply added the individual trading positions (the sum of which was $53,090). A quick check will reveal that if we had assumed that all three assets were perfectly positively corre-

---

[17]This is a standard relationship from modern portfolio theory in which the standard deviation or risk of a portfolio of three assets is equal to the square root of the sum of the variances of returns on each of the three assets individually plus two times the covariances among each pair of these assets. With three assets there are three covariances. Here we use the fact that a correlation coefficient times the standard deviations on each pair of assets equals the covariance between each pair of assets. Note that *DEAR* is measured in dollars and has the same dimensions as a standard deviation.

TABLE 10–3   Portfolio *DEAR* Spreadsheet

	Interest Rate Risk National Amounts (U.S. $ millions equivalents)									FX Risk		Total	
	1 Month	1 Year	2 Years	3 Years	4 Years	5 Years	7 Years	10 Years	Interest DEAR	Spot FX	FX DEAR	Portfolio Effect	Total DEAR
Australia											AUD		
Belgium											BEF		
Canada											CAD		
Denmark											DKK		
France	19			−30				11	48		FFR		48
Germany	−19			30				−11	27		DEM		27
Italy											LIR		
Japan											YEN		
Netherlands											NLG		
Spain											ESB		
Sweden											SEK		
Switzerland											CHF		
United Kingdom											GBP		
ECU											ECU		
United States						10		10	76		USD		76
Total						10		10	151				151
						Portfolio effect			(62)				(62)
RISK	DATA	PRINT	CLOSE			Total *DEAR* ($ 000s)			89				89

Source: J. P. Morgan, *RiskMetrics* (New York: 1994).

lated (i.e., $\rho_{ij} = 1$), then *DEAR* for the portfolio would have been $53,090. Clearly, even in abnormal market conditions, assuming that asset returns are perfectly correlated will exaggerate the degree of trading risk exposure.

Table 10–3 shows the type of spreadsheet used by banks such as J. P. Morgan to calculate *DEAR*. As you can see, in this example positions can be taken in 15 different country (currency) bonds in eight different maturity buckets.[18] There is also a column for FX risk (and, if necessary, equity risk) in these different country markets.

In the example in Table 10–3, while the bank is holding offsetting long and short positions in both German and French bonds, the bank is still exposed to trading risk of $48,000 and $27,000, respectively (as can be seen from the column Interest *DEAR*). This is because the French yield curve is more volatile than the German and shocks at different maturity buckets are not equal. The *DEAR* figure for a U.S. bond position of long $20 million is $76,000. As can be seen, adding these three positions yields a *DEAR* of $151,000. However, this ignores the fact that German, French, and U.S. yield shocks are not perfectly correlated. Taking into account these offsetting effects (the "portfolio effect") results in a total *DEAR* of only $89,000. This would be the number reported to JPM's senior management. The 1998 annual report of J. P. Morgan showed that DEAR increased throughout most

---

[18]Bonds held with different maturity dates (e.g., six years) are split into two and allocated to the nearest two of the eight maturity buckets (here, five years and seven years) using three criteria:

1. The sum of the current market *value* of the two resulting cash flows must be identical to the market value of the original cash flow.
2. The market *risk* of the portfolio of two cash flows must be identical to the overall market risk of the original cash flow.
3. The two cash flows have the same *sign* as the original cash flow.

See J. P. Morgan, RiskMetrics—Technical document, November 1994. pp. 35–36.

of the year, reaching a high of $55 million around the time of the Russian bond default crisis.

Currently, the number of markets covered by JPM's traders and the number of correlations among those markets require the daily production and updating of over 450 volatility estimates (σ) and correlations (ρ). These data are updated daily.

Concept Questions

1. Why is market risk measurement important for FIs?
2. What is the ultimate objective of market risk measurement models?
3. Referring to the example on page 185, what is the *DEAR* for this bond if (σ) had been 15 bp?
4. Referring to the example on page 188, what is the *DEAR* of the portfolio if the returns on the three assets are independent of each other?

Historic or Back Simulation Approach

A major criticism of RiskMetrics is the need to assume a symmetric (normal) distribution for all asset returns. Clearly, for some assets, such as options and short-term securities (bonds), this is highly questionable. For example, the most an investor can lose if he or she buys a call option on an equity is the call premium; however, the investor's potential upside returns are unlimited. In a statistical sense, the returns on call options are nonnormal since they exhibit a positive skew.[19]

Because of these and other considerations discussed below, the large majority of FIs that have developed market risk models have employed a historic or back simulation approach. The advantages of this approach are that (1) it is simple, (2) it does not require that asset returns be normally distributed, and (3) it does not require that the correlations or standard deviations of asset returns be calculated.

The essential idea is to take the current market portfolio of assets (FX, bonds, equities, etc.) and revalue them on the basis of the actual prices (returns) that existed on those assets yesterday, the day before that, and so on. Frequently, the FI will calculate the market or value risk of its current portfolio on the basis of prices (returns) that existed for those assets on each of the last 500 days. It would then calculate the 5 percent worst case, that is, the portfolio value that has the 25th lowest value out of 500. That is, on only 25 days out of 500, or 5 percent of the time, would the value of the portfolio fall below this number based on recent historic experience of exchange rate changes, equity price changes, interest rate changes, and so on.

Consider the following simple example in Table 10–4, where a U.S. FI is trading two currencies: the Japanese yen and the Swiss franc. At the close of trade on December 1, 2000, it has a long position in Japanese yen of 500,000,000 and a long position in Swiss francs of 20,000,000. It wants to assess its *VAR*. That is, if tomorrow is that one bad day in 20 (the 5 percent worst case), how much does it stand to lose on its total foreign currency position? As shown in Table 10–4, six steps are required to calculate the *VAR* of its currency portfolio. It should be noted that the same methodological approach would be followed to calculate the *VAR* of any asset, liability, or derivative (bonds, options, etc.) as long as market prices were available on those assets over a sufficiently long historic time period.

---

[19]For a normal distribution, its skew (which is the third moment of a distribution) is zero.

TABLE 10–4   Hypothetical Example of the Historic or Back Simulation Approach Using Two Currencies as of December 1, 2000

	Yen	Swiss Franc
Step 1. Measure Exposures		
1. Closing position on December 1, 2000	500,000,000	20,000,000
2. Exchange rate on December 1, 2000	¥130/$1	Swf 1.4/$1
3. U.S. $ equivalent position on December 1, 2000	3,846,154	14,285,714
Step 2. Measure Sensitivity		
4. 1.01 × current exchange rate	¥131.3	Swf 1.414
5. Revalued position in $s	3,808,073	14,144,272
6. Delta of position ($s) (measure of sensitivity to a 1% adverse change in exchange rate, or row 5 minus row 3)	− 38,081	− 141,442

Step 3. Measure risk of December 1, 2000, closing position using exchange rates that existed on each of the last 500 days

November 30, 2000	Yen	Swiss Franc
7. Change in exchange rate (%) on November 30, 2000	0.5%	0.2%
8. Risk (delta × change in exchange rate)	−19,040.5	−28,288.4
9. Sum of risks = −$47,328.9		

Step 4. Repeat Step 3 for each of the remaining 499 days

November 29, 2000
⋮

April 15, 1999
⋮

November 30, 1998
⋮

Step 5. Rank days by risk from worst to best

DATE	*RISK ($)*
1. May 6, 1999	− $105,669
2. Jan 27, 2000	− $103,276
3. Dec 1, 1998	− $ 90,939
⋮	⋮
25. Nov 30, 2000	− $ 47,328.9
⋮	⋮
499. April 8, 2000	+ $ 98,833
500. July 28, 1999	+ $108,376

Step 6. VAR (25th worst day out of last 500)

VAR = − $47,328.9 (November 30, 2000)

• *Step 1: Measure exposures.* Convert today's foreign currency positions into dollar equivalents using today's exchange rates. Thus, in evaluating the FX position of the FI on December 1, 2000, it has a long position of $3,846,154 in yen and $14,285,714 in Swiss francs.

• *Step 2: Measure sensitivity.* Measure the sensitivity of each FX position by calculating its delta, where delta measures the change in the dollar value of each FX position if the yen or the Swiss franc depreciates (declines in value) by 1 percent against the dollar. As can be seen from Table 10–4, line 6, the delta for the Japanese yen position is −$38,081, and for the Swiss franc position it is −$141,442.

• *Step 3: Measure risk.* Look at the actual percentage changes in exchange rates, yen/$ and Swf/$, on each of the past 500 days. Thus, on November 30, 2000, the yen declined in value against the dollar over the day by 0.5 percent while the Swiss franc declined in value against the dollar by 0.2 percent. (It might be noted that if the currencies were to appreciate in value against the dollar, the sign against the number in row 7 of Table 10–4 would be negative; that is, it takes fewer units of foreign currency to buy a dollar than it did the day before). As can be seen in row 8, combining the delta and the actual percentage change in each FX rate means a total loss of $47,328.9 if the FI had held the current ¥ 500,000,000 and Swf 20,000,000 positions on that day (November 30, 2000).

• *Step 4: Repeat Step 3.* Step 4 repeats the same exercise for the yen and Swiss franc positions but using actual exchange rate changes on November 29, 2000; November 28, 2000; and so on. That is, we calculate the FX losses and/or gains on each of the past 500 trading days, excluding weekends and holidays, when the FX market is closed. This amounts to going back in time over two years. For each of these days the actual change in exchange rates is calculated (row 7) and multiplied by the deltas of each position (the numbers in row 6 of Table 10–4). These two numbers are summed to attain total risk measures for each of the past 500 days.

• *Step 5: Rank days by risk from worst to best.* These risk measures can then be ranked from worst to best. Clearly the worst-case loss would have occurred on this position on May 6, 1999, with a total loss of $105,669. While this "worst-case scenario" is of interest to FI managers, we are interested in the 5 percent worst case, that is, a loss that does not occur more than 25 days out of the 500 days (25 ÷ 500 equals 5 percent). As can be seen, in our example, the 25th worst loss out of 500 occurred on November 30, 2000. This loss amounted to $47,328.9.

• *Step 6: VAR.* If it is assumed that the recent past distribution of exchange rates is an accurate reflection of the likely distribution of FX rate changes in the future—that exchange rate changes have a "stationary" distribution—then the $47,328.9 can be viewed as the FX value at risk *(VAR)* exposure of the FI on December 1, 2000. That is, if tomorrow (in our case December 2, 2000) is a bad day in the FX markets, and given the FI's position of long yen 500 million and long Swf 20 million, the FI can expect to lose $47,328.9 (or more) with a 5 percent probability. This *VAR* measure can then be updated every day as the FX position changes and the delta changes. For example, given the nature of FX trading, the positions held on December 5, 2000, could be very different from those held on December 1, 2000.

The Historic (Back Simulation) Model versus RiskMetrics

One obvious benefit of the historic or back simulation approach is that we do not need to calculate standard deviations and correlations (or assume normal distributions for asset returns) to calculate the portfolio risk figures in row 9 of Table 10–4.[20] A second advantage is that it directly provides a worse-case scenario number, in our example, a loss of $105,669—see step 5. RiskMetrics, since it as-

---

[20]The reason for this is that the historic or back simulation approach uses actual exchange rates on each day which implicitly include correlations or comovements with other exchange rates and asset returns on that day.

sumes asset returns are normally distributed—that returns can go to plus and minus infinity—provides no such worst-case scenario number.[21]

The disadvantage of the back simulation approach is the degree of confidence we have in the 5 percent *VAR* number based on 500 observations. Statistically speaking, 500 observations are not very many, and so there will be a very wide confidence band (or standard error) around the estimated number ($47,328.9 in our example). One possible solution to the problem is to go back in time more than 500 days and estimate the 5 percent *VAR* based on 1,000 past observations (the 50th worst case) or even 10,000 past observations (the 500th worst case). The problem is that as one goes back farther in time, past observations may become decreasingly relevant in predicting *VAR* in the future. For example, 10,000 observations may require the FI to analyze FX data going back 40 years. Over this period we have moved through many very different FX regimes: from relatively fixed exchange rates in the 1950–70 period, to relatively floating exchange rates in the 1970s, to more managed floating rates in the 1980s and 1990s. Clearly, exchange rate behavior and risk in a fixed exchange-rate regime will have little relevance to an FX trader or market risk manager operating and analyzing risk in a floating-exchange rate regime.

This seems to confront the market risk manager with a difficult modeling problem. There are, however, at least two approaches to this problem. The first is to weight past observations in the back simulation unequally, giving a higher weight to the more recent past observations.[22] The second is to use a Monte Carlo simulation approach that generates additional observations that are consistent with recent historic experience. The latter approach in effect amounts to simulating or creating artificial trading days and FX rate changes.

*The Monte Carlo Simulation Approach**

To overcome the problems imposed by a limited number of actual observations, additional observations (in our example, FX changes) can be generated. Normally, the simulation or generation of these additional observations is structured to reflect returns or rates that reflect the probability with which they have occurred in recent historic time periods. The first step is to calculate the historic variance–covariance matrix (Σ) of FX changes. This matrix is then decomposed into two symmetric matrices, A and A'. The only difference between A and A' is that the numbers in the rows of A become the numbers in the columns of A'. This decomposition[23] then allows us to generate "scenarios" for the FX position by multiplying the A' matrix by a random number vector z: 10,000 random values of z are drawn for each FX exchange rate.[24] The A' matrix, which reflects the historic correlations among FX rates, results in realistic FX scenarios being generated when multiplied by the

---

[21]The 5 percent number in RiskMetrics tells us that we will lose more than this amount on 5 days out of every 100; it does not tell us the maximum amount we can lose. As noted in the text, theoretically, with a normal distribution, this could be an infinite amount.

[22]See J. Boudoukh, M. Richardson, and X. R. Whitelaw, "The Best of Both Worlds: A Hybrid Approach to Calculating Value at Risk," New York University, Finance Department, Working Paper, 1998.

[23]The technical term for this procedure is the Cholesky decomposition, where $\Sigma = AA'$.

[24]Technically, let y be an FX scenario; then $y = A'z$. For each FX rate, 10,000 values of z are randomly generated to produce 10,000 values of y. The y values are then used to revalue the FX position and calculate gains and losses.

randomly drawn values of z. The *VAR* of the current position is then calculated as in Table 10–4 above, except that in the Monte Carlo approach the *VAR* is the 500th worst simulated loss out of 10,000.[25]

Regulatory Models: The BIS Standardized Framework

The development of internal market risk models by FIs such as JPM and Chase was done partly in response to proposals by the Bank for International Settlement (BIS) in 1993 to regulate the market risk exposures of banks by imposing capital requirements on their trading portfolios.[26] After refining these proposals over a number of years, the BIS (including the Federal Reserve) decided on a final approach to measuring market risk and the capital reserves necessary for an FI to hold to withstand and survive market risk losses. Since January 1998 banks in the countries that are members of the BIS can calculate their market risk exposures in one of two ways. The first is to use a simple standardized framework (to be discussed below). The second, with regulatory approval, is to use their own internal models, which are similar to the models described above. However, if an internal model is approved for use in calculating capital requirements for the FI, it is subject to regulatory audit and certain constraints. Before looking at these constraints, we examine the BIS standardized framework for, respectively, fixed-income securities, foreign exchange, and equities.

Fixed Income

We can examine the BIS standardized framework for measuring the market risk on the fixed-income (or debt security) trading portfolio by using the example it provides (see Table 10–5). As can be seen, the FI holds long and short positions in various quality debt issues, with maturities ranging from one month to over 20 years. To ameliorate the risk of this trading portfolio, the BIS has proposed two capital charges: (1) a specific risk charge and (2) a general market risk charge.

The specific risk charge is meant to measure the risk of a decline in the liquidity or credit risk quality of the trading portfolio over the FI's holding period. As can be seen, Treasuries have a zero risk weight, while junk bonds (e.g., 10–15 year nonqualifying corporate debt) have a risk weight of 8 percent. As shown in Table 10–5, multiplying the absolute dollar values of all the long and short positions in these instruments by the specific risk weights produces a total specific risk charge of $229.

The general market risk charges or weights reflect the product of the modified durations and interest rate shocks expected for each maturity.[27] This results in a general market risk charge of $66 for the whole fixed-income portfolio.

However, this $66 tends to underestimate interest rate or price risk exposure since it is assumed that long and short positions in the same time band, but in different instruments, can perfectly offset each other. For example, the FI is short 10–15 year U.S. Treasuries with a market risk charge of $67.50 and is long 10–15

---

[25]See, for example, J. P. Morgan, *RiskMetrics,* Technical Document, 4th ed., 1997.

[26]BIS, Basle Committee on Banking Supervision, "The Supervisory Treatment of Market Risks," Basle, Switzerland, April 1993; and "Proposal to Issue a Supplement to the Basle Accord to Cover Market Risks," Basle, Switzerland, April 1995.

[27]For example, for 15–20 year Treasuries in Table 10–5, the modified duration is assumed to be 8.75 years, and the expected interest rate shock is 0.60 percent. Thus, $8.75 \times 0.6 = 5.25$, which is the general market risk weight for these securities shown in Table 10–5. Multiplying 5.25 by the $1,500 long position in these securities results in a general market risk charge of $78.75.

TABLE 10–5   BIS Market Risk Calculation
Debt Securities, Sample Market Risk Calculation

Time Band	Issuer	Position ($)	Specific Risk Weight (%)	Specific Risk Charge	General Market Risk Weight (%)	General Market Risk Charge
0–1 month	Treasury	5,000	0.00%	0.00	0.00%	0.00
1–3 months	Treasury	5,000	0.00	0.00	0.20	10.00
3–6 months	Qual Corp	4,000	0.25	10.00	0.40	16.00
6–12 months	Qual Corp	(7,500)	1.00	75.00	0.70	(52.50)
1–2 years	Treasury	(2,500)	0.00	0.00	1.25	(31.25)
2–3 years	Treasury	2,500	0.00	0.00	1.75	43.75
3–4 years	Treasury	2,500	0.00	0.00	2.25	56.25
3–4 years	Qual Corp	(2,000)	1.60	32.00	2.25	(45.00)
4–5 years	Treasury	1,500	0.00	0.00	2.75	41.25
5–7 years	Qual Corp	(1,000)	1.60	16.00	3.25	(32.50)
7–10 years	Treasury	(1,500)	0.00	0.00	3.75	(56.25)
10–15 years	Treasury	(1,500)	0.00	0.00	4.50	(67.50)
10–15 years	Non Qual	1,000	8.00	80.00	4.50	45.00
15–20 years	Treasury	1,500	0.00	0.00	5.25	78.75
> 20 years	Qual Corp	1,000	1.60	16.00	6.00	60.00
Specific risk				229.00		
Residual general market risk						66.00

Calculation of Capital Charge

	Charge
1. Specific Risk	229.00

2. Vertical Offsets within Same Time Bands

Time Band	Longs	Shorts	Residual*	Offset	Disallowance	Charge
3–4 years	56.25	(45.00)	11.25	45.00	10.00%	4.50
10–15 years	45.00	(67.50)	(22.50)	45.00	10.00	4.50

3. Horizontal Offsets within Same Time Zones
Zone 1

	Longs	Shorts	Residual	Offset	Disallowance	Charge
0–1 month	0.00					
1–3 months	10.00					
3–6 months	16.00					
6–12 months		(52.50)				
Total zone 1	26.00	(52.50)	(26.50)	26.00	40.00%	10.40
Zone 2						
1–2 years		(31.25)				
2–3 years	43.75					
3–4 years	11.25					
Total zone 2	55.00	(31.25)	23.75	31.25	30.00%	9.38
Zone 3						
4–5 years	41.25					
5–7 years		(31.50)				
7–10 years		(56.25)				
10–15 years		(22.50)				
15–20 years	78.75					
>20 years	60.00					
Total zone 3	180.00	(111.25)	68.75	111.25	30.00%	33.38

continued

year junk bonds with a risk charge of $45. However, because of basis risk—that
is, the fact that the rates on Treasuries and junk bonds do not fluctuate exactly
together—we cannot assume that a $45 short position in junk bonds is hedg-
ing an equivalent ($45) risk value of U.S. Treasuries of the same maturity. Thus,
the BIS requires additional capital charges for basis risk, called vertical offsets or

---

TABLE 10–5   *(concluded)*

Time Band	Longs	Shorts	Residual*	Offset	Disallowance	Charge
4. Horizontal Offsets between Time Zones						
Zones 1 and 2	23.75	(26.50)	(2.75)	23.75	40.00%	9.50
Zones 1 and 3	68.75	(2.75)	66.00	2.75	150.00%	4.12
5. Total Capital Charge						
Specific risk						229.00
Vertical disallowances						9.00
Horizontal disallowances						
Offsets within same time zones						53.16
Offsets between time zones						13.62
Residual general market risk after all offsets						66.00
Total						370.78

---

*Residual amount carried forward for additional offsetting as appropriate.

Note: Qual Corp is an investment grade debt issue (e.g., rated BBB and above). Non Qual is a below investment grade debt issue (e.g., rated BB and below), that is, a "junk bond."

disallowance factors. In our case, we disallow 10 percent of the $45 short position in junk bonds in hedging $45 of the long Treasury bond position. This results in an additional capital charge of $4.5.[28] In addition, the debt trading portfolio is divided into three maturity zones: zone 1 (1 month to 12 months), zone 2 (over 1 year to 4 years), and zone 3 (over 4 years to 20 years plus). Again because of basis risk, long and short positions of different maturities in these zones will not perfectly hedge each other. This results in additional (horizontal) disallowance factors of 40 percent (zone 1), 30 percent (zone 2), and 30 percent (zone 3). Finally, any residual long or short position in each zone can only partly hedge an offsetting position in another zone. This leads to a final set of offsets or disallowance factors between time zones. As can be seen, summing the specific risk charges ($229), the general market risk charge ($66), and the basis risk or disallowance charges ($75.78) produces a total risk or capital charge of $370.78.

Foreign Exchange

The standardized model or framework requires the FI to calculate its net exposure in each foreign currency—yen, DM, and so on—and then convert this into dollars at the current spot exchange rate. As shown in Table 10–6, the FI is net long (million dollar equivalent) $50 yen, $100 DM, and $150 £s while being short $20 French francs and $180 Swiss francs. Its total currency long position is $300, and its total short position is $200. The BIS standardized framework imposes a capital requirement equal to 8 percent times the maximum absolute value of the aggregate long or short positions. In this example, 8 percent times $300 million = $24 million. This assumes some partial but not complete offsetting of currency risk by holding opposing long or short positions in different currencies.

Equities

As discussed in the context of the RiskMetrics market value model, there are two sources of risk in holding equities: a firm specific, or unsystematic, risk element and

---

[28]Intuitively, this implies that long-term U.S. Treasury rates and long-term junk bond rates are approximately 90 percent correlated. However, in the final plan, it was decided to cut vertical disallowance factors in half. Thus, a 10 percent disallowance factor becomes a 5 percent disallowance factor, and so on.

**TABLE 10–6   Example of the BIS Standardized Framework Measure of
Foreign Exchange Risk**

Once a bank has calculated its net position in each foreign currency, it converts each position into its
reporting currency and calculates the risk (capital) measure as in the following example, in which the
position in the reporting currency (dollars) has been excluded:

Yen *	*DM*	*GB*	*Fr fr*	*SW fr*
+ 50	+100	+150	−20	−180

$$\underbrace{\hspace{6cm}}_{+300} \qquad \underbrace{\hspace{4cm}}_{-200}$$

The capital charge would be 8 percent of the higher of the longs and shorts (i.e., 300).

*All currencies in $ equivalents.
Source: BIS, 1993.

a market, or systematic, risk element. The BIS proposes to charge for unsystematic
risk by adding the long and short positions in any given stock and applying a 4 percent charge against the gross position in the stock (this is called the *x* factor). Suppose stock number 2, in Table 10–7, was IBM. The FI has a long $100 million and
short $25 million position in that stock. Its gross position that is exposed to unsys-
tematic (firm-specific) risk is $125, which is multiplied by 4 percent, to give a cap-
ital charge of $5 million.

Market or systematic risk is reflected in the net long or short position (this is the
so-called y factor). In the case of IBM, this is $75 million ($100 long minus $25
short). The capital charge would be 8 percent against the $75 million, or $6 million.
The total capital charge (*x* factor + *y* factor) is $11 million for this stock.

This approach is very crude, basically assuming the same β for every stock and
not fully taking into account the benefits from portfolio diversification.

The BIS Regulations and Large Bank Internal Models

As discussed above, the BIS capital requirement for market risk exposure introduced in January 1998 allows large banks (subject to regulatory permission) to use
their own internal models to calculate market risk instead of the standardized framework. However, the required capital calculation has to be relatively conservative
compared to that produced internally. This can be seen by calculating the BIS capital requirements under RiskMetrics. In particular for capital requirement reporting:

1. In calculating *DEAR*, an adverse change in rates has to be defined as being
   in the 99th percentile rather than in the 95th percentile (multiply σ by 2.33
   rather than by 1.65 as under RiskMetrics).
2. The minimum holding period is 10 days (this means that RiskMetrics'
   daily *DEAR* would have to be multiplied by $\sqrt{10}$).

The proposed capital charge or requirement will be the *higher* of:

1. The previous day's *VAR* (value at risk or *DEAR* $\times$ $\sqrt{10}$)
2. The average daily *VAR* over the previous 60 days times a multiplication
   factor with a minimum value of 3 (i.e., Capital charge = $(DEAR) \times (\sqrt{10})$
   $\times$ (3)).

Table 10–7   BIS Capital Requirement for Equities
Illustration of *x* plus *y* Methodology

Under the proposed two-part calculation, there would be separate requirements for the position in each individual equity (i.e., the gross position) and for the net position in the market as a whole. Here we show how the system would work for a range of hypothetical portfolios, assuming a capital charge of 4 percent for the gross positions and 8 percent for the net positions.

Stock	Sum of Long Positions	Sum of Short Positions	Gross Position (sum of cols. 1 and 2)	4 Percent of Gross	Net Position (difference between cols. 1 and 2)	8 Percent of Net	Capital Required (gross + net)
1	100	0	100	4	100	8	12
2	100	25	125	5	75	6	11
3	100	50	150	6	50	4	10
4	100	75	175	7	25	2	9
5	100	100	200	8	0	0	8
6	75	100	175	7	25	2	9
7	50	100	150	6	50	4	10
8	25	100	125	5	75	6	11
9	0	100	100	4	100	8	12

Columns heading span: *x* Factor (Gross Position, 4 Percent of Gross); *y* Factor (Net Position, 8 Percent of Net).

Source: BIS, 1993.

In general, the multiplication factor will make required capital significantly higher than VAR produced from private models.

However, to reduce the burden of capital needs, an additional type of capital can be raised by FIs to meet the capital charge (or requirement). For example, suppose the portfolio *DEAR* was $10 million using the 1 percent worst case (or 99th percentile).

The minimum capital charge would be:[29]

$$\text{Capital charge} = (\$10 \text{ million}) \times (\sqrt{10}) \times (3) = \$94.86 \text{ million}$$

There are three types of capital that can be held to meet this requirement. As explained in greater detail in Chapter 20, capital provides an internal insurance fund to protect an FI and its depositors against losses. The three types of capital are called Tier 1, Tier 2, and Tier 3. Tier 1 capital is essentially retained earnings and common stock, Tier 2 is essentially long-term subordinated debt (over five years), and Tier 3 is short-term subordinated debt with an original maturity of at least two years. Thus, the $94.86 million in the example above can be raised by any of the three capital types subject to the two following limitations: (1) Tier 3 capital is limited to 250 percent of Tier 1 capital, and (2) Tier 2 capital may be substituted for Tier 3 capital up to the same 250 percent limit. For example, suppose Tier 1 capital was $27.10 million and the bank issued short-term Tier 3 debt of $67.76 million. Then the 250

[29]The idea of a minimum multiplication factor of 3 is to create a scheme that is "incentive compatible." Specifically, if FIs using internal models constantly underestimate the amount of capital they need to meet their market risk exposures, regulators can punish those FIs by raising the multiplication factor to as high as 4. Such a response may effectively put the FI out of the trading business. The degree to which the multiplication factor is raised above 3 depends on the number of days an FI's model underestimates its market risk over the preceding year. For example, an underestimation error that occurs on more than 10 days out of the past 250 days will result in the multiplication factor being raised to 4.

percent limit would mean that no more Tier 3 (or Tier 2) debt could be issued to meet a target above $94.86 ($27.1 × 2.5 = $67.76) without additional Tier 1 capital being added. This capital charge for market risk would be added to the capital charge for credit risk to get the bank's total capital requirement. The different types of capital and capital requirements are discussed in more detail in Chapter 20.

Concept Questions

1. What is the BIS standardized framework for measuring market risk?
2. What is the effect of using the 99th percentile (1 percent worst case) rather than the 95th percentile (5 percent worst case) on the measured size of an FI's market risk exposures?

Summary

In this chapter we analyzed the importance of measuring an FI's market risk exposure. This risk is likely to continue to grow in importance as more and more loans and previously illiquid assets become marketable and as the traditional franchises of commercial banks, insurance companies, and investment banks shrink. Given the risks involved, both private FI management and regulators are investing increasing resources in models to measure and track market risk exposures. We analyzed in detail three different approaches FIs have used to measure market risk: RiskMetrics, the historic (or back simulation) approach, and the Monte Carlo simulation approach. The three different approaches were also compared in terms of simplicity and accuracy. Market risk is also of concern to regulators. Beginning in January 1998, banks in the United States and other major countries have had to hold a capital requirement against the risk of their trading positions. The novel feature of the regulation of market risk is that the Federal Reserve and other central banks have given large FIs the option to calculate capital requirements based on their own internal models rather than based on the regulatory model.

Questions and Problems

1. What is meant by *market risk?*
2. Why is the measurement of market risk important to the manager of a financial institution?
3. What is meant by *daily earnings at risk (DEAR)?* What are the three measurable components? What is the price volatility component?
4. Follow Bank has a $1 million position in a five-year, zero-coupon bond with a face value of $1,402,552. The bond is trading at a yield to maturity of 7.00 percent. The historical mean change in daily yields is 0.0 percent, and the standard deviation is 12 basis points.

    a. What is the modified duration of the bond?

    b. What is the maximum adverse daily yield move given that we desire no more than a 5 percent chance that yield changes will be greater than this maximum?

    c. What is the price volatility of this bond?

    d. What is the daily earnings at risk for this bond?

5. What is meant by value at risk (*VAR*)? How is *VAR* related to *DEAR* in J. P. Morgan's RiskMetrics model? What would be the *VAR* for the bond in problem (4) for a 10-day period? With what statistical assumption is our analysis taking liberties? Could this treatment be critical?

6. The *DEAR* for a bank is $8,500. What is the *VAR* for a 10-day period? A 20-day period? Why is the *VAR* for a 20-day period not twice as much as that for a 10-day period?

7. The mean change in the daily yields of a 15-year, zero-coupon bond has been five basis points (bp) over the past year with a standard deviation of 15 bp. Use these data and assume that the yield changes are normally distributed.

    a. What is the highest yield change expected if a 90 percent confidence limit is required; that is, adverse moves will not occur more than one day in 20?

    b. What is the highest yield change expected if a 95 percent confidence limit is required?

8. In what sense is duration a measure of market risk?

9. Bank Alpha has an inventory of AAA-rated, 15-year zero-coupon bonds with a face value of $400 million. The bonds currently are yielding 9.5 percent in the over-the-counter market.

   a. What is the modified duration of these bonds?

   b. What is the price volatility if the potential adverse move in yields is 25 basis points?

   c. What is the *DEAR*?

   d. If the price volatility is based on a 90 percent confidence limit and a mean historical change in daily yields of 0.0 percent, what is the implied standard deviation of daily yield changes?

10. Bank Two has a portfolio of bonds with a market value of $200 million. The bonds have an estimated price volatility of 0.95 percent. What are the *DEAR* and the 10-day *VAR* for these bonds?

11. Bank of Southern Vermont has determined that its inventory of 20 million German deutsche marks (DM) and 25 million British pounds (BP) is subject to market risk. The spot exchange rates are $0.40/DM and $1.28/BP, respectively. The σ's of the spot exchange rates of the DM and BP, based on the daily changes of spot rates over the past six months, are 65 bp and 45 bp, respectively. Determine the bank's 10-day *VAR* for both currencies. Use adverse rate changes in the 95th percentile.

12. Bank of Alaska's stock portfolio has a market value of $10,000,000. The beta of the portfolio approximates the market portfolio, whose standard deviation (σ_m) has been estimated at 1.5 percent. What is the five-day *VAR* of this portfolio using adverse rate changes in the 99th percentile?

13. Jeff Resnick, vice president of operations of Choice Bank, is estimating the aggregate *DEAR* of the bank's portfolio of assets consisting of loans (L), foreign currencies (FX), and common stock (EQ). The individual *DEAR*s are $300,700, $274,000, and $126,700, respectively. If the correlation coefficients (ρ_{ij}) between L and FX, L and EQ, and FX and EQ are 0.3, 0.7, and 0.0, respectively, what is the *DEAR* of the aggregate portfolio?

14. Calculate the *DEAR* for the following portfolio with and without the correlation coefficients.

Assets	Estimated DEAR	$(\rho_{S,\,FX})$	$(\rho_{S,\,B})$	$(\rho_{FX,\,B})$
Stocks (S)	$300,000	− 0.10	0.75	0.20
Foreign Exchange (FX)	$200,000			
Bonds (B)	$250,000			

What is the amount of risk reduction resulting from the lack of perfect positive correlation between the various asset groups?

15. What are the advantages of using the back simulation approach to estimate market risk? Explain how this approach would be implemented.

16. Export Bank has a trading position in Japanese yen and Swiss francs. At the close of business on February 4, the bank had ¥ 300,000,000 and Swf 10,000,000. The exchange rates for the most recent six days are given below:

Exchange Rates per U.S. Dollar at the Close of Business

	2/4	2/3	2/2	2/1	1/29	1/28
Japanese yen	112.13	112.84	112.14	115.05	116.35	116.32
Swiss francs	1.4140	1.4175	1.4133	1.4217	1.4157	1.4123

   a. What is the foreign exchange (FX) position in dollar equivalents using the FX rates on February 4?

   b. What is the definition of delta as it relates to the FX position?

   c. What is the sensitivity of each FX position; that is, what is the value of delta for each currency on February 4?

   d. What is the daily percentage change in exchange rates for each currency over the five-day period?

   e. What is the total risk faced by the bank on each day? What is the worst-case day? What is the best-case day?

   f. Assume that you have data for the 500 trading days preceding February 4. Explain how you would identify the worst-case scenario with a 95 percent degree of confidence?

   g. Explain how the 5 percent value at risk (*VAR*) position would be interpreted for business on February 5.

   h. How would the simulation change at the end of the day on February 5? What variables and/or processes in the analysis may change? What variables and/or processes will not change?

17. What is the primary disadvantage of the back simulation approach in measuring market risk? What effect does the inclusion of more observation days have as a remedy for this disadvantage? What other remedies can be used to deal with the disadvantage?

18. How is Monte Carlo simulation useful in addressing the disadvantages of back simulation? What is the primary statistical assumption underlying its use?

19. In the BIS standardized framework for regulating risk exposure for the fixed-income portfolios of banks, what do the terms *specific risk* and *general market risk* mean? Why does the capital charge for general market risk tend to underestimate the true interest rate or price risk expo-

sure? What additional offsets or disallowance factors are included in the analysis?

20. An FI has the following bonds in its portfolio: long one-year U.S. Treasury bills, short three-year Treasury bonds, long three-year AAA-rated corporate bonds, and long 12-year B-rated (nonqualifying) bonds worth $40, $10, $25, and $10 million, respectively (market values). Using Table 10–5, determine the following:

  a. Charges for specific risk.
  b. Charges for general market risk.
  c. Charges for basis risk: vertical offsets within same time bands only (i.e., ignoring horizon effects).
  d. What is the total capital charge using the information from parts (a) through (c)?

21. Explain how the capital charge for foreign exchange risk is calculated in the BIS standardized model. If an FI has an $80 million long position in deutsche marks, a $40 million short position in British pounds, and a $20 million long position in French francs, what will be the capital charge required against FX market risk?

22. Explain the BIS capital charge calculation for unsystematic and systematic risk for an FI which holds various amounts of equities in its portfolio. What would be the total capital charge required for an FI which holds the following portfolio of stocks? What criticisms can be

levied against this treatment of measuring the risk in the equity portfolio?

Company	Long	Short
Texaco	$45 millon	$25 million
Microsoft	$55 million	$12 million
Robeco	$20 million	
Cifra		$15 million

23. What conditions were introduced by BIS in 1998 to allow large banks to use internally generated models for the measurement of market risk? What types of capital can be held to meet the capital charge requirements?

24. Dark Star Bank has estimated its average *VAR* for the previous 60 days to be $35.5 million. *DEAR* for the previous day was $30.2 million.

  a. Under the latest BIS standards, what is the amount of capital required to be held for market risk?
  b. Dark Star has $15 million of Tier 1 capital, $37.5 million of Tier 2 capital, and $55 million of Tier 3 capital. Is this amount of capital sufficient? If not, what minimum amount of new capital should be raised? Of what type?

CREDIT RISK

Individual Loan Risk

Introduction

In this first of two chapters on credit risk, we look at different approaches to measuring credit or default risk on individual loans (and bonds). In the next chapter we look at methods for evaluating the risk of loan portfolios, or loan concentration risk. Methods for hedging and managing credit risk are left to Chapters 24 to 27. Measurement of the credit risk on individual loans or bonds is crucial if an FI is to (1) price a loan or value a bond correctly and (2) set appropriate limits on the amount of credit it extends to any one borrower or the loss exposure it accepts from any particular counterparty. For example, in recent years Japanese FIs have suffered losses from an overconcentration of loans in real estate and in Asia. Indeed, in 1998 the bad loans of Japanese banks were conservatively estimated to exceed 20 trillion yen, with a majority of banks reporting losses as a result of having to write off these loans. In addition, Japanese life insurers were heavily exposed through their 14 trillion yen loan exposure to Japanese banks.

Before we look at the measurement of credit risk, we first look at the types of loans—as well as the characteristics of those loans—made by U.S. FIs.

Credit Quality Problems

Junk Bond
A bond rated as speculative or less than investment grade by bond-rating agencies such as Moody's.

Over the past two decades the credit quality of many FIs' lending and investment decisions has raised a great deal of attention. In the 1980s there were tremendous problems with bank loans to less developed countries (LDCs) as well as thrift and bank residential and farm mortgage loans. In the early 1990s attention switched to the problems of commercial real estate loans—to which banks, thrifts, and insurance companies were all exposed—as well as **junk bonds.** More recently concerns have been raised about the rapid growth in low-quality auto loans and credit cards as well as the effects on U.S. FIs of the financial crises in Asian countries such as Korea, Indonesia, Thailand, and Malaysia.

Nevertheless, over most of the 1990s the asset quality of U.S. banks has continued to improve even in the face of a prolonged spurt in the growth of loans (see Figure 11–1). This improvement in asset quality—measured by the decline in the ratio of nonperforming loans to loans[1] from 3.9 percent in 1991 to less than 1 percent in 1998—reflects, in part, the continued expansion of the U.S. economy as well as improvements in the way FIs measure and manage credit risk (see below).

Credit quality problems, in the worst case, can result in FI insolvency. Or they can result in such a significant drain on capital and net worth that they adversely affect an FI's growth prospects and ability to compete with other domestic and international FIs.

However, credit risk doesn't apply only to traditional areas of lending and bond investing. As banks and other FIs have expanded into credit guarantees and other off-balance-sheet activities (see Chapter 13), new types of credit risk exposure have arisen, causing concern among managers and regulators. Thus, credit risk analysis is now important for a whole variety of contractual agreements between FIs and counterparties.[2]

---

[1]Nonperforming loans are loans that are 90 days or more past due or are not accruing interest.

[2]This is one of the reasons for bank regulators' setting capital requirements against credit risk (see Chapter 20).

FIGURE 11–1

Loan Growth and Asset Quality

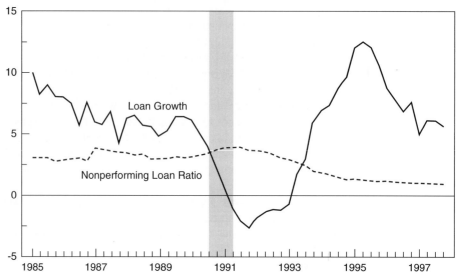

Loan growth is measured as the simple change from its year-ago level.
Shaded area represents a business recession.
Source: Federal Reserve Bank of St. Louis, *Monetary Trends,* April 1998.

Concept Questions

1. What are some of the credit quality problems faced by FIs over the last two decades?
2. What are some of the newer, nontraditional activities that create credit risk for today's FIs?

Types of Loans

Although most FIs make loans, the types of loans made and the characteristics of those loans differ considerably. In this section we concentrate on analyzing the major types of loans made by U.S. commercial banks. Remember from Chapters 1 through 5, however, that other FIs, such as thrifts, finance companies, and insurance companies, are also heavily engaged in lending, especially in the real estate area. We also discuss important aspects of their loan portfolios.

Table 11–1 shows a recent breakdown of the aggregate loan portfolio of U S. commercial banks into four broad classes: commercial and industrial (C&I), real estate, individual, and all other. We briefly look at each of these loan classes in turn.

Commercial and Industrial Loans

The broad figures in Table 11–1 disguise a great deal of heterogeneity in the commercial and industrial loan portfolio. Indeed, commercial loans can be made for periods as short as a few weeks to as long as eight years or more. They can be made in quite small amounts such as $100,000 to small businesses or in packages as large as $10 million or more to major corporations. In addition, they can be secured or unsecured. A **secured loan** is one backed by specific assets of the borrower; if the borrower defaults, the lender has a first lien or claim on those assets. In the terminology

Secured Loan
A loan that is backed by a first claim on certain assets (collateral) of the borrower if default occurs.

TABLE 11–1   Types of U.S. Bank Loans, January 1998
(in billions of dollars)

	Amount	*Percent*
Total loans*	$3,009	100.0%
C&I	857	28.5
Real estate	1,228	40.8
Individual	509	16.9
Other	415	13.8

*Excluding interbank loans.
Source: Federal Reserve Bulletin, April 1998, Table 1.26.

Unsecured Loan
A loan that only has a general claim to the assets of the borrower if default occurs.

Spot Loan
The loan amount is withdrawn by the borrower immediately.

Loan Commitment
A credit facility with a maximum size and a maximum period of time over which the borrower can withdraw funds.

of finance, secured debt is senior to an **unsecured loan,** or junior debt, that has only a general claim on the assets of the borrower if default occurs. As we explain later in this chapter, there is normally a trade-off between the security or collateral backing of a loan and the loan interest rate or risk premium charged by the lender on a loan.[3]

In addition, loans can be made at either fixed rates of interest or floating rates. A fixed-rate loan has the rate of interest set at the beginning of the contract period. This rate remains in force over the loan contract period no matter what happens to market rates. Suppose, for example, IBM borrowed $10 million at 10 percent for one year but the bank's cost of funds rose over the course of the year. Because this is a fixed-rate loan, the bank bears all the interest rate risk. This is why many loans have floating-rate contractual terms. The loan rate can be periodically adjusted according to a formula so that the interest rate risk is transferred in large part from the bank to the borrower. As might be expected, longer-term loans are more likely to be made under floating-rate contracts than are relatively short-term loans.

Finally, loans can be made either spot or under commitment. A **spot loan** is made by the bank, and the borrower uses or takes down the whole loan amount immediately. With a **loan commitment,** by contrast, the lender makes an amount of credit available such as $10 million; the borrower has the option to take down any amount up to the $10 million at any time over the commitment period. In a fixed-rate loan commitment, the interest rate to be paid on any takedown is established at the time the loan commitment contract originates. In a floating-rate commitment, the borrower pays the loan rate in force at the time at which the loan is actually taken down. For example, suppose the $10 million IBM loan was made under a one-year loan commitment. At the time the loan commitment was originated (say, January 2001), IBM borrows nothing. Instead, it waits until six months has passed (say, June 2001) before it takes down the whole $10 million. IBM would pay the loan rate in force as of June 2001. We discuss the special features of loan commitments more fully in Chapter 13.

To get some idea of the basic characteristics of C&I loans, the Federal Reserve surveys more than 400 banks each quarter. Table 11–2 shows the major characteristics in a recent lending survey. As you can see, there were more short-term (under one year) C&I loans than long-term loans. Also, short-term loans are less likely to

[3]A recent empirical study has confirmed such a trade-off; see A. Berger and G. Udell, "Lines of Credit, Collateral and Relationship Lending in Small Firm Finance," *Journal of Business* 68 (July 1995), pp. 351–82.

TABLE 11–2   Characteristics of Commercial Loan Portfolios, November 3–7, 1997

	Long-Term Loans	*Short-Term Loans (under one year)*
Amount outstanding	$4.213 billion	$134.78 billion
Average size of loan	$327,000	$787,000
Weighted-average maturity	57 months	321 days
Percent of which made under commitment	52.8%	75.7%
Percent of loans secured by collateral	60.7%	33.4%
Most common pricing	Prime rate	Fed funds rate

Source: *Federal Reserve Bulletin,* February 1998, Table 4.23.

be made under commitment than long-term loans and are less likely to be backed or secured by collateral.

Finally, as we noted in Chapter 1, commercial loans are declining in importance in bank loan portfolios. The major reason for this has been the rise in nonbank loan substitutes, especially commercial paper. Commercial paper is a short-term debt instrument issued by corporations either directly or via an underwriter to purchasers in the financial markets, such as money market mutual funds. By using commercial paper, a corporation can sidestep banks and the loan market while raising funds at rates that often are below those banks charge. Moreover, since only the largest corporations can tap the commercial paper market, banks are left facing a pool of increasingly smaller and more risky borrowers in the C&I loan market. This makes credit risk evaluation more important today than ever before. As of January 1998, the total commercial paper outstanding was $970 billion compared to C&I loans of $857 billion.

Real Estate Loans

Real estate loans include primarily mortgage loans but also some revolving home equity loans (approximately 8 percent of the real estate loan portfolio).[4] We show the distribution of mortgage debt for U.S. banks for the third quarter of 1997 in Table 11–3.

As you can see, for banks (as well as thrifts), residential mortgages are still the largest component of the real estate loan portfolio; until recently, however, commercial real estate mortgages were the fastest growing component of real estate loans. Moreover, commercial real estate loans make up more than 80 percent of life insurance companies' real estate portfolios.

As with C&I loans, the characteristics of residential mortgage loans differ widely. These characteristics include the size of loan, the ratio of the loan to the property's price, the loan price or loan value ratio, and the maturity of the mortgage. Other important characteristics are the mortgage interest (or commitment) rate and fees and charges on the loan, such as commissions, discounts, and points paid by the

---

[4]Under home equity loans, borrowers use their homes as collateral backing for loans. For recent trends in home equity lending, see *Federal Reserve Bulletin,* April 1998, pp. 241–53.

TABLE 11–3   The Distribution of U.S. Commercial Bank Real Estate Mortgage Debt, Third Quarter 1997

	Percent
One- to four-family residences	76.5%
Multifamily residences	6.2
Commercial	15.5
Farm	1.8
	100.0%

Source: *Federal Reserve Bulletin*, April 1998, Table 1.54.

FIGURE 11–2

ARMs' Share of Total Loans Closed, 1992–1997

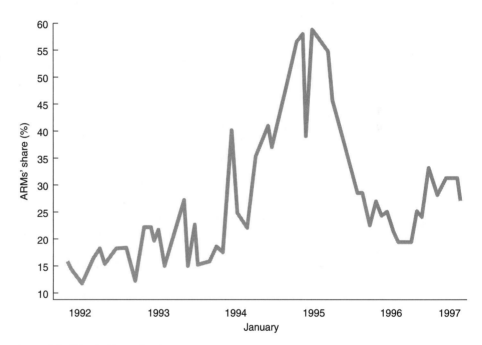

Source: Federal Housing Finance Board.

Adjustable Rate Mortgage (ARM)
A mortgage whose interest rate adjusts with movements in an underlying market index interest rate.

borrower or the seller to obtain the loan.[5] In addition, the mortgage rate differs according to whether the mortgage has a fixed rate or a floating rate, also called an adjustable rate. **Adjustable rate mortgages (ARMs)** have their contractual rates periodically adjusted to some underlying index, such as the T-bond rate. The proportion of fixed-rate to adjustable rate mortgages in FI portfolios varies with the interest rate cycle. In low-interest-rate periods, borrowers prefer fixed-rate to adjustable rate mortgages. As a result, the proportion of ARMs to fixed-rate mortgages can vary considerably over the rate cycle. In Figure 11–2, note the behavior of ARMs over one recent interest rate cycle—1992 to 1997—when interest rates rose and then fell.

Table 11–4 includes a summary of the major contractual terms on conventional fixed-rate mortgages as of January 1998.

---

[5]Points are a certain percentage of the face value of the loan paid up front, as a fee, by the borrower to the lender.

TABLE 11–4   Contractual Terms on Conventional New Home Mortgages, January 1998
(in thousands of dollars)

Purchase price	184.1
Amount of loan	142.3
Loan to value ratio (percent)	80.5%
Maturity (years)	28.5
Fees and charges (percent of loan amount)	0.91%
Contract rate (percent)	7.13%

Source: *Federal Reserve Bulletin,* April 1998, Table 1.53.

Residential mortgages are very long-term loans with an average maturity of approximately 28 years. To the extent that house prices can fall below the amount of the loan outstanding—that is, the loan to value ratio rises—the residential mortgage portfolio can also be susceptible to default risk. For example, during the collapse in real estate prices in Houston, Texas, in the late 1980s, many house prices actually fell below the prices of the early 1980s. This led to a dramatic surge in the proportion of mortgages defaulted on and eventually foreclosed by banks and thrifts.

Individual (Consumer) Loans

Another major type of loan is the individual or consumer loan, such as personal and auto loans. Commercial banks, finance companies, retailers, savings banks, and oil companies also provide consumer loan financing through credit cards such as Visa, MasterCard, and proprietary credit cards issued by Sears and AT&T. The Contemporary Perspectives box on p. 209 shows how a typical credit card transaction works. The five largest credit card issuers and their outstanding balances in 1997 are shown in Table 11–5.

In Table 11–6 are the three major classes of consumer loans at U.S. banks. The largest class of loans is revolving consumer loans, which include credit card debt. With a **revolving loan,** the borrower has a credit line on which to draw as well as to repay up to some maximum over the life of the credit contract. In recent years, banks have normally faced default rates between 3 and 7 percent on their credit card outstandings. These default rates are significantly higher than those on commercial loans (see Figure 11–3). Such relatively high default rates again point to the importance of risk evaluation prior to the credit decision. The other major class of consumer loans is for new or used automobile purchases. Finally, other consumer loans include fixed-term consumer loans such as 24-month personal loans as well as loans to purchase mobile homes.

In Table 11–7 we show indicative rates on car, personal, mobile home, and credit card loans as of November 1997. These rates differ widely depending on features such as collateral backing, maturity, default rate experience, and noninterest rate fees. In addition, competitive conditions in each market as well as regulations such as state-imposed **usury ceilings** all affect the rate structure for consumer loans.

Other Loans

The other loans category can include a wide variety of borrowers and types, including other banks, nonbank financial institutions (such as call loans to investment

Revolving Loan
A credit line on which a borrower can both draw and repay many times over the life of the loan contract.

Usury Ceilings
State-imposed ceilings on the maximum rate FIs can charge on consumer and mortgage debt.

Contemporary Perspectives

PAYMENT FLOWS IN A TYPICAL
CREDIT CARD TRANSACTION

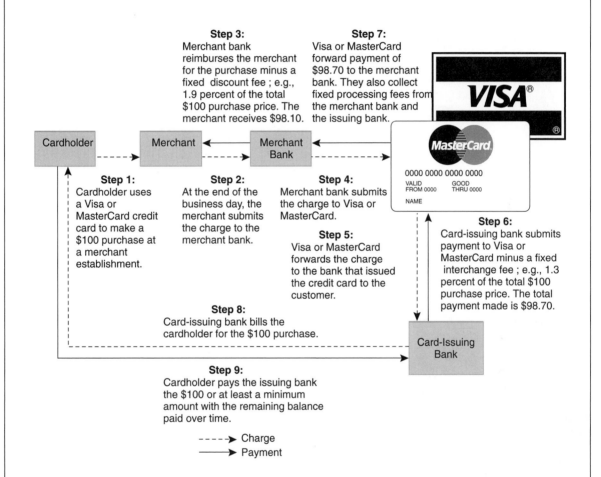

Step 3:
Merchant bank reimburses the merchant for the purchase minus a fixed discount fee ; e.g., 1.9 percent of the total $100 purchase price. The merchant receives $98.10.

Step 7:
Visa or MasterCard forward payment of $98.70 to the merchant bank. They also collect fixed processing fees from the merchant bank and the issuing bank.

Step 1:
Cardholder uses a Visa or MasterCard credit card to make a $100 purchase at a merchant establishment.

Step 2:
At the end of the business day, the merchant submits the charge to the merchant bank.

Step 4:
Merchant bank submits the charge to Visa or MasterCard.

Step 5:
Visa or MasterCard forwards the charge to the bank that issued the credit card to the customer.

Step 6:
Card-issuing bank submits payment to Visa or MasterCard minus a fixed interchange fee ; e.g., 1.3 percent of the total $100 purchase price. The total payment made is $98.70.

Step 8:
Card-issuing bank bills the cardholder for the $100 purchase.

Step 9:
Cardholder pays the issuing bank the $100 or at least a minimum amount with the remaining balance paid over time.

- - - -► Charge
———► Payment

A typical credit card transaction involves the cardholder, the merchant, the merchant's bank, Visa or MasterCard, and the depository institution that issued the credit card. In most cases, the merchant will seek authorization for the purchase from the cardholder's bank via a computer hookup provided by Visa or MasterCard or an independent company such as Nabanco. The issuing bank maintains information on the cardholder's credit limit and can authorize a transaction in as little as two seconds, according to a Visa official.

During the processing of credit card transactions, fixed fees are charged to the merchant, the merchant's bank, and the card issuer. The merchant's bank subtracts a "discount" fee of 1.9 percent of the total purchase price as compensation for providing credit card processing services to the merchant. An "interchange" fee of 1.3 percent of the total purchase price is paid to the depository institution that issued the credit card. Finally, Visa and MasterCard charge fixed processing fees to the merchant bank and the card issuers for using their computerized transactions settlement systems.

Source: GAO (1994) (GAO/GGD-94-23), p. 57.

TABLE 11–5   Biggest Credit Card Issuers as of June 1997

Card Issuer	Total Outstanding Balances, billions of dollars	Change from Year Earlier, percent
Citicorp	$45.8	+7%
MBNA America	39.1	+35%
Chase/Chemical	26.3	+12%
First USA	24.6	+31%
First Chicago NBD	17.1	−2%

Source: The Nilson Report.

TABLE 11–6   Types of Consumer Loan at Commercial Banks, December 1997

	Percent
Automobile	33.5%
Revolving	42.8%
Other	23.7%
	100.0%

Source: *Federal Reserve Bulletin,* April 1998, Table 1.55.

TABLE 11–7   Interest Rate Terms on Consumer Loans, November 1997

	Percent
48-month car loan	8.96%
24-month personal loan	14.50%
Credit card	15.65%

Source: *Federal Reserve Bulletin,* April 1998, Table 1.56.

banks), state and local governments, foreign banks, and sovereign governments.[6] We discuss sovereign loans in Chapter 16.

Concept Questions

1. What are the four major types of loans made by U.S. commercial banks? What are the basic distinguishing characteristics of each type of loan?
2. Will more ARMs be originated in high- or low-interest-rate environments? Explain your answer.
3. In Table 11–7, explain why credit card loan rates are much higher than car loan rates.

---

[6]A call loan is a loan contract enabling the lender (e.g., the bank) to request repayment of a loan at any time in the contract period. A noncallable loan leaves the timing of the repayment in the hands of the borrower subject to the limit of the maturity of the loan. For example, most broker loans to investment banks are callable within the day and have to be repaid immediately at the bank lender's request.

FIGURE 11–3

*Credit Card Losses,
1995–1997*

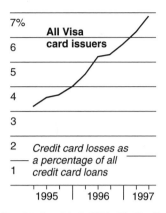

Source: *New York Times,* October 22, 1997, p. D1. Copyright © 1997 by The New York Times. Reprinted by permission.

The Return on a Loan

The Contractually Promised Return on a Loan

The previous description of loans makes it clear that a number of factors impact the promised return an FI achieves on any given loan. These factors include:

1. The interest rate on the loan.
2. Any fees relating to the loan.
3. The credit risk premium on the loan.
4. The collateral backing of the loan.
5. Other nonprice terms (especially compensating balances and reserve requirements).

Compensating Balance
A proportion of a loan that a borrower is required to hold on deposit at the lending institution.

Compensating balances are a proportion of a loan that a borrower cannot actively use for expenditures. Instead, these balances have to be kept on deposit at the FI. For example, a borrower facing a 10 percent compensating balance requirement on a $100 loan would have to place $10 on deposit (traditionally on demand deposit) with the bank and could use only $90 of the $100 borrowed. This requirement raises the effective cost of loans for the borrower since the deposit rate earned on compensating balances is less than the borrowing rate. Thus, compensating balance requirements act as an additional source of return on lending for an FI.[7] Consequently, while credit risk may be the most important factor ultimately affecting the return on a loan, these other factors should not be ignored by FI managers in evaluating loan profitability and risk. Indeed, FIs can compensate for high credit risk in a number of ways other than charging a higher explicit interest rate or risk premium on a loan or restricting the amount of credit available. In particular, higher fees, high compensating balances, and increased collateral backing all offer implicit and indirect methods of compensating an FI for lending risk.

Next, we look at an example of how the promised return on a C&I loan may vary by choosing specific noninterest rate terms. Suppose a bank makes a spot one-year, $1 million loan. The loan rate is set at

---

[7]They also create a more stable supply of deposits and thus mitigate liquidity problems.

$$\text{Base lending rate} = 12\% = L$$
$$\text{plus}$$
$$\text{Risk premium} = \underline{2\% = m}$$
$$14\% = L + m$$

LIBOR
The London Interbank Offered Rate, which is the rate for interbank dollar loans in the offshore or Eurodollar market of a given maturity.

Prime Lending Rate
The base lending rate periodically set by banks.

The base lending rate (L) could reflect the bank's marginal cost of funds, such as the commercial paper rate, the federal funds rate, or **LIBOR**—the London Interbank Offered Rate. Alternatively, it could reflect the **prime lending rate.** As shown in Table 11–2, the prime rate is most commonly used in "pricing" longer-term loans, while the fed funds rate is most commonly used in pricing short-term loans. Traditionally, the prime rate was the rate charged to the bank's lowest risk customers. Now, it is more of a base rate to which positive or negative risk premiums can be added. In other words, the best and largest borrowers now commonly pay below prime rate to be competitive with the commercial paper market.[8]

Suppose the bank also:

1. Charges a $\frac{1}{8}$ percent loan origination fee (f) to the borrower.
2. Imposes a 10 percent compensating balance requirement (b) to be held as noninterest-bearing demand deposits.
3. Pays reserve requirements (R) of 10 percent imposed by the Federal Reserve on the bank's demand deposits, including any compensating balances.

Then the contractually promised gross return on the loan, k, per dollar lent would equal[9]

$$1 + k = 1 + \frac{f + (L + m)}{1 - [b(1 - R)]}$$

This formula may need some explanation. The numerator is the promised gross cash inflow to the FI per dollar, reflecting fees plus interest. In the denominator, for every \$1 in loans the FI lends, it retains b as noninterest-bearing compensating balances. Thus, $1 - b$ is the cash outflow from the bank, ignoring reserve requirements. However, since b (compensating balances) are held by the borrower at the bank as demand deposits, the Federal Reserve requires the bank to hold noninterest-bearing reserves at the rate R against these compensating balances. Thus, the net benefit from compensating balances has to take into account noninterest-bearing reserve requirements. The net outflow by the bank per \$1 of loans is $1 - [b(1 - R)]$ or, 1 minus the reserve adjusted compensating balance requirement.

Plugging in the numbers from our example into this formula, we have[10]

---

[8]For more information on the prime rate, see P. Nabar, S. Park, and A. Saunders, "Prime Rate Changes: Is There an Advantage in Being First?" *Journal of Business* 66 (1993), pp. 69–92; and L. Mester and A. Saunders, "When Does the Prime Rate Change?" *Journal of Banking and Finance* 19 (1995), pp. 743–64.

[9]This formula ignores present value aspects that could easily be incorporated. For example, fees are earned in up-front undiscounted dollars while interest payments and risk premiums are normally paid on loan maturity and thus should be discounted by the bank's cost of funds.

[10]If we take into account the present value effects on the fees and the interest payments and assume that the bank's discount rate (d) was $12\frac{1}{2}$ percent, then the $L + m$ term needs to be discounted by $1 + d = 1.125$ while fees (as up-front payments) are undiscounted. In this case, k is 13.81 percent.

$$1 + k = 1 + \frac{.00125 + (.12 + .02)}{1 - [(.10)(.9)]}$$

$$1 + k = 1 + \frac{.14125}{.91}$$

$$1 + k = 1.1552 \text{ or } k = 15.52\%$$

This is, of course, greater than the simple promised interest return on the loan, $L + m = 14\%$.

In the special case where fees (f) are zero and the compensating balance (b) is zero:

$$f = 0$$
$$b = 0$$

the contractually promised return formula reduces to

$$1 + k = 1 + (L + m)$$

That is, the credit risk premium (m) is the fundamental factor driving the promised return on a loan once the base rate on the loan is set.

Note that as credit markets have become more competitive, both origination fees (f) and compensating balances (b) are becoming less important. For example, where compensating balances are still charged, the bank may now require them to be held as time deposits, and they earn interest. As a result, borrowers' opportunity losses from compensating balances have been reduced to the difference between the loan rate and the compensating balance time-deposit rate. Further, in most non-domestic dollar loans made offshore, compensating balance requirements are very rare.[11]

The Expected Return on a Loan

The promised return on the loan ($1 + k$) that the borrower and lender contractually agreed on includes both interest rate and noninterest rate features such as fees. Therefore, it may well differ from the expected and, indeed, actual return on a loan. Default risk is the risk of the borrower being unable or unwilling to fulfill the terms promised under the loan contract. It is usually present to some degree or other in all loans. Thus, at the time the loan is made, the expected return [$E(r)$] per dollar loaned is related to the promised return by

$$E(r) = p(1 + k)$$

where p is the probability of repayment of the loan. To the extent that p is less than 1, default risk is present. This means the FI manager must (1) set the risk premium (m) sufficiently high to compensate for this risk and (2) recognize that setting

---

[11]For a number of interesting examples using similar formulas, see J. R. Brick, *Commercial Banking: Text and Readings* (Haslett, Mich.: Systems Publications Inc., 1984), chapter 4. If compensating balances held as deposits paid interest at 8 percent ($r_d = 8\%$), then the numerator (cash flow) of the bank in the example would be reduced by $b \times r_d$, where $r_d = .08$ and $b = .1$. In this case, the $k = 14.64$ percent. This assumes that the reserve requirement on compensating balances held as time deposits (R) is 10 percent. However, while currently reserve requirements on demand deposits are 10 percent, the reserve requirement on time deposits is 0 percent (zero). Recalculating but assuming $R = 0$ and interest of 8 percent on compensating balances, we find $k = 14.81$ percent.

high risk premiums as well as high fees and base rates may actually reduce the probability of repayment (p). That is, k and p are not independent. Indeed, over some range, they may be negatively related. As a result, FIs usually have to control for credit risk along two dimensions: the price or promised return dimension $(1 + k)$ and the quantity or credit availability dimension. In general, the quantity dimension controls credit risk differences on retail loans more than the price dimension does compared to wholesale loans. We discuss the reasons for this in the next section. That is followed by a section that evaluates different ways in which FI managers can assess the appropriate size of m, the risk premium on a loan. This is the key to pricing wholesale loan and debt risk exposures correctly.

Concept Questions

1. Calculate the promised return (k) on a loan if the base rate is 13 percent, the risk premium is 2 percent, the compensating balance requirement is 5 percent, fees are $\frac{1}{2}$ percent, and reserve requirements are 10 percent.
2. What is the expected return on this loan if the probability of default is 5 percent?

Retail versus Wholesale Credit Decisions

Retail

Because of their small dollar size in the context of an FI's overall investment portfolio and the higher costs of collecting information on household borrowers, most loan decisions made at the retail level tend to be reject or accept decisions. All borrowers who are accepted are often charged the same rate of interest and by implication the same risk premium. For example, a wealthy individual borrowing from a bank to finance the purchase of a Rolls-Royce is likely to be charged the same auto loan rate as a less wealthy individual borrowing to finance the purchase of a Honda. In the terminology of finance, retail customers are more likely to be sorted or rationed by loan quantity restrictions than by price or interest rate differences. Residential mortgage loans provide another good example. While two borrowers may be accepted for mortgage loans, an FI discriminates between them according to the loan to value ratio—the amount it is willing to lend relative to the market value of the house being acquired—rather than by setting a different mortgage rate.[12]

Wholesale

Credit Rationing
Restrictions on the quantity of loans made available to an individual borrower.

Generally, at the retail level an FI controls its credit risks by **credit rationing** rather than by using a range of interest rates or prices. At the wholesale level, FIs use both interest rates and credit quantity to control credit risk. Thus, when banks quote a prime lending rate (L) to certain business borrowers, lower-risk customers are charged a lending rate below the prime lending rate. More risky borrowers are charged an additional markup on prime, or a default risk premium (m), to compensate the FI for the additional risk involved.

---

[12]However, as the cost of information falls and comprehensive databases on individual households' creditworthiness are developed, the size of a loan for which a single interest rate becomes optimal will shrink.

FIGURE 11–4

The Relationship Between the Promised Loan Rate and the Expected Return on the Loan

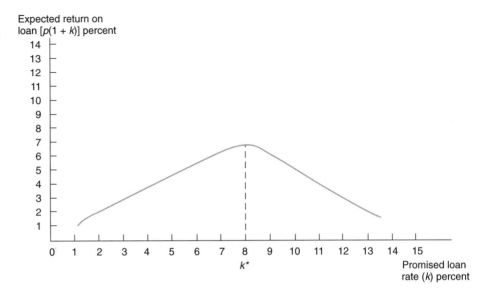

Even though over some range of credit demand FIs may be willing to loan funds to lower-quality wholesale borrowers as long as they are compensated by high enough interest rates, too high lending rates can backfire on the FI, as discussed earlier. For example, a borrower charged 15 percent for a loan—a prime rate of 10 percent plus a risk premium of 5 percent—may be able to repay only by using the funds to invest in highly risky investments with some small chance of a big payoff. However, by definition, many high-risk projects fail to pay off and the borrower may default. In an extreme case, the FI receives neither the promised interest nor the original principal lent. This suggests that very high contractual interest rate charges on loans may actually reduce an FI's expected return on loans because high interest rates induce the borrower to invest in risky projects.[13] Alternatively, only borrowers with risky projects may be interested in borrowing at high interest rates, with low-risk borrowers dropping out of the potential borrowing pool at high-rate levels. This lowers the average quality of the pool of potential borrowers. We show these effects in Figure 11–4.[14]

At very low contractual interest rates (k), borrowers do not need to take high risks in their use of funds and those with relatively safe investment projects use bank financing. As interest rates increase, borrowers with fairly safe low-return projects no longer think it is profitable to borrow from FIs. Alternatively, they may switch to higher-risk investment projects to have a chance of being able to pay off the loan. In terms of Figure 11–4, when interest rates rise above k^*, the additional expected return earned by the FI through higher interest rates (k) is increasingly offset by an increase in the expected default risk on the loan ($1 - p$). In other words, an FI charging wholesale borrowers loan rates in the 9 to 15 percent region can earn a *lower* expected return than will an FI charging 8 percent.

---

[13]In the context of the previous section, a high k on the loan reflecting a high base rate (L) and risk premium (m) can lead to a lower probability of repayment (p) and thus a lower $E(r)$ on the loan, where $E(r) = p(1 + k)$. Indeed, for very high k, the expected return on the loan can become negative.

[14]See also J. Stiglitz and A. Weiss, "Credit Rationing in Markets with Imperfect Information," *American Economic Review* 71 (1981). pp. 393–410.

This relationship between interest rates and the expected returns on loans suggests that beyond some interest rate level it may be best for the FI to *credit ration* its wholesale loans; that is, not to make loans or make fewer loans. Rather than seeking to ration by price by charging higher and higher risk premiums to borrowers, the FI can establish an upper ceiling on the amounts it is willing to lend to maximize its expected returns on lending. In the context of Figure 11–4, borrowers may be charged interest rates up to 8 percent, with the most risky borrowers also facing more restrictive limits or ceilings on the amounts they can borrow at any given interest rate.

Concept Questions

1. Can a bank's return on its loan portfolio increase if it cuts its loan rates?
2. What might happen to the expected return on a wholesale loan if a bank eliminates its fees and compensating balances in a low-interest-rate environment?

Measurement of Credit Risk

To calibrate the default risk exposure of its credit and investment decisions as well as to assess its credit risk exposure in off-balance-sheet contractual arrangements such as loan commitments, an FI manager needs to measure the probability of borrower default. The ability to do this largely depends on the amount of information the FI has about the borrower. At the retail level, much of the information needs to be collected internally or purchased from external credit agencies. At the wholesale level, these information sources are bolstered by publicly available information such as certified accounting statements, stock and bond prices, and analysts' reports. Thus, for a publicly traded company, more information is produced and is available to an FI than is available for a small, single-proprietor corner store. The availability of more information along with the lower average cost of collecting such information, allows FIs to use more sophisticated and usually more quantitative methods in assessing default probabilities for large borrowers compared to small borrowers. However, advances in technology and information collection are making quantitative assessments of even smaller borrowers increasingly feasible and less costly.[15]

In principle, FIs can use very similar methods and models to assess the probabilities of default on both bonds and loans. Even though loans tend to involve fewer lenders to any single borrower as opposed to multiple bondholders, in essence both loans and bonds are contracts that promise fixed (or indexed) payments at regular intervals in the future. Loans and bonds stand ahead of the borrowing firm's equity holders in terms of the priority of their claims if things go wrong. Also, bonds, like loans, include **covenants** restricting or encouraging various actions to enhance the probability of repayment. A common restrictive covenant included in many bond and loan contracts limits the amount of dividends a firm can pay to its equity holders. Clearly, for any given cash flow, a high dividend payout to stockholders means that less is available for repayments to bondholders and lenders. Moreover, bond yields, like wholesale loan rates, usually reflect risk premiums that vary with

Covenants
Restrictions written into bond and loan contracts either limiting or encouraging the borrower's actions that affect the probability of repayment.

---

[15]These advances include database services and software for automating credit assessment provided by companies such as Dun & Bradstreet.

the perceived quality of the borrower and the collateral or security backing of the debt. Given this, FIs can use many of the following models that analyze default risk probabilities either in making lending decisions or when considering investing in corporate bonds offered either publicly or privately.[16]

Concept Questions

1. Is it more costly for an FI manager to assess the default risk exposure of a publicly traded company or a small, single-proprietor firm? Explain your answer.
2. How do loan covenants help protect an FI against default risk?

Default Risk Models

Economists, bankers, and analysts have employed many different models to assess the default risk on loans and bonds. These vary from the relatively qualitative to the highly quantitative. Further, these models are not mutually exclusive in that an FI manager may use more than one to reach a credit pricing or loan quantity rationing decision. As the Contemporary Perspectives box on p. 218 shows and as will be discussed below in more detail, a great deal of time and effort have recently been expended by FIs in building highly technical credit risk evaluation models. Many of these models use ideas and techniques similar to the market risk models discussed in Chapter 10. We analyze a number of models in three broad groups: qualitative models, credit scoring models, and newer models.

Qualitative Models

In the absence of publicly available information on the quality of borrowers, the FI manager has to assemble information from private sources—such as credit and deposit files—and/or purchase such information from external sources—such as credit rating agencies. This information helps a manager make an informed judgment on the probability of default of the borrower and price the loan or debt correctly.

In general, the amount of information assembled varies with the size of the potential debt exposure and the costs of collection. However, a number of key factors enter into the credit decision. These include (1) *borrower-specific* factors that are idiosyncratic to the individual borrower and (2) *market-specific* factors that have an impact on all borrowers at the time of the credit decision. The FI manager then weights these factors to come to an overall credit decision. Because of their reliance on the subjective judgment of the FI manager, these models are often called expert systems.

---

[16]For more discussion of the similarities between bank loans and privately placed debt, see M. Berlin and L. Mester, "Debt Covenants and Renegotiation," *Journal of Financial Intermediation* 2 (1992). pp. 95–133; M. Carey et al., "The Economics of Private Placement: A New Look," *Financial Markets, Institutions and Instruments* 2, no. 3 (1993); and M. Carey et al., "Does Corporate Lending by Banks and Finance Companies Differ? Evidence on Specialization in Private Debt Contracting," *Journal of Finance* 53 (June 1998), pp. 845–78.

MODEL BEHAVIOUR

Banks' credit-risk models are mind-bogglingly complex. But the question they try to answer is actually quite simple: how much of a bank's lending might plausibly turn bad? Armed with the answer, banks can set aside enough capital to make sure they stay solvent should the worst happen.

No model, of course, can take account of every possibility. Credit-risk models try to put a value on how much a bank should realistically expect to lose in the 99.9% or so of the time that passes for normality. This requires estimating three different things: the likelihood that any given borrower will default; the amount that might be recoverable if that happened; and the likelihood that the borrower will default at the same time others are doing so.

This last factor is crucial. In effect, it will decide whether some unforeseen event is likely to wreck the bank. Broadly speaking, the less likely it is that many loans will go bad at the same time—that is, the lower the correlation of the individual risks—the lower the risk will be of a big loss from bad loans.

None of this is easy to do. Many of the banking industry's brightest rocket scientists have been given over to the task. Credit Suisse Financial Products has launched "CreditRisk+", which attempts to provide an actuarial model of the likelihood that a loan will turn bad, much as an insurance firm would produce a forecast of likely claims. McKinsey, a consultancy, has a model that links default probabilities to macroeconomic variables, such as interest rates and growth in GDP. J. P. Morgan's "CreditMetrics" applies a theoretical model of when borrowers default, using credit ratings for bonds and drawing on another model developed by KMV, a Californian firm, which calculates the risk that a firm will default by looking at changes in the price of its shares.

With the help of Taylor-series expansions, Gamma integrals, negative binomial distributions and so forth (we'll spare you the details), the models go from calculating the probability that any one borrower will default, to estimating the chances that Wal-Mart, say, will default at the same time as Woolworth or that loans to French property developers will go bad at the same time as loans to Air France. This leads to a series of loss probabilities for the bank's entire portfolio of loans. This will indicate the maximum loss that the bank needs to prepare for by setting aside capital.

Last year's model

Credit-risk models have evolved from "value-at-risk" models, which were developed to estimate how much of a bank's trading portfolio—foreign exchange, cash, securities and derivatives—it could lose in a single day because of adverse movements in financial prices. These models have been criticised for assuming that past correlations in the prices of different assets will hold in future and for making simplistic assumptions about the range of possible price changes. They also fail when prices for the underlying assets become unavailable—when a stockmarket suspends trading, for example. These criticisms apply just as well to credit-risk models.

Value-at-risk models have one big advantage over credit-risk models, however. They generally deal with assets that are publicly traded, so there is a vast amount of data for the models to crunch. It is far harder to come up with data on the market value of loans or on how much of the value of bad loans banks eventually recover. That leaves it uncertain whether the results cranked out by credit-risk models are statistically valid. The models are clever, all right. But how much relation they bear to reality may not be clear until after the next recession.

FIGURE 11–5

The Relationship Between the Cost of Debt, the Probability of Default, and Leverage

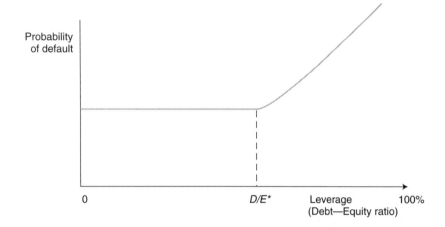

Borrower-Specific Factors

Implicit Contract
Long-term customer relationship between a borrower and lender based on reputation.

Reputation.   The borrower's reputation involves the borrowing-lending history of the credit applicant. If, over time, the borrower has established a reputation for prompt and timely repayment, this enhances the applicant's attractiveness to the FI. A long-term customer relationship between a borrower and lender forms an **implicit contract** regarding borrowing and repayment that extends beyond the formal explicit legal contract on which borrower-lender relationships are based. The importance of reputation, which can be established only over time through repayment and observed behavior, works to the disadvantage of small, newer borrowers. This is one of the reasons why initial public offerings of debt securities by small firms often require higher yields than do offerings of older, more seasoned firms.[17]

Leverage
The ratio of a borrower's debt to equity.

Leverage.   A borrower's **leverage** or capital structure—the ratio of debt to equity—affects the probability of its default. This is the case because large amounts of debt, such as bonds and loans, increase the borrower's interest charges and pose a significant claim on its cash flows. As shown in Figure 11–5, relatively low debt–equity ratios may not significantly impact the probability of debt repayment. Yet beyond some point, the risk of bankruptcy increases, as does the probability of some loss of interest or principal for the lender. Thus, highly leveraged firms, such as firms recently engaged in leveraged buyouts (LBOs) financed in part by FIs' provision of junk bonds or below–investment grade debt, may find it necessary to pay higher risk premiums on their borrowings if they are not rationed in the first place.[18]

Volatility of Earnings.   As with leverage, a highly volatile earnings stream increases the probability that the borrower cannot meet fixed interest and principal charges for any given capital structure. Consequently newer firms or firms in

---

[17]For the link between bank finance and the cost of initial public offerings of securities, see C. James and P. Weir, "Borrowing Relationships, Intermediation, and the Costs of Issuing Public Securities," *Journal of Financial Economics* 28 (1992), pp. 149–71.

[18]However, S. J. Grossman and O. D. Hart argue that high debt (leverage) may be a signal of managerial efficiency and may in fact lower bankruptcy risk. Similar arguments have been made about the efficiency incentives for managers in junk bond–financed LBOs. That is, firms with a lot of debt have to be "lean and mean" to meet their repayment commitments. See "Corporate Financial Structure and Managerial Incentives," in *The Economics of Information and Uncertainty*, ed. J. McCall (Chicago: Chicago University Press, 1982).

high-tech industries with a high earnings variance over time are less attractive credit risks than are those with long and more stable earnings histories.

Collateral.   As discussed earlier, a key feature in any lending and loan-pricing decision is the degree of collateral or assets backing the security of the loan. Many loans and bonds are backed by specific assets should a borrower default on repayment obligations. Mortgage bonds give the bondholder first claim to some specific piece of property of the borrower, normally machinery or buildings; debentures give a bondholder a more general and more risky claim to the borrower's assets. Subordinated debentures are even riskier because their claims to the assets of a defaulting borrower are junior to those of both mortgage bondholders and debenture bondholders. Similarly, loans can be either secured (collateralized) or unsecured (uncollateralized).[19]

Market-Specific Factors

The Business Cycle.   The position of the economy in the business cycle phase is enormously important to an FI in assessing the probability of borrower default. For example, during recessions, firms in the consumer durable goods sector that produce autos, refrigerators, or houses do relatively badly compared to those in the nondurable goods sector producing tobacco and foods. People cut back on luxuries during a recession but are less likely to cut back on necessities such as food. Thus, corporate borrowers in the consumer durable goods sector of the economy are especially prone to default risk. Because of cyclical concerns, FIs are more likely to increase the relative degree of credit rationing in recessionary phases. This has especially adverse consequences for smaller borrowers with limited or no access to alternative credit markets such as the commercial paper market.[20]

The Level of Interest Rates.   High interest rates indicate restrictive monetary policy actions by the Federal Reserve. FIs not only find funds to finance their lending decisions scarcer and more expensive but also must recognize that high interest rates are correlated with higher credit risk in general. As discussed earlier, high interest rate levels may encourage borrowers to take excessive risks and/or encourage only the most risky customers to borrow.

So far, we have delineated just a few of the qualitative borrower and economy-specific factors an FI manager may take into account in deciding on the probability of default on any loan or bond.[21] Rather than letting such factors enter into the decision process in a purely subjective fashion, the FI manager may weight these

---

[19]However, collateralized loans are still subject to some default risk unless these loans are significantly overcollateralized; that is, assets are pledged with market values exceeding the face value of the debt instrument. There is also some controversy as to whether posting collateral signifies a high- or low-risk borrower. Arguably, the best borrowers do not need to post collateral since they are good credit risks, whereas only more risky borrowers need to post collateral. That is, posting collateral may be a signal of more rather than less credit risk. See, for example, A. Berger and G. Udell, "Lines Of Credit, Collateral and Relationship Lending in Small Firm Finance," *Journal of Business,* 1995.

[20]For a good discussion of the sensitivity of different U.S. industries' default rates to the business cycle, see J. D. Taylor, "Cross-Industry Differences in Business Failure Rates: Implications for Portfolio Management," *Commercial Lending Review,* 1998, pp. 36–46.

[21]More generally, J. F. Sinkey identifies five Cs of credit that should be included in any subjective (qualitative) credit analysis: character (willingness to pay), capacity (cash flow), capital (wealth), collateral (security), and conditions (economic conditions). See *Commercial Bank Financial Management—In the Financial Services Industry,* 5th ed. (New York: Macmillan, 1998).

factors in a more objective or quantitative manner. We discuss quantitative credit scoring models used to measure credit risk next.

Concept Questions

1. Make a list of 10 key borrower characteristics you would assess before making a mortgage loan.
2. How should the risk premium on a loan be affected if there is a reduction in a borrower's leverage?

Credit Scoring Models

Credit scoring models use data on observed borrower characteristics either to calculate the probability of default or to sort borrowers into different default risk classes. By selecting and combining different economic and financial borrower characteristics, an FI manager may be able to:

1. Numerically establish which factors are important in explaining default risk.
2. Evaluate the relative degree or importance of these factors.
3. Improve the pricing of default risk.
4. Be better able to screen out bad loan applicants.
5. Be in a better position to calculate any reserves needed to meet expected future loan losses.

To employ credit scoring models in this manner, the manager must identify objective economic and financial measures of risk for any particular class of borrower. For consumer debt, the objective characteristics in a credit scoring model might include income, assets, age, occupation, and location. For corporate debt, financial ratios such as the debt-equity ratio are usually key factors. After data are identified, a statistical technique quantifies or scores the default risk probability or default risk classification.

Credit scoring models include these three broad types: (1) linear probability models, (2) logit models, and (3) linear discriminant analysis. Next we take a brief look at each of these models and their major strengths and weaknesses.

Linear Probability Model and Logit Model.   The linear probability model uses past data, such as accounting ratios, as inputs into a model to explain repayment experience on old loans. The relative importance of the factors used in explaining past repayment performance then forecasts repayment probabilities on new loans; that is, can be used for assessing p, the probability of repayment discussed earlier in this chapter (a key input in setting the credit premium on a loan or determining the amount to be lent).

Briefly, we divide old loans (i) into two observational groups: those that defaulted ($Z_i = 1$) and those that did not default ($Z_i = 0$). Then we relate these observations by linear regression to a set of j causal variables (X_{ij}) that reflect quantitative information about the ith borrower, such as leverage or earnings. We estimate the model by linear regression of this form.[22]

---

[22]G. Turvey, "Credit Scoring for Agricultural Loans: A Review with Applications," *Agricultural Finance Review* 51 (1991), pp. 43–54.

$$Z_i = \sum_{j=1}^{n} \beta_j X_{ij} + \text{error}$$

where β_j is the estimated importance of the *j*th variable (leverage) in explaining past repayment experience.

If we then take these estimated β_js and multiply them by the observed X_{ij} for a prospective borrower, we can derive an expected value of Z_i for the prospective borrower. That value can be interpreted as the probability of default for the borrower: $E(Z_i) = (1 - p_i) =$ expected probability of default, where p_i is the probability of repayment on the loan.

For example, suppose there were two factors influencing the past default behavior of borrowers: the leverage or debt-equity ratio (*D/E*) and the sales-asset ratio (S/A). Based on past default (repayment) experience, the linear probability model is estimated as

$$Z_i = .5(D/E_i) + .1(S/A_i)$$

Assume a prospective borrower has a *D/E* = .3 and an *S/A* = 2.0. Its expected probability of default (Z_i) can then be estimated as

$$Z_i = .5(.3) + .1(2.0) = .35$$

While this technique is straightforward as long as current information on the X_{ij} is available for the borrower, its major weakness is that the estimated probabilities of default can often lie outside the interval 0 to 1. The logit model overcomes this weakness by restricting the estimated range of default probabilities to lie between 0 and 1.[23]

Concept Question

Suppose the estimated linear probability model looked as follows:
$Z = 0.3 X_1 + 0.1 X_2 +$ error, where

$X_1 =$ Debt-equity ratio and $X_2 =$ Total assets–working capital ratio

Suppose, for a prospective borrower, $X_1 = 1.5$ and $X_2 = 3.0$. What is the projected probability of default for the borrower?

Linear Discriminant Models.   While linear probability and logit models project a value for the expected probability of default if a loan is made, discriminant models divide borrowers into high or low default risk classes contingent on their observed characteristics (X_j).

For example, consider the discriminant analysis model developed by E. I. Altman for publicly traded manufacturing firms in the United States. The indicator variable Z is an overall measure of the default risk classification of the borrower. This in turn depends on the values of various financial ratios of the borrower (X_j)

---

[23]Essentially this is done by plugging the estimated value of Z_i from the linear probability model (in our example, $Z_i = .35$) into the following formula:

$$F(Z_i) = \frac{1}{1 + e^{-Z_i}}$$

where e is exponential (equal to 2.718) and $F(Z_i)$ is the logistically transformed value of Z_i.

and the weighted importance of these ratios based on the past observed experience of defaulting versus nondefaulting borrowers derived from a discriminant analysis model.[24]

Altman's discriminant function takes the form

$$Z = 1.2X_1 + 1.4X_2 + 3.3X_3 + 0.6X_4 + 1.0X_5$$

where

X_1 = Working capital/total assets ratio
X_2 = Retained earnings/total assets ratio
X_3 = Earnings before interest and taxes/total assets ratio
X_4 = Market value of equity/book value of long-term debt ratio
X_5 = Sales/total assets ratio

The higher the value of Z, the lower the default risk classification of the borrower.[25] Thus, low or negative values of Z may be evidence of the borrower being a member of a relatively high default risk class.

Suppose that the financial ratios of a potential borrowing firm took the following values:

$$X_1 = .2$$
$$X_2 = 0$$
$$X_3 = -.20$$
$$X_4 = .10$$
$$X_5 = 2.0$$

The ratio X_2 is zero and X_3 is negative, indicating that the firm has had negative earnings or losses in recent periods. Also, X_4 indicates that the borrower is highly leveraged. However, the working capital ratio (X_1) and the sales/assets ratio (X_5) indicate that the firm is reasonably liquid and is maintaining its sales volume. The Z score provides an overall score or indicator of the borrower's credit risk since it combines and weights these five factors according to their past importance in explaining borrower default. For the borrower in question

$$Z = 1.2 (.2) + 1.4(0) + 3.3(-.20) + 0.6(.10) + 1.0 (2.0)$$
$$Z = 0.24 + 0 - .66 + 0.06 + 2.0$$
$$Z = 1.64$$

According to Altman's credit scoring model, any firm with a Z score less than 1.81 should be placed in the high default risk region.[26] Thus, the FI should not make a loan to this borrower until it improves its earnings.

There are, however, a number of problems in using the discriminant analysis model to make credit risk evaluations.[27] The first problem is that this model usually discriminates only between two extreme cases of borrower behavior: no default and default. In the real world there are various gradations of default, from nonpayment

---

[24]E. I. Altman. "Managing the Commercial Lending Process," in *Handbook of Banking Strategy,* eds. R. C. Aspinwall and R. A. Eisenbeis (New York: John Wiley & Sons, 1985), pp. 473–510.

[25]Working capital is current assets minus current liabilities.

[26]Discriminant analysis models produce such a switching point, $Z = 1.81$. This is the mean difference between the average Z scores of the defaulting firms and the nondefaulting firms. For example, suppose the average Z for nondefaulting firms was 2.01 and for defaulting firms it was 1.61. The mean of these two scores is 1.81. See Turvey, "Credit Scoring," for more details.

[27]Most of these criticisms also apply to the linear probability and logic models.

or delay of interest payments (nonperforming assets) to outright default on all promised interest and principal payments. This suggests that a more accurate or finely calibrated sorting among borrowers may require defining more classes in the discriminant analysis model.

The second problem is that there is no obvious economic reason to expect the weights in the discriminant function—or, more generally, the weights in any credit scoring model—to be constant over any but very short periods. The same concern also applies to the variables (X_j). Specifically, due to changing real and financial market conditions, other borrower-specific financial ratios may come to be increasingly relevant in explaining default risk probabilities. Moreover, the linear discriminant model assumes that the X_j variables are independent of one another.[28]

The third problem is that these models ignore important hard-to-quantify factors that may play a crucial role in the default or no default decision. For example, the reputational characteristics of the borrower and the implicit contractual nature of long-term borrower-lender relationships could be important borrower-specific characteristics, as could macrofactors such as the phase of the business cycle. These variables are often ignored in credit scoring models. Moreover, credit scoring models rarely use publicly available information, such as the prices in asset markets in which the outstanding debt and equity of the borrower are already traded.[29]

A fourth problem relates to default records kept by FIs. Currently, there is no centralized database on defaulted business loans—for proprietary and other reasons. While some task forces are currently under way by consortiums of commercial banks, insurance companies, and consulting firms to construct such databases, it may well be many years before sufficient databases are developed.[30] This constrains the ability of many FIs to use traditional credit scoring models (and quantitative models in general) for business loans—although their use for smaller consumer loans, such as credit card loans where much better centralized data bases exist is well established.

The third, or newer group, of credit risk models that follow use *financial theory* and more widely available *financial market* data to make inferences about default probabilities on debt and loan instruments. Consequently, these models are most relevant in evaluating lending to larger borrowers in the corporate sector. This is the area in which a great deal of current research is taking place by FIs, as noted in the Contemporary Perspectives box on p. 218 and in Appendixes 11–A and 11–B. Below we consider a number of these newer approaches or models of credit risk, including:

1. The term structure of credit risk approach
2. Mortality rate approach

---

[28]Recent work in nonlinear discriminant analysis has sought to relax this assumption. Moreover, work with neural networks, which are complex computer algorithms seeking links or correlations between the X_j variables to improve on Z classifications shows some promise. See P. K. Coats and L. F. Fant, "Recognizing Financial Distress Patterns: Using a Neural Network Tool," *Financial Management,* Summer 1993, pp. 142–55; and "New Tools for Routine Jobs," *The Financial Times,* September 24, 1994.

[29]For example, S. C. Gilson, K. John, and L. Lang show that three years of low or negative stock returns can usefully predict bankruptcy probabilities. In fact, this market-based approach is supplementary to the market-based information models discussed in later sections of this chapter. See "An Empirical Study of Private Reorganization of Firms in Default," *Journal of Financial Economics,* 1990, pp. 315–53.

[30]A recent, successful example of such a database is "1986–1992 Credit-Loss Experience Study: Private Placement Bonds," *Society of Actuaries,* Schaumberg, IL, 1996. For an analysis of these data, see Mark Carey, "Credit Risk in Private Debt Portfolios," *Journal of Finance,* June 1998, pp. 1363–1387.

3. RAROC models
4. Option models (including the KMV credit monitor model)
5. CreditMetrics (see Appendix 11–A)
6. Credit Risk+ (see Appendix 11–B)

While some of these models focus on different aspects of credit risk, they are all linked by a strong reliance on modern financial theory and financial market data.[31]

Concept Questions

1. Suppose $X_3 = .5$ in the preceding discriminant model example. Show how this would change the default risk classification of the borrower.
2. What are two problems in using discriminant analysis to evaluate credit risk?

Newer Models of Credit Risk Measurement and Pricing

Term Structure Derivation of Credit Risk

One market-based method of assessing credit risk exposure and default probabilities is to analyze the risk premiums inherent in the current structure of yields on corporate debt or loans to similar risk-rated borrowers. Rating agencies categorize corporate bond issuers into at least seven major classes according to perceived credit quality. The first four quality ratings—AAA, AA, A, and BBB—indicate investment quality borrowers. For example, the Office of the Comptroller of the Currency, which regulates national banks, restricts the ability of banks to purchase securities rated outside these classes. By comparison, insurance company regulators have permitted these FIs to purchase noninvestment grade securities with ratings such as BB, B, and CCC, but with restrictions on the aggregate amounts they can include in their portfolios. These three classes are known as high-yield or junk bonds. Different quality ratings are reflected in the degree to which corporate bond yields exceed those implied by the Treasury (credit risk–free) yield curve.

Treasury Strips and Zero-Coupon Corporate Bonds
Bonds that are created or issued bearing no coupons and only a face value to be paid on maturity. As such, they are issued at a large discount from face value. (Also called deep-discount bonds.)

Look at the spreads shown in Figure 11–6 for zero-coupon corporate (grade B) bonds over similar maturity zero-coupon Treasuries (so-called Treasury strips). Because **Treasury strips and zero-coupon corporate bonds** are single-payment discount bonds, it is possible to extract required credit risk premiums and implied probabilities of default from actual market data on interest rates. That is, the spreads between risk-free discount bonds issued by the Treasury and discount bonds issued by corporate borrowers of differing quality reflect perceived credit risk exposures of corporate borrowers for single payments at different times in the future.

Next, we look at the simplest case of extracting an implied probability of default for an FI considering buying one-year bonds from or making one-year loans to a risky borrower. Then, we consider multiyear loans and bonds. In each case, we show that we can extract a market view of the credit risk—the expected probability of default—of an individual borrower.

Probability of Default on a One-Period Debt Instrument.   Assume that the FI requires an expected return on a one-year corporate debt security at least equal to

---

[31]For further details on these newer models, see A. Saunders, *Credit Risk Measurement: New Approaches to Value at Risk and Other Paradigms* (John Wiley and Sons: New York, 1999).

FIGURE 11–6

Corporate and Treasury Discount Bond Yield Curves

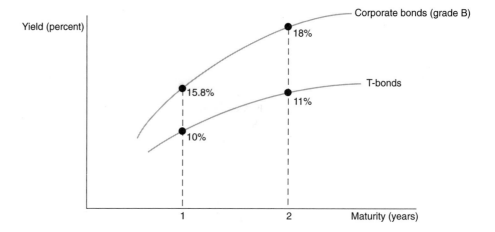

the risk-free return on Treasury bonds of one year's maturity. Let p be the probability that the corporate debt, both principal and interest, will be repaid in full; therefore, $1 - p$ is the probability of default. If the borrower defaults, the FI is assumed to get nothing. By denoting the promised return on the one-year corporate security as $1 + k$ and that on the credit risk-free Treasury security as $1 + i$, the FI manager would just be indifferent between corporate and Treasury securities when[32]

$$p(1 + k) = 1 + i$$

or, the expected return on corporate securities is equal to the risk-free rate. Suppose, as shown in Figure 11–6, the interest rate in the market for one-year zero-coupon Treasuries and one-year zero-coupon grade B corporate bonds are, respectively,

$$i = 10\%$$

and

$$k = 15.8\%$$

This implies that the probability of repayment on the security as perceived by the market is

$$p = \frac{1 + i}{1 + k} = \frac{1.100}{1.158} = .95$$

If the probability of repayment is .95, this implies a probability of default $(1 - p)$ equal to .05. Thus, in this simple one-period framework, a probability of default of 5 percent on the corporate bond (loan) requires the FI to set a risk premium (ϕ) of 5.8 percent[33]

$$\phi = k - i = 5.8\%$$

---

[32]This assumes that the FI manager is not risk averse; that is, this is a risk-neutral valuation method and the probabilities so derived are called risk-neutral probabilities. In general these will differ from probabilities estimated from historic data on defaults. See, Saunders, ibid, Chapter 6..

[33]In the real world a bank could partially capture this required spread in higher fees and compensating balances rather than only in the risk premium. In this simple example, we are assuming away compensating balances and fees. However, they could easily be built into the model. For additional information on this model, see A. Ginzburg, K. J. Maloney, and R. Wilner, "Risk Rating Migration and the Valuation of Floating Rate Debt," Citicorp Working Paper, March 1994; and R. Litterman and T. Iben, "Corporate Bond Valuation and the Term Structure of Credit Spreads," *Journal of Portfolio Management,* 1989, pp. 52–64.

Clearly, as the probability of repayment (*p*) falls and the probability of default (1 − *p*) increases, the required spread ɸ between *k* and *i* increases.

This analysis can easily be extended to the more realistic case where the FI does not expect to lose all interest and all principal if the corporate borrower defaults.[34] Realistically, the FI lender can expect to receive some partial repayment even if the borrower goes into bankruptcy. For example, Altman and Kishore estimated that when firms defaulted on their bonds in 1997, the investor lost on average around 45 cents on the dollar.[35] As discussed earlier in this chapter, many loans and bonds are secured or collateralized by first liens on various pieces of property or real assets should a borrower default. Let γ be the proportion of the loan's principal and interest that is collectible on default, where in general γ is positive. For example, in the bond case, γ is approximately .55 (that is, 1 minus the loss rate).

The FI manager would set the expected return on the loan to equal the risk-free rate in the following manner:

$$[\gamma(1 + k) \times (1 - p)] + [p(1 + k)] = 1 + i$$

The new term here is $\gamma(1 + k) \times (1 - p)$; this is the payoff the FI expects to get if the borrower defaults.

As might be expected, if the loan has collateral backing such that γ > 0, the required risk premium on the loan will be less for any given default risk probability (1 − *p*). Collateral requirements are a method of controlling default risk; they act as a direct substitute for risk premiums in setting required loan rates. To see this, solve for the risk premium ɸ between *k* (the required yield on risky corporate debt) and *i* (the risk-free rate of interest):

$$k - i = \phi = \frac{(1 + i)}{(\gamma + p - p\gamma)} - (1 + i)$$

If *i* = 10 percent and *p* = .95 as before but the FI can expect to collect 90 percent of the promised proceeds if default occurs (γ = .9), then the required risk premium ɸ = 0.6 percent.

Interestingly, in this simple framework, γ and p are perfect substitutes for each other. That is, a bond or loan with collateral backing of γ = .7 and *p* = .8 would have the same required risk premium as one with γ = .8 and *p* = .7. An increase in collateral γ is a direct substitute for an increase in default risk (i.e., a decline in *p*).

Probability of Default on a Multiperiod Debt Instrument.*

We can extend this type of analysis to derive the credit risk or default probabilities occurring in the market for longer-term loans or bonds.

Suppose the FI manager wanted to find out the probability of default on a two-year bond. To do this, the manager must estimate the probability that the bond will default in the second year conditional on the probability that it does not default in the first year. The probability that a bond will default in any one year is clearly

---

[34]See J. B. Yawitz, "Risk Premia on Municipal Bonds," *Journal of Financial and Quantitative Analysis* 13 (1977), pp. 475–85; and J. B. Yawitz, "An Analytical Model of Interest Rate Differentials and Different Default Recoveries," *Journal of Financial and Quantitative Analysis* 13 (1977), pp. 481–90.

[35]E. I. Altman and V. M. Kishore, "Defaults and Returns on High-Yield Bonds: Analysis through 1997," Working Paper, New York University Salomon Center, January 1998. More recent studies by Citicorp, Sand P. and Fitch suggest that the default loss on loans (so-called loss-given-default) may be even lower in the 20 to 25 percent range (see Saunders, ibid, Chapter 4).

Marginal Default Probability
The probability that a borrower will default in any given year.

conditional on the fact that the default hasn't occurred earlier. The probability that a bond will default in any one year is the **marginal default probability** for that year. For the one-year loan, $1 - p_1 = .05$ is the marginal and total or cumulative probability (Cp) of default in year 1. However, for the two-year loan, the marginal probability of default in the second year $(1 - p_2)$ can differ from the marginal probability of default in the first year $(1 - p_1)$. Later in this chapter we discuss ways in which p_2 can be estimated by the FI manager, but for the moment suppose that $1 - p_2 = .07$. Then

$$1 - p_1 = .05 = \text{marginal probability of default in year 1}$$
$$1 - p_2 = .07 = \text{marginal probability of default in year 2}$$

Cumulative Default Probability
The probability that a borrower will default over a specified multiyear period.

The probability of the borrower surviving—not defaulting at any time between now (time 0) and the end of period 2—is $p_1 \times p_2 = (.95)(.93) = .8835$. The **cumulative default probability** at some time between now and the end of year 2 is

$$Cp = 1 - [(p_1)(p_2)]$$
$$Cp = 1 - [(.95)(.93)] = .1165$$

There is an 11.65 percent probability of default over this period.

We have seen how to derive the one-year probability of default from yield spreads on one-year bonds. We now want to derive the probability of default in year 2, year 3, and so on. Look at Figure 11–6; as you can see, yield curves are rising for both Treasury issues and corporate issues. We want to extract from these yield curves the *market's expectation* of the multiperiod default rates for corporate borrowers classified in the grade B rating class.[36]

No Arbitrage
The inability to make a profit without taking risk.

Look first at the Treasury yield curve. The condition of efficient markets and thus **no arbitrage** profits by investors requires that the return on buying and holding the two-year Treasury discount bond to maturity just equal the expected return from investing in the current one-year discount T-bond and reinvesting the principal and interest in a new one-year discount T-bond at the end of the first year at the expected one-year **forward rate.** That is,

$$(1 + i_2)^2 = (1 + i_1)(1 + f_1) \tag{1}$$

Forward Rate
A one-period rate of interest expected on a bond issued at some date in the future.

The term on the left side is the return from holding the two-year discount bond to maturity. The term on the right side results from investing in two successive one-year bonds, where i_1 is the current one-year bond rate and f_1 is the expected one-year bond rate or forward rate next year. Since we can observe directly from the T-bond yield curve the current required yields on one- and two-year Treasuries, $i_1 = 10$ percent and $i_2 = 11$ percent, we can directly infer the market's expectation of the one-year T-bond rate next period or the one-year forward rate, f_1:

$$1 + f_1 = \frac{(1 + i_2)^2}{(1 + i_1)} = \frac{(1.11)^2}{(1.1)} = 1.12 \tag{2}$$
$$\text{or} \quad f_1 = 12\%$$

---

[36]To use this model, one has to place borrowers in a rating class. One way to do this for unrated firms would be to use the Z score model to calculate a Z ratio for this firm. E. I. Altman has shown that there is a high correlation between Z scores and Standard & Poor's and Moody's bond ratings. Once a firm is placed in a bond rating group (e.g., B) by the Z score model, the term structure model can be used to infer the expected (implied) probabilities of default for the borrower at different times in the future. See "Valuation, Loss Reserves, and Pricing of Commercial Loans," *Journal of Commercial Bank Lending*, August 1993, pp. 9–25.

TABLE 11–8   Treasury and Corporate Rates and Rate Spreads

	Current One-Year Rate	*Expected One-Year Rate*
Treasury	10.0%	12.0%
Corporate (B)	15.8	20.2
Spread	5.8	8.2

The expected rise in one-year rates from 10 percent (i_1) this year to 12 percent (f_1) next year reflects investors' perceptions regarding inflation and other factors that directly affect the time value of money.

We can use the same type of analysis with the corporate bond yield curve to infer the one-year forward rate on corporate bonds (grade B in this example). The current yield curve indicates that appropriate one-year discount bonds are yielding k_1 equal to 15.8 percent and two-year bonds are yielding $k_2 = 18$ percent. The one-year rate expected on corporate securities (c_1) one year into the future reflects the market's default risk expectations for this class of borrower as well as the more general time value factors also affecting f_1:

$$1 + c_1 = \frac{(1 + k_2)^2}{1 + k_1} = \frac{(1.18)^2}{1.158} = 1.202 \qquad (3)$$

$$\text{or} \quad c_1 = 20.2\%$$

We summarize these calculations in Table 11–8. As you can see, the expected spread between one-year corporate bonds and Treasuries in one year's time is higher than the spread for current one-year bonds. The expected rates on one-year bonds can generate an estimate of the expected probability of repayment on one-year corporate bonds in one year's time, or what we have called p_2.

Since

$$p_2 (1 + c_1) = 1 + f_1$$

then

$$p_2 = \left[\frac{1 + f_1}{1 + c_1}\right] = \frac{[1.12]}{[1.202]} = .9318$$

Thus, the expected probability of default in year 2 is

$$1 - p_2 = 1 - .9318 = .0682$$
$$\text{or} \quad 6.82\%$$

In a similar fashion, the one-year rates expected in two years' time can be derived from the Treasury and corporate term structures so as to derive p_3, and so on.

The probabilities we have estimated are marginal probabilities conditional on default not occurring in a prior period. We also discussed the concept of the *cumulative probability* of default that would tell the FI the probability of a loan or bond investment defaulting over a particular time period. In the example developed earlier, the cumulative probability that corporate grade B bonds would default over the next two years is

$$Cp = 1 - [(p_1)(p_2)]$$
$$Cp = 1 - [(.95)(.9318)] = 11.479\%$$

As with the credit scoring approach, using this model creates some potential problems. Its principal advantages are that it is clearly forward looking and based on market expectations. Moreover, if there are liquid markets for Treasury and corporate discount bonds—such as Treasury strips and corporate zeros—then we can easily estimate expected future default rates and use them to value and price loans.[37] However, while the market for Treasury strips is now quite deep, the market for corporate discount bonds is quite small. Although a discount yield curve for corporate bonds could be extracted mathematically from the corporate bond coupon yield curve, these bonds are not very actively traded. Given this, the FI manager might have to consider an alternative way to use bond or loan data to extract default rate probabilities for all but the very largest corporate borrowers. We consider a further possible alternative next.

Concept Question

What is the difference between the marginal default probability and the cumulative default probability?

Mortality Rate Derivation of Credit Risk

Rather than extracting *expected* default rates from the current term structure of interest rates, the FI manager may analyze the *historic* or past default risk experience, the **mortality rates,** of bonds and loans of a similar quality. Consider calculating p_1 and p_2 using the mortality rate model.[38] Here p_1 is the probability of a grade B bond or loan surviving the first year of its issue; thus $1 - p_1$ is the **marginal mortality rate,** or the probability of the bond or loan dying or defaulting in the first year of issue. While p_2 is the probability of the loan surviving in the second year given that default has not occurred during the first year, $1 - p_2$ is the marginal mortality rate for the second year. Thus, for each grade of corporate borrower quality, a marginal mortality rate (MMR) curve can show the historical default rate experience of bonds in any specific quality class in each year after issue on the bond or loan.

Note in Figure 11–7 that as grade B bonds age, their probability of dying in each successive year increases. Of course, in reality, any shape to the mortality curve is possible. It is possible that MMRs can be flat, decline over time, or show a more complex functional form. These marginal mortality rates can be estimated from actual data on bond and loan defaults. Specifically, for grade B quality bonds (loans):

$$MMR_1 = \frac{\text{Total value of grade B bonds defaulting in year 1 of issue.}}{\text{Total value of grade B bonds outstanding in year 1 of issue.}}$$

$$MMR_2 = \frac{\text{Total value of grade B bonds defaulting in year 2 of issue.}}{\begin{array}{l}\text{Total value of grade B bonds oustanding in year 2 of issue}\\ \text{adjusted for defaults, calls, sinking fund redemptions, and}\\ \text{maturities in the prior year.}\end{array}}$$

Mortality Rate
Historic default rate experience of a bond or loan.

Marginal Mortality Rate
The probability of a bond or loan dying (defaulting) in any given year of issue.

---

[37]For a recent commercial application of these ideas to valuing and pricing loans, see the Loan Analysis System (LAS) developed by KPMG Peat Marwick, as discussed in S. D. Aguais, "Creating Value from Both Loan Structure and Price," *Commercial Lending Review,* 1998, pp. 1–10.

[38]For further reading, see Altman, "Measuring Corporate Bond Mortality"; Altman and Kishore, "Defaults and Returns on High-Yield Bonds"; and Saunders, Credit Risk Measurement, Chapter 7.

FIGURE 11–7

*Hypothetical Marginal
Mortality Rate Curve for
Grade B Corporate Bonds*

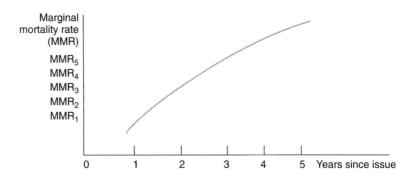

TABLE 11–9   Comparison of Syndicated Bank Loan versus Corporate Bond Mortality Rates Based on Original Issuance Principal Amounts, 1991–1996

Years after issue		1 Year		2 Years		3 Years	
		Bank	*Bond*	*Bank*	*Bond*	*Bank*	*Bond*
Aaa	Marginal	0.00%	0.00%	0.00%	0.00%	0.00%	0.00%
	Cumulative	0.00%	0.00%	0.00%	0.00%	0.00%	0.00%
Aa	Marginal	0.00%	0.00%	0.00%	0.00%	0.00%	0.00%
	Cumulative	0.00%	0.00%	0.00%	0.00%	0.00%	0.00%
A	Marginal	0.00%	0.00%	0.12%	0.00%	0.00%	0.00%
	Cumulative	0.00%	0.00%	0.12%	0.00%	0.12%	0.00%
Baa	Marginal	0.04%	0.00%	0.00%	0.00%	0.00%	0.00%
	Cumulative	0.04%	0.00%	0.04%	0.00%	0.04%	0.00%
Ba	Marginal	0.17%	0.00%	0.60%	0.38%	0.60%	2.30%
	Cumulative	0.17%	0.00%	0.77%	0.38%	1.36%	2.67%
B	Marginal	2.30%	0.81%	1.86%	1.97%	2.59%	4.99%
	Cumulative	2.30%	0.81%	4.11%	2.76%	6.60%	7.61%
Caa	Marginal	15.24%	2.65%	7.44%	3.09%	13.03%	4.55%
	Cumulative	15.24%	2.65%	21.55%	5.66%	31.77%	9.95%

Table 11–9 shows the estimated mortality and cumulative default rates for samples of over 4,000 publicly traded corporate bonds and (rated) syndicated bank loans over the 1991–96 period. From Table 11–9 it can be seen that (1) mortality rates are higher the lower the rating of the bond or loan and (2) in general, syndicated loans appear to have higher mortality rates than similarly rated corporate bonds.

The mortality rate approach has a number of conceptual and applicability problems. Probably the most important of these is that like the credit scoring model, it produces historic or backward-looking measures. Also, the estimates of default rates and therefore implied future default probabilities tend to be highly sensitive to the period over which the FI manager calculates the MMRs. In addition, the estimates tend to be sensitive to the number of issues and the relative size of issues in each investment grade.[39]

Concept Questions

1. In Table 11–9, the CMR over 3 years for Caa rated bonds is 9.95 percent. Check this calculation using the individual year MMRs.
2. Why would any FI manager buy loans that have a CMR of 31.77 percent? Explain your answer.

RAROC Models

A popular model to evaluate (and price) credit risk based on market data is the RAROC model. RAROC (risk-adjusted return on capital) was pioneered by Bankers Trust and has now been adopted by virtually all the large banks in the United States and Europe, although with some significant proprietary differences between them.

The essential idea behind RAROC is that rather than evaluating the actual or promised annual ROA on a loan (as on p. 212) that is, net interest and fees divided by the amount lent, the lending officer balances expected interest and fee income against the loan's risk. Thus, rather than dividing loan income by assets lent, it is divided by some measure of asset (loan) risk:

$$RAROC = \frac{\text{One year income on a loan}}{\text{Loan (asset) risk or risk captial}}$$

A loan is approved only if RAROC is sufficiently high relative to a benchmark cost of capital for the bank. Alternatively, if the RAROC on an existing loan falls below a bank's RAROC benchmark, the lending officer should seek to adjust the loan's terms to make it "profitable" again.

One problem in estimating RAROC is the measurement of loan risk (the denominator in the RAROC equation). Chapter 9 on duration showed that the percentage change in the market value of an asset such as a loan ($\Delta L/L$) is related to the duration of the loan and the size of the interest rate shock ($\Delta R/1 + R$):

$$\frac{\Delta L}{L} = -D_L \frac{\Delta R}{1 + R}$$

The same concept is applied here, except that interest rate shocks are replaced by credit quality (or credit risk premium) shocks.

We can thus rewrite the duration equation with the following interpretation:

ΔL	$=$	$-D_L$	$\times$	L	$\times$	$(\Delta R/1 + R)$
(dollar capital risk exposure or loss amount)		(duration of the loan)		(risk amount or size of loan)		(expected maximum change in the credit premium or risk factor on the loan)

---

[39]For example, even though the estimates in Table 11–9 are based on over 4,000 observations of both bonds and loans, these estimates still have quite wide confidence bands. See P. H. McAllister and J. J. Mingo, "Commercial Loan Risk Management, Credit Scoring and Pricing: The Need for a New Shared Data Base," *Journal of Commercial Lending,* May 1994, pp. 6–20.

FIGURE 11–8

Hypothetical Frequency Distribution of Yield Spread Changes for All AAA Bonds in 2000

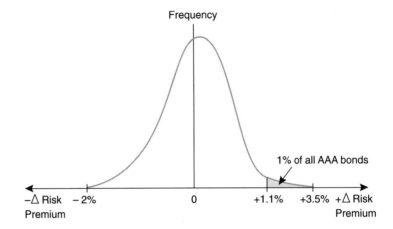

    While the loan's duration (say, 2.7 years) and the loan amount (say, $1 million) are easily estimated, it is more difficult to estimate the maximum change in the credit risk premium on the loan over the next year. Since publicly available data on loan risk premiums are scarce, we turn to publicly available corporate bond market data to estimate premiums. First, an S&P credit rating (AAA, AA, A, and so on) is assigned to a borrower. Thereafter, the risk premium changes of all the bonds traded in that particular rating class over the last year are analyzed. The ΔR in the RAROC equation equals

$$\Delta R = \text{Max} \, [\Delta(R_i - R_G) > 0]$$

where $\Delta (R_i - R_G)$ is the change in the yield spread between corporate bonds of credit rating class i (R_i) and matched duration treasury bonds (R_G) over the last year. In order to consider only the worst-case scenario, the maximum change in yield spread is chosen, as opposed to the average change.

    As an example, we evaluate the credit risk of a loan to a AAA borrower. Assume there are currently 400 publicly traded bonds in that class (i.e., bonds issued by firms of a rating type similar to that of the borrower). The first step is to evaluate the actual changes in the credit risk premiums ($R_i - R_G$) on each of these bonds for the past year (in this example, the year 2000). These (hypothetical) changes are plotted in the frequency curve of Figure 11–8. They range from a fall in the risk premiums of negative 2 percent to an increase of 3.5 percent. Since the largest increase may be a very extreme (unrepresentative) number, the 99 percent worst-case scenario is chosen (i.e., only 4 bonds out of 400 had risk premium increases exceeding the 99 percent worst case). For the example shown in Figure 11–8 this is equal to 1.1 percent.

    The estimate of loan (or capital) risk, assuming that the current average level of rates (R) on AAA bonds is 10 percent, is

$$\Delta L = D_L \times L \times \frac{\Delta R}{1 + R}$$
$$= -(2.7)(\$1 \text{ million})\left(\frac{.011}{1.1}\right)$$
$$= -\$27,000$$

Thus, while the face value of the loan amount is $1 million, the risk amount or change in the loan's market value due to a decline in its credit quality is $27,000.

To determine whether the loan is worth making, the estimated loan risk is compared to the loan's income (spread over the FI's cost of funds plus fees on the loan). Suppose the projected (one-year) spread plus fees is as follows:

$$\text{Spread} = 0.2\% \times \$1 \text{ million} = \$2,000$$
$$\text{Fees} = 0.1\% \times \$1 \text{ million} = \underline{\$1,000}$$
$$\$3,000$$

The loan's RAROC is

$$RAROC = \frac{\text{One-year income on loan}}{\text{Loan risk (or capital risk)}(\Delta L)} = \frac{\$3,000}{\$27,000} = 11.1\%$$

Note that this calculation can be either forward looking, comparing the projected income over the next year on the loan with ΔL, or backward looking, comparing the actual income generated on the loan over the past year with ΔL.

If the 11.1 percent exceeds the bank's internal RAROC benchmark (based on its cost of funds), the loan will be approved. If it is less, the loan will be rejected outright or the borrower will be asked to pay higher fees and/or a higher spread to increase the RAROC to acceptable levels.

Other banks have adopted different ways of calculating ΔL in their versions of RAROC. Some banks, usually the largest ones with very good loan default databases, divide one-year income by the product of an unexpected loss rate and the proportion of the loan that cannot be recaptured on default. Thus:

$$RAROC = \frac{\text{One-year income per dollar loaned}}{\text{Unexpected loss rate} \times \text{Proportion of loan lost on default}}$$

Suppose expected income per dollar lent is 0.3 cents. or .003. The 99th percentile historic (extreme case) loss rate for borrowers of this type is 4 percent and the dollar proportion of loans of this type that cannot be recaptured is 80 percent. Then[40]

$$RAROC = \frac{.003}{(.04)(.8)} = \frac{.003}{(.032)} = 9.375\%$$

Concept Question

Describe the basic concept behind RAROC models.

Option Models of Default Risk*

Theoretical Framework. In recent years, following the pioneering work of Merton, Black, and Scholes and others, we now recognize that when a firm raises funds by issuing bonds or increasing its bank loans, it holds a very valuable default or repayment option.[41] That is, if a borrower's investment projects fail so that it cannot repay the bondholder or the bank, it has the option of defaulting on its debt

---

[40]In other versions of this approach, such as that used by Bank of America, the denominator can be adjusted for the degree of correlation of the loan with the rest of the portfolio. See, for example, Edward Zaik, et al., "RAROC at Bank of America: From Theory to Practice," *Journal of Applied Corporate Finance,* Summer 1996, pp. 83–93.

[41]R. C. Merton, "On the Pricing of Corporate Debt: The Risk Structure of Interest Rates," *Journal of Finance* 29 (1974), pp. 449–70; and F. Black and M. Scholes, "The Pricing of Options and Corporate Liabilities," *Journal of Political Economy* 81 (1973), pp. 637–59.

FIGURE 11–9

The Payoff Function to Corporate Borrowers (Stockholders)

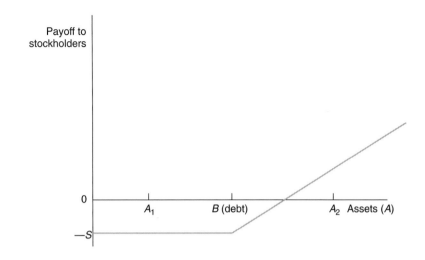

repayment and turning any remaining assets over to the debtholder. Because of limited liability for equity holders, the borrower's loss is limited on the downside by the amount of equity invested in the firm.[42] On the other hand, if things go well, the borrower can keep most of the upside returns on asset investments after the promised principal and interest on the debt have been paid. This relatively simple idea has been turned into a credit monitoring model by the KMV Corporation. Reputedly, many of the largest U.S. banks are now using this model to look at the expected default risk frequency (EDF) of large corporations.[43] Before we look at the KMV Model, we will take a closer look at the theory underlying the option approach to default risk estimation.

The Borrower's Payoff from Loans. Look at the payoff function for the borrower in Figure 11–9 where S is the size of the initial equity investment in the firm, B is the value of outstanding bonds or loans (assumed for simplicity to be issued on a discount basis), and A is the market value of the assets of the firm.

If the investments in Figure 11–9 turn out badly, the limited-liability stockholder–owners of the firm will default on the firm's debt, turn its assets (such as A_1) over to the debt holders, and lose only their initial stake in the firm (S). By contrast, if the firm does well and the assets of the firm are valued highly (A_2), the firm's stockholders will pay off the firm's debt ($0B$) and keep the difference ($A_2 - B$). Clearly, the higher A_2 is relative to B, the better off are the firm's stockholders. Given that borrowers face only a limited downside risk of loss of their equity investment but a very large potential upside return if things turn out well, equity is analogous to buying a call option on the assets of the firm.

The Debt Holder's Payoff from Loans. Consider the same loan or bond issue from the perspective of the bank or bondholder. The maximum amount the bank or

---

[42]Given limits to losses in personal bankruptcy, a similar analysis can be applied to retail and consumer loans.

[43]See KMV Corporation Credit Monitor, KMV Corporation, San Francisco, 1994; S. P. Choudhury, "Choosing the Right Box of Credit Tricks," *Risk Magazine,* November 1997; and, A. Saunders, Credit Risk Measurement, Chapter 3.

FIGURE 11–10

Payoff Function to the Debt Holder (the Bank) from a Loan

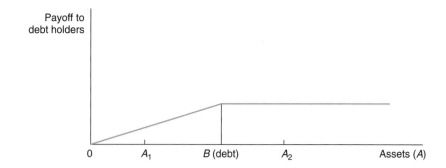

bondholder can get back is *B,* the promised payment. However, the borrower who possesses the default or repayment option would rationally repay the loan only if *A* > *B;* that is, if the market value of assets exceeds the value of promised debt repayments. A borrower whose asset value falls below *B* would default and turn over any remaining assets to the debt holders. Thus, the payoff function to the debt holder is shown in Figure 11–10.

After investment has taken place, if the value of the firm's assets resembles points to the right of *B,* the face value of the debt—such as A_2—the debt holder or bank will be paid off in full and receive *B.* On the other hand, if asset values fall in the region to the left of *B*—such as A_1—the debt holder will receive back only those assets remaining as collateral, thereby losing $B - A_1$. Thus, the value of the loan from the perspective of the lender is always the minimum of *B* or *A,* or min [*B,A*]. That is, the payoff function to the debt holder is similar to writing a put option on the value of the borrower's assets with *B,* the face value of debt as the *exercise price.* If *A* > *B,* the loan is repaid and the debt holder earns a small fixed return (similar to the premium on a put option), which is the interest rate implicit in the discount bond. If *A* < *B,* the borrower defaults and the debt holder stands to lose both interest and principal. In the limit, default for a firm with no assets left results in debt holders losing all their principal and interest. In actuality, if there are also costs of bankruptcy, the debt holder can potentially lose even more than this.

Applying the Option Valuation Model to the Calculation of Default Risk Premiums.   Merton has shown that in the context of the preceding options framework, it is quite straightforward to express the market value of a risky loan made by a lender to a borrower as[44]

$$F(\tau) = Be^{-i\tau} [(1/d)N(h_1) + N(h_2)] \tag{7}$$

where

τ = The length of time remaining to loan maturity; that is, $\tau = T - t$ where *T* is the maturity date and time *t* is today.

d = The borrower's leverage ratio measured as $Be^{-i\tau}/A$ where the market value of debt is valued at the rate *i,* the risk-free rate of interest.

$N(h)$ = A value computed from the standardized normal distribution statistical tables. This value reflects the probability that a deviation exceeding the calculated value of *h* will occur.

---

[44]See Merton, "On the Pricing of Corporate Debt."

$$h_1 = -[\tfrac{1}{2}\sigma^2\tau - ln(d)\,]/\sigma\sqrt{\tau}$$
$$h_2 = -[\tfrac{1}{2}\sigma^2\tau + ln(d)\,]/\sigma\sqrt{\tau}$$

σ^2 = Measures the asset risk of the borrower. Technically, it is the variance of the rate of change in the value of the underlying assets of the borrower.

More important, written in terms of a yield spread, this equation reflects an equilibrium default risk premium that the borrower should be charged:

$$k(\tau) - i = (-1/\tau)ln[N(h_2) + (1/d)N(h_1)] \tag{8}$$

where

$k(\tau)$ = Required yield on risky debt
ln = Natural logarithm
i = Risk-free rate on debt of equivalent maturity (here, one period)

Thus, Merton has shown that the lender should adjust the required risk premium as d and σ^2 change, that is, as leverage and asset risk change.

An Option Model Example.[45]   Let

B = \$100,000
τ = 1 year
i = 5 percent
d = 90% or .9
σ = 12%

That is, suppose we can measure the market value of a firm's assets (and thus $d = Be^{-i\tau}/A$) as well as the volatility of those assets (σ). Then, substituting these values into the equations for h_1 and h_2 and solving for the areas under the standardized normal distribution, we find that

$$N(h_1) = .174120$$
$$N(h_2) = .793323$$

where

$$h_1 = \frac{-[\tfrac{1}{2}(.12)^2 - ln(.9)]}{.12} = -.938$$

and

$$h_2 = \frac{-[\tfrac{1}{2}(.12)^2 + ln(.9)]}{.12} = +.818$$

The current market value of the loan is

$$
\begin{aligned}
L(t) &= Be^{-i\tau}[N(h_2) + (1/d)N(h_1)] \\
&= \frac{\$100,000}{1.05127}[.793323 + (1.1111)(.17412)] \\
&= \frac{\$100,000}{1.05127}[.986788] \\
&= \$93,866.18
\end{aligned}
$$

and the required risk spread or premium is

---

[45]This numerical example is based on D. F. Babbel, "Insuring Banks against Systematic Credit Risk," *Journal of Futures Markets* 9 (1989), pp. 487–506.

$$k(\tau) - i = \left(\frac{-1}{\tau}\right)ln[N(h_2) + (1/d)N(h_1)]$$
$$= (-1)ln[.986788]$$
$$= 1.33\%$$

Thus, the risky loan rate $k(\tau)$ should be set at 6.33 percent when the risk-free rate (i) is 5 percent.

Theoretically, this model is an elegant tool for extracting premiums and default probabilities; it also has important conceptual implications regarding which variables to focus on in credit risk evaluation [e.g., the firm's market value of assets (A) and asset risk (σ^2)]. Even so, this model has a number of real-world implementation problems. Probably the most significant is the fact that neither the market value of a firm's assets (A) nor the volatility of the firm's assets (σ^2) is directly observed.

The KMV model in fact recognizes this problem by using the option pricing model (OPM) to extract the implied market value of assets (A) and the asset volatility of a given firm's assets (σ^2).[46] Using the implied value of σ for assets and A, the market value of assets, the likely distribution of possible asset values of the firm relative to its current debt obligations can be calculated over the next year.[47] As shown in Figure 11–11, the expected default frequency (EDF) reflects the probability that the market value of the assets of the firm (A) will fall below the promised repayments on debt liabilities (B) in one year. Simulations by KMV have shown that this outperforms both Z score–type models and S&P rating changes as predictors of corporate failure and distress.[48] An example for Venture Stores Inc., that filed for Chapter 11 bankruptcy protection in January 1998, is shown in Figure 11–12.

Concept Questions

1. Which is the only credit risk model discussed in this section that is really forward looking?
2. How should the posting of collateral by a borrower affect the risk premium on a loan?

---

[46]It does this by using the equity (stock market) value of the firm's shares (E) and the volatility of the value of the firm's shares (σ_E). Since equity can be viewed as a call option on the firm's assets and the volatility of a firm's equity value will reflect the leverage adjusted volatility of its underlying assets, we have in general form

$$\bar{E} = f(A, \sigma, \bar{B}, \bar{r}, \bar{\tau})$$

and

$$\bar{\sigma}_E = g(\sigma)$$

where the bars denote values that are directly measurable. Since we have two equations in two unknowns (A, σ), we can directly solve for both A and σ and use these to calculate the EDF (Expected Default Frequency).

[47]Suppose the value of the firm's assets (A) at the time zero is $100 million and the value of its debt is $80 million. Suppose that the implied volatility (σ) of asset values was estimated at $12.12 million, and it is assumed that asset-value changes are normally distributed. The firm becomes distressed only if the value of its assets falls to $80 million or below (falls by $20 million). Such a fall is equal to 1.65σ, i.e., $1.65 \times$ $12.12 million = $20 million. From statistics, we know that the area of the normal distribution (in each tail) lying ± 1.65 σ from the mean is theoretical 5 percent. Thus, the KMV model would suggest a theoretical 5 percent probability of the firm going into distress over the next year (by time 1). However, KMV calculates empirical EDF's since we do not know the true distribution of asset values (A) over time. Essentially, it asks the question—in practice how many firms that started the year with asset values 1.65σ distance from default (see Figure 11–11) actually defaulted at the end of the year? This value may or may not equal 5 percent.

[48]KMV provides monthly EDFs for over 6,000 U.S. companies and 20,000 companies worldwide.

FIGURE 11–11

Expected Default Frequency Using the KMV Model

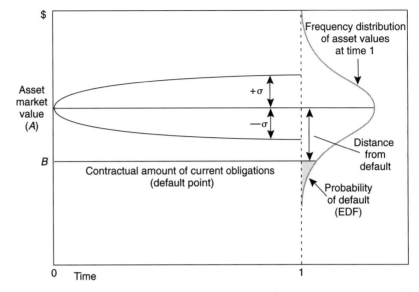

Source: KMV Corporation Credit Monitor. Reprinted by permission of KMV Corporation.

FIGURE 11–12

The KMV and S&P Ratings for Venture Stores Inc.

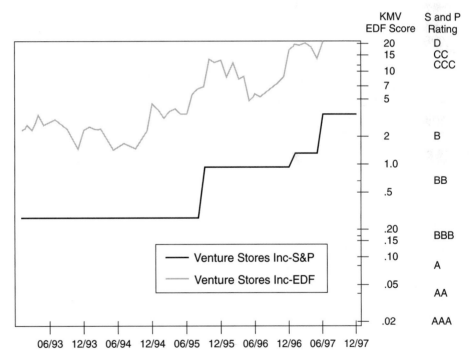

Source: KMV Corporation, San Francisco, California.

3. What are three major problems with the Z score model of credit risk evaluation?

4. How should the risk premium on a loan be affected if there is a reduction in a borrower's leverage and the underlying volatility of its earnings?

5. What is the link between the implied volatility of a firm's assets and its expected default frequency?

Summary

This chapter discussed different approaches to measuring credit or default risk on individual loans (bonds). The different types of loans made by FIs and some of their basic characteristics were first examined. The expected return on a loan was shown to depend on factors such as origination fees, compensating balances, interest rates, and maturity. The various models to assess default risk include both qualitative and quantitative models. The qualitative models usually contain both firm-specific factors such as reputation and leverage and market-specific factors such as the business cycle and the level of interest rates. Quantitative models such as the linear

probability model, the logit model, and the linear discriminant model were shown to provide credit scores that can rank or classify loans by expected default risk. The more rigorous of the quantitative models make use of both financial theory and financial data. These include the term structure and mortality rate models as well as the RAROC (risk-adjusted return on capital) and option-based models. (Two additional models, CreditMetrics and Credit Risk+, are discussed in the Appendixes to this chapter.) In the next chapter we look at methods to evaluate the risk of loan portfolios, or loan concentration risk.

Questions and Problems

1. Why is credit risk analysis an important component of bank risk management? What recent activities by FIs have made the task of credit risk assessment more difficult for both bank managers and regulators?

2. Differentiate between a secured loan and an unsecured loan. Who bears most of the risk in a fixed-rate loan? Why would bankers prefer to charge floating rates, especially for longer-maturity loans?

3. How does a spot loan differ from a loan commitment? What are the advantages and disadvantages of borrowing through a loan commitment?

4. Why is commercial lending declining in importance in the United States? What effect does this decline have on overall commercial lending activities?

5. What are the primary characteristics of residential mortgage loans? Why does the ratio of adjustable rate mortgages to fixed-rate mortgages in the economy vary over the interest rate cycle? When would the ratio be highest?

6. What are the three major classes of consumer loans at U.S. banks? How do revolving loans differ from automobile and other consumer installment loans?

7. How does the credit card transaction process assist in the credit monitoring function of financial institutions? Which major parties receive a fee in a typical credit card transaction? Do the services provided warrant the payment of these associated fees?

8. What are compensating balances? What is the relationship between the amount of compensating balance requirement and the return on the loan to the FI?

9. County Bank offers one-year loans with a stated rate of 9 percent but requires a compensating balance of 10 percent. What is the true cost of this loan to the borrower? How does the cost change if the compensating balance is 15 percent? If the compensating balance is 20 percent?

10. Metrobank offers one-year loans with a 9 percent stated or base rate, charges a 0.25 percent loan origination fee, imposes a 10 percent compensating balance requirement, and must pay a 6 percent reserve requirement to the Federal Reserve. The loans typically are repaid at maturity.

    a. If the risk premium for a given customer is 2.5 percent, what is the simple promised interest return on the loan?

    b. What is the contractually promised gross return on the loan per dollar lent?

    c. Which of the fee items has the greatest impact on the gross return?

11. Why are most retail borrowers charged the same rate of interest, implying the same risk premium or class? What is credit rationing? How is it used to control credit risks with respect to retail and wholesale loans?

12. Why could a lender's expected return be lower when the risk premium is increased on a loan? In addition to the risk premium, how can a lender increase the expected return on a wholesale loan? A retail loan?

13. What are covenants in a loan agreement? What are the objectives of covenants? How can these covenants be negative? Affirmative?

14. Identify and define the borrower-specific and market-specific factors which enter into the credit decision. What is the impact of each factor on the risk premium?

    a. Which of these factors is more likely to affect adversely small businesses rather than large businesses in the credit assessment process by lenders?

    b. How does the existence of a high debt ratio typically affect the risk of the borrower? Is it possible that high leverage may reduce the risk of bankruptcy (or the risk of financial distress)? Explain.

    c. Why is the volatility of the earnings stream of a borrower important to a lender?

15. Why is the degree of collateral as specified in the loan agreement of importance to the lender? If the book value of the collateral is greater than or equal to the amount of the loan, is the credit risk of the lender fully covered? Why or why not?

16. Why are FIs consistently interested in the expected level of economic activity in the markets in which they operate? Why is monetary policy of the Federal Reserve System important to FIs?

17. What are the purposes of credit scoring models? How could these models possibly assist an FI manager in better administering credit?

18. Suppose the estimated linear probability model is $Z = 1.1X_1 + .6X_2 + .5X_3 +$ error, where $X_1 = 0.75$ is the borrower's debt/equity ratio, $X_2 = 0.25$ is the volatility of borrower earnings, and $X_3 = 0.15$ is the borrower's profit ratio.

    a. What is the projected probability of repayment for the borrower?

    b. What is the projected probability of repayment if the debt/equity ratio is 3.5?

    c. What is a major weakness of the linear probability model?

19. Describe how a linear discriminant analysis model works. Identify and discuss the criticisms which have been made regarding the use of this type of model to make credit risk evaluations.

20. MNO, Inc., a publicly traded manufacturing firm in the United States, has provided the following financial information in its application for a loan.

Assets		Liabilities and Equity	
Cash	$ 20	Accounts Payable	$ 30
Accounts Receivables	$ 90	Notes Payable	$ 90
Inventory	$ 90	Accruals	$ 30
		Long-term debt	$150
Plant and equipment	$500	Equity	$400
Total assets	$700	Total liabilities and equity	$700

Also assume sales = $500, cost of goods sold = $360, taxes = $56, interest payments = $40, and net income = $44; the dividend payout ratio is 50 percent, and the market value of equity is equal to the book value.

    a. What is the Altman discriminant function value for MNO, Inc.? Recall that:

    Net working capital = current assets minus current liabilities.

    Current assets = Cash + Accounts receivable + Inventories.

    Current liabilities = Accounts payable + Accruals + Notes payable.

    EBIT = Revenues − Cost of goods sold − depreciation.

    Taxes = (EBIT − Interest) (Tax rate).

    Net income = EBIT − Interest − Taxes.

    Retained earnings = Net income (1 − dividend payout ratio)

    b. Should you approve MNO, Inc.'s, application to your bank for a $500 capital expansion loan?

    c. If sales for MNO were $300, the market value of equity was only half of book value, and the cost of goods sold and interest were unchanged, what would be the net income for MNO? Assume the tax credit can be used to offset other tax liabilities incurred by other divisions of the firm. Would your credit decision change?

    d. Would the discriminant function change for firms in different industries? Would the function be different for retail lending in different geographic sections of the country? What are the implications for the use of these types of models by FIs?

21. Consider the coefficients of Altman's Z-score. Can you tell by the size of the coefficients which ratio appears most important in assessing creditworthiness of a loan applicant? Explain.

22. If the rate on one-year T-bills currently is 6 percent, what is the repayment probability for each of the following two securities? Assume that if the loan is defaulted, no payments are expected. What is the market-determined risk premium for the corresponding probability of default for each security?

    a. One-year AA rated bond yielding 9.5 percent.

    b. One-year BB rated bond yielding 13.5 percent.

23. A bank has made a loan charging a base lending rate of 10 percent. It expects a probability of default of 5 percent. If the loan is defaulted, it expects to recover 50 percent of its money through the sale of its collateral. What is the expected return on this loan?

24. Assume that a one-year T-Bill is currently yielding 5.5 percent and a AAA-rated discount bond with similar maturity is yielding 8.5 percent.

    a. If the expected recovery from collateral in the event of default is 50 percent of principal and interest, what is the probability of repayment of the AAA-rated bond? What is the probability of default?

    b. What is the probability of repayment of the AAA-rated bond if the expected recovery from collateral in the case of default is 94.47 percent of principal and interest? What is the probability of default?

    c. What is the relationship between the probability of default and the proportion of principal and interest which may be recovered in case of default on the loan?

25. What is meant by the phrase *marginal default probability?* How does this term differ from *cumulative default probability?* How are the two terms related?

26. Calculate the term structure of default probabilities over three years using the following spot rates from the Treasury and corporate bond (pure discount) yield curves. Be sure to calculate both the annual marginal and the cumulative default probabilities.

	Spot 1 year	Spot 2 year	Spot 3 year
Treasury bonds	5.0%	6.1%	7.0%
BBB-rated bonds	7.0%	8.2%	9.3%

27. The bond equivalent yields for U.S. Treasury and A-rated corporate bonds with maturities of 93 and 175 days are given below:

	93 days	175 days
U.S. Treasury	8.07%	8.11%
A-rated corporate	8.42%	8.66%
Spread	0.35%	0.55%

    a. What are the implied forward rates for both an 82-day Treasury and an 82-day A-rated bond beginning in 93 days? Use daily compounding on a 365-day year basis.

    b. What is the implied probability of default on A-rated bonds over the next 93 days? Over 175 days?

    c. What is the implied default probability on an 82-day A-rated bond to be issued in 93 days?

28. What is the mortality rate of a bond or loan? What are some of the problems with using a mortality rate approach to determine the probability of default of a given bond issue?

29. The following is a schedule of historical defaults (yearly and cumulative) experienced by an FI manager on a portfolio of commercial and mortgage loans.

Loan Type	*Years after Issuance*				
	1 Year	2 Years	3 Years	4 Years	5 Years
Commercial:					
Annual default	0.00%	_____	0.50%	_____	0.30%
Cumulative default	_____	0.10%	_____	0.80%	_____
Mortgage:					
Annual default	0.10%	0.25%	0.60%	_____	0.80%
Cumulative default	_____	_____	_____	1.64%	_____

    a. Complete the blank spaces in the table.

    b. What are the probabilities that each type of loan will not be in default after five years?

    c. What is the measured difference between the cumulative default (mortality) rates for commercial and mortgage loans after four years?

30. The table below shows the dollar amounts of outstanding bonds and corresponding default amounts for every year over the past five years. Note that the default figures are in millions, while those outstanding are in billions. The outstanding figures reflect default amounts and bond redemptions.

Loan Type	*Years after Issuance*				
	1 Year	2 Years	3 Years	4 Years	5 Years
A-rated: Annual					
default (millions)	0	0	0	$ 1	$ 2
Outstanding					
(billions)	$100	$95	$93	$91	$88
B-rated: Annual					
default (millions)	0	$ 1	$ 2	$ 3	$ 4
Outstanding					
(billions)	$100	$94	$92	$89	$85
C-rated: Annual					
default (millions)	$ 1	$ 3	$ 5	$ 5	$ 6
Outstanding					
(billions)	$100	$97	$90	$85	$79

What are the annual and cumulative default rates of the above bonds?

31. What is RAROC? How does this model use the concept of duration to measure the risk exposure of a loan? How is the expected change in the credit premium measured? What precisely is ΔL in the RAROC equation?

32. A bank is planning to make a loan of $5,000,000 to a firm in the steel industry. It expects to charge an up-front fee of 1.5 percent and a servicing fee of 50 basis points. The loan has a maturity of 8 years with a duration of 7.5 years. The cost of funds (the RAROC benchmark) for the bank is 10 percent. Assume the bank has estimated the maximum change in the risk premium on the steel manufacturing sector to be approximately 4.2 percent, based on two years of historical data. The current market interest rate for loans in this sector is 12 percent.

    a. Using the RAROC model, estimate whether the bank should make the loan.

    b. What should be the duration in order for this loan to be approved?

    c. Assuming that the duration cannot be changed, how much additional interest and fee income will be necessary to make the loan acceptable?

    d. Given the proposed income stream and the negotiated duration, what adjustment in the loan rate would be necessary to make the loan acceptable?

33. A firm is issuing two-year debt in the amount of $200,000. The current market value of the assets is $300,000. The risk-free rate is 6 percent, and the standard deviation of the rate of change in the underlying assets of the borrower is 10 percent. Using an options framework, determine the following:

    a. The current market value of the loan.

    b. The risk premium to be charged on the loan.

34. A firm has assets of $200,000 and total debts of $175,000. Using an option pricing model, the implied volatility of the firm's assets is estimated at $10,730. Under the KMV method, what is the expected default frequency (assuming a normal distriubtion for assets)?

35. Carman County Bank (CCB) has outstanding a $5,000,000 face value, adjustable rate loan to a company that has a leverage ratio of 80 percent. The current risk-free rate is 6 percent, and the time to maturity on the loan is exactly ½ year. The asset risk of the borrower, as measured by the standard deviation of the rate of change in the value of the underlying assets, is 12 percent. The normal density function values are given below:

h	N(h)	h	N(h)
−2.55	0.0054	2.50	0.9938
−2.60	0.0047	2.55	0.9946
−2.65	0.0040	2.60	0.9953
−2.70	0.0035	2.65	0.9960
−2.75	0.0030	2.70	0.9965

    a. Use the Merton option valuation model to determine the market value of the loan.

    b. What should be the interest rate for the last six months of the loan?

The questions and problems that follow refer to Appendixes 11A and 11B.

Refer to the example information in Appendix 11A.

36. From Table 11A–1, what is the probability of a loan upgrade? A loan downgrade?

    a. What is the impact of a rating upgrade or downgrade?

    b. How is the discount rate determined after a credit event has occurred?

    c. Why does the probability distribution of possible loan values have a negative skew?

    d. How do the capital requirements of the CreditMetrics approach differ from those of the BIS and the Federal Reserve System?

37. A five-year fixed-rate loan of $100 million carries a 7 percent annual interest rate. The borrower is rated BB. Based on hypothetical historical data, the probability distribution given below has been determined for various

ratings upgrades, downgrades, status quo, and default possibilities over the next year. Information also is presented reflecting the forward rates of the current Treasury yield curve and the annual credit spreads of the various maturities of BBB bonds over Treasuries.

Rating	Probability Distribution	New Loan Value plus Coupon $	t	Forward Rate Spreads at time t $r_t\%$	$s_t\%$
AAA	0.01%	$114.82	1	3.00%	0.72%
AA	0.31%	$114.60	2	3.40%	0.96%
A	1.45%	$114.03	3	3.75%	1.16%
BBB	6.05%		4	4.00%	1.30%
BB	85.48%	$108.55			
B	5.60%	$ 98.43			
CCC	0.90%	$ 86.82			
Default	0.20%	$ 54.12			

    a. What is the present value of the loan at the end of the one-year risk horizon for the case where the borrower has been upgraded from BB to BBB?

    b. What is the mean (expected) value of the loan at the end of year one?

    c. What is the volatility of the loan value at the end of year one?

    d. Calculate the 5 percent and 1 percent VARs for this loan assuming a normal distribution of values.

    e. Estimate the "approximate" 5 percent and 1 percent VARs using the actual distribution of loan values and probabilities.

    f. How do the capital requirements of the 1 percent VARs calculated in parts (*d*) and (*e*) above compare with the capital requirements of the BIS and the Federal Reserve System?

    g. Go to the J. P. Morgan Web site (www.jpmorgan.com/RiskManagement/CreditMetrics/). What data set information is provided for use with CreditMetrics?

38. How does the Credit Risk+ model of Credit Suisse Financial Products differ from the CreditMetrics model of J. P. Morgan?

39. An FI has a loan portfolio of 10,000 loans of $10,000 each. The loans have an historical average default rate of 4 percent, and the severity of loss is 40 cents per $1.

    a. Over the next year, what are the probabilities of having default rates of 2, 3, 4, 5, and 8 percent?

    b. What would be the dollar loss on the portfolios with default rates of 4 and 8 percent?

    c. How much capital would need to be reserved to meet the 1 percent worst-case loss scenario? What proportion of the portfolio's value would this capital reserve be?

APPENDIX 11A*
CREDITMETRICS

CreditMetrics, was introduced in 1997 by J. P. Morgan and its co-sponsors (Bank of America, Union Bank of Switzerland, etc.) as a value at risk (*VAR*) framework to apply to the valuation and risk of nontradable assets such as loans and privately placed bonds.[1] Thus, while RiskMetrics seeks to answer the question, If tomorrow is a bad day, how much will I lose on tradable assets such as stocks, bonds, and equities? CreditMetrics asks, If next year is a bad year, how much will I lose on my loans and loan portfolio?

With RiskMetrics (see Chapter 10) we answer this question by looking at the market value or price of an asset and the volatility of that asset's price or return in order to calculate a probability (e.g., 5 percent) that the value of that asset will fall below some given value tomorrow. In the case of RiskMetrics, this involves multiplying the estimated standard deviation of returns σ on that asset by 1.65 and then revaluing the current market value of the position (*P*) downward by 1.65σ.

That is, *VAR* for one day (or *DEAR*) is

$$VAR = P \times 1.65 \times \sigma$$

Unfortunately, for loans, since they are not publicly traded, we observe neither *P* (the loan's market value) nor σ (the volatility of loan value over the horizon of interest—assumed to be 1 year for loans and bonds under CreditMetrics).

However, using (1) available data on a borrower's credit rating, (2) the probability of that rating changing over the next year (the rating transition matrix), (3) recovery rates on defaulted loans, and (4) yield spreads in the bond market, it is possible to calculate a hypothetical *P* and σ for any nontraded loan or bond and thus a *VAR* figure for individual loans and the loan portfolio.

Consider the example of a five-year fixed-rate loan of $100 million made at 6 percent annual interest.[2] The borrower is rated BBB.

Rating Migration

Based on historic data collected by S&P, Moody's, and other bond analysts, it is estimated that the probability of a BBB borrower staying at BBB over the next year is 86.93 percent. There is also some probability that the borrower of the loan will be upgraded (e.g., to A), and there is some probability that

it will be downgraded (e.g., to CCC) or even default. Indeed, there are eight possible transitions the borrower can make over the next year, seven of which involve upgrades, downgrades, and no rating changes and one which involves default. The estimated probabilities of these are shown in Table 11A–1.

Valuation

The effect of rating upgrades and downgrades is to impact the required credit risk spreads or premiums on loans and thus the implied market value (or present value) of the loan. If a loan is downgraded, the required credit spread premium should rise (remember, the loan rate in our example is fixed at 6 percent) so that the present value of the loan to the FI should fall; the reverse is true for a credit rating upgrade.

Technically, since we are revaluing the five-year $100 million, 6 percent loan at the end of the first year after a credit event has occurred during that year, then (measured in $ millions)

$$P = 6 + \frac{6}{(1 + r_1 + s_1)} + \frac{6}{(1 + r_2 + s_2)^2} + \frac{6}{(1 + r_3 + s_3)^3} + \frac{106}{(1 + r_4 + s_4)^4}$$

where the r_i are the risk-free rates on T-bonds expected to exist one year, two years, and so on, into the future (i.e., they reflect forward rates from the current Treasury yield curve—see Chapter 26) and s_i are annual credit spreads for loans of a particular rating class of one year, two years, three years, and four years maturity (the latter are derived from observed spreads in the corporate bond market over Treasuries). The first coupon or interest payment of $6 million in the above example is

TABLE 11A–1   One-Year Transition Probabilities for BBB-Rated Borrower

Rating	Transition Probability	
AAA	0.02%	
AA	0.33%	
A	5.95%	
BBB	86.93% ←	Most likely to stay in same class
BB	5.30%	
B	1.17%	
CCC	0.12%	
Default	0.18%	

[1]See CreditMetrics, *Technical Document,* New York, April 2, 1997; and Saunders, Credit Risk Measurement, Chapter 4.

[2]This example is based on the one used in the CreditMetrics *Technical Document,* April 2, 1997.

TABLE 11A–2   Value of the Loan at the End of 1 Year under Different Ratings

Year-End Rating	Loan Value ($) (including first year coupon)
AAA	109.37
AA	109.19
A	108.66
BBB	107.55
BB	102.02
B	98.10
CCC	83.64
Default	51.13

FIGURE 11A–1

Distribution of Loan Values on a 5-Year BBB Loan at the End of Year 1

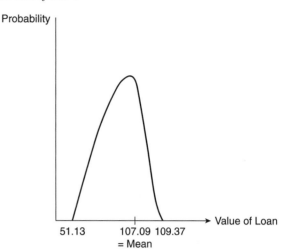

undiscounted and can be viewed as being similar to the accrued interest earned on a bond or a loan.

Suppose the borrower gets upgraded during the next year from BBB to A.

Then the present value or market value of the loan to the FI at the end of the one-year risk horizon (in millions) is

$$P = 6 + \frac{6}{(1.0372)} + \frac{6}{(1.0432)^2} + \frac{6}{(1.0493)^3} + \frac{6}{(1.0532)^4}$$
$$= \$108.66$$

That is, at the end of the first year, if the loan borrower is upgraded from BBB to A, the $100 million (book value) loan has a market value to the FI of $108.66 million. (This is the value the FI would theoretically be able to obtain if it "sold" the loan, with the accrued first year coupon of 6, to another FI at the year 1 horizon at the fair market price or value). Table 11A–2 shows the value of the loan if other credit events occur. Note that the loan has a maximum market value of $109.37 (if the borrower is upgraded to AAA) and a minimum value of $51.13 if the borrower defaults. The minimum value is the estimated recovery value of the loan if the borrower declares bankruptcy.

The probability distribution of loan values is shown in Figure 11A–1. As can be seen, the value of the loan has a fixed upside and a long downside (i.e., a negative skew). It is clear that the value of the loan is not symmetrically (or normally) distributed. Thus CreditMetrics produces two VAR measures:

1. Based on the normal distribution of loan values
2. Based on the actual distribution of loan values

Calculation of VAR

Table 11A–3 shows the calculation of the *VAR* based on each approach for both the 5 percent worst-case and the 1 percent worst-case scenarios.

The first step in calculating *VAR* is to calculate the mean of the loan's value, or its expected value, at year 1, which is the sum of each possible loan value at the end of year 1 times its transition probability. As can be seen, the mean value of the loan is $107.09 (also see Figure 11A–1). However, the FI is concerned about losses or volatility in value. In particular, if next year is a bad year, how much can it expect to lose? We could define a bad year as occurring once every 20 years (the 5 percent *VAR*) or once every 100 years (the 1 percent *VAR*)— this is similar to market risk *VAR* except that for credit risk the horizon is longer: 1 year rather than 1 day as under market risk *DEAR*.

Assuming that loan values are normally distributed, the variance of loan value around its mean is $8.9477 (squared) and its standard deviation or volatility is the square root of the variance equal to $2.99. Thus the 5 percent *VAR* for the loan is 1.65 × $2.99 = $4.93 million, while the 1 percent *VAR* is 2.33 × $2.99 = $6.97 million. However, this is likely to underestimate the actual or true *VAR* of the loan because, as shown in Figure 11A–1, the distribution of the loan's value is clearly nonnormal. In particular, it demonstrates a negative skew or a long-tail downside risk. Using the actual distribution of loan values and probabilities, we can see from Table 11A–3 that there is a 6.77 percent probability that the loan value will fall below $102.02, implying an "approximate" 5 percent actual *VAR* of over $107.09 − $102.02 = $5.07 million, and that there is a 1.47 percent probability that the loan value will fall below $98.10, implying an "approximate" 1 percent actual *VAR* of over $107.09 − $98.10 = $8.99. These actual *VARs* could be made less approximate by using linear interpolation to get the exact 5 percent and 1 percent *VAR* measures. For example, since the 1.47 percentile equals 98.10 and the 0.3 percentile equals 83.64, then, using linear interpolation, the 1.00 percentile equals $92.29. This suggests an actual 1 percent *VAR* of $107.09 − 92.29 = $14.80.

TABLE 11A–3   VAR Calculations for the BBB Loan

Year-End Rating	Probability of State, %	New Loan Value plus Coupon, $	Probability Weighted Value, $	Difference of Value from Mean, $	Probability Weighted Difference Squared
AAA	0.02%	$109.37	$ 0.02	$ 2.28	0.0010
AA	0.33	109.19	0.36	2.10	0.0146
A	5.95	108.66	6.47	1.57	0.1474
BBB	86.93	107.55	93.49	0.46	0.1853
BB	5.30	102.02	5.41	(5.06)	1.3592
B	1.17	98.10	1.15	(8.99)	0.9446
CCC	0.12	83.64	1.10	(23.45)	0.6598
Default	0.18	51.13	0.09	(55.96)	5.6358

Mean = $107.09   Variance = 8.94777

σ = Standard deviation = $2.99

Assuming Normal Distribution $\begin{cases} 5\% \text{ VAR} = 1.65 \times \sigma = \$4.93 \\ 1\% \text{ VAR} = 2.33 \times \sigma = \$6.97 \end{cases}$

Assuming Actual Distribution* $\begin{cases} 5\% \text{ VAR} = 95\% \text{ of actual distribution} = \$107.09 - \$102.02 = \$5.07 \\ 1\% \text{ VAR} = 99\% \text{ of actual distribution} = \$107.09 - \$ 98.10 = \$8.99 \end{cases}$

*5% VAR approximated by 6.77% VAR (i.e., 5.3% + 1.17% + 0.12% + 0.18%) and 1% VAR approximated by 1.47% VAR (i.e., 1.17% + 0.12% + 0.18%).

Capital Requirements

It is interesting to compare these *VAR* figures with the capital reserves against loans currently required by the Federal Reserve and the BIS. While these requirements are explained in more detail in Chapter 20, they basically amount to a requirement that a bank (or thrift) hold an 8 percent ratio of the book value of the loan as a capital reserve against unexpected losses. In our example of a $100 million face (book) value BBB loan, the capital requirement would be $8 million. This contrasts to the two market-based *VAR* measures developed above. Using the 1 percent *VAR* based on the normal distribution, a capital requirement of $6.97 million would be required (i.e., less than the BIS requirement), while using the 1 percent *VAR* based on the iterated value from the actual distribution, a

$14.80 million capital requirement would be required (which is much greater than the BIS capital requirement).

It should be noted that under the CreditMetrics approach every loan is likely to have a different *VAR* and thus a different implied capital requirement. This contrasts to the current BIS regulations, where all private sector loans of different ratings (AAA through CCC) and different maturities are subject to the same 8 percent capital requirement. Thus, an important objective of the CreditMetrics sponsors is to get regulators to move toward accepting "internal model"–based measures of capital requirements for credit risk similar to the way in which they have accepted internal model–based measures for market risk capital requirements (implemented in January 1998)—see Chapter 10.

APPENDIX 11B*
CREDIT RISK+

Credit Risk+ is a model developed by Credit Suisse Financial Products (CSFP).[1] Unlike CreditMetrics, which seeks to develop a full *VAR* framework, Credit Risk+ attempts to estimate the expected loss of loans and the distribution of those losses, with a focus on calculating the FI's required capital reserves to meet losses above a certain level.

[1] See Credit Suisse Financial Products, "Credit Risk+: Credit Risk Management Framework," October 1997, New York/London, and Saunders, Credit Risk Measurement, Chapter 7.

The key ideas come from the insurance literature (especially fire insurance), where the losses incurred by an insurer reflect two things: (1) the probability of a house burning down (what an insurer calls the "frequency" of the event) and (2) the value of the house lost if it burns down (what the insurer calls "severity of the loss"). We can apply the same idea to loans where the loss distribution on a portfolio of loans reflects the combination (or product) of the frequency of loan defaults and their severity. This framework is shown in Figure 11B–1.

Unlike CreditMetrics, which assumes that there is a fixed probability of a loan defaulting in the next period (defined by its historic transition probability), it is assumed in its simplest form that (1) the probability of any individual loan defaulting in the portfolio of loans is random and (2) the correlation between the defaults on any pair of loans is zero (i.e., individual loan default probabilities are independent). This framework is therefore most appropriate for analyzing the default risk on large portfolios of small loans (e.g., small business loans, mortgages, and consumer loans) rather than portfolios which contain a few large loans. The model's assumptions about the probability (frequency) of default are shown in Figure 11B–2.

When the probability of default on individual loans is small and this probability is independent across loans in the portfolio, the frequency distribution of default rates can be modeled by a Poisson distribution. Below we look at an example.

FIGURE 11B–1

CreditRisk+ Model of the Determinants of Loan Losses

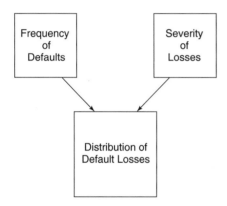

Assume that:

1. The FI makes 100 loans of $100,000 each.
2. Historically 3 percent (3 of 100) of loans have defaulted on average.
3. On default, the severity of loss on each of these loans is the same at 20 cents per $1 (or $20,000 per $100,000 loan).

The Frequency Distribution of Default Rates

From the Poisson distribution, we can easily generate the probability of different numbers of defaults (in a 100-loan portfolio) occurring:

$$\text{Probability of } n \text{ defaults } = \frac{e^{-m}m^n}{n!}$$

Where e is exponential (2.71828), m is the historic average number of defaults (3 of 100 or 3 percent) for loans of this type, and $n!$ is n factorial where n is the number of loans for which we are trying to determine the probability of default.

For example, the probability of 3 of 100 loans defaulting over the next year is

$$\frac{(2.71828)^{-3} \times 3^3}{1 \times 2 \times 3} = .224$$

That is, there is a 22.4 percent probability of 3 loans defaulting. We can also determine the probability of 4 of the 100 loans defaulting:

$$\frac{(2.71828)^{-3} \times 3^4}{1 \times 2 \times 3 \times 4} = .168$$

or 16.8 percent.

The frequency distribution of default rates is shown in Figure 11B–3.

FIGURE 11B–2

The Frequency of Default on a Loan Assumed by CreditRisk

Default Rate

Possible path of default rate

Frequency of default rate outcomes

0

1 Year

FIGURE 11B–3

Frequency Distribution of Default Rates from Example

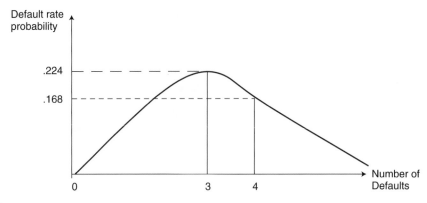

FIGURE 11B–4

Frequency Distribution of Losses on Loan Portfolio from Example

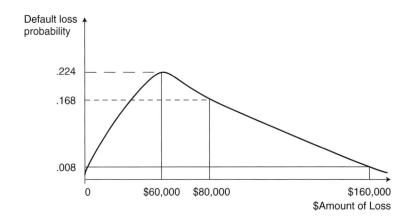

We can multiply these default numbers by loss severity to get the distribution of dollar *losses* on the loan:

Dollar loss of 3 loans defaulting = 3 × 20c × $100,000
= $60,000

Dollar loss of 4 loans defaulting = 4 × 20c × $100,000
= $80,000

The distribution of dollar losses is shown in Figure 11B–4.

As under CreditMetrics, we may ask what the 1 percent worst-case loss scenario (i.e., the 99th worst year's loss out of 100 years) is. From the Poisson distribution, the probability of having 8 losses per 100 loans is approximately 1 percent; thus, there is a 1 percent chance of losing $160,000.[2] In the framework of Credit Risk+ the FI would hold a capital reserve to meet the difference between the unexpected (1 percent) loss rate and the average or expected loss rate (the losses associated with three defaults), with expected losses being covered by loan loss provisions and pricing. In our example the capital

reserve would be $160,000 − $60,000 = $100,000, or approximately 1 percent of the value of the portfolio. One reason why capital reserves are low in this case is that the severity of loss is assumed to be low and equal in each case (i.e., only 20 percent). If, for example, each of the loans in the portfolio lost 80 cents on default, the required capital reserve would rise to 4 percent of the loan portfolio's value. Moreover, in general, the severity of the losses themselves has a distribution. For example, if a loan defaults, the FI might lose 20 cents in $1, while if loan 2 defaults, it may lose 30 cents in $1, and so on. Allowing for a distribution in the severity of losses as well as in the number of defaults can be easily built into the Credit Risk+ framework, as can allowing the mean default rate itself to be variable (see the CSFP technical document for more details).[3]

---

[2]In actual practice, the probability of eight losses is 0.8 percent.

[3]Similarly, allowing the mean default rate to shift (have a distribution) can also be incorporated into the model. This allows the FI to analyze unexpected loan losses in recessions versus expansions.

CHAPTER 12

CREDIT RISK

Loan Portfolio and Concentration Risk

Simple Models of Loan Concentration Risk 249

Loan Portfolio Diversification and Modern Portfolio Theory (MPT) 251
- KMV Portfolio Manager Model 253
- Partial Applications of Portfolio Theory 255
- Loan Loss Ratio-Based Models 257
- Regulatory Models 257

Introduction

The models discussed in the previous chapter describe alternative ways by which an FI manager can measure the default risks on individual debt instruments such as loans and bonds. In this chapter we concentrate on the ability of an FI manager to measure credit risk in a loan (asset) portfolio context and to benefit from loan (asset) portfolio diversification. Additionally, we look at the potential use of loan portfolio models in setting maximum concentration (borrowing) limits for certain business or borrowing sectors (e.g., sectors identified by their SIC codes). We also discuss regulatory methods for measuring default risk. In particular, the FDIC Improvement Act of 1991 required bank regulators to incorporate credit concentration risk into their evaluation of bank insolvency risk. Moreover, a debate currently is being conducted among bankers and regulators about how this could be done. One possibility is that banks will be allowed to use their own "internal" models, such as CreditMetrics and Credit Risk+ (discussed in the Chapter 11 Appendixes) and KMV's Portfolio Manager (discussed later in this chapter), to calculate their capital requirements against insolvency risk from excessive loan concentrations. Further the National Association of Insurance Commissioners (NAIC) has developed limits for different types of assets and borrowers in insurers' portfolios—a so-called pigeonhole approach.

Simple Models of Loan Concentration Risk

Two simple models are widely employed by bankers to measure credit risk concentration beyond the purely subjective model of "we have already lent too much to

TABLE 12–1   A Hypothetical Rating Migration or Transition Matrix

		Risk Grade at End of Year			
		1	*2*	*3*	*D**
Risk grade at	1	.85	.10	.04	.01
beginning of year	2	.12	.83	.03	.02
	3	.03	.13	.80	.04

*D = default.

this borrower."[1] The first is called migration analysis, where lending officers track S&P, Moody's, or their own internal credit ratings of certain pools of loans or certain sectors—for example, machine tools. If the credit ratings of a number of borrowers in a sector or rating class decline faster than has been historically experienced, then lending to that sector or class will be curtailed.

Loan Migration Matrix
Measures the probability of a loan being upgraded, downgraded, or defaulting over some period.

A **loan migration matrix** (or transition matrix) seeks to reflect the historic experience of a pool of loans in terms of their credit-rating migration over time. As such, it can be used as a benchmark against which the credit migration patterns of any new pool of loans can be compared.

Table 12–1 shows a hypothetical credit migration matrix or table in which loans are graded into 3 rating classes (most FIs use 9 or 10 rating classes). In the rows are the grades at which the portfolio of loans began the year, and in the columns are the grades at which they ended the year. The numbers in the table are called transition probabilities, reflecting the average experience (proportions) of loans that began the year, say, as grade 2 remaining grade 2 at the end of the year, being upgraded to a 1, being downgraded to a 3, or defaulting (*D*).

For example, looking at loans that began the year at grade 2, historically (on average) 12 percent have been upgraded to 1, 83 percent have remained at 2, 3 percent have been downgraded to 3, and 2 percent have defaulted by the end of the year. Suppose that the FI is evaluating the credit risk of its current portfolio of loans of grade 2 rated borrowers and that over the last few years a much higher percentage (say, 5 percent) of loans has been downgraded to 3 and a higher percentage (say, 3 percent) has defaulted than is implied by the historic transition matrix. The FI may then seek to restrict its supply of lower-quality loans (e.g., those rated 2 and 3), concentrating more of its portfolio on grade 1 loans.[2] At the very least, it should seek higher credit risk premiums on lower-quality (graded) loans. Not only is migration analysis used to evaluate commercial loan portfolios, it is widely used to analyze credit card portfolios and consumer loans as well.[3]

A second simple model is for management to set some firm external limit on the maximum amount of loans that can be made to an individual borrower or sector. For example, suppose management is unwilling to permit losses exceeding

---

[1]See Board of Governors of the Federal Reserve, "Revisions to Risk Based Capital Standards to Account for Concentration of Credit Risk and Risks of Non Traditional Activities," Section 305, FDICIA, Washington, D.C., March 26, 1993.

[2]The theory underlying the use of the average one-year transition matrix (based on historic data) as a benchmark is that actual transactions will fluctuate randomly around these average transitions. In the terminology of statistics, actual transitions follow a stable Markov (chain) process.

[3]See, for example, J. Kallberg and A. Saunders, "Markov Chain Approaches to the Analysis of Payment Behavior of Retail Credit Customers," *Financial Management,* 1983, pp. 5–14.

10 percent of an FI's capital to a particular sector. If it is estimated that the amount lost per dollar of defaulted loans in this sector is 50 cents, then the maximum loans to a single borrower as a percent of capital, defined as the concentration limit, is

$$\text{Concentration limit} = \text{Maximum loss as a percent capital} \times \frac{1}{\text{Loss rate}}$$
$$= 10\% \times [\,1/.5\,]$$
$$= 20\%$$

Bank regulators in recent years have limited loan concentrations to *individual borrowers* to a maximum of 10 percent of a bank's capital.

Concept Questions

1. What would the concentration limit be if the loss rate on bad loans is 25 cents on the dollar?
2. What would the concentration limit be if the maximum loss (as a percent of capital) is 15 percent instead of 10 percent?

Next we look at the use of more sophisticated portfolio theory–based models to set concentration limits. While these models have a great deal of potential, data availability and other implementation problems have, until recently, hindered their use. The basic idea is to select the portfolio of loans that maximizes the return on the loan portfolio for any given level of risk (or that minimizes the degree of portfolio risk for any given level of returns).

Loan Portfolio Diversification and Modern Portfolio Theory (MPT)

To the extent that an FI manager holds widely traded loans and bonds as assets or, alternatively, can calculate loan or bond returns, portfolio diversification models can be used to measure and control the FI's aggregate credit risk exposure. Suppose the manager can estimate the expected returns of each loan or bond ($\bar{R}_i$) in the FI's portfolio.

After calculating the individual security return series, the FI manager can compute the expected return ($\bar{R}_p$) on a portfolio of assets as

$$\bar{R}_P = \sum_{i=1}^{N} X_i \bar{R}_i \tag{1}$$

In addition, the variance of returns or risk of the portfolio (σ_p^2) can be calculated as

$$\sigma_p^2 = \sum_{i=1}^{n} X_i^2 \, \sigma_i^2 + \sum_{i=1}^{n} \sum_{\substack{j=1 \\ i \neq j}}^{n} X_i X_j \sigma_{ij} \tag{2}$$

or[4]

$$\sigma_p^2 = \sum_{i=1}^{n} X_i^2 \, \sigma_i^2 + \sum_{i=1}^{n} \sum_{\substack{j=1 \\ i \neq j}}^{n} X_i X_j \rho_{ij} \sigma_i \sigma_j \tag{3}$$

---

[4] The correlation coefficient reflects the joint movement of asset returns or default risks in the case of loans and lies between the values $-1 \leq \rho \leq +1$, where ρ is the correlation coefficient. As can be seen from Equations (2) and (3), the covariance between any two assets (σ_{ij}) is related to the correlation coefficient (ρ_{ij}) by $\sigma_{ij} = \rho_{ij} \, \sigma_i \, \sigma_j$.

FIGURE 12–1

*FI Portfolio
Diversification*

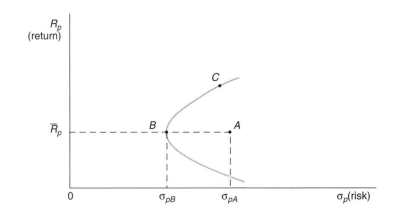

where

$\bar{R}_p$ = The expected or mean return on the asset portfolio

Σ = Summation sign

$\bar{R}_i$ = The mean return on the ith asset in the portfolio

X_i = The proportion of the asset portfolio invested in the ith asset (the desired concentration amount)

σ_i^2 = The variance of returns on the ith asset

σ_{ij} = The covariance of returns between the ith and jth assets

ρ_{ij} = The correlation between the returns on the ith and jth assets

The fundamental lesson of modern portfolio theory is that by taking advantage of its size, an FI can diversify away considerable amounts of credit risk as long as the returns on different assets are imperfectly correlated.[5]

Consider the σ_p^2 in Equation 2. If many loans have negative default covariances or correlations (ρ_{ij} are negative)—that is, when one borrower's loans do badly and another's do well—the sum of the individual credit risks of loans viewed independently will overestimate the risk of the whole portfolio. This is what we meant in Chapter 6 when we stated that by pooling funds, FIs can take advantage of the law of large numbers in their investment decisions.

Look at the advantages of diversification in Figure 12–1. Note that A is an undiversified portfolio with heavy investment concentration in just a few loans or bonds. By fully exploiting diversification potential with bonds or loans whose returns are negatively correlated or that have a low positive correlation with those in the existing portfolio, the FI manager can lower the credit risk on the portfolio from σ_{pA} to σ_{pB} while earning the same expected return. That is, portfolio B is the efficient (lowest risk) portfolio associated with portfolio return level $\bar{R}_p$. By varying the required portfolio return level $\bar{R}_p$ up and down, the manager can identify a whole frontier of efficient portfolio mixes of loans. Each portfolio mix is efficient in the sense that it offers the lowest risk level to the FI manager at each possible level of portfolio returns. However, as you can see in Figure 12–1, of all possible efficient portfolios that can be generated, portfolio B produces the lowest possible risk level for the FI manager. That is, it maximizes the gains from diversifying across all

---

[5]One objection to using modern portfolio theory for loans is that the returns on individual loans are not normally or symmetrically distributed. In particular, most loans have limited upside returns and long-tail downside risks (see the discussion in Chapter 11, Appendix A, on CreditMetrics and Chapter 9 in Saunders, *Credit Risk Measurement*).

available loans so that the manager cannot reduce the risk of the portfolio below σ_{pB}. For this reason, σ_{pB} is usually labeled the **minimum risk portfolio.**

Minimum Risk Portfolio
Combination of assets that reduces the variance of portfolio returns to the lowest feasible level.

Even though B is clearly the minimum risk portfolio, it does not generate the highest returns. Consequently, portfolio *B* may be chosen only by the most risk-averse FI managers, those whose sole objective is to minimize portfolio risk regardless of the portfolio's return. Most portfolio managers have some desired return-risk trade-off in mind; they are willing to accept more risk if they are compensated with higher expected returns.[6] One such possibility would be portfolio *C* in Figure 12–1. This is an efficient portfolio in that the FI manager has selected loan proportions (X_i) so as to produce a portfolio risk level that is a minimum for that higher expected return level. This portfolio dominates all other portfolios that can produce the same expected return level.

Portfolio theory is a highly attractive tool. Still, over and above the intuitive concept that diversification is generally good, a question arises as to its applicability for banks, insurance companies, and thrifts. These FIs often hold significant amounts of regionally specific nontraded or infrequently traded loans and bonds.

KMV Portfolio Manager Model

Despite the nontraded aspect of many loans, a great deal of recent research has gone into developing modern portfolio theory models for loans. Below we look at one approach developed by KMV Corporation called **Portfolio Manager**.

KMV Portfolio Manager
A model that applies modern portfolio theory to the loan portfolio.

Any model that seeks to estimate an efficient frontier for loans as in Figure 12–1 and thus the optimal or best proportions (X_i) in which to hold loans made to different borrowers needs to determine and measure three things [see Equations (1), (2), and (3)]: the expected return on a loan to borrower i (R_i), the risk of a loan to borrower i (σ_i), and the correlation of default risks between loans made to borrowers i and j (ρ_{ij}).

KMV measures each of these as follows:

$$R_i = AIS_i - E(L_i) = AIS_i - [EDF_i \times LGD_i]$$

$$\sigma_i = UL_i = \sigma_{Di} \times LGD_i = \sqrt{EDF_i(1 - EDF_i)} \times LGD_i$$

ρ_{ij} = correlation between the systematic return components of the equity returns of borrower i and borrower j.

Each of these needs some explanation.

Return on the loan (R_i).   The return on a loan is measured by the so-called annual all-in-spread (AIS), which measures annual fees earned on the loan by the FI plus the annual spread between the loan rate paid by the borrower and the FI's cost of

[6]The point that is chosen depends on the risk aversion of managers and the degree of separation of ownership from control. If the FI is managed by agents who perform the task of maximizing the value of the firm, they act as risk-neutral agents. They would know that stockholders, who are well diversified, could, through homemade diversification, hold the shares of many firms to eliminate borrower-specific risk. Thus, managers would seek to maximize expected return subject to any regulatory constraints on risk-taking behavior (i.e., they probably would pick a point in region *C* in Figure 12–1). However, if managers are risk averse because of their human capital invested in the FI and make lending decisions based on their own risk preferences rather than those of the stockholders, they are likely to choose a relatively low-risk portfolio, something closer to the minimum risk portfolio. For more on agency issue and bank risk taking, see A. Saunders, E. Strock, and N. G., Travlos, "Ownership Structure, Deregulation, and Bank Risk Taking," *Journal of Finance* 45 (1990), pp. 643–54.

funds. Deducted from this is the expected loss on the loan [$E(L_i)$]. This expected loss is equal to the product of the expected probability of the borrower defaulting over the next year, or its expected default frequency (EDF_i)—as discussed in Chapter 11—times the amount lost by the FI if the borrower defaults [the loss given default or LGD_i].

Risk of the Loan (σ_i).   The risk of the loan reflects the volatility of the loan's default rate (σ_{Di}) around its expected value times the amount lost given default (LGD_i). The product of the volatility of the default rate and the LGD is called the "unexpected" loss on the loan (UL_i) and is a measure of the loan's risk or σ_i. To measure the volatility of the default rate, assume that loans can either default or repay (no default); then defaults are "binomially" distributed, and the standard deviation of the default rate for the ith borrower (σ_{Di}) is equal to the square root of the probability of default times 1 minus the probability of default ($\sqrt{(EDF)(1 - EDF)}$).

Correlation (ρ_{ij}).   To measure the unobservable default risk correlation between any two borrowers, the KMV Portfolio Manager model uses the systematic return components of the stock or equity returns of the two borrowers and calculates a correlation that is based on the historical comovement between those returns. According to KMV, default correlations tend to be low and lie between .002 and .15. This makes intuitive sense. For example, what is the probability that both IBM and General Motors will go bankrupt at the same time? For both firms, their asset values would have to fall below their debt values at the same time over the next year! The likelihood of this is small except in a very severe or extreme recession. The generally low (positive) correlations between the default risks of borrowers is also good news for FI managers in that it implies that by spreading loans across many borrowers, they can reduce portfolio risk significantly.[7] Reportedly, a number of large banks are using the KMV model (and other similar models) to actively manage their loan portfolios. Nevertheless, some banks are reluctant to use such models if it involves selling or trading loans made to their long-term customers. In the view of some bankers, active portfolio management harms the long-term relationships bankers have built up with their customers. As a result, gains from diversification have to be offset against loss of reputation.

Concept Questions

1. How does KMV measure the return on a loan?
2. If EDF = 0.1 percent and LGD = 50 percent, what is the unexpected loss (σ_i) on the loan?
3. How does KMV calculate loan default correlations?

---

[7]The Portfolio Manager model of KMV also can be used to assess the risk of extending more loans to any one borrower. If more loans are extended to one borrower, fewer loans can be made to others (assuming a fixed amount of loans). Technically, since the risk of the loan portfolio is

$$UL_p^2 = \sum_{i=1}^{n} X_i^2 UL_i^2 + \sum_{i=1}^{n} \sum_{\substack{j=1 \\ i \neq j}}^{n} X_i X_j UL_i UL_j \rho_{ij}$$

The "risk contribution" of a small amount of additional loans to borrower i can be calculated as

$$\text{Risk contribution} = \frac{dUL_p^2}{dX_i}$$

Partial Applications of Portfolio Theory

Loan Volume–Based Models.   Although, as discussed above, full application of modern portfolio theory is often difficult for depository institutions lacking information on market prices of assets, sufficient loan volume data may be available to allow managers to construct modified portfolio models to analyze the overall concentration or credit risk exposure of the FI.[8] Such loan volume data include:

1. *Commercial bank call reports.* These reports to the Federal Reserve classify loans as real estate, agriculture, commercial and industrial (C&I), depository institutions, individuals, state and political subdivisions, and international. Produced for individual banks, these data can be aggregated to get estimates of the national allocation of loans among categories or types.

2. *Shared national credit.* A national database on commercial and industrial loans that breaks loan volume into two-digit Standard Industrial Classification (SIC) codes. For example, loans made to SIC code 49 are loans to public utilities. Because this database provides a national picture of the allocation of loans across sectors, it is analogous to the market portfolio or basket of commercial and industrial loans.

These data therefore provide *market benchmarks* against which an individual bank can compare its own internal allocations of loans across major lending sectors such as real estate and C&I. For example, the Shared National Credit (SNC) database provides a market benchmark of the allocation of loans across various industries or borrowers.

By comparing its own allocation, or the proportions (X_{ij}), it allocates to loans in any specific area with the national allocations across borrowers (X_i), where i designates different loan groups, the jth FI can measure the extent to which it deviates from the market portfolio benchmark. This indicates the degree to which it has developed *loan concentrations* or relatively undiversified portfolios in various areas.

For example, consider Table 12–2. In this table we evaluate the first level of the loan asset allocation problem, which is the amount to be lent to each major loan sector or type. Here we show hypothetical numbers for four types of loans: real estate, commercial and industrial, individual, and others. Column (1) shows the loan allocation proportions at the national level for all banks; this is the market portfolio

TABLE 12–2   Allocation of the Loan Portfolio to Different Sectors
(in percentages)

	(1) National	(2) Bank A	(3) Bank B
Real estate	10%	15%	10%
C&I	60	75	25
Individuals	15	5	55
Others	15	5	10
	100%	100%	100%

---

[8]This partial application of portfolio theory was first suggested by L B. Morgan, "Managing a Loan Portfolio Like an Equity Fund," *Bankers Magazine,* January–February 1989, pp. 228–35.

allocation. Column (2) lists the allocations assumed to be chosen by bank A, and Column (3) shows the allocations chosen by bank B.

Note that bank A has concentrated loans more heavily in C&I lending than the national average, while bank B has concentrated loans more heavily in lending to individuals. To calculate the extent to which each bank deviates from the national benchmark, we use the standard deviation of bank A's and bank B's loan allocations from the national benchmark. Of course, the national benchmark may be inappropriate as the relevant market portfolio for a very small regional bank, insurance company, or thrift. In this case, the FI could construct a regional benchmark from the call report data of banks (or similar data collected by insurance company and thrift regulators) in a given regional area such as the American Southwest or, alternatively, a peer group benchmark of banks of a similar asset size and location.

We calculate the relative measure of loan allocation deviation as[9]

$$\sigma_j = \sqrt{\frac{\sum_{i=1}^{4} (X_{ij} - X_i)^2}{N}} \tag{4}$$

where

σ_j = Standard deviation of bank j's asset allocation proportions from the national benchmark
X_{ij} = Asset allocation proportions of the jth bank
X_i = National asset allocations
N = Number of observations or loan categories, $N = 4$

The relevant calculation for the example in Table 12–2 is shown in Table 12–3. As you can see, bank B deviates significantly from the national benchmark due to its heavy concentration in individual loans. This is not necessarily bad; a bank may specialize in this area of lending because of its comparative advantage in information collection and monitoring of personal loans (perhaps due to its size or location). The standard deviation simply provides a manager with a measure of the degree to which an FI's loan portfolio composition deviates from the national average or benchmark. Nevertheless, to the extent that the national composition of a loan portfolio represents a more diversified market portfolio because it aggregates

TABLE 12–3   **Measures of Loan Allocation Deviation from the National Benchmark Portfolio**

	Bank A	*Bank B*
$(X_{1j} - X_1)^2$	$(.05)^2 = .0025$	$(0)^2 = 0$
$(X_{2j} - X_2)^2$	$(.15)^2 = .0225$	$(-.35)^2 = .1225$
$(X_{3j} - X_3)^2$	$(-.10)^2 = .01$	$(.4)^2 = .16$
$(X_{4j} - X_4)^2$	$(-.10)^2 = .01$	$(-.05)^2 = .0025$
$\sum_{i=1}^{n} (X_{ij} - X_i)^2$	$\sum_{i=1}^{4} = .045$	$\sum_{i=1}^{4} = .285$
	$\sigma_A = 10.61\%$	$\sigma_B = 26.69\%$

---

[9]For small samples such as this, it is really more appropriate for the divisor of Equation (4) to be $N - 1$ rather than N.

across all banks, the asset proportions derived nationally (the X_i) are likely to be closer to the *most efficient portfolio composition* than the X_{ij} of the individual bank. This partial use of modern portfolio theory provides an FI manager with a feel for the relative degree of loan concentration carried in the asset portfolio. Finally, although the preceding analysis has referred to the loan portfolio of banks, any FI can use it for any asset group or, indeed, the whole asset portfolio, whether the asset is traded or not. The key data needed are those of a peer group of regional or national financial institutions faced with similar investment decision choices.

Loan Loss Ratio–Based Models

A second partial application of MPT is a model based on historic loan loss ratios.[10] This model involves estimating the systematic loan loss risk of a particular (SIC) sector relative to the loan loss risk of a bank's total loan portfolio. This systematic loan loss can be estimated by running a time-series regression of quarterly losses of the ith sector's loss rate on the quarterly loss rate of a bank's total loans:

$$\left(\frac{\text{Sectoral losses in the } i\text{th sector}}{\text{Loans to the } i\text{th sector}}\right) = \alpha + \beta_i \left(\frac{\text{Total loan losses}}{\text{Total Loans}}\right)$$

where β measures the systematic loss sensitivity of the ith sector loans. For example, if the regression results show that the consumer sector has a β of 0.2 and the real estate sector has a β of 1.4, this suggests that loan losses in the real estate sector are systematically higher relative to the total loan losses of the bank (by definition, the loss rate β for the whole loan portfolio is 1). Similarly, loan losses in the consumer sector are systematically lower relative to the total loan losses of the bank. Consequently, it may be prudent for the bank to maintain lower concentration limits for the real estate sector as opposed to the consumer sector, especially as the economy moves toward a recession and total loan losses start to rise. The implication of this model is that sectors with lower βs could have higher concentration limits than high β sectors—since low β loan sector risks (loan losses) are less systematic, that is, are more diversifiable in a portfolio sense.[11]

Regulatory Models

As noted in the introduction to this chapter, bank and insurance regulators have also been investigating ways of measuring concentration risk. After examining various quantitative approaches, the Federal Reserve in 1994 came out with a final ruling on its proposed measure of credit concentration risk. The method adopted is largely subjective and is based on examiner discretion. The reasons given for rejecting the more technical models are that (1) current methods for identifying concentration risk are not sufficiently advanced to justify their use and (2) insufficient data are available to estimate more quantitative-type models, although the development of models like KMV (as well as CreditMetrics and Credit Risk+, discussed in the Appendixes in Chapter 11) may make bank regulators change their minds.

---

[10]See E. P. Davis, "Bank Credit Risk," Bank of England, Working Paper Series no. 8, April 1993.

[11]This type of approach suggests a possible extension to factor analysis (on the lines of multifactor models). Basically, it involves regressing SIC sector losses against various factors (market risk, interest rate risk, etc.) to see which sectors have the greatest (least) factor sensitivity. See also J. Neuberger, "Conditional Risk and Return in Bank Holding Company Stocks: A Factor-GARCH Approach." Federal Reserve Bank of San Francisco, Working Paper, May 1994.

Life and property-casualty insurance regulators have also been concerned with excessive industry sector and borrower concentrations. The Model Act established by the National Association of Insurance Commissioners (NAIC) for state regulators (remember that insurance companies are regulated at the state level—see Chapter 2) sets maximums on the investments an insurer can hold in securities or obligations of any single issuer.[12] These so-called general diversification limits are set at 3 percent for life-health insurers and 5 percent for property-casualty insurers—implying that life-health companies must hold securities of a minimum of 33 different issuers, while for PC companies the minimum is 20. The rationale for such a simple rule comes from modern portfolio theory, which shows that *equal* investments across approximately 15 or more stocks can provide significant gains from diversification, that is, a lowering of portfolio risk or the variance of returns.

Concept Questions

1. Suppose the returns on different loans were independent; would there be any gains from loan portfolio diversification?
2. How would you find the minimum risk loan portfolio in a modern portfolio theory framework?
3. Should FI managers select the minimum risk loan portfolio? Why or why not?
4. Explain the reasoning behind the Federal Reserve's 1994 decision to rely more on a subjective rather than a quantitative approach to measuring credit concentration risk. Is that view valid today?

Summary

This chapter discussed the various approaches available to an FI manager to measure credit portfolio and concentration risk. It showed how portfolio diversification can reduce the loan risk exposure of an FI. Two simple models to reduce loan concentration risk were also discussed: migration analysis, which relies on rating changes to provide information on desirable and undesirable loan concentrations, and a model that sets concentration limits based on an FI's capital exposure to different lending sectors. The application of the fully fledged MPT model to the credit (loan) concentration issue was also analyzed as was the KMV Portfolio Manager model. In addition, a model that applies portfolio theory to loan loss ratios in different sectors to determine loan concentrations was discussed. Finally, the approaches of regulators, such as the Federal Reserve and the NAIC, to measuring loan concentrations were described.

Questions and Problems

1. How do loan portfolio risks differ from individual loan risks?
2. What is migration analysis? How do FIs use it to measure credit risk concentration? What are its shortcomings?
3. What does loan concentration risk mean?
4. A manager decides not to lend to any firm in sectors that generate losses in excess of 5 percent of equity.

   a. If the average historical losses in the automobile sector total 8 percent, what is the maximum loan a manager can lend to a firm in this sector as a percentage of total capital?
   b. If the average historical losses in the mining sector total 15 percent, what is the maximum loan a manager can make to a firm in this sector as a percentage of total capital?

---

[12]See Investments of Insurers Model Act, NAIC, draft, Washington D.C., August 12, 1994.

5. An FI has set a maximum loss of 12 percent of total capital as a basis for setting concentration limits on loans to individual firms. If it has set a concentration limit of 25 percent to a firm, what is the expected loss rate for that firm?

6. Explain how modern portfolio theory can be applied to lower the credit risk of an FI's portfolio.

7. The Bank of Tinytown has two $20,000 loans which have the following characteristics: Loan A has an expected return of 10 percent and a standard deviation of returns of 10 percent. The expected return and standard deviation of returns for loan B are 12 percent and 20 percent, respectively.

    a. If the covariance between A and B is .015 (1.5 percent), what are the expected return and the standard deviation of this portfolio?

    b. What is the standard deviation of the portfolio if the covariance is −.015 (−1.5 percent)?

    c. What role does the covariance, or correlation, play in the risk reduction attributes of modern portfolio theory?

8. Why is it difficult for small banks and thrifts to measure credit risk using modern portfolio theory?

9. What is the minimum risk portfolio? Why is this portfolio usually not the portfolio chosen by FIs to optimize the return-risk trade-off?

10. The obvious benefit to holding a diversified portfolio of loans is to spread risk exposures so that a single event does not result in a great loss to the bank. Are there any benefits to not being diversified?

11. A bank vice president is attempting to rank, in terms of the risk-reward trade-off, the loan portfolios of three loan officers. How would you rank the three portfolios? The portfolios have the following information:

Portfolio	Expected Return	Standard Deviation
A	10%	8%
B	12%	9%
C	11%	10%

12. CountrySide Bank uses the KMV Portfolio Manager model to evaluate the risk-return characteristics of the loans in its portfolio. A specific $10 million loan earns 2 percent per year in fees, and the loan is priced at a 4 percent spread over the cost of funds for the bank. Because of collateral considerations, the loss to the bank if the borrower defaults will be 20 percent of the loan's face value. The expected probability of default is 3 percent. What is the anticipated return on this loan? What is the risk of the loan?

13. What databases are available that contain loan information at the national and regional levels? How can they be utilized to analyze credit concentration risk?

14. Information concerning the allocation of loan portfolios to different market sectors is given below:

Allocation of Loan Portfolios in Different Sectors (%)

Sectors	National	Bank A	Bank B
Commercial	30%	50%	10%
Consumer	40%	30%	40%
Real Estate	30%	20%	50%

Bank A and Bank B would like to estimate how much their portfolios deviate from the national average.

    a. Which bank is further away from the national average?

    b. Is a large standard deviation necessarily bad for a bank using this model?

15. Assume that the averages for national banks engaged primarily in mortgage lending have their assets diversified in the following proportions: 20 percent residential, 30 percent commercial, 20 percent international, and 30 percent mortgage-backed securities. A local bank has the following ratios: 30 percent residential, 40 percent commercial, and 30 percent international. How does the local bank differ from national banks?

16. Using regression analysis on historical loan losses, a bank has estimated the following:

$$X_C = 0.002 + 0.8X_L, \text{ and } X_h = 0.003 + 1.8X_L$$

where X_C = loss rate in the commercial sector, X_h = loss rate in the consumer (household) sector, and X_L = loss rate for its total loan portfolio.

    a. If the bank's total loan loss rates increase by 10 percent, what are the expected loss rate increases in the commercial and consumer sectors?

    b. In which sector should the bank limit its loans and why?

17. What reasons did the Federal Reserve Board offer for recommending the use of subjective evaluations of credit concentration risk instead of quantitative models?

18. What rules on credit concentrations has the National Association of Insurance Commissioners proposed? How are they related to modern portfolio theory?

19. An FI is limited to holding no more than 8 percent of the securities of a single issuer. What is the minimum number of securities it should hold to meet this requirement? What if the requirements are 2 percent, 4 percent, and 7 percent?

OFF-BALANCE-SHEET ACTIVITIES

Introduction

Off-balance-sheet activities can involve risks that add to an FI's overall risk exposure. Indeed, the failure of the U.K. investment bank Barings, the legal problems of Bankers Trust (relating to swap deals involving Procter & Gamble and Gibson Greeting Cards), and the $1.5 billion in losses and eventual bankruptcy of Orange County in California have all been linked to FI off-balance-sheet activities in derivatives. For example, in May 1998 Credit Suisse First Boston paid $52 million to Orange County to settle a lawsuit alleging that they had been in part responsible for that county's investments in risky securities and derivatives transactions. Twenty other banks and securities firms have been similarly sued. The Contemporary Perspectives box on p. 261 lists some other big losses for FIs from trading in derivatives. However, off-balance-sheet activities can also be used to hedge or reduce the interest rate, credit, and foreign exchange risks of FIs. That is, off-balance-sheet

Contemporary Perspectives

SOME BIG LOSSES ON DERIVATIVES

- December 1996: NatWest Bank finds losses of £77 million caused by mispricing of derivatives in its investment-banking arm. Former trader Kyriacos Papouis blamed for loss, caused by two years of unauthorized trading by him, but NatWest Markets chief Martin Owen resigned over the incident.
- March 1997: Damian Cope, a former trader at Midland Bank's New York branch, was banned by the Federal Reserve Board over the falsification of books and records relating to his interest-rate derivatives trading activities. Midland parent HSBC said the amount of money involved was not significant.
- November 1997: Chase Manhattan found to have lost up to $200 million on trading emerging-market debt; part of the problem was reportedly due to exposure to emerging markets through complex derivatives products.

- January 1998: Union Bank of Switzerland reported sitting on unquantified derivatives losses; UBS pledged full disclosure at a later date.
- August–September 1998: Long-Term Capital Management, a hedge fund with an exposure exceeding $1.25 trillion in derivatives and other securities, had to be rescued by a consortium of commercial and investment banks that infused an additional $3.65 billion of equity into the fund.

———————
Source: Dan Atkinson, "UBS Pledged Derivatives Explanation," *Manchester Guardian,* 1998; and update by author.

activities have both risk-increasing and risk-reducing attributes. In addition, off-balance-sheet activities are now an important source of fee income for many FI's.[1]

Off-Balance-Sheet Activities and FI Solvency

One of the most important choices facing an FI manager is the relative scale of an FI's on- and off-balance-sheet activities. On-balance-sheet activities are those most of us are aware of because they appear on the published asset and liability balance sheets of financial institutions. For example, a bank's deposits and holdings of bonds and loans are on-balance-sheet activities. By comparison, off-balance-sheet activities are less obvious and often are invisible to all but the best informed investor or regulator. In accounting terms, off-balance-sheet items usually appear below the bottom line, frequently just as footnotes to accounts. In economic terms, however, off-balance-sheet items are *contingent* assets and liabilities that affect the future, rather than the current, shape of an FI's balance sheet. As such, they have a direct impact on the future profitability and solvency performance of the FI. Consequently, efficient management of these off-balance-sheet items is central to controlling overall risk exposure in a modern FI.

From a valuation perspective, off-balance-sheet assets and liabilities have the potential to produce positive or negative *future* cash flows. As a result, the true value of an FI's capital or net worth is not simply the difference between the market value of assets and that of liabilities on its balance sheet today but also reflects the

———————
[1]This fee income can have both direct (e.g., a fee from the sale of a letter of credit) and indirect (through improved customer relationships) effects that have a positive income impact in other product areas. In cases where customers feel aggrieved with respect to derivatives purchased from a dealer FI, off-balance-sheet activities can have important negative reputational effects that have an adverse impact on the future flow of fees and other income (see "Bankers Trust Clients Complaining," *New York Times,* January 20, 1995, p. D1).

difference between the current market value of off-balance-sheet or contingent assets and liabilities.

In this section we show how off-balance-sheet activities can affect the risk exposure and performance of an FI. The following section describes different types of off-balance-sheet activities and the risks associated with each one.

An item or activity is an **off-balance-sheet (OBS) asset** if, when a contingent event occurs, the off-balance-sheet item moves onto the asset side of the balance sheet. Conversely, an item or activity is an **OBS liability** if, when the contingent event occurs, the off-balance-sheet item moves onto the liability side of the balance sheet. As we discuss in more detail later, FIs sell various performance guarantees, especially guarantees that their customers will not default on their financial and other obligations. Examples of such guarantees include letters of credit and standby letters of credit. If a customer default occurs, the bank's contingent liability (its guaranty) becomes an actual liability and moves onto the liability side of the balance sheet.

Since off-balance-sheet items are contingent assets and liabilities and move onto the balance sheet with a probability less than 1, their valuation is difficult and often highly complex. Because many off-balance-sheet items involve option features, the most common methodology has been to apply contingent claims/option pricing theory models of finance. For example, one relatively simple way to estimate the value of an OBS position in options is by calculating the **delta of an option**—the sensitivity of an option's value to a unit change in the price of the underlying security, which is then multiplied by the notional value of the option's position. (The delta of an option lies between 0 and 1.) Thus, suppose an FI has bought call options on bonds with a face or **notional value** of $100 million and the delta is calculated at .25.[2] Then the contingent asset value of this option position would be $25 million:

$$d = \text{Delta of an option} = \frac{\text{Change in the option's price}}{\text{Change in price of underlying security}} = \frac{dO}{dS} = .25$$

$$F = \text{Notional or face value amount of options} = \$100 \text{ million}$$

Delta equivalent or Contingent asset value = Delta × Face value of option = .25 × $100 million = $25 million. Of course, to figure the value of delta for the option, one needs an option pricing model such as Black-Scholes or a binomial model. In general, the delta of the option varies with the level of the price of the underlying security as it moves in and out of the money;[3] that is, $0 < d < 1$.[4] Note that if the FI sold options, they would be valued as a contingent liability.[5]

Off-Balance-Sheet (OBS) Asset
When an event occurs, this item moves onto the asset side of the balance sheet.

Off-Balance-Sheet Liability
When an event occurs, this item moves onto the liability side of the balance sheet.

Delta of an Option
The change in the value of an option for a small unit change in the price of the underlying security.

Notional Value of an OBS Item
The face value of an OBS item.

[2]A 1 cent change in the price of the bonds underlying the call option leads to a 0.25 cent (or quarter cent) change in the price value of the option.

[3]For example, for an in-the-money call option the price of the underlying security exceeds the option's exercise price. For an out-of-the money call option, the price of the underlying security is less than the option's exercise price. In general, the relationship between the value of an option and the underlying value of a security is nonlinear. Thus, using the delta method to derive the market value of an option is at best an approximation. To deal with the nonlinearity of payoffs on options, some analysts take into account the gamma as well as the delta of the option (gamma measures the change in delta as the underlying security price varies). For example, the standardized model of the BIS used to calculate the market risk of options incorporates an option's delta, its gamma, and its vega (a measure of volatility risk). See Bank for International Settlements, *Standardized Model for Market Risk,* 1996. See also J. P. Morgan, *RiskMetrics,* 4th ed., 1996.

[4]In the context of the Black-Scholes model, the value of the delta on a call option is $d = N(d_1)$, where $N(.)$ is the cumulative normal distribution function and $d_1 = [In(S/X) + (r + \sigma^2/2\tau]/\sigma\sqrt{\tau}$.

[5]Note that a cap or a floor is a complex option—that is, a collection of individual options (see Chapter 25).

Loan commitments and letters of credit are also off-balance-sheet activities that have option features.[6] Specifically, when the holder of a loan commitment or credit line decides to draw on that credit line, this person is exercising an *option to borrow.* When the buyer of a guaranty defaults, this buyer is exercising a *default* option. Similarly, when the counterparty to a derivatives transaction is unable or unwilling to meet its obligation to pay (e.g., in a swap), this is considered an exercise of a default option.

With respect to swaps, futures, and forwards, a common approach is to convert these positions into an equivalent value of the underlying assets. For example, a $20 million, 10-year, fixed–floating interest rate swap in which a bank receives 20 semi-annual fixed interest rate payments of 8 percent per annum (i.e., 4 percent per half year) and pays floating rate payments every half year indexed to LIBOR, can be viewed as the equivalent, in terms of valuation, of an on-balance-sheet position in two $20 million bonds. That is, the bank can be viewed as being long $20 million (holding an asset) in a 10-year bond with an annual coupon of 8 percent per annum and short $20 million (holding a liability) in a floating rate bond of 10 years maturity whose rate is adjusted every six months.[7] The market value of the swap can be viewed as the present value difference between the cash flows of the fixed-rate bond and the expected cash flows on the floating-rate bond. This market value is usually a very small percent of the notional value of the swap. In our example of a $20 million swap the market value is about 3 percent of this figure, or $600,000.[8]

Given this, we can calculate, in an approximate sense, the current or market value of each OBS asset and liability and their effect on an FI's solvency.

Consider Tables 13–1 and 13–2. In Table 13–1 the value of the FI's net worth *(E)* is calculated in the traditional way as the difference between the market values of its on-balance-sheet assets *(A)* and liabilities *(L).* As we discussed in Chapter 8,

$$E = A - L$$
$$10 = 100 - 90$$

Under this calculation, the market value of the stockholders' equity stake in the FI is 10 and the ratio of the FI's capital to assets (or capital-assets ratio) is 10 percent. Regulators and FIs often use the latter ratio as a simple measure of solvency (see Chapter 20 for more details).

TABLE 13–1   Traditional Valuation of an FI's Net Worth

Assets		Liabilities	
Market value of assets *(A)*	100	Market value of liabilities *(L)*	90
		Net worth *(E)*	10
	100		100

---

[6]See S. I. Greenbaum, H. Hong, and A. Thakor, "Bank Loan Commitments and Interest Rate Volatility," *Journal of Banking and Finance* 5 (1981), pp. 497–510; and T. Ho and A. Saunders, "Fixed Rate Loan Commitments, Takedown Risk, and the Dynamics of Hedging with Futures," *Journal of Financial and Quantitative Analysis* 18 (1983), pp. 499–516.

[7]An interest rate swap does not normally involve principal payments on maturity, in the case above the two principal amounts on the fixed- and floating-rate bonds cancel each other out.

[8]This is based on calculations by J. Kambhu, F. Keane, and C. Benadon, "Price Risk Intermediation in the Over-The-Counter Derivatives Markets: Interpretation of a Global Survey," Federal Reserve Bank of New York, *Economic Policy Review,* April 1996, pp. 1–15.

TABLE 13–2   Valuation of an FI's Net Worth with On- and Off-Balance-Sheet Activities Valued

Assets		Liabilities	
Market value of assets *(A)*	100	Market value of liabilities *(L)*	90
		Net worth *(E)*	5
Market value of contingent assets *(CA)*	50	Market value of contingent liabilities *(CL)*	55
	150		150

A truer picture of the FI's economic solvency should take into account both its visible on-balance-sheet and invisible OBS activities. Specifically, the FI manager needs to value contingent or future assets and liability claims as well as current assets and liabilities. In our example, the current market value of the FI's contingent assets *(CA)* is 50 while the current market value of its contingent liabilities *(CL)* is 55. Since the market value of contingent liabilities exceeds the market value of contingent assets by 5, this difference is an additional obligation, or claim, on the net worth of the FI. That is, stockholders' true net worth *(E)* is really

$$
\begin{aligned}
E &= (A - L) + (CA - CL) \\
&= (100 - 90) + (50 - 55) \\
&= 5
\end{aligned}
$$

rather than 10, as it was when we ignored off-balance-sheet activities. Thus, economically speaking, contingent assets and liabilities are contractual claims that directly impact the value of the FI. Indeed, from both the stockholders' and regulators' perspectives, large increases in the value of off-balance-sheet liabilities can render an FI economically insolvent just as effectively as can losses due to mismatched interest rate gaps and default or credit losses from on-balance-sheet activities. For example, in 1998, J. P. Morgan had to recognize $587 million in currency swaps as nonperforming, of which $489 million were related to currency swaps with SK, a Korean investment company. Two of those swaps involved the exchange of Thai baht for Japanese yen in which SK would benefit if the Thai baht rose in value. As it turned out, soon after the contract was entered into, the baht collapsed and SK disputed the legality of the contract.[9]

Concept Questions

1. Define a contingent asset and a contingent liability.
2. Suppose an FI had a market value of assets of 95 and a market value of liabilities of 88. In addition, it had contingent assets valued at 10 and contingent liabilities valued at 7. What is the FI's true net worth position?

Returns and Risks of Off-Balance-Sheet Activities

In the 1980s, rising losses on loans to less developed and Eastern European countries, rising interest rate volatility, and squeezed interest margins for on-balance-sheet lending due to nonbank competition induced many larger commercial banks to seek profitable OBS activities. By moving activities off the balance sheet, banks hoped to earn increased fee income to offset declining margins or spreads on their

---

[9]See "J. P. Morgan in Korean Battle on Derivatives," *New York Times,* February 27, 1998, p. D1.

traditional intermediation business. At the same time, they could avoid regulatory costs or taxes since reserve requirements, deposit insurance premiums, and capital adequacy requirements were not levied on off-balance-sheet activities. Thus, banks had both earnings and regulatory tax-avoidance incentives to move activities off their balance sheets.[10]

The dramatic growth in OBS activities resulted in the Federal Reserve introducing a tracking scheme in 1983. As part of their quarterly call reports, banks began filling out schedule L, on which they listed the notional size and variety of their off-balance-sheet activities. We show these off-balance-sheet activities and their distribution and growth for 1991–97 in Table 13–3.

In Table 13–3 notice the relative growth of off-balance-sheet activities. By the end of 1997, the notional or face value of off-balance-sheet bank activities was $28,409 billion compared to $4,869 billion of on-balance-sheet activities. Table 13–4 shows how the growth of derivative contracts accelerated over the 1991–97 period. While, as noted above, the notional value of OBS items overestimates their current market or contingent claims values, the growth of these activities is still nothing short of phenomenal.

From Tables 13–3, and 13–4 you can see that the major types of off-balance-sheet activities for U.S. banks are:

- Loan commitments.
- Standby letters of credit and letters of credit.
- Futures, forward contracts, swaps, and options.
- When issued securities.
- Loans sold.

Larger thrifts and insurance companies engage in most of these OBS activities as well.[11]

In the next section we analyze these off-balance-sheet activities in more detail, with particular attention being paid to the types of risk exposure an FI faces when engaging in such activities. As we discussed earlier, precise market valuation of these contingent assets and liabilities can be extremely difficult because of their complex contingent claim features and option aspects. At a very minimum, FI managers should understand not only the general features of the risk exposure associated with each major OBS asset and liability but also how each one can impact the return and profitability of an FI.

Loan Commitments

These days, most commercial and industrial loans are made by firms taking down prenegotiated lines of credit or loan commitments rather than borrowing spot loans (see Chapter 11's discussion on C&I loans).[12]

---

[10]For a modeling of the incentives to go off balance sheet due to capital requirements, see G. G. Pennacchi, "Loan Sales and the Cost of Bank Capital," *Journal of Finance* 43 (1988), pp. 375–96. Also, Chapter 26 goes into further details on incentives relating to loan sales.

[11]See, for example, M. K. Hassan and W. H. Sackley, "Determinants of Thrift Institution Off-Balance-Sheet Activities: An Empirical Investigation," Working Paper 70148, Department of Finance, University of New Orleans, LA.

[12]For example, see ibid.: S. Figlewski, "The Use of Futures and Options by Life Insurance Companies," *Best's Review,* 1989; and R. L. Shockley and A. V. Thakor, "Bank Loan Commitment Contracts: Data, Theory and Tests," *Journal of Money, Credit and Banking,* 2d (November 1997) (Part 1), pp. 517–34.

TABLE 13–3   Aggregate Volume of Off-Balance-Sheet Commitments and Contingencies by U. S. Commercial Banks, Annual Data as of December
(in billions of dollars)

	1991	1992	1993	1994	1995	1996	1997	Percentage Distribution 1997*
Commitments to lend	$1,183.4	$ 1,272.0	$ 1,455.3	$ 1,768.3	$ 2,157.4	$ 2,528.7	$ 2,966.9	10.4%
Future and forward contracts (exclude FX)								
On commodities and equities	24.9	26.3	43.9	54.3	115.0	101.6	101.2	0.4
On interest rates	1,226.5	1,738.1	2,496.7	3,434.3	3,063.1	3,201.2	4,170.9	14.7
Notional amount of credit derivatives								
Bank is guarantor	3.4	4.1	10.4	7.6	4.1	14.1	14.7	0.0
Bank is beneficiary	3.0	4.5	8.0	8.4	7.9	14.5	24.1	0.1
Standby contracts and other option contracts								
Written option contracts on interest rates	427.6	504.7	950.2	1,024.4	1,261.7	1,588.6	2,148.0	7.6
Purchased option contracts on interest rates	426.5	508.0	818.8	1,015.0	1,223.8	1,567.6	2,046.7	7.2
Written option contracts on foreign exchange	236.3	245.7	263.3	341.4	406.6	529.9	764.9	2.7
Purchased option contracts on foreign exchange	226.7	249.1	254.5	312.0	409.9	502.6	711.5	2.5
Written option contracts on commodities	40.1	30.9	50.3	77.5	111.6	106.8	159.6	0.6
Purchased option contracts on commodities	36.0	29.4	46.3	71.1	102.6	97.1	129.8	0.5
Commitments to buy FX (includes $U.S.), spot, and forward	2,624.1	3,015.5	3,689.4	4,620.4	4,525.4	5,000.8	5,844.2	20.6
Standby LCs and foreign office guarantees								
To U.S. addresses								
To non-U.S. addresses	37.0	34.5	32.2	35.7	39.6	44.5	45.5	0.2
(Amount of these items sold to others via participations)								
Commercial LCs	29.7	28.1	28.0	32.5	31.9	30.9	31.7	0.1
Participations in acceptances sold to others	0.8	0.8	0.9	0.8	1.1	1.2	1.3	0.0
Participations in acceptances bought from others	0.3	0.2	0.2	0.2	0.3	0.2	0.2	0.0
Securities borrowed	9.1	10.8	21.4	14.6	17.9	25.5	24.6	0.1
Securities lent	66.4	96.4	127.0	140.4	149.8	208.0	288.3	1.0
Other significant commitments and contingencies	13.7	8.7	7.8	3.5	3.6	14.0	10.3	0.0
Memoranda								
Notional value of all outstanding interest rate swaps	1,755.9	2,122.0	2,946.3	4,451.1	5,546.8	7,069.4	8,904.5	31.3
Mortgages sold, with recourse								
Outstanding principal balance of mortgages sold or swapped	18.5	10.7	8.8	7.5	9.4	11.4	12.1	0.0
Amount of recourse exposure on these mortgages	9.2	6.3	4.9	4.2	5.6	8.2	8.3	0.0
Total, including memoranda items	$8,510.8	$10,072.3	$13,365.5	$17,409.1	$19,195.1	$22,666.8	$28,409.3	100.0%
Total assets (on-balance-sheet items)	$3,402.2	$ 3,476.4	$ 3,673.7	$ 3,972.9	$ 4,312.7	$ 4,578.3	$ 4,869.4	

FX = Foreign exchange, LC = Letter of credit.

*1997 figures are as of September.

Sources: Call reports (OCC, Ogilvie, April 1995), Comptroller of the Currency, and FDIC.

TABLE 13–4   Derivatives by Contract Product ($ Billions)*

	91 Q4	92 Q4	93 Q4	94 Q4	95 Q4	96 Q1	96 Q2	96 Q3	96 Q4	97 Q1	97 Q2	97 Q3
Futures and forwards	$3,876	$4,780	$ 6,229	$ 8,109	$ 7,399	$ 7,653	$ 8,138	$ 8,304	$ 8,041	$ 8,866	$ 9,165	$ 9,465
Swaps	2,071	2,417	3,260	4,823	5,945	6,336	6,727	7,288	7,601	7,950	8,723	9,563
Options	1,393	1,568	2,384	2,841	3,516	3,858	4,171	4,227	4,393	5,052	5,411	5,961
Credit derivatives										19	26	39
Total	7,340	8,765	11,873	15,773	16,860	17,847	19,036	19,819	20,035	21,887	23,325	25,028

*In billions of dollars, notional value of futures, total exchange traded options, total over-the-counter options, total forwards, and total swaps. Note that data after 1994 do not include spot FX in the total notional amount of derivatives.

Credit derivatives were reported for the first time in the first quarter of 1997. Currently, the Call Report does not differentiate credit derivatives by product, which have therefore been added as a separate category. As of 1997, credit derivatives have been included in the sum of total derivatives in this table.

Note: Numbers may not add due to rounding.

Source: Call reports.

A bank's loan commitment agreement is a contractual commitment to loan to a firm a certain maximum amount (say, $10 million) at given interest rate terms (say, 12 percent). The length of time over which the borrower has the option to take down this loan is also defined in the loan commitment agreement. In return for making this loan commitment, the bank may charge an up-front fee of, say, ⅛ percent of the commitment size, or $12,500 in this example. In addition, the bank has to stand ready to supply the full $10 million at any time over the commitment period—say, one year. Meanwhile, the borrower has a valuable option to take down any amount between $0 and $10 million. The bank also may charge the borrower a **back-end fee** on any unused balances in the commitment line at the end of the period.[13] In this example, if the borrower takes down only $8 million in funds over the year and the fee on *unused* commitments is ¼ percent, the bank will generate additional revenue of ¼ percent times $2 million, or $5,000.

See Figure 13–1 for a summary of the structure of this loan commitment. Note that only when the borrower actually draws on the commitment do the loans made under the commitment appear on the balance sheet. Thus, when the $8 million loan is taken down exactly halfway through the one-year commitment period, only the balance sheet *six months later* will show a new $8 million loan being created. When the $10 million commitment is made at time 0, nothing shows on the balance sheet. Nevertheless, the bank must stand ready to make the full $10 million in loans on any day within the one-year commitment period; that is, at time 0 a new contingent claim on the resources of the bank was created.

This raises the question: What contingent risks are created by the loan commitment provision? At least four types of risk are associated with the extension of loan commitments: interest rate risk, take-down risk, credit risk, and aggregate funding risk.

Interest Rate Risk.   Interest rate risk is a contingent risk emanating from the fact that the bank precommits to make loans available to a borrower over the commitment period at either (1) some fixed interest rate as a fixed-rate loan commitment or (2) some variable rate as a variable-rate loan commitment. Suppose the bank precommits to lend $10 million at 12 percent over the year and its cost of funds rises. The cost of funds may well rise to a level that makes the spread between the 12 percent commitment rate and the cost of funds negative or very small. Moreover, 12 percent may be much less than the rate the customer would have to pay if forced to borrow on the spot loan market under current interest rate conditions. When rates do rise over the commitment period, the FI stands to lose on its portfolio of

Back-End Fee
The fee imposed on the unused component of a loan commitment.

FIGURE 13–1

The Structure of a Loan Commitment

¹³This can be viewed as an excess capacity charge; see A. V. Thakor and G. Udell, "An Economic Rationale for the Pricing Structure of Bank Loan Commitments," *Journal of Banking and Finance* 11 (1987), pp. 271–90.

fixed-rate loan commitments as borrowers exercise to the full their very valuable options to borrow at below-market rates.[14]

One way the FI can control this risk is by making commitment rates float with spot loan rates, for example, by making loan commitments indexed to the prime rate. If the prime rate rises over the commitment period, so does the cost of commitment loans to the borrower—the borrower pays the market rate in effect at the time of drawing on the commitment. Nevertheless, this fixed formula rate solution does not totally eradicate interest rate risk on loan commitments. For example, if the prime rate rises 1 percent but the cost of funds rises 1.25 percent, the spread between the indexed commitment loan and the cost of funds narrows by .25 percent. This spread risk is often called **basis risk.**[15]

Basis Risk
The variable spread between a lending rate and a borrowing rate or between any two interest rates or prices.

Take-Down Risk.   Another contingent risk is take-down risk. Specifically, in making the loan commitment, the FI must always stand ready to provide the maximum of the commitment line—$10 million in our example. The borrower has the flexible option to borrow anything between $0 and the $10 million ceiling on any business day in the commitment period. This exposes the FI to a degree of future liquidity risk or uncertainty. The FI can never be absolutely sure when, during the commitment period, the borrower will arrive and demand the full $10 million or some proportion thereof in cash.[16] To some extent, at least, the back-end fee on unused amounts is designed to create incentives for the borrower to take down lines in full to avoid paying this fee. However, in actuality, many lines are only partially drawn upon.[17]

Credit Risk.   FIs also face a degree of contingent credit risk in setting the interest or formula rate on a loan commitment. Specifically, the FI often adds a risk premium based on its current assessment of the creditworthiness of the borrower. For example, the borrower may be judged as a AA credit risk paying 1 percent over

---

[14]In an options sense, the loans are in the money to the borrower.

[15]Basis risk arises because loan rates and deposit rates are not perfectly correlated in their movements over time.

[16]Indeed, the borrower could come to the bank and borrow different amounts over the period ($1 million in month 1, $2 million in month 2, etc.). The only constraint is the $10 million ceiling. See Ho and Saunders, "Fixed Rate Loan Commitments," for a modeling approach to take-down risk. We discuss this liquidity risk aspect of loan commitments more in Chapter 17.

[17]See A. Melnick and S. Plaut, "Loan Commitment Contracts, Terms of Lending, and Credit Allocations," *Journal of Finance* 41 (1986), pp. 425–36; R. L. Shockley and A. V. Thakor, "Bank Loan Commitment Contracts: Data, Theory and Tests," ibid; and E. Asarnow and J. Marker, "Historical Performance of the U.S. Corporate Loan Market 1988–1993," *Journal of Commercial Lending,* Spring 1995, pp. 13–22. Asarnow and Marker show that the average take-down rates vary widely by borrower credit rating, from a take-down rate of only 0.1 percent by a AAA borrower to a 20 percent for BBB and 75 percent for CCC.

It is quite easy to show how the unique features of loan commitments affect the promised return $(1 + k)$ on a loan. In Chapter 11 we developed a model for determining $(1 + k)$ on a spot loan. This can be extended by allowing for partial take-down and the up-front and back-end fees commonly found in loan commitments. Let

L = Interest on the loan = 12%
m = Risk premium = 2%
f_1 = Up-front fee on the whole commitment = 1/8%
f_2 = Back-end fee on the unused commitment = 1/4%
b = Compensating balance = 10%
R = Reserve requirements = 10%
t = Expected (average) take-down rate $(0 < t < 1)$ on the loan commitment = 75%

prime rate. However, suppose that over the one-year commitment period the borrowing firm gets into difficulty; its earnings decline so that its creditworthiness is downgraded to BBB. The problem for the FI is that the credit risk premium on the commitment had been preset to the AA level for the one-year commitment period. To avoid being exposed to dramatic declines in borrower creditworthiness over the commitment period, most FIs include an adverse material change in conditions clause under which the FI can cancel or reprice a loan commitment. However, exercising such a clause is really a last resort tactic for an FI because it may put the borrower out of business and result in costly legal claims for breach of contract.[18]

Aggregate Funding Risk.   Many large borrowing firms, such as GM, Ford, and IBM, take out multiple commitment or credit lines with many banks as insurance against future credit crunches.[19] In a credit crunch, the supply of credit to borrowers is restricted, possibly due to restrictive monetary policy actions of the Federal Reserve. Another cause is an increased aversion toward lending by FIs, that is, a shift to the left in the loan supply function at all interest rates. In such credit crunches, borrowers with long-standing loan commitments are unlikely to be as credit constrained as are those without loan commitments. However, this also implies that aggregate demands by borrowers to take down loan commitments are likely to be greatest when the FI's borrowing and funding conditions are most costly and difficult. In difficult credit conditions, this aggregate commitment take-down effect can raise the cost of funds above normal levels as many FIs scramble for funds to meet their commitments to customers. This is similar to the *externality* effect common in many markets when all participants simultaneously act together and affect the costs of each individual participant adversely.

The four contingent risk effects just identified—interest rate risk, take-down risk, credit risk, and aggregate funding risk—all appear to imply that loan commitment activities increase the insolvency exposure of FIs that engage in such activities. However, an opposing view holds that loan commitment contracts may make an FI less risky than it would be if it had not engaged in them. This view maintains that to be able to charge fees and sell loan commitments or equivalent credit rationing insurance, the bank must convince borrowers that it will still be around to

---

Then the general formula for the promised return $(1 + k)$ of the loan commitment is

$$1 + k = 1 + \frac{f_1 + f_2(1 - t) + (L + m)t}{t - [bt(1 - R)]}$$

$$1 + k = 1 + \frac{.00125 + .0025(.25) + (.12 + .02).75}{.75 - [(.10)(.75)(.9)]}$$

$$1 + k = 1 + \frac{.106875}{.682500} = 1.1566 \quad \text{or} \quad k = 15.66\%$$

This formula closely follows that in John R. Brick, *Commercial Banking: Text and Readings* (Haslett, MI: S.P.I., 1984), chapter 4. Note that for simplicity we have used undiscounted cash flows. Taking into account the time value of money means that we would need to discount both f_2 and $L + m$ since they are paid at the end of the period. If the discount factor (cost of funds) is $d = 10$ percent, then $k = 14.25$ percent.

[18]Potential damage claims can be enormous if the borrower goes out of business and attributes this to the cancellation of loans under the commitment contract. There are also important reputational costs to take into account in canceling a commitment to lend.

[19]Recent research by Donald P. Morgan, "The Credit Effects of Monetary Policy: Evidence Using Loan Commitments," *Journal of Money, Credit, and Banking* 30 (February 1998), pp. 102–18, has found evidence of this type of insurance effect. Specifically in credit crunches, spot loans may decline but loans made under commitment do not.

provide the credit needed in the *future*.[20] To convince borrowers in a credible fashion that an FI will be around to meet its future commitments, managers may have to adopt *lower*-risk portfolios *today* than otherwise. By adopting lower-risk portfolios, they increase the probability of meeting all long-term on- and off-balance-sheet obligations. Interestingly, empirical studies have confirmed that banks making more loan commitments have lower on-balance-sheet portfolio risk characteristics than do those with relatively low levels of commitments, that is, safer banks have a greater tendency to make loan commitments.[21]

Commercial Letters of Credit and Standby Letters of Credit

Letters of Credit
Contingent guarantees sold by an FI to underwrite the trade or commercial performance of the buyer of the guaranty.

Standby Letters of Credit
Guarantees issued to cover contingencies that are potentially more severe and less predictable than contingencies covered under trade-related or commercial letters of credit.

In selling commercial **letters of credit** (LCs) and **standby letters of credit** (SLCs) for fees, FIs add to their contingent future liabilities. Both LCs and SLCs are essentially *guarantees* sold by an FI to underwrite the *performance* of the buyer of the guaranty (such as a corporation). In economic terms, the FI that sells LCs and SLCs is selling insurance against the frequency or severity of some particular future occurrence. Further, similar to the different lines of insurance sold by property-casualty insurers, LC and SLC contracts have differences in the severity and frequency of their risk exposures. We look next at the risk exposure to an FI from engaging in LC and SLC off-balance-sheet activities.

Commercial Letters of Credit. Commercial letters of credit are widely used in both domestic and international trade. For example, they ease the shipment of grain between a farmer in Iowa and a purchaser in New Orleans or the shipment of goods between a U.S. importer and a foreign exporter. The FI's role is to provide a formal guaranty that payment for goods shipped or sold will be forthcoming in the future regardless of whether the buyer of the goods defaults on payment. We show a very simple LC example in Figure 13–2 for an international transaction between a U.S. importer and a German exporter.

Suppose the U.S. importer sent an order for $10 million worth of machinery to a German exporter, as shown by arrow 1 in Figure 13–2. However, the German exporter may be reluctant to send the goods without some assurance or guaranty of being paid once the goods are shipped. The U.S. importer may promise to pay for the goods in 90 days, but the German exporter may feel insecure either because it knows little about the creditworthiness of the U.S. importer or because the U.S. importer has a low credit rating (say, A or BBB). To persuade the German exporter to ship the goods, the U.S. importer may have to turn to a large U.S. bank with which it has developed a long-term customer relationship. The U.S. bank can better appraise the creditworthiness of the U.S. importer due to its role as a lender and monitor. It can issue a contingent payment guaranty—that is, a letter of credit to the German exporter on the importer's behalf—in return for a letter of credit fee paid by the U.S. importer. In our example, the bank would send an LC to the German exporter guaranteeing payment for the goods in 90 days regardless of whether the importer defaults on its obligation to the German exporter (see arrow 2

---

[20]A. W. A. Boot and A. V. Thakor, "Off-Balance-Sheet Liabilities. Deposit Insurance, and Capital Regulation," *Journal of Banking and Finance* 15 (1991), pp. 825–46.

[21]See, for example, R. B. Avery and A. N. Berger, "Loan Commitments and Bank Risk Exposure," *Journal of Banking and Finance* 15 (1991), pp. 173–92.

FIGURE 13–2

A Simple Letter of Credit Transaction

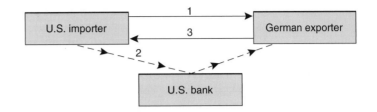

in Figure 13–2). Implicitly, the bank is replacing the credit risk of the U.S. importer with its own credit risk guaranty. For this substitution to work effectively, in guaranteeing payment, the bank has to have a higher credit standing or better credit quality reputation than the U.S. importer. Once the bank issues the LC and sends it to the German exporter, the exporter ships the goods to the U.S. importer, as shown by arrow 3. In 90 days' time, the U.S. importer pays the German exporter for the goods sent with a very high probability and the bank keeps the fee as profit. The fee is, perhaps, 10 basis points of the face value of the letter of credit, or $10,000 in this example.

There is a small probability that the U.S. importer will be unable to pay the $10 million in 90 days and will default. Then the bank would be obliged to make good on its guaranty. The cost of such a default could mean a payment of $10 million by the bank, although the bank would have a creditor's claim against the assets of the importer to offset this loss. Clearly, the LC fee should exceed the expected default risk on the LC, which is equal to the probability of default times the expected net payout on the LC, after adjusting for its ability to reclaim assets from the defaulting importer and any monitoring costs.[22]

Standby Letters of Credit. Standby letters of credit perform an insurance function similar to that of commercial and trade letters of credit. However, the structure and type of risks covered are different. FIs may issue standby letters of credit to cover contingencies that are potentially more *severe,* less *predictable* or frequent, and not necessarily trade related.[23] These include performance bond guarantees whereby an FI may guarantee that a real estate development will be completed in some interval of time. Alternatively, the FI may offer default guarantees to back an issue of commercial paper (CP) or municipal revenue bonds to allow issuers to achieve a higher credit rating and a lower funding cost than otherwise.

Without credit enhancements, for example, many firms would be unable to borrow in the CP market or would have to borrow at a higher funding cost. P1 borrowers, who offer the highest-quality commercial paper, normally pay 40 basis points less than P2 borrowers, the next quality grade. By paying a fee to a bank of perhaps 25 basis points, an FI guarantees to pay commercial paper purchasers' principal and interest on maturity if the issuing firm itself is unable to pay. The SLC backing of commercial paper issues normally results in the paper being placed in the lowest default risk class (P1) and the issuer saving up to 15 basis points on issuing costs—

---

[22]Hassan finds that stockholders view commercial letter of credit activities by banks as risk reducing. See M. K. Hassan, "The Market Perception of the Riskiness of Large U.S. Bank Commercial Letters of Credit," *Journal of Financial Services Research* 6 (1992), pp. 207–21.

[23]G. O. Koppenhaver uses a similar definition to distinguish between LCs and SLCs. See "Standby Letters of Credit," Federal Reserve Bank of Chicago, *Economic Perspectives,* 1987, pp. 28–38.

40 basis points (the P2 – P1 spread) minus the 25-basis-point SLC fee equals 15 basis points.

Note that in selling the SLCs, banks are directly competing with another of their off-balance-sheet products, loan commitments. Rather than buying an SLC from a bank to back a CP issue, the issuing firm might pay a fee to a bank to supply a loan commitment. This loan commitment would match the size and maturity of the commercial paper issue, for example, a $100 million ceiling and 45 days maturity. If, on maturity, the commercial paper issuer has insufficient funds to repay the commercial paper holders, the issuer has the right to take down the $100 million loan commitment and to use those funds to meet CP repayments. Often, the up-front fees on such loan commitments are less than those on SLCs; therefore, many CP-issuing firms prefer to use loan commitments.

Finally, remember that banks are not the only issuers of SLCs. Not surprisingly, performance bonds and financial guarantees are an important business line of property-casualty insurers.

Derivative Contracts: Futures, Forwards, Swaps, and Options

FIs can be users of derivative contracts for hedging and other purposes or dealers who act as counterparties in trades with customers for a fee. It has been estimated that only 600 U.S. banks are users of derivatives, with five big dealer banks, such as Bankers Trust and Citigroup (formerly Citicorp), accounting for some 70 percent of the derivatives held by the user banks.[24]

Contingent credit risk is likely to be present when FIs expand their positions in forward, futures, swaps, and option contracts. This risk relates to the fact that the counterparty to one of these contracts may default on payment obligations, leaving the FI unhedged and having to replace the contract at today's interest rates, prices, or exchange rates. Further, such defaults are most likely to occur when the counterparty is losing heavily on the contract and the FI is in the money on the contract. As noted earlier, J. P. Morgan suffered significantly increased default exposure on its derivative positions in 1998. This type of default risk is much more serious for forward (and swap) contracts than for futures contracts. The reason for this is that forward contracts[25] are nonstandard contracts entered into bilaterally by negotiating parties such as two banks and all cash flows are required to be paid at one time (on contract maturity). Thus, they are essentially over-the-counter (OTC) arrangements with no external guarantees if one or the other party defaults on the contract. For example, a forward foreign exchange contract that promises to deliver £10 million in three months' time at the exchange rate of $1.70 to £1 might be defaulted on by the contract seller if it costs $1.90 to purchase £1 for delivery when the forward contract matures. By contrast, futures contracts are standardized contracts guaranteed by organized exchanges such as the New York Futures Exchange (NYFE). Futures contracts, like forward contracts, make commitments about the delivery of foreign exchange (or some other asset) at some future date. If a counterparty defaults on a futures contract, however, the exchange assumes the position and the payment obligations of the defaulting party. For example, when Barings, the British merchant bank, was unable to meet its margin calls on Nikkei Index futures traded on the

---

[24]See J. F. Sinkey, Jr., and D. Carter, "The Determination of Hedging and Derivative Activities by U.S. Banks," American Finance Association, January 1995.

[25]Conceptually, a swap contract can be viewed as a succession of forward contracts.

Singapore futures exchange (SIMEX) in 1995, the exchange stood ready to assume Barings' futures contracts and ensure that no counterparty lost money. Thus, unless the exchange itself is threatened by a systematic financial market collapse, futures are essentially default risk free.[26] In addition, default risk is reduced by the daily marking to market of contracts. This prevents the accumulation of losses and gains that occurs with forward contracts. These differences are discussed in more detail in Chapter 23.

The same is true for option contracts purchased or sold by an FI. If these are standardized options traded on exchanges, such as bond options, they are virtually default risk free.[27] If they are specialized options purchased over the counter such as interest rate caps (see Chapter 24), then some element of default risk exists.[28] Similarly, swaps are OTC instruments normally susceptible to counterparty risk (see Chapter 25).[29] In general, default risk on OTC contracts increases with the time to maturity of the contract and the fluctuation of underlying prices, interest rates, or exchange rates.[30] Most empirical evidence suggests that derivative contracts have generally reduced FI risk or left it unaffected.[31]

Forward Purchases and Sales of When Issued Securities

When Issued (WI) Trading
Trading in securities prior to their actual issue.

Very often banks and other FIs—especially investment banks—enter into commitments to buy and sell securities before issue. This is called **when issued (WI) trading.** These off-balance-sheet commitments can expose an FI to future or contingent interest rate risk.

Good examples of when issued commitments are those taken on in new T-bills in the week prior to the announcement of T-bill auction results. Every Tuesday, on behalf of the Treasury, the Federal Reserve announces the auction size of new three- and six-month bills to be allotted the following Monday (see Figure 13–3).

Between the time the total auction size is announced on Tuesday and the time the bill allotments are announced on the following Monday, major T-bill dealers sell

[26]More specifically, there are at least four reasons why the default risk of a futures contract is less than that of a forward contract: (1) daily marking to market of futures, (2) margin requirements on futures that act as a security bond, (3) price limits that spread out over time extreme price fluctuations, and (4) default guarantees by the futures exchange itself.

[27]Note that the options can still be subject to interest rate risk; see our earlier discussion of the delta on a bond option.

[28]Under an interest rate cap, in return for a fee the seller promises to compensate the buyer if interest rates rise above a certain level. If rates rise a lot more than expected, the cap seller may have an incentive to default to truncate the losses. Thus selling a cap is similar to a bank selling interest rate risk insurance (see Chapter 24 for more details).

[29]In a swap, two parties contract to exchange interest rate payments or foreign exchange payments. If interest rates (or foreign exchange rates) move a lot, one party can be faced with considerable future loss exposure, creating incentives to default.

[30]Reputational considerations and the need for future access to markets for hedging deter the incentive to default (see Chapter 25 as well).

[31]See, for example, L. Angbazo, "Commercial Bank Net Interest Margins, Default Risks, Interest Rate Risk and Off-Balance-Sheet Banking," *Journal of Banking and Finance 21* (January 1997), pp. 55–87, who finds no link between interest rate risk and FI's use of derivatives; and G. Gorton and R. Rosen, "Banks and Derivatives," Working Paper, University of Pennsylvania, Wharton School, February 1995. Gorton and Rosen find that swap contracts have generally reduced the systemic risk of the U.S. banking system. Nevertheless, B. Hirtle, "Derivatives, Portfolio Composition and Bank Holding Company Interest Rate Risk Exposure," *Journal of Financial Services Research,* 1997, pp. 243–266, finds that the use of interest rate derivatives corresponded to greater interest rate risk exposure during the 1991–94 period for U.S. bank holding companies.

Figure 13–3

T-Bill Auction Time Line

Tuesday	Monday
Size of	Allotment of bills
auction announced	among bidders

WI contracts. Normally, large investment banks and commercial banks are major T-bill dealers (currently approximately 40 in number). They sell the yet-to-be-issued T-bills for forward delivery to customers in the secondary market at a small margin above the price they expect to pay at the primary auction. This can be profitable if the primary dealer gets all the bills needed at the auction at the appropriate price or interest rate to fulfill these forward WI contracts. A primary dealer that makes a mistake regarding the tenor of the auction faces the risk that the commitments entered into to deliver T-bills in the WI market can be met only at a loss. For example, an overcommitted dealer may have to buy bills from other dealers at a loss right after the auction results are announced to meet the WI T-bill delivery commitments made to its customers.[32]

Loans Sold

We discuss the types of loans FIs sell, their incentives to sell, and the way in which they can be sold in more detail in Chapter 26. Increasingly, banks and other FIs originate loans on their balance sheets, but rather than holding them to maturity, they quickly sell them to outside investors. These outside investors include other banks, insurance companies, mutual funds, and even corporations. In acting as loan originators and loan sellers, FIs are operating more in the fashion of loan brokers than as traditional asset transformers (see Chapter 6).

Recourse
The ability to put an asset or loan back to the seller if the credit quality of that asset deteriorates.

When an outside party buys a loan with absolutely no **recourse** to the seller of the loan if the loan eventually goes bad, loan sales have no off-balance-sheet contingent liability implications for FIs. Specifically, *no recourse* means that if the loan sold by the FI does go bad, the buyer of the loan has to bear the full risk of loss. In particular, the buyer cannot put the bad loan back to the seller or originating bank. Suppose the loan is sold with recourse. Then loan sales present a long-term contingent credit risk to the seller. Essentially, the buyer of the loan holds a long-term option to put the loan back to the seller, which can be exercised if the credit quality of the purchased loan deteriorates. In reality, the recourse or nonrecourse nature of loan sales is often ambiguous. For example, some have argued that banks generally are willing to repurchase bad no recourse loans to preserve their reputations with their customers.[33] Obviously, reputational concerns may extend the size of a selling bank's contingent liabilities for off-balance-sheet activities.[34]

---

[32]This problem occurred when Salomon Brothers cornered or squeezed the market for new two-year Treasury bonds in 1990. Under the auction rules, no bidder could bid for or attain more than 35 percent of an issue. However, by bidding using customers' names (without their knowledge) in addition to bidding under its own name, Salomon vastly exceeded the 35 percent limit. This put extreme pressure on other dealers, who were unable to meet their selling commitments.

[33]G. Gorton and G. Pennacchi, "Are Loan Sales Really Off Balance Sheet?" in *Off-Balance-Sheet Activities,* ed. J. Ronen, A. Saunders, and A. C. Sondhi (New York: Quorum Books, 1989), pp. 19–40. We discuss loan sales in more detail in Chapter 26.

[34]However, C. Pavel finds that there is little relationship between bank loan sales and bank risk. See C. Pavel, "Loan Sales Have Little Effect on Bank Risk," *Economic Perspectives,* Federal Reserve Bank of Chicago, May–June 1988, pp. 23–31.

Concept Questions

1. What are the four risks related to loan commitments?
2. What is the major difference between a commercial letter of credit and a standby letter of credit?
3. What is meant by counterparty risk in a forward contract?
4. Which is more risky for the bank, loan sales with recourse or loan sales without recourse?

Schedule L and Nonschedule L Off-Balance-Sheet Risks

So far we have looked at five different off-balance-sheet activities that banks have to report to the Federal Reserve each quarter as part of their Schedule L section of the call report. Remember that many other FIs engage in these activities as well. Thus, thrifts, insurance companies, and investment banks all engage in futures, forwards, swaps, and options transaction of varying forms. Life insurers are heavily engaged in making loan commitments in commercial mortgages, property-casualty companies underwrite large amounts of financial guarantees, and investment banks engage in when issued securities trading. Moreover, the five activities just discussed are not the only off-balance-sheet activities that can create contingent liabilities or risks for an FI. Next, we introduce two others briefly; we discuss them at greater length in later chapters.

Settlement Risk

FIs send the bulk of their wholesale dollar payments along wire transfer systems such as Fedwire and the Clearing House InterBank Payments System (CHIPS). Fedwire is a domestic wire transfer network owned by the Federal Reserve, while CHIPS is an international and private network owned by 140 or so participating or member banks. Currently, over $1.7 trillion a day is transferred across these two networks.

Unlike the domestic Fedwire system, funds or payment messages sent on the CHIPS network *within* the day are provisional messages that become final and are settled only at the *end* of the day. Say that bank X sends a fund transfer payment message to bank Z at 11 AM EST. The actual cash settlement and the physical transfer of funds between X and Z take place at the end of the day, normally through transferring cash held in reserve accounts at the Federal Reserve banks. Because the transfer of funds is not finalized until the end of the day, bank Z—the message-receiving bank—faces an *intraday* or within-day settlement risk. Specifically, bank Z may assume that the funds message received at 11 AM from bank X is for good funds and then on-lend them to Bank Y at 11:15 AM. However, if bank X does not deliver (settle) the promised funds at the end of the day, bank Z may be pushed into a serious net funds deficit position when it is unable to meet its payment commitment to bank Y. Conceivably, its net debtor position may be large enough to exceed its capital and reserves, rendering it technically insolvent. Such a disruption might occur only if a major fraud were discovered in bank X's books during the day and it was closed the same day by bank regulators. That would make payment to bank Z impossible to complete at the end of the day. Alternatively, bank X might be transmitting funds it does not have in the hope of keeping its "name in the market" to be able to raise funds later in the day. However, other banks may revise their credit

FIGURE 13–4

One-Bank and Multibank Holding Company Structures

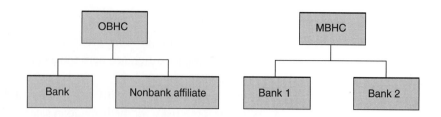

limits for this bank during the day, making it unable to deliver all the funds it promised to bank Z.

The essential feature of settlement risk is that bank Z is exposed to a within-day or intraday credit risk that does not appear on its balance sheet. The balance sheet at best summarizes only the end of day closing position or book of a bank. Thus, intraday settlement risk is an additional form of off-balance-sheet risk facing FIs participating on private wholesale wire transfer system networks. (See Chapter 14 for a more detailed analysis of this risk and recent policy changes designed to reduce this risk.)

Affiliate Risk

Many FIs operate as holding companies. A holding company is a corporation that owns the shares (normally more than 25 percent) of other corporations. For example, Citigroup is a one-bank holding company (OBHC) that owns all the shares of Citibank. Certain permitted nonbank activities such as data processing are engaged in through separately capitalized affiliates or companies also owned by Citigroup. Similarly, a number of other holding companies are multibank holding companies (MBHCs) that own shares in a number of different banks. First InterState is an MBHC that holds shares in banks in more than 10 states. Look at these two organizational structures in Figure 13–4.

Legally, in the context of OBHCs, the bank and the nonbank affiliate are separate companies, as are bank 1 and bank 2 in the context of MBHCs. Thus, in Figure 13–4, if the nonbank affiliate and bank 2 fail, they should have no effect on the financial resources of the bank in the OBHC or on bank 1 in the MBHC. This is the essence of the principle of corporate separateness underlying a legal corporation's limited liability in the United States. In reality, the failure of an affiliated firm or bank can impact another bank in a holding company structure in a number of ways. We discuss two ways next. First, *creditors* of the failed affiliate may lay a claim to the surviving bank's resources on the grounds that operationally, in name or in activity, it is not really a separate company from the failed affiliate. This "estoppel argument" made under the law is based on the idea that the customers of the failed institution are relatively unsophisticated in their financial affairs. They probably don't distinguish between the failing corporation and its surviving affiliate due to name similarity or some similar reason.[35] Second, *regulators* have tried to enforce a source of strength doctrine in recent years for large multibank holding company failures. Under this doctrine, directly challenging the principle of corporate

---

[35]For example, suppose the failing nonbank affiliate was called Town Data Processing and the affiliated bank was called Town Bank.

separateness, the resources of sound banks may be used to support failing banks. However, regulators have generally been prevented from doing this by the courts.[36]

If either of these breaches of corporate separateness are legally supported, the risks of a nonbank affiliate or an affiliated bank's activities impose a further contingent off-balance-sheet liability on a healthy bank. This is true not only for banks but also potentially true for many other FIs such as insurance companies, investment banks, and financial service conglomerates that adopt holding company organizational structures in which corporate separateness is in doubt.[37]

Concept Questions

1. What is the source of settlement risk on the CHIPS payments system?
2. What are two major sources of affiliate risk?

The Role of OBS Activities in Reducing Risk

This chapter has emphasized that OBS activities may add to the riskiness of an FI's activities. Indeed, most contingent assets and liabilities have various characteristics that may accentuate the default and/or interest rate risk exposures of FIs. Even so, FIs use some OBS instruments—especially forwards, futures, options, and swaps—to reduce or manage their interest rate risk, foreign exchange risk, and credit risk exposures in a manner superior to that which would exist in their absence.[38] When used to hedge on-balance-sheet interest rate, foreign exchange, and credit risks, these instruments can actually work to reduce the overall insolvency risk of FIs. Although we do not fully describe the role of these instruments as hedging vehicles in reducing an FI's insolvency exposure until Chapters 23 through 25, you can now recognize the inherent danger in the overregulation of off-balance-sheet activities and instruments. For example, despite the risk that a counterparty might default on a forward foreign exchange contract, this risk is very small. It is probably much lower than the insolvency risk faced by an FI that does not use forward contracts to hedge foreign exchange assets against undesirable fluctuations in exchange rates. (See Chapters 15 and 23 for some examples of this.) As the regulatory costs of hedging rise, such as through the imposition of special capital requirements or restrictions on the use of such instruments (see Chapter 20), FIs may have a tendency to underhedge, resulting in an increase rather than a decrease in FI insolvency risk.

Finally, fees from off-balance-sheet activities provide a key source of noninterest income for many FIs, especially the largest and most creditworthy. You can see the importance of such noninterest incomes for large banks in Table 14–1 in the next

---

[36]Nevertheless, the attempts by regulators to impose the source of strength doctrine appear to have had an adverse effect on the equity values of holding companies operating with a larger number of subsidiaries. Also, the number of subsidiaries of holding companies has fallen each year since 1987, the first year in which the Fed tried to impose the source of strength doctrine (Hawkeye BanCorp of Iowa). See J. Houston, "Corporate Separateness and the Organizational Structure of Bank Holding Companies," Working Paper, Department of Finance, University of Florida–Gainesville, April 1993.

[37]A good example is the failure of Drexel Burnham Lambert in February 1991. For a good discussion of affiliate risk in this case, see W. S. Haraf, "The Collapse of Drexel Burnham Lambert: Lessons for Bank Regulators," *Regulation,* Winter 1991, pp. 23–25.

[38]As we discuss in Chapter 23, there are strong tax disincentives to using derivatives for purposes other than direct hedging.

chapter. Thus, increased OBS earnings can potentially compensate for increased OBS risk exposure and actually reduce the probability of insolvency for some FIs.[39]

Concept Questions

1. While recognizing that OBS instruments may add to the riskiness of an FI's activities, explain how they also work to reduce the overall insolvency risk of FIs.
2. Other than hedging and speculation, what reasons do FIs have for engaging in OBS activities?

Summary

This chapter showed that the net worth or economic value of an FI as a going concern is linked not only to the value of its traditional on-balance-sheet activities but also to the contingent asset and liability values of its off-balance-sheet activities. The risks and returns of several off-balance-sheet items were discussed in detail; loan commitments; commercial and standby letters of credit; derivative contracts such as futures, options, and swaps; forward purchases; and sales of when issued securities and loans sold. In all cases, it is clear that these instruments have a major impact on the future profitability and risk of an FI. Two other risks associated with off-balance-sheet activities—settlement risk and affiliate risk—were also discussed. The chapter concluded by pointing out that although off-balance-sheet activities can be risk increasing, they can also be used to hedge on-balance-sheet exposures, resulting in lower risks as well as generating fee income to the FI.

Questions and Problems

1. Classify the following items as (i) on-balance-sheet assets, (ii) on-balance-sheet liabilities, (iii) off-balance-sheet assets, (iv) off-balance-sheet liabilities, or (v) capital account.

   a. Loan commitments.
   b. Loan loss reserves.
   c. Letter of credit.
   d. Bankers acceptance.
   e. Rediscounted bankers acceptance.
   f. Loan sales without recourse.
   g. Loan sales with recourse.
   h. Forward contracts to purchase.
   i. Forward contracts to sell.
   j. Swaps.
   k. Loan participations.
   l. Securities borrowed.
   m. Securities lent.

   n. Loss adjustment expense account (PC insurers).
   o. Net policy reserves.

2. How does one distinguish between an off-balance-sheet asset and an off-balance-sheet liability?

3. Contingent Bank has the following balance sheet in market value terms ($ millions):

Assets		Liabilities	
Cash	$ 20	Deposits	$220
Mortgages	$220	Equity	$ 20
Total assets	$240	Total liabilities and equity	$240

In addition, the bank has contingent assets with $100 million market value and contingent liabilities with $80 million market value. What is the true stockholder net worth? What does the term *contingent* mean?

---

[39]In addition, by allowing risk-averse managers to hedge risk, derivatives may induce the managers to follow more value-maximizing investment strategies. That is, derivatives may allow manager-stockholder agency conflicts over the level of risk taking to be reduced. See, for example, D. R. Nance, C. W. Smith, Jr., and C. W. Smithson, "On the Determinants of Corporate Hedging," *Journal of Finance,* 1993, pp. 267–84.

4. Why are contingent assets and liabilities like options? What is meant by the delta of an option? What is meant by the term *notional value?*

5. An FI has purchased options on bonds with a notional value of $500 million and has sold options on bonds with a notional value of $400 million. The purchased options have a delta of 0.25, and the sold options have a delta of 0.30. What is (*a*) the contingent asset value of this position, (*b*) the contingent liability value of this position, and (*c*) the contingent market value of net worth?

6. What factors explain the growth of off-balance-sheet activities in the 1980s and 1990s among U.S. FIs?

7. What role does Schedule L play in reporting off-balance-sheet activities? Refer to Table 13–3. What was the annual growth rate over the six-year period 1991–97 in the notional value of off-balance-sheet items compared to on-balance-sheet items? Which contingencies have exhibited the most rapid growth?

8. What are the characteristics of a loan commitment which a bank may make to a customer? In what manner and to whom is the commitment an option? What are the various possible pieces of the option premium? When does the option or commitment become an on-balance-sheet item for the bank and the borrower?

9. A bank makes a loan commitment of $2,500,000 with an up-front fee of 50 basis points and a back-end fee of 25 basis points on the unused portion of the loan. The take-down on the loan is 50 percent.

    a. What total fees does the bank earn when the loan commitment is negotiated?

    b. What are the total fees earned by the bank at the end of the year, that is, in future value terms? Assume the cost of capital for the bank is 6 percent.

10. A bank has issued a one-year loan commitment of $2,000,000 for an up-front fee of 25 basis points. The back-end fee on the unused portion of the commitment is 10 basis points? The bank requires a compensating balance of 5 percent as demand deposits. The bank's cost of funds is 6 percent, the interest rate on the loan is 10 percent, and reserve requirements on demand deposits are 8 percent. The customer is expected to draw down 80 percent of the commitment at the beginning of the year.

    a. What is the expected return on the loan without taking future values into consideration?

    b. What is the expected return using future values? That is, the net fee and interest income are evaluated at the end of the year when the loan is due.

    c. How is the expected return in part (*b*) affected if the reserve requirements on demand deposits are zero?

    d. How is the expected return in part (*b*) affected if compensating balances are paid a nominal interest rate of 5 percent?

    e. What is the expected return using future values but with the funding of demand deposits replaced by certificates of deposit which have an interest rate of 5.5 percent and no reserve requirements?

11. Suburb Bank has issued a one-year loan commitment of $10,000,000 for an up-front fee of 50 basis points. The back-end fee on the unused portion of the commitment is 20 basis points. The bank requires a compensating balance of 10 percent on demand deposits, has a cost of funds of 7 percent, will charge an interest rate on the loan of 9 percent, and must maintain reserve requirements on demand deposits of 10 percent. The customer is expected to draw down 60 percent of the commitment.

    a. What is the expected return on this loan?

    b. What is the expected return per annum on the loan if the draw-down on the commitment does not occur until the end of 6 months?

12. How is an FI exposed to interest rate risk when it makes loan commitments? In what way can an FI control for this risk? How does basis risk affect the implementation of the control for interest rate risk?

13. How is an FI exposed to credit risk when it makes loan commitments? How is credit risk related to interest rate risk? What control measure is available to an FI for the purpose of protecting against credit risk? What is the realistic opportunity to implement this control feature?

14. How is an FI exposed to takedown risk and aggregate funding risk? How are these two contingent risks related?

15. Do the contingent risks of interest rate, takedown, credit, and aggregate funding tend to increase the insolvency risk of an FI? Why or why not?

16. What is a letter of credit? How is a letter of credit like an insurance contract?

17. A German bank issues a three-month letter of credit on behalf of its customer in Germany, who is planning to import $100,000 worth of goods from the United States. It charges an up-front fee of 100 basis points.

    a. What up-front fee does the bank earn?

    b. If the U.S. exporter decides to discount this letter of credit after it has been accepted by the German bank, how much will the exporter receive, assuming that the interest rate currently is 5 percent and that 90 days remain before maturity?

    c. What risk does the German bank incur by issuing this letter of credit?

18. How do standby letters of credit differ from trade letters of credit? With what other types of FI products do SLCs compete? What types of FIs can issue SLCs?

19. A corporation is planning to issue $1,000,000 of 270-day commercial paper for an effective yield of 5 percent. The

corporation expects to save 30 basis points on the interest rate by using either an SLC or a loan commitment as collateral for the issue.

    a. What are the net savings to the corporation if a bank agrees to provide a 270-day SLC for an up-front fee of 20 basis points to back the commercial paper issue?

    b. What are the net savings to the corporation if a bank agrees to provide a 270-day loan commitment to back the issue? The bank will charge 10 basis points for an up-front fee and 10 basis points for a back-end fee for any unused portion of the loan. Assume the loan is not needed.

20. Explain how the use of derivative contracts such as forwards, futures, swaps, and options creates contingent credit risk for an FI. Why do OTC contracts carry more contingent credit risk than do exchange-traded contracts? How is the default risk of OTC contracts related to the time to maturity and the price and rate volatilities of the underlying assets?

21. What is meant by when issued trading? Explain how forward purchases of when issued government T-bills can expose FIs to contingent interest rate risk.

22. Distinguish between loan sales with and without recourse. Why would banks want to sell loans with recourse? Explain how loan sales can leave banks exposed to contingent interest rate risks.

23. The manager of Shakey Bank sends a $2 million funds transfer payment message via CHIPS to the Trust Bank at 10 AM. Trust Bank sends a $2 million funds transfer message via CHIPS to Hope Bank later that same day. What type of risk is inherent in this transaction? How will the risk become reality?

24. Explain how settlement risk is incurred in the interbank payment mechanism and how it is another form of off-balance sheet risk.

25. What is the difference between a one-bank holding company and a multibank holding company? How does the principle of corporate separateness ensure that a bank is safe from the failure of its affiliates?

26. Discuss how the failure of an affiliate can affect the holding company or its affiliates even if the affiliates are structured separately.

27. Defend the statement that although off-balance-sheet activities expose FIs to several forms of risks, they also can alleviate the risks of banks.

28. Go to the FDIC Web site (HYPERLINK http://www.fdic.gov) and find the total amount of unused commitments and letters of credit and the notional value of interest rate swaps of FDIC-insured commercial banks for the most recent year available.

OPERATIONAL AND TECHNOLOGY RISK

Introduction

In Chapters 7 through 13 we concentrated on the financial risks that arise as FIs perform their asset-transformation and/or brokerage functions on or off the balance sheet. However, financial risk is only one part of the risk profile of a modern FI. Like regular corporations, FIs have a real or production side to their operations that results in additional costs and revenues. In this chapter we focus on factors that impact the operational returns and risks of FIs and on the importance of managers optimally controlling labor, capital, and other input sources and costs. In particular, well-managed FIs can use operational cost savings to augment profits and thus reduce the probability of insolvency.

What Are the Sources of Operational Risk?

These are at least five sources of operational risk:[1]

1. Employees (e.g., human error and internal fraud)
2. Technology (e.g., technological failure and deteriorating systems)
3. Customer relationships (e.g., contractual disputes)
4. Capital assets (e.g., destruction by fire or other catastrophes)
5. External (e.g., external fraud)

Increasingly important to the profitability and riskiness of modern FIs has been item 2: technology.

Technological Innovation and Profitability

Central to FIs' real or operating decisions are the costs of the inputs or the factors used in producing services both on and off the balance sheet. The two most important factors are labor (tellers, credit officers, etc.) and capital (buildings, machinery, furniture, etc.). Crucial to the efficient management and combination of these inputs resulting in financial outputs at the lowest possible cost is *technology.* Broadly defined, technology includes computers, visual and audio communication systems, and other information technology (IT). In recent years U.S. banks alone have spent $20 billion per annum in technologically related expenditures.

An efficient technological base for an FI can result in:

1. Lower costs by combining labor and capital in a more efficient mix.
2. Increased revenues by allowing a broader array of financial services to be produced or innovated and sold to customers.

The importance of an FI's operating costs and the efficient use of technology impacting these costs is clearly demonstrated by this simplified profit function:

Earnings or profit before taxes = (Interest income − Interest expense)
+ (Other income − Noninterest expense) − Provision for loan losses

In Table 14–1 we break down the profit data for U.S. banks over the 1991–97 (third quarter) period into the different components impacting profits. For example, in 1996, you can see that interest income of $312,783 million and interest expense of $150,007 million produced net interest income of $162,776 million. However, U.S. banks also had total other income of $93,667 million (including service charges of $16,937 million) and noninterest expenses of $160,713 million (including other operating expenses of $93,659 million). Thus, banks' net other income was −$67,046. After taking into account provisions for loan losses of $16,278 million, and net securities gains and losses ($1,114 million), income before taxes or gross profits of U.S. banks was $80,566 million, and after-tax net profits were $52,357 million. Underscoring the importance of operating costs is the fact that noninterest expenses amount to 107 percent of interest expense and were 2 times gross profits in 1996.

Technology is important because well-chosen technological investments have the potential for increasing both the FI's net interest margin, or the difference between interest income and interest expense, and other net income. Therefore, it can directly improve profitability, as these examples show:

---

[1]See, for example, D. Hoffman and M. Johnson, "Operating Procedures," *Risk Magazine,* October 1996, pp. 60–63.

TABLE 14–1   **Earnings and Other Data for All Insured Banks**
(in millions of dollars)

Financial Data	R1987	R1988	R1989	R1990	R1991	R1992	R1993	R1994	R1995	R1996	1997*
Interest income	$244,784	$272,351	$316,362	$319,987	$289,440	$256,524	$244,595	$257,829	$302,663	$312,783	$250,915
Interest expense	144,975	165,001	204,581	204,703	167,693	122,494	105,531	111,278	148,441	150,007	121,110
Net interest income	99,809	107,350	111,781	115,284	121,747	134,030	139,064	146,551	154,222	162,776	129,805
Provision for loan losses	37,711	17,486	31,034	32,206	34,351	26,775	16,597	10,963	12,550	16,278	14,269
Miscellaneous	33,132	36,084	41,347	44,184	48,062	53,097	61,062	60,939	66,395	76,730	—
Service charges	8,735	9,455	10,235	11,423	12,818	14,117	14,869	15,337	16,045	16,937	—
Total other income	41,867	45,539	51,582	55,607	60,880	67,214	75,931	76,276	82,440	93,667	77,326
Personnel expenses	45,333	46,878	49,293	52,030	53,536	55,487	58,460	60,600	63,440	67,054	—
Other operating expenses	53,333	55,127	59,265	64,350	72,425	77,351	81,834	83,634	86,231	93,659	—
Noninterest expenses	97,666	102,005	108,558	116,380	125,961	132,838	140,294	144,234	149,671	160,713	125,556
Net securities gains or losses	1,441	275	794	476	2,897	3,957	3,042	1,571	545	1,114	947
Income before taxes	5,741	33,672	24,569	22,780	25,214	45,589	61,146	67,059	74,986	80,566	68,280
Taxes	5,407	10,016	9,550	7,720	8,274	14,500	19,925	22,420	26,176	28,209	24,353
Net earnings	2,536	24,468	15,307	15,705	17,927	31,502	43,295	44,624	48,810	52,357	43,927
Average total assets ($ billion)	2,922	3,048	3,188	3,339	3,380	3,441	3,565	3,880	4,313	4,578	4,869
Return on assets (%)	0.09	0.80	0.48	0.47	0.53	0.92	1.21	1.15	1.13	1.19	1.24

R = Revised.

*Through the third quarter.

Source: Federal Reserve Board and FDIC.

1. *Interest income* can increase if the FI sells a broader array of financial services due to technological developments. These may include cross selling of financial products by having the computer match customers and telemarketing of financial service products such as life insurance and bank products directly and over the Internet.

2. *Interest expense* can be reduced if access to markets for liabilities is directly dependent on the FI's technological capability. For example, Fedwire and CHIPS link the domestic and international interbank lending markets; they are based on interlocking computer network systems. Moreover, the ability of an FI to originate and sell commercial paper is increasingly computer driven. Thus, failure to invest in the appropriate technology may lock an FI out of a lower-cost funding market.[2]

3. *Other income* increases when fees for FI services, especially those from off-balance-sheet activities, are linked to the quality of the FI's technology. For example, letters of credit are now commonly electronically originated by customers: swaps, caps, options, and other complex derivatives are usually screen traded and valued using high-powered computers and algorithms. FIs could not offer innovative derivative products to customers without investments in suitable IT.

4. *Noninterest expenses* can be reduced if the collection and storage of customer information as well as the processing and settlement of numerous financial products are computer based rather than paper based. This is particularly true of security-related back-office activities.

---

[2]Not only corporations sell commercial paper. In recent years approximately 75 percent of all commercial paper has been sold by financial firms such as bank holding companies, investment banks, and finance companies. Thus, commercial paper is now an important source of funds for many FIs.

Concept Questions

1. What are some of the advantages of an efficient technological base for an FI? How can it be used to directly improve profitability?
2. Looking at Table 14–1, determine if noninterest expenses have been increasing or decreasing as a percent of total bank costs over the 1987–97 period.

The Impact of Technology on Wholesale and Retail Banking

Our previous discussion established that modern technology has the potential to directly affect all profit-producing areas of a modern FI. Next, we describe some specific technology-based products found in modern retail and wholesale banking. Note that this is far from a complete list.

Wholesale Banking Services

Probably the most important area where technology has had an impact on wholesale or corporate customer services is in banks' ability to provide cash management or working capital services. Cash management services include "services designed to collect, disburse and transfer funds—on a local, regional, national or international basis—and to provide information about the location and status of those funds."[3] Cash management service needs have largely resulted from (1) corporate recognition that excess cash balances result in a significant opportunity cost due to lost or forgone interest and (2) a corporation's need to know its cash or working capital position on a real-time basis. Among the services modern banks provide to improve the efficiency with which corporate clients manage their financial positions are:

1. *Controlled disbursement accounts.* These checking accounts are debited early each day so that corporations can get an early insight into their net cash positions.
2. *Account reconciliation.* A checking feature that provides a record of which of the firm's checks have been paid by the bank.
3. *Wholesale lockbox.* A centralized collection service for corporate payments to reduce the delay in check clearing, or the **float.**
4. *Electronic lockbox.* Same as item 3 but receives on-line payments for public utilities and similar corporate clients.
5. *Funds concentration.* Redirects funds from accounts in a large number of different banks or branches to a few centralized accounts at one bank.
6. *Electronic funds transfer.* Includes overnight payments via CHIPS or Fedwire, automated payment of payrolls or dividends via automated clearinghouses (ACHs), and automated transmission of payments messages by SWIFT, an international electronic message service owned and operated by U.S. and European banks that instructs banks to make particular payments.
7. *Check deposit services.* Encoding, endorsing, microfilming, and handling checks of customers.
8. *Electronic initiation of letters of credit.* Allows customers in a network to access bank computers to initiate letters of credit.

Float
The interval between the deposit of a check and when funds become available for depositor use—that is, the time it takes a check to clear at a bank.

---

[3]Salomon Brothers, "Transaction Processing: Raising the Technological Hurdle," U.S. Equity Research (Commercial Banks), January 6, 1997, p. 5.

9. *Treasury management software.* Allows efficient management of multiple currency portfolios for trading and investment purposes.[4]

10. *Electronic data interchange.* A specialized application of electronic mail that allows businesses to transfer and transact invoices, purchase orders, and shipping notices automatically, using banks as clearinghouses.

Retail Banking Services

Retail customers have also demanded efficiency and flexibility in their financing of transactions. Using only checks or holding cash is often more expensive and time-consuming than making use of retail-oriented electronic payments technology and, increasingly, the Internet. Some of the most important retail product innovations are:

1. *Automated teller machines (ATMs).* These give customers 24-hour access to their checking accounts. This can include payment of bills as well as withdrawals of cash. In addition, if the bank's ATMs are part of a bank network such as CIRRUS, retail depositors can gain direct nationwide, and in many cases international, access to their deposit accounts by using the ATMs of other banks in the network to draw on their accounts.[5]

2. *Point-of-sale debit cards.* For customers who choose not to use cash, checks, or credit cards for purchases, using debit card/point-of-sale terminals (POS) allows them to buy merchandise while the merchant avoids the check float and any delay in credit card receivables since the bank offering the debit card/POS service immediately and directly transfers funds from the customer's bank account to the merchant's bank account at the time of card use. Unlike check or credit card purchases, the use of a debit card results in an immediate deduction of funds from the customers' checking accounts and transfer to the merchant's account.[6] Moreover, the customer never runs up a debit to the card issuer as is common with a credit card.

3. *Home banking.* Usually connects customers to their deposit and brokerage accounts as well as providing a bill-paying service, all via personal computers.

4. *Preauthorized debits/credits.* Includes direct payment into bank accounts of payroll checks as well as direct debits of mortgage payments and utility bills.

5. *Telephone bill paying.* Allows direct transfer of funds from the customer's bank account to outside parties either by voice command or by touch-tone telephone.

6. *E-mail billing.* Uses the Internet to bill customers, thus saving postage and paper.[7]

7. *On-line banking.* Retail banking and investment services offered via the Internet.[8] In some cases this involves building a new on-line Internet only "bank."[9]

---

[4]Computerized pension fund management and advisory services could be added to this list.

[5]Using another bank's ATM usually results in an "access fee" to the customer which averages $1 but can be as high as $5. See J. J. McAndrews, "ATM Surcharges," *Current Issues in Economics and Finance,* Federal Reserve Bank of New York, April 1998.

[6]In the case of bank-supplied credit cards, the merchant normally gets compensated very quickly but not instantaneously by the credit card issuer (usually one or two days). The bank then holds an account receivable against the card user. However, even a short delay can represent an opportunity cost for the merchant.

[7]For example, the U.S. Postal Service estimates that $2.4 billion was spent on postage for bills and bank statements in 1995 and that electronic billing will save $900 million of that within 10 years. See "Paying Bills Without Any Litter," *New York Times,* July 5, 1996, pp. D1–D3.

[8]In October 1998, Citigroup announced a new Internet service covering all areas of retail financial services. This will require it to scrap its existing computer systems and build a whole new infrastructure. The new service will be known as E-Citi (see *New York Times,* October 5, 1998, pp. C1–C4.)

[9]An example of an Internet bank is Security First Network Bank of Atlanta.

8. *Smart-cards (store-value cards).* A card that has a chip storage device, usually in the form of a strip, that allows the customer to store and use money for various transactions. These have become increasingly popular at universities.[10-12] One set of projections for Worldwide Smart Card growth between 1994–2000 suggests that the number of cards will grow from 440 million to 3,800 million.

Concept Questions

1. Describe some of the wholesale banking services provided to corporate customers that have been improved by technology.
2. Describe some of the automated retail payment products available today. What advantages do these products offer the retail customer?

The Effect of Technology on Revenues and Costs

In the last section we described an extensive yet incomplete list of current products or services being built around a strong technological base and, increasingly, the Internet. Technological advances allow an FI to offer such products to its customers and potentially to earn higher profits. The investment of resources in many of these products is risky, however, because product innovations may fail to attract sufficient business relative to the initial cash outlay and the future costs related to these investments once they are in place. In the terminology of finance, a number of technologically based product innovations may turn out to be *negative* net present value projects due to uncertainties over revenues and costs and over how quickly rivals mimic or copy any innovation. Another factor is agency conflicts, in which managers undertake growth-oriented investments to increase the size of an FI; such investments may be inconsistent with stockholders' value-maximizing objectives. As a result, losses on technological innovations and new technology could weaken an FI because scarce capital resources were invested in value-decreasing products.[13]

This raises the question: Is there direct or indirect evidence that technology investments updating the operational structure of FIs have either increased revenues

---

[10]Another example is Mondex, under which employees of Wells Fargo Bank use store-value cards at nearby merchants. See Barbara A. Good, "Electronic Money," Federal Reserve Bank of Cleveland, Working Paper 97-16, 1997.

[11]It might be noted that the provision of electronic funds and the public and policy issues that arise relating to their provision fall under Regulation E of the Federal Reserve.

[12]In addition to cash management services, technology also enhances the ability of FIs to offer security services (e.g., local and global custody and transfer).

[13]Standard capital budgeting techniques can be applied to technological innovations and new FI products. Let

I_o = Initial capital outlay for developing an innovation or product at time 0
R_i = Expected net revenues or cash flows from product sales in future years i, $i = 1 \ldots N$
d = FI's discount rate reflecting its risk-adjusted cost of capital

Thus, a negative net present value (NPV) project would result if

$$I_0 > \frac{R_1}{(1 + d)} + \ldots + \frac{R_N}{(1 + d)^N}$$

Clearly, the profitability of any product innovation is negatively related to the size of the initial setup and development costs (I_o) and the bank's cost of capital (d) and positively related to the size of the stream of expected net cash flows (R_i) from selling the services.

or decreased costs? As you will note, most of the direct or indirect evidence has concerned the effects of size on financial firms' operating costs; indeed, it is the largest FIs that appear to be investing most in IT and other technological innovations.

We begin by looking at the evidence on the product revenue side and then on the operating cost side. However, before looking at these revenue and cost aspects, we should stress that the success of a technologically related innovation cannot be evaluated independently from regulation and regulatory changes. To a large extent, the success of the retail and wholesale cash management products just described depends on trends in FI consolidation and interstate banking (see Chapter 22). For example, historically restrictions on U.S. banks' ability to branch across state lines created problems for large corporations with national and international franchises; these firms needed to consolidate and centralize their deposit funds for working capital purposes. Thus, innovations such as wholesale lockboxes and funds concentration were products that eased this problem. It is more than coincidence that cash management services have never reached the same degree of customer attraction in Europe that they have reached in the United States. One reason for this is that nationwide branching and banking is far more prevalent in European countries. As a result, the introduction of full interstate banking for banks since 1997, as well as the rapid consolidation in the U.S. financial services industry (e.g., the merger of large banks and the development of national branch systems), may well reduce the demand for such services in the United States in the future.

Technology and Revenues

One potential benefit of technology is that it allows an FI to cross-market both new and existing products to customers. Such joint selling doesn't require the FI to produce all the services sold within the same branch or financial services outlet. For example, a commercial bank may link up with an insurance company to jointly market each other's loan, credit card, and insurance products. This arrangement has proved popular in Germany, where the second and third largest banks (Dresdner and Commerzbank) have developed sophisticated cross-marketing arrangements with large insurance companies. In the United States, Citicorp's merger with Travelers to create Citigroup was explicitly designed to cross-market banking, insurance, and securities products in over 100 countries. However, as the Contemporary Perspectives box on p. 288 shows, it may take 10 or more years to integrate computer systems to a sufficient degree to achieve this objective.

Technology also increases the rate of innovation of new products. In recent years, there have been many notable failures as well as successes. For example, despite large investments by banks, product innovations such as POS/debit cards have found it hard to find a sufficiently large market in the United States. On the other hand, telephone bill paying and preauthorized debits and credits, including direct payroll systems, are proving to be high-growth areas in modern banking.

For example, home banking might reasonably be viewed—to date—as a negative NPV product for banks such as BankAmerica. Considerable resources (I_o) were sunk into its development in the 1980s at a time when banks' cost of capital (d) was high. The realized net revenue streams (R_t) from home banking have been extremely disappointing so far—although, as is described in the text and Figure 14–1, home banking will become increasingly important as the Internet takes a hold in determining the size and direction of retail financial service transactions.

CLASH OF TECHNOLOGIES IN MERGER

Citicorp and Travelers' Computers Not on Speaking Terms

Saul Hansell

If you have an insurance policy with the Travelers Group, don't expect your local agent to be able to help you with your Citicorp credit card any time soon.

Despite the promised synergies that are to result from the planned $84 billion merger the two companies announced last week, it would likely take the better part of a decade, at best, before the computer and data base systems of the combined company can be fully integrated.

Technology experts point out that Citicorp itself has been trying for 10 years to merge the computers that run its banks in 100 countries into one happy family, and that work is far from done. Meanwhile, the computers in Travelers insurance company are barely on speaking terms with the machines in its Salomon Smith Barney brokerage or its Commercial Credit finance company.

In any merger of big companies, which tend to have vast, aging mainframe computer systems, integration is hard work. For Citigroup, as the combined companies plan to call themselves, the task would be even more onerous because their computer departments are already operating at full speed on other projects.

"This is the mother of all high wire acts," said Colin Crook, who retired three years ago as Citicorp's chief technology officer. "They are working like the blazes on what they are already doing, yet the payoffs from integration can be quite significant."

The technological benefits might eventually include mining the customer data bases of one business unit to seek ways of tailoring sales pitches to those customers for the products of a sibling Citigroup unit. Moreover, the larger company can share the costs of developing sophisticated new capabilities, like Internet-based marketing and

transaction systems. And ultimately, there may be opportunities to cut costs by consolidating computer and network operations.

But first things first. Travelers still has at least a year to go before Salomon Brothers, which it bought only last fall, is fully integrated into Smith Barney. Citicorp, meanwhile, is in the middle of a year-long sprint to finish its long-delayed global system consolidation.

Like many big corporations, both companies are consumed with the vast and tedious task of examining every system they run to make sure they are ready for the introduction of a new European currency next year and that computers will be able to handle dates after the year 2000.

"We just don't have the bandwidth to look at the new deal," said a technology executive at one of the companies, who voiced his exasperation only on condition of anonymity.

Travelers and Citicorp both said it was too early to discuss their plans for technology—or any other aspect of the merger. The deal, after all, was struck largely through personal negotiations between Sanford I. Weill, the Travelers chairman, and John S. Reed, the chairman of Citicorp. It could take a month or two before Mr. Reed and Mr. Weill, who will be co-chief executives of Citigroup, announce who will hold the next tier of management positions. Only then could any technical planning begin.

Yet, analysts say that any delays could actually benefit information technology managers at Travelers and Citicorp by allowing them to each finish their current projects.

"It is very important for Citibank to get the current system changes completed," said Diane Glossman, a bank

Finally, we cannot ignore the issue of *service quality.* For example, while ATMs may potentially lower bank operating costs compared to employing full-service tellers, the inability of machines to address customers' concerns and questions flexibly may drive retail customers away. That is, revenue losses may counteract any cost-savings effects. The survival of small banks in the face of growing nationwide branching may well be due in part to customers' belief that overall service quality is higher with tellers who provide a human touch rather than the ATMs more common at bigger banks. Nevertheless, Figure 14–1 shows how the combination of the Internet, the growth of personal computers, and the creation of specialized retail FI customer software by firms such as Microsoft and Intuit will certainly reduce the

Contemporary Perspectives

analyst with Lehman Brothers. "If they try to combine Travelers and Citibank at the same time they will have a bowl of spaghetti, rather than something workable."

Citibank and Travelers say their deal is mainly about finding ways to grow rather than cutting costs. But the challenge will be finding common ground between Citicorp's traditional emphasis on advanced technology and Travelers' preference for low-cost, no-frills systems.

From the days in the 1970's when Mr. Reed led the development of the automated teller machine, Citicorp has seen technological innovations as a centerpiece of its strategy. But as a result, executives of each line of business within the company have wielded jealous control over their computer systems, creating fiefs of incompatible technologies.

For more than a decade the company has been trying to make sense of its sprawling collection of incompatible systems, with the pressure increasing more recently as Mr. Reed mandated that Citibank become able to offer the same banking services in each of nearly 100 countries. Some 200 data centers have been merged into 20, and 100 networks into 11.

Last fall, Citicorp took a $889 million charge for a revamping that would eliminate 9,000 jobs and centralize many of its operating centers: The company has hired AT&T to further merge its data networks into a single global system.

The dominant Travelers technology culture was developed as Mr. Weill built the Shearson brokerage empire through dozens of mergers. Mr. Weill left Shearson, after selling it to American Express, but he bought it back into the company that is now Travelers. Most of the computers that run Salomon Smith Barney today, in fact, are the old Shearson systems.

Shearson's approach has been to have simple, cheap and efficient systems on central mainframe computers. This made completing mergers easier but sacrificed the kind of fancy features favored by Salomon, which before it was acquired last year by Travelers' Smith Barney unit had emphasized advanced technology that put considerable power and flexibility into the hands of its traders. Smith Barney says that while it originally moved Salomon stock traders to its old mainframe system, it is slowly adding back some of the advanced functions of Salomon's systems. But it will take another year before the two brokerage firms are fully integrated.

Still, most of the insurance, banking and brokerage systems at Citicorp and Travelers will be able to run as they are now for years to come. This will potentially give the companies breathing room to finish their current projects and get their plans in order.

Some argue that merging computers centers and data networks together—even for products as dissimilar as insurance and banking—can ultimately produce big savings. But care must be taken, they say.

"In a classic bank merger you have to be brutal and ruthless," said Mr. Crook. "In this case you have to get costs out by being more thoughtful in the way you architect your systems. It's not a game for the bewildered."

ability of small banks and thrifts to maintain franchise value based on service quality.[14]

Technology and Costs

Traditionally, FIs have considered the major benefits of technological advances to be on the cost side rather than the revenue side. After a theoretical look at how

---

[14]For example, Intuit's Quicken personal finance software has the ability to receive electronic bills.

FIGURE 14–1

*Evolution of Future Retail
Banking Delivery*

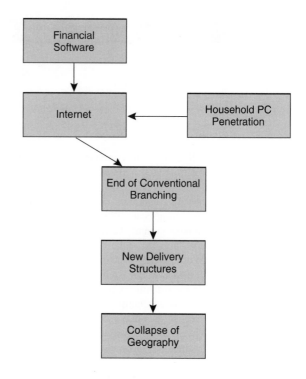

technology favorably or unfavorably affects an FI's costs, we look at the direct and
indirect evidence of technology-based cost savings for FIs. In general, technology
may favorably affect an FI's cost structure by allowing it to exploit either
economies of scale or economies of scope.

Economies of Scale.   As financial firms grow bigger, generally the potential scale
and array of the technology in which they can invest will expand. As noted above,
the largest FIs have the biggest expenditures on technology-related innovations. If
enhanced or improved technology lowers an FI's average costs of financial service
production, then bigger FIs may have an **economy of scale** advantage over smaller
financial firms. Economies of scale imply that the unit or average cost of producing
FI services in aggregate or some specific service such as deposits or loans falls as
the size of the FI expands.

> **Economies of Scale**
> As the output of an FI in-
> creases, its average costs
> of production fall.

In Figure 14–2 we show three different-sized FIs. The average cost of producing an FI's output of financial services is measured as

$$AC_i = \frac{TC_i}{S_i}$$

where

AC_i = Average costs of the ith bank
TC_i = Total costs of the ith bank
S_i = Size of the bank measured by assets, deposits, or loans.[15]

---

[15]It is arguable that the size of a modern FI should be measured by including off-balance-sheet assets
(contingent value) as well.

FIGURE 14–2

Economies of Scale in FIs

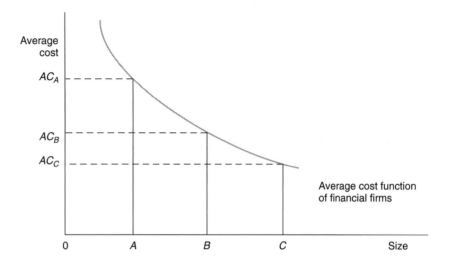

FIGURE 14–3

The Effects of Technological Improvement

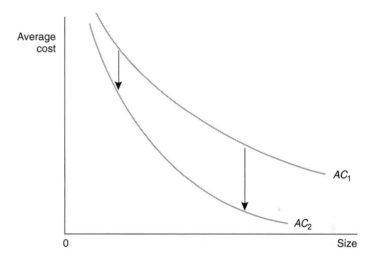

As you can see in Figure 14–2, the largest FI (size *C*) has a lower average cost of producing financial services than do smaller firms such as *B* and *A*. This means that at any given price for financial service firm products, firm *C* can make a bigger profit than either *B* or *A*. Alternatively, firm *C* can undercut *B* and *A* in price and potentially gain a larger market share. The long-run implication of economies of scale on the FI sector is that larger and most cost-efficient FIs will drive out smaller FIs, leading to increased large-firm dominance and concentration in financial services production. Such an implication is reinforced if time-related technological improvements increasingly benefit larger FIs over smaller FIs. For example, satellite technology and supercomputers, in which enormous technological advances are being made, may be available to only the largest FIs. The effect of improving technology over time, which is biased toward larger projects, is to shift the *AC* curve downward over time but with a bigger downward shift for large-sized FIs (see Figure 14–3).

AC_1 is the hypothetical *AC* curve prior to technological innovations. AC_2 reflects the cost-lowering effects of technology on FIs of all sizes but with the greatest benefit accruing to those of the largest size.

As noted earlier, technological investments are risky; if they do not cover their costs of development through future revenues, they reduce the value of the FI and its net worth. On the cost side, large-scale investments may result in excess capacity problems and integration problems as well as cost overruns and cost control problems. Then small FIs with simple and easily managed computer systems and/or those leasing time on large FIs' computers without bearing the fixed costs of installation and maintenance may have an average cost advantage. In this case, large-sized FIs' technological investments result in higher average costs of financial service production, causing the industry to operate under conditions of **diseconomies of scale** (Figure 14–4). Diseconomies of scale imply that small FIs are more cost efficient than bigger FIs and that in a freely competitive environment for financial services, small FIs prosper.

Diseconomies of Scale
As the output of an FI increases, its average costs of production increase.

At least two other possible shapes for the *AC* function exist; we show them in Figure 14–5. In panel (a) of Figure 14–5 the financial services industry reflects economies of scale at first and then diseconomies of scale as firms grow larger. This suggests a best or most efficient size for an FI at point S* and implies that too much technology investment can be as bad as too little. In panel (b) of Figure 14–5, we have constant returns to scale. Any potential cost-reducing effects of technology are spread evenly over FIs of all sizes. That is, technology investments are neutral rather than favoring one size of FI over another.

Economies of Scope.   While technological investments may have good or bad effects on FIs in general and these effects may well differ across FIs of different size, technology tends to be applied more in some product areas than in others. That is, FIs are multiproduct firms producing services of different technological intensity.

FIGURE 14–4

Diseconomies of Scale

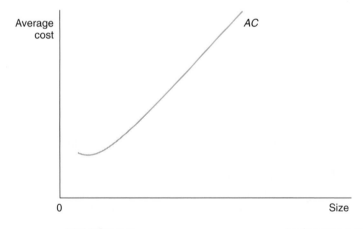

FIGURE 14–5

Other Average Cost Functions

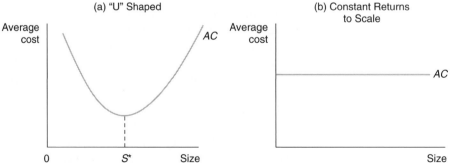

Moreover, technological improvements or investments in one financial service area (such as lending) may have incidental and synergistic benefits in lowering the costs of producing financial services in other areas (such as securities underwriting and brokerage). Specifically, computerization allows the storage and joint use of important information on customers and their needs. The simple *economy of scale* concept ignores these interrelationships among products and the "jointness" in the costs of producing financial products. In particular, the ability of FIs to generate synergistic cost savings across products is called *economies of scope* as opposed to economies of scale.

Technology may allow an FI to jointly use its input resources, such as capital and labor, to produce a set of financial services at a lower cost than would be the case if financial service products were produced independently of one another. Technically, let X_1 and X_2 be two financial products; each has one firm producing it as a specialized producer. That is, firm A produces on X_1 and no X_2, and firm B produces only X_2 and no X_1. The average cost functions *(AC)* of these firms are

$$AC_A[X_1, 0] \text{ and } AC_B[0, X_2]$$

Economies of Scope
The ability of FIs to generate synergistic cost savings through joint use of inputs in producing multiple products.

Economies of scope exist if these firms merge and jointly produce X_1 and X_2, and this joint production results in

$$AC_{A + B}[X_1, X_2] < AC_A[X_1, 0] + AC_B[0, X_2]$$

That is, the cost of joint production via cost synergies is less than the separate and independent production of these services.

As an example, let TC_B be the total cost of a specialized bank producing lending services to a corporate client. Suppose the total operating costs of producing these services is $50,000 for a loan volume (L_B) of $10 million. Such costs include information collection and monitoring as well as account maintenance and processing. Thus, the average cost (AC_B) of loan production for the bank is

$$AC_B = \frac{TC_B}{L_B} = \frac{\$50,000}{\$10,000,000} = .005 = \tfrac{1}{2}\%$$

At the same time, a specialized investment bank is selling commercial paper for the same corporate customer. The total cost *(TC_s)* of the securities firm running the commercial paper operation is $10,000 for a $1 million issue (P_S). These costs include the cost of underwriting the issue as well as the costs of placing the issue with outside buyers. Thus,

$$AC_S = \frac{TC_S}{P_S} = \frac{\$10,000}{\$1,000,000} = .01 = 1\%$$

Consequently, the total average cost *(TAC)* of separately producing the loan services through the bank and the commercial paper issuance through the securities firm is

$$TAC = \frac{\$60,000}{\$11,000,000} = 0.54\%$$

Suppose, instead, a single financial services firm produced both $10 million of lending services and $1 million commercial paper issuance services for the same customer. For corporate customers, loans and commercial paper are a source of funds substitutes. For a financial services firm to originate a loan and to originate commercial paper requires very similar expertise both in funding that issue and in credit risk assessment and monitoring. To the extent that most loans are quickly sold after origination, loan origination is very similar to the sale of commercial paper to outside buyers by the original underwriter. Common technologies in the loan and commercial paper production functions suggest that a single financial services firm simultaneously (or jointly) producing both loan and commercial paper services for the same client should be able to do this at a lower average cost compared with the separate production of these services with specialized FIs.

That is, if AC_{FS} is the total average cost of a nonspecialized financial services firm, then economies of scope imply that

$$AC_{FS} < TAC = 0.54\%$$

That is, the average cost of jointly producing many financial services may be less than the average cost of producing these products separately.

Diseconomies of Scope
The costs of joint production of FI services are higher than they would be if they were produced independently.

Nevertheless, **diseconomies of scope** may occur instead. This is where FIs find costs actually higher from joint production of services than if they were produced independently. For example, suppose an FI purchases some very specialized information-based technology to ease the loan production and processing function. Any excess capacity this system has could be employed by the FI in other service areas. However, this process could be a relatively inefficient technology for other service areas and add to the overall costs of production compared to using a specialized technology for each service or product area.

Concept Questions

1. What are two risk factors involved in an FI's investment of resources in innovative technological products?
2. What is the link between interstate banking restrictions and the retail demand for electronic payment services?
3. Does the existence of economies of scale for FIs mean that in the long run small FIs cannot survive?
4. If there are diseconomies of scope, do specialized FIs have a relative cost advantage or disadvantage over product-diversified FIs?
5. Make a list of the potential economies of scope or cost synergies if a commercial bank merged with an investment bank.

Testing for Economies of Scale and Economies of Scope

To test for economies of scale and economies of scope, FIs must clearly specify both the inputs into their production process and the cost of those inputs. Basically the two approaches to analyzing the cost functions of FIs are the production and the intermediation approaches.

The Production Approach

The production approach views FIs' outputs of services as having two underlying inputs: labor and capital. If w = Wage costs of labor, r = Rental costs of capital, and y = Output of services, the total cost function (C) for the FI is

$$C = f(y, w, r,)$$

The Intermediation Approach

The intermediation approach views the output of financial services as being produced by labor and capital as well as the funds the intermediary uses to produce intermediated services. Thus, deposit costs would be an input in banking and the thrift industry, while premiums or reserves would be inputs in insurance:

$$C = f(y, w, r, k)$$

where k reflects the cost of funds for the FI.

Concept Questions

1. Describe the basic concept behind the production approach to testing for economies of scale and economies of scope.
2. How does the intermediation approach differ from the production approach?

Empirical Findings on Cost Economies of Scale and Scope and Implications for Technology Expenditures

A large number of studies have examined cost economies of scale and scope in different financial service industry sectors.[16] We summarize some of these in Table 14–2.

With respect to banks, most of the early studies failed to find economies of scale beyond the smallest bank size. More recently, better data sets and improved methodologies have suggested that economies of scale may exist for banks up to the $10 billion to $25 billion size range. Many large-regional and superregional banks fall in this size range. With respect to economies of scope either among deposits, loans, and other traditional banking product areas or between on-balance-sheet products and off-balance-sheet products such as loan sales, the evidence is at best very weak that cost complementarities exist. Similarly, the smaller number of studies of nonbank financial service firms such as thrifts, insurance companies, and securities firms almost always report neither economies of scale nor economies of scope.[17]

---

[16]Good reviews are found in J. A. Clark, "Economies of Scale and Scope at Depository Financial Institutions: A Review of the Literature," Federal Reserve Bank of Kansas City, *Economic Review,* September–October 1988, pp. 16–33; L. Mester, "Efficient Production of Financial Services: Scale and Scope Economies," Federal Reserve Bank of Philadelphia, *Economic Review,* January–February 1987, pp. 15–25; and A. Berger, W. C. Hunter, and S. B. Timme, "The Efficiency of Financial Institutions: A Review and Preview of Research Past, Present and Future," *Journal of Banking and Finance* 17 (1993), pp. 221–49. Three major production function forms have been tested: The Cobb-Douglas, the trans-log, and the Box-Cox flexible functional form. For more details on the specific characteristics of these functions and estimation issues, see the references in Table 14–2.

[17]A. Berger, D. Humphrey, and L. B. Pulley, "Do Consumers Pay for One-Stop Banking? Evidence from an Alternative Revenue Function," *Journal of Banking and Finance* 20 (1996), pp. 1601–21, looks at revenue economies of scope (rather than cost economies of scope) between loans and deposits over the 1978–90 period, and finds no evidence of revenue economies of scope.

Economies of Scale and Scope and X-Inefficiencies

Finally, a number of very recent studies have looked at the *dispersion* of costs in any given size class rather than looking at the shape of the average cost functions. These efficiency studies find quite dramatic cost differences of 20 percent or more among banks, thrifts, and insurance companies in any given size class ($100 million asset size class, $200 million asset size class, etc.). Moreover, these studies find that only a small part of the cost differences among FIs in any size class can be attributed to economies of scale or scope.[18] This suggests that cost inefficiencies related to managerial ability and other hard-to-quantify factors (so-called *X-inefficiencies*) may better explain cost differences and operating cost efficiencies among financial firms than technology related investments per se.

Thus, there is an absence of any strong direct evidence that bigger multiproduct financial service firms enjoy cost advantages over smaller, more specialized financial firms. Also, economies of scope and scale do not explain many of the cost differences among FIs of the same size. These empirical findings raise questions about the benefits of technology investments and technological innovation. While a majority of the studies in Table 14–2 are concerned with testing for economies of scope and scale rather than the benefits of technology, these results are consistent with the relatively low payoff from technological innovation. To the extent that benefits arise to large FIs, they may well be on the revenue generation/new product innovation side rather than on the cost side. Indeed, recent studies looking at output and input efficiencies for banks and insurance companies derived from revenue and profit functions found that large FIs tend to be more efficient in revenue generation than smaller FIs and that such efficiencies may well offset scope and scale cost inefficiencies related to size.[19]

The Professional Perspectives boxes by A. Berger and L. Mester show current thinking by two Fed economists on the importance of efficiency and scale and scope economies in banking. Finally, the real benefits of technological innovation may be long term and dynamic, related to the evolution of the U.S. payments system away from cash and checks and toward electronic means of payment. Such benefits are difficult to pick up in traditional economy of scale and scope studies, which are largely static and ignore the more dynamic aspects of efficiency gains. This dynamic technological evolution not only has affected the fundamental role of FIs in the financial system but also has generated some new and subtle types of risks for FIs and their regulators. In the next section we take a closer look at the effects of technology on the payments system.

Concept Questions

1. What does the empirical evidence in Table 14–2 reveal about economies of scale and scope?
2. What conclusion is suggested by recent studies that have focused on the dispersion of costs across banks of a given asset size?

[18]See Allen N. Berger and Loretta J. Mester, "Inside the Black-Box: What Explains Differences in the Efficiencies of Financial Institutions," *Journal of Banking and Finance* 21 (1997) pp. 895–947, for an extensive review of these efficiency studies.

[19]See Berger and Mester, "Inside the Black-Box" and J. David Cummins, Sharon Tennyson, and Mary A. Weiss, "Efficiency, Scale Economies and Consolidation in the U.S. Life Insurance Industry," *Journal of Banking and Finance,* February 1999, pp. 325–357.

TABLE 14–2   Economies of Scale and Scope in Financial Service Firms— The Evidence

	Economies of Scale beyond Small Levels of Output (size)	Economies of Scope among Outputs
Domestic Banks		
Benston et al., 1983	No	No
Berger et al., 1987	No	No
Gilligan and Smirlock, 1984	No	Yes
Gilligan, Smirlock, and Marshall, 1984	No	Yes
Kolari and Zardkoohi, 1987	No	No
Lawrence, 1989	No	Yes
Lawrence and Shay, 1986	No	No
Mester, 1990	Yes	No
Noulas et al., 1990	Yes	?
Shaffer, 1988	Yes	?
Hunter et al., 1990	Yes	No
McAllister and McManus, 1993	No	?
Pulley and Humphrey, 1993	?	Yes
Jagtiani and Khanthavit, 1996	Yes	Yes
Foreign Banks		
Yoshika and Nakajima, 1987 (Japan)	Yes	?
Kim, 1987 (Israel)	Yes	Yes
Saunders and Walter, 1991 (Worldwide)	Yes	No
Ruthenberg, 1994 (European Community)	No	?
McKillop, Glass, and Morikawa, 1996 (Japan)	Yes	No
Allen and Rai, 1996 (Worldwide)	Yes	No
Thrifts		
Mester, 1987	No	No
LeCompte and Smith, 1990	No	No
Life Insurance		
Fields and Murphy, 1989	Yes	No
Fields, 1988	No	?
Grace and Timme, 1992	Yes	?
Cummins et al., 1998	Yes	?
Securities Firms		
Goldberg et al., 1991	No	No

Technology and the Evolution of the Payments System

To better understand the changing nature of the U.S. payments system, look at Tables 14–3 to 14–5. As you can see, while nonelectronic methods—mostly checks—accounted for 75 percent of noncash transactions, this represented only 11 percent of the dollar *value* of noncash transactions. By comparison, electronic methods of payment—automated clearinghouses (ACH), credit cards, debit cards, and wire transfer systems—accounted for only 25 percent in volume but 89 percent in value. Wire transfer systems alone accounted for 87 percent of all dollar transactions measured in value.

Also, as can be seen from Tables 14–4 and 14–5, the use of electronic methods of payment is far higher in other major developed countries. For example, in Europe and Japan electronic transactions account for over 70 percent of total transactions measured by number of transactions. To some extent, the United States is now starting to catch up with these countries. The speed with which this "electronic

TABLE 14–3   The U.S. Payment System: Volume, Value, and Average Transaction Amount, 1996*

	Volume, billions	Percent	Value, billions	Percent	Transaction Average Value
Debit card	2.6	3%	$ 97	0%	$ 37
Credit card	16	19	983	.1	61
Check	65	75	74,879	11	1,158
ACH	3	3.5	9,998	1.5	3,283
Wire transfer	.1	0	580,681	87	4,266,577
	86.6		666,638		

*Numbers have been rounded off and may not sum to total.

Source: Bank for International Settlements, *Statistics on Payment Systems in the Group of Ten Countries,* Basle, December 1997.

TABLE 14–4   Annual Number and Composition of Noncash Transactions Per Person, 1996

	Total*	Check	Credit Card	Debit Card	ACH and Giro
United States	326	244	61	10	11
Canada	151	62	45	23	21
Europe	126	31	5	16	74
Japan	40	2	3	.1	35

* Data have been rounded off so that they will add to the total.

Source: Bank for International Settlements, *Statistics on Payment Systems in the Group of Ten Countries,* Basle, December 1997. Japanese data are from estimates by D. Humphrey.

TABLE 14–5   Annual Number of Paper and Electronic Noncash Transactions Per Person, 1996

	Paper*	Electronic†	% Electronic
United States	244	82	25%
Canada	62	89	59
Europe	38	88	70
Japan‡	10	30	75

*Checks and paper giro.

†Credit and debit card, ACH, and electronic giro.

‡See notes to Table 14–4.

payments" gap will be closed will in large part depend on two factors: the speed with which the trend towards consolidation and automated banking continues and the degree and speed of technological innovation.

The two wire systems that dominate the U.S. payments system are Fedwire and the Clearing House Interbank Payments System (CHIPS). Fedwire is a wire transfer network linking more than 10,000 domestic banks with the Federal Reserve System. Banks use this network to make deposit and loan payments, transfer book

Professional Perspectives

SCALE AND SCOPE ECONOMIES

Loretta J. Mester
Federal Reserve Bank of Philadelphia

The banking industry has been undergoing a significant restructuring over the last several years. Since the mid-80s, the number of commercial banks has fallen by about 5,000 as a result of failures and especially mergers, and average bank asset size has increased. Recently, several large banking organizations have merged—for example, Chemical and Chase and Nationsbank and BankAmerica. A chief concern of the Federal Reserve and other bank regulators, who must approve mergers, is that restructuring could lead to a financial services industry that is too concentrated—one in which a handful of very large institutions could exert monopoly power. But we also recognize that restructuring might lead to an industry much more efficient in delivering financial services; that would help promote the safety and soundness of the industry.

To help analyze this issue, economists at the Fed and elsewhere have studied the banking industry's cost structure and, in particular, *scale and scope economies*. The degree of scale economies measures the percentage change in a firm's cost of production given a percent increase in the level of all its products. Scale economies are said to exist when increasing the scale of operations reduces the average cost of production. Thus, a financial institution can become more efficient by increasing its operating scale until such economies are exhausted. Because a financial institution produces multiple outputs, in addition to identifying the optimal scale of operations, it is also important to determine the optimal combination of products to minimize production cost. Is it more efficient to have financial "supermarkets" or financial "boutiques"?

The degree of scope economies measures the percentage change in production costs if a bank's products were produced by specialized firms as opposed to a single firm. If this measure is positive, scope economies exist and it is more efficient to have the bank produce multiple products than to have several specialized banks producing the products. If the measure is negative, there are scope diseconomies and it is more efficient to have specialized banks.

Empirical studies of the banking industry using data from the 1980s suggested there were significant scale economies for banks with assets up to $100 million or so; that is, scale economies were exhausted at a small size. But recent studies that used data from the 1990s have found scale economies at much larger institutions—up to at least

$25 billion in assets. The difference in results between the earlier and later studies partly reflects improvements in the methods used to measure scale economies—in particular, accounting for the bank's choice of risk and financial capital. But there also appears to have been a real increase in the efficient scale of commercial banks between the 1980s and 1990s, as improvements in technology and the relaxation of geographic restrictions on competition, among other changes, have occurred. The empirical evidence shows there does not seem to be much in the way of scope economies or diseconomies, suggesting that banks that offer a variety of financial services and banks that offer just a few should be equally cost efficient. Thus, the empirical work suggests that the current consolidation trend could lead to a more efficient industry, as banks merge to attain a larger and more efficient size.

Biographical Summary

Loretta J. Mester is a vice president and economist at the Federal Reserve Bank of Philadelphia, which she joined in 1985. Dr. Mester provides economic forecasts, policy analysis, and regulatory analysis for the bank's senior management involved in monetary policymaking and bank regulatory policymaking. In addition, she conducts research on the organizational structure and production technologies of financial institutions, the theory of the banking firm, agency theory, and regulatory issues in banking, and her work has been published in professional journals. Dr. Mester is also an adjunct assistant professor of finance at the Wharton School of the University of Pennsylvania and a senior fellow in the Wharton Financial Institutions Center.

In addition, she is an associate editor of *Journal of Banking and Finance, Journal of Financial Intermediation, Journal of Money, Credit, and Banking,* and *Journal of Financial Services Research* and an editor of *Journal of Productivity Analysis.*

Dr. Mester received her M.A. and Ph.D. in economics from Princeton University, where she held a National Science Foundation Fellowship. She earlier received her B.A. in mathematics and economics from Barnard College of Columbia University.

EFFICIENCY IN BANKING

Allen N. Berger
Board of Governors of the Federal Reserve System
Wharton Financial Institutions Center

Bank efficiency is an important topic because it is both a powerful motivation for, and an important consequence of, changes in the banking industry. Bank merger and acquisition (M&A) participants often cite efficiency gains as their primary motivation for consolidation. Inefficiency has also been found to be a leading cause of bank failure.

A bank is fully efficient if it produces the output level and mix that maximizes profits and does so at the minimum possible cost. However, most banks are not fully efficient. There are a number of sources of inefficiency in banking. Many studies have investigated cost scale inefficiency—whether the costs per unit of output are unnecessarily high for particular bank sizes. The results generally suggest that the average cost curve in banking has a relatively flat U shape. In the 1980s, banks of medium size, $100 million to $5 billion in assets, had the lowest unit costs, while smaller and larger banks were somewhat less efficient. However, these inefficiencies usually did not amount to more than about 5 percent of costs, indicating that cost scale economies were relatively unimportant.

More recent analysis suggests that scale economies have increased substantially in the 1990s, possibly as a result of lower open-market interest rates, removal of geographic restrictions on competition, elimination of regulatory ceilings on deposit interest rates, and improvements in physical technology and applied financial management techniques.

As a best guess, cost efficiency appears to improve up to about $10 billion to $25 billion in assets, although the data on banks larger than this are simply too sparse to draw firm conclusions. In addition, there may be scale economies in terms of better risk diversification and higher revenues from providing a better or broader mix of financial services from very large banking organizations, but again this is difficult to determine based on the existing data in which there are very few large organizations.

Another area of research has been cost scope efficiencies. Here, the goal is to determine whether it is cheaper to produce two or more outputs jointly in one consolidated firm or to produce them separately in multiple specializing firms. The results suggest that cost scope inefficiencies are quite small.

The most important origin of cost problems in banking is X-inefficiency, or differences in managerial ability to control costs for any given scale or scope of production. On average, banks have costs that are about 20 percent above the efficient frontier. That is, the average bank has costs about 20 percent higher than those of a "best-practice" firm producing the same output. Most of this is operational inefficiency, such as branch offices that use excessive labor, as opposed to financial inefficiency, where excessive interest rates are paid for funds.

Recently, researchers have used bank profits to measure inefficiency. Profits include revenue or output inefficien-

entry securities among themselves, and act as payment agents on behalf of large corporate customers, including other financial service firms. CHIPS is operated as a private network. At the core of the system are approximately 105 large U.S. and foreign banks acting as correspondent banks for a larger number of domestic and international banks in clearing mostly international payments (foreign exchange, Eurodollar loans, certificates of deposit).

Together, these two wire transfer networks have been growing at around 8 percent per annum. Indeed, since 1997 the combined value of payments sent over these two networks has often exceeded $2.5 trillion a day.[20] Another way to see the tremendous growth in these wire transfer payment networks is to compare their dollar payment values to bank reserves, as we do in Table 14–6. Thus, the value of wire

---

[20]For example, in 1997, the average daily Fed funds value was $1.149 trillion and the average daily CHIPS value was $1.443 trillion.

Professional Perspectives

cies as well as cost or input inefficiencies. As noted above, full efficiency requires that the bank produce the profit-maximizing level and mix of output as well as minimizing costs for that output. A surprising result is that revenue inefficiencies may be as large as or larger than cost inefficiencies. The inclusion of revenues also makes larger firms tend to be more efficient, perhaps because of the benefits of diversification.

Given that the banking industry is consolidating rapidly, an important application of efficiency analysis is the estimation of the efficiency effects of M&As. Research has found very little cost efficiency gains on average from consolidation but does find improvements in profit efficiency. Profit efficiency includes revenue benefits from improving product mix, and can reflect the benefits of improved diversification. In part, the increase in profit efficiency is manifested in a portfolio shift from securities into consumer loans and business loans. This is consistent with the hypothesis that improved diversification of risks associated with M&As from an improved mix of geographic areas, industries, loan types, or maturity structures might allow consolidated banks to shift their output mixes into higher-risk investments with higher expected revenues. Greater diversification protects shareholders and uninsured creditors, so there need be no costly increase in equity capital or rise in the costs of uninsured purchased funds.

This research has also uncovered some of the conditions that tend to predict the largest efficiency gains from M&As. Efficiency gains are the most pronounced when the participating banks are relatively inefficient before the consolidation. This is consistent with the hypothesis that M&As may "wake up" inefficient management.

The opinions expressed do not necessarily reflect those of the Board of Governors or its staff.

Biographical Summary
Allen N. Berger is a senior economist with the Board of Governors of the Federal Reserve System and a senior fellow at the Wharton Financial Institutions Center. Mr. Berger is editor of *Journal of Money, Credit and Banking,* editor of *Journal of Productivity Analysis,* associate editor of *Journal of Banking and Finance,* and associate editor of *Journal of Financial Services Research.* He has coorganized research conferences at the Wharton School, New York University, the Board of Governors, and the Atlanta and New York Federal Reserve Banks and has coedited special issues of *Journal of Banking and Finance, Journal of Money, Credit, and Banking,* and *European Journal of Operational Research.* Mr. Berger has published over 60 professional economics and finance articles, including papers in the *Journal of Political Economy, American Economic Review, Journal of Financial Economics, Journal of Monetary Economics, Journal of Business, Review of Economics and Statistics,* and *Brookings Papers on Economic Activity.* His research covers a variety of topics related to financial institutions. He received his Ph.D. in economics from the University of California, Berkeley, in 1983.

transfers increased more than 100-fold relative to bank reserves over the 1970–97 period. [21] Table 14–7 shows the importance of wholesale wire transfer systems (for 1996) in other countries. Measured as a percent of local gross domestic product (GDP), Switzerland has the biggest system. In 1999 as a result of the single currency (the euro) and the European Monetary Union, a single wholesale wire transfer system for Europe will emerge, linking all countries that are members of the European Monetary Union. The transactional system is called TARGET (Trans-European Automated Real-Time Gross-Settlement Express Transfer).

---

[21]This increase has been aided by a steep decline in bank reserves in recent years. For example, in 1994 bank reserves were $25 billion versus $10.6 billion in 1997. Part of this is due to the development of "sweep accounts" in which customers can automatically switch funds from high-reserve requirement checking accounts into low-reserve requirement savings accounts. As a result, both banks and customers benefit: banks, through lower reserve requirements and customers through higher interest payments.

TABLE 14–6   Ratio of Fedwire and CHIPS Dollar Payments to Bank Reserves

	The Ratio of Average Daily Fedwire and CHIPS Payments ($) to Bank Reserves
1970	2
1980	17
1983	38
1985	42
1990	80
1994	81
1997	243

Source: David B. Humphrey, "Future Directions in Payment Risk Reduction," *Journal of Cash Management*, 1988; Federal Reserve figures; and estimates by D. Humphrey.

TABLE 14–7   Wholesale Wire Transfer Systems in Different Countries, 1996

	Number of transactions, thousands	*Annual Value of transactions, U.S. $ billions*	*Ratio of transactions value to GDP (at annual rate)*
Japan			
FEYCS	9,403	78,788	17.1
BOJ-NET	3,781	357,336	77.7
Netherlands			
Interpay	1,586,100	1,376	3.5
8007-S.W.I.F.T.	2,099	8,112	20.7
FA	600	5,304	13.5
Sweden			
RIX	310	10,146	46.6
Bank Giro System	264,880	313	1.4
Switzerland			
SIC	108,407	28,658	104.6
DTA/LSV	85,796	221,611	1.2
United Kingdom			
CHAPS	14,395	45,104	38.9
BACS	2,476,000	1,954	1.7
Check/credit	2,136,000	1,960	1.7
United States			
Fedwire	82,600	249,140	32.9
CHIPS	53,500	331,541	43.8

Source: The Bank for International Settlements, *Statistics on Payment Systems in the Group of Ten Countries,* Basle, December 1997, Table 10b. p. 125.

Risks That Arise in a Wire Transfer Payment System

At least six important risks have arisen along with the growth of wire transfer systems. Some we touched on while discussing off-balance-sheet activities in Chapter 13; here we go into more detail.

Daylight Overdraft Risk.   Some analysts and regulators view settlement or daylight overdraft risk as one of the greatest potential sources of instability in the financial markets today. To understand daylight overdrafts better, look at

FIGURE 14–6

Daylight Overdrafts on Fedwire

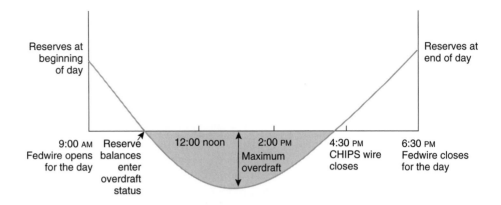

Figure 14–6. It shows a typical daily pattern of net wire payment transfers—payment messages sent (debits) minus payment messages received (credits)—for a large money center bank using Fedwire.

Under the Federal Reserve Act, banks must maintain cash reserves on deposit at the Fed; Fedwire settlement occurs at the end of the banking day at 6:30 PM EST. At that time, the Federal Reserve adjusts each member bank's reserve account to reflect that bank's net debit (credit) position with other banks.[22] Under current regulations, the end-of-day reserve position of a member bank cannot be negative. However, what is true at the end of the day is not true during the day; that is, the Fed allows banks to run real-time **daylight overdrafts** (or negative intraday balances) on their reserve accounts. These negative reserve balances arise under the current payments system because large banks and their customers often send payment messages repaying overnight loans and making interest payments at the beginning of the banking day and borrow funds (i.e., receive payment messages) toward the end of the banking day. For periods during the day, banks frequently run daylight overdrafts on their reserve accounts at the Fed by having their payment outflow messages exceed their payment inflow messages (see Figure 14–6).

Daylight Overdraft
When a bank's reserve account at the Fed becomes negative within the banking day.

In effect, the Fed is implicitly lending banks within-day reserves. There are two other important institutional aspects to this process. First, until recently, the Federal Reserve did not charge banks an explicit interest rate or fee for these daylight overdrafts. As a result, neither banks nor their large corporate customers had any incentive to economize on these transactions. Daylight Fedwire overdrafts were effectively free and therefore oversupplied.[23] Second, under Regulation J, the Federal Reserve guarantees payment finality for every wire transfer message. Therefore, if the representative bank in Figure 14–6 were to fail at 12:00 noon, the Federal Reserve would be liable for all the Fedwire transactions made by that bank until 12 noon. This eliminates any risk that a payment message receiving bank or its customers would be left short of funds at the end of the day. Essentially, the Federal Reserve bears the Fedwire credit risk of bank failures by granting overdrafts without charging a market interest rate.

---

[22]Technically, CHIPS transactions settle on Fedwire by 4:30 PM, before Fedwire closes.

[23]Beginning in 1993, a small per annum interest charge (penalty) was levied on a bank's daily overdraft amount in excess of a deductible amount (10 percent of its regulatory capital). The interest charge is an annualized 15 basis points. As a result, this interest charge is very small. For example, it is estimated that only 90 financial institutions had to pay a penalty exceeding $100 over any two-week period in 1995. See H. W. Richards, "Daylight Overdraft Fees and the Federal Reserves Payment System Risk Policy, *Federal Reserve Bulletin,* December 1995, pp. 1065–77.

Book Entry Securities
Securities held in computerized account form rather than in paper form.

A good example of how technological failure or malfunctions can expose the Federal Reserve and the financial system to massive settlement risk exposure occurred in November 1985 at the Bank of New York. The Bank of New York (BONY) is a major dealer in government securities and uses Fedwire to pay for securities. Since the vast majority of U.S. Treasury securities are **book entry securities** (i.e., computerized accounts rather than paper claims), these would usually be transferred by securities Fedwire at the same time payments were made on cash Fedwire.[24] The problem occurred on November 20–21, 1985. On November 20, BONY had a very large number of securities transactions, too extensive for its clearing and settlement software to handle in an efficient fashion. Indeed, because of a software breakdown, it was still processing November 20 transactions the next day. As a result, BONY could not make any new securities deliveries the next day and therefore receive federal funds as payments. Its daylight overdraft on its reserve account started to build up throughout the day. Even though the Fed extended the hours of Fedwire, the software problem was still not solved late into the evening of the 21st. When settlement finally occurred early in the morning of the 22nd, the Federal Reserve had to extend a one-day loan to BONY equal to nearly two-thirds of BONY's total domestic and worldwide assets and over 24 times the size of its primary equity capital. Clearly, failure to extend the loan would have resulted in a large number of settlement failures by BONY and other banks. The fact that the loan size was so enormous relative to BONY's capital is symptomatic of the type of risk exposure that can potentially arise on wire transfer networks and the sensitivity of banks to operational and technological breakdowns.[25]

Indeed, the risk of failure of a major government securities dealer such as BONY or Chase to settle its transactions on Fedwire has arisen again as part of general concerns surrounding the so-called Millennium bug, or the Y2K problem which involves the inability of computers to read correctly computer-coded payments that rely on the last two digits of any year. Specifically, the fear is that a computer system will read all transactions for January, 2000, as January, 1900, since it will interpret the "00" year digits as referring to 1900 rather than 2000. Currently, the securities industry in the United States is spending $6 billion to fix this problem, and many are lobbying for financial markets to be closed on Friday, December 31, 1999. Instead, one estimate is that if a major government securities dealer's computers failed to operate for one day (due to the bug), the Federal Reserve might have to extend a loan as large as $100 billion to that dealer to help it balance its books.[26]

On CHIPS, net payment flows often take on a daily pattern similar to that in Figure 14–6 except that, as a privately owned pure net settlement system, the beginning-of-day position must be zero for all banks. As on Fedwire, big banks often run a daylight overdraft, but this is generally larger and more pronounced early in the morning than it is on Fedwire. Again, large banks then seek to borrow funds in the afternoon to cover net debit positions created earlier in the day. While CHIPS does not charge banks explicit fees for running daylight overdrafts, a bank failing to settle at the end of the day is treated very differently than it is on Fedwire. On Fedwire, all payments are in good funds—the Federal Reserve guarantees the finality of any wire transfer at the time it is made. By contrast, on CHIPS, since it is a private network, all within-day transfers are provisional and become final only on

---

[24]Technically, there are two Fedwires: one for securities and one for cash and reserve transfers.

[25]This description of the BONY crisis is based on R. J. Herring, "Innovations to Enhance Liquidity: The Implications for Systemic Risk" (University of Pennsylvania, Wharton School, October 1992).

[26]See "An Extra Day to Fine Tune 1000 Years" *New York Times,* January 19, 1998, p. D5.

settlement among CHIPS members at the end of the day. In this case, if a bank (bank Z) with a daylight overdraft were to fail, CHIPS might have to resolve this by unwinding all of the failing bank's transactions over that day with the other $(N - 1)$ remaining banks. Bank Z's individual failure could result in a systemic crisis in the banking and financial system among the remaining $(N - 1)$ banks in the system.

In particular, suppose bank Y would have been in a net creditor position at the end of the banking day if the failing bank had settled. Bank Y may find that after bank Z's failure and any CHIPS unwinding of message transactions, it too cannot settle its transactions with the other remaining banks. As a result, all its transactions with those banks have to unwound.[27] Such a process would have to continue until all banks could settle their transactions with each other. While no settlement failure has occurred recently on CHIPS,[28] any such failure could be potentially disastrous, with financial ramifications far exceeding those of the October 1987 stock market crash.[29]

To lower this settlement risk problem and to introduce an element of payment finality, the members of CHIPS have contributed to a special escrow fund. This fund became operational in October 1990. CHIPS members can use this fund to replace the message commitments of any failed bank, therefore preventing the potentially disastrous unwinding effects just described. However it's estimated that this fund is sufficient to cover only the failure of its two largest financial institution members.[30] At the end of the day, it would probably be left to the Federal Reserve and other central banks to mount a rescue scheme to prevent an international failure contagion from spreading throughout the domestic and international financial system. Of course, this implies yet another subsidy from U.S. regulators and taxpayers to the private domestic and international banking system.

Because of these concerns, the FDICIA, passed in 1991, required the Federal Reserve to implement Regulation F, under which banks, thrifts, and foreign banks must develop internal procedures or benchmarks to limit their settlement and other credit exposures to depository institutions with which they do business (so-called correspondent banks). Accordingly, since December 1992, banks must normally limit their exposure to an individual corespondent to no more than 25 percent of the correspondent bank's capital. However, for adequately capitalized banks, this can be raised to 50 percent, while no set benchmark is required for well-capitalized banks. Thus, the most solvent banks now find it easier to transact on the wire transfer networks and run daylight overdrafts than less well-capitalized banks.[31] In addition, as

---

[27]This would leave only $N - 2$ banks.

[28]There was a failure in 1974 by the Herstatt Bank of Germany.

[29]Simulations by D. B. Humphrey of CHIPS unwinding following an assumed bank failure show that up to 50 banks might be unable to meet their payment obligations on CHIPS following any one bank's failure to settle, implying a massive systematic collapse of the payment system. See "Payments Finality and Risk Settlement Failure," in *Technology and the Regulation of Financial Markets: Securities, Futures, and Banking,* ed. A. Saunders and L. J. White (Lexington, Mass.: Lexington Books, 1986), pp. 97–120. Interestingly, in a paper conducting similar simulations for Italy (P. Angelini, G. Maresca, and D. Russo, "An Assessment of Systemic Risk in the Italian Clearing System," *Bank of Italy,* Discussion Paper No. 207, 1993), these systemic costs were much lower. This was largely due to the lower importance of wholesale wire transfers in Italy. For example, there are only 288 participants, versus 10,000 on Fedwire. In fact, only the failure of 4 out of 288 banks triggers a systemic crisis in simulations for January 1992.

[30]See CSC, *Sustaining Stable Financial Markets throughout the Millennium* Computer Sciences Corp. (Waltham, Mass., 1998).

[31]See Federal Reserve Board of Governors press release, July 14, 1992, for more details.

long as the benchmarks are adhered to, regulators' exposure to settlement risk is reduced.[32]

International Technology Transfer Risk.   In recent years the United States has been at the forefront in making technology investments and financial service innovations in the payments system. For example, the United States has been a major pioneer of ATMs. Yet such networks have grown relatively slowly in countries such as Germany, Italy, and Belgium, often because of prohibitive charges imposed for the use and leasing of domestic telephone lines (see Table 14–8).

This suggest that U.S. financial service firms have often been unable to transfer profitably domestic technological innovations to international markets to gain competitive advantage, at least in the short term.[33] By contrast, foreign financial service firms entering the U.S. market gain direct access to and knowledge of U.S. technology–based products at a very low cost. For example, since the passage of the International Banking Act in 1978, foreign banks have had direct access to U.S. Fedwire.

Crime and Fraud Risk.   The increased replacing of checks and cash as methods of payment or exchange by wire transfers has raised new problems regarding theft, data snooping, and white-collar crime. Because huge sums are transferred across the wire networks each day and some bank employees have specialized knowledge of personal identification numbers (PINS) and other entry codes, the incentive for white-collar crime appears to have increased. For example, a manager at the Sri Lankan branch of the now defunct BCCI reportedly stole a computer chip from a telex machine in the bank's Oman branch and used it to transfer $10 million from three banks in the United States and Japan to his own account in Switzerland.[34] In the future, greater bank and regulatory resources will have to be spent on surveillance and employee monitoring as well as on developing fail-safe and unbreakable entry codes to wire transfer accounts, especially as a number of countries have passed data privacy laws.

Surprisingly, however, a recent study on the problems arising with U.S. on-line banking found that only 1 percent of those problems could be attributed to employee sabotage or internal fraudulent attacks.[35]

Regulatory Risk.   The improvement in FIs' computer and telecommunications networks also enhances the power of FIs vis-à-vis regulators, effectively aiding regulatory avoidance. Thus, as implied earlier, regulation not only can affect the profitability of technological innovations, it also can either spur or hinder the rate and types of innovation.[36,37] For example, each state in the United States imposes usury

---

[32]One way to eliminate payment systems risk is to go to continuous real-time gross settlement (RTGS) rather than end-of-day settlement. Such a system is used in Switzerland. However, arguably such a system imposes a danger of payment system gridlock. See New York Clearing House Association, January 1995; and W. R. Emmons, "Recent Developments in Wholesale Payment Systems," *Federal Reserve Bank of St. Louis Review,* November–December 1997, pp. 23–43.

[33]Long-term benefits may yet be realized due to telecommunications deregulation globally and through better customer recruitment and marketing of products in foreign environments.

[34]Office of Technology Assessment, *U.S. Banks and International Telecommunications,* chapter 5, pp. 27–35.

[35]General Accounting Office, *Electronic Banking: Experiences Reported by Banks in Implementing On-line Banking,* January 1998, GAO/GGD 98–34.

TABLE 14–8   Cash Dispensers and ATMs

	1991	*1992*	*1993*	*1994*	*1995*
Number of Machines per 1,000,000 Inhabitants					
Belgium	105	109	119	313	360
Canada	467	510	554	578	595
France	284	305	325	356	395
Germany	161	235	308	361	436**
Italy	204	245	266	326	378
Japan	795	870	935	978	1,013
Netherlands	222	260	291	324	355
Sweden	258	254	255	259	267
Switzerland	347	387	439	481	532
United Kingdom	309	316	321	334	358
United States	331	342	367	418	467
Number of Transactions per Inhabitant					
Belgium	8.1	8.8	9.1	11.9	14.2
Canada	33.6	36.0	37.5	41.0	45.9
France	11.0	12.0	13.3	14.2	15.7
Germany	—	—	—	11.5	13.4**
Italy*	2.9	3.6	4.1	4.6	5.3
Japan	2.4	3.0	3.3	3.6	3.8
Netherlands	13.7	17.2	20.4	23.8	27.5
Sweden	24.1	25.1	28.3	30.7	31.8
Switzerland	6.6	7.4	8.3	9.1	10.3
United Kingdom	18.5	19.8	20.6	22.1	25.2
United States	25.3	28.2	29.0	31.8	36.9
Average Value of Transactions (U.S. $)†					
Belgium	117.4	113.2	110.3	125.2	137.5
Canada‡	56.7	55.5	53.5	51.2	51.3
France	82.7	86.1	77.0	76.4	81.3
Germany	—	—	—	157.6	196.6**
Italy	239.2	245.4	196.8	195.3	194.4
Japan	356.5	355.4	392.9	419.3	450.6
Netherlands	92.2	98.5	96.4	97.9	108.4
Sweden	120.6	128.6	101.2	104.7	112.6
Switzerland	224.6	225.1	207.8	217.8	242.1
United Kingdom	81.0	83.0	72.7	71.2	77.3
United States	67.0	66.9	70.0	67.2	67.7

*Estimated figures referring to the whole system.

**Increase partly due to new data source.

†Converted at yearly average exchange rates.

‡Average value of a cash withdrawal only.

Source: The Bank for International Settlements, *Statistics on Payment Systems in the Group of 10 Countries,* Basle, December 1996, Table 5, p. 117.

---

[36]A further example of regulatory risk impacts on technology and operating costs in general is the cost of converting European banks' systems from local currencies into the euro. This may cost European banks $150 billion or more. See "A Year before the Millennium Bug, There's the Euro Problem," *New York Times,* March 9, 1998, p. 1.

[37]The importance of accounting for technological change in the design of regulatory policies has been emphasized by the Chairman of the Federal Reserve. See Alan Greenspan, "Technological Change and the Design of Bank Supervising Policies," in *33rd Annual Conference on Bank Structure and Competition* (Federal Reserve Bank of Chicago, May 1997), pp. 1–8.

Usury Ceiling
Cap or ceiling on consumer and mortgage interest rates imposed by state governments.

ceilings on banks. **Usury ceilings** place caps and controls on the fees and interest rates that bankers can charge on credit cards, consumer loans, and residential mortgages. Because credit card operations are heavily communications based and do not need to be located directly in an FI's market, the two states that now dominate the credit card market are South Dakota and Delaware. These two states are among the most liberal regarding credit card fee and interest rate usury regulations.[38] A further example of regulatory avoidance has been the growth of banking in the relatively unregulated Cayman Islands. The 500 or more banks located there do most of their banking business via public and private telecommunications networks.[39] The growth of telecommunications networks and improvements in technology have changed, perhaps irreversibly, the balance of power between large multinational FIs and governments—both local and national—in favor of the former. This shift in power also creates incentives for countries to lower their regulations to attract entrants; that is, it increases the incentives for competitive deregulation. This trend may be potentially destabilizing to the market in financial services, with the weakest regulators attracting the most entrants.[40]

Tax Avoidance.   The development of international wire networks as well as international financial service firm networks has enabled FIs to shift funds and profits through internal pricing mechanisms, thereby minimizing their overall U.S. tax burden and maximizing their foreign tax credits. For example, prior to 1986, many large U.S. banks paid almost no corporate income taxes, despite large reported profits, by rapidly moving profits and funds across different tax regimes. This raised considerable public policy concerns and was a major reason underlying the 1986 tax reforms in the United States. These reforms imposed a minimum corporate income tax rate of 20 percent on U.S. banks and limited their ability to use foreign tax credits to offset their domestic income tax burdens.

Competition Risk.   As financial services become more technologically based, they are increasingly facing competition from nontraditional financial service suppliers such as AT&T. For example, in addition to offering its own enhanced credit card in competition with bank-supplied credit cards, AT&T owns a finance company.[41] Also, once established, financial services technology can easily be purchased by nonfinancial firms. Thus, General Motors has also established a credit card operation linked to the purchase of its vehicles at a discount. Currently, banks issue less than half of all new credit cards; much of the new business is going to nontraditional firms such as AT&T and General Motors. As a result, technology

---

[38]For example, Citigroup, the U.S. financial services firm with the largest credit card franchise, has located its credit card operations in South Dakota. See also I. Walter and A. Saunders for a discussion of trends in financial service firms leaving New York: "Global Competitiveness of New York City as a Financial Center." Occasional Papers in Business and Finance, Stern Business School, New York University, 1992.

[39]A major reason for the growth in Cayman Islands banking was the desire of large U.S. banks to avoid or reduce the cost of the Federal Reserve's noninterest-bearing reserve requirements. Many attribute its current popularity to drug or crime-related secret money transactions. See I. Walter, *Secret Money: The World of International Financial Secrecy* (London: George Allen and Unwin, 1985).

[40]A closely associated risk for regulators is that increased use of international wire transfer systems weakens the power of central banks to control the domestic money supply.

[41]AT&T's universal card began operation in March 1990. It is both a credit card and a calling card. Its finance company subsidiary—AT&T Capital Corp—does leasing, project financing, and small business lending.

exposes existing FIs to the increased risk of erosion of their franchises as costs of entry fall and the competitive landscape changes.[42]

Concept Questions

1. Describe the six risks faced by FIs with the growth of wire transfer payment systems.
2. Why do daylight overdrafts create more of a risk problem for banks on CHIPS than on Fedwire?
3. What steps have the members of CHIPS taken to lower settlement or daylight overdraft risk?

Summary

This chapter analyzed the operating cost side of FIs' activities, including the effects of the growth of technology-based innovations. The impact of technology was first examined separately for wholesale and retail services before an analysis was presented of its impact on cost and revenues. While technology-based investments can potentially result in new product innovations and lower costs, the evidence for such cost savings is mixed. Moreover, new and different risks appear to have been created by modern technology. These include settlement or daylight overdraft risk, international technology transfer risk, crime or fraud risk, regulatory avoidance risk, taxation avoidance, risk, and competition risk.

Questions and Problems

1. Explain how technological improvements can increase an FI's interest and noninterest income and reduce interest and noninterest expenses. Use some specific examples.
2. Table 14–1 shows data on earnings, expenses, and assets for all insured banks. Calculate the annual growth rates in the various income, expense, earnings, and asset categories from 1987 to 1997. If part of the growth rates in assets, earnings, and expenses can be attributed to technological change, in what areas of operating performance has technological change appeared to have the greatest impact? What growth rates are more likely to be caused by economywide economic activity?
3. Compare the effects of technology on a bank's wholesale operations with the effects of technology on a bank's retail operations. Give some specific examples.
4. What are some of the risks inherent in being the first to introduce a financial innovation?
5. The operations department of a major FI is planning to reorganize several of its back-office functions. Its current operating expense is $1,500,000, of which $1,000,000 is for staff expenses. The FI uses a 12 percent cost of capital to evaluate cost-saving projects.

   a. One way of reorganizing is to outsource overseas a portion of its data entry functions. This will require an initial investment of approximately $500,000 after taxes. The FI expects to save $100,000 in annual operating expenses. Should it undertake this project, assuming that this change will lead to permanent savings?

   b. Another option is to automate the entire process by installing new state-of-the-art computers and software. The FI expects to realize more than $500,000 per year in after-tax savings, but the initial investment will be approximately $3,000,000. In addition, the life of this project is limited to seven years, at which time new computers and software will need to be installed. Using this seven-year planning horizon, should it invest in this project? What level of after-tax savings would be necessary to make this plan comparable in value creation to the plan in part *(a)?*

---

[42]For an excellent overview of the issues relating to the risks of payment systems, see D. Hancock and D. B. Humphrey, "Payment Transactions, Instruments and Systems: A Survey," *Journal of Banking and Finance* 21 (December 1997), pp. 1573–1624.

6. City Bank upgrades its computer equipment every five years to keep up with changes in technology. Its next upgrade is two years from today and is budgeted to cost $1,000,000. Management is considering moving up the date by two years to install some new computers with a breakthrough software that could generate significant cost savings. The cost for this new equipment also is $1,000,000. What should be the savings per year to justify moving up the planned upgrade by two years? Assume a cost of capital of 15 percent.

7. What is the link between technology risk and regulation?

8. Distinguish between economies of scale and economies of scope.

9. What information on the operating costs of FIs does the measurement of economies of scale provide? If economies of scale exist, what implications do they have for regulators?

10. What information on the operating costs of FIs is provided by the measurement of economies of scope? What implications do economies of scope have for regulators?

11. Buy Bank had $130 million in assets and $20 million in expenses before the acquisition of Sell Bank, which had assets of $50 million and expenses of $10 million. After the merger, the bank had $180 million in assets and $35 million in costs. Did this acquisition generate either economies of scale or economies of scope?

12. What are diseconomies of scale? What are the risks of large-scale technological investments, especially to large FIs? Why are small FIs willing to outsource production to large FIs against which they are competing? Why are large FIs willing to accept outsourced production from smaller FI competition?

13. A bank with assets of $2 billion and costs of $200 million has acquired an investment banking firm subsidiary with assets of $40 million and expenses of $15 million. After the acquisition, the costs of the bank are $180 million and the costs of the subsidiary are $20 million. Does the resulting merger reflect economies of scale or economies of scope?

14. What are diseconomies of scope? How could diseconomies of scope occur?

15. A survey of a local market has provided the following average cost data: Mortgage Bank A (MBA) has assets of $3 million and an average cost of 20 percent. Life In-
surance Company B (LICB) has assets of $4 million and an average cost of 30 percent. Corporate Pension Fund C (CPFC) has assets of $4 million and an average cost of 25 percent. For each firm, average costs are measured as a proportion of assets. MBA is planning to acquire LICB and CPFC with the expectation of reducing overall average costs by eliminating the duplication of services.

   a. What should be the average cost after acquisition for the bank to justify this merger?

   b. If Bank A plans to reduce operating costs by $500,000 after the merger, what will be the average cost of the new firm?

16. What is the difference between the production approach and the intermediation approach to estimating cost functions of FIs?

17. What are some of the conclusions of empirical studies on economies of scale and scope? How important is the impact of cost reductions on total average costs? What are X-inefficiencies? What role do these factors play in explaining cost differences among FIs?

18. Why does the United States lag behind most other industrialized countries in the proportion of annual electronic noncash transactions per capita? What factors probably will be important in causing the gap to decrease?

19. What are the differences between the Fedwire and CHIPS payment systems?

20. What is a daylight overdraft? How do an FI's overdraft risks incurred during the day differ for each of the two competing electronic payment systems, Fedwire and CHIPS? What provision has been taken by the members of CHIPS to introduce an element of insurance against the settlement risk problem?

21. How does Regulation F of the 1991 FDICIA reduce the problem of daylight overdraft risk?

22. Why do FIs in the United States face a higher degree of international technology risk than do the FIs in other countries, especially Europe?

23. How have crime and fraud risk and the avoidance of regulation been made easier by rapid technological improvements in the electronic payment systems?

24. What are usury ceilings? How does technology create regulatory risk?

25. How has technology altered the competition risk of FIs?

FOREIGN EXCHANGE RISK

Introduction

The globalization of the U.S. financial services industry has caused FI managers to be increasingly exposed to foreign exchange (FX) risk. Such risks can arise directly through trading in foreign currencies, making foreign currency loans (a loan in sterling to a corporation), buying foreign-issued securities (U.K. sterling gilt-edged bonds or German mark government bonds), or issuing foreign currency–denominated debt (sterling certificates of deposit) as a source of funds. In this chapter we evaluate risks faced by FIs when assets and liabilities are denominated in foreign (as well as in domestic) currencies and when FIs take major positions as traders in the spot and forward foreign currency markets.

Sources of Foreign Exchange Risk Exposure

In recent years the nation's largest commercial banks have been major players in foreign currency trading and dealing, with large money center banks such as Citigroup and Chase also taking significant positions in foreign currency assets and liabilities (see also Chapter 10 on trading or market risk). Table 15–1 shows the outstanding (dollar value) of U.S. banks' foreign assets and liabilities for the period

TABLE 15–1   **Liabilities to and Claims on Foreigners Reported by Banks in the United States, Payable in Foreign Currencies**
(millions of dollars, end of period)

				1996		1997		
Item	*1993*	*1994*	*1995*	*June*	*December*	*March*	*June*	*September*
Banks' liabilities	$78,259	$89,284	$109,713	$111,651	$103,383	$109,238	$109,433	$118,477
Banks' claims	62,017	60,689	74,016	65,825	66,018	72,589	84,665	89,568
Deposits	20,993	19,661	22,696	20,890	22,467	24,542	26,503	28,961
Other claims	41,024	41,028	51,320	44,935	43,551	48,047	58,162	60,607
Claims of banks' domestic customers*	12,854	10,878	6,145	7,554	10,978	9,357	11,292	10,210

Note: Data on claims exclude foreign currencies held by U.S. monetary authorities.

*Assets owned by customers of the reporting bank located in the United States that represent claims on foreigners held by reporting banks for the accounts of the domestic customers.

Source: *Federal Reserve Bulletin*, Table 3.16, various issues.

TABLE 15–2   **Weekly U.S. Bank Positions in Foreign Currencies and Foreign Assets and Liabilities, September 1997**
(in currency of denomination)

	(1) *Assets*	*(2)* *Liabilities*	*(3)* *FX Bought**	*(4)* *FX Sold**	*(5)* *Net Position†*
Canadian dollars (millions)	82,156	71,754	272,658	271,655	11,405
German marks (millions)	275,079	274,374	2,188,964	2,177,715	11,954
Japanese yen (billions)	24,979	24,295	180,804	184,456	−2,968
Swiss francs (millions)	33,194	45,512	637,016	652,715	−28,017
British pounds (millions)	73,248	76,550	395,007	386,919	4,786

*Includes spot, future and forward contracts.

†Net Position = (Assets − Liabilities) + (FX Bought − FX Sold).

Source: *Treasury Bulletin*, December 1997, pp. 98–102.

1993 to September 1997. The September 1997 figure for foreign assets (claims) was 89.6 billion, with foreign liabilities of $118.4 billion. As you can see both foreign currency liabilities and assets have been growing in recent years. In Table 15–2, we give a more detailed breakdown of the foreign currency positions of all U.S. banks in five major currencies as of September 1997.

Spot Market for FX
The market in which foreign currency is traded for immediate delivery.

Forward Market for FX
The market in which foreign currency is traded for future delivery.

In Table 15–2, columns (1) and (2) refer to U.S. banks' financial portfolio activities: the holding of assets and the issuing of liabilities denominated in foreign currencies. Columns (3) and (4) refer to foreign currency trading activities: the **spot** and **forward foreign exchange** contracts bought and sold in each major currency. As you can see, foreign currency trading dominates direct portfolio investments. Even though the aggregate trading positions appear very large—180,804 billion yen being bought by U.S. banks—their overall or net exposure positions can be relatively small.

FIs' overall FX exposure in any given currency can be measured by their net position exposure, which is measured in column (5) of Table 15–2 as

$$\text{Net exposure}_i = (\text{FX assets}_i - \text{FX liabilities}_i) + (\text{FX bought}_i - \text{FX sold}_i)$$
$$\text{Net exposure}_i = \text{Net foreign assets}_i + \text{Net FX bought}_i$$

where

$$i = i\text{th currency}$$

Net Exposure
The degree to which a
bank is net long (positive)
or net short (negative) in a
given currency.

Net Long in a Currency
Holding more assets
than liabilities in a
given currency.

Clearly, an FI could match its foreign currency assets to its liabilities in a given currency and match buys and sells in its trading book in that foreign currency to avoid FX risk. Or it could offset an imbalance in its foreign asset–liability portfolio by an opposing imbalance in its trading book so that its **net exposure** position in that currency would be zero.

Notice in Table 15–2 that U.S. banks had positive net FX exposures in three of the five major currencies in September 1997. A *positive* net exposure position implies a U.S. FI is overall **net long in a currency** and faces the risk that the foreign currency will fall in value against the U.S. dollar, the domestic currency. A *negative* net exposure position implies that a U.S. FI is *net short* in a foreign currency and faces the *risk* that the foreign currency could rise in value against the dollar. Thus, failure to maintain a fully balanced position in any given currency exposes a U.S. FI to fluctuations in the FX rate of that currency against the dollar.

Even though we have given the FX exposures for U.S. banks only, most large nonbank FIs also have some FX exposure through asset–liability holdings or currency trading. The absolute sizes of these exposures are smaller than those for major U.S. money center banks. The reasons for this are threefold: smaller asset sizes, prudent person concerns,[1] and regulations.[2] For example, U.S. pension funds invest approximately 14 percent of their asset portfolios in foreign securities, and U.S. life insurance companies generally hold less than 10 percent of their assets in foreign securities. Interestingly, U.S. FIs' holdings of overseas assets are less than those of FIs in Japan and Britain. For example, in Britain pension funds have traditionally invested over 20 percent of their funds in foreign assets.

Foreign Exchange Rate Volatility and FX Exposure

As we discussed in Chapter 10 on market risk, we can measure the potential size of an FI's FX exposure by analyzing the asset, liability, and currency trading mismatches on its balance sheet and the underlying volatility of exchange rate movements. Specifically,

Dollar loss/gain in currency i = [Net exposure in foreign currency i measured in U.S. dollars] × Shock (volatility) to the $/Foreign currency i exchange rate

The greater the FI's net exposure in a foreign currency and the greater that foreign currency's exchange rate volatility,[3] the greater the potential dollar loss or gain to an FI's earnings [i.e., the greater its daily earnings at risk (*DEAR*)]. The underlying

---

[1]Prudent person concerns are especially important for pension funds.

[2]For example, New York State restricts foreign asset holdings of New York–based life insurance companies to less than 10 percent of their assets.

[3]In the case of RiskMetrics the shock or (volatility) measure would equal 1.65 times the historic volatility (standard deviation) of the currency's exchange rate with the dollar. This shock, when multiplied by the net exposure in that currency (measured in dollars), provides an estimate of the loss exposure of the FI if tomorrow is that "one bad day in twenty" (see Chapter 10 for more details).

causes of FX volatility will reflect fluctuations in the demand for and supply of a country's currency. That is, conceptually, an FX rate is like the price of any good and will appreciate in value relative to other currencies when demand is high or supply is low and will depreciate in value when demand is low or supply is high. For example, in October 1998 the dollar fell (depreciated) in value on one day from 121yen/$ to 112yen/$ or by over 7 percent. The major reason for this was the purchase of yen by hedge funds and the sale of dollars to repay Japanese banks for the yen loans they had borrowed at low interest rates earlier in 1998. See Chapter 10 for more details on measuring FX exposure.

We next take a closer look at the underlying determinants and risks of the two components of an FI's net exposure in a foreign currency: its foreign currency trading book and its foreign financial asset and liability book.

Concept Questions

1. How is the net foreign currency exposure of an FI measured?
2. If a bank is long in deutsche marks (DM), does it gain or lose if the dollar appreciates in value against the DM?
3. A bank has £10 million in assets and £7 million in liabilities. It has also bought £52 million in foreign currency trading. What is it net exposure in pounds?

Foreign Currency Trading

The FX markets of the world have become the largest of all financial markets, with a turnover often exceeding $3 trillion a day. London has the largest market, followed by New York and Tokyo.[4] Moreover, the market is essentially a 24-hour market, moving among Tokyo, London, and New York over the day. Therefore, FX trading risk exposure continues into the night even when other bank operations are closed. This clearly adds to the risk from holding mismatched FX positions. An FI's position in the FX markets generally reflects four trading activities.

FX Trading Activities

1. The purchase and sale of foreign currencies to allow customers to partake in and complete international commercial trade transactions.
2. The purchase and sale of foreign currencies to allow customers (or the FI itself) to take positions in foreign real and financial investments.
3. The purchase and sale of foreign currencies for hedging purposes to offset customer (or FI) exposure in any given currency.
4. The purchase and sale of foreign currencies for speculative purposes through forecasting or anticipating future movements in FX rates.

In the first two activities, the FI normally acts for a fee as an *agent* of its customers and does not assume the FX risk itself. Citibank (now Citigroup) is the dominant supplier of FX to retail customers in the United States. In the third activity, the FI acts defensively as a hedger to reduce FX exposure. Thus, risk exposure essen-

---

[4]On a global basis approximately 30 percent of trading in FX occurs in London, 16 percent in New York, and 10 percent in Tokyo. The remainder is spread throughout the world.

Open Position
An unhedged position in a particular currency.

tially relates to **open positions** taken as a principal for speculative purposes, the fourth activity. This is usually done by an FI taking an unhedged position in a foreign currency in its FX trading with other FIs. FIs can make speculative trades directly with other FIs or arrange them through specialist FX brokers. The Federal Reserve Bank of New York estimates that approximately 44 percent of speculative or trades are done through specialized brokers who receive a fee for arranging trades between FIs. Speculative trades can be instituted through a variety of FX instruments. Spot currency trades are the most common, with FIs seeking to make a profit on the difference between buy and sell prices or on movements in the bid–ask prices over time. However, FIs can also take speculative positions in foreign exchange forward contracts, futures, and options. As the Contemporary Perspectives box on p. 317 shows, increasingly banks are having to compete with specialist hedge funds operated by investors such as Joseph Lewis and George Soros who put on huge bets regarding currency movements that arguably trigger the movements themselves. While Soros's activities are well known, little is known about the Englishman Joseph Lewis, who makes most of his trades from his base in Bermuda. The collapse of Long-Term Capital Management in the fall of 1998 and the activities of hedge fund operators such as Soros and Lewis have raised demands in Congress and elsewhere for greater regulation and oversight of their FX trading and other activities.

The Profitability of Foreign Currency Trading

Remember from the previous section that most profits or losses on foreign trading come from open position taking or speculation in currencies. Fees from market making—the bid–ask spread—or from acting as agents for retail or wholesale customers generally provide only a secondary or supplementary revenue source.

Note the trading income from FX trading for some large U.S. banks in Table 15–3. As can be seen, total trading income has remained steady over recent years. The dominant FX trading banks are Citibank (Citigroup) and Chase (incorporating the former Chemical Bank). A major reason for the slow growth of profits in this area has been the decline in the volatility of FX rates among major European countries that has more than offset the greater volatilities of Asian currencies. This decline in European FX volatility is the result of two forces. The first is the reduction in inflation rates in these countries, and the second is the fixity of exchange rates among European countries as they move toward full monetary union and the replacement of local currencies with the "euro." Specifically, in May 1998, 11 counties in the European Union[5] fixed their exchange rates with each other and on January 1, 1999, all FIs and stock exchanges in these countries began using euros (electronically). On January 1, 2002, the euro will go into physical circulation, and on July 1, 2002, local currencies will no longer be accepted. While, as noted above, there has been increased FX volatility in many emerging-market countries, such as those of Thailand, Indonesia, and Malaysia[6] the importance of these currencies in the FX trading activities of major FIs remains small.

---

[5]These countries were Austria, Belgium, Finland, France, Germany, Ireland, Italy, Luxemburg, Netherlands, Portugal, and Spain.

[6]For example, in 1997 these currencies fell over 50 percent in value relative to the dollar. In the fall of 1998 Malaysia introduced capital controls and restrictions on trading in its currency.

Table 15–3   Foreign Exchange Trading Income of Major U.S. Banks

	1988	1989	1990	1991	1992	1993	1994	1995	1996	1997[1]
1. Bank of America[2]	$ 135.0	$ 143.2	$ 207.0	$ 246.0	$ 300.0	$ 325.0	$ 237.0	$ 303.0	$ 316.0	$ 312.0
2. Bankers Trust[3]	153.9	296.5	425.0	272.0	331.0	191.0	(54.0)	36.0	178.0	205.0
3. Chase Manhattan Bank	249.7	227.0	217.2	215.0	327.0	354.4	280.0	241.0	444.0	572.0
4. Chemical Bank	143.2	153.9	207.2	289.0	363.0	302.0	152.9	291.0	—	—
5. Manufacturers Hanover	103.0	95.0	106.0	—	—	—	—	—	—	—
6. Citibank[4]	616.0	471.0	657.0	709.0	1,005.0	995.0	573.0	1,053.0	864.0	924.0
7. Continental Bank Corp.[5]	20.9	(1.0)	187.0	18.0	13.0	17.0	—	—	—	—
8. First Chicago NBD[6]	148.6	75.9	102.8	95.1	109.5	105.0	42.0	106.0	63.0	NR*
9. Bank of New York[7]	30.9	29.0	47.6	71.0	66.0	54.2	27.0	42.0	57.0	87.0
10. Marine Midland	5.0	3.3	3.4	3.1	3.2	7.3	3.6	3.8	3.8	NR*
11. J. P. Morgan & Co.	186.8	191.0	309.0	218.3	359.6	304.4	131.0	253.0	320.0	270.0
12. Republic New York Corp.	35.4	55.0	77.3	81.4	102.6	111.6	91.0	113.1	98.0	86.3
Total	$1,828.4	$1,740.7	$2,378.2	$2,217.9	$2,980.2	$2,766.9	$1,483.5	$2,441.9	$2,343.8	$2,456.3

*NR=Not reported.

[1]Through third quarter.

[2]Millions of dollars, exclusive of translation income.

[3]1987 figures adjusted downward by $80 million due to revaluation of open options.

[4]Includes translation gains and losses.

[5]1987, 1988, and 1989 only; prior years for Continental Illinois.

[6]1994 and prior years for First Chicago.

[7]1988 and prior years for Irving Trust.

Source: Annual reports, 10-Qs, call report data.

Concept Questions

1. What are the four major FX trading activities?
2. In which trades do FIs normally act as agents, and in which trades as principals?
3. What is the source of most profits or losses on foreign exchange trading? What foreign currency activities provide a secondary source of revenue?

Foreign Asset and Liability Positions

The second dimension of an FI's foreign exchange exposure results from any mismatches between its foreign financial asset and foreign financial liability portfolios. As discussed in Chapter 7, an FI is long a Foreign currency if its assets in that currency exceed its liabilities, while it is short a foreign currency if its liabilities in that currency exceed its assets. Foreign financial assets might include Swiss franc–denominated bonds, British pound gilt-edged securities, or even peso-denominated Mexican bonds. Foreign financial liabilities might include issuing British pound CDs or a yen-denominated bond in the Euromarkets to raise yen finance. The globalization of financial markets has created an enormous range of possibilities for raising finance in currencies other than the home currency. This is important for FIs that wish not only to diversify their source and use of funds but also to exploit imperfections in foreign banking markets that create opportunities for higher returns on assets or lower funding costs.

Contemporary Perspectives

WHEN SPECULATORS POUNCE

Traders like Joseph C. Lewis have the power to further aggravate a nation's economic weakness when they attack its currency. These are two instances that Mr. Lewis acknowledges produced some of his biggest trading windfalls.

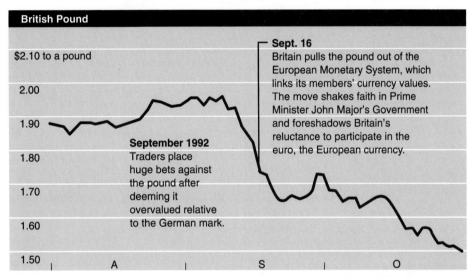

British Pound

$2.10 to a pound

Sept. 16
Britain pulls the pound out of the European Monetary System, which links its members' currency values. The move shakes faith in Prime Minister John Major's Government and foreshadows Britain's reluctance to participate in the euro, the European currency.

September 1992
Traders place huge bets against the pound after deeming it overvalued relative to the German mark.

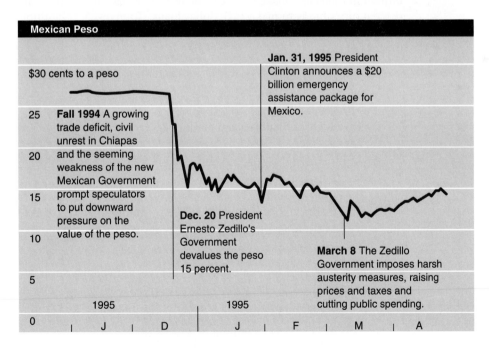

Mexican Peso

$30 cents to a peso

Jan. 31, 1995 President Clinton announces a $20 billion emergency assistance package for Mexico.

Fall 1994 A growing trade deficit, civil unrest in Chiapas and the seeming weakness of the new Mexican Government prompt speculators to put downward pressure on the value of the peso.

Dec. 20 President Ernesto Zedillo's Government devalues the peso 15 percent.

March 8 The Zedillo Government imposes harsh austerity measures, raising prices and taxes and cutting public spending.

The Return and Risk of Foreign Investments

To understand the extra dimension of return and risk from adding foreign currency assets and liabilities to an FI's portfolio, consider the following simple example:

Assets	Liabilities
$100 million U.S. loans (one year) in dollars	$200 million U.S. CDs (one year) in dollars
$100 million equivalent U.K. loans (one year) (loans made in sterling)	

The U.S. FI is raising all its liabilities in dollars but investing 50 percent in U.S. dollar assets and 50 percent in U.K. pound sterling assets.[7] In this example, the FI has matched the duration of its assets and liabilities ($D_A = D_L = 1$ year) but mismatched the currency composition of its asset and liability portfolios. Suppose the promised one-year U.S. CD rate is 8 percent, to be paid in dollars at the end of the year. Suppose one-year, credit risk–free loans in the United States are yielding only 9 percent. The FI would face a positive spread of 1 percent from investing domestically. Suppose, however, that credit risk–free one-year loans are yielding 15 percent in the United Kingdom.

To invest in the United Kingdom, the FI decides to take 50 percent of its $200 million in funds and make one-year maturity U.K. sterling loans while keeping 50 percent of its funds to make U.S. dollar loans. To invest $100 million overseas in one-year loans in the United Kingdom, the U.S. FI has to undertake the following transactions:

1. At the beginning of the year, sell $100 million for pounds on the spot currency markets. If the exchange rate is $1.60 to £1, this translates into $100 million/1.6 = £62.5 million.
2. Take the £62.5 million and make one-year U.K. loans at a 15 percent interest rate.
3. At the end of the year, sterling revenue from these loans will be £62.5(1.15) = £71.875 million.[8]
4. Repatriate these funds back to the United States at the end of the year. That is, the U.S. bank sells the £71.875 million in the foreign exchange market at the spot exchange rate that exists at that time, the end of the year spot rate.

Suppose the spot foreign exchange rate has not changed over the year; it remains fixed at $1.60/£1. Then the dollar proceeds from the U.K. investment will be

£71.875 million × $1.60/£1 = $115 million or, as a return,

$$\frac{\$115 \text{ million} - \$100 \text{ million}}{\$100 \text{ million}} = 15\%$$

[7]For simplicity, we ignore the leverage or net worth aspects of the FI's portfolio.
[8]No default risk is assumed.

Given this, the weighted return on the bank's portfolio of investments will be

$$(.5)(.09) + (.5)(.15) = .12 \text{ or } 12\%$$

This exceeds the cost of the bank's CDs by 4 percent (12% − 8%). However, suppose that at the end of the year the British pound had fallen in value relative to the dollar, or the U.S. dollar had appreciated in value relative to the pound. The returns on the U.K. loans could be far less than 15 percent even in the absence of interest rate or credit risk. For example, suppose the exchange rate had fallen from $1.60/£1 at the beginning of the year to $1.45/£1 at the end of the year when the bank needed to repatriate the principal and interest on the loan. At an exchange rate of $1.45/£1, the pound loan revenues at the end of the year translate into

$$£71.875 \text{ million} \times \$1.45/£1 = \$104.22 \text{ million}$$

or as a return on the original dollar investment of

$$\frac{\$104.22 - \$100}{\$100} = .0422 = 4.22\%$$

The weighted return on the bank's asset portfolio would be

$$(.5)(.09) + (.5)(.0422) = .0661 = 6.61\%$$

Here the bank would actually make a loss or have a negative interest margin on its balance sheet investments of −1.39 percent since its cost of funds is 8 percent.

The reason for the loss is that the depreciation of the pound from $1.60 to $1.45 has offset the attractive high yield on British pound sterling loans relative to domestic U.S. loans. If the pound had instead appreciated against the dollar over the year—say, to $1.70/£1—then the U.S. bank would have generated a dollar return from its U.K. loans of

$$£71.875 \times \$1.70 = \$122.188 \text{ million}$$

or a percentage return of 22.188 percent.

Then the U.S. bank would receive a double benefit from investing in the United Kingdom: a high yield on the domestic British loans plus an appreciation in sterling over the one-year investment period.

Risk and Hedging

Since a manager cannot know in advance what the pound/dollar spot exchange rate will be at the end of the year, a portfolio imbalance or investment strategy where the bank is *net long* $100 million in pounds (or £62.5 million) is risky. As we discussed, the British loans would generate a return of 22.188 percent if the pound appreciated from $1.60 to $1.70 but would produce a return of only 4.22 percent if the pound depreciated in value against the dollar to $1.45.

There are in principle two major ways in which an FI manager can better control the scale of its FX exposure: on-balance-sheet hedging and off-balance-sheet hedging.

Hedging on Balance Sheet.   Suppose that instead of funding the $100 million investment in 15 percent British loans with U.S. CDs, the FI manager funds the British loans with $100 million equivalent one-year pound sterling CDs at a rate of 11 percent. Now the balance sheet of the bank would look like this:

Assets	Liabilities
$100 million U.S. loans (9%)	$100 million U.S. CDs (8%)
$100 million U.K. loans (15%) (loans made in sterling)	$100 million U.K. CDs (11%) (deposits raised in sterling)

This is a situation when the bank has a matched maturity and currency foreign asset–liability book. We might now consider the bank's profitability or spreads between the return on assets and the cost of funds under two scenarios: first when the pound depreciates in value against the dollar over the year from $1.60/£1 to $1.45/£ and second when the pound appreciates in value over the year from $1.60/£1 to $1.70/£1.

The Depreciating Pound.   When the pound falls in value to 1.45/£1, the return on the British loan portfolio is 4.22 percent. Consider now what happens to the cost of $100 million in pound liabilities in dollar terms.

1. At the beginning of the year, the bank borrows $100 million equivalent in sterling CDs for one year at a promised interest rate of 11 percent. At an exchange rate of $1.60/£, this is a sterling equivalent amount of borrowing of $100/1.6 = £62.5 million.
2. At the end of the year, the bank has to pay back the sterling CD holders their principal and interest, £62.5 (1.11) = £69.375 million.
3. If the pound had depreciated to $1.45/£ over the year, the repayment in dollar terms would be £69.375 × $1.45/£1 = $100.59 million, or a dollar cost of funds of 0.59 percent.

Thus, at the end of the year:

Average return on assets

$$(0.5)(0.9) + (0.5)(0.422) = .0661 = 6.61\%$$
U.S. asset return + U.K. asset return = Overall return

Average cost of funds

$$(0.5)(.08) + (0.5)(.0059) = .04295 = 4.295\%$$
U.S. cost of funds + U.K. cost of funds = Overall cost

Net return
Average return on assets − Average cost of funds
6.61% − 4.295% = 2.315%

The Appreciating Pound.   When the pound appreciates over the year from $1.60/£1 to $1.70/£1, the return on British loans is equal to 22.188. Now consider the dollar cost of British one-year CDs at the end of the year when the U.S. FI has to pay the principal and interest to the CD holder:

$$£69.375 × \$1.70/£1 = \$117.9375 \text{ million}$$

or a dollar cost of funds of 17.9375 percent. Thus, at the end of the year:

Average return on assets

$$(0.5)(.09) + (0.5)(.22188) = .15594 \text{ or } 15.594\%$$

Average cost of funds

$$(0.5)(.08) + (0.5)(.179375) = .12969 \text{ or } 12.969\%$$

Net return

$$15.594 - 12.969 = 2.625\%$$

Thus, by directly matching its foreign asset and liability book, an FI can lock in a positive return or profit spread whichever direction exchange rates change over the investment period. Moreover, even if domestic U.S. banking is not very profitable due to an assumed 1 percent spread between the return on assets and the cost of funds, the bank could be quite profitable overall. It could lock in a positive spread—if it exists—between deposit rates and loan rates in overseas markets. In our example, there was a 4 percent positive spread between British one-year loan rates and deposit rates.

Note that for such imbalances in domestic spreads and foreign spreads to continue over long periods of time, there would have to be significant barriers to entry facing financial service firms in overseas markets. Specifically, if real and financial capital is free to move, banks will increasingly withdraw from the U.S. market and reorient their operations toward the United Kingdom. Reduced competition would widen loan deposit interest spreads in the United States, while increased competition would contract U.K. spreads, until the profit opportunities from overseas activities disappeared. We discuss banks' abilities, and limits on their abilities, to engage in cross-border financial and real investments further in Chapter 23.[9]

Hedging with Forwards.   Instead of matching its $100 million foreign asset position with $100 million of foreign liabilities, the FI may have chosen to remain unhedged on the balance sheet.[10] Instead, it could hedge by taking a position in the forward market for foreign currencies, especially the one-year forward market for selling sterling for dollars. We discuss the nature and use of forward contracts by FI managers more extensively in Chapter 24; however, here we introduce them to

---

[9]In the background of the previous example was the implicit assumption that the FI was also matching the durations of its foreign assets and liabilities. In our example, it was issuing one-year duration sterling CDs to fund one-year duration sterling loans. Suppose instead that it still had a matched book in size ($100 million) but funded the one-year 15 percent British loans with three-month 11 percent sterling CDs:

$$D_{\pounds A} - D_{\pounds L} = 1 - .25 = .75 \text{ years}$$

Thus, sterling assets have a longer duration than do sterling liabilities.

If British interest rates were to change over the year, the market value of sterling assets would change by more than the market value of sterling liabilities. This effect should be familiar from Chapter 9. More importantly, the bank would no longer be locking in a fixed return by matching the size of its foreign currency book since it would have to take into account its potential exposure to capital gains and losses on its sterling assets and liabilities due to shocks to British interest rates. In essence, an FI is hedged against both foreign exchange rate risk and foreign interest rate risk only if it matches both the size and the durations of its foreign assets and liabilities in a specific currency. For a detailed discussion of this risk, see T. Grammatikos, A. Saunders, and I. Swary, "Returns and Risks of U.S. Bank Foreign Currency Activities," *Journal of Finance* 41 (1986), pp. 670–81; and K. C. Mun and G. E. Morgan, "Should Interest and Foreign Exchange Risk Management Be Integrated in International Banking?" Working Paper, Virginia Polytechnic Institute, 1994.

[10]An FI could also hedge its on-balance-sheet FX risk by taking off-balance-sheet positions in futures, swaps, and options on foreign currencies. Such strategies are discussed in detail in Chapters 24 through 26.

show how they can insulate the FX risk of the bank in our example. Any forward position taken would not appear on the balance sheet; it would appear as a contingent off-balance-sheet claim, which we described in Chapter 13 as an item below the bottom line. The role of the forward FX contract is to offset the uncertainty regarding the future spot rate on sterling at the end of the one-year investment horizon. Instead of waiting until the end of the year to transfer sterling back into dollars at an unknown spot rate, the FI can enter into a contract to sell forward its *expected* principal and interest earnings on the loan, at today's known **forward exchange rate** for dollars/pounds, with delivery of sterling funds to the buyer of the forward contract taking place at the end of the year. Essentially, by selling the expected proceeds on the sterling loan forward, at a known exchange rate today, the FI removes the future spot exchange rate uncertainty and thus the uncertainty relating to investment returns on the British loan. Consider the following transactional steps when the FI hedges its FX risk by selling its one-year sterling loan proceeds forward:

Forward Exchange Rate
The exchange rate agreed to today for future (forward) delivery of a currency.

1. The U.S. bank sells $100 million for pounds at the *spot* exchange rate *today* and receives $100 million/$1.6/£1 = £62.5 million.
2. The bank then immediately lends the £62.5 million to a British customer at 15 percent for one year.
3. The bank also sells the expected principal and interest proceeds from the sterling loan forward for dollars at today's forward rate for one-year delivery. Let the current forward one-year exchange rate between dollars and pounds stand at $1.55/£1 or at a 5 cent discount to the spot pound; as a percentage discount

$$(\$1.55 - \$1.60)/\$1.6 = -3.125\%$$

This means that the forward buyer of sterling promises to pay

$$£62.5 \text{ million } (1.15) \times \$1.55/£ = £71.875 \times \$1.55/£1 = \$111.406 \text{ million}$$

to the FI seller in one year when the bank delivers the £71.875 million proceeds of the loan to the FI seller.

4. In one year, the British borrower repays the loan to the bank plus interest in sterling (£71.875 million).
5. The bank delivers the £71.875 million to the buyer of the one-year forward contract and receives the promised $111.406 million.

Consider the economics of this transaction, barring a default on the loan by the sterling borrower or a reneging on the forward contract by the forward buyer of pounds. The bank knows from the very beginning of the investment period that it has locked in a guaranteed return on the British loan of

$$\frac{\$111.406 - \$100}{\$100} = .11406 = 11.406\%$$

Specifically, this return is fully hedged against any dollar/pound exchange rate changes over the one-year holding period of the loan investment. Given this return on British loans, *the overall expected return* on the bank's asset portfolio would be

$$(.5)(.09) + (.5)(.11406) = .10203 \text{ or } 10.203\%$$

Since the cost of funds for the bank's $200 million U.S. CDs is an assumed 8 percent, it has been able to lock in a risk-free return spread over the year of 2.203 percent regardless of spot exchange rate fluctuations between the initial overseas (loan) investment and repatriation of the foreign loan proceeds one year later.

In this example, it is profitable for the FI to increasingly get out of domestic U.S. loans and into hedged foreign U.K. loans, since the hedged dollar return on foreign loans of 11.406 percent is so much higher than domestic loans' 9 percent. As the FI seeks to invest more in British loans, it needs to buy more spot sterling. This drives up the spot price of sterling in dollar terms to more than $1.60/£1. In addition, the bank would sell more sterling forward (the proceeds of these sterling loans) for dollars, driving down the forward rate to below $1.55/£1. The outcome would be a widening of the forward-spot rate spread on sterling, making forward hedged sterling investments less attractive than before. This process would go on until the 8 percent cost of bank funds just equals the forward hedged return on British loans. That is, no further profits could be made by borrowing in U.S. dollars and making forward contract–hedged investments in U.K. loans. This eventual equality between the cost of domestic funds and the hedged return on foreign assets looks like this:

$$1 + r_{ust}^D = \frac{1}{S_t} \times [1 + r_{ukt}^L] \times F_t$$

where

$1 + r_{ust}^D$ = 1 plus the interest cost of U.S. CDs for the bank at time t

S_t = $/£ spot exchange rate at time t

$1 + r_{ukt}^L$ = 1 plus the interest return on U.K. loans at time t

F_t = $/£ forward exchange at time t

Suppose r_{ust}^D = 8 percent and r_{ust}^L = 15 percent, as in our preceding example. As the bank moves into more British loans, suppose the spot exchange rate for buying pounds rises from $1.60/£1 to $1.63/£1. In equilibrium, the forward exchange rate would have to fall to $1.5308/£1 to eliminate completely the attractiveness of British investments to the U.S. FI manager. That is

$$(1.08) = \left(\frac{1}{1.63}\right)[1.15](1.5308)$$

This is a *no-arbitrage* relationship in the sense that the hedged dollar return on foreign investments just equals the bank's dollar cost of domestic CDs. We can also express this relationship as

$$\frac{r_{ust}^D - r_{ukt}^L}{1 + r_{ukt}^L} \simeq \frac{F_t - S_t}{S_t}$$

$$\frac{.08 - .15}{1.15} \simeq \frac{1.5308 - 1.63}{1.63}$$

$$-.0609 \simeq -.0609$$

Interest Rate Parity Theorem
The discounted spread between domestic and foreign interest rates equals the percentage spread between forward and spot exchange rates.

That is, the discounted spread between domestic and foreign interest rates would be reflected, in equilibrium, in a similar percentage spread between forward and spot exchange rates. In this form, the relationship is called the **interest rate parity theorem** (IRPT). The implication of this relationship is that in a competitive market for deposits, loans, and foreign exchange, the potential profit opportunities from overseas investment for the FI manager are likely to be small and fleeting.[11]

---

[11]Note that in a fully competitive market for loans and deposits (and free movement of exchange rates), not only would the U.S. deposit rate equal the hedged return on U.K. loans (8 percent in our example), but the U.S. loan rate (for risk-free loans) would also be driven into equality with the U.S. CD rate, that is, would fall from 9 percent to 8 percent.

That is, long-term violations of this relationship are likely to occur only if there are major imperfections in international deposit, loan, and other financial markets, including barriers to cross-border financial flows.

Multicurrency Foreign Asset–Liability Positions

So far, we have used a one-currency example of a matched or mismatched foreign asset–liability portfolio. Many FIs, including banks, mutual funds, and pension funds, hold multicurrency asset–liability positions. As for multicurrency trading portfolios, diversification across many asset and liability markets can potentially reduce the risk of portfolio returns and the cost of funds.

To the extent that domestic and foreign interest rates or stock returns for equities do not move strongly together over time, potential gains from asset–liability portfolio diversification can offset the risk of mismatching individual currency asset–liability positions.

Real Interest Rate
The difference between a nominal interest rate and the expected rate of inflation.

Theoretically speaking, the one-period nominal interest rate (r_i) on fixed-income securities in any particular country has two major components. First, the **real interest rate** reflects underlying real sector demands and supplies for funds in that currency. Second, the *expected inflation rate* reflects an extra amount of interest lenders demand from borrowers to compensate the lenders for the erosion in the principal (or real) value of the funds they lend due to inflation in goods prices expected over the period of the loan. Formally:[12]

$$r_i = rr_i + i_i^e$$

where

> r_i = The nominal interest rate in country i
> rr_i = The real interest rate in country i
> i_i^e = The expected one-period inflation rate in country i

If real savings and investment demand and supply pressures, as well as inflationary expectations, were closely linked or integrated across countries, we would expect to find that nominal interest rates are highly correlated across financial markets. For example, if due to a strong demand for investment funds, German real interest rates rise, there may be a capital outflow from other countries toward Germany. This may lead to rising real and nominal interest rates in other countries as policymakers and borrowers try to mitigate the size of their capital outflows. On the other hand, if the world capital market is not very well integrated, quite significant nominal and real interest deviations may exist before equilibrating international flows of funds materialize. Foreign asset or liability returns are likely to be relatively weakly correlated, and significant diversification opportunities exist.

In Table 15–4 we list the correlations among the returns on long-term bonds in major bond markets for 1967–1994. Looking at correlations between foreign bond market monthly returns and U.S. bond market monthly returns, you can see that the correlations across bond markets vary from a high of .3119 between the United States and Japan to a low of .1856 between the United States and Germany. Further,

---

[12]This equation is often called the Fisher equation after the economist who first publicized this hypothesized relationship among nominal rates, real rates, and expected inflation. As shown, we ignore the small cross product term between the real rate and the expected inflation rate.

TABLE 15–4   Correlations of Long-Term Government Bond Annual Returns in Local Currencies, January 1967–June 1994

	United States	United Kingdom	Germany	Japan
United States	1.00	.1856	.2521	.3119
United Kingdom	.1856	1.00	.3095	.2217
Germany	.2521	.3095	1.00	.3706
Japan	.3119	.2217	.3706	1.00

Source: Data from Ibbotson Associates.

while these correlations are all positive, they are generally quite low compared to similar correlations computed for stock returns among the same countries.[13]

Concept Questions

1. The cost of one-year U.S. dollar CDs is 8 percent, one-year U.S. dollar bank loans yield 10 percent, and U.K. sterling loans yield 15 percent. The dollar/pound spot exchange is \$1.50/£1, and the one-year forward exchange rate is \$1.48/£1. Are one-year U.S. dollar loans more or less attractive than U.K. sterling loans?
2. What are two ways in which an FI manager can control FX exposure?
3. Suppose the one-year expected inflation rate in the United States is 8 percent and nominal one-year interest rates are 10 percent. What is the real rate of interest?

Summary

This chapter analyzed the sources of FX risk faced by modern FI managers. Such risks arise through mismatching foreign currency trading and/or foreign asset–liability positions in individual currencies. While such mismatches can be profitable if FX forecasts prove to be correct, unexpected outcomes and volatility can impose significant losses on an FI. They threaten its profitability and ultimately its solvency in a similar fashion to interest rate, off-balance-sheet, and technology risks. This chapter discussed possible ways to mitigate such risks, including direct hedging through matched foreign asset–liability books, hedging through forward contracts, and hedging through foreign asset and liability portfolio diversification.

Questions and Problems

1. What are the four FX risks faced by FIs?
2. What is the spot market for FX? What is the forward market for FX? What is the position of being net long in a currency?
3. X-IM Bank has DM 14 million in assets and DM 23 million in liabilities and has sold DM 8 million in foreign currency trading. What is the net exposure for X-IM?

For what type of exchange rate movement does this exposure put the bank at risk?
4. What two factors directly affect the profitability of an FI's position in a foreign currency?
5. The following are the foreign currency positions of an FI, expressed in dollars.

---

[13]From the Fisher relationship, low correlations may be due to weak correlations of real interest rates over time and/or inflation expectations.

Currency	Assets	Liabilities	FX Bought	FX Sold
Deutsche mark (DM)	$125,000	$50,000	$10,000	$15,000
British pound (£)	50,000	22,000	15,000	20,000
Japanese yen (¥)	75,000	30,000	12,000	88,000

   a. What is the FI's net exposure in deutsche marks?

   b. What is the FI's net exposure in British pounds?

   c. What is the FI's net exposure in Japanese yen?

   d. What is the expected loss or gain if the DM exchange rate appreciates by 1 percent?

   e. What is the expected loss or gain if the £ exchange rate appreciates by 1 percent?

   f. What is the expected loss or gain if the ¥ exchange rate appreciates by 2 percent?

6. What are the four FX trading activities undertaken by FIs? How do FIs profit from these activities? What are the reasons for the slow growth in FX profits at major U.S. banks?

7. City Bank issued $200 million of one-year CDs in the United States at a rate of 6.50 percent. It invested part of this money, $100 million, in the purchase of a one-year bond issued by a U.S. firm at an annual rate of 7 percent. The remaining $100 million was invested in a one-year Brazilian government bond paying an annual interest rate of 8 percent. The exchange rate at the time of the transactions was Brazilian real 1/$.

   a. What will be the net return on this $200 million investment in bonds if the exchange rate between the Brazilian real and the U.S. dollar remains the same?

   b. What will be the net return on this $200 million investment if the exchange rate changes to real 1.20/$?

   c. What will the net return on this $200 million investment be if the exchange rate changes to real 0.80/$?

8. Sun Bank USA has purchased a 16 million one-year deutsche mark loan that pays 12 percent interest annually. The spot rate for deutsche marks is DM1.60/$. Sun Bank has funded this loan by accepting a British pound (BP)–denominated deposit for the equivalent amount and maturity at an annual rate of 10 percent. The current spot rate of the British pound is $1.60/£.

   a. What is the net interest income earned in dollars on this one-year transaction if the spot rates at the end of the year are DM1.70/$ and $1.85/£?

   b. What should be the BP to US $ spot rate in order for the bank to earn a net interest margin of 4 percent?

   c. Does your answer to part (*b*) imply that the dollar should appreciate or depreciate against the pound?

9. Bank USA recently made a one-year $10 million loan that pays 10 percent interest annually. The loan was funded with a deutsche mark–denominated one-year deposit at an annual rate of 8 percent. The current spot rate is DM1.60/$.

   a. What will be the net interest income in dollars on the one-year loan if the spot rate at the end of the year is DM1.58/$?

   b. What will be the net interest return on assets?

   c. How far can the DM appreciate before the transaction will result in a loss for Bank USA?

10. What motivates FIs to hedge foreign currency exposures? What are the limitations to hedging foreign currency exposures?

11. What are the two primary methods of hedging FX risk for an FI? What two conditions are necessary to achieve a perfect hedge through on-balance-sheet hedging? What are the advantages and disadvantages of off-balance-sheet hedging in comparison to on-balance-sheet hedging?

12. North Bank has been borrowing in the U.S. markets and lending abroad, thus incurring foreign exchange risk. In a recent transaction, it issued a one-year $2 million CD at 6 percent and funded a loan in deutsche marks at 8 percent. The spot rate for the deutsche mark was DM1.45/$ at the time of the transaction.

   a. Information received immediately after the transaction closing indicated that the deutsche mark will depreciate to DM1.47/$ by year end. If the information is correct, what will be the realized spread on the loan? What should have been the bank interest rate on the loan to maintain the 2 percent spread?

   b. The bank had an opportunity to sell one-year forward marks at DM1.46. What would have been the spread on the loan if the bank had hedged forward its foreign exchange exposure?

   c. What would have been an appropriate change in loan rates to maintain the 2 percent spread if the bank intended to hedge its exposure using forward contracts?

13. A bank purchases a six-month $1 million Eurodollar deposit at an annual interest rate of 6.5 percent. It invests the funds in a six-month Swedish krone bond paying 7.5 percent per year. The current spot rate is $0.18/SK.

   a. The six-month forward rate on the Swedish krone is being quoted at $0.1810/SK. What is the net spread earned on this investment if the bank covers its foreign exchange exposure using the forward market?

   b. What forward rate will cause the spread to be only 1 percent per year?

   c. Explain how forward and spot rates will both change in response to the increased spread.

   d. Why will a bank still be able to earn a spread of 1 percent knowing that interest rate parity usually eliminates arbitrage opportunities created by differential rates?

14. Explain the concept of interest rate parity. What does this concept imply about the long-run profit opportunities from investing in international markets? What market conditions must prevail for the concept to be valid?

15. Assume that annual interest rates are 8 percent in the United States and 4 percent in Germany. An FI can borrow (by issuing CDs) or lend (by purchasing CDs) at these rates. The spot rate is $0.60/DM.

    a. If the forward rate is $0.64/DM, how could the bank arbitrage using a sum of $1 million? What is the expected spread?

    b. What forward rate will prevent an arbitrage opportunity?

16. How does the lack of perfect correlation of economic returns between international financial markets affect the risk-return opportunities for FIs holding multicurrency assets and liabilities? Referring to Table 15–4, which country pairings seem to have the highest correlation of returns on long-term government bonds?

17. What is the relationship between the real interest rate, the expected inflation rate, and the nominal interest rate on fixed-income securities in any particular country? Referring to Table 15–4, what factors may be the reasons for the relatively low correlation coefficients?

18. What is economic integration? What impact does the extent of economic integration of international markets have on the investment opportunities for FIs?

19. An FI has $100,000 of net positions outstanding in deutsche marks (DM) and −$30,000 in French Francs (FF). The standard deviation of the net positions as a result of exchange rate changes is 1 percent for the DM and 1.3 percent for the FF. The correlation coefficient between the changes in exchange rates of the DM and the FF is 0.80.

    a. What is the risk exposure to the FI of fluctuations in the DM/$ rate?

    b. What is the risk exposure to the FI of fluctuations in the FF/$ rate?

    c. What is the risk exposure if both the DM and the FF positions are combined?

20. A money market mutual fund manager is looking for some profitable investment opportunities and observes the following one-year interest rates on government securities and exchange rates: $r_{US} = 12\%$, $r_{UK} = 9\%$, $S = \$1.50/£$, $f = \$1.6/£$, where S is the spot exchange rate and f is the forward exchange rate. Which of the two types of government securities would constitute a better investment?

SOVEREIGN RISK

Introduction

In the 1970s, American and other countries' commercial banks rapidly expanded their loans to Eastern European, Latin American, and other less developed countries (LDCs). This was largely to meet their demand for funds beyond those provided by the World Bank and the International Monetary Fund (IMF), to aid their development, and to allow commercial banks to recycle petrodollar funds from huge dollar holders such as Saudi Arabia. In many cases, loans appear to have been made with little judgment regarding the credit quality of the sovereign country in which the borrower resided or whether that body was a government-sponsored organization (such as Pemex) or a private corporation. The debt repayment problems of Poland and other Eastern European countries at the beginning of the 1980s and the **debt moratoria** announced by the Mexican and Brazilian governments in the fall of

Debt Moratoria
Delay in repaying interest and/or principal on debt.

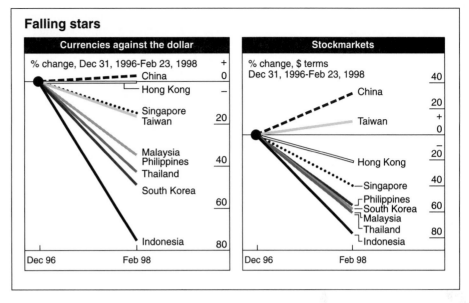

Falling stars

Source: "Collapsing Foreign Currency and Stockmarket Values for Asian Countries in 1997," *The Economist,* March 7, 1998, p. 4. © 1998. The Economist Newspaper Group, Inc. Reprinted with permission. Further reproduction prohibited.

1982 had a major and long-lasting impact on commercial banks' balance sheets and profits.

Notwithstanding their experience with LDC lending a decade earlier, U.S. and other FIs began once again to invest considerable amounts in these emerging market countries in the late 1980s to early 1990s. However, in the face of rising trade deficits and declining foreign exchange reserves, as the result of an overvalued peso, Mexico devalued the peso on December 20, 1994.[1] The Mexican devaluation—as with the Mexican loan moratorium 12 years earlier—had devastating short-term repercussions on the Mexican capital market as well as adversely and contagiously impacting other emerging markets. These effects were dampened only when the Clinton administration, along with the IMF, put together an international aid package for Mexico amounting to some $50 billion. Specifically, the United States provided loan guarantees, over three to five years, that would amount to up to $20 billion to help restructure Mexican debt. The IMF and the Bank for International Settlements provided loans of $17.8 billion and $10 billion, respectively. Mexican oil revenues were promised as collateral for the U.S. financial guarantees.[2] By January 1997 the Mexican economy had improved to such an extent that the Mexican government was able to pay back all its loans in full to the U.S. government.[3]

More recently, we have seen a financial collapse in a number of emerging-market countries in Asia. Beginning with Thailand in July 1997 and followed by Indonesia, Malaysia, the Philippines, and South Korea, these countries suffered major currency and financial market collapses. Figure 16–1 shows the declines in currency and stock market values that occurred in these countries in 1997.

---

[1]Mexico's foreign exchange reserves fell from $25 billion at the end of 1993 to $6 billion at the end of 1994.

[2]See *New York Times,* February 1, 1995, p. 1.

[3]See "Mexico Will Close Out Its Debt to U.S.," *The Wall Street Journal,* January 16, 1997, p. A10.

FIGURE 16–2

*Foreign Banks' Share of
Asian Debt in June 1997*

Foreign banks' share of total Asian debt at the end of
June 1997, excluding Singapore and Hong Kong.

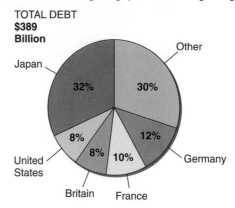

Source: Bank for International Settlements, June 1997.

While these collapses had a number of effects, a common impact was apparent. Specifically, foreign banks—especially those from Japan, Germany, France, and the United States—were exposed to a significant risk of default because of the large amount of foreign (hard) currency loans they had extended to banks and corporations in those countries. As can be seen from Figure 16–2, in June 1997 (just before the beginning of the Thai crisis in July 1997) foreign banks had $389 billion in loans and other debt outstanding to emerging market Asian countries. While most of those loans were made to private companies, many of those companies had either implicit or explicit guarantees from their own governments. This crisis is still being resolved (as will be discussed in greater detail in this chapter) through bailouts of governments and loan restructuring packages for local banks and companies. For example, South Korea was provided with an IMF organized package amounting to $57 billion, with foreign lender banks also agreeing to restructure $24 billion in short-term foreign currency debt of Korean banks and companies into longer-term loans of one to three years in maturity.

These experiences have confirmed the importance of assessing the country or sovereign risk of a borrowing country in making lending or other investment decisions such as buying foreign bonds or equities.

In this chapter, we first define sovereign or country risk. We then look at measures of country risk to use as screening devices before making loans or other investment decisions. Finally, in the Appendix to this chapter, we look at the ways banks have reacted to their sovereign risk problems, by entering into **multiyear restructuring agreements (MYRAs),** debt-equity swaps, loan sales, and **Brady bond** conversions as mechanisms to alleviate their sovereign risk problems.

MYRA
A multiyear restructuring agreement that is the official terminology for a sovereign loan rescheduling.

Brady Bond
A bond that is swapped for an outstanding loan to a LDC.

Rescheduling
Changing the contractual terms of a loan such as its maturity and interest payments.

Credit Risk versus Sovereign Risk

To understand the difference between the sovereign risk and the credit risk on a loan or a bond, consider what happens to a domestic firm that refuses or is unable to repay its loans. The lender probably will seek to work out the loan with the borrower by **rescheduling** its promised interest and principal payments on the loan into the future. Ultimately, continued inability or unwillingness to pay probably would result in bankruptcy proceedings and eventual liquidation of the firm's assets. Consider next a dollar loan made by a U.S. bank to a private Indonesian corporation. Suppose this first-class corporation always maintained its debt repayments in the past. However, the Indonesian economy and the Indonesian government's dollar reserve position are in bad shape. As a result, the government refuses to allow any further debt repayment to be made in dollars to outside creditors. This puts the Indonesian borrower automatically into default even though, when viewed on its own, the company is a good credit risk. The Indonesian government's decision is a *sovereign risk event* in large part independent of the credit standing of the individual loan to the borrower. Further, unlike in the United States, where the lender might seek a legal remedy in the local bankruptcy courts, there is no international bankruptcy court to which the lender can take the Indonesian government. That is, the lenders' legal remedies to offset a sovereign country's default or moratoria decisions are very limited. For example, lenders can and have sought legal remedies in U.S. courts, but such decisions pertain only to Indonesian government or Indonesian corporate assets held in the United States itself.

This situation suggests that making a lending decision to a party residing in a foreign country is a *two-step* decision. First, lenders must assess the underlying *credit quality* of the borrower, as would be done for a normal domestic loan, including setting an appropriate credit risk premium or credit ceiling (see Chapter 11). Second, lenders must assess the *sovereign risk quality* of the country in which the borrower resides. Should the credit risk or quality of the borrower be assessed as good but the sovereign risk be assessed as bad, the loan should not be made. In international lending or foreign bond investment decisions, considerations of sovereign risk should dominate considerations of private credit risk.

Concept Questions

1. What is the difference between credit risk and sovereign risk?
2. In deciding to lend to a party residing in a foreign country, what two considerations must an FI weigh?

Debt Repudiation versus Debt Rescheduling

There is a good deal of misunderstanding regarding the nature of a sovereign risk event. In general, a sovereign country's (negative) decisions on its debt obligations or the obligations of its public and private organizations may take two forms:

Repudiation
Outright cancellation of all current and future debt obligations by a borrower.

Repudiation. **Repudiation** is an outright cancellation of all a borrower's current and future foreign debt and equity obligations. Since the Second World War, only China (1949), Cuba (1961), and North Korea (1964) have followed this course.[4] Repudiations on debt obligations were far more common before the Second World War, as we discuss later in this chapter.

Rescheduling. Rescheduling has been the most common form of sovereign risk event. Specifically, a country (or a group of creditors in that country) declares a moratorium or delay on its current and future debt obligations and

----
[4]With respect to equity, repudiation can include direct nationalization of private sector assets.

then seeks to ease credit terms through a rescheduling of the contractual terms such as debt maturity and/or interest rates. Such delays may relate to the principal and/or the interest on the debt (South Korea in January 1998 was a recent example of debt rescheduling).

One of the interesting questions of international banking is why we have generally witnessed international debtor problems being met by reschedulings in the post–Second World War period, whereas a large proportion of debt problems were met with repudiations before the Second World War. A fundamental reason given for this difference in behavior is that until recently, most postwar international debt has been in *bank loans,* while before the war it was mostly in the form of foreign *bonds.*[5]

International loan rather than bond finance makes rescheduling more likely for reasons related to the inherent nature of international loan versus bond contracts. First, there are generally fewer banks in any international lending syndicate compared to thousands of geographically dispersed bondholders. The relatively small number of lending parties makes renegotiation or rescheduling easier and less costly than occurs when a borrower or a bond trustee has to get thousands of bondholders to agree to changes in the contractual terms on a bond.[6]

Second, many international loan syndicates comprise the same groups of banks, which adds to bank cohesiveness in loan renegotiations and increases the probability of consensus being reached. For example, Citigroup was chosen the lead bank negotiator by other banks in five major loan reschedulings in the 1980s,[7] as well as in both the Mexican and South Korean reschedulings.

Third, many international loan contracts contain cross-default provisions that state that if a country were to default on just one of its loans, all the other loans it has outstanding would automatically be put into default as well. Cross-default clauses prevent a country from selecting a group of weak lenders for special default treatment and make the outcome of any individual loan default decision potentially very costly for the borrower.

A further set of reasons why rescheduling is likely to occur on loans relates to the behavior of governments and regulators in lending countries. One of the overwhelming public policy goals in recent years has been to prevent large bank failures in countries such as the United States, Japan, Germany, and the United Kingdom. Thus, government-organized rescue packages for LDCs arranged either directly or indirectly via World Bank/IMF guarantees or the Brady Plan are ways of subsidizing large banks and/or reducing the incentives for LDCs to default on their loans. To the extent that banks are viewed as special (see Chapter 6), domestic governments may seek political and economic avenues to reduce the probability of foreign sovereign borrowers defaulting on or repudiating their debt contracts. Governments and regulators appear to view the social costs of default on international bonds as less worrisome than those on loans. The reason for this is that bond defaults are likely to be more geographically and numerically dispersed in their effects, and bondholders do not play a key role in the provision of liquidity services to the domestic and world economy. It should also be noted that the tendency of the IMF/governments

---

[5]See B. Eichengreen and R. Portes, "The Anatomy of Financial Crises," in *Threats to International Financial Stability,* ed. R. Portes and A. K. Swoboda (Cambridge: Cambridge University Press, 1987), pp. 10–15.

[6]In January 1998 the rescheduling of South Korean loans required the agreement of just over 100 banks.

[7]See Grammatikos and Saunders, "Additions to Bank Loan Loss Reserves."

to bail out countries and thus, indirectly, bank lenders such as the major U.S., Japanese, and European banks has not gone without criticism. Specifically, it has been argued that unless banks and countries are ultimately punished, they will have no incentives to avoid similar risks in the future. This is one reason why sovereign debt crises keep reoccurring (see the Contemporary Perspectives box on p. 336).

Concept Questions

1. What is the difference between debt repudiation and debt rescheduling?
2. Provide four reasons why we see sovereign loans being rescheduled rather than repudiated.

Country Risk Evaluation

In evaluating sovereign risk, an FI can use alternative methods varying from the highly quantitative to the very qualitative. Moreover, as in domestic credit analysis, an FI may rely on outside evaluation services or develop its own internal evaluation models. Of course, to make a final assessment, many models and sources may be used together because different measures of country risk are not mutually exclusive.

We begin by looking at two country risk assessment services available to outside investors and FIs: the *Euromoney Index* and the *Institutional Investor Index*. We then look at ways in which an FI manager might make internal risk assessments regarding sovereign risk.

Outside Evaluation Models

The Euromoney Index.   When originally published in 1979, the *Euromoney Index* was based on the spread in the Euromarket of the required interest rate on that country's debt over **LIBOR,** adjusted for the volume and maturity of the issue. More recently, this has been replaced by an index based on a large number of economic and political factors weighted subjectively according to their perceived relative importance in determining country risk problems.

LIBOR
The London Interbank Offered Rate. The rate charged on prime interbank loans on the Eurodollar market.

The Institutional Investor Index.   Normally published twice a year, this index is based on surveys of the loan officers of major multinational banks. These officers give subjective judgmental scores regarding the credit quality of given countries. Originally the score was based on 10, but since 1980 it has been based on 100, where a score of 0 indicates certainty of default and 100 indicates no possibility of default. The *Institutional Investor* then weighs the scores received from the officers surveyed by the exposure of each bank to the country in question. For the *Institutional Investor's* country credit ratings as of March 1998, see Table 16–1. Note the large falls in Thailand (−8.8), South Korea (−7.0), and Malaysia (−3.0) compared to their ratings one year earlier.

Internal Evaluation Models

Statistical Models.   By far, the most common approach has been to develop sovereign country risk-scoring models based on key economic ratios for each country similar to the domestic credit risk-scoring models discussed in Chapter 11.

An FI analyst begins by selecting a set of macro- and microeconomic variables and ratios that might be important in explaining the probability of a country

TABLE 16–1 Institutional Investor's 1998 Country Credit Ratings

Rank Sept. 1997	Rank March 1998	Country	Institutional Investor credit rating	Six-month change	One-year change
1	1*	Switzerland	92.6	0.4	0.1
2	2*	United States	92.6	0.5	1.4
4	3	Germany	92.3	1.0	0.8
3	4	Japan	90.8	-0.7	-0.5
5	5	Netherlands	90.5	-0.1	0.8
6	6*	France	89.3	0.9	1.1
7	7*	United Kingdom	89.3	0.9	0.9
8	8	Luxembourg	88.3	0.4	1.0
9	9	Austria	87.4	0.9	2.8
10	10	Norway	87.3	1.5	2.6
12	11	Denmark	83.4	0.8	1.8
13	12	Canada	83.1	1.0	2.3
11	13	Singapore	82.9	-1.3	-1.0
14	14	Belgium	82.0	0.7	1.3
15	15	Ireland	78.0	1.3	2.3
17	16	Finland	77.9	1.3	3.0
19	17	Spain	77.3	1.8	2.6
18	18	Sweden	77.1	0.9	2.8
20	19	Italy	76.6	1.2	2.3
16	20	Taiwan	75.5	-1.2	-1.6
21	21	Australia	73.7	0.4	1.5
22	22	New Zealand	73.4	0.3	1.7
23	23	Portugal	72.7	1.5	3.1
25	24	Malaysia	64.5	-2.2	-3.0
24	25	South Korea	64.4	-5.3	-7.0
30	26	Iceland	63.9	2.4	3.8
27	27	Chile	63.2	-0.3	1.2
26	28	Hong Kong	62.9	-1.0	-2.0
29	29	Malta	62.1	-0.6	-1.3
31	30	United Arab Emirates	61.4	1.3	0.6
28	31	Czech Republic	60.7	-2.4	-2.1
33	32	China	57.6	-0.2	-0.4
34	33	Cyprus	57.2	0.0	0.4
35	34	Kuwait	55.8	0.8	1.6
37	35	Slovenia	55.5	1.5	3.4
36	36	Saudi Arabia	55.4	0.6	1.7
38	37	Greece	53.7	0.7	2.4
39	38	Oman	53.2	0.2	0.4

Rank Sept. 1997	Rank March 1998	Country	Institutional Investor credit rating	Six-month change	One-year change
74	71	Latvia	34.0	1.4	4.9
78	72*	Sri Lanka	33.6	1.5	0.4
68	73*	Zimbabwe	33.6	-0.2	1.3
69	74	Peru	33.5	-0.2	1.5
77	75	Papua New Guinea	33.2	0.9	0.7
73	76	Swaziland	33.1	-0.2	1.3
80	77	Lithuania	32.9	1.8	5.5
72	78	Paraguay	32.8	-0.7	0.8
75	79	Vietnam	32.7	0.2	0.2
76	80	Lebanon	32.5	0.1	1.0
79	81	Ghana	31.4	-0.1	0.8
88	82	Russia	31.2	3.7	7.7
81	83	Jamaica	30.1	0.4	2.6
86	84	El Salvador	29.0	1.5	5.1
85	85	Libya	28.3	0.5	-0.4
82	86	Seychelles	28.2	-1.3	0.9
86	87	Iran	28.1	0.6	2.0
89	88	Pakistan	27.5	0.3	-0.2
84	89	Bangladesh	27.2	-1.3	-0.2
90	90	Guatemala	27.0	0.2	2.9
83	91*	Kenya	26.7	-1.9	-1.2
91	92*	Ecuador	26.7	0.4	0.1
92	93	Bolivia	26.5	0.3	1.6
98	94	Kazakstan	26.4	2.4	5.5
94	95	Dominican Republic	25.8	1.0	3.3
93	96	Nepal	25.5	-0.4	0.3
96	97	Algeria	25.1	0.6	1.9
95	98†	Gabon	24.7	0.2	0.6
97	99	Syria	24.7	0.4	-0.3
99	100	Bulgaria	22.9	0.7	0.4
102	101	Myanmar	21.7	0.7	0.4
100	102	Senegal	21.6	0.4	1.8
104	103	Côte d'Ivoire	21.4	1.3	2.5
103	104	Uganda	21.2	1.1	3.5
105	105	Ukraine	20.5	0.7	2.9
106	106*	Burkina Faso	20.1	0.4	2.4
101	107*	Malawi	20.1	-0.9	0.3
108	108	Honduras	19.8	0.9	1.5

Rank Sept. 1997	Rank March 1998	Country	Institutional Investor credit rating	Six-month change	One-year change	Rank Sept. 1997	Rank March 1998	Country	Institutional Investor credit rating	Six-month change	One-year change
41	39	Qatar	53.1	0.9	0.7	107	109	Uzbekistan	19.6	0.1	2.5
40	40	Israel	52.5	-0.4	0.3	110	110	Tanzania	19.3	0.6	1.2
32	41	Thailand	52.3	-7.6	-8.8	109	111	Cameroon	18.5	-0.3	0.4
46	42	Hungary	52.2	2.5	4.6	113	112*	Ethiopia	17.5	0.4	1.5
44	43*	Botswana	51.9	0.7	2.4	115	113*	Zambia	17.5	1.5	1.4
45	44*	Poland	51.9	1.7	4.0	114	114	Togo	17.4	0.5	0.7
42	45	Mauritius	51.8	-0.1	0.9	111	115*	Benin	17.3	-0.1	1.3
43	46	Indonesia	49.9	-1.9	-1.7	117	116*	Grenada	17.3	2.3	4.4
47	47	Bahrain	49.8	0.1	0.1	111	117	Mali	16.7	-0.7	0.0
48	48	Tunisia	48.0	0.1	1.7	118	118	Guinea	16.4	1.5	2.6
49	49	Colombia	46.9	-0.3	-0.8	119	119	Mozambique	16.1	1.5	1.2
51	50*	South Africa	46.5	0.1	0.5	116	120	Nigeria	15.2	-0.1	0.4
50	51*	India	46.5	-0.4	0.2	124	121	Nicaragua	13.5	0.0	1.6
54	52	Mexico	45.2	1.7	2.6	121	122	Belarus	12.9	-1.3	-1.6
55	53	Uruguay	44.6	1.2	2.9	122	123	Haiti	12.7	-1.3	1.3
56	54	Trinidad and Tobago	43.5	0.6	3.8	123	124	Angola	12.5	-1.1	0.0
53	55	Philippines	43.3	-1.0	1.0	126	125	Cuba	12.2	0.9	1.4
52	56	Slovakia	43.1	-1.7	-0.8	125	126	Albania	11.1	-0.5	-3.2
57	57	Barbados	42.3	-0.6	0.4	120	127	Congo Republic	10.7	-3.5	-3.3
58	58	Argentina	41.6	0.3	1.7	128	128	Georgia	10.6	1.1	1.1
59	59	Morocco	41.5	0.6	1.8	127	129	Yugoslavia	10.2	0.0	0.3
60	60	Egypt	41.3	1.6	4.6	129	130	Sudan	7.6	-1.5	-2.8
63	61	Estonia	38.9	2.0	5.3	130	131	Iraq	7.4	-0.5	-0.9
61	62	Brazil	38.7	-0.8	-0.1	131	132	Liberia	7.0	-0.4	0.1
62	63	Turkey	37.8	-0.8	-3.0	132	133	Congo (formerly Zaire)	6.8	-0.2	-1.3
—	64	Namibia	36.4	—	—	134	134	Afghanistan	6.1	-0.2	-0.2
65	65	Venezuela	36.1	0.7	3.0	133	135	Sierra Leone	5.7	-0.8	-0.9
71	66	Croatia	36.0	2.4	6.7	135	136	North Korea	5.1	0.4	-0.7
64	67	Costa Rica	35.8	-0.2	1.3						
66	68	Jordan	35.5	0.6	1.7						
70	69	Panama	34.9	1.3	4.7						
67	70	Romania	34.5	0.4	1.8			Global average rating	41.2	0.2	1.1

*Order determined by actual results before rounding.

†Actual tie.

Source: *Institutional Investor*, March 1998.

Contemporary Perspectives

HAIRCUT TIME: THE ASIAN BAILOUT HAS TO HURT

Thomas L. Friedman

Treasury Secretary Robert Rubin better hurt somebody fast. Citibank would do. Or maybe his old partners at Goldman Sachs. Or maybe his old competitors at J. P. Morgan. Or better yet, all of them. But he better hurt somebody, fast.

Because if Mr. Rubin can't show that as part of the U.S.-led I.M.F. bailout of Korea, Indonesia and Thailand, the U.S., European and Japanese banks that lent these countries money won't also pay a price for their mistakes, he can forget about getting any more money out of Congress for the I.M.F. Forget it. Congress returns next week, and you can already hear the tom-toms beating: "No More Money For The I.M.F. Let The Asians Go Bust."

Mr. Rubin needs to do two things if he wants to save U.S. funding for the $40 billion I.M.F. bailout: He needs to speak to America and draw blood on Wall Street. He needs to explain to Americans precisely why the Asian bailout is valid. And he needs to make sure that any American bank that was involved in loans to Asia, and now wants to share in the I.M.F. bailout, takes a haircut. And I'm not just talking about a trim.

So far the Clinton team has failed miserably to make a convincing argument as to why the U.S. should make its overdue deposit to the I.M.F.—$17.9 billion—and why this won't end up as welfare for Asian tycoons and U.S. bankers. (Most Americans don't even realize that the I.M.F. is a credit union for countries. The U.S. doesn't "give" the I.M.F. anything. The U.S. deposits funds in the I.M.F. bank, and the I.M.F. pays the U.S. interest and then lends money to troubled economies.)

Consider Korea. Korea's private banks borrowed $92 billion from foreign banks. Those foreign banks are saying to Korea that they will extend the loans, to get the Koreans past the short-term debt crunch so they don't have to declare bankruptcy, but only on the condition that the Korean Government take over responsibility for that bank debt and pay it back with even higher interest over the long term. An I.M.F. loan now gives Korea the cushion to take the deal.

Opponents of such a workout argue that Korea is much better off letting private companies go bust and having them bought out or restructured by more prudent and efficient managers, and that the world is better off letting the foreign banks also get burned so they will be less reckless in the future. Those are not ridiculous arguments.

What U.S. officials mumble in response are two arguments. One is that the collapse of huge economies like South Korea or Indonesia could present a real national security problem for the U.S. Maybe.

The more compelling argument is the domino theory—that if huge economies like Korea, Thailand and Indonesia are allowed to just go bankrupt, they will take down other emerging markets, from Asia to Latin America, and likely drag down Japan. And if the world's second-largest economy goes down, that will seriously impact U.S. interest rates and markets. And it won't just be Billionaire Bob who takes a hit, but also Joe Sixpack's pension fund, mutual fund and, maybe, job. Millions of workers in developing countries would also be ruined.

This domino argument may be exaggerated, but testing it by seeing what would happen if the Asian tigers were left to melt down would be the greatest roll of the dice of the post-cold-war era. It is reasonable that the U.S. Treasury Secretary wouldn't want to take that risk.

So what to do? The U.S. must insist that it will contribute to an I.M.F. bailout only if both borrowers and lenders being bailed out receive no more than 75 cents on the dollar for any money invested and lost. The U.S. also has to use its influence to try to insure that, in restructuring a country's debts, that country is not forced to pay exorbitant additional interest. The worst thing would be that the I.M.F. bails out a country and Western banks profit even more from their own mistakes.

It's a fine line. People need to be hurt, so they think twice in the future. But not killed, if there is a chance they can recover and grow again.

An I.M.F. bailout that makes reckless banks and investors whole again will never fly. An I.M.F. bailout that punishes both reckless banks and investors, but still leaves them some space and buys them some time to make real business and governance reforms, is both good economics and good politics.

rescheduling. Then the analyst uses past data on rescheduling and nonrescheduling countries to see which variables best discriminate between those countries that rescheduled their debt and those that did not. This helps the analyst identify a set of key variables that best explain rescheduling and a group of weights indicating the relative importance of these variables. In domestic credit risk analysis we can employ discriminant analysis to calculate a Z score rating of the probability of corporate bankruptcy. Similarly in sovereign risk analysis we can develop a Z score to measure the probability of a country rescheduling (see Chapter 11 for discussion of the Z score model).[8]

The first step in this country risk analysis (CRA) is to pick a set of variables that may be important in explaining rescheduling probabilities. In many cases analysts select more than 40 variables. Here we identify the variables most commonly included in sovereign risk probability models.[9]

The Debt Service Ratio (DSR)

$$DSR = \frac{\text{Interest plus amortization on debt}}{\text{Exports}}$$

Debt Service Ratio
The ratio of a country's interest and amortization obligations to the value of its exports.

An LDC's exports are its primary way of generating dollars and other hard currencies. The larger the debt repayments in hard currencies are in relation to export revenues, the greater the probability that the country will have to reschedule its debt. Thus, there should be a *positive* relationship between the size of the **debt service ratio** and the probability of rescheduling. Figure 16–3 shows the scheduled debt service ratios of various geographic regions. Note that the regions with the poorest countries, such as South Asia, Sub-Saharan Africa, and Latin America, tend to have the highest DSRs.

FIGURE 16–3

Actual Debt Service Ratios, 1990 and 1995*: Interest and Principal Paid as a Percentage of Exports of Goods and Services

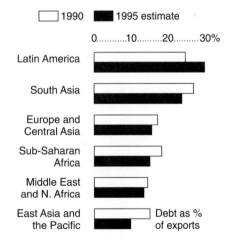

*Total debt service as percent of exports of goods and services.

Sources: World Bank; and *The Economist*, April 6, 1995, p. 110. © 1995 The Economist Newspaper Group, Inc. Reprinted with permission. Further reproduction prohibited.

---

[8]Alternatively, analysts could employ linear probability, logit, or probit models.

[9]See, for example, K. Saini and P. Bates, "Statistical Techniques for Determining Debt-Serving Capacity for Developing Countries: Analytical Review of the Literature and Further Empirical Results," Federal Reserve Bank of New York Research Paper no. 7818, September 1978.

The Import Ratio (IR)

$$IR = \frac{\text{Total imports}}{\text{Total foreign exchange reserves}}$$

Many LDCs have to import manufactured goods since they cannot produce them without an adequately advanced infrastructure. In times of famine, even food becomes a vital import. To pay for imports, the LDC has to run down its stock of hard currencies—its foreign exchange reserves. The greater its need for imports—especially vital imports—the quicker a country can be expected to deplete its foreign exchange reserves. Since the first use of reserves is to buy vital imports, the greater the ratio of imports to foreign exchange reserves, the higher the probability that the LDC will have to reschedule its debt repayments. This is the case because the repayment of foreign debtholders is generally viewed by countries as being less important than supplying vital goods to the domestic population. Thus, the **import ratio** and the probability of rescheduling should be *positively* related.

Import Ratio
The ratio of a country's imports to its total foreign currency reserves.

Investment Ratio (INVR)

$$INVR = \frac{\text{Real investment}}{\text{GNP}}$$

Investment Ratio
The ratio of a country's real investment to its GNP.

The **investment ratio** measures the degree to which a country is allocating resources to real investment in factories, machines, and so on, rather than to consumption. The higher this ratio is, the more productive the economy should be in the future and the lower the probability that the country will need to reschedule its debt: this implies a *negative* relationship between *INVR* and the probability of rescheduling. An opposing view is that a higher investment ratio allows an LDC to build up its investment infrastructure. The higher ratio puts it in a stronger bargaining position with external creditors since the LDC would be less reliant on funds in the future and less scared about future threats of credit rationing by FIs should it request a rescheduling. This view argues for a *positive* relationship between the investment ratio and the probability of rescheduling, especially if the LDC invests heavily in import competing industries.[10]

Variance of Export Revenue (VAREX)

$$VAREX = \sigma^2_{ER}$$

An LDC's export revenues may be highly variable due to two risk factors. Quantity risk means that the production of the raw commodities the LDC sells abroad—for example, coffee or sugar—is subject to periodic gluts and shortages. Price risk means that the international dollar prices at which the LDC can sell its exportable commodities are subject to high volatility as world demand for and supply of a commodity such as copper vary. The more volatile an LDC's export earnings, the less certain creditors can be that at any time in the future it will be able to meet its repayment commitments. That is, there should be a positive relationship between σ^2_{ER} and the probability of rescheduling.

---

[10]See S. Acharya and I. Diwan, "Debt Conversion Schemes of Debtor Countries as a Signal of Creditworthiness: Theory and Evidence," Working Paper, Stern School of Business, New York University, June 1987.

Domestic Money Supply Growth (MG)

$$MG = \frac{\Delta M}{M}$$

The faster the domestic growth rate of an LDC's money supply [$\Delta M/M$, which measures the change in the money supply (ΔM) over its initial level (M)], the higher the domestic inflation rate and the weaker that country's currency becomes in domestic and international markets.[11] When a country's currency loses credibility as a medium of exchange, real output is often adversely impacted, and increasingly the country has to rely on hard currencies for both domestic and international payments. These inflation, output, and payment effects suggest a *positive* relationship between domestic money supply growth and the probability of rescheduling.

We can summarize the expected relationships among these five key economic variables and the probability of rescheduling (p) for any country as

$$p = f(DSR,\ IR,\ INVR,\ VAREX,\ MG\ \dots)$$
$$+ \quad ++\text{ or}- \quad + \quad +$$

After selecting the key variables, the FI manager normally places countries into two groups or populations:

$$P_1 = \text{Bad (reschedulers)}$$
$$P_2 = \text{Good (nonreschedulers)}$$

Then the manager uses a statistical methodology such as discriminant analysis to identify which of these variables best discriminates between the population of rescheduling borrowers and that of nonrescheduling borrowers. Once the key variables and their relative importance or weights have been identified, the discriminant function can classify as good or bad current sovereign loans or sovereign loan applicants using currently observed values for the *DSR, IR,* and so on. Again, the methodology is very similar to the credit scoring models discussed in Chapter 11.

Problems with Statistical CRA Models. Even though this methodology has probably been one of the most common forms of CRA used by FIs, it is fraught with problems. Next we discuss six of the major problems of using traditional CRA models and techniques. We do not imply in any way that these techniques should not be used but instead indicate that FI managers should be aware of the potential pitfalls in using such models.

Measurement of Key Variables. Very often the FI manager's information on a country's *DSR* or *IR* is out of date because of delays in collection of data and errors in measurement. For example, the Bank for International Settlements (BIS) collects aggregate loan volume data for countries; frequently, this information is six months old or more before it is published. This example illustrates the problem: Citigroup may know today the current amount of its outstanding loans to Indonesia, but it is unlikely to know with any great degree of accuracy Indonesia's total outstanding external loans and debt with every other lender in the world.

Moreover, these measurement problems are compounded by forecast errors when managers use these statistical models to predict the probabilities of rescheduling with future or projected values of key variables such as *DSR* and *IR.*

---

[11]The purchasing power parity (PPP) theorem argues that high relative inflation rates lead to a country's currency depreciating in value against other currencies.

340   *Part II   Measuring Risk*

FIGURE 16–4

*A Corruption Index for
Selected Countries, 1997*

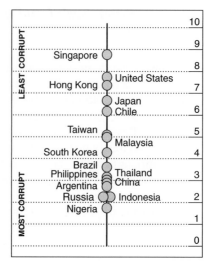

Source: Transparency International; and *The Economist,* March 7, 1998. © 1998 The Economist Newspaper Group, Inc. Reprinted with permission. Further reproduction prohibited.

Population Groups.   Usually, analysts seek to find variables that distinguish between only two possible outcomes: reschedulers and nonreschedulers. In actuality, a finer distinction may be necessary—for example, a distinction between those countries announcing a moratorium only on interest payments and those announcing a moratorium on both interest and principal payments. Thus, Peru, which in the early 1980s limited its total debt repayments to a small proportion of its export revenues, should be viewed as a worse risk than a country that delayed the interest payments on its debt for a few months due to short-term foreign exchange shortages.

Political Risk Factors.   Traditionally, CRA statistical credit scoring models incorporate only economic variables. While there may a strong correlation between an economic variable such as money supply growth and rescheduling, the model may not capture very well purely political risk events such as *strikes, elections, corruption,* and *revolutions.* For example, the election of a strongly nationalist politician may reduce the probability of repayment and increase the probability of rescheduling. Similarly, a considerable part of the debt repayment and banking crisis problems in Southeast Asia has been attributed to "cronyism" and corruption. Quantitative measures of political risk, such as the degree of corruption, may have to be included to get better predictive power. Figure 16–4 shows a corruption "index" for selected countries in 1997.

Portfolio Aspects.   Traditional CRA considers each country separately. However, many large banks with LDC or sovereign risk exposures hold a portfolio of LDC loans. In a portfolio context, the risk of holding a well-diversified portfolio of LDC sovereign loans may be smaller than that of having a portfolio heavily concentrated in nonoil-producing LDC loans. In particular, the lender may distinguish between those key risk indicator variables having a *systematic* effect on the probability of repayment across a large number of sovereign countries and those variables having an *unsystematic* effect by impacting only one or a few countries.

One way to address this problem is to employ a portfolio framework for sovereign risk analysis. Such an analysis would identify those indicator variables that have a *systematic* impact across all borrowers' probability of repayment and those that tend to be country specific (or *unsystematic*).[12] The indicator variables that the FI manager should really be concerned with are the *systematic* variables since they cannot be diversified away in a multisovereign loan portfolio. By comparison, unsystematic or country specific risks can be diversified away. Consider this model:

$$X_i = a_i + b_i \overline{X} + e_i$$

where

X_i = A key variable or country risk indicator for country i (e.g., the *DSR* for country i)

$\overline{X}$ = A weighted index of this key risk indicator across all countries to which the lender makes loans (e.g., the *DSR* for each country weighted by the shares of loans for each country in the bank's portfolio)

e_i = Other factors impacting X_i for any given country

Expressing this equation in variance terms:

$$\underset{\text{Total risk}}{VAR(X_i)} = \underset{\text{Systematic risk}}{b_i^2 VAR(\overline{X})} + \underset{\text{Unsystematic risk}}{VAR(e_i)}$$

From this equation, you can see that the total risk or variability of any given risk indicator for a country, such as the *DSR* for Nigeria, can be divided into a nondiversifiable *systematic* risk element that measures the extent to which that country's *DSR* moves in line with the *DSR*s of all other debtor countries and an unsystematic risk element that impacts the *DSR* for Nigeria independently. The greater the size of the *unsystematic* element relative to the systematic risk element, the less important this variable is to the lender since it can be diversified away by holding a broad array of LDC loans.

L. S. Goodman found that for the 1970–83 period, the *DSR* had a high systematic element across countries, as did export revenue variance (*VAREX*).[13] This implies that when one LDC country was experiencing a growing debt burden relative to its exports, so were all others. Similarly, when commodity prices or world demand collapsed for one debtor country's commodity exports, the same occurred for other debtor countries as well. A possible reason for the high systematic risk of the *DSR* is the sensitivity of this ratio to rising nominal and real interest rates in the developed (or lending) countries. As we discussed in Chapter 15, international interest rates tend to be positively correlated over time. A possible reason for the high systematic risk of the export variance is the tendency of prices and world demands for commodities to reflect simultaneously economic conditions such as recessions and expansions in developed countries.

By comparison, money supply growth ($\Delta M/M$) and the import ratio appear to have low systematic elements.[14] This is not surprising since control over the money supply and the use of domestic reserves are relatively discretionary variables for

---

[12]See L. S. Goodman, "Diversifiable Risks in LDC Lending: A 20/20 Hindsight View," *Studies in Banking and Finance* 3 (1986), pp. 249–62.

[13]Ibid.

[14]Ibid.

LDC governments. Thus, while Argentina may choose a money supply growth rate of 50 percent per annum, the Chilean government may choose a target rate of 10 percent per annum. Similarly, the Argentinean and Chilean economies may have very different demands for imports and the scale of vital imports may differ quite widely across LDCs. Using this type of analysis allows an FI manager to focus on relatively few variables, such as the *DSR*s and export variances, that affect the risk of the LDC sovereign loan portfolio.

In a further study[15] of systematic risk versus nonsystematic risk, for 54 LDCs over the 1974–87 period looking at *Institutional Investor* ratings of a country as the risk indicator variable, it was found that the systematic versus nonsystematic risk components varied from 97 percent versus 3 percent for Argentina to 41 percent versus 59 percent for Russia. This would suggest, all else being equal, that an FI should hold more Russian than Argentinean loans—although the experience of banks in 1998 with Russian defaults may call into question the appropriateness of the portfolio approach and especially the ability of FIs to diversify away unsystematic sovereign risk in a contagious crisis such as that which occurred in 1998.

Incentive Aspects.   CRA statistical models often identify variables based on rather loose or often nonexistent analyses of the borrower or lender's incentives to reschedule. Rarely are the following questions asked: What are the *incentives* or *net benefits* to an LDC seeking a rescheduling? What are the incentives or net benefits to an FI that grants a rescheduling? That is, what determines the demand for rescheduling by LDCs and the supply of rescheduling by FIs? Presumably, only when the benefits outweigh the costs for both parties does rescheduling occur. Consider the following benefits and costs of rescheduling for borrowers on the one hand and FIs on the other.

Borrowers
Benefits
- By rescheduling its debt, the borrower lowers the present value of its future payments in hard currencies to outside lenders. This allows it to increase its consumption of foreign imports and/or increase the rate of its domestic investment.

Costs
- By rescheduling now, the borrower may close itself out of the market for loans in the future. As a result, even if it encounters high-growth investment opportunities in the future, it may be difficult or impossible to finance them.
- Rescheduling may result in significant interference with the borrower's international trade since it would be difficult to gain access to instruments such as letters of credit without which trade may be more costly.[16]

Lenders
Benefits
- After a loan has already been made, a rescheduling is much better than a borrower default. With a rescheduling, the FI lender may anticipate some

[15]See M. Palmer and T. B. Sanders, "A Model for Diversifying International Loan Portfolios," *Journal of Financial Services Research,* 1996, pp. 359–71.
[16]See Chapter 13 on letters of credit.

present value loss of principal and interest on the loan; with an outright default, the FI stands to lose all its principal and future interest repayments.

- The FI can renegotiate fees and various other collateral and option features into a rescheduled loan.
- There may be tax benefits to a FI taking a recognized write-down or loss in value on a rescheduled LDC loan portfolio.[17]

Costs

- Through rescheduling, loans become similar to long-term bonds or even equity, and the FI often becomes locked into a particular loan portfolio structure.
- Those FIs with large amounts of rescheduled loans are subject to greater regulatory attention. For example, in the United States, such FIs may be placed on the regulators' problem list of FIs.[18]

All these relevant economic incentive considerations go into the demand for and the supply of rescheduling; however, it is far from clear how the simple statistical models just described incorporate this complex array of incentives. At a very minimum, statistical models should clearly reflect the underlying theory of rescheduling.[19]

Stability.   A final problem with simple statistical CRA models is that of stability. The fact that certain key variables may have explained rescheduling in the past does not mean that they will perform or predict well in the future. Over time, new variables and incentives affect rescheduling decisions, and the relative weights on the key variables change. This suggests that the FI manager must continuously update the CRA model to incorporate all currently available information and ensure the best predictive power possible.

Using Market Data to Measure Risk: The Secondary Market for LDC Debt

Since the mid-1980s, a secondary market for trading LDC debt has developed among large commercial and investment banks in New York and London. The volume of trading has grown dramatically from around $2 billion per year in 1984 to over $5.3 trillion in 1997 (trade in Brazilian debt alone accounted for $1.44 trillion), with trading often taking place in the high-yield (or junk bond) departments of the participating banks.[20]

These markets provide quoted prices for LDC loans and other debt instruments that an FI manager can use for CRA. Before we look at how this might be done, we describe the structure and development of the markets for LDC loans and related debt instruments, including the determinants of market demand and supply.

---

[17]For example, in 1998 Deutsche Bank took a loan loss provision of nearly $800 million against its Asian loan portfolio (see *New York Times,* January 30, 1998, p. D1).

[18]The problem list singles out banks for special regulatory attention. Normally, examiners rate a problem list bank as 4 or 5 on a rating scale of 1 to 5, where 1 is good and 5 is bad.

[19]See J. Bulow and K. Rogoff, "A Constant Recontracting Model of Sovereign Debt," *Journal of Political Economy* 97 (1989), pp. 155–78.

[20]See *The Economist,* March 22, 1997, p. 5.

The Structure of the Market.   This secondary market has considerably enhanced the liquidity of LDC loans on bank and other FI balance sheets.[21] The following are the market players that sell and buy LDC loans and debt instruments.

Sellers

- Large FIs willing to accept write-downs of loans on their balance sheets.
- Small FIs wishing to disengage themselves from the LDC loan market.
- FIs willing to swap one country's LDC debt for another's to rearrange their portfolios of country risk exposures.

Buyers

- Wealthy investors, hedge funds, FIs, and corporations seeking to engage in debt-equity swaps or speculative investments.
- FIs seeking to rearrange their LDC balance sheets by reorienting their LDC debt concentrations.

Consider the quote sheet from Salomon Brothers in Table 16–2 for May 2, 1988.

As you can see in Table 16–2—a relatively early stage of LDC loan market development—FIs such as investment banks and major commercial banks act as market makers, quoting two-way bid-ask prices for LDC debt.[22] Thus, an FI or an investor could have bought $100 of Peruvian loans from Salomon for $9 in May 1988, or at a 91 percent discount from face value. However, if selling the same loans to Salomon, the investor would have received only $7 per $100, or a 93 percent discount. The bid-ask spreads for certain countries were very large in this period; for example, Sudan's $2 bid and $10 ask was indicative of a serious lack of market demand for the sovereign loans of many countries.

In recent years there have been a large number of changes in the structure of the market. Now there are four market segments: Brady bonds, sovereign bonds, performing loans, and nonperforming loans.

Brady Bonds.   The first segment of the market (and the largest) is that for Brady bonds. These reflect programs under which the U.S. and other banks exchange their dollar loans for dollar bonds issued by the relevant countries. These bonds have a much longer maturity than that promised on the original loans and a lower promised original coupon (yield) than the interest rate on the original loan. However, the principal is usually collateralized through the issuing country purchasing U.S. treasury bonds, and holding them in a special-purpose escrow account. Should that country default on its Brady bonds, the buyers of the bonds could access the dollar bonds held as collateral. These loan for bond restructuring programs, also called debt for debt swaps, were developed under the auspices of the U.S. Treasury's 1989 Brady

---

[21]LDC loans change hands when one creditor assigns the rights to all future interest payments and principal payments to a buyer. In most early market transactions, the buyer had to get the permission of the sovereign debtor country before the loan could be assigned to a new party. The reason for this was that the country might have concerns as to whether the buyer was as committed to any new money deals as part of restructuring agreements as the original lender. Most recent restructuring agreements, however, have removed the right of assignment from the borrower (the sovereign country). This has increased liquidity in the LDC loan market.

[22]Major market makers include the Dutch ING bank, as well as Lehman, Citigroup, J. P. Morgan, Bankers Trust, and Merrill Lynch.

TABLE 16–2   Indicative Prices for Less Developed Country Bank Loans

Country	Indicative Cash Prices		Swap Index		Trading Commentary
	Bid	*Offer*	*Sell*	*Buy*	
Algeria	$91.00	$93.00	5.22	6.71	Longer-dated paper resurfacing as cash substitute in swaps.
Argentina	29.00	30.00	0.66	0.67	Less volume this period; consolidation exercise slows note trades.
Bolivia	10.00	13.00	0.52	0.54	Minimal current activity.
Brazil	53.00	54.00	1.00	1.02	Rally topping out as supply catches up with auction interest.
Chile	60.50	61.50	1.19	1.22	Market firm and rising as deal calendar fills.
Colombia	67.00	68.00	1.42	1.47	Resurgence of interest as high-quality exit.
Costa Rica	13.00	16.00	0.54	0.56	Market building reserves of patience to deal with this name again.
Dominican Republic	17.00	20.00	0.57	0.59	Trading picks up at lower levels.
Ecuador	31.00	33.00	0.66	0.70	Occasional swaps surfacing.
Honduras	25.00	28.00	0.63	0.65	Viewed as expensive on a relative value basis.
Ivory Coast	30.00	33.00	0.67	0.70	Newly sighted by fee swappers.
Jamaica	33.00	36.00	0.70	0.73	Slow but serious inquiry continues.
Mexico	52.50	53.50	0.99	1.01	Prices continue upward drift on lower, lumpy flow.
Morocco	50.00	51.00	0.94	0.96	Fee swappers oblige sellers by jumping into the wider breach versus Latins.
Nicaragua	3.00	4.00	0.48	0.49	Avoided by the surviving court tasters.
Nigeria	28.50	30.50	0.66	0.68	Retail stonewalls dealer interest.
Panama	20.00	23.00	0.59	0.61	Recent bidding stirs the mud.
Peru	7.00	9.00	0.51	0.52	Debt-for-debt workouts and debt-for-goods deals continue.
Philippines	52.00	53.00	0.98	1.00	Prices drift higher with good interest in non-CB names.
Poland	43.25	44.50	0.83	0.85	Somewhat slower trading this period.
Romania	82.00	84.00	2.61	2.94	Bidding improves on expectations of 1988 principal payments.
Senegal	40.00	45.00	0.78	0.85	Trading talk more serious.
Sudan	2.00	10.00	0.48	0.52	Still on the mat.
Turkey	97.50	99.00	18.80	47.00	CTLDs remain well bid.
Uruguay	59.50	61.50	1.16	1.22	Remains a patience-trying market.
Venezuela	55.00	55.75	1.04	1.06	Trading stronger as uptick in Chile brings swaps back into range.
Yugoslavia	45.50	47.00	0.86	0.89	More frequent trading.
Zaire	19.00	23.00	0.58	0.61	New interest develops.

Source: Salomon Brothers Inc., May 2, 1988.

Plan and other international organizations such as the IMF. Once loans were swapped for bonds by banks and other FIs, they could be sold on the secondary market. For example, in November 1996, the 30-year Venezuelan discount bonds with a remaining life of 23.4 years had a bid price of $78.12 per $100 of face value. These bonds have their principal repayments collateralized by U.S. Treasury bonds maturing in March 2020.

Approximately $136 billion of LDC loans were converted into bonds under the Brady Plan.

Sovereign Bonds.   The second segment of the LDC debt market is that for sovereign bonds. Beginning in May 1996, as the debt position and economies of some LDCs improved, a number started buy-back or repurchase programs for their Brady bonds. As shown in Table 16–3, by June 1997 six countries had repurchased or

TABLE 16–3 Brady Bond Repurchases
Brady bonds, swapped or bought back by governments, in billions of dollars

Country	Date	Amount
Mexico	May '96	$ 2.90
Philippines	Sept. '96	0.68
Mexico	Sept. '96	1.24
Mexico	Feb. '97	1.10
Ecuador	April '97	0.25
Poland	May '97	1.70
Brazil	June '97	2.80
Total swapped or bought back		$ 10.67
Total Brady bond market		$136.20

Source: Wall Street Journal reports; Santandar Investment; and *Wall Street Journal,* June 6, 1997.

swapped $10 billion of Brady bonds with newly issued sovereign bonds. The difference between a Brady bond and a sovereign bond is that a Brady bond's value partly reflects the value of the U.S. Treasury bond collateral underlying the principal and/or interest on the issue. By contrast, sovereign bonds are uncollateralized and their price or value reflects the credit risk rating of the country issuing the bonds. The benefit to the country is the "saving" from not having to pledge U.S. Treasury bonds as collateral. The cost is the higher interest spreads required on such bonds. Thus, the $2.8 billion June 1997 issue by Brazil of 30-year dollar-denominated bonds was sold at a yield spread of nearly 4 percent over U.S. Treasuries at the time of issue.

Performing Loans.   The third segment of the LDC debt market is that for performing LDC loans. Performing loans are original or restructured outstanding sovereign loans on which the sovereign country is currently maintaining promised payments to lenders or debt holders. Any discounts from $100 reflect expectations that these countries may face repayment problems in the future.

Nonperforming Loans.   The fourth and final segment of the LDC market is that for nonperforming loans. Nonperforming loans reflect the secondary market prices for the sovereign loans of countries where there are no interest or principal payments currently being made. These are normally traded at very deep discounts from $100.

LDC Market Prices and Country Risk Analysis.   By combining LDC debt prices with key variables, FI managers can potentially predict future repayment problems. For example, in the markets for which LDC debt is quite heavily traded, such as Mexico and Brazil, these prices reflect market consensus regarding the current and expected future cash flows on these loans and, implicitly, the probability of rescheduling or repudiation of these loans. Because market prices on LDC loans have been available monthly since 1985, the FI manager might construct a statistical CRA model to analyze which key economic and political variables or factors have driven changes in secondary market prices. Basically, this would involve regressing periodic changes in the prices of LDC debt in the secondary market on a set of key variables such as those described earlier in this section. In Table 16–4,

---

TABLE 16–4   Variables Affecting Secondary Market Prices

The following regression equation is estimated:

$$P_{it} = \beta_1 \times \text{Intercept} + \beta_2 \times \text{TDGNP}_{it} + \beta_3 \times \text{TDEX}_{it} + \beta_4 \times \text{NETDS}_{it} + \beta_5 \times \text{NIRES}_{it} +$$
$$\beta_6 \times \text{INT}_t + \beta_7 \times \text{ARR}_{it} + \beta_8 \times \text{USP}_t + \beta_9 \times \text{BDUM}_{it} + \beta_{10} \times \text{PDUM}_t +$$
$$\beta_{11} \times \text{CONVDUM}_{it} + U_{it}$$

where

TDGNP	= Ratio of total long-term debt to GNP
TDEX	= Ratio of total long-term debt to exports
NETDS	= Ratio of net exports to debt service
NIRES	= Ratio of net imports to hard currency reserves
INT	= Monthly London Interbank Offered Rate (a short-term interest rate)
ARR	= Level of incurred payment arrears
USP	= Cumulative developing country specific loan provisioning by U.S. Banks
BDUM	= Unity for Brazil from January to December of 1987 and zero otherwise to capture the effects of the debt moratorium
PDUM	= Unity for Peru over the whole sampling period and zero otherwise to account for the unilateral limitation of debt service payments
CONVDUM	= Unity for all months in which a country maintained legislation for debt-to-equity conversions

Parameter	Estimate	t-Statistic
Intercept	88.51760	13.47
TDGNP	−18.11610	−4.75
TDEX	−0.10437	−3.57
NETDS	−0.30754	−0.50
NIRES	5.79548	1.28
INT	0.22825	0.30
ARR	−0.00574	−2.68
USP	−0.00100	−13.69
BDUM	−10.92820	−6.61
PDUM	−36.07240	−8.31
CONVDUM	−5.43157	−6.75
Degrees of freedom: 309		
Adjusted R^2: 0.96		

Source: E. Boehmer and W. L. Megginson, "Determinants of Secondary Market Prices for Developing Country Syndicated Loans," *Journal of Finance* 45 (1990), pp. 1517–40.

consider the results of a study by E. Boehmer and W. L. Megginson of the factors driving the secondary market prices of 10 LDC countries' loans over a 32-month period, July 1985–July 1988.

As you can see, the most significant variables affecting LDC loan sale prices over this period were a country's debt service ratios (TDGNP and TDEX), its import ratio (NIRES), its accumulated debt arrears (ARR), and the amount by which banks had already made loan loss provisions against these LDC loans (USP). Also important were variables that reflect debt moratoria for Peru and Brazil (PDUM and BDUM) and that indicate whether a debt-equity swap program was in place. Interestingly, debt-equity swap programs appear to depress prices. (We discuss these programs in more detail in the Appendix.)

Once managers have estimated a statistical model, they can use the estimate of parameters β_1, β_2, ... β_n along with forecasts for a given LDC's debt service and other key variables to derive predicted changes in LDC asset prices. That is, this approach might allow the FI manager to come up with another set of forecasts regarding changes in sovereign risk exposure to a number of sovereign debtors.

This approach is subject to many of the same criticisms as the traditional statistical models of country risk prediction. Specifically, the parameters of the model may be unstable; managers can measure variables, such as the *DSR* and the import ratio, only with error; and the LDC loan market may not be price efficient.[23] In addition, the link between these key variables and the change in secondary market price is something of a black box in terms of links to the underlying theoretical incentives of borrowers and lenders to engage in future reschedulings or repudiations of their debt obligations.

Concept Questions

1. Are the credit ratings of countries in the *Institutional Investor* rating scheme forward looking or backward looking?
2. What variables are most commonly included in sovereign risk prediction models? What does each one measure?
3. What are the major problems involved with using traditional CRA models and techniques?
4. Which sovereign risk indicators are the most important for a large FI, those with a high or those with a low systematic element?
5. Why is the supply of Brady bonds in decline?

Summary

This chapter reviewed the problems FIs face from sovereign or country risk exposures. Sovereign risk is the risk of a foreign government limiting or preventing domestic borrowers in its jurisdiction from repaying the principal and interest on debt owned to external lenders. In recent years this risk has caused enormous problems for U.S. banks lending to LDCs, and Latin American and Asian countries. We reviewed various models for country risk analysis (CRA), including those produced by external monitoring agencies such as *Euromoney* and the *Institutional Investor* and those that could be constructed by an FI manager for internal evaluation purposes. Such statistical CRA models have problems and pitfalls. An alternative approach using secondary market prices on LDC loans and bonds was also described. In the appendix, we analyze the advantages and disadvantages of using four alternative mechanisms for dealing with problem sovereign credits from the perspective of the lender: debt-equity swaps, MYRAs, loan sales, and debt-debt swaps.

---

[23]However, in S. H. Lee, H. M. Sung, and J. L. Urrutia, "The Behavior of Secondary Market Prices of LDC Syndicated Loans," *Journal of Banking and Finance* 20 (1996), pp. 537–54, it is shown that returns on LDC loans traded in the secondary market conform to those expected to exist in an efficient market.

Questions and Problems

1. What risks are incurred in making loans to borrowers based in foreign countries? Explain.

2. What is the difference between debt rescheduling and debt repudiation?

3. Identify and explain at least four reasons why rescheduling debt in the form of loans is easier than rescheduling debt in the form of bonds.

4. What two country risk assessment models are available to investors? How is each model compiled?

5. What types of variables normally are used in a CRA Z-score model? Define the following ratios and explain how each is interpreted in assessing the probability of rescheduling.

   a. Debt service ratio.

   b. Import ratio.

   c. Investment ratio.

   d. Variance of export revenue.

   e. Domestic money supply growth.

6. What are the shortcomings introduced by using traditional CRA models and techniques? How does each of the problems impact the estimation techniques? In each case, what adjustments are made in the estimation techniques to compensate for the problems?

7. An FI manager has calculated the following values and weights to assess the credit risk and likelihood of having to reschedule the loan. From the Z-score calculated from these weights and values, is the manager likely to approve the loan? Validation tests of the Z-score model indicated that scores below 0.500 were likely to be nonreschedulers, while scores above 0.700 indicated a likelihood of rescheduling. Scores between 0.500 and 0.700 do not predict well.

Variable	Country Value	Weight
DSR	1.25	0.05
IR	1.60	0.10
INVR	0.60	0.35
VAREX	0.15	0.35
MG	0.02	0.15

8. Countries A and B have exports of $2 and $6 billion, respectively. The total interest and amortization on foreign loans for both countries are $1 and $2 billion, respectively.

   a. What is the debt service ratio (DSR) for each country?

   b. Based only on this ratio, to which country should lenders charge a higher risk premium?

   c. What are the shortcomings of using only these ratios to determine your answer in (b)?

9. Explain the following relation:

$$p = f(IR, INVR)$$
$$+, + \text{ or } -$$

   p = Probability of rescheduling

   IR = Total imports/Total foreign exchange reserves

   $INVR$ = Real investment/GNP

10. What is systematic risk in terms of sovereign risk? Which of the variables often used in statistical models tend to have high systematic risk? Which variables tend to have low systematic risk?

11. What are the benefits and costs of rescheduling to the following?

    a. A borrower.

    b. A lender.

12. How do price and quantity risks affect the variability of a country's export revenue?

13. The average σ^2_{ER} (or VAREX = variance of export revenue) of a group of countries has been estimated at 20 percent. The individual VAREX of two countries in the group, Holland and Singapore, has been estimated at 15 percent and 28 percent, respectively. The regression of individual country VAREX on the average VAREX provides the following beta (coefficient) estimates:

$$\beta_H = \text{Beta of Holland} = 0.80;$$
$$\beta_S = \text{Beta of Singapore} = 0.20.$$

    a. Based only on the VAREX estimates, which country should be charged a higher risk premium? Explain.

    b. If FIs include unsystematic risk in their estimation of risk premiums, how would your conclusions to (a) be affected? Explain.

14. Who are the primary sellers of LDC debt? Who are the buyers? Why are FIs often both sellers and buyers of LDC debt in the secondary markets?

15. Identify and describe the four market segments of the secondary market for LDC debt.

The following questions and problems are based on material presented in Appendix 16A.

16. What are the risks to an investing company participating in a debt-equity swap?

17. Chase Bank holds a $200 million loan to Argentina. The loans are being traded at bid-offer prices of 91–93 per 100 in the London secondary market.

    a. If Chase has an opportunity to sell this loan to an investment bank at a 7 percent discount, what are the savings after taxes compared to the revenue selling the loan in the secondary market? Assume the tax rate is 40 percent.

b. The investment bank in turn sells the debt at a 6 percent discount to a real estate company planning to build apartment complexes in Argentina. What is the profit after taxes to the investment bank?

c. The real estate company converts this loan into pesos under a debt-equity swap organized by the Argentinean government. The official rate for dollar to peso conversion is P1.05/$. The free market rate is P1.10/$. How much did the real estate company save by investing in Argentina through the debt-equity swap program as opposed to directly investing $200 million using the free market rates?

d. How much would Chase benefit from doing a local currency debt-equity swap itself? Why doesn't the bank do this swap?

18. Zlick Company plans to invest $20 million in Chile to expand its subsidiary's manufacturing output. Zlick has two options. It can convert the $20 million at the current exchange rate of 410 pesos to a dollar (i.e., P410/$), or it can engage in a debt-equity swap with its bank City Bank by purchasing Chilean debt and then swapping that debt into Chilean equity investments.

a. If City Bank quotes bid-offer prices of 94–96 for Chilean loans, what is the bank expecting to receive from Zlick Corporation (ignore taxes)? Why would City Bank want to dispose of this loan?

b. If Zlick decides to purchase the debt from City Bank and convert it to equity, it will have to exchange it at the official rate of P400/$. Is this option better than investing directly in Chile at the free market rate of P410/$?

c. What official exchange rate will cause Zlick to be indifferent between the two options?

19. What is concessionality in the process of rescheduling a loan?

20. Which variables typically are negotiation points in an LDC multiyear restructuring agreement (MYRA)? How do changes in these variables provide benefits to the borrower and to the lender?

21. How would the restructuring, such as rescheduling, of sovereign bonds affect the interest rate risk of the bonds? Is it possible that such restructuring would cause the bank's cost of capital not to change? Explain.

22. A bank is in the process of renegotiating a loan. The principal outstanding is $50 million and is to be paid back in two installments of $25 million each, plus interest of 8 percent. The new terms will stretch the loan out to five years with no principal payments except for interest payments of 6 percent for the first three years. The principal will be paid in the last two years in payments

of $25 million along with the interest. The cost of funds for the bank is 6 percent for both the old loan and the renegotiated loan. An up-front fee of 1 percent is to be included for the renegotiated loan.

a. What is the present value of the existing loan for the bank?

b. What is the present value of the rescheduled loan for the bank?

c. Is the concessionality positive or negative for the bank?

23. A bank is in the process of renegotiating a three-year nonamortizing loan. The principal outstanding is $20 million, and the interest rate is 8 percent. The new terms will extend the loan to 10 years at a new interest rate of 6 percent. The cost of funds for the bank is 7 percent for both the old loan and the renegotiated loan. An up-front fee of 50 basis points is to be included for the renegotiated loan.

a. What is the present value of the existing loan for the bank?

b. What is the present value of the rescheduled loan for the bank?

c. What is the concessionality for the bank?

d. What should be the up-front fee to make the concessionality zero?

24. A $20 million loan outstanding to the Nigerian government is currently in arrears with City Bank. After extensive negotiations, City Bank agrees to reduce the interest rates from 10 percent to 6 percent and to lengthen the maturity of the loan to 10 years from the present 5 years remaining to maturity. The principal of the loan is to be paid at maturity. There will be no grace period, and the first interest payment is expected at the end of the year.

a. If the cost of funds is 5 percent for the bank, what is the present value of the loan prior to the rescheduling?

b. What is the present value of the rescheduled loan to the bank?

c. What is the concessionality of the rescheduled loan if the cost of funds remains at 5 percent and an up-front fee of 5 percent is charged?

d. What up-front fee should the bank charge to make the concessionality equal zero?

25. A bank was expecting to receive $100,000 from its customer based in Germany. Since the customer has problems repaying the loan immediately, the bank extends the loan for another year at the same interest rate of 10 percent. However, in the rescheduling agreement, the bank reserves the right to exercise an option for receiving the payment in deutsche marks, equal to DM181,500.

a. If the cost of funds to the bank is also assumed to be 10 percent, what is the value of this option built into the agreement if only two possible exchange rates are expected at the end of the year, DM1.75/$ or DM1.55/$, with equal probability?

   b. How would your answer differ if the probability of the DM being DM1.75/$ is 70 percent and that of DM1.55/$ is 30 percent?

   c. Does the currency option have more or less value as the volatility of the exchange rate increases?

26. What are the major benefits and costs of loan sales to an FI?

27. What are the major costs and benefits of converting debt to Brady bonds for an FI?

APPENDIX 16A:
MECHANISMS FOR DEALING WITH SOVEREIGN RISK EXPOSURE

In Chapter 16, we identified methods and models FI managers could use to measure sovereign risk exposure before making credit decisions. In this appendix, we take a closer look at the benefits and costs of using four alternative mechanisms to deal with problem sovereign credits once they have arisen. The four mechanisms are:

1. Debt for equity swaps.
2. Restructuring of loans (MYRAs).
3. Sale of LDC loans on the secondary market.
4. Debt for debt swaps (Brady bonds).

While restructuring keeps the loans in the portfolio, the other three mechanisms change the fundamental nature of the FI's claim itself or remove it from the balance sheet.

In this appendix we take a detailed look at the mechanics of loan restructuring and debt for equity swaps. As we have already described LDC loan sales and debt for debt swaps (e.g., Brady bonds), we only summarize their benefits and costs here. Discussing each of these mechanisms, especially their benefits and costs, is important since an FI can choose among the four in dealing with a problem sovereign loan or credit.

Debt-Equity Swaps

The market for LDC loan sales has a close link to debt-equity swap programs arranged by certain LDCs, such as Chile and Mexico, with outside investors that wish to make equity investments in debtor countries.[1] Indeed, while banks are the major sellers of LDC loans, important buyers are parties that wish to engage in long-term equity or real investments in those debtor countries. For example, the 1985 Mexican debt-equity swap program allowed Mexican dollar loans to be swapped for Mexican equity in certain priority investment areas. These were the motor industry, tourism, and the chemical

industry. A good example of an FI exploiting the opportunities of the Mexican debt-equity swap program was American Express bank, which built seven hotels in Mexico as a result of debt-equity swaps.[2] The estimated annual amount of debt-equity swaps is currently around $10 billion.

To demonstrate the costs and benefits of a debt-equity swap for the FI and other parties participating in the transaction, we present a hypothetical example. Suppose that in November 2000, Citibank had $100 million loans outstanding to Chile and could have sold those loans on the secondary market for a bid price of $91 million, or $91 per $100. The advantage to Citibank from selling loans is removing these loans from its books and freeing up funds for other investments. However, Citibank has to accept a loss of $9 million on the loan. Given that the rest of the bank is profitable, this loss can be offset against other profits of the bank. Further, if the corporate tax rate is 34 percent, then Citibank's after-tax loss will be $9(1 − .34) million = $5.94 million.

If this loan were sold to Salomon Brothers for $91 million, as a market maker Salomon would turn around and reoffer it to an outside buyer at a slightly higher price—say, $93 million (or $93 per $100 of face value). Suppose IBM wants to build a computer factory in Chile and buys the $100 million face value loan from Salomon for $93 million for the purpose of financing its investments in Chile. Thus, Salomon earns a profit of $93 million − $91 million = $2 million, while IBM knows that Chile has a debt for equity swap program. This means that at a given exchange rate, the Chilean government would allow IBM to convert the $100 million dollar loan it has purchased into local currency or pesos. However, the Chilean government would be willing to do this only if there were something in it for that government. Thus, it may be willing to convert the dollars into pesos only at a 5 percent discount from

---

[1]For more details, see R. Grosse, "The Debt/Equity Swap in Latin America—In Whose Interest?" *Journal of International Financial Management and Accounting* 4 (Spring 1992), pp. 13–39.

[2]Countries which have recently employed debt-equity swap programs include Argentina, Brazil, Chile, Costa Rica, Ecuador, Jamaica, Mexico, Uruguay, and Venezuela.

FIGURE 16A–1

*Debt-Equity Swaps and
Loan Sales*

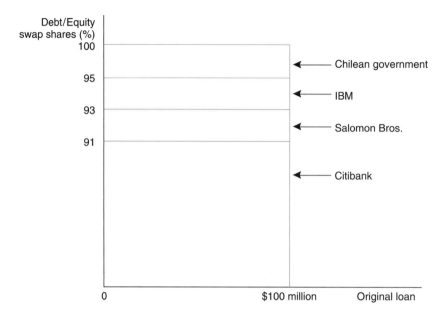

the true free market dollar/peso exchange rate. Suppose the free market exchange rate were 380 Chilean pesos to the U.S. dollar; then the Chilean government would convert the dollars only at 361 pesos to the U.S. dollar. Thus IBM would have to bear a 5 percent discount on the face value of the purchased loan—when converting the $100 million loan at the Chilean Central Bank, that is, IBM would receive $95 million equivalent in pesos.[3] Remember that IBM had originally bought the loan for only $93 million on the secondary market. Thus, its net savings from this debt-equity conversion program is $2 million.[4] However, note that the $95 million is in pesos that have to be invested in Chilean equity, such as real estate for factories. In general, debt-equity swap investors face long periods before they can repatriate dividends (12 years in the Mexican case) and often large withholding taxes (55 percent in the Mexican case). Moreover, they face the risk of future expropriation or nationalization of those assets as well as peso currency risk. Thus, the $2 million spread reflects IBM's expectations about such risks.

Finally, what does the Chilean government get out of this debt-equity swap program? On the one hand, it has retired relatively expensive hard-currency dollar debt with local currency pesos at a discount. Implicitly, the Chilean government has retired a $100 million face value debt at a cost of $95 million in pesos; the difference reflects the debt-equity swap official exchange rate (361 pesos/$1) and the true exchange rate (380 pesos/$1). The cost to Chile is printing $95 million more in pesos. This may lead to a higher domestic inflation

rate as well as increased foreign ownership and control of Chilean real assets as a result of IBM's equity purchases.

We depict the division of the original $100 million face value loan among the four parties as a result of the loan sale and debt–equity swap in Figure 16A–1. As you can see, Citibank gets 91 percent of the original face value of the loan; Salomon Brothers, 2 percent; IBM, 2 percent; and Chile, 5 percent. That is, the 9 percent discount from face value accepted by Citibank is shared among three parties: the investment bank, the corporation involved in the debt-equity swap, and the sponsoring country's government.

One puzzle from the preceding example is why Citibank doesn't sidestep both the investment bank and IBM and engage in a local currency debt for equity swap itself. That is, why doesn't Citibank directly swap its $100 million loan to Chile for the $95 million equivalent of local equity? The problem is that in the United States, Federal Reserve Regulation K places restrictions on the ability of U.S. banks to buy real equity or engage in commerce in overseas countries.[5] If a U.S. bank can buy and hold Chilean real assets, this might lower its potential losses from restructuring its LDC loan portfolio. Nevertheless, note that while a loan sale directly removes a problem loan from the balance sheet, a debt for equity

---

[3]In practice, debt-equity swaps convert into pesos at an official rate. This official rate is often less attractive than the rate quoted in official or unofficial parallel markets for private transactions.

[4]That is, in general, the swap is cheaper than direct local borrowing if this is an available alternative.

---

[5]Limited amounts of equity purchases are allowed to specialized U.S. bank subsidiaries called Edge Act corporations. Such corporations have been established since 1919 under the Edge Act to allow banks to finance international transactions. In 1987, the Federal Reserve approved bank acquisitions of 100 percent stakes in nonfinancial companies in 33 extremely poor LDCs as part of debt-equity swaps. Unfortunately, most of these countries do not operate debt-equity programs or have very little equity that is attractive. However, the American Express bank example of building seven hotels in Mexico illustrates a bank engaging in a direct debt-equity swap.

swap replaces that problem with a risky long-term peso-denominated equity position on the balance sheet. Thus, it is far from certain that the liquidity of the balance sheet has been improved through such a transaction.

Multiyear Restructuring Agreements (MYRAs)

If a country is unable to keep its payments on a loan current and an FI chooses to maintain the loan on its balance sheet rather than selling it or swapping it for equity or debt, the loan and its contractual terms will be rescheduled under a multiyear restructuring agreement (MYRA). A good example of a MYRA was the January 1998 agreement reached between South Korea and its major creditors to restructure $24 billion of short-term dollar loans that had been made by banks and corporations (and that were coming due in March 1998). Many of these loans had interest rates as high as 20 percent and maturities of 90 days or less.

As with the loan sale, the debt-equity swap, and the debt for debt swap, the crucial question for an FI is how much it is willing to concede or give up to the borrower in the sovereign loan rescheduling process. The benefits and costs of this policy depend on a number of ingredients that are usually built into any MYRA, including:

1. The *fee* charged by the bank to the borrower for the costs of restructuring the loan. This fee may be as high as 1 percent of the face value of the loan if a large lending syndicate is involved in the negotiations.
2. The *interest rate* charged on the new loan. This is generally lower than the rate on the original loan to ease the repayment cash flow problems of the borrower. In the South Korean case, if the loan was rescheduled for one year, the new interest was LIBOR plus 2.25 percent; if it was rescheduled for two years, the new loan interest rate was LIBOR plus 2.5 percent; and if it was rescheduled for three years, the new interest rate was 2.75 percent.
3. A *grace period* may be involved before interest and/or principal payments begin on the new loan. This gives the borrower time to accumulate hard currency reserves to meet its debt interest and principal obligations in the future. In the South Korean case, no grace period was set.
4. The *maturity* of the loan is lengthened, normally to stretch out the interest and principal payments over a longer period. In the South Korean case the restructured loan maturities were set at between one and three years.
5. *Option and guarantee features* are often built into the MYRA to allow the lender (and sometimes the borrower) to choose the currency for repayment of interest and principal,[6] and/or to protect the lenders against default in the future. In the case of the South Korean

---

[6]For example, the lender may choose to be repaid in dollars or in yen. Such option features add value to the cash flow stream for either the borrower or the lender, depending on who can exercise the currency option.

loans, the government had to guarantee repayment of the $24 billion.

The following simple example demonstrates how these factors determine the degree of **concessionality** (the net cost) of a MYRA to an FI. In general, the net cost or degree of concessionality can be defined as:

$$\text{Concessionality} = [\text{Present value of} - [\text{Present value of} \\ \text{original loan}] \quad \text{restructured loan}] \\ = PV_o - PV_R$$

The lower the present value of the restructured loan relative to the original loan, the greater the *concessions* the bank has made to the borrower, that is, the greater the cost of loan restructuring.

Suppose the original loan was $100 million for two years and, under the terms of the original loan agreement, the borrower was required to pay back $50 million principal at the end of the first year and $50 million at the end of the second year. That is, the loan was amortized equally over the two-year period. The interest rate charged on the loan was 10 percent, and the bank's cost of funds was 8 percent. The present value of the original loan (PV_O) is

$$PV_O = \frac{(A_1 + I_1)}{(1 + d)} + \frac{(A_2 + I_2)}{(1 + d)^2}$$

where

A_i = Principal paid back in year $i = 1,2$
I_i = Interest paid in year $i = 1,2$
d = Bank cost of funds (discount rate)

Thus:

$$PV_O = \frac{(50 + 10)}{(1.08)} + \frac{(50 + 5)}{(1.08)^2} = \$102.71 \text{ million}$$

That is, the present value of the loan is $102.71 million with a gross return of $102.71/$100, or 2.71 percent.

Suppose a borrowing country is unable to meet its promised principal amortization and interest payments of $60 million and $55 million in years 1 and 2. To prevent default, the bank negotiates a MYRA that has the following terms:

Maturity = 6 years
Principal amortization = 4 years (25 percent per year)
Grace period = 2 years
Loan rate = 9 percent (assumed to be constant)
Bank's discount rate = 10 percent
Up-front fee = 1 percent
Guarantees and options = None

We look at each of these features of the MYRA in turn.

- *Maturity.* The maturity has been increased from two to six years to allow the principal to be paid off over a longer time.

FIGURE 16A–2

*Principal Repayments
(Amortization Schedule)
on the Old Loan and the
MYRA*

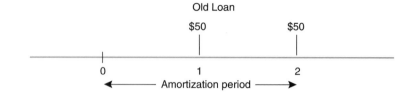

- *Amortization.* The principal is to be paid off over the last four years of the six-year period at 25 percent per year, or $25 million per year.
- *Grace period.* For the first two years of the restructured loan agreement, no principal payments are required of the borrower.

See Figure 16A–2 for a summary of these three features.

- *Loan interest rate.* The loan interest rate is lowered from 10 to 9 percent for the six-year period. Because no grace period is granted for interest payments, all appropriate interest payments have to be made on time.[7]
- *Bank cost of funds.* The bank's cost of funds or discount rate has increased to 10 percent to reflect depositors' and investors' concerns about the bank's solvency in light of its risky sovereign lending policies.
- *Up-front fee.* The bank charges an up-front fee, assumed to be equal to 1 percent of the face value of the loan, as compensation for the legal-contractual costs involved in the MYRA.
- *Guarantee and option features.* For simplicity, no special guarantees or currency conversion options for principal or interest are included in the MYRA.[8]

The present value of the restructured loan (PV_R) is[9]

$$PV_R = F + \frac{I_1}{(1+d)} + \frac{I_2}{(1+d)^2} + \frac{(A_3 + I_3)}{(1+d)^3}$$
$$+ \frac{(A_4 + I_4)}{(1+d)^4} + \frac{(A_5 + I_5)}{(1+d)^5} + \frac{(A_6 + I_6)}{(1+d)^6}$$

Substituting in the values from the previous example:

$$PV_R = 1 + \frac{9}{(1.10)} + \frac{9}{(1.10)^2} + \frac{(25+9)}{(1.10)^3}$$
$$+ \frac{(25+6.75)}{(1.10)^4} + \frac{(25+4.5)}{(1.10)^5} + \frac{(25+2.25)}{(1.10)^6}$$
$$= \$97.55 \text{ million}$$

The present value of the loan has fallen to $97.55 million. Therefore:

$$
\begin{aligned}
\text{Bank concessionality} &= PV_o - PV_R \\
&= \$102.71 - \$97.55 \\
&= \$5.16 \text{ million}
\end{aligned}
$$

In present value terms, the bank has given up $5.16 million in the MYRA. This value is very sensitive to the revised contractual terms and in particular to *d*, the bank's discount rate. Suppose bank investors viewed the bank as being "too big to fail," believing that regulators would always bail out the bank if it got into trouble. Such a belief would mean that even with the onset of sovereign loan problems, the required returns on bank debt and equity (i.e., the bank's cost of funds) might remain unchanged at *d* = 8 percent.

Replacing the discount rate *d* = 10 percent with *d* = 8 percent in the preceding MYRA, we recalculate the PV_R as $104.63 million. In present value terms, the bank actually gains from the restructuring by $104.63 − $102.71 = $1.92 million.[10]

Also, as we noted earlier, many MYRAs contain option features that usually allow the lending bank to choose the

---

[7]This assumption could easily be relaxed.

[8]We discuss the incorporation of such option features and their effects on the net cost of the MYRA later in this appendix.

[9]This assumes that the FI rationally expects the borrower to maintain the restructured payments schedule.

[10]That the required return on a bank's equity and debt might not rise has some support from the findings of J. Madura and E. Zarruk that the announcement of the Brady Plan (debt for debt swaps) had a positive effect on bank equity values. See "Impact of the Debt Reduction Plan on the Value of LDC Debt," *International Review of Economics and Finance* 1 (1992), pp. 177–87.

FIGURE 16A–3

The Value of a Currency Option to the FI (Lender)

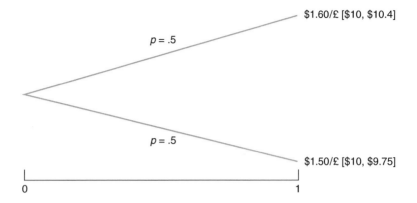

$1.60/£ [$10, $10.4]

$p = .5$

$p = .5$

$1.50/£ [$10, $9.75]

0   1

currency in which it wishes to receive interest or principal. Occasionally, the borrower receives this option, but in most actual MYRAs this is rare. For example, in the 1985 Mexican MYRA, non-U.S. banks received the option of switching one-half of their loans from dollars to their local currencies (yen, sterling, etc.). An FI that has this option reduces the degree of concessionality it makes under the MYRA. To illustrate the value of currency and interest rate options to the FI, we use another simple example (see Figure 16A–3).

Suppose a lender makes a one-year loan to an LDC borrower. At the end of the year the lender has the option of being paid either $10 million or £6.5 million; that is, the lender can be paid either in dollars or in pounds. Also, suppose the pound's expected spot exchange rate in dollars at the end of the year is equally likely to be either $1.50 or $1.60. If it chooses to be repaid in dollars, the bank will receive $10 million regardless of the exchange rate. If the exchange rate at the end of the year is $1.60/£, the lender choosing to be repaid in British pounds receives £6.5 million. This could be converted into $10.4 million in the foreign exchange market (£6.5 × 1.6). Since this is more than $10 million, the bank would elect to be paid in pounds and receive the equivalent of $10.4 million. If the exchange rate at the end of the year is $1.50/£, then by choosing pounds the lender will end up with the equivalent of only $9.75 million, which is less than the $10 million to be repaid in dollars. The bank would be better off choosing to be repaid in dollars. Consequently, one exchange rate outcome would yield $10.4 million and the other would yield $10 million. Because either exchange rate outcome is assumed to be equally likely, the lender should expect to receive a cash flow of $10.2 million (½ × $10.4 + ½ × $10).

In Figure 16A–3, $p = .5$ reflects the equal probabilities that the exchange rate could be $1.60 or $1.50 in one year's time. In the upper arm of the probability tree, if the exchange rate rises to $1.60/£1, the bank will choose payment in pounds rather than dollars—£6.5 × 1.6 = $10.4 million is bigger than the $10 million payment in dollars. If the exchange rate is $1.50/£1—the lower arm of the probability tree—the lender

will choose dollars since £6.5 × 1.5 = $9.75 million is less than the $10 million payment in dollars.

Thus, the value of the option is the discounted value of the expected cash flow in one year's time minus the cash flow without the option. That is, since the option pays off in one year's time, we need to discount it to derive its present value at the time of the MYRA. If the discount rate is 10 percent, then

$$\text{Option value} = \frac{[\frac{1}{2}(10.4) + \frac{1}{2}(10)] - 10}{(1.1)}$$

$$= \frac{0.2}{1.1}$$

$$= \$0.1818 \text{ million}$$

Consequently, the inclusion of this type of currency option clause in a MYRA reduces the value of the lender's concessionality by $181,818. Further, the more volatile are exchange rates, the greater is the value of such a currency option to the lender and the more costly it is to the borrower.[11]

Loan Sales

We described a third mechanism for dealing with problem sovereign loans—LDC loan sales—earlier in this chapter. Here we summarize the main benefits and costs to the FI. The first major benefit is that a sale removes these loans from the balance sheet and as such frees up resources for other investments. Second, being able to sell these loans at a discount or loss signifies that the bank is sufficiently strong in the rest of its balance sheet to bear the cost. In fact, a number of studies

---

[11]In the context of concessionality, the value of this option should be added to PV_R to get the value of the restructured loan as a whole. In the case of guarantees, the contingent claims value of these guarantees would be added to PV_R. In general, there is always some probability of a guarantor defaulting on his or her obligations, so that the contingent claim value is less than the face value of a guarantee.

have found that announcements of banks taking reserve additions against LDC loans—prior to their charge-off and sale—has a positive effect on bank stock prices.[12] Third, part of the loan sale loss is shared with the government because such losses provide a tax write-off for the lender.

The major cost is that of the loss itself—the tax-adjusted difference between the face value of the loan and its market value at the time of the sale.

Debt for Debt Swaps (Brady Bonds)

The fourth mechanism is a debt for debt swap. The primary benefit of debt for debt swaps is that they transform an LDC loan into a highly marketable and liquid instrument—a bond. For example, FIs trade and clear Brady bonds (the most common debt for debt swap) in a similar fashion to most

---

[12]See, for example, Grammatikos and Saunders, "Additions to Bank Loan Loss Reserves."

Eurobonds with relatively low transactions cost, small bid–ask spreads, and an efficient clearing and settlement system (via Euroclear and Cedel). In addition, because of full or partial collateral backing, these bonds are normally senior in status to any remaining LDC loans or sovereign bonds of that country. The major cost is that when the bond is swapped for the loan, it usually has a longer stated maturity. Also, the swap of loan face value for debt face value is often less than dollar for dollar. Moreover, posting U.S. dollar debt as collateral can be very expensive for an LDC country with minimal hard currency exchange reserves.

Concept Questions

1. What are four alternative mechanisms for dealing with problem sovereign loans?
2. What are the major benefits and costs of each of the mechanisms in question (1)?
3. Which alternative is most popular among FI managers today?

CHAPTER 17

LIQUIDITY RISK

Introduction

In Chapters 7 through 16 you saw how the major problems of interest rate risk, credit risk, market risk, off-balance-sheet risk, operational and technology risk, foreign exchange risk, and sovereign risk can threaten the solvency of an FI. In this chapter we look at the problems created by liquidity risk.

Unlike the preceding risks that threaten the very solvency of an FI, liquidity risk is a normal aspect of the everyday management of an FI. Only in extreme cases do liquidity risk problems develop into solvency risk problems. Moreover, some FIs are more exposed to liquidity risk than others. At one extreme banks and thrifts are highly exposed, and in the middle are life insurance companies that are moderately exposed. At the other end are mutual and pension funds and property-casualty insurance companies with relatively low exposure. We examine the reasons for these differences in this chapter.

Causes of Liquidity Risk

Liquidity risk arises for two reasons: a liability-side reason and an asset-side reason. The liability-side reason arises whenever an FI's liability holders, such as depositors and insurance policyholders, seek to cash in their financial claims immediately. When liability holders demand cash by withdrawing deposits, there is a need for the FI to borrow additional funds or sell off assets to meet the withdrawal. The most liquid asset of all is cash; FIs use this asset to pay off directly claimholders who seek to withdraw funds. However, FIs tend to minimize their holdings of cash reserves as assets because those reserves pay no interest. To generate interest revenues, most FIs invest in less liquid and/or longer maturity assets. While most assets can be turned into cash eventually, for some assets this can be done only at a high cost when the asset must be liquidated immediately. The price the asset holder has to accept for immediate sale may be far less than it would be if there were a longer horizon over which to negotiate a sale. As a result, some assets may be liquidated only at low **fire-sale prices,** thus threatening the solvency of the FI. Alternatively, rather than liquidating assets, an FI may seek to purchase or borrow additional funds.

Fire-Sale Price
The price received for an asset that has to be liquidated (sold) immediately.

The second source of liquidity risk arises on the asset side as a result of lending commitments. As we described in Chapter 13, a loan commitment allows a borrower to take down funds from an FI (over a commitment period) on demand. When a loan commitment is taken down, the FI has to fund it on the balance sheet immediately; this creates a demand for liquidity. As with liability withdrawals, an FI can meet such a liquidity need by running down its cash assets, selling off other liquid assets, or borrowing additional funds.

To analyze the differing degree of importance of liquidity risk across FIs, we next analyze liquidity risk problems faced by banks and thrifts, insurance companies, and mutual and pension funds.

Concept Questions

1. What are the sources of liquidity risk?
2. Why is cash more liquid than loans for an FI?

Liquidity Risk at Banks and Thrifts

Liability-Side Liquidity Risk

As discussed in Chapter 1, typically a depository institution's balance sheet has a large amount of short-term liabilities, such as demand deposits and other transaction accounts, funding relatively long-term assets. Demand deposit accounts and other transaction accounts are contracts that give the holders the right to put their claims back to the bank on any given day and demand immediate repayment of the face value of their deposit claims in cash.[1] Thus, an individual demand deposit account holder with $10,000 in an account can turn up and demand cash immediately as readily as can a corporation with $100 million in its demand deposit account. In theory, at least, a bank that has 20 percent of its liabilities in demand deposits and

---

[1]Accounts with this type of put option include demand deposits, NOW accounts (checking accounts with minimum balance requirements), and money market accounts (checking accounts with minimum balance and number-of-checks-written restrictions). We describe these accounts in more detail in Chapter 18. Many savings account contracts give a bank some powers to delay withdrawals by requiring a certain number of days of prior notification of withdrawal or by imposing penalty fees such as loss of interest.

TABLE 17–1   Assets and Liabilities of U.S. Banks, August 1997
(in billions of dollars)

	Assets			Liabilities*	
Total securities	$1,027.7	21.97%	Total deposits	$3,029.0	70.99%
Total loans	3,083.4	65.91	Borrowings	750.4	17.59
Total cash assets	281.6	6.02	Other liabilities	487.4	11.42
Other assets	285.6	6.10	Total liabilities	$4,266.8	
Total assets	$ 4,678.3				

*Excluding bank equity capital.

Source: *Federal Reserve Bulletin,* November 1997, Table 1.26.

Core Deposits
Those deposits that provide a bank with a long-term funding source.

Deposit Drains
The amount by which cash withdrawals exceed additions; a net cash outflow.

other transaction accounts must stand ready to pay out that amount by liquidating its assets on any banking day. Table 17–1 shows an aggregate balance sheet of the assets and liability of U.S. commercial banks. As seen in this table, total deposits are approximately 71 percent of total liabilities (with 16.7 percent demand deposits and transaction accounts). By comparison, cash assets are only 6 percent of total assets. Also note that borrowed funds are 17.6 percent of total liabilities.

In reality, a depository institution knows that in normal times only a small proportion of depositors withdraw funds from their accounts, or put their account claims back to the bank, on any given day. Normally, most demand deposits act as **core deposits** on a day-by-day basis, providing a relatively long-term source of funds for an FI. Moreover, deposit withdrawals may in part be offset by the receipt of new deposits (and income generated on bank assets and off-balance-sheet activities). Specifically, over time, a depository institution manager can predict the probability distribution of net **deposit drains** on any given normal banking day.[2] Consider the two possible distributions shown in Figure 17–1.

As shown in panel (*a*) of Figure 17–1, the distribution is assumed to be strongly peaked at the 5 percent net deposit withdrawal level. That is, this FI expects approximately 5 percent of its net deposit funds to be withdrawn on any given day with the highest probability. In panel (*a*) a net deposit drain means that a bank would be receiving insufficient additional deposits (and other cash inflows) to offset deposit withdrawals. For the banking industry to be growing, most banks would have a mean or average deposit drain where new deposit funds more than offset deposit withdrawals. Thus, the peak of the net deposit drain probability distribution would be at a point to the left of zero. See the −2 percent in panel (*b*), where the bank would be receiving net cash inflows with the highest probability.

The bank in panel (*a*) has a mean or expected net positive drain on deposits, and so its new deposit funds and other cash flows are expected to be insufficient to offset deposit withdrawals. The liability side of its balance sheet would be contracting. See Table 17–2 for a simple example of an actual 5 percent net drain of deposit accounts (or, in terms of dollars, a drain of $5 million).

---

[2]Apart from predictable daily seasonality to deposit flows, there are other seasonal variations, many of which are to a greater or lesser degree predictable. For example many retail banks face above average deposit outflows around the end of the year and in the summer (due to Christmas and the vacation season). Also, many rural banks face a deposit inflow-outflow cycle that closely matches the agricultural cycle of the local crop or crops. In the planting and growing season deposits tend to fall, while in the harvest season deposits tend to rise (as crops are sold).

FIGURE 17–1

Distribution of Net Deposit Drains

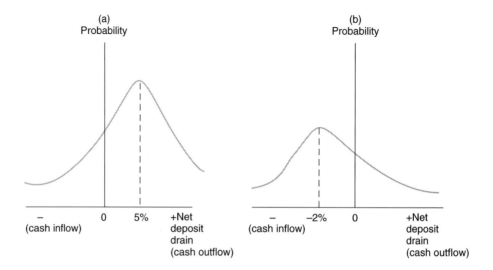

TABLE 17–2   The Effect of Net Deposit Drains on the Balance Sheet
(in millions of dollars)

		Before the Drain				After the Drain	
Assets		*Liabilities*		*Assets*		*Liabilities*	
Assets	100	Deposits	70	Assets	100	Deposits	65
		Borrowed funds	10			Borrowed funds	10
		Other liabilities	20			Other liabilities	20
	100		100		100		95

The two major ways in which the bank can meet this $5 million drain on deposits are liability management and/or reserve asset management.

Traditionally, bankers have relied on reserve asset management as the primary mechanism of adjustment. Today, many banks—especially the largest banks with access to the money market and other nondeposit markets for funds—rely on liability management to deal with the risk of cash shortfalls. A more extensive discussion of liability management techniques of liquidity management is left to Chapter 18. Here we briefly discuss the alternative methods of liquidity risk management.

Liability Management.   If a manager uses liability management, the bank turns to markets for purchased funds, such as the federal funds market and/or the repurchase agreement markets, which are interbank markets for short-term loans. Alternatively, the bank could issue additional fixed-maturity wholesale certificates of deposit or even sell some notes and bonds.[3] As long as the total amount of these funds equaled $5 million, the bank in Table 17–2 could fully fund its net deposit drain. However, this can be expensive for the bank since it is paying *market rates* for funds in the wholesale money market to offset net drains on low-interest-bearing

---

[3]The discount window is also a source of funds, but in emergency situations only. See the section on bank runs, the discount window, and deposit insurance in this chapter and Chapter 19 for more discussion of the role of the discount window.

TABLE 17–3   Adjusting to a Deposit Drain through Liability Management
(in millions of dollars)

Assets		*Liabilities*	
Assets	100	Deposits	65
		Borrowed funds	15
		Other liabilities	20
	100		100

deposits.[4] Thus, the higher the cost of purchased funds is, relative to the rates earned on assets, the less attractive liability management becomes. Table 17–3 shows the bank's balance sheet if it responds to deposit drains by using liability management techniques and markets.

Note that liability management has allowed the bank to maintain its overall balance sheet size of $100 million without disturbing the size and composition of the asset side of the balance sheet. That is, all the adjustments to the deposit drain take place on the liability side of the balance sheet. In other words, effective liability management can insulate the asset side of the balance sheet from normal drains in deposit accounts. This is one of the reasons for the enormous growth in recent years of bank liability management techniques and associated purchased fund markets such as fed funds, repurchase agreements, and CDs. (We describe and discuss these instruments in more detail in Chapter 18.)

Reserve Asset Adjustment.   Instead of meeting the net deposit drain by borrowing in the wholesale money markets, the bank could liquidate some assets. Traditionally, banks have held cash reserves at the Federal Reserve and in their vaults for this very purpose. The Federal Reserve sets minimum reserve requirements for the cash reserves banks must hold. (Currently, the Fed requires 3 percent on the first $47.8 million and 10 percent on the rest of a bank's demand deposit and transaction account holdings.)[5] Even so, banks still tend to prudently hold excess reserve assets to meet liquidity drains. As an example, the United Kingdom has no official central bank–designated cash reserve requirements; even so, banks still hold 1 percent or more of their assets in cash reserves.

Suppose, in our example, that on the asset side of the balance sheet the bank normally held 9 percent of its assets in cash. We depict the situation before the net drain in liabilities in Table 17–4. As depositors withdraw $5 million in deposits, the bank can meet this directly by running down the cash held in its vaults or by withdrawing cash reserves called correspondent balances on deposit at other banks or at the Federal Reserve. If the reduction of $5 million in deposit liabilities is met by a $5 million reduction in cash assets held by the bank, the balance sheet will be as shown in Table 17–5.

When the bank uses its cash reserve assets as the adjustment mechanism, both sides of its balance sheet contract; in this example, the bank's size shrinks from $100 to $95 million. The cost to the bank from using reserve asset adjustment, apart

---

[4]While checking accounts pay no explicit interest, transaction accounts such as NOW and money market accounts do. However, the rates paid are normally sticky and lie below purchased fund rates (see Chapter 18).

[5]The $47.8 million figure is adjusted annually along with the growth in bank deposits. The first $4.7 million of the $47.8 million is not subject to reserve requirements (the figures are as of January 1998).

TABLE 17–4   Composition of the Bank's Balance Sheet
(in millions of dollars)

Assets		Liabilities	
Cash	9	Deposits	70
Other assets	91	Borrowed funds	10
		Other liabilities	20
	100		100

TABLE 17–5   Reserve Asset Adjustment to Deposit Drain
(in millions of dollars)

Assets		Liabilities	
Cash	4	Deposits	65
Other assets	91	Borrowed funds	10
		Other liabilities	20
	95		95

from shrinkage in bank size,[6] is that it has to hold excess noninterest-bearing assets on its balance sheet.[7] Thus, the cost is the forgone return (or opportunity cost) from being unable to invest these funds in loans and other higher income earning assets.

Finally, note that while reserve asset adjustment and liability management are alternative strategies for meeting deposit drains, a bank can also combine the two methods by using some liability management and some reserve asset adjustment to meet any given deposit drain.

Asset-Side Liquidity Risk

Just as deposit drains can cause a bank liquidity problems, so can the exercise by borrowers of their loan commitments and other credit lines. In Table 17–6, $5 million of a loan commitment is exercised on a particular day. As a result, $5 million in additional loans has to be funded on the balance sheet.[8] Consider panel (*a*) in Table 17–6, the balance sheet before the commitment exercise, and panel (*b*), the balance sheet afterward. In particular, the exercise of the loan commitment means that the bank needs to provide $5 million in loans immediately to the borrower (other assets rise from $91 to $96 million). This can be done either by liability management (borrowing an additional $5 million in the money market and on-lending those funds to the borrower) or by reserve adjustment (running down the bank's own cash assets from $9 million to $4 million). We present these two policies in Table 17–7.

Measuring a Bank's Liquidity Exposure

Sources and Uses of Liquidity.   As discussed, a bank's liquidity risk can arise from a drain on deposits or new loan demands and the subsequent need to meet

---

[6]There is no empirical evidence showing a significant correlation between a bank's asset size and profits.

[7]Banks could hold highly liquid interest-bearing assets such as T-bills, but these are still less liquid than cash and immediate liquidation may result in some small capital value losses.

[8]Larger banks with more extensive commercial loan portfolios tend to be more susceptible to this type of note than are smaller retail (or consumer) -oriented banks.

TABLE 17–6   The Effects of a Loan Commitment Exercise
(in millions of dollars)

(a) Before				(b) After			
Cash	9	Deposits	70	Cash	9	Deposits	70
Other assets	91	Borrowed funds	10	Other assets	96	Borrowed funds	10
		Other liabilities	20			Other liabilities	20
	100		100		105		100

TABLE 17–7   Adjusting the Balance Sheet to a Loan Commitment Exercise
(in millions of dollars)

(a) Liability Management				(b) Cash Reserve Asset Adjustment			
Cash	9	Deposits	70	Cash	4	Deposits	70
Other assets	96	Borrowed funds	15	Other assets	96	Borrowed funds	10
		Other liabilities	20			Other liabilities	20
	105		105		100		100

TABLE 17–8   Net Liquidity Position
(in millions of dollars)

Sources of Liquidity	
1. Total cash-type assets	$ 2,000
2. Maximum borrowed funds limit	12,000
3. Excess cash reserves	500
Total	$14,500
Uses of Liquidity	
1. Funds borrowed	$ 6,000
2. Federal Reserve borrowing	1,000
Total	7,000
Total net liquidity	$ 7,500

those demands through liquidating assets or borrowing funds. Therefore, an FI manager must be able to measure the liquidity position on a daily basis, if possible. A useful tool is a net liquidity statement that lists the sources and uses of liquidity and thus provides a measure of an FI's net liquidity position. Look at such a statement for a hypothetical U.S. money center bank in Table 17–8.

The bank has three primary sources of liquidity: First, its cash-type assets such as T-bills can be sold immediately with little price risk and low transaction costs; second, the maximum amount of funds it can borrow on the money/purchased funds market (this *internal* guideline is based on the manager's assessment of the credit limits the purchased or borrowed funds market is likely to impose on the bank); and third, any excess cash reserves over and above those held to meet regulatory imposed reserve requirements. As you can see, the bank's total sources of liquidity are $14,500 million. Compare this to the bank's *uses* of liquidity, in particular the amount of borrowed or money market funds it has already utilized (e.g., fed funds, RPs borrowed) and the amount it has already borrowed from the Federal Reserve through discount window loans. These add up to $7,000 million. As a result, the bank has a positive net liquidity position of $7,500 million. The position can be easily tracked on a day-by-day basis.

Peer Group Ratio Comparisons.   Another way to measure an FI's liquidity exposure is to compare certain key ratios and balance sheet features of the bank, such as its loans–deposits, borrowed funds–total assets, and commitments to lend–assets ratios, with those of banks of a similar size and geographic location. A high ratio of loans-deposits and borrowed funds–total assets means that the bank is placing a heavy reliance on the short-term money market rather than core deposits to fund loans. This could mean future liquidity problems if the bank is at or near its borrowing limits in the purchased funds market. Similarly, a high ratio of loan commitments to assets indicates a need for a high degree of liquidity to fund any unexpected takedowns of these loans. That is, high-commitment banks often face more liquidity risk exposure than do low-commitment banks.

Liquidity Index.   A third way to measure liquidity risk is by using the liquidity index. Developed by Jim Pierce at the Federal Reserve, this index measures the potential losses suffered by an FI from a sudden or fire-sale disposal of assets compared to a fair market value established under normal market (sale) conditions—which might take a lengthy period of time as a result of a careful search and bidding process. The greater the differences between immediate fire-sale asset prices (P_i) and fair market prices (P_i^*), the less liquid the FI's portfolio of assets. That is, define an index I such that

$$I = \sum_{i=1}^{N} [(w_i)(P_i/P_i^*)]$$

where w_i is the percent of each asset in the FI's portfolio:

$$\sum_{i=1}^{N} w_i = 1$$

For example, suppose an FI has two assets: 50 percent in one-month Treasury bills and 50 percent in real estate loans. If the FI has to liquidate its T-bills today (P_1), it will receive $99 per $100 of face value; if it can wait to liquidate them on maturity (in one month's time), it will receive $100 per $100 of face value ($P_1^*$). If the FI had to liquidate its real estate loans today, it would receive $85 per $100 of face value ($P_2$), while liquidation at the end of one month would be expected to produce $92 per $100 of face value ($P_2^*$). Thus, the one-month liquidity index value for this FI's asset portfolio would be

$$\begin{aligned} I &= (\tfrac{1}{2}) \, [(.99/1.00)] + \tfrac{1}{2}[(.85/.92)] \\ &= 0.495 + 0.462 \\ &= 0.957 \end{aligned}$$

The liquidity index will always lie between 0 and a maximum of 1. The liquidity index for this FI could also be compared to similar indexes calculated for a peer group of similar FIs.

Financing Gap and the Financing Requirement.   A fourth way to measure liquidity risk exposure is to measure the bank's financing gap. As we discussed earlier,

TABLE 17–9   The Financing Requirement of a Bank
(in millions of dollars)

Assets		Liabilities	
Loans	$25	Core deposits	$20
Liquid assets	5	Financing requirement	
		(borrowed funds)	10
Total	$30	Total	$30
		Financing gap	(5)

Financing Gap
The difference between a bank's average loans and average (core) deposits.

even though demand depositors can withdraw their funds immediately, in normal circumstances they don't. On average, most demand deposits stay at banks for quite long periods—often two years or more.[9] Thus, a banker often thinks of the average deposit base, including demand deposits, as a core source of funds that over time can fund a bank's average amount of loans.

We define a **financing gap** (Fgap) as:

$$\text{Financing gap} = \text{Average loans} - \text{Average deposits}$$

If this financing gap is positive, the bank has to fund it by running down its cash and liquid assets and/or borrowing funds on the money market. Thus:

$$\text{Financing gap} = -\text{Liquid assets} + \text{Borrowed funds}$$

We can write this relationship as

$$\text{Financing gap} + \text{Liquid assets} = \text{Financing requirement (borrowed funds)}$$

Financing Requirement
The financing gap plus a bank's liquid assets.

As expressed in this fashion, the liquidity and managerial implications of the **financing requirement** are that some level of core deposits and loans and some amount of liquid assets determine the bank's borrowing or purchased fund needs. In particular, the larger a bank's financing gap and liquid asset holdings, the larger the amount of funds it needs to borrow on the money markets and the greater its exposure to liquidity problems from that reliance.

We present an example of the relationship between the financing gap, liquid assets, and the borrowed fund financing requirement in Table 17–9. See also the following equation:

$$\underset{(5)}{\text{Financing gap}} + \underset{(5)}{\text{Liquid assets}} = \underset{(10)}{\text{Financing requirement}}$$

A rising financing gap can warn of future liquidity problems for a bank since it may indicate increased deposit withdrawals (core deposits falling below 20 in Table 17–9) and rising loans due to increased exercise of loan commitments (loans rising above 25). If the bank does not reduce its liquid assets—they stay at 5—the manager will have to resort to more money market borrowings. As these borrowings rise, sophisticated lenders in the money market may be concerned about the creditworthiness of the bank. They may react by imposing higher risk premiums for borrowed funds or establishing stricter credit limits by not rolling over funds lent to the bank. If the banker's financing requirements exceed such limits, the bank is effectively

---

[9]See Federal Reserve Board of Governors, "Risk-Based Capital and Interest Rate Risk," press release, July 30, 1992.

insolvent. A good example of an excessive financing requirement resulting in bank insolvency was the failure of Continental Illinois in 1984.[10] This also indicates a need for FI managers to engage in active liquidity planning to avoid such crises.

Liquidity Planning.   Liquidity planning is a key component of forecasting (and being able to deal with) liquidity problems. Specifically, it allows managers to make important borrowing decisions before relatively predictable events occur. Such forward planning can lower the cost of funds (by determining an optimal funding mix) and minimize the amount of excess reserves a bank needs to hold.

A liquidity plan will have a number of components. First, it will delineate managerial details and responsibilities. These include assigning responsibilities to key management personnel during a liquidity crisis, including identifying those managers responsible for interacting with regulatory agencies such as the Federal Reserve, the FDIC, and OTS. It will also specify areas of managerial responsibility in disclosing information to the public—including depositors. Second, it will include a detailed list of those fund providers that are most likely to withdraw as well as the seasonality of fund withdrawals. For example, in a crisis, financial institutions such as mutual funds and pension funds are likely to withdraw funds more quickly from banks and thrifts than correspondent banks and small business corporations. In turn, correspondent banks and small corporations are likely to withdraw funds more quickly than individual depositors. This makes liquidity exposure sensitive to the effects of future changes in funding composition. Further, FIs such as banks and thrifts face particularly heavy seasonal withdrawals of deposits in the quarter before Christmas. Third, it will identify the size of potential deposit and fund runoffs over various time horizons in the future (one week, one month, one quarter, etc.) as well as alternative private market funding sources to meet such runoffs, (e.g., emergency loans from other FIs as well as the Federal Reserve). Fourth, the plan will involve internal limits on separate subsidiaries' and branches' borrowings as well as bounds for acceptable risk premiums to pay in each market (fed funds, RPs, CDs, etc.). In addition, it will detail a sequencing of assets for disposal in anticipation of various degrees or intensities of deposit/fund withdrawals. Such a plan may evolve from the asset–liability management committee of an FI and be relayed to various key departments of the FI—for example, the money desk and the treasury department—which play vital day-to-day roles in liability funding.

Liquidity Risk, Unexpected Deposit Drains, and Bank Runs

Under normal conditions and with appropriate forward planning, net deposit withdrawals and the exercise of loan commitments pose few liquidity problems for banks because borrowed funds availability or excess cash reserves are adequate to meet anticipated needs. For example, even in December and the summer vacation

---

[10]Continenal Illinois, headquartered in Chicago, had a very small core deposit base due to restriction on bank branching within the state. As a result, it had to rely extensively on borrowed funds such as fed funds, RPs, and Eurodollar deposits (wholesale CDs from the offshore Euromarkets). As these borrowings grew, there were increased concerns about the bank's ability to meet its payment commitments—especially in view of a worsening loan portfolio. This resulted in the eventual refusal of a number of large money market lenders (such as Japanese banks) to renew or roll over their borrowed funds held by Continental Illinois on maturity. With the rapid withdrawal of such borrowed funds, Continental Illinois was unable to survive and was eventually taken over by the FDIC. For good detailed descriptions of the Continental Illinois failure, see I. Swary, "Stock Market Reaction to Regulatory Action in the Continental Illinois Crisis," *Journal of Business* 59 (1986), pp. 451–73; and L. Wall and D. R. Peterson, "The Effect of Continental Illinois' Failure on the Performance of Other Banks," *Journal of Monetary Economics,* 1990, pp. 77–99.

season, when net deposit withdrawals are high, banks anticipate these *seasonal* effects through holding larger than normal excess cash reserves or borrowing more than they normally do on the wholesale money markets.

Major liquidity problems can arise, however, if deposit drains are abnormally *large* and unexpected. Such deposit withdrawal shocks may occur for a number of reasons, including:

1. Concerns about a bank's solvency relative to other banks.
2. Failure of a related bank leading to heightened depositor concerns about the solvency of other banks (the contagion effect).
3. Sudden changes in investor preferences regarding holding nonbank financial assets (such as T-bills) relative to deposits.

Bank Run

A sudden and unexpected increase in deposit withdrawals from a bank.

Any sudden unexpected surge in net deposit withdrawals risks triggering a **bank run** that would eventually force a bank into insolvency.[11] The Contemporary Perspectives box on page 368 discusses recent runs on banks (and cake shops) in Hong Kong.

Deposit Drains and Bank Run Liquidity Risk.   At the core of bank run liquidity risk is the fundamental and unique nature of the *demand deposit contract*. Specifically, demand deposit contracts are first come, first served contracts in the sense that a depositor's place in line matters in withdrawing funds. In particular, a depositor either gets paid in full or gets nothing. To see this, suppose a bank has 100 depositors who each deposited $1. Suppose each has a reason to believe—correctly or incorrectly—that the bank has assets valued at only $90 on its balance sheet (see Table 17–10).

As a result, each depositor has an incentive to go to the bank quickly to withdraw his or her $1 deposit because the bank pays off depositors sequentially by liquidating its assets. If it has $90 in assets, it can pay off, in full, only the first 90 depositors in the line. The 10 depositors at the end of the line will get *nothing at all*. Thus, demand deposits are in essence either full pay or no pay contracts. We show the sequential nature of deposit withdrawals, and the importance of being first in line, for our troubled bank in Figure 17–2.

TABLE 17–10   Bank Run Incentives

	Assets		*Liabilities*
Assets	$90	Deposits	$100 (100 × $1 each)

FIGURE 17–2

Place in Line Matters for Bank Depositors

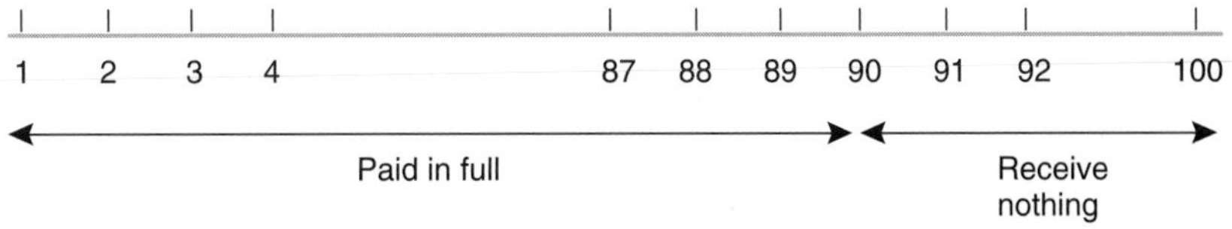

Footnotes:

[11]For more analysis regarding the details of bank runs, see D. W. Diamond and P. H. Dybvig, "Bank Runs, Deposit Insurance, and Liquidity," *Journal of Political Economy* 91 (1983), pp. 401–19; and G. Kaufman, "Bank Contagion: Theory and Evidence," *Journal of Financial Services Research* 8 (1994), pp. 123–50.

Contemporary Perspectives

IN HONG KONG, RUNS ON BANKS AND CAKES

Edward A. Gargan

First it was bank runs. Then cake runs. And then arcade runs.

A series of small-scale panics have been afflicting Hong Kong the last month, a sign, perhaps, of deeper problems.

It started with rumors that the **International Bank of Asia** was in trouble, dragged down by the crisis ricocheting through Asia. Crowds thundered to the bank, harried managers threw up their hands and armored trucks arrived with hundreds of millions of Hong Kong dollars. Customers got their money—and in the end, the bank carried on.

Then the air was rife with hints that the Saint Honore Cake Shops, owned in part by Yaohan, a dying Japanese company, was about to go under. Once again crowds stampeded, cashing in gift certificates that the shops had sold. Cakes leaped from shelves (and shelves collapsed), bakers worked overtime—300,000 eggs, 2.23 tons of flour and 1.34 tons of butter in 24 hours—and Saint Honore carried on.

And just when people had started to eat all the cakes they had stashed in their cupboards, a rumor red alert went out on Whimsy amusement arcades, which were also partly owned by Yaohan. Engulfed in clanging bells, bongs and the electronic beeps of computer games, customers jammed their way into the arcades to use promotional tickets they had won through years of plugging rolls of coins into the machines.

While it may be tempting to dismiss these incidents as nothing more than minor rumor-mongering, they are widely seen here as signs of broader distress brought about by the financial panic sweeping Asia and by Hong Kong's own problems. The former British colony is barely five months from its takeover by China, and the people of Hong Kong are still uncertain about what their new master intends.

"Things somehow do seem a little fragile," said Diahann Brown, a fund manager with Thornton Management. "Hong Kong is in good shape basically, but weird things do happen here."

Hong Kong's pattern of solid growth is fraying, with the Government estimating a slowdown from this year's 5.5 percent growth in gross domestic product to 5 percent next year. Private economists are less sanguine. Ian Perkins, chief economist of the Hong Kong General Chamber of Commerce, projects a growth rate of 4 percent next year, a lethargic pace not seen here in more than a decade.

"Weaker growth in domestic consumption will be the chief culprit," Mr. Perkins said, "although there will also be slower growth in capital investment."

And joblessness, almost unknown here, is beginning to creep up.

Yaohan's chain of department stores shut its doors late last month, throwing 2,700 people out of work. Real estate agencies across the territory are closing and investment houses and brokerage firms are dismissing staff members in droves.

And while the rate of unemployment remains low, 2.3 percent in September and October, up 0.1 percent from the preceding two-month period, most analysts think it will continue to head up.

In many respects, Hong Kong would appear to be in great financial shape. It has one of the globe's strongest

Because demand deposit contracts pay off in full only a certain proportion of depositors when a bank's assets are valued at less than its deposits—and because depositors realize this—any line outside a bank encourages other depositors to join immediately even if the depositor doesn't need cash today for normal consumption purposes.[12] Thus, even the bank's core depositors who don't really need to withdraw deposits for consumption needs, on observing a sudden increase in the lines at their bank, rationally seek to withdraw their funds immediately.

As a bank run develops, the demand for net deposit withdrawals grows. The bank may initially meet this by running down its cash reserves, selling off liquid or readily marketable assets such as T-bills and T-bonds, and seeking to borrow in the

---

[12]Here we are assuming no deposit insurance or discount window. The presence of deposit insurance and the discount window alters the incentives to engage in a bank run, as we describe later in this chapter and in Chapter 19.

Contemporary Perspectives

banking sectors. Its companies are not wallowing in debt. The Government runs a fat surplus. Interest rates are high, but both housing and office space is in short supply. And Chinese companies wanting to raise money are generally able to descend on the local stock exchange and walk away handsomely.

But the smell on Hong Kong's streets is still sour.

"We are moving from expansion to slowing in the economic cycle," said Miron Mushkat, the director of economics and strategy for Indocam Asia Asset Management. "Largely it's externally induced but transmitted through asset prices, which will dampen domestic demand. From a regional perspective, because of Korea, we cannot close the chapter on this."

Real estate, long the bulwark of the economy and the stock market, has been jolted by the stock market's decline—from a high of 16,673 in August to 10,754 today, after plummeting below 9,000 last month—with home buyers proving to be noticeably skittish.

Fueled by last year's strong economy, the number of real estate agents here soared to 25,000 (double the number of lawyers and doctors combined), from 18,000 in 1996. But with buyers reluctant to spend for new apartments and many people deciding to put off moves, real estate agencies are shutting down and layoffs are spreading.

And, said Michael Choi Ngai-min, the managing director of Hong Kong Property Services, "The worst is to come."

He estimated that if the market did not recover, more than a third of the territory's real estate agents would be out of work by January. Goodfortune Realty, one of the bigger agencies, collapsed recently, closing all 23 of its offices and laying off all 240 employees. Even brokerage firms and banks are laying off staff. Peregrine Investments Holdings, an investment bank, slashed 275 jobs from its work force of about 2,000 at the end of November.

Hotels and restaurants have been hit hard, too.

"In the last few weeks business has been down 10 to 20 percent," said Tommy Cheung, the president of the Association of Restaurant Managers. "That's a big drop. There have been more closings in recent months than in the same period of last year."

Hotels are laying off staff, and the local airline, Cathay Pacific, is running partly empty flights and is losing money on what used to be some of its most lucrative routes, particularly flights to and from Japan.

The carrier on Wednesday deferred options to acquire 13 new aircraft in 1998 and 1999. It was believed that the decision was made because of the sharp drop in visitors.

The Hong Kong Government remains resolutely upbeat, with the chief executive appointed by Beijing to administer the territory, the shipping tycoon Tung Chee-hwa, repeatedly boasting about Hong Kong's strong economy.

But to a 46-year-old woman who sold sweaters at one of the Yaohan department stores, which are now closed, that strength is hard to see.

"I'm not sure what I will do," said the woman, who would only give her surname, Wong, as she prepared for the store's closing last month. "For someone like me there isn't much future now. Even if I get another job, will it be as good as this one? I don't think it will."

Source: *New York Times*, December 19, 1997, p. 3. Copyright © 1997 by The New York Times. Reprinted by permission.

---

money markets. As a bank run increases in intensity, more depositors join the withdrawal line, and a liquidity crisis develops. Specifically, the bank would find it difficult, if not impossible, to borrow on the money markets at virtually any price. Also, it would have sold off all its liquid assets, cash, and bonds as well as any loans that are saleable (see Chapter 27). All the bank is likely to have left is relatively illiquid loans on the asset side of the balance sheet to meet depositors' claims for cash. However, these loans can be sold or liquidated only at very large discounts from face value. For example, the Resolution Trust Corporation, which until 1995 disposed of assets formerly held by failed thrifts, found it difficult to dispose of some commercial real estate loans at almost any price!

A bank needing to liquidate long-term assets at fire-sale prices to meet continuing deposit drains faces the strong possibility that the proceeds from such asset sales will be insufficient to meet depositors' cash demands. The bank's liquidity problem would turn into a solvency problem; that is, the bank would have to close its doors.

Bank Panic
A systemic or contagious
run on the deposits of the
banking industry as a
whole.

The incentives for depositors to run first and ask questions later creates a fundamental instability in the banking system such that an otherwise sound bank can be pushed into insolvency and failure by unexpectedly large depositor drains and liquidity demands. This is especially so in periods of contagious runs or **bank panics,** when depositors lose faith in the banking system as a whole and engage in a run on all banks by not materially discriminating among them according to their asset qualities.[13]

Bank Runs, the Discount Window, and Deposit Insurance

Regulators have recognized the inherent instability of the banking system due to the all or nothing payoff features of the deposit contract. As a result, regulatory mechanisms are in place to ease the liquidity problems of banks and to deter bank runs and panics. The two major liquidity risk insulation devices are deposit insurance and the discount window. We discuss these in detail in Chapter 19. As we describe there, deposit insurance has effectively deterred bank panics since 1933, although the provision of deposit insurance has not been without other costs.

Concept Questions

1. List two benefits and two costs of using (*a*) liability management and (*b*) reserve or cash assets to meet a deposit drain.
2. What are the three major sources of bank liquidity? What are the two major uses?
3. Which factors determine the financing requirement of an FI?

Liquidity Risk and Life Insurance Companies

Banks and thrifts are not the only FIs exposed to liquidity risk or run problems. Similar to banks, life insurance companies hold some cash reserves to meet policy cancellations and other working capital needs. In the normal course of business, premium income and returns on the asset portfolio are sufficient to meet the cash outflows required when policyholders cash in or surrender their policies early. As with banks, the distribution or pattern of premium income minus policyholder liquidations is normally predicable. When premium income is insufficient, a life insurer can sell off some of its relatively liquid assets, such as government bonds. Here bonds act as a buffer or reserve asset fund for the insurer. As with banks, concerns about the solvency of the insurer or insurance company in general can result in a run where new premium income dries up and existing policyholders seek to cancel their policies by cashing them in for their **surrender values.**[14] To meet

Surrender Value
The amount received by
an insurance policyholder
when cashing in a policy
early.

---

[13]See Kaufman, "Bank Contagion," for an excellent review of the nature and causes of bank runs and panics. There is strong evidence of contagious bank runs or panics in 1930–32 in the United States. See A. Saunders and B. Wilson, "Informed and Uninformed Depositor Runs and Panics: Evidence from the 1929–33 Period, *Journal of Financial Intermediation* 5 (1996), pp. 409–23.

[14]A surrender value is usually some proportion or percent less than 100 percent of the face value of the insurance contract.

Some insurance companies have also faced run problems resulting from their sale of guaranteed investment contracts (GICs). A GIC, similar to a long-term, fixed-rate bank deposit, is made by an investor with an insurance company. As market interest rates rose, many investors withdrew their funds and reinvested elsewhere in higher-return investments. This created both liquidity and refinancing problems for life insurers that supplied such contracts and eventually led to restrictions on withdrawals.

exceptional demands for cash, a life insurer could be forced to liquidate the less liquid assets in its portfolio, such as commercial mortgage loans and other securities, at potentially fire-sale prices.[15] As with banks, forced asset liquidations can push an insurer into insolvency. A good example of an insurance company run occurred in 1991 on First Executive Corporation, a large California-based insurer. Losses on its junk bond portfolio raised regulator and policyholder concerns about the quality of its balance sheet. New policyholder premiums dried up, and existing policyholders engaged in a run by seeking to cash in their policies for whatever surrender values they could get. To deter the run, the California state insurance regulator placed limits on the ability of existing policyholders to surrender their policies.[16]

Concept Questions

1. What is likely to be a life insurance company's first source of liquidity when premium income is insufficient?
2. Can a life insurance company be subjected to a run? If so, why?

Liquidity Risk and Property-Casualty Insurers

As discussed in Chapter 2, property-casualty insurers sell policies insuring against certain contingencies impacting either real property or individuals. Unlike life insurers, the contingencies (and policy coverages) are relatively short term, often one to three years. As a result, PC insurers' assets tend to be shorter term and more liquid than those of life insurers. Also, contracts and premium-setting intervals are usually relatively short term as well, and so problems caused by policy surrenders are less severe. Their greatest exposure arises if policyholders cancel or fail to renew policies because of insolvency risk, pricing, or competitive reasons. This may result in their premium cash inflow, when added to their investment returns, being insufficient to meet policy claims. Or large unexpected claims may materialize and exceed the flow of premium income and income returns from assets. Disasters such as Hurricane Andrew in 1991 and the blizzard of the century in 1996 have caused severe liquidity crises and failures among smaller PC insurers.[17]

Concept Questions

1. What is the greatest cause of liquidity exposure faced by property-casualty insurers?
2. Is the liquidity risk of property-casualty insurers in general greater or less than that of life insurers?

---

[15]Life insurers also provide a considerable amount of loan commitments, especially in the commercial property area. As a result, they face asset-side loan commitment liquidity risk in a similar fashion to banks.

[16]State guaranty schemes also deter policyholder runs. In general, the level of coverage and the value of the guarantees are less than deposit insurance. We discuss these guaranty schemes in Chapter 19. See also H. L. DeAngelo, L. DeAngelo, and S. Gilson, "The Collapse of First Executive Corporation: Junk Bonds, Adverse Publicity, and the 'Run on the Bank' Phenomenon," *Journal of Financial Economics* 36 (1994), pp. 287–336.

[17]Also, claims may arise in so-called long-tail lines where a contingency takes place during the policy period but a claim is not lodged until many years later. As mentioned in Chapter 2, one example is the claims regarding damage caused by asbestos contact.

Mutual Funds

Mutual funds sell shares as liabilities to investors and invest the proceeds in assets such as bonds and equities. Mutual funds are open-ended and closed-ended. **Closed-end funds** issue a fixed number of shares as liabilities; unless the issuing fund chooses to repurchase them, the quantity of outstanding shares does not change. As discussed in Chapter 4, by far the majority of U.S. mutual funds are **open-end funds;** that is, they can issue an unlimited supply of shares to investors. Open-end funds must also stand ready to buy back previously issued shares from investors at the current market price for the fund's shares.

We show the supply function of open-ended mutual fund shares in Figure 17–3. Thus, at a given market price—0P in Figure 17–3—the supply of open-end fund shares is perfectly elastic. The price at which an open-end mutual fund stands ready to sell new shares or redeem existing shares is the **net asset value** (NAV) of the fund. NAV is the current or market value of the fund's assets divided by the number of shares in the fund. A mutual fund's willingness to provide instant liquidity to shareholders while investing funds in equities, bonds, and other long-term instruments could expose it to liquidity problems similar to those of banks, thrifts, and life insurance companies when withdrawals (or cashing in of mutual fund shares) rise to abnormally and unexpectedly high levels. However, the fundamental difference in the way mutual fund contracts are valued compared to bank deposit and insurance policy contracts mitigates the incentives for mutual fund shareholders to engage in runs. Specifically, if a mutual fund were to be liquidated, its assets would be distributed to mutual fund shareholders on a pro rata basis rather than the first come, first served basis employed under deposit and insurance contracts.

To illustrate this difference, we can directly compare the incentives for mutual fund investors to engage in a run with those of bank depositors. In Table 17–11 we show a simple balance sheet of an open-ended mutual fund and a bank. When they perceive a bank's assets are valued below its liabilities, depositors have an incentive to engage in a run on the bank to be first in line to withdraw. In the example in Table 17–11, only the first 90 bank depositors would receive a dollar back for each dollar deposited. The last 10 would receive nothing at all.

Now consider the mutual fund with 100 shareholders who invested a total of $100 but whose assets are worth $90. If these shareholders tried to cash in their shares, *none* would receive $1 back. Instead, a mutual fund values its balance sheet liabilities on a market value basis: the price of any share liquidated by an investor is

$$P = \frac{\text{Value of assets}}{\text{Shares outstanding}} = \text{NAV (net asset value)}$$

Thus, unlike deposit contracts that have fixed face values of $1, the value of a mutual fund's shares reflects the changing value of the fund's assets divided by the number of shares outstanding. In Table 17–11, the value of each shareholder's claim would be

$$P = \frac{\$90}{100} = \$.9$$

That is, each mutual fund shareholder participates in the fund's loss of asset value on a *pro rata* or proportional basis. Technically, whether first or last in line, each shareholder who cashes in shares on any given day would receive the net asset value of the mutual fund. In this case, it is 90 cents, representing a loss of 10 cents

FIGURE 17–3

The Supply of Shares of an Open-End Mutual Fund

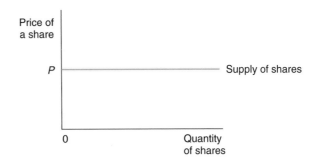

TABLE 17–11   Run Incentives of Bank Depositors versus Mutual Fund Investors

Bank			Mutual Fund		
Assets		*Liabilities*	*Assets*		*Liabilities*
Assets	$90	$100 Deposits (100 depositors with $1 deposits)	Assets	$90	$100 Shares (100 shareholders with $1 shares)

per share. All mutual fund shareholders realize this and know that asset losses are shared among investors on a pro rata basis; there is no overall advantage to being first in line to withdraw, unlike the case for bank deposits.

This is not to say that mutual funds bear no liquidity risk, but rather that the incentives for mutual fund shareholders to engage in runs that produce the extreme form of liquidity problems faced by banks, thrifts, and life insurance companies are generally absent.[18] This has led some academics to argue for a restructuring of deposit contracts in a form more similar to mutual fund or equity contracts. This might also obviate the need for deposit insurance to deter bank runs.[19] The Contemporary Perspectives box on page 374 shows some recent regulatory concerns about the liquidity of emerging-market mutual funds.[20]

---

[18]A sudden surge of mutual fund shareholder redemptions might require a mutual fund manager to sell off some of its less marketable bonds and equities at fire-sale prices. For example, in 1994, Piper Jafray—a funds adviser—injected $10 million of its own funds to defray a liquidity problem at the Institutional Government Income mutual fund.

[19]See C. S. Jacklin, "Demand Deposits, Trading Restrictions, and Risk Sharing," in *Contractual Arrangements for Intertemporal Trade,* ed. E. Prescott and N. Wallace (Duluth: University of Minnesota, 1987). A common argument against this is that since deposits are money and money is the unit of account in the economy, equity-type contracts could pose a problem if the value of a deposit were to fluctuate from day to day. However, note that money market mutual funds offer depositlike contracts as well. As their NAV varies, they solve the fluctuating share value problem by setting the value of each share at $1 but allowing the number of shares an individual holds to fluctuate so that the value of the individual's overall holdings moves in line with asset values, while the price of each money market mutual fund share remains at $1. A similar policy could be adopted for deposits at banks.

[20]Relatedly, a number of hedge funds, such as Long-Term Capital Management, faced severe liquidity problems when trying to unwind large positions in many assets markets at the end of 1998. For example, some mortgage-backed securities markets (see Chapter 28) were insufficiently "deep" to be able to absorb the massive sale of hedge fund assets without major price dislocations.

Contemporary Perspectives

SEC OFFICIAL SEES SMALL-MARKET FUND LIQUIDITY RISK

A top U.S. mutual funds regulator said Tuesday he is concerned about potential liquidity problems confronting the growing number of mutual funds investing in emerging and other small markets.

"I have fears that we could see problems with some kinds of markets . . . It does concern me," said Barry Barbash, director of the division of investment management of the U.S. Securities & Exchange Commission.

Liquidity means the ability of a fund to buy and sell the securities it owns on short notice—an eventuality that can arise if mutual fund investors suddenly want their money back. Liquidity can be hard to come by, though, in markets with limited numbers of active buyers and sellers. "The problem can arise in any sort of market that is smaller," Barbash said.

In search of superior returns, a growing number of mutual funds have poured money into small markets, such as emerging economies and small- and micro-cap stocks.

In the $3 trillion mutual fund business, with about 40,000 funds worldwide, potential liquidity problems at small-market funds likely do not pose a risk to the entire industry.

The risk faced by emerging country funds is that a political, military or other surprise—whether in Russia, China or Latin America—could frighten investors, leading to a wave of share redemption requests.

In an illiquid market, that could cause big problems, Barbash said, adding that it may only be a matter of time before the mutual fund industry finds out just how big.

"At some point there will be a test and we'll see what happens."

Emerging country funds are not the only type of mutual funds that could be vulnerable to a liquidity crunch.

Micro-capitalization stock funds in the United States and other highly specialized funds run such risks, too.

_____

Source: *The Reuters Business Report,* November 12, 1996.

Concept Questions

1. What would be the impact on their liquidity needs if banks offered deposit contracts of an open-ended mutual fund type rather than the traditional all or nothing demand deposit contract?
2. How do the incentives of mutual fund investors to engage in runs compare with the incentives of bank depositors?

Summary

Liquidity risk, as a result of heavier than anticipated liability withdrawals or loan commitment exercise, is a common problem faced by FI managers. Well-developed policies for holding liquid assets or having access to markets for purchased funds are normally adequate to meet liability withdrawals. However, very large withdrawals can cause asset liquidity problems that can be compounded by incentives for liability claimholders to engage in runs at the first sign of a liquidity problem. These incentives for depositors and life insurance policyholders to engage in runs can push normally sound FIs into insolvency. Mutual funds are able to avoid runs because liabilities are marked to market so that losses are shared equally among liability holders. Since such insolvencies have costs to society as well as to private shareholders, regulators have developed mechanisms such as deposit insurance and the discount window to alleviate liquidity problems. We discuss these mechanisms in detail in Chapter 19.

Questions and Problems

1. How does the degree of liquidity risk differ for different types of financial institutions?

2. What are the two reasons why liquidity risk arises? How does liquidity risk arising from the liability side of the balance sheet differ from liquidity risk arising from the asset side of the balance sheet? What is meant by fire-sale prices?

3. What are core deposits? What role do core deposits play in predicting the probability distribution of net deposit drains?

4. The probability distribution of the net deposit drain of an FI has been estimated to have a mean of 2 percent and a standard deviation of 1 percent. Is this bank increasing or decreasing in size? Explain.

5. How is the bank's distribution pattern of net deposit drains affected by the following?
   a. The holiday season.
   b. Summer vacations.
   c. A severe economic recession.
   d. Double-digit inflation.

6. What are two ways in which an FI can offset the liquidity effects of a net deposit drain of funds? How do the two methods differ? What are the operational benefits and costs of each method?

7. What are three ways in which an FI can offset the effects of asset-side liquidity risk such as the drawing down of a loan commitment?

8. An FI with the following balance sheet (in millions) expects a net deposit drain of $15 million.

Assets		Liabilities and Equity	
Cash	$10	Deposits	$68
Loans	$50	Equity	$ 7
Securities	$15		
Total assets	$75	Total liabilities and equity	$75

   Show the FI's balance sheet if the following conditions occur.
   a. The bank purchases liabilities to offset this expected drain.
   b. The reserve-asset adjustment method is used to meet the expected drain.

9. AllStarBank has the following balance sheet (in millions):

Assets		Liabilities and Equity	
Cash	$ 30	Deposits	$110
Loans	$ 90	Borrowed funds	$ 40
Securities	$ 50	Equity	$ 20
Total assets	$170	Total liabilities and equity	$170

   AllStarBank's largest customer decides to exercise a $15 million loan commitment. How will the new balance sheet appear if AllStar uses the following liquidity risk strategies?
   a. Asset management.
   b. Liability management.

10. An FI has assets of $10 million consisting of $1 million in cash and $9 million in loans. The FI has core deposits of $6 million, subordinated debt of $2 million, and equity of $2 million. Increases in interest rates are expected to cause a net drain of $2 million in core deposits over the year.
    a. The average cost of deposits is 6 percent, and the average yield on loans is 8 percent. The FI decides to reduce its loan portfolio to offset this expected decline in deposits. What will be the effect on net interest income and the size of the FI after the implementation of this strategy?
    b. If the interest cost of issuing new short-term debt is expected to be 7.5 percent, what would be the effect on net interest income of offsetting the expected deposit drain with an increase in interest-bearing liabilities?
    c. What will be the size of the FI after the drain using this strategy?
    d. What dynamic aspects of bank management would further support a strategy of replacing the deposit drain with interest-bearing liabilities?

11. Define each of the following four measures of liquidity risk. Explain how each measure would be implemented and utilized by an FI.
    a. Sources and uses of liquidity.
    b. Peer group ratio comparisons.
    c. Liquidity index.
    d. Financing gap and financing requirement.

12. An FI has $10 million in T-bills, a $5 million line of credit to borrow in the repo market, and $5 million in excess cash reserves (above reserve requirements) with the Fed. The FI currently has borrowed $6 million in fed funds and $2 million from the fed discount window to meet seasonal demands.
    a. What is the bank's total available (sources of) liquidity?
    b. What is the bank's current total uses of liquidity?
    c. What is the net liquidity of the bank?
    d. What conclusions can you derive from the result?

13. An FI has the following assets in its portfolio: $20 million in cash reserves with the Fed, $20 million in T-bills, $50 million in mortgage loans, and $10 million in fixed

assets. If the assets need to be liquidated at short notice, the FI will receive only 99 percent of the fair market value of the T-bills and 90 percent of the fair market value of the mortgage loans. Estimate the liquidity index using the above information.

14. Conglomerate Corporation has acquired Acme Corporation. To help finance the takeover, Conglomerate will liquidate the overfunded portion of Acme's pension fund. The face values and current and one-year future liquidation values of the assets that will be liquidated are given below.

Liquidation Values

Asset	Face Value	$t = 0$	$t = 1$
IBM stock	$10,000	$ 9,900	$10,500
GE bonds	$ 5,000	$ 4,000	$ 4,500
Treasury securities	$15,000	$13,000	$14,000

Calculate the one-year liquidity index for these securities.

15. Plainbank has $10 million in cash and equivalents, $30 million in loans, and $15 million in core deposits.
    a. Calculate the financing gap.
    b. What is the financing requirement?
    c. How can the financing gap be used in the day-to-day liquidity management of the bank?

16. How can an FI's liquidity plan help reduce the effects of liquidity shortages? What are the components of a liquidity plan?

17. What is a bank run? What are some possible withdrawal shocks that could initiate a bank run? What feature of the demand deposit contract provides deposit withdrawal momentum that can result in a bank run?

18. The following is the balance sheet of an FI in millions:

Assets		Liabilities and Equity	
Cash	$ 2	Demand deposits	$50
Loans	$50		
Plant and equipment	$ 3	Equity	$ 5
Total	$55	Total	$55

The asset-liability management committee has estimated that the loans, whose average interest rate is 6 percent and whose average life is three years, will have to be discounted at 10 percent if they are to be sold in less than two days. If they can be sold in four days, they will have to be discounted at 8 percent. If they can be sold later than a week, the FI will receive the full market value. Loans are not amortized; that is, the principal is paid at maturity.

a. What will be the price received by the FI for the loans if they have to be sold in (i) two days and (ii) four days.
b. In a crisis, if depositors all demand payment on the first day, what amount will they receive? What will they receive if they demand to be paid within the week? Assume no deposit insurance.

19. What government safeguards are in place to reduce liquidity risk for banks?

20. What are the first, second, and third levels of defense against liquidity risk for a life insurance company? How does liquidity risk for a property-casualty insurer differ from that for a life insurance company?

21. How is the liquidity problem faced by mutual funds different from that faced by banks and insurance companies? How does the liquidity risk of an open-end mutual fund compare with that of a closed-end fund?

22. A mutual fund has the following assets in its portfolio: $40 million in fixed-income securities and $40 million in stocks at current market values. In the event of a liquidity crisis, the fund can sell the assets at 96 percent of market value if they are disposed of in two days. The fund will receive 98 percent if the assets are disposed of in four days. Two shareholders, A and B, own 5 percent and 7 percent of equity (shares), respectively.

a. Market uncertainty has caused shareholders to sell their shares back to the fund. What will the two shareholders receive if the mutual fund must sell all the assets in two days? In four days?
b. How does this situation differ from a bank run? How have bank regulators mitigated the problem of bank runs?

23. A mutual fund has $1 million in cash and $9 million invested in securities. It currently has 1 million shares outstanding.

a. What is the net asset value (NAV) of this fund?
b. Assume that some of the shareholders decide to cash in their shares of the fund. How many shares at its current NAV can the fund take back without resorting to a sale of assets?
c. As a result of anticipated heavy withdrawals, the fund sells 10,000 shares of IBM stocks currently valued at $40. Unfortunately, it receives only $35 per share. What is the net asset value after the sale? What are the cash assets of the fund after the sale?
d. Assume that after the sale of IBM shares, 100,000 shares are sold back to the fund. What is the current NAV? Is there a need to sell more securities to meet this redemption?

MANAGING RISK

LIABILITY AND LIQUIDITY MANAGEMENT

Introduction

Depository institutions as well as life insurance companies are especially exposed to liquidity risk (see Chapter 17). The essential feature of this risk is that an FI's assets are relatively illiquid in the face of sudden withdrawals (or nonrenewals) of liability claims. The classic case is a bank run where depositors demand cash as they withdraw their claims from a bank and the bank is unable to meet those demands because of the relatively illiquid nature of its assets. For example, it could have a large portfolio of nonmarketable small business or real estate loans.

To reduce the risk of a liquidity crisis, FIs can insulate their balance sheets from liquidity risk by efficiently managing their liquid asset positions or managing the liability structure of their portfolios. We address both management issues. In reality, an FI manager can optimize over both liquid asset and liability structures to insulate the FI against liquidity risk.

Liquid Asset Management

A liquid asset can be turned into cash quickly and at a low transactions cost with little or no loss in principal value (see the discussion in Chapter 17 on the liquidity index). Specifically, a liquid asset is traded in a thick market where even large transactions in that asset do not move the market price or move it very little. Good examples of liquid assets are newly issued Treasury bills, Treasury notes, and Treasury bonds. The ultimate liquid asset is, of course, cash. While it is obvious that an FI's liquidity risk can be reduced by holding large amounts of assets such as cash, T-bills, and T-bonds, FIs usually face a return or interest earnings penalty from doing this. Because of their high liquidity and low default risks, such assets often bear low returns that reflect their essentially risk-free nature. By contrast, illiquid assets often have to promise additional return or liquidity premiums to compensate an FI for the relative lack of marketability and often greater default risk of the instrument.

On the other hand, holding relatively small amounts of liquid assets exposes an FI to enhanced illiquidity and *run risk problems.* Excessive illiquidity risk can result in insolvency and can even lead to contagious effects that negatively impact other FIs (see Chapter 17). Consequently, regulators have often imposed minimum liquid asset reserve requirements on FIs. In general, these liquid asset requirements differ in nature and scope across FIs and even across countries. They depend on the illiquidity risk exposure perceived for the type of FI and other regulator objectives that relate to minimum liquid asset requirements.

Specifically, regulators often set minimum liquid asset requirements for at least two other reasons beyond simply ensuring that FIs can meet expected and unexpected liability withdrawals. These two reasons are monetary policy reasons and taxation reasons.

Monetary Policy Reasons

Many countries set minimum liquid asset reserve requirements with the objective of strengthening monetary policy. Specifically, setting a minimum ratio of liquid reserve assets to deposits limits the ability of banks and bank-related institutions to expand lending and enhances the central bank's ability to control the money supply. In this context, requirements that depository institutions hold minimum ratios of liquid assets to deposits allow the central bank to gain greater control over the money supply and its growth as part of its overall macro-control objectives.

Taxation Reasons

Another reason for minimum requirements on FI liquid asset holdings is to force FIs to invest in government financial claims rather than private sector financial claims.

That is, minimum required liquid asset reserve requirements are an indirect way in which governments can raise additional "taxes" from FIs. Requiring banks to hold cash in the vault or cash reserves at the central bank (when there is no interest rate compensation paid) involves a resource transfer from banks to the central bank. In fact, the profitability of many central banks is contingent on the size of the **reserve requirement tax,** which can be viewed as a levy on banks under their jurisdiction. The tax or cost effect is increased further if inflation erodes the purchasing power value of those balances.

Reserve Requirement Tax
The cost of holding reserves that pay no interest at the central bank. This cost is increased further if inflation erodes the purchasing power value of these reserve balances.

Concept Questions

1. Why do regulators set minimum liquid asset requirements for FIs?
2. Can we view reserve requirements as a tax when the consumer price index (CPI) is falling?

The Composition of the Liquid Asset Portfolio

The composition of an FI's liquid asset portfolio, especially among cash and government securities, is determined partly by earnings considerations and partly by the type of minimum liquid asset reserve requirements imposed by the central bank. In many countries, such as the United Kingdom, reserve ratios have historically been imposed to encompass both cash and liquid government securities such as T-bills.[1] Thus, a 20 percent **liquid assets ratio** would require a bank to hold cash plus government securities in a ratio of $1 to $5 of deposits. Also, many states in the United States impose liquid asset ratios on life insurance companies and savings banks that require minimum cash and government securities holdings in their balance sheets. By contrast, the minimum liquid asset requirements on banks in the United States have been cash based and have excluded government securities. Currently, banks in the United States are required to hold a 10 percent minimum cash reserve ratio against demand deposits above $47.8 million and 3 percent against deposits exceeding $4.7 million and under $47.8 million. No reserve requirements are currently charged on the first $4.7 million of demand deposits.[2] As a result, government securities are less useful in that they are not given official reserve status and at the same time yield lower promised returns than loans. Nevertheless, many banks view government securities holdings as performing a useful secondary or **buffer reserve** function. In times of liquidity crisis, when significant drains on cash reserves occur, these securities can be turned into cash quickly and with very little loss of principal value because of the deep nature of the markets in which these assets are traded.

Liquid Assets Ratio
A minimum ratio of liquid assets to total assets set by the central bank.

Buffer Reserves
Nonreserve assets that can be quickly turned into cash.

Concept Question

1. In general, would it be better to hold 3-month T-bills or 10-year T-notes as buffer assets? Explain.

---

[1] The United Kingdom no longer imposes minimum reserve requirements on banks.

[2] As of 1998 these were the requirements. These deposit break-point figures are adjusted by the Federal Reserve at the end of each year to reflect the growth of deposits. Specifically, these figures are adjusted by 80 percent of the change in transaction accounts held by all depository institutions. The reserve ratio was also reduced from 12 percent to 10 percent for transaction accounts in April 1992.

Return-Risk Trade-Off for Liquid Assets

In optimizing its holdings of liquid assets, an FI has to trade the benefit of cash immediacy for lower returns. In addition, the FI manager's choice is one of constrained optimization in the sense that liquid asset reserve requirements imposed by regulators set a minimum bound on the level to which liquid reserve assets can fall in the balance sheet. Thus, an FI facing little risk of liquidity withdrawals and holding only a small amount of liquid assets for prudential reasons will find that it is forced to hold more than is privately optimal due to minimum reserve restrictions imposed by regulators.

In the next section we examine the risk-return trade-off in running a liquid asset position and the constraints imposed on this position by regulation by looking at a detailed example of FI liquidity management. This example is for U.S. banks under the current minimum reserve requirements imposed by the Federal Reserve. However, many of the issues and trade-offs are readily generalizable to any FI facing liability withdrawal risk under conditions where minimum liquid asset reserve ratios are imposed by regulators.

The Liquid Asset Reserve Management Problem for U.S. Banks

The issues involved in the optimal management of a liquid asset portfolio are illustrated by the problems faced by the money desk manager in charge of a U.S. bank's reserve position. In the context of U.S. bank regulation, we concentrate on a bank's management of its cash reserves, defined as vault cash and cash deposits held by the bank at the Federal Reserve.[3] In 1998 banks in the United States had to hold a 3 percent cash reserve against the first $47.8 million of transaction accounts (such as demand deposits) and 10 percent against the rest.[4] Historically, banks in the United States also had to hold a reserve ratio against time deposits; however, this was reduced from 3 percent to 0 percent at the beginning of 1991.[5]

While knowing the target reserve ratio—here assumed to be 10 percent of demand deposits—the bank reserve manager requires two additional pieces of information to manage the position. First, over what period's deposits do they compute the bank's reserve requirement? Second, over what period or periods do they have to maintain the target reserve requirement just computed?

The U.S. system is complicated by the fact that the period for which the bank manager computes the required reserve target differs from the period during which the reserve target is maintained or achieved. We describe the computation and maintenance periods for bank reserves next.

---

[3]However, banks that are not members of the Federal Reserve System—mostly very small banks—may maintain reserve balances with a Federal Reserve Bank indirectly (on a pass-through basis) with certain approved institutions, such as correspondent banks.

[4]The Garn-St. Germain Depository Institutions Act of 1982 (Public Law 97-320) required that the first $2 million of reservable liabilities (transaction accounts, nonpersonal time deposits, and Eurocurrency liabilities) of each depository institution be subject to a zero percent reserve requirement. The Federal Reserve adjusts the amount of reservable liabilities subject to this zero percent reserve requirement each year for the succeeding calendar year by 80 percent of the percentage increase in the total reservable liabilities of all depository institutions, measured on an annual basis as of June 30. In 1998 this figure was $4.7 million.

[5]Personal savings deposits also have a zero reserve requirement.

TABLE 18–1   Demand Deposits of ABC Bank
(in millions of dollars)

Date	
Tuesday, July 21	$ 1,420
Wednesday, July 22	1,410
Thursday, July 23	1,360
Friday, July 24	1,200
Saturday, July 25	1,200
Sunday, July 26	1,200
Monday, July 27	1,250
Tuesday, July 28	1,240
Wednesday, July 29	1,290
Thursday, July 30	1,320
Friday, July 31	1,350
Saturday, August 1	1,350
Sunday, August 2	1,350
Monday, August 3	1,340
Total	$18,280
Daily average demand deposits	$ 1,305.7

Reserve Computation Period
Period over which required reserves are calculated.

Computation Period.   A U.S. bank reserve manager has to think of the world as being divided into two-week periods for the purposes of bank reserve management. The **reserve computation period** always begins on a Tuesday and ends on a Monday 14 days later. Consider ABC bank's reserve manager who wants to assess the bank's minimum cash reserve requirement target. Let's suppose that the manager knows the bank's demand deposit position at the close of the banking day on each of the 14 days over the period Tuesday, July 21, to Monday, August 3. Of course, in reality, the manager knows these deposit positions with certainty only at the very end of the two-week period. Consider the realized demand deposit positions of ABC bank in Table 18–1.

The first thing to note in Table 18–1 is that the minimum daily average reserves a bank must maintain in the reserve maintenance period are computed as a percent of the daily average demand deposits held by the bank over the two-week computation period. For simplicity, if we assume the reserve ratio is 10 percent,[6] then

$$\begin{array}{ccc} \text{Minimum daily average} & & \text{Daily average demand} \\ \text{reserves in the reserve} & = \dfrac{\text{Reserve}}{\text{ratio}} \times & \text{deposits in the reserve} \\ \text{maintenance period} & & \text{computation period} \end{array}$$

$$\$130.57 \text{ million} = 10\% \times \$1{,}305.7 \text{ million}$$

That is, the ABC bank must maintain a daily average minimum of $130.57 million in reserves (vault cash plus deposits held by the bank at the Federal Reserve) over the reserve maintenance period. Note that this daily average target is calculated by taking the 14-day average of demand deposits even though the bank is closed for 4 of the 14 days (two Saturdays and two Sundays). Effectively, Friday's deposit fig-

---

[6]The true reserve requirements would be
$$[4.7 \times 0] + [(48.7 - 4.7) \times .03] + [(1305.7 - 48.7) \times .10] = \$127.02 \text{ million}$$

ures count three times compared to other days in the business week. This means that a bank manager who can engage in a strategy whereby deposits are lower on Fridays, on average, can lower the bank's reserve requirements. This may be important if required liquid asset reserve holdings are above the level that is optimal from the bank's perspective to handle liquidity drains due to expected and unexpected deposit withdrawals.

One strategy employed in the past is for a bank to send deposits offshore on a Friday, when a reduction in deposits effectively counts for $3/14$ths of the two-week period, and to bring them back on the following Monday, when an increase counts for just $1/14$th of the two-week period. This action effectively reduces the average demand deposits in the balance sheet of the bank over the 14-day period by $2/14$ths times the amount sent offshore and thus the reserves it needs to hold. Analysts have labeled this the **weekend game.**[7]

A second strategy is for the bank to offer its customers "sweep accounts" in which high reserve ratio demand deposits are "swept" out of customers' accounts on Friday into higher interest-bearing savings accounts. On Monday (or in many cases when the depositor needs funds in his/her checking account) these funds are swept back. The effective result is lower average balances in a bank's demand deposit accounts and thus lower required reserve holdings at the Federal Reserve.

Note that the $130.57 million figure is a minimum reserve target. The bank manager may hold excess cash reserves above this minimum level if the privately optimal or prudential level for the bank exceeds the regulatory specified minimum level because this bank is especially exposed to deposit withdrawal risk. In addition, the bank manager may hold some buffer reserves in the form of government securities that can be turned into cash quickly if deposit withdrawals are unusually high or to preempt the early stages of a bank run.

Maintenance Period.   We have computed a daily average minimum cash reserve requirement for ABC bank but have yet to delineate exactly the two-week period over which the bank manager has to maintain this $130.57 million daily average reserve target. Suppose that the **reserve maintenance period** was set as the same two-week period over which reserve requirements were computed (July 21 to August 3). Obviously, this **contemporaneous reserve accounting system** would impose an extreme level of stress on the bank reserve manager, who would not know the exact reserve target until the two-week period was over on August 3. Implicitly, on any day before then, the manager would face reserve target uncertainty. For example, on Monday, July 27, the manager knows the deposit levels for 7 of the 14 days but is unclear about what deposits are going to be for the last 7 days. The manager can estimate deposits based on projections of deposit flows from deposit behavior observed over the first seven days, but these estimates will always be subject to error. Required reserves are the product of the reserve ratio and average daily deposits over a 14-day period, and the latter are not fully observed with certainty until the end of the period. Thus, the manager must face some uncertainty about the true level of the reserve target. Of course, as the days pass and the end of the 14 days approaches, the degree of uncertainty about the true reserve target diminishes;

Weekend Game
Lowering deposit balances on Fridays since that day's figures count three times for reserve accounting purposes.

Reserve Maintenance Period
Period over which actual reserves have to meet or exceed the required reserve target.

Contemporaneous Reserve Accounting System
When the reserve computation and reserve maintenance periods overlap.

---

[7]In fact, the weekend game is a special case of bank window dressing, which means undertaking transactions in a manner that reduces reported deposits below their true or actual figures. For a discussion of window dressing in banking and the incentives for bankers to window dress, see L. Allen and A. Saunders, "Bank Window Dressing: Theory and Evidence," *Journal of Banking and Finance* 16 (1992), pp. 585–624.

there is a gradual resolution of uncertainty about the true reserve target for the bank as the period evolves.[8]

Because the manager would not know the true minimum reserve target until the two weeks are up on August 3, regulators have set the two-week reserve maintenance period to be later than the computation period, to make the achievement of reserve targets easier than if the two-week reserve maintenance period ran exactly synchronous to the two-week reserve calculation period (e.g., full contemporaneous reserve accounting). Two forms of reserve maintenance period have been used by the regulators. In the partial contemporaneous reserve accounting system, regulators give bank managers a two-day leeway, or grace period; the 14-day maintenance period for meeting the reserve targets begins two days after the start and ends two days after the end of two-week reserve computation period. In the lagged reserve accounting system, regulators give bank managers a 17-day grace period; the 14-day maintenance period begins 17 days after the end of the computation period (a lag of 30 days between the beginning of the reserve computation period and the beginning of the reserve maintenance period). We next show an example of the partial contemporaneous reserve accounting system followed by the lagged reserve accounting system.

In our example, the reserve computation period runs from Tuesday, July 21, to Monday, August 3, but the reserve maintenance period under 2-day lagged contemporaneous reserve accounting runs from Thursday, July 23, to Wednesday, August 5. As a result, for the last two days of the reserve maintenance period, August 4 and 5, the bank manager knows the minimum reserve target (here $130.57 million per day) with absolute certainty. However, for the first 12 days of the reserve maintenance period, the manager would still be uncertain about the final daily average target. We show this almost contemporaneous reserve accounting system in Figure 18–1.

Basically, the reserve manager has two days, August 4 and August 5, to correct any major undershooting or overshooting of the required reserve target over the preceding 12 days when there was target uncertainty.

Table 18–2 looks at ABC bank's reserve position at the close of the day on August 3, when the final reserve target can be calculated with certainty and there are two days left in the reserve maintenance period to make adjustments to reserves held to meet the required target.

FIGURE 18–1

Almost Contemporaneous Reserve Requirements

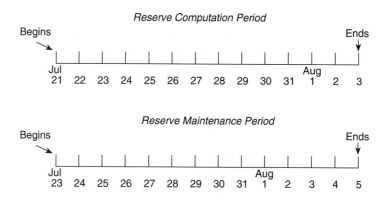

[8]For a further discussion of this resolution of uncertainty, see P. A. Spindt and J. R. Hoffmeister, "The Micromechanics of the Federal Funds Market: Implications for Day of the Week Effects in Funds Rate Variability," *Journal of Financial and Quantitative Analysis* 23 (1988), pp. 401–16.

TABLE 18–2   ABC Bank's Daily Reserve Positions over the July 23–August 5 Reserve Maintenance Period
(in millions of dollars)

Date		
Thursday, July 23	$129	
Friday, July 24	130	
Saturday, July 25	130	
Sunday, July 26	130	
Monday, July 27	128	
Tuesday, July 28	127	
Wednesday, July 29	132	
Thursday, July 30	131	
Friday, July 31	129	
Saturday, August 1	129	
Sunday, August 2	129	
Monday, August 3	130	[Last day of the reserve computation period]
Tuesday, August 4	?	
Wednesday, August 5	?	[Last day of the reserve maintenance period]

On the close of the Monday, August 3, banking day, the average daily cash reserve position of the ABC bank (over the first 12 days of the reserve maintenance period) was $1,554 million/12 = $129.5 million. However, based on deposits held over the full reserve computation period, the manager must hold an average reserve level of $130.57 million per day over the full 14-day reserve maintenance period. Thus, as of that Monday evening, the manager can easily calculate that over the preceding 12 days the minimum reserve target was short by $130.57 million − $129.5 million = $1.07 million per day, or cumulatively 12 × $1.07 million = $12.84 million.

This presents the manager with a clear target for the two remaining days of the reserve maintenance period: Tuesday, August 4, and Wednesday, August 5. The manager must hold an average of $130.57 on each of those days plus make up the cumulative shortfall of $12.84 million over the previous 12 days. The bank manager must hold a total average of

$$\frac{\$130.57 + \$130.57 + \$12.84}{2} = \$136.99 \text{ million}$$

over the last two days of the reserve maintenance period. While the manager could hold different amounts of reserves on each of these two days, such as $131.99 million on Tuesday and $141.99 million on Wednesday, they must average to at least $136.99 so that over the full 14-day period the manager can meet the regulatory imposed minimum reserve ratio target.[9]

---

[9]While the $130.57 million daily average is the sum of the vault cash and deposits held by the ABC bank at the central bank, the vault cash component is in fact given at the time the reserve maintenance period begins. The vault cash component is calculated over a two-week period that ends two weeks prior to the beginning of the reserve computation period. For example, suppose vault cash had been $10 million on average during the period ending two weeks before the reserve computation period started. This means that the true or real target for the bank manager is to maintain reserves on deposit at the Federal Reserve equal to a daily average of $130.57 million − $10 million = $120.57 million over the 14-day reserve maintenance period. That is, effectively, the minimum reserve target is really a minimum target for deposits held on reserve at the Federal Reserve (the central bank).

In the lagged accounting reserve system, the reserve maintenance period runs from Thursday, August 20, to Wednesday, September 2.

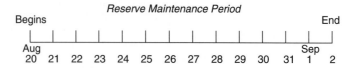

Reserve Maintenance Period

This system provides a manager with ample time to plan the $130.57 million average reserves required per day during the maintenance period.

In the United States, the lagged reserve accounting system was in place before 1984. In 1984, the regulators moved to the 2-day lagged (partial) contemporaneous reserve accounting (as shown in Figure 18–1). Beginning July 30, 1998, regulators switched back to the lagged reserve accounting system described above with a 17-day lag between the end of the computation period and the start of the maintenance period.

An interesting question is why would regulators require any form of contemporaneous reserve accounting system since it imposes such a burden on the reserve manager? Also, fine-tuning by reserve managers during the last two days of the computation period often leads to higher volatility in the Fed funds market. The answer is that lagged reserve accounting inhibits the ability of regulators to affect monetary policy under a regime of monetary targeting. That is, if regulators use reserve requirements as a tool for achieving monetary targets, such as M1 and M2, a lagged reserve system is ineffective because of the delay between reserve requirement calculation and the reserve maintenance period. Indeed, this was the argument used when regulators adopted the partial contemporaneous reserve system in 1984.

The recent (1998) ruling to move back to a lagged reserve accounting system has also been justified because regulators no longer use reserve requirements as the only instrument to affect monetary policy. The emphasis now has shifted to using more interest rate tools, primarily the discount and federal funds rates. In addition, since reserve requirements are now imposed only on demand deposits, their sensitivity to interest rate movements as well as the ability of banks to engage in sweep programs, make it less likely that reserve requirements can serve as an effective tool to control M1.

Undershooting/Overshooting of the Reserve Target

Undershooting. What happens if, at the end of the reserve maintenance period (on August 5 or September 2nd from the previous examples) the bank holds less than the regulatory required daily minimum reserve ratio—that is, less than the $130.57 daily average million in our example? The Federal Reserve allows the bank to make up to a 4 percent daily average error without penalty.[10] Thus, if the bank is 4 percent in the red on its reserve target to the tune of 4 percent × $130.57 million = $5.22 million, it has to make this up in the next two-week reserve maintenance period.[11] If the reserve shortfall exceeds 4 percent, the bank is liable to explicit and

---

[10]The carryover was changed from 2 percent to 4 percent on September 3, 1992. See Federal Reserve Board of Governors (1992). CSC no. 92–35, Attachment Docket no. R–0750, p. 5.

[11]This means that the allowable deficiency over the full 14 days would be

$$\$130.57 \text{ million} \times .04 \times 14 = \$73.08 \text{ million}$$

implicit penalty charges from the Federal Reserve. The explicit charges include the imposition of a penalty interest rate charge equal to the central bank's discount rate plus a 2 percent markup, while the implicit charges can include more frequent monitoring, examinations, and surveillance if bank regulators view the undershooting of the reserve requirements as reflecting an unsafe and unsound practice by the bank's manager. Such a view is likely to be taken only if the bank consistently undershoots its reserve targets.

In undershooting the target, the bank manager has to weigh the explicit and implicit costs of undershooting against any potential benefits. Specifically, it may be beneficial to undershoot if the privately optimal or prudential reserve position of the bank is less than the regulatory set minimum and/or there are very high opportunity costs of meeting the reserve requirement targets. There may be high opportunity costs of meeting reserve targets if interest rates and loan demands are high so that the cost of forgone loans on future profits may be significant.

For a bank below the reserve target, there are two principal ways to build up reserves to meet the target as the reserve maintenance period comes to an end: (1) by liquidating assets through selling off some buffer assets such as Treasury bills or (2) by borrowing in the interbank market for reserves, especially in the federal funds and repurchase agreement markets, which we describe later. The bank manager is likely to choose the least costly method of meeting any reserve deficiency, such as borrowing fed funds if this rate is less than the cost of selling off liquid assets. The manager may be reluctant to fund the whole gap in this manner, however, if the costs of adjusting to an undershooting are high and the privately optimal amount of reserves is less than the regulatory required minimum amount.

In the past, such cost considerations led some bank managers to use the Federal Reserve's discount window to borrow the required funds to meet reserve shortfalls. The reason for this is that the cost of borrowing from the discount window is the discount rate, an administered rate set by the Federal Reserve. Since this rate is not market determined and is adjusted at a maximum of only once a week (and usually much less frequently than that), it usually lies below fed funds and government security rates and offers a very attractive borrowing cost to a bank with deficient reserves as the reserve maintenance period comes to an end. However, discount window loans are really meant to be used by banks on a need rather than a profit basis, that is, by banks that are solvent but face sudden liquidity crises due to deposit withdrawals caused by seasonality in deposit flows or some other similar lender of last resort need. Specifically, discount window borrowings are not meant to be a cheap source of funds to meet reserve requirements or because the interbank federal funds rate is more costly than the Federal Reserve's discount rate.[12] Despite this, it is evident that discount window borrowings do increase when market rates rise well above the discount rate and tend to fall when the market rate–discount rate spread narrows. Thus, some bank managers appear to be gaming the Federal Reserve by claiming that their borrowings are due to sudden liquidity needs when in fact they reflect borrowings to arbitrage the spread between the discount rate and market rates and to profit from the lender of last resort discount window facility.

---

[12]For more on the use of fed funds versus the discount window as a borrowing source, see T. Ho and A. Saunders, "A Micro Model of the Federal Funds Market," *Journal of Finance* 40 (1985), pp. 977–88; and M. Smirlock and J. Yawitz, "Asset Returns, Discount Rate Changes, and Market Efficiency," *Journal of Finance* 40 (1985), pp. 1141–58.

Finally, note that any such gaming behavior is extremely dangerous not only on ethical grounds but also on economic grounds; if a bank is caught, it could theoretically lose its bank charter. At best, bank managers seeking to exploit the availability of cheap discount window finance are likely to borrow on a highly randomized basis that is difficult for central bank regulators to detect.

Overshooting.   The cost of overshooting, or holding cash reserves in excess of the minimum required level, depends on whether the bank perceives its prudent level of reserves to meet expected and unexpected deposit withdrawals to be above or below the regulatory imposed minimum reserve requirement.

If its required minimum reserves are above what managers perceive as optimal, the first 4 percent of excess reserves can be carried forward and the Federal Reserve allows them to count toward meeting the reserve requirement in the next two-week maintenance period. After that, any excess reserves held above the required minimum plus 4 percent are a drag on bank earnings, since every dollar that is held as excess reserves in cash or central bank deposits earns no interest and could have been lent out at the bank lending rate. For example, if the bank's lending rate to its best customers is 12 percent, the bank and its shareholders have suffered an opportunity cost of 12 percent for every dollar of excess cash reserves held by the bank.

By contrast, if the bank manager perceives that its required minimum level of reserves is below what it privately needs for expected and unexpected deposit withdrawal exposure, the FI would overshoot the required minimum reserve target. This policy would maintain the liquidity position of the bank at a prudently adequate level. In choosing to overshoot the target, the manager must consider the least cost instrument in which to hold such reserves.

Thus, while some excess reserves might be held in highly liquid noninterest-bearing cash form, at least part of any excess reserve position might be held in buffer assets such as short-term securities or Treasury bills that earn interest but are not quite as liquid as cash. The proportions held between cash and Treasury bills depend in large part on yield spreads.

For example, suppose the loan rate is 12 percent, the T-bill rate is 7 percent, and the interest earned on excess cash holdings is 0 percent. The opportunity cost, or forgone return to the bank, from holding excess reserves in cash form or T-bill form is

$$\text{Opportunity cost cash} = 12\% - 0\% = 12\%$$
$$\text{Opportunity cost T-bills} = 12\% - 7\% = 5\%3$$

Thus, T-bills have a significantly lower opportunity cost than cash, and the manger has to weigh the 7 percent net opportunity cost saving of holding excess reserves in T-bill form against the ease with which such instruments can be sold and turned into cash to meet liability withdrawals or liquidity crunches. Table 18–3 shows excess cash reserves of U.S. banks between 1990 and 1998. As you can see, because of their opportunity cost, excess reserves are invariably kept at very low levels of around 3 to 4 percent of required reserves.

Liquidity Management as a Knife Edge Management Problem.   The management of an FI's liquidity position is something of a knife edge situation because holding too many liquid assets penalizes a bank's earnings and thus its stockholders.

TABLE 18–3   Reserves and Excess Reserves of U.S. Banks
(in millions of dollars)

	1990	1994*	1998†
Total reserves	$59,120	$61,319	$47,503
Required reserves	57,456	60,171	45,719
Excess reserves	1,664	1,158	1,784

*December.
†January.
Source: *Federal Reserve Bulletin,* (various issues).

An FI manager who holds excessive amounts of liquid assets is unlikely to survive for long. Similarly, a manager who excessively undershoots the reserve target faces enhanced risks of liquidity crises and regulatory intervention. Again, such a manager's tenure at the FI may be relatively short-lived.

Concept Questions

1. In addition to the target reserve ratio, what other pieces of information does the bank reserve manager require to manage the bank's reserve requirement position?
2. For a bank that undershoots its reserve target, what ways are available to a reserve manager to build up reserves to meet the target?
3. Since 1998, U.S. banks have operated under a lagged reserve accounting system in which the reserve computation period ends 17 days before the reserve maintenance period begins. Does the reserve manager face any uncertainty at all in managing a bank's reserve position? Explain your answer.
4. What explains the decline in the level of required reserves held by banks between 1994 and 1998 (see Table 18–3)?

Liability Management

Liquidity and liability management are closely related: One aspect of liquidity risk control is to build up a prudential level of liquid assets. Another aspect is to manage the FI's liability structure so that it reduces the need for large amounts of liquid assets to meet liability withdrawals. However, excessive use of purchased funds can result in a liquidity crisis if investors lose confidence in the bank and refuse to roll over such funds.

Funding Risk and Cost

Unfortunately, constructing a low-cost, low-withdrawal-risk liability portfolio is more difficult than it sounds because those liabilities, or sources of FI funds, that are the most subject to withdrawal risk are often the least costly. That is, an FI has to trade off the benefits of attracting liabilities at a low funding cost with a high chance of withdrawal against liabilities with a high funding cost and low liquidity. For example, demand deposits are relatively low funding cost vehicles for banks but can

FIGURE 18–2

Funding Risk versus Cost

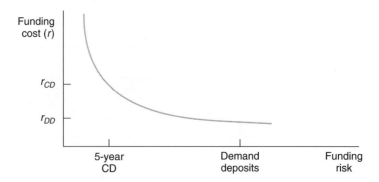

be withdrawn instantaneously.[13] By contrast, a five-year, fixed-term certificate of deposit may have a relatively high funding cost but can be withdrawn before the five-year maturity is up only after the payment of a substantial interest rate penalty.

Thus, in structuring the liability, or funding, side of the balance sheet, the FI manager faces a trade-off along the lines suggested in Figure 18–2.

Although we have discussed commercial banks' funding risk, thrifts and other FIs face a similar trade-off.[14] For example, investment banks can finance through overnight funds (RPs and broker deposits) or longer-term sources such as notes and bonds, while finance companies have a choice between commercial paper and longer-term notes and bonds.

In the next section we look at the spectrum of liabilities available to a bank manager in seeking to actively impact liquidity risk exposure through the choice of liability structure.

Concept Questions

1. How are liquidity and liability management related?
2. Describe the trade-off faced by an FI manager in structuring the liability side of the balance sheet.

Choice of Liability Structure

In this section, we take a more detailed look at the withdrawal risk and funding cost characteristics of the major liabilities available to a modern bank manager.

Demand Deposits

Withdrawal Risk.   Demand deposits have a high degree of withdrawal risk. Withdrawals can be instantaneous and largely expected by the bank manager, such as preweekend cash withdrawals, or unexpected, as occurs during economic crisis situations (so-called bank runs; see Chapter 17).

---

[13]Depositors do not always exercise this option; therefore, some demand deposits behave like longer-term core deposits.

[14]The trade-off faced by thrifts is essentially the same as that faced by banks with the exception of thrifts' access to borrowings from Federal Home Loan banks, while banks tend to have more direct access to the federal funds and repurchase agreement markets.

Costs.   In the United States, demand deposits have paid zero explicit interest since the 1930s by law. This does not mean that they are a costless source of funds for banks or that banks have no price or interest mechanisms available to control partially the withdrawal risk associated with these contracts.

Despite the zero explicit interest paid on demand deposit accounts, competition among banks and FIs has resulted in the payment of implicit interest, or payments of interest in kind, on these accounts. Specifically, in providing demand deposits that are checkable accounts, a bank has to provide a whole set of associated services from provision of checkbooks, to clearing of checks, to sending out statements with cleared checks. Because such services absorb real resources of labor and capital, they are costly for banks to provide. One way in which banks can recapture these costs is through charging fees, such as 10 cents a check cleared. To the extent that these fees do not cover the bank's cost of providing such services, the depositor receives a subsidy or an implicit interest payment. For example, if it costs the bank 15 cents to clear a check, the customer receives a 5 cent subsidy. We can calculate such implicit yields for each service or an average implicit interest rate for each demand deposit account. For example, an average implicit interest rate for a bank's demand deposits might be calculated as

$$\begin{array}{c} \text{Average implicit} \\ \text{interest rate} \\ \text{(IIR)} \end{array} = \frac{\begin{array}{c}\text{Bank's average management} \\ \text{costs per account per annum}\end{array} - \begin{array}{c}\text{Fees earned per} \\ \text{account per annum}\end{array}}{\text{Average annual size of account}}$$

Suppose that

$$\begin{array}{r}\text{Bank's average management costs per account per annum} = \$150 \\ \text{Fees earned per account per annum} = \$100 \\ \text{Average annual size of account} = \$1,200\end{array}$$

Then

$$IIR = \frac{\$150 - \$100}{\$1,200} = 4.166\%$$

The payment of implicit interest means that the bank manager is not absolutely powerless to mitigate deposit withdrawals, especially if rates on competing instruments are rising. In particular, the FI could lower check-clearing fees, which would in turn raise implicit interest payments to depositors. Such payments are payments in kind or subsidies and are not paid in actual dollars and cents as is interest earned on competing instruments. Nevertheless, implicit payments of interest are tax free while explicit interest payments are taxable. Finally, demand deposits have an additional cost in the form of noninterest-bearing reserve requirements the bank has to hold at the Federal Reserve.

Interest-Bearing Checking Accounts

Withdrawal Risk.   Since 1980 banks in the United States have been able to offer to noncorporate customers checkable deposits that pay interest and are withdrawable on demand; they are called negotiable order of withdrawal accounts or **NOW accounts.**[15] The major distinction between these instruments and traditional demand

NOW Account
Negotiable order of withdrawal account that is like a demand deposit account but has a minimum balance requirement.

---

[15]There are also Super-Now accounts that have very similar features to NOW accounts but require a larger minimum balance.

deposits is that the depositor has to maintain a minimum account balance to earn interest. If the minimum balance falls below some level, such as $500, these accounts formally convert to a status equivalent to demand deposits and earn no interest. The payment of explicit interest and the existence of minimum balance requirements make them potentially less prone to withdrawal risk than demand deposits. Nevertheless, they are still highly liquid instruments from the depositor's perspective.

Costs.   Like demand deposits, the bank can affect the potential withdrawability of these accounts through the payment of implicit interest or fee subsidies such as not charging the full cost of check clearance. However, the manager has two other ways to impact the yield paid to the depositor. The first is varying the minimum balance requirement. If the minimum balance requirement is lowered—say, from $500 to $250—a larger portion of a NOW account becomes subject to interest payments and thus the explicit return and attractiveness of these accounts increases.[16] The second is to vary the explicit interest rate payment itself, such as increasing it from 5 to 5¼ percent. Thus, the bank manager has three pricing mechanisms to increase or decrease the attractiveness, and therefore impact the withdrawal rate, of NOW accounts: implicit interest payments, minimum balance requirements, and explicit interest payments.[17]

For example, consider a depositor who holds on average $250 per month for the first three months of the year, $500 per month for the next three months, and $1,000 per month for the final six months of the year in a NOW account. The NOW account pays 5 percent per annum if the minimum balance is $500 or more. The depositor writes an average of 50 checks per month and pays a service fee of 10 cents for each check, but it costs the bank 15 cents to process each check. The account holder's gross interest return, consisting of implicit plus explicit interest, is

$$\begin{aligned}
\text{Gross interest return} &= \text{Explicit interest} + \text{Implicit interest} = \$500\,(.05)(.25) \\
&\quad + \$1000\,(.05)(.5) + (\$.15 - \$.10)(50)(12) \\
&= \$6.25 + \$25 + \$30 = \$61.25
\end{aligned}$$

Suppose the minimum balance was lowered from $500 to $250 and check service fees were lowered from 10 cents to 5 cents per check. Then

$$\begin{aligned}
\text{Gross interest return} &= \$250(.05)(.25) + \$500(.05)(.25) + \$1000(.05)(.5) \\
&\quad + (\$.15 - \$.05)(50)(12) \\
&= \$3.125 + \$6.25 + \$25 + \$60 \\
&= \$94.375
\end{aligned}$$

Table 18–4 shows the minimum balance requirement and sample fees of a group of New York banks that link fee payment to the size of a minimum balance. Specifically, if a customer fails to meet the minimum balance, he or she pays a fixed fee plus a per check fee. If the account exceeds the minimum balance, the fixed fee

---

[16]Subject to any regulatory requirement on the minimum balance.

[17]As transactions accounts, these deposits are also subject to reserve requirements at the same rate as on demand deposits as well as deposit insurance premiums. Given a 5 percent NOW account interest rate, a 10 percent reserve ratio, and a 27-basis-point deposit insurance premium and ignoring implicit interest, the effective cost of the marginal dollar of NOW accounts to the issuing bank is

$$\text{Effective cost} = [r_{NOW}/1 - R] + \text{Premium} = [.05/.90] + .0027 = .0583 \text{ or } 5.83\%$$

TABLE 18–4   Minimum Balance and Fees for Select New York City Banks, April 1998

Name	Minimum balance to avoid fees	Fees if balance not met		Bounced-check fee	Stop-payment fee	Use of other banks' ATM	Use of ATM card as a debit card	Changes in the last year
		Monthly	Per check					
Bank of New York	$2,000	$9	35 cents	$15	$15	$1*	35 cents*	Raised monthly fee from $8 plus 25 cents per check. Raised ATM fee from 75 cents.
Chase Manhattan	$1,500	$9.50	50 cents	$15	$15	$1*	50 cents*	Lowered minimum balance from $3,000.
Citibank	$6,000†	$9.50	50 cents	$30	0‡	$1*	0	Raised minimum balance from $2,000. Increased bounced-check fee from $25.
Fleet Bank	$1,500	$9.50§	35 cents	$30	$15	$1.50#	25 cents	Raised bounced-check fee from $25. Raised minimum balance from $1,200 and monthly fee from $8.
Republic Bank	$1,500**	$7.50	30 cents	$15	$15	0	0	No changes.

*Fee waived if minimum balance is met.
†Includes all Citibank credit and debt accounts.
‡Will go to $25 next month.
§Monthly fee is $7.50 if customer uses direct deposit for paycheck.
#Waived if balance is at least $10,000.
**All deposit accounts.
Source: *New York Times,* April 26, 1998, Money and Business section, p. 9. Copyright © 1998 by The New York Times, Reprinted by permission.

and the per check fees are reduced to zero. This creates strong incentives for a customer to maintain a relatively high average balance at the bank to generate high implicit interest payments (returns).

Passbook Savings

Withdrawal Risk.   Passbook savings are generally less liquid than demand deposits and NOW accounts for two reasons. First they are noncheckable and usually involve physical presence at the bank for withdrawal. Second, the bank has the legal power to delay payment or withdrawal requests for as long as one month. While this is rarely done and withdrawal requests are normally met with immediate cash payment, the legal right to delay provides an important withdrawal risk control to bank managers.

Costs.   Since these accounts are noncheckable, any implicit interest rate payments are likely to be small; thus, the principal costs to the bank are the explicit interest payments on these accounts. In recent years, banks have normally paid slightly higher explicit rates on passbook savings than on NOW accounts.

Money Market Deposit Accounts (MMDAs)

Withdrawal Risk.   Introduced in 1982 under the Garn-St. Germain Act, MMDAs are an additional liability instrument banks can use to control their overall with-

MMDAs
Money market deposit
accounts are retail savings
accounts with some
limited checking account
features.

drawal risk—in particular, the risk of funds disintermediating from banks and flowing to money market mutual funds (MMMFs) (see Chapter 4). To make banks competitive with the money market mutual funds offered by groups such as Vanguard and Fidelity, **MMDAs** have to be liquid but are not as liquid as demand deposits and NOW accounts. In the United States, MMDAs are checkable but are subject to restrictions on the number of checks written on each account per month, the number of preauthorized automatic transfers per month, and the minimum denomination of the amount of each check. For example, a customer with an MMDA may make a maximum of six preauthorized transfers, of which no more than three can be checks of at least $500 each. In addition, MMDAs impose minimum balance requirements on depositors.

Costs.   The major cost of MMDAs and the pricing mechanism to control withdrawal risk is the explicit interest rate paid to depositors. Since MMDAs are in direct competition with MMMFs, the bank manager can affect their net withdrawal rate by varying the rate paid on such accounts. In particular, while the rate paid by MMMFs on their shares directly reflects the rates earned on the underlying money market assets in which the portfolio manager invests, such as commercial paper, bankers acceptances, repurchase agreements, and T-bills, the rates paid on MMDAs by bank managers are not directly based on any underlying portfolio of money market assets. In general, bank managers have considerable discretion to alter the rates paid on MMDAs and thus the spread on MMMF–MMDA accounts. This can directly impact the rate of withdrawals and withdrawal risk on such accounts. Allowing MMDA rates to have a large negative spread with MMMFs increases the net withdrawal rate on such accounts.

Retail Time Deposits and CDs

Withdrawal Risk.   By contractual design, time deposits and retail certificates of deposit reduce the withdrawal risk of bank issuers. Retail CDs are fixed-maturity instruments with face values under $100,000. In a world of no early withdrawal requests, the bank knows the exact scheduling of interest and principal payments to depositors holding such deposit claims, since these payments are contractually specified. As such, the bank manager can directly control fund inflows and outflows by varying the maturities of the time deposits and CDs it offers to the public. In general, banks offer time deposits and CDs with maturities varying from two weeks to eight years.

In cases where depositors wish to withdraw before the maturity of a time deposit or CD contract, banks are empowered by regulation to impose penalties on a withdrawing depositor, for example, penalties equal to a certain number of months' interest depending on the maturity of the deposit. However, while this does impose a friction or transactions cost on withdrawals, it is unlikely to stop withdrawals when the depositor has exceptional liquidity needs. Also, withdrawals may increase if the bank is perceived to be insolvent, despite the presence of interest penalties and the existence of deposit insurance coverage up to $100,000. Nevertheless, under normal banking conditions, these instruments have relatively low withdrawal risk compared to transaction accounts such as demand deposits and NOW accounts and can be used as an important liability management tool to control withdrawal/liquidity risk.

Costs.   Similar to passbook savings, the major costs of these accounts are explicit interest payments. Short-term CDs are often competitive with T-bills, and their rates are set with the T-bill rate in mind. Note that depositors who buy CDs are subject to state and local taxes on their interest payments, whereas T-bill investors do not pay state and local taxes on T-bill interest income.[18] Finally, time deposits and CDs do not at present require the bank to hold noninterest-bearing reserves at the central bank.

Wholesale CDs

Withdrawal Risk.   Wholesale CDs were innovated by banks in the early 1960s as a contractual mechanism for giving the depositor liquidity without imposing withdrawal risk on the bank. The unique feature of these liability instruments is not so much their large minimum denomination size of $100,000 or more but the fact that they are **negotiable instruments.** That is, they can be resold by title assignment in a secondary market to other investors. This means, for example, that if IBM bought a $1 million three-month CD from Chase and for unexpected liquidity reasons needs funds after only one month has passed, it can sell this deposit to another outside investor in the secondary market. This does not impose any obligation on Chase in terms of an early funds withdrawal request. Thus, a depositor can sell a relatively liquid instrument without causing adverse withdrawal risk exposure for the bank. Essentially, the only withdrawal risk is that these wholesale CDs may not be rolled over and reinvested by the holder of the deposit claim on maturity.[19]

Negotiable Instrument
An instrument where ownership can be transferred in the secondary market.

Costs.   The rates banks pay on these instruments are competitive with other wholesale money market rates, especially those on commercial paper and T-bills. This competitive rate aspect is enhanced by the highly sophisticated nature of investors in such CDs, such as money market mutual fund managers, and the fact that these deposits are not covered by explicit deposit insurance guarantees beyond the first $100,000. To the extent that these CDs are offered by large banks perceived as being too big to fail, the required credit risk premium on CDs is less than that required for similar quality instruments issued by the nonbank private sector (e.g., commercial paper). In addition, required interest yields on CDs reflect investors' perceptions of the depth of the secondary market for CDs. In recent years, the liquidity of the secondary market in CDs appears to have diminished as dealers have

---

[18]Thus, the marginal investor would be indifferent between Treasury bills and insured bank CDs when

$$r_{TB} = r_{CD}(1 - T_L)$$

where r_{TB} is the rate on T-bills, r_{CD} is the CD rate, and T_L is the local income tax rate. Suppose, the average local tax rate is 8 percent. Then, if the T-bill rate is 3 percent, insured CDs would have to pay

$$r_{CD} = r_{TB}/(1 - T_L) = 3.00\%/(1 - .08) = 3.26\%$$

[19]Wholesale CDs are also offered offshore, in which case they are called Eurodollar CDs. Eurodollar CDs may sell at slightly different rates from domestic CDs because of differences in demand and supply for CDs between the domestic market and the Euromarket and differences in credit risk perceptions of depositors buying a CD from an overseas branch (e.g., Chase in London) rather than a domestic branch (Chase in New York). To the extent that it is believed that banks are too big to fail, a guaranty that only extends to domestic branches, a higher risk premium may be required of overseas CDs. Indeed, FDICIA passed in 1991, has severely restricted the ability of the FDIC to rescue overseas depositors of a failed U.S. bank.

withdrawn and the credit risk problems of the largest banks have increased. This has increased the relative cost of issuing such instruments by banks.[20]

Federal Funds

Withdrawal Risk.   The liabilities just described are all deposit liabilities, reflecting deposit contracts issued by banks in return for cash. However, banks not only fund their assets through issuing deposits but also can borrow in various markets for purchased funds. Since the funds generated from these purchases are borrowed funds and are not deposits, they are subject to neither reserve requirements (like demand deposits and NOW accounts) nor deposit insurance premium payments to the FDIC (like all the domestic deposits described earlier).[21] The largest market available for banks for purchased funds is the federal funds market. While banks with excess reserves can invest some of this excess in liquid assets such as T-bills and short-term securities, an alternative is to lend excess reserves for short intervals to other banks seeking increased short-term funding. The interbank market for excess cash reserves is called the federal funds market. In the United States, federal funds are short-term uncollateralized loans made by one bank to another; more than 90 percent of such transactions have maturities of one day. The bank that purchases funds shows them as a liability on its balance sheet, while the bank that sells them shows them as an asset.

For the liability-funding bank, there is no risk that the fed funds borrowed can be withdrawn within the day, although there is settlement risk at the end of each day (see Chapter 14). However, there is some risk that they will not be rolled over by the lending bank the next day if this is desired by the borrowing bank. In reality, this has occurred only in periods of extreme crisis such as the failure of Continental Illinois in 1984. Nevertheless, since fed funds are uncollateralized loans, fed funds–selling banks normally impose maximum bilateral limits or credit caps on a fed funds–borrowing bank. This may constrain the ability of a bank to expand its federal funds–borrowing position very rapidly if this is part of its overall liability management strategy.

Costs.   The cost for the purchasing bank is the federal funds rate. The federal funds rate can vary considerably both within the day and across days, although rate variability has fallen since the introduction of lagged reserve accounting in July 1998.

---

[20]In addition, for all the liability instruments considered so far (with the exception of Euro CDs), the bank may have to pay an FDIC insurance premium depending on its perceived riskiness (see Chapter 19). For example, consider a bank issuing CDs at 3.26 percent, at which rate a depositor might just be indifferent to holding T-bills at 3.00 percent, given a local tax rate of 8 percent. However, the cost to the bank of the CD issue is not 3.26 percent but rather

$$\text{Effective CD cost} = 3.26\% + \text{Insurance premium} = 3.26\% + .27\% = 3.53\%$$

where 27 basis points is the assumed size of the deposit insurance premium. Thus, deposit insurance premiums add to the cost of deposits as a source of funds. However, in 1998, the insurance premium was set by the FDIC at zero for most banks, with only the very riskiest banks having to pay 27 basis points.

[21]Foreign deposits are not subject to deposit insurance premiums. However, in the exceptional event of a very large bank failure where all deposits are protected, under the 1991 FDICIA, the FDIC is required to levy a charge on surviving large banks proportional to their total asset size. To the extent that assets are partially funded by foreign liabilities, this is an implied premium on foreign deposits.

Repurchase Agreements (RPs)

Withdrawal Risk.   RPs are collateralized federal funds transactions. In a federal funds transaction, the bank with excess reserves sells fed funds for one day to the purchasing bank. The next day, the purchasing bank returns the fed funds plus one day's interest reflecting the fed funds rate. Since there is a credit risk exposure to the selling bank in that the purchasing bank may be unable to repay the fed funds the next day, that bank may seek collateral backing for the one-day loan of fed funds. In an RP transaction, the funds-selling bank receives government securities as collateral from the funds-purchasing bank. That is, the funds-purchasing bank temporarily exchanges securities for cash.[22] The next day, this transaction is reversed, with the funds-purchasing bank sending back the fed funds borrowed plus interest (the RP rate): it receives in return or repurchases its securities used as collateral in the transaction.

As with the fed funds market, the RP market is a highly liquid and flexible source of funds for banks that need to increase their liabilities and offset deposit withdrawals. Moreover, like fed funds, these transactions can be rolled over each day. The major liability management flexibility difference between fed funds and RPs is that a fed funds transaction can be entered into at any time in the banking day as long as the Fedwire is open (see Chapter 14).[23] In general, it is difficult to effect an RP borrowing late in the day since the fed funds–sending bank has to be satisfied with the type and quality of the securities collateral proposed by the funds-borrowing bank. While this collateral is normally T-bills, T-notes, T-bonds, and mortgage-backed securities, their maturities and other features, such as callability and coupons, may be unattractive to the funds seller. Negotiations over the collateral package can delay RP transactions and make them more difficult to arrange than simple uncollateralized fed fund loans.

Costs.   Because of their collateralized nature, RP rates normally lie below federal funds rates. Also, RP rates generally show less fluctuation than do fed funds rates. This is in part due to the lesser intraday flexibility of RPs relative to fed fund transactions.

Other Borrowings

While fed funds and RPs have been the major sources of borrowed funds, banks have utilized a host of other borrowing sources to supplement their liability management flexibility. We describe these briefly in the following sections.

Bankers Acceptances.   Banks often convert off-balance-sheet letters of credit into on-balance-sheet bankers acceptances (BAs) by discounting the letter of credit when it is presented by the holder for acceptance. Further, these BAs may then be resold to money market investors. Thus, BA sales to the secondary market are an additional funding source.

---

[22]Since Treasury securities are of a book-entry form, the title to ownership is transferred along a securities Fedwire, in a similar manner to cash transfers.

[23]Normally, Fedwire closes at 6:30 PM EST.

Commercial Paper.   Although a bank itself cannot issue commercial paper, its parent holding company can; that is, Citigroup can issue commercial paper but Citibank cannot. This provides banks owned by holding companies—most of the largest banks in the United States—with an additional funding source. Specifically, when the bank itself finds funding tight, it can utilize the funds downstreamed from its holding company's issue of commercial paper. Indeed, Citigroup is one of the largest issuers of commercial paper in the United States. Note that funds downstreamed to an affiliated bank are subject to reserve requirements, detracting from the attractiveness of this mechanism as a regular funding source.

Medium-Term Notes.   A number of banks in search of more stable sources of funds with low withdrawal risk have begun to issue medium-term notes, often in the five- to seven-year range. These notes are additionally attractive because they are subject to neither reserve requirements nor deposit insurance premiums.

Discount Window Loans.   As discussed earlier, banks facing temporary liquidity crunches can borrow from the central bank's discount window at the discount rate.

Concept Questions

1. Describe the withdrawal risk and funding cost characteristics of some of the major liabilities available to a modern bank manager.
2. Since transaction accounts are subject to both reserve requirements and deposit insurance premiums, whereas fed funds are not, why shouldn't a bank fund all of its assets through fed funds? Explain your answer.
3. What are the major differences between fed funds and repurchase agreements?

Liquidity and Liability Structures for U.S. Banks

In this section we summarize the preceding discussion by looking at some balance sheet data for U.S. banks. In Table 18–5 we show the liquid asset–nonliquid asset composition of insured U.S. banks in 1997 versus 1960. We use 1960 as a benchmark year since the next year (1961) is widely viewed as the date when banks first began to actively manage their liabilities, with Citibank's innovation of wholesale CDs.

As you can see, the ratio of traditional liquid to illiquid assets has declined since 1960, with cash plus securities in 1997 comprising 28 percent of the asset balance sheet of insured banks versus 52 percent in 1960. However, it is arguable that such a comparison misrepresents and overstates the fall in bank asset liquidity, since bank loans themselves have become significantly more liquid over this 30-year period. As we discuss in Chapters 27 and 28, bank loans are increasingly being securitized and/or sold in secondary markets. This has fundamentally altered the illiquidity of bank loan portfolios and has made them more similar to securities than hitherto. The more liquid the loan portfolio, the less the need for large amounts of traditional liquid assets, such as cash and securities, to act as buffer reserves against unexpected liability withdrawals.

TABLE 18–5 **Liquid Assets versus Nonliquid Assets for Insured Commercial Banks, 1960 and 1997**

	Percentage	
Assets	*1960*	*1997*
Cash	20%	6.0%
Government and agency securities	24	15.4
Other securities*	8	6.6
Loans†	46	65.9
Other assets	2	6.1
	100%	100%

*Other securities = state and local, mortgage-backed, plus others.

†Loans = C&I, mortgage, consumer, and others.

Source: *Federal Reserve Bulletin,* various issues.

Table 18–6 **Liability Structure of Insured Commercial Banks, 1960 and 1997**

	Percentage	
Liabilities	*1960*	*1997*
Transaction accounts	61%	15.2%
Retail CDs and time deposits	29	36.5
Wholesale CDs and time deposits	0	13.0
Borrowings and other liabilities	2	26.5
Bank capital	8	8.8
	100%	100%

Source: *Federal Reserve Bulletin,* various issues.

In Table 18–6 we look at a breakdown of the liability composition of banks over the 1960 to 1997 period. The most striking feature of Table 18–6 has been the shift by banks away from funds sources with relative high withdrawal risk—transaction accounts (demand deposits and NOW accounts) and retail savings and time deposit accounts—to accounts or instruments over which a bank has greater potential control concerning the supply—for example, liability managed accounts. Specifically, the sum of transaction and retail savings and time deposit accounts fell from 90 percent in 1960 to 51.7 percent in 1997. By contrast, wholesale CDs and time deposits plus borrowed funds (fed funds, RPs, plus other borrowed funds) have expanded from 2 percent in 1960 to 39.5 percent in 1997. However, having a liability management strategy that reduces liability withdrawal risk doesn't come without a cost. As implied in Figure 18–2, there is often a trade-off between withdrawal risk and funding cost. As banks have sought to reduce their withdrawal risk by relying more on borrowed and wholesale funds, this has added to their interest expense.

Finally, too heavy a reliance on borrowed funds can be a risky strategy in itself. Even though withdrawal risk may be reduced if lenders in the market for borrowed funds have confidence in the borrowing bank, perceptions that the bank is risky can lead to nonrenewals of fed fund and RP loans and the nonrollover of wholesale CDs and other purchased funds as they mature. The best example of a bank that failed partly due to excessive reliance on large CDs and purchased funds was Continental Illinois in 1984 with more than 80 percent of its funds borrowed from wholesale lenders. Consequently, excessive reliance on borrowed funds may be as bad an overall liability management strategy as excessive reliance on transaction accounts and passbook savings. Thus, a well-diversified portfolio of liabilities may be the best strategy to balance withdrawal risk and funding cost considerations.

Concept Questions

1. Looking at Table 18–5, how has the ratio of traditional liquid to illiquid assets changed over the 1960–1997 period?
2. Looking at Table 18–6, how has the liability composition of banks changed over the 1960–97 period?

Liability and Liquidity Risk Management in Insurance Companies

Insurance companies use a variety of sources to meet liquidity needs. As discussed in Chapters 2 and 17, liquidity is required to meet claims on the insurance policies these FIs have written as well as unexpected surrenders of those policies. These contracts therefore represent a potential future liability to the insurance company. Ideally, liquidity management in insurance companies is conducted so that funds needed to meet claims on insurance contracts written can be met with premiums received on new and existing contracts. However, a high frequency of claims at a single point in time could force insurers to liquidate assets at something less than their fair market value (e.g., an unexpectedly severe hurricane season).

Insurance companies can reduce their exposure to liquidity risk by diversifying the distribution of risk in the contracts they write. For example, property-casualty insurers can diversify across the types of disasters they cover [e.g., in 1996 the top two property-casualty insurance companies (in terms of premiums sold) held policies for 18 different business lines from commercial auto liability (where they wrote 10.9 percent of all industry premiums) to homeowners multiple peril (where they wrote 35.1 percent of all industry premiums)].[24]

Alternatively, insurance companies can meet liquidity needs by holding relatively marketable assets to cover claim payments. Assets, such as government and corporate bonds and corporate stock, usually can be quickly liquidated at close to their fair market values in financial markets to pay claims on insurance policies when premium income is insufficient. For example, at the end of 1997 life insurance companies held 81.2 percent of their assets in the form of government securities and corporate securities (see Chapter 2). Because of the less predictable timing of claims against property-casualty insurers (i.e., fires, earthquakes, and floods), those insurers typically hold more bonds and common stock than do life insurance

---

[24]See *Best's Review,* August 1997.

companies. In 1997 property-casualty companies held 89.5 percent of their assets in the form of these assets.

Concept Questions

1. Discuss two strategies insurance companies can use to reduce liquidity risk.
2. Why would property-casualty insurers hold more short-term liquid assets to manage liquidity risk than life insurers hold?

Liability and Liquidity Risk Management in Other FIs

Other FIs (such as securities firms, investment banks, and finance companies) may experience liquidity risk if they rely on short-term financing (such as commercial paper or bank loans) and investors become reluctant to roll those funds over. Remember from Chapter 3 that the main sources of funding for securities firms are repurchase agreements, bank call loans,[25] and short positions in securities. Liquidity management for these FIs entails the ability to have sufficient cash and other liquid resources at hand to underwrite (purchase) new securities from quality issuers before reselling those securities to other investors. It also entails the ability of a securities firm to act as a market maker, which requires it to finance an inventory of securities in its portfolio. Similarly, in Chapter 5 we saw finance companies fund assets mainly with commercial paper and long-term debt. Liquidity management for these FIs entails the ability to fund loan requests and loan commitments of sufficient quality without delay.

A good example of a securities firm being subjected to a liquidity crisis was the experience of Drexel Burnham Lambert in 1989. Throughout the 1980s Drexel Burnham Lambert captured the bulk of the junk bond market by promising investors that it would act as a dealer for junk bonds in the secondary market. Investors were therefore more willing to purchase junk bonds because Drexel provided an implied guarantee that it would buy the securities back or find another buyer at market prices if an investor needed to sell. However, the junk bond market experienced extreme difficulties in 1989 as the prices of these securities fell reflecting the economy's move into a recession. Serious concerns about the creditworthiness of Drexel's junk bond–laden asset portfolio led creditors to deny Drexel extensions of its vital short-term commercial paper financings, and Drexel had to declare bankruptcy. Drexel's sudden collapse makes it very clear that access to short-term purchased funds is crucial to the health of securities firms.[26]

Concept Questions

1. What is a bank call loan?
2. Give two reasons why an investment bank needs liquidity.

---

[25]A bank call loan means that a lending bank can call in the loan from an investment bank with very little notice.

[26]For additional discussion of the failure of Drexel Burnham Lambert, see W. S. Haraf, "The Collapse of Drexel Burnham Lambert: Lessons for Bank Regulators," *Regulation,* Winter 1991, pp. 22–25.

Summary

Liquidity and liability management issues are intimately linked for the modern FI. Many factors, both cost and regulatory, impact on a FI manager's choice of the amount of liquid assets to hold. An FI's choice of liquidity is something of a knife edge situation, trading off the costs and benefits of undershooting or overshooting regulatory specified (and prudentially specified) reserve asset targets.

An FI can manage its liabilities in a fashion that affects the overall withdrawal risk of its funding portfolio and therefore the need for liquid assets to meet such withdrawals. However, reducing withdrawal risk often comes at a cost because liability sources that are easier to control from a withdrawal risk perspective are often more costly for the FI to utilize.

Questions and Problems

1. What are the benefits and costs to an FI of holding large amounts of liquid assets? Why are Treasury securities considered good examples of liquid assets?

2. How is an FI's liability and liquidity risk management problem related to the maturity of its assets relative to its liabilities?

3. Consider the assets (in millions) of two banks, A and B. Both banks are funded by $120 million in deposits and $20 million in equity. Which bank has the stronger liquidity position? Which bank probably has a higher profit?

Bank A Assets		*Bank B Assets*	
Cash	$ 10	Cash	$ 20
Treasury securities	$ 40	Consumer loans	$ 30
Commercial loans	$ 90	Commercial loans	$ 90
Total assets	$140	Total assets	$140

4. What concerns motivate regulators to require FIs to hold minimum amounts of liquid assets?

5. How do liquid asset reserve requirements enhance the implementation of monetary policy? How are reserve requirements a tax on FIs?

6. Rank-order the liquidity of the financial assets cash, corporate bonds, NYSE-traded stocks, and T-bills.

7. Define the reserve computation period, the reserve maintenance period, and the contemporaneous reserve accounting system.

8. City Bank has estimated that its average daily demand deposit balance over the recent 14-day computation period was $225 million. The average daily balance with the Fed over the 14-day maintenance period was $11 million, and the average daily balance of vault cash over the two-week period prior to the computation period was $7 million.

a. Under the rules effective in 1998, what is the amount of average daily reserves required to be held during the reserve maintenance period for these demand deposit balances?

b. What is the average daily balance of reserves held by the bank over the maintenance period? By what amount were the average reserves held higher or lower than the required reserves?

c. If the bank had transferred $20 million of its deposits every Friday over the two-week computation period to one of its offshore facilities, what would be the revised average daily reserve requirement?

9. Assume that the 14-day reserve computation period for problem (8) above extended from May 18 through May 31.

a. What is the corresponding reserve maintenance period under the rules effective in 1998?

b. Given your answers to parts (a) and (b) of problem (8), what would the average required reserves need to be for the last two days of the maintenance period for the bank to be in reserve compliance?

10. The average demand deposit balance of a local bank during the most recent reserve computation period is $225 million. The amount of average daily reserves at the Fed during the reserve maintenance period is $16 million, and the average daily vault cash corresponding to the maintenance period is $4 million.

a. What is the average daily reserve balance required to be held by the bank during the maintenance period?

b. Is the bank in compliance with the reserve requirements?

c. What amount of reserves can be carried over to the next maintenance period either as excess or as shortfall?

d. If the local bank has an opportunity cost of 6 percent, what is the effect on the income statement from this reserve period?

11. The following demand deposits and cash reserves at the Fed have been documented by a bank for computation of its reserve requirements (in millions) under two-day lagged contemporaneous reserve accounting.

	Monday 10th	Tuesday 11th	Wednesday 12th	Thursday 13th	Friday 14th
Demand deposits	$200	$300	$250	$280	$260
Reserves at Fed	20	22	21	18	27

	Monday 17th	Tuesday 18th	Wednesday 19th	Thursday 20th	Friday 21st
Demand deposits	$280	$300	$270	$260	$250
Reserves at Fed	20	35	21	18	28

	Monday 24th	Tuesday 25th	Wednesday 26th	Thursday 27th	Friday 28th
Demand deposits	$240	$230	$250	$260	$270
Reserves at Fed	19	19	21	19	24

The average vault cash for the computation period has been estimated to be $2 million per day.

   a. What level of average daily reserves is required to be held by the bank during the maintenance period?

   b. Is the bank in compliance with the requirements?

   c. What amount of required reserves can be carried over to the following computation period?

   d. If the average cost of funds to the bank is 8 percent per year, what is the effect on the income statement for this bank for this reserve period?

12. Prior to February 1984, (and since 1998) reserve requirements in the United States were (are) computed on a lagged reserve accounting system. Under lagged reserve accounting, the reserve computation period preceded the reserve maintenance period by two weeks pre 1984 (and by 17 days post-1998).

   a. Contrast a contemporaneous reserve accounting (CRA) system with a lagged reserve accounting (LRA) system.

   b. Under which accounting system, CRA or LRA, are bank reserves higher? Why?

   c. Under which accounting system, CRA or LRA, is bank uncertainty higher? Why?

   d. Why did the Fed move from LRA to CRA in 1984?

13. What is the "weekend game"? Contrast the bank's ability and incentive to play the weekend game under LRA as opposed to CRA.

14. Under CRA, when is the uncertainty about the reserve requirement resolved? Discuss the feasibility of making large reserve adjustments during this period of complete information.

15. What is the relationship between funding cost and funding or withdrawal risk?

16. An FI has estimated the following annual costs for its demand deposits: management cost per account = $140, average account size = $1,500, average number of checks processed per account per month = 75, cost of clearing a check = $0.10, fees charged to customer per check = $0.05, and average fee charged per customer per month = $8.

   a. What is the implicit interest cost of demand deposits for the FI?

   b. If the FI has to keep an average of 8 percent of demand deposits as required reserves with the Fed, what is the implicit interest cost of demand deposits for the FI?

   c. What should be the check-clearing fees to reduce the implicit interest cost to 3 percent? Ignore the reserve requirements.

17. A NOW account requires a minimum balance of $750 for interest to be earned at an annual rate of 4 percent. An account holder has maintained an average balance of $500 for the first six months and $1,000 for the remaining six months. She writes an average of 60 checks per month and pays $0.02 per check, although it costs the bank $0.05 to clear a check.

   a. What average return does the account holder earn on the account?

   b. What is the average return if the bank lowers the minimum balance to $400?

   c. What is the average return if the bank pays interest only on the amount in excess of $400? Assume that the minimum required balance is $400.

   d. How much should the bank increase its check-clearing fee to ensure that the average interest it pays on this account is 5 percent? Assume that the minimum required balance is $750.

18. Rank-order the following liabilities, with respect first to funding risk and then to funding cost.

   a. Money market mutual funds.

   b. Demand deposits.

   c. Certificates of deposit.

   d. Federal funds.

   e. Bankers acceptances.

   f. Eurodollar deposits.

   g. Money market demand deposits.

   h. NOW accounts.

   i. Wholesale CDs.

   j. Passbook savings.

   k. Repos.

   l. Commercial paper.

19. How is the withdrawal risk different for federal funds and repurchase agreements?

20. How does the cash balance, or liquidity, of an FI determine the types of repurchase agreements into which it will enter?

21. How does the cost of MMMFs differ from the cost of MMDAs? How is the spread useful in managing the withdrawal risk of MMDAs?

22. Why do wholesale CDs have minimal withdrawal risk to the issuing bank?

23. What characteristics of fed funds may constrain a bank's ability to use fed funds to expand quickly its liquidity?

24. What does a low fed funds rate indicate about the level of bank reserves? Why does the fed funds rate have higher than normal variability around the last two days in the reserve maintenance period?

25. What trends have been observed between 1960 and 1997 in regard to liquidity and liability structures of commercial banks? What changes have occurred in the management of assets that may cause the measured trends to be overstated?

26. What are two primary methods that insurance companies can use to reduce their exposure to liquidity risk?

DEPOSIT INSURANCE AND OTHER LIABILITY GUARANTEES

Introduction

In Chapter 17, we discussed the liquidity risks faced by FIs, and in Chapter 18 we described ways in which FIs can better manage that risk. Because of concerns about the asset quality or solvency of an FI, liability holders such as depositors and life insurance policyholders have incentives to engage in runs, that is, to withdraw all their funds from an FI. As we discussed in Chapter 17, the incentive to run is accentuated in banks, thrifts, and insurance companies by the sequential servicing rule used to meet liability withdrawals. As a result, deposit and liability holders who are first in line to withdraw funds get preference over those last in line.

While a run on an unhealthy FI is not necessarily a bad thing—it can discipline the performance of managers and owners—there is a risk that runs on bad FIs can become contagious and spread to good or well-run FIs. In contagious run or panic conditions, liability holders do not bother to distinguish between good and bad FIs but instead seek to turn their liabilities into cash or safe securities as quickly as possible. This has a major contractionary effect on the supply of credit as well as the money supply.

Moreover, a contagious run on FIs can have other serious social welfare effects. In particular, a major run on banks can have an adverse effect on the level of savings and therefore inhibit the ability of individuals to transfer wealth through time to protect themselves against major risks such as future ill health and falling income in old age.

Because of such wealth, money supply, and credit supply effects, government regulators of financial service firms have introduced guaranty programs to deter runs by offering liability holders varying degrees of failure protection. Specifically, if a liability holder believes a claim is totally secure even if the FI is in trouble, there is no incentive to run. The liability holder's place in line no longer affects getting his or her funds back. Regulatory guaranty or insurance programs for liability holders deter runs and thus deter contagious runs and panics.

Federally backed insurance programs include the Federal Deposit Insurance Corporation (FDIC) (created in 1933) for banks and thrifts, the Securities Investors Protection Corporation (SIPC) (created in 1970) for securities firms, and the Pension Benefit Guaranty Corporation (PBGC) (created in 1974) for private pension funds.[1] In addition, because of their state rather than federal regulation, state-organized guaranty funds back up most life and property-casualty insurance companies.

We analyze deposit insurance funds for banks and thrifts and then look at the special features of the guaranty funds for other FIs.

The History of Bank and Thrift Guaranty Funds

The FDIC

The FDIC was created in 1933 in the wake of the banking panics of 1930–33, when some 10,000 commercial banks failed. The original level of individual depositor insurance coverage at commercial banks was $2,500, which was increased to $100,000 in 1980. Between 1945 and 1980, commercial bank deposit insurance

---

[1]Until its insolvency in 1989, FSLIC (the Federal Savings and Loan Insurance Corporation) insured the deposits of most thrifts. Since 1989, both banks and thrifts have been insured under the umbrella of the FDIC, as we discuss later in this chapter.

clearly worked; there were no runs or panics, and the number of individual bank failures was very small (see Figure 19–1).

Beginning in 1980, however, bank failures accelerated, with more than 1,039 failures in the decade ending in 1990, peaking at 221 in 1988. This number of failures was actually larger than that for the entire 1933–79 period. Moreover, the costs to the FDIC were often larger than those for the mainly small bank failures in 1933–79. As the number and costs of these closures mounted in the 1980s, the FDIC fund became rapidly weakened. Any insurance fund becomes insolvent if the premiums collected and the reserves built up from investing premiums are insufficient to offset the cost of failure claims. The FDIC's resources were virtually depleted by early 1991, when it was given permission to borrow $30 billion from the Treasury. Even then, it ended 1991 with a deficit of $7 billion. In response to this crisis, Congress passed the FDIC Improvement Act (FDICIA) in December 1991 to restructure the bank insurance fund and prevent its potential insolvency.

Since 1991 there has been a dramatic turnaround in the fund's finances and a drop in bank failures—partially in response to record profit levels in banks. Specifically, at the end of 1997, the FDIC's Bank Insurance Fund (BIF) had reserves of $28 billion and the number of bank failures had fallen to zero. In 1996 there were 5 failures, in 1995 there were 6 failures, and in 1994 there were 13 failures. The fund's reserves now stand at a record high, with reserves exceeding 1.35 percent of insured deposits.

The FSLIC and Its Demise

FSLIC covered savings and loan associations (S&Ls); other thrifts, such as mutual savings banks, often chose to be insured under the FDIC rather than FSLIC.[2] Like the FDIC, this insurance fund was in relatively good shape until the end of the 1970s. Beginning in 1980, the fund's resources were rapidly depleted as more and more thrifts failed and had to be closed or merged. The causes of these failures were many, including fraud, risky lending, declining real estate values, and insider loans. A major reason was thrifts' exposure to interest rate risk due to their massive duration mismatches of assets and liabilities in 1979–82. In this period, interest rates rose to historically high levels, resulting in a major fall in the market values of thrifts' long-term fixed-rate mortgage portfolios. Between 1980 and 1988, 514 thrifts failed, at an estimated cost of $42.3 billion. Moreover, between 1989 and 1992, an additional 734 thrifts failed, at a cost of $78 billion. As a result of these failures, by 1989 the FSLIC fund had a negative net worth—its present value of liabilities exceeded its assets—variously estimated at between $40 and $80 billion. Lacking the resources to close and resolve failing thrifts, the FSLIC had to follow a policy of forbearance toward the closure of failed and failing thrifts. This meant that many bad thrifts stayed open and their losses continued to accumulate.

In August 1989, Congress passed the Financial Institutions Reform, Recovery, and Enforcement Act (FIRREA), largely in response to the deepening crisis in the

---

[2]As we discussed in Chapter 1, credit union depositors enjoy a degree of coverage similar to that of bank, S&L, and savings bank depositors via coverage through the National Credit Union Insurance Fund (established in 1971). See Edward J. Kane and Robert Hendershott, "The Federal Deposit Insurance Fund That Didn't Put a Bite on U.S. Taxpayers," *Journal of Banking and Finance* 20, no. 5 (1996), pp. 1305–27. Christine A. McClatchey and Gordon V. Karels, "Deposit Insurance and Risk-Taking Behavior in the Credit Union Industry," University of Nebraska, Working Paper, 1996, look at whether credit unions increased their risk-taking behavior after credit union deposits became federally insured. They find that asset quality and liquidity improved over the period following the institution of deposit insurance.

FIGURE 19–1

Number of Failed Banks by Year, 1934–1997

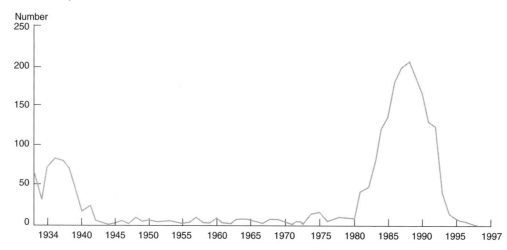

Source: FDIC annual reports and statistics on banking.

FIGURE 19–2

FDIC, BIF, and SAIF

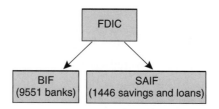

thrift industry and the growing insolvency of FSLIC. This act completely restructured the savings bank fund and transferred its management to the FDIC.[3] At the same time, the restructured savings bank insurance fund became the Savings Association Insurance Fund (SAIF). FDIC manages SAIF separately from the commercial bank fund, which is now called the Bank Insurance Fund (BIF). (At the end of 1997, SAIF had $9.3 billion in reserves, representing 1.32 percent of insured deposits.) We present the organizational structure of FDIC and these funds in Figure 19–2.

Finally, the *Resolution Trust Corporation* (RTC), an agency created by FIRREA in 1989, began resolving failed savings and loan assets through liquidations and restructuring of troubled savings banks by recapitalizations and mergers. The FIRREA gave the RTC $50 billion to undertake this task, supplemented by a further $18 billion in December 1993. By the date of its termination (December 31, 1995), the RTC had resolved 747 thrift institution failures at an estimated cost of $90.1 billion.[4]

---

[3]At that time, FSLIC ceased to exist.

[4]D.P. Ely and N. P. Varaiya argue that this cost ($90.1 billion) is an underestimate since it ignores the opportunity cost to taxpayers of providing "equity" to the RTC to resolve these failures. When this opportunity cost is added in, the total cost of the RTC resolutions rises to between $112 and $146 billion. (See D. P. Ely and N. P. Varaiya, "Opportunity Costs Incurred by the RTC in Cleaning up S and L Insolvencies," *Quarterly Review of Economics and Finance* 36, no. 3 (1996), pp. 291–310.

Arguably, FIRREA and FDICIA, along with record profitability in the banking and thrift industries, have engineered a dramatic turnaround in the prospects of the BIF and SAIF funds as we move into the next millennium.

Concept Questions

1. What events led to Congress's passing of the FDIC Improvement Act (FDICIA)?
2. What events brought about the demise of the FSLIC?
3. What is (or was) the RTC?

The Causes of the Depository Fund Insolvencies

There are two not necessarily independent views of why depository institution insurance funds became insolvent in the 1980s. In addition, some factors offer better explanations of FSLIC insolvency than of FDIC insolvency, especially as the FSLIC insolvency was far worse than the FDIC insolvency.

The Financial Environment

One view is that a number of external events or shocks adversely impacted U.S. banks and thrifts in the 1980s. The first was the dramatic rise in interest rates in the 1979–82 period. As we noted earlier, this rise in rates had a major negative effect on those thrifts funding long-term, fixed-rate mortgages with short-term deposits. The second event was the collapse in oil, real estate, and other commodity prices, which particularly harmed oil, gas, and agricultural loans in the southwestern United States. The third event was increased competition at home and abroad, which eroded the value of bank and thrift charters during the 1980s (see Chapters 21 to 23).[5]

Moral Hazard

A second view is that these financial environment effects were catalysts for, rather than causes of, the crisis. At the heart of the crisis was deposit insurance itself, especially some of its contractual features. Although deposit insurance had deterred depositors and other liability holders from engaging in runs prior to 1980, in so doing it had also removed or reduced depositor discipline. Deposit insurance allowed banks to borrow at rates close to the risk-free rate and, if they chose, to undertake high-risk asset investments. Bank managers knew that insured depositors had little incentive to restrict such behavior either through fund withdrawals or by requiring risk premia on deposit rates since they were fully insured by the FDIC if a bank failed. Given this scenario, losses on oil, gas, and real estate loans in the 1980s are viewed as the outcome of bankers exploiting underpriced or mispriced risk under the deposit insurance contract. When the provision of insurance encourages rather than discourages risk taking, this is called **moral hazard** because it increases the scope of the risk exposure faced by insurers.[6]

Moral Hazard
The loss exposure faced by an insurer when the provision of insurance encourages the insured to take more risks.

---

[5]The value of a bank or thrift charter is the present value of expected profits from operating in the industry. As expected profits fall, so does the value of a bank or thrift charter.

[6]The precise definition of moral hazard is that it is the loss exposure of an insurer (the FDIC) that results from the character or circumstances of the insured (here, the bank).

In the absence of depositor discipline (as will be explained below), regulators could have priced risk taking by bankers either through charging explicit deposit insurance premiums linked to bank risk taking or by charging **implicit premiums** through restricting and monitoring the risky activities of banks. This could potentially have substituted for depositor discipline; those banks that took more risk would have paid directly or indirectly for this risk-taking behavior. However, from 1933 until January 1, 1993, regulators levied deposit insurance premiums based on bank deposit size rather than on a risk basis. The 1980s were also a period of deregulation and capital adequacy forbearance rather than stringent activity regulation and tough capital requirements. Moreover, for the FSLIC, the number of bank examinations and examiners actually fell between 1981 and 1984.[7] Finally, prompt corrective action for undercapitalized banks did not begin until the end of 1992 (see Chapter 20).

Concept Questions

1. What two basic views are offered to explain why depository institution insurance funds became insolvent during the 1980s?
2. Why was interest rate risk less of a problem for banks than for thrifts in the early 1980s?

Panic Prevention versus Moral Hazard

A great deal of attention has been focused on the moral hazard reason for the collapse of the bank and thrift insurance funds in the 1980s. The less bank owners have to lose from taking risks, the greater are their incentives to take excessively risky asset positions. When asset investment risks or gambles pay off, bank owners make windfall gains in profits. If they fail, however, the FDIC, as the insurer, bears most of the costs, given that owners of banks—like owners of regular corporations—have limited liability. It's a heads I win, tails I don't lose (much) situation.

Note that even without deposit insurance, the limited liability of bank owners or stockholders always creates incentives to take risk at the expense of fixed claimants such as depositors and debtholders.[8] The only difference between banks

---

[7]L. J. White points to a general weakness of thrift supervision and examination in the 1980s. The number of examinations fell from 3,210 in 1980 to 2,347 in 1984, and examinations per billion dollars of assets fell from 5.41 in 1980 to 2.4 in 1984. See L. J. White, *The S and L Debacle* (New York: Oxford University Press, 1991), p. 89.

[8]See K. John, T. John, and L. W. Senbet, "Risk Shifting Incentives of Depository Institutions: A New Perspective on Federal Deposit Insurance Reform," *Journal of Banking and Finance* 36, (1991), pp. 335–67. Thus, one possible policy to reduce excessive bank risk taking would be to eliminate limited liability for bank stockholders. A study by L. J. White found that bank failures in private banking systems with unlimited liability, such as that which existed in 18th-century Scotland, were rare. Indeed, in the United States, double liability existed for bank stockholders prior to the introduction of deposit insurance; that is, on failure, the stockholders would lose their initial equity contribution and be assessed by the receiver an extra amount equal to the par value of their stock, which would be used to pay creditors (over and above the liquidation value of the bank's assets). See L. J. White, "Scottish Banking and Legal Restrictions Theory: A Closer Look," *Journal of Money Credit and Banking* 22 (1990), pp. 526–36. For a discussion of double liability in pre-1933 United States, see A. Saunders and B. Wilson, "If History Could Be Re-Run: The Provision and Pricing of Deposit Insurance in 1933," *Journal of Financial Intermediation* 4 (1995), pp. 396–413; and J. R. Macey and G. P. Miller, "Double Liability of Bank Shareholders: History and Implications," *Wake Forest Law Review* 27 (1992), pp. 31–62.

FIGURE 19–3

*Bank Run Risk versus
Moral Hazard Risk
Trade-Off*

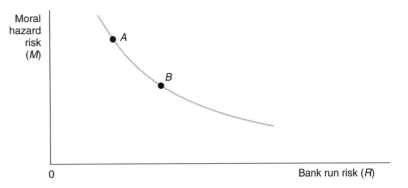

**Actuarially Fairly
Priced Insurance**
Insurance pricing based
on the perceived risk of
the insured.

and firms is that mispriced deposit insurance, when risk taking is not **actuarially
fairly priced** in **insurance** premiums, adds to the incentives of bank stockholders
to take additional risk.

Nevertheless, even though mispriced deposit insurance potentially accentuates
bank risk taking, we have also seen from Figure 19–1 that deposit insurance effectively deterred bank panics and runs of the 1930–33 kind in the postwar period. That
is, deposit insurance has ensured a good deal of stability in the credit and monetary
system.

This suggests that ideally, regulators should design the deposit insurance contract with the trade-off between moral hazard risk and bank panic or run risk in
mind. For example, by providing 100 percent coverage of all depositors and reducing the probability of runs to zero, the insurer may be encouraging a significant degree of moral hazard risk-taking behavior among certain banks. On the other hand,
a very limited degree of deposit insurance coverage might encourage runs and panics, although moral hazard behavior itself would be less evident. We depict the potential trade-off between bank run risk and moral hazard risk in Figure 19–3.

In the 1980s, the insurance contract wound up at a point such as *A* in Figure
19–3, where depositors had little incentive to engage in runs and bank owners and
managers had strong incentives to engage in moral hazard risk-taking behavior.[9] By
restructuring the deposit insurance contract, it may be possible to reduce moral hazard risk quite a bit without a very large increase in bank run risk. Such a point might
be *B* in Figure 19–3. To some extent, these were the objectives behind the passage
of the FDIC Improvement Act (FDICIA) of 1991 and the depositor preference

---

[9]At this point, note that managers may not have the same risk-taking incentives as owners. This is especially true if managers are compensated through wage and salary contracts rather than through shares and
share option programs. Where managers are on fixed-wage contracts, their preferences in regard to risk lean
toward being risk averse. That is, they are unlikely to exploit the same type of moral hazard incentives that
stockowner-controlled banks would. This is because managers have little to gain if their banks do exception-
ally well (their salaries are fixed) but probably will lose their jobs and human capital investments in a bank
if they fail. A study by A. Saunders, E. Strock, and N. Travlos showed that stockowner-controlled banks tend
to be more risky than manager-controlled banks. Thus, understanding the agency structure of the bank is
important in identifying which banks are most likely to exploit risk-taking (moral hazard) incentives. See
A. Saunders, E. Strock, and N. Travlos, "Ownership Structure, Deregulation, and Bank Risk Taking," *Journal of Finance* 45 (1989), pp. 643–54. Moreover, as pointed out by K. John, A. Saunders, and L. Senbet in
"A Theory of Bank Regulation and Management Compensation," Working Paper, Salomon Center, New
York University, February 1998, deposit insurers might usefully take into account managerial compensation
structures and incentives in setting deposit insurance premiums.

legislation contained in the Omnibus Budget Reconciliation Act of 1993, discussed later in this chapter. Of course, Figure 19–3 is only illustrative. We don't know the actual shape of the moral hazard bank run risk trade-off as the deposit insurance contract changes; however, we expect the relationship to be inverse, and pricing bank risk taking more explicitly should discourage moral hazard behavior.[10]

Concept Questions

1. Historically, what effect has deposit insurance had on bank panics and runs?
2. How would levying actuarially fairly priced deposit insurance premiums on banks change the trade-off in Figure 19–3?
3. If the FDIC provided deposit insurance free of charge to banks and covered all depositors, roughly where would we be on the trade-off curve in Figure 19–3?

Controlling Bank Risk Taking

There are three ways in which a deposit insurance contract could be structured to reduce moral hazard behavior:

1. Increase stockholder discipline.
2. Increase depositor discipline.
3. Increase regulator discipline.

Specifically, redesigning the features of the insurance contract can either directly impact bank owners' and stockholders' risk-taking incentives or indirectly affect their risk-taking incentives by altering the behavior of depositors and regulators. In the wake of the insolvency of the FDIC, in 1991, the FDIC Improvement Act (FDICIA) was passed with the objective of increasing discipline in all three areas.

Stockholder Discipline

Insurance Premiums.   One approach toward making stockholders' risk taking more expensive is to link FDIC insurance premiums to the risk profile of the bank. Below we look at ways in which this might be done, including the risk-based premium scheme adopted by the FDIC since 1993.

Theory.   A major feature of the pre-1993 FDIC deposit insurance contract was the flat deposit insurance premium levied on banks and thrifts. Specifically, each year a bank paid a given sum or premium to the FDIC based on a fixed proportion of its domestic deposits. [11] Until 1989, the premium was 8.33 cents per $100 in domestic

---

[10]E. Kane, "Three Paradigms for the Role of Capitalization Requirements in Insured Financial Institutions," *Journal of Banking and Finance,* 19 June 1995, pp. 431–60, models the trade-off between the level of risk taking eventually undertaken by banks, contractual features of deposit insurance, and capital regulation as the outcome of a "bargaining game" among three different groups of agents (with different preferences regarding risk-taking) and the "agency conflicts" among these groups. The groups are bank stockholders, bank managers, and the providers of insurance guarantees (the FDIC).

[11]In actual practice, premiums are levied and paid semiannually.

deposits.[12] As the FDIC fund became increasingly depleted, the level of the premium was raised several times but its risk-insensitive nature was left unaltered. By 1993 the premiums banks had to pay had risen to 23 cents per $100 of their domestic deposits, almost a tripling of their premiums since 1988.[13]

To see why a flat or size-based premium schedule does not discipline a bank's risk taking, consider two banks of the same domestic deposit size, as shown in Table 19–1. Banks A and B have domestic deposits of $100 million and would pay the same premium to the FDIC (.0023 × $100 million = $230,000 per annum). However, their risk-taking behavior is completely different. Bank A is excessively risky, investing all its assets in real estate loans. Bank B is almost risk fee, investing all of its assets in government T-bills. We graph the insurance premium rates paid by the two banks compared to their asset risk in Figure 19–4.

In Figure 19–4, note that under the pre-1993 flat premium schedule, banks A and B would have been charged the same deposit insurance premium based on a bank's domestic deposit size. Critics of flat premiums argue that the FDIC should act more like a private property-casualty insurer. Under normal property-casualty insurance premium setting principles, insurers charge those with higher risks higher premiums. That is, low-risk parties (such as bank B) do not generally subsidize high-risk parties (such as bank A) as they did under the pre-1993 FDIC premium pricing scheme. If premiums increased as bank risk increased, banks would have reduced incentives to take risks. Therefore, the ultimate goal might be to price risk in an actuarially fair fashion, similar to a private property-casualty insurer, so that premiums reflect the expected private costs or losses to the insurer from the provision of deposit insurance.

TABLE 19–1   Flat Deposit Insurance Premiums and Risk Taking

Bank A				Bank B			
Assets		*Liabilities*		*Assets*		*Liabilities*	
Real estate loans	100	Domestic deposits	100	T-bills	100	Domestic deposits	100

FIGURE 19–4

Premium Schedules Relative to Risk

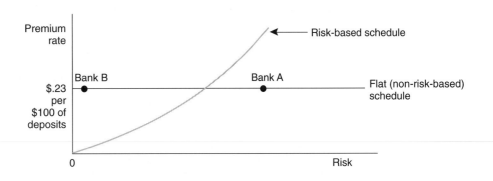

[12]In the pre-1980 period, the FDIC was able to rebate some of these premiums as it felt it had adequate reserves at the time. See S. A. Buser, A. H. Chen, and E. J. Kane, "Federal Deposit Insurance, Regulatory Policy, and Optimal Bank Capital," *Journal of Finance* 36 (1981), pp. 51–60.

[13]This was also the rate for thrifts insured under SAIF.

FIGURE 19–5

Deposit Insurance as a Put Option (0D = bank's deposits; 0A = bank's assets; 0P = premium paid by bank)

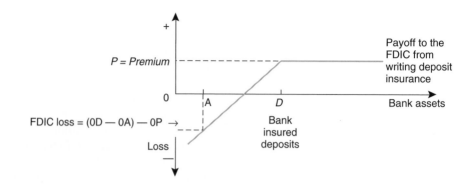

Note that there are arguments against imposing an actuarially fair risk-based premium schedule. If the deposit insurer's mandate is not to act as if it were a private cost minimizing insurer such as a PC insurance company, because of social welfare considerations, some type of subsidy to banks and thrifts can be justified. Remember that the FDIC is a quasi-government agency, and broader banking market stability concerns and savers' welfare concerns might arguably override private cost minimizing concerns and require subsidies.[14] Other authors have argued that if an actuarially fair premium is imposed on a banking system that is fully competitive, banking itself cannot be profitable. That is, some subsidy is needed for banks to profitably exist.[15] However, while U.S. banking is competitive, it probably deviates somewhat from the perfectly competitive model.

Calculating the Actuarially Fair Premium.   Economists have suggested a number of approaches for calculating the fair premium that a cost-minimizing insurer should charge. One approach would be to set the premium equal to the expected severity times the frequency of losses due to bank failure plus some load or markup factor. This would exactly mimic the approach toward premium setting in the property-casualty industry. However, the most common approach has been to view the FDIC's provision of deposit insurance as virtually identical to the FDIC writing a put option on the assets of the bank that buys the deposit insurance.[16,17] We depict the conceptual idea underlying the option pricing model (OPM) approach in Figure 19–5.

In this framework, the FDIC charges a bank a premium 0P to insure a bank's deposits (0D). If the bank does well and the market value of the bank's assets is greater than 0D, its net worth is positive and it can continue in business. The FDIC would face no charge against its resources, and would keep the premium paid to it

[14]Most of the deposit insurance literature, however, assumes that the objective of the FDIC should be to minimize cost; see S. Acharya and J. F. Dreyfus, "Optimal Bank Reorganization Policies and the Pricing of Federal Deposit Insurance," *Journal of Finance* 44 (1988), pp. 1313–34. Also, the FDIC Improvement Act generally confirms cost minimization as an important objective defining FDIC's policies.

[15]See Y. S. Chan, S. I. Greenbaum, and A. V. Thakor, "Is Fairly Priced Deposit Insurance Possible?" *Journal of Finance* 47 (1992), pp. 227–46; and Buser, Chen, and Kane, "Federal Deposit Insurance," ibid.

[16]See, for example, R. C. Merton, "An Analytic Derivation of the Cost of Deposit Insurance and Loan Guarantees: An Application of Modern Option Pricing Theory," *Journal of Banking and Finance* 1 (1977), pp. 3–11; and E. Ronn and A. K. Verma, "Pricing Risk-Adjusted Deposit Insurance: An Option-Based Model," *Journal of Finance* 41 (1986), pp. 871–96.

[17]There is a third approach that views deposit insurance premiums being set as the outcome of an agency conflict among three groups of self-interested parties: bank stockholders, bank managers, and bank regulators. See E. J. Kane "Three Paradigms," op cit.

FIGURE 19–6

*Average Deposit
Insurance Liability,
OPM Estimates*

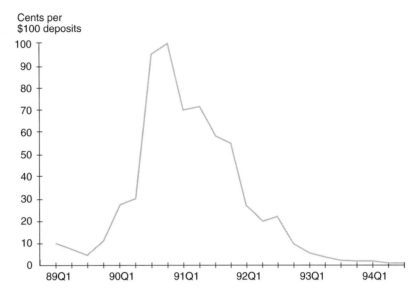

Source: Federal Reserve Bank of San Francisco, Newsletter 95–08.

by the bank (0*P*). If the bank is insolvent, possibly because of a bad or risky asset portfolio, such that the value of the bank's assets (0*A*) falls below 0*D,* and its net worth is negative, the bank owners will "put the bank" back to the FDIC. If this happens, the FDIC will pay out to the insured depositors an amount 0*D* and will liquidate the bank's assets (0*A*). As a result, the FDIC bears the cost of the insolvency (or negative net worth) equal to (0*D* − 0*A*) minus the insurance premiums paid by the bank (0*P*).

When valued in this fashion as a simple European put option, the FDIC's cost of providing deposit insurance increases with the level of asset risk (σ^2_A) and with the bank's leverage (*D/A*). That is, the actuarially fair premium (0*P*) is equivalent to the premium on a put option and as such should be positively related to both asset risk (σ^2_A) and leverage risk (*D/A*).[18] One OPM estimate of the average fair insurance premium based on the option pricing model for 300 banks is shown in Figure 19–6 for 1989–94.[19] The decline in average fair premia after 1991 reflects a decline in bank asset volatility and improvements in bank leverage risk (*D/A*) since 1991.

---

[18]In Merton, "An Analytic Derivation," the value of a deposit insurance guaranty is shown to be the same as the Black-Scholes model for a European put option of maturity *T* (where *T* is the time period until the next premium assessment):

$$0P(T) = De^{-rT}\phi(X_2) - A\phi(X_1)$$
$$\text{where: } X_1 = \{ \log (D/A) - (r + \sigma^2_A/2)T \}/\sigma_A \sqrt{T}$$
$$X_2 = X_1 + \sigma_A \sqrt{T}$$

and ϕ is the standard normal distribution.

Other authors have relaxed many of Merton's assumptions, including (1) allowing for partial deposit insurance coverage (Ronn and Verma, "Pricing Risk-Adjusted Deposit Insurance"), (2) closure taking place when *D* < *A* (i.e., forbearance) rather than *D* = *A* (Ronn and Verma, and Acharya and Dreyfus, "Optimal Bank Reorganization"), (3) surveillance and monitoring involving costs (R. C. Merton, "On the Cost of Deposit Insurance When There Are Surveillance Costs," *Journal of Business* 51 (1978), pp. 439–52), and (4) the option being American rather than European, that is, closure exercisable at any time during the insurance contract period rather than at the end (Merton, "On the Cost").

[19]See M. Levonian and F. Furlong, "Reduced Deposit Insurance Risk," Federal Reserve Bank of San Francisco Weekly Letter, no. 95–08, February 24, 1995.

Even though the option pricing model is a conceptually and theoretically elegant tool, it is difficult to apply in practice—expecially as asset risk (σ^2_A) is not directly observable. Such risk can be proxied by using the variance of a bank's stock market returns; however, only 300 banks have their stocks traded on the three major exchanges (AMEX, NASDAQ, and NYSE), and there are over 9,000 banks. Even so, the option model framework is useful because it indicates that both leverage and asset quality (or risk) are important elements that should enter into any deposit insurance pricing model. Next, we look at the risk-based deposit insurance premium scheme introduced by the FDIC in January 1993; it is directly linked to both bank leverage and asset quality.

Concept Questions

1. Bank A has a ratio of deposits to assets of 90 percent and a variance of asset returns of 10 percent. Bank B has a ratio of deposits to assets of 85 percent and a variance of asset returns of 5 percent. Which bank should pay the higher insurance premium?
2. If deposit insurance is similar to a put option, who exercises that option?
3. If you are managing a bank that is technically insolvent but has not yet been closed by the regulators, would you invest in Treasury bonds or real estate development loans? Explain your answer.

Implementing Risk-Based Premiums.   The FDIC Improvement Act (FDICIA) required the FDIC to establish risk-based premiums by January 1, 1994. The FDIC now has to base premiums on:[20]

1. Different categories and concentrations of assets.
2. Different categories and concentrations of liabilities—insured, uninsured, contingent, and noncontingent.
3. Other factors that affect the probability of loss.
4. The deposit insurer's revenue needs.[21]

The FDIC first introduced a risk-based deposit insurance program on January 1, 1993. Under this program, which applied equally to all depository-insured institutions, a bank or thrift's risk would be ranked along a capital adequacy dimension and a supervisory dimension. That is, rankings were partly based on regulators' judgments regarding asset quality, loan underwriting standards, and other operating risks. Since each dimension had three categories, a bank or thrift was placed in any one of nine cells. See Table 19–2 (panel A) for the original structure of premiums.

The best banks, those in cell 1 that were well capitalized and healthy, paid an annual insurance premium of 23 cents per $100 of deposits, while the worst banks paid 31 cents. At the time of the risk-based premiums' introduction, the FDIC estimated that about 75 percent of the then over 12,000 insured commercial banks and savings banks (with 51 percent of the bank deposit base) and 60 percent of the 2,300 insured thrifts (with approximately 43 percent of the thrift deposit base) were in the

---

[20]The FDIC is also allowed to reinsure up to 10 percent of an insured institution's risk and to use reinsurance prices to set the insured's premiums.

[21]In particular, it cannot cut premiums until the fund's reserves exceed 1.25 percent of insured deposits. Since 1996 this target level has been exceeded by both BIF and SAIF.

TABLE 19–2   Shifting the Deposit Insurance Burden

A. The fee structure for deposit insurance, effective January 1, 1993.

Supervisory Groups

Capital Category	Healthy[1]	Supervisory Concern[2]	Substantial Supervisory Concern[3]
Well capitalized[4]	**23** cents per $100	**26** cents per $100	**29** cents per $100
Adequately capitalized[5]	**26** cents per $100	**29** cents per $100	**30** cents per $100
Undercapitalized[6]	**29** cents per $100	**30** cents per $100	**31** cents per $100

B. The fee structure for deposit insurance, effective January 1, 1997.

Supervisory Groups

Capital Category	Healthy[1]	Supervisory Concern[2]	Substantial Supervisory Concern[3]
Well capitalized[4]	**0** cents per $100	**3** cents per $100	**17** cents per $100
Adequately capitalized[5]	**3** cents per $100	**10** cents per $100	**24** cents per $100
Undercapitalized[6]	**10** cents per $100	**24** cents per $100	**27** cents per $100

Note: Numbers in cells show premiums (bold type)

[1]Financially sound and only a few weaknesses.

[2]Weaknesses that if not corrected could result in significant risk to the fund.

[3]Substantial probability of loss to the fund unless effective corrective action is taken.

[4]Total risk based $\geq$ 10 percent, Tier 1 risk based $\geq$ 6 percent, Tier 1 leverage $\geq$ 5 percent.

[5]Total risk based $\geq$ 8 percent, Tier 1 risk based $\geq$ 4 percent, Tier 1 leverage $\geq$ 4 percent.

[6]Does not meet the capital criteria for well or adequately capitalized depository institutions.

Source: From the *New York Times,* September 16, 1992, p. D2. Copyright © 1992 by The New York Times. Reprinted by permission; and Tara Rice, Comptroller of the Currency, January 1997.

group paying the lowest premium. Only about 220 banks (2 percent of all insured commercial and savings banks) and 160 thrifts (7 percent of all insured thrifts) were in the group paying the highest insurance premiums. The average assessment rate in 1993 was 23.2 cents per $100 of deposits. However, the improving solvency position of the FDIC (and of the banks and thrifts it insures) has resulted in a considerable reduction in insurance premiums. Specifically, since 1996 over 90 percent of banks have had to pay the statutory minimum premium, which has fallen to zero. Thrifts have faced a similar reduction in their premiums since 1997. The 1997 fee structure is shown in Table 19–2 (panel B), with the average assessment rate equal to 0.3 cents per $100 of deposits.[22]

Increased Capital Requirements and Stricter Closure Rules.   A second way to reduce stockholders' incentives to take excessive risks would be to (1) require higher capital—lower leverage—ratios (so that stockholders have more at stake in taking risky investments) and (2) impose stricter bank closure rules. The moral hazard risk-taking incentives of bank owners increase as their capital or net worth approaches zero and their leverage increases. For those thrifts allowed to operate in

---

[22]Beginning in January 1997, all insured banks also had to pay a charge of 1.3 cents per $100 of deposits to help pay off the bonds (so-called FICO bonds) issued to aid the FDIC's restructuring operations in the 1990s.

Capital Forbearance
Regulators allowing an FI
to continue operating even
when its capital funds are
fully depleted.

the 1980s with virtually no book equity capital and with negative net worth, the risk-taking incentives of their owners were enormous.

By failing to close such thrifts, regulators exhibited excessive **capital forbearance.** In the short term, forbearance may save the insurance fund some liquidation costs. In the long run, owners of bad banks or thrifts have continuing incentives to grow and take additional risks in the hope of a large payoff that could turn the institution around. This strategy potentially adds to the future liabilities of the insurance fund and to the costs of bank liquidation. We now know that huge additional costs were the actual outcome of the regulators' policy of capital forbearance in the thrift industry in the 1980s.

As we discuss in Chapter 20, a system of risk-based capital requirements mandates that those banks and thrifts taking greater on- and off-balance-sheet credit and interest rate risks must hold more capital. Thus, risk-based capital is supporting risk-based deposit insurance premiums by increasing the cost of risk taking for bank stockholders.[23] In addition, the 1991 FDIC Improvement Act has sought to increase significantly the degree of regulatory discipline over bank stockholders by introducing a prompt corrective action program. This has imposed five capital zones for banks and thrifts, with progressively harsher mandatory actions being taken by regulators as capital ratios fall. Under this carrot and stick approach, a bank or thrift is placed into receivership within 90 days of the time when its capital falls below some positive book value level, that is, when it is critically undercapitalized (currently 2 percent of assets for banks).

To the extent that the book value of capital approximates true net worth or the market value of capital, this enhances stockholder discipline by imposing additional costs on bank owners for risk taking. It also increases the degree of coinsurance, in regards to risks taken, between bank owners and regulators.[24]

Concept Question

Do we need both risk-based capital requirements and risk-based premiums to discipline shareholders?

Depositor Discipline

An alternative, more indirect route to disciplining riskier banks is to create conditions for a greater degree of depositor discipline. Depositors could either require higher interest rates and risk premiums on deposits or ration the amount of deposits they are willing to hold in riskier banks.

Critics argue that under the current insurance contract, neither insured depositors nor uninsured depositors have sufficient incentives to discipline riskier banks. To understand these arguments, we consider the risk exposure of both insured and uninsured depositors under the current deposit insurance contract.

Insured Depositors.   When the deposit insurance contract was introduced in 1933, the level of coverage per depositor was $2,500. This coverage cap has

---

[23]On the assumption that new equity is more costly to raise than deposits for banks.

[24]Looking at the implementation of prompt corrective action between December 1992 and December 1995, the GAO found that regulators closed or merged all but 2 of 25 critically undercapitalized banks within the required 90-day time frame. See GAO, "Bank and Thrift Regulation: Implementation of FDICIA's Prompt Regulatory Action Provisions," GAO/GGO, 97–18 (November 1996).

TABLE 19–3   Deposit Ownership Categories

Individual ownership, such as a simple checking account.

Joint ownership, such as the savings account of a husband and wife.

Revocable trusts, in which the beneficiary is a qualified relative of the settlor, and the settlor has the ability to alter or eliminate the trust.

Irrevocable trusts, where the beneficial interest is not subject to being altered or eliminated.

Interests in employee benefit plans where the interests are vested and thus are not subject to being altered or eliminated.

Public units, that is, accounts of federal, state, and municipal governments.

Corporations and partnerships.

Unincorporated businesses and associations.

Individual retirement accounts (IRAs).

Keogh accounts.

Executor or administrator accounts.

Accounts held by banks in an agency or fiduciary capacity.

Source: U.S. Department of the Treasury, "Modernizing the Financial System; Recommendations for Safer More Competitive Banks," Washington, D.C.: February 1991.

gradually risen through the years, reaching $100,000 in 1980. The $100,000 cap concerns a depositor's beneficial interest and ownership of deposited funds. In actuality, by structuring deposit funds in a bank or thrift in a particular fashion, a depositor can achieve many times the $100,000 coverage cap on deposits. To see this, consider the different categories of deposit fund ownership available to an individual shown in Table 19–3.

IRA and Keogh Accounts
Private pension plans held by individuals with banks or other FIs.

A married couple with one daughter, where both husband and wife had **individual retirement accounts (IRA)** and **Keogh** private pension plans at the bank, could garner a total coverage cap of $800,000 as a family: his individual deposit account, her individual deposit account, their joint deposit account, their daughter's deposit account held in trust, his IRA account, his Keogh account, her IRA account, and her Keogh account. When the range of ownership is expanded in this fashion, the coverage cap for a family can rapidly approach $1 million or more.

Note that this coverage ceiling is *per bank;* wealthy and institutional investors can employ **deposit brokers** to spread their funds over many banks up to the permitted cap. In this way, all their deposits become explicitly insured. For example, a wealthy individual with $1 million in deposits could hire a deposit broker such as Merrill Lynch to split the $1 million into 10 parcels of $100,000 and deposit those funds at 10 different banks. During the 1980s, the greatest purchasers of brokered deposits were the most risky banks that had no, or limited, access to the borrowed funds market. These risky banks attracted brokered deposits by offering higher interest rates than did relatively healthy banks. In fact, a high proportion of brokered deposits held by a bank became an early warning signal of its future failure risk. Neither the depositors nor the fund brokers were concerned about the risk of these funds because every parcel of $100,000 was fully insured, including interest accrued up until time of failure.[25]

Deposit Brokers
Break up large deposits into smaller units at different banks to ensure full coverage by deposit insurance.

In 1984, the FDIC and FSLIC introduced a joint resolution intending to deny insurance coverage to funds invested by deposit brokers. After extensive congressional hearings, this resolution was ultimately rejected; however, in 1989

---

[25]Technically, principal on deposits plus accrued interest up to $100,000 is covered.

Congress passed the Financial Institutions Reform, Recovery, and Enforcement Act (FIRREA). It specified that insured financial institutions that failed to meet capital standards would be prohibited from accepting brokered deposits as well as from soliciting deposits by offering interest rates significantly higher than prevailing rates. The FDIC Improvement Act (FDICIA) of 1991 formalized these restrictions by allowing access to brokered deposits only to banks and thrifts in Zone 1 capital range. Under the prompt corrective action plan, this means banks with total risk-based capital ratios exceeding 10 percent. Banks outside this range are generally precluded unless they receive specific approval from the FDIC. These restrictions became effective in June 1992.[26]

Finally, the FDIC Improvement Act left the insured depositor coverage cap unchanged at $100,000. While lowering the coverage cap would increase the incentives of depositors to monitor and run from more risky banks, it would also increase the number of bank failures and the probability of panics. Thus, the gains to the FDIC from covering a smaller dollar amount of deposits per head would have to be weighed against the possibility of more failures, with their attendant liquidation costs. This suggests that setting the optimal level of the insurance cap per depositor per bank is a far from easy problem[27]

Uninsured Depositors.   The primary intention of deposit insurance is to deter bank runs and panics. A secondary and related objective has been to protect the smaller, less informed saver against the reduction in wealth that would occur if that person were last in line when a bank fails. Under the current contract, the small, less informed depositor is defined by the $100,000 ceiling. Theoretically at least larger, informed depositors with more than $100,000 on deposit are at risk if a bank fails. As a result, these large uninsured depositors should be sensitive to bank risk and seek to discipline more risky banks by demanding higher interest rates on their deposits or withdrawing their deposits completely. Until recently, the manner in which bank failures have been resolved meant that both large and small depositors were often fully protected against losses. This was especially so where large banks got

Too Big to Fail Banks
Regulators view these banks as being too big to be closed and liquidated without imposing a systemic risk to the banking and financial system.

into trouble and were viewed as **too big to fail.** That is, they were too big to be liquidated by regulators either because of the draining effects on the resources of the insurance fund or for fear of contagious or systemic runs spreading to other major banks. Thus, although uninsured depositors tended to lose in small bank failures, in large bank failures the failure resolution methods employed by regulators usually resulted in implicit 100 percent deposit insurance. As a result, for large banks in particular, neither small nor large depositors had sufficient incentives to impose market discipline on riskier banks.

To understand these arguments, we look at the major ways bank failures were resolved before the passage of the FDIC Improvement Act in 1991. We also look at the post-1992 procedures required under the FDICIA and the Depositor Preference legislation under the Omnibus Budget Reconciliation Act of 1993 to create greater

---

[26]There were certain other provisions limiting coverage to an individual, including coverage of certain pension fund accounts (other than IRA and Keogh) and investment accounts. So-called pass-through insurance, where a bank manages pension funds on behalf of a large number of savers, such as investing in bank investment contracts (BIC) is fully covered by FDIC insurance up to $100,000 per head only if the bank is eligible to issue brokered deposits and/or meets the highest capital standards.

[27]For a modeling of this problem, see J. F. Dreyfus, A. Saunders, and L. Allen, "Deposit Insurance and Regulatory Forbearance: Are Caps on Insured Deposits Optimal?" *Journal of Money, Credit and Banking* 26 (August 1994), part 1, pp. 412–38.

exposure for uninsured depositors and creditors and to reduce the FDIC's failure resolution costs.

Failure Resolution Procedures Pre-FDICIA.   Pre-FDICIA, the three failure resolution methods were the payoff method, the purchase and assumption method, and the open assistance method. Before the passage of the FDICIA in 1991, the FDIC had to use liquidation (**the payoff method**) unless an alternative method was judged by the FDIC to cost less. This method of choosing the closure policy is "a less than liquidation cost requirement" and contrasts with a true "least-cost resolution" policy where the lowest-cost method of all closure methods available would be selected.[28] Not until the passage of the FDICIA was the least-cost resolution required of the FDIC. In addition, prior to 1991, the less than liquidation cost requirement could be overridden and the bank kept open in a restructured form if its continued operation was deemed essential for the local community. The FDICIA also repealed this "essentiality" provision.

Next, we look in more detail at the three principal methods of failure resolution employed by the FDIC. We also discuss how the FDICIA and the Depositor Preference legislation of 1993 have changed the FDIC's strategy and, most importantly, the potential effects of these changes on increasing depositor discipline.

- **The payoff method (liquidation).** Historically, the payoff method has resolved most small bank failures where a merger was unavailable or too costly or where the bank's loss to the community would impose few local social costs. Under a payoff closure, regulators liquidate the assets of the bank and pay off the insured depositors in full (insured deposit payoff). They could also transfer these deposits in full to another local bank (insured deposit transfer). In Table 19–4, compare the relative sizes of these two payoff methods over the 1986–97 period.[29] On liquidation, uninsured depositors and the FDIC, which assumes the claims of the insured depositors, had pro rata claims to the remaining value of the failed bank's assets up until 1993. However, with the passage of the 1993 Depositor Protection legislation, the FDIC and *domestic* uninsured depositors have been given priority over *foreign* uninsured depositors (e.g., in overseas branches of a failed bank) as well as over creditors supplying federal funds on the interbank market. This reduces the FDIC's potential liability.[30]

To understand who gains and who potentially loses under the payoff (liquidation) method, consider the simple example of a failed bank in Table 19–5. The failed bank's liquidation value of assets is only $80 million. It has $50 million in outstanding claims held by small insured depositors whose claims individually are $100,000 or less and $50 million in uninsured domestic depositor claims that individually exceed $100,000. The net worth of the failed bank is negative $20 million.

On closure, the insured depositors receive a $50 million payoff in full.[31] The FDIC liquidates the $80 million in assets and shares it on an equal, or pro rata,

Payoff Method of Closure
Liquidating the bank and paying off the bank's depositors.

---

[28]See R. S. Carnell, "A Partial Antidote to Perverse Incentives: The FDIC Improvement Act of 1991." Paper presented at a Conference on Rebuilding Public Confidence through Financial Reform, Ohio State University, Columbus, June 25, 1992.

[29]There were five payoffs in 1993 and zero in 1994–97. The remaining resolutions during 1996–97 were all purchase and assumptions (P&As).

[30]The FDIC has estimated savings of up to $1 billion over the 1993–98 period. However, this ignores the greater incentives of uninsured foreign depositors and bank creditors to engage in runs.

[31]Instead of a payoff in full, in an insured deposit transfer their deposits are transferred in full to another local bank.

TABLE 19–4   **Summary Statistics for Banks Resolved by the Federal Deposit Insurance Corporation by Type of Resolution, 1986–1997**

Type of Resolution	Bank Resolved, 1986–1997		Estimated Losses to the Bank Insurance Fund		Assets Recorded at Time of Resolution		Losses as a Percentage of Assets*	Average Asset Size of Resolved Banks (millions of dollars)*
	Number of Banks	*(percentage of total)*	*(millions of dollars)*	*(percentage of total)*	*(millions of dollars)*	*(percentage of totals)*		
Payoffs and transfers								
Deposit payoff	75	6	$ 1,337	4	$ 3,969	2	34	$52.9
Deposit transfer	153	12	2,865	10	9,725	4	29	63.6
Subtotal	228	18	4,202	14	13,694	6	31	60.1
Purchases and assumption								
Toal bank	291	23	9,802	32	72,120	32	14	247.8
Insured deposits only	90	7	2,470	8	23,176	10	11	257.5
Clean and other	596	48	12,103	40	102,670	45	12	172.5
Subtotal	977	78	24,375	80	197,966	87	12	202.6
Assistance transactions	54	4	1,860	6	16,914	7	11	313.2
Total	1,259	100	$30,437	100	$228,574	100	13	$181.6

Notes: Sample includes commercial and savings banks insured by the Bank Insurance Fund that were resolved between 1986 and 1995. Assets are those recorded at time of resolution.

*Figures represent averages for each type of resolution.

Source: Congressional Budget Office analysis based on Federal Deposit Insurance Corporation, *Failed Bank Cost Analysis,* 1985–1995; and FDIC Historical Statistics, 1996.

TABLE 19–5   **Failed Bank Balance Sheet**
(in millions of dollars)

Assets		Liabilities	
Asset (liquidation value)	$ 80	Insured deposits	$ 50
		Uninsured domestic deposits	50
	$ 80		$100

basis with the uninsured domestic depositors. Since the FDIC owns 50 percent of deposit claims and the uninsured domestic depositors own the other 50 percent, each gets $40 million on the liquidation of the bank's assets.

The allocation of the $20 million net worth loss of the bank among the three parties or claimants follows:[32]

	Loss
Insured depositors	$ 0
FDIC	10
Uninsured domestic depositors	10
	$20

[32]We do not show the value of the equity holders' claims or those of foreign uninsured depositors and creditors in this example. Since they have junior claims to these three parties (the FDIC, the insured depositors, and uninsured domestic depositors), their claims are reduced to zero on failure.

Table 19–6   A Traditional or Clean P&A Transaction

Assets		Liabilities		
Good assets	$ 80	Insured depositors	$ 50	
				→ Good bank (acquirer)
FDIC cash infusion	20	Uninsured depositors	50	
	$100		$100	

The negative $20 million net worth loss of the bank is shared pro rata by the FDIC and the uninsured domestic depositors.[33] From this example, it is clear that if the payoff method were always used to resolve bank failures, uninsured depositors would have very strong incentives to monitor bank risk taking. They would also discipline owners by requiring higher risk premiums on their deposits and/or withdrawing their deposits from riskier banks.

While regulators have frequently used the payoff method, this has been mostly for small failing banks (see the relatively small average asset size of these banks in Table 19–5). They have used the second and third closure methods described next most often for large failing banks. As will become clear, these methods impose much less discipline on uninsured depositors.

Purchase and Assumption (P&A)
Merger of a failed bank with a healthy bank.

• **Purchase and assumption (P&A).**   As shown in Table 19–4, there are three types of purchase and assumption resolutions. That most commonly used prior to the FDIC Improvement Act was the traditional "clean" P&A method; beginning in 1987, regulators tried total bank P&As. Since 1992 (and post-FDICIA), the FDIC has used insured deposit P&As in an increasing number of cases.

Under a traditional "clean" purchase and assumption, a stronger healthy bank purchases and assumes both the insured and uninsured deposits of the failed bank as well as its remaining good assets, mostly securities. The difference between the total deposits of the failed bank and the market value of the failed bank's good assets is met by a cash infusion from the FDIC minus any takeover premium the acquiring bank is willing to pay. For large bank failures, total or whole bank P&As transferred all assets, good and bad, with a lower initial FDIC cash infusion but with an option for the acquiring bank to put back uncollectible bad assets (up to some limit) to the FDIC at a later date. Insured deposit P&As will be discussed later in this chapter, as they have significantly altered the degree of risk borne by uninsured depositors post-FDICIA.

To understand the mechanics of a traditional clean P&A and who bears the losses, we look at a P&A of the same bank discussed in the *payoff* (liquidation) example earlier (see Table 19–6).

The clean P&A transfers all depositors, insured and uninsured (both domestic and foreign), as well as other liabilities to the acquiring bank. Thus, neither the insured nor the uninsured depositors lose. The full $20 million loss is borne by the FDIC through its cash injection to clean up the failed bank's bad assets prior to the merger with the acquiring bank minus any premium it can obtain from the

---

[33]In insured deposit transfers, when the insured deposits of the failed bank are transferred to another bank and its assets are liquidated, the acquirer of the insured deposits sometimes pays a premium to the FDIC reflecting the value of picking up new deposit customers. Any such premium would lower the costs of liquidation to the FDIC.

acquiring bank.[34] For example, a bank in New York may pay a premium to acquire a failing bank in Florida because Florida is a high-growth market.

To summarize the losses of the three parties in a traditional clean P&A:

Loss (in millions)	
Insured depositors	0
Uninsured depositors	0
FDIC	$20 (minus any merger premium)
	Total $20

Clearly, with a clean P&A, large uninsured depositors are de facto insured depositors.

Open Assistance
Provision of FDIC loans or capital funds to keep a large failing bank open as part of a restructuring plan.

• **Open assistance.** The third main method of closure regulators used is open assistance (see Table 19–4). When very large banking organizations fail, such as Continental Illinois in 1984 with $36 billion in assets and First City Bancorporation of Texas in 1987 with $11 billion in assets, it is often difficult, if not impossible, to find a bank sound and big enough to engage in a P&A. Moreover, regulators fear that smaller correspondent banks will be hurt by a large bank's closure and that big depositors and investors might lose confidence in all large U.S. banks if they used payoff and liquidation. Open bank assistance can take the form of promissory notes, net worth certificates, cash, infusions of equity, and so on. An example of open assistance was the commitment of $870 million by the FDIC to an investor group headed by Robert Abboud to take over control of First City Bancorporation of Texas in September 1987. However, failure to close and liquidate a bad bank sends a strong and undesirable signal to large uninsured depositors at other big banks that their deposits are safe and that regulators will not permit big banks to fail. That is, all large uninsured depositors with big banks are really implicitly 100 percent insured, thereby alleviating depositors from any monitoring/market discipline responsibilities.[35] Such an implicit guaranty to uninsured depositors at large banks is often called the too big to fail guaranty.[36]

In 1987, the Competitive Equality Banking Act allowed for a new form of open bank assistance called the bridge bank. Two examples of bridge banks were First Republic Bancorp ($33.7 billion) and MCorp ($15.4 billion). In these cases, the

---

[34]In recent years, regulators have held auctions to select the acquiring bank. However, the bank that bids the highest premium does not always win; the FDIC takes into account the quality of the bidder as well. For example, a low-quality bank that acquires a failed bank in an auction might become a bigger problem bank in the future.

[35]For example, in the final restructuring arrangement for Continental Illinois, all depositors were protected; the FDIC assumed a large amount of problem loans and infused $1 billion new capital into the bank with a part convertible into a direct ownership interest. By taking an equity stake in the failed bank, the FDIC stood to gain, with outside equity owners, from any improvement in the performance of the bank as well. Indeed, in a number of open assistance programs, the FDIC held (holds) long-term options or warrants that allow it to share in the upside of improved bank performance (if any). Nevertheless, the incentive to impose market discipline has still been eliminated for large uninsured depositors.

[36]O'Hara and Shaw and Mei and Saunders seek to calculate the value of such a too big to fail guarantee. O'Hara and Shaw find significant value while Mei and Saunders find little value from such guarantees. See M. O'Hara and W. Shaw, "Deposit Insurance and Wealth Effects: The Value of Being Too Big to Fail," *Journal of Finance* 45 (1990), pp. 1587–1600; and J. P. Mei and A. Saunders, "Bank Risk and Too Big to Fail Guarantees: An Asset Pricing Perspective," *Journal of Real Estate Finance and Economics* 10 (1995), pp. 199–224.

TABLE 19–7   Least-Cost Resolutions (LCR) Requirements under FDICIA

The FDIC must:
- Consider and evaluate all possible resolution alternatives by computing and comparing their costs on a present value basis, using realistic discount rates.
- Select the least costly alternative based on the evaluation.
- Document the evaluation and the assumption on which it is based, including any assumptions with regard to interest rates, asset recovery rates, asset holding costs, and contingent liabilities.
- Retain documentation for at least five years.

Source: GAO, 1992 Bank Resolutions, GAO/GGD-94–197, p. 14.

FDIC took over the bank and managed its operations prior to sale. A bridge bank can last as long as five years. Technically, bridge banks are government-run banks.

Failure Resolution Policies Post-FDICIA.   In the wake of the FDIC's growing deficit, the FDICIA sought to pass more of the costs of insured bank failures on to uninsured depositors, thereby enhancing their incentives to monitor banks and to control risk through interest rates and/or in their deposit placement decisions.

The FDICIA required that a least-cost resolution (LCR) strategy be put in place by the FDIC. In applying the LCR strategy, the FDIC evaluates failure resolution alternatives on a present value basis and documents their assumptions in deciding which method to use (see Table 19–7). These decisions can be audited by the General Accounting Office, the government's audit watchdog.

However, there was a very important and controversial exemption to using least-cost resolution in all cases. Specifically, a systemic risk exemption applies where a large bank failure could cause a threat to the whole financial system. Then methods that could involve the full protection of uninsured depositors as well as insured depositors could be used. This appears to allow the "too big to fail" guaranty to large bank uninsured depositors prevalent in the pre-1991 system to carry over after the passage of the FDICIA. However, the act has restricted when this systemic risk exemption can be used. Such an exemption is allowed only if a two-thirds majority of the boards of the Federal Reserve and the FDIC recommend it to the secretary of the Treasury and if the secretary of the Treasury, in consultation with the president of the United States, agrees. Further, any cost of such a bailout of a big bank would have to be shared among all other banks by charging them an additional deposit insurance premium based on their size as measured by their domestic and foreign deposits as well as their borrowed funds, excluding subordinated debt. Because large banks have more foreign deposits and borrowed funds, they will have to make bigger contributions (per dollar of assets) than smaller banks to any future bailout of a large bank.

Nevertheless, some concern has been raised about the continuance of the too big to fail (TBTF) guarantee even in its more restricted form. With the growing wave of bank and financial service firm mergers, it is argued that more and more FIs are likely to be covered by TBTF guarantees.[37] If we use the same asset-size cutoff

---

[37]Indeed, the Federal Reserve–organized $3.5 billion bank bailout of the Long-Term Capital Management (LTCM) hedge fund has been described by some as a TBTF bailout because the fund was allowed to continue operations largely on the basis of the size of its exposure both in capital market instruments and in derivatives of over $1.25 trillion in nominal value. The fear here was that allowing LTCM to liquidate its positions at a massive loss could cause a number of banks that had lent money to the fund to fail or be significantly undercapitalized once losses were written off. Others have argued that this was not really a TBTF bailout in the conventional sense since no government money was directly involved.

FIGURE 19–7

*Failed Commercial Banks
by Uninsured Depositor
Treatment, 1986–1997*

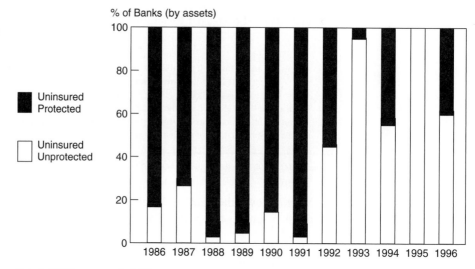

Note: In 1997 there were no bank failures.
Source: Federal Reserve Bank of Minneapolis and Federal Deposit Insurance Corp., 1997

(adjusted for inflation) that the Comptroller of the Currency used in specifying the 11 banks that were to be protected as being TBTF after the Continental Illinois failure in 1984, we find that today this amounts to an asset size of around $38 billion. As of 1998, 21 banking organizations had assets exceeding this figure, representing 38 percent of all uninsured deposits.[38]

With the exception of the systemic risk exemption the least-cost resolution strategy requires the FDIC to employ the method that imposes most failure costs on the uninsured depositors. To this end, the FDIC has been increasingly using an **insured depositor transfer** (IDT) or "haircut" method to resolve a number of post-1991 failures. For example, in 60 out of 122 failures in 1992, the FDIC imposed initial losses or haircuts on uninsured depositors ranging from 13 to 69 percent. The size of the haircut depends mostly on the FDIC-estimated value of the failed bank's assets. The total dollar size of 1992 haircuts taken by uninsured depositors was $80 million. Figure 19–7 shows the increased propensity of uninsured depositors to be left unprotected (and thus subject to haircuts) since 1986. We describe a simplified form of the IDT or haircut method next. This allows us to compare the cost of this new approach to that of previous methods such as the traditional P&A and payoff methods.

Insured Depositor Transfer
Uninsured depositors take a loss or haircut on failure equal to the difference between their deposit claims and the estimated value of the failed bank's assets minus insured deposits.

In Table 19–8, the failed bank in panel *a* has only $80 million in good assets to meet the $50 million in deposit claims of insured depositors and the $50 million in claims of the uninsured depositors.[39] Under an IDT in panel *b,* the FDIC would transfer the $80 million in assets to an acquiring bank along with the full $50 million in small insured deposits but only $30 million of the $50 million in uninsured deposits.[40] Notice that the uninsured depositors get protection only against losses up

---

[38]See Federal Reserve Bank of Minneapolis, Annual Report, 1997 ("Fixing FDICIA: A Plan to Address the Too-Big-To-Fail Problem").

[39]That is, it has $20 million negative net worth.

[40]Unlike in a P&A, it would not inject cash into the failed bank prior to a merger with the acquiring bank.

TABLE 19–8   An Insured Depositor Transfer Resolution

(a) Failed				(b) Insured Depositor Transfer				
Assets		*Liabilities*		*Assets*		*Liabilities*		
Good assets	$80	Insured deposits	$50	Good assets	$80	Insured deposits	$50	Merger
							$\rightarrow$	with good
		Uninsured deposits	50			Uninsured deposits	30	bank
	$80		$100		$80		$80	

to the difference between the estimated value of the failed bank's assets and its insured deposits. In effect, the uninsured depositors are subject to a haircut to their original deposit claims of $20 million (or, as a percentage, 40 percent of the value of their deposit claims on the failed bank). After the IDT, the uninsured depositors own $30 million in deposits in the acquiring bank and $20 million in receivership claims on the bad assets of the failed bank. Only if the FDIC as receiver can recover some value from the $20 million in bad assets will the loss to the uninsured be less than $20 million.

To summarize the losses of the three parties under the IDT:

Loss (in millions)		
Insured depositors	=	0
FDIC	=	0
Uninsured depositors	=	$20

As you can see from this simple example, the uninsured depositors bear all the losses and now have a much stronger incentive than before to monitor and control the actions of bank owners through imposing market discipline via interest rates and the amount of funds deposited.[41]

Concept Questions

1. In Table 19–5, how would the losses of the bank be shared if insured deposits were 30 and uninsured deposits were 70?
2. List four factors that might influence an acquirer to offer a large premium when bidding for a failed bank.
3. Make up a simple balance sheet example to show a case where the FDIC can lose even when it uses an IDT to resolve a failed bank.

---

[41]For evidence that uninsured creditors (in this case, bank bondholders) impose market discipline on riskier banks, see M. J. Flannery and S. M. Sorescu, "Evidence of Bank Market Discipline in Subordinated Debenture Yields: 1983–1991," *Journal of Finance* 51, no. 4, pp. 1347–77.

Regulatory Discipline

To bolster increased stockholder and depositor discipline, the FDICIA imposed additional regulatory discipline. The act perceived two areas of regulatory weakness: (1) the frequency and thoroughness of examinations and (2) the forbearance shown to weakly capitalized banks in the pre-1991 period.

Examinations.   First, the act required improved accounting standards for banks, including working toward the market valuation of balance sheet assets and liabilities. This would improve the ability of examiners to monitor banks' net worth positions off-site and is consistent with monitoring the true net worth of the bank (see Chapters 8 and 9). Second, beginning in December 1992, the act required an annual on-site examination of every bank.[42] Third, private accountants were given a greater role in monitoring a bank's performance with independent audits being mandated. This is similar to the United Kingdom, where the 1987 Bank Act required an enhanced role for private auditors as a backup for regulatory examiners.

Capital Forbearance.   The introduction of prompt corrective action capital zones (see Chapter 20), along with the mandatory actions required of regulators in each of those zones (including closure), is symptomatic of a movement toward a regulatory policy based on rules rather than discretion. Such rules clearly direct the regulators to act in a certain manner even if they are reluctant to do so out of self-interest or for other reasons. The weakness of such rules is that if a policy is bad, then bad policy becomes more effective.[43]

Concept Question

What additional measures were mandated by the FDICIA to bolster stockholder and depositor discipline?

Non-U.S. Deposit Insurance Systems

Deposit insurance systems are increasingly being adopted worldwide. See Appendix 19A for a description of systems in the European Union and G-10 countries. Many of these systems offer quite different degrees of protection to depositors compared to the United States. In response to the single banking and capital market in Europe, the EC has proposed establishing a single deposit insurance system covering all European Community–located banks, to be introduced at the end of 1999. This would insure deposit accounts up to 20,000 ECUs. However, depositors would be subject to a 10 percent deductible in order to create incentives for them to

---

[42]Although the timing of examinations is secret, M. Flannery and J. Houston, in "Market Responses to Federal Examinations of U.S. Bank Holding Companies," GSBA University of Florida, October 1993, mimeograph, find that examinations have a positive effect on bank equity values since an examination is seen as certifying (or reducing uncertainty surrounding) reported accounting values of banks, for example, the size of nonperforming loans. See, also, R.DeYoung et al., "Could Publication of Bank CAMEL Ratings Improve Market Discipline?" Comptroller of the Currency, 1998, mimeograph.

[43]Similar arguments have been made in the area of monetary policy, where proponents (such as monetarist Milton Friedman) have argued for a rules based policy built around a constant growth rate of the money supply. However, most central bankers prefer discretion in deciding on the timing and size of monetary policy actions such as their open market operations.

monitor banks. Currently, the United Kingdom insures up to £20,000 with a 10 percent deductible and Germany provides virtually 100 percent insurance to depositors (each nonbank depositor is insured up to 30 percent of a bank's capital). The idea underlying the EC plan is to create a level playing field for banks across all European Community countries.

Japan also has a deposit insurance system that was established in 1971. Currently, the Japanese banking system appears to be going through a similar experience to U.S. banks and thrifts in the 1930s and 1980s, with record bad debts (over $600 billion in 1998) and bank failures. The effect on its deposit insurance fund has also been similar to the United States in the 1980s, with a rapidly declining reserve fund that has limited its ability to deal with the crisis. As the Contemporary Perspectives box on p. 430 explains, this has led to a government "bailout" to the tune of some $500 billion.

The Discount Window

Deposit Insurance versus the Discount Window

The previous sections have described how a well-designed deposit insurance system might impose stockholder, depositor, and manager discipline. Such a system can potentially stop bank runs and extreme liquidity problems arising in the banking system without introducing significant amounts of moral hazard risk-taking behavior among insured institutions.

Whether the FDICIA (and the Depositor Preference legislation) has priced risk accurately enough to stop all but the most egregious cases of moral hazard, only time, as well as the next recession, will tell. It has certainly increased the incentives of bank owners, uninsured depositors, and regulators to monitor and control bank risk. As such, the changes made under the act are considerable improvements over the old deposit insurance contract.

However, deposit insurance isn't the only mechanism by which regulators mitigate bank liquidity risk. A second mechanism has been the central banks' provision of a lender of last resort facility through the discount window.

The Discount Window

Discount window
Central bank lender of last resort facility.

Traditionally, central banks such as the Federal Reserve have provided a **discount window** facility to meet the short-term, nonpermanent liquidity needs of banks.[44] For example, suppose a bank has an unexpected deposit drain close to the end of a reserve requirement period and cannot meet its reserve target. It can seek to borrow from the central bank's discount window facility. Alternatively, short-term seasonal liquidity needs due to crop planting cycles can also be met through discount window loans. Normally, such loans are made by a bank discounting short-term high-quality paper such as Treasury bills and bankers acceptances with the central bank. The rate at which such paper is discounted is called the discount rate and is set by the central bank. In the United States the central bank has traditionally set the

---

[44]In times of extreme crisis, the discount window can meet the liquidity needs of securities firms as well (as was the case during the stock market crash of October 19, 1987).

Contemporary Perspectives

THE TIMID JAPANESE BANKING BAILOUT JUST MIGHT DO THE JOB

Michael M. Weinstein

The law the Japanese Parliament recently passed to rescue broken-down banks commits several blunders. It does not require insolvent banks to close. It does not require banks to disclose losses. It does not require wobbly banks that accept taxpayer money to lend to credit-worthy borrowers—the primary purpose of a bailout. The obvious prediction is that Japan will remain credit-starved, dragging down other economies in Asia and beyond.

But the obvious may be wrong. The law takes the important step of injecting public money into failing banks. Despite its flaws, the measure might pry open clogged credit lines and channel money to companies in need of a fresh start. As Adam Posen of the Institute for International Economics, author of a new book on the Japanese economy, says, "The bill will succeed despite itself."

Japan's banks are buried in bad loans and confront an economy that has slipped into recession. Thus they are loath to lend even to reliable customers. But if banks do not lend, companies cannot invest, and the economy cannot grow.

The crisis has been worsened by an accounting system that lets banks mask losses. Fanciful financial reports have scared away investors and creditors. Worse, the phantom bookkeeping pretends that borrowers can repay impossibly big loans.

Japan needs to have its banks wipe bad loans from their books so borrowers can start fresh. To that end, the law creates three pots of public money totaling about $500 billion, more than 10 percent of Japan's annual output. America's bailout of savings and loans in the 1980's cost about 2 or 3 percent of output.

The first pot, about $150 billion, will pay off depositors at banks that close. Their assets will be transferred to a Government agency for resale to private investors, much the way the Resolution Trust Corporation worked in the United States.

The second pot, also around $150 billion, will be used to nationalize insolvent banks the Government decides to keep open. The Government will run these banks until private owners take over, mirroring the way the Roosevelt Administration handled the 1930's banking crisis.

The third, most-controversial pot has no American parallel. It will pump about $200 billion into private banks the Government deems shaky but solvent. In return, the Government will get stock. The idea is that the taxpayer money will build up the banks' capital so they can resume lending.

Daniel K. Tarullo, formerly President Clinton's top adviser on international economic policy, is unconvinced the plan will work. "There is no clear mechanism for moving the $500 billion out the door of Government and into banks," he says. "Banks have to ask for assistance. But by asking for assistance, the bank managers identify themselves as incompetent, invoke intrusive Government

discount rate below market rates, such as the overnight federal funds rates (see Table 19–9).[45]

The Discount Window Does Not Substitute for Deposit Insurance

There are a number of reasons why bank access to the discount window is unlikely to deter bank runs and panics the way deposit insurance does. The first reason is that to borrow from the discount window, a bank needs high-quality liquid assets to pledge as collateral. By definition, highly illiquid banks are unlikely to have such assets available to discount. The second reason is that borrowing is not automatic unlike deposit insurance coverage, once premiums are paid. Specifically, banks gain

---

[45]However, as the level of market rates drops, it is possible for fed fund rates to lie below the discount rate. This occurred in October 1992, when fed funds were 2.96 percent and the discount rate was 3 percent.

Contemporary Perspectives

monitoring and put their jobs in jeopardy. That is hardly an incentive to play along."

Critics ask why the Government should bail out supposedly solvent banks. Besides, nothing in the law forces banks that take public money to write down loans to feasible levels. Mr. Tarullo points out that the ruling party has a history of letting banks serving agriculture and construction—its core supporters—do as they want.

The legislation is vague, critics point out, relying on bureaucrats to fill in the blanks. That might have worked fine when the finance and other ministries were all powerful. But now they are largely discredited, and the ability of the bureaucrats to discipline private markets is dubious.

The threat is that insolvent banks, operating under the cover of a bogus accounting system and a compliant Government, will limp along, draining resources from productive parts of the economy. Mr. Tarullo paints a picture of continued drift.

Perhaps, Mr. Posen says, . . . Parliament should have forced banks that take public money to write down old loans and use the cash to issue new loans. But, he says, there are good reasons to believe all this will happen anyway.

He argues that the discipline of international capital markets, which have largely shut off Japan's banks, will force banks to take the Government bailout. Yesterday, three major Japanese banks were reported to be preparing applications.

Mr. Posen also predicts that these banks will be forced by public pressure and new political forces to pass along cash to worthy borrowers.

He points out that the law was not written according to Japanese custom by bureaucrats in the Finance Ministry but was drafted, at the request of Cabinet officials, by a younger generation of Parliament leaders.

American officials have been clamoring for the Japanese to clean up their bank mess—no matter how. The bailout passed by the Parliament will waste lots of taxpayer money. It will not dispense justice. It will not by itself turn the Japanese economy around—fiscal measures will also be needed. But by throwing serious money into blocked credit lines, the law takes an essential step toward ending Japan's immediate crisis.

Source: *New York Times,* October 22, 1998, p. C2. Copyright © 1998 by The New York Times. Reprinted by permission.

TABLE 19–9   The Spread between the Discount Rate and the Fed Funds Rate

	1994	*1998 (Jan)*
Federal funds	4.21	5.56
Discount window	3.60	5.00

Source: *Federal Reserve Bulletin,* various issues.

access to the window only on a "need to borrow" basis. If the central bank considers that a borrowing request emanates from a profit motive because the discount rate is set below money market interbank rates, the borrowing request will be refused. That is, discount window loans are made at the discretion of the central bank. Third, discount window loans are meant to provide temporary liquidity for inherently solvent banks, not permanent long-term support for otherwise insolvent banks.

This narrow role of the discount window was confirmed in the 1991 FDICIA, which limited the discretion of the Federal Reserve to make extended loans to troubled banks. Specifically, discount window loans to troubled, undercapitalized banks are limited to no more than 60 days in any 120-day period unless both the FDIC and the institution's primary regulator certify that the bank is viable. Additional extensions of up to 60 days are allowed subject to regulator certification. Finally, any discount window advances to undercapitalized banks that eventually fail would lead to the Federal Reserve having to compensate the FDIC for incremental losses caused by the delay in keeping the troubled bank open longer than necessary.[46] Consequently, the discount window is a partial but not a full substitute for deposit insurance as a liquidity stabilizing mechanism.

Concept Question

Is a bank's access to the discount window as effective as deposit insurance in deterring bank runs and panics? Why or why not?

Other Guaranty Programs

As discussed in Chapter 17, other FIs are also subject to liquidity crises and liability holder runs. To deter such runs and protect small claimholders, guaranty programs have appeared in other sectors of the financial services industry. We describe these programs and their similarities to and differences from deposit insurance next.

PC and Life Insurance Companies

Both life insurance companies and property-casualty insurance companies are regulated at the state level (see Chapter 2). Unlike banks and thrifts, no federal guaranty fund exists for either life or PC insurers. Beginning in the 1960s, most states began to sponsor state guaranty funds for firms selling insurance in that state. By 1991 all states had established such funds. These state guaranty funds have a number of important differences from deposit insurance. First, while these programs are sponsored by state insurance regulators, they are actually run and administered by the private insurance companies themselves.

Second, unlike SAIF or BIF, where the FDIC established a permanent reserve fund through banks paying annual premiums in excess of payouts to resolve failures, no such permanent guaranty fund exists for the insurance industry, with the sole exception of the PC and life guaranty funds for the state of New York. This means that contributions are paid into the guaranty fund by surviving firms only after an insurance company has failed.

Third, the size of the required contributions surviving insurers make to protect policyholders in failed insurance companies differs widely across states. In those states that have guaranty funds, each surviving insurer is normally levied a pro rata amount, according to the size of its statewide premium income. This amount either helps pay off small policyholders after the assets of the failed insurer have been liquidated or acts as a cash injection to make the acquisition of a failed insurer at-

---

[46]In practice, the Fed would be penalized by a loss in the interest income on discount window loans made to banks that eventually fail.

tractive. The definition of small policyholders generally varies across states from $100,000 to $500,000.[47]

Finally, because there is no permanent fund and the annual pro rata contributions are often legally capped (often at 2 percent of premium income), there is usually a delay before small policyholders get the cash surrender values of their policies or other payment obligations are met from the guaranty fund. This contrasts with deposit insurance, where insured depositors normally receive immediate coverage of their claims. For example, the failure of Executive Life Insurance in 1991 left approximately $117.3 million in outstanding claims in Hawaii. But the Hawaii life insurance guaranty fund can raise only $13.1 million a year due to legal caps on surviving firms' contributions. This means that it will take up to nine years for surviving firms to meet the claims of Executive Life policyholders in Hawaii. In the failure of Baldwin United in 1983, the insurers themselves raised additional funds, over and above the guaranty fund, to satisfy policyholders' claims.

Thus, the private nature of insurance industry guaranty funds, their lack of permanent reserves, and low caps on annual contributions mean that they provide less credible protection to claimants than do the bank and thrift insurance funds. As a result, the incentives for insurance policyholders to engage in a run if they perceive that an insurer has asset quality problems or insurance underwriting problems is quite strong even in the presence of such guaranty funds.

The Securities Investor Protection Corporation

Since the passage of the Securities Investor Protection Act in 1970 and the creation of the Securities Investor Protection Corporation (SIPC), securities firm customers have been given specific but limited protection against insolvencies. Basically, customers receive pro rata shares of a liquidated securities firm's assets with SIPC satisfying remaining claims up to a maximum of $500,000 per individual. Since its inception, the SIPC has had to intervene in approximately 1 percent of the 20,000 security dealers–brokers that have failed or ceased operations. Most of these firms had less than 1,000 customers, with the biggest loss involving 6,500 customers (and a payout of $31.7 million) following the failure of Bell and Beckwith. Thus, compared to the banking and insurance funds, SIPC losses have been very small. In 1997 the fund's reserves stood at $1.082 billion and the premium rate was a flat assessment of $150 per member. However, some concerns have been raised regarding the adequacy of this fund in the wake of increased stock and bond market volatility and the growth of highly complex derivative instruments.[48]

The Pension Benefit Guaranty Corporation

In 1974, the Employee Retirement Income Security Act (ERISA) established the pension Benefit Guaranty Corporation (PBGC). Currently, the PBGC protects the

---

[47]Since insurance industry guaranty fund premiums are size based, they are similar to the pre-1993 flat insurance premiums under deposit insurance. Indeed, similar types of moral hazard behavior (related to fixed-premium, risk-insensitive insurance) have been found for property-casualty companies. See, for example, S.-J. Lee, D. Mayers and C. W. Smith, Jr., "Guaranty Funds and Risk-Taking Behavior: Evidence from the Insurance Industry," *Journal of Financial Economics* 44 (1997), pp. 3–24.

[48]See U.S. General Accounting Office, *Securities Investor Protection,* GAO/GGD-92-109, September 1992.

retirement benefits of more than 41 million workers and has 58,000 insured pension plan sponsors. Prior to 1974, an employee's pension benefits with a private corporation had very limited backing from that firm's assets. The establishment of the PBGC insured pension benefits against the underfunding of plans by corporations.

When the PBGC was created in 1974, the single-employer premium was a flat-rate $1 per plan participant. Congress raised the premium to $2.60 in 1979 and to $8.50 in 1986. In 1987, the basic premium was raised to $16 and an additional variable-rate premium was imposed on underfunded plans up to a maximum of $50. In 1991, Congress set the maximum at $72 per participant for underfunded plans and $19 per participant for fully funded plans.

However, despite these premiums, the PBGC entered into a deficit of $2.7 billion at the end of 1992. This reflects the fact that unlike the FDIC, it has no monitoring power over the pension plans it insures. Thus, it cannot restrict the risk taking of plan managers through portfolio restrictions or implicit insurance premiums.[49]

Partly in response to the growing PBGC deficit, the 1994 Retirement Protection Act was passed. Under the act, the $72 premium cap was phased out in 1997. As a result, underfunded programs are now subject to even higher premiums (80 percent of underfunded plans were at the cap in 1997). It is estimated that this will eliminate the PBGC's deficit within 10 years. Thus, like the FDIC in 1993, the PBGC has switched to an overtly risk-based premium scheme.

Concept Questions

1. How do state-sponsored guaranty funds for insurance companies differ from deposit insurance?
2. What specific protection against insolvencies does the Securities Investor Protection Corporation provide to securities firm customers?

Summary

In recent years, bank and other financial services industry guaranty programs have been weakened and in some cases rendered insolvent. This has led to a major restructuring of a number of schemes, including the introduction of risk-related premiums, risk-based capital, and increased market and regulatory discipline on FI owners and liability holders. The objective of such restructurings is to lower the cost to the government and taxpayers from resolving FI failures. The guaranty programs examined included the FDIC, FSLIC, SIPC, PBGC, and state insurance guaranty funds.

Questions and Problems

1. What is a contagious run? What are some of the potentially serious adverse social welfare effects of a contagious run? Do all types of FIs face the same risk of contagious runs?

2. How does federal deposit insurance help mitigate the problem of bank runs? What other elements of the safety net are available to banks in the United States?

3. What major changes did the Financial Institutions Reform, Recovery, and Enforcement Act of 1989 make to the FDIC and the FSLIC? What federal agency was created by FIRREA, and for what purpose was it created?

4. Contrast the two views on, or reasons why, depository institution insurance funds became insolvent in the 1980s.

---

[49]To the extent that regulation restricts the asset and liability activities of a firm or FI, it is similar to imposing an implicit premium or tax on the activities of the firm.

5. What is moral hazard? How did the fixed-rate deposit insurance program of the FDIC contribute to the moral hazard problem of the savings and loan industry? What other changes in the S&L environment during the 1980s encouraged the developing instability of that industry?

6. How does a risk-based insurance program solve the moral hazard problem of excessive risk taking by FIs? Is an actuarially fair premium for deposit insurance always consistent with a competitive banking system?

7. What are three suggested ways in which a deposit insurance contract could be structured to reduce moral hazard behavior?

8. What are some ways of imposing stockholder discipline to prevent them from engaging in excessive risk taking?

9. How is the provision of deposit insurance by the FDIC similar to the FDIC writing a put option on the assets of a bank that buys the insurance? What two factors drive the premium of the option?

10. What is capital forbearance? How does a policy of forbearance potentially increase the costs of financial distress to the insurance fund as well as the stockholders?

11. Under what conditions may the implementation of minimum capital guidelines, either risk-based or nonrisk-based, fail to impose stockholder discipline as desired by regulators?

12. What four factors were provided by FDICIA as guidelines to assist the FDIC in the establishment of risk-based deposit insurance premiums? What has happened to the level of deposit insurance premiums since the risk-based program was implemented in 1993? Why?

13. Why did the fixed-rate deposit insurance system fail to induce insured and uninsured depositors to impose discipline on risky banks in the United States in the 1980s?

    a. How is it possible to structure deposits in a bank to reduce the effects of the insured ceiling?

    b. What are brokered deposits? Why are brokered deposits considered more risky than non-brokered deposits by bank regulators?

    c. How did FIRREA and FDICIA change the treatment of brokered deposits from an insurance perspective?

    d. What trade-offs were weighed in the decision to leave the deposit insurance ceiling at $100,000?

14. What is the too-big-to-fail doctrine? What factors caused regulators to act in a way that caused this doctrine to evolve?

15. What failure resolution methods were available to regulators before the passage of FDICIA in 1991? What was the "essentiality" provision?

16. What procedural steps are involved under the payoff method of failure resolution?

17. How was the FDIC's potential liability reduced by the 1993 depositor protection legislation? How does this method of failure resolution encourage uninsured depositors to monitor more closely a bank's risk taking?

18. What are the three types of purchase and assumption failure resolution?

    a. How does the "clean" P&A differ from the "total bank" P&A?

    b. How are the uninsured depositors treated differently in a clean P&A as opposed to the payoff method of failure resolution?

    c. How does the open assistance process solidify the too-big-to-fail guaranty?

19. What are some of the essential features of the FDICIA of 1991 with regard to the resolution of failing banks?

    a. What is the least-cost resolution (LCR) strategy?

    b. When can the systemic risk exemption be used as an exception to the LCR policy of bank closure methods?

    c. What procedural steps must be taken to gain approval for using the systemic risk exemption?

    d. What are the implications to the other banks in the economy of the implementation of this exemption?

20. What is the primary goal of the FDIC in employing the LCR strategy?

    a. How is the insured depositor transfer method implemented in the process of failure resolution?

    b. Why does this method of failure resolution encourage uninsured depositors to more closely monitor the strategies of bank managers?

21. The following is a balance sheet of a commercial bank in $millions.

Assets		Liabilities and Equity	
Cash	$ 5	Insured Deposits	$30
Loans	$40	Uninsured Deposits	$10
		Equity	$ 5
Total assets	$45	Total liabilities and equity	$45

The bank experiences a run on its deposits after it declares that it will write off $10 million of its loans as a result of nonpayment. The bank has the option of meeting the withdrawals by first drawing down on its cash and then by selling off its loans. A fire sale of loans in one day can be accomplished at a 10 percent discount. They can be sold at a 5 percent discount if they are sold in two days. The full market value will be obtained if they are sold after two days.

a. What is the amount of loss to the insured depositors if a run on the bank occurs on the first day? On the second day?

b. What amount do the uninsured depositors lose if the FDIC uses the insured depositor transfer method to close the bank immediately? The assets will be sold after the two-day period.

22. A bank with insured deposits of $55 million and uninsured deposits of $45 million has assets valued at only $75 million. What is the cost of failure resolution to insured depositors, uninsured depositors, and the FDIC if the following occur?

   a. The payoff method is used.

   b. A purchase and assumption is arranged with no purchase premium.

   c. A purchase and assumption is arranged with a $5 million purchase premium.

   d. A purchase and assumption is arranged with a $25 million purchase premium.

   e. An insured depositor transfer method is used.

23. A commercial bank has $150 million in assets at book value. The insured and uninsured deposits are valued at $75 and $50 million, respectively, and the book value of equity is $25 million. As a result of loan defaults, the market value of the assets has decreased to $120 million. What is the cost of failure resolution to insured depositors, uninsured depositors, shareholders, and the FDIC if the following occur?

   a. A payoff method is used to close the bank.

   b. A purchase and assumption method with no purchase premium paid is used.

   c. A purchase and assumption method is used with $10 million paid as a purchase premium.

   d. An insured depositor transfer method is used.

24. In what ways did FDICIA enhance the regulatory discipline to help reduce moral hazard behavior? What has the operational impact of these directives been?

25. Match the following policies with their intended consequences:

   Policies:

   a. Lower FDIC insurance levels

   b. Stricter reporting standards

   c. Risk-based deposit insurance

   Consequences:

   1. Increased stockholder discipline

   2. Increased depositor discipline

   3. Increased regulator discipline

26. Why is access to the discount window of the Fed less of a deterrent to bank runs than deposit insurance?

27. How do insurance guaranty funds differ from deposit insurance? What impact do these differences have on the incentive for insurance policyholders to engage in a contagious run on an insurance company?

28. What was the purpose of the establishment of the Pension Benefit Guaranty Corporation (PBGC)?

   a. How does the PBGC differ from the FDIC in its ability to control risk?

   b. How is the 1994 Retirement Protection Act expected to reduce the deficits currently experienced by the PBGC?

APPENDIX 19A
DEPOSIT-INSURANCE SCHEMES FOR COMMERCIAL BANKS IN THE EU AND G-10 COUNTRIES

A: Administration of and Membership in the System

Country	Name of Guarantee/Insurance System	Year First Established	Date Current System Took Effect	Administration of System: Government or Industry	Agency Responsible for Administering System	Membership: Voluntary or Compulsory
Austria	Deposit Guarantee System	1979	July 1, 1995	Industry	Sectoral Associations	Compulsory
Belgium	Guarantee Scheme for Deposits with Credit Institutions	1974	January 1, 1995	Government/Industry—joint	Herdiscontering-en Waarborginstituut-Institut de Reescompte et de Garantie	Compulsory
Canada	Canada Deposit Insurance System	1967	1967	Government (crown corporation)	Canada Deposit Insurance Corporation	Compulsory
Denmark	Deposit Insurance Fund	1987	July 17, 1995	Government	Deposit Insurance Fund	Compulsory
Finland	Guarantee Fund of Commercial Banks and Postipankki Ltd.	1966	July 1, 1995	Industry	Guarantee Fund of Commercial Banks and Postipankki Ltd.	Compulsory
France	Deposit Guarantee Fund	1980	No information	Industry	French Bankers' Association	Compulsory
Germany	Deposit Protection Fund of the Federal Association of German Banks	1966	1976	Industry	Federal Association of German Banks	Voluntary
Greece	Deposit Guarantee Fund	1995	July 1, 1995	Government/industry—joint	Deposit Guarantee Fund	Compulsory
Ireland	Deposit Protection Account (Central Bank)	1989	July 1, 1995	Government	Central Bank of Ireland	Compulsory
Italy	Fonds Interbancario Di Tutela Dei Deposit	1987	1987	Industry	Independently Administered	Voluntary
Japan	Deposit Insurance Corporation	1971	No information	Government/industry—joint	Deposit Insurance Corporation	Compulsory
Luxembourg	Association pour la Garantie des Depots, Luxembourg (AGDL)	1989	October 1995	Industry	AGDL	Compulsory
Netherlands	Collective Guarantee System	1979	July 1, 1995	Government/industry—joint	De Netherlandsche Bank N.V.	Compulsory
Portugal	Deposit Guarantee Fund	1992	1994	Government	Deposit Guarantee Fund	Compulsory
Spain	Deposit Guarantee Fund	1977	End of 1995	Government/industry—joint	Fondo de Garantia de Depositos	Compulsory
Sweden	Swedish Deposit-Guarantee Scheme	1974	January 1, 1996	Government	The Bank Support Authority	Compulsory
Switzerland	Deposit Guarantee Scheme	1982	July 1, 1993	Industry	Swiss Banker's Association	Voluntary
United Kingdom	Deposit Protection Fund	1982	July 1, 1995	Government	Deposit Protection Board	Compulsory
United States	Bank Insurance Fund	1933	January 1, 1996	Government	Federal Deposit Insurance Corporation	Compulsory
European Union (EC Directive on Deposit-Guarantee Schemes)	Determined within each member state	Adopted on May 30, 1994	July 1, 1995	Only directs that each member state shall ensure within its territory that one or more deposit guarantee schemes are introduced and officially recognized	Determined with each member state	Compulsory

Part B: Coverage or Protection

Country	Extent Amount of Coverage	Interbank Deposits Covered	Deposits of Foreign Branches of Domestic Banks Covered	
			Branches located in EU Country	Branches located in Non-EU Country
Austria	ATS 260,000 (per physical person-depositor)	No	Yes	Yes
Belgium	15,000 ECU until Dec. 1999 20,000 ECU thereafter	No	Yes	No
Canada	Can $60,000 (per depositor)	Yes	No	No
Denmark	300,000 DKK or 42,000 ECU (per depositor)	No	Yes	Yes
Finland	100 percent (per depositor)	No	Yes	Yes
France	FF 400,000 (per depositor)	No	Yes	No, except for EEA countries
Germany	100% up to a limit of 30% of the bank's liable capital (per depositor)	No	Yes	Yes
Greece	20,000 ECU (per depositor)	No	Yes	Yes
Ireland	90% of deposit—maximum compensation is 15,000 ECU	No	Yes	Yes
Italy	100% of first 200 million lira and 75% of next 800 million lira (per deposit)	No	Yes	Yes
Japan	10 million yen (per depositor)	No	No	No
Luxembourg	Lux F 500,000 (per depositor), only natural persons	No	No	No
Netherlands	20,000 ECU (per depositor): compensation paid in guilders	No	Yes	No
Portugal	100% up to 15,000 ECU 75%—15,000–30,000 ECU 50%—30,000–45,000 ECU (per depositor)	No	Yes	No
Spain	Pias 1.5 million (per depositor): to be increased to 20,000 ECU	No	Yes	Yes
Sweden	SEK 250,000 (per depositor)	No	Yes	No
Switzerland	SF 30,000 (per depositor)	No	No	No
United Kingdom	90% of protected deposits, with the maximum amount of deposits protected for each depositor being £20,000 (unless the sterling equivalent of ECU 20,000 is greater). Thus, the most an individual can collect in a bank failure is £18,000 (per depositor) or ECU 20,000 if greater.	No	Yes, throughout EEA	No
United States	100,000 USD (per depositor)	No	No	No
European Union	The aggregate deposits of each depositor must be covered up to ECU 20,000. Until December 31, 1999, member states in which deposits are not covered up to ECU 20,000 may retain the maximum amount laid down on their guarantee schemes, provided that this amount is not less than ECU 15,000 (per depositor).	No	If located within the EU, but until December 13, 1999, not to exceed the maximum amount laid down in their guarantee scheme within the territory of the host member state. If the host member state has greater coverage, a branch may voluntarily supplement its coverage	This issue is determined by each member state

Deposits of Domestic Branches of Foreign Banks Covered		Foreign-Currency Denominated Deposits Covered	Non-Resident Depositors Covered
Branches of EU Banks	Branches of Non-EU Banks		
Yes, amount depends on home country	Yes	Yes	Yes
Yes	Yes	Yes, but only deposits expressed in ECU or another EU currency	Yes
Yes	Yes	No	Yes
Yes	Yes	Yes	Yes
Yes	Yes	Yes	Yes
Yes	Yes	Yes, but only deposits expressed in ECU or another EU currency	No information
Yes	Yes	Yes	Yes
Yes	Yes	Yes	Yes
No	Yes	Yes	Yes
Yes	Yes	Yes	Yes
No	No	No	Yes
Yes	Yes	Yes	Yes
Yes	Yes	Yes	Yes
Yes	Yes	Yes	Yes
Yes	Yes	Yes	Yes
Yes	Yes	Yes	Yes
Yes	Yes	Yes	Yes
Yes	Yes	Yes, but only deposits in other EEA currencies and the ECU, as well as sterling	Yes
No, unless engaged in retail deposit-taking activities	No, unless engaged in retail deposit-taking activities	Yes	Yes
Yes, either by having coverage equivalent to the directive or by joining the host-country deposit-guarantee scheme if it is more favorable for the extra coverage	NA	Yes, if denominated in ECU or currencies of member states of EU.	Yes, determined within each member state

Part C: Funding

Country	Ex ante or Ex post Funding	Fund Minimum Reserve Level
Austria	Ex post, system organized as an incident-related guarantee facility	NA
Belgium	Ex ante, but in case of insufficient reserves, banks may be asked to pay, each year if necessary, an exceptional additional contribution up to 0.04 percent.	No
Canada	Ex ante	No
Denmark	Ex ante	Yes, 3 billion DKK
Finland	Ex ante	No
France	Ex post	NA
Germany	Ex ante; however, additional assessments may be made if necessary to discharge the fund's responsibilities; these contributions are limited to twice the annual contribution	No
Greece	Ex ante	No
Ireland	Ex ante	No, but see information under "Premium Rate" column
Italy	Ex post; banks commit ex ante; however contributions are ex post	NA
Japan	Ex ante	No
Luxembourg	Ex post	NA
Netherlands	Ex post	NA
Portugal	Ex ante. However, the payment of the annual contributions may be partly replaced, with a legal maximum of 75%, by the commitment to deliver the amount due to the fund at any moment it proves necessary	No
Spain	Ex ante	No
Sweden	Ex ante	No
Switzerland	Ex post	NA
United Kingdom	Ex ante: banks make initial contributions of £10,000 when a bank is first authorized, further contributions if the fund falls below £3 million, not exceeding £300,000 per bank based on the insured deposit base of the banks involved, and special contributions, again based on the insured deposit base of the banks involved, but with no contribution limit.	Yes, the fund is required by law to maintain a level of £5 million to £6 million, but the DPB can decide to borrow to meet its needs
United States	Ex ante	Yes, 1.25 percent of insured deposits
European Union	Determined within each member state	Determined within each member state

Base for Premium	Premium Rate	Risk-Based Premiums
The deposit guarantee system shall obligate its member institutions, in case of paying out of guaranteed deposits, to pay without delay pro rata amounts which shall be computed according to the share of the remaining member institution at the preceding balance sheet date compared to the sum of such guaranteed deposits of the deposit guarantee system	See adjacent column to left	NA
Total amount of customers' deposits which qualify for reimbursement and which are expressed in BEF, ECU, or another EU currency	0.02 percent	No
Insured deposits	One-sixth of one percent	No
Deposits	Max 0.2 percent	No
Total assets	Between 0.01 and 0.05 percent	No
The contribution consists of two parts: (1) a fixed part, irrespective of the size of the bank, equal to 0.1% of any claim settled and with a FFR 200,000 ceiling and (2) a proportional part, varying according to a regressive scale relative to the size of the bank contributing, based on deposits and one-third credits.	See adjacent column to left.	NA
Balance sheet item "Liabilities to Customers"	0.03 percent	No
Total deposits	0–200 billion GRD 2% 200–500 billion GRD 1% 500–1000 billion GRD 0.4% Above 1,000 billion GRD 0.1%	No
Total deposits excluding interbank deposits and deposits represented by negotiable certificates of deposit	0.2 percent, with a minimum of £20,000	No
Maximum limit for funding the whole system: 4,000 billion lire. Contributions are distributed among participants on the basis of (Deposits + Loans − Own Funds) with a correction mechanism linked to deposit growth	See adjacent column to left	NA
Insured deposits	0.012 percent	No
Banks' premiums based on percentage of loss to be met	See adjacent column to left	NA
Amount repaid in compensation to insured is apportioned among participating institutions. However, the contribution in any one year shall not exceed 5% per an institution's own funds and per all institutions' own funds	See adjacent column to left	NA
Guaranteed deposits	0.08 to 0.12 percent	Yes
Deposits	Maximum 2 Pias per thousand. Premiums will be interrupted when the fund reaches 2%	No
Covered deposits	0.25 percent	Yes
Two Components: Fixed fee in relation to gross profit; Variable fee depending on share of total protected deposits of an individual bank.	See adjacent column to left	NA
All deposits in EEA currencies less deposits by credit institutions; financial institutions, insurance undertakings, directors, controllers and managers, secured deposits, CDs, deposits by other group companies, and deposits which are part the bank's own funds	Initial contributions are 0.01 percent. The rate of other contributions depends on the sum required to be raised	No
Domestic deposits	0 to 0.27 percent, subject to a flat minimum of $2,000 for the highest rated banks	Yes
Determined within each member state	Determined within each member state	Determined within each member state

Description: The EU and the seven-member European Free Trade Association (EFTA)—except Switzerland—form European Economic Area (EEA), a single market of 18 countries. In addition to the EU countries, it includes Iceland, Liechtenstein, and Norway. EFTA includes Austria, Finland, Iceland, Norway, Sweden, Switzerland, and Liechtenstein. The EEA was initially established in May 1992 and came fully into effect in January 1994.

Source: J. R. Barth, D. E. Nolle, and T. N. Rice, "Commercial Banking Structure, Regulations, and Performance: An International Comparison," *Managerial Finance* 23 (November 1997).

CAPITAL ADEQUACY

Introduction

Chapters 7 to 17 examined the major areas of risk exposure facing a modern FI manager. These risks can emanate from both on-and off-balance-sheet (OBS) activities and can be either domestic or international in source. To ensure survival, an FI manager needs to protect the institution against the risk of insolvency, that is, shield it from risks sufficiently large to cause the institution to fail. The primary means of protection against the risk of insolvency and failure is an FI's capital. This leads to the first function of capital, namely:

1. To absorb unanticipated losses with enough margin to inspire confidence and enable the FI to continue as a going concern.

In addition, capital protects nonequity liability holders—especially those uninsured by an external guarantor such as the FDIC—against losses. This leads to the second function of capital:

2. To protect uninsured depositors, bondholders, and creditors in the event of insolvency and liquidation.

When FIs fail, regulators such as the FDIC have to intervene to protect insured claimants (see Chapter 19). The capital of an FI offers protection to insurance funds and ultimately the taxpayers who bear the cost of insurance fund insolvency. This leads to the third function of capital:

3. To protect FI insurance funds and the taxpayers.

Finally, just as for any firm, equity or capital is an important source of finance or funds for an FI. In particular, subject to regulatory constraints, FIs have a choice between debt and equity to finance new projects and business expansion. Thus, the traditional factors that affect a business firm's choice of a capital structure—for instance, the tax deductibility of the interest on debt or the private costs of failure or insolvency—also interpose on the FI's capital decision.[1] This leads to a fourth function of capital:

4. To acquire the plant and other real investments necessary to provide financial services.[2]

In the following sections, we focus mostly on the first three functions concerning the role of capital in reducing insolvency risk. First, we look briefly at the fourth function—equity capital—and its cost as a funding source.

The Cost of Equity Capital as a Funding Source

Just as an FI competes for funds in the market for fixed-income securities by offering claims such as deposits in competition with Treasury bills, Treasury bonds, and commercial paper, it must also compete in the market for equity capital. As we discussed in the preceding chapters, a bank's profitability reflects the net cash flows from its on- and off-balance-sheet activities. In turn, the value of a bank's stocks or equities sold in the capital market reflects the current and expected future dividends to be paid by the FI from its earnings, as for all firms. Thus:

$$P_0 = \frac{D_1}{(1+k)} + \frac{D_2}{(1+k)^2} + \ldots + \frac{D_\infty}{(1+k)^\infty} \tag{1}$$

where

P_0 = Current price of the stock
D_i = Dividends expected in year $i = 1 \ldots n$
k = Discount rate or required return on the stock

[1]See S. A. Ross, R. W. Westerfield, and B. D. Jordan, *Fundamentals of Corporate Finance* (Chicago: Irwin/McGraw-Hill, 1998).

[2]A fifth function might be added. This would focus on the role of capital regulation in restraining the rate of asset growth.

We can also reexpress this as a price/earnings (P/E) ratio. To see this, suppose dividends are growing at a constant annual rate (g), so that

$$D_1 = (1 + g) D_0$$
$$D_2 = (1 + g)^2 D_0$$

Then, Equation 1 reduces to[3]

$$P_0 = \frac{D_0(1 + g)}{k - g} \qquad (2)$$

This is the well-known dividend growth model of stock price determination. Dividing both sides of Equation (2) by current earnings per share (E), we have

$$\frac{P_0}{E_0} = \frac{D_0/E_0(1 + g)}{k - g} \qquad (3)$$

The P/E Ratio
The price of a share per dollar of earnings.

Thus, the **P/E ratio,** or the price of a share per dollar of earnings, would be greater; the higher the dividend payout ratio (D/E), the higher the growth in dividends (g) and the lower the required return on the firm's equity (k).[4] For any firm (including FIs), the higher the P/E ratio, the more investors are willing to pay for a dollar of earnings and the more attractive and cheaper equity is to issuers.

Capital and Insolvency Risk

Capital

To see how capital protects an FI against insolvency risk, we have to define *capital* more precisely. The problem is that there are many definitions of capital: what an economist defines as capital may differ from an accountant's definition, which in turn can differ from the definition used by regulators. Specifically, the economic definition of a bank's capital or owners' equity stake in an FI is the difference between the market values of its assets and those of its liabilities. This is also called the **net worth** of an FI (see Chapter 8). While this is the economic meaning of capital, regulators have found it necessary to adopt different definitions of capital that depart by a greater or lesser degree from economic net worth. The concept of an FI's economic net worth is really a *market value accounting* concept. With the exception of the investment banking industry, regulatory defined capital and required leverage ratios are based in whole or in part on historical or **book value** accounting concepts.

Net worth
A measure of an FI's capital that is equal to the difference between the market value of its assets and the market value of its liabilities.

Book Value
Asset and liability values are based on their historical costs.

We begin by taking a look at the role of economic capital or net worth as an insulation device against two major types of risk: credit risk and interest rate risk. We then compare this market value concept with the book value concept of capital. Because it can actually distort the true solvency position of an FI, the book value of

---

[3]See F. K. Reilly and K. C. Brown, *Investment Analysis and Portfolio Management,* 5th ed. (Chicago: Dryden, 1998). The 20-year simple average annual dividend growth rate (g) for 50 banks followed by Salomon Brothers over the 1974–94 period was 7.1 percent. However, this growth rate varied over time. For example, during the 1989–93 period the growth rate was 5.1 percent, whereas in 1994 it was 25.3 percent. See Salomon Brothers, *U.S. Equity Research: Commercial Banks,* December 1994.

[4]This is subject to $k > g$. In 1994, the average dividend payout ratio (D/E) for the 50 banks followed by Salomon Brothers was 35.8 percent. The historical 12-year average dividend payout ratio was 32.6 percent. See Salomon Brothers, *U.S. Equity Research,* December 1994.

capital concept can be misleading to managers, owners, liability holders, and regulators alike. We also examine some possible reasons why FI regulators continue to rely on book value concepts in the light of such economic value transparency problems and rulings by the Financial Accounting Standards Board (such as *FASB Statement 115*). Finally, we take a detailed look at the actual minimum capital requirements imposed by regulators in commercial banking, thrift or savings banking, PC and life insurance, and investment banking.

The Market Value of Capital

Market Value or Marking to Market
Allowing balance sheet values to reflect current rather than historical prices.

To see how economic net worth or equity insulates an FI against risk, consider the following example. In Table 20–1 we have a simple balance sheet where all the assets and liabilities of an FI are valued in **market value** terms at current prices on a **mark-to-market** basis (see Chapter 8). On a mark-to-market or market value basis, the economic value of the FI's equity is $10 (million), which is the difference between the market value of its assets and that of liabilities. On a market value basis, the FI is economically solvent and would impose no failure costs on depositors or regulators if it were liquidated today. Let's consider the impact of two classic types of FI risk on this FI's net worth: credit risk and interest rate risk.

Market Value of Capital and Credit Risk.   In Table 20–1, an FI has $20 (million) in long-term loans. (For simplicity we drop the $ sign and million notation in the rest of the example.) Suppose that due to a recession a number of these borrowers get into cash flow problems and are unable to keep up their promised loan repayment schedules. A decline in the current and expected future cash flows on loans lowers the market value of the loan portfolio held by the FI below 20. Suppose loans are really worth only 12; that means the market value of the loan portfolio has fallen from 20 to 12. Look at the revised market value balance sheet in Table 20–2.

The loss of 8 in the market value of loans appears on the liability side of the balance sheet as a loss of 8 to an FI's net worth. That is, the loss of asset value is

TABLE 20–1   An FI's Market Value Balance Sheet
(in millions of dollars)

Assets		Liabilities	
Long-term securities	$ 80	Liabilities (short-term, floating-rate deposits)	$ 90
Long-term loans	20	Net worth	10
	$100		$100

TABLE 20–2   The Market Value Balance Sheet after a Decline in the Value of Loans
(in millions of dollars)

Assets		Liabilities	
Long-term securities	$80	Liabilities	$90
Long-term loans	12	Net worth	2
	$92		$92

TABLE 20–3   A Major Decline in the Value of the Loan Portfolio
(in millions of dollars)

Assets		*Liabilities*	
Long-term securities	$80	Liabilities	$90
Long-term loans	8	Net worth	−2
	$88		$88

charged against the equity owners' capital or net worth. As you can see, the liability holders (depositors) are fully protected in that the total market value of their claims is still 90. This is the case because debt holders are senior claimants and equity holders are junior claimants. That is, equity holders bear losses on the asset portfolio first. In fact, in our example, liability holders are hurt only when losses on the loan portfolio exceed 10, the net worth of the FI. Let's consider a larger credit risk shock such that the market value of the loan portfolio plummets from 20 to 8, a loss of 12 (see Table 20–3).

This larger loss has rendered the FI insolvent; the market value of its assets (88) is now less than the value of its liabilities (90). The owners' net worth stake has been completely wiped out—reduced from 10 to −2, making net worth negative. As a result, liability holders are hurt, but only a bit. Specifically, the first 10 of the 12 loss in value of the loan portfolio is borne by the equity holders. Only after the equity holders are wiped out do the liability holders begin to lose. In this example, the economic value of their claims on the FI has fallen from 90 to 88, or a loss of 2 (a percentage loss of 2.22 percent). After insolvency and the liquidation of the remaining 88 in assets, the depositors would get only 88/90 on the dollar, or 97.77 cents per $1 of deposits. Note here that we are ignoring deposit insurance.[5]

If the FI's net worth had been larger—say 15 rather than 10 in the previous example—the liability holders would have been fully protected against the loss of 12.[6] This example clearly demonstrates the concept of net worth or capital as an insurance fund protecting liability holders, such as depositors, against insolvency risk. The larger the FI's net worth is relative to the size of its assets, the more insolvency protection or insurance there is for liability holders and liability guarantors such as the FDIC. This is why regulators focus on capital requirements such as the ratio of net worth to assets in assessing the insolvency risk exposure of an FI and in setting risk-based deposit insurance premiums (see Chapter 19).

Market Value of Capital and Interest Rate Risk.   Consider the same market value balance sheet in Table 20–1 after a rise in interest rates. As we discuss in Chapter 8, rising interest rates reduce the market value of the bank's long-term fixed-income securities and loans while floating-rate instruments, if instantaneously repriced, find their market values largely unaffected. Suppose the rise in interest rates reduces the market value of the FI's long-term securities investments from 80 to 75 and the market value of its long-term loans from 20 to 17. Because all deposit liabilities are assumed to be short-term floating-rate deposits, their market values are unchanged at 90.

---

[5]In the presence of deposit insurance, the insurer, such as FDIC, would bear some of the depositors' losses; for details, see Chapter 19.

[6]In this case, the 12 loss reduces net worth to +3.

TABLE 20–4   The Market Value Balance Sheet after a Rise in Interest Rates
(in millions of dollars)

Assets		*Liabilities*	
Long-term securities	$75	Liabilities	$90
Long-term loans	17	Net worth	2
	$92		$92

After the shock to interest rates, the market value balance sheet might look like it does in Table 20–4. The loss of 8 in the market value of the FI's assets is once again reflected on the liability side of the balance sheet by a fall in FI net worth from 10 to 2. Thus, as for increased credit risk, losses in asset values due to adverse interest rate changes are borne first by the equity holders. Only if the fall in the market value of assets exceeded 10 would the liability holders, as senior claimants to the FI's assets, be adversely affected.

These examples show that market valuation of the balance sheet produces an economically accurate picture of the net worth, and thus the solvency position, of an FI. Credit risk and interest rate risk shocks that result in losses in the market value of assets are borne directly by the equity holders in the sense that such losses are charges against the value of their ownership claims in the FI. As long as the owners' capital or equity stake is adequate, or sufficiently large, liability holders (and implicitly regulators that back the claims of liability holders) are protected against insolvency risk. That is, if an FI were closed by regulators before its economic net worth became zero, neither liability holders nor those regulators guaranteeing the claims of liability holders would stand to lose. Thus, many academics and analysts have advocated the use of market value accounting and market value of capital closure rules for all FIs, especially in the light of the book value of capital rules associated with the savings and loan disaster.[7]

For example, the Financial Accounting Standards Board (*FASB*) *Statement No. 115* technically requires securities classified as "available for sale" to be marked to market. By comparison, no similar marked-to-market requirement exists on the liabilities side. In the absence of any contrary ruling by regulators, this would require FI capital (net worth) positions to be adjusted downward if interest rates rose. However, as discussed later in this chapter, federal bank regulators in December 1994 exempted banks from the need to adjust their net worth positions for capital losses on securities, thereby reconfirming their preference for book value–based capital rules. The rationale is that they might be forced to close too many banks in the face of temporary spikes in interest rates.

The Book Value of Capital

We contrast market value or economic net worth with book value of capital or net worth. As we discuss in later sections, book value capital and capital rules based on

---

[7]See, for example, G. J. Benston and G. C. Kaufman, "Risk and Solvency Regulation of Depository Institutions: Past Policies and Current Options," Monograph Series in Finance and Economics, 1988–1 (New York University, Salomon Brothers Center, 1988); and L. J. White, *The S and L Debacle* (New York: Oxford University Press, 1991).

TABLE 20–5 **Book Value of an FI's Assets and Liabilities**
(in millions of dollars)

Assets		Liabilities	
Long-term securities	$ 80	Short-term liabilities	$ 90
Long-term loans	20	Net worth	10
	$100		$100

book values are most commonly used by FI regulators. In Table 20–5, we use the same initial balance sheet we used in Table 20–1 but assume that assets and liabilities are now valued at their historical book values.

In Table 20–5, the 80 in long-term securities and the 20 in long-term loans reflect the historic or original book values of those assets. That is, they reflect the values when the loans were made and the bonds were purchased, which may have been many years ago. Similarly, on the liability side, the 90 in liabilities reflects their historical cost, and net worth or equity is now the book value of the stockholders' claims rather than the market value of those claims. For example, the book value of capital—the difference between the book values of assets and liabilities—usually comprises the following four components in banking:

1. *Par value of shares.* The face value of the common stock shares issued by the FI (the par value is usually $1 per share) times the number of shares outstanding.
2. *Surplus value of shares.* The difference between the price the public paid for common stock or shares when originally offered (e.g., $5 share) and their par values (e.g., $1) times the number of shares outstanding.
3. *Retained earnings.* The accumulated value of past profits not yet paid out in dividends to shareholders. Since these earnings could be paid out in dividends, they are part of the equity owners' stake in the FI.
4. *Loan loss reserve.* A special reserve set aside out of retained earnings to meet expected and actual losses on the portfolio.

Consequently, book value of capital = Par value + Surplus + Retained earnings + Loan loss reserves. As the example in Table 20–5 is constructed, the book value of capital equals 10. However, invariably, the *book value of equity does not equal the market value of equity* (the difference between the market value of assets and that of liabilities).

You can see this by examining the effects of the same credit and interest rate shocks on the FI's capital position but assuming book value accounting methods.

The Book Value of Capital and Credit Risk. Suppose that some of the 20 in loans are in difficulty regarding repayment schedules. We assumed in Table 20–2 that the revaluation of cash flows leads to an immediate downward adjustment of the loan portfolio's market value from 20 to 12, a market value loss of 8. By contrast, under historic book value accounting methods such as Generally Accepted Accounting Principles (GAAP), FIs have greater discretion in reflecting or timing problem loan loss recognition on their balance sheets and thus in the impact of such losses on capital. Indeed, FIs may well resist writing down the values of bad assets as long as possible to try to present a more favorable picture to depositors and

TABLE 20–6   The Effect of a Loan Loss Chargeoff against the Book Value of Equity
(in millions of dollars)

Assets		Liabilities	
Long-term securities	$80	Liabilities	$90
Long-term loans	17	Equity (loss of 3 on loan loss reserve)	7
	$97		$97

regulators. Such resistance may be expected if managers believe their jobs could be threatened when they recognize such losses. Only pressure from regulators such as bank, thrift, or insurance examiners may force loss recognition and write-downs in the values of problem assets. For example, in recent years on-site examinations of property insurance companies have taken place as infrequently as once every three years with regulators analyzing off-site balance sheet information after delays as long as 18 months. While bank on-site examinations are more frequent, there is still a tendency to delay writing down the book values of loans. A good international example is the delay shown by Japanese banks in recognizing loan losses incurred over the 1996–98 period, as a result of the Asian crisis and an economic recession domestically. As of 1998 the collective bad debts of Japanese banks were conservatively estimated to exceed $600 billion, most of which remains on their balance-sheets at original book values. Moreover, even when loans are declared substandard by examiners, they usually remain on the balance sheet at book value. A problem loan may require a write-down of only 50 percent, while only an outright loss requires a full 100 percent charge-off against the bank's equity position.

Suppose that in our example of historical book value accounting the FI is forced to recognize a loss of 3 rather than 8 on its loan portfolio. The 3 is a charge against the 10 of stockholders' book equity value. Technically, the 3 loss on assets would be charged off against the loan loss reserve component of equity.[8] The new book value balance sheet is shown in Table 20–6.

Book Value of Capital and Interest Rate Risk.   Although book value accounting systems do recognize credit risk problems, albeit only partially and usually with a long and discretionary time lag, their failure to recognize the impact of interest rate risk is more extreme.

In our market value accounting example in Table 20–5, a rise in interest rates lowered the market values of long-term securities and loans by 8 and led to a fall in the market value of net worth from 10 to 2. In a book value accounting world, when all assets and liabilities reflect their original cost of purchase, the rise in interest rates has no effect on the value of assets, liabilities, or the book value of equity. That is, the balance sheet remains unchanged; Table 20–5 reflects the position both before and after the interest rate rise. Consider those thrifts that, even though interest rates rose dramatically in the early 1980s, still reported long-term fixed-rate

---

[8]Banks normally get a tax shelter against the cost of the write-off, thus reducing its cost. If losses exceed the bank's loan loss reserves, the bank is likely to use its retained earnings as its next line of defense.

mortgages at historical book values and therefore a positive book capital position. Yet on a market value net worth basis, their mortgages were worth far less than the book values shown on their balance sheets. Indeed, more than half of the firms in the industry were economically insolvent—many massively so.[9]

The Discrepancy between the Market and Book Values of Equity

The degree to which the book value of an FI's capital deviates from its true economic market value depends on a number of factors, especially:

1. *Interest rate volatility.* The higher the interest rate volatility, the greater the discrepancy.

2. *Examination and enforcement.* The more frequent the on-site and off-site examinations and the stiffer the examiner/regulator standards regarding charging off problem loans, the smaller the discrepancy.

In actual practice, for large publicly traded FIs, we can get a good idea of the discrepancy between book values (*BV*) and market values (*MV*) of equity even when the FI itself doesn't mark its balance sheet to market.

Specifically, in an efficient capital market, investors can value the shares of an FI by doing an as-if market value calculation of the assets and liabilities of the FI. This valuation is based on its current and future net earnings or dividend flows (see the section on the cost of equity capital). The stock price of the FI reflects this valuation and thus the market value of its shares outstanding. The market value of equity per share is therefore

$$MV = \frac{\text{Market value of shares outstanding}}{\text{Number of shares}}$$

By contrast, the historical or book value of the FI's equity per share (*BV*) is equal to

$$BV = \frac{\begin{array}{c}\text{Par value} \\ \text{of equity}\end{array} + \begin{array}{c}\text{Surplus} \\ \text{value}\end{array} + \begin{array}{c}\text{Retained} \\ \text{earnings}\end{array} + \begin{array}{c}\text{Loan loss} \\ \text{reserves}\end{array}}{\text{Number of shares}}$$

Market to Book Ratio
Shows the discrepancy between the stock market value of an FI's equity and the book value of its equity.

The ratio *MV/BV* is often called the **market to book ratio** and shows the degree of discrepancy between the market value of an FI's equity capital as perceived by investors in the stock market and the book value of capital on its balance sheet.

The lower this ratio, the more the book value of capital *overstates* the true equity or economic net worth position of an FI as perceived by investors in the capital market. To see the size of some of these differences, look at Figure 20–1, which shows the average *MV/BV* ratio for all available banks whose stocks were traded over the 1914–96 period.

Given such discrepancies, why do regulators and FIs continue to oppose the implementation of market value accounting? As noted above, the foremost accounting standards body, the Financial Accounting Standards Board, has recommended such a move, as has the Securities and Exchange Commission.

---

[9]See White, *The S and L Debacle.*

FIGURE 20–1

Average Market Value (MV) to Book Value (BV) of Banks, 1914–1996

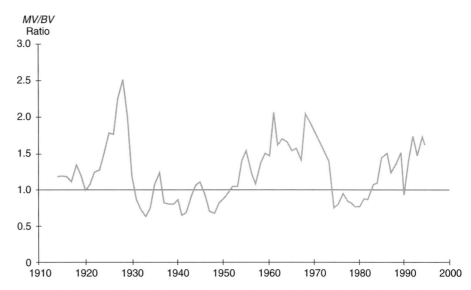

Source: A. Saunders and B. Wilson, "Bank Capital Structure: An Analysis of the Charter Value Hypotheses," a Salomon Center, New York University Working Paper, 1996 (updated).

Arguments against Market Value Accounting

The first argument against market value (*MV*) accounting is that it is difficult to implement, especially for small commercial banks and thrifts with large amounts of nontraded assets such as small loans in their balance sheets. When it is impossible to get accurate market prices or values for assets, marking to market may be done only with error. A counterargument to this is that the error with market valuation of nontraded assets is still likely to be less than that using original book or historical valuation since the market value approach does not require all assets and liabilities to be traded. As long as current and expected cash flows on an asset or liability and an appropriate discount rate can be specified, approximate market values can always be imputed (see CreditMetrics, described in Appendix 11A). Further, with the growth of loan sales and asset securitization (see Chapters 27 and 28), indicative market prices are available on an increasing variety of loans.[10]

The second argument against market value accounting is that it introduces an unnecessary degree of variability into an FI's earnings—and thus net worth—as paper capital gains and losses on assets are passed through the income statement. Critics argue that reporting unrealized capital gains and losses is distortionary if the FI actually plans to hold these assets to maturity. Insurers and bankers argue that in many cases they do hold loans and other assets to maturity and therefore never actually realize capital gains or losses. Further, regulators have argued that they may be forced to close banks too early under the prompt corrective action requirements imposed by FDICIA (discussed later in this chapter)—especially if an interest rate spike is only temporary and capital losses on securities can be quickly turned into capital gains as rates fall again (e.g., if interest rates are mean reverting, as much

---

[10]Recently, Congress also proposed a number of initiatives to securitize small business loans using a public agency similar to the Government National Mortgage Association (GNMA), the public agency that facilitates residential mortgage securitizations.

empirical evidence shows). The counterargument is that FIs are increasingly trading, selling, and securitizing assets rather than holding them to maturity. Further, the failure to reflect capital gains and losses from interest rate changes means that the FI's equity position fails to reflect its true interest rate risk exposure.

The third argument against market value accounting is that FIs are less willing to take on longer-term asset exposures, such as commercial mortgage loans and C&I loans, if these assets have to be continuously marked to market to reflect changing credit quality and interest rates. For example, as shown in Chapter 8, long-term assets are more interest rate sensitive than are short-term assets. The concern is that market value accounting may interfere with FIs' special functions as lenders and monitors (see Chapter 6) and may even result in (or accentuate) a major credit crunch. Of the three arguments against market value accounting, this one is probably the most persuasive to regulators concerned about small business finance and economic growth.[11]

Concept Questions

1. Why is an FI economically insolvent when its net worth is negative?
2. What are the four major components of a banks' book equity?
3. Is book value accounting for loan losses backward looking or forward looking?
4. What does a market to book ratio that is less than 1 imply about an FI's performance?

Capital Adequacy in the Commercial Banking and Thrift Industry

Actual Capital Rules

We have just discussed the advantages and disadvantages of book- and market-based measures of an FI's capital. As noted, most FI regulators have chosen some form of book value accounting standard to measure an FI's capital adequacy. The major exception is the SEC. Along with the NYSE and major stock exchanges, the SEC imposes on securities firms, retail brokers, and specialists a capital or net worth rule that is to all intents and purposes, a market value accounting rule.

Next, we examine the capital adequacy rules imposed in key FI sectors: (1) commercial banking and thrifts, (2) PC insurance, (3) securities firms, and (4) life insurance. Because many of these rules currently differ considerably across financial firms, the current wave of consolidation of the U.S. financial industry into financial conglomerates—or universal banks—on German or British lines is likely to be more difficult than it would be if market value accounting rules were adopted across all sectors of the financial services industry. Nevertheless, there is a clear movement toward similar risk-based capital rules in banking, the thrift industry, and insurance (both PC and life), as will be discussed in more detail in the remainder of this chapter.

---

[11]This was a particularly sensitive issue in the early 1990s, when a credit crunch was already perceived to exist and the proportion of C&I loans in bank portfolios was falling (also see Chapter 1).

The FDIC Improvement Act of 1991 required that banks and thrifts adopt essentially the same capital requirements. While there are some minor differences, the two industries have converged toward a level playing field as far as capital requirements are concerned. Given this, we concentrate on describing the recent evolution of capital requirements in commercial banking.

Since 1987, U.S. commercial banks have faced two different capital requirements: a capital-assets (leverage) ratio and a risk-based capital ratio that is in turn subdivided into a Tier 1 capital risk-based ratio and a total capital (Tier 1 plus Tier II capital) risk-based ratio. We describe these in more detail next.

The Capital-Assets Ratio (or Leverage Ratio)

Leverage Ratio
Ratio of an FI's core capital to its assets.

The capital-assets or **leverage ratio** measures the ratio of a bank's book value of primary or core capital to its assets. The lower this ratio is, the more leveraged the bank is. Primary or core capital is a bank's common equity (book value) plus qualifying cumulative perpetual preferred stock plus minority interests in equity accounts of consolidated subsidiaries.

With the passage of the FDIC Improvement Act in 1991, a bank's capital adequacy is assessed according to where its leverage ratio (L) places in one of five target zones. The leverage ratio is

$$L = \frac{\text{Core capital}}{\text{Assets}}$$

Note the target zones in column 3 of Table 20–7. If a bank's leverage ratio is greater than 5 percent, it is well capitalized. If it is 4 percent or more, it is adequately capitalized; under 4 percent, it is undercapitalized; under 3 percent, significantly undercapitalized; and 2 percent or under, critically undercapitalized.

Associated with each zone is a mandatory set of actions as well as a set of discretionary actions that regulators have to take. The idea here is to put teeth into minimum capital requirements and limit the ability of regulators to show forbearance to the worst capitalized banks. Analysts blame such forbearance and regulator discretion for the size of the losses borne by taxpayers due to the widespread collapse of

TABLE 20–7   Specifications of Capital Categories for Prompt Corrective Action
(in percent)

Zone	*(1)* Total Risk-Based Ratio		*(2)* Tier I Risk-Based Ratio		*(3)* Tier I Leverage Ratio		Capital Directive/Other
1. Well capitalized	10% or above	and	6% or above	and	5% or above	and	Not subject to a capital directive to meet a specific level for any capital measure
2. Adequately capitalized	8% or above	and	4% or above	and	4% or above	and	Does not meet the definition of well capitalized
3. Undercapitalized	Under 8%	or	Under 4%	or	Under 4%		
4. Significantly undercapitalized	Under 6%	or	Under 3%	or	Under 3%		
5. Critically undercapitalized	2% or under	or	2% or under	or	2% or under		

Source: Federal Reserve Board of Governors, September 10, 1993.

thrifts and the Federal Savings and Loan Insurance Corporation (FSLIC) in the 1980s and the technical insolvency of the FDIC in 1991.

Since December 18, 1992, under the FDICIA legislation, regulators must take specific actions—**prompt corrective action** (PCA)—whenever a bank falls outside the zone 1 or well-capitalized category. Most important, a receiver must be appointed when its book value of capital to assets (leverage) ratio falls to 2 percent or under.[12] That is, receivership is mandatory even before the book value ratio falls to 0 percent.

Unfortunately, the leverage ratio has three problems as a measure of capital adequacy:

1. *Market value.* Even if a bank is closed when its leverage ratio falls below 2 percent, a 2 percent book capital–asset ratio could be consistent with a massive *negative* market value net worth. That is, there is no assurance that depositors and regulators (including taxpayers) are adequately protected against losses. Many thrifts that were closed with low book capital values in the 1980s had negative net worths on a market value basis exceeding 30 percent.

2. *Asset risk.* By taking the denominator of the leverage ratio as total assets, it fails to take into account, even partially, the different credit and interest rate risks of the assets that comprise total assets.

3. *Off-balance-sheet activities.* Despite the massive growth in bank off-balance-sheet activities, no capital is required to be held to meet the potential insolvency risks involved with such contingent assets and liabilities.

Risk-Based Capital Ratios

In light of the weaknesses of the simple capital-assets ratio just described, U.S. bank regulators formally agreed with other member countries of the Bank for International Settlements (BIS) to implement two new risk-based capital ratios for all commercial banks under their jurisdiction. The BIS phased in and fully implemented these risk-based capital ratios on January 1, 1993, under what has become known as the **Basel (or Basle) Agreement.**

Regulators currently enforce the Basel Agreement alongside the traditional leverage ratio. To be adequately capitalized, a bank has to hold a minimum total capital (Tier I core capital plus Tier II supplementary capital) to risk-adjusted assets ratio of 8 percent; that is,

$$\textbf{Total risk-based capital ratio} = \frac{\text{Total capital (Tier I + Tier II)}}{\text{Risk-adjusted assets}} \geq 8\%$$

In addition, the Tier I core capital component of total capital has its own minimum guideline:

$$\textbf{Tier I (core) capital ratio} = \frac{\text{Core capital (Tier I)}}{\text{Risk-adjusted assets}} \geq 4\%$$

Prompt Corrective Action
Mandatory actions that have to be taken by regulators as a bank's capital ratio falls.

Basel Agreement
The requirement to impose risk-based capital ratios on banks in major industrialized countries.

Total Risk-Based Capital Ratio
The ratio of the total capital to the risk-adjusted assets of an FI.

Tier I Core Capital Ratio
The ratio of core capital to the risk-adjusted assets of an FI.

---

[12]Admittedly, there are a number of loopholes and delaying tactics managers and stockholders might exploit, especially through the courts. This loss of discretion in closure is also one reason why bank regulators have resisted *FASB Statement No. 115,* as described earlier.

TABLE 20–8   Summary of Prompt Corrective Action Provisions of the Federal Deposit Insurance Corporation Improvement Act of 1991

Zone	Mandatory Provisions	Discretionary Provisions
1. Well capitalized		
2. Adequately capitalized	1. No brokered deposits except with FDIC approval	
3. Undercapitalized	1. Suspend dividends and management fees	1. Order recapitalization
	2. Require capital restoration plan	2. Restrict interaffiliate transactions
	3. Restrict asset growth	3. Restrict deposit interest rates
	4. Approval required for acquisitions, branching, and new activities	4. Restrict certain other activities
	5. No brokered deposits	5. Any other action that would better carry out prompt corrective action
4. Significantly undercapitalized	1. Same as for Zone 3	1. Any Zone 3 discretionary actions
	2. Order recapitalization*	2. Conservatorship or receivership if fails to submit or implement plan or recapitalize pursuant to order
	3. Restrict interaffiliate transactions*	
	4. Restrict deposit interest rates*	3. Any other Zone 5 provisions if such action is necessary to carry out prompt corrective action
	5. Pay of officers restricted	
5. Critically undercapitalized	1. Same as for Zone 4	
	2. Receiver/conservator within 90 days*	
	3. Receiver if still in Zone 5 four quarters after becoming critically undercapitalized	
	4. Suspend payments on subordinated debt*	
	5. Restrict certain other activities	

*Not required if primary supervisor determines action would not serve purpose of prompt corrective action or if certain other conditions are met.

Source: Federal Reserve Board of Governors, September 10, 1993.

That is, of the 8 percent total risk-based capital ratio, a minimum of 4 percent has to be held in core or primary capital.[13]

Apart from their use to define adequately capitalized banks, risk-based capital ratios also define—along with the traditional leverage ratio—well capitalized, undercapitalized, significantly undercapitalized, and critically undercapitalized banks as part of the prompt corrective action program under the FDIC Improvement Act. As with the simple leverage ratio, for both the total risk-based capital ratio and the Tier I risk-based capital ratios, these five zones assess capital adequacy and the actions regulators are mandated to take (see Tables 20–7 and 20–8).

Unlike the simple capital-asset (leverage) ratio, however, the calculation of these risk-based capital adequacy measures is quite complex. Their major innovation is to distinguish among the different credit risks of assets on the balance sheet as well as the credit risk inherent in instruments off the balance sheet through the use of a risk-adjusted assets denominator in these capital adequacy ratios. In a very rough fashion, these capital ratios mark to market the on- and off-balance-sheet positions of the bank to reflect its credit risk.[14] We discuss the limitations of these new risk-based ratios after we take a closer look at their calculation.

---

[13]The difference between the 8 percent and the 4 percent can be made up with noncore or other capital sources; see the description in Table 20–9.

[14]As we discussed in Chapter 10, market risk was integrated into the risk-based capital requirements in 1998 in the form of an "add-on" to the 8 percent ratio for credit risk.

Calculating Risk-Based Capital Ratios

A bank's capital is the numerator of the risk-based capital ratios. We begin by looking at the definition of Tier I and Tier II capital—the numerator of these ratios—and then look at the definition of risk-adjusted assets—the denominator.

Capital.   A bank's capital is divided into Tier I and Tier II. Tier I capital is primary or core capital and must be a minimum of 4 percent of a bank's risk-adjusted assets, while Tier II, or supplementary capital, is the make-weight such that

$$\text{Tier I capital} + \text{Tier II capital} \geq 8\% \text{ of risk-adjusted assets}$$

Tier I Capital.   Look at the definitions of Tier I core capital and Tier II supplementary capital in Table 20–9.

Tier I capital is closely linked to a bank's book value of equity reflecting the concept of the core capital contribution of a bank's owners.[15] Basically, it includes the book value of common equity, plus an amount of perpetual (nonmaturing) preferred stock, plus minority equity interest held by the bank in subsidiaries, minus goodwill. Goodwill is an accounting item that reflects the excess a bank pays over market value in purchasing or acquiring other banks or subsidiaries.

Tier II Capital.   Tier II capital is a broad array of secondary capital resources. Tier II includes a bank's loan loss reserves up to a maximum of 1.25 percent of risk-adjusted assets plus various convertible and subordinated debt instruments with maximum caps.

Risk-Adjusted Assets.   Risk-adjusted assets are the denominator of the risk-based capital ratios. Two components comprise risk-adjusted assets:

$$\text{Risk-adjusted assets} = \text{Risk-adjusted on-balance-sheet assets} + \text{Risk-adjusted off-balance-sheet assets}$$

Next, we look at each component separately.

Risk-Adjusted On-Balance-Sheet Assets.   Under the risk-based capital plan, each bank assigns its assets to one of four categories of credit risk exposure: 0 percent, 20 percent, 50 percent, or 100 percent. In Table 20–10 we list the key categories and assets in these categories. The main features are that cash assets, U.S. T-bills, notes, and bonds of all maturities, and GNMA (Ginnie Mae) mortgage-backed securities—mortgage securitization packages backed by a government agency—are all zero risk based. In the 20 percent class are U.S. agency-backed securities, municipal issued general obligation bonds, FHLMC and FNMA mortgage-backed securities, and interbank deposits.[16] In the 50 percent class are regular residential mortgage loans and other municipal (revenue) bonds. Finally, all other loans, such as C&I, consumer, and credit card, are in the 100 percent risk category. To figure the

---

[15]However, loan loss reserves are assigned to Tier II capital on the basis that they often reflect losses that have already occurred rather than losses or insolvency risks that may occur in the future.

[16] The Federal Home Loan Mortgage Corporation (FHLMC) and Federal National Mortgage Association (FNMA) are quasi-government or government-backed mortgage securitization agencies. (See Chapter 28 for more details on these agencies.) It is also currently being proposed that privately backed (issued) mortgage-backed securities and other securitization issues that are rated AAA also be placed in the 20 percent rather than 100 percent class as at present. See A. J. Taddei, "Banking Regulators Publish Recourse Capital Proposals," *The Financier* 4, no. 5, December 1997.

TABLE 20–9   **Summary Definition of Qualifying Capital for Bank Holding Companies**

Components	*Minimum Requirements*
Core capital (Tier I)	Must equal or exceed 4 percent of weighted-risk assets
Common stockholders' equity	No limit
Qualifying cumulative and noncumulative perpetual preferred stock	Limited to 25 percent of the sum of common stock, minority interests, and qualifying perpetual preferred stock
Minority interest in equity accounts of consolidated subsidiaries	Organizations should avoid using minority interests to introduce elements not otherwise qualifying for Tier I capital
Less: Goodwill*	
Supplementary capital (Tier II)	Total of Tier II is limited to 100 percent of Tier I†
Allowance for loan and lease losses	Limited to 1.25 percent of weighted-risk assets
Perpetual preferred stock	No limit within Tier II
Hybrid capital instruments, perpetual debt, and mandatory convertible securities	No limit within Tier II
Subordinated debt and intermediate-term preferred stock (original weighted-average maturity of five years or more)	Subordinated debt and intermediate-term preferred stock are limited to 50 percent of Tier I; amortized for capital purposes as they approach maturity†
Revaluation reserves (equity and buildings)	Not included; organizations encouraged to disclose; may be evaluated on a case-by-case basis for international comparisons and taken into account in making an overall assessment of capital
Deductions (from sum of Tier I and Tier II)	
Investments in unconsolidated subsidiaries	
Reciprocal holdings of banking organizations' capital securities	As a general rule, one-half of the aggregate investments would be deducted from Tier I capital and one-half from Tier II capital‡
Other deductions (such as other subsidiaries or joint ventures) as determined by supervisory authority	On a case-by-case basis or as a matter of policy after formal rule making
Total capital (Tier I + Tier II − Deductions)	Must equal or exceed 8 percent of weighted-risk assets

*Goodwill on the books of bank holding companies before March 12, 1988, would be grandfathered.

†Amounts in excess of limitations are permitted but do not qualify as capital.

‡A proportionately greater amount may be deducted from Tier I capital if the risks associated with the subsidiary so warrant.

Source: Federal Reserve Board of Governors press release, January 1989, Attachment II.

risk-adjusted assets of the bank, we would multiply the dollar amount of assets it has in each category by the appropriate risk weight.

Consider the balance sheet in Table 20–11 as an example. Then the risk-adjusted value of the bank's on-balance-sheet assets would be

$$\sum_{i=1}^{n} w_i a_i$$

where

w_i = Risk weight of the ith asset
a_i = Dollar (book) value of the ith asset on the balance sheet

Thus, in our example:

Risk-adjusted on-balance-sheet assets = 0(5) + 0(5) + 0(10) + .2(10) + .2(5) + .5(30) + 1(35) = 0 + 0 + 0 + 2 + 1 + 15 + 35 = $53 million

While the simple book value of on-balance-sheet assets is $100 million, its risk-adjusted value is $53 million.

TABLE 20–10   Summary of the Risk-Based Capital Standards for On-Balance-Sheet Items

Risk Categories
Category 1 (0% weight)
Cash, Federal Reserve Bank balances, securities of the U.S. Treasury, OECD governments, and some U.S. agencies.
Category 2 (20% weight)
Cash items in the process of collection. U.S. and OECD interbank deposits and guaranteed claims. Some non-OECD bank and government deposits and securities. General obligation municipal bonds. Some mortgage-backed securities. Claims collateralized by the U.S. Treasury and some other government securities.
Category 3 (50% weight)
Loans fully secured by first liens on one- to four-family residential properties. Other (revenue) municipal bonds.
Category 4 (100% weight)
All other on-balance-sheet assets not listed above, including loans to private entities and individuals, some claims on non-OECD governments and banks, real assets, and investments in subsidiaries.

Source: Federal Reserve Board of Governors press release, January 1989, Attachment III.

TABLE 20–11   A Bank's Balance Sheet
(in millions of dollars)

Weight		Assets	Liabilities	
	Cash	$ 5	Total Tier I plus	
0%	T-Bills,	5	Tier II capital	$ 10
	T-Notes and T-bonds	10		
20%	General obligation municipal bonds,	10	Liabilities	90
	FNMA securities	5		
50%	Residential mortgages	30		
100%	Other loans	35		
		$100		$100

Risk-Adjusted Off-Balance-Sheet Activities. The risk-adjusted value of assets is only one component of the capital ratio denominator; the other is the credit risk-adjusted value of the bank's off-balance-sheet activities. The calculation of the risk-adjusted values of the off-balance-sheet activities involves some initial segregation of these activities. In particular, the calculation of the credit risk exposure or the risk-adjusted asset amounts of contingent or guaranty contracts such as letters of credit differs from the calculation of the risk-adjusted asset amounts for foreign exchange and interest rate forward, option, and swap contracts. We consider the risk-adjusted asset value of off-balance-sheet guaranty type contracts and contingent contracts and then derivative or market contracts.

The Risk-Adjusted Asset Value of Off-Balance-Sheet Contingent Guaranty Contracts. The beginning step in calculating the risk-adjusted asset values of these off-balance-sheet items is to convert them into credit equivalent amounts—

TABLE 20–12   Conversion Factors for Off-Balance-Sheet Contingent or Guaranty Contracts

Sale and repurchase agreements and assets sold with recourse that are not included on the balance sheet (100%)
Direct credit substitute standby letters of credit (100%)
Performance-related standby letters of credit (50%)
Unused portion of loan commitments with original maturity of more than one year (50%)
Commercial letters of credit (20%)
Bankers acceptances conveyed (20%)
Other loan commitments (10%)

Source: Federal Reserve Board of Governors press release, January 1989, Attachment IV.

amounts equivalent to an on-balance-sheet item. Consider the appropriate conversion factors in Table 20–12.[17]

From Table 20–12 note that standby letter of credit guarantees issued by banks to back commercial paper have a 100 percent conversion factor rating; this means they have the same credit risk as on-balance-sheet loans. Similarly, sale and repurchase agreements and assets sold with recourse are also given a 100 percent conversion factor rating. Future performance-related SLCs and unused loan commitments of more that one year have a 50 percent conversion factor. Standard trade-related commercial letters of credit and bankers acceptances sold have a 20 percent conversion factor. Other loan commitments, those with less than one year to run, impose no credit risk on the bank and have a 0 percent credit conversion factor. To see how off-balance-sheet activities are incorporated into the risk-based ratio, we can extend the example of the bank in Table 20–12. Assume that in addition to having $53 million in risk-adjusted assets on its balance sheet, it also has the following off-balance-sheet contingencies or guarantees:

1. $80 million two-year loan commitments to large U.S. corporations.
2. $10 million standby letters of credit backing an issue of commercial paper.
3. $50 million commercial letters of credit.

To find out the risk-adjusted asset value for these off-balance-sheet items, we follow a two-step process. In the first step we multiply the dollar amount outstanding of these items to derive the **credit equivalent amounts** using the conversion factors (CF) listed in Table 20–12.

Credit Equivalent Amount
The credit risk exposure of an off-balance-sheet item calculated by multiplying the face value of an OBS instrument by a conversion factor.

OBS Item	Face Value		Conversion Factor		Credit Equivalent Amount
Two-year loan commitment	$80	×	.5	=	$40
Standby letter of credit	10	×	1.0	=	10
Commercial letter of credit	50	×	.2	=	10

Thus, the credit equivalent amounts of loan commitments, standby letters of credit, and commercial letters of credit are, respectively, $40, $10, and $10 million.

[17]Appropriate here means those used by the regulators and required to be used by banks rather than being equal to conversion factors that might be calculated from a contingent asset valuation (option) model. Indeed, regulators used no such valuation model in deriving the conversion factors in Table 20–12.

These conversion factors convert an off-balance-sheet item into an equivalent credit or on-balance-sheet item.

In the second step we multiply these credit equivalent amounts by their appropriate risk weights. The appropriate risk weight in each case depends on the underlying counterparty to the off-balance-sheet activity such as a municipality, a government, or a corporation. For example, if the underlying party being guaranteed were a municipality issuing general obligation (GO) bonds, and a bank issued an off-balance-sheet standby letter of credit backing the credit risk of the municipal GO issue, then the risk weight would be .2. However, in our example, the counterparty being guaranteed is a *private agent* in all three cases; a corporate loan commitment, a guaranty underlying commercial paper, and a commercial letter of credit. Thus, the appropriate risk weight in each case is 1. Note that if the counterparty had been the central government, the risk weight would be zero. The appropriate risk weights for our example follow:

OBS Item	Credit Equivalent Amount, $ millions		Risk Weight (w_i)		Risk-Adjusted Asset Amount, $ millions
Two-year loan commitment	$40	×	1.0	=	$40
Standby letter of credit	10	×	1.0	=	10
Commercial letter of credit	10	×	1.0	=	10
					$60

The bank's risk-adjusted asset value of its OBS contingencies and guarantees is $60 million.

The Risk-Adjusted Asset Value of Off-Balance-Sheet Market Contracts or Derivative Instruments.   In addition to having OBS contingencies and guarantees, modern FIs heavily engage in buying and selling OBS futures, options, forwards, swaps, caps, and other derivative securities contracts for interest rate and foreign exchange management and hedging reasons as well as buying and selling such products on behalf of their customers (see Chapter 13). Each of these positions potentially exposes banks to **counterparty credit risk,** that is, the risk that the counterparty (or other side of a contract) will default when suffering large actual or potential losses on its position. Such defaults mean that a bank would have to go back to the market to replace such contracts at (potentially) less favorable terms.

Counterparty Credit Risk
The risk that the other side of a contract will default on payment obligations.

Under the risk-based capital ratio rules, we make a major distinction between exchange-traded derivative security contracts (e.g., Chicago Board of Trade's exchange-traded options) and over-the-counter traded instruments (e.g., forwards, swaps, caps, and floors). The credit or default risk of exchange-traded derivatives is approximately zero because when a counterparty defaults on its obligations, the exchange itself adopts the counterparty's obligations in full. However, no such guarantees exist for bilaterally agreed, over-the-counter contracts originated and traded outside organized exchanges. Hence, most OBS futures and options positions have no capital requirements for a bank while most forwards, swaps, caps, and floors do.[18]

---

[18]This may create some degree of preference among banks for using exchange-traded hedging instruments rather than over-the-counter instruments because using the former may save a bank costly capital resources.

The calculation of the risk-adjusted asset values of OBS market contracts also requires a two-step approach. First, we calculate a conversion factor to create credit equivalent amounts. Second, we multiply the credit equivalent amounts by the appropriate risk weights.

Specifically, we convert the notional or face values of all nonexchange-traded swap, forward, and other derivative contracts into credit equivalent amounts. The credit equivalent amount itself is divided into a *potential exposure* element and a *current exposure* element. That is:

$$\text{Credit equivalent amount} = \text{Potential exposure} + \text{Current exposure}$$
$$\text{of OBS derivative} \quad\quad (\$) \quad\quad\quad (\$)$$
$$\text{security items (\$)}$$

Potential Exposure
The risk of a counterparty to a derivative securities contract defaulting in the future.

The **potential exposure** component reflects the credit risk if the counterparty to the contract defaults in the *future*. The probability of such an occurrence depends on the future volatility of either interest rates for an interest rate contract or exchange rates for an exchange rate contract. The Bank of England and the Federal Reserve carried out an enormous number of simulations and found that FX rates were far more volatile than interest rates.[19] Thus, the potential exposure conversion factors in Table 20–13 are larger for foreign exchange contracts than for interest rate contracts. Also, note the larger potential exposure credit risk for longer-term contracts of both types.

Current Exposure
The cost of replacing a derivative securities contract at today's prices.

In addition to calculating the potential exposure of an OBS market instrument, a bank has to calculate its **current exposure** with the instrument. This reflects the cost of replacing a contract if a counterparty defaults today. The bank calculates this replacement cost or current exposure by replacing the rate or price that was initially in the contract with the current rate or price for a similar contract and recalculates all the current and future cash flows that would have been generated under current rate or price terms.[20] The bank would discount any future cash flows to give a current present value measure of the replacement cost of the contract. Since each swap

TABLE 20–13   Credit Conversion Factors for Interest Rate and Foreign Exchange Contracts in Calculating Potential Exposure

Remaining Maturity	*(1) Interest Rate Contracts*	*(2) Exchange Rate Contracts*
1. One year or less	0	1.0%
2. One to five years	0.5%	5.0%
3. Over five years	1.5%	7.5%

Source: Federal Reserve Board of Governors press release, August 1995, Section II.

[19]The Bank of England and the Federal Reserve employed a Monte Carlo simulation approach in deciding on the size of the appropriate conversion factors. See C. W. Smith, C. W. Smithson, and D. S. Wilford, *Managing Financial Risk* (New York: Ballinger Publishing Company, 1990), pp. 225–56.

[20]For example, suppose a two-year forward foreign exchange contract was entered into in January 1999 at $1.55/£. In January 2000, the bank has to evaluate the credit risk of the contract, which now has one year remaining. To do this, it replaces the agreed forward rate $1.55/£ with the forward rate on current one-year forward contracts, $1.65/£. It then recalculates its net gain or loss on the contract if it had to be replaced at this price. This is the contract's replacement cost.

or forward is in some sense unique, this involves a considerable computer processing task for the FI's management information systems. Indeed, specialized service firms are likely to perform this task for smaller banks.[21]

Once the current and potential exposure amounts are summed to produce the credit equivalent amount for each contract, we multiply this dollar number by a risk weight to produce the final risk-adjusted asset amount for OBS market contracts. In general, the appropriate risk weight is .5, or 50 percent. That is:

Risk-adjusted asset value of OBS market contracts = Total credit equivalent amount × .5 (risk weight)

Continuing our example of calculating the risk-based capital ratio for a bank, suppose the bank had taken one interest rate hedging position in the fixed-floating interest rate swap market for 4 years with a notional dollar amount of $100 million and one two-year forward $/£ foreign exchange contract for $40 million. We calculate the credit equivalent amount for each item or contract as:

Type of Contract (remaining maturity)	Notional Principal	×	Potential Exposure Conversion Factor	=	Potential Exposure	Replacement Cost	Current Exposure	=	Credit Equivalent Amount
4-year fixed–floating interest rate swap	$100	×	.005	=	$.5	$ 3	$3		$3.5
Two-year forward foreign exchange contract	$ 40	×	.05	=	$2	$−1	$0		$2

Potential Exposure + Current Exposure

Let's look closely at these calculations. For the 4-year fixed–floating interest rate swap, the notional value (contract face value) of the swap is $100 million. Since this is a long-term, over-one-year, less-than-five-year interest rate market contract, its face value is multiplied by .005 to get a potential exposure or credit risk equivalent value of $0.5 million (see column 1 of Table 20–13). We add this potential exposure to the replacement cost (current exposure) of this contract to the bank. The replacement cost reflects the cost of having to enter into a new 4-year fixed–floating swap agreement at today's interest rates for the remaining life of the swap. Assuming that interest rates today are less favorable, on a present value basis, the cost of replacing the existing contract for its remaining life would be $3 million. Thus, the total credit equivalent amount—current plus potential exposures—for the interest rate swap is $3.5 million.

Next, we can look at the foreign exchange two-year forward contract of $40 million face value. Since this is an over-one-year, less-than-five-year foreign exchange contract, the potential (future) credit risk is $40 million × .05, or $2 million [see column (2) in Table 20–13]. However, its replacement cost is *minus* $1 million. That is, in this example our bank actually stands to gain if the counterparty defaults.

[21]One large New York money center bank has to calculate, on average, the replacement cost of more than 6,000 different forward contracts alone.

Exactly why the counterparty would do this when it is in the money is unclear. However, regulators cannot permit a bank to gain from a default by a counterparty as this might produce all types of perverse risk-taking incentives. Consequently, if the replacement cost of a contract is negative, as in our example, current exposure has to be set equal to zero (as shown). Thus, the sum of potential exposure ($2) and current exposure ($0) produces a total credit equivalent amount of $2 million for this contract.

Since the bank has just two OBS derivative contracts, summing the two credit equivalent amounts produces a total credit equivalent amount of $3.5 + $2 = $5.5 million for the bank's OBS market contracts. The next step is to multiply this credit equivalent amount by the appropriate risk weight. Specifically, to calculate the risk-adjusted asset value for the bank's OBS derivative or market contracts, we multiply the credit equivalent amount by the appropriate risk weight, which for virtually all over-the-counter derivative security products is .5, or 50 percent:

$$
\begin{array}{lcccc}
\text{Risk-adjusted} & = & \$5.5\text{ million} & \times & 0.5 & = \$2.75\text{ million} \\
\text{asset value of} & & \text{(credit equivalent} & & \text{(risk weight)} & \\
\text{OBS deliveries} & & \text{amount)} & & &
\end{array}
$$

The Risk-Adjusted Asset Value of Off-Balance-Sheet Derivative Instruments with Netting.* One criticism of the above method is that it ignores the netting of exposures. In response, the Fed has adopted a proposal put forward by the BIS that allows netting of off-balance-sheet derivative contracts as long as the bank has a bilateral netting contract that clearly establishes a legal obligation by the counterparty to pay or receive a single net amount on the different contracts. This rule has been effective since October 1, 1995.[22]

Provided that such written contracts are clearly documented by the bank, the new rules require the estimation of *net current exposure* and *net potential exposure* of those positions included in the bilateral netting contract. The sum of the net current exposure and the net potential exposure equals the total credit equivalent amount.

The new rules define net current exposure as the net sum of all positive and negative replacement costs (or mark-to-market values of the individual derivative contracts). If the sum of the replacement costs is positive, then the net current exposure equals the sum. If it is negative, the net current exposure is zero.

The net potential exposure is defined by a formula that adjusts the gross potential exposure estimated earlier:

$$
A_{\text{net}} = (0.4 \times A_{\text{gross}}) + (0.6 \times \text{NGR} \times A_{\text{gross}})
$$

where A_{net} is the net potential exposure (or adjusted sum of potential future credit exposures), A_{gross} is the sum of the potential exposures of each contract, and NGR is the ratio of net current exposure to gross current exposure. The 0.6 is the amount of potential exposure that is reduced as a result of netting.[23]

The same example used in the previous section (without netting) will be used to show the effect of netting on the total credit equivalent amount. Here we assume that both contracts are with the same counterparty.

---

[22]See Federal Reserve Board of Governors press release, August 29, 1995, p. 17.

[23]The original Fed proposal had ratios of 50/50, but these were reduced to 40/60 after public comments were received.

Type of Contract Remaining Maturity	Potential Exposure	Replacement Cost	Current Exposure
4-year fixed–floating interest rate swap	$0.5	$ 3	$ 3
Two-year forward foreign exchange contract	$2	$−1	$−0

$$A_{gross} = \$2.5 \quad \text{Net current exposure} = \$2 \quad \text{Current exposure} = \$3$$

The net current exposure is just the sum of the positive and negative replacement costs—that is, $\$+3$ and $\$-1 = \$2$. The gross potential exposure (A_{gross}) is the sum of the individual potential exposures $= \$2.5$. To determine the net potential exposure, the following formula is used:

$$A_{net} = (0.4 \times A_{gross}) + (0.6 \times \text{NGR} \times A_{gross})$$

$$\text{NGR} = \text{Net current exposure} / \text{Current exposure} = 2/3$$

$$\begin{aligned} A_{net} &= (0.4 \times 2.5) + (0.6 \times 2/3 \times 2.5) \\ &= \$2 \end{aligned}$$

$$\begin{aligned} \text{Total credit equivalent} &= \text{Net potential exposure} + \text{Net current exposure} \\ &= 2 + 2 = \$4 \end{aligned}$$

$$\begin{aligned} \text{Risk-adjusted asset value of OBS market contracts} &= \text{Total credit equivalent amount} \times 0.5 \text{ (risk weight)} \\ &= 4 \times 0.5 = \$2 \end{aligned}$$

As can be seen, using netting reduces the risk-adjusted asset value from $2.75 million to $2 million.

Calculating the Overall Risk-Based Capital Position of a Bank.   We can now calculate our bank's overall capital adequacy in the light of the risk-based capital requirements. From our example, we have calculated:

1. Tier I plus Tier II capital = $10 million
2. Risk-adjusted assets on balance sheet = $53 million
3. Risk-adjusted assets off balance sheet =
   a. Contingent/Guaranty items = $60 million
   b. Market contracts/Derivative securities (assuming no netting) = $2.75 million

Thus, the total risk-based capital ratio is

$$\frac{\text{Total capital}}{\text{Risk-adjusted assets}} = \frac{(1)}{(2) + (3a) + (3b)} = \frac{10}{53 + 60 + 2.75} = \frac{10}{115.75}$$
$$= 8.64\%$$

Since the minimum risk-based capital ratio required is 8 percent, this bank has adequate capital, exceeding the required minimum by 0.64 percent.[24]

Interest Rate Risk, Market Risk, and Risk-Based Capital.   From a regulatory perspective, a risk-based capital ratio is adequate only as long as a bank is not ex-

---

[24]With netting, the total capital–risk adjusted assets ratio would have been 10/115, or 8.70 percent.

posed to undue interest rate or market risk. The reason is that the risk-based capital ratio takes into account only the adequacy of a bank's capital to meet both its on- and off-balance-sheet credit risks. Not explicitly accounted for is the insolvency risk emanating from interest rate risk (duration mismatches) and market (trading) risk.

To meet these criticisms, the Federal Reserve (along with the Bank for International Settlements) developed additional capital requirement proposals for interest rate risk (see Chapter 9) and market risk (see Chapter 10). As is discussed in Chapter 10, since 1998 banks have had to calculate an "add-on" to the 8 percent risk-based capital ratio to reflect their exposure to market risk. There are two approaches available to banks to calculate the size of this add-on: (1) the standardized model proposed by regulators and (2) the bank's own internal market risk model. To date, no formal add-on has been required for interest-rate risk.

Criticisms of the Risk-Based Capital Ratio.   The risk-based capital requirement seeks to improve on the simple leverage ratio by (1) more systematically accounting for credit risk differences among assets, (2) incorporating off-balance-sheet risk exposures, and (3) applying a similar capital requirement across all the major banks (and banking centers) in the world. Unfortunately, it has a number of conceptual and applicability weaknesses in achieving these objectives.

1. *Risk weights.* It is unclear how closely the four risk weight categories reflect true credit risk. For example, residential mortgage loans have a 50 percent risk weight, while commercial loans have a 100 percent risk weight. Taken literally, these relative weights imply that commercial loans are exactly twice as risky as mortgage loans.[25]

2. *Balance sheet incentive problems.* The fact that different assets have different risk weights may induce bankers to engage in balance sheet asset allocation games (or what is often called "regulatory arbitrage"). For example, given any amount of total capital, a bank can always increase its reported risk-based capital ratio by reducing its risk-adjusted assets, the denominator of the ratio. There are a number of interesting opportunities for an FI manager to do this. For example, residential mortgages have a 50 percent risk weight, while GNMA mortgage-backed securities have a 0 percent risk weight. Suppose a bank pooled all its mortgages and then sold them to outside investors. If it then replaced the mortgages sold by buying GNMA securities backing similar pools of mortgages to those sold, it could significantly reduce its risk-adjusted asset amount. Overall, the incentives and opportunities for balance sheet games have increased, especially if bank managers believe certain asset and OBS risks are either over- or underpriced in terms of the risk-based capital weights.

3. *Portfolio aspects.* The new plan also ignores credit risk portfolio diversification opportunities. As we discuss in Chapter 12, when returns on assets have negative or less than perfectly positive correlations, an FI may lower its portfolio risk through diversification. As constructed, the new capital adequacy plan is essentially a linear risk measure that ignores correlations or covariances among assets and asset

---

[25]R. B. Avery and A. Berger show evidence that these risk weights do a good job in distinguishing between failing and nonfailing banks. See "Risk-Based Capital and Deposit Insurance Reform," *Journal of Banking and Finance* 15 (1991), pp. 847–74. However, David S. Jones and Kathleen Kuester King, in "The Implementation of Prompt Corrective Action: An Assessment," *Journal of Banking and Finance,* 1995, find that risk-based capital would have done a poor job in identifying failing banks over the 1981–89 period if it had been used for prompt corrective action purposes.

group credit risks—such as between residential mortgages and commercial loans.[26] That is, the banker weights each asset separately by the appropriate risk weight and then sums those numbers to get an overall measure of credit risk. No account is taken of the covariances among asset risks between different counterparties (or risk weights).

4. *Bank specialness.* Giving private sector commercial loans the highest credit risk weighting may reduce the incentive for banks to make such loans relative to holding other assets. This may reduce the amount of bank loans to business, as well as the degree of bank monitoring, and have associated negative externality effects on the economy. That is, one aspect of banks' special functions—bank lending—may be muted.[27]

5. *All commercial loans have equal weight.* Loans made to a AAA-rated company have a credit risk weight of 1, as do loans made to a CCC company. That is, within a risk-weight class such as commercial loans, no account is taken of credit risk quality differences. This may create perverse incentives for banks to pursue lower-quality customers, thereby increasing the risk of a bank.[28]

6. *Other risks.* While market risk exposure was integrated into the risk-based capital requirements in 1998, the BIS plan does not yet account for other risks, such as interest rate risk, foreign exchange rate risk, asset concentration risk, and operating risk. A more complete risk-based capital requirement would include these risks.[29]

7. *Competition.* As a result of tax and accounting differences across banking systems as well as in safety net coverages, the 8 percent risk-based capital requirement has not created a level competitive playing field across banks. This is different from what proponents of the scheme claim. In particular, Japan and the United States have very different accounting, tax, and safety net rules that significantly affect the comparability of U.S. and Japanese bank risk-based capital ratios.[30]

---

[26]In a portfolio context, it assumes that asset and OBS risks are independent of each other.

[27]This effect has been of great concern and controversy. Indeed, the high-risk weight given to commercial loans relative to securities has been blamed in part for inducing a credit crunch and a reorientation of bank portfolios away from commercial loans toward securities in the early 1990s. See C. Jacklin, "Bank Capital Requirements and Incentives for Lending," Working Paper, Stanford University, February 1993; and J. Haubich and P. Wachtel, "Capital Requirements and Shifts in Commercial Bank Portfolios," Federal Reserve Bank of Cleveland, *Economic Review* 29 (3rd quarter, 1994), pp. 2–15. However A. Berger and G. Udell, "Did Risk-Based Capital Allocate Bank Credit and Cause a Credit Crunch in the U.S.?" *Journal of Money Credit and Banking* 26 (August 1994), dispute these findings.

[28]One possible argument in support of the same risk weight for all commercial loans is that if the bank holds a well-diversified commercial loan portfolio, the unsystematic risk of each individual loan will be diversified away, leaving only systematic credit risk. However, the betas or systematic risk sensitivity of loans may still differ across loans. Giving the same weight to all loans is also one of the reasons for the development of private sector credit risk measurement models such as CreditMetrics and CreditRisk+, discussed in the appendixes to Chapter 11. These models develop analytical techniques to measure the capital requirements required against individual loans as well as portfolios of loans. These models have been proposed as alternatives to the BIS approach for measuring a bank's capital requirements (see also Saunders, Credit Risk Measurement, ibid.).

[29]Interestingly, the risk-based capital schemes for property-casualty and life insurers (discussed later in this chapter) have more complete coverage of risks than does the bank scheme.

[30]H. S. Scott and S. Iwahara, "In Search of a Level Playing Field," Group of Thirty, Washington, D.C., 1994, argue that these distortions are so large that they render meaningful comparisons impossible. Indeed, many analysts have argued that a majority of the largest Japanese banks would have violated the 8 percent rule in 1998 under U.S. accounting and regulatory practices. This is one of the major reasons for the bailout plan announced by the Japanese government in October 1998. See "The Timid Japanese Bailout Just Might Do the Job," *New York Times,* October 22, 1998, p. C2.

Concept Questions

1. What are the major strengths of the risk-based capital ratios?
2. You are an FI manager with a total risk-based capital ratio of 6 percent. Discuss four strategies to meet the required 8 percent ratio in a short period of time without raising new capital.
3. Why isn't a capital ratio levied on exchange-traded derivative contracts?
4. What are three problems with the simple leverage ratio measure of capital adequacy?
5. What is the difference between Tier I and Tier II capital?
6. Identify one asset in each of the four risk-weight categories.

Capital Requirements for Other FIs

Securities Firms

Unlike the book value capital rules employed by bank and thrift regulators, the capital requirements for broker-dealers set by the SEC's Rule 15C 3–1 in 1975 are close to a market value accounting rule. Essentially, broker-dealers have to calculate a market value for their net worth on a day-to-day basis and ensure that their net worth–assets ratio exceeds 2 percent:

$$\frac{\text{Net worth}}{\text{Assets}} \geq 2\%$$

The essential idea is that if a broker-dealer has to liquidate all assets at near market values, a capital cushion of 2 percent should be sufficient to satisfy all customer liabilities, such as brokerage accounts held with the firm.[31]

Specifically, to compute net capital, the broker-dealer calculates book net worth and then makes a number of adjustments: (1) subtracting all assets such as fixed assets not readily convertible into cash and (2) subtracting securities that cannot be publicly offered or sold. Moreover, the dealer must make other deductions, or haircuts, reflecting potential market value fluctuations in assets. For example, the net capital rule requires haircuts on illiquid equities of up to 40 percent and on debt securities generally between 0 and 9 percent. Finally, other adjustments are required to reflect unrealized profits and losses, subordinated liabilities, contractual commitments, deferred taxes, options, commodities and commodity futures, and certain collateralized liabilities.

Thus, broker-dealers must make significant adjustments to the book value of net worth—the difference between the book values of assets and liabilities—to reach a market value net worth figure. This figure must exceed 2 percent of assets.

Life Insurance

In 1993 the life insurance industry adopted a model risk-based capital scheme. Although similar in nature to that adopted by banks and thrifts, it is more extensive in that it also covers other types of risk (discussed later in this chapter). While capital requirements are imposed at the state level, they are heavily influenced by

---

[31]If a broker-dealer fails with negative net worth, the SIPC provides guarantees of up to $500,000 per customer (see Chapter 19).

recommendations from the National Association of Insurance Commissioners (NAIC). We describe the NAIC model next.

The model begins by identifying four risks faced by the life insurer:

$C1$ = Asset risk
$C2$ = Insurance risk
$C3$ = Interest rate risk
$C4$ = Business risk

C1: Asset Risk.   Asset risk reflects the riskiness of the asset portfolio of the life insurer. It is similar in spirit to the risk-adjusted asset calculations for banks and thrifts in that a credit risk weight is multiplied by the dollar or face value of the assets on the balance sheet. Table 20–14 shows the relative asset risk weights for life and PC insurers.

Thus, an insurer with $100 million in common stocks would have a risk-based capital requirement of $30 million, while for one with $100 million in BBB corporate bonds only $1 million would be required.

Mortality Risk
The risk of death.

Morbidity Risk
The risk of ill health.

C2: Insurance Risk.   Insurance risk captures the risk of adverse changes in **mortality risk** and **morbidity risk.** As we discuss in Chapter 2, through mortality tables life insurers have an extremely accurate idea of the probabilities of an insured dying in any given year. However, epidemics such as AIDS can upset these predictions drastically. As a result, insurers adjust insurance in force for the current level of reserves and multiply the resulting number by an insurance risk factor. Similar calculations are carried out for accident and health insurance, which covers morbidity (ill health) risk.

C3: Interest Rate Risk.   Interest rate risk in part reflects the liquidity of liabilities and their probability or ease of withdrawal as interest rates change. For example,

TABLE 20–14   Risk-Based Capital (RBC) Factors for Selected Assets

	Insurer	
Asset	*Life*	*Property-Casualty*
Bonds		
U.S. government	0.0%	0.0%
NAIC 1: AAA-A*	0.3	0.3
NAIC 2: BBB	1.0	1.0
NAIC 3: BB	4.0	2.0
NAIC 4: B	9.0	4.5
NAIC 5: CCC	20.0	10.0
NAIC 6: In or near default	30.0	30.0
Residential mortgages (whole loans)	0.5†	5.0
Commercial mortgages	3.0†	5.0
Common stock	30.0	15.0
Preferred stock—bond factor for same NAIC category plus:	2.0	2.0

*Includes agencies and most collateralized mortgage obligations.

†Mortgage factors are for loans in good standing. These factors will be adjusted for a company's default experience relative to the industry.

Source: Salomon Brothers, *Insurance Strategies,* August 2, 1993.

guaranteed investment contracts (GICs) have similar characteristics to long-term, fixed-rate bank deposits and are often highly sensitive to interest rate movements. As we also discuss in Chapter 17, illiquidity problems have led to a number of insurer insolvencies in recent years. With respect to interest rate risk, insurers must divide liabilities into three risk classes: low risk (0.5 percent risk-based capital requirement), medium risk (1 percent capital requirement), and high risk (2 percent capital requirement).

C4: Business Risk.   As we discuss in Chapter 19, states have organized guaranty funds that partially pay for insurer insolvencies by levying a charge on surviving firms. Thus, the capital requirement for business risk is set to equal the maximum potential assessment by state guaranty funds (2 percent for life and annuity premiums and 0.5 percent for health premiums for each surviving insurer). Also, company-specific fraud and litigation risks may require an additional capital charge.

After calculating $C1$, $C2$, $C3$ and $C4$, the life insurance manager computes a risk-based capital measure (RBC) based on the following equation:

$$RBC = \sqrt{(C1 + C3)^2 + C2^2} + C4$$

As calculated, the RBC is the minimum required capital for the life insurer. The insurer compares this risk-based capital measure to the actual capital and surplus (total capital) held:

$$\frac{\text{Total surplus and capital}}{\text{Risk-based capital } (RBC)}$$

If this ratio is greater than 1, the life insurance manager is meeting or is above the minimum capital requirements. If the ratio falls below 1, the manager will be subject to regulatory scrutiny.[32]

Property-Casualty Insurance

The model risk-based capital requirements—introduced by the National Association of Insurance Commissioners in 1994—are quite similar to the life insurance industry's RBC except that there are six (instead of four) risk categories, including three separate asset risk categories. The risk weights for these different types of assets are shown in Table 20–14 next to the weight for similar assets held by life insurance companies. As can be seen, the risk weights in some areas—especially common stock—are lower than those for life insurers because of the relatively smaller exposures of PC companies to this type of asset risk. The six different types of risk and the calculation of RBC (to be compared with a PC insurer's total capital and surplus) are shown in Table 20–15.

The calculation of RBC assumes that risks $R1$ to $R5$ are independent of each other—that is, have a zero correlation coefficient, whereas investments in PC affiliates (risk $R0$) are assumed to be perfectly correlated with the net risk of the $R1$ to

[32]NAIC testing found that 87 percent of the industry had a total surplus and capital-*RBC* ratio above 1 at the time of the RBC ratio's introduction. This description of the life insurance risk-based capital ratio is based on L. S. Goodman, P. Fischer, and C. Anderson, "The Impact of Risk-Based Capital Requirements on Asset Allocation for Life Insurance Companies," *Insurance Executive Review,* Fall 1992, pp. 14–21; and P. J. Bouyoucos, M. H. Siegel, and E. B. Raisel, "Risk-Based Capital for Insurers: A Strategic Opportunity to Enhance Franchise Value," Goldman Sachs, Industry Resource Group, September 1992.

TABLE 20–15   Calculation of Total Risk-Based Capital (*RBC*)

Risk	Type	Description
R0	Asset	*RBC* for investments (common and preferred) in property-casualty affiliates
R1	Asset	*RBC* for fixed income
R2	Asset	*RBC* for equity—includes common and preferred stocks (other than in property-casualty affiliates) and real estate
R3	Credit	*RBC* for reinsurance recoverables and other receivables
R4	Underwriting	*RBC* for loss and loss adjustment expense (LAE) reserves plus growth surcharges
R5	Underwriting	*RBC* for written premiums plus growth surcharges

$$RBC = R0 + \sqrt{R1^2 + R2^2 + R3^2 + R4^2 + R5^2}$$

TABLE 20–16   Risk-Based Capital (*RBC*) Charges for Typical Company

Risk	Description	RBC Charge (millions)
R0	Affiliated property-casualty	$ 10
R1	Fixed income	5
R2	Common stock	10
R3	Credit	10
R4	Reserve	40
R5	Premium	25
Total charges before covariance		$100

$$RBC = 10 + \sqrt{5^2 + 10^2 + 10^2 + 40^2 + 25^2} = \$59.50$$

Source: Salomon Brothers, *Insurance Strategies,* August 2, 1993.

*R*5 components.[33] If the total capital and surplus of a PC insurer exceed the calculated *RBC,* the insurer is viewed as being adequately capitalized. For example, suppose a PC insurer had total capital and surplus of $60 million and its *RBC* charge was calculated as $59.5 million (as shown in Table 20–16); it would have a capital–*RBC* ratio exceeding 1 (i.e., 60/59.5 = 1.008) and be adequately capitalized.[34]

Concept Questions

1. How do the capital requirements for securities firms differ from the book value capital rules employed by bank and thrift regulators?
2. What types of risks are included by the NAIC in estimating the *RBC* of life insurance firms?
3. How do the NAIC's model risk-based capital requirements for PC insurers differ from the life insurance industry's *RBC?*

[33]See Alfred Weinberger, *Insurance Strategies,* Salomon Brothers, August 2, 1993.
[34]For a critical evaluation of the NAIC's *RBC* plan, see J. Commins, S. E. Harrington, and R. Klein, "Insolvency Exercise, Risk-Based Capital and Prompt Corrective Action in Property-Liability Insurance," *Journal of Banking and Finance,* 1995.

Summary

This chapter reviewed the role of an FI's capital in insulating it against credit, interest rate, and other risks. According to economic theory, capital or net worth should be measured on a market value basis as the difference between the market values of assets and liabilities. In actuality, regulators use book value accounting rules. While a book value capital adequacy rule accounts for credit risk exposure in a rough fashion, it overlooks the effects of interest rate changes and interest rate exposure on net worth. We analyzed the specific capital rules adopted by the regulators of banks and thrifts,

insurance companies, and securities firms and discussed their problems and weaknesses. In particular, we looked at how bank, thrift, PC, and life insurance regulators are now adjusting book value–based capital rules to account for different types of risk as part of their imposition of risk-based capital adequacy ratios. As a result, actual capital requirements in banks, life insurance companies, PC insurance companies, and thrifts are moving closer to the market value–based net worth requirements of broker-dealers.

Questions and Problems

1. Identify and briefly discuss the importance of the four functions of an FI's capital.

2. Why are regulators concerned with the levels of capital held by an FI compared to a nonfinancial institution?

3. What is the P/E ratio? How do three performance variables affect the P/E ratio according to the dividend growth model?

4. Peoples Bank has reported net income of $3.60 per share for the most recent year. The bank's dividend-payout ratio is 30 percent, the growth in dividends in 7.5 percent, and the required return by shareholders is 10 percent.

   a. What is the year-end price of the stock?

   b. What is the year-end price/earnings ratio?

   c. What is the year-end price/earnings ratio for each of the following incremental changes in the above assumptions?

      1. The growth rate is 9 percent

      2. The dividend payout rate is 40 percent

      3. The required return on equity is 9 percent

   d. What is the year-end price/earnings ratio if all three assumptions are changed?

5. What are the differences between the economic definition of capital and the book value definition of capital?

   a. How does economic value accounting recognize the adverse effects of credit and interest rate risk?

   b. How does book value accounting recognize the adverse effects of credit and interest rate risk?

6. A financial intermediary has the following balance sheet (in millions) with all assets and liabilities in market values:

Assets		Liabilities and Equity	
6 percent semiannual four-year Treasury-notes (par value $12)	$10	5 percent two-year subordinated debt (par value $25)	$20
7 percent annual 3-year AA-rated bonds (par-$15)	15		
9 percent annual 5-year BBB rated bonds (par-$15)	15	Equity capital	20
Total assets	$40	Total liabilities and equity	$40

   a. Under FASB Statement No. 115, what would be the effect on equity capital (net worth) if interest rates increased by 30 basis points? The T-notes are held for trading purposes; the rest are all classified as held to maturity.

   b. Under FASB Statement No. 115, how are the changes in the market value of assets adjusted in the income statements and balance sheets of FIs?

7. Why is the market value of equity a better measure of a bank's ability to absorb losses than book value of equity?

8. State Bank has the following year-end balance sheet (in millions):

Assets		Liabilities and Equity	
Cash	$ 10	Deposits	$ 90
Loans	90	Equity	10
Total assets	$100	Total liabilities and equity	$100

The loans primarily are fixed-rate, medium-term loans, while the deposits are either short-term or variable-rate deposits. Rising interest rates have caused the failure of a key industrial company, and as a result, 3 percent of the loans are considered to be uncollectable and thus have no economic value. One-third of these uncollectable loans will be charged off. Further, the increase in interest rates has caused a 5 percent decrease in the market value of the remaining loans. What is the impact on the balance sheet after the necessary adjustments are made according to the following?

   a. Book value accounting.

   b. Market value accounting.

   c. What is the new market to book value ratio if State Bank has $1 million shares outstanding?

9. What are the arguments for and against the use of market value accounting for FIs?

10. How is the leverage ratio for a bank defined?

11. What is the significance of prompt corrective action as specified by the FDICIA legislation?

12. Identify and discuss the weaknesses of the leverage ratio as a measure of capital adequacy.

13. What is the Basle Agreement?

14. What is the major feature in the estimation of credit risk under the 1988 Basle capital requirements?

15. What is the total risk-based capital ratio?

16. Identify the five zones of capital adequacy and explain the mandatory regulatory actions corresponding to each zone.

17. What are the definitional differences between Tier I and Tier II capital?

18. What components are used in the calculation of risk-adjusted assets?

19. Explain the process of calculating risk-adjusted on-balance-sheet assets.

   a. What assets are included in the four categories of credit risk exposure?

   b. What are the appropriate risk-weights for each category?

20. National Bank has the following balance sheet (in millions) and has no off-balance-sheet activities.

Assets		Liabilities and Equity	
Cash	$ 20	Deposits	$ 980
Treasury bills	40	Subordinated debentures	40
Residential mortgages	600	Common stock	40
Other loans	430	Retained earnings	30
Total assets	$1,090	Total liabilities and equity	$1,090

   a. What is the leverage ratio?

   b. What is the Tier I capital ratio?

   c. What is the total risk-based capital ratio?

   d. In what capital category would the bank be placed?

21. Onshore Bank has $20 million in assets, with risk-adjusted assets of $10 million. Tier I capital is $500,000, and Tier II capital is $400,000. How will each of the following transactions affect the value of the Tier I and total capital ratios? What will be the new values of each ratio be?

   a. The bank repurchases $100,000 of common stock.

   b. The bank issues $2,000,000 of CDs and uses the proceeds for loans to homeowners.

   c. The bank receives $500,000 in deposits and invests them in T-bills.

   d. The bank issues $800,000 in common stock and lends it to help finance a new shopping mall.

   e. The bank issues $1,000,000 in nonqualifying perpetual preferred stock and purchases general obligation municipal bonds.

   f. Homeowners pay back $4,000,000 of mortgages, and the bank uses the proceeds to build new ATMs.

22. Explain the process of calculating risk-adjusted off-balance-sheet contingent guaranty contracts.

   a. What is the basis for differentiating the credit equivalent amounts of contingent guaranty contracts?

   b. On what basis are the risk weights for the credit equivalent amounts differentiated?

23. Explain how off-balance-sheet market contracts, or derivative instruments, differ from contingent guaranty contracts.

   a. What is counterparty credit risk?

   b. Why do exchange-traded derivative security contracts have no capital requirements?

   c. What is the difference between the potential exposure and the current exposure of over-the-counter derivative contracts?

   d. Why are the credit conversion factors for the potential exposure of foreign exchange contracts greater than they are for interest rate contracts?

   e. Why do regulators not allow banks to benefit from positive current exposure values?

24. What is the process of netting off-balance-sheet derivative contracts? What requirement is necessary to allow a bank to calculate this exposure? How is net current exposure defined? How does net potential exposure differ from net current exposure?

25. How does the risk-based capital measure attempt to compensate for the limitations of the static leverage ratio?

26. Identify and discuss the problems in the risk-based capital approach to measuring capital adequacy.

27. What is the contribution to the asset base of the following items under the Basle requirements? Under the U.S. capital-assets rule?

    a. $10 million cash reserves.

    b. $50 million 91-day U.S. Treasury bills.

    c. $25 million cash items in the process of collection.

    d. $5 million U.K. government bonds.

    e. $5 million Australian short-term government bonds.

    f. $1 million general obligation municipal bonds.

    g. $40 million repurchase agreements (against U.S. Treasuries).

    h. $500 million 1–4 family home mortgages.

    i. $500 million commercial and industrial loans.

    j. $100,000 performance–related standby letters of credit to a blue chip corporation.

    k. $100,000 performance-related standby letters of credit to a municipality issuing general obligation bonds.

    l. $7 million commercial letter of credit to a foreign corporation.

    m. $3 million five-year loan commitment to an OECD government.

    n. $8 million bankers acceptance conveyed to a U.S. corporation.

    o. $17 million three-year loan commitment to a private agent.

    p. $17 million three-month loan commitment to a private agent.

    q. $30 million standby letter of credit to back a corporate issue of commercial paper.

    r. $4 million five-year interest rate swap with no current exposure (the counterparty is a private agent).

    s. $4 million five-year interest rate swap with no current exposure (the counterparty is a municipality).

    t. $6 million two-year currency swap with $500,000 current exposure (the counterparty is a private agent).

The bank balance sheet information below is for questions 28 through 31.

28. What is the bank's risk-adjusted asset base?

29. What are the bank's Tier I and total risk-based capital requirements?

30. Using the leverage ratio requirement, what is the minimum regulatory capital required to keep the bank in the well-capitalized zone?

31. What is the bank's capital adequacy level if the par value of its equity is $150,000, the surplus value of equity is $200,000, and the qualifying perpetual preferred stock is $50,000? Does the bank meet Basle (Tier I) capital standards? Does the bank comply with the well-capitalized leverage ratio requirement?

On-Balance-Sheet Items	Category	Face Value
Cash	1	$ 121,600
Short-term government securities (<92 days)	1	5,400
Long-term government securities (>92 days)	1	414,400
Federal Reserve stock	1	9,800
Repos secured by federal agencies	2	159,000
Claims on U.S. depository institutions	2	937,900
Short-term (<1 year) claims on foreign banks	2	1,640,000
General obligation municipals	2	170,000
Claims on or guaranteed by federal agencies	2	26,500
Municipal revenue bonds	3	112,900
Loans	4	6,645,700
Claims on foreign banks (>1 year)	4	5,800

Off-Balance-Sheet Items	Conversion Factor	Face Value
U.S. Government Counterparty		
Loan commitments:		
<1 year	0%	$ 300
1–5 years	50%	1,140
Standby letters of credit:		
Performance-related	50%	200
Other	100%	100
U.S. depository insitution counterparty		
(risk weight category 2)		
Loan commitments:		
<1 year	0%	1,000
>1 year	50%	3,000
Standby letters of credit		
Performance-related	50%	200
Other	100%	56,400
Commercial letters of credit	20%	400
State and local government counterparty		
(risk weight category 3)		
Loan commitments:		
>1 year	50%	100
Standby letters of credit		
Nonperformance-related	50%	135,400
Corporate customer counterparty		
Loan Commitments		
<1 year	0%	2,980,000
>1 year	50%	3,046,278
Standby letters of credit		
Performance-related	50%	101,543
Other	100%	485,000
Commercial letters of credit	20%	78,978
Note issuance facilities	50%	20,154
Forward agreements	100%	5,900
Interest rate market contracts		
(Current exposure assumed to be zero.)		
<1 year (notional amount)	0%	2,000
>1–5 years (notional amount)	.5%	5,000

32. How does the leverage ratio test impact the stringency of regulatory monitoring of bank capital positions?

33. Third Bank has the following balance sheet (in millions) with the risk weights in parentheses.

Assets		Liabilities and Equity	
Cash (0%)	$ 20	Deposits	$175
OECD interbank deposits (20%)	25	Subordinated debt (2.5 years)	3
Mortgage loans (50%)	70	Cumulative preferred stock	5
Consumer loans (100%)	70	Equity	2
Total assets	$185	Total liabilities and equity	$185

In addition, the bank has $30 million in performance-related standby letters of credit (SLCs), $40 million in two-year forward FX contracts that are currently in the money by $1 million, and $300 million in six-year interest rate swaps that are currently out of the money by $2 million. Credit conversion factors follow:

Performance-related standby LCs	50%
1–5 year foreign exchange contracts	5%
1–5 year interest rate swaps	0.5%
5–10 year interest rate swaps	1.5%

a. What are the risk-adjusted on-balance-sheet assets of the bank as defined under the Basle Accord?

b. What is the total capital required for both off- and on-balance-sheet assets?

c. Does the bank have enough capital to meet the Basle requirements? If not, what minimum Tier I or total capital does it need to meet the requirement?

34. Third Fifth Bank has the following balance sheet (in millions) with the risk weights in parentheses.

Assets		Liabilities and Equity	
Cash (0%)	$ 20	Deposits	$130
Mortgage loans (50%)	50	Subordinated debt (>5 years)	5
Consumer loans (100%)	70	Equity	5
Total assets	$140	Total liabilities and equity	$140

In addition, the bank has $20 million in commercial standby letters of credit and $40 million in 10-year forward contracts that are in the money by $1 million.

a. What are the risk-adjusted on-balance-sheet assets of the bank as defined under the Basle Accord?

b. What is the total capital required for both off- and on-balance-sheet assets?

c. Does the bank have sufficient capital to meet the Basle requirements? How much in excess? How much short?

35. According to SEC Rule 15C 3–1, what adjustments must securities firms make in the calculation of the book value of net worth?

36. A securities firm has the following balance sheet (in millions):

Assets		Liabilities and Equity	
Cash	$ 40	5-day commercial paper	$ 20
Debt securities	300	Bonds	550
Equity securities	500	Debentures	300
Other assets	60	Equity	30
Total assets	$900	Total liabilities and equity	$900

The debt securities have a coupon rate of 6 percent, have 20 years remaining until maturity, and trade at a yield of 8 percent. The equity securities have a market value equal to book value, and the other assets represent building and equipment which was recently appraised at $80 million. The company has 1 million shares of stock outstanding and its price is $35 per share. Is this company in compliance with SEC Rule 15C 3–1?

37. An investment bank specializing in fixed-income assets has the following balance sheet (in millions). Amounts are in market values, and all interest rates are annual unless indicated otherwise.

Assets		Liabilities and Equity	
Cash	$0.50	5% 1-year Eurodollar deposits	$ 5.0
8% 10-year Treasury-notes semi-annual (par value $16m)	15.0	6% 2-year subordinated debt (par = $10 million)	10.0
		Equity	0.5
Total assets	$15.5	Total liabilities and equity	$15.5

Assume that the haircut for all assets is 15 basis points and for all liabilities, 25 basis points (per annum).

a. Does the investment bank have sufficient liquid capital to cushion any unexpected losses per the net capital rule?

b. What should the FI do to maintain the net minimum required liquidity?

c. How does the net capital rule for investment banks differ from the capital requirements imposed on commercial banks and other depository institutions?

38. Identify and define the four risk categories incorporated into the life insurance risk-based capital model.

39. A life insurance company has estimated the following capital requirements for each of the risk classes: asset risk ($C1$) = $5 million, insurance risk ($C2$) = $4 million, interest rate risk ($C3$) = $1 million, and business risk ($C4$) = $3 million.

    a. What is the required risk-based capital for the life insurance company?

    b. If the total surplus and capital held by the company is $9 million, does it meet the minimum requirements?

    c. How much capital must be raised to meet the minimum requirements?

40. How do the risk categories in the risk-based capital model for property-casualty insurance companies differ from those for life insurance companies? What are the assumed relationships between the risk categories in the model?

41. A property-casualty insurance company has estimated the following required charges for its various risk classes (in millions):

Risk	Description	RBC Charge
R0	Affiliated P/C	$ 2
R1	Fixed income	3
R2	Common stock	4
R3	Reinsurance	3
R4	Loss adjustment expense	2
R5	Written premiums	3
Total		$17

    a. What is the *RBC* charge per the model recommended by the NAIC?

    b. If the firm currently has $7 million in capital, what should be its surplus to meet the minimum capital requirement?

PRODUCT DIVERSIFICATION

Introduction

The U.S. financial system has traditionally been structured on separatist or segmented product lines. Regulatory barriers and restrictions have often inhibited the ability of an FI operating in one area of the financial services industry to expand its product set into other areas. This might be compared with FIs operating in Germany, Switzerland, and the United Kingdom, where a more **universal FI** structure allows any single financial services organization to offer a far broader range of

Universal FI
An FI that can engage in a broad range of financial service activities.

476

TABLE 21–1   The Largest Financial Service Firms in the World

	Assets, billions
Citigroup*	$698
Tokyo Mitsubishi	691
UBS/Swiss Bank*	663
Deutsche Bank	570
Nationsbank/BankAmerica*	570
Sumitomo Bank	482
Sanwa Bank	444
HSBC Holdings	401
Chase Manhattan	336
ING	278

*Pending completion of merger.

Source: Reuters, and *New York Times,* April 7, 1998, p. 8. Copyright © 1998 by The New York Times, reprinted by permission.

banking, insurance, securities, and other financial services products.[1] However, the recent merger between Citicorp and Travelers to create the new Citigroup (See Figure 21–1), the largest universal bank or financial conglomerate in the world, indicates that the importance of regulatory barriers in the United States is receding. Indeed, as consolidation in the U.S. and global financial services industry proceeds apace, we are likely to see an acceleration in the creation of very large, globally oriented multiproduct financial service firms. Table 21–1 shows the largest financial service firms in the world (measured by assets) in 1998.

In this chapter, we first analyze the problems and risks that can arise, and have arisen historically, for U.S. FIs constrained to limited financial service sectors or franchises as well as the potential benefits from greater product expansion of the Citigroup kind. Second, we analyze the existing set of laws and regulations restricting product expansions for banks, insurance companies, and securities firms in the United States and elsewhere. In addition, we look at barriers to product expansion between the financial sector and the real or commercial sector of the economy. Third, we evaluate the advantages and disadvantages of allowing U.S. FIs to adopt more universal franchises, as appears to be the current trend.

Risks of Product Segmentation

Historically, many U.S. financial service firms have faced return and risk problems due to constraints on product diversification. Arguably, product expansion restrictions have affected commercial banks the most. For example, to the extent that regulations have limited the franchise of banks to traditional areas such as deposit taking and commercial lending, banks have been increasingly susceptible to nonbank competition on both the liability and asset sides of their balance sheets. Specifically, the growth of **money market mutual funds** (MMMFs) that offer checking account–like deposit services with high liquidity, stability of value, and an attractive

Money Market Mutual Funds (MMMFs)
Mutual funds that offer high liquidity, check-writing ability, and a money market return to smaller individual investors.

---

[1]For a thorough analysis of universal banking systems overseas, see A. Saunders and I. Walter, *Universal Banking in the U.S.?* (New York: Oxford University Press, 1994); and A. Saunders and I. Walter eds., *Financial System Design: Universal Banking Considered* (Burr Ridge, Ill.: McGraw-Hill/Irwin, 1996).

FIGURE 21–1

*The Merger of Travelers
Group and Citicorp*

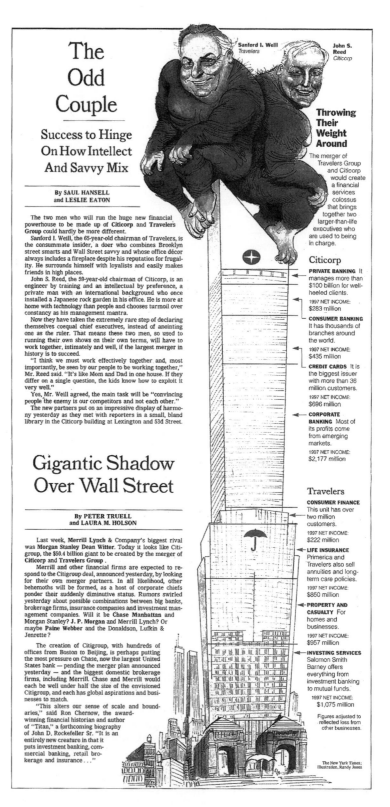

Source: *New York Times,* April 7, 1998, p. D1. Illustration, Randy Jones return have proved to be very strong competition for bank deposit and transaction account products.[2]

From virtually no assets in 1972, MMMFs had acquired more than $1,016 billion by January 1998; compared to small time deposits and money market accounts of approximately $1,649 billion in commercial banks.

In addition, until recently banks have been threatened by the growth of annuities offered by the life insurance industry. Annuities are a savings product that have many of the same features as bank CDs. In 1998, fixed and variable annuities were selling at the rate of over $110 billion a year.[3]

On the asset side of the balance sheet, the commercial and industrial (C&I) loans of banks have faced increased competition from the dynamic growth of the commercial paper market as an alternative source of short-term finance for large- and middle-sized corporations. For example, in January 1988, C&I loans outstanding were $565 billion versus $380 billion of commercial paper: in January 1998, C&I loans were $865 billion versus $967 billion of commercial paper outstanding. In addition, relatively unregulated finance companies are taking an increasing share of the business credit market. In January 1998, the ratio of finance company business credit to bank C&I loans was approximately 42 percent.

These trends have meant that the economic value of narrowly defined bank franchises have declined. In particular, product line restrictions inhibit the ability of an FI to optimize the set of financial services it can offer, potentially forcing it to adopt a more risky set of activities than it would adopt if it could fully diversify.[4]

Product restrictions also limit the ability of FI managers to adjust flexibly to shifts in the demand for financial products by consumers and to shifts in costs due to technology and related innovations. We analyze the advantages and disadvantages of increased product line diversification in more detail after we look more closely at the major laws and regulations segmenting the U.S. financial services industry and ways in which U.S. FIs have tried to ameliorate the effects of such regulations, culminating in the merger of Citicorp and Travelers in 1998.

Concept Questions

1. Offer support for the claim that product expansion restrictions have affected commercial banks more than any other type of financial services firm.
2. What sources of competition have had an impact on the asset side of banks' balance sheets?

---

[2]As we discuss in Chapter 4, MMMFs collect small savers' funds and invest in a diversified portfolio of short-term money market instruments. This allows the small saver indirect access to the wholesale money market and to the relatively more attractive rates in those markets.

[3]An annuity is a contract where the purchaser makes one or more payments up front to receive a fixed or variable flow of payments over time. These instruments are normally tax sheltered. As will be discussed below, the Supreme Court upheld the legality of banks selling these instruments in 1996.

[4]While it is true that banks earned very high profits in the 1993–98 period, this was in large part due to relatively low interest rates for deposits, high interest rates for consumer loans, and falling default rates, especially in the commercial lending area. The increased profitability of banks in the 1990s may well be more cyclical than secular.

Segmentation in the U.S. Financial Services Industry

Commercial and Investment Banking Activities

Since 1863 the United States has passed through several phases in regulating the links between the commercial and investment banking industries. Simply defined, commercial banking is the activity of deposit taking and commercial lending, while investment banking is the activity of underwriting, issuing, and distributing securities. Early legislation, such as the 1863 National Bank Act, prohibited nationally chartered banks from engaging in corporate securities activities such as underwriting and the distribution of corporate bonds and equities. However, as the United States industrialized and the demand for corporate finance grew, the largest banks, such as National City Bank (today's Citigroup), found ways around this restriction by establishing state-chartered affiliates in which to do the underwriting. By 1927 these bank affiliates were underwriting approximately 30 percent of the corporate securities being issued. In that year the Comptroller of the Currency, the regulator of national banks, relaxed the controls on national banks underwriting securities within the bank, thereby allowing them to pursue an even greater market share of securities underwritings.

After the 1929 stock market crash, the United States entered a major recession and some 10,000 banks failed between 1930 and 1933. A commission of inquiry established in 1932 began looking into the causes of the crash. The Pecora Commission pointed to banks' securities activities and the inherent abuses and conflicts of interest that arise when commercial and investment banking activities were mixed as a major cause. Today, many question the Pecora Commission's findings, believing that the slow growth in bank reserves and the money supply by the Federal Reserve lay at the heart of the post crash recession.[5]

Nonetheless, the commission's findings resulted in new legislation, the 1933 Banking Act, or the Glass-Steagall Act, which was named after the two congressmen who most strongly promoted the legislation.

The Glass-Steagall Act sought to impose a rigid separation between commercial banking—taking deposits and making commercial loans—and investment banking—underwriting, issuing, and distributing stocks, bonds, and other securities. Sections 16 and 21 of the act limit the ability of banks and securities firms to engage directly in each other's activities, while Sections 20 and 32 limit the ability of banks and securities firms to engage indirectly in such activities through separately established affiliates. For important excerpts from these sections of the act, see Table 21–2.

Nevertheless, the act defined three major securities underwriting exemptions. First, commercial banks were to continue to underwrite new issues of Treasury bills, note, and bonds. Thus, the largest commercial banks today, such as Chase, actively compete with securities firms such as Goldman Sachs in government bond auctions.

---

[5]For a major critique of the facts underlying the Pecora Commission's findings and the Glass-Steagall Act, see G. J. Benston, *The Separation of Commercial and Investment Banking: The Glass-Steagall Act Revisited and Reconsidered* (New York: St. Martins Press, 1989); and G. J. Benston, "Universal Banking," *Journal of Economic Perspectives* 8 (1994), pp. 121–43. For a monetary explanation of the 1930–33 contraction, see M. Freidman and A J. Schwartz, *A Monetary History of the United States, 1867–1960* (Princeton, N.J.: Princeton University Press, 1963).

**TABLE 21–2   Excerpts from the Banking Act of 1933 Relating
to Securities Activities**

Section 16

The business of dealing in securities and stock by the (national) association (bank) shall be limited to purchasing and selling such securities and stock without recourse, solely upon the order, and for the account of, customers, and in no case for its own account, and the association shall not underwrite any issues of securities or stock: Provided (specific securities qualified for the association's own investment account). . . . The limitations and restriction herein contained are to dealing in, underwriting and purchasing for its own account. (Section 5 extends these restrictions to Federal Reserve member banks.)

Section 20

No member bank shall be affiliated in any manner . . . with any corporation, association, business trust, or other similar organization engaged principally in the issue, flotation, underwriting, public sale, or distribution at wholesale or retail or through syndicate participation of stocks, bonds, debentures, notes, or other securities.

Section 21

It shall be unlawful . . . for any person, firm, corporation, association, business trust, or other similar organization, engaged in the business of issuing, underwriting, selling, or distributing, at wholesale or retail, or through syndicate participation, stock, bonds, debentures, notes, or other securities, to engage at the same time to any extent whatever in the business of receiving deposits subject to check or to repayment upon presentation of a passbook, certificate of deposit, or other evidence of debt or upon request of the depositor.

Section 32

No officer, director, or employee of any corporation or unincorporated association, no partner or employee of any partnership, and no individual, primarily engaged in the issue, flotation, underwriting, public sale, or distribution, at wholesale or retail, or through syndicate participation, of stocks, bonds, or other similar securities shall serve at the same time as an officer, director, or employee of any member bank except in limited classes of cases in which the Board of Governors of the Federal Reserve may allow such service by general regulations when in the judgment of said Board it would not unduly influence the investment policies of such member bank or the advice it gives its customers regarding investments.

Source: G. G. Kaufman and L. R. Mote, "Glass-Steagall: Repeal by Regulatory and Judicial Interpretation:" *Banking Law Journal,* September–October 1990, pp. 388–421.

Second, commercial banks were allowed to continue underwriting municipal general obligation (GO) bonds.[6]

Third, commercial banks were allowed to continue engaging in private placements of all types of bonds and equities, corporate and otherwise. In a **private placement,** a bank seeks to find a large buyer or investor for a new securities issue. As such, the bank acts as an agent for a fee. By comparison, in a public offering of securities, a bank would normally act as a direct principal and have an underwriting stake in the issue. This principal position, such as in **firm commitment underwriting,** involves buying securities from the issuer at one price and seeking to resell them to the public at a slightly higher price. Failure to sell these securities can result in a major loss to the underwriter of publicly issued securities. Thus, the

Private Placement
The placement of a whole issue of securities with a single or a few large investors by a bank acting as a placing agent.

Firm Commitment Underwriting
An underwriter buys securities from an issuer and reoffers them to the public at a slightly higher price.

---

[6]A municipal general obligation bond is a bond issued by a state, city, or local government whose interest and principal payments are backed by the full faith and credit of that local government, that is, its full tax and revenue base.

act distinguished between the private placement of securities, which was allowed, and public placement, which was not.

For most of the 1933–63 period, commercial banks and investment banks generally appeared to be willing to abide by the letter and spirit of the Glass-Steagall Act. However, since 1963, both have sought to erode Glass-Steagall and enter into each other's activity areas.

For commercial banks, such as the large money center banks (e.g., J. P. Morgan and Bankers Trust), the usual procedure has been to challenge "gray" areas in the act and to leave it to the courts to decide on the validity of the activity. Thus, between 1963 and 1987, banks challenged restrictions on municipal revenue bond underwriting, commercial paper underwriting, discount brokerage, managing and advising open- and closed-end mutual funds, underwriting mortgage-backed securities, and selling annuities.[7]

In most cases, the courts have eventually upheld these activities.[8]

In the face of this onslaught and de facto erosion of the act by legal interpretation, in April 1987 the Federal Reserve Board allowed commercial bank holding companies—such as Citicorp, the parent of Citibank—to establish separate **Section 20 affiliates.** In these Section 20 affiliates, bank holding companies can conduct all their ineligible or gray area securities activities, such as commercial paper underwriting, mortgage-backed securities underwriting, and municipal revenue bond underwriting. Note the organizational structure of a bank holding company, its bank, and the Section 20 subsidiary or investment bank in Figure 21–2 for J. P. Morgan.

Legally, these Section 20 subsidiaries do not violate Section 20 of the Glass-Steagall Act, which restricts bank–securities firm affiliations as long as the revenue generated from the Section 20 subsidiaries' ineligible securities activities amounts to less than 50 percent of the total revenues they generate; that is, a majority of a Section 20 subsidiary's revenue does *not* come from ineligible security activities. To avoid legal challenges, the Federal Reserve initially set the revenue limit at a very conservative 5 percent of total revenue. In recent years this limit has been raised to 10 percent, and most recently, in 1996, to 25 percent.

Section 20 Affiliate
A securities subsidiary of a bank holding company through which a banking organization can engage in investment banking activities.

FIGURE 21–2

A Bank Holding Company and Its Bank and Section 20 Subsidiary

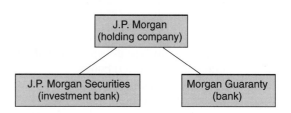

---

[7]Municipal revenue bonds are more risky than municipal GO bonds, since their interest and principal are guaranteed only by the revenue from the projects they finance. One example would be the revenue from road tolls if the bond funded the building of a new section of highway.

[8]To see the type of issues involved, discount brokerage was held to be legal since it was not viewed as being the same as full-service brokerage supplied by securities firms. In particular, a full-service brokerage combines both the agency function of securities purchase along with investment advice (e.g., hot tips). By contrast, discount brokers only carry out the agency function of buying and selling securities for clients; they do not give investment advice. For further discussion of these issues, see M. Clark and A. Saunders, "Judicial Interpretation of Glass-Steagall: The Need for Legislative Action," *The Banking Law Journal* 97 (1980), pp. 721–40; and "Glass-Steagall Revisited: The Impact on Banks, Capital Markets, and the Small Investor," *The Banking Law Journal* 97 (1980), pp. 811–40.

Firewalls
Legal barriers separating
the activities of a bank
from those of its
subsidiaries.

Moreover, initially the Fed placed very stringent **firewalls** or barriers, amounting to 28 in number, between the bank and its Section 20 securities affiliate to protect the bank from the risks of the affiliate's securities activities. These firewalls were both legal and economic in nature.[9] However, in 1997, the Fed recognized the potential costs from such firewalls in limiting synergies between a bank and its Section 20 affiliate, and choose to relax a number of them. Table 21–3 shows the initial set of firewalls (as established in 1987 and 1989) and the actions taken by the Federal Reserve in 1997 to relax many of them. With the relaxation of firewalls, bank holding companies have also seen an advantage in acquiring investment banks rather than establishing their Section 20 subsidiaries, de novo. By buying existing investment banks and converting them into Section 20 subsidiaries, a banking organization can instantly acquire underwriting expertise and a distributional network for new underwriting. Some of the biggest of these mergers include Bankers Trust's April 1997 acquisition of Alex Brown for $1.7 billion, NationsBank's 1997 purchase of Montgomery Securities for more than $1 billion, U.S. Bancorp's December 1997

TABLE 21–3 **Section 20 Firewalls Enacted in 1987 and 1989 and Federal Reserve Board Action Taken for Each One in 1997.**

Firewall	1997 Action Taken
I. Capital Adequacy Conditions	
1. Deduction of investment in subsidiary from bank holding company capital. Deduction of extensions of credit from holding company capital.	1. Eliminated the investment deduction from bank holding company capital but required holding company to maintain adequate capital as a condition for operating a Section 20 subsidiary.
2. Prior approval requirement for investments in subsidiaries.	2. Restriction repealed.
3. Requirement of capital plan before commencing new activities.	3. Restriction eliminated as superfluous since Board analysis is normal part of Board authority.
4. Capital adequacy requirement for underwriting subsidiary.	4. Board seeking comment on necessity, since no such restriction is imposed on other subsidiaries and capital requirements are still required at holding company level.
II. Credit Extensions to Customers of Underwriting Subsidiary	
5. Restriction on credit enhancement by underwriting subsidiary.	5. Restriction eliminated.
6. Restriction on funding purchases of securities by nonunderwriting subsidiary to underwriting subsidiary customers.	6. Restriction retained, but comments on need sought.
7. Restrictions on extensions of credit for repayment of underwritten securities.	7. Restriction eliminated.
8. Procedures for extensions of credit for repayment of underwritten securities.	8. Firewall eliminated.
9. Restriction on thrift subsidiaries to follow same restrictions as bank subsidiaries in dealings with underwriting subsidiary.	9. Restriction became superfluous with passage of Home Owners' Loan Act.
10. Restrictions on industrial revenue bonds consistent with firewalls 5 through 9.	10. Restrictions changed as in firewalls 5 through 9.
11. Loan documentation and exposure limits adopted for all bank and thrift subsidiaries.	11. Restriction retained.
12. Procedures for limiting exposure to one customer.	12. Restriction retained, but comment sought.

[9]For banks and their Section 20 securities affiliates, some 28 firewalls were established (see General Accounting Office, "Bank Powers: Issues Relating to Banks Selling Insurance," GAO/GGO 90–113, Washington, D.C.; U.S. Government Printing Office, 1990). The idea of a firewall is to insulate or protect the bank (and thus the deposit insurance fund) from the risk's of nonbank activities.

TABLE 21–3   (continued)

Firewall	1997 Action Taken
III. Limitations to Maintain Separateness of an Underwriting Affiliate's Activity	
13. Interlocks restriction on directors, officers, or employees of a bank or thrift subsidiary with underwriting subsidiary.	13. Retained but amended to majority restriction. Eliminated separate subsidiary office requirement.
IV. Disclosure by the Underwriting Subsidiary	
14. Customer disclosure on distinctness of bank/thrift and underwriting subsidiaries.	14. Restriction retained.
V. Marketing Activities on Behalf of an Underwriting Subsidiary	
15. Restriction on advertising bank connections with underwriting subsidiary.	15. Restriction eliminated.
16. Cross-marketing and agency activities by banks.	16. Restriction eliminated.
VI. Investment Advice by Bank/Thrift Affiliates	
17. Restriction on comments by bank/thrift affiliates on value of underwriting subsidiary services.	17. Restriction retained.
18. Restriction on fiduciary purchases during underwriting period or from market maker.	18. Restriction eliminated.
VII. Extensions of Credit and Purchases and Sales of Agents	
19. Restrictions on purchases as principal during underwriting period or from market maker.	19. Restriction eliminated.
20. Restriction on underwriting and dealing in affiliates securities.	20. Restriction eliminated.
21. Prohibition on extensions of credit to Section 20 subsidiary.	21. Restriction eliminated except for intraday extensions of credit.
22. Financial assets restrictions on bank or thrift to purchase or sell such assets of or to an underwriting subsidiary for its own account.	22. Restriction eliminated.
VIII. Limitations on Transfers of Information	
23. Disclosure of nonpublic information restricted across subsidiaries.	23. Restriction retained.
IX. Reports	
24. Reports to Federal Reserve required quarterly from underwriting subsidiaries.	24. Restriction retained.
X. Transfer of Activities and Formation of Subsidiaries of an Underwriting Subsidiary to Engage in Underwriting and Dealing	
25. Scope of order complete.	25. Restriction eliminated
XI. Limitations on Reciprocal Arrangements and Discriminatory Treatment	
26. Prohibition on reciprocity arrangements.	26. Restriction eliminated.
27. Prohibition of discriminatory treatment based on customer's use of affiliate services.	27. Restriction retained, but comment requested.
XII. Requirement for Supervisory Review before Commencement of Activities	
28. Infrastructure review required.	28. Restriction retained.

Source: *Federal Reserve Bulletin*, January 1997.

acquisition of Piper Jaffray for $730 million, and Bank of America's June 1997 purchase of Robert Stephens for $540 million (resold to Bank of Boston for $800 million in April 1998). In all cases the banks stated that one motivation for these acquisitions was the desire to establish a presence in the securities business as laws separating investment banking and commercial banking are falling. Also noted as a motivation in these acquisitions was the opportunity to expand business lines, taking advantage of economies of scale and scope to reduce overall costs and merge the customer bases of the respective commercial and investment banks involved in the acquisitions.

TABLE 21–4   Permissible Securities Activities of U.S. Commercial Banking Organizations

	When Permissible
Underwriting and dealing	
U.S. Treasury securities	Always
U.S. agency securities	Always*
Commercial paper	1987
Mortgage and other asset-backed securities	1987
Municipal securities	
General obligation	Always
Some revenue bonds	1968
All revenue bonds	1987
Corporate bonds	1989
Corporate equity	1990
Private placements of bonds and equity securities	Always
Sponsor closed-end funds	1974
Deposits with returns tied to stock market performance	1987
Underwriting and dealing in securities offshore	Always
Mergers and acquisitions	Always
Trust investments	
Individual accounts	Always
IRA commingled accounts	1982
Automatic investment service	1974
Dividend investment service	Always
Financial advising and managing	
Closed-end funds	1974
Mutual funds	1974
Brokerage	Always
Securities swaps	Always
Research advice to investors	
Separate from brokerage	Always
Combined with brokerage	
Institutional	1986
Retail	1987

*Agency securities became permissible on a case-by-case basis shortly after the agencies came into being.

Source: J. P. Morgan, "Glass-Steagall: Overdue for Repeal," April 1995. Adapted from: George G. Kaufman, *The U.S. Financial Systems: Money, Markets, and Institutions* (Englewood Cliffs, N.J.: Prentice Hall, 1995), p. 395.

In Table 21–4 we list the currently permissible securities activities of U.S. commercial bank organizations. Note that these activities include underwriting of both corporate debt (bonds) and equities.

The erosion of the product barriers between commercial banking and investment banking has also been helped by the fact that more than 20 states allow state-chartered banks to engage in securities activities beyond those permitted by Glass-Steagall for national banks and recent rulings by the Office of the Comptroller of the Currency (OCC), the primary regulator of national banks. Specifically, in 1996 the OCC ruled that it was willing to permit national banks on a "case-by-case" basis to establish direct subsidiaries to undertake nonbanking activities such as securities underwriting. The Contemporary Perspectives box on p. 486 shows the case of Zions Bancorporation, the first banking organization to take advantage of this ruling. Moreover, some 17 foreign banks can engage in securities activities because they were legally engaged in such activities prior to the passage of the International

Contemporary Perspectives

NEW DOOR OPENS FOR BANKS TO ENTER SECURITIES MARKET

The Zions Bancorporation won approval today to use a new system to underwrite municipal revenue bonds, opening another door for banks into securities markets.

In April, Zions became one of the first banks to apply under a regulatory system established last year by the Office of the Comptroller of the Currency. The system allows national banks to establish or expand subsidiaries to market new products and services, which could include securities and insurance products.

In the past, national banks had to create separate and cumbersome bank holding companies, which are regulated by the Federal Reserve, not the Comptroller of the Currency, to underwrite securities. Today's ruling by the Office of the Comptroller opens the door for small and midsize banks to underwrite all types of municipal revenue bonds without taking the expensive step of creating a holding company.

The ruling will "increase the depth of bank involvement in municipal revenue bonds and bring a local supplier to many parts of the country," said Jim McLaughlin, the director of regulatory affairs at the American Bankers Association.

Brokerage firms and other financial service companies have criticized the new system saying it lets banks move into their markets without giving other financial firms the same access to banking markets.

"What is needed is a comprehensive overhaul of the Depression-era laws regulating banking, securities and insurance activities," said James Spellman, a spokesman for the Securities Industry Association.

Zions, based in Sale Lake City, will expand an existing subsidiary that has co-managed about $7.9 billion in general obligation and housing revenue bonds so far this year. A general obligation bond is paid off from the tax revenue of a municipality. With a municipal revenue bond, however, the principal and interest are paid by the revenue from a particular project, like a stadium or an airport, for which the bonds were sold.

The bank still needs approval from the National Association of Securities Dealers before it can start handling bonds sold to support water and sewage systems, schools and other revenue needs.

The new subsidiary cannot earn more than 25 percent of its income from underwriting municipal revenue bonds, the same limit imposed on bank holding companies' securities activities. The subsidiary must also maintain separate records, have a name that is different from that of the parent bank and maintain adequate capital levels. And the new division must comply with the Federal rules governing broker-dealers.

Because Zions is the first bank to successfully use the new system, its application will establish a model that other banks can follow.

Grandfathered Affiliate
An existing affiliate that is allowed to continue operating even after the passage of restrictive laws regarding new entrants into an activity area.

Banking Act of 1978. This act imposes the Glass-Steagall Act restrictions on the securities activities of all new foreign bank entrants to the United States. However, all foreign banks established prior to 1978 had their securities activities in the United States **grandfathered.**[10]

The erosion of the product barriers between the commercial and investment banking industries has not been all one way. Large investment banks such as Merrill Lynch have increasingly sought to offer banking products. For example, in the late 1970s, Merrill Lynch innovated the cash management account (CMA), which allowed investors to own a money market mutual fund with check-writing privileges into which bond and stock sale proceeds could be swept on a daily basis. This allows the investor to earn interest on cash held in a brokerage account. In addition,

---

[10]Prior to 1978, foreign banks entering the United States were largely regulated by state laws. Since these state laws often allowed more extensive securities activities than did federal laws, a number of major foreign banks engaged in securities activities through affiliates.

many investment banks act as deposit brokers. As we discussed in Chapter 19, deposit brokers charge a fee to break large deposits into $100,000 deposit units and place them in banks across the country. Finally, investment banks have been major participants as traders and investors in the secondary market for LDC and other loans (see Chapters 16 and 27).

In sum, while the Glass-Steagall Act remains the defining piece of legislation concerning the mixing of commercial and investment banking, it is fast being eroded through homemade deregulation by banks and securities firms,[11] and a pro-deregulatory stance by the primary regulator of bank holding companies (the Federal Reserve) and the primary regulator of national banks (the OCC).

Banking and Insurance

Traditionally, there have been very strong barriers restricting the entry of banks into insurance. Insurance activities can be either of the property-casualty kind (home-owners insurance, auto insurance) or of the life/health kind (term life insurance). Moreover, we must make a distinction between a bank selling insurance as an agent by selling others' policies for a fee and a bank acting as an insurance underwriter and bearing the direct risk of underwriting losses.

In general, the risks of insurance agency activities are quite low in loss potential compared to insurance underwriting. Certain types of insurance tend to have natural synergistic links to bank lending products, for example, credit life insurance, mortgage insurance, and auto insurance.[12]

Nevertheless, banks are under very stringent restrictions when selling and underwriting almost every type of insurance. For example, national banks have been restricted to offering credit-related life, accident, health, or unemployment insurance. Moreover, they can act as insurance agents only in small towns of less than 5,000 people (see Table 21–5).[13] Further, the Bank Holding Company Act of 1956 (and its 1970 amendments) places severe restrictions on bank holding companies establishing separately capitalized insurance affiliates and on insurance companies acquiring banks. The Garn-St. Germain Depository Institutions Act of 1982 sets out these restrictions explicitly (see Table 21–6). Most states also have taken quite restrictive actions regarding the insurance activities of state-chartered banks. A few states—most notably Delaware—have passed liberal laws allowing state-chartered banks to underwrite and broker various types of property-casualty and life insurance. This has encouraged large bank holding companies such as Chase to enter Delaware and establish state-chartered banking subsidiaries with their own insurance affiliates.

Nevertheless, as with banking and securities activities, these barriers between banking and insurance are currently under attack from a number of directions. One area where banks have successfully survived legal challenges is in the area of annuities. In 1986, Nationsbank started selling annuities and was aggressively challenged in court. In the meantime, a large number of other banks began offering annuities as well. In 1995, the Supreme Court upheld the legality of banks selling

---

[11]While the 1991 Treasury Report to Congress recommended eliminating most of the restrictive provisions of the Glass-Steagall Act, the resulting piece of legislation—the FDIC Improvement Act of 1991—did not materially change the Glass-Steagall Act's provisions.

[12]See Saunders and Walter, *Universal Banking,* for an elaboration of these arguments.

[13]This was supported by a Supreme Court ruling in 1994.

TABLE 21–5   Insurance Activities Permitted to National Banks under Incidental Powers Provision of National Banking Act

Insurance Activity	Interpretive Letter or Provisions
Credit life insurance	12 C.F.R. 2.6
Credit health and accident insurance, credit disability insurance, and mortgage life and disability insurance	12 C.R.R. 2.3(3)(c)
Underwriting credit life insurance	OCC Interpretative Letter No. 377
Debt cancellation contracts—obligate the bank to cancel an unpaid debt on borrower's death	12 C.F.R. 7.7495
Involuntary unemployment insurance	OCC Interpretative Letter No. 283
Vendors single interest insurance—a type of credit-related property insurance protecting a bank against loss or damage to personal property in which the bank has a security interest	OCC Interpretative Letter No. 283
Sell and underwrite title insurance	OCC Interpretative Letter No. 386 and OCC Interpretative Letter No. 377.
Sell fixed- and variable-rate annuities	OCC Interpretative Letter No. 331 and 499
Sell municipal bond insurance	OCC Interpretative Letter No. 338
Enter into percentage leases with insurance agencies—space is leased to an insurance agency in return for a share of the agency's sales	OCC Interpretative Letter No. 274
Joint marketing programs to sell or rent customer lists to insurance agencies and to refer customers, provide administrative services, and provide insurance free as an inducement for a bank customer to take another bank service	OCC Interpretative Letter No. 316 12 C.F.R. 7.7200 OCC Interpretative Letter No. 566
Insurance for bank officers, including blanket bond and D&O insurance, and to affiliate with an insurance company providing D&O insurance.	12 C.F.R. 7.7115 Unpublished OCC Letter October 22, 1986 OCC Interpretative Letter No. 554

Source: Robert Eisenbeis, "Banks and Insurance Activities." Paper presented at Salomon Center, New York University Conference on Universal Banking, February 1995.

TABLE 21–6   Bank Holding Companies Insurance Activities

A. Acting as agent, broker, or principal (i.e., underwriter) for credit-related life, accident, health, or unemployment insurance.
B. For bank holding company finance subsidiaries, acting as agent or broker for credit-related property insurance in connection with loans and exceeding $10,000 ($25,000 in the case of a mobile home loan) made by finance company subsidiaries of bank holding companies.
C. Acting as agent for any insurance activity in a place with a population not exceeding 5,000 or with insurance agency facilities that the bank holding company demonstrates to be inadequate.
D. Any insurance agency activity engaged in by a bank holding company or its subsidiaries on May 1, 1982 (or approved as of May 1, 1982), including (1) insurance sales at new locations of the same bank holding company or subsidiaries in the state of the bank holding company's principal place of business or adjacent states, or any states in which insurance activities were conducted by the bank holding company or any of its subsidiaries on May 1, 1982, or (2) insurance coverages functionally equivalent to those engaged in or approved by the Board as of May 1, 1982.
E. Acting, on behalf of insurance underwriters, as supervisor of retail insurance agents who sell fidelity insurance and property and casualty insurance on bank holding company assets or group insurance for the employees of a bank holding company or its subsidiaries.
F. Any insurance agency activity engaged in by a bank holding company (or subsidiary) having total assets of $50 million or less, except that life insurance and annuities sold under this provision must be authorized by (A), (B), or (C).
G. Any insurance agency activity that is performed by a registered bank holding company, which was engaged in the insurance activity prior to January 1, 1971, pursuant to the approval of the Board.

Note: These are the seven statutory exemptions to the Bank Holding Company Act's prohibition on insurance activities under Title VI of the Garn-St. Germain Depository Institution Act of 1982, Public Law 97–320 (October 15, 1982).

Source: S. D. Felgren, "Banks as Insurance Agencies: Local Constraints and Competitive Advances," Federal Reserve Bank of Boston, *New England Economic Review,* September–October 1985, pp. 34–39.

annuities, arguing they should be viewed more as investment products rather than as insurance products. It is estimated that such sales add close to $1 billion a year to bank profits.

Beginning in the early 1980s, several insurance companies and commercial firms also found indirect ways to engage in banking activities. This was through the organizational mechanism of establishing **nonbank bank** subsidiaries. The 1956 Bank Holding Company Act legally defined a bank as an organization that both accepts demand deposits and makes commercial and industrial loans and severely limited the ability of an insurance company or commercial firm to acquire such a bank. An insurance company could get around this restrictive provision by buying a full-service bank and then divesting its demand deposits or commercial loans. This converted the bank into a nonbank bank. In 1987, Congress passed the Competitive Equality Banking Act (CEBA) in an attempt to block the nonbank bank loophole. This essentially prevented the creation of any new nonbank banks by redefining a bank as any institution that accepts and is accepted for deposit insurance coverage. This meant that any new nonbank bank established after 1987 would have to forgo deposit insurance coverage, making it very difficult to raise deposits. Although nonbank banks established prior to 1987 were grandfathered by CEBA, their growth rates were capped.[14]

However, the greatest challenge to the Bank Holding Company Act's restrictions on bank–insurance company affiliations has come from the 1998 merger between Citicorp and Travelers to create the largest financial services conglomerate in the world. As can be seen in Figure 21–1, the primary activity of Travelers was insurance (life and property-casualty), while the primary activity of Citicorp was banking (both also were engaged in securities activities: Citicorp through its Section 20 subsidiary and Travelers through its earlier acquisition of Smith–Barney and Salomon Brothers). Under the Bank Holding Company Act, the Federal Reserve has up to five years to formally approve the merger. The Federal Reserve gave initial approval in September 1998. However, final approval is unlikely given the current provisions of the Bank Holding Company Act, unless Citicorp gives up its banking license and/or Travelers divests itself of its insurance underwriting activities. Both possibilities seem unlikely since the declared objective of the merger is to create a financial conglomerate that "cross-sells" bank and insurance products to 100 million customers globally to maximize the potential revenue gains from "one-stop shopping." Because of the unwillingness of either Travelers or Citicorp to give up their core activities, it may require a change in the Bank Holding Company Act itself to permit this merger and similar mergers to proceed toward final approval.[15]

Commercial Banking and Commerce

The 1863 National Bank Act severely limited the ability of nationally chartered banks, which were the nation's largest, to expand into commercial activities by

Nonbank Bank
A bank divested of its commercial loans and/or demand deposits.

---

[14]Specifically, nonbank banks established before March 5, 1987, were allowed to continue in business but were limited to a maximum growth in assets of 7 percent during any 12-month period beginning one year after the act's passage. It also permitted those nonbank banks that were allowed to remain in business to engage only in the activities in which they were engaged as of March 1987 and limited the cross-marketing of products and services by nonbank banks and affiliated companies.

[15]As noted earlier, insurance is state-regulated. Since Travelers is headquartered in Connecticut, any challenge from an insurance regulator is most likely to come from that state.

taking direct equity stakes in firms. Today the provisions of the National Bank Act limit participation by national banks in nonbank subsidiaries to those activities permitted by statute or regulation. Banks can engage only in commercial sector activities "incidental to banking" and even then, only through service or subsidiary corporations. However, broader powers to take equity stakes exist when a borrower is in distress. In this case, national banks have unlimited powers to acquire corporate stock and hold it for up to 10 years. Nevertheless, corporate stocks or equities are conspicuously absent from most bank balance sheets (see Chapter 1).

While the direct holding of equity by national banks has been constrained as far back as 1863, restrictions on the commercial activities of bank holding companies are more recent phenomena. In particular, the 1970 amendments to the 1956 Bank Holding Company Act required bank holding companies to divest themselves of nonbank-related subsidiaries over a 10-year period following the amendment. When Congress passed the amendments, bank holding companies owned some 3,500 commercial sector subsidiaries ranging from public utilities to transportation and manufacturing firms. Nevertheless, bank holding companies today can still hold up to 4.9 percent of the voting shares in any commercial firm without regulatory approval.[16]

The 1956 Bank Holding Company Act also effectively restricts acquisitions of banks by commercial firms (as is true for insurance companies). To date, the major vehicle for commercial firm entry into commercial banking has been nonbank banks and nonbank financial service firms that offer banking-type services.

Nonbank Financial Service Firms and Commerce

In comparison with the barriers separating banking and either securities, insurance, or commercial sector activities, the barriers among nonbank financial service firms and commercial firms are generally much weaker. Indeed, in recent years, nonbank financial service firms and commercial firms have faced few barriers to entering into and exiting from various areas of nonbank financial service activity. For example, Travelers faced few regulatory barriers in acquiring the securities firms Smith–Barney (in 1996) and Salomon Brothers (in 1997). Moreover, in 1997 it also acquired a single S&L. Indeed, under the Savings and Loan Holding Company Act of 1968, any corporation or insurance firm can legally acquire *one* savings and loan institution. This is in direct contrast to the Bank Holding Company Act, which prohibits bank acquisitions. Nevertheless, as Figure 21–3 shows, not all commercial firms–nonbank acquisitions have been successful. Two notable failures have been the acquisition of Shearson–Lehman by American Express (since broken up) and the acquisition and breakup of the Sears financial "Supermarket" (as shown in Figure 21–3).

Concept Questions

1. What was the rationale for the passage of the Glass-Steagall Act in 1933? What permissible underwriting activities did it identify for commercial banks?
2. Why do you think that there is a 25 percent rather than a 50 percent maximum ceiling on the revenues earned from the ineligible underwriting activities of a Section 20 subsidiary?

---

[16]Under the Bank Holding Company Act, *control* is defined as when a holding company has an equity stake exceeding 25 percent in a subsidiary bank or affiliate.

FIGURE 21–3

The Sears Financial Su-
permarket: A Timeline

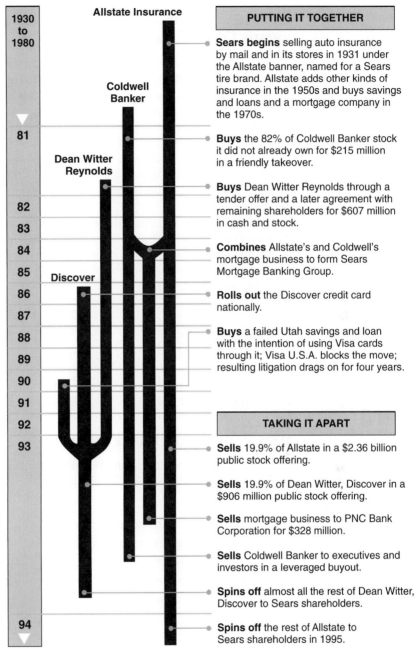

PUTTING IT TOGETHER

Sears begins selling auto insurance by mail and in its stores in 1931 under the Allstate banner, named for a Sears tire brand. Allstate adds other kinds of insurance in the 1950s and buys savings and loans and a mortgage company in the 1970s.

Buys the 82% of Coldwell Banker stock it did not already own for $215 million in a friendly takeover.

Buys Dean Witter Reynolds through a tender offer and a later agreement with remaining shareholders for $607 million in cash and stock.

Combines Allstate's and Coldwell's mortgage business to form Sears Mortgage Banking Group.

Rolls out the Discover credit card nationally.

Buys a failed Utah savings and loan with the intention of using Visa cards through it; Visa U.S.A. blocks the move; resulting litigation drags on for four years.

TAKING IT APART

Sells 19.9% of Allstate in a $2.36 billion public stock offering.

Sells 19.9% of Dean Witter, Discover in a $906 million public stock offering.

Sells mortgage business to PNC Bank Corporation for $328 million.

Sells Coldwell Banker to executives and investors in a leveraged buyout.

Spins off almost all the rest of Dean Witter, Discover to Sears shareholders.

Spins off the rest of Allstate to Sears shareholders in 1995.

Source: Company reports: *Hoover's Handbook;* Bloomberg Financial Market. Copyright © 1995 by The New York Times Company. Reprinted by permission (updated).

3. Does a bank that currently specializes in making consumer loans but makes no commercial loans qualify as a nonbank bank?

4. How do the provisions of the National Bank Act of 1863 affect the participation of today's national banks in establishing nonbank subsidiaries?

Activity Restrictions in the United States versus Other Countries

We have just described the barriers to product expansion and financial conglomeration in the United States. Although many of the barriers are being eroded, those that remain fall most heavily on this nation's commercial banks. This is shown in Appendix 21A, which compares the range of activities permitted to U.S. commercial banks with the range of product activities permitted to banks in other major industrialized countries and financial centers. Figure 21–4 shows the highly diversified product structure of the Swiss universal bank Credit Suisse. With the possible exception of Japan, U.S. banks are still the most constrained of all the major industrialized countries in terms of the range of nonbank product activities permitted.[17]

This has created considerable pressure on Congress to bring U.S. banks' activity powers in line with those of their global competitors and counterparts.

In the next section, we look at the issues that have been raised and will continue to be raised whenever the question of expanded product (or more universal) powers for banks and other FIs arise.

Concept Questions

1. How does the range of product activities permitted for U.S. commercial banks compare to that of banks in other major industrialized countries?
2. How are the product activities of U.S. commercial banks likely to change in the future?

Issues Involved in the Expansion of Product Powers

Whether the debate concerns bank expansion into securities activities, insurance, or commerce, similar issues arise. These include:

1. Safety and soundness issues.
2. Economy of scale and scope issues.
3. Conflict of interest issues.
4. Deposit insurance issues.
5. Regulatory oversight issues.
6. Competition issues.

In this section, we evaluate these issues in the context of banks entering into securities activities.

Consider the three alternative organizational structures for linking banking and securities activities in Figure 21–5. The bank holding company structure in panel (c) of the figure is the organizational form within which we will evaluate the six issues

---

[17]Many of Japan's postwar regulations were modeled on those of the United States. Thus, Article 65 in Japan separates commercial banking from investment banking in a similar fashion to the Glass-Steagall Act. However, Japan has recently passed a major deregulation law that will considerably weaken the historic barriers between commercial and investment banking in that country. See T. Ito, T. Kiso, and H. Uchibori, "The Impact of the Big Bang on the Japanese Financial System." Fuji Research Paper No. 9, Fuji Research Institute Corporation, Tokyo, Japan, May 1998.

FIGURE 21–4

The Structure of a Universal Bank: CS Holding Group

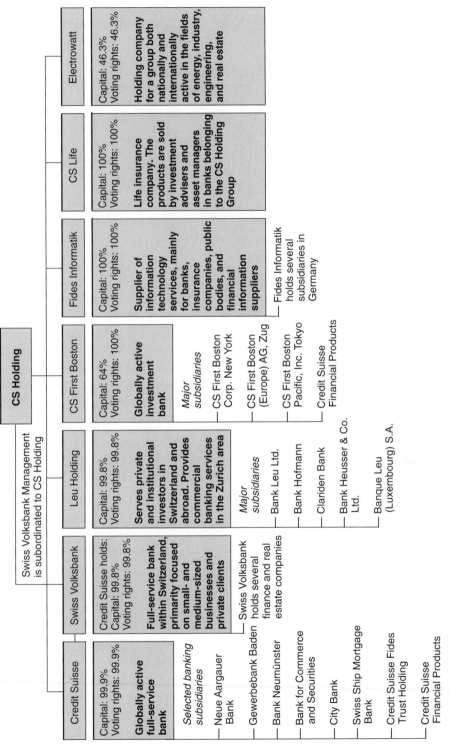

Source: Ernst Kilgus and Alfred Mettler, Swiss Banking School, November 1994.

FIGURE 21–5

Alternative Organizational Forms for Nonbank Product Expansions of Banking Organizations

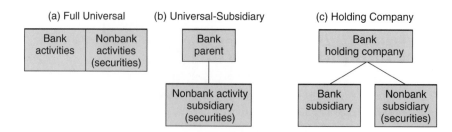

just identified. This is the form already adopted by the Federal Reserve to accommodate most bank organization expansions into nonbank activities—for example, the creation of Section 20 subsidiaries to engage in limited amounts of ineligible securities activities.

In Figure 21–5, panel (a) shows the fully integrated universal bank, where banking and securities activities are conducted in different departments. This is typical of the way in which large banks in Germany, such as Deutsche Bank, engage in securities activities. Panel (b) shows the universal subsidiary model where a bank engages in securities activities through a separately owned securities affiliate. This is typical of the way in which commercial banks such as Barclay's in the United Kingdom and Toronto Dominion in Canada conduct their securities activities. This is also the model adopted in 1996 by the OCC to allow U.S. nationally chartered banks to expand their nonbank activities. Note that the degree of bank-nonbank integration is much less with the holding company model [panel (c)] than with either the full or subsidiary universal banking model.[18]

For example, in the universal subsidiary model, the bank holds a direct ownership stake in the securities subsidiary. By comparison, in the holding company model, the bank and securities subsidiary are separate companies with their own equity capital; their link is that their equity is held by the same parent company, the bank holding company (such as J. P. Morgan).[19]

Safety and Soundness Concerns

With respect to the securities activities of commercial banks and the possible effects on their safety and soundness, two key questions arise: How risky is securities underwriting? and if losses occur for a securities subsidiary, can this cause the affiliated bank to fail?

The Risk of Securities Underwriting.   To understand the risk of securities underwriting, you must understand the mechanics of firm commitment securities offerings. While some corporate securities are offered on a **best-efforts** basis in which the underwriter does not guarantee a price to the insurer and acts more like a placing or distribution agent, the dominant form of underwriting in the United States is a firm commitment offering.

Best-Efforts Underwriting
An underwriting where the investment banker acts as an agent rather than as a principal that bears risk.

---

[18]For a comparative analysis of these three models, see Saunders and Walter, *Universal Banking.* The Japanese do not allow holding company structures for fear of recreating the *zaibatsu,* finance and commercial conglomerates that dominated the pre-Second World War Japanese economy. See T. Hoshi, "Back to the Future: Universal Banking in Japan," paper presented at the Salomon Center, New York University Conference on Universal Banking, February 1995.

[19]In general, the advantages of the full universal is greater resource flexibility and integration of commercial bank and investment bank product lines. Its perceived disadvantages include greater monopoly power and greater potential conflicts of interest.

In a firm commitment offering, the underwriter purchases securities directly from the issuing firm (say, at $99 per share) and then reoffers them to the public or the market at large at a slightly higher price, say, $99.50. The difference between the underwriter's buy price ($99) and the public offer price ($99.50) is the spread that compensates the underwriter for accepting the principal risk of placing the securities with outside investors as well as any administrative and distribution costs associated with the underwriting. In our simple example of a $0.50 spread, the maximum revenue the underwriter can gain from underwriting the issue is $0.50 × the number of shares issued. Thus, if 1 million shares were offered, the maximum gross revenue for the underwriting would be $0.50 × 1,000,000 = $500,000. Note that once the public offering has been made and the price has been specified in the prospectus, the underwriter cannot raise the price over the offering period. In this example, the underwriter could not raise the price above $99.50 even after determining that the market valued the shares more highly.[20]

While the upside return from underwriting is normally capped, by comparison, the downside risk can be very large.

The downside risk arises if the underwriter overprices the public offering, setting the public offer price higher than outside investors' valuations. As a result, the underwriter will be unable to sell the shares during the public offering period and will have to lower the price to get rid of the inventory of unsold shares, especially as this inventory often is financed through issuing commercial paper or RP agreements. In our example, if the underwriter has to lower the offering price to $99, the gross revenue from the underwriting will be zero, since this is the price paid to the issuing firm. Any price less than $99 generates a loss. For example, suppose that the issue can be placed only at $97; the underwriter's losses will be $2 × 1,000,000 shares = $2 million.

There are a number of possible reasons why an underwriter may take a big loss or big hit on an underwriting. The first is simply overestimating the market's demand for the shares. The second is that in the short period between setting the public offering price and seeking to sell the securities to the public, there may be a major drop in security values in general.

The classic example of this second type of underwriting risk was the sale of British Petroleum (BP) shares in October 1987 in the period surrounding the October 19, 1987, stock market crash. Underwriters set the bid price of the shares at £3.265 and the offer price at £3.30 on October 15, 1987, four days before the crash, and four large U.S. investment banks (such as Goldman Sachs) agreed to underwrite 22 percent of the issue or 505,800,000 shares. However, in the week following the October 19, 1987, crash, BP's share price fell to a low of £2.65—so that the underwriters faced a loss of as much as $0.615 per share (£3.265 minus £2.65), or a loss of £311 million. Note that the maximum gross revenue the U.S. underwriters could have made if all shares had been sold at the originally planned offer price of £3.30 was [£3.30 − £3.265) × 505.8 million], or £17,703,000. We show this profit and loss trade-off in Figure 21–6.

As you can see, firm commitment underwriting involves a potential payoff with a limited upside gain (£17,703,000) and a very large downside loss. As such, it is similar to the risks involved in *writing put* options on assets.[21]

---

[20]The offering period is usually a maximum of 10 business days.

[21]The premium on the put could be thought of as similar to the maximum revenue that could be earned on an underwriting.

FIGURE 21–6

Profit-Loss Function for
BP Share Underwriting

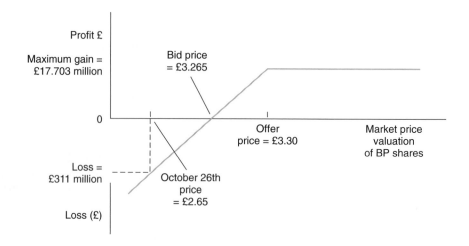

Of course, the big hit described in the BP case is unusual for three reasons. First, most new issues are underpriced rather than overpriced. Second, in the United States the offer period is usually much shorter than in the BP example, and third, stock market crashes are fortunately rare. However, it is very much this bit hit scenario that regulators are concerned about when it comes to the question of allowing banks to engage in securities underwriting through an affiliate.[22]

If Underwriting Losses Occur for the Securities Affiliate, Can This Cause a Bank to Fail?   Proponents of allowing banking organizations to expand their securities activities argue that the answer to this question is no, as long as the bank subsidiary is sufficiently insulated from the risk problems of the securities affiliate. As noted earlier, in a bank holding company structure, the bank is legally a separate corporation from the securities affiliate. As shown in Figure 21–7, its only link to its securities affiliate is indirect, through the holding company that owns a controlling equity stake in both the bank and securities affiliate. However, even this indirect link raises the concern that the effects of losses by the securities affiliate could threaten the safety of the bank unless firewalls or regulatory barriers are introduced to insulate the bank against such losses (see Figure 21–7.).

There are at least three ways a bank could be harmed by losses of a securities affiliate in a holding company structure. First, a bank holding company might be tempted to drain capital and funds from the bank by requiring excessive dividends and fees from the bank (this is called upstreaming). The holding company could then downstream these funds to protect the failing securities affiliate from insolvency. As a result, the bank would be weakened at the expense (or because) of the securities affiliate.

Currently, the Federal Reserve closely monitors bank dividend payments to holding company owners and must restrict dividend payments of the bank if it is undercapitalized under the prompt corrective action plan (see Chapter 20). Also, Section 23B of the 1982 Federal Reserve Act limits the size of management and

---

[22]Similarly, in underwriting insurance, concerns relate to the effects of earthquakes and other such catastrophes on a bank subsidiary.

FIGURE 21–7

The Role of Firewalls in Protecting Banks

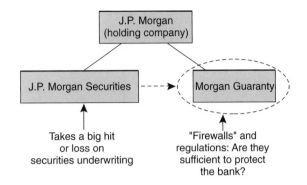

other fees banks can pay for services provided by the holding company to those normally established by the market for such services.[23]

A second way in which a bank could be harmed is through interaffiliate loans. For example, the holding company may induce the bank to extend loans to the securities affiliate to keep it afloat even though such loans are excessively risky. To prevent this, the Federal Reserve Act limits bank loans to any single nonbank affiliate to 10 percent of a bank's capital. If bank capital is approximately 5 percent of bank assets, this limits loans to an affiliate to $.05 \times .1$ of bank assets, or 0.5 percent of bank assets. Prior to 1997, firewalls prohibited a bank from lending anything at all to its securities affiliates (see Table 21–3).[24]

The third way in which a bank may be affected is through a contagious confidence problem. Specifically, if an affiliated securities firm gets into difficulty, it may result in a negative information signal to financial service consumers and investors regarding the quality of the management of the holding company and its bank affiliate. Such negative information can create incentives for large depositors and investors to withdraw their money from the bank in the manner described in Chapter 19. This bank run possibility seems more likely to occur if the bank and its securities affiliate share similar names and logos, which in general they do.

Obviously, a big hit taken by the securities affiliate can potentially threaten the safety and solvency of the affiliated bank, especially through the confidence effect. However, at least two countervailing risk-reducing effects may enhance the safety and soundness of a bank indirectly linked to a securities affiliate in a holding company framework. The first effect is a *product diversification benefit*. A well-diversified financial services firm (bank holding company) potentially enjoys a far more stable earnings and profit stream over time than does a product-specialized bank. As demand and cost shifts reduce earnings in one activity area, such as banking, offsetting demand and cost shifts may take place in other activity areas, such as securities or insurance, increasing bank holding company earnings. Advocates argue that a more stable and diversified earnings stream for the holding company enables it to act as a source of strength in keeping the affiliated bank well capitalized.

---

[23]Nevertheless, in 1994 alone there were at least seven cases of bank holding companies infusing funds into mutual funds they managed, including $50.5 million by BankAmerica Corp. into its Pacific Horizon Prime MMMF to prevent fund holders from taking losses. So far, the Fed has not taken any punitive action against these banks. See also E. J. Kane, "What Is the Value-Added Large U.S. Banks Find in Offering Mutual Funds?" Working Paper, Boston College, November 1994.

[24]This also holds for the sale of assets by the affiliate to the bank.

In the academic literature, a number of empirical studies have evaluated the gains from bank activity diversification by looking at the correlations of accounting earnings between segmented financial firms or industries and analyzing correlations between firms' stock market returns. Essentially, the lower these correlations are, the greater are the potential gains from activity diversification and the lower is the coefficient of variation (COV)—the standard deviation divided by the mean—of a banking organization's earnings flows. Other studies have sought to evaluate the potential effects of activity diversification on the risk of failure of banks (ROF) and simulate the effects of bank–nonbank mergers (MS) on bank risk. We summarize the findings of a number of these COV, ROF, and MS studies in Table 21–7.

As you can see from Table 21–7, the majority of the studies find that bank holding company risk could be reduced by expansion into nonbank product lines. However, the optimal proportion of investment in individual nonbank product lines often falls in the 5 to 25 percent range. This suggests that excessive product expansion in some nonbank lines could actually increase the total risk exposure of a banking organization.

TABLE 21–7   Review of Selected Studies of the Risk of Nonbank Activities*

Study	Time Period	Methodology[†]	Nonbank Activities Reduce BHC Risk
Accounting Industry Data			
Heggestad (1975)	1953–67	COV	Yes. Impermissible activities: insurance agents and brokers, and real estate agents, brokers, managers, holdings, and investment companies, and lessors of R.R., oil, and mining properties. Banking is among the riskiest activities based on the coefficient variation in profits. [Studies activities of one bank holding company (BHC) prior to 1970 BHC Act amendments.]
Johnson and Meinster (1974)	1954–69 (annual data)	COV	Yes. Impermissible activities: insurance agents and brokers, portfolio holding and investment companies, and real estate agents, analysis brokers and managers. Studies 13 activities. Portfolio analysis based on earnings and cash flow concludes there are diversification benefits into nonbank activities but that the benefits are sensitive to the percentage of assets in each activity.
Wall and Eisenbeis (1984)	1970–80	COV	Yes. Impermissible activities: S&Ls, security brokers and dealers, life insurance, general merchandise stores, lessor of R.R. property. Permissible activities personal and business credit agency. Banking neither highest nor lowest risk based on coefficient of variation. Results are sensitive to time period.
Wall, Reichart, and Mohanty (1993)	1981–89	COV	Yes, for insurance and real estate. The securities brokerage industry does not enter the efficient portfolio.
Accounting Firm Data			
Jessee and Seelig (1977)		COV	No. Risk reduction is not related to share of nonbank investment.
Meinster and Johnson (1979)	1973–77	ROF	Yes. BHCs effectively diversified but slightly increased probability of capital impairment with debt financing. (Sample of only two BHCs in seven permissible activities of leasing, consumer finance, mortgage banking, bank management consulting, financial services, and foreign bank services.)
Litan (1985)	1978–83	COV	As likely to reduce volatility of BHC income as to increase it. (Sample of 31 large BHCs.)
Wall (1986)	1976–84	ROF	Nonbank activity either decreases BHC risk slightly or has no impact. The positive relationship between nonbank risk and BHC risk, BHC leverage, and bank risk is consistent with the possibility that management preferences influence the riskiness of the BHC's subsidiaries and determine the use of leverage to influence overall risk.
Boyd and Graham (1986)	1971–83 (1971–77 and 1978–83)	ROF	Entire period: no significant relationship between nonbank activity and any risk or return measures. Less stringent policy period (1971–77): no nonbank activity is positively related to risk. More stringent policy period (1978–83): weak negative relationship between nonbank activity and risk.

TABLE 21–7   *(concluded)*

Study	Time Period	Methodology[†]	Nonbank Activities Reduce BHC Risk
Boyd and Graham (1988)	1971–84 (annual data)	COV/ROF/ MS	Study covers six impermissible activities. Yes for life insurance. The standard deviation and bankruptcy risk measures indicate risk is likely to increase for real estate development, securities firms, and property-casualty insurance activities and increase slightly for other real estate and insurance agency and brokerage activities. BHC is lowest-risk activity.
Brewer (1988)	1979–85	COV	Yes. One standard deviation increase in investment in nonbank subsidiaries leads to 6-basis-point drop in BHC risk (approximately 7 percent).
Industry and Firm Data			
Stover (1982)	1959–68	Wealth- maximization debt capacity	Yes. Impermissible activities: S&Ls, investment banking, land development, fire and casualty insurance. Measures equity returns and diversification benefits of 14 permissible and impermissible activities in wealth-maximization model.
Boyd, Hanweek, and Pithyachanyakul (1980)	1971–77	COV/ROF	Yes, but limited. Permissible activities: mortgage banking, factoring, consumer finance, credit card, loan servicing, investment advisers, leasing (except auto), community welfare, data processing, credit life, accident and health insurance agents, and underwriters and management consulting. No (any investment increases probability of bankruptcy). Permissible activities: commercial and sales finance, industrial banks, trust services, auto leasing. (Study covered only permissible activities.)
Market Data Industry Data			
Eiseman (1976)	1961–68 (monthly data)	Industry (portfolio) selection model (COV)	Yes. Banking is minimum-risk activity. Lowest-risk BHC includes permissible activity of sales finance and impermissible activities of insurance and investment banking. Highest-risk BHC includes permissible activity of data processing. Studies 20 activities.
Firm Data			
Wall (1984)	Select dates	Bond returns	No significant effect.
Wall and Eisenbeis (1984)	Select dates (monthly data)	Bond returns	No. (Study covered only permissible activity of discount brokerage.)
Boyd and Graham (1988)	1974–84 (annual data)	COV/ROF/ MS	Studies six impermissible activities. Yes for life insurance, insurance agency and brokerage, and property-casualty insurance. Risk likely to increase for real estate development and securities firms and increase slightly for other real estate. Based on standard deviation, bankruptcy, and beta risk measures BHC is not lowest-risk activity. Insurance agency and brokerage and property and casualty insurance are lowest-risk activities.
Brewer (1988)	1979–83 (daily data)	COV	Yes. One standard deviation increase in investment in nonbank subsidiaries leads to an 8 to 11 percent basis point drop in BHC risk. Results are sensitive to the time period studied.
Brewer, Fortier, and Pavel (1988)	1980, 1982 and 1986 and 1979–83	COV/MS	Yes. Impermissible activities of insurance agents and brokers, property and casualty and life insurance underwriting. Investment of 5 percent or less for any of the tested activities would not increase the variance of the BHC significantly; the investment of 25 percent or more for all but the above listed activities would increase the riskiness of the BHC significantly. Examination of the impact of total investment in nonbank activities regardless of the specific activities finds increases in nonbank activity tend to lower BHC risk significantly.
Saunders and Walter (1994)	1984–88	COV/MS	Yes. Looks at 250,000 possible merger combinations among the largest FIs in the United States. Finds that a full multiple activity universal bank with optimal investments in different financial service activities can lower risk by as much as one-third compared to specialized banks.

*Permissible activities refer to those nonbank activities currently permissible, whether or not they were permissible at the time of the study. Impermissible activities also include activities not yet ruled upon by the Board at the time of the study.

†COV—analysis of coefficient of variation of rates of return of banking and nonbanking activities.

  ROF—risk of failure (bankruptcy analysis).

  MS—simulated merger analysis.

Source: From "Bank Risk from Nonbank Activities," by E. Brewer, D. Fortier, and C. Pavel, in *Economic Perspective,* July–August 1988, pp. 14–26. Reprinted by permission of the Federal Reserve Bank of Chicago; and A. Saunders and I. Walter, *Universal Banking in the U.S.?* (New York: Oxford University Press, 1994), chapter 6.

In addition to the potential risk-reducing gains of product diversification, by diversifying its earnings stream geographically, a bank holding company can generate additional risk reduction gains when there are regional imperfections in the costs of raising debt and equity (see Chapter 22).

Economies of Scale and Scope

A second issue concerning the expansion of banks into securities and other nonbank activities is the potential for additional economies of scale and scope. As we discuss in Chapter 14, there appears to be economy of scale opportunities for financial firms up to $25 billion in asset size. However, most studies find cost-based economies of scope are negligible, although revenue-based economies may arise for the largest FIs. Arguably, the remaining, post-1997, firewalls between banks and their Section 20 investment banking affiliates covering finance, management and cross marketing limit potential economies of scope and related revenue and cost synergies. Greater economies might be generated only in a more integrated universal banking structure of the German kind with few if any cross marketing and finance firewalls between the bank and its nonbank product activities.[25]

Conflicts of Interest

A third issue—the potential for conflicts of interest—lies at the very heart of opposition to an expansion of banking powers into other financial service areas. Indeed, concerns regarding conflicts of interest provided the main foundation for the passage of the Glass-Steagall Act in 1933.[26]

The two principal questions that arise are (1) what are the potential conflicts of interest arising from the expansion of banks' securities activities? and (2) what type of incentive structures change *potential* conflicts into *actual* conflicts?

Six Potential Conflicts of Interest.   We discuss the six most common potential conflicts of interest identified by regulators and academics below.[27]

Salesperson's Stake.   Critics argue that when banks have the power to sell nonbank products, managers no longer dispense dispassionate advice to their customers about which product to buy. Instead, they have a salesperson's stake in pushing the bank's own products, often to the disadvantage of the customer. For example, in April 1998 NationsBank agreed to pay $7 million to settle charges that it misled customers who bought two bond funds sponsored by the bank in association with Morgan Stanley Dean Witter in 1993 and 1994. These two bond funds exhibited dramatic declines in value in 1994, with many elderly people losing money believing they had invested in insured CDs.

---

[25]See T. F. Huertas, "Redesigning Regulation: The Future of Finance in the United States," Jackson Hole, Wyoming, August 22, 1987, mimeographed. Nevertheless, Saunders and Walter, *Universal Banking,* could find no evidence of cost economies of scope for the world's 100 largest banks, many of which are universal banks.

[26]See Benson, *The Separation of Commercial and Investment Banking.*

[27]See A. Saunders, "Conflicts of Interest: An Economic View," in *Deregulating Wall Street,* ed. I. Walter (New York: John Wiley & Sons, 1985), pp. 207–30; E. J. Kelly, "Conflicts of Interest: A Legal View," in *Deregulating Wall Street,* pp. 231–54; R. S. Kroszner and R. G. Rajan, "Is the Glass-Steagall Act Justified? A Study of U.S. Experience with Universal Banking before 1933," *The American Economic Review,* September 1994; and M. Puri, "Commercial Banks in Investment Banking: Conflict of Interest or Certification Role?" *Journal of Financial Economics* 40 (1996), pp. 373–401.

Stuffing Fiduciary Accounts.   Suppose a bank is acting as a securities underwriter and is unable to place these securities in a public offering. To avoid being exposed to potential losses, the bank may stuff these unwanted securities in accounts that are managed by its own trust department and over which it has discretionary investment powers.

Bankruptcy Risk Transference.   Assume that a bank has a loan outstanding to a firm whose credit or bankruptcy risk has increased to the private knowledge of the banker. With this private knowledge, the banker may have an incentive to induce the firm to issue bonds underwritten by the bank's securities affiliate to an unsuspecting public. The proceeds of this bond issue could then be used to pay down the bank loan. As a result, the bank would have transferred the issuing firm's credit risk from itself to less-informed outside investors, while the securities affiliate also earned an underwriting fee.

Third-Party Loans.   To ensure that an underwriting goes well, a bank may make cheap loans to third-party investors on the implicit condition that this loan finance is used to purchase securities underwritten by its securities affiliate.

Tie-Ins.   A bank may use its lending powers to coerce or tie in a customer to the products sold by its securities affiliate. For example, it may threaten credit rationing unless the customer agrees to let the bank's securities affiliate do its securities underwritings.

Information Transfer.   In acting as a lender, the bank may become privy to certain inside information about its customers or rivals. This information could also flow from the securities affiliate to the bank. Such conflicts are potentially present when M and A activity is involved along with new security issues and loan originations. The Contemporary Perspective box on p. 502 documents one such "conflict of interest" dispute involving ADT Inc. and Chase.

Potential Conflicts of Interest and Their Actual Exploitation.   On their own, and unquestionably accepted, these conflicts appear to be extremely troublesome. Remember, however, that there are specific and general checks and balances that mitigate their exploitation. Many of these conflicts are likely to remain potential rather than actual conflicts of interest. Specifically, many of these conflicts, such as tie-ins and third-party loans, breach existing bank regulations and laws.[28] Also, internal barriers or **Chinese walls** in most banks prohibit internal information transfers where they potentially conflict with the best interests of the customer. Further, sales of debt issues to a less-informed public to pay down bank loans may result in future lawsuits against the underwriter once investors discover their losses.[29]

More generally, conflicts of interest are exploitable only under three conditions. First, markets for bank services are uncompetitive so that banks have monopoly power over their customers, for example, in making loans. Second, information flows between the customer and the bank are imperfect or asymmetric so that the bank possesses an information advantage over its customers. Third, the bank places

Chinese Wall
An internally imposed barrier within an organization that limits the flow of confidential client information among departments or areas.

---

[28]Involuntary tie-ins are illegal under various sections of the Clayton Act, the Sherman Antitrust Act, and the Bank Holding Company Act.

[29]In particular, the underwriter may be accused of lack of due diligence in not disclosing information in the new issue's prospectus.

Contemporary Perspectives

ADT VS. CHASE: TESTING LIMITS OF BANK'S ROLE IN TAKEOVERS

ADT Inc., continuing to resist a hostile $3.5 billion bid by Western Resources, will drag the takeover battle into the courtroom on Monday, saying that Chase Manhattan Bank violated fiduciary and contractual obligations by allying itself with Western.

Whatever the merits of the case, the wrangling between ADT and Chase in State Supreme Court in Manhattan may well portend the pitfalls that await those commercial banks that are aggressively pushing into Wall Street's domain, providing investment banking services, merger advice and underwriting, as well as loans.

The commercial banks are much larger and have many more clients than investment banks and law firms and are therefore exposed to far more potential conflicts of interest. ADT contends in the lawsuit that it filed on Feb. 10 that Chase Manhattan, which was ADT's lender and financial adviser, used confidential information in providing financing and advice for Western's attempted takeover.

ADT . . . contends that Chase's alliance with Western Resources contradicted oral statements by Chase executives in 1993 that the bank would never back a hostile bid for ADT . . . Chase's response states that no such oral promises were made and that under New York law the bank "owes no fiduciary duties" to ADT. Finally, Chase says that its actions on behalf of Western do not harm ADT shareholders and that ADT managers, fearing for their jobs, are merely trying to obstruct Western's effort to acquire ADT . . .

"This is an indication of how life has gotten complex for everyone in the financial world," said Harvey Goldschmid, a professor of corporate law at Columbia University Law School. "It means they're going to have to be very careful. The banks have to build impregnable walls between the mergers and acquisitions work and the traditional banking relationships, otherwise they run the risk of being accused of using confidential information . . ."

Stephen J. Ruzika, president of ADT, contends in an affidavit that Chase's involvement with the Western bid contradicted statements made to him by Chase executives in 1993, when he was negotiating a $500 million loan agreement. Mr. Ruzika's affidavit states that Chase, which aggressively sought to be ADT's financial adviser as well as a lender, assured him that the bank would not "fund or otherwise assist a hostile takeover effort." ADT provided the bank with sensitive documents and discussed corporate strategy. In similar cases, courts have ruled that banks, unlike lawyers and investment banks, do not owe a fiduciary duty to a borrower. But ADT contends that there was a relationship of trust and confidence that went well beyond that of a simple borrower-lender connection.

The Chase Manhattan executives named by Mr. Ruzika, however, have denied that the conversations took place and have stated that impregnable walls existed between its investment bankers who worked with Western Resources and its lending officers who dealt with ADT and acquired confidential information about the company.

Source: *New York Times,* February 27, 1997, p. 35. Copyright © 1997 by The New York Times, reprinted by permission.

a relatively low value on using its reputation as an asset. The discovery of having exploited a conflict can result in considerable market and regulatory penalties.[30] Nevertheless, as noted above, in recent years some banks, such as the former Nationsbank, have been subject to a number of lawsuits alleging overzealous selling tactics and incomplete information disclosure that amount to conflicts of interest.

---

[30]R. G. Rajan models these incentives in "A Theory of the Costs and Benefits of Universal Banking," C. R. S. P. Working Paper no. 346, University of Chicago, 1992. See also G. Kanatas and J. Qi, "Underwriting by Commercial Banks: Conflicts of Interest vs. Scope Economics," University of South Florida 1996, mimeograph. For an assessment of the reputational costs of exploiting conflicts of interest, see R. Smith and I. Walter, *Street Smarts: Leadership, Conduct and Shareholder Value in the Securities Industry* (Boston: Harvard Business School Press, 1997).

Deposit Insurance

A possible argument against expanded powers is that the explicit and implicit protection given to banks by deposit insurance coverage give banks a competitive advantage over other financial service firms (see Chapter 19). For example, because bank deposits up to $100,000 are covered by explicit deposit insurance, the banks are able to raise funds at subsidized, lower-cost rates than are available to traditional securities firms. This may allow them to pass on these lower costs in cheaper loans to their affiliates, although, as noted earlier such interaffiliate loans are restricted to 10 percent of the bank's capital. Nevertheless, there still may be an indirect deposit insurance–related advantage to banking organizations undertaking securities activities compared to traditional securities firms. This may result if bank regulators regard certain large banking organizations as being too big to fail (TBTF), thereby encouraging these institutions to take excessive risks such as placing aggressive underwriting bids for new issues. This effect would limit the underwriting shares of traditional investment banks, especially as TBTF guarantees do not appear to exist for them—as shown by the failure of Drexel Burnham Lambert in February 1990. Consequently, TBTF guarantees tend to give banks some unfair competitive advantages.[31]

Regulatory Oversight

Currently, most bank holding companies with extensive nonbank subsidiaries face a diffuse and multilayered regulatory structure that would potentially hinder the monitoring and control of conflicts of interest abuses and excessive risk taking if banks were allowed to expand their securities activities further. Specifically, for a bank holding company such as Chase, the Federal Reserve is the primary regulator. For its bank subsidiary, the Comptroller of the Currency, which is the charterer of national banks, shares regulatory oversight with the Federal Reserve and the FDIC. For its Section 20 securities subsidiary, the primary regulator is the SEC, although the Federal Reserve also has some oversight powers. It is far from clear that such a complex and overlapping regulatory structure is efficient from a public policy perspective.[32]

This is the case because it can lead to waste of monitoring and surveillance resources as well as unnecessary fights over bureaucratic turf. Furthermore, coordination problems can weaken monitoring and surveillance efficiency. Thus, a case can be made for subsuming all regulatory power in a single regulatory body if banks' securities powers are extended further.[33]

---

[31]This point has also been made with respect to bank sales of mutual funds. See Kane, "What Is the Value-Added?" One way to reduce this problem would be to subject uninsured depositors in a TBTF bailout to a loss (or haircut). This would create incentives for them to impose market discipline on even the biggest banks (see, Federal Reserve Bank of Minneapolis, Annual Report 1997, "Fixing FDICIA: A Plan to Address the Too-Big-To-Fail Problem.")

[32]In the context of allowing banks to expand into insurance activities (as in the Citigroup case), the problem of aligning the differences between (largely) federal bank regulations and state-based insurance regulations would have to be faced as well.

[33]Despite numerous attempts in recent years to reform and rationalize the regulatory structure through Congress, none has been successful. For a criticism of the structure of U.S. regulation, see General Accounting Office, "Bank Oversight Structure," GAO/GGO–97–23, November 1997.

Competition

The final issue concerns the effects of bank product expansions on competition in investment banking product lines. In securities underwriting, there are three primary reasons for believing that bank expansions would enhance competition. There is also one reason for believing that it would do the reverse, that is, increase both market concentration and the monopoly power of commercial banks over customers.

Procompetitive Effects.   The three potential procompetitive effects of banks' entry into securities activities are discussed below.

Increased Capital Market Access for Small Firms.   Most large investment banks are headquartered in New York and the Northeast. As a result, small U.S. firms based in the Midwest and Southwest have often had a more difficult time accessing national capital markets compared with firms of a similar size in the Northeast. Consequently, the entry of regional and superregional banks into securities underwriting through securities affiliates could potentially expand the national capital market access of smaller firms.[34]

Lower Commissions and Fees.   Greater competition for securities underwritings should work to reduce the underwriter's spread. That is, it should reduce the spread between the new issue bid price paid to the issuing firm and the offer price at which those securities are resold to the market. This potentially raises the new issue proceeds for the issuing firm by raising the underwriter's bid price. (Such an effect was claimed when banks expanded their municipal bond underwritings, although this has been disputed.)[35] In recent years, the spreads on investment grade debt underwritings fell from approximately 78 basis points in 1986 to 66 basis points in 1996. Similarly, the spread on equity underwritings fell from 334 basis points in 1986 to 224 basis points in 1996. At the end of 1996, banks' Section 20 subsidiaries had over a 20 percent share of new issue underwritings of debt and a 0.88 percent share for equity. There is some empirical evidence to support the view that part of the reason for the decline in debt underwriting spreads is due to enhanced competition to underwrite securities issues emanating from the entry of Section 20 subsidiaries into this market.[36]

Reduce the Degree of Underpricing of New Issues.   The greatest risk to the underwriter is to price a new issue too high relative to the market's valuation of that security. That is, underwriters stand to lose when they overprice new issues. Given this, there is an incentive for underwriters to underprice new issues by setting the public offer price (OP) below the price established for the security in the secondary market once trading begins (P). The investment banker stands to gain through

---

[34]Some support for this can be found in A. Gande, M. Puri, A. Saunders, and I. Walter, "Bank Underwriting of Debt Securities: Modern Evidence," *Review of Financial Studies* 10, No. 4, 1997, pp. 1175–1201. They find that the size of debt issues underwritten by Section 20 subsidiaries is significantly smaller than those underwritten by investment banks.

[35]For a review of this debate and the evidence, see W. L. Silber, "Municipal Revenue Bond Costs and Bank Underwriting: A Survey of the Evidence." Monograph Series in Finance and Economics, Salomon Center for the Study of Financial Institutions, New York University, 1979

[36]See A. Gande, Puri, and A. Saunders, "Bank Entry, Competition and the Market for Corporate Securities Underwriting," *Journal of Financial Economics,* forthcoming, 1999. See also "Banks Push Into Securities Squeezes Fees," *The Wall Street Journal,* December 16, 1997.

underpricing as it increases the probability of selling out the issue without affecting the fixed underwriting spread. That is, a spread of $.50 at a bid-offer price spread of $93 and $93.50 produces the same gross revenue (spread) of $.50 per share to the underwriter as a bid-offer price spread of $97 and $97.50. The major difference is that a lower offer price increases the demand for the shares by investors and the probability of selling the whole issue to the public very quickly. Both the underwriter and the outside investor may benefit from underpricing; the loser is the firm issuing the securities, which garners lower proceeds than it would have if the offer price had been set at a higher price reflecting a more accurate market valuation. In the preceding example, the issuer receives only $93 per share rather than $97. Consequently, the underpricing of new issues is an additional cost of securities issuance borne by issuing firms. Most empirical research on the underpricing of U.S. new issues, or **initial public offerings** (IPOs), has found that they are underpriced in the range of 8 to 48 percent depending on the sample and time period chosen.[37] In contrast, **secondary issues** tend to be underpriced by less than 3 percent.[38]

If a major cause of IPO underpricing is a lack of competition among existing investment banks, then bank entry and competition should lower the degree of underpricing and increase the new issue proceeds for firms. Nevertheless, many economists argue that monopoly power is not the primary reason for the underpricing of new issues; in their view, underpricing reflects a risk premium that has to be paid to investors and investment bankers for information imperfections. That is, it is a risk premium for the information advantage possessed by issuers who better know the true quality of their firm's securities and its assets.[39]

If this is so, bank entry may only reduce the degree of underpricing to the extent that it reduces the degree of information imperfection among issuers and investors. This might reasonably be expected given the specialized role of banks as delegated monitors (see Chapter 6).[40]

Anticompetitive Effects. While bank entry may be procompetitive in the short term, there still exists considerable concern about potential anticompetitive behavior in the long term. The big bank holding companies, measured by either capital or assets, are many times larger than the biggest securities firms—or insurance firms, for that matter (see Table 21–1). They may aggressively compete for business in the short run, trying to force traditional investment banks out of business. If successful, they would assume quasi-oligopoly positions, market concentration may rise, and in

IPO (Initial Public Offering)
A corporate equity or debt security offered to the public for the first time through an underwriter.

Secondary Issues
A new issue of equity or debt of firms whose securities are already traded in the market.

[37]See the review of some 20 studies of underpricing by A. Saunders, "Why Are So May Stock Issues Underpriced?" Federal Reserve Bank of Philadelphia, *Business Review,* March–April 1990, pp. 3–12.

[38]See C. F. Loderer, D. P. Sheehan, and G. B. Kadler, "The Pricing of Equity Offerings," *Journal of Financial Economics,* 1991, pp. 35–37.

[39]See F. Beatty and J. Ritter, "Investment Banking, Reputation, and the Underpricing of Initial Public Offerings," *Journal of Financial Economics* 15 (1986), pp. 213–32; and K. Rock, "Why New Issues Are Underpriced," *Journal of Financial Economics* 15 (1986), pp. 187–212. Also see C. Muscerella and M. R. Vetsuypens, "A Simple Test of Baron's Model of IPO Underpricing," *Journal of Financial Economics* 24 (1989), pp. 125–36. They found out that when investment banks themselves (such as Morgan Stanley) went public, their stocks were also underpriced. This tends to support an information role in underpricing—although the average underpricing of investment banks was less than that found on average for other firms.

[40]However, firewalls limit the efficiency with which the delegated monitor can transfer information to its affiliate. See M. Puri, "Conflicts of Interest, Intermediation and the Pricing of Underwritten Securities," *Journal of Financial Economics,* 1999.

the long run prices for investment banking services would rise rather than fall. Such a long-run outcome would outweigh any short-term procompetitive benefits.[41]

Concept Questions

1. What are some of the issues that tend to arise in response to bank expansion into securities, insurance, and commercial activities?
2. Explain how firm commitment underwriting of securities is similar to writing put options on assets.
3. Describe three ways in which the losses of a securities affiliate in a holding company structure could be transmitted to a bank.
4. In addition to the six potential conflicts of interest discussed in this section, can you think of any additional possible conflicts that might arise if commercial banks were allowed to expand their investment banking activities?
5. What are three potential procompetitive effects cited in support of banks' expansion into securities activities? What reason is given to support the opposite claim (i.e., that bank expansion would not enhance competition)?

Summary

Traditionally, the U.S. financial system has been structured on segmented product lines. Unlike most other countries, commercial banking, investment banking, and insurance activities have been separated by several legislative acts, including the Glass-Steagall Act of 1933 and the Bank Holding Company Act of 1956. These restrictions on product or activity expansion have had some significant costs. Most important has been the loss of potential risk-reducing gains that arise from both regional and product diversification, as well as gains from the potential generation of cost and revenue synergies. However, a set of important public policy or social welfare concerns relate to conflicts of interest, safety and soundness, competition, and regulation. Nevertheless, in recent years, there has been a dramatic breakdown in many of the regulatory barriers to financial service conglomeration. Part of this has been due to "homemade" deregulation by financial service firms (e.g., the Citicorp and Travelers merger to create Citigroup) and part has been due to deregulatory efforts by the Federal Reserve and the OCC. As a result, the U.S. financial system is rapidly converging toward a "universal banking"–type system similar to those that exist in a number of major European countries. In such a system bank, insurance, and securities products are increasingly cross-sold by large conglomerate (universal) financial service firms with the objective of maximizing revenue and cost synergies and reducing risk through diversification.

Questions and Problems

1. How does product segmentation reduce the risks of FIs? How does it increase the risks of FIs?
2. In what ways have other FIs taken advantage of the restrictions on product diversification imposed on commercial banks?
3. How does product segmentation reduce the profitability of FIs? How does product segmentation increase the profitability of FIs?
4. What general prohibition regarding the activities of commercial banking and investment banking did the Glass-Steagall Act impose? What investment banking activities have been permitted for U.S. commercial banks?
5. What restrictions are placed on Section 20 subsidiaries of U.S. commercial banks that make investment banking activities other than those permitted by the Glass-Steagall Act less attractive? How does this differ from banking activities in other countries?

---

[41]One possible reason for slow development of the German corporate bond market is that German universal banks wish to preserve their monopoly power over corporate debt. This may best be done by encouraging corporate loans rather than bond issues.

6. A section 20 subsidiary of a major U.S. bank is planning to underwrite corporate securities and expects to generate $5 million in revenues. It currently underwrites U.S. Treasury securities and general obligation municipal bonds, earning annual fees of $40 million.

   a. Is the bank in compliance with the laws regulating the revenue generation of Section 20 subsidiaries?

   b. The bank plans to increase its private placement activities and expects to generate $11 million in revenue. Is it in compliance with the revenue generation requirements?

   c. If it plans to increase underwriting of corporate securities and generate $11 million in revenues, is it in compliance? If not, what should it do to ensure that it is in compliance?

7. Review the Section 20 firewall provisions in Table 21–3. Explain in general terms what impact the actions of the Federal Reserve Board in 1997 should have on the strategic implementation of Section 20 activities.

8. The Garn-St. Germain Act of 1982 and several subsequent banking laws have clearly established the separation of banking and insurance firms. What are the likely reasons for maintaining this separation?

9. What types of insurance products are commercial banks permitted to offer?

10. How have nonbanks managed to exploit the loophole in the Bank Holding Company Act of 1956 and engage in banking activities? What law closed this loophole?

11. What are the differences in the risk implications of a firm commitment securities offering versus a best-efforts offering?

12. An FI is underwriting the sales of 1 million shares of Ultrasonics, Inc., and is quoting a bid–ask price of $6.00–6.50.

    a. What are the fees earned by the FI if a firm commitment method is used to underwrite the securities?

    b. What are the fees if it uses the best-efforts method and a commission of 50 basis points is charged?

    c. How would your answer be affected if it manages to sell the shares only at $5.50 using the firm commitment method? The commission for best efforts is still 50 basis points.

13. What is the maximum possible underwriter's fee on both the best-efforts and firm commitment underwriting contracts on an issue of $12 million shares at a bid price of $12.45 and an offer price of $12.60? What is the maximum possible loss? The best-efforts underwriting commission is 75 basis points.

14. A Section 20 affiliate agrees to underwrite a debt issue for one of its clients. It has suggested a firm commitment offering for issuing 100,000 shares of stock. The bank

quotes a bid-ask spread of $97–$97.50 to its customers on the issue date.

   a. What are the total underwriting fees generated if all the issue is sold? If only 60 percent is sold?

   b. Instead of taking a chance that only 60 percent of the shares will be sold on the issue date, a bank suggests a price of $95 to the issuing firm. It expects to quote a bid-ask spread of $95–$95.40 and sell 100 percent of the issue. From the FI's perspective, which price is better if it expects to sell the remaining 40 percent at the bid price of $97 under the first quote?

15. What are the reasons why the upside returns from firm commitment securities offerings are not symmetrical in regard to the downside risk? How is underwriting on a firm commitment basis similar to writing a put option on a firm's assets?

16. Why is the underwriting loss in the British Petroleum case unusual? Why do losses of this nature warrant consideration by regulatory agencies?

17. What are three ways in which the failure of a securities affiliate in a holding company organizational form could negatively affect a bank? How has the Fed attempted to prevent a breakdown of the firewalls between banks and affiliates in these situations?

18. What are two operational strategies to reduce the risk to the safety and soundness of a bank resulting from a securities affiliate failure or many other types of financial distress?

19. What do empirical studies reveal about the effect of activity diversification on the risk of failure of banks?

20. What role does bank activity diversification play in the ability of a bank to exploit economies of scale and scope? What remains as the limitation to creating potentially greater benefits?

21. What six conflicts of interest have been identified as potential roadblocks to the expansion of banking powers into the financial services area?

22. What are some of the legal, institutional, and market conditions that lessen the likelihood that an FI can exploit conflicts of interest from the expansion of commercial banks into other financial service areas?

23. Under what circumstances could the existence of deposit insurance provide an advantage to banks in competing with other traditional securities firms?

24. In what ways does the current regulatory structure argue against providing additional securities powers to the banking industry? Does this issue just concern banks?

25. What are the potential procompetitive effects of allowing banks to enter more fully into securities underwriting? What is the anticompetitive argument or position?

APPENDIX 21A
PERMISSIBLE BANKING ACTIVITIES AND BANK OWNERSHIP IN THE EU AND G-10 COUNTRIES

Country and Bank Supervisor(s)	Securities[1]
Austria Federal Ministry of Finance	Unrestricted; conducted either directly in bank or through subsidiaries. No firewalls mandated.
Belgium Banking and Finance Commission	Permitted; conducted directly in bank or through subsidiaries. No restrictions on bonds. However, a bank may not underwrite stock issues. No firewalls mandated.
Canada Office of the Superintendent of Financial Institutions	Permitted; conducted only through subsidiaries. No firewalls mandated.
Denmark Danish Financial Supervisory Authority	Unrestricted; conducted directly in bank or through subsidiaries. Firewalls are mandated.
Finland Financial Supervision	Unrestricted; conducted directly in bank or through subsidiaries. No firewalls mandated.
France Credit Institutions Committee, Bank Regulatory Commission, and Banking Commission	Unrestricted; conducted directly in bank or through subsidiaries. No firewalls mandated.
Germany Federal Banking Supervisory Office and Deutsche Bundesbank	Unrestricted; conducted directly in bank. No firewalls mandated.
Greece Bank of Greece	Permitted; underwriting may be conducted directly in bank, whereas dealing and brokerage must be conducted through subsidiaries. However, the selling of mutual funds products directly by banks is permitted. Some firewalls are mandated. For example, persons responsible for the management of a bank cannot hold similar positions in a securities firm.
Ireland Central Bank of Ireland	Unrestricted; conducted directly in bank or through subsidiaries. No firewalls are mandated.
Italy Bank of Italy	Unrestricted; conducted directly in bank or through subsidiaries. However, for brokering and dealing in securities listed on an Italian exchange other than Italian government and government-guaranteed securities, only through a special subsidiary. Firewalls are mandated.
Japan Ministry of Finance (primary responsibility) and Bank of Japan	Restricted; only bonds (not equities) and only through securities subsidiaries. A bank can own more than 50% of a securities firm only with permission from the Ministry of Finance and Fair Trade Commission. Firewalls are mandated.
Luxembourg Luxembourg Monetary Institute	Unrestricted; conducted directly in bank or through subsidiaries. No firewalls mandated.

Insurance[2]	Real Estate[3]
Permitted; conducted only through subsidiaries. However, a bank may broker insurance policies.	Unrestricted; conducted directly in bank or through subsidiaries. The total book value of a bank's investment in real estate, plant and equipment, and furniture and fixtures must not exceed liable capital.
Permitted; conducted directly in the bank for those activities licensed by the Insurance Supervisory Authority and through insurance companies (subsidiaries) in which banks can own either controlling or minority participating interests if certain framework conditions are fulfilled.	Restricted; investments limited to real estate used in the exercise of the bank's activities. May serve as an agent and manager of real estate for clients as well as engage in real estate leasing through subsidiaries.
Permitted; conducted only through subsidiaries.	Permitted; conducted only through subsidiaries.
Permitted; conducted only through subsidiaries.	Permitted; banks are permitted to hold real estate to a book value not exceeding 20% of the bank's own funds. Real estate in which the bank performs banking activities is not included in this 20% limitation. Mortgage-credit activity is permitted only through subsidiaries.
Restricted; only selling of insurance policies as an agent is permitted.	Permitted; may hold real estate and shares in real estate firms up to 13% of the bank's total assets directly in bank or through subsidiaries.
Permitted; sale of insurance products/services may be conducted directly in bank, but underwriting must be done through subsidiaries.	Permitted; conducted directly in bank or through subsidiaries but limited to 10% of the bank's net income.
Restricted; conducted as principal only through insurance subsidiaries, which are supervised by the Insurance Supervisory Office. Insurance regulation does not allow any business other than insurance business being carried out by an insurance firm. However, a bank may conduct insurance activities as agent without restrictions.	Permitted; investment in equity and real estate, calculated at book value, may not exceed a bank's liable capital, but unlimited through subsidiaries.
Restricted; selling of limited combined bank/insurance products by banks is permitted, but selling of separate insurance products by banks is not. The latter is allowed through bank subsidiaries.	Restricted; direct investment in real estate is limited to 50% of own funds for purposes of conducting banking activities. Real estate investment for commercial purposes is not permitted. The setting up of a subsidiary engaging in real estate management requires Bank of Greece permission. Subsidiaries engaging in real estate development are considered nonfinancial firms and are regulated according to the EC Second Banking Directive.
Prohibited.[4]	Unrestricted.
Permitted; sale of insurance products/services may be conducted directly in bank, but underwriting must be done through subsidiaries.	Restricted; generally limited to bank premises.
Prohibited.	Restricted; generally limited to bank premises.
Permitted; a bank employee may obtain an insurance license and thereby sell insurance product/services as an agent of insurance firms within the bank. However, a bank is allowed to carry out insurance activities through a subsidiary or by taking an equity stake in an insurance firm, with prior approval.	Unrestricted; conducted directly in bank or through subsidiaries.

Country and Bank Supervisor(s)	*Securities*[1]
Netherlands Bank of Netherlands	Unrestricted; conducted directly in bank or through subsidiaries. No firewalls mandated.
Portugal Bank of Portugal	Unrestricted; conducted either directly in bank or through subsidiaries. However, for the organized stock exchanges, brokerage and dealer activities must be conducted through subsidiaries. No firewalls mandated.
Spain Bank of Spain	Unrestricted; conducted directly in bank or through subsidiaries, but banks do not have direct access to official stock exchanges. No firewalls mandated.
Sweden Financial Supervisory Authority	Unrestricted; conducted directly in bank or through subsidiaries. No firewalls mandated.
Switzerland Swiss Federal Banking Commission	Unrestricted; conducted directly in bank or through subsidiaries. No firewalls mandated.
United Kingdom Bank of England	Unrestricted; conducted directly in bank or through subsidiaries. However, gilt-edged (government bond) market making must be conducted through a subsidiary. No firewalls mandated.
United States Federal Reserve System, Comptroller of the Currency, Federal Deposit Insurance Corporation, and state authorities.	Restricted; national and state member banks generally are prohibited from underwriting or dealing in corporate debt and equity instruments or securities. They may, however, engage in discount and full-service brokerage as well as serve as agent for issues in privately placing securities. State nonmember banks are subject to the same restriction as national banks unless the FDIC determines the activity would not pose a significant risk to the deposit insurance fund. Bank holding companies may on a case-by-case basis be permitted to underwrite and deal in corporate debt and equity securities through a Section 20 subsidiary so long as the subsidiary's revenues for these activities do not exceed 25% of total gross revenues. Firewalls are mandated, but lowered in 1997.
European Union[5]	Not applicable; permissibility is subject to home country authorization and limited host country regulation, primarily notification requirements. (A single EU "passport" exists.)

Insurance[2]	*Real Estate*[3]
Permitted; sale of insurance products/services may be conducted directly in bank, but underwriting must be done through subsidiaries. More generally, an insurance company is not allowed to pursue the business of a bank within one corporation (Insurance Companies Supervision Act).	Permitted; but real estate other than bank premises may not exceed 25% of the actual own funds of the bank.
Permitted; conducted only through subsidiaries for underwriting and selling as principal. May sell as agent directly in bank.	Restricted; generally limited to holding bank premises. Moreover, net value of fixed assets shall not exceed own funds.
Permitted; sale of insurance products/services may be conducted directly in bank, but underwriting must be done through subsidiaries.	Restricted; generally limited to bank premises. Real estate and other immobilized tangible assets are limited to 70% of own funds. Banks may also hold such assets in payment of debts for up to 3 years.
Permitted; bank may directly sell only insurance products/services. However, both banks and insurance firms are allowed to form financial groups as long as the two activities are conducted in different firms.	Restricted; generally limited to bank premises.
Permitted; conducted only through subsidiaries.	Unrestricted; investments in a single real estate project are limited to equivalent of 20% of the bank's capital. However, the Swiss Federal Banking Commission can allow this limit to be exceeded.
Permitted; sales of insurance products/services may be conducted directly in bank, but underwriting only through subsidiaries. However, the bank's investment in the subsidiary must be deducted from the bank's capital when calculating its capital adequacy if bank ownership share in the subsidiary exceeds 20%.	Unrestricted; conducted directly in bank or through subsidiaries.
Restricted; banks generally may engage in credit life and disability insurance underwriting and agency activities. National banks, in addition, may engage in general insurance agency activities in towns below 5,000 in population.	Restricted; banks generally are restricted to investment in premises or that which is necessary for the transaction of their business.
Not applicable; permissibility is subject to home country regulation.	Not applicable; permissibility is subject to home country and host country regulation.

Country and Bank Supervisor(s)	Commercial Bank Investment in Nonfinancial Firms
Austria	
Federal Ministry of Finance	Unrestricted; complies with the EC Second Banking Directive. Subject to this limitation, a bank may own 100% of the equity in a nonfinancial firm[6]
Belgium	
Banking and Finance Commission	Restricted; single share holding may not exceed 10% of bank's own funds and such share holding on an aggregate basis may not exceed 35% of own funds. More restrictive than the EC Second Banking Directive during a transition period.[6]
Canada	
Office of the Superintendent of Financial Institutions	Restricted; limited to 10% of outstanding shares of a nonfinancial firm, with aggregate holdings not to exceed 70% of bank capital.
Denmark	
Danish Financial Supervisory Authority	Permitted; complies with the EC Second Banking Directive. However, a bank may not hold a permanent decisive participation in nonfinancial firms.[6]
Finland	
Financial Supervision	Unrestricted; complies with the EC Second Banking Directive. Subject to this limitation, a bank may own 100% of the equity in any nonfinancial firm.[6]
France	
Credit Institutions Committee, Bank Regulatory Commission, and Banking Commission	Unrestricted; complies with EC Second Banking Directive. Subject to this limitation, a bank may own 100% of the equity in any nonfinancial firm.[6]
Germany	
Federal Banking Supervisory Office and Deutsche Bundesbank	Unrestricted; complies with EC Second Banking Directive. Subject to this limitation, a bank may own 100% of the equity in any nonfinancial firm.[6]
Greece	
Bank of Greece	Unrestricted; complies with EC Second Banking Directive. Subject to this limitation, a bank may own 100% of the equity in any nonfinancial firm.[6]
Ireland	
Central Bank of Ireland	Unrestricted; complies with EC Second Banking Directive. Subject to this limitation, a bank may own 100% of the equity in any nonfinancial firm.[6]
Italy	
Bank of Italy	Restricted; more restrictive than the EC Second Banking Directive. Most banks are subject to an overall investment limit of 15% of own funds (7.5% in the case of unlisted firms) and to a concentration limit of 3% of own funds in each holding in nonfinancial firms or groups. Some banks, due to their size and proven stability, are subject to less stringent limits (overall and concentration limits of, respectively, 50% and 6% for leading banks and 60% and 15% for specialized banks). Consistency with the principle of separation between banking and commerce is ensured by a further investment limit of 15% of invested firms' capital for all banks.[6]
Japan	
Ministry of Finance (primary responsibility) and Bank of Japan	Restricted; a single bank's ownership is limited to 5% of a single firm's shares, including other banks (Article 9, Anti-Monopoly Law).
Luxembourg	
Luxembourg Monetary Institute	Unrestricted; complies with EC Second Banking Directive. Subject to this limitation, a bank may own 100% of the equity in any nonfinancial firm.[6]
Netherlands	
Bank of Netherlands	Unrestricted; complies with EC Second Banking Directive. Subject to this limitation, a bank may own 100% of the equity in any nonfinancial firm.[6] However, a declaration of nonobjection from the minister of finance (or the Nederlandsche Bank on behalf of the minister) is required for any bank investment exceeding 10% of the capital of a nonfinancial firm.

Definitions: Unrestricted–A full range of activities in the given category can be conducted directly in the bank.
Permitted–A full range of activities can be conducted, but all or some must be conducted in subsidiaries.
Restricted–Less than a full range of activities can be conducted in the bank or subsidiaries.
Prohibited–The activity cannot be conducted in either the bank or subsidiaries.

	Geographical Branching Restrictions on Commercial Banks within Country		
Nonfinancial Firm Investment in Commercial Banks	*Domestic Banks*	*Nondomestic Banks*	*Prior Regulatory Approval Required*
Unrestricted; complies with the EC Second Banking Directive.[7]	None	None	No
Unrestricted; complies with the EC Second Banking Directive. However, the Banking and Finance Commission examines the "fit and proper" character of those shareholders holding at least 5% of the bank's capital.	None	None	Yes
Restricted; limited to 10% of outstanding shares. Since no shareholders may exceed this 10% limit, Canada is attempting to ensure that banks are widely held.	None	Limited restrictions	Yes
Unrestricted; complies with the EC Second Banking Directive.[7] However, a bank may not without supervisory authority have engagement with a firm that through its ownership of shares or otherwise directly or indirectly has a decisive influence on the bank.	None	None	No
Unrestricted; complies with the EC Second Banking Directive.[7] In the case of commercial banks, a firm is not allowed to vote at the annual meeting with more than 5% of the total voting rights presented at the meeting.	None	None	No
Unrestricted; complies with the EC Second Banking Directive.[7]	None	None	No
Unrestricted; complies with the EC Second Banking Directive.[7]	None	None	No
Unrestricted; complies with the EC Second Banking Directive.[7]	None	None	Yes
Unrestricted. However, advance notification is required for any application of more that 5% of the voting rights in a bank and prior approval is required for any acquisition of 10% or more of the total shares or voting rights or any holding or interest that confers a right to appoint or remove directors.[5]	None	None	No
Restricted; more restrictive than the EC Second Banking Directive. Persons who engage in significant business activity in sectors other than banking and finance are forbidden from acquiring an equity stake which, when added to those already held, would result in a holding exceeding 15% of the voting capital of a bank or in control of the bank.[7]	None	None	No
Restricted; total investment is limited to firm's capital or net assets. The Anti-Monopoly Law prohibits establishment of a holding company whose main business is to control the business activities of other domestic companies through the holding of ownership.	None	None	Yes
Restricted; nonfinancial firms may legally be the majority shareholders in banks. However, general policy is to discourage nonfinancial groups or private persons from being major shareholders in banks.	None	None	Yes
Unrestricted; complies with the EC Second Banking Directive.[7] However, a declaration of nonobjection from the minister of finance (or the Nederlandsche Bank on behalf of the minister) is required for an investment exceeding 5% of a bank's capital.	None	None	No

[1]Securities activities include underwriting, dealing, and brokering all kinds of securities and all aspects of the mutual fund business.

[2]Insurance activities include underwriting and selling insurance products/services as principal and as agent.

[3]Real estate activities include investment, development, and management.

[4]However, three commercial banks are authorized to engage in assurance activities.

Country and Bank Supervisor(s)	Commercial Bank Investment in Nonfinancial Firms
Portugal Bank of Portugal	Permitted; complies with the EC Second Bank Directive. However, a bank may not control more than 25% of the voting rights of a nonfinancial firm.[6]
Spain Bank of Spain	Unrestricted; complies with EC Second Banking Directive. Subject to this limitation, a bank may own 100% of the equity in any nonfinancial firm.[6]
Sweden Financial Supervisory Authority	Restricted; investments on an aggregated basis are limited to 40% of a bank's own funds. Ownership in a firm is limited to 5% of this base (i.e., 1.5% in a firm or group of firms related to each other). Furthermore, ownership in a firm must not exceed 5% of the total voting power in the firm concerned. These limits do not apply when a bank has to protect itself against credit losses. In this case the bank must sell when market conditions are appropriate.[6]
Switzerland Swiss Federal Banking Commission	Unrestricted, a single participation is limited to the equivalent of 20% of the bank's capital. However, the Swiss Federal Banking Commission can allow this limit to be exceeded.
United Kingdom Bank of England	Unrestricted; complies with EC Second Banking Directive. Subject to this limitation, a bank may own 100% of the equity in any nonfinancial firm. However, an ownership share of more than 20% requires that the investment be deducted from the bank's capital when calculating its capital adequacy on a risk basis. Otherwise, the investment is treated as a commercial loan for the risk-based calculation.
United States Federal Reserve System, Comptroller of the Currency, Federal Deposit Insurance Corporation, and state authorities	Restricted; national and state member banks generally are prohibited from making direct equity investment in voting or nonvoting stock. State nonmember banks generally are limited to investments that are permissible for national banks. Bank holding companies are limited to an investment not to exceed 25 percent of a nonfinancial firm's capital.

EU Banks

European Union[5]	Unrestricted; the EC Second Banking Directive (Article 12) limits "qualifying investments" to no more than 15% of a bank's own funds for investment in a single firm and to no more than 60% for all investment in nonfinancial firms. In exceptional circumstances, these limits may be exceeded, but the amount by which the limits are exceeded must be covered by a bank's own funds, and these own funds may not be included in the solvency ratio calculation.
A qualifying investment is defined as a direct or indirect holding in an undertaking equal to at least 10% of its capital or voting rights or permitting the exercise of significant influence over its management.

[5]The EU members are Austria (January 1, 1995), Belgium (original member), Denmark (January 1, 1973), Finland (January 1, 1995), France (original member), Germany (original member), Greece (January 1, 1981), Ireland (January 1, 1973), Italy (original member), Luxembourg (original member), the Netherlands (original member), Portugal (January 1, 1986), Spain (January 1, 1986), Sweden (January 1, 1995), and the United Kingdom (January 1, 1973).

[6]The EC Second Banking Directive (Article 12) limits "qualifying investments" to no more than 15% of a bank's own funds for investments in a single nonfinancial firm and to no more than 60% for aggregate investments in nonfinancial firms. In exceptional circumstances these limits may be exceeded, but the amount by which the limits are exceeded must be covered by a bank's own funds and these own funds may not be included in the solvency ratio calculation. A qualifying

Nonfinancial Firm Investment in Commercial Banks	Geographical Branching Restrictions on Commercial Banks within Country		
	Domestic Banks	Nondomestic Banks	Prior Regulatory Approval Required
Unrestricted; complies with the EC Second Banking Directive.[7]	None	None	No
Permitted; complies with the EC Second Banking Directive. However, a nonfinancial firm cannot hold more than 20% of the shares of a new bank during the first five years of its existence.[5] Specified shareholder thresholds require authorization by the Bank of Spain before additional investment.	None	None	No for EU banks. Non-EU banks require authorization by the Ministry of Economy.
Restricted; ownership is limited to 50% except under certain circumstances when a bank is near insolvency and there is a need for external capital injection. In the latter case, greater ownership may be permitted, based upon suitability of new owners.[7]	None	None	Yes
Unrestricted; a nonfinancial firm may own 100% of the equity in a bank.	None	None	Yes but only for nondomestic banks
Unrestricted; complies with the EC Second Banking Directive. However, a firm would have to make application to the Bank of England to become a shareholder controller and receive the Bank's nonobjection.	None. But need to comply with the local requirements and have adequate systems and controls for the function.	None. However, a bank must make an application to open a branch unless passporting into the United Kingdom under the EC Second Banking Directive.	Yes (see adjacent column).
Restricted; a nonfinancial firm may make equity investments in banks and bank holding companies. However, the investment must not exceed 25% of the bank's capital to avoid becoming a bank holding company. In other words, banks may be acquired only by companies that limit their activities to those deemed to be closely related to banking by the Federal Reserve Board.	No	Same restrictions that apply to domestic banks.	Yes
Non-EU Banks			
Unrestricted; subjects qualifying investments to regulatory consent based only on the suitability of shareholders.	None. (A single EU "passport" exists).	Restricted; branches are fully regulated by the authorities of the EU member state in which they are situated and do not have access to the single EU "passport" to provide services or establish subsidiary branches throughout the EU.	

investment is defined as a direct or indirect holding in an undertaking equal to at least 10% of its capital or voting rights or permitting the exercise of significant influence over its management.

[7]The EC Second Banking Directive (Article 11) subjects qualifying investments to regulatory consent based only on the suitability of shareholders.

Source: J. R. Barth, D. E. Nolle, and T. N. Rice, "Commercial Banking Structure, Regulation and Performance: An International Comparison," Office of the Comptroller of the Currency. Economic working Paper 97–6, March 1997 (updated). For France and Japan a source was the Institute of International Bankers, 1995.

GEOGRAPHIC DIVERSIFICATION

Domestic

Introduction

Just as product expansion (see Chapter 21) may enable an FI to reduce risk and increase returns, so may geographic expansion. Geographic expansions can have a number of dimensions. In particular, they can be either domestic within a state or region or international by participating in an overseas market. Also, expansions can be effected through opening a new office or branch or by acquiring another FI. In this chapter we trace the potential benefits and costs to an FI from expanding domestically—especially through mergers and acquisitions—and then go on to look at international or cross-border expansions in Chapter 23. In particular, we look at the reasons underlying the current merger wave among U.S. financial service firms that is dramatically changing the structure of the U.S. financial system as we move into the new millennium.

Domestic Expansions

De Novo Office
A newly established office.

In the United States, the ability of FIs to expand domestically has historically been constrained by regulation. By comparison, no special regulations have inhibited the ability of commercial firms such as General Motors, IBM, and Sears from establishing new or **de novo offices,** factories, or branches anywhere in the country. Nor have they been prohibited from acquiring other firms—as long as they are not banks. While securities firms and insurance companies have faced relatively few restrictions in expanding their business domestically, other FIs, especially banks, have faced a complex and changing network of rules and regulations. While such regulations may inhibit expansions, they also create potential opportunities to increase an FI's returns. In particular, regulations may create locally uncompetitive markets with monopoly economic rents that new entrants can potentially exploit. Thus, for the most innovative FIs, regulation can provide profit opportunities as well as costs. As a result, regulation both inhibits and creates incentives to engage in geographic expansions.[1]

In addition, the economic factors that impact commercial firm expansion and acquisition decisions are likely to impact the decisions of FIs as well. Two major groups of factors are cost and revenue synergies and firm/market-specific attractions, such as the specialized skills of an acquired firm's employees and the markets of the firm to be acquired. Thus, the attractiveness of a geographic expansion, whether through acquisition, branching, or opening a new office, depends on a broad set of factors encompassing:

1. Regulation and the regulatory framework.
2. Cost and revenue synergies.
3. Firm- or market-specific factors.

We start by considering how the first factor—regulation—impacts an FI's geographic expansion decision. Specifically, we briefly discuss the restrictions applying to insurance companies and thrifts; then we look in more detail at regulations affecting commercial banks.

Concept Questions

1. Explain why regulation both inhibits and provides incentives to an FI to engage in geographic expansion.
2. What three basic factors influence the attractiveness of geographic expansion to an FI?

---

[1]E. Kane has called this interaction between regulation and incentives the regulatory dialectic. See "Accelerating Inflation, Technological Innovation, and the Decreasing Effectiveness of Banking Regulation," *Journal of Finance* 36 (1981), pp. 335–67. Expansions that are geographic market extensions involving firms in the same product areas are part of a broader set of horizontal mergers.

Regulatory Factors Impacting Geographic Expansion

Insurance Companies

As we discussed in Chapter 2, insurance companies are state-regulated firms. By establishing a subsidiary in one state, an insurance company normally has the opportunity to sell insurance anywhere in that state and often to market the product nationally by telemarketing and direct sales. To deliver a financial service effectively, however, it is often necessary to establish a physical presence in a local market. To do this, insurance companies establish subsidiaries and offices in other states. This is usually easy since the initial capital requirement for establishing a new subsidiary is set at relatively low levels by state regulators. Thus, most large insurance companies, such as Aetna, Allstate, and Prudential, have a physical presence in virtually every state in the union.

Thrifts

The ability of thrifts to branch or expand geographically—whether intrastate (within a state) or interstate (between states)—was under the power of the Federal Home Loan Bank Board until 1989. Since 1989, the ability to branch has been under the power of the Office of Thrift Supervision (OTS) as part of the 1989 FIRREA legislation. Historically, the policy was that a federally chartered thrift could not branch across state lines. In the 1980s, a considerable loosening of these restrictions occurred. Both the Garn-St. Germain Act of 1982 and the Financial Institutions Reform, Recovery, and Enforcement Act (FIRREA) of 1989 allowed sound banks and thrifts to acquire failing thrifts across state lines and to run them as separate subsidiaries or convert them into branches. Finally, in 1992 the OTS announced that it was willing to allow interstate branching for all federally chartered S&Ls. By 1993 interstate S&Ls controlled 25 percent of all S&L assets and had established over 1,200 branches across state lines. Table 22–1 summarizes the loosening of interstate branching and acquisition activity regulation for thrifts.

Commercial Banks

Restrictions on Intrastate Banking.   At the beginning of the century most U.S. banks were **unit banks** with a single office. Improving communications and customer needs resulted in a rush to branching in the first two decades of the 20th century. Increasingly, this movement ran into opposition from the smallest unit banks and the largest money center banks. The smallest unit banks perceived a competitive threat to their retail business from the bigger branching banks; money center banks feared a loss of valuable correspondent business such as check clearing and other payment services. As a result, several states restricted the ability of banks to branch within the state. Indeed, some states prohibited intrastate branching per se, effectively constraining a bank to unit status. Over the years and in a very piecemeal fashion, states have liberalized their restrictions on within state branching. As we show in Table 22–2 column (1), by 1994 only one state (Iowa) had not deregulated intrastate banking.

Restrictions on Interstate Banking.   The defining piece of legislation affecting interstate branching until 1997 was the McFadden Act, passed in 1927 and amended

Unit Bank
A bank with a single office.

TABLE 22–1   Relaxation of Geographic Expansion Restrictions for S&Ls

1982	The *Garn-St. Germain Act* allows interstate branching with the acquisition of failed S&Ls by out-of-state S&Ls.
1989	The Office of Thrift Supervision (OTS) assumes power to regulate interstate branching for federally chartered thrifts as part of the *Financial Institutions Reform, Recovery, and Enforcement Act of 1989,* allowing healthy thrifts to be acquired across state lines by holding companies. The Resolution Trust Company is placed in charge of resolving failed thrifts, at times overriding state branching laws.
1992	OTS allows interstate branching for all federally chartered thrifts.

Source: S. Cebonoyan et al., unpublished Working Paper, University of Maryland, School of Business, Baltimore, 1998.

---

in 1933. The McFadden Act and its amendments restricted nationally chartered banks' branching ability to the same extent allowed to state-chartered banks. Because states prohibit interstate banking for state-chartered banks in general, nationally chartered banks were similarly prohibited.[2]

Between 1927 and 1997 (see later), given the prohibition on interstate branching, bank organizations expanding across state lines largely relied on establishing subsidiaries rather than branches. Some of the biggest banking organizations established **multibank holding companies** for that purpose. A multibank holding company (MBHC) is a parent company that acquires more than one bank as a direct subsidiary. While MBHCs had been around in the early part of the 20th century, the 1927 restrictions on interstate branching gave the bank acquisition movement an added impetus. By 1956, some 47 multibank holding companies were established, many owning banks in two or more states.[3]

In 1956, Congress recognized the potential loophole to interstate banking posed by the MBHC movement and passed the Douglas Amendment to the Bank Holding Company Act. This act permitted MBHCs to acquire bank subsidiaries only to the extent allowed by the laws of the state in which the proposed bank target resided. Because states prohibited out-of-state bank acquisitions, this essentially curtailed the growth of the MBHC movement until the emergence and expansion of regional banking pacts (see later). Any MBHCs with out-of-state subsidiaries established prior to 1956 were **grandfathered;** that is, MBHCs were allowed to keep them. (One such example was First Interstate.)

The passage of the 1956 Douglas Amendment did not close all potential interstate banking loopholes. Since the amendment pertained to MBHC acquisitions, it still left open the potential for **one-bank holding company** (OBHC) geographic extensions. An OBHC is a parent bank holding company that has a single bank subsidiary and a number of other nonbank subsidiaries. By creating an OBHC and establishing across state lines various nonbank subsidiaries that sell financial services such as consumer finance, leasing, and data processing, a bank could almost replicate an out-of-state banking presence. However, doing interstate banking in this fashion is far more expensive than establishing either direct branches or full-service subsidiaries. Nevertheless, one-bank holding expansions are excellent examples of

Multibank Holding Company (MBHC)
A parent banking organization that owns a number of individual bank subsidiaries.

Grandfathered Subsidiary
A subsidiary established prior to the passage of a restrictive law and not subject to that law.

One-Bank Holding Company
A parent banking organization that owns one bank subsidiary and nonbank subsidiaries.

---

[2]It is arguable, contrary to conventional wisdom, that the McFadden Act actually enlarged the geographic expansion powers of nationally chartered banks since the prime regulator of nationally chartered banks had restricted national bank branching even within a state until the act's passage.

[3]By 1990, there were 157 interstate multibank holding companies with the growth reflecting the presence of regional banking pacts. This will be discussed later in this chapter.

TABLE 22–2   The States Remove Restrictions on Geographic Expansion Pre-1994

State	Intrastate Branching Deregulated	Interstate Banking Deregulated
Alabama	1981	1987
Alaska	Before 1970	1982
Arizona	Before 1970	1986
Arkansas	1994	1989
California	Before 1970	1987
Colorado	1991	1988
Connecticut	1980	1983
Delaware	Before 1970	1988
District of Columbia	Before 1970	1985
Florida	1988	1985
Georgia	1983	1985
Hawaii	1986	—
Idaho	Before 1970	1985
Illinois	1988	1986
Indiana	1989	1986
Iowa	—	1991
Kansas	1987	1992
Kentucky	1990	1984
Louisiana	1988	1987
Maine	1975	1978
Maryland	Before 1970	1985
Massachusetts	1984	1983
Michigan	1987	1986
Minnesota	1993	1986
Mississippi	1986	1988
Missouri	1990	1986
Montana	1990	1993
Nebraska	1985	1990
Nevada	Before 1970	1985
New Hampshire	1987	1987
New Jersey	1977	1986
New Mexico	1991	1989
New York	1976	1982
North Carolina	Before 1970	1985
North Dakota	1987	1991
Ohio	1979	1985
Oklahoma	1988	1987
Oregon	1985	1986
Pennsylvania	1982	1986
Rhode Island	Before 1970	1984
South Carolina	Before 1970	1986
South Dakota	Before 1970	1983
Tennessee	1985	1985
Texas	1988	1987
Utah	1981	1984
Vermont	1970	1988
Virginia	1978	1985
Washington	1985	1987
West Virginia	1987	1988
Wisconsin	1990	1987
Wyoming	1988	1987

Note: Before the passage of the 1994 Riegle-Neal Act, Iowa had not deregulated intrastate branching and Hawaii had not deregulated interstate banking.

Source: J. Jayaratne and P. E. Strahan, "The Benefits of Branching Deregulation," *Economic Policy Review,* Federal Reserve Bank of New York, December 1997, pp. 13–29.

Kane's regulatory dialectic—blocking one path to geographic expansion simply resulted in banks exploiting a loophole elsewhere if they believed it was net profitable to do so.[4]

The OBHC movement grew tremendously from 117 banking organizations in 1956 to 1,318 in 1970, with all manner of financial and nonfinancial subsidiaries established both within the home state of the affiliated bank and across state lines. For example, some OBHCs even had ownership stakes in supermarket chains and railroads.

In 1970 Congress again acted, recognizing that bankers had creatively innovated yet another loophole to interstate banking restrictions. The 1970 Bank Holding Company Act Amendments effectively restricted the nonbank activities an OBHC could engage in to those "closely related to banking," as defined by the Federal Reserve under Section 4(c)(8) of the act. Further, acquisitions of nonbank subsidiaries after 1970 were subject to the approval of the Federal Reserve. Initially, the act permitted only six nonbank activities, including consumer finance and credit cards. Moreover, subsidiaries engaged in activities not closely related to banking had to be divested by 1980.

Thus, the year 1970 and the passage of the Bank Holding Company Act amendments are probably the low point of interstate banking in the United States. Since that time, five developments have resulted in the virtual erosion of interstate banking restrictions. We describe these developments next.

Regional and National Banking Pacts.   Maine took the first step in eroding interstate banking restrictions in 1978 by passing a law that exploited a loophole in the Douglas Amendments of 1956. This loophole occurred because the law prohibited the acquisition of a bank across state lines unless directly permitted by the state in which the proposed target bank resided. To increase employment in and growth of its financial services industry, Maine passed a law allowing banks from any other state to enter and acquire local banks even if the banks in Maine could not engage in such acquisitions in other states. This nationwide nonreciprocal bank acquisition law led to a rapid acquisition of Maine's banking assets by out-of-state bank holding companies. Indeed, by 1988, some 85 percent of bank assets in Maine were held by out-of-state banking organizations such as Citicorp.

Regional or Interstate Banking Pact
An agreement among states describing the conditions for entrance of out-of-state banks by acquisition.

In the early 1980s other states in New England sought to follow Maine's example by enacting their own **interstate banking pacts.** However, these laws were often more restrictive in that they allowed banks from only a certain geographic region—in one case, New England—to enter their banking markets by acquisition. In particular, acquisitions by out-of-state banks from New York and California were generally prohibited. This created some concern about the legality of these more restrictive regional pacts until Connecticut's restrictive law was upheld by the U.S. Supreme Court in the face of a challenge to its legality by New York–based Citicorp in 1984.

By 1994, all states but Hawaii had passed some form of interstate banking law or pact. There were three general types of interstate banking laws:

Nationwide (N). Nationwide laws allowed an out-of-state bank to acquire an in-state target bank even if the acquirer's home state did not give banks from the target's state similar acquisition powers.

---

[4]Kane, "Accelerating Inflation."

Nationwide reciprocal (NR). An out-of-state acquirer could purchase a target bank as long as the acquirer's state allowed other banks from the target's state to enter by acquisition as well. Big banking states such as New York and California had such laws.

Regional reciprocal (RR). These regional banking pacts allowed banks from a regional group of states to acquire a target bank in a given state as long as there was reciprocity, that is, as long as home state banks could acquire targets in other regional pact states and vice versa. For example, Wisconsin's regional reciprocal law allowed entry by acquisition for banks from Iowa, Illinois, Indiana, Kentucky, Michigan, Minnesota, Missouri, and Ohio as long as those states reciprocated by allowing acquisitions by Wisconsin banks in their markets.

In Table 22–2, column (2), we show the condition of interstate banking laws before passage of the Riegle-Neal Act of 1994 (see later).

Purchase of Troubled Banks.   The acquisition of failing or troubled banks across state lines has been a second way that interstate banking barriers have been eroded. Following the passage of the Garn-St. Germain Act in 1982, the bankruptcy of the FSLIC, and the depletion of the FDIC's reserves, regulators increasingly turned to out-of-state acquisitions to resolve bank failures. Thus, for example, in 1987, Chemical Bank (which has itself been acquired by Chase) acquired Texas Commerce and gained a foothold in the Texas banking market. Through its Texas Commerce unit, Chemical Bank acquired most of the banks of the failed First City Bancorporation of Texas in January 1993.

In addition, the 1982 Garn-St. Germain Act allowed banks to acquire failing thrifts as well as banks; through this mechanism, Citicorp acquired thrifts in growing banking markets such as California and Florida. Finally, the passage of FIRREA in August 1989 extended the interstate acquisition powers of banks to encompass healthy thrifts as well.

Nonbank Banks.   A third way interstate banking barriers were eroded came in the establishment of nonbank banks (described in Chapter 21). Until 1987, a large U.S. bank could acquire a full-service out-of-state bank, divest it of its commercial loans, and legally operate it as a nonbank bank specializing in consumer finance.[5] However, the Competitive Equality Banking Act (CEBA) effectively put an end to this loophole in 1987, although it grandfathered existing nonbank banks.

Expansion in OBHC Activities.   Increasingly, after 1970, banks could virtually replicate a full interstate banking presence by establishing out-of-state nonbank subsidiaries. For example, in 1994 Norwest Corporation, a bank holding company from Minneapolis, had mortgage subsidiaries in 49 states and more than 770 consumer lending subsidiaries in 46 states. Moreover, while the 1970, Section 4(c)(8) of the Bank Holding Company Act amendments specified that permitted nonbank activities of bank holding companies had to be "closely related to banking" (as defined by the Federal Reserve), the permitted list had grown close to 60 by 1998 compared to only 6 in 1970.

---

[5]For the purposes of the 1956 Bank Holding Company Act's restrictions on MBHC acquisitions, the definition of a bank was an institution that accepted demand deposits and made commercial and industrial loans. By stripping a bank of its commercial loans, it turned into a nonbank bank that was not subject to restrictions on interstate banking.

Riegle-Neal Interstate Banking and Branching Efficiency Act of 1994.   It had long been recognized that nationwide banking expansion through multibank holding companies was potentially far more expensive than through branching. Separate corporations and boards of directors have to be established for each bank in an MBHC, and it is hard to achieve the same level of economic and financial integration as with branches. Moreover, most of the major banking competitor countries, such as Japan, Germany, France, and the United Kingdom, have nationwide branching.

In the fall of 1994 the U.S. Congress finally passed an interstate banking law under which U.S. and nondomestic banks were allowed to branch interstate by consolidating out-of-state bank subsidiaries into a branch network and/or acquiring banks and thus the branches of banks by merger and acquisition beginning on June 1, 1997. While the law is quiet on the ability of banks to establish de novo (new) branches in other states—essentially leaving it to individual states to pass laws allowing de novo branching—it became possible under the new law for a New York bank to acquire by purchase the branch system of a California bank.[6]

The implication of the Riegle-Neal Act is that full interstate banking—with the exception of de novo branching—became a reality in the United States in 1997. Further details of the Riegle-Neal Act are provided in Table 22–3.[7]

The relaxation of the branching restrictions, along with recognition of the potential cost, revenue, and risk benefits from geographic expansions (discussed next), has set off a wave of consolidation in the U.S. banking system. This consolidation trend has been particularly evident among the largest U.S. banks in a wave of "megamergers." Table 22–4 shows some of the biggest mergers between 1995 and 1998 that are reshaping the U.S. banking industry into a nationwide banking system along European and Canadian lines.

Concept Questions

1. What was the difference between the interstate banking restrictions imposed under the 1956 Bank Holding Company Act and those passed under the 1970 amendments to the Bank Holding Company Act?
2. What are some of the ways in which interstate banking barriers have been eroded?
3. What were the main features of the Riegle-Neal Interstate Banking and Branching Efficiency Act of 1994?

Cost and Revenue Synergies Impacting Geographic Expansion

One reason for an FI expanding (or not expanding) geographically by acquisition relates to the regulations defining its merger opportunities. Other reasons relate to the exploitation of potential cost and revenue synergies from merging (as well as the associated diversification of risk benefits). We look at these potential gains next.

---

[6]One state—Montana (until 2001)—has opted out of allowing interstate banking. Virtually all other states that pursued laws have "opted in."

[7]The reason for the restriction on de novo branching is to protect smaller community banks' franchise values. If you can branch only by acquisition, the franchise values of small banks will be greater than when larger banks have the alternative of branching de novo.

TABLE 22–3   Key Dates for the Riegle-Neal Interstate Banking and Branching Efficiency Act of 1994

Date	Event	Summary
September 24, 1994, to May 31, 1997	Interstate bank merger and branch acquisition early opt-in	A state may "opt in early" to allow interstate merger transactions, including branch acquisitions, to occur prior to June 1, 1997.
	Interstate bank merger opt-out	A state may "opt out" to prohibit interstate merger transactions entirely.
Any time after date of enactment	Interstate de novo branching opt-in	A state may expressly permit out-of-state banks to establish de novo branches within its limits.
One year after date of enactment and thereafter	Interstate banking	A bank holding company may acquire banks located in any state. States do not have the ability to opt out. However, the acquiring institution is not permitted to control more than 10 percent of nationwide deposits or 30 percent of deposits in the state entered.
June 1, 1997, and thereafter	Interstate bank mergers	Banks in different states may merge unless one of the states has opted out of interstate merger transactions by June 1, 1997.
	Interstate branching acquisitions	Banks may acquire an existing branch in another state if the law of that state permits it.

Source: Office of the Comptroller of the Currency.

Cost Synergies

A common reason given for bank mergers is the potential cost synergies that may result from economies of scale, economies of scope, or managerial efficiency sources (often called **X efficiencies** because they are difficult to pin down in a quantitative fashion). For example, in 1996, Chase Manhattan and Chemical Bank merged, creating the (then) largest banking organization in the United States, with assets of $300 billion. It was estimated that annual cost savings from the merger would be $1.5 billion, to be achieved by consolidating certain operations and eliminating redundant costs, including the elimination of some 12,000 positions from a combined staff of 75,000 in 39 states and 51 countries. Wells Fargo's $11.2 billion merger with First Interstate, also in 1996, was expected to reap cost savings of up to $1 billion per year through the elimination of branches and layoffs. The cutbacks would eliminate 365 of the 430 First Interstate branches in California and result in the layoff of 5,100 of the approximately 6,000 employees.

While the Chase–Chemical and Wells Fargo–Interstate mergers are interesting examples of **megamergers**, they are still essentially mergers in the same or closely related banking markets.[8] By comparison, the two largest pure bank mergers in 1998—those between Banc One and First Chicago and between NationsBank and Bank of America were clearly geographic extension mergers with little or no geographic overlap. For example, a major aim of the Bank One and First Chicago merger was to generate an enhanced national presence and economies of scale in the credit card business. Before the merger, Banc One and First Chicago were the third

X Efficiency
Cost savings due to the greater managerial efficiency of the acquiring bank.

Megamerger
The merger of two large banks.

---

[8]Indeed, it is worth noting that in merging, Chase–Chemical chose a New York State bank charter rather than a national bank charter (see Chapter 1 for a discussion of state versus national charters).

TABLE 22–4   The New Shape of U.S. Banking
Major Mergers, 1995–1998

	1995–1996			1996–1997			1997–1998		
	Capital, $million	*Assets, $million*	*Capital– Assets, %*	*Capital, $million*	*Assets, $million*	*Capital– Assets, %*	*Capital, $million*	*Assets, $million*	*Capital– Assets, %*
Chemical	$11,436	$ 82,296	6.25% ⎤	(Chase Manhattan Corp)					
Chase	8,444	121,173	6.97 ⎦	$21,095	$336,099	6.28%	$22,594	$365,521	6.18%
Citicorp	19,239	256,853	7.49	20,109	281,018	7.16	21,096	310,897	6.78 ⎤
Travelers	15,853	302,344	5.24	17,942	345,948	5.19	20,893	386,555	5.40 ⎦
BankAmerica	14,820	232,446	6.38	17,181	250,753	6.85	17,200	260,159	6.65
NationsBank	11,074	187,298	5.91	12,662	185,794	6.82 ⎤			⎤
Boatmen's	2,666	33,704	7.91 ⎤			⎟			⎟
Fourth Financial	592	7,456	7.94 ⎦	3,359	41,200	8.15 ⎟			⎬
Barnett Banks	2,491	41,631	5.98	3,289	41,456	7.93 ⎦	13,593	310,602	4.37 ⎦
First Union	4,479	96,740	4.63 ⎤						
First Fidelity	2,301	35,366	6.51 ⎦	7,790	140,127	5.56	10,215	157,274	6.49 ⎤
CoreStates	2,165	29,729	7.28 ⎤						⎟
Meridian	1,191	14,740	8.08 ⎦	3,725	45,651	8.16 ⎤			⎬
Signet	779	11,100	7.02	857	11,751	7.29 ⎦	3,756	48,461	7.75 ⎦
Banc One	7,824	90,176	8.68	8,107	102,034	7.95	8,701	115,901	7.51 ⎤
First Chicago NBD	7,890	122,002	6.47	9,318	104,619	8.91	8,541	114,096	7.48 ⎦
Wells Fargo	3,505	50,316	6.97 ⎤						
First Interstate	3,431	58,071	5.91 ⎦	6,572	108,888	6.04	6,100	97,456	6.25
Bank of Boston	3,392	47,397	7.16 ⎤	(BankBoston)					
Baybanks	884	12,066	7.33 ⎦	4,954	62,306	7.95	4,971	69,268	7.18
National City	2,524	36,199	6.97 ⎤						
Integra	998	14,391	6.93 ⎦	4,010	50,856	7.88	3,609	54,683	6.60 ⎤
First of America	1,575	23,600	6.67	1,573	22,062	7.13	1,727	21,079	8.19 ⎦
Wachovia	3,625	44,964	8.06	3,963	46,886	8.45 ⎤			
Central Fidelity	739	10,822	6.83	778	10,556	7.37 ⎦	5,465	65,397	8.35
US Bancorp	2,417	31,865	7.58	2,628	33,421	7.86 ⎤			
First Bank System	1,989	33,874	5.87	2,354	36,489	6.45 ⎦	5,028	71,295	7.05

Source: *The Banker,* May 1998, p. 5.

and fifth largest credit card companies. Their merger has created the second largest credit card bank (behind Citigroup), with 40 million accounts and over $56 billion in loans outstanding. It is also perceived that the enhanced scale of the new bank's credit card business will allow it to invest in even more innovative computer technology.

Another example of a market extension megamerger that has both geographic and cost synergy dimensions was the Bank of America purchase of Continental Bank. In this case, the retail-oriented, California-based Bank of America acquired the wholesale-oriented, Chicago-based Continental Bank. The objective of Bank of

America was to sell fee-based services—especially those with a strong technology base—to Continental's corporate customers.[9] Research has shown that corporate customers stay very loyal to a bank even after acquisition.

In a comprehensive study, A. Berger and D. Humphrey used data from 1981 to 1989 to analyze the cost savings from megamergers, which they defined as when the acquirer's and the target bank's assets exceeded $1 billion. They could find very little evidence of potential gains from economies of scale and scope. Indeed, the cost savings they could find were related to improved managerial efficiency (X efficiency).[10,11] In a more recent study of nine megamergers by Rhoades[12] (seven of the nine occurring since 1990), large cost savings were found. Specifically, four of the nine mergers showed significant cost efficiency gains relative to a peer group of nonmerged banks and seven of the nine showed a significant improvement in their return on assets. Interestingly, where cost efficiency gains were *not* realized, the major problems came from integrating data processing and operating systems.

Revenue Synergies

The revenue synergies argument has three dimensions. First, revenues may be enhanced by acquiring a bank in a growing market.

Second, the acquiring bank's revenue stream may become more stable if the asset and liability portfolio of the target institution exhibits different credit, interest rate, and liquidity risk characteristics from the acquirer.[13] For example, real estate loan portfolios showed very strong regional cycles in the 1980s. Specifically, U.S. real estate declined in value in the Southwest, followed by the Northeast, followed by California with a long and variable lag. Thus, a geographically diversified real estate portfolio may be far less risky than one in which both acquirer and target specialize in a single region.[14] Recent studies confirm risk diversification gains from geographic expansions.[15]

Third, there is an opportunity for revenue enhancement by expanding into markets that are less than fully competitive. That is, banks may be able to identify and expand geographically into those markets where *economic rents* potentially exist but where such entry will not be viewed as being potentially anticompetitive by regulators. Arguably, one of the great potential benefits of the Nationsbank and

---

[9]These services include derivatives, FX trading, and cash management (such as lockboxes).

[10]X efficiencies are those cost savings not directly due to economies of scope or economies of scale. As such, they are usually attributed to superior management skills and other difficult-to-measure managerial factors. To date, the explicit measurement of what comprises these efficiencies remains to be established in the empirical banking literature.

[11]A. Berger and D. B. Humphrey, "Megamergers in Banking and the Use of Cost Efficiency as an Antitrust Defense," *The Anti Trust Bulletin* 37 (1992), pp. 541–600.

[12]S. A. Rhoades, "The Efficiency Effects of Bank Mergers: An Overview of Case Studies of Nine Mergers," *Journal of Banking and Finance* 22, No. 3 (1998), pp. 273–92.

[13]See B. Esty et al., "Interest Rate Exposure and Bank Mergers," *Journal of Banking and Finance,* February 1999, Vol. 23, pp. 255–285, for evidence on the opposing interest rate risk exposures of acquirers and targets.

[14]As a result, the potential revenue diversification gains for more geographically concentrated mergers such as Bank of America and Security Pacific are likely to be relatively low; for example, both were heavily exposed to California real estate loans.

[15]M. Levonian, "Interstate Banking and Risk," Federal Reserve Bank of San Francisco, *Weekly Letter* 94–26 (1994); W. Lee, "The Value of Risk Reduction to Investors," unpublished Research Paper 9312, Federal Reserve Bank of New York, 1993; and P. S. Rose, "The Diversification and Cost Effects of Interstate Banking," *The Financial Review,* 13 (May 1996), pp. 431–51.

FIGURE 22–1

The Branching Presence of BankAmerica as a Result of Its Merger with Nationsbank

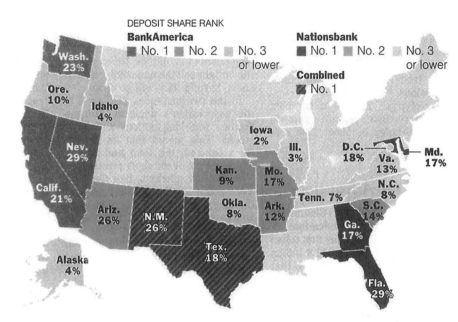

DEPOSIT SHARE RANK

BankAmerica   **Nationsbank**
■ No. 1 ■ No. 2 ▨ No. 3 or lower   ■ No. 1 ■ No. 2 ▨ No. 3 or lower

Combined
▨ No. 1

Source: *New York Times,* April 14, 1998, p. D1. Copyright © 1998 by The New York Times. Reprinted by permission.

BankAmerica merger is the potential for enhanced revenue diversification due to the lack of overlap of the branch networks of the two systems due to the merger. The new bank will have a branching presence in 22 states and an 8.3 percent share of federally insured banking deposits (see Figure 22–1).

To the extent that geographic expansions of the NationsBank–BankAmerica kind are viewed as enhancing the monopoly power of an FI, regulators may act to prevent a merger unless the merger produces potential efficiency gains that cannot be reasonably achieved by other means.[16] In recent years, the ultimate enforcement of antimonopoly laws and guidelines has fallen to the U.S. Department of Justice. In particular, the Department of Justice has laid down guidelines regarding the acceptability or unacceptability of acquisitions based on the potential increase in concentration in the market in which an acquisition takes place, with the cost-efficiency exception just noted.[17]

---

[16]U.S. Department of Justice, "Horizontal Merger Guidelines," April 2, 1982. In should also be added that the Riegle-Neal Act of 1994 placed a maximum 10 percent cap on the market share of the national (insured) deposit base held by any bank. As of 1998, the national insured deposit base was $3.5 trillion. This suggests that the new BankAmerica may be limited by this cap if it seeks further acquisitions beyond its current 8.3 percent national market share.

[17]The Federal Reserve also has the power to approve or disapprove mergers among state member banks and bank holding companies. The Comptroller of the Currency has similar powers over nationally chartered banks. The Federal Reserve's criteria are similar to those of the Department of Justice in that they take into account the HHI (market concentration index). However, it also evaluates the risk effects of the merger. The Department of Justice has powers to review the decisions made by the bank regulatory agencies. For example, in 1990 and 1991, the Department of Justice successfully challenged two mergers approved by the Federal Reserve Board. These two mergers eventually went ahead only after the acquiring bank had divested some branches and offices. The two mergers were First Hawaiian's acquisition of First Interstate of Hawaii and the Society–Ameritrust merger. See D. Palia, "Recent Evidence of Bank Mergers," *Financial Markets, Instruments, and Institutions* 3, no. 5 (1994), pp. 36–59, for further details.

The HHI
An index or measure of market concentration based on the squared market shares of market participants.

These merger guidelines are based on a measure of market concentration called the Herfindahl-Hirschman Index (**HHI**). This index is created by taking the percentage market shares of each firm in a market, squaring them, and then adding these squared shares. Thus, in a market where a single firm had a 100 percent market share, the HHI would be

$$HHI = (100)^2 = 10,000$$

Alternatively, in a market in which there was an infinitely large number of firms of equal size, then

$$HHI = 0$$

Thus, the HHI must lie between 0 and 10,000.

Whether a merger will be challenged under the Department of Justice guidelines depends on the postmerger HHI level. As you can see in Table 22–5, the Department of Justice defines a *concentrated* market as having a postmerger HHI ratio of 1,800, a moderately concentrated market as having a ratio of 1,000 to 1,800, and an unconcentrated market as having a ratio of less than 1,000. In either a concentrated or a moderately concentrated market, postmerger HHI increases of 100 or more may be challenged.[18] For example, consider a market that has three banks with the following shares:

Bank A = 50%
Bank B = 46%
Bank C = 4%

The premerger HHI for the market is

TABLE 22–5   1982 Department of Justice Horizontal Merger Guidelines

Postmerger Market Concentration	Level of Herfindahl-Hirschman Index	Postmerger Change in Herfindahl-Hirschman Index and Likelihood of a Challenged Merger
Highly concentrated	Greater than 1,800	Greater than 100—likely to be challenged 50 to 100—depends on other factors* Less than 50—unlikely to be challenged
Moderately concentrated	1,000–1,800	Greater than 100—likely to be challenged; other factors considered* Less than or equal to 100—unlikely to be challenged
Unconcentrated	Less than 1,000	Any increase—unlikely to be challenged

*In addition to the postmerger concentration of the market and the size of the resulting increase in concentration, the department will consider the presence of the following factors in deciding whether to challenge a merger: ease of entry; the nature of the product and its terms of sale; market information about specific transactions; buyer market characteristics; conduct of firms in the market; and market performance. [For a detailed explanation of these factors see Sections III(B) and III(C) of the 1982 Department of Justice Merger Guidelines.]

Source: Department of Justice, Merger Guidelines, 1982.

---

[18]In practice, it is only when the change exceeds 200 in banking that a challenge may occur. This is the case because banking is generally viewed as being more competitive than most industries. See Department of Justice, "Horizontal Merger Guidelines."

$$HHI = (50)^2 + (46)^2 + (4)^2 = 2{,}500 + 2{,}116 + 16 = 4{,}632$$

Thus, the market is highly concentrated according to the Department of Justice guidelines.

Suppose Bank A wants to acquire Bank C so that the postacquisition market would exhibit the following shares:[19]

$$A + C = 54\%$$
$$B = 46\%$$

The postmerger HHI would be

$$HHI = (54)^2 + (46)^2 = 2{,}916 + 2{,}116 = 5{,}032$$

Thus, the increase or change in the HHI ($\triangle$HHI) postmerger is

$$\triangle HHI = 5032 - 4632 = 400$$

Since the increase is 400, which is more than the 100 benchmark defined in the Department of Justice guidelines, the market is heavily concentrated and the merger could be challenged.[20]

Interestingly, comparing asset concentrations by bank size, the recent merger wave in banking appears to have reduced the national asset share of the very smallest banks (under $100 million) from 16.1 percent in 1984 to 5.7 percent in 1997 while increasing the relative size of the very biggest banks (over $10 billion) from 34.5 percent in 1984 to 60.2 percent in 1997. The relative market shares of intermediate-sized banks appear to have remained relatively stable (see Table 22–6). However, even though the degree of concentration of assets among the largest banks has increased, the percentage share exhibited by the largest U.S. banks is still well below the shares attained by the largest Canadian and European banks in their domestic markets.

Concept Questions

1. What recent bank mergers have been motivated by cost synergies?
2. What are the three dimensions of revenue synergy gains?
3. Suppose five firms in a banking market each have a 20 percent share. What is the HHI?

---

[19]Here we consider the effect on the HHI of a within-market acquisition; similar calculations can be carried out for between-market acquisitions.

[20]There are two problems of interpretation of the HHI in the context of banking and financial services. First, what is the relevant geographic scope of the market for financial services—national, regional, or city? Second, once that market is defined, do we view banks, thrifts, and insurance companies as separate or unique lines of business, or are they competing in the same financial market? That is, what defines the institutional scope of the market? In the case of financial services, it has been traditional to define markets on functional, or line of business, criteria, so that commercial banking is a separate market from savings (thrift) banking and other financial services. Further, the relevant market area has usually been defined as highly localized: the standard metropolitan statistical areas (SMSAs) or rural areas (non-SMSAs). Unfortunately, such definitions become increasingly irrelevant in a world of greater geographic and product expansions. Indeed, the use of HHIs should increasingly be based on regional or national market lines and include a broad financial service firm definition of the marketplace. Indeed, in recent years the Federal Reserve has often included one-half of thrift deposits in calculating bank market HHIs.

TABLE 22–6   U.S. Bank Asset Concentration, 1984 versus 1997

	1997				1984			
	Number	Percent of Total	Assets	Percent of Total	Number	Percent of Total	Assets	Percent of Total
All FDIC-insured Commercial Banks	9,308		4,771,200		14,483		2,508,871	
1. Under $100 million	6,047	65.0%	$ 273,400	5.7%	12,044	83.2%	$ 404,223	16.1%
2. $100 million–$1 billion	2,888	31.0	711,000	14.9	2,161	14.9	513,912	20.5
3. $1–$10 billion	306	3.3	916,000	19.2	254	1.7	725,947	28.9
4. $10 billion or more	67	0.7	2,870,800	60.2	24	0.2	864,789	34.5

Source: General Accounting Office, *Interstate Banking,* GAO/GGD, 95–35, December 1994, p. 101; and *FDIC Quarterly Banking Profile,* September, 1997.

Other Market- and Firm-Specific Factors Impacting Geographic Expansion Decisions

In addition to regulation and cost and revenue synergies, other factors may impact an acquisition decision. For example, an acquiring bank may be concerned about the solvency and asset quality of a potential target bank in another region. Thus, important factors influencing the acquisition decision may include the target bank's leverage and capital ratio, its loss reserves, and the amount of nonperforming loans in its portfolio.

A study by R. P. Beatty, A. M. Santomero, and M. L. Smirlock analyzed the factors potentially impacting the attractiveness of bank mergers and identified some 13 factors or variables, many of them bank specific. In particular, they analyzed 149 bank acquisitions over the period 1984–85; they measured the attraction of the merger by the size of the **merger premium** the acquiring bank was willing to pay for a target bank. Analytically, we measure this premium by the ratio of the purchase price of the target bank's equity to its book price or the market to book ratio (see Chapter 20).

Merger Premium
The ratio of the purchase price of a target bank's equity to its book value.

The variables analyzed, their average values, and the expected direction of their effect on the merger premium appear in Table 22–7, panel (a), with the regression results in panel (b). As you can see, 6 of the 13 variables are bank-specific variables measuring the quality of the bank and 3 variables are regulatory variables reflecting the degree of barriers to entry into the market of the target bank. Two variables are market structure variables reflecting the possibilities of revenue synergies and rents from entry as measured by the market HHI and the deposit share of the target bank. Panel (b) indicates that the highest merger premiums are paid for well-managed banks in relatively uncompetitive environments.[21]

In a recent review of a number of studies that analyzed the determinants of merger bid premiums (the ratio of the purchase price of a target bank's equity to its book value), Darius Palia found some support for the Beatty, Santomero, and Smir-

---

[21]R. P. Beatty, A. M. Santomero, and M. L. Smirlock, "Bank Merger Premiums: Analysis and Evidence," the Salomon Center Monograph Series in Economics and Finance, New York University, 1987.

TABLE 22–7   Determinants of Bank Merger Premiums

(a) Variable Definitions and Expected Coefficient Signs

	Variable	Definition	Average	Expected Sign
Bank Variables	TREAS	Ratio of U.S. Treasury investments to total assets	.203	−
	LNTOAST	Ratio of net loans to total assets	.482	?
	PROV	Ratio of loan loss provision to net loans	.007	+
	CHARGOFF	Ratio of loan write-offs to net loans	.008	−
	ROEQ	Ratio of net income to equity capital	.091	+
	CAPDEV	(ratio of loan loss allowance plus equity capital to assets) − .06	.030	−
Regulatory Variables	UNIT	Equals 1 if acquired bank located in unit bank state and zero otherwise	.276	+
	MULTI	Equals 1 if state law permits multi-bank holding companies and zero otherwise	.002	?
	ELECT	Equals 1 if state law permits statewide electronic banking and zero otherwise	.397	−
Market Structure Variables	MS	Ratio of bank's total deposits to those of the market; its market share	.179	+
	HERF	The Herfindahl index of that target bank's market	.253	+
Other Variables	PURCH	Equals 1 if the acquisition was a purchase of the acquired bank	.609	?
	COMB	Equals 1 if the acquisition involved a combination of cash and equity shares	.166	?

(b) Bank Merger Premium Regression Equation Results*

$$
\begin{aligned}
\text{Premium} = \ & 1.927^{*\dagger} && - .771\,\text{TREAS}^{*\dagger} && - .574\,\text{LNTOAST}^{*\dagger} && + 10.438\,\text{PROV} \\
& (9.27) && (-2.76) && (-1.96) && (1.41) \\
& - 6.684\,\text{CHARGOFF} && - 1.786\,\text{CAPDEV}^{*\dagger} && + .510\,\text{ROEQ}^{*\dagger} && + .096\,\text{UNIT}^{*\dagger} \\
& (-1.08) && (-1.76) && (2.10) && (1.66) \\
& - .506\,\text{MULTI} && - .061\,\text{ELECT} && - .306\,\text{MS}^{*\dagger} && + .392\,\text{HERF}^{*\dagger} \\
& (-1.26) && (-1.19) && (-1.66) && (1.70) \\
& - .176\,\text{PURCH}^{*\dagger} && - .171\,\text{COMB}^{*\dagger} \\
& (-2.85) && (-2.2)
\end{aligned}
$$

$R^2 = .121$ number of observations = 264   F-statistic = $2.68^{*\dagger}$

*T-statistics in parentheses below estimated coefficients.

†Coefficient on variable or test statistic significant at the 10 percent level.

Source: R. P. Beatty, A. M. Santomero, and M. L. Smirlock, "Bank Merger Premiums: Analysis and Evidence," *The Salomon Center Monograph Series on Economics and Finance,* 1987. Reprinted by permission.

---

lock findings.[22] Specifically, other empirical studies appear to confirm that premiums are higher (1) in states with the most restrictive regulations and (2) for target banks with high-quality loan portfolios. Palia also concludes that the growth rate of the target bank has little effect on bid premiums, while the results for the effects on bid premiums of target bank profitability and capital adequacy are rather mixed.

---

[22]Palia, "Recent Evidence of Bank Mergers," ibid.

Concept Questions

1. Suppose you are a manager of a bank looking at another bank as a target for acquisition. What three characteristics of the target bank would most attract you?
2. Given the same scenario as in question (1), what three characteristics would most discourage you?

The Success of Geographic Expansions

As you can see, a variety of regulatory and economic factors impact the attractiveness of geographic expansions to an FI manager. In this section, we evaluate some of the empirical evidence on the success of market extension mergers. There are at least two levels at which such an evaluation can be done: First, how did investors react when an interstate bank merger was announced? Second, once interstate bank mergers have taken place, do they produce, in aggregate, the expected gains in efficiency and profitability?

Investor Reaction

Abnormal Returns
Risk-adjusted stock returns above expected levels.

Researchers have conducted a number of studies on both nonbank and bank mergers, looking at the announcement effects of mergers on bidding and target firms' share values. They measure the announcement effect by the reaction of investors in the stock market to the news of a merger event. In particular, economists have been interested in whether a merger announcement generates positive **abnormal returns**—risk-adjusted stock returns above normal levels—for the bidding and/or target firms. Unlike commercial firms, where the typical study finds that only target firms' shareholders gain from merger announcements through significantly positive abnormal returns, studies in banking find that occasionally both the acquiring bank and the target bank gain.[23] For example, M. Millon-Cornett and S. De studied interstate merger proposals during the period 1982–86. They found that on the day of the merger announcement, bidding bank stockholders enjoyed positive abnormal returns of 0.65 percent while target bank shareholders enjoyed 6.08 percent abnormal returns. They also found that bidding bank returns were higher for those banks seeking to acquire targets in states with more restrictive banking pact laws, that prohibited nationwide entry and where the target bank was not a failed bank. Studies by A. Desai and R. Stover and C. James and P. Weir also report significant abnormal returns for bidding bank stockholders even for intrastate mergers. Nevertheless, other studies—for example, by G. Hawawini and I. Swary—find negative returns for bidding banks.[24] Table 22–8 summarizes these and other findings.

---

[23]See, for example, N. Travlos, "Corporate Takeover Bids, Methods of Payment, and Bidding Firm Stock Returns," *Journal of Finance* 42 (1987), pp. 943–63.

[24]M. Millon-Cornett and S. De, "Common Stock Returns in Corporate Takeover Bids: Evidence of Interstate Bank Mergers: *Journal of Banking and Finance* 15 (1991), pp. 273–95; A. Desai and R. Stover, "Bank Holding Company Acquisitions, Stockholders Returns, and Regulatory Uncertainty," *Journal of Financial Research* 8 (1985), pp. 145–56; C. James and P. Weir, "Returns to Acquirers and Competition in the Acquisition Market: The Case of Banking," *Journal of Political Economy* 95 (1983), pp. 355–70; and G. Hawawini and I. Swary, *Mergers and Acquisitions in the U.S. Banking Industry* (Amsterdam: North Holland, 1990), p. 211.

TABLE 22–8   Summary of Event Studies

Study	Sample	Definition of Event*	Definition of Market†	Target's Excess Returns‡	Acquirer's Excess Returns
Baradwaj, Dubofsky, and Fraser, 1991	108 interstate (July 1981–87)	1	Nasdaq value weighted	N/A	Negative
Baradwaj, Fraser, and Furtado, 1990	23 hostile 30 nonhostile (1980–87)	1	OTC equally weighted	Positive	Negative
Cornett and De, 1991a	152 interstate 152 acquirers 37 targets (1982–86)	1,4 5	Equally weighted, value weighted	Positive	Positive
Cornett and De, 1991b	132 interstate 132 acquirers 36 targets (1982–86)	1,4 5	Equally weighted, value weighted	Positive	Positive
Cornett and Tehranian, 1992	30 mergers (1982–87)	10	Equally weighted	Positive	Negative
Desai and Stover, 1985	18 BHCs (1976–82)	1,2 3	Equally weighted	N/A	Positive
Dubofsky and Fraser, 1989	101 mergers (1973–83)	1	Equally weighted, value weighted	N/A	Positive (before June 1981), negative (after June 1981)
Hannan and Wolken, 1989	43 acquirers 69 targets (1982–87)	1	Wilshire Index	Positive	Negative
Hawawini and Swary 1990	78 acquirers 123 targets (1971–86)	1,2	Nasdaq value weighted	Positive	Negative
James and Weir, 1987a	60 mergers (1972–83)	1	Equally weighted	N/A	Positive
Kaen and Tehranian, 1989	33 New Hampshire mergers (June 1979–87)	1,7 9	Nasdaq equally weighted bank index	N/A	Zero
Lobue, 1984	37 BHCs (N/A)	3	OTC general market index and OTC banking index	N/A	Positive
Neely, 1987	26 mergers (1979–85)	1,5	Creates bank index from S&P	Positive	Negative
Palia, 1994	48 mergers (1984–87)	1	Nasdaq value weighted	N/A	Negative
Sushka and Bendeck, 1988	41 mergers (1972–85)	2	Uses mean adjusted returns model	N/A	Negative
Trifts and Scanlon, 1987	21 interstate 14 acquirers 17 targets (1982–85)	1	S&P 500 index	Positive	Negative
Wall and Gup, 1989	23 mergers (June 1981–83)	1	Value weighted	N/A	Negative

*The event dates among the various studies are coded (for easy presentation) as follows: 1 = *Wall Street Journal* announcement date; 2 = Federal Reserve Board approval date; 3 = acquisition completion date; 4 = Dow Jones News Wire announcement date; 5 = *New York Times* announcement date; 6 = American Banker announcement date; 7 = Cates MergerWatch announcement date; 8 = American Banker announcement date; 9 = Union Leader announcement date; 10 = Shearson Lehman Brothers' Bank Merger and Acquisition study announcement date.

†Whenever the study specifies that Nasdaq stocks have been included in the market portfolio, we explicitly specify so. Otherwise, we present the market portfolio as an equally weighted and/or value weighted portfolio. Other market portfolios (such as the Standard & Poor's 500 Index) are also presented.

‡We do not present the actual excess returns earned because many studies provide results for a larger number of differing event windows (which are not comparable). Accordingly, we present whether the excess returns were positive or negative. N/A stands for not available or not examined.

Source: Darius Palia, "Recent Evidence of Bank Mergers," *Financial Markets, Instruments, and Institutions* 3, no. 5 (1994), pp. 36–59.

Postmerger Performance

Even though the expectation, on announcement, might be favorable for enhanced profitability and performance as a result of an interstate geographic expansion, are such mergers actually proving successful in the postmerger period? M. Millon-Cornett and H. Tehranian have looked at the postacquisition performance of large bank mergers between 1982 and 1987. Using operating cash flow (defined as earnings before depreciation, goodwill, interest on long-term debt, and taxes) divided by assets as a performance measure, they found that merged banks tended to outperform the banking industry. They found that superior performance resulted from improvements in these banks' ability to (1) attract loans and deposits, (2) increase employee productivity, and (3) enhance asset growth. K. Spong and J. D. Shoenhair studied the postmerger performance of banks that merged interstate in 1985, 1986, and 1987; they found that acquired banks either maintained or increased earnings and demonstrated some success in controlling and reducing overhead and personnel costs. The acquired banks also tended to become more active lenders.[25] J. Boyd and S. Graham[26] looked at small bank mergers (merged banks have combined total deposits less than $400 million) from 1989 through 1991. Comparing industry-adjusted return on assets (ROA) before versus after a merger, they found that 1989 mergers saw large ROA increases, 1991 mergers saw decreases, and 1990 mergers were somewhere in the middle. However, for all years the merged banks outperformed the banking industry. Finally, deLong found that mergers that "focused" activities but diversified geographically, over the 1988–95 period, improved the performance of the merging firms more than any other type of financial service firm mergers.

Thus, both the announcement effect studies and the postmerger performance studies generally support the existence of gains from domestic geographic expansions by U.S. commercial banks.

Concept Questions

1. If the abnormal returns for target banks are usually positive, does this mean that managers of acquiring banks tend to overpay the shareholders of the target bank?
2. In general, what do studies of the announcement effect and postmerger performance conclude?

---

[25]M. Millon-Cornett and H. Tehranian, "Changes in Corporate Performance Associated with Bank Acquisitions," *Journal of Financial Economics* 31 (1992), pp. 211–34; and K. Spong and J. D. Shoenhair, "Performance of Banks Acquired on an Interstate Basis," Federal Reserve Bank of Kansas City, *Financial Industry Perspectives,* December 1992, pp. 15–23.

[26]J. D. Boyd and S. L. Graham, "Consolidation in U.S. Banking: Implications for Efficiency and Competitive Risk," *Bank Mergers and Acquisitions,* eds. T. Amihud and G. Miller (Amsterdam: Kluwer, 1998); and G. deLong, "Domestic and International Bank Mergers: The Gains from Focusing versus Diversifying," Ph.D. dissertation, Stern School of Business, New York University, 1998.

Summary

Domestic geographic expansions are one way in which an FI can improve its return-risk performance. This chapter reviewed the various restrictions existing in the United States that inhibit geographic expansions for different types of FIs. While, traditionally, commercial banks have faced the most restrictions on their geographic expansions (especially in their branching activities), these restrictions have recently been removed. Partly as a result of this and other factors relating to cost and revenue synergies, the U.S. financial system is now in a dramatic period of consolidation. This consolidation has resulted in a number of megamergers among large FIs and the movement of the United States toward a nationwide banking system similar to those that exist in Canada and major European countries.

Questions and Problems

1. How do limitations on geographic diversification affect an FI's profitability?

2. How are insurance companies able to offer services in states beyond their state of incorporation?

3. In what way did the Garn-St Germain Act and FIRREA provide incentives for the expansion of interstate branching?

4. Why were unit and money center banks opposed to bank branching in the early 1900s?

5. In what ways did the banking industry continuously succeed in maintaining interstate banking activities during the 50-year period beginning in the early 1930s? What legislative efforts did regulators use to respond to each foray by banks into previously prohibited banking and commercial activities?

6. What is the difference between an MBHC and an OBHC?

7. What is an interstate banking pact? How did the three general types of interstate banking pacts differ in their encouragement of interstate banking?

8. What significant economic events during the 1980s provided the incentive for the Garn-St Germain Act and FIRREA to allow further expansion of interstate banking?

9. What is a nonbank bank? What legislation allowed the creation of nonbank banks? What role did nonbank banks play in the further development of interstate banking activities?

10. How did the development of the nonbank bank competitive strategy further clarify the meaning of the term *activities closely related to banking?* In a more general sense, how has this strategy assisted the banking industry in its attempts to provide services and products outside the strictly banking environment?

11. How did the provisions of the Riegle-Neal Interstate Banking and Branching Efficiency Act of 1994 allow for full interstate banking? What are the expected profit performance effects of interstate banking? What has been the impact on the structure of the banking and financial services industry?

12. Bank mergers often produce hard to quantify benefits called X efficiencies and costs called X inefficiencies. Give an example of each.

13. What does the Berger and Humphrey study reveal about the cost savings from bank mergers? What differing results are revealed by the Rhoades study?

14. What are the three revenue synergies that may be obtained by an FI from expanding geographically?

15. What is the Herfindahl-Hirschman Index? How is it calculated and interpreted?

16. City Bank currently has a 60 percent market share in banking services, followed by NationsBank with 20 percent and State Bank with 20 percent.

    a. What is the concentration ratio as measured by the Herfindahl-Hirschman Index (HHI)?

    b. If City Bank acquires State Bank, what will the new HHI be?

    c. Assume that the Justice Department will allow mergers as long as the changes in HHI do not exceed 1,400. What is the minimum amount of assets that City Bank will have to divest after it merges with State Bank?

17. The Justice Department has been asked to review a merger request for a market with the following four FIs:

Bank	Assets
A	$ 12 million
B	$ 25 million
C	$102 million
D	$ 3 million

    a. What is the HHI for the existing market?

    b. If bank A acquires bank D, what will be the impact on the market's level of concentration?

c. If bank C acquires bank D, what will be the impact on the market's level of concentration?

d. What is likely to be the Justice Department's response to the two merger applications?

18. The Justice Department measures market concentration using the HHI of market share. What problems does this measure have for (*a*) multiproduct FIs and (*b*) FIs with global operations?

19. What factors other than market concentration does the Justice Department consider in determining the acceptability of a merger?

20. What are some plausible reasons for the percentage of small banks decreasing and the percentage of large banks increasing while the percentage of intermediate banks has stayed constant since 1984?

21. According to empirical studies, what factors have the highest impact on merger premiums as defined by the ratio of a target bank's purchase price to book value?

22. What are the results of studies that have examined the mergers of banks, including postmerger performance? How do they differ from the studies examining mergers of nonbanks?

23. What are some of the important firm-specific financial factors that influence the acquisition of an FI?

24. How has the performance of merged banks compared to that of bank industry averages?

25. What are some of the benefits for banks engaging in geographic expansion?

GEOGRAPHIC
DIVERSIFICATION
International

Introduction

Many FIs can diversify domestically, but only the very largest can aspire to diversify beyond national frontiers. In this chapter we analyze recent trends toward the globalization of FI franchises and examine the potential return-risk advantages and disadvantages of such expansions. While FIs from some countries, such as the United States, are currently seeking to expand internationally as fast as possible, others, most notably those from Japan, are contracting their international operations. In the Contemporary Perspectives box on p. 538, the case of Travelers, the U.S. financial conglomerate that has merged with Citicorp, acquiring a stake in Nikko, the third largest Japanese securities firm, is discussed, while in the Contemporary Perspectives box on p. 542, the inclination of Japanese banks to shrink their international operations is described.

Global and International Expansions

There are at least three ways an FI can establish a global or international presence: (1) selling financial services from its domestic offices to foreign customers, such as a loan originated in the New York office of Chase made to a Brazilian manufacturer, (2) selling financial services through a branch, agency, or representative office established in the foreign customer's country, such as making a loan to the Brazilian

Contemporary Perspectives

TRAVELERS DEAL WITH NIKKO

$1.6 Billion Investment in Securities Venture

Peter Truell

With the world's most powerful financial companies rushing to build global franchises, **Travelers Group** Inc. and the **Nikko Securities** Company are expected to announce today an extensive partnership in the securities business, with Travelers investing about $1.6 billion to acquire as much as a quarter of Japan's third-largest brokerage firm.

The deal—which would also involve the Travelers brokerage subsidiary, Salomon Smith Barney, in forming a Japanese joint venture with Nikko—is to be announced in Tokyo by Sanford I. Weill, the chairman of Travelers, and Masashi Kaneko, the president of Nikko, at the end of the Japanese business day, executives involved in the negotiations said yesterday.

The last year has seen a blizzard of deal-making by Mr. Weill and Travelers, which acquired Salomon Inc. for $9 billion late last year, and then in April agreed to merge with **Citicorp** to form Citigroup in a pending $70 billion transaction. Competitors wonder how efficiently all these companies will work together.

A Travelers' investment in Nikko would be the first instance of a foreign company's buying a sizable stake in one of Japan's marquee financial names. It comes as Japan is preparing to open its financial markets in response to international pressure and to try to counter a prolonged economic downturn.

The investment, which would make Travelers the biggest shareholder in Nikko, shows how quickly national borders are breaking down in financial markets; even Japan, historically a protected market dominated almost exclusively by local brokerage firms, is now eager to embrace Wall Street investment and management.

Under the agreement, Nikko would join with Salomon's Japanese business to create Nikko Salomon Smith Barney Ltd., a joint venture, into which Nikko would put its capital markets and international businesses. The new joint venture company's chief executive would be Toshiharu Koyama, the head of Salomon's business in Japan, and it would be 51 percent owned by Nikko and 49 percent by Salomon, with each firm contributing six board members, according to the executives involved in the negotiations.

But Travelers through its investment in Nikko would be the more powerful partner. It would, under the accord to be announced today, buy 9.5 percent of Nikko's common stock, which has a current market value of about $540 million, and would also buy Nikko bonds that would be convertible into a further interest of about 15 percent of the brokerage firm, to give it about a 25 percent stake in the firm. Nikko is also expected to buy Travelers' shares in the open market to strengthen the link between the two companies.

Both companies declined to make any comment on their pending alliance over the weekend.

The Nikko investment carries big risks for Travelers, but also holds out the prospect of huge rewards if the joint venture works well and Travelers becomes the first Amer-

customer through Chase's branch in Brazil, and (3) selling financial services to a foreign customer through subsidiary companies in the foreign customer's country, such as Chase buying a Brazilian bank and using that wholly owned bank to make loans to the Brazilian customer. Note that these three methods of global activity expansion are not mutually exclusive; an FI could use all three simultaneously to expand the scale and scope of its operations.

U.S. banks, insurance companies, and securities firms have all expanded abroad in recent years, often through branches and subsidiaries; this has been reciprocated by the entrance and growth until recently of foreign FIs in U.S. financial service markets. Table 23–1 shows that 15 banks had more than 48 percent of their assets outside their home countries. These include a number of European banks as well as U.S. banks such as Bankers Trust, J. P. Morgan, and Citigroup. Noticeably absent (as implied by the Contemporary Perspectives box on p. 542) are Japanese banks even though, based on size of assets, they are among the largest in the world.

Contemporary Perspectives

ican financial company to get extensive access to Japanese investors, who are currently estimated to have about $10 trillion of investments—mostly invested in bank and savings deposits that yield less than 1 percent a year. Others are racing to try to reach the same goal in other ways; earlier this year, **Merrill Lynch** & Company bought some of the branches of the recently defunct Yamaichi Securities, and hired many of its former executives.

The Travelers' move, which is much larger than the Merrill Lynch investment, also comes soon after the big Japanese brokerage firms—Nomura, Daiwa and Nikko—have been found guilty of, and sanctioned for, paying bribes to sokaiya, as Japan's racketeers are known.

After weeks of examining Nikko, Travelers, and particularly its Salomon Smith Barney subsidiary, is betting that the Japanese firm has since cleaned up its operations and that Nikko will readily adapt to American standards of business practice and accounting in the new joint venture. Salomon and Nikko have, one insider said, already hired Davis, Polk & Wardell to write a new compliance code for the venture.

But it is unlikely that the culture of Japan's securities firms can be changed overnight. Until recently, industry analysts said, they did business in a cozy, protected and often corrupt world.

In March, Moody's Investors Service, the credit rating agency, lowered its rating for the senior debt of Nikko Securities, citing its concerns about the "relatively slow pace

of introducing new products, rationalizing its expense base, and implementing efficient management tools."

In addition, Japan's financial markets are a complex web of entrenched relationships; it is unclear, for example, how the Mitsubishi Bank, which has historically been close to Nikko Securities, may react to Travelers' move.

But the pending alliance shows how eager Mr. Weill and his colleagues are to get access to the financial markets of the world's second largest economy, and its tens of millions of savers. Japanese investors are more interested in overseas investments, in part because their own institutions have generally offered them low-yielding investments and have been mired in scandal.

Under the pending agreement, Salomon would group its 700 employees in Japan with more than 600 from Nikko to form the core of the joint venture. Nikko would also merge its main international operations—in New York, London and Hong Kong—with those of Salomon Smith Barney. The new joint venture would begin operating in January 1999. Nikko, meanwhile, would retain its asset management and its network of offices in Japan that deal with ordinary investors. But these offices would offer financial products marketed by Travelers and later Citigroup.

Next, we concentrate on the global growth of banking. We begin with U.S. bank expansions abroad and the factors motivating these expansions and then move on to foreign bank expansions into the United States.

U.S. Banks Abroad

While some U.S. banks, such as Chase and J. P. Morgan, have had offices abroad since the beginning of the century, the major phase of growth began in the early 1960s after the passage of a law restricting domestic U.S. banks' ability to lend to U.S. corporations that wanted to make investments overseas. The major law restricting this activity, the Overseas Direct Investment Control Act of 1964, was eventually repealed; however, it created incentives for U.S. banks to establish offices offshore to service the overseas funding and other business needs of their U.S. clients. This offshore funding and lending in dollars created the beginnings of a

TABLE 23–1   The World's Most Active International Banks

Global Survey Ranking	World Ranking	Country of Origin and Date of Figures for Business Overseas	Business Overseas 1996–1997, %	Business Overseas 1995–1996, %	Total Assets, $m	Income Overseas 1996–1997, %	Income Overseas 1995–1996, %	Staff Overseas 1993–1996, %	Staff Overseas 1995–1996, %	USA Total Assets June 1997, $m
1	94	Standard Chartered UK, 12/96	74.34	73.11	71,554	83.43	80.87	88.69	89.00	5,827
2	22	Credit Suisse Group Switzerland, 12/96	74.21	68.72	389,300	47.60	41.42	32.36	29.08	189,804
3	10	Union Bank of Switzerland Switzerland, 12/96	71.00	67.00	324,756	NA	NA	26.00	24.00	78,884
4	3	Credit Agricole Indosuez France, 12/96	70.30	NA	477,336	61.00	56.00	59.00	NA	133,654
5	28	Swiss Bank Corporation Switzerland, 12/96	64.60	58.00	267,339	39.20	36.40	34.40	33.60	53,866
6	1	HSBC Holdings UK, 12/96	62.80	64.80	401,686	63.80	62.40	55.80	54.30	38,833
7	5	Citicorp USA, 12/96	59.63	57.62	281,018	56.65	57.36	51.67	56.27	Domestic
8	26	Comp. Financière de Paribas France, 12/96	55.61	50.00	290,720	45.86	28.68	31.98	NA	56,315
9	41	Crédit Lyonnais France, 12/96	52.50	46.40	310,040	41.00	44.00	35.00	34.00	44,000
10	153	Creditanstalt–Bankverein Austria, 12/96	52.31	49.92	62,774	16.76	14.38	20.57	16.31	17,669
11	115	Erste Bank Austria, 12/96	50.98	49.33	69,228	NA	NA	3.00	3.00	2,399
12	23	J.P. Morgan USA, 12/96	50.92	46.15	222,026	59.22	55.40	NA	NA	Domestic
13	56	Bankers Trust USA, 12/95	49.50	48.30	104,002	28.00	NA	27.3	NA	Domestic
14	8	ABN AMRO Bank Netherlands, 12/96	49.39	44.00	341,396	52.81	48.29	50.83	45.70	61,313
15	141	Allied Irish Banks Ireland, 12/96	48.83	51.12	43,936	49.44	50.00	50.37	49.00	11.167

NA = not available.
Source: *The Banker,* February 1998, p. 41, reprinted by permission of *The Banker,* London, England.

market we now call the Eurodollar market. The term *Eurodollar transaction* usually denotes a banking transaction booked externally to the boundaries of the United States, often through an overseas branch or subsidiary.[1]

Table 23–2 shows the aggregate size of U.S. bank activities abroad through direct and holding company subsidiaries as well as the different types of activities those subsidiaries engage in. As can be seen, the number of foreign subsidiaries of U.S. banks grew from 622 and $159 billion in assets in 1987 to 849 and $491 billion in assets in 1996. That is, in less than a decade the assets of U.S. bank subsidiaries abroad tripled. We examine the factors encouraging and deterring U.S. banks' international expansions next. Many of these factors are important to U.S. insurance companies and securities firms' international expansion decisions as well.

---

[1]That is, the definition of a Euro transaction is more general than "a transaction booked in Europe." In fact, any deposit in dollars taken externally to the United States normally qualifies that transaction as a Euro transaction.

TABLE 23–2 U.S. Bank Subsidiaries Abroad in 1987 and 1996

Primary Activity	1987					1996				
	No. of Subsidiaries	Total Assets	Net Income	Percent of ROA	Subsidiaries with Profit	No. of Subsidiaries	Total Assets	Net Income	Percent of ROA	Subsidiaries with Profit
Commercial finance	36	2813.1	54.3	1.93	63.3	28	7264.5	67.8	0.93	75.0
Consumer finance	26	4175.3	68.5	1.64	76.9	10	8391.9	135.2	1.61	73.7
Foreign bank	116	67761.3	325.7	0.46	72.4	104	129653.4	1912.8	1.48	85.6
Insurance underwriting	3	262.3	1.9	7.27	100.0	11	3481.9	103.2	2.96	90.9
Leasing	82	6751.9	−44.8	−0.66	65.9	88	12112.5	404.0	3.34	87.6
Nonbank credit agency	70	5654.7	45.2	0.8	76.7	158	41078.7	436.7	1.06	69.0
Other holding companies	85	27685.4	279.9	1.01	67.1	181	56744.1	3008.4	5.12	72.4
Securities	103	33192.9	−317.1	−0.96	68.0	113	220373.8	1340.4	0.61	90.3
All foreign subsidiaries with total assets of $1 million or more	622	159226.7	577.4	0.36	70.6	849	491806.1	7796.5	1.59	77.9

Total assets and net income are in millions of dollars. ROA and percent of subsidiaries with profits are in percentage points.

Source: G. Whalen, "The Securities Activities of The Foreign Subsidiaries of U.S. Banks: Evidence on Risk And Returns," White Paper 98–2, OCC, Washington, D.C., February 1998, Table 1.

JAPAN BANKS THAT VENTURED ABROAD COME BACK HOME

When Hokuriku Bank Ltd., a small lender based in the central Japanese city of Toyama, announced it was "coming back home" and shutting its branches in New York, London and Hong Kong, it was the latest in a wave of Japanese banks to withdraw from overseas.

And it was yet another sign that many Japanese lenders, saddled with trillions of yen worth of bad loans and pressed to reduce their assets, are shrinking from their role as major players in international finance.

"We were the princes of capital, and we believed we were almighty," said Kaneo Muromachi, senior managing director and head of the international division of Sanwa Bank Ltd., recalling the late 1980s, when Japanese banks expanded around the world.

Today, as lenders increasingly compete with foreign banks at home and Japan deregulates its financial markets, withdrawal from overseas is increasingly an option.

The list of banks that have pulled back from the global arena this year includes some of the biggest names in Japanese finance: Hokkaido Takushoku Bank Ltd., one of 10 nationwide lenders, Nippon Credit Bank Ltd., one of three long-term credit banks, and Ashikaga Bank Ltd., one of the largest regional lenders.

Last week, Sumitomo Bank Ltd., Japan's second-largest bank, said it was considering selling Sumitomo Bank of California, the state's fifth-largest bank.

Other Japanese lenders are slimming down their businesses in the United States and Europe while expanding or maintaining their Asian branches.

In the six years to 1987, Japanese banks doubled their loan assets at overseas branches, to 40.6 trillion yen ($313.03 billion) from 19.4 trillion yen. By 1986, they had become the world's biggest lenders, according to the Bank for International Settlements.

Then, in 1990, the Japanese asset bubble burst. During the last seven years the benchmark Nikkei 225-stock index has lost almost 60 percent of its value, while property prices have plunged 70 percent in urban centers.

That has left banks, which count profits they see on stock holdings as capital, with big dents in their capital-to-assets ratio. It also left them with an estimated 28 trillion yen worth of bad loans as of the end of March.

The deputy director of the Finance Ministry's banking bureau, Sei Nakai, said the ministry, which regulates the industry, would step in before any bank defaulted on foreign clients.

Even the top 19 nationwide banks, which had a total of 364 overseas branches or offices at the end of March, will not all be able to maintain their positions abroad, analysts say.

Source: *Herald Tribune,* December 10, 1997, p. 2. Bloomberg News.

Factors Encouraging U.S. Bank Expansions Abroad.   While regulation of off-shore lending was the original impetus for the early growth of the Eurodollar market and the associated establishment of U.S. branches and subsidiaries abroad, other regulatory and economic factors have also impacted the growth of U.S. offshore banking. These factors are discussed next.

The Dollar as an International Medium of Exchange.   The growth of international trade after the Second World War and the use of the dollar as an international medium of exchange encouraged foreign corporations and investors to demand dollars. A convenient way to do this was by using U.S. banks' offshore offices to intermediate such fund flows between the United States and foreign demand. Today, trade-related transactions underlie much of the activity in the Eurodollar market.[2]

---

[2]The decline in the dollar relative to the yen and mark in recent years has weakened the role of the dollar as the international medium of exchange.

However, with the emergence of the new single "euro" currency in 1999, the importance of the dollar as the "international medium of exchange" may well decline, especially among major European corporations.

Political Risk Concerns.   Political risk concerns among countries from Asia, the old Eastern or Communist bloc, and Latin America have led to enormous flows of dollars offshore, often to U.S. branches and subsidiaries in the Cayman Islands and the Bahamas, where there are very stringent bank secrecy rules. The Contemporary Perspectives box on p. 546 discusses the role that centers such as the Cayman Islands play in offshore banking.

Domestic Activity Restrictions.   As we discussed in Chapter 21, U.S. banks have faced considerable activity restrictions at home regarding their securities, insurance, and commercial activities. However, with certain exceptions, Federal Reserve regulations allow U.S. banking offices abroad to engage in the permitted banking activities of the foreign country even if such activities are not permitted in the United States. For example, U.S. banks setting up subsidiaries overseas can engage in leasing real property, act as general insurance agents, and underwrite and deal in foreign corporate securities (up to a maximum commitment of $2 million). Moreover, in a recent study Whalen[3] has shown that many of these nonbanking activities produce revenue flows that have a low or negative correlation with the revenues from domestic banking. That is, international expansions appear to produce important revenue-risk diversification benefits for U.S. banks.

Technology and Communications Improvements.   The improvements in telecommunications and other communications technologies such as CHIPS (the international payment system) as well as the development of proprietary communication networks by large FIs have allowed U.S. parent banks to extend and maintain real-time control over their overseas operations at a decreasing cost. The decreasing operating costs of such expansions have made it feasible to locate offices in an even wider array of international locations.

Factors Deterring U.S. Expansions Abroad.   However, there are also a number of potential factors deterring international expansion, as discussed next.

Capital Constraints.   The phasing in of the 1993 risk-based capital requirements over the 1988–92 period meant that a number of large global U.S. banks, such as Chase, had to scale back their activities to be in a position to meet the 8 percent target. However, this constraint is currently nonbinding given the large excess capital positions of U.S. banks (see Chapter 20).

Emerging Market Problems.   The financial collapse of Mexico in 1994 and the problems of other emerging-market countries such as Korea, Thailand, and Indonesia in 1997 and 1998 have made many U.S. banks more cautious in expanding outside traditional overseas markets despite the existence of an increasingly favorable regulatory environment. For example, the 1994 **NAFTA** agreement has given U.S. (and Canadian) banks greater powers to expand into Mexico. See Table 23–3 for

NAFTA
The North American Free
Trade Agreement.

---

[3]See G. Whalen, "The Securities Activities of the Foreign Subsidiaries of U.S. Banks: Evidence of Risk and Returns," White Paper 98–2, OCC, Washington, D.C., February 1998.

TABLE 23–3   The NAFTA Agreement and U.S. Banks

- Any bank chartered in Canada or the United States, including Canadian or U.S. banks owned by nondomestic banks, may establish a bank subsidiary in Mexico that may expand in Mexico without geographic restriction. Canadian and U.S. banks, however, may not branch directly into Mexico.
- Banks from Mexico and Canada may establish direct branches and subsidiaries in the United States subject to the same geographic restrictions imposed on direct branches of other nondomestic banks and on other U.S. chartered banks, respectively.
- Banks from the United States and Mexico that are not controlled by investors from other countries may establish Schedule II bank subsidiaries in Canada, which subsidiaries enjoy nationwide branching powers. Mexican and U.S. banks may not branch directly into Canada.

Notes:

1. Nondomestic banks cannot open branches but are allowed to establish Schedule II subsidiary banks in Canada. Schedule II subsidiary banks owned by banks from the United States or Mexico have the same nationwide branching privileges as domestic Canadian banks. Schedule II banks owned by banks from other countries must seek government approval to open additional branches. This geographic restriction on Schedule II subsidiaries will be eliminated when the latest round of GATT comes into effect.

2. Mexico does not permit nondomestic banks to establish domestic branches. However, nondomestic banks can establish representative offices and offshore branches and take minority interests in local banking institutions. In addition, under NAFTA, banks from the United States and Canada, including U.S. and Canadian banks owned by banks from other countries, are allowed to establish bank subsidiaries with the same nationwide branching privileges as Mexican banks.

Source: Institute of International Bankers, *1994 Global Survey of Regulatory and Market Developments in Banking, Securities and Insurance,* September 1994, p. 17.

details on the NAFTA agreement.[4] The December 1997 agreement by 100 countries reached under the auspices of the World Trade Organization (WTO) is also an important step toward dismantling the regulatory barriers inhibiting the entry of U.S. FIs into emerging-market countries.[5]

Competition.   In the mid-1990s, U.S. banks faced extensive and increasing competition from Japanese banks for overseas business. Aiding the Japanese banks was their access to a large domestic savings base at a relatively low funding cost, the relatively slow pace of deregulation in the Japanese domestic financial markets, and their size. However, in recent years, as the Japanese economy has moved into recession and the bad debts of Japanese banks have mounted, the main competitive threat to U.S. banks has come from European banks.

For example, for most of the 1990s, Japan has had 9 of the 10 largest banks, measured by asset size, in the world. While large size doesn't necessarily mean high profits,[6] it gives a bank a greater ability to diversify across borders (and products) and to attract business by aggressively cutting fees and spreads in selected areas.

Aiding the competitive position of European banks has been the passage of the European Community (EC) Second Banking Directive, which has created a single banking market in Europe. Under the Directive, European banks are allowed to

---

[4]For an excellent discussion of the potential effects of NAFTA on U.S. banks, securities firms, and insurance companies, see R. S. Sczudio, "NAFTA: Opportunities Abound for U.S. and Canadian Financial Institutions," *Bankers Magazine,* July–August 1993, pp. 28–32.

[5]See, *New York Times,* "Accord Is Reached to Lower Barriers in Global Finance," December 12, 1997, p. A1.

[6]In fact, Credit Lyonnais is a good example of why large size does not necessarily correlate with high profitability. In spring 1995, the French government had to bail out the bank by shifting its bad loans into a newly created entity. In addition, most Japanese banks have had severe problems with bad loans in recent years, which has meant a reduced tendency to expand abroad further.

branch and acquire banks throughout the European Community—that is, they have a single EC passport.[7] While the Second Banking Directive didn't come fully into effect until the end of 1992, it had been announced as early as 1988. As a result, there has been a cross-border merger wave among European banks that has paralleled the current U.S. domestic merger and acquisition wave.[8] In addition, a number of European banks have formed strategic alliances that will enable retail bank customers to open new accounts, access account information, and make payments to third parties through any of the branches of the member banks in the alliance. This greater consolidation in European banking has created more intense competition for U.S. and other overseas banks in European wholesale markets as well as making it more difficult for them to penetrate European retail markets.

Foreign Banks in the United States

Just as U.S. banks can profitably expand into overseas markets, foreign banks have historically viewed the United States as an attractive market for entry.

Organizational Form.   The five primary forms of entry by foreign banks into the U.S. market are discussed next.

Subsidiary.   A foreign bank subsidiary has its own capital and charter; it operates in the same way as any U.S. domestic bank, with access to both retail and wholesale markets.

Branch.   A branch bank is a direct expansion of the parent bank into an overseas or U.S. banking market. As such, it is reliant on its parent bank, such as Sumitomo Bank in Japan, for capital support; normally, it has access to both wholesale and retail deposit and funding markets.

Agency.   An agency is a restricted form of entry; this organizational form restricts access of funds to those borrowed on the wholesale and money markets. A special case of an agency is a New York Agreement Company that has both agency functions and limited investment banking functions.

Edge Act Corporation.   An Edge Act Corporation is a specialized organizational form open to U.S. domestic banks since 1919 and to foreign banks since 1978. These banks specialize in international trade-related banking transactions or investments.

Representative Office.   Even though a representative office books neither loans nor deposits in the United States, it acts as a loan production office, generating loan business for its parent bank at home. This is the most limited organizational form for a foreign bank entering the United States.[9]

---

[7]Direct branching by non-EC banks into member states was not governed by the Second Banking Directive but the laws of each member state. Currently, all EC countries allow foreign banks to branch.

[8]See A. Cybo-Ottone and M. Murgia, "Mergers and Acquisitions in the European Banking Markets," *Journal of Banking and Finance,* forthcoming.

[9]Also note the existence of International Banking Facilities (IBF) in the United States since 1981. These are specialized vehicles that are allowed to take deposits from and make loans to foreign (non-U.S.) customers only. As such, they are essentially offshore banking units that operate onshore. Most are located in New York, Illinois, and California and are generally free of U.S. bank regulation and taxes.

GRAND CAYMAN FIGHTS OFF ILLICIT IMAGE

George Graham

A travel tip for visitors to the Cayman Islands: don't mention how much you enjoyed Tom Cruise in The Firm. The film, in which Cruise's Mafiosi employers use the Caribbean islands for their illicit financial dealings, still rankles in Cayman.

Cayman has been trying hard to establish itself as a *bona fide* financial centre whose attraction lies in the sophistication of its banking, accounting, and legal infrastructure, not in a "no questions asked" attitude.

"We want to focus on keeping our jurisdiction a quality jurisdiction for quality money. Our message must be clear: dirty money is not welcome here," said Mr. John Owen, governor of the British dependent territory.

With 47 of the world's 50 largest banks now operating in Grand Cayman, the island would appear to have made its point with the financial sector. More than $500bn of deposits now make it by some measures the world's fifth largest financial centre.

"We are comparing ourselves more to places like New York and London than to other offshore centres," said Mr. Jürg Kaufmann, executive director of Swiss Bank Corp's Cayman affiliate and president of the Cayman Islands Bankers' Association.

"All we can say is we believe the Cayman Islands to be a legitimate jurisdiction only interested in good quality business. We've been telling as many people as we can and I think we've been able to convince the professionals," said Mr. Gerald Williams, managing director of the Cayman operation of Coutts, the private banking arm of the UK's National Westminster Bank.

With a broader public, however, the image embodied in The Firm is harder to shake off.

Over the last 10 years, Cayman has taken a series of legislative steps to tackle criminal financial activities.

A mutual legal assistance treaty with the US, signed in 1986 and ratified in 1990, provides for the exchange of information between law enforcement agencies.

Legislation in 1992 made the laundering of drug money a criminal offence and obliged banks to report suspicious transactions. Last year, Cayman followed that by becoming the first Caribbean country to extend its money laundering legislation to cover all serious crimes—though with tax offences explicitly excluded.

In this area Cayman has been well ahead of Bermuda, which a decade ago would probably have been considered a much more cautious and restrictive jurisdiction, let alone territories with more rudimentary regulatory structures such as Anguilla or St. Vincent.

"We are proud of the fact that the new criminal proceeds law is a flag-flying operation. It states exactly what sort of business we are prepared to look at and what we are not," said Mr. Peter Larder, managing director of CIBC Bank and Trust Co, a subsidiary of Canada's CIBC group and one of Cayman's largest banks. "Smaller jurisdictions may not be ready to cast aside the more questionable kinds of business."

Trends and Growth.   Table 23–4 shows the rapid expansion of foreign banks in the United States. In 1980 foreign banks had $166.7 billion in assets (10.8 percent of the size of total U.S. bank assets). This activity reached a peak in 1992, when foreign banks had $514.3 billion in assets (16.4 percent of the size of U.S. assets). Since 1997, there has been a modest retrenchment in the asset share of foreign banks in the United States. In 1997, their U.S. assets totaled $601.8 billion (14.7 percent of the size of U.S. assets). This recent retrenchment reflects a number of factors, including the highly competitive market for wholesale banking in the United States, a decline in average U.S. loan quality, capital constraints on Japanese banks at home and their poor lending performance at home and the introduction of the Foreign Bank Supervision and Enhancement Act (FBSEA) of 1991, which tightened regulations on foreign banks in the United States (discussed below). Whether this retrenchment is temporary or permanent remains to be seen and may depend on the competitive effects of recent regulatory actions in the United States and the

Contemporary Perspectives

Detective Inspector Brian Gibbs, who served for 30 years with London's Metropolitan Police before setting up Cayman's financial investigations unit in 1989, says he has received around 500 reports of suspicious transactions since the drug money laundering legislation came into effect in 1992, and 80 per cent of those were subsequently identified as crime-related.

Two local banks which had been involved in a series of US and Canadian investigations have been closed down, and almost every bank now operating in Cayman is a subsidiary of a major international banking group.

As a result, Cayman is no longer reckoned to be a choice venue for money launderers. Local lawyers say that they used to receive a steady stream of two or three injunctions a month seeking to freeze assets held in Cayman, but that has dried to a trickle.

Cayman's bankers, too, say it is now extremely rare for someone to arrive in their offices with a suitcase full of cash, and they are unanimous that anyone who did would be sent packing.

Cash couriers do still arrive—one was arrested recently by Cayman customs officers with $80,000 strapped to his body—but local officials say they are more likely to try to filter the cash through real estate agents or company managers than directly through a bank.

One critical problem for Cayman—and still more so for smaller offshore financial centres—is supervisory resources. The island government has now merged its financial services supervision department with its currency board to create a separate monetary authority.

But the government is still seeking a permanent head for the authority. Mrs. Jennifer Dilbert, the longtime inspector of financial services, moved to the private sector to head Deutsche Morgan Grenfell's Cayman operation, and Mr. John Fleming, who succeeded her, resigned recently, leaving Mr. Mitchell Scott as acting managing director.

Mr. Michael Foot, head of banking supervision at the Bank of England, warned the Cayman government this week that effective supervision will require a substantial commitment of resources.

"The maintenance of adequate provisions against money laundering doesn't come cheap," he told a Cayman conference on the prevention of money laundering this week.

That is a price that Cayman will have to pay if it is to fulfil its ambition of competing not with Anguilla and the Bahamas but with London and New York.

Source: *Financial Times,* January 10, 1997. Reprinted with permission from the January 10, 1997, issue of Financial Times.

restructuring of the Japanese financial system (especially in regards to their problem loans domestically and to other Asian countries).[10]

Regulation of Foreign Banks in the United States.   Before 1978, foreign branches and agencies entering the United States were licensed mostly at the state level. As such, their entry, regulation, and oversight were almost totally confined to the state level. Beginning in 1978 with the passage of the International Banking Act (IBA) and the more recent passage of the Foreign Bank Supervision Enhancement

---

[10]J. Peek, E. Rosengren, and F. Kasirye, "The Poor Performance of Foreign Subsidiaries: Were the Problems Acquired or Created?" *Journal of Banking and Finance,* forthcoming, find that many foreign banks acquiring U.S. banks have been hurt by the fact that the target banks already had problems at the time of acquisition. Moreover, they find that the changes in strategy introduced by foreign owners were generally insufficient in raising the performance of foreign banks relative to U.S. domestically owned peer banks.

TABLE 23–4   U.S. and Foreign Bank Assets, 1980–1997

	Bank Assets Held in United States (billions of dollars)	
	U.S.-Owned	*Foreign-Owned*
1980	$1,537.0	$166.7
1985	2,284.8	175.5
1990	3,010.3	389.6
1991	3,068.7	467.3
1992	3,138.4	514.3
1993	3,204.6	427.9
1994	3,409.9	471.1
1995	3,660.6	530.1
1996	3,812.6	601.8
1997	4,083.6	642.3

Source: *Federal Reserve Bulletin,* various issues, Tables 1.25 and 1.26.

Act (FBSEA), Title II of the FDICIA, of December 1991, federal regulators have been exerting increasing control over foreign banks operating in the United States.

The International Banking Act of 1978

Pre-IBA.   Before its passage in 1978, foreign agencies and branches entering the United States with state licenses had some competitive advantages and disadvantages relative to most domestic banks. On the one hand, as state-licensed organizations, they were not subject to the Federal Reserve's reserve requirements, Federal Reserve audits and exams, interstate branching restrictions (the McFadden Act), or restrictions on corporate securities underwriting activities (the Glass-Steagall Act). However, they had no access to the Federal Reserve's discount window (i.e., lender of last resort), no direct access to Fedwire and thus the fed funds market, and no access to FDIC deposit insurance.

Their inability to gain access to deposit insurance effectively precluded them from the U.S. retail banking markets and its deposit base. As a result, prior to 1978, foreign banks in the United States largely concentrated on wholesale banking.

Post-IBA.   The unequal treatment of domestic and foreign banks regarding federal regulation and lobbying by domestic banks regarding the unfairness of this situation provided the impetus for Congress to pass the International Banking Act in 1978. The fundamental regulatory philosophy underlying the IBA was one of **national treatment.** This philosophy attempted to lay down a level playing field for both domestic and foreign banks in U.S. banking markets. As a result of this act, foreign banks were required to hold Federal Reserve-specified reserve requirements if their worldwide assets exceeded $1 billion, made subject to Federal Reserve examinations, and made subject to both the McFadden and Glass-Steagall Acts. With respect to the latter, an important grandfather provision was inserted into the act that allowed foreign banks established in the United States prior to 1978 to keep their illegal interstate branches and securities-activity operations. That is, interstate and

National Treatment
Regulating foreign banks in the same fashion as domestic banks or creating a level playing field.

security activity restrictions were applied only to new foreign banks entering the United States after 1978.[11]

If anything, the passage of the IBA accelerated the expansion of foreign bank activities in the United States. A major reason for this was that for the first time, the IBA gave foreign banks access to the Federal Reserve's discount window (lender of last resort facility), Fedwire, and FDIC insurance.

In particular, access to FDIC insurance allowed entry into retail banking. For example, in 1979 alone foreign banks acquired four large U.S. banks (Crocker, National Bank of North America, Union Planters, and Marine Midland). In addition, in the early 1980s the Bank of Tokyo, Mitsubishi Bank, and Sanwa Bank invested $1.3 billion in California bank acquisitions. Overall, Japanese banks owned over 25 percent of California bank assets at the end of the 1980s. (By the end of the 1990s, many of these Japanese-owned California banks assets were up for sale.)

The Foreign Bank Supervision Enhancement Act (FBSEA) of 1991.   Along with the growth of foreign bank assets in the United States came concerns about foreign banks' rapidly increasing share of U.S. banking markets as well as about the weakness of regulatory oversight of many of these institutions. This latter concern was compounded by three events that focused attention on the weaknesses of foreign bank regulation. The first event was the collapse of the Bank of Credit and Commerce International (BCCI), which had a highly complex international organizational structure based in the Middle East, the Cayman Islands, and Luxembourg and had undisclosed ownership stakes in two large U.S. banks (see Figure 23–1). BCCI was not subject to any consolidated supervision by a home country regulator; this quickly became apparent after its collapse, when massive fraud, insider lending abuses, and money-laundering operations were discovered. The second event was the issuance of more than $1 billion in unauthorized letters of credit to Saddam Hussein's Iraq by the Atlanta agency of the Italian Banca Nazionale del Lavoro. The third event was the unauthorized taking of deposit funds by the U.S. representative office of the Greek National Mortgage Bank of New York.

These events and related concerns led to the passage of the Foreign Bank Supervision Enhancement Act (FBSEA) of 1991. The objective of this act was to extend federal regulatory authority over foreign banking organizations in the United States, especially where these organizations have entered using state licenses. The act had five main features that have significantly enhanced the powers of federal bank regulators over foreign banks in the United States.[12]

1. *Entry.* Under FBSEA, the Fed's approval is now needed to establish a subsidiary, branch, agency, or representative office in the United States. The approval applies to both a new entry and an entry by acquisition. To get Fed approval, a number of standards have to be met, two of which are mandatory. First, the foreign bank must be subject to comprehensive supervision on a consolidated basis by a home

---

[11]For example, in 1978, some 60 foreign banks had branches in at least three states. As noted earlier, the McFadden Act prevented domestic banks from engaging in interstate branching.

[12]See S. Bellanger, "Stormy Weather: The FBSEA's Impact on Foreign Banks," *Bankers Magazine,* November–December 1992, pp. 25–31; M. Gruson, "Are Foreign Banks Still Welcome in the United States?" *Bankers Magazine,* September–October 1992, pp. 16–21; and GAO, "Foreign Banks: Implementation of the Foreign Bank Supervision and Enhancement Act of 1991," GAO/GGD–96–187, September 1996, Washington, D.C.

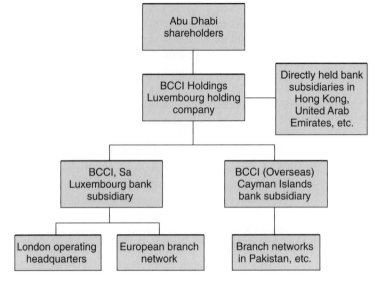

Source: U.S. General Accounting Office, *International Banking,* GAO/GGD–94–68 (1994), p. 17.

country regulator.[13] Second, that regulator must furnish all the information needed by the Federal Reserve to evaluate the application. Both standards are aimed at avoiding the lack of disclosure and lack of centralized supervision associated with BCCI's failure.

2. *Closure.* The act also gives the Federal Reserve power to close a foreign bank if its home country supervision is inadequate, if it has violated U.S. laws, or if it is engaged in unsound and unsafe banking practices.

3. *Examination.* The Federal Reserve has the power to examine each office of a foreign bank, including its representative offices. Further, each branch or agency has to be examined at least once a year.

4. *Deposit taking.* Only foreign subsidiaries with access to FDIC insurance can take retail deposits under $100,000. This effectively rolls back the provision of the IBA that gave foreign branches and agencies access to FDIC insurance.

5. *Activity powers.* Beginning on December 19, 1992, state-licensed branches and agencies of foreign banks could not engage in any activity not permitted to a federal branch.[14]

Overall, the FBSEA considerably increased the Federal Reserve's authority over foreign banks and added to the regulatory burden or costs of entry into the United States. Indeed, between 1993 and 1995 federal bank supervisors issued 40 formal enforcement actions against foreign banks operating in the United States. In the most serious case, the Japanese Daiwa bank was ordered to cease its U.S. bank-

---

[13]A requirement for consolidated supervision has also been proposed by the Bank for International Settlements in its "Minimum Standards for the Supervision of International Banking Groups and Their Cross Border Establishments," Basel, Switzerland, June 1992.

[14]See M. Gruson, "Non-Banking Investments and Activities of Foreign Banks in the United States," paper presented at the Salomon Center, New York University, Conference on Universal Banking, February 23–24, 1995.

ing operations. Underlying its forced closure were losses by a single bond trader that had been concealed by Daiwa's management from U.S. regulators for over six weeks, and that amounted to over $1 billion. In January 1996 Daiwa's U.S. bank assets were sold to Sumitomo Bank of Japan, and in February 1996 Daiwa paid a fine of $340 million to the U.S. authorities for settlement of charges against the bank. This sent a strong signal regarding the willingness of the authorities to take a tough stand against errant foreign banks.

Concept Questions

1. What regulatory and economic factors have encouraged the growth of U.S. offshore banking? What factors have deterred U.S. offshore banking?
2. What are the primary forms of entry by foreign banks into the U.S. market?
3. What impact did the passage of the International Banking Act of 1978 have on foreign bank activities in the United States?

Advantages and Disadvantages of International Expansion

So far, we have laid out the historical and recent trends affecting the geographic expansion of FIs both into and outside the United States. Here we summarize the advantages and disadvantages of international expansions to the individual FI seeking to generate additional returns or better diversify its risk.

Advantages

These are the six major advantages of international expansion:[15]

Risk Diversification.   As with domestic geographic expansions, an FI's international activities potentially enhance its opportunity to diversify the risk of its earning flows. Often, domestic earnings flows from financial services are strongly linked to the state of that economy. Therefore, the less integrated the economies of the world are, the greater is the potential for earnings diversification through international expansions.[16] International expansions can also reduce risk if the FI can undertake activities that are not permitted domestically but that have a low, or negative, correlation with domestic activities.

---

[15]See, for example, L. Goldberg and A. Saunders, "The Causes of U.S. Bank Expansion Overseas: The Case of Great Britain," *Journal of Money Credit and Banking* 12 (1980), pp. 630–44; Goldberg and Saunders, "The Growth of Organizational Forms of Foreign Banks in the U.S.," *Journal of Money Credit and Banking* 13 (1981), pp. 365–74; Goldberg and Saunders, "The Determinants of Foreign Banking Activity in the United States," *Journal of Banking and Finance* 5 (1981), pp. 17–32; C. W. Hultman and L. R. McGee, "Factors Affecting the Foreign Banking Presence in the United States," *Journal of Banking and Finance* 13 (1989), pp. 383–96; and L. M. Aguilar, "A Current Look at Foreign Banking in the United States and Seventh District," Federal Reserve Bank of Chicago, *Economic Perspectives,* 1994, pp. 20–28.

[16]G. Whalen, in "The Securities Activities–" provides empirical evidence on the benefits of international expansions as a mechanism of reducing risk. For example, he finds that for 1987–96 domestic bank and foreign insurance underwriting had a return correlation that was highly negative: −0.56.

Economies of Scale.   To the extent that economies of scale exist, by expanding its activities beyond domestic boundaries, an FI can potentially lower its average operating costs.

Innovations.   An FI can generate extra returns from new product innovations if it can sell such services internationally rather than just domestically. For example, consider complex financial innovations, such as securitization, caps, floors, and options, that FIs have innovated in the United States and sold to new foreign markets with few domestic competitors. It has been argued that the increasing dominance of U.S. securities firms in Japan is attributable to their comparative advantage and knowledge on risk management techniques and the use of derivatives compared to domestic Japanese securities firms.[17] However, the large losses incurred by many of these U.S. securities firms from trading in Asian and Russian markets in 1998 raise doubts about the size of any such comparative advantage.

Funds Source.   International expansion allows an FI to search for the cheapest and most available sources of funds. This is extremely important given the very thin profit margins in domestic and international wholesale banking. Also, it reduces the risk of fund shortages (credit rationing) in any one market.

Customer Relationships.   International expansions also allow an FI to maintain contact with and service the needs of domestic multinational corporations. Indeed, one of the fundamental factors determining the growth of FIs abroad has been the parallel growth of foreign direct investment and foreign trade by globally oriented multinational corporations from the FI's home country.[18]

Regulatory Avoidance.   To the extent that domestic regulations such as activity restrictions and reserve requirements impose constraints or taxes on the operations of an FI, seeking out low regulatory tax countries can allow an FI to lower its net regulatory burden and to increase its potential net profitability.

Disadvantages

These are the three major disadvantages of international expansion:

Information/Monitoring Costs.   While global expansions give an FI the potential opportunity to better diversify its geographic risk, the absolute level of exposure in areas such as lending can be high, especially if the FI fails to diversify in an optimal fashion. For example, the FI may fail to choose a loan portfolio combination

---

[17]In 1998, Merrill Lynch absorbed 30 branches and 2,000 employees of the defunct Yamaichi Securities (traditionally the fourth largest domestic securities firm in Japan). In the same year Travelers (and its Salomon Securities subsidiary) bought a 25 percent share in Nikko Securities (traditionally the third largest securities firm in Japan). The comparative advantage of US. FIs over Japanese FIs in risk management is discussed in "Rich Pickings for the Gaijin," *The Economist,* May 16, 1998, p. 83.

[18]R. Seth et al. "Do Banks Follow their Customers Abroad?" *Financial Markets, Instruments and Institutions* (1998, No. 4.), find that the customer relationship is getting weaker as banks and firms become more global. For example, they find that foreign banks in the United States from Japan, Canada, the Netherlands, and the United Kingdom allocated a majority of their loans to non–home country borrowers over the 1981–92 period.

on the efficient lending frontier (see Chapter 12). Foreign activities may also be more risky for the simple reason that monitoring and information collection costs are often higher in overseas markets. For example, Japanese and German accounting standards differ significantly from the generally accepted accounting principles (GAAP) used by U.S. firms. In addition, language, legal, and cultural problems can impose further transaction costs on international activities. Finally, because the regulatory environment is controlled locally and regulation imposes a different array of net costs in each market, a truly global FI faces the problem of having to master the various rules and regulations in each market.

Nationalization/Expropriation.   To the extent that an FI expands by establishing a local presence through investing in fixed assets such as branches or subsidiaries, an FI faces the political risk that a change in government may lead to the nationalization of those fixed assets.[19] Further, if overseas FI depositors take losses following a nationalization, they may seek legal recourse from the FI in U.S. courts rather than from the nationalizing government. For example it took many years to resolve the outstanding claims of depositors in Citicorp's branches in Vietnam following the Communist takeover and expropriation of those branches.[20]

Fixed Costs.   The fixed costs of establishing overseas organizations may be extremely high. A U.S. FI seeking an organizational presence in the Tokyo banking market faces real estate prices significantly higher than those in New York. Such relative costs can be even higher if an FI chooses to enter by buying a Japanese bank rather than establishing a strategic alliance (as in the Travelers–Nikko Securities case). The reason is the considerable cost of acquiring Japanese equities measured by price-earnings ratios despite recent falls in the Nikkei Index. These relative cost considerations become even more important if there is uncertainty about the expected volume of business to be generated and thus revenue flows from foreign entry. The failure of U.S. acquisitions to realize expected profits following the 1986 "big bang" deregulation in the United Kingdom is a good example of unrealized revenue expectations vis-à-vis the high fixed costs of entry and the costs of maintaining a competitive position.[21]

Concept Questions

1. What are the major advantages of international expansion to an FI?
2. What are the major disadvantages of international expansion to an FI?
3. Comparing the advantages and disadvantages discussed above, why do you think so few U.S. banks have established branches in the Ukraine?

---

[19]Such nationalizations have occurred with some frequency in African countries.

[20]See G. Dufey and I. Giddy, "Eurocurrency Deposit Risk," *Journal of Banking and Finance* 8 (1984), pp. 567–89.

[21]The low return to U.S. banks in London following the United Kingdom's "big bang" in 1986 can be seen in Table 23–2. For example, the return on US. banks' foreign subsidiaries securities activities (assets) in 1987 were −0.96 percent. However, U.S. banks and securities firms have fared better in the Canadian "big bang" deregulation of securities business (see "Canada's Borrowing with Its Fat Fees Lures Wall Street," *New York Times,* April 15, 1995, p. D1).

Summary

In this chapter, we examined the potential return-risk advantages and disadvantages to FIs from international geographic expansions. While regulatory considerations and costs are fundamental to such decisions, several other economic factors play an important role in the net return or benefit-cost calculus for any given FI. For example, considerations such as earnings diversification, economies of scale and scope, extending customer relationships, and better exploiting financial service innovations, add to the potential benefits from international geographic expansions. However, there are also costs or risks of such expansions such as monitoring costs, expropriation of assets, and the fixed costs of market entry. Managers need to carefully weigh each of these factors before making a geographic expansion decision, whether international or domestic.

Questions and Problems

1. What are three ways in which an FI can establish a global or international presence?

2. How did the Overseas Direct Investment Control Act of 1964 assist in the growth of global banking activities? How much growth in assets occurred from the mid-1980s to the mid-1990s? Which types of bank subsidiaries seemed to receive the greatest benefits?

3. What is a Eurodollar transaction? What are Eurodollars?

4. Identify and explain the impact of at least four factors that have encouraged global U.S. bank expansion.

5. What was the initial impact of the implementation of the risk-based capital requirements on the international activities of some major U.S. banks?

6. What effect have the problems of emerging-market economies in the late 1990s had on the global expansion of traditional banking activities by U.S. banks?

7. What factors gave Japanese banks significant advantages in competing for international business for an extended period through the mid-1990s? What are the advantages of size in a competitive market? Does size necessarily imply high profitability?

8. What is the European Community (EC) Second Banking Directive? What impact has the Second Banking Directive had on the competitive banking environment in Europe?

9. Identify and discuss the various ways in which foreign banks can enter the U.S. market. What are international banking facilities?

10. What factors have led to a slowdown—indeed, a decrease—in the relative growth of the proportion of U.S. banking assets which are controlled by foreign banks?

11. What was the fundamental philosophical focus of the International Banking Act (IBA) of 1978?

    a. What advantages and disadvantages did foreign banks have relative to domestic banks before the passage of this legislation?

    b. What requirements were placed on foreign banks by the IBA?

    c. What was the likely effect of the IBA on the growth of foreign bank activities in the United States? Why?

12. What events led to the passage of the Foreign Bank Supervision Enhancement Act (FBSEA) of 1991? What was the main objective of this legislation?

13. What were the main features of FBSEA? How did FBSEA encourage cooperation with the home country regulator? What was the effect of the FBSEA on the Federal Reserve and on foreign banks?

14. What are the major advantages of international expansion to FIs? Explain how each advantage can affect the operating performance of FIs.

15. What are the difficulties of expanding globally? How can each of these difficulties create negative effects on the operating performance of FIs?

FUTURES AND FORWARDS

Introduction

In Chapter 13 we described the growth in FIs' off-balance-sheet activities. A major component of this has been the growth of derivative contracts such as futures and forwards. While a significant amount of derivatives reflect the trading activity of large banks and other FIs, many FIs (of all sizes) have used these instruments to hedge their asset-liability risk exposures. Indeed, as will be discussed in this chapter, derivative contracts—such as futures and forwards—potentially allow an

FI to manage (or hedge) its interest rate, foreign exchange (FX), and credit risk exposures and even its exposure to catastrophes such as hurricanes.

Table 24–1 lists the derivative contract holdings of all commercial banks, and specifically, the 25 largest U.S. banks, as of December 1997. The table shows notional (dollar) contract volumes for these 25 banks exceeding $24 trillion, while the other 450 bank and trust companies with derivatives activity report notional contract volumes of $356 billion. Table 24–1 shows the breakdown of those positions into futures and forwards, swaps, options, and credit derivatives. As can be seen, swaps ($9.56 trillion) are the largest group of derivatives, followed by futures and forwards ($9.47 trillion) and options ($5.96 trillion). The replacement cost of these derivative contracts for the top 25 derivative users is reported at $156 billion, while credit exposure is $312 billion (or 96.8 percent of the capital of these banks).[1]

The rapid growth of derivatives use by both FIs and firms has been controversial. As will be discussed in this chapter and the following two chapters, when employed appropriately, derivatives can be used to hedge (or reduce an FI's risk). However, when misused, derivatives can increase the risk of an FI's insolvency. A number of recent scandals involving FIs firms, and municipalities (such as Orange County) has led to a tightening of the accounting (reporting) requirements for derivative contracts. Specifically, as described in the Contemporary Perspectives box on p. 560, the Financial Accounting Standards Board (FASB) requires all derivatives to be marked to market and mandates that losses and gains be immediately transparent on FIs' and firms' financial statements by the year 2000.

In this chapter, we look at the role futures and forward contracts play in managing an FI's interest rate, FX, and credit risk exposures as well as their role in hedging natural catastrophes. We look at option-type derivatives and swaps in Chapters 25 and 26.

Forward and Futures Contracts

To understand the essential nature and characteristics of forward and futures contracts, we can compare them with spot contracts. We show appropriate time lines for each of the three contracts in Figure 24–1.

Spot Contracts

A spot contract is an agreement between a buyer and a seller at time 0, when the seller of the asset agrees to deliver the asset immediately and the buyer of the asset agrees to pay for that asset immediately.[2] Thus, the unique feature of a spot market is the immediate and simultaneous exchange of cash for securities, or what is often called *delivery versus payment*. A spot bond quote of $97 for a 20-year maturity bond would be the price the buyer would have to pay the seller, per $100 of face value, for immediate delivery of the 20-year bond.

---

[1] See Chapter 20 for a discussion of how the credit exposure of derivatives is calculated for regulatory reporting.

[2] Technically, physical settlement and delivery may take place one or two days after the contractual spot agreement in bond markets. In equity markets, delivery and cash settlement normally occur three business days after the spot contract agreement.

TABLE 24–1 Derivative Contracts: Notional Amount and Credit Equivalent Exposure of the 25 Commercial Banks and Trust Companies with the Most Derivative Contracts, September 1997

(in millions of dollars)

Rank	Bank Name	Total Assets	Derivative Contracts					Replacement Cost of All Contracts	RBC Add-on	Credit Exposure from All Contracts	Credit Exposure to Capital Ratio
			Futures and Forwards	Total Swaps	Total Options	Credit Derivatives	Total Derivatives				
1	Chase Manhattan Bank	$ 291,529	$3,176,381	$3,455,313	$ 999,928	$ 4,886	$7,636,508	$ 35,376	$ 39,618	$ 74,994	308.2
2	Morgan Guaranty Tr Co	201,145	1,465,381	2,873,646	1,741,057	23,592	6,103,678	56,798	46,558	103,356	736.9
3	Citibank NA	253,929	1,572,070	609,964	676,148	4,343	2,862,525	24,052	21,238	45,290	184.2
4	Bankers Trust Co	106,152	837,325	867,474	391,282	2,439	2,098,520	15,923	16,175	32,098	400.1
5	Nationsbank of NC NA	186,021	245,931	403,826	1,092,708	353	1,742,817	3,379	6,103	9,482	61.8
6	Bank of America NT and SA	235,952	943,508	518,075	168,956	204	1,630,743	7,892	10,828	18,720	83.4
7	First NB of Chicago	56,109	599,537	309,368	341,063	0	1,249,968	3,804	7,600	11,404	19.2
8	Republic NB of New York	51,350	158,848	42,843	105,438	251	307,380	3,458	2,374	5,833	159.5
9	Bank of New York	57,537	56,219	15,301	140,228	0	211,748	1,192	1,041	2,232	40.4
10	Bankboston NA	60,188	83,438	20,333	51,231	700	155,702	528	619	1,147	21.4
11	First Union NB of NC	109,113	35,414	60,335	19,510	6	115,265	542	500	1,042	11.0
12	State Street Bank & TC	35,892	105,544	3,645	755	0	109,944	976	989	1,965	100.1
13	Fleet National Bank	50,059	5,113	19,641	34,890	0	59,644	164	271	435	7.9
14	Wells Fargo Bank Na	89,529	7,172	18,998	30,286	0	56,455	285	223	508	6.5
15	Mellon Bank NA	37,806	31,994	12,974	6,333	0	51,300	405	373	778	18.0
16	Citibank South Dakota	14,757	12,278	13,378	11,928	0	37,584	103	55	158	7.6
17	Keybank NA	68,989	9,275	18,680	8,710	0	36,664	180	152	333	4.9
18	Nationsbank of Texas NA	54,012	2,487	13,401	18,461	0	34,348	170	177	347	8.2
19	Citibank Nevada NA	9,673	3,257	11,264	16,395	0	30,916	93	83	175	11.8
20	National City Bank	11,500	3,086	20,210	5,430	0	28,726	123	160	283	27.3
21	PNC Bank NA	57,649	6,071	9,981	11,523	0	27,573	153	77	230	4.0
22	Marine Midland Bank	31,196	3,222	10,544	9,396	0	23,162	61	36	97	3.8
23	Corestates Bank NA	44,430	4,518	11,869	5,844	0	22,231	182	116	298	6.6
24	Banc One NA	24,941	0	19,941	953	10	20,903	110	127	237	7.6
25	Chase Manhattan USA	27,176	8,967	8,675	765	0	18,407	108	58	166	5.1
	Total 25 commercial banks	$2,166,632	$9,377,033	$9,369,679	$5,889,216	$36,783	$24,672,712	$156,057	$155,552	$311,610	96.8[a]
	Other 450 commercial banks	$1,565,410	$ 88,261	$ 193,864	$ 71,383	$ 2,096	$ 355,605	$ 2,234	$ 1,761	$ 3,995	N/A
	Total for all banks	$3,732,042	$9,465,294	$9,563,543	$5,960,600	$38,880	$25,028,316	$158,292	$157,313	$315,604	6.4

[a]Average.

Source: Office of the Comptroller of the Currency.

557

FIGURE 24–1

Contract Time Lines

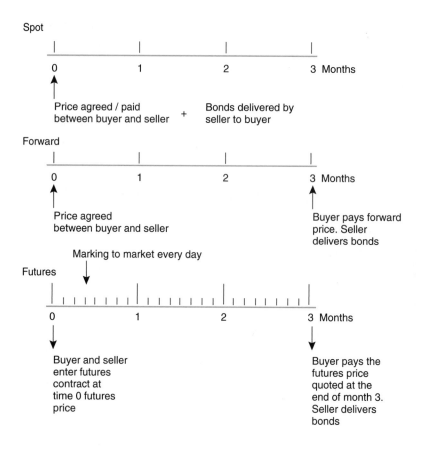

Forward Contracts

A forward contract is a contractual agreement between a buyer and a seller at time 0 to exchange an asset for cash at a later date. For example, in a three-month forward contract to deliver 20-year bonds, the buyer and seller would agree on a price and quantity today (time 0) but the delivery (or exchange) of the 20-year bond for cash would not occur until three months hence. If the forward price agreed to at time 0 was $97 per $100 of face value, in three months' time the seller would deliver $100 of 20-year bonds and receive $97 from the buyer. This is the price the buyer would have to pay and the seller would have to accept no matter what happened to the spot price of 20-year bonds during the three months between the time when the contract was entered into and the time when the bonds were delivered for payment.

Futures Contracts

Marking to Market
The process by which the prices on outstanding futures contracts are adjusted each day to reflect current futures market conditions.

A futures contract is normally arranged through an organized exchange. It is an agreement between a buyer and a seller at time 0 that an asset will be exchanged for cash at a later date. As such, a futures contract is very similar to a forward contract. The difference is that whereas the price of a forward contract is fixed over the life of the contract ($97 per $100 of face value for three months), futures contracts are **marked to market** daily. This means the contract's price is adjusted each day as the futures price for the contract changes. Therefore, actual daily cash settlements occur between the buyer and seller in response to this marking-to-market process. This can be compared to a forward contract, where the whole cash payment from buyer to seller occurs at the end of the contract period.[3]

Concept Questions

1. What is the difference between a futures contract and a forward contract?
2. What are the major differences between a spot contract and a forward contract?

Forward Contracts and Hedging Interest Rate Risk

Naive Hedge
When a cash asset is hedged on a direct dollar-for-dollar basis with a forward or futures contract.

To see the usefulness of forward contracts in hedging the interest rate risk of an FI, we consider a simple example of a **naive hedge.** Suppose an FI portfolio manager holds a 20-year $1 million face value bond on the balance sheet. At time 0, these bonds are valued by the market at $97 per $100 face value, or $970,000 in total. Assume the manager receives a forecast that interest rates are expected to rise by 2 percent from their current level of 8 to 10 percent over the next three months. Knowing that rising interest rates mean that bond prices will fall, the manager stands to make a capital loss on the bond portfolio. Having read Chapters 8 and 9, the manager is an expert in duration and has calculated the weighted-average life of the 20-year maturity bonds to be exactly 9 years. Thus, the manager can predict a capital loss or change in bond values (ΔP) from the duration equation of Chapter 9.[4]

$$\frac{\Delta P}{P} = -D \times \frac{\Delta R}{1 + R}$$

where

ΔP = Capital loss on bonds = ?
P = Initial value of bond position = $970,000
D = Duration of the bonds = 9 years
ΔR = Change in forecast yield = .02
$1+R$ = 1 plus the current yield on 20-year bonds = 1.08

$$\frac{\Delta P}{\$970,000} = -9 \times \left[\frac{.02}{1.08}\right]$$

$$\Delta P = -9 \times \$970,000 \times \left[\frac{.02}{1.08}\right] = -\$161,666.67$$

As a result, the FI portfolio manager would expect to make a capital loss on the bond portfolio of $161,666.67 (as a percentage loss ($\Delta P/P$) = 16.67%) or as a fall in price from $97 per $100 face value to $80.833 per $100 face value. To offset this loss—in fact, to reduce the risk of capital loss to zero—the manager may hedge this position by taking an off-balance-sheet hedge, such as selling $1 million face value

---

[3]Aside from the marking-to-market process, the two major differences between forwards and futures are that (1) forwards are tailor-made contracts while futures are standardized contracts and (2) forward contracts are bilateral contracts subject to counterparty default risk, while the default risk on futures is significantly reduced by the futures exchange guaranteeing to indemnify counterparties against credit or default risk.

[4]For simplicity, we ignore issues relating to convexity here.

BOARD GIVES FINAL APPROVAL TO NEW RULE ON DERIVATIVES

Melody Petersen

The nation's accounting rule makers said yesterday that they had given final approval to a new rule that will force companies to record the value of derivatives in their financial statements.

The move was immediately criticized by the banking industry and other groups, which have complained so loudly in Washington about the rule in recent months that a bill has been introduced to weaken the power of the private rule-making body, known as the Financial Accounting Standards Board.

Edmund L. Jenkins, the chairman of the accounting board, said that the new rule was needed to help protect investors in cases where companies might be investing heavily in derivatives that could result in huge losses. He added that the intense criticism had made it even more important for the board to act.

Several years ago, the accounting board decided to weaken another proposed rule on the accounting of employee stock options after companies complained to Congress.

"If the board had backed down on derivatives, I think it would have made it very difficult for the board to be an effective standard-setter in the future," Mr. Jenkins said. "It is crucial that we have independent standard-setting."

The seven members of the accounting board voted unanimously to approve the new rule during balloting that concluded late last week.

Derivatives are complicated financial contracts between two or more parties where the contract's value is tied to an underlying asset or pre-existing index. Companies use derivatives such as swaps and futures contracts to reduce the risk they face from fluctuating foreign currencies or interest rates.

The new rule will require companies to record the market value of the derivatives on their balance sheets and to include the gains or losses on those contracts as income. Most companies must start using the rule in January 2000—a month that company executives are already worried about because of the potential havoc that the millennium date could have on computers.

Banks and other companies said that the rule was not practical. They said that companies already provided enough information on derivatives in notes that must be included with financial statements.

Last year, Alan Greenspan, the chairman of the Federal Reserve, sided with the banks and urged the accounting board to refrain from dramatic rules changes. Mr. Greenspan warned that the new rule could keep companies from using derivatives and could "constrain prudent risk management practices."

But at times, companies have created more risk for themselves by entering into derivative contracts. For example, **Procter & Gamble** lost tens of millions of dollars in 1994 on derivative contracts that were tied to interest rates.

---

of 20-year bonds for forward delivery in three months' time.[5] Suppose at time 0 the portfolio manager can find a buyer willing to pay $97 for every $100 of 20-year bonds delivered in three months' time.

Now consider what happens to the FI portfolio manager if the gloomy forecast of a 2 percent rise in interest rates proves to be true. The portfolio manager's bond position has fallen in value by 16.67 percent, equal to a capital loss of $161,667. After the rise in interest rates, the manager can buy $1 million face value of 20-year bonds in the spot market at $80.833 per $100 of face value, a total cost of $808,333, and deliver those bonds to the forward contract buyer. Remember that the forward

---

[5]Since a forward contract involves delivery of bonds in a future time period, it does not appear on the balance sheet, which records only current and past transactions. Thus, forwards are one example of off-balance-sheet items (see Chapter 13).

Contemporary Perspectives

"Unfortunately, there are some who have been trying to force the F.A.S.B. to not issue this standard, preventing valuable information from reaching investors," Mr. Jenkins said. "We must avoid placing the interests of any particular group over the consumers' interests."

All publicly held companies must follow the rules of the Financial Accounting Standards Board, a privately financed group based in Norwalk, Conn. The Securities and Exchange Commission can sanction any company that does not abide by the board's rules.

Under a bill introduced by Representative Richard H. Baker, any accounting rule proposed by the accounting board would have to be approved by Federal regulators at the S.E.C. The bill by Mr. Baker, a Louisiana Republican, would also make it easier for companies to challenge the new accounting rules in court.

Senator Lauch Faircloth, a North Carolina Republican, has introduced another bill that would exempt banks from using the new derivatives rule unless banking regulators give their approval.

In a statement yesterday, the International Swaps and Derivatives Association, a group that includes banks and other companies, said the new rule was "a flawed product adopted in a process that ignored widespread dissent."

But Mr. Jenkins said that the board had considered the comments by the banks and other companies during more than 140 meetings it had on the proposed rule. In response to the comments, the board delayed the rule's effective date by two years and agreed that companies meeting certain requirements would not have to include the changes in a derivative's value in income.

The accounting board was created in 1972 as a private sector body, Mr. Jenkins said, to try to keep politics and the "self-serving objectives of special interest groups" out of the rule-making process.

Many investor groups, government officials and companies have urged Congress not to change the process of setting the nation's accounting rules, which are widely considered to be the strongest in the world.

Source: *New York Times,* June 2, 1998, p. D2. Copyright © 1998 by The New York Times. Reprinted by permission.

contract buyer agreed to pay $97 per $100 of face value for the $1 million of face value bonds delivered, or $970,000. As a result, the portfolio manager makes a profit on the forward transaction of

$$\underset{\substack{\text{(price paid by} \\ \text{forward buyer to} \\ \text{forward seller)}}}{\$970,000} - \underset{\substack{\text{(cost of purchasing} \\ \text{bonds in the spot market} \\ \text{at } t = \text{month 3 for delivery} \\ \text{to the forward buyer)}}}{\$808,333} = \$161,677$$

Immunized
Fully hedged or protected against adverse movements in interest rates (or other asset prices).

As you can see, the on-balance-sheet loss of $161,667 is exactly offset by the off-balance-sheet gain of $161,667 from selling the forward contract. Thus, the FI's net interest rate exposure is zero; in the parlance of finance, it has **immunized** its assets against interest rate risk.

Concept Questions

1. Explain how a naive hedge works.
2. What does it mean to say that an FI has immunized its portfolio against a particular risk?

Hedging Interest Rate Risk with Futures Contracts

Even though some hedging of interest rate risk does take place using forward contracts—such as forward rate agreements commonly used by insurance companies and banks prior to mortgage loan originations—most FIs hedge interest rate risk either at the micro level (called microhedging) or at the macro level (called macrohedging) using futures contracts. See Figure 24–3, later in the chapter, for a list of interest rate futures contracts currently available. Before looking at futures contracts, we explain the difference between microhedging and macrohedging and between routine hedging and selective hedging.

Microhedging

Microhedging
Using a futures (forward) contract to hedge a specific asset or liability.

An FI is **microhedging** when it employs a futures or a forward contract to hedge a particular asset or liability risk. For example, earlier we considered a simple example of microhedging asset-side portfolio risk, where an FI manager wanted to insulate the value of the institution's bond portfolio fully against a rise in interest rates. An example of microhedging on the liability side of the balance sheet might be when an FI is attempting to lock in a cost of funds to protect the FI against a possible rise in short-term interest rates by taking a short (sell) position in futures contracts on CDs or T-bills. In microhedging, the FI manager often tries to pick a futures or forward contract whose underlying deliverable asset is closely matched to the asset (or liability) position being hedged. In the earlier example, we had an unrealistic example of exact matching of the asset in the portfolio with the deliverable security underlying the forward contract (20-year bonds). Such exact matching cannot be achieved often, and this produces a residual unhedgable risk termed **basis risk.** We discuss basis risk in detail later in this chapter; it arises mainly because the prices of the assets or liabilities that an FI wishes to hedge are imperfectly correlated over time with the prices on the futures or forward contract used to hedge risk.

Basis Risk
A residual risk that arises because the movement in a spot (cash) asset's price is not perfectly correlated with the movement in the price of the asset delivered under a futures or forward contract.

Macrohedging

Macrohedging
Hedging the entire duration gap of an FI.

Macrohedging occurs when an FI manager wishes to use futures or other derivative securities to hedge the entire balance sheet duration gap. This contrasts to microhedging, where an FI manager identifies specific assets and liabilities and seeks out individual futures and other derivative contracts to hedge those individual risks. Note that macrohedging and microhedging can lead to quite different hedging strategies and results. In particular, a macrohedge takes a whole portfolio view and allows for individual asset and liability interest sensitivities or durations to net each other out. This can result in a very different aggregate futures position than the one established when an FI manager disregards this netting or portfolio effect and hedges individual asset and liability positions on a one-to-one basis.[6]

---

[6]P. H. Munter, D. K. Clancy, and C. T. Moores found that macrohedges provided better hedge performance than microhedges in a number of different interest rate environments. See "Accounting for Financial Futures: A Question of Risk Reduction," *Advances in Accounting* 3 (1986), pp. 51–70. See also R. Stoebe, "Macrohedging Bank Investment Portfolios," *Bankers Magazine,* November–December 1994, pp. 45–48.

FIGURE 24–2

*The Effects of Hedging on
Risk and Return*

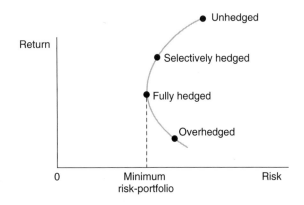

FIGURE 24–2

*The Effects of Hedging on
Risk and Return*

Routine Hedging versus Selective Hedging

Routine Hedging
Seeking to hedge all
interest rate risk exposure.

Routine hedging occurs when an FI reduces its interest rate or other risk exposure
to its lowest possible level by selling sufficient futures to offset the interest rate risk
exposure of its whole balance sheet or cash positions in each asset and liability. For
example, this might be achieved by macrohedging the duration gap, as described
next. However, since reducing risk also reduces return, not all FI managers seek
to do this. In Figure 24–2 we show the trade-off between return and risk and the
minimum-risk fully hedged portfolio.[7]

Hedging Selectively
Only partially hedging the
gap or individual assets
and liabilities.

Rather than a fully hedged position, many FIs choose to bear some interest rate
risk as well as credit and FX risks because of their comparative advantage as FIs
(see Chapter 6). One possibility is that an FI may choose to **hedge selectively** its
portfolio. For example, an FI manager may generate expectations regarding future
interest rates before deciding on a futures position. As a result, the manager may
selectively hedge only a proportion of its balance sheet position. Alternatively, the
FI manager may decide to remain unhedged or even to overhedge by selling more
futures than required by the cash position, although regulators may view the latter
as speculative. Thus, the fully hedged position—and the minimum-risk portfolio—
becomes one of several choices depending in part on managerial interest rate
expectations, managerial objectives, and the nature of the return-risk trade-off from
hedging. Finally, an FI may selectively hedge in an attempt to arbitrage profits
between a spot asset's price movements and movements in a futures price.

Macrohedging with Futures

How many futures contracts an FI should buy or sell depends on the size and direction of its interest rate risk exposure and the return-risk trade-off from fully or selectively hedging that risk. In Chapter 9, we showed that an FI's net worth exposure
to interest rate shocks was directly related to its leverage adjusted duration gap as
well as its asset size. Again, this is

$$\Delta E = -[D_A - kD_L] \times A \times \frac{\Delta R}{1 + R}$$

where

---

[7]The minimum-risk portfolio is not shown as zero here because of basis risk that prevents perfect hedging.
In the absence of basis risk, a zero-risk position becomes possible.

$$\Delta E = \text{Change in an FI's net worth}$$
$$D_A = \text{Duration of its asset portfolio}$$
$$D_L = \text{Duration of its liability portfolio}$$
$$k = \text{Ratio of an FI's liabilities to assets } (L/A)$$
$$A = \text{Size of an FI's asset portfolio}$$
$$\frac{\Delta R}{1 + R} = \text{Shock to interest rates}$$

To see how futures might fully hedge a positive or negative portfolio duration gap, consider the following example for an FI where

$$D_A = 5 \text{ years}$$
$$D_L = 3 \text{ years}$$

Suppose the FI manager receives information from an economic forecasting unit that rates are expected to rise from 10 to 11 percent; that is,

$$\Delta R = 1\% = .01$$
$$1 + R = 1.10$$

and the FI's initial balance sheet is:

Assets (in millions)	Liabilities (in millions)
A = $100	L = $ 90
	E = $\underline{\quad 10}$
$\overline{\$100}$	$\overline{\$100}$

The FI manager wants to calculate the potential loss to the FI's net worth (E) if the forecast of rising rates proves to be true. As we showed in Chapter 9:

$$\Delta E = -(D_A - kD_L) \times A \times \frac{\Delta R}{1 + R}$$

so that

$$\Delta E = -(5 - (.9)(3)) \times \$100 \times \frac{.01}{1.1} = -\$2.09 \text{ million}$$

The bank could expect to lose $2.09 million in net worth if the interest rate forecast turns out to be correct. Since the FI started with a net worth of $10 million, the loss of $2.09 million is almost 21 percent of its initial net worth position. Clearly, as this example illustrates, the impact of the rise in interest rates could be quite threatening to the FI and its insolvency risk exposure.

The Risk-Minimizing Futures Position.   The FI manager's objective to hedge fully the balance sheet exposure would be fulfilled by constructing a futures position such that if interest rates do rise by 1 percent to 11 percent, as in the prior example, the FI will make a gain on the futures position to just offset the loss of balance sheet net worth of $2.09 million.

When interest rates rise, the price of a futures contract falls, since its price reflects the value of the underlying bond that is deliverable against the contract. How much a bond price falls when interest rates rise depends on its duration. Thus, we would expect the price of the 20-year T-bond futures contract to be more sensitive to interest rate changes than the price of the 3-month T-bill futures contract since the former futures price reflects the price of the 20-year T-bond deliverable on contract maturity. Thus, the sensitivity of the price of a futures contract depends on the duration of the deliverable bond underlying the contract, or

$$\frac{\Delta F}{F} = -D_F \frac{\Delta R}{1 + R}$$

where

ΔF = Change in dollar value of futures contracts
F = Dollar value of the initial futures contracts
D_F = Duration of the bond to be delivered against the futures contracts such as a 20-year, 8 percent coupon T-bond
ΔR = Expected shock to interest rates
$1 + R$ = 1 plus the current level of interest rates

This can be rewritten as

$$\Delta F = -D_F \times F \times \frac{\Delta R}{1 + R}$$

The left side of this expression (ΔF) shows the dollar gain or loss on a futures position when interest rates change. To see this dollar gain or loss more clearly, we can decompose the initial dollar value position in futures contracts, F, into its two component parts:

$$F = N_F \times P_F$$

The dollar value of the outstanding futures position depends on the number of contracts bought or sold (N_F) and the price of each contract (P_F).

Futures contracts are homogeneous in size. Thus, futures exchanges sell T-bond futures in minimum units of $100,000 of face value; that is, one T-bond futures ($N_F = 1$) = $100,000. T-bill futures are sold in larger minimum units: one T-bill future ($N_F = 1$) = $1,000,000.

The price of each contract quoted in the newspaper is the price per $100 of face value for delivering the underlying bond. Looking at Figure 24–3, a price quote of $116^{25}/_{32}$ on October 24, 1997, for the T-bond futures contract maturing in December 1997 means that the buyer would be required to pay $116,781.25 if this were the price on contract maturity for one T-bond contract and the 20-year, 8 percent T-bonds were delivered by the seller in December.[8]

In actuality, the seller of the futures contract has a number of alternatives other than an 8 percent coupon 20-year bond that can be delivered against the T-bond futures contract. If only one type of bond could be delivered, a shortage or squeeze might develop, making it very hard for the short side or seller to deliver. In fact, the seller has quite flexible delivery options; apart from delivering the 20-year, 8 percent coupon bond, the seller can deliver bonds that range in maturity from 15 years

---

[8]In practice, the futures price changes day to day and gains or losses would be generated for the seller/buyer over the period between when the contract is entered into and when it matures. See our later discussion of this unique marking-to-market feature.

Note that the FI could sell contracts in T-bonds maturing at later dates. However, while contracts exist for up to two years into the future, longer-term contracts tend to be infrequently traded and therefore relatively illiquid.

FIGURE 24–3

Futures Contracts on Interest Rates.

INTEREST RATE

TREASURY BONDS (CBT)-$100,000; pts. 32nds of 100%

	Open	High	Low	Settle	Change	Lifetime High	Lifetime Low	Open Interest
→ Dec	116-11	117-02	115-27	116-25	+ 15	118-18	100-08	663,835
→ Mr98	116-08	116-23	115-20	116-15	+ 15	118-07	104-21	69,513
June	115-31	116-09	115-23	116-02	+ 13	117-15	104-03	9,338
Sept	....	....	....	115-26	+ 15	115-21	103-22	2,006
Dec	....	....	....	115-17	+ 15	116-10	103-13	4,704

Est vol 600,000; vol Thu 736,678; open int 749,452, +24,677.

TREASURY BONDS (MCE)-$50,000; pts. 32nds of 100%

	Open	High	Low	Settle	Change	Lifetime High	Lifetime Low	Open Interest
Dec	115-29	117-01	115-28	116-30	+ 18	118-17	105-20	17,086

Est vol 5,050; vol Thu 7,394; open int 17,114, −34.

TREASURY NOTES (CBT)-$100,000; pts. 32nds of 100%

	Open	High	Low	Settle	Change	Lifetime High	Lifetime Low	Open Interest
Dec	110-16	110-27	110-07	110-22	+ 5	111-29	104-10	370,503
Mr98	109-31	110-16	109-31	110-12	+ 5	111-18	105-24	18,858

Est vol 110,001; vol Thu 169,180; open int 389,363, −5,096.

5 YR TREAS NOTES (CBT)-$100,000; pts. 32nds of 100%

	Open	High	Low	Settle	Change	Lifetime High	Lifetime Low	Open Interest
Dec	107-18	07-255	107-12	07-225	+ 3.5	108-19	04-005	230,795
Mr98	107-18	107-22	107-12	107-20	+ 3.5	108-10	106-07	4,311

Est vol 64,500; vol Thu 82,438; open int 235,106, −2,435.

2 YR TREAS NOTES (CBT)-$200,000; pts. 32nds of 100%

	Open	High	Low	Settle	Change	Lifetime High	Lifetime Low	Open Interest
Dec	103-20	103-23	103-17	103-21	+ .7	03-305	02-265	37,829

Est vol 3,000; vol Thu 4,436; open int 37,849, −852.

30-DAY FEDERAL FUNDS (CBT)-$5 million; pts. of 100%

	Open	High	Low	Settle	Change	Lifetime High	Lifetime Low	Open Interest
Oct	94.495	94.500	94.495	94.500	....	94.510	93.900	7,781
Nov	94.43	94.44	94.43	94.44	....	94.46	93.88	7,318
Dec	94.36	94.39	94.36	94.39	+ .01	94.43	93.78	4,367
Ja98	94.32	94.36	94.32	94.36	+ .01	94.43	93.97	2,384
Feb	94.32	94.35	94.32	94.35	+ .01	94.44	93.84	1,657

Est vol 2,222; vol Thu 6,406; open int 23,872, +1,430.

MUNI BOND INDEX (CBT)-$1,000; times Bond Buyer MBI

	Open	High	Low	Settle	Change	Lifetime High	Lifetime Low	Open Interest
Dec	119-22	120-21	119-21	120-13	+ 14	122-19	109-22	21,222
Mr98	118-13	119-06	118-13	119-03	+ 14	119-19	116-29	134

Est vol 8,000; vol Thu 6,593; open int 21,356, +464.
The index: Close 120-20; Yield 5.69.

TREASURY BILLS (CME)-$1mil.; pts. of 100%

	Open	High	Low	Settle	Chg	Discount Settle	Discount Chg	Open Interest
Dec	95.03	95.08	95.02	95.05	+ .01	4.95	− .01	4,455
→ Mr98	95.04	95.10	95.04	95.10	+ .03	4.90	− .03	4,453
June	....	....	....	95.02	+ .04	4.98	− .04	384

Est vol 1,112; vol Thu 1,463; open int 9,304, +271.

LIBOR-1 MO. (CME)-$3,000,000; points of 100%

	Open	High	Low	Settle	Chg	Discount Settle	Discount Chg	Open Interest
Nov	94.30	94.32	94.27	94.32	+ .02	5.68	− .02	40,920
Dec	94.16	94.16	94.11	94.15	+ .01	5.86	− .01	13,527
Mr98	94.20	94.20	94.16	94.22	+ .04	5.79	− .04	753

Est vol 6,616; vol Thu 13,432; open int 61,090, −1,792.

EURODOLLAR (CME)-$1 million; pts. of 100%

	Open	High	Low	Settle	Chg	Yield Settle	Yield Chg	Open Interest
Nov	94.15	94.19	94.15	94.18	+ .02	5.82	− .02	24,505
Dec	94.15	94.18	94.11	94.17	+ .03	5.83	− .03	552,891
Mr98	94.10	94.14	94.05	94.13	+ .04	5.87	− .04	423,088
June	94.03	94.07	93.97	94.06	+ .04	5.94	− .04	347,330
Sept	93.96	94.01	93.90	93.97	+ .03	6.03	− .03	255,889
Dec	93.86	93.90	93.79	93.86	+ .02	6.14	− .02	227,954
Mr99	93.85	93.88	93.78	93.85	+ .02	6.15	− .02	162,382
June	93.76	93.85	93.76	93.82	+ .02	6.18	− .02	143,533
Sept	93.77	93.82	93.73	93.78	+ .01	6.22	− .01	109,540
Dec	93.65	93.75	93.65	93.72	+ .02	6.28	− .02	89,014
Mr00	93.70	93.76	93.65	93.73	+ .03	6.27	− .03	72,091
June	93.67	93.73	93.62	93.70	+ .03	6.30	− .03	59,129
Sept	93.64	93.70	93.59	93.67	+ .03	6.33	− .03	50,880
Dec	93.54	93.64	93.54	93.61	+ .03	6.39	− .03	41,290
Mr01	93.54	93.64	93.54	93.61	+ .03	6.39	− .03	37,775
June	93.51	93.61	93.45	93.58	+ .03	6.42	− .03	34,930
Sept	93.48	93.58	93.42	93.55	+ .03	6.45	− .03	34,496
Dec	93.41	93.51	93.36	93.48	+ .03	6.52	− .03	18,297
Mr02	93.41	93.51	93.36	93.48	+ .03	6.52	− .03	18,874
June	93.38	93.48	93.33	93.45	+ .03	6.55	− .03	14,500
Sept	93.35	93.45	93.30	93.42	+ .03	6.58	− .03	12,826
Dec	93.34	93.38	93.32	93.36	+ .03	6.64	− .03	7,826
Mr03	93.34	93.38	93.32	93.36	+ .03	6.64	− .03	6,565
June	93.31	93.35	93.29	93.33	+ .03	6.67	− .03	5,654
Sept	93.28	93.32	93.26	93.30	+ .03	6.70	− .03	5,608
Dec	93.25	93.25	93.19	93.23	+ .03	6.77	− .03	5,091
Mr04	....	....	....	93.23	+ .03	6.77	− .03	4,486
June	....	....	....	93.20	+ .03	6.80	− .03	6,283
Sept	....	....	....	93.17	+ .03	6.83	− .03	4,395
Dec	....	....	....	93.10	+ .03	6.90	− .03	4,523
Mr05	....	....	....	93.10	+ .03	6.90	− .03	2,262
June	....	....	....	93.06	+ .03	6.94	− .03	2,510
Sept	....	....	....	93.03	+ .03	6.97	− .03	2,361
Dec	....	....	....	92.97	+ .03	7.03	− .03	1,712
Mr06	....	....	....	92.97	+ .03	7.03	− .03	2,731
June	....	....	....	92.93	+ .03	7.07	− .03	1,882
Sept	....	....	....	92.90	+ .03	7.10	− .03	1,781
Dec	....	....	....	92.84	+ .03	7.16	− .03	1,514
Mr07	....	....	....	92.84	+ .03	7.16	− .03	1,503

Est vol 586,535; vol Thu 895,549; open int 2,804,348, −11,233.

Source: *The Wall Street Journal,* October 27, 1997, p. C14. Reprinted by permission of The Wall Street Journal,

Conversion Factor
A factor used to figure the invoice price on a futures contract when a bond other than the benchmark bond is delivered to the buyer.

upward. Often, up to 25 different bonds may qualify for delivery. When a bond other than the 20-year benchmark bond is delivered, the buyer pays a different invoice price for the futures contract based on a **conversion factor** that calculates the price of the deliverable bond if it were to yield 8 percent divided by face value. Suppose $100,000 worth of 18-year, 10 percent semiannual coupon Treasury bonds were valued at a yield of 8 percent. This would produce a fair present value of the bond of approximately $119,000. The conversion factor for the bond would be 1.19 (or $119,000/$100,000). This means the buyer would have to pay the seller the conversion factor of 1.19 times the published futures price of $116,781.25. That is, the futures price would be $138,969.69.[9]

We can now solve the problem of how many futures contracts to sell to fully macrohedge an FI's on-balance-sheet interest rate risk exposure. We have shown that:

[9]In practice, the seller exploits the delivery option by choosing the cheapest bond to deliver, that is, bonds whose conversion factor is most favorable (being based on an 8 percent yield) relative to the true price of the bond to be delivered (which reflects the actual level of yields). See S. Figlewski, *Hedging with Financial Futures for Institutional Investors: From Theory to Practice* (Cambridge, Mass.: Ballinger, 1986)

1. *Loss on balance sheet.* The loss of net worth for an FI when rates rise is equal to

$$\Delta E = -(D_A - kD_L)A \frac{\Delta R}{1 + R}$$

2. *Gain off balance sheet on futures.* The gain off balance sheet from selling futures is equal to[10]

$$\Delta F = -D_F(N_F \times P_F) \frac{\Delta R}{1 + R}$$

Fully hedging can be defined as selling a sufficient number of futures contracts (N_F) so that the loss of net worth on the balance sheet (ΔE) when rates rise is just offset by the gain from off-balance-sheet selling of futures when rates rise, (ΔF), or

$$\Delta F = \Delta E$$

Substituting in the appropriate expressions for each:

$$-D_F(N_F \times P_F)\frac{\Delta R}{1 + R} = -(D_A - kD_L)A \frac{\Delta R}{1 + R}$$

canceling $\Delta R/1 + R$ on both sides:[11]

$$D_F (N_F \times P_F) = (D_A - kD_L) A$$

Solving for N_F (the number of futures to sell):

$$N_F = \frac{(D_A - kD_L)A}{D_F \times P_F}$$

From the equation for N_F, we can now solve for the correct number of futures positions to sell (N_F) in the context of our earlier example where the bank was exposed to a balance sheet loss of net worth (ΔE) amounting to $2.09 million when interest rates rose. In that example:

$$D_A = 5 \text{ years}$$
$$D_L = 3 \text{ years}$$
$$k = .9$$
$$A = \$100 \text{ million}$$

Thus, the N_F equation reads

$$N_F = \frac{(5 - (.9)(3)) \, \$100 \text{ million}}{D_F \times P_F}$$

Suppose the current futures price quote is $97 per $100 of face value for the benchmark 20-year, 8 percent coupon bond underlying the nearby futures contract, the minimum contract size is $100,000, and the duration of the deliverable bond is 9.5 years:

---

[10]When futures prices fall, the buyer of the contract compensates the seller, here the FI. Thus, the FI gains when the prices of futures fall.

[11]This amounts to assuming that the interest changes of the cash asset position match those of the futures position; that is, there is no basis risk. This assumption is relaxed later.

$$D_F = 9.5 \text{ years}$$
$$P_F = \$97,000$$

Inserting these numbers into the expression for N_F, we can now solve for the number of futures to sell:[12]

$$
\begin{aligned}
N_F &= \frac{(5 - (.9)(3)) \times \$100 \text{ million}}{9.5 \times \$97,000} \\
&= \frac{\$230,000,000}{\$921,500} \\
&= 249.59 \text{ contracts to be sold}
\end{aligned}
$$

Since the FI cannot sell a part of a contract, the number of contracts should be rounded down to the nearest whole number, or 249 contracts.[13] Next, we double-check that selling 249 T-bond futures contracts will indeed hedge the FI against a sudden increase in interest rates from 10 to 11 percent, or a 1 percent interest rate shock.

On Balance Sheet.   You have already seen that when rates rise by 1 percent, the FI takes a net worth loss (ΔE) of $2.09 million on the balance sheet:

$$\Delta E = -(D_A - kD_L)A \frac{\Delta R}{1 + R}$$

$$-\$2.09 \text{ million} = -(5 - (.9)(3)) \times \$100 \text{ million} \times \left(\frac{.01}{1.1}\right)$$

Off Balance Sheet.   The value of the off-balance-sheet futures position (ΔF) falls by approximately $2.09 million when the FI sells 249 futures contracts in the T-bond futures market. Such a fall in value of the futures contracts means a positive cash flow to the futures seller as the buyer compensates the seller for a lower futures price through the marking-to-market process. This requires a cash flow from the buyer's margin account to the seller's margin account as the price of a futures contracts falls.[14] The change in the value of the futures position is

---

[12]For further discussions of this formula, see Figlewski, *Hedging with Financial Futures,* and E. Brewer, "Bank Gap Management and the Use of Financial Futures," Federal Reserve Bank of Chicago, *Economic Perspectives,* March–April 1985. Also note that if the FI intends to deliver any bond other than the 20-year benchmark bond, the P_F has to be multiplied by the appropriate conversion factor (c). If $c = 1.19$, then $P_F = 97 \times 1.19 = \$115.43$ per $100 of face value and the invoice price per contract would be $115,430.

[13]The reason for rounding down rather than rounding up is technical. The target number of contracts to sell is that which minimizes interest rate risk exposure. By slightly underhedging rather than overhedging, the FI can generate the same risk exposure level but the underhedging policy produces a slightly higher return (see Figure 24–2).

[14]An example of marking to market might clarify how the seller gains when the price of the futures contract falls. Suppose on day 1 the seller entered into a 90-day contract to deliver 20-year T-bonds at $P = \$97$. The next day, because of a rise in interest rates, the futures contract, which now has 89 days to maturity, is trading at $96 when the market closes. Marking to market requires the prices on all contracts entered into on the previous day(s) to be marked to market at each night's closing (settlement) price. As a result, the price of the contract is lowered to $96 per $100 of face value, but in return for this lowering of the price from $97 to $96, the buyer has to compensate the seller to the tune of $1 per $100 of face value. Thus, given a $100,000 contract, there is a cash flow payment of $1,000 on that day from the buyer to the seller. Note that if the price had risen to $98, the seller would have had to compensate the buyer $1,000. The marking-to-market process goes on until the futures contract matures. If, over the period, futures prices have mostly fallen, then the seller accumulates positive cash flows on the futures position. It is this accumulation of cash flows that can be set off against losses in net worth on the balance sheet.

$$\Delta F = -D_F(N_F \times P_F)\frac{\Delta R}{1 + R}$$

$$= -9.5(249 \times \$97{,}000)\left(\frac{.01}{1.1}\right)$$

$$= -\$2.086 \text{ million}$$

Thus, as the seller of the futures, the FI makes a gain of $2.086 million. As a result, the net gain/loss on and off the balance sheet is

$$\Delta E - \Delta F = -\$2.09 + \$2.086 = -\$0.004 \text{ million}$$

This small remaining net loss of $.004 million to equity or net worth reflects the fact that the FI couldn't achieve the perfect hedge—even in the absence of basis risk—as it needed to round down the number of futures to the nearest whole contract from 249.59 to 249 contracts. Table 24–2 summarizes the key features of the hedge.

Suppose instead of using the 20-year T-bond futures to hedge, it had used the three-month T-bill futures.[15] We can use the same formula to solve for N_F in the case of T-bill futures:

$$N_F = \frac{(D_A - kD_L)A}{D_F \times P_F}$$

$$= \frac{(5 - (.9)(3))\,\$100 \text{ million}}{D_F \times P_F}$$

Assuming that $P_F = \$97$ per $100 of face value or $970,000 per contract (the minimum contract size of a T-bill future is $1,000,000) and $D_F = .25$ (the duration of a three-month T-bill that is the discount instrument deliverable under the contract).[16] Then

$$N_F = \frac{(5 - (.9)(3))\,\$100 \text{ million}}{.25 \times \$970{,}000} = \frac{\$230{,}000{,}000}{\$242{,}500}$$

$$N_F = 948.45 \text{ contracts to be sold}$$

TABLE 24–2   On- and Off-Balance-Sheet Effects of a Macrohedge Hedge

	On Balance Sheet	Off Balance Sheet
Begin hedge $t = 0$	Equity value of $10 million exposed to impact of rise in interest rates.	Sell 249.59 T-bond futures contracts at $97,000. Underlying T-bond coupon rate is 8%.
End hedge $t = 1$ day	Interest rates rise on assets and liabilities by 1%. Opportunity loss on-balance-sheet: $$\Delta E = -[5 - .9(3)] \times \$100\text{m} \times \frac{.01}{1.1}$$ $$= -\$2.09 \text{ million}$$	Buy 249.59 T-bond futures (closes out futures position). Real gain on futures hedge: $$-\Delta F = -\left[-9.5 \times (249.59 \times \$97{,}000) \times \frac{.01}{1.1}\right]^*$$ $$= \$2.09 \text{ million}$$

*Assuming no basis risk and no contract "rounding."

[15]As Figure 24–3 shows, three-month T-bill futures are an alternative interest rate futures contract to the long-term bond futures contract.

[16]We assume the same futures price ($97) here for purposes of comparison. Of course, the actual prices of the two futures contracts are very different (see Figure 24–3).

Rounding down to the nearest whole contract, $N_F = 948$.

As this example illustrates, we can hedge an FI's on-balance-sheet interest rate risk when its $D_A > kD_L$ by selling either T-bond or T-bill futures. In general, fewer T-bond than T-bill contracts need to be sold—in our case, 948 T-bill versus 249 T-bond contracts. This suggests that on a simple transaction cost basis, the FI might normally prefer to use T-bond futures. However, other considerations can be important, especially if the FI holds the futures contracts until the delivery date. The FI needs to be concerned about the availability of the deliverable set of securities and any possible supply shortages or squeezes. Such liquidity concerns may favor T-bills.[17]

The Problem of Basis Risk

Because spot bonds and futures on bonds are traded in different markets, the shift in yields $\Delta R/1 + R$ affecting the values of the on-balance-sheet cash portfolio may differ from the shift in yields ($\Delta R_F/1 + R_F$) affecting the value of the underlying bond in the futures contract; that is, spot and futures prices or values are not perfectly correlated. This lack of perfect correlation has been called *basis risk*. In the previous section, we assumed a simple world of no basis risk in which $\Delta R/1 + R = \Delta R_F/1 + R_F$. Let's suppose this is not the case. How can the formula to solve for the risk minimizing N_F be fixed to account for greater or less rate volatility and hence price volatility in the futures market relative to the spot or cash market? Returning to our on-balance-sheet exposure, we have

$$\Delta E = -(D_A - kD_L) \times A \times \Delta R/1 + R$$

and, for the off-balance-sheet futures position,

$$\Delta F = -D_F (N_F \times P_F) \times \Delta R_F/1 + R_F$$

setting

$$\Delta E = \Delta F$$

and solving for N_F, we have

$$N_F = \frac{(D_A - kD_L) \times A \times \Delta R/1 + R}{D_F \times P_F \times \Delta R_F/1 + R_F}$$

Dividing the top and bottom of the RHS by $\Delta R/1 + R$ and letting the ratio $(\Delta R_F/1 + R_F)/(\Delta R/1 + R) = b$, we have

$$N_F = \frac{(D_A - kD_L)A}{D_F \times P_F \times b}$$

The only difference between this and the previous formula is an adjustment for basis risk (b), which measures the degree to which the futures price (yields) moves more or less than spot bond price (yields). In our example, let $b = 1.1$. This means

---

[17]However, when rates change, the loss of net worth on the balance sheet and the gain on selling the futures are instantaneous; therefore, delivery need not be a concern. Indeed, because of the daily marking-to-market process, an FI manager can close out a futures position by taking an exactly offsetting position. That is, a manager who had originally sold 100 futures contracts could close out a position on any day by buying 100 contracts. Because of the unique marking-to-market feature, the marked-to-market price of the contracts sold equals the price of any new contracts bought on that day.

that for every 1 percent change in discounted spot rates ($\Delta R/1 + R$), the implied rate on the deliverable bond in the futures market moves by 1.1 percent. That is, futures prices are more sensitive to interest rate shocks than are spot market prices. Solving for N_F we have

$$N_F = \frac{(5 - (.9)(3))\ \$100\ \text{million}}{9.5 \times \$97{,}000 \times 1.1}$$

$$= 226.9\ \text{contracts}$$

or 226 contracts rounding down. This compares to 249 when we assumed equal rate shocks in both the cash and futures markets ($\Delta R/1 + R = \Delta R_F/1 + R_F$). The reason that we need fewer contracts is that futures rates and prices are more volatile, so that selling fewer futures would be sufficient to provide the same change in ΔF (the value of the futures position) than before when we implicitly assumed $b = 1$.

Note that if futures rates or prices had been less volatile than spot rates or prices, we would have had to sell more than 249 contracts to get the same dollar gain in the futures position as was lost in net worth on the balance sheet so that $\Delta E = \Delta F$.

Next, we look at the important issue of measuring the basis risk adjustment in the preceding formula. One method is to look at the ratio between $\Delta R/1 + R$ and $\Delta R_F/1 + R_F$ today. Since this is only one observation, we might better analyze their relationship by investigating their relative behavior in the recent past. We can do this by running an ordinary least squares linear regression of implied futures rate changes on spot rate changes with the slope coefficient of this regression giving an estimate of the degree of comovement of the two rates over time. We discuss this regression procedure in greater detail next in connection with calculating basis risk when hedging with FX futures.[18]

Concept Questions

1. What is the difference between microhedging and macrohedging and between routine hedging and selective hedging?
2. Regarding the example that concludes on page 569, suppose the FI had the reverse duration gap; that is, the duration of its assets was shorter ($D_A = 3$) than the duration of its liabilities ($D_A = 5$). (This might be the case of a bank that borrows with long-term notes or time deposits to finance floating-rate loans.) How should it hedge using futures?
3. Regarding the example that concludes on page 571, how many futures should have been sold using the 20-year bond and 3-month T-bill contracts, if the basis risk measure $b = .8$?

Hedging Foreign Exchange Risk

Just as forwards and futures can hedge an FI against losses due to interest rate changes, they can also hedge against foreign exchange risk.

---

[18]Another problem with the simple duration gap approach to determining N_F is that it is assumed that yield curves are flat. This could be relaxed by using duration measures that allow for nonflat yield curves (see Chapter 9).

Forwards

In Chapter 15 we analyzed how an FI uses forward contracts to reduce the risks due to FX fluctuations when it mismatched the sizes of its foreign asset and liability portfolios. In that chapter we considered the simple case of an FI that raised all its liabilities in dollars while investing half of its assets in British pound sterling–denominated loans and the other half in dollar-denominated loans. Its balance sheet looks as follows:

Assets	*Liabilities*
U.S. loans ($) $100 million	U.S. CDs $200 million
U.K. loans (£) $100 million	

All assets and liabilities are of a one-year maturity and duration. Because the bank is net long in pound sterling assets, it faces the risk that over the period of the loan, the pound will depreciate against the dollar so that the proceeds of the pound loan (along with the dollar loan) will be insufficient to meet the required payments on the maturing dollar CDs. Then the bank will have to meet such losses out of its net worth; that is, its insolvency risk will increase.

In Chapter 15 we showed that by selling both the pound loan principal and interest forward one year at the known forward exchange rate at the beginning of the year, the FI could hedge itself against losses on its pound loan position due to changes in the dollar/pound exchange rate over the succeeding year. Note the hedging strategy for hedging (£100 million) of British pound sterling loans with forwards in Figure 24–4.

Futures

Instead of using FX forward contracts to hedge foreign exchange risk, the FI could use FX futures contracts.

Consider a U.S.-based FI wishing to hedge a one-year British pound loan of £100 million principal plus £15 million interest (or £115 million) against the risk of the pound falling in value against the dollar over the succeeding year.

Suppose the FI wished to hedge this loan position on October 24, 1997. On that day, there were two British pound futures contracts outstanding: a contract expiring in December 1997 (the "nearby" contract) and a contract expiring in March 1998. Thus, the futures market did not allow the FI to institute a long-term one-year hedge that day. The longest maturity contract available matured in just over five months (March 1998). Thus, the FI could use futures only by rolling over the hedge into a new futures contract on maturity. Considerations such as the transactions costs from

FIGURE 24–4

Hedging a Long Position in Pound Assets through Sale of Pounds Forward

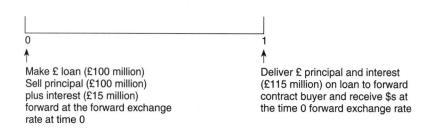

Make £ loan (£100 million)
Sell principal (£100 million)
plus interest (£15 million)
forward at the forward exchange
rate at time 0

Deliver £ principal and interest
(£115 million) on loan to forward
contract buyer and receive $s at
the time 0 forward exchange rate

having to roll over the hedge and uncertainty regarding the prices of new futures contracts may make hedging through forwards or swaps relatively more attractive to those FIs that want to lock in a longer-term hedge (see Chapter 26).

However, let's suppose the FI still wants to hedge fully via the futures markets. How many futures should it sell? The answer to this question is that is should sell the amount that produces a sufficient profit on the pound futures contracts to just offset any exchange-rate losses on the pound loan portfolio should the pound fall in value relative to the dollar. There are two cases to consider:

1. The futures dollar/pound price is expected to change in exactly the same fashion as the spot dollar/pound price over the course of the year. That is, futures and spot price changes are perfectly correlated; there is no basis risk.
2. Futures and spot prices, while expected to change in the same direction, are not perfectly correlated (there is basis risk).

Perfect Correlation between Spot and Futures Prices.   On October 24, 1997, *The Wall Street Journal* reported:

$$S_t = \text{Spot exchange rate (\$/£): \$1.634 per £1}$$
$$f_t = \text{Futures price (\$/£) for the nearby contract}$$
$$\text{(December 1997): \$1.6304 per £1}$$

Suppose the FI made a £100 million loan at 15 percent interest and wished to hedge fully the risk that the dollar value of the proceeds would be eroded by a declining British pound sterling over the year. Also, suppose that the FI manager receives a forecast that in one year's time the spot and futures will be

$$S_{t+1} = \$1.584 \text{ per £1}$$
$$f_{t+1} = \$1.5804 \text{ per £1}$$
$$\text{So that over the year, } \Delta S_t = -5 \text{ cents}$$
$$\Delta f_t = -5 \text{ cents}$$

For a manager who believes this forecast of a depreciating pound against the dollar, the correct full-hedge strategy would be to cover the £115 million expected earnings on the British loan by selling or shorting £115 million of British pound futures contracts on October 24, 1997. We are assuming here that the FI manager continuously rolls over the futures position into new futures contracts and will get out of futures on October 24, 1998.

The size of each British pound futures contract is £62,500. Therefore, the number (N_F) of futures to be sold is

$$N_F = \frac{£115,000,000}{£62,500} = \frac{\text{Size of long position}}{\text{Size of a pound futures contract}}$$
$$= 1,840 \text{ contracts to be sold}$$

Next, look at whether losses on the long asset position (the British loan) would just offset gains on the futures should the FI sell 1,840 British pound futures contracts and should spot and futures prices change in the direction and amount expected.

Loss on British Pound Loan.   The loss on the British pound loan in dollars would be

$$[\text{£ Principal} + \text{Interest}] \times \Delta S_t$$
$$[\text{£115 million}] \times [\$1.634/\text{£} - \$1.584/\text{£}] = \$5.75 \text{ million}$$

That is, the dollar value of the British pound loan proceeds would be $5.75 million less should the pound depreciate from $1.634/£ to $1.584/£ in the spot market over the year.

Gain on Futures Contracts

$$[N_F \times \text{£62,500}] \times \Delta f_t$$
$$[1,840 \times \text{£62,500}] \times [\$1.6304/\text{£} - \$1.5804/\text{£}] = \$5.75 \text{ million}$$

By selling 1,840 futures contracts of £62,500 each, the seller makes $5.75 million as the futures price falls from $1.6304/£ at the contract initiation on October 24, 1997 to $1.5804/£ at the futures position termination on October 24, 1998. This cash flow of $5.75 million results from the marking to market of the futures contract. As the futures price falls due to the daily marking to market, the pound futures contract buyer has the contract repriced to a lower level in dollars to be paid per pound but has to compensate the seller out of his or her margin account for the difference between the original contract price and the new lower marked-to-market contract price. Thus, over the one year, the buyer compensates the seller by a net of 5 cents per £1 of futures purchased, that is, $1.6304/£1 minus $1.5804/£1 as the futures price falls, or a total of 5 cents $\times$ the number of contracts (1,840) $\times$ the pound size of each contract (62,500). Note that on October 24, 1998, when the principal and interest on the pound loan are paid by the borrower, the FI seller of the pound futures terminates its position in 1,840 short contracts by taking an opposing position of 1,840 long in the same contract. This effectively ends any net cash flow implications from futures positions beyond this date.

Finally, in this example we have ignored the interest income effects of marking to market In reality, the $5.75 million from the futures position would be received by the FI seller over the course of the year. As a result, this cash flow can be reinvested at the current short-term dollar interest rate to generate a cash flow of more than $5.75 million. Given this, an FI hedger can sell slightly fewer contracts in anticipation of this interest income. The number of futures that could be sold, below the 1,840 suggested, would depend on the level and pattern of short-term rates over the hedging horizon as well as the precise expected pattern of cash flows from marking to market. In general, the higher the level of short-term interest, the more an FI manager could **tail the hedge** in this fashion.[19]

Tail the Hedge
Reducing the number of futures contracts that are needed to hedge a cash position because of the interest income that is generated from reinvesting the marked-to-market cash flows generated by the futures contract.

Imperfect Correlation between Spot and Futures Prices (Basis Risk).   Suppose, instead, the FI manager did not believe that the spot exchange rate and futures price on the dollar/pound contract would fall by exactly the same amount. Instead, let the forecast for one year's time be

$$S_{t+1} = 1.584/\text{£}1$$
$$f_{t+1} = \$1.6004/\text{£}1$$

So that, in expectation, over the succeeding year

---

[19]See Figlewski, *Hedging with Financial Futures,* for further discussion. One way to do this is to discount the calculated hedge ratio (the optimal number of futures to sell per $1 of cash position) by a short-term interest rate such as the federal funds rate.

$$\Delta S_t = -5 \text{ cents}$$
$$\Delta f_t = -3 \text{ cents}$$

This means that the dollar/pound futures price is expected to depreciate less than will the spot dollar/pound. This basis risk arises because spot and futures contracts are traded in different markets with different demand and supply functions. Given this, even though futures and spot prices are normally highly correlated, this correlation is often less than 1.

Because futures prices and spot prices do not always move exactly together, this can create a problem for an FI manager seeking to hedge the long position of £115 million with pound futures. Suppose the FI manager ignored the fact that the spot pound is expected to depreciate faster against the dollar than the futures price for pounds and continued to believe that selling 1,840 contracts would be the best hedge. That manager could be in for a big (and nasty) surprise in one year's time. To see this, consider the loss on the cash asset position and the gain on the futures position under a new scenario where the dollar/pound spot rate falls by 2 cents more than dollar/pound futures over the year.

Loss on British Pound Loan.   The expected fall in the spot value of the pound by 5 cents over the year results in a loss of

$$[£115 \text{ million}] \times [\$1.634/£ - \$1.584/£] = \$5.75 \text{ million}$$

Gain on Futures Position.   The expected gain on the futures position is

$$[1,840 \times £62,500] \times [\$1.6304/£ - \$1.6004/£] = \$3.45 \text{ million}$$

Thus, the net loss to the FI is

Net loss = Loss on British pound loan − Gain on British pound futures
Net loss = \$5.75 − \$3.45
Net loss = \$2.3 million

Such a loss would have to be charged against the FI's profits and implicitly its net worth or equity. As a result, the FI manager needs to take into account the lower sensitivity of futures prices relative to spot exchange rate changes by selling more than 1,840 futures contracts to hedge fully the British pound loan risk.

To see how many more contracts are required, we need to know how much more sensitive spot exchange rates are relative to futures prices. Let h be the ratio of ΔS_t to Δf_t.

$$h = \frac{\Delta S_t}{\Delta f_t}$$

Then, in our example,

$$h = \frac{\$.05}{\$.03} = 1.66$$

That is, spot rates are 66 percent more sensitive than futures prices, or—put slightly differently—for every 1 percent change in futures prices, spot rates change by 1.66 percent.[20]

---

[20]Of course, this can always be expressed the other way around—a 1 percent change in spot prices leads on average to only a 0.6 percent change in futures prices.

Hedge Ratio
The dollar value of futures contracts that should be sold per $ of cash position exposure.

An FI manager could use this ratio, h, as a **hedge ratio** to solve the question of how many futures should be sold to hedge the long position in the British pound when the spot and futures prices are imperfectly correlated. Specifically, the value of h means that for every £1 in the long asset position, £1.66 futures contracts should be sold. To see this, let's look at the FI's losses on its long asset position in pound loans relative to the gains on its selling pound futures.

Loss on British Pound Loans.   As before, its losses are

$$[£115 \text{ million}] \times [\$1.634/£ - \$1.584/£] = \$5.75 \text{ million}$$

Gains on British Pound Futures Position.   Taking into account the degree to which spot exchange rates are more sensitive than futures prices—the hedge ratio (h)—means that we can solve for the number of futures (N_F) to sell as

$$N_f = \frac{\text{Long asset position} \times h}{\text{Size of one futures contract}}$$

$$N_f = \frac{£115 \text{ million} \times 1.66}{£62,500} = 3,054.4 \text{ contracts}$$

or, rounding down to the nearest whole contract, 3,054 contracts. Selling 3,054 British pound futures results in expected profits of

$$[3,054 \times £62,500] \times [\$1.6304/£ - \$1.6004/£] = \$5.73 \text{ million}$$

The difference of $0.02 million between the loss on British pound loans and the gain on the pound futures is due to rounding.

Estimating the Hedge Ratio

In the previous example, we showed that the number of FX futures that should be sold to hedge fully foreign exchange rate risk exposure depends crucially on expectations regarding the correlation between the change in the dollar/pound spot rate (ΔS_t) and the change in its futures price (Δf_t). When

$$h = \frac{\Delta S_t}{\Delta f_t} = \frac{\$.05}{\$.05} = 1$$

there is no basis risk. Both the spot and futures are expected to change together by the same absolute amount, and the FX risk of the cash position should be hedged dollar for dollar by selling FX futures. When basis risk is present, the spot and futures are expected to move imperfectly together:

$$h = \frac{\Delta S_t}{\Delta f_t} = \frac{\$.05}{\$.03} = 1.66$$

The FI must sell a greater number of futures than it has to when basis risk is absent.

Unfortunately, without perfect foresight, we cannot know exactly how exchange rates and futures prices will change over some future time period. If we did, we would have no need to hedge in the first place! Thus, a common method to calculate h is to look at the behavior of ΔS_t relative to Δf_t over the *recent past* and to use this past behavior as a prediction of the appropriate value of h in the future. One

FIGURE 24–5

Monthly Changes in ΔS_t and Δf_t in 200X

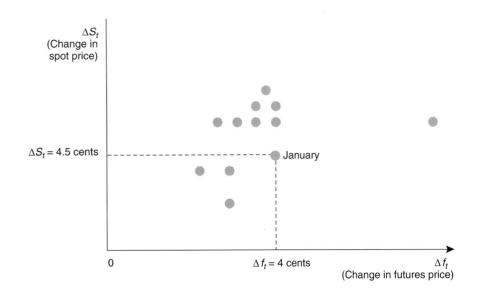

way to estimate this past relationship is to run an ordinary least squares regression of recent changes in spot prices on recent changes in futures prices.[21]

Consider Figure 24–5, where we plot hypothetical monthly changes in the spot pound/dollar exchange rate (ΔS_t) against monthly changes in the futures pound/dollar price (Δf_t) for the year 200X. Thus, we have 12 observations from January through December.

For information purposes, the first observation (January) is labeled in Figure 24–5. In January, the dollar/pound spot rate rose by 4.5 cents and the dollar/pound futures price rose by 4 cents. Thus, the pound appreciated in value over the month of January but the spot exchange rate rose by more than the futures price did. In some other months, as implied by the scatter of points in Figure 24–5, the futures price rose by more than the spot rate did.

An ordinary least squares (OLS) regression fits a line of best fit to these monthly observations such that the sum of the squared deviations between the observed values of ΔS_t and its predicted values (as given by the line of best fit) are minimized. This line of best fit reflects an intercept term α and a slope coefficient β. That is,

$$\Delta S_t = \alpha + \beta \, \Delta f_t + u_t$$

where the u_t are the regression's residuals (the differences between actual values of ΔS_t and its predicted values based on the line of best fit).

Definitionally, β, or the slope coefficient, of the regression equation is equal to

$$\beta = \frac{\text{Cov} \, (\Delta S_t, \Delta f_t)}{\text{Var} \, (\Delta f_t)}$$

---

[21]When we calculate h (the hedge ratio), we could use the ratio of the most recent spot and futures price changes. However, this would amount to basing our hedge ratio estimate on *one* observation of the change in S_t and f_t. This is why the regression model, which uses many past observations, is usually preferred by market participants.

that is, the covariance between the change in spot rates and change in futures prices divided by the variance of the change in futures prices. Suppose ΔS_t and Δf_t moved perfectly together over time. Then

$$\text{Cov } (\Delta S_t, \Delta f_t) = \text{Var } (\Delta f_t)$$
$$\text{and } \beta = 1$$

If spot rate changes are greater than futures price changes, then $\text{Cov } (\Delta S_t, \Delta f_t) > \text{Var } (\Delta f_t)$ and $\beta > 1$. Conversely, if spot rate changes are less sensitive than futures price changes over time, then $\text{Cov } (\Delta S_t, \Delta f_t) < \text{Var } (\Delta f_t)$ and $\beta < 1$.

Moreover, the value of β, or the estimated slope of the regression line, has theoretical meaning as the hedge ratio (h) that minimizes the risk of a portfolio of spot assets and futures contracts.[22] Put more simply, we can use the estimate of β from the regression model as the appropriate measure of h (the hedge ratio) to be used by the FI manager. For example, suppose we used the 12 observations on ΔS_t and Δf_t in 200X to estimate an OLS regression equation (the equation of the line of best fit in Figure 24–5). This regression equation takes the form

$$\Delta S_t = 0.15 + 1.2 \, \Delta f_t$$

Thus

$$\alpha = 0.15$$
$$\beta = 1.2$$

Using $\beta = 1.2$ as the appropriate risk minimizing hedge ratio h for the portfolio manager, we can solve our earlier problem of determining the number of futures contracts to sell to protect the FI from FX losses on its £115 million loan:

$$N_F = \frac{\text{Long position in £ assets} \times \beta \text{ (the estimated value of the hedge ratio } h \text{ using past data)}}{\text{Size of one £ futures contract}}$$

$$N_F = \frac{£115 \text{ million} \times 1.2}{£62,500} = 2,208 \text{ contracts}$$

Thus, using the past relationship between ΔS_t and Δf_t as the best predictor of their future relationship over the succeeding year dictates that the FI manager sell 2,208 contracts.

The degree of confidence the FI manager may have in using such a method to determine the appropriate hedge ratio depends on how well the regression line fits the scatter of observations. The standard measure of the goodness of fit of a regression line is the R^2 of the equation, where the R^2 is the square of the correlation coefficient between ΔS_t and Δf_t:

$$R^2 = \rho^2 = \left[\frac{(\text{Cov } (\Delta S_t, \Delta f_t))}{\sigma_{\Delta S_t} \times \sigma_{\Delta f_t}} \right]^2$$

The term in brackets [ ] is the statistical definition of a correlation coefficient. If changes in the spot rate (ΔS_t) and changes in the futures price (Δf_t) are perfectly correlated, then

$$R^2 = \rho^2 = (1)^2 = 1$$

---

[22]For proof of this, see L. H. Ederington, "The Hedging Performance of the New Futures Markets," *Journal of Finance* 34 (1979), pp. 157–70.

and all observations between ΔS_t and Δf_t lie on a straight line. By comparison, an $R^2 = 0$ indicates that there is no statistical association at all between ΔS_t and Δf_t.

Hedging Effectiveness
The (squared) correlation between past changes in spot asset prices and futures prices.

Since we are using futures contracts to hedge the risk of loss on spot asset positions, the R^2 of the regression measures the degree of **hedging effectiveness** of the futures contract. A low R^2 would mean that we might have little confidence that the slope coefficient β from the regression is actually the true hedge ratio. As the R^2 approaches 1, our degree of confidence increases in the use of futures contracts, with a given hedge ratio (h) estimate, to hedge our cash asset-risk position.

Concept Questions

1. Circle an observation in Figure 24–5 that shows futures price changes exceeding spot price changes.
2. Suppose that $R^2 = 0$ in a regression of ΔS_t on Δf_t. Would you still use futures contracts to hedge? Explain your answer.
3. In running a regression of ΔS_t on Δf_t, the regression equation is $\Delta S_t = .51 + .95 \Delta f_t$ and $R^2 = .72$. What is the hedge ratio? What is the measure of hedging effectiveness?

Hedging Credit Risk with Futures and Forwards

In Chapter 12, we demonstrated that by diversifying their loan portfolios across different borrowers, sectors, and regions, FIs could diversify away much of the borrower-specific or unsystematic risk of the loan portfolio. Of course, the ability of an FI manager to diversify sufficiently depends in part on the size of the loan portfolio under management. Thus, the potential ability to diversify away borrower-specific risk increases with the size of the FI.

In recent years, however, new types of derivative instruments have been developed (including forwards, options, and swaps) to better allow FIs to hedge their credit risk. As discussed in the Contemporary Perspectives box on p. 580, the market for these instruments is developing very quickly. Credit derivatives can be used to hedge the credit risk on individual loans or bonds or on portfolios of loans and bonds. The emergence of these new derivatives is important since more FIs fail due to credit risk exposures than to either interest rate or FX risk exposures. We discuss credit forward contracts below. In Chapter 25 we discuss credit options, and in Chapter 26 we discuss credit swaps.

Credit Forward Contracts and Credit Risk Hedging

Credit Forward
An agreement that hedges against an increase in default risk on a loan after the loan terms have been determined and the loan has been issued.

A **credit forward** is a forward agreement that hedges against an increase in default risk on a loan (a decline in the credit quality of a borrower) after the loan rate is determined and the loan is issued. Common buyers of credit forwards are insurance companies, and common sellers are banks. The credit forward agreement specifies a credit spread (a risk premium above the risk-free rate to compensate for default risk) on a benchmark bond issued by a bank borrower. For example, suppose the benchmark bond of the borrower was rated BBB at the time a loan was originated from a bank and it had an interest spread over a U.S. Treasury bond of the same maturity of 2 percent. Then $S_F = 2$ percent defines the credit spread on which the credit forward contract is written. Figure 24–6 illustrates the payment pattern on a credit

NEW YORK OVERTAKEN IN CREDIT HEDGE MARKET

George Graham

London has overtaken New York as the leading centre for the fast growing market in credit derivatives, which allow banks to insure against the risk that their borrowers will not repay them.

The first credit derivatives were created in New York in 1992, but a survey by the British Bankers Association says the London market is already larger than New York, with contracts outstanding covering $20bn of loans. That is estimated to be about half the world market.

Large banks have started to pour money into credit derivatives which they see as one of the most exciting new opportunities to boost trading and manage their risks.

Banks can use credit derivatives to hedge themselves against changes in a borrower's credit-worthiness, in the same way that traditional derivatives such as interest or exchange rate swaps and options enable them to hedge against market fluctuations.

Dealers contacted by the BBA said the London market was likely to grow to more than $100bn by 2000—a number which still pales beside the $46,000bn of traditional interest rate and foreign exchange derivatives. But even in London, the biggest participants are all US institutions, such as Chase Manhattan, or Japanese securities houses, such as Daiwa and Nomura.

Although banks spend millions of dollars hedging interest rate and currency risks, most banking disasters still result from old-fashioned credit problems.

Usually banks have run into trouble by lending too much to one risky sector, such as Latin American governments in the 1980s or Japanese property developers in the 1990s.

Bankers believe credit derivatives will give them a more sophisticated way of managing their credit risks.

Emerging market debt is expected to be the biggest application for credit derivatives, but leading dealers also believe European monetary union will open up a new market.

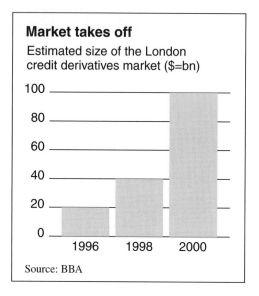

Market takes off
Estimated size of the London credit derivatives market ($=bn)

Source: BBA

Because the euro will eliminate currency risk in the European monetary union area, credit risk will become the only factor separating one government's bond interest rate from another's.

The earliest credit derivatives were known as default swaps. In effect, a bank pays an insurance premium to another bank, which promises to pay up if a borrower defaults on its loan.

But the fastest growing segment is now credit spread derivatives which allow banks to trade smaller shifts in a borrower's credit rating, short of outright default.

Source: *Financial Times,* November 20, 1996, p. 1. Reprinted with permission from the November 20, 1996 issue of Financial Times.

forward. In Table 24–3, S_T is the actual credit spread on the bond when the credit forward matures, that is, one year after the loan was originated and the credit forward contract was entered into, *MD* is the modified duration on the benchmark BBB bond, and *A* is the principal amount of the forward agreement.

From the payment pattern established in the credit forward agreement, Table 24–3 shows that the credit forward buyer (an insurance company) bears the risk of an increase in default risk on the benchmark bond of the borrowing firm, while the credit forward seller (the bank lender) hedges itself against an increase in the

TABLE 24–3   Payment Pattern on a Credit Forward

Credit Spread at End of Forward Agreement	Credit Spread Seller (Bank)	Credit Spread Buyer (Counterparty)
$S_T > S_F$	Receives $(S_T - S_F) \times MD \times A$ Pays	Pays $(S_T - S_F) \times MD \times A$ Receives
$S_F > S_T$	$(S_F - S_T) \times MD \times A$	$(S_F - S_T) \times MD \times A$

borrower's default risk. That is, if the borrower's default risk increases so that when the forward agreement matures the market requires a higher credit spread on the borrower's benchmark bond, S_T, than that originally agreed to in the forward contract, S_F, (i.e., $S_T > S_F$), the credit forward buyer pays the credit forward seller, which is the bank, $(S_T - S_F) \times MD \times A$. For example, suppose the credit spread between BBB bonds and U.S. Treasury bonds widened to 3 percent from 2 percent over the year, the modified duration (*MD*) of the benchmark BBB bond was five years, and the size of the forward contract *A* was $10,000,000. Then the gain on the credit forward contract to the seller (the bank) would be $(3\% - 2\%) \times 5 \times \$10,000,000 = \$500,000$. This amount could be used to offset the loss in market value of the loan due to the rise in the borrower's default risk. However, if the borrower's default risk and credit spread decrease over the year, the credit forward seller pays the credit forward buyer $(S_F - S_T) \times MD \times A$. (However, the maximum loss on the forward contract (to the bank seller) is limited, as will be explained below.)

Figure 24–6 illustrates the impact on the bank from hedging the loan.[23] If the default risk on the loan increases, the value of the loan falls below its value at the beginning of the hedge period. However, the bank hedged the change in default risk by selling a credit forward contract. Assuming the credit spread on the borrower's benchmark bond also increases (so that $S_T > S_F$), the bank receives $(S_T - S_F) \times MD \times A$ on the forward contract. If the characteristics of the benchmark bond (i.e., change in credit spread, modified duration, and principal value) are the same as those of the bank's loan to the borrower, the loss on the balance sheet is offset completely by the gain (off the balance sheet) from the credit forward, in our example a $500,000 market value loss in the loan would be offset by a $500,000 gain from selling the credit forward contract.

If the default risk does not increase or decreases (so that $S_T < S_F$), the bank selling the forward contract will pay $(S_F - S_T) \times MD \times A$ to the credit forward buyer (the insurance company). However, importantly, this payout by the bank is limited to a maximum. This is when S_T falls to zero; that is, the default spread on BBB bonds falls to zero or the original BBB bonds of the borrower are viewed as having the same default risk as Treasury bonds (in other words, the credit spread or rate on the benchmark bond cannot fall below the risk-free rate). In this case the maximum loss on the credit forward $[S_F - (0)] \times MD \times A$ mirrors (offsets) the maximum and limited upside gain (return) on the loan. Anyone familiar with options will

[23]For additional discussion, see J. D. Finnerty, "Credit Derivatives, Infrastructure Finance, and Emerging Market Risk, *The Financier, ACMT,* February 1996, pp. 64–75.

FIGURE 24–6

Impact on Bank of Hedging a Loan with a Credit Forward Contract

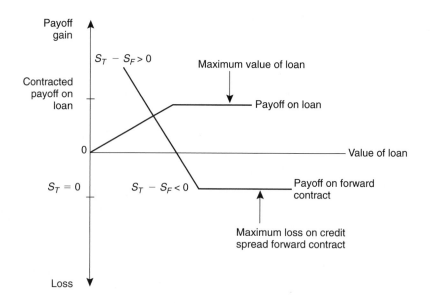

recognize that (as was discussed in Chapter 11) when the bank makes a loan, it is similar to writing a put option. In selling a credit forward, the payoff is similar to buying a put option (see Chapter 25 as well).

Futures Contracts and Catastrophe Risk

In recent years, the Chicago Board of Trade (CBOT) has also introduced futures and options for catastrophe insurance. In this chapter we will discuss catastrophe insurance futures, and in the next chapter we will discuss catastrophe insurance options. The essential idea of catastrophe futures is to allow property-casualty insurers to hedge the extreme losses that occur after major hurricanes, such as Hurricane Andrew in 1992, which resulted in damage of over $10 billion and losses exceeding 20 percent of 1992 premium income on the properties directly affected. Since in a catastrophe the ratio of insured losses to premiums rises (i.e., the so-called loss ratio increases), the payoff on a catastrophe futures contract is directly linked to the loss ratio. Specifically, on settlement, the payoff to the buyer of the futures is equal to the nominal value of the futures contract (which is $25,000) times the actual loss ratio incurred by insurers. Suppose that on maturity of the futures contract the loss ratio was 1.5. This means that the payoff to the insurance company futures hedger would be 1.5 × $25,000 = $37,500. Also suppose that three months earlier (before the catastrophe occurred) the market expected the loss ratio to be only 0.8. Thus, the insurer would have been able to pay 0.8 × $25,000 = $20,000 to buy the futures contract. Because actual losses exceeded expected losses, the insurer makes a profit of $37,500 − $20,000 = $17,500 on each contract. These profits on futures contracts can be used to help offset the huge payouts on hurricane insurance contracts.[24]

[24]For more details on catastrophe insurance futures, see J. D. Cummins and H. Geman, "Pricing Catastrophe Insurance Futures and Call Spreads: An Arbitrage Model," *Journal of Fixed Income,* March 1995, pp. 46–57.

Concept Questions

1. Why are credit forwards useful for hedging the credit risk of an FI's portfolio?
2. What are some of the practical problems an FI manager may face when using catastrophe futures to hedge losses on insurance lines?

Futures and Forward Policies of Regulators

As described earlier in the Contemporary Perspectives box on p. 560, the main regulator of accounting standards (the FASB) requires all FIs (and firms) to reflect the mark-to-market value of their derivative positions in their financial statements beginning January 1, 2000. This means that they will have to immediately recognize all gains and losses on such contracts and disclose those gains and losses to shareholders and regulators.

The main bank regulators—the Federal Reserve, the FDIC, and the Comptroller of the Currency—have also issued uniform guidelines for trading in futures and forwards.[25] These guidelines require a bank to (1) establish internal guidelines regarding its hedging activity, (2) establish trading limits, and (3) disclose large contract positions that materially affect bank risk to shareholders and outside investors. Overall, the policy of regulators is to encourage the use of futures for hedging and discourage their use for speculation, although on a practical basis it is often difficult to distinguish between the two.

Finally, as noted in Chapter 20, futures contracts are not subject to risk-based capital requirements; by contrast, OTC forward contracts are potentially subject to capital requirements. Other things being equal, the risk-based capital requirements favor the use of futures over forwards.

Summary

In this chapter we analyzed the risk-management role of futures and forwards. We saw that while they are close substitutes, they are not perfect substitutes. A number of characteristics, such as maturity, liquidity, flexibility, marking to market, and capital requirements, differentiate these products and make one or the other more attractive to any given FI manager. These products might be used to partially or fully hedge at least four types of risk commonly faced by an FI: interest rate risk, foreign exchange risk, credit risk, and catastrophe risk. An FI can engage in microhedging or macrohedging as well as engage in selective or routine hedging. In all cases, perfect hedging is shown to be difficult because of basis risk. Finally, accounting rules require FIs to disclose the market values of their (off-balance-sheet) derivatives positions.

Questions and Problems

1. What are derivative contracts? What is the value of derivative contracts to the managers of FIs? Which type of derivative contracts had the highest volume among all U.S. banks as of September 1997?

2. What has been the regulatory result of some of the misuses by FIs of derivative products?

3. What are some of the major differences between futures and forward contracts? How do these contracts differ from spot contracts?

---

[25]See B. C. Gendreau, "The Regulation of Bank Trading in Futures and Forward Markets," in *Below the Bottom Line: The Use of Contingencies and Commitments by Commercial Banks* (Washington, D.C.: Federal Reserve Board of Governors, 1982).

4. What is a naive hedge? How does a naive hedge protect an FI from risk?

5. An FI holds a 15-year, par value, $10,000,000 bond that is priced at 104 with a yield to maturity of 7 percent. The bond has a duration of eight years, and the FI plans to sell it after two months. The FI's market analyst predicts that interest rates will be 8 percent at the time of the desired sale. Because most other analysts are predicting no change in rates, two-month forward contracts for 15-year bonds are available at 104. The FI would like to hedge against the expected change in interest rates with an appropriate position in a forward contract. What will this position be? Show that if rates rise 1 percent as forecast, the hedge will protect the FI from loss.

6. Contrast the position of being short with that of being long in futures contracts.

7. Suppose an FI purchases a Treasury bond futures contract at 95.

   a. What is the FI's obligation at the time the futures contract is purchased?

   b. If an FI purchases this contract, in what kind of hedge is it engaged?

   c. Assume that the Treasury bond futures price falls to 94. What is the loss or gain?

   d. Assume that the Treasury bond futures price rises to 97. Mark to market the position.

8. Long Bank has assets that consist mostly of 30-year mortgages and liabilities that are short-term time and demand deposits. Will an interest rate futures contract the bank buys add to or subtract from the bank's risk?

9. In each of the following cases, indicate whether it would be appropriate for an FI to buy or sell a forward contract to hedge the appropriate risk.

   a. A commercial bank plans to issue CDs in three months.

   b. An insurance company plans to buy bonds in two months.

   c. A thrift is going to sell Treasury securities next month.

   d. A U.S. bank lends to a French company; the loan is payable in francs.

   e. A finance company has assets with a duration of six years and liabilities with a duration of 13 years.

10. The duration of a 20-year, 8 percent coupon Treasury bond selling at par is 10.292 years. The bond's interest is paid semiannually, and the bond qualifies for delivery against the Treasury bond futures contract.

    a. What is the modified duration of this bond?

    b. What is the impact on the Treasury bond price if market interest rates increase 50 basis points?

    c. If you sold a Treasury bond futures contract at 95 and interest rates rose 50 basis points, what would be the change in the value of your futures position?

    d. If you purchased the bond at par and sold the futures contract, what would be the net value of your hedge after the increase in interest rates?

11. What are the differences between a microhedge and a macrohedge for an FI? Why is it generally more efficient for FIs to employ a macrohedge than a series of microhedges?

12. What are the reasons why an FI may choose to hedge selectively its portfolio ?

13. Hedge Row Bank has the following balance sheet (in millions):

Assets	$150	Liabilities	$135
		Equity	$ 15
Total	$150	Total	$150

The duration of the assets is six years, and the duration of the liabilities is four years. The bank is expecting interest rates to fall from 10 percent to 9 percent over the next year.

   a. What is the duration gap for Hedge Row Bank?

   b. What is the expected change in net worth for Hedge Row Bank if the forecast is accurate?

   c. What will be the effect on net worth if interest rates increase 100 basis points?

   d. If the existing interest rate on the liabilities is 6 percent, what will be the effect on net worth of a 1 percent increase in interest rates?

14. For a given change in interest rates, why is the sensitivity of the price of a Treasury bond futures contract greater than the sensitivity of the price of a Treasury bill futures contract?

15. What is the meaning of the Treasury bond futures price quote 101–13?

16. What is meant by fully hedging the balance sheet of an FI?

17. Tree Row Bank has assets of $150 million, liabilities of $135 million, and equity of $15 million. The asset duration is six years, and the duration of the liabilities is four years. Market interest rates are 10 percent. Tree Row Bank wishes to hedge the balance sheet with Treasury bond futures contracts, which currently have a price quote of $95 per $100 face value for the benchmark 20-year, 8 percent coupon bond underlying the contract.

   a. Should the bank go short or long on the futures contracts to establish the correct macrohedge?

b. How many contracts are necessary to hedge fully the bank?

c. Verify that the change in the futures position will offset the change in the cash balance sheet position for a change in market interest rates of plus 100 basis points and minus 50 basis points.

d. If the bank had hedged with Treasury bill futures contracts which had a market value of $98 per $100 of face value, how many futures contracts would have been necessary to hedge fully the balance sheet?

e. What additional issues should be considered by the bank in choosing between T-bonds and T-bills futures contracts?

18. Reconsider Tree Row Bank in problem 17 but assume that the cost rate on the liabilities is 6 percent.

a. How many contracts are necessary to hedge fully the bank?

b. Verify that the change in the futures position will offset the change in the cash balance sheet position for a change in market interest rates of plus 100 basis points and minus 50 basis points.

c. If the bank had hedged with Treasury bill futures contracts which had a market value of $98 per $100 of face value, how many futures contracts would have been necessary to hedge fully the balance sheet?

19. What is basis risk? What are the sources of basis risk?

20. How would your answers for part (b) in problem 17 change if the relationship of the price sensitivity of futures contracts to the price sensitivity of underlying bonds were $b = 0.92$?

21. A mutual fund plans to purchase $500,000 of 30-year Treasury bonds in four months. These bonds have a duration of 12 years and are priced at 96–08. The mutual fund is concerned about interest rates changing over the next four months and is considering a hedge with T-bond futures contracts that mature in six months. The T-bond futures contracts are selling for 98–24 and have a duration of 8.5 years.

a. If interest rate changes in the spot market exactly match those in the futures market, what types of futures position should the mutual fund create?

b. How many contracts should be used?

c. If the implied rate on the deliverable bond in the futures market moves 12 percent more than the change in the discounted spot rate, how many futures contracts should be used to hedge the portfolio?

d. What causes futures contracts to have different price sensitivity than assets in the spot markets?

22. Consider the following balance sheet (in millions) for an FI:

Assets	Liabilities
Duration = 10 years $950	Duration = 2 years $860
	Equity 90

a. What is the FI's duration gap?

b. What is the FI's interest rate risk exposure?

c. How can the FI use futures and forward contracts to put on a macrohedge?

d. What is the impact on the FI's equity value if the relative change in interest rates is an increase of 1 percent? That is $\Delta R/(1 + R) = 0.01$.

e. Suppose that the FI in part (c) macrohedges using Treasury bond futures that are currently priced at 96. What is the impact on the FI's futures position if the relative change in all interest rates is an increase of 1 percent? That is $\Delta R/(1 + R) = 0.01$. Assume that the deliverable Treasury bond has a duration of nine years.

f. If the FI wants a perfect macrohedge, how many Treasury bond futures contracts does it need?

Refer again to problem 22.

23. How does consideration of basis risk change your answers to problem 22?

a. Compute the number of futures contracts required to construct a perfect macrohedge if

$$[\Delta R_f/(1 + R_f)/\Delta R/(1 + R)] = b = 0.90$$

b. Explain what is meant by $b = 0.90$.

c. If $b = 0.90$, what information does this provide on the number of futures contracts needed to construct a perfect macrohedge?

24. An FI is planning to hedge its $100 million bond instruments with a cross hedge using Euromark interest rate futures. How would the FI estimate

$$b = [\Delta R_f/(1 + R_f)/\Delta R/(1 + R)]$$

to determine the exact number of Euromark futures contracts to hedge?

25. Village Bank has $240 million worth of assets with a duration of 14 years and liabilities worth $210 million with a duration of 4 years. In the interest of hedging interest rate risk, Village Bank is contemplating a macrohedge with interest rate futures contracts now selling for 102–21. If the spot and futures interest rates move together, how many futures contracts must Village Bank sell to hedge fully the balance sheet?

26. Assume that an FI has assets of $250 million and liabilities of $200 million. The duration of the assets is six years, and the duration of the liabilities is three years.

The price of the futures contract is $115,000, and its duration is 5.5 years.

a. What is the number of futures contracts needed to construct a perfect hedge if $b = 1.10$?

b. If $\Delta R_f/(1 + R_f) = 0.0990$, what is the expected $\Delta R/(1 + R)$?

27. Suppose an FI purchases a $1 million 91-day Eurodollar futures contract trading at 98.50.

a. If the contract is reversed two days later by purchasing the contract at 98.60, what is the net profit?

b. What is the loss or gain if the price at reversal is 98.40?

28. What factors may make the use of swaps or forward contracts preferable to the use of futures contracts for the purpose of hedging long-term foreign exchange positions?

29. An FI has an asset investment in German marks. The FI expects the exchange rate of $/DM to increase by the maturity of the asset.

a. Is the dollar appreciating or depreciating against the mark?

b. To fully hedge the investment, should the FI buy or sell deutsche mark futures contracts?

c. If there is perfect correlation between changes in the spot and futures contracts, how should the FI determine the number of contracts necessary to hedge the investment fully?

30. What is meant by tailing the hedge? What factors allow an FI manager to tail the hedge effectively?

31. What does the hedge ratio measure? Under what conditions is this ratio valuable in determining the number of futures contracts necessary to hedge fully an investment in another currency? How is the hedge ratio related to basis risk?

32. What technique is commonly used to estimate the hedge ratio? What statistical measure is an indicator of the confidence that should be placed in the estimated hedge ratio? What is the interpretation if the estimated hedge ratio is greater than one? Less than one?

33. An FI has assets denominated in British pounds sterling of $125 million and sterling liabilities of $100 million.

a. What is the FI's net exposure?

b. Is the FI exposed to a dollar appreciation or depreciation?

c. How can the FI use futures or forward contracts to hedge its FX rate risk?

d. What is the number of futures contracts that must be utilized to hedge fully the FI's currency risk exposure?

e. If the British pound falls from $1.60/£ to $1.50/£, what will be the impact on the FI's cash position?

f. If the British pound futures price falls from $1.55/£ to $1.45/£, what will be the impact on the FI's futures position?

g. Using the information in parts (e) and (f), what can you conclude about basis risk?

34. Refer to problem 33, part (f).

a. If the British pound futures price fell from $1.55/£ to $1.43/£, what would be the impact on the FI's futures position?

b. Does your answer to part (a) differ from your answer to part (f) in problem 33? Why or why not?

c. How would you fully hedge the FX risk exposure in problem 33 using the new futures price change?

35. An FI is planning to hedge its one-year $100 million deutsche mark (DM)–denominated loan against exchange rate risk. The current spot rate is $0.60/DM. A 1-year DM futures contract is currently trading at $0.58/DM. DM futures are sold in standardized units of DM62,500.

a. Should the FI be worried about the DM appreciating or depreciating?

b. Should it buy or sell futures to hedge against exchange rate exposure?

c. How many futures contracts should it buy or sell if a regression of past changes in spot prices on changes in future prices generates an estimated slope of 1.4?

d. Show exactly how the FI is hedged if it repatriates its principal of DM100 million at year end and the spot price of DM at year end is $0.55/DM.

36. An FI has made a loan commitment of DM10 million that is likely to be taken down in six months. The current spot rate is $0.60/DM.

a. Is the FI exposed to the dollar's depreciating or appreciating? Why?

b. If the spot rate six months from today is $0.64/DM, what amount of dollars is needed if the loan is taken down and the FI is unhedged?

c. If it decides to hedge using DM futures, should the FI buy or sell DM futures?

d. A six-month DM futures contract is available for $0.61/DM. What net amount would be needed to fund the loan at the end of six months if the FI had hedged using the DM10 million futures contract? Assume that futures prices are equal to spot prices at the time of payment (i.e., at maturity).

37. A U.S. FI has assets denominated in deutsche marks (DM) of 75 million and liabilities of 125 million. The spot rate is $0.6667/DM, and one-year futures are available for $0.6579/DM.

a. What is the FI's net exposure?

b. Is the FI exposed to dollar appreciation or depreciation?

c. If the DM spot rate falls from $0.6667/DM to $0.6897/DM, how will this impact the FI's currency exposure? Assume no hedging.

d. What is the number of futures contracts necessary to fully hedge the currency risk exposure of the FI? The contract size is DM62,500 per contract.

e. If the DM futures price falls from $0.6579/DM to $0.6349/DM, what will be the impact on the FI's futures position?

38. What is a credit forward? How is it structured?

39. What is the gain on the purchase of a $20,000,000 credit forward contract with a modified duration of seven years if the credit spread between a benchmark Treasury bond and a borrowing firm's debt decreases 50 basis points?

40. How is selling a credit forward similar to buying a put option?

41. A property-casualty (PC) insurance company purchased catastrophe futures contracts to hedge against loss during the hurricane season. At the time of purchase, the market expected a loss ratio of 0.75. After processing claims from a severe hurricane, the PC actually incurred a loss ratio of 1.35. What amount of profit did the PC make on each $25,000 futures contract?

42. What is the primary goal of regulators in regard to the use of futures by FIs? What guidelines have regulators given to banks for trading in futures and forwards?

OPTIONS, CAPS, FLOORS, AND COLLARS

Introduction

Just as there is a wide variety of forward and futures contracts available for an FI to use in hedging, there is an even wider array of option products, including exchange-traded options, over-the-counter options, options embedded in securities, and caps, collars, and floors.

In this chapter we mostly concentrate on the use of fixed-income or interest rate options to hedge interest rate risk. We also discuss the role of options in hedging foreign exchange and credit risks as well as catastrophe risk. We start by reviewing the four basic options strategies: buying a call, writing a call, buying a put, and writing a put.[1]

Basic Features of Options

In describing the features of the four basic option strategies FIs might employ, we discuss their return payoffs in terms of interest rate movements. Specifically, we consider bond options whose payoff values are inversely linked to interest rate movements in a manner similar to bond prices and interest rates in general (see Chapter 8).

Buying a Call Option on a Bond

Call Option

Gives a purchaser the right (but not the obligation) to buy the underlying security from the writer of the option at a prespecified exercise price on a prespecified date.

The first strategy of buying a call option on a bond is shown in Figure 25–1. A **call option** gives the purchaser the right (but not the obligation) to buy the underlying security—a bond—at a prespecified exercise or strike price (X). In return, the buyer of the call option must pay the writer or seller an up-front fee known as a call premium (C). This premium is an immediate negative cash flow for the buyer of the call, who potentially stands to make a profit if the underlying bond's price rises above the exercise price by an amount exceeding the premium.

As shown in Figure 25–1, if the price of the bond underlying the option rises to price $0B$, the buyer makes a profit of 0π, which is the difference between the bond price ($0B$) and the exercise price of the option ($0X$) minus the call premium (C). If it rises to $0A$, the buyer of the call has broken even in that the profit from exercising the call ($0A - 0X$) just equals the premium payment for the call (C).

FIGURE 25–1

Payoff Function for the Buyer of a Call Option on a Bond

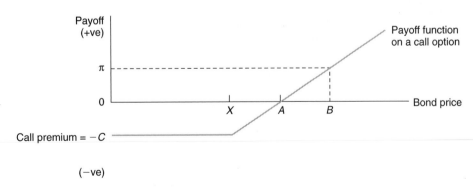

[1]There are two basic option contracts: puts and calls. However, an FI could potentially be a buyer or seller (writer) of each.

Notice two important things about bond call options in Figure 25–1:

1. As interest rates fall, bond prices rise and the potential for a positive (+ve) payoff for the buyer of the call option on a bond increases.
2. As interest rates rise, bond prices fall and the potential for a negative (−ve) payoff (loss) for the buyer of the call option increases. However, the losses of the buyer are truncated by the amount of the up-front premium payment (C) made to purchase the call option.

Thus, unlike interest rate futures, whose prices and payoffs move symmetrically with changes in the level of rates, the payoffs on bond call options move asymmetrically with interest rates (see Chapter 24).

Writing a Call Option on a Bond

The second strategy is writing a call option on a bond. In writing a call option on a bond, the writer or seller receives an up-front fee or premium and must stand ready to sell the underlying bond to the purchaser of the option at the exercise price X. Note the payoff from writing a call option on a bond in Figure 25–2.

There are two important things to notice about this payoff function:

1. When interest rates *rise* and bond prices *fall*, there is an increased potential for the writer of the call to receive a positive payoff or profit. However, this profit has a maximum equal to the call premium (C) charged up front to the buyer of the option.
2. When interest rates fall and bond prices rise, the writer has an increased potential to take a loss. Since bond prices are theoretically unbounded in the upward direction, although they must return to par at maturity, these losses could be very large.

In Figure 25–2, a fall in interest rates and a rise in bond prices to 0B results in the writer of the option losing 0π.

Put Option
Gives a purchaser the right (but not the obligation) to sell the underlying security to the writer of the option at a prespecified exercise price on a prespecified date.

Buying a Put Option on a Bond

The third strategy is buying a put option on a bond. The buyer of a **put option** on a bond has the right (but not the obligation) to sell the underlying bond to the writer of the option at the agreed exercise price (X). In return for this option, the buyer of the put option pays a premium to the writer (P). We show the potential payoffs to the buyer of the put option in Figure 25–3. Note that:

FIGURE 25–2

Payoff from Writing a Call Option on a Bond

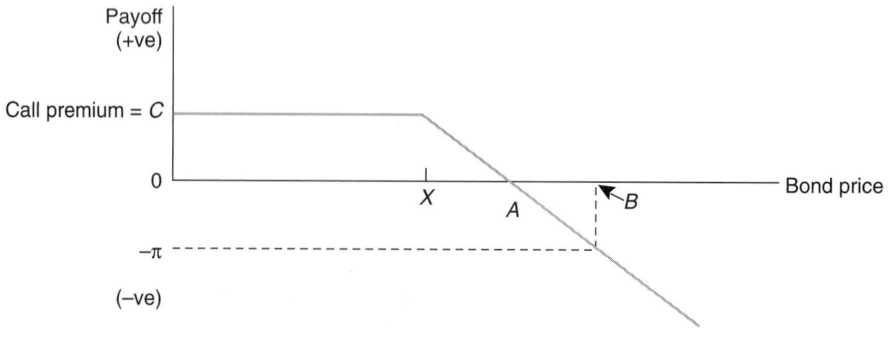

1. When interest rates rise and bond prices fall, the buyer of the put has an increased probability of making a profit from exercising the option. Thus, if bond prices fall to 0*D*, the buyer of the put option can purchase bonds in the bond market at that price and put them (sell them) back to the writer of the put at the higher exercise price (0*X*). As a result, the buyer makes a profit, after deducting the cost of the put premium (*P*), of πp in Figure 25–3.

2. When interest rates fall and bond prices rise, the probability of the buyer of a put losing increases. However, the maximum loss is limited to the size of the up-front put premium (*P*).

Writing a Put Option on a Bond

The fourth strategy is writing a put option on a bond. In writing a put option on a bond, the writer or seller receives a fee or premium (*P*) in return for standing ready to buy bonds at the exercise price (*X*) if the buyer of the put chooses to exercise the option to sell. See the payoff function for writing a put option on a bond in Figure 25–4. Note that:

1. If interest rates rise and bond prices fall, the writer of the put is exposed to potentially large losses (e.g., $-\pi p$, if bond prices fall to 0*D* in Figure 25–4).

2. If interest rates fall and bond prices rise, the writer has an enhanced probability of making a profit. However, the writer's maximum profit is constrained to be equal to the put premium (*P*).

FIGURE 25–3

Buying a Put Option on a Bond

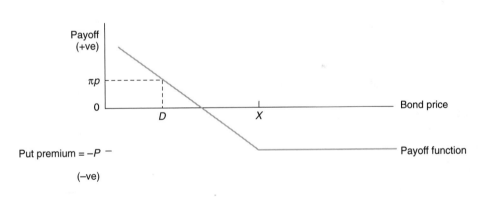

FIGURE 25–4

Writing a Put Option on a Bond

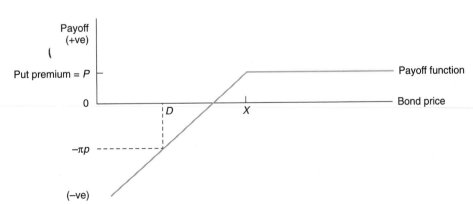

Concept Questions

1. How do interest rate increases affect the payoff from buying a call option on a bond? How do they affect the payoff from writing a call option on a bond?
2. How do interest rate increases affect the payoff from buying a put option on a bond? How do they affect the payoff from writing a put option on a bond?

Writing versus Buying Options

For many smaller FIs, the relevant strategy set is constrained to buying rather than writing options. There are two reasons for this, one economic and the other regulatory. However, as we note later, large FIs such as money center banks often both write and buy options including caps, floors, and collars that are complex forms of interest rate options.

Economic Reasons for Not Writing Options

In writing an option, the upside profit potential is truncated, whereas the payoffs on the downside losses are not. While such risks may be offset by writing a large number of options at different exercise prices and/or hedging an underlying portfolio of bonds, the downside risk exposure of the writer may still be significant. To see this, look at Figure 25–5, where an FI is long in a bond in its portfolio and seeks to hedge the interest rate risk on that bond by writing a bond call option.

As you can see, writing the call may hedge the FI when rates fall and bond prices rise; that is, the increase in the value of the bond is offset by losses on the written call. When the reverse occurs and interest rates rise, the FI's profits from writing the call may be insufficient to offset the loss on its bonds. This is the case because the upside profit (per call written) is truncated and is equal to the premium income (C).

By contrast, hedging the FI's risk by buying a put option on a bond offers the manager a much more attractive alternative. You can see this from Figure 25–6, the gross payoff of the bond and the payoff from buying a put option on a bond, and in Figure 25–7, the net payoff or the difference between the bond and option payoff.

FIGURE 25–5

Writing a Call Option to Hedge the Interest Rate Risk on a Bond

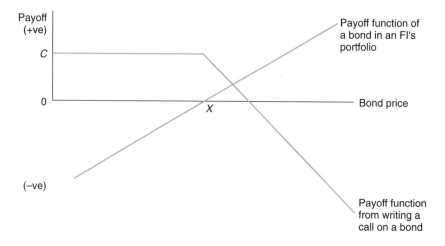

Note that:

1. Buying a put option truncates the downside losses on the bond following interest rate rises to some maximum amount and scales down the upside profits by the cost of bond price risk insurance—the put premium—leaving some positive upside profit potential.

2. The combination of being long in the bond and buying a put option on a bond mimics the payoff function of buying a call option (compare Figures 25–1 and 25–7).

Regulatory Reasons

There are also regulatory reasons why FIs buy options rather than write options. Regulators view writing options, especially naked options that do not identifiably hedge an underlying asset or liability position, as risky because of the unlimited loss potential. Indeed, in the past, bank regulators prohibited banks from writing puts or calls in certain areas of risk management.

Concept Questions

1. What are some of the economic reasons for an FI not to write options?
2. What are some regulatory reasons why an FI might choose to buy options rather than write options?

FIGURE 25–6

Buying a Put Option to Hedge the Interest Rate Risk on a Bond

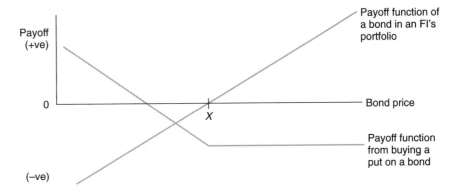

FIGURE 25–7

Net Payoff of Buying a Bond Put and Investing in a Bond

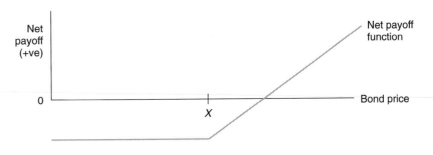

The Mechanics of Hedging a Bond or Bond Portfolio

You have seen how buying a put option on a bond can potentially hedge the interest rate risk exposure of an FI that holds bonds as part of its asset investment portfolio. In this section, we use a simple example to demonstrate how buying a put option works mechanically as a hedging device and how an FI manager can calculate the fair value of the premium to pay for buying a put option on a bond.

In calculating the fair value of an option, two alternative models can be used: the binomial model and the Black-Scholes model. The Black-Scholes model produces a closed-form solution to the valuation of call and put options. Although it works well for stocks, the Black-Scholes model has two major problems when employed to value bond options. First, it assumes that short-term interest rates are constant, which they generally are not. Second, it assumes a constant variance of returns on the underlying asset.[2] The problem with applying the Black-Scholes formula to bonds is the way bond prices behave between issuance and maturity.[3] This is shown in Figure 25–8, where a bond is issued at par, that is, at 100 at time of issue. If interest rates fall, its price may rise above 100, and if interest rates rise, its price may fall below 100. However, as the bond approaches maturity, all price paths must lead to 100, the face value of the bond or principal paid by the issuer on maturity. Because of this **pull-to-par,** the variance of bond prices is nonconstant over time, rising at first and then falling as the bond approaches maturity. We evaluate the mechanics of hedging using bond put options in a simple binomial framework next.

Pull-to-Par
The tendency of the variance of a bond's price or return to decrease as maturity approaches.

Hedging with Bond Options Using the Binomial Model

Let's suppose that an FI manager has purchased a zero-coupon bond with exactly two years to maturity. A zero-coupon bond, if held to maturity, pays its face value of

---

[2]The Black-Scholes formulas for a put and a call are

$$P = Xe^{-rT}N[-D + \sigma\sqrt{T}] - SN[-D]$$
$$C = SN[D] - Xe^{-rT}N[D - \sigma\sqrt{T}]$$

where
      S = Price of the underlying asset
      X = Exercise price
      T = Time to option expiration
      r = Instantaneous riskless interest rate

$$D = \frac{ln(S/X) + (r + \sigma^2/2)T}{\sigma\sqrt{T}}$$

  $ln[\,.\,]$ = Natural logarithm
     σ = Volatility of the underlying asset
  $N[\,.\,]$ = Cumulative normal distribution function, that is, the probability of observing a value less than the value in brackets when drawing randomly from a standardized normal distribution

[3]There are models that modify Black-Scholes to allow for nonconstant variance. These include Merton, who allows variance to be time dependent; Ball and Tourous, who allow bond prices to change as a stochastic process with a variance that first increases and then decreases (the Brownian bridge process); and the Schaefer-Schwartz model, which assumes that the standard deviation of returns is proportional to a bond's duration. See R. C. Merton, "On the Pricing of Corporate Debt: The Risk Structure of Interest Rates," *Journal of Finance* 29 (1974), pp. 449–70; C. Ball and W. N. Tourous, "Bond Price Dynamics and Options," *Journal of Financial and Quantitative Analysis* 18 (1983), pp. 517–31; and S. Schaefer and E. S. Schwartz, "Time Dependent Variance and the Pricing of Bond Options," *Journal of Finance* 42 (1987), pp. 1113–28.

FIGURE 25–8

The Variance of a Bond's Price

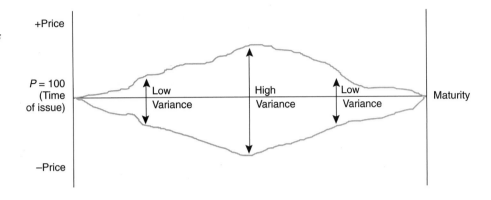

$100 on maturity in two years. Assume that the FI manager pays $80.45 per $100 of face value for this zero-coupon bond. This means that if held to maturity, the FI's annual yield to maturity (R_2) from this investment would be

$$P_2 = \frac{100}{(1 + R_2)^2}$$

$$80.45 = \frac{100}{(1 + R_2)^2}$$

$$(1 + R_2)^2 = \frac{100}{80.45}$$

$$1 + R_2 = \sqrt{\frac{100}{80.45}}$$

$$R_2 = \sqrt{\frac{100}{80.45}} - 1 = .115 = 11.5\%$$

Now, fearing unexpected deposit withdrawals, the FI manager may be forced to liquidate and sell this two-year bond before maturity. As we discuss in Chapter 17, Treasury securities are important liquidity sources for an FI. We assume here that the manager may have to sell the bond at the end of the first year. Because of uncertainty about future interest rates, the FI manager faces the risk that if interest rates rise over the next year, the bond will have to be sold at a low price if it is liquidated early at the end of the first year.

Suppose that the current yield on one-year discount bonds (R_1) is $R_1 = 10$ percent. Also, assume a forecast that next year's one-year interest rate (r_1) will rise to either 13.82 percent or 12.18 percent.

If one-year interest rates rise from $R_1 = 10$ percent this year to $r_1 = 13.82$ percent next year, the FI manager will be able to sell the zero-coupon bond with one year remaining to maturity for only a price of

$$P_1 = \frac{100}{(1 + r_1)} = \frac{100}{(1.1382)} = \$87.86$$

If, on the other hand, one-year interest rates rose to 12.18 percent, the manager could expect to sell the bond with one year remaining to maturity for

$$P_1 = \frac{100}{(1 + r_1)} = \frac{100}{(1.1218)} = \$89.14$$

In these equations, r_1 stands for the two possible one-year rates that might arise one year into the future.[4] That is:

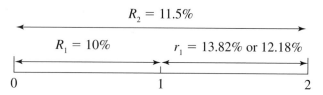

Assume the manager believes that one-year rates (r_1) one year from today will be 13.82 percent or 12.18 percent with an equal probability. This means that the expected one-year rate one year from today would be

$$[E(r_1)] = .5\,(.1382) + .5\,(.1218) = .13 = 13\%$$

Thus, the expected price if the bond has to be sold at the end of the first year is[5]

$$E(P_1) = \frac{100}{(1.13)} = \$88.5$$

Assume that the FI manager wants to ensure that the bond sale produces at least $88.5 per $100; otherwise the FI has to find alternative and very costly sources of liquidity (for example, the FI having to borrow from the central bank's discount window and incurring the direct and indirect penalty costs involved).

One way for the bank to ensure that it receives at least $88.5 on selling the bond at the end of the year is to buy a put option on the bond at time 0 with an exercise price of $88.5 at time 1. If the bond is trading below $88.5 at the end of year—say, at $87.86—the FI can exercise its option and put the bond back to the writer of the option, who will have to pay the FI $88.5. If, however, the bond is trading above the $88.5 level—say, at $89.14—the FI does not have to exercise its option and instead can sell the bond in the open market for $89.14.

What premium should the FI manager pay for buying this put option or bond insurance at time 0? To calculate this, look at Figure 25–9, which shows the possible paths of the zero-coupon bond's price from purchase to maturity over the two-year period.[6] The FI manager purchased the bond at $80.45 with two years to maturity. Given expectations of rising rates, there is a 50 percent probability that the bond with one year left to maturity will trade at $87.86 and a 50 percent probability that it will trade at $89.14. Note that between $t = 1$, or one year left to maturity, and

---

[4]If one-year bond rates next year equaled the one-year bond rate this year, $R_1 = r_1 = 10$ percent, then the bond could be sold for $P_1 = \$90.91$.

[5]The interest rates assumed in this example are consistent with arbitrage-free pricing under current term structure conditions. [See T. S. Y. Ho and S. B. Lee, "Term Structure Movements and Pricing Interest Rate Contingent Claims," *Journal of Finance* 61 (1986), pp. 1001–29.] That is, the expectations theory of interest rates implies that the following relationship must hold:

$$(1 + R_2)^2 = (1 + R_1) \times (1 + E(r_1))$$

As you can easily see, when the interest rates from our example are inserted, $R_1 = 10\%$, $R_2 = 11.5\%$, $E(r_1) = 13\%$, this equation holds. Also, the two interest rates (prices) imply that the current volatility of one-year interest rates is 6.3 percent. That is, from the binomial model, $\sigma = \frac{1}{2}ln\,[r_u/r_d]$, such that $\sigma = \frac{1}{2}ln[13.82/12.18] = .063$ or 6.3%.

[6]This example is based on R. Litterman and T. Iben, "Corporate Bond Valuation and the Term Structure of Credit Spreads," *Journal of Portfolio Management,* 1989, pp. 52–64.

maturity ($t = 2$), there must be a pull to par on the bond; that is, all paths must lead to a price of $100 on maturity.

Figure 25–9 shows the binomial tree or lattice. We show the value of the option in Figure 25–10.

The option in Figure 25–10 can be exercised only at the end of year 1 ($t = 1$). If the zero-coupon bond with one year left to maturity trades at $87.86, the option is worth $88.5 − $87.86 in time 1 dollars, or $0.64. If the bond were trading at $89.14, the option would have no value since the bond could be sold at a higher value than the exercise price of $88.5 on the open market. This suggests that in time 1 dollars, the option is worth

$$.5\,(0.64) + .5\,(0) = \$0.32$$

FIGURE 25–9

Binomial Model of Bond Prices: Two-Year Zero-Coupon Bond

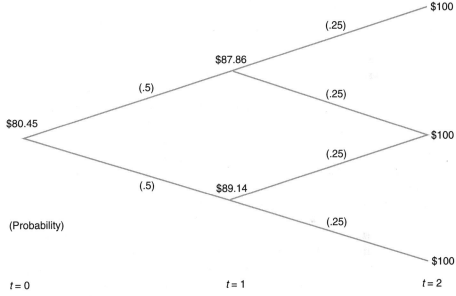

FIGURE 25–10

The Value of a Put Option on the Two-Year Zero-Coupon Bond

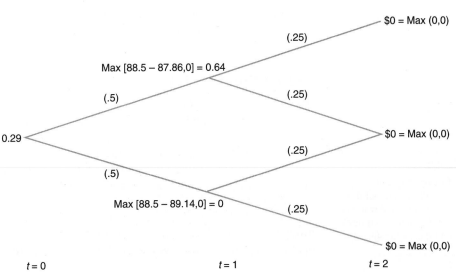

However, the FI is evaluating the option and paying the put premium at time $t = 0$, that is, one year before the date when the option might be exercised. Thus, the fair value of the put premium (P) the FI manager should be willing to pay is the discounted present value of the expected payoff from buying the option. Since one-year interest rates (R_1) are currently 10 percent, this implies:

$$P = \frac{\$0.32}{1 + R_1} = \frac{\$0.32}{(1.1)} = \$0.29$$

or approximately 29 cents per $100 bond option purchased.

Further, as you can easily see, the option becomes increasingly valuable as the variability of interest rates increases. Conceptually, the branches of the binomial tree diagram become more widely dispersed as variability increases. For example, suppose one-year interest rates on the upper branch were expected to be 14.82 percent instead of 13.82 percent. Then, the price on a one-year, zero-coupon bond associated with a one-year yield of 14.82 percent is $87.09 and the value of the put option with the same exercise price of $88.5 is

$$P = \frac{.5(1.41) + .5(0)}{1.1}$$

$$= 64 \text{ cents}$$

Thus, the familiar result from option pricing theory holds:

$$\frac{\delta P}{\delta \sigma} > 0$$

That is, the value of the put option increases with an increase in underlying variance of asset returns.

Concept Questions

1. What are two common models used to calculate the fair value of a bond option? Which is preferable, and why?
2. Referring to the example that concludes this section, calculate the value of the option if the exercise price (X) = $88.

Actual Bond Options

We have presented a simple example of how FIs may use bond options to hedge exposure to liability withdrawal and forced liquidation of assets in a world of interest rate variability. In actuality, FIs have a wide variety of over-the-counter (OTC) and exchange-traded options available. In Figure 25–11, we show exchange-traded interest rate options on the Chicago Board Options Exchange (CBOE). However, these contracts are rarely traded. In actual practice, most pure bond options trade over-the-counter.

This is not because interest rate or bond options aren't used, although the **open interest** is relatively small, but because the preferred method of hedging is an option on an interest rate futures contract. See these **futures options** on bonds in

Open Interest
The outstanding stock of put or call contracts.

Futures Option
An option contract that when exercised results in the delivery of a futures contract as the underlying asset.

FIGURE 25–11

Interest Rate Options, October 24, 1997

CBOE INTEREST OPTIONS

Friday, October 24, 1997

OPTIONS ON SHORT-TERM INTEREST RATES (IRX)

Strike	Calls-Last			Puts-Last		
Price	Nov	Dec	Jan	Nov	Dec	Jan
52 ½	....	3/16	....	....	....	.....

Total call volume 80   Total call open int. 1
Total put volume 0   Total put open int. 391
IRX levels: high 50.40; Low 49.80; Close 50.10, +0.40

30 YEAR TREASURY YIELD OPTION (TYX)

Strike	Calls-Last			Puts-Last		
Price	Nov	Dec	Jan	Nov	Dec	Jan
60	3 1/4	....	....	....	....	13/16
62½	1 7/8	2 1/8	2 ½	7/8	....	....
65	7/16	7/8	1 ½	2 9/16	....	....
70	.....	.....	.....	7 1/8	....	....

Total call volume 150   Total call open int. 2,846
Total put volume 145   Total put open int. 1,866
TYX levels: high 63.55; Low 62.65; Close 62.92, -0.28

Source: *The Wall Street Journal*, October 27, 1997, p. C14. Reprinted by permission of The Wall Street Journal, © 1997 Dow Jones & Company, Inc. All rights reserved worldwide.

Figure 25–12. Bond or interest rate futures options are generally preferred to options on the underlying bond because they combine the favorable liquidity, credit risk, homogeneity, and marking-to-market features of futures with the same asymmetric payoff functions as regular puts and calls (see Chapter 24).

Specifically, when the FI hedges by buying put options on futures, if interest rates rise and bond prices fall, the exercise of the put results in the FI delivering a futures contract to the writer at an exercise price higher than the cost of the bond future currently trading on the futures exchange. The futures price itself reflects the price of the underlying deliverable bond such as a 20 year, 8 percent coupon T-bond; see Figure 25–12. As a result, a profit on futures options may be made to offset the loss on the market value of bonds held directly in the FI's portfolio. If interest rates fall while bond and futures prices rise, the buyer of the futures option will not exercise the put, and the losses on the futures put option are limited to the put premium. Thus, if on October 24, 1997, the FI had bought one $100,000 November 1997 T-bond futures put option at a strike price of $117 but did not exercise the option, the FI's loss equals the put premium of 34/64 per $100, or $531.25 per $100,000 contract. Offsetting these losses, however, would be an increase in the market value of the FI's underlying bond portfolio. Unlike futures positions in Chapter 24 a new upside profit potential remains when interest rates fall and FIs use put options on futures to hedge interest rate risk.

Concept Questions

1. Why are bond or interest rate futures options generally preferred to options on the underlying bond?
2. If an FI hedges by buying put options on futures and interest rates rise (i.e., bond prices fall), what is the outcome?

FIGURE 25–12

Futures Options on Interest Rates, October 24, 1997

INTEREST RATE

T-BONDS (CBT)
$100,000; points and 64ths of 100%

Strike	Calls-Settle			Puts-Settle		
Price	Nov	Dec	Mar	Nov	Dec	Mar
115	1-49	2-18	....	c1	0-33	....
→ 116	0-50	1-37	2-49	0-02	0-53	2-19
→ 117	0-08	1-03	....	0-34	1-17	....
118	0-01	0-41	1-54	1-19	1-56	3-22
119	c1	0-24	....	2-17	2-38	....
120	c1	0-15	1-11	3-17	3-29	4-42

Est. vol. 170,000;
Th vol. 140,797 calls; 111,659 puts
Op. Int. Thur 613,857 calls; 525,772 puts

T-NOTES (CBT)
$100,000; points and 64ths of 100%

Strike	Calls-Settle			Puts-Settle		
Price	Nov	Dec	Mar	Nov	Dec	Mar
108	2-26	2-47	2-57	0-01	0-04	0-35
109	1-26	1-53	2-12	0-01	0-09	0-53
110	0-24	1-03	1-37	0-01	0-23	1-13
111	0-05	0-32	1-07	0-24	0-52	1-47
112	0-01	0-13	0-49	1-22	1-32	2-23
113	0-01	0-04	0-32	....	2-23	....

Est vol 35,000 Th 23,575 calls 15,647 puts
Op Int Thur 227,566 calls 233,255 puts

5 YR TREAS NOTES (CBT)
$100,000; points and 64ths of 100%

Strike	Calls-Settle			Puts-Settle		
Price	Nov	Dec	Mar	Nov	Dec	Mar
10650	....	1-19	....	0-01	0-06	0-32
10700	0-44	0-56	1-19	0-01	0-12	0-43
10750	0-13	0-35	1-00	0-02	0-22	0-56
10800	0-03	0-19	0-49	0-22	0-38	1-09
10850	0-01	0-10	0-38	0-52	0-61	....
10900	0-01	0-05	0-26	1-20	1-23	....

Est vol 12,000 Th 3,375 calls 8,948 puts
Op Int Thur 51,702 calls 62,802 puts

MUNI BOND INDEX (CBT)
$1,000; times Bond Buyer MBI

Strike	Calls-Settle			Puts-Settle		
Price	Oct	Dec	Mar	Oct	Dec	Mar
118	....	....	....	....	0-42	....
119	1-26	2-18	....	0-01	0-56	....
120	0-01	1-58	2-50	....	1-22	....
121	0-01	0-52	....	....	....	....
122	0-01	0-33	....	....	....	....
123	....	0-27	....	....	....	....

Est vol 700 Th 0 calls 1,500 puts
Op Int Thur 4,937 calls 13,181 puts

EURODOLLAR (CME)
$ million; pts. of 100%

Strike	Calls-Settle			Puts-Settle		
Price	Nov	Dec	Jan	Nov	Dec	Jan
9375	....	0.42	....	0.00	0.01	0.02
9400	0.18	0.19	0.20	0.01	0.02	0.07
9425	0.02	0.03	0.07	0.10	0.11	0.19
9450	0.00	0.01	0.02	0.33	0.34	....
9475	....	0.00	....	....	0.58	....
9500	....	0.00	....	....	0.83	....

Est. vol. 141,659;
Th vol. 124,856 calls; 91,478 puts
Op. Int. Thur 1,288,073 calls; 1,288,371 puts

1 YR. MID-CURVE EURODLR (CME)
$1,000,000 contract units; pts. of 100%

Strike	Calls-Settle			Puts-Settle		
Price	Nov	Dec	Jan	Nov	Dec	Jan
9325	....	0.63	....	0.00	0.02	....
9350	0.38	0.41	....	0.02	0.05	0.07
9375	0.18	0.22	0.25	0.07	0.11	0.15
9400	0.05	0.10	0.13	0.19	0.24	....
9425	0.01	0.04	0.05	0.40	0.43	....
9450	....	0.01	....	....	....	....

Est vol 21,445 Th 16,650 calls 10,835 puts
Op Int Thur 151,639 calls 165,131 puts

2 YR. MID-CURVE EURODLR (CME)
$1,000,000 contract units; pts. of 100%

Strike	Calls-Settle			Puts-Settle		
Price	Dec	Mar	....	Dec	Mar	....
9325	....	....	....	0.02	0.08	....
9350	0.29	0.38	....	0.07	0.15	....
9375	0.14	0.23	....	0.17	0.25	....
9400	0.05	0.12	....	....	....	....
9425	0.01	0.06	....	....	....	....
9450	0.01	....	....	....	....	....

Est vol 450 Th 0 calls 0 puts
Op Int Thur 22,515 calls 22,855 puts

EUROMARK (LIFFE)
$1 million; pts. of 100%

Strike	Calls-Settle			Puts-Settle		
Price	Nov	Dec	Jan	Nov	Dec	Jan
9575	0.43	0.44	0.19	....	0.01	0.06
9600	0.19	0.21	0.06	0.01	0.03	0.18
9625	0.03	0.05	0.02	0.10	0.12	0.39
9650	0.01	0.01	....	0.33	0.33	0.62
9675	....	....	....	0.57	0.57	0.87
9700	....	....	....	0.82	0.82	1.12

Vol Fr 9,749 calls 4,179 puts
Op Int Thur 361,763 calls 305,900 puts

LONG GILT (LIFFE)
£50,000; 64ths of 100%

Strike	Calls-Settle			Puts-Settle		
Price	Nov	Dec	Jan	Nov	Dec	Jan
117	1-50	2-08	2-24	....	0-22	0-40
118	0-50	1-26	1-47	....	0-40	0-63
119	....	0-54	1-13	0-14	1-04	1-29
120	....	0-29	0-51	1-14	1-43	2-03
121	....	0-15	0-32	2-14	2-29	2-48
122	....	0-08	0-19	3-14	3-22	3-35

Vol Fr 2,500 calls 816 puts
Op Int Thur 66,360 calls 37,310 puts

GERMAN GOVT BOND (LIFFE)
$250,000 marks; pts. of 100%

Strike	Calls-Settle			Puts-Settle		
Price	Nov	Dec	Jan	Nov	Dec	Jan
1.13	1.13	1.35	1.06	....	0.22	0.66
10150	0.63	0.97	0.79	....	0.34	0.89
10200	0.13	0.66	0.56	....	0.53	1.16
10250	....	0.41	0.39	0.37	0.78	1.49
10300	....	0.24	0.26	0.87	1.11	1.86
10350	....	0.13	0.16	1.37	1.50	2.26

Vol Fr 28,239 calls 22,791 puts
Op Int Thur 274,045 calls 317,538 puts

Source: *The Wall Street Journal,* October 27, 1997, p. C15. Reprinted by permission of The Wall Street Journal, © 1997 Dow Jones & Company, Inc. All rights reserved worldwide.

Using Options to Hedge Interest Rate Risk on the Balance Sheet*

Our previous simple example showed how a bond option could hedge the interest rate risk on an underlying bond position in the asset portfolio. Next, we determine the put option position that can hedge the interest rate risk of the whole balance sheet; that is, we analyze macrohedging rather than microhedging.

In Chapter 8 we showed that an FI's net worth exposure to an interest rate shock could be represented as

$$\Delta E = -(D_A - kD_L) \times A \times \frac{\Delta R}{1 + R}$$

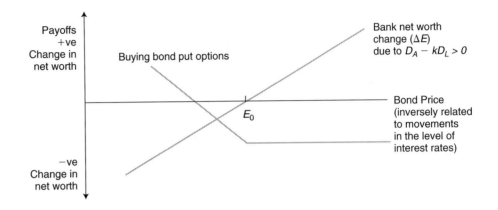

where

$$\Delta E = \text{Change in the FI's net worth}$$
$$(D_A - kD_L) = \text{FI's duration gap}$$
$$A = \text{Size of the FI's assets}$$
$$\frac{\Delta R}{1 + R} = \text{Size of the interest rate shock}$$
$$k = \text{FI's leverage ratio } (L/A)$$

Let's say we wish to determine the optimal number of put options to buy to insulate the FI against moving rates—given that it has a positive duration gap (see Figure 25–13). That is, we want to adopt a put option position to generate profits that just offset the loss in net worth due to a rate shock (where E_o is the bank's initial equity (net worth) position in Figure 25–13).

Let ΔP be the total change in the value of the put position in T-bonds. This can be decomposed into

$$\Delta P = (N_p \times \Delta p) \tag{1}$$

where N_p is the number of \$100,000 put options on T-bond contracts to be purchased (the number for which we are solving) and Δp is the change in the dollar value for each \$100,000 face value T-bond put option contract.

The change in the dollar value of each contract (Δp) can be further decomposed into

$$\Delta p = \frac{dp}{dB} \times \frac{dB}{dR} \times \Delta R \tag{2}$$

This decomposition needs some explanation. The first term (dp/dB) shows how the value of a put option changes for each \$1 dollar change in the underlying bond. This is called the delta of an option (δ) and lies between 0 and 1. For put options, the delta has a negative sign since the value of the put option falls when bond prices rise. The second term (dB/dR) shows how the market value of a bond changes if interest rates rise by one basis point. This value of a basis point term can be linked to duration. Specifically, we know from Chapter 9 that

$$\frac{dB}{B} = -MD \times dR \tag{3}$$

That is, the percentage change in the bond's price for a small change in rates is proportional to the bond's modified duration (*MD*). Equation (3) can be rearranged by cross multiplying as

$$\frac{dB}{dR} = -MD \times B \tag{4}$$

Thus, the term dB/dR is equal to minus the modified duration on the bond (MD) times the current market value of the T-bond (B) underlying the put option contract. As a result, we can rewrite Equation (2) as

$$\Delta p = [(-\delta) \times (-MD) \times B \times \Delta R] \tag{5}$$

where ΔR is the shock to interest rates (i.e., the number of basis points by which rates change). Since from Chapter 9 we know that $MD = D/1 + R$, we can rewrite equation (5) as

$$\Delta p = \left[-(\delta) \times (-D) \times B \times \frac{\Delta R}{1 + R} \right] \tag{6}$$

Thus, the change in the total value of a put position (ΔP) is

$$\Delta P = N_p \times \left[\delta \times D \times B \times \frac{\Delta R}{1 + R} \right] \tag{7}$$

The term in square brackets is the change in the value of one $100,000 face-value T-bond put option as rates change, and Np is the number of put option contracts.

To hedge net worth exposure, we require the profit on the off-balance-sheet put options to just offset the loss of on-balance-sheet net worth when rates rise (or bond prices fall). That is:

$$\Delta P = \Delta E$$

$$N_P \times \left[\delta \times D \times B \times \frac{\Delta R}{1 + R} \right] = [D_A - kD_L] \times A \times \frac{\Delta R}{1 + R}$$

Canceling $\Delta R/1 + R$ on both sides, we get

$$N_p \times [\delta \times D \times B] = [D_A - kD_L] \times A$$

Solving for N_p—the number of put options to buy—we have

$$N_P = \frac{[D_A - kD_L] \times A}{[\delta \times D \times B]} \tag{8}$$

Suppose, as in Chapter 24, $D_A = 5$, $D_L = 3$, $k = .9$, and $A = \$100$ million so that

$$N_P = \frac{\$230,000,000}{[\delta \times D \times B]} \tag{9}$$

Suppose δ of the put option is .5, which indicates that the option is close to being in the money, and $D = 8.82$ and that the current market value of $100,000 face value of long-term Treasury bonds $B = \$97,000$.[7]

Solving for N_p, the number of put option contracts to buy is

$$N_p = \frac{\$230,000,000}{[.5 \times 8.82 \times \$97,000]} = \frac{\$230,000,000}{\$427,770}$$

$$= 537.7 \text{ contracts}$$

---

[7]Note that since both the delta and D of the put option and bond have negative signs, their product will be positive: $(-.5) \times (-8.82) = +4.41$. Thus, these negative signs are not shown in the equation to calculate N_p.

If we slightly underhedge, this can be rounded down to 537 contracts.

The total premium cost to the FI of buying these puts is the price (premium) of each put times the number of puts:

$$\text{Cost} = N_p \times \text{Put premium per contract}$$

Suppose that T-bond put option premiums are quoted at $2\frac{1}{2}$ per $100 of face value for the nearby contract or $2,500 per $100,000 put contract; then the cost of macro-hedging the gap with put options will be

$$\text{Cost} = 537 \times \$2,500 = \$1,342,500$$

or just over $1.3 million. Remember, the total assets of the bank were assumed to be $100 million.

Concept Questions

1. If interest rates fall, are you better off purchasing call or put options on T-bonds, and why?
2. In the example above, what number of put options should you purchase if $\delta = .25$ and $D = 6$?

Using Options to Hedge Foreign Exchange Risk

Just as an FI can hedge a long position in bonds against interest rate risk through bond options or futures options on bonds, a similar opportunity is available to microhedge long or short positions in a foreign currency asset against foreign exchange rate risk.

To see this, suppose that an FI bought, or is long in, a sterling asset in October 1997. This sterling asset is a one-month T-bill paying £100 million in November 1997. Since the FI's liabilities are in dollars, it may wish to hedge the FX risk that the pound sterling will depreciate over the forthcoming month. Suppose that if the pound were to fall from the current exchange rate of $1.634/£1, the bank would make a loss on its British T-bill investment when measured in dollar terms. For example, if the pound depreciated from $1.634/£ in October 1997 to $1.4939/£ in November 1997, the £100 million asset would be worth only $149.39 million on maturity instead of the expected $163.4 million when it was purchased in October. If the foreign exchange rate depreciation is sufficiently severe, the bank might be unable to meet its dollar liability commitments used to fund the T-bill purchase. To offset this exposure, the bank may buy one-month put options on sterling at an exercise price of $1.60/£1. Thus, if the exchange rate does fall to $1.4939/£ at the end of the month, the FI manager can put the £100 million proceeds from the T-bill on maturity to the writer of the option. Then the bank receives $160 million instead of the $149.39 million if the pounds were sold at the open market spot exchange rate at the end of the month. If the pound actually appreciates in value, or does not depreciate below $1.60/£1, the option expires unexercised and the proceeds of the £100 million asset will be realized by the FI manager by a sale of pounds for dollars in the spot foreign exchange market one month into the future (see Figure 25–14).

The cost of this one-month hedge and the number of put options required to hedge depend on the premium and the exchange on which it is traded. Figure 25–15 shows the cost of buying a one-month European option on the British pound on the Philadelphia Options Exchange. As you can see, the premium cost of a November

FIGURE 25–14

Hedging FX Risk by Buying a Put Option on Sterling

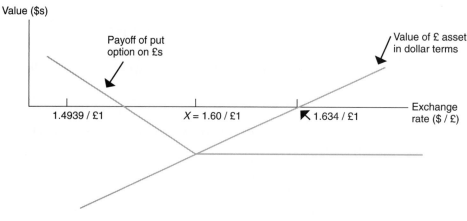

FIGURE 25–15

Currency Put Options, October 24, 1997

PHILADELPHIA OPTIONS
Friday, October 24, 1997

		Calls		Puts	
		Vol.	Last	Vol.	Last
ADollr				69.40	
50,000 Australian Dollar EOM-cents per unit.					
73½	Oct	40	0.06	.....	.....
Australian Dollar				69.40	
50,000 Australian Dollars-cents per unit.					
70	Mar	.....	.....	10	1.20
British Pound				163.39	
31,250 British Pounds-cents per unit.					
→ 158	Nov	.....	.....	10	0.20
Canadian Dollar				71.81	
50,000 Canadian Dollars-cents per unit.					
73½	Dec	.....	.....	6	1.60
German Mark				56.20	
62,500 German Marks EOM-European style.					
56	Oct	.....	.....	300	0.20
62,500 German Marks EOM-European style.					
56½	Oct	300	0.25	.....	.....
62,500 German Marks-European Style.					
56	Dec	.....	....	16	0.60
62,500 German Marks-cents per unit.					
54	Mar	5	2.90	.....	.....
55	Dec	.....	.....	10	0.37
55	Mar	.....	.....	1	0.83
55½	Dec	.....	.....	10	0.45
56	Nov	.....	.....	229	0.43
56	Dec	.....	.....	30	0.73
56	Mar	.....	.....	20	1.19
57	Dec	2	0.51	5	1.16
58	Dec	20	0.23	.....	.....
Japanese Yen				82.01	
6,250,000 J. Yen EOM-European style.					
82	Oct	.....	.....	20	0.28
6,250,000 J. Yen EOM-European style.					
82½	Oct	80	0.50	80	0.65
6,250,000 J. Yen EOM 100ths of a cent per unit.					
80½	Oct	.....	.....	400	0.12
6,250,000 J. Yen EOM 100ths of a cent per unit.					
82	Oct	.....	.....	200	0.46

		Calls		Puts	
		Vol.	Last	Vol.	Last
6,250,000 J. Yen-100ths of a cent per unit.					
80½	Dec	.....	.....	400	0.58
81½	Nov	.....	.....	10	0.52
81½	Dec	.....	.....	194	1.05
82	Dec	.....	.....	350	1.18
82	Mar	.....	.....	37	1.80
83	Dec	2	1.42	.....	.....
84	Nov	2	0.42	.....	.....
84	Dec	3	0.88	.....	.....
94	Dec	6	0.05	.....	.....
6,2500,000 J. Yen-European Style.					
82	Nov	.....	.....	20	0.60
Swiss Franc				68.07	
62,500 Swiss Francs EOM-cents per unit.					
68	Oct	.....	.....	100	0.23
62,500 Swiss Francs-European Style.					
66	Dec	10	2.23	.....	.....
67	Nov	66	1.16	.....	.....
68	Nov	20	0.90	.....	.....
68	Dec	10	1.00	.....	.....
68½	Dec	.....	.....	20	1.12
69	Nov	32	0.22	.....	.....
70	Nov	.....	.....	34	1.70
71	Nov	.....	.....	48	2.89
71	Dec	.....	....	5	3.12
72	Dec	.....	....	5	4.00
62,500 Swiss Francs-cents per unit.					
66	Mar	.....	.....	5	0.66
67	Mar	.....	.....	5	1.04
68	Mar	.....	.....	5	1.55
68½	Nov	.....	.....	25	1.08
69	Nov	.....	.....	34	1.05
69	Mar	.....	.....	1	1.92
Call vol 4,716				Open Int 132,287	
Put vol 8,636				Open Int 131,826	

Source: *The Wall Street Journal*, October 27, 1997, p. C24. Reprinted by permission of *The Wall Street Journal*, © 1997 Dow Jones & Company, Inc. All Rights Reserved Worldwide.

1997 put option (as of October 24, 1997) with a strike price of 158 or ($1.58 per £) was 0.20 cents per pound or ($.002 per £). Since each contract has a size of £31,250, the dollar premium cost per put contract would be $62.50. If the bank wished to microhedge its whole £100 million position in the sterling assets, it would need to buy[8]

---

[8]These cost calculations are based on the fact that there was no put option on the pound available on October 24, 1997, with a $1.60/£ strike price. Thus, it is assumed that the FI hedges using the put option with a strike price of $1.58/£.

$$\frac{£100,000,000}{£31,250} = 3,200 \text{ contracts (puts)}$$

Thus, the total premium cost of this put position would be $200,000 ($62.50 × 3,200 contracts). This is the cost of buying foreign currency risk insurance in the options market against a major fall in the value of the pound.

As with bonds, instead of taking a direct position in an option on the underlying pound asset, the bank could have bought put options on foreign currency futures contracts. A put position in one foreign currency futures contract with expiration in November 1997 and exercise price of $1.61/£ would have cost the bank a premium of $.0032 per pound on October 24, 1997. Since each pound sterling futures option contract is £62,500 in size, the cost would have been $200 per contract. If we ignore the question of basis risk—that is, the imperfect correlation between the dollar/pound exchange rate on the spot and futures on options markets—the optimal number of futures options purchased would be[9]

$$\frac{£100,000,000}{£62,500} = 1,600 \text{ contracts}$$

with a total premium cost of $320,000.[10] The futures option contracts for foreign currencies traded on the Chicago Mercantile Exchange (CME) are shown in Figure 25–16.

Concept Questions

1. What is the difference between options on foreign currency and options on foreign currency futures?
2. If an FI has to hedge a $5,000,000 liability exposure in German marks (DM), what options should it purchase to hedge this position? Using Figure 25–15, how many contracts of German mark options should it purchase (assuming no basis risk) if it wants to hedge against the DM falling in value against the dollar given a current exchange rate of $0.56/DM1 (or 1.78 DM/$1).

Hedging Credit Risk with Options

Options also have a potential use in hedging the credit risk of an FI. Although FIs are always likely to be willing to bear some credit risk as part of the intermediation process (i.e., exploit their comparative advantage to bear such risk), options may allow them to modify that level of exposure selectively. In Chapter 24 we stated that an FI could seek an appropriate credit risk hedge by selling credit forward contracts. Rather than using credit forwards to hedge, an FI has at least two alternative credit option derivatives with which it can hedge its on-balance-sheet credit risk.

A **credit spread call option** is a call option whose payoff increases as the risk premium or yield spread on a specified benchmark bond of the borrower increases

Credit Spread Call Option
A call option whose payoff increases as a yield spread increases above some stated exercise spread.

---

[9]On October 24, 1997, there were no put options available for an FI hedger with a strike price of $1.60/£. Thus, it is assumed that the FI uses the put option with the nearest available strike price, that is, the contract with a strike price of $1.61/£.

[10]There are a number of reasons why the cost of the two option positions should differ, including differences in strike prices, basis risk, market liquidity, and contract maturity and the American-style nature of the futures option, which may be exercised before the expiration date, versus the European-style nature of the cash option, which may be exercised only on the expiration date.

FIGURE 25–16

Futures Options on Currencies, October 27, 1997

CURRENCY

JAPANESE YEN (CME)
12,500,000 yen; cents per 100 yen

Strike Price	Calls-Settle Nov	Dec	Jan	Puts-Settle Nov	Dec	Jan
8150	.....	.....	.....	0.36	0.86	.....
8200	1.16	1.70	.....	0.51	1.05	1.12
8250	0.86	1.42	.....	0.71	1.27	.....
8300	0.62	1,17	.....	0.97	1.52	1.48
8350	0.44	0.96	.....	1.29	1.80	.....
8400	0.31	0.78	.....	1.66	2.12	1.96

Est vol 6,166 Th 6,373 calls 2,578 puts
Op int Thur 61,249 calls 46,962 puts

DEUTSCHEMARK (CME)
125,000 marks; cents per mark

Strike Price	Calls-Settle Nov	Dec	Jan	Puts-Settle Nov	Dec	Jan
5550	1.05	1.29	.....	0.15	0.40	0.56
5600	0.69	0.96	.....	0.29	0.56	0.73
5650	0.41	0.70	.....	0.51	0.80	.....
5700	0.23	0.49	0.89	0.83	1.09	.....
5750	0.12	0.34	0.70	1.22	1.43	1.51
5800	0.07	0.23	.....	.....	1.82	.....

Est vol 2,580 Th 5,524 call 2,797 puts
Op int Thur 39,055 calls 50,636 puts

CANADIAN DOLLAR (CME)
100,000 Can.$; cents per Can.$

Strike Price	Calls-Settle Nov	Dec	Jan	Puts-Settle Nov	Dec	Jan
7100	.....	1.06	.....	0.03	0.08	.....
7150	.....	0.66	.....	0.08	0.17	.....
7200	.....	0.37	.....	0.24	0.38	.....
7250	0.08	0.19	.....	0.59	0.70	.....
7300	0.03	0.09	.....	1.04	1.09	.....
7350	0.02	0.04	.....	1.53	1.54	.....

Est vol 716 Th 1,504 calls 297 puts
Op int Thur 13,695 calls 7,027 puts

BRITISH POUND (CME)
62,500 pounds; cents per 100 pound

Strike Price	Calls-Settle Nov	Dec	Jan	Puts-Settle Nov	Dec	Jan
→ 16100	2.36	3.00	.....	0.32	0.96	1.82
16200	1.64	2.36	2.76	0.60	1.32	.....
16300	1.06	1.82	2.28	1.02	1.78	.....
16400	0.64	1.38	1.86	1.60	.....	.....
16500	0.38	1.00	1.50	2.34	.....	.....
16600	0.20	0.72	1.20	.....	3.36	.....

Est vol 1,048 Th 367 calls 306 puts
Op int Thur 26,946 calls 24,903 puts

SWISS FRANC (CME)
125,000 francs; cents per franc

Strike Price	Calls-Settle Nov	Dec	Jan	Puts-Settle Nov	Dec	Jan
6750	1.26	1.56	2.28	0.19	0.50	0.61
6800	0.88	1.24	.....	0.31	0.67	.....
6850	0.57	0.96	.....	0.50	0.89	.....
6900	0.36	0.74	.....	0.79	1.17	.....
6950	0.21	0.56	.....	1.14	1.48	.....
7000	0.13	0.41	.....	1.56	1.83	.....

Est vol 958 Th 1,807 calls 395 puts
Op int Thur 19,854 calls 15,547 puts

BRAZILLIAN REAL (CME)
100,000 Braz. Reals; $ per reals

Strike Price	Calls-Settle Nov	Dec	Jan	Puts-Settle Nov	Dec	Jan
895	.....	.....	.....	.....	.....	.....
900	.....	.....	.....	0.01	.....	.....
905	.....					
910	.....					
915	.....					
920	.....					

Est vol 6,645 Th 0 call 2,900 puts
Op int Thur 0 calls 26,330 puts

MEXICAN PESO (CME)
500,000 new Mex. Peso; $ per MP

Strike Price	Calls-Settle Nov	Dec	Jan	Puts-Settle Nov	Dec	Jan
1212	.....	.....	.....	.....	0.35	.....
1225	.....	2.27	.....	0.05	0.65	.....
1238	.....	.....	.....	.....	1.02	.....
1250	.....	0.70	.....	.....	1.60	5.00
1262	.....	0.35	.....	.....	2.45	.....
1275	.....	0.17	.....	.....	3.52	.....

Est vol 1,656 Th 669 calls 1,779 puts
Op int Thur 18,568 calls 16,445 puts

Source: *The Wall Street Journal,* October 27, 1997, p. C15. Reprinted by permission of *The Wall Street Journal,* © 1997 Dow Jones & Company, Inc. All Rights Reserved Worldwide.

above some exercise spread, S. An FI concerned that the risk on a loan to that borrower will increase can purchase a credit spread call option to hedge the increased credit risk.

Figure 25–17 illustrates the payoffs from the credit spread call option to the FI as a function of the credit spread. As the credit spread increases on an FI's loan to a borrower, the value of the loan, and consequently the FI's net worth, decreases. However, if the credit risk characteristics of the benchmark bond (i.e., change in credit spread) are the same as those on the FI's loan, the loss of net worth on the balance sheet is offset by a gain from the credit spread call option. If the required credit spread on the FI's loan decreases (perhaps because the credit quality of the borrower improves over the loan period), the value of the FI's loan will increase (up to some maximum value) but the credit spread call option will expire out of the money. As a result, the FI will suffer a maximum loss equal to the required (call) premium on the credit option which will be offset by the market value gain of the loan in the portfolio (which is reflected in a positive increase in the FI's net worth).[11]

Digital Default Option
An option that pays the par value of a loan in the event of default.

A **digital default option** is an option that pays a stated amount against the possibility of a loan default (the extreme case of increased credit risk). As shown in Figure 25–18, the FI can purchase a default option covering the par value of a loan (or

---

[11]For additional discussion, see J. D. Finnerty, "Credit Derivatives, Infrastructure Finance, and Emerging Market Risk, *The Financier, ACMT,* February 1996, pp. 64–75.

FIGURE 25–17

Buying Credit Spread Call Options to Hedge Credit Risk

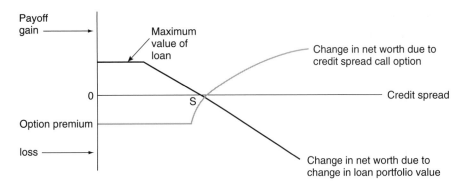

FIGURE 25–18

Buying a Digital Default Option to Hedge Credit Risk

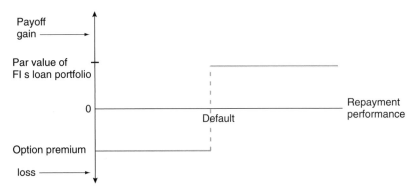

loans) in its portfolio. If there is a loan default, the option writer pays the FI the par value of the defaulted loans. If the loans are paid off in accordance with the loan agreement, however, the default option expires unexercised. As a result, the FI will suffer a maximum loss on the option equal to the premium (cost) of buying the default option from the writer (seller).

Hedging Catastrophe Risk with Call Spread Options

Catastrophe (CAT) Call Spread
A call option on the loss ratio incurred in writing catastrophe insurance with a capped (or maximum) payout.

In 1993 the CBOT introduced **catastrophe (CAT) call spread** options to hedge the risk of unexpectedly high losses being incurred by property-casualty insurers as a result of catastrophes such as hurricanes. The basic idea can be seen in Figure 25–19. For an option premium the insurer can hedge a range of loss ratios that may occur (remember that the loss ratio is the ratio of losses incurred divided by premiums). In the example in the figure, the insurer buys a call spread to hedge the risk that the loss ratio on its catastrophe insurance may be anywhere between 50 percent and 80 percent. If the loss ratio ends up below 50 percent (perhaps because of a mild hurricane season), the insurance company loses the option premium. For loss ratios between 50 percent and 80 percent it receives an increasingly positive payoff. For loss ratios above 80 percent the amount paid by the writers of the option to the buyer (the insurer) is capped at the 80 percent level.[12]

---

[12]For more information, see J. D. Cummins and H. Geman, "Pricing Catastrophe Insurance Futures and Call Spreads: An Arbitrage Approach," ibid.

FIGURE 25–19

*Catastrophe Call Spread
Options*

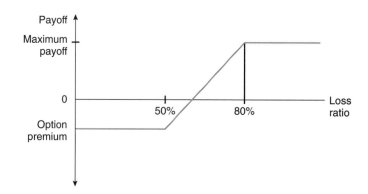

Concept Questions

1. What is the difference between a credit spread call option and a digital default option?
2. What is the difference between the payoff on the catastrophe call spread option in Figure 25–19 and the payoff of a standard call option on a stock?

Caps, Floors, and Collars

Cap
A call option on interest rates, often with multiple exercise dates.

Buying a **cap** means buying a call option or a succession of call options on interest rates. Specifically, if interest rates rise above the cap rate, the seller of the cap—usually a bank—compensates the buyer—for example, another FI—in return for an up-front premium. As a result, buying an interest rate cap is like buying insurance against an (excessive) increase in interest rates. The exercise dates in a cap agreement can be one or many.

Floor
A put option on interest rates, often with multiple exercise dates.

Buying a **floor** means buying a put option on interest rates. If interest rates fall below the floor rate, the seller of the floor compensates the buyer in return for an up-front premium. As with caps, there can be one or many exercise dates.

Collar
A position taken simultaneously in a cap and a floor.

A **collar** occurs when an FI takes a simultaneous position in a cap and a floor, such as buying a cap and selling a floor. Thus, these three over-the-counter instruments are special cases of options; FI managers use them like bond options and bond futures options to hedge the interest rate risk of FI's portfolios.

In general, FIs purchase interest rate caps if they are exposed to losses when interest rates rise. Usually, this happens if they are funding assets with floating-rate liabilities such as notes indexed to LIBOR (or some other cost of funds) and they have fixed-rate assets or they are net long in bonds, or—in a macrohedging context—their duration gap is $D_A - kD_L > 0$. By contrast, FIs purchase floors when they have fixed costs of debt and have variable rates (returns) on assets, are net short in bonds, or $D_A - kD_L < 0$. Finally, FIs purchase collars when they are concerned about excessive volatility of interest rates and to finance cap or floor positions.

Caps

For simplicity, let us assume that a bank buys a 9 percent cap at time 0 from another bank with a notional face value of $100 million. In return for paying an up-front premium, the seller of the cap stands ready to compensate the buying bank whenever the interest rate index defined under the agreement is above the 9 percent cap

FIGURE 25–20

Hypothetical Path of Interest Rates

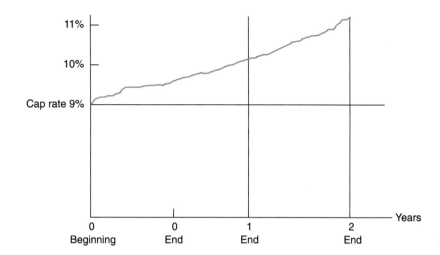

rate on the dates specified under the cap agreement. This effectively converts the cost of the bank's floating-rate liabilities into fixed-rate liabilities. In this example, we assume that the purchasing bank buys a cap at time 0 with cap exercise dates at the end of the first year and the end of the second year. That is, the cap has a three-year maturity from initiation until the final exercise dates, with exercise dates at the end of year 1 and year 2.[13]

Thus, the buyer of the cap would demand two cash payments from the seller of the cap if rates lie above 9 percent at the end of the first year and at the end of the second year on the cap exercise dates. In practice, cap exercise dates usually closely correspond to payment dates on liabilities, for example, coupon dates on floating-rate notes. Consider one possible scenario in Figure 25–20.

In Figure 25–20, the seller of the cap has to pay the buyer of the cap the amount shown in Table 25–1. In this scenario, the cap-buying bank would receive $3 million (undiscounted) over the life of the cap to offset any rise in the cost of liability funding or market value losses on its bond/asset portfolio. However, the interest rates in Figure 25–20 are only one possible scenario. Consider the possible path to interest rates in Figure 25–21.

In this interest scenario, rates fall below 9 percent at the end of the first year to 8 percent and at the end of the second year to 7 percent on the cap exercise dates. Thus, the cap seller makes no payments. This example makes it clear that buying a cap is similar to buying a call option on interest rates in that when the option expires out of the money because the interest rate is below the cap level, the cap seller makes no payments to the buyer. Conceptually, buying this cap is like buying a complex call option on an interest rate or a put option on a bond price with a single exercise price or interest rate and two exercise dates: the end of year 1 and the end of year 2.

The problem for the FI manager is to calculate the fair value of this 9 percent cap in the face of interest rate uncertainty. In particular, the FI manager does not

---

[13]There is no point exercising the option at the end of year 0 (i.e., having three exercise dates) since interest rates for year 0 are set at the beginning of that year and are contractually set throughout. As a result, the bank does not bear interest rate uncertainty until the end of year 0 (i.e., interest uncertainty exists only in years 1 and 2).

FIGURE 25–21

Hypothetical Path of Interest Rates

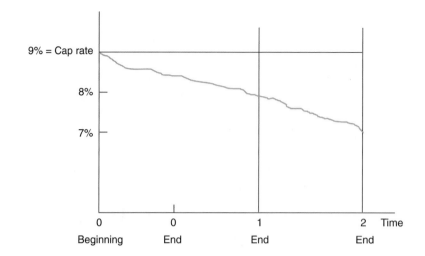

TABLE 25–1 Payments under the Cap

End of Year	Cap Rate	Actual Interest Rate	Interest Differential	Payment by Seller to Buyer
1	9%	10%	1%	$1 million
2	9%	11%	2%	$2 million
Total				$3 million

know whether interest rates will be 10 percent at the end of year 1 or 8 percent. Similarly, the manager does not know whether interest rates will be 11 percent or 7 percent at the end of year 2. Nevertheless, to buy interest rate risk insurance in the form of a cap, the manager has to pay an up-front fee or premium to the seller of the cap. Next, we solve for the fair value of the cap premium in the framework of the binomial model introduced earlier to calculate the premium on a bond option.[14]

Consider Figure 25–22, the binomial tree for the cap contract entered into at the beginning of year 0 and where the cap is exercised at the end of the first year and the end of the second year.[15] The current (time 0) value of the cap or the fair cap premium would be the sum of the present value of the cap option exercised at the end of year 1 plus the present value of the cap option exercised at the end of year 2:

$$\text{Fair premium} = P = PV \text{ of year 1 option} + PV \text{ of year 2 option}$$

***PV* of Year 2 Option.** At the end of year 2, there are three possible interest rate scenarios: 11 percent, 9 percent, and 7 percent. With a cap exercise price of 9 percent and the 9 percent or 7 percent scenarios realized, the cap would have no value to the buyer. In other words, it would expire out of the money. The only interest rate scenario where the cap has exercise value to the buyer at the end of the second year

---

[14]For more details and examples, see R. C. Stapleton and M. Subrahmanyam, "Interest Rate Caps and Floors," in *Financial Options: From Theory to Practice,* ed. S. Figlewski (Burr Ridge, IL: Business One-Irwin, 1990), pp. 220–80.

[15]Interest rates are normally set at the *beginning* of each period and paid at the *end* of each period.

FIGURE 25–22

*Interest Rate Cap at
9 Percent Cap Rate*

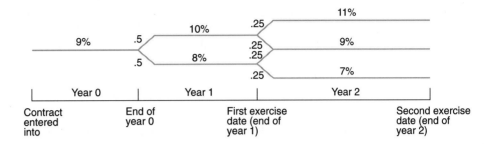

is if rates rise to 11 percent. With rates at 11 percent, the interest differential would be 11 percent minus 9 percent, or 2 percent. But since there is only a 25 percent probability that interest rates will rise to 11 percent at the end of the second year, the expected value of this interest differential is

$$.25 \times 2\% = 0.5\%$$

With a $100 million cap, therefore, the expected cash payment at the end of year 2 would be $0.5 million. However, to calculate the fair value of the cap premium in current dollars, the expected cash flow at the end of year 2 has to be discounted back to the present (time 0).

$$PV_2 = \frac{0.5}{(1.09)(1.1)(1.11)} = .3757$$

where 9 percent, 10 percent, and 11 percent are the appropriate one-year discount rates for payments in years 0, 1, and 2. Thus, the fair present value of the option at the end of year 2 is .3757 or $375,700, given the $100 million face value of the cap.

***PV* of Year 1 Option.**   We can also derive the present value of the option exercised at the end of the first year. At the end of year 1, there are two interest rate scenarios: Interest rates could rise to 10 percent or fall to 8 percent. If rates fall to 8 percent, the 9 percent cap has no value to the buyer. However, if rates rise to 10 percent, this results in a positive interest differential of 1 percent at the end of year 1. However, the expected interest differential is only .5 of 1 percent since this is the probability that rates will rise from 9 percent to 10 percent between the beginning of year 0 and end of year 1:

$$.5 \times 1\% = 0.5\%$$

In dollar terms, with a $100 million cap, the expected value of the cap at the end of year 1 is $0.5 million. To evaluate the time 0 or present value of a cap exercised at the end of time period 1, this expected cash flow has to be discounted back to the beginning of time 0 using the appropriate one-year discount rates. That is:

$$PV_1 = \frac{0.5}{(1.09)(1.1)} = .417$$

or $417,000, given the $100 million face value of the cap. As a result, the fair value of the premium the bank should be willing to pay for this cap is

$$
\begin{aligned}
\text{Cap premium} &= PV_1 + PV_2 \\
&= \$417,000 + \$375,700 \\
&= \$792,700
\end{aligned}
$$

That is, under the interest rate scenarios implied by this simple binomial model, the bank should pay no more than $792,700 or 0.792 percent of notional face value in buying the cap from the seller.

Floors

A floor is a put option or a collection of put options on interest rates. Here the FI manager who buys a floor is concerned about falling interest rates. Perhaps the FI is funding liabilities at fixed rates and has floating-rate assets, or maybe it is short in some bond position and will lose if it has to cover the position with higher-priced bonds after interest rates fall. In a macrohedging sense, the FI could face a duration gap where the duration of assets is less than the leverage adjusted duration of liabilities ($D_A - kD_L < 0$). For an example of the payoff from buying a floor, see Figure 25–23.

In this simple example, the floor is set at 4 percent and the buyer pays an up-front premium to the seller of the floor. While caps can be viewed as buying a complex call option on interest rates, a floor can be viewed as buying a complex put option on interest rates. In our example, the floor has two exercise dates: the end of year 1 and the end of year 2.

If the interest scenario in Figure 25–23 were the actual interest rate path followed, the payments from the seller to the buyer would be as shown in Table 25–2. However, since the buyer of the cap is uncertain about the true path of interest rates—rates could rise and not fall—such profits are only probabilistic. That is , the buyer would have to use a model similar to the binomial model for caps to calculate the fair up-front premium to be paid for the floor at time 0.

FIGURE 25–23

A 4 Percent Floor

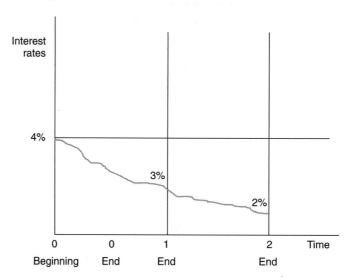

TABLE 25–2   Hypothetical Floor Payments

End of Year	Cap Rate	Actual Interest Rate	Interest Differential	Payment by Seller to Buyer
1	4%	3%	1%	$1 million
2	4%	2%	2%	$2 million
Total				$3 million

Collars

Financial institutions whose managers are very risk averse and overly concerned about the exposure of their portfolios to increased interest rate volatility may seek to protect themselves against such increases. One method of hedging such risk is through buying a cap and a floor together. This is usually called a collar. In Figure 25–24 we illustrate the essential risk-protection features of a collar when an FI buys a 9 percent cap and a 4 percent floor.

The shaded areas in Figure 25–24 show the interest rate payment regions (> 9 percent or < 4 percent) where the cap or floor is in the money and the buyer potentially receives either a cap or a floor payment from the seller. If interest rates fall in the range of 4 through 9 percent, the buyer of the collar receives no compensation from the seller. In addition, the buyer has to pay two up-front premiums: one for the cap and one for the floor to the cap and floor sellers. As is clear, buying a collar is similar to simultaneously buying a complex put and call bond option, or straddle.

An alternative and more common use of a collar is to finance the cost of purchasing a cap. In our earlier example of the $100 million cap, the fair cap premium (pc) was $792,000 or 0.792 percent of the notional face value (NV_c) of the cap. That is, the cost (C) of the cap was

$$C = NV_c \times pc$$
$$= \$100 \text{ million} \times .00792$$
$$= \$792,000$$

To purchase the cap, the bank has to pay this premium to the cap seller in up-front dollars.

Many large banks more exposed to rising interest rates than falling interest rates—perhaps because they are heavily reliant on interest sensitive sources of liabilities—seek to finance a cap by selling a floor at the same time.[16] In so doing, they generate up-front revenues; this floor premium can finance the cost of the cap purchase or the cap premium. Nevertheless, they give up potential profits if rates fall rather than rise. Indeed, when rates fall, the floor is more likely to be triggered and the bank will have to compensate the buyer of the floor.

FIGURE 25–24

Payoffs from a Collar

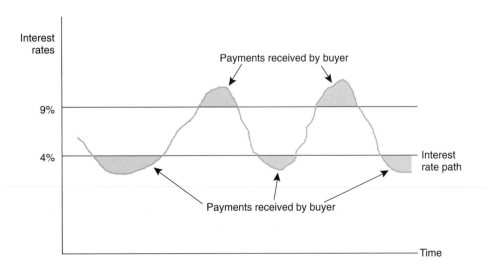

[16]In this context, the sale of the floor is like the sale of any revenue-generating product.

614 Part III Managing Risk

After a bank buys a cap and sells a floor, its net cost of the cap is[17]

$$C = (NV_c \times pc) - (NV_f \times pf)$$
$$C = \text{Cost of cap} - \text{Revenue on floor}$$

where

NV_f = Notional principal of the floor
P_f = Premium rate on the floor

Suppose that while buying the cap the bank sold a two-year $100 million notional face value floor at a premium of .75 percent. The net up-front cost of purchasing the cap is reduced to

$$C = (\$100 \text{ million} \times .00792) - (\$100 \text{ million} \times .0075) = \$42,000$$

Note that if the bank is willing to raise the floor exercise interest rate and thereby expose itself to increasing losses if rates fall, it can generate higher premiums on the floor it sells. Like any option, as the exercise price or rate moves from being out of the money when current rates are above the floor to being in the money when current rates are below the floor, the floor buyer would be willing to pay a higher premium to the writer (the bank). Given this, the buyer of the cap could set the floor rate with notional face values of $100 million each so that the floor premium earned by the FI just equals the cap premium paid:

$$C = (\$100 \text{ million} \times .00792) - (\$100 \text{ million} \times .00792)$$
$$C = 0$$

When $pc = pf$, the cap buyer-floor seller can reduce the cap's net cost of purchase to zero. Indeed, if the cap buyer bought a very out-of-the-money cap and sold a very in-the-money floor, as shown in Figure 25–25, the net cost of the cap purchase could actually be negative. In recent years, FIs have offered a number of cap-floor innovations as financial products to customers.

In Figure 25–25, the current interest rate is 7 percent while the cap rate is 10 percent. Thus, rates would have to rise at least 3 percent for the cap buyer to receive a payment at the end of year 1. By contrast, the 8 percent floor is already 1 percent above the current 7 percent rate. If rates stay the way they are until the end of year 1, the bank seller of the floor is already exposed to a 1 percent notional face value loss in writing the floor.

If the out-of-the-money cap can be bought at a premium of .792 percent but the in-the-money floor is sold at a premium of .95 percent, the (net) cost of the cap purchase is

$$C = (NV_c \times pc) - (NV_f \times pf)$$
$$= \$792,000 - \$950,000$$
$$= -\$158,000$$

Raising the floor exercise rate and thus the floor premium can also be combined with mismatching the notional principal amounts of the cap and the floor to produce a zero net cost financing for the cap. That is, there is no reason why both the floor and cap agreements have to be written against the same notional face values ($NV_c = NV_f = \$100$ million).

[17]See K. C. Brown and D. J. Smith, "Recent Innovations in Interest Rate Risk Management and the Reintermediation of Commercial Banking," *Financial Management* 17 (1988), pp. 45–58.

FIGURE 25–25

In-the-Money Floor and Out-of-the-Money Cap

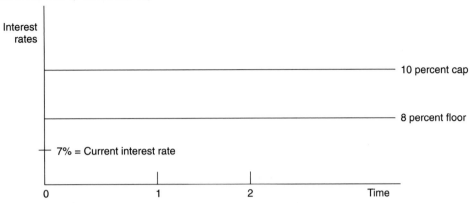

Suppose the out-of-the-money cap can be bought at a premium of .792 percent and the in-the-money floor can be sold at a .95 percent premium. An FI manager might want to know what notional principal on the floor (or contract size) is necessary to finance a $100 million cap purchase at zero net up-front cost. That is:

$$C = (NV_c \times pc) - (NV_f \times pf) = 0$$
$$= (\$100 \text{ million} \times .00792) - (NV_f \times .0095) = 0$$

Solving for NV_f,

$$NV_f = \frac{(\$100 \text{ million} \times .00792)}{.0095} = \frac{(NV_c \times pc)}{pf}$$

$$= \$83.37 \text{ million}$$

Clearly, the higher premium rate on the floor requires a lower notional face value floor amount to generate sufficient premium income up front to finance the cap's purchase. In general, to fund fully the cap purchase ($C = 0$), the relationship between premium rates and notional value should be[18]

$$\frac{NV_f}{NV_c} = \frac{pc}{pf}$$

---

[18]As shown earlier in this chapter, it is possible to macrohedge a gap position of an FI using put options. A cap is economically equivalent to a call option on an interest rate or a put option on a bond. However, the major difference is that the cap is a complex option in that there are multiple exercise dates. For example, in our simple model of the determination of the fair cap premium, there were two exercise dates: the end of year 1 and the end of year 2. However, we showed that we could decompose the value of the cap as a whole into the value of the (end of) year 1 option and the value of the (end of) year 2 option. Both of these options would have their own deltas (δ) because of the different maturity of these options. Thus, the change in the total value of the cap (ΔC) position would equal

$$\Delta C = N_c \times \{[\delta_1 \times (D \times B)] + [\delta_2 \times (D \times B)]\} \times \Delta R/1 + R$$

where N_c—the number of $100,000 cap contracts—is calculated by solving

$$N_c = \frac{[D_A - kD_L] \times A}{\{[\delta_1 \times (D \times B)] + [\delta_2 \times (D \times B)]\}}$$

Concept Questions

1. Referring to the example that concludes on page 611, suppose that in year 2 the highest and lowest rates were 12 percent and 6 percent instead of 11 percent and 7 percent. Calculate the fair premium on the cap.

2. Assume two exercise dates at the end of year 1 and the end of year 2. Suppose the bank buys a floor of 4 percent at time 0. The binomial tree suggests that rates at the end of year 1 could be 3 percent ($p = .5$) or 5 percent ($p = .5$) and at the end of year 2 rates could be 2 percent ($p = .25$), 4 percent ($p = .5$), or 6 percent ($p = .25$). Calculate the fair value of the floor premium.

3. A bank buys a $100 million cap at a premium of .75 percent and sells a floor at a .85 percent premium. What size floor should be sold so that the net cost of the cap purchase is zero?

Caps, Floors, Collars, and Credit Risk

One important feature of buying caps, collars, and floors for hedging purposes is the implied credit risk exposure involved that is absent for exchange-traded futures and options. Since these are multiple exercise over-the-counter contracts, the buyer of these instruments faces a degree of counterparty credit risk. To see this, consider the cap example just discussed. Suppose the writer of the cap defaulted on the $1 million due at the end of the first year if interest rates rose to 10 percent. The buyer not only would fail to collect on this in-the-money option but also would lose a potential payment at the end of year 2. In general, a default in year 1 would mean that the cap buyer would have to find a replacement contract for year 2 (and any succeeding years thereafter) at the cap rate terms or premiums prevailing at the end of year 1 rather than at the beginning of year 0. These cap rates may be far less favorable than those under the original cap contract (reflecting the higher interest rate levels of time 1). In addition, the buyer could incur further transaction and contracting costs in replacing the original contract. Because of the often long-term nature of cap agreements, occasionally extending up to 10 years, only FIs that are the most creditworthy are likely to be able to write and run a large cap/floor book without the backing of external guarantees such as standby letters of credit. As we discuss in the next chapter, swaps have similar credit risk exposures due to their long-run contractual nature and their OTC origination.

Concept Question

1. Why are only the most creditworthy FIs able to write a large cap/floor book without external guarantees?

Summary

In this chapter we evaluated a wide range of option-type contracts that are available to FI managers to hedge the risk exposures of individual assets, portfolios of assets, and the balance sheet gap itself. We illustrated how these options—some of which are exchange traded and some of which are sold OTC—can hedge the interest rate, credit, FX, and catastrophe risks of FIs. In particular, we described how the unique nature of the asymmetric payoff function of option-type contracts often makes them more attractive to FIs than other hedging instruments, such as forwards and futures.

Questions and Problems

1. How does using options differ from using forward or futures contracts?

2. What is a call option?

3. What must happen to interest rates for the purchaser of a call option on a bond to make money? How does the writer of the call option make money?

4. What is a put option?

5. What must happen to interest rates for the purchaser of a put option on a bond to make money? How does the writer of the put option make money?

6. Consider the following:

    a. What are the two ways to use call and put options on T-bonds to generate positive cash flows when interest rates decline? Verify your answer with a diagram.

    b. Under what balance sheet conditions can an FI use options on T-bonds to hedge its assets and/or liabilities against interest rate declines?

    c. Is it more appropriate for FIs to hedge against a decline in interest rates with long calls or short puts?

7. In each of the following cases, identify what risk the manager of an FI faces and whether that risk should be hedged by buying a put or a call option.

    a. A commercial bank plans to issue CDs in three months.

    b. An insurance company plans to buy bonds in two months.

    c. A thrift plans to sell Treasury securities next month.

    d. A U.S. bank lends to a French company with a loan payable in francs.

    e. A mutual fund plans to sell its holding of stock in a German company.

    f. A finance company has assets with a duration of six years and liabilities with a duration of 13 years.

8. Consider an FI that wishes to use bond options to hedge the interest rate risk in the bond portfolio.

    a. How does writing call options hedge the risk when interest rates decrease?

    b. Will writing call options fully hedge the risk when interest rates increase? Explain.

    c. How does buying a put option reduce the losses on the bond portfolio when interest rates rise?

    d. Diagram the purchase of a bond call option against the combination of a bond investment and the purchase of a bond put option.

9. What are the regulatory reasons why FIs seldom write options?

10. What are the problems of using the Black-Scholes option pricing model to value bond options? What is meant by the term *pull to par*?

11. An FI has purchased a two-year, $1,000 par value zero-coupon bond for $867.43. The FI will hold the bond to maturity unless it needs to sell the bond at the end of one year for liquidity purposes. The current one-year interest rate is 7 percent, and one-year rates in one year are forecast to be either 8.04 percent or 7.44 percent with equal likelihood. The FI wishes to buy a put option to protect itself against a capital loss if the bond needs to be sold in one year.

    a. What was the yield on the bond at the time of purchase?

    b. What is the market-determined, implied one-year rate one year before maturity?

    c. What is the expected sale price if the bond has to be sold at the end of one year?

    d. Diagram the bond prices over the two-year horizon.

    e. If the bank buys a put option with an exercise price equal to your answer in part (c), what will be its value at the end of one year?

    f. What should be the premium on the put option today?

    g. Diagram the values of the put option on the two-year zero-coupon bond.

    h. What would have been the premium on the option if the one-year interest rates at the end of one year were expected to be 8.14 percent and 7.34 percent?

12. A pension fund manager anticipates the purchase of a 20-year, 8 percent coupon Treasury bond at the end of two years. Interest rates are assumed to change only once every year at year end, with an equal probability of a 1 percent increase or a 1 percent decrease. The Treasury bond, when purchased in two years, will pay interest semiannually. Currently the Treasury bond is selling at par.

    a. What is the pension fund manager's interest rate risk exposure?

    b. How can the pension fund manager use options to hedge that interest rate risk exposure?

    c. What prices are possible on the 20-year T-bonds at the end of year 1 and year 2?

    d. Diagram the prices over the two-year period.

    e. If options on $100,000, 20-year, 8 percent coupon Treasury bonds (both puts and calls) have a strike price of 101, what are the possible (intrinsic) values of the option position at the end of year 1 and year 2?

    f. Diagram the possible option values.

g. What is the option premium? (Use an 8 percent discount factor.)

13. Why are options on interest rate futures contracts preferred to options on cash instruments in hedging interest rate risk?

14. Consider Figure 25–12. What are the prices paid for the following futures option:

    a. March T-bond calls at 116.

    b. March five-year T-note puts at 107.50 (10750).

    c. January Eurodollar calls at 94.50 (9450).

15. Consider Figure 25–12 again. What happens to the price of the following?

    a. A call when the exercise price increases.

    b. A call when the time until expiration increases.

    c. A put when the exercise price increases.

    d. A put when the time to expiration increases.

16. An FI manager writes a call option on a T-bond futures contract with an exercise price of 114 at a quoted price of 0–55.

    a. What type of opportunities or obligations does the manager have?

    b. In what direction must interest rates move to encourage the call buyer to exercise the option?

17. What is the delta of an option (δ)?

18. An FI has a $100 million portfolio of six-year Eurodollar bonds which have an 8 percent coupon. The bonds are trading at par and have a duration of five years. The FI wishes to hedge the portfolio with T-bond options that have a delta of −0.625. The underlying long-term Treasury bonds for the option have a duration of 10.1 years and trade at a market value of $96,157 per $100,000 of par value. Each put option has a premium of $3.25.

    a. How many bond put options are necessary to hedge the bond portfolio?

    b. If interest rates increase 100 basis points, what is the expected gain or loss on the put option hedge?

    c. What is the expected change in market value on the bond portfolio?

    d. What is the total cost of placing the hedge?

    e. Diagram the payoff possibilities.

    f. How far must interest rates move before the payoff on the hedge will exactly offset the cost of placing the hedge?

    g. How far must interest rates move before the gain on the bond portfolio will exactly offset the cost of placing the hedge?

    h. Summarize the gain, loss, and cost conditions of the hedge on the bond portfolio in terms of changes in interest rates.

19. Corporate Bank has $840 million of assets with a duration of 12 years and liabilities worth $720 million with a duration of 7 years. The bank is concerned about preserving the value of its equity in the event of an increase in interest rates and is contemplating a macrohedge with interest rate options. The call a put options have a delta (δ) of 0.4 and −0.4, respectively. The price of an underlying T-bond is 104−³⁄₆₄ths, and its modified duration is 7.6 years.

    a. What type of option should Corporate Bank use for the macrohedge?

    b. How many options should be purchased?

    c. What is the effect on the economic value of the equity if interest rates rise 50 basis points?

    d. What will be the effect on the hedge if interest rates rise 50 basis points?

    e. What will be the cost of the hedge if each option has a premium of $0.875?

    f. Diagram the economic conditions of the hedge.

    g. How much must interest rates move against the hedge for the increased value of the bank to offset the cost of the hedge?

    h. How much must interest rates move in favor of the hedge, or against the balance sheet, before the payoff from the hedge will exactly cover the cost of the hedge?

    i. Formulate a management decision rule regarding the implementation of the hedge.

20. An FI has a $200 million asset portfolio which has an average duration of 6.5 years. The average duration of its $160 million in liabilities is 4.5 years. The FI uses put options on T-bonds to hedge against unexpected interest rate increases. The average delta (δ) of the put options has been estimated at −0.3, and the average duration of the T-bonds is 7 years. The current market value of the T-bonds is $96,000.

    a. What is the modified duration of the T-bonds if the current level of interest rates is 10 percent?

    b. How many put option contracts should it purchase to hedge its exposure against rising interest rates? The face value of the T-bonds is $100,000.

    c. If interest rates increase 50 basis points, what will be the change in value of the equity of the FI?

    d. What will be the change in value of the T-bond option hedge position?

    e. If put options on T-bonds are selling at a premium of $1.25 per face value of $100, what is the total cost of hedging using options on T-bonds?

    f. Diagram the spot market conditions of the equity and the option hedge.

g. What must the change in interest rates be before the change in value of the balance sheet (equity) will offset the cost of placing the hedge?

h. How much must interest rates change before the payoff of the hedge will exactly cover the cost of placing the hedge?

i. Given your answer in part (*g*), what will be the net gain or loss to the FI?

21. A mutual fund plans to purchase $10,000,000 of 20-year T-bonds in two months. These bonds have a duration of 11 years. The mutual fund is concerned about interest rates changing over the next four months and is considering a hedge with a two-month option on a T-bond futures contract. Two-month calls with a strike price of 105 are priced at 1–25, and puts of the same maturity and exercise price are quoted at 2–09. The delta of the call is .5 and the delta of the put is −.7. The current price of a deliverable T-bond is $103–08 per $100 of face value, and its modified duration is nine years.

a. What type of option should the mutual fund purchase?

b. How many options should it purchase?

c. What is the cost of those options?

d. If rates change +/−50 basis points, what will be the impact on the price of the desired T-bonds?

e. What will be the effect on the value of the hedge if rates change +/− 50 basis points?

f. Diagram the effects of the hedge and the spot market value of the desired T-bonds.

g. What must the change in interest rates be to cause the change in value of the hedge to exactly offset the change in value of the T-bonds?

22. An FI must make a single payment of 500,000 Swiss francs in six months at the maturity of a CD. The FI's in-house analyst expects the spot price of the franc to remain stable at the current $0.80/Sf. But as a precaution, the analyst is concerned that it could rise as high as $0.85/Sf or fall as low as $0.75/Sf. Because of this uncertainty, the analyst recommends that the FI hedge the CD payment using either options or futures. Six-month call and put options on the Swiss franc with an exercise price of $0.80/Sf are trading at 4 cents and 2 cents, respectively. A six-month futures contract on the Swiss franc is trading at $0.80/Sf.

a. Should the analysts be worried about the dollar depreciating or appreciating?

b. If the FI decides to hedge using options, should the FI buy put or call options to hedge the CD payment? Why?

c. If futures are used to hedge, should the FI buy or sell Swiss franc futures to hedge the payment? Why?

d. What will be the net payment on the CD if the selected call or put options are used to hedge the payment? Assume the following three scenarios: the spot price in six months will be $0.75, $0.80, or $0.85/Sf. Also assume that the options will be exercised.

e. What will be the net payment if futures had been used to hedge the CD payment? Use the same three scenarios as in part (*d*).

f. Which method of hedging is preferable after the fact?

23. An American insurance company issued $10 million of one-year, zero-coupon GICs (guaranteed investment contracts) denominated in deutsche marks at a rate of 5 percent. The insurance company holds no DM-denominated assets and has neither bought nor sold marks in the foreign exchange market.

a. What is the insurance company's net exposure in deutsche marks?

b. What is the insurance company's risk exposure to foreign exchange rate fluctuations?

c. How can the insurance company use futures to hedge the risk exposure in part (*b*)? How can it use options to hedge?

d. If the strike price is $0.6667/DM and the spot price is $0.6452/DM, what is the intrinsic value (on expiration) of a call option on deutsche marks? What is the intrinsic value (on expiration) of a deutsche mark put option? (*Note:* Deutsche mark futures options traded on the Chicago Mercantile Exchange are set at DM125,000 per contract.)

e. If the June delivery call option premium is 0.32 cents per mark and the June delivery put option is 10.7 cents per mark, what is the dollar premium cost per contract? Assume that today's date is April 15.

f. Why is the call option premium lower than the put option premium?

24. An FI has made a loan commitment of DM10 million that is likely to be taken down in six months. The current spot rate is $0.60/DM.

a. Is the FI exposed to the dollar depreciating or the dollar appreciating? Why?

b. If it decides to hedge using DM futures, should it buy or sell DM futures?

c. If the spot rate six months from today is $0.64/DM, what dollar amount is needed in six months if the loan is taken down?

d. A six-month DM futures contract is available for $0.61/DM. What is the net amount needed at the end of six months if the FI has hedged using the DM10 million of futures contracts? Assume that futures prices are equal to spot prices at the time of payment, that is, at maturity.

e. If it decides to use options to hedge, should it purchase call or put options?

f. Call and put options with an exercise price of $0.61/DM are selling for $0.02 and $0.03, respectively. What would be the net amount needed by the FI at the end of six months if it had used options instead of futures to hedge this exposure?

25. What is a credit spread call option?

26. What is a digital default option?

27. How do the cash flows to the lender differ for a credit spread call option hedge from the cash flows for a digital default option?

28. What is a catastrophe call option? How do the cash flows of this option affect the buyer of the option?

29. What are caps? Under what circumstances would the buyer of a cap receive a payoff?

30. What are floors? Under what circumstances would the buyer of a floor receive a payoff?

31. What are collars? Under what circumstances would an FI use a collar?

32. How is buying a cap similar to buying a call option on interest rates?

33. Under what balance sheet circumstances would it be desirable to sell a floor to help finance a cap? When would it be desirable to sell a cap to help finance a floor?

34. Use the following information to price a three-year collar by purchasing an in-the-money cap and writing an out-of-the-money floor. Assume a binomial options pricing model with an equal probability of interest rates increasing 2 percent or decreasing 2 percent per annum.

Current rates are 7 percent, the cap rate is 7 percent, and the floor rate is 4 percent. The notional value is $1 million. All interest payments are annual payments as a percent of notional value, and all payments are made at the end of year 1 and the end of year 2.

35. Use the following information to price a three-year collar by purchasing an out-of-the-money cap and writing an in-the-money floor. Assume a binomial options pricing model with an equal probability of interest rates increasing 2 percent or decreasing 2 percent per annum.

Current rates are 4 percent, the cap rate is 7 percent, and the floor rate is 4 percent. The notional value is $1 million. All interest payments are annual payments as a percent of notional value, and all payments are made at the end of year 1 and the end of year 2.

36. Contrast the total cash flows associated with the collar position in question 34 against the collar in question 35. Do the goals of banks that utilize the collar in question 34 differ from those that put on the collar in question 35? If so, how?

37. An FI has purchased a $200 million cap (i.e., call options on interest rates) of 9 percent at a premium of 0.65 percent of face value. A $200 million floor (i.e., put options on interest rates) of 4 percent is also available at a premium of 0.69 percent of face value.

a. If interest rates rise to 10 percent, what is the amount received by the FI? What are the net savings after deducting the premium?

b. If the FI also purchases a floor, what are the net savings if interest rates rise to 11 percent? What are the net savings if interest rates fall to 3 percent?

c. If, instead, the FI sells (writes) the floor, what are the net savings if interest rates rise to 11 percent? What if they fall to 3 percent?

d. What amount of floors should it sell to compensate for its purchase of caps, given the above premiums?

38. What credit risk exposure is involved in buying caps, floors, and collars for hedging purposes?

SWAPS

Introduction

The market for swaps has grown enormously in recent years; the notional value of swap contracts outstanding of U.S. commercial banks was $9.6 trillion in 1997. Commercial banks and investment banks are major participants in the market as dealers, traders, and users for proprietary hedging purposes. In particular, a dealer can act as an intermediary or third party by putting a swap together and/or creating an OTC secondary market for swaps. The massive growth of the swap market has raised regulatory concerns regarding the credit risk exposures of banks engaging in this market. It was one of the motivations behind the introduction of the 1992 BIS-sponsored risk-based capital adequacy reforms described in Chapter 20. In addition, in recent years there has been a growth in exotic swap products such as "inverse floater" swaps that have raised considerable controversy—especially since the bankruptcy of Orange County and the legal suits filed against swap-selling banks and investment banks. Indeed, as discussed in the Contemporary Perspectives box

621

PAYING A PRICE FOR THE FAILURE

The bankruptcy of Orange County, Calif., in late 1994 led to a series of criminal and civil lawsuits as the county and its bondholders sought to recover losses. Here is the status of some of the major lawsuits and criminal inquiries.

Civil Settlements

LeBoeuf, Lamb, Greene & McRae $45 million
Announced in April. The county sued the law firm over its role as a bond adviser.

Credit Suisse First Boston $52.5 million
Announced last month. A brokerage firm that Orange County said had sold it risky and inappropriate investments.

KPMG Peat Marwick $75 million
Also last month. The county accused the accounting firm of failing to detect and warn it of the riskiness of the investments sold to it by the various brokerage firms.

Merrill Lynch $400 million
Announced yesterday. The agreement ended a lawsuit that argued that Merrill sold investments that were barred by California law and misrepresented how risky there were.

Criminal Cases

Robert L. Citron $100,000
Pled guilty in April 1995 to securities fraud. Mr. Citron, the former county treasurer, was sentenced to one year in jail and a $100,000 fine.

Robert S. Rubino   No fine
Pled guilty in September 1996 to violating a public records law. The conviction of Mr. Rubino, the former county budget director, was cleared from his record after serving 200 hours of community service and two years of probation.

Mathew R. Raabe $10,000
Convicted in May 1997 of misappropriation of funds and deceiving investors. Mr. Raabe, the deputy county treasurer, was sentenced to a three-year jail term and a fine, but he is free pending an appeal.

Merrill Lynch $30 million
Announced settlement in June 1997. The firm agreed to settle a criminal investigation by the county district attorney into its role in underwriting bonds.

Actions by the Securities and Exchange Commission

Orange County and several officials   No fine
Announced January 1996. The county, its Board of Supervisors, Mr. Citron and Mr. Raabe agreed not to violate securities laws again.

Credit Suisse First Boston $870,000
Announced January 1998. The firm and two former employees agreed to pay a fine for misleading investors.

Pending

Merrill Lynch may still be subject to an S.E.C. enforcement action.

Seventeen other firms, including Morgan Stanley, Bear, Stearns, Paine Webber and Standard & Poor's, still face lawsuits by the county.

_____

above, the legal costs and reputational damage emanating from the Orange County bankruptcy have been huge.

The five generic types of swaps, in order of their quantitative importance, are interest rate swaps, currency swaps, commodity swaps, equity swaps, and credit swaps.[1] While the instrument underlying the swap may change, the basic principle of a swap agreement is the same in that there is a restructuring of asset or liability cash flows in a preferred direction by the transacting parties. Next, we consider the role of the two major generic types of swap—interest rate and currency—in

_____

[1]There are also *swaptions,* which are options to enter into a swap agreement at some preagreed contract terms (e.g., a fixed rate of 10 percent) at some time in the future in return for the payment of an up-front premium.

hedging FI risk. We then go on to examine the newest and fastest growing type of swap: the credit swap.

Interest Rate Swaps

Interest Rate Swap
An exchange of fixed interest payments for floating interest payments by two counterparties.

By far the largest segment of the global swap market is comprised of **interest rate swaps.** Conceptually, an interest rate swap is a succession of forward contracts on interest rates arranged by two parties.[2] As such, it allows an FI to put in place a long-term hedge sometimes for as long as 15 years. This reduces the need to roll over contracts if reliance had been placed on futures or forward contracts to achieve such long-term hedges.

Swap Buyer
By convention, makes the fixed-rate payments in an interest rate swap transaction.

In a swap, the **swap buyer** agrees to make a number of fixed interest rate payments on periodic settlement dates to the **swap seller.** The seller of the swap in turn agrees to make floating-rate payments to the buyer of the swap on the same periodic settlement dates. The fixed-rate side—by convention, the swap buyer—generally has a comparative advantage in making fixed-rate payments, while the floating-rate side—by convention, the swap seller—generally has a comparative advantage in making variable or floating-rate payments. In undertaking this transaction, the FI that is the fixed-rate payer is seeking to transform the variable-rate nature of its liabilities into fixed-rate liabilities to better match the fixed returns earned on its assets. Meanwhile, the FI that is the variable-rate payer seeks to turn its fixed-rate liabilities into variable-rate liabilities to better match the variable returns on its assets.

Swap Seller
By convention, makes the float-rate payments in an interest rate swap.

To explain the role of a swap transaction in hedging FI interest rate risk, we use a simple example. Consider two FIs: The first is a money center bank that has raised $100 million of its funds by issuing four-year medium-term notes with 10 percent annual fixed coupons rather than relying on short-term deposits to raise funds (see Table 26–1). On the asset side of its portfolio, the bank makes commercial and industrial (C&I) loans whose rates are indexed to annual changes in the London Interbank Offered Rate (LIBOR). As we discussed in Chapter 11, banks currently index most large commercial and industrial loans to either LIBOR or the federal funds rate in the money market.

As a result of having floating-rate loans and fixed-rate liabilities in its asset-liability structure, the money center bank has a negative duration gap: the duration of its assets is shorter than that of its liabilities.

$$D_A - kD_L < 0$$

TABLE 26–1   Money Center Bank Balance Sheet

Assets		Liabilities	
C&I loans (rate indexed to LIBOR) =	$100 million	Medium-term notes (coupons fixed) =	$100 million

[2]See C. W. Smith, C. W. Smithson, and D. S. Wilford, *Managing Financial Risk* (Cambridge, Mass.: Ballinger Publishing, 1990). For example, a four-year swap with annual swap dates involves four net cash flows between the parties to a swap. This is essentially similar to arranging four forward contracts: a one-year, a two-year, a three-year, and a four-year contract.

TABLE 26–2   The Savings Bank Balance Sheet

Assets	Liabilities
Fixed-rate mortgages = $100 million	Short-term CDs (one year) = $100 million

One way for the bank to hedge this exposure would be to shorten the duration or interest rate sensitivity of its liabilities by transforming them into short-term floating-rate liabilities that better match the duration characteristics of its asset portfolio. To do this, it can sell an interest rate swap—that is, enter into a swap agreement to make the floating-rate payment side of a swap agreement.

The second party in the swap is a thrift institution (savings bank) that is heavily invested in $100 million worth of fixed-rate residential mortgages of long duration. To finance this residential mortgage portfolio, the savings bank has had to rely on short-term certificates of deposit with an average duration of one year (see Table 26–2). On maturity, these CDs have to be rolled over at the current market rate.

Consequently, the savings bank's asset-liability balance sheet structure is the reverse of the money center bank's; that is,

$$D_A - kD_L > 0$$

The savings bank could hedge its interest rate risk exposure by transforming the short-term floating-rate nature of its liabilities into fixed-rate liabilities that better match the long-term maturity/duration structure of its assets. One way to do this is to buy a swap—take the fixed payment side of a swap agreement.

The opposing balance sheet and interest rate risk exposures of the money center bank and the savings bank provide the necessary conditions for an interest rate swap agreement between the two parties. This swap agreement can be arranged directly between the parties. However, it is likely that an FI—another bank or an investment bank—would act as either a broker or an agent, receiving a fee to bring the two parties together or to intermediate fully by accepting the credit risk exposure and guaranteeing the cash flows underlying the swap contract. By acting as a principal as well as an agent, the FI can add a credit risk premium to the fee. However, the credit risk exposure of a swap to an FI is somewhat less than that on a loan (this is discussed later in this chapter). Conceptually, when a third-party FI fully intermediates the swap, that FI is really entering into two separate swap agreements: one with the bank and one with the savings banks.

Plain Vanilla
Standard agreement without any special features.

For simplicity, we consider a **plain vanilla** fixed–floating rate swap where a third-party intermediary acts as a simple broker or agent by bringing together two banks with opposing interest rate risk exposures to enter into a swap agreement or contract. In this example, the notional value of the swap is $100 million—equal to the assumed size of the money center bank's medium-term note issue—and the maturity of four years is equal to the maturity of the bank's note liabilities. The annual coupon cost of these note liabilities is 10 percent, and the bank's problem is that the variable return on its assets may be insufficient to cover the cost of meeting these coupon payments if market interest rates, and therefore asset returns, *fall.* By comparison, the fixed returns on the thrift's mortgage asset portfolio may be insufficient to cover the interest cost of its CDs if market rates *rise.* As a result, the swap agreement might dictate that the thrift should send fixed payments of 10 percent per

FIGURE 26–1

*Fixed–Floating
Rate Swap*

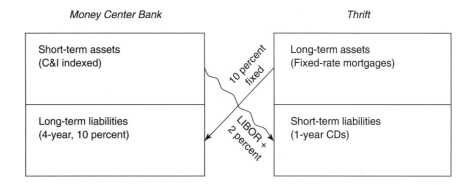

annum of the notional $100 million value of the swap to the bank to allow the bank to cover fully the coupon interest payments on its note issue. In return, the bank sends annual payments indexed to one-year LIBOR to help the thrift cover the cost of refinancing its one-year renewable CDs. Suppose that one-year LIBOR is currently 8 percent and the bank agrees to send annual payments at the end of each year equal to one-year LIBOR plus 2 percent to the thrift.[3] We depict this fixed–floating rate swap transaction in Figure 26–1.

In analyzing this swap, one has to distinguish between how it should be priced at time 0 (now), that is, how the exchange rate of fixed (10 percent) for floating (LIBOR + 2 percent) is set when the swap agreement is initiated, and the actual realized cash flows on the swap. As we discuss later in this chapter, *fair pricing* on initiation of the swap depends on the market's expectations of future short-term rates, while realized cash flows on the swap depend on the actual market rates (here, LIBOR) that materialized over the life of the swap contract.

Realized Cash Flows on an Interest Rate Swap

We assume that the realized or actual path of interest rates (LIBOR) over the four-year life of the contract would be similar to Figure 26–2. Given this actual path of LIBOR, we can see that at the end of each year's settlement date for the four-year swap, the rates would be:

End of Year	LIBOR
1	9%
2	9%
3	7%
4	6%

Money Center Bank Payments to the Savings Bank.   The money center bank's variable payments to the thrift were indexed to these rates by the formula

$$(\text{LIBOR} + 2\%) \times \$100 \text{ million}$$

---

[3]These rates implicitly assume that this is the cheapest way each party can hedge its interest rate exposure. For example, LIBOR + 2 percent is the cheapest way in which the money center bank can transform its fixed-rate liabilities into floating-rate liabilities.

FIGURE 26–2

Actual Path of One-Year LIBOR over the Four Years of the Swap Agreement

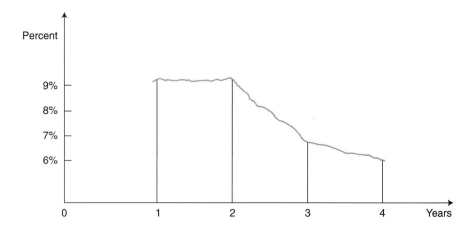

TABLE 26–3   **Realized Cash Flow on the Swap Agreement**
(in millions of dollars)

End of Year	One-Year LIBOR	One-Year LIBOR +2 percent	Cash Payment by MCB	Cash Payment by Savings Bank	Net Payment Made by MCB
1	9%	11%	$11	$10	+1
2	9	11	11	10	+1
3	7	9	9	10	−1
4	6	8	8	10	−2
Total			39	40	−1

Savings Bank Payments to the Money Center Bank.   By contrast, the fixed annual payments the thrift made to the bank were the same each year: 10% × $100 million. We summarize the actual or realized cash flows among the two parties over the four years in Table 26–3. As you can see in the table, the savings bank's net gains from the swap in years 1 and 2 are $1 million per year. The enhanced cash flow offsets the increased cost of refinancing its CDs in a higher interest rate environment—that is, it is hedged against rising rates. By contrast, the money center bank makes net gains on the swap in years 3 and 4, when rates fall; thus, the bank is hedged against falling rates. The positive cash flow from the swap offsets the decline in the variable returns on the money center bank's asset portfolio. Overall, the money center bank made a net dollar gain of $1 million in nominal dollars; its true realized gain would be the present value of this amount.

In effect, the bank has transformed its four-year fixed-rate liability notes into a variable-rate liability (a floating-rate swap payment to the savings bank). Meanwhile, the thrift has transformed its variable-rate liability of one-year CDs into a fixed-rate liability (a 10 percent fixed-rate swap payment to the bank).

In this example, note that in the absence of default/credit risk, only the money center bank is really fully hedged. This is the case because the annual 10 percent payments it receives from the savings bank at the end of each year allow it to meet the promised 10 percent coupon rate payments to its note holders regardless of the return it gets on its variable-rate assets. By contrast, the savings bank receives variable-rate payments based on LIBOR plus 2 percent. However, it is quite possible that the CD rate the savings bank has to pay on its deposit liabilities doesn't exactly track the LIBOR-indexed payments sent by the bank. That is, the savings bank is subject to basis risk exposure on the swap contract. There are two possible sources of this basis risk. First, CD rates do not exactly match the movements of LIBOR rates over time, since the former are determined in the domestic money market and the latter in the overseas Eurodollar market. Second, the credit/default risk premium on the savings bank's CDs may increase over time; thus, the +2 percent add-on to LIBOR may be insufficient to hedge the savings bank's cost of funds. The savings bank might be better hedged if it required the bank to send it floating payments based on U.S. domestic CD rates rather than LIBOR. To do this, the bank would probably require additional compensation since it would then be bearing basis risk. Its asset returns would be sensitive to LIBOR movements while its swap payments were indexed to U.S. CD rates.

Off-Market Swaps
Swaps that have nonstandard terms that require one party to compensate another.

Swaps can always be molded or tailored to the needs of the transacting parties as long as one party is willing to compensate the other party for accepting nonstandard terms or **off-market swap** arrangements, usually in the form of an up-front fee or payments. Relaxing a standardized swap can include special interest rate terms and indexes as well as allowing for varying notional values underlying the swap.

For example, in the case we just considered, the notional value of the swap was fixed at $100 million for each of the four annual swap dates. However, swap notional values can be allowed either to decrease or to increase over a swap contract's life. This flexibility is useful when one of the parties has heavy investments in mortgages (in our example, the savings bank) and the mortgages are fully amortized. Fully amortized means that the annual and monthly cash flows on the mortgage portfolio reflect repayments of both principal and interest such that the periodic payment is kept constant (see Chapter 28). Fixed-rate mortgages normally have larger payments of interest than principal in the early years, with the interest component falling as mortgages approach maturity. One possibility would be for the savings bank to enter into a mortgage swap to hedge the amortizing nature of the mortgage portfolio or alternatively to allow the notional value of the swap to decline at a rate similar to the decline in the principal component of the mortgage portfolio.[4]

Another example of a special type of interest rate swap is the inverse floater swap, which was engineered by major FIs as part of structured note finance deals to lower the cost of finance to various government agencies. Such arrangements have resulted in enormous problems for investor groups such as municipal authorities and corporations that are part of the overall swap deal.

A structured note–inverse floater swap arrangement is shown in Figure 26–3.

In this arrangement, a government agency issues notes (say, $100 million) to investors with a coupon that is equal to 7 percent minus LIBOR—that is, an (inverse)

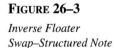

FIGURE 26–3

Inverse Floater Swap–Structured Note

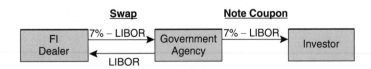

[4]For further details of nonstandard swaps, see P. A. Abken, "Beyond Plain Vanilla: A Taxonomy of Swaps," Federal Reserve Bank of Atlanta, *Economic Review,* March–April 1991, pp. 21–29; and C. James and C. Smith, "The Use of Index Amortizing Swaps by Banc One," *Journal of Applied Corporate Finance* 7, no. 5 (Fall 1994), pp. 54–59.

floating coupon. The novel features of this coupon is that when market rates fall (and thus LIBOR is low), the coupon received by the investor is large.

The government agency then converts this spread liability (7 percent − LIBOR) into a LIBOR liability by entering into a swap with an FI dealer (e.g., a bank such as Bankers Trust). In effect, the cost of the $100 million note issue is LIBOR to the agency plus any fees relating to the swap.

The risk of these notes to the investor is very clear. If LIBOR is 2 percent, then the investor will receive coupons of 7 percent − 2 percent = 5 percent, which is an excellent spread return if the investor can borrow at close to LIBOR (e.g., the Orange County situation). However, consider what happens if, as in 1994, interest rates rise. If LIBOR rises from 2 to 8 percent, the promised coupon becomes 7 percent − 8 percent = −1 percent. Since negative coupons can't be paid, the actual coupon paid to the investor is 0 percent. However, if the investor borrowed funds to buy the notes at LIBOR, the cost of funds is 8 percent. Thus, the investor is facing an extremely large negative spread and loss.

Macrohedging with Swaps*

The duration model shown in Chapters 24 and 25 to estimate the optimal number of futures and options contracts to hedge an FI's duration gap also can be applied to estimate the optimal number of swap contracts. For example, an FI manager might wish to know how many 10-year (or 5-year) swap contracts are needed to hedge its overall risk exposure.

Assume that an FI (such as a thrift) has a positive duration gap so that it has positive net worth exposure to rising interest rates:

$$\Delta E = -(D_A - kD_L)A \frac{\Delta R}{1 + R} > 0$$

As discussed above, the thrift can seek to hedge by paying fixed and receiving floating. However, there are many different maturity swaps available. As will be shown below, the size of the notional value of the interest rate swaps entered into will depend on the maturity (duration) of the swap contract. Suppose the FI manager chooses to hedge with 10-year swaps.

In terms of valuation, a 10-year swap arrangement can be considered in terms of bond equivalent valuation. That is, the fixed-rate payments on a 10-year swap are formally equivalent to the fixed payments on a 10-year T-bond. Similarly, the floating-rate payments on a 10-year swap with *annual* payments can be viewed as equivalent to floating coupons on a bond where coupons are repriced (to LIBOR) every year. That is, how the value of the swap changes (ΔS) when interest rates ($\Delta R/1+R$) rise will depend on the relative interest sensitivity of 10-year bonds to 1-year bonds, or in duration terms, $(D_{10} - D_1)$.[5] In general,

$$\Delta S = -(D_{\text{fixed}} - D_{\text{float}}) \times N_S \times \frac{\Delta R}{1 + R}$$

where

$$\Delta S = \text{Change in the market value of the swap contract}$$

---

[5] Although principal payments on bonds are not swapped on maturity, this does not matter since the theoretical payment and receipt of principal values cancel each other out.

$(D_{fixed} - D_{float})$ = Difference in durations between a government bond that has the same maturity and coupon as the fixed-payment leg of the swap and a government bond that has the same duration as the swap-payment interval (e.g., annual floating payments)

N_s = Notional value of swap contracts

$\dfrac{\Delta R}{1 + R}$ = Shock to interest rates

Note that as long as $D_{fixed} > D_{float}$, then when interest rates rise, the market (present) value of fixed-rate payments will fall by more than will the market (present) value of floating-rate payments; in market (or present value) terms, the fixed-rate payers gain when rates rise and lose when rates fall.

To solve for the optimal notional value of swap contracts, we set

$$\Delta S = \Delta E$$

The gain on swap contracts entered into off the balance sheet just offsets the loss in net worth on the balance sheet when rates rise. Substituting values for ΔS and ΔE, we have

$$-(D_{fixed} - D_{float}) \times N_s \times \frac{\Delta R}{1 + R} = -(D_A - kD_L) \times A \times \frac{\Delta R}{1 + R}$$

Canceling out the common terms, we have

$$(D_{fixed} - D_{float}) \times N_s = (D_A - kD_L) \times A$$

Solving for N_s, we have

$$N_s = \frac{(D_A - kD_L) \times A}{D_{fixed} - D_{float}}$$

Suppose $D_A = 5$, $D_L = 3$, $k = .9$, and $A = \$100,000,000$. Also, assume the duration of a current 10-year fixed-rate T-bond with the same coupon as the fixed rate on the swap is seven years, while the duration of a floating-rate bond that reprices annually is one year:[6]

$$D_{fixed} = 7 \text{ and } D_{float} = 1$$

Then

$$N_S = \frac{(D_A - kD_L) \times A}{D_{fixed} - D_{float}} = \frac{\$230,000,000}{(7 - 1)} = \$38,333,333$$

If each swap contract is \$100,000 in size,[7] then the number of swap contracts into which the FI should enter will be \$38,333,333/\$100,000 = 383.33, or 383 contracts, rounding down.

If the FI engaged in a longer-term swap—for example, 15 years—such that $D_{fixed} = 9$ and $D_{float} = 1$, then the notional value of swap contracts would fall to \$230,000,000/(9 − 1) = \$28,750,000. If each swap contract is \$100,000 in size, the FI should enter into 287 swap contracts. While it may seem logical that fewer

---

[6]See Chapter 8 for a discussion of the duration on floating-rate bonds.

[7]The notional value of swap contracts can take virtually any size since they are individually tailored OTC contracts.

contracts are preferable in the sense of saving on fees and other related costs of hedging, this advantage is offset by the fact that longer-term swaps have greater counterparty default or credit risk (discussed later in this chapter).

Concept Questions

1. In the example that concludes on page 627, which of the two FIs has its liability costs fully hedged and which is only partially hedged? Explain your answer.
2. What are some nonstandard terms that might be encountered in an off-market swap?
3. In the hedging example that concludes on page 630, what is the notional size of the swap contract if $D_{fixed} = 5$ and swap contracts require payment every six months?

Pricing an Interest Rate Swap*

We now discuss fair pricing of the swap at the time the parties enter into the swap agreement. As with much of financial theory, there are important no-arbitrage conditions that should hold in setting rates in a fixed-floating rate swap agreement. The most important no-arbitrage condition is that the expected present value of the cash flow payments made by the fixed-rate payer, the buyer, should equal the expected present value of the cash flow payments made by the seller.

$$\text{Expected fixed-payment } PV = \text{Expected floating-payment } PV$$

If this no-arbitrage condition doesn't hold, one party usually has to compensate the other with an up-front payment equal to the difference between the two expected present values of the cash flows.

On-the-Run Issues
New issues of Treasury securities.

The fixed-rate payment of the swap is usually priced off the newly issued or **on-the-run** yield curve of U.S. Treasury notes and bonds. Thus, if four-year Treasuries are currently yielding 10 percent, a quote of 10.25 percent (bid) and 10.35 percent (offer) would mean that the commercial or investment bank acting as a swaps dealer is willing to buy or become the fixed-rate payer in a swap agreement at a contractual swap rate of 10.25 percent. It is also willing to take the other side of the swap (become the fixed-rate receiver) if the swap fixed rate is set higher at 10.35 percent. The 10-basis-point spread is the dealer's spread or the return for intermediating the swap. As discussed earlier, in intermediating, the FI has to cover the credit risk assumed in the swap transaction and cover its costs of search and intermediation as well. In the next subsection we develop an example of how a swap might be priced.

Pricing a Swap: An Example*

We develop an example of swap pricing under simplified assumptions by applying the no-arbitrage condition and pricing swaps off the Treasury yield curve. This provides an understanding of why expected cash flows from the swap agreement can differ from actual or realized cash flows. It also explains why when yield curves slope upward, the fixed-rate payer (swap buyer) faces an inherent credit risk in any swap contract.

Assume that in a four-year swap agreement, the fixed-rate payer makes fixed-rate payments at the end of each year. Also assume that while these payments are made at the end of each year, interest rates are determined at the beginning of each year.[8] That is:

Since this is a four-year swap agreement, the fixed-rate payer knows in advance the annual interest rate to pay each year:

$$\bar{R}_1 = \bar{R}_2 = \bar{R}_3 = \bar{R}_4 = Fixed$$

Treasury Par Yield Curve
The yield curve that reflects newly issued bonds whose coupons and yields are the same (i.e., the bonds are priced at par or 100).

Let R be priced off the current **Treasury** bond **par yield curve** for four-year on-the-run Treasury note issues. See the assumed current par yield curve in Figure 26–4.

Suppose that newly issued four-year Treasury bonds are currently yielding 10 percent and that the fixed-rate payments on the swap are set at 10 percent for each of the four years:

$$R_i = 10\% \qquad\qquad i = 1, \dots , 4$$

Here we ignore the usual markup in the swap market over Treasuries for simplicity.

For the no-arbitrage condition to hold, the present value of these fixed payments made must equal the expected stream of variable one-year payments received from the floating-rate payer. If we assume that the expectations theory of interest rates holds, we can extract the expected one-year rates (payments) from the Treasury yield curve. We wish to determine:

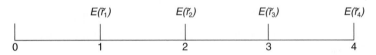

Figure 26–4

T-bond Par Yield Curve

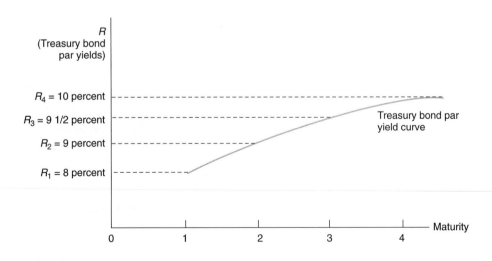

---

[8]This is not always the case.

Where $E(\bar{r}_i)$ are the expected one-year (forward) interest payments to be made at the end of years 1, 2, 3, and 4, respectively.

Extracting these expected one-year forward rates is a little awkward. We begin by extracting the spot or zero-coupon discount bond yield curve from the coupon par yield curve on Treasury bonds; then we derive expected one-year forward rates from this zero-coupon yield curve. The reason we need to extract the zero-coupon discount yield curve is that this yield curve reflects the time value of money for single payments (bonds) at 1 year's, 2 years', 3 years', and 4 years' time. Unfortunately, the yield to maturity on a coupon bond is a complex weighted average of the time value of money discount yields on zero-coupon bonds. Specifically, a yield to maturity on a coupon bond is the internal rate of return on that bond or the single interest rate (yield) that equates the promised cash flows on the bond to its price. Such a yield is not the same as the time value of money. For example, assuming annual coupon payments, the 10 percent yield to maturity on the four-year T-bond is a complex average of the yields to maturity on a one-year, two-year, three-year, and four-year zero-coupon discount bond.

To see this, consider the cash flows on the four-year coupon par value Treasury bond:

$$100 = P_4 = \frac{10}{(1 + R_4)} + \frac{10}{(1 + R_4)^2} + \frac{10}{(1 + R_4)^3} + \frac{110}{(1 + R_4)^4}$$

and the yield to maturity on this par bond, $R_4 = 10$ percent. Thus:

$$P_4 = \frac{10}{(1.1)} + \frac{10}{(1.1)^2} + \frac{10}{(1.1)^3} + \frac{110}{(1.1)^4} = 100$$

Conceptually, this coupon bond could be broken down and sold as four separate zero-coupon bonds with one year, two years, three years, and four years to maturity. This is similar to how the U.S. Treasury currently creates zero-coupon bonds through its **Treasury Strips** program.[9] That is:

Treasury Strip
A zero-coupon or deep-discount bond

$$P_4 = \frac{\dfrac{10}{(1 + R_4)} + \dfrac{10}{(1 + R_4)^2} + \dfrac{10}{(1 + R_4)^3} + \dfrac{110}{(1 + R_4)^4}}{\text{Coupon bond value}}$$

$$= \frac{\dfrac{10}{(1 + d_1)} + \dfrac{10}{(1 + d_2)^2} + \dfrac{10}{(1 + d_3)^3} + \dfrac{110}{(1 + d_4)^4}}{\text{Sum of separate zero-coupon bond values}}$$

The first relationship is the value of the coupon bond as a whole, while the second is the value of four stripped coupon and principal discount bonds of 10, 10, 10, and 110, each sold separately to different investors. The time values of money for single payments in each of the four years, or required discount yields are d_1, d_2, d_3, and d_4. Further, this equation confirms that the yield to maturity on the four-year coupon bond, when sold as a whole bond (R_4), is a complex average of the discount rates on four different zero-coupon bonds—d_1, d_2, d_3, and d_4—where the d_is are discount yields on single payment bonds of i year to maturity, $i = 1, 2, 3$, and 4:

---

[9]Apart from semiannual rather than annual coupon stripping, the other major difference in practice is that the final coupon payment of 10 is separated and sold independently from the 100 face value, even though both are paid at the same time and have the same time value of money.

$$P_1^D = \frac{10}{(1 + d_1)}$$

$$P_2^D = \frac{10}{(1 + d_2)^2}$$

$$P_3^D = \frac{10}{(1 + d_3)^3}$$

$$P_4^D = \frac{110}{(1 + d_4)^4}$$

$$\text{and } P_4 = \sum_{i=1}^{4} P_i^D$$

where the P_i^D represent the market values of the four different stripped or zero-coupon bonds. The no-arbitrage condition requires that the values of the four zero-coupon bonds sum to the price of the four-year Treasury coupon bond (P_4) when sold as a whole.

To derive the expected forward one-year rates implied by the yield curve, we need to calculate the discount yields themselves: d_1, d_2, d_3, and d_4.

Solving the Discount Yield Curve.* To calculate the discount yields, we use a process of forward iteration. From Figure 26–4, which shows the T-bond yield curve, we note that one-year par value coupon Treasury bonds are currently yielding 8 percent:

$$P_1 = \frac{108}{(1 + R_1)} = \frac{108}{1.08} = 100$$

$$R_1 = 8\%$$

Because the one-year coupon bond has exactly one year left to maturity, and thus only one final payment of interest (8) and principal (100), its valuation is exactly the same as a one-year zero-coupon bond with one payment at the end of the year. Thus, by definition, under no arbitrage,

$$R_1 = d_1 = 8\%$$

Once we have solved for d_1, we can go on to solve for d_2 by forward iteration.

Specifically, from the par coupon yield curve we can see that two-year coupon-bearing bonds are yielding 9 percent:

$$P_2 = \frac{9}{(1 + R_2)} + \frac{109}{(1 + R_2)^2} = \frac{9}{(1.09)} + \frac{109}{(1.09)^2} = 100$$

$$R_1 = 9\%$$

The no-arbitrage condition between coupon bonds and zero-coupon bonds implies that

$$P_2 = \frac{9}{(1.09)} + \frac{109}{(1.09)^2} = \frac{9}{(1 + d_1)} + \frac{109}{(1 + d_2)^2} = 100$$

Since we have solved for $d_1 = 8$ percent, we can directly solve for d_2:

$$100 = \frac{9}{(1.08)} + \frac{109}{(1 + d_2)^2}$$

$$d_2 = 9.045\%$$

Similarly, we know from the current par T-bond yield curve that three-year coupon-bearing bonds are yielding $9\frac{1}{2}$ percent. Also, no arbitrage requires

$$P_3 = \frac{9\frac{1}{2}}{(1 + R_3)} + \frac{9\frac{1}{2}}{(1 + R_3)^2} + \frac{109\frac{1}{2}}{(1 + R_3)^3}$$

$$= \frac{9\frac{1}{2}}{(1 + d_1)} + \frac{9\frac{1}{2}}{(1 + d_2)^2} + \frac{109\frac{1}{2}}{(1 + d_3)^3} = 100$$

$$R_3 = 9\frac{1}{2}\%$$

To solve for d_3, the yield on a three-year zero-coupon bond, we have

$$100 = \frac{9\frac{1}{2}}{(1.08)} + \frac{9\frac{1}{2}}{(1.09045)^2} + \frac{109\frac{1}{2}}{(1 + d_3)^3}$$

Thus, since d_1 and d_2 have already been determined, $d_3 = 9.58$ percent.

Finally, to solve for the discount rate on a four-year zero-coupon bond (d_4), we know that

$$P_4 = 100 = \frac{10}{(1 + R_4)} + \frac{10}{(1 + R_4)^2} + \frac{10}{(1 + R_4)^3} + \frac{110}{(1 + R_4)^4}$$

$$= \frac{10}{(1 + d_1)} + \frac{10}{(1 + d_2)^2} + \frac{10}{(1 + d_3)^3} + \frac{110}{(1 + d_4)^4}$$

$$R_4 = 10\%$$

To solve for d_4, we have:

$$100 = \frac{10}{(1.08)} + \frac{10}{(1.09045)^2} + \frac{10}{(1.0958)^3} + \frac{110}{(1 + d_4)^4}$$

As a result, since d_1, d_2, and d_3 were solved, $d_4 = 10.147$ percent.

In Figure 26–5 we plot the derived zero-coupon discount bond yield curve alongside the coupon par yield curve. As you can see, the derived zero-coupon yield curve slopes upward faster than does the coupon bond yield curve. This result is a mathematical relationship and comes from the no-arbitrage derivation of the zero-coupon curve from the T-bond par yield curve. There is an intuitive explanation for this result as well. Remember that $R_4 = 10$ percent, the yield to maturity or internal rate of return on a four-year coupon bond, can conceptually be viewed as a complex weighted average of the discount rates on four successive one-year zero-coupon bonds (d_1, d_2, d_3, and d_4).

Since R_4 at 10 percent is higher than $d_1 = 8$ percent, $d_2 = 9.045$ percent, and $d_3 = 9.58$ percent, then d_4 (10.147 percent) must be above R_4 (10 percent) if R_4 is to be a weighted average of the individual zero-coupon discount rates. This same reasoning applies to why $R_3 < d_3$ and $R_2 < d_2$.

Note, however, that if the coupon yield curve were flat, then $R_i = d_i$ for every maturity. If the coupon yield curve were downward sloping, the discount or zero-coupon yield curve would lie below the coupon yield curve (for the converse reason used to explain why it must be above when the coupon yield curve is rising). We can now solve for the expected one-year floating rates implied by the zero-coupon yield curve.

We are assuming that floating interest rate payments are made at the end of each year based on the one-year interest rates that are set at the beginning of each

FIGURE 26–5

*Discount Yield Curve
versus Par Yield Curve*

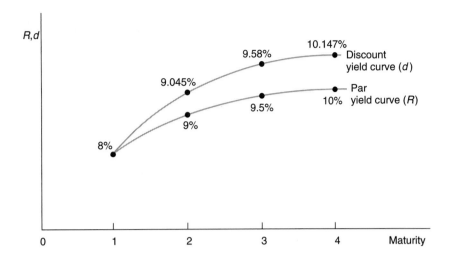

year. We can use the zero-coupon bond yield curve to derive the expected one-year forward rates that reflect the expected floating swap payments at the end of each year.

**Solving for the Implied Forward Rates/Floating Payments
on a Swap Agreement.***

End of Year 1 Payment.   The expected end of year 1 payment $E(\tilde{r}_1)$ must be equal to the current one-year rate set for one-year discount bonds at time 0 since floating rates paid at the end of a period are assumed to depend on rates set or expected at the beginning of that period. That is, the expected first-year floating payment equals the current one-year discount rate.

$$E(\tilde{r}_1) = d_1 = 8 \text{ percent}$$

End of Year 2 Payment.   To determine the end of year 2 payment, we need to solve the expected one-year interest rate or forward rate in year 2. This is the rate that reflects expected payments at the end of year 2. We know that no arbitrage requires[10]

$$(1 + d_2)^2 = (1 + d_1)(1 + E(\tilde{r}_2))$$

That is, the yield from holding a two-year zero-coupon bond to maturity must equal the expected yield from holding the current one-year zero-coupon bond to maturity times the expected yield from investing in a new one-year zero-coupon bond in year 2. Rearranging this equation, we have

$$(1 + E(\tilde{r}_2)) = \frac{(1 + d_2)^2}{(1 + d_1)}$$

Since we have already solved for d_2 = 9.045 percent and d_1 = 8 percent, we can solve for $E(\tilde{r}_2)$:

---

[10]Under the pure expectations theory of interest rates.

$$1 + E(\tilde{r}_2) = \frac{(1.09045)^2}{(1.08)}$$

$$E(\tilde{r}_2) = 10.1\%$$

End of Year 3 Payment.   In a similar fashion,

$$(1 + E(\tilde{r}_3)) = \frac{(1 + d_3)^3}{(1 + d_2)^2}$$

Substituting in the d_2 and d_3 values from the zero-coupon bond yield curve, we have

$$1 + E(\tilde{r}_3) = \frac{(1.0958)^3}{(1.09045)^2}$$

$$E(\tilde{r}_3) = 10.658\%$$

End of Year 4 Payment.   Using the same procedure,

$$1\ 1\ E(\tilde{r}_4)\ 5\ \frac{(1\ 1\ d_4)^4}{(1\ 1\ d_3)^3}\ 5\ \frac{(1.10147)^4}{(1.0958)^3}$$

$$E(\tilde{r}_4)\ 5\ 11.866\%$$

These four expected one-year payments by the floating-rate payer are plotted against the fixed-rate payments by the buyer of the swap in Figure 26–6. Although expecting to pay a net payment $[\bar{R} - E(\tilde{r}_1)]$ of 2 percent to the floating-rate seller in the first year, the fixed-rate payer expects to receive net payments of 0.1 percent, 0.658 percent, and 1.866 percent from the floating-rate seller in years 2, 3, and 4. This has important credit risk implications. It implies that when the yield curve is upward sloping, the fixed-rate payer can expect not only to pay more than the floating-rate payer in the early years of a swap agreement but also to receive higher cash flows from the seller or floating-rate payer in the later years of the swap agreement. Thus, the fixed-rate payer faces the risk that if expected rates are actually realized, the floating-rate payer may have an incentive to default toward the end of the swap agreement as a net payer. In this case the swap buyer might have to replace the swap at less favorable market conditions in the future.[11]

Finally, note that in this section we have been comparing expected cash flows in the swap agreement under no-arbitrage conditions. If the term structure shifts after the swap has been entered into, then realized one-year rates (and payments) will not equal expected rates for the floating-rate payer. In our example, if the term structure shifts, then

$$r_2 \neq E(\tilde{r}_2)$$
$$r_3 \neq E(\tilde{r}_3)$$
$$r_4 \neq E(\tilde{r}_4)$$

where r_2, r_3, and r_4, are realized or actual one-year rates on new one-year discount bonds issued in years 2, 3, and 4, respectively. Of course, the floating-rate payer has to make payments on actual or realized rates rather than expected rates, as we discussed in the first section of this chapter.

---

[11]This example is based on the discussion in C. W. Smith, C. W. Smithson, and L. M. Wakeman, "The Market for Interest Rate Swaps," *Financial Management* 17 (1988), pp. 34–44.

FIGURE 26–6

Fixed and Expected
Floating Swap Payments

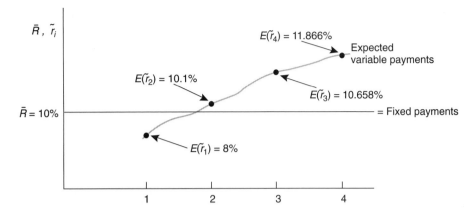

Concept Questions

1. What is the most important no-arbitrage condition in setting rates in a fixed–floating rate swap agreement?
2. Suppose the current par T-bond yield curve slopes downward and $R_1 = 12$ percent, $R_2 = 11$ percent, $R_3 = 10$ percent, and $R_4 = 9$ percent. Derive d_1, d_2, d_3, and d_4.
3. The current T-bond par yield curve shows $R_1 = 8$ percent, $R_2 = 9$ percent, and $R_3 = 11$ percent. Suppose you enter a \$100 million three-year swap as the floating-rate paying party. What do you expect to receive over the three years? What do you expect to pay?

Currency Swaps

Just as swaps are long-term contracts that can hedge interest rate risk exposure, they can also be used to hedge currency risk exposures of FIs. In the following section, we consider a simple plain vanilla example of how currency swaps can immunize FIs against exchange rate risk when they mismatch the currencies of their assets and liabilities.

Fixed-Fixed Currency Swaps

Consider a U.S. bank with fixed-rate assets all denominated in dollars. However, it is financing part of its asset portfolio with a £50 million issue of four-year medium-term British pound sterling notes that have a fixed annual coupon of 10 percent. By comparison, there is a U.K. bank that has all its assets denominated in sterling; however, it is partly funding those assets with a \$100 million issue of four-year medium-term dollars notes with a fixed annual coupon of 10 percent.

These two banks are exposed to opposing currency risks. The U.S. bank is exposed to the risk that the dollar will depreciate against the pound over the next four years, making it more costly to cover the annual coupon interest payments and the principal repayment on its pound-denominated notes. On the other hand, the U.K. bank is exposed to the dollar appreciating against the pound, making it more difficult to cover the dollar coupon and principal payments on its four-year \$100 million note issue out of the sterling cash flows on its assets.

One solution to these exposures is for the U.K. and U.S. banks to enter into a currency swap under which the U.K. bank undertakes to send annual payments in pounds to cover the coupon and principal repayments of the U.S. bank's sterling note issue, while the U.S. bank would send annual dollar payments to the U.K. bank to cover the interest and principal payments on its dollar note issue.[12] In so doing, the U.K. bank has transformed fixed-rate dollar liabilities into fixed-rate sterling liabilities that better match the sterling fixed-rate cash flows from its asset portfolio. Similarly, the U.S. bank has transformed fixed-rate sterling liabilities into fixed-rate dollar liabilities that better match the fixed-rate dollar cash flows from its asset portfolio. In undertaking this exchange of cash flows, the two parties normally agree on a fixed exchange rate for the cash flows at the beginning of the period.[13] In this example, the fixed exchange rate would be $2/£1. We summarize the currency swap in Figure 26–7 and the realized cash flows in Table 26–4.

In this example, both liabilities bear a fixed 10 percent interest rate. This is not a necessary requirement for the fixed-fixed currency swap agreement. For example, suppose that U.S. bank's note coupons were 5 percent per annum, while U.K. bank's note coupons were 10 percent. The swap dollar payments of the U.S. bank in Table 26–4 would remain unchanged, but the U.K. bank's sterling payments would be reduced by £2.5 million (or $5 million) in each of the four years. This difference could be met either by some up-front payment by the U.K. bank to the U.S. bank, reflecting the difference in the present value of the two fixed cash flows, or by annual payments that result in zero net present value differences among the fixed-fixed

FIGURE 26–7

Fixed-Fixed Pound/ Dollar Currency Swap

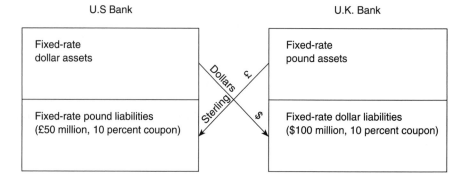

TABLE 26–4   Cash Flows under the Fixed-Fixed Currency Swap Agreement

	Cash Flow Payments			
End of Year	*U.S. Bank ($s)*	*U.K. Bank (£s)*	*Payments by U.K. Bank in $s (at $2/£1 exchange rate)*	*Net Cash Flow ($s)*
1	$ 10	£ 5	$ 10	0
2	10	5	10	0
3	10	5	10	0
4	110	55	110	0

---

[12]In a currency swap, it is usual to include both principal and interest payments as part of the swap agreement. For interest rate swaps, it is usual to include just interest rate payments. The reason for this is that both principal and interest are exposed to FX risk.

[13]As with interest rate swaps, this exchange rate reflects the contracting parties' expectations in regard to future exchange rate movements.

currency swap participants' payments. Also note that if the exchange rate changed from the rate agreed in the swap (\$2/£1), either one or the other side would be losing in the sense that a new swap might be entered into at an exchange rate more favorable to one party. Specifically, if the dollar were to appreciate against the pound over the life of the swap, the agreement would become more costly for the U.S. bank. If, however, the dollar depreciated, the U.K. bank would find the agreement increasingly costly over the swap's life.

By combining an interest rate swap of the fixed-floating type described earlier with a currency swap, we can also produce a fixed-floating currency swap that is a hybrid of the two plain vanilla swaps we have considered so far.

Fixed-Floating Currency Swaps

Consider a U.S. bank that holds mostly floating-rate short-term U.S. dollar-denominated assets. It has partly financed this asset portfolio with a £50 million, four-year note issue with fixed 10 percent annual coupons denominated in sterling. By comparison, a U.K. bank with mostly long-term fixed-rate assets denominated in sterling has partly financed this portfolio with \$100 million short-term dollar-denominated Euro CDs whose rates reflect changes in one-year LIBOR plus a 2 percent premium. As a result, the U.S. bank is faced with both an interest rate risk and a foreign exchange risk. Specifically, if dollar short-term rates fall and the dollar depreciates against the pound, it may face a problem in covering its promised fixed-coupon and principal payments on the pound-denominated note. Consequently, it may wish to transform its fixed-rate, pound-denominated liabilities into variable-rate, dollar-denominated liabilities. The U.K. bank also faces interest rate and foreign exchange rate risk exposure. If U.S. interest rates rise and the dollar appreciates against the pound, the U.K. bank will find it more difficult to cover its promised coupon and principal payments on its dollar-denominated CDs out of the cash flows from its fixed-rate pound asset portfolio. Consequently, it may wish to transform its floating-rate, short-term, dollar-denominated liabilities into fixed-rate pound liabilities.

Each bank can achieve its objective of liability transformation by engaging in a fixed-floating currency swap. Each year, the two banks swap payments at some prearranged dollar/pound exchange rate, assumed to be \$2/£1. The U.K. bank sends fixed payments in pounds to cover the cost of the U.S. bank's pound note issue, while the U.S. bank sends floating payments in dollars to cover the U.K. bank's floating-rate dollar CD costs.

Given the realized LIBOR rates in column (2), we show the relevant payments among the contracting parties in Table 26–5. As you can see from Table 26–5, the realized cash flows from the swap result in a net nominal payment of \$2 million by the U.S. bank to the U.K. bank over the life of the swap.

Concept Questions

1. Referrring to the fixed-fixed currency swap in Table 26–4, if the net cash flows are zero, why does either bank enter into the swap agreement?
2. Referring to Table 26–5, suppose that the U.S. bank had agreed to make floating payments of LIBOR + 1 percent instead of LIBOR + 2 percent. What would its net payment have been to the U.K. bank over the four-year swap agreement?

TABLE 26–5   Fixed-Floating Currency Swap
(in millions of dollars)

Year	LIBOR	LIBOR + 2 percent	Floating Rate Payment by U.S. Bank ($s)	Fixed Rate Payment by U. K. Bank		Net Payment by U.S. Bank ($s)
				(£s)	($ at $2/£1)	
1	9%	11%	$ 11	£ 5	$ 10	$+1
2	7	9	9	5	10	−1
3	8	10	10	5	10	0
4	10	12	112	55	110	+2
Total net payment						$+2

Credit Swaps

In recent years the fastest growing types of swaps have been those developed to better allow FIs to hedge their credit risk. This is important for two reasons. First, credit risk is still more likely to cause an FI to fail than is either interest rate risk or FX risk. Second, credit swaps allow FIs to maintain long-term customer lending relationships without bearing the full credit risk exposure from those relationships.

Below we look at two types of credit swap: (1) the total return swap and (2) the pure credit swap.

Total Return Swaps

Total Return Swap
A swap involving an obligation to pay interest at a specified fixed or floating rate for payments representing the total return on a specified amount.

Although FIs spend significant resources attempting to evaluate and price expected changes in a borrower's credit risk over the life of a loan, a borrower's credit situation (credit quality) sometimes deteriorates unexpectedly after the loan terms are determined and the loan is issued. A lender can use a total return swap to hedge this possible change in credit risk exposure. A **total return swap** involves swapping an obligation to pay interest at a specified fixed or floating rate for payments representing the total return on a loan or a bond (interest and principal value changes) of a specified amount.

For example, suppose that an FI lends $100 million to a Brazilian manufacturing firm at a fixed rate of 10 percent. If the firm's credit risk increases unexpectedly over the life of the loan, the market value of the loan and consequently the FI's net worth will fall. The FI can hedge an unexpected increase in the borrower's credit risk by entering into a total return swap in which it agrees to pay a total return based on an annual fixed rate (f) plus changes in the market value of Brazilian government debt (changes in the value of these bonds reflect the political and economic events in the firm's home country and thus will be correlated with the credit risk of the Brazilian borrowing firm). In return, the FI receives a variable market rate payment of interest annually (e.g., one-year LIBOR rate). Figure 26–8 and Table 26–6 illustrate the cash flows associated with the typical total return swap for the FI.

Using the total return swap, the FI agrees to pay a fixed rate of interest annually and the capital gain or loss on the market value of the Brazilian bond over the period of the hedge. In Figure 26–8, P_0 denotes the market value of the bond at the beginning of the swap period and P_T represents the market value of the bond at the end of the swap period. If the Brazilian bond decreases in value over the period of the hedge ($P_0 > P_T$), the FI pays a relatively small (possibly negative) amount to the

FIGURE 26–8

Cash Flows on a Total Return Swap

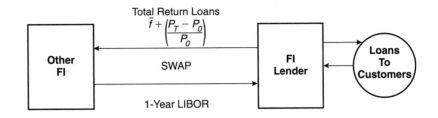

TABLE 26–6   Cash Flows on a Total Return Swap

	Annual Cash Flow For Year 1 through Final Year	Additional Payment by FI	Total Return
Cash inflow on swap to FI lender	1-year LIBOR (11%)	—	1-year LIBOR (11%)
Cash outflow on swap to other FI	Fixed rate ($\bar{f}$) (12%)	$P_T - P_0$ (90 − 100)	$\left[\bar{f} + \dfrac{P_T - P_0}{P_0}\right]$
			$\left(12\% + \dfrac{90-100}{100} = 12\% - 10\% = 2\%\right)$
		Net profit	9%

counterparty equal to the fixed payment on the swap minus the capital loss[14] on the bond. For example, suppose the Brazilian bond was priced at par ($P_0 = 100$) at the beginning of the swap period. At the end of the swap period or the payment date, the Brazilian bond had a secondary market value of 90 ($P_T = 90$) due to an increase in the Brazilian country's risk. Suppose that the fixed-rate payment as part of the total return swap was 12 percent; then the FI would send to the swap counterparty the fixed rate of 12 percent minus 10 percent (the capital loss on the Brazilian bond), or a total of 2 percent, and would receive in return a floating payment (e.g., LIBOR = 11 percent) from the counterparty to the swap. Thus, the net profit on the swap to the FI lender is 9 percent (11 percent minus 2 percent) times the notional amount of the swap contract. This gain can be used to offset the loss of market value of the loan to the Brazilian firm. This example is illustrated in Table 26–6.[15]

Note that hedging credit risk in this fashion allows the bank to maintain its customer relationship with the Brazilian firm (and perhaps earn fees from selling other financial services to that firm) without bearing a large amount of credit risk exposure. Moreover, since the Brazilian bond remains on the FI's balance sheet, the Brazilian firm may not even know its bond is being hedged. This would not be the case if the FI sought to reduce its risk by selling all or part of the bond (see Chapter 27). Finally, the swap does not completely hedge credit risk in this case. Specifically, basis risk is present to the extent that the credit risk of the Brazilian firm is imperfectly correlated with Brazilian country risk.

---

[14]Total return swaps are typically structured so that the capital gain or loss is paid at the end of the swap. However, an alternative structure does exist in which the capital gain or loss is paid at the end of each interest period during the swap.

[15]For additional discussion, see J. D. Finnerty, "Credit Derivatives, Infrastructure Finance, and Emerging Market Risk," *The Financier, ACMT,* February 1996, pp. 64–75.

Pure Credit Swaps

While total return swaps can be used to hedge credit risk exposure, they contain an element of interest rate risk as well as credit risk. For example, in Table 26–6, if the LIBOR rate changes due to Federal Reserve monetary policy, the *net* cash flows on the total return swap will also change—even though the credit risks of the underlying loans (and bonds) have not changed.

Pure Credit Swap
A swap by which a FI receives the par value of loan on default in return for paying a periodic swap fee.

To strip out the "interest rate" sensitive element of total return swaps, an alternative swap has been developed called a **"pure" credit swap.**

In this case, as shown in Figure 26–9, the FI lender will send (each swap period) a fixed fee or payment (like an insurance premium) to the FI counterparty. If the FI lender's loan or loans do not default, it will receive nothing back from the FI counterparty. However, if the loan or loans default, the FI counterparty will cover the default loss by making a default payment that is often equal to the par value of the original loan (e.g., $P_0 = \$100$) minus the secondary market value of the defaulted loan (e.g., $P_T = \$40$); that is, the FI counterparty will pay $P_0 - P_T$ (or $60, in this example).[16] As can be seen, a pure credit swap is like buying credit insurance and/or a multiperiod credit option.

Swaps and Credit Risk Concerns

The growth of the OTC swap market was one of the major motivating factors underlying the imposition of the BIS risk-based capital requirements in January 1993 (see Chapter 20). The fear was that in a long-term OTC swap-type contract, the out-of-the-money counterparty would have incentives to default to deter future and current losses. Consequently, the BIS requirements imposed a required capital ratio for banks against their holdings of both interest rate and currency swaps (and, more recently, other types of swaps, including credit swaps). Many analysts have argued that these capital requirements work against the growth of the swap market since they can be viewed as a cost or tax on market participants.

Not only regulators have a heightened awareness of credit risk; so do market participants. Both Merrill Lynch and Salomon Brothers (now Salomon Smith Barney) are heavy participants as intermediaries in the swap market; for example, they act as counterparty guarantors to both the fixed and floating sides in swaps. To do this successfully and to maintain market share, a high if not the highest credit rating is increasingly required. For example, both Merrill Lynch and Salomon Brothers were rated only single As in 1993. To achieve a AAA rating, they established separately capitalized subsidiaries in which to conduct their swap business. Merrill Lynch had to invest $350 million and Salomon, $175 million in these swap subsidiaries.

FIGURE 26–9

A Pure Credit Swap

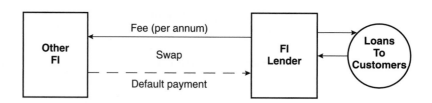

---

[16]While a pure credit swap is like a default option (e.g., the digital default option in Chapter 25), a key difference is that the fee (or premium) payments on the swap are paid over the life of the swap, whereas for a default option the whole fee (premium) is paid up front.

This raises some questions: What exactly is the default risk on swaps? Is it high or low? Is it the same as or different from the credit risk on loans? In fact, there are three major differences between the credit risk on swaps and the credit risk on loans. As a result, the credit risk on a swap is generally much less than that on a loan.[17] We discuss these differences next.

Netting and Swaps.   One factor that mitigates the credit risk on swaps is the netting of swap payments. On each swap payment date, a fixed payment is made by one party and a floating payment is made by the other. However, in general, each party calculates the net difference between the two payments, and a single payment for the net difference is made by one party to the other. This netting of payments implies that the default exposure of the in-the-money party is limited to the net payment rather than either the total fixed or floating payment. Further, when two parties have large numbers of contracts outstanding against each other, they tend to net across contracts. This process, called *netting by novation*—often formalized through a master netting agreement in the United States—further reduces the potential risk of loss if some contracts are in the money and other are out of the money to the same counterparty.[18] However, note that netting by novation hasn't been fully tested in all international courts of law. For example, in 1990 a number of U.K. municipal authorities engaged in swaps with U.S. and U.K. banks and investment banks. These municipal authorities, after taking major losses on some swap contracts, defaulted on further payments. The U.K. High Court supported the municipal authorities' right to default by stating that their entering into such swaps had been outside their powers of authority in the first place. This still has not stopped these municipal authorities from seeking to collect on in-the-money swaps. .

Payment Flows Are Interest and Not Principal.   While currency swaps involve swaps of interest and principal, interest rate swaps involve swaps of interest payments only measured against some notional principal value. This suggests that the default risk on such swaps is less than that on a regular loan, where both interest and principal are exposed to credit risk.

Standby Letters of Credit.   In cases where swaps are made between parties of different credit standing, such that one party perceives a significant risk of default by the other party, then the poor-quality credit risk party may be required to buy a standby letter of credit (or another form of performance guaranty) from a third-party high-quality (AAA) FI such that if default occurs, the standby letter of credit will provide the swap payments in lieu of the defaulting party. Further, increasingly,

---

[17]As with loans, swap participants deal with the credit risk of counterparties by setting bilateral limits on the notional amount of swaps entered into (similar to credit rationing on loans) as well as adjusting the fixed and/or floating rates by including credit risk premiums. For example, a low credit quality fixed-rate payer may have to pay an additional spread to a high credit quality floating-rate payer. For a discussion on pricing swap default risk, see E. H. Sorensen and T. F. Bollier, "Pricing Swap Default Risk," *Financial Analyst's Journal,* May–June 1994, pp. 23–33.

[18]In January 1995, FASB Interpretation No. 39 (FIN 39) established the right of setoff under a master netting agreement. Also, since 1995, the BIS has allowed banks to use bilateral netting of swap contracts in calculating these risk-based capital requirements (see Chapter 20). It is estimated that this reduces banks' capital requirements against swaps by up to 40 percent. See also D. Hendricks, "Netting Agreements and the Credit Exposures of OTC Derivatives Portfolios," Federal Reserve Bank of New York, *Quarterly Review,* Spring 1994.

low-quality counterparties are required to post collateral in lieu of default. This collateral is an incentive mechanism working to deter swap defaults.[19]

Concept Questions

1. What is the link between preserving "customers relationships" and credit derivatives such as total return swaps?
2. Is there any difference between a digital default option (see Chapter 25) and a pure credit swap?
3. Are swaps as risky as equivalent-sized loans?

Summary

This chapter evaluated the role of swaps as risk-management vehicles for FIs. We analyzed the major types of swaps: interest rate and currency swaps as well as credit swaps. Swaps have special features of long maturity, flexibility, and liquidity that make them attractive alternatives relative to shorter-term hedging vehicles such as the futures, forwards, options, and caps discussed in Chapters 24 and 25. However, even though the credit risk of swaps is less than that of loans, because of their OTC nature and long maturities, their credit risk is still generally greater than that for other OTC derivative instruments such as floors and caps. Also, the credit risk on swaps compares unfavorably with that on exchange-traded futures and options, whose credit risk is approximately zero.

Questions and Problems

1. Explain the similarity between a swap and a forward contract.
2. Forwards, futures, and options contracts had been used by FIs to hedge risk for many years before swaps were invented. If FIs already had these hedging instruments, why did they need swaps?
3. Distinguish between a swap buyer and a swap seller. In which markets does each have the comparative advantage?
4. An insurance company owns $50 million of floating-rate bonds yielding LIBOR plus 1 percent. These loans are financed by $50 million of fixed-rate guaranteed investment contracts (GICs) costing 10 percent. A finance company has $50 million of auto loans with a fixed rate of 14 percent. The loans are financed by $50 million in CDs at a variable rate of LIBOR plus 4 percent.
   a. What is the risk exposure of the insurance company?
   b. What is the risk exposure of the finance company?
   c. What would the cash flow goals of each company be if they were to enter into a swap arrangement?
   d. Which company would be the buyer and which company would be the seller in the swap?
   e. Diagram the direction of the relevant cash flows for the swap arrangement.
   f. What are reasonable cash flow amounts, or relative interest rates, for each of the payment streams?
5. In a swap arrangement, the variable-rate swap cash flow streams often do not fully hedge the variable-rate cash flow streams from the balance sheet due to basis risk.
   a. What are the possible sources of basis risk in an interest rate swap?
   b. How could the failure to achieve a perfect hedge be realized by the swap buyer?
   c. How could the failure to achieve a perfect hedge be realized by the swap seller?
6. A commercial bank has $100 million of floating-rate loans yielding the T-bill rate plus 2 percent. These loans are financed by $200 million of mortgages with a fixed rate of 13 percent. They are financed by $200 million in CDs with a variable rate of T-bill rate plus 3 percent.

---

[19]One solution being considered by market participants (such as the International Association of Swap Dealers) is to use collateral to mark to market a swap contract in a way similar to that in which futures are marked to market to prevent credit risk building up over time. Remember, a swap contract is like a succession of forwards. A survey by Arthur Andersen showed that approximately $6.9 billion was posted as collateral against a net replacement value of $77.9 billion of swaps. (See "A Question of Collateral," *Euromoney,* November 1995, pp. 46–49.)

a. Discuss the type of interest rate risk each FI faces.

b. Propose a swap that would result in each FI having the same type of asset and liability cash flows.

c. Show that this swap would be acceptable to both parties.

d. What are some of the practical difficulties in arranging this swap?

7. Bank 1 can issue five-year CDs at an annual rate of 11 percent fixed or at a variable rate of LIBOR plus 2 percent. Bank 2 can issue five-year CDs at an annual rate of 13 percent fixed or at a variable rate of LIBOR plus 3 percent.

    a. Is a mutually beneficial swap possible between the two banks?

    b. Where is the comparative advantage of the two banks?

    c. What is the net quality spread?

    d. What is an example of a feasible swap?

8. First Bank can issue one-year floating-rate CDs at prime plus 1 percent or fixed-rate CDs at 12.5 percent. Second Bank can issue one-year floating-rate CDs at prime plus 0.5 percent or fixed-rate CDs at 11 percent.

    a. What is a feasible swap with all the benefits going to First Bank?

    b. What is a feasible swap with all the benefits going to Second Bank?

    c. Diagram each situation.

    d. What factors will determine the final swap arrangement?

9. Two multinational corporations enter their respective debt markets to issue $100 million of two-year notes. Firm A can borrow at a fixed annual rate of 11 percent or a floating rate of LIBOR plus 50 basis points, repriced at the end of the year. Firm B can borrow at a fixed annual rate of 10 percent or a floating rate of LIBOR, repriced at the end of the year.

    a. If firm A is a positive duration gap insurance company and firm B is a money market mutual fund, in what market(s) should each firm borrow to reduce its interest rate risk exposure?

    b. In which debt market does firm A have a comparative advantage over firm B?

    c. Although firm A is riskier than firm B and therefore must pay a higher rate in both the fixed-rate and floating-rate markets, there are possible gains to trade. Set up a swap to exploit firm A's comparative advantage over firm B. What are the total gains from the swap trade? Assume a swap intermediary fee of 10 basis points.

    d. The gains from the swap trade can be apportioned between firm A and firm B through negotiation. What terms of trade would give all the gains to firm A? What terms of trade would give all the gains to firm B?

    e. Assume swap pricing that allocates all the gains from the swap to firm A. If A buys the swap from B and pays the swap intermediary's fee, what are the end-of-year net cash flows if LIBOR is 8.25 percent?

    f. If A buys the swap in part (*e*) from B and pays the swap intermediary's fee, what are the end-of-year net cash flows if LIBOR is 11 percent? Be sure to net swap payments against cash market payments for both firms.

    g. If all barriers to entry and pricing inefficiencies between firm A's debt markets and firm B's debt markets were eliminated, how would that affect the swap transaction?

10. What are off-market swap arrangements? How are these arrangements negotiated?

11. Describe how an inverse floater works to the advantage of an investor who receives coupon payments of 10 percent minus LIBOR if LIBOR is currently at 4 percent. When is it a disadvantage to the investor? Does the issuing party bear any risk?

12. An FI has $500 million of assets with a duration of nine years and $450 million of liabilities with a duration of three years. The FI wants to hedge its duration gap with a swap that has fixed-rate payments with a duration of six years and floating-rate payments with a duration of two years. What is the optimal amount of the swap to effectively macrohedge against the adverse effect of a change in interest rates on the value of the FI's equity?

13. The following information is available on a three-year swap contract. One-year maturity notes are currently priced at par and pay a coupon rate of 5 percent annually. Two-year maturity notes are currently priced at par and pay a coupon rate of 5.5 percent annually. Three-year maturity notes are currently priced at par and pay a coupon rate of 5.75 percent annually. The terms of a three-year swap of $100 million notional value are 5.45 percent annual fixed-rate payments in exchange for floating-rate payments tied to the annual discount yield.

    a. If an insurance company buys this swap, what can you conclude about the interest rate risk exposure of the company's underlying cash position?

    b. What are the end-of-year cash flows expected over the three-year life of the swap? (**Hint:** Be sure to convert par value coupon yields to discount yields and then solve for the implied forward rates.)

    c. What are end-of-year actual cash flows that occur over the three-year life of the swap if $d_2 = 4.95$ percent and $d_3 = 6.1$ percent (where d_i are discount yields)?

14. A German bank issues a $100 million, three-year Eurodollar CD at a fixed annual rate of 7 percent. The proceeds of the CD are lent to a German company for three years at a fixed rate of 9 percent. The spot exchange rate is DM1.50/$.

a. Is this expected to be a profitable transaction?

b. What are the cash flows if exchange rates are unchanged over the next three years?

c. What is the risk exposure of the bank's underlying cash position?

d. How can the German bank reduce that risk exposure?

e. If the U.S. dollar is expected to appreciate against the DM to DM1.65/$, D1.815/$, and DM2.00/$ over the next three years, what will be the cash flows on this transaction?

f. If the German bank swaps U.S.$ payments for DM payments at the current spot exchange rate, what are the cash flows on the swap? What are the cash flows on the entire hedged position? Assume that the U.S.$ appreciates at the rates in part (*e*).

g. What are the cash flows on the swap and the hedged position if actual spot exchange rates are as follows:

> End of year 1: DM1.55/US$
>
> End of year 2: DM1.47/US$
>
> End of year 3: DM1.48/US$

h. What would be the bank's risk exposure if the fixed-rate German loan was financed with a floating-rate U.S. $100 million, three-year Eurodollar CD?

i. What type(s) of hedge is appropriate if the German bank in part (*h*) wants to reduce its risk exposure?

j. If the annual Eurodollar CD rate is set at LIBOR and LIBOR at the end of years 1, 2, and 3 is expected to be 7 percent, 8 percent, and 9 percent, respectively, what will be the cash flows on the bank's unhedged cash position? Assume no change in exchange rates.

k. What are the cash flows on the bank's unhedged cash position if exchange rates are as follows:

> End of year 1: DM1.55/US$
>
> End of year 2: DM1.47/US$
>
> End of year 3: DM1.48/US$

l. What are both the swap and the total hedged position cash flows if the bank swaps out its floating rate U.S.$ CD payments in exchange for 7.75 percent fixed-rate DM payments at the current spot exchange rate of DM1.50/$?

m. Use the following spot rates for par value coupon bonds to forecast expected future spot rates. (*Hint:* Forecast expected future spot rates using implied forward rates.)

> one-year 7 percent
>
> two-year 8.5 percent
>
> three-year 9.2 percent

n. Use the rate forecasts in part (*m*) to calculate the cash flows on an 8.75 percent fixed–floating rate swap of U.S. dollars to German deutsche marks at DM1.50/$.

15. Use the following balance sheet information (in millions) to construct a swap hedge against interest rate risk exposure.

Assets		Liabilities and Equity	
Rate-sensitive assets	$ 50	Rate-sensitive liabilities	$ 75
Fixed-rate assets	150	Fixed-rate liabilities	100
		Net worth	25
Total assets	$200	Total liabilities and equity	$200

Rate-sensitive assets are repriced quarterly at the 91-day Treasury bill rate plus 150 basis points. Fixed-rate assets have five years until maturity and are paying 9 percent annually. Rate-sensitive liabilities are repriced quarterly at the 91-day Treasury bill rate plus 100 basis points. Fixed-rate liabilities have two years until maturity and are paying 7 percent annually. Currently, the 91-day Treasury bill rate is 6.25 percent.

a. What is the bank's current net interest income? If Treasury bill rates increase 150 basis points, what will be the change in the bank's net interest income?

b. What is the bank's repricing or funding gap? Use the repricing model to calculate the change in the bank's net interest income if interest rates increase 150 basis points.

c. How can swaps be used as an interest rate hedge in this example?

16. Use the following information to construct a swap of asset cash flows for the bank in problem 16. The bank is a price taker in both the fixed-rate market at 9 percent and the rate-sensitive market at the T-bill rate plus 1.5 percent. A securities dealer is a price taker in a fixed-rate market paying 8.5 percent and a floating-rate market paying the 91-day T-bill rate plus 1.25 percent. All interest is paid annually.

a. If the securities dealer is running a long book, what is its interest rate risk exposure?

b. How can the bank and the securities dealer use a swap to hedge their respective interest rate risk exposures?

c. What are the total potential gains to the swap trade?

d. Consider the following two-year swap of asset cash flows: An annual fixed-rate asset cash inflow of 8.6 percent in exchange for a floating-rate asset cash inflow of T-bill plus 125 basis points. The total swap intermediary fee is 5 basis points. How are the swap gains apportioned between the bank and the securities dealer if they each hedge their interest rate risk exposures using this swap?

e. What are the swap net cash flows if T-bill rates at the end of the first year are 7.75 percent and at the end of the second year are 5.5 percent?

f. What are the sources of the swap gains to trade?

g. What are the implications for the efficiency of cash markets?

17. Consider the following currency swap of coupon interest on the following assets:

    5 percent (annual coupon) fixed-rate U.S. $1 million bond

    5 percent (annual coupon) fixed-rate bond denominated in deutsche marks (DM)

    Spot exchange rates: DM1.5/$

    a. What is the face value of the DM bond if the investments are equivalent at spot rates?

    b. What are the end-of-year cash flows, assuming no change in spot exchange rates? What are the net cash flows on the swap?

    c. What are the cash flows if spot exchange rates fall to DM0.50/$? What are the net cash flows on the swap?

    d. What are the cash flows if spot exchange rates rise to DM 2.25/$? What are the net cash flows on the swap?

    e. Describe the underlying cash position that would prompt the FI to hedge by swapping dollars for deutsche marks.

18. Consider the following fixed–floating rate currency swap of assets:

    5 percent (annual coupon) fixed-rate U.S. $1 million bond. Floating-rate DM1.5 million bond set at LIBOR annually. Currently LIBOR is 4 percent. Face value of swap is DM1.5 million. Spot exchange rates: DM1.5/$.

    a. What are the end-of-year cash flows assuming no change in the spot exchange rates? What are the net cash flows on the swap at the spot exchange rates?

    b. If the 1-year forward rate is DM1.538 per U.S.$, what are the end-of-year net cash flows on the swap? Assume LIBOR is unchanged.

    c. If LIBOR increases to 6 percent, what are the end-of-year net cash flows on the swap? Evaluate at the forward rate.

19. What is a total return swap?

20. Give two reasons why credit swaps have been the fastest growing form of swaps in recent years.

21. How does a "pure" credit swap differ from a total return swap? How does it differ from a digital default option?

22. Why is the credit risk on a swap lower than the credit risk on a loan?

23. What is netting by novation?

24. A U.S. thrift has most of its assets in the form of French franc–denominated floating-rate loans. Its liabilities consist mostly of fixed-rate dollar-denominated CDs. What type of currency risk and interest rate risk does this FI face? How might it use a swap to eliminate some of those risks?

LOAN SALES AND OTHER CREDIT RISK MANAGEMENT TECHNIQUES

Introduction

Traditionally, banks and other FIs have relied on a number of contractual mechanisms to control the credit risks of lending. These have included (1) requiring higher interest rate spreads and fees on loans to more risky borrowers, (2) restricting or rationing loans to more risky borrowers, (3) requiring enhanced seniority (collateral) for the bank over the assets of risky borrowers, (4) diversifying across different types of risky borrowers, and (5) placing more restrictive covenants on risky borrowers' actions, such as restrictions on the use of proceeds from asset sales, new debt issues, and dividend payments. These traditional mechanisms for controlling or managing credit risk were described in Chapter 11 and 12.

In this and the following chapter on securitization, we describe the growing role of loan sales and other newer types of techniques (such as the good bank–bad bank structure) increasingly used by FI managers to control credit risk.

We have already discussed in Chapters 24 through 26 the increasing use of credit derivatives in the forward, options, and swaps markets to manage credit risk—for example, the use of digital put options to control the credit risk of an individual loan or portfolio loans. In addition, FIs are increasingly requiring borrowers to hedge their own risks, especially when the FI makes floating-rate loans to borrowers. When interest rates rise, the borrower of a floating-rate loan may have greater difficulty meeting interest rate payments. However, if the borrower has hedged the risk of rising rates in the derivatives market (e.g., by selling interest rate futures or receiving floating payments–paying fixed payments in an interest rate swap), the borrower is in a far better position to meet its contractual payments to the FI. As a result, the credit risk exposure of the FI is reduced.[1]

While loan sales have been in existence for many years, the use of loan sales (by removing existing loans from the balance sheet) is increasingly being recognized as a valuable additional tool in an FI manager's portfolio of credit risk management techniques.

Loan Sales

Correspondent Banking
A relationship entered into between a small bank and a big bank in which the big bank provides a number of deposit, lending, and other services.

Highly Leveraged Transaction (HLT) Loan
A loan made to finance a merger and acquisition: a leveraged buyout results in a high leverage ratio for the borrower.

Banks and other FIs have sold loans among themselves for over 100 years. In fact, a large part of **correspondent banking** involves small banks making loans that are too big for them to hold on their balance sheets—for lending concentration, risk, or capital adequacy reasons—and selling parts of those loans to large banks in bigger cities with which they have a long-term deposit-lending correspondent relationship. In turn, the bigger city banks often sell parts of their loans called *participations* to smaller banks. Even though this market has existed for many years, it grew slowly until the early 1980s, when it entered a period of spectacular growth, largely due to expansion in **highly leveraged transaction (HLT) loans** to finance leveraged buyouts (LBOs) and mergers and acquisitions (M&As). Specifically, the volume of loans sold by U.S. banks grew from less than $20 billion in 1980 to $285 billion in 1989. Between 1990 and 1994 the volume of loan sales fell almost equally dramatically, along with the decline in LBOs and M&As as a result of the credit crunch associated with the 1990–91 recession. In 1994, the volume of loan sales had fallen to approximately $20 billion.

In recent years, the volume of loan sales has expanded again, partly due to an expanding economy and a resurgence in M&As. Figure 27–1 shows the growth in loan sales over the 1994–97 period.

---

[1]In addition, the floating-rate loans may enable the FI to better hedge its own duration gap exposure.

FIGURE 27–1

Recent Trends in the Loan Sales Market

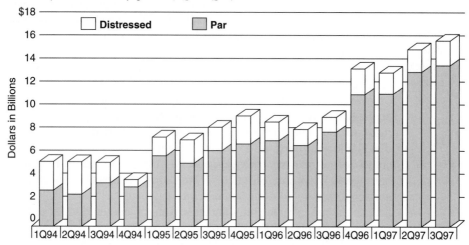

Source: Loan Pricing Corporation, *Gold Sheets,* November 10, 1997, p. 23.

In this chapter we describe the structure of the market for bank loan sales and then examine reasons why banks and other FIs seeks to buy and sell loans. Finally, we discuss the potential for loan sales growth in the future.

Concept Question

1. Explain the main reason behind the explosion in loan sales in the 1980s.

The Bank Loan Sales Market

Definition of a Loan Sale

A bank loan sale occurs when a bank originates a loan and sells it either with or without recourse to an outside buyer. If the loan is sold without recourse, not only is it removed from the bank's balance sheet but the bank has no explicit liability if the loan eventually goes bad. Thus, the buyer (and not the FI that originated the loan) bears all the credit risk. If, however, the loan is sold with **recourse,** under certain conditions the buyer can put the loan back to the selling bank; therefore, the bank retains a contingent credit risk liability. In practice, most loans are sold without recourse because a loan sale is technically removed from the balance sheet only when the buyer has no future credit risk claim on the bank. Importantly, loan sales involve no creation of new types of securities such as the pass-throughs, CMOs, and MBBs described in Chapter 28; as such, they are a primitive form of securitization in that loan selling creates a secondary market for loans.

Recourse
The ability of a loan buyer to sell the loan back to the originator if it goes bad.

Types of Loan Sales

The U.S. loan sales market has three segments: two involve the sale and trading of domestic loans, while the third involves emerging-market loan sales and trading. Since we fully described emerging-market loan sales in Chapter 16 on sovereign risk, we concentrate on the domestic loan sales market here.

Traditional Short Term.   In the traditional short-term segment of the market, banks sell loans with short maturities, often one to three months. This market has characteristics similar to commercial paper issued by corporations in that loan sales have similar maturities and issue size. Loan sales, however, usually have yields that are 1 to 10 basis points above those of commercial paper of a similar rating. In particular, the loan sales market in which a bank originates and sells a short-term loan of a corporation is a close substitute for the issuance of commercial paper—either directly or through dealers—for the 1,000 or so largest U.S. corporations. The key characteristics of the short-term loan sales market are:

> Secured by assets of the borrowing firm.
>
> Loans to investment grade borrowers or better.
>
> Short term (90 days or less).
>
> Yields closely tied to the commercial paper rate.
>
> Sold in units of $1 million and up.

Until 1984 and the emergence of the HLT and LDC loan markets, these were the predominant loan sales. The growth of the commercial paper market (and its accessibility by over 20,000 corporations), as well as the increased ability of banks (through their Section 20 securities affiliates) to underwrite commercial paper (see Chapter 21), has also reduced the importance of this market segment.

HLT Loan Sales.   With the growth in mergers and acquisitions and LBOs, especially during the period 1985–89, a new segment in the loan sales market appeared. What constitutes an HLT loan has often caused dispute. However, in October 1989 the three U.S. federal bank regulators adopted a definition of an HLT loan as one that (1) involves a buyout, acquisition, or recapitalization and (2) doubles the company's liabilities and results in a leverage ratio higher than 50 percent, results in a leverage ratio higher than 75 percent, or is designated as an HLT by a syndication agent.

HLT loans mainly differ according to whether they are nondistressed (bid price exceeds 95 cents per $1 of loans) or distressed (bid price is less than 95 cents per $1 of loans or the borrower is in default).[2]

Virtually all HLT loans have the following characteristics:

> Are term loans (TLs).
>
> Are secured by assets of the borrowing firm (usually senior secured).
>
> Have a long maturity (often three- to six-year maturities).
>
> Have floating rates tied to LIBOR, the prime rate, or a CD rate (normally 200 to 275 basis points above these rates).
>
> Have strong covenant protection.

Nevertheless, HLTs tend to be quite heterogeneous with respect to the size of the issue, the interest payment date, interest indexing, and prepayment features.

After origination, some HLT borrowers, such as Macy's and El Paso Electric, suffered periods of **financial distress.** As a result, a distinction is usually made between the markets for distressed and nondistressed HLTs.

Approximately 20 banks and securities firms make a market in this debt either as brokers or (less commonly) as broker-dealers, including Bankers Trust, Bear

Financial Distress
A period when a borrower is unable to meet a payment obligation to lenders and other creditors.

---

[2]See Walter J. Blumenthal, "Loan Trading: A New Business Opportunity for Your Bank," *Commercial Lending Review,* Winter 1997–1998, pp. 26–31.

Stearns, CIBC, Prudential Securities, and Goldman Sachs. Most of these FIs view trading in this debt as similar to trading in junk bonds.[3]

Types of Loan Sales Contracts

There are two basic types of loan sale contracts or mechanisms by which loans can be transferred between seller and buyer: participations and assignments. Currently, assignments comprise the bulk of loan sales trading.

Participation in a Loan
Buying a share in a loan syndication with limited, contractual control and rights over the borrower.

Participations.   The unique features of **participations in loans** are:

> The holder (buyer) is not a party to the underlying credit agreement so that the initial contract between loan seller and borrower remains in place after the sale.

> The loan buyer can exercise only partial control over changes in the loan contract's terms. The holder can only vote on material changes to the loan contract, such as the interest rate or collateral backing.

The economic implication of these features is that the buyer of the loan participation has a double risk exposure: a risk exposure to the borrower and a risk exposure to the loan selling bank. Specifically, if the selling bank fails, the loan participation bought by an outside party may be characterized as an unsecured obligation of the bank rather than as a true sale if there are grounds for believing that some explicit or implicit recourse existed between the loan seller and the loan buyer. Alternatively, the borrower's claims against a failed selling bank may be set off against its loans from that bank, reducing the amount of loans outstanding and adversely impacting the buyer of a participation in those loans. As a result of these exposures, the buyer bears a double monitoring cost as well.

Assignment
Buying a share in a loan syndication with some contractual control and rights over the borrower.

Assignments.   Because of the monitoring costs and risks involved in participations, loans are sold on an assignment basis in more than 90 percent of the cases on the U.S. domestic market. The key features of an **assignment** are:

> All rights are transferred on sale, meaning the loan buyer now holds a direct claim on the borrower.

> Transfer of U.S. domestic loans is normally associated with a Uniform Commercial Code filing (as proof that a change of ownership has been perfected).

While ownership rights are generally much clearer in a loan sale by assignment, frequently contractual terms limit the seller's scope regarding to whom the loan can be sold. In particular, the loan contract may require either the bank agent or the borrower to agree to the sale and/or the sale may be restricted to a certain class of institutions, such as those that meet certain net worth/net asset size conditions. (A bank agent is a bank that distributes interest and principal payments to lenders in loan syndications with multiple lenders.)

Currently, the trend appears to be toward loan contracts being originated with very limited assignment restrictions. This is true in both the U.S. domestic and the

---

[3]In a recent study comparing the determinants of the yield spreads on HLT loans versus those on high-yield (junk) bonds, it was found that the spreads on HLT loans behaved more like investment grade bonds than like high-yield bonds. A possible reason for this is that HLT loans tend to be more senior in bankruptcy and to have greater collateral backing than do high-yield bonds. See L. Angbazo, Jianping Mei, and Anthony Saunders, "Credit Spreads in the Market for Highly Leveraged Transaction Loans," *Journal of Banking and Finance,* 22, 1998, pp. 1249–82.

emerging-market loan sales markets. The most tradable loans are those that can be assigned without buyer restrictions. Even so, one has to distinguish between floating-rate and fixed-rate assignment loans. In floating-rate loans, most loan sales by assignment occur on the loan's repricing date, which may be two or four times a year, due to complexities for the agent bank in calculating and transferring accrued interest—especially given the heterogeneous nature of floating-rate loan indexes such as fed funds plus, T-bond plus, and LIBOR plus. In addition, the nonstandardization of **accrued interest** payments in fixed-rate loan assignments (trade date, assignment date, coupon payment date) adds complexity and friction to this market. Moreover, while the bank agent may have a full record of the initial owners of the loans, it does not always have an up-to-date record of loan ownership changes and related transfers following trades. This means that great difficulties often occur for the borrower, bank agent, and loan buyer in ensuring that the current holder of the loan receives the interest and principal payments due.

Finally, the buyer of the loan often needs to verify the original loan contract and establish the full implications of the purchase regarding the buyer's rights to collateral if the borrower defaults.

Because of these contractual problems, trading frictions, and costs, some loan sales take as long as three months to complete; reportedly, up to 50 percent eventually fail to be completed at all. In many cases, the incentive to renege on a contract arises because market prices move away from those originally agreed so that the counterparty finds reasons to delay the completion of a loan sale and/or eventually refuses to complete the transaction.[4]

Accrued Interest
The loan seller's claim to part of the next interest payment on the loan.

The Buyers and the Sellers

The Buyers.   Out of the wide array of potential buyers, some are concerned with only a certain segment of the market for regulatory and strategic reasons. In particular, HLT loans interest investment banks, hedge funds, and **vulture funds**.

Investment banks are predominantly involved because they (1) utilize investment skills similar to those used in junk bond trading and (2) were often closely associated with the HLT borrower in underwriting the original junk bond/HLT deals. As such, large investments banks—for example, First Boston, Merrill Lynch, and Goldman Sachs—are relatively more informed agents in this market either as market makers or in taking short-term positions on movements in the discount from par.

Vulture funds are specialized hedge funds established to invest in distressed loans. They include funds run by entrepreneurs such as George Soros and Sam Zell. These investments can be active, especially for those seeking to use the loans purchased for bargaining in a restructuring deal; this generates a restructuring outcome and thus returns that strongly favor the loan purchaser. Alternatively, such loans may be held as passive investments, as high-yield securities in a well-diversified portfolio of distressed securities. Many vulture funds are in fact managed by investment banks.

For the nondistressed HLT market and the traditional U.S. domestic loan sales market, the five major buyers are other domestic banks, foreign banks, insurance companies and pension funds, closed-end bank loan mutual funds, and nonfinancial corporations.

Vulture Fund
A specialized fund that invests in distressed loans.

---

[4]See "In Distress but Booming," *The Independent,* February 19, 1993. However, in recent years, completion of a trade within 10 days (or T + 10) has become an increasing convention.

Other Domestic Banks.   Interbank loan sales are at the core of the traditional market and have revolved around correspondent banking relationships. Restrictions on nationwide banking also traditionally led to banks seeking to purchase loans from other regions to better diversify their loan portfolios.

The traditional interbank market, however, has been shrinking. This is due to at least three factors. First, the traditional correspondent banking relationship is breaking down in a more competitive and increasingly consolidated banking market. Second, concerns about counterparty risk and moral hazard have increased (e.g., Penn Square, a small bank, made bad loan sales to its larger correspondent bank, Continental Illinois, in the early 1980s). Third, the barriers to nationwide banking were largely eroded with the passage of the Riegle-Neal Interstate Branching and Efficiency Act of 1994. Nevertheless, as explained in the Professional Perspectives box on p. 657, some small banks find the loan sales market enormously useful in allowing them to regionally diversify their loan portfolios.

Foreign Banks.   Foreign banks remain the dominant buyer of domestic U.S. loans. In recent years they have purchased over 40 percent of loans sold. The loan sales market allows foreign banks to achieve a well-diversified domestic U.S. loan portfolio without developing a costly nationwide banking network. However, renewed interest in asset **downsizing,** especially among Japanese banks (see Chapter 23), has meant that this source of demand has started to contract.

Downsizing
Shrinking the asset size of an FI.

Insurance Companies and Pension Funds.   Subject to meeting liquidity and quality or investment grade regulatory restrictions, insurance companies (such as Aetna) and pension funds are important buyers of long-term maturity loans.

Closed-End Bank Loan Mutual Funds.   First established in 1988, these leveraged mutual funds, such as Merrill Lynch Prime Fund, invest in domestic U.S. bank loans. While they purchase loans on the secondary market, such as loan resales, the largest funds have also moved into primary loan syndications because of the attractive fee income available. Indeed, some money center banks, such as Chase, have actively encouraged closed-end fund participation in primary loan syndications.

Nonfinancial Corporations.   There are some corporations that buy loans, but this activity is limited mostly to the financial services arms of the very largest U.S. and European companies (e.g., GE Capital and ITT Finance) and amounts to no more than 5 percent of total U.S. domestic loan sales.[5]

The Sellers.   The sellers of domestic loans and HLT loans are major money center banks, foreign banks, investment banks, and the U.S. government and its agencies.

Major Money Center Banks.   Loan selling has been dominated by the largest money center banks. In recent years, market concentration on the loan-selling side has been accentuated by the growth of HLTs (and the important role major money center banks have played in originating loans in HLT deals) as well as the growth in real estate loan sales. In recent years, large money center banks have engaged in large (real estate) loan sales directly or have formalized such sales through the mechanism of a "good bank–bad bank" structure.

---

[5]Nonfinancial corporations are bigger buyers in the emerging-market loan sales market as part of debt-equity swaps (see Chapter 16).

Good Bank–Bad Bank.   Bad banks are special-purpose vehicles organized to liquidate portfolios of nonperforming loans. The principal objective in their creation is to maximize asset values by separating good loans (in the "good bank") from bad loans (in the "bad bank"). Recent examples of bad banks include Grant Street National Bank (established by Mellon bank), National Loan Bank (established by Chemical), and National Asset Bank (established by First Interstate).[6]

For example, Mellon Bank wrote down the face value of $941 million in real estate loans and sold them to a specially created bad bank subsidiary—Grant Street National Bank—for $577 million. This special-purpose bad bank was funded by bond issues and common and preferred stock.

Managers of the bad bank were given equity (junior preferred stock) as an incentive mechanism to generate maximum values in liquidating the loans purchased from Mellon (i.e., achieving a market resale value greater than $577 million).

There are at least five reasons for believing that loan sales through a bad bank vehicle will be value enhancing compared to the originating bank itself retaining (and eventually selling) these loans:

1. The bad bank enables bad assets to be managed by loan workout specialists.
2. The good bank's reputation and access to deposit and funding markets tend to be improved once bad loans are removed from the balance sheet.
3. Because the bad bank doesn't have any short-term deposits (i.e., is a self-liquidating entity), it can follow an optimal disposition strategy for bad assets, as it is not overly concerned with liquidity needs.
4. As in the case of Mellon's bad bank, contracts for managers can be created to maximize their incentives to generate enhanced values from loan sales.
5. The good bank–bad bank structure reduces information asymmetries about the value of the good bank's assets (the so-called lemons problem), thus potentially increasing its attractiveness to risk-averse investors.

Foreign Banks.   To the extent that foreign banks are sellers rather than buyers of loans, these loans come out of branch networks such as Japanese-owned banks in California or through their market-making activities. One of the major market makers in the U.S. loan sales market (especially the HLT market) is ING Bank.

Investment Banks.   Investment banks, such as Bear Stearns, act as loan sellers either as part of their market-making function or as active traders. Again, these loan sales are generally confined to large HLT transactions.

The U.S. Government and Its Agencies.   In recent years the U.S. government and its agencies have shown an increased willingness to engage in loan sales. This has been aided by the passage of the 1996 Federal Debt Improvements Act, which authorizes federal agencies to sell delinquent and defaulted loan assets. Figure 27–2 shows an advertisement by the FDIC of a sale of assets in February 1997 resulting from its takeover and management of failed banks. The Department of Housing and Urban Development has also been an increasingly large seller of mortgage loans on multifamily apartment properties. However, the largest loan sales by a government agency to date were made by the Resolution Trust Corporation (RTC). Established in 1989, and disbanded at the end of 1995, the RTC had to resolve more than 700

---

[6]This technique has also been used outside the United States. For example, in 1998 the good bank–bad bank structure was adopted by the Indonesian government as a way of resolving the bad debt crisis in the domestic banking industry.

FIGURE 27–2

*Loan Sale Announcement
by the FDIC*

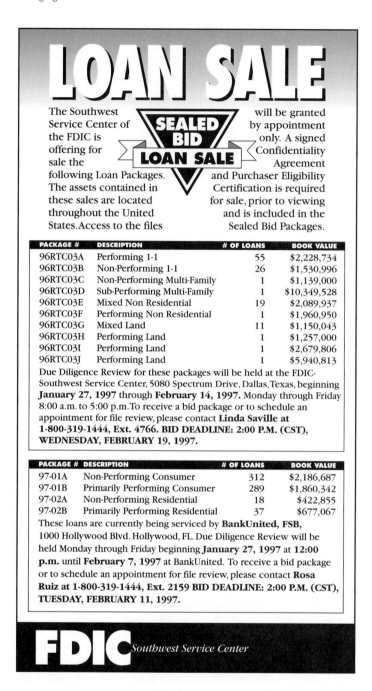

LOAN SALE

SEALED BID LOAN SALE

The Southwest Service Center of the FDIC is offering for sale the following Loan Packages. The assets contained in these sales are located throughout the United States. Access to the files will be granted by appointment only. A signed Confidentiality Agreement and Purchaser Eligibility Certification is required for sale, prior to viewing and is included in the Sealed Bid Packages.

PACKAGE #	DESCRIPTION	# OF LOANS	BOOK VALUE
96RTC03A	Performing 1-1	55	$2,228,734
96RTC03B	Non-Performing 1-1	26	$1,530,996
96RTC03C	Non-Performing Multi-Family	1	$1,139,000
96RTC03D	Sub-Performing Multi-Family	1	$10,349,528
96RTC03E	Mixed Non Residential	19	$2,089,937
96RTC03F	Performing Non Residential	1	$1,960,950
96RTC03G	Mixed Land	11	$1,150,043
96RTC03H	Performing Land	1	$1,257,000
96RTC03I	Performing Land	1	$2,679,806
96RTC03J	Performing Land	1	$5,940,813

Due Diligence Review for these packages will be held at the FDIC-Southwest Service Center, 5080 Spectrum Drive, Dallas, Texas, beginning **January 27, 1997** through **February 14, 1997.** Monday through Friday 8:00 a.m. to 5:00 p.m. To receive a bid package or to schedule an appointment for file review, please contact **Linda Saville at 1-800-319-1444, Ext. 4766. BID DEADLINE: 2:00 P.M. (CST), WEDNESDAY, FEBRUARY 19, 1997.**

PACKAGE #	DESCRIPTION	# OF LOANS	BOOK VALUE
97-01A	Non-Performing Consumer	312	$2,186,687
97-01B	Primarily Performing Consumer	289	$1,860,342
97-02A	Non-Performing Residential	18	$422,855
97-02B	Primarily Performing Residential	37	$677,067

These loans are currently being serviced by **BankUnited, FSB,** 1000 Hollywood Blvd. Hollywood, FL. Due Diligence Review will be held Monday through Friday beginning **January 27, 1997** at **12:00 p.m.** until **February 7, 1997** at BankUnited. To receive a bid package or to schedule an appointment for file review, please contact **Rosa Ruiz at 1-800-319-1444, Ext. 2159 BID DEADLINE: 2:00 P.M. (CST), TUESDAY, FEBRUARY 11, 1997.**

FDIC *Southwest Service Center*

problem savings banks through merger, closure, or conservatorship. With respect to the U.S. commercial and industrial loan sale market, RTC dispositions had a relatively moderate supply-side effect largely because the bulk of RTC's asset sales were real estate assets (such as multi-family mortgages). The tendency of the RTC was to combine good and bad loans into loan packages and sell them at auction to bidders. For example, in an April 21, 1995, auction, it offered to the highest bidder a package of 29 different commercial assets for sale—located in New Jersey, New York, and Pennsylvania—with aggregate estimated market values of $7.5 million. Bidders had only four days to enter bids on this asset package.

SMALL BANK PURCHASES BIG LOANS

Lawrence G. Goldberg and Jean LeGrand

Recently a community bank with less than $80 million in assets bought a piece of a $2.7 billion loan. The loan is to an auto-parts company based in Detroit—but the community bank is located near Miami.

This purchase reflects a radical change in banking practice. Traditionally, a small bank has been a neighborhood bank, in the most literal sense. Because the only loans a small bank could originate were in its own neighborhood, it was tied closely to the local economy—for better or for worse. If the local economy depended upon the steel industry, so did the local bank. The only way a small bank could diversify its commercial loan portfolio was by buying into loans originated by a larger correspondent—usually a medium-sized bank in the same, or a nearby town. Only slight geographic diversification and limited industry diversification could be obtained in this way.

Now, however, small banks have another option. A nationwide loan market has developed in the last few years, giving smaller banks the ability to build better diversified portfolios. This new market is called the syndicated loan market, because large loans are shared (syndicated) by a large number of banks. Typically one of the largest "money center" banks originates these large loans and takes a leadership role in distributing the loan to the syndicate. Although there are many variations, the process often works like this:

BIGCO asks MONEYBANK for a large loan, say for half a billion dollars or more. MONEYBANK commits to making the loan, explaining that it will not keep the entire loan for itself (because MONEYBANK too prefers to diversify) but rather will offer portions of the proposed loan to other banks. MONEYBANK prepares an offering package including descriptive information about BIGCO operations, as well as historical and projected financial statements and sends the package to other banks known to be active in the market. Each recipient of the package must then make its own determination as to whether it wishes to sign up for a piece of the loan. Recipients respond to MONEYBANK by a predetermined date, specifying how much of the loan they would be willing to take; if there is a strong demand for the loan, however, they may receive a lesser allocation.

The Miami-area bank, Kislak National Bank, purchases loans in the syndicated market to put excess funds to work quickly and at attractive returns, and to reduce its sensitivity to the cyclical local economy. Previously the bank worked closely with an affiliated mortgage banking company and was heavily concentrated in real-estate loans; now its portfolio has a better balance, as the bank manages its purchase of syndicated loans according to strict diversification guidelines whereby no industry may represent more than 7.5% of the portfolio. To offset real estate concentrations elsewhere in the bank's loan portfolio, no real estate loans are permitted in the syndicated loan portfolio. Low start-up costs have enabled the bank's syndicated loan portfolio to achieve significant profitability in the first 12 months of operation.

Access to the nationwide syndicated loan market gives smaller banks more flexibility and opportunity. Now community banks can manage their loan portfolios according to the best principles of portfolio management, mitigating risk through diversification. Small banks can now participate in a national loan market. Kislak, along with an affiliated bank, is the only bank in this size range to get into this market, but others may follow in the future.

Biographical Summary

Lawrence G. Goldberg is professor of finance at the University of Miami and is on the board of directors of Kislak National Bank.

Jean LeGrand is president, Gulfstream Associates, Inc., a consulting firm headquartered in Sarasota, Florida. She is a consultant to Kislak National Bank. Previously she was managing director at First Chicago, in charge of discount loan trading.

Concept Questions

1. Which loans should have the highest yields: (*a*) loans sold with recourse or (*b*) loans sold without recourse?

2. Which have higher yields, junk bonds or HLT loans? Explain your answer.

3. Describe the two basic types of loan sale contracts by which loans can be transferred between seller and buyer.

4. What institutions are the major buyers in the traditional U.S. domestic loan sales market? What institutions are the major sellers in this market?

Why Banks and Other FIs Sell Loans

In the introduction to this chapter we argued that a major reason for FIs to sell loans is to manage their credit risk better. Loan sales remove assets (and credit risk) from the balance sheet as well as allow an FI to achieve better asset diversification. However, other than credit risk management, there are a number of economic and regulatory reasons that encourage FIs to sell loans. These are discussed below.

Reserve Requirements

Regulatory requirements, such as noninterest-bearing reserve requirements that a bank has to hold at the central bank, are a form of tax that adds to the cost of funding the loan portfolio. Taxes such as reserve requirements create an incentive for banks to remove loans from the balance sheet by selling them without recourse to outside parties.[7]

Fee Income

A bank can often report any fee income earned from originating (and then selling) loans as current income, whereas interest earned on direct lending can be accrued (as income) only over time. As a result, originating and quickly selling loans can boost a bank's reported income under current accounting rules.

Capital Costs

Like reserve requirements, the capital adequacy requirements imposed on banks are a burden as long as required capital exceeds the amount the bank believes to be privately beneficial. For tax reasons, debt is a cheaper source of funds than equity capital. Thus, banks struggling to meet a required capital (K) to assets (A) ratio can boost this ratio by reducing assets (A) rather than boosting capital (K) (see Chapter 20). One way to downsize or reduce A and boost the K/A ratio is through loan sales.

Liquidity Risk

In addition to credit risk and interest rate risk, holding loans on the balance sheet can increase the overall illiquidity of a bank's assets. This illiquidity is a problem because bank liabilities tend to be highly liquid. Asset illiquidity can expose a bank to harmful liquidity squeezes whenever depositors unexpectedly withdraw their deposits. To mitigate a liquidity problem, a bank's management can sell some of its

---

[7]Under current reserve requirement regulations (Regulation D, amended May 1986), bank loan sales with recourse are regarded as a liability and hence are subject to reserve requirements. The reservability of loan sales extends to when a bank issues a credit guaranty as well as a recourse provision. Loans sold without recourse (or credit guarantees by the selling bank) are free of reserve requirements. With the elimination of reserve requirements on nontransaction accounts, the lowering of reserve requirements on transaction accounts in 1991, and the innovation of deposit sweep accounts (see Chapter 18), the reserve tax effect is likely to become a less important feature driving bank loan sales (as well as the recourse/nonrecourse mix) in the future.

loans to outside investors. Thus, the bank loan sales market has created a secondary market in loans that has significantly reduced the illiquidity of bank loans held as assets on the balance sheet.

Glass-Steagall and Securities Law Interpretations

Loan origination and sales are also a substitute for securities underwriting, whose revenues are currently restricted to 25 percent of a Section 20 subsidiary's total revenues.[8] Indeed, loan sales (and trading) are normally undertaken by banks in their Section 20 subsidiaries. Since loan sales are viewed as "eligible" activities (unlike debt securities underwriting), the scale of these activities is not subject to the revenue cap. Nevertheless, as the revenue cap of securities underwriting gets raised (it was raised from 10 percent in 1996 to 25 percent), the relative advantage of loan sales over securities underwriting gets diminished. It might also be noted that case law has been almost unanimous in deciding that a loan or loan participation sold by one bank to another financial institution is not a security for the purposes of Federal Securities Acts or the Glass-Steagall Act (or state securities laws). For example, in *Reves* v. *Ernst & Young,* a family resemblance test was laid down by the Supreme Court. Essentially, the family resemblance test presumes that all debt notes are securities unless they bear a strong family resemblance to certain types of loans, including commercial loans. The *Reves* decision requires focusing not on what is distributed but to whom and how it is distributed. In particular, a loan sale offering to sophisticated institutional investors is unlikely to be viewed as a security. Indeed, in a June 1992 Court of Appeals decision regarding a Security Pacific Loan Participation, the family resemblance test was upheld. Specifically, Security Pacific was held not liable to reimburse institutions that purchased a short-term interest in loans made by Security Pacific to the now bankrupt Integrated Resources Inc. under a loan participation sales program. The court held that sophisticated investors were bound by a disclaimer in the master participation agreement exonerating Security Pacific from any duty to pass on the unfavorable information that it possessed about the financial condition of Integrated to the loan participation buyer.

Concept Questions

1. What are some of the economic and regulatory reasons why FIs choose to sell loans?
2. How can an FI use its loans to mitigate a liquidity problem?

Factors Deterring Loan Sales Growth in the Future

The loan sales market has gone through a number of up and down phases in recent years (as discussed above). However, notwithstanding the value of loan sales as a credit risk management tool, there remain a number of factors that will both spur and deter the market's growth and development in future years. We first discuss factors that may deter the market's growth.

---

[8]Underwriting is the origination, sale, and distribution of a security or loan.

Access to the Commercial Paper Market

With the advent of Section 20 subsidiaries in 1987, large banks have enjoyed much greater powers to underwrite commercial paper (and other securities) directly without legal challenges by the securities industry that underwriting by banks is contrary to the Glass-Steagall Act. This has meant that the need to underwrite or sell short-term bank loans as an imperfect substitute for commercial paper underwriting is now much less important. In addition, more and more smaller middle market firms are gaining direct access to the commercial paper market. As a result, they have less need to rely on bank loans to finance their short-term expenditures.

Customer Relationship Effects

As the banking industry consolidates and expands the range of financial services sold, customer relationships are likely to become even more important than they are today. To the extent that a loan customer (borrower) views the sale of its loan by its banker as an adverse statement about the customer's value to the bank, loan sales can harm revenues generated by the bank as customers take their business elsewhere.

Legal Concerns

Fraudulent Conveyance
When a transaction such as a sale of securities or transference of assets to a particular party is ruled illegal.

A number of legal concerns are hampering the loan sale market's growth, especially for distressed HLT loans. In particular, while banks are normally secured creditors, this status may be attacked by other creditors if the firm enters bankruptcy. For example, **fraudulent conveyance** proceedings have been brought against the secured lenders to Revco, Circle K, Allied Stores, and RJR Nabisco. Such legal suits are one of the factors that have slowed the growth of the distressed loan market. Indeed, in many of the most recent HLT sales, buyers have demanded a put option feature that allows the loan buyer to put the loan back to the seller at the purchase price if a transaction is proved to be fraudulent under the Uniform Fraudulent Conveyance Act. Further, a second type of distressed-firm risk may result if, in the process of a loan workout, the bank lender acts more like an equity owner than an outside debtor. For example, the bank may get involved in the day-to-day running of the firm and make strategic investment and asset sales decisions. This could open up claims that the bank's loans should be treated like equity rather than secured debt. That is, the bank's loans may be subordinated in the claims priority ranking.

Concept Questions

1. What are some of the factors that are likely to deter the growth of the loan sales market in the future?
2. What are some specific legal concerns that have hampered the growth of the loan sales market?

Factors Encouraging Loan Sales Growth in the Future

There are at least six factors that point to an increasing volume of loan sales in the future. These are in addition to the credit risk "hedging" value of loan sales.

BIS Capital Requirements

The BIS 8 percent risk-based capital rules regarding a 100 percent risk weighting of commercial loans mean that bankers will continue to have strong incentives to sell commercial loans to other FIs and investors, downsize their balance sheets, and boost bank capital ratios.

Market Value Accounting

The Securities and Exchange Commission and the Financial Accounting Standards Board (FASB) have both advocated the replacement of book value accounting with market value accounting for financial services firms. In addition, the proposed capital requirements for interest rate risk and the current capital requirements for market risk have moved banks toward a market value accounting framework. The trend towards the marking to market of assets will make bank loans look more like securities and thus make them easier to sell and/or trade.

Asset Brokerage and Loan Trading

The greater emphasis of large money center banks as well as investment banks on trading and trading income suggests that significant attention will still be paid to those segments of the loan sales market where price volatility is high and thus potential trading profits can be made. Most HLT loans have floating rates so that their underlying values are in large part insulated from swings in the level of interest rates (unlike fixed-income securities such as Treasury bonds). Nevertheless, the low credit quality of many of these loans and their long maturities create an enhanced potential for credit risk volatility. As a result, a short-term three-month secured loan to a AAA-rated company is unlikely to show significant future credit risk volatility compared to an eight-year HLT loan to a distressed company. This suggests that trading in loans to below investment grade companies will always be attractive for banks that use their specialized credit monitoring skills as asset traders rather than as asset transformers in participating in the market.

Government Loan Sales

With the passage of the 1996 Federal Debt Collection Improvements Act and the continued downsizing of federal government employees, there is a strong likelihood that the sale of loans by the government and its agencies will increase in the future.

Credit Ratings

There is a growing trend toward the "credit rating" of loans offered for sale. Unlike bonds, a loan credit rating reflects more than the financial soundness of the underlying borrowing corporation. In particular, the value of the underlying collateral can change a loan's credit rating up to one full category above a standard bond rating.[9] As more loans are rated, their attractiveness to secondary market buyers is likely to increase.

Purchase and Sale of Foreign Bank Loans

With over $600 billion in doubtful and troubled loans on their books in 1998, Japanese banks present a huge potential market for the sale of distressed loans. Indeed, a number of banks and investment banks have established funds to buy up some of these bad loans. For example, in April 1998 Goldman Sachs announced a $4 billion

---

[9]See L. S. Alex, "How S and P Rates Commercial Loans: Implications for Bank Portfolios," *Commercial Lending Review*, Winter 1997–1998, pp. 32–37.

fund to buy troubled loans from Japanese banks. In the same month it did its first deal, purchasing $100 million in loans from the Bank of Tokyo–Mitsubishi.[10]

Concept Questions

1. What are some of the factors that are likely to encourage loan sales growth in the future?
2. Why have the FASB and the SEC advocated that financial services firms replace book value accounting with market value accounting?

Summary

Loan sales provide a primitive alternative to the full securitization of loans through bond packages. In particular, they provide a valuable off-balance-sheet tool to an FI that wishes to manage its credit risk exposure better. The new loan sales market grew rapidly in the 1980s and allowed banks to sell off short-term and long-term loans of both high and low credit quality. There are a number of important factors that suggest that the loan sales market will continue to grow.

Questions and Problems

1. What is the difference between loans sold with recourse and loans sold without recourse from the perspective of both sellers and buyers?

2. A bank has made a three-year $10 million loan that pays annual interest of 8 percent. The principal is due at the end of the third year.
   a. The bank is willing to sell this loan with recourse at an interest rate 8.5 percent? What price should it receive for this loan?
   b. The bank has the option to sell this loan without recourse at a discount rate of 8.75 percent. What price should it receive for this loan?
   c. If the bank expects a 0.5 percent probability of default on this loan, is it better to sell this loan with or without recourse? It expects to receive no interest payments or principal if the loan is defaulted.

3. What are some of the key features of short-term loan sales?

4. Why are yields higher on loan sales than on commercial paper issues with similar maturity and issue size?

5. What are highly leveraged transactions? What constitutes the federal regulatory definition of an HLT?

6. How do the characteristics of an HLT loan differ from those of a short-term loan which is sold?

7. What is a possible reason why the spreads on HLT loans perform differently than do the spreads on junk bonds?

8. City Bank has made a 10-year, $2 million HLT loan that pays an annual interest of 10 percent. The principal is expected at maturity.
   a. What should City Bank expect to receive from the sale of this loan if the current market interest rate on loans of this risk is 12 percent?
   b. The price of loans of this risk is currently being quoted in the secondary market at bid-offer prices of 88–89 cents (on each dollar). Translate these quotes into actual prices for the above loan.
   c. Do these prices reflect a distressed or nondistressed loan? Explain.

9. What is the difference between loan participations and loan assignments?

10. What are the difficulties in completing a loan assignment?

11. Who are the buyers of U.S. loans, and why do they participate in this activity?
   a. What are vulture funds?
   b. What are three reasons why the interbank market has been shrinking?
   c. What are reasons why a small bank would be interested in participating in a loan syndication?

---

[10]See "Goldman Has $4 Billion to Spend on Japanese Loan Portfolios," *Times of London,* April 7, 1998, p. 19.

12. Who are the sellers of U.S. loans, and why do they participate in this activity?

    a. What is the purpose of a bad bank?

    b. What are the reasons why loan sales through a bad bank will be value-enhancing?

    c. What impact has the 1996 Federal Debt Improvements Act had on the loan sale market?

13. In addition to managing credit risk, what are some other reasons for the sale of loans by FIs?

14. How have banks used loan sales to circumvent Glass-Steagall limitations? What is the legal position of this type of transaction?

15. What are factors that may deter the growth of the loan sales market in the future? Discuss.

16. An FI is planning the purchase of a $5 million loan to raise the existing average duration of its assets from 3.5 years to 5 years. It currently has total assets worth 20 million, $5 million in cash (0 duration), and $15 million in loans. All the loans are fairly priced.

    a. Assuming it uses the cash to purchase the loan, should it purchase the loan if its duration is seven years?

    b. What asset duration loans should it purchase to raise its average duration to five years?

17. In addition to hedging credit risk, what are five factors that are expected to encourage loan sales in the future? Discuss the impact of each factor.

SECURITIZATION

Introduction

Along with futures, forwards, options, swaps, and loan sales, asset securitization—the packaging and selling of loans and other assets backed by securities—is a mechanism that FIs have used to hedge their interest rate exposure gaps. In addition, the process of securitization has allowed FI asset portfolios to become more liquid, provided an important source of fee income (with FIs acting as servicing agents for the assets sold), and helped reduce the effects of regulatory taxes such as capital requirements, reserve requirements, and deposit insurance premiums. Thus, in 1998 over 47 percent of all residential mortgages were securitized, compared with less than 15 percent in 1980. Moreover, as discussed in the Contemporary Perspectives box on p. 666, many other types of loans and assets are being securitized (including the assets of rock and roll artists), with the worldwide value of outstanding securitized issues rapidly approaching $500 billion.

In this chapter we investigate the role of securitization in improving the return-risk trade-off for FIs. We describe the three major forms, or vehicles, of asset securitization and analyze their unique characteristics. The major forms of asset securitization are the pass-through security, the collateralized mortgage obligation (CMO), and the asset-backed security. Chapter 27 dealt with a more primitive form of asset securitization—loan sales—whereby loans are sold or traded to other investors and no new securities are created.

The Pass-Through Security

While many different types of loans and assets on FIs' balance sheets are currently being securitized, the original use of securitization came as a result of government-sponsored programs to enhance the liquidity of the residential mortgage market. These programs indirectly subsidize the growth of home ownership in the United States.

Given this, we begin by analyzing the securitization of residential mortgage loans. Three government agencies or government-sponsored enterprises are directly involved in the creation of mortgage-backed pass-through securities. Informally, they are known as Ginnie Mae, Fannie Mae, and Freddie Mac.

GNMA

The Government National Mortgage Association, or "Ginnie Mae," began in 1968 when it split off from FNMA. GNMA is a directly owned government agency with two major functions. The first is sponsoring mortgage-backed securities programs by FIs such as banks, thrifts, and mortgage bankers. The second is acting as a guarantor to investors in mortgage-backed securities regarding the timely pass-through of principal and interest payments on their sponsored bonds. In other words, GNMA provides **timing insurance,** which we describe more fully later in this chapter. In acting as a sponsor and payment-timing guarantor, GNMA supports only those pools of mortgages that comprise mortgage loans whose default or credit risk is insured by one of three government agencies: the Federal Housing Administration (FHA), the Veterans Administration (VA), and the Farmers Home Administration (FMHA). The mortgage loans insured by these agencies are targeted at groups that might otherwise be disadvantaged in the housing market, such as low-income families, young families, and veterans. As such, the maximum mortgage under the FHA/VA/FMHA–GNMA securitization program is capped.

Timing Insurance
A service provided by a sponsor of pass-through securities (such as GNMA) guaranteeing the bondholder interest and principal payments at the calendar date promised.

FNMA

Originally created in 1938, the Federal National Mortgage Association, or "Fannie Mae," is the oldest of the three mortgage-backed security sponsoring agencies. While it is now a private corporation owned by shareholders with stock traded on major exchanges, in the minds of many investors it still has implicit government

BONDS THAT ROCK AND ROLL

Fancy investing in a security whose payoff depends on how much beer is sold in British pubs? How about a bond to be paid by collections of overdue parking fines in New York City? If you'd prefer, you can purchase the rights to a slice of the revenues from old Italian films, or the amounts raised by selling executive suites in Denver's new stadium, or the royalties earned by pop stars such as David Bowie and Rod Stewart. There is barely a cash flow anywhere, it seems, that cannot be reassembled into a bond-like security that the most conservative of investors might buy.

Putting such strange instruments together has become one of the hottest businesses on Wall Street. New issues of asset-backed securities rose by a quarter last year, to $484 billion (see chart). This year's growth rate is expected to be at least as rapid, and the value of new asset-backed securities may for the first time exceed that of traditional corporate bonds. Mostly, that is good news, as securitisation can reduce the cost of borrowing. Yet amid the enthusiasm, the risks may be overlooked. The fact that new sorts of security can be created does not always mean they should be.

It is easy to see why securitisation has become so popular. Issuers gain instant access to money for which they would otherwise have to wait months or years, and they can shed some of the risk that their expected revenues will not materialise. Investment bankers are able to finance their customers without extending loans that tie up large amounts of capital. And investors can hold a new sort of asset, less risky than unsecured bonds, so they can diversify their portfolios and thus reduce their risk.

Those, at least, are the theoretical benefits. Turning them into reality can be tricky. In fact, for all the current excitement about rock-star bonds and the like, it is striking that the vast majority of asset-backed securities are American and involve a few types of assets, such as mortgage and credit-card loans, which generate relatively predictable amounts of cash at predictable times. Much of this year's growth is expected to come from banks securitising loans that are already on their books and from an increase in American-style securitisation in other markets, especially European. Yet even that is by no means certain: two previous attempts to introduce Europeans to asset-backed securities failed, even though American investment banks spent a fortune trying to make them work.

Even traditional sorts of asset-backed securities sometimes spring nasty surprises. Investors in mortgage-backed securities have repeatedly taken hits when borrowers repaid in larger numbers than computer models had predicted. And in the past year, AutoBond Acceptance, a car lender, saw profits drop and Green Tree Financial, which lends on mobile homes, reported a loss, after default and pre-payment rates were higher than expected. The securities continued to perform, because investors had purchased only a portion of the expected payments rather than the whole lot.

These failures illustrate how difficult securitisation can be even with relatively straightforward assets. It is harder still to make securities out of such things as music royalties and patent licence fees.

Most traditional securitisations involve cash flows that have been earned, but are not yet received; the main risk is that the cash will flow earlier or later than promised, or not at all. When lots of similar receivables are bundled together in an asset-backed security, the average rates of default, late payment and pre-payment are predictable, so both issuers and investors can be relatively confident of their ability to value the security properly.

Many of the more exotic asset-backed securities, by contrast, are based not on earned-but-uncollected cash, such as monthly mortgage payments, but on forecasts

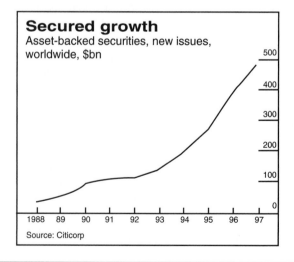

Secured growth
Asset-backed securities, new issues, worldwide, $bn

500
400
300
200
100
0

1988 89 90 91 92 93 94 95 96 97

Source: Citicorp

Contemporary Perspectives

of future earnings. Henry Morriello, a partner at Kaye Scholer, a law firm in New York, reckons that at least five years of sales data are necessary to have much confidence about future streams of music revenues, which is why established rockers such as Messrs Bowie and Stewart have been able to do deals; it would be much harder to predict royalties for shorter-lived acts, such as the Spice Girls. Even so, music fans and cinema-goers are fickle, so the past may not be a reliable guide to the future.

Some of the new financial instruments also confront investors with a problem largely absent from traditional asset-backed securities: moral hazard. In this case, that means that the issuer's own actions can have a considerable impact on the value of the securities. Once a pool of mortgages is securitised there is little that the original lender can do to alter its value. The value of PolyGram's recent $650m securitisation of ticket, video and merchandising revenues, however, depends heavily upon how hard the company promotes its upcoming films. There may be moral issues of a different sort as well. "What happens to record sales if the star is caught molesting kids?" asks Paul Taylor, of Duff & Phelps, a bond-rating agency.

Odd couples

One reason investors love securities which pool assets is that they limit risk by minimising the loss if something awful happens to any one asset. This is harder to do with royalties, film revenues and patent licenses: One rock star's royalty stream differs from another's in a way that two 25-year mortgages rarely do. Although Rod Stewart is reported to have securitised his royalties, that is only half true; he merely received a $15m loan secured against future royalties. Bankers hope to bundle this with other loans to entertainers and fully securitise it, but this is proving hard to do. Just negotiating the simpler deal announced last week took more than a year.

Complicating matters further, it is not always clear whether the issuer of such one-off securities actually owns the cash flow being securitised. There can be huge legal problems in establishing ownership of patents and royalties, points out Joseph Donovan of Prudential Securities. Sometimes, ownership is shared among several people or companies, not all of whom may want to be part of the securitisation.

Together these factors are an obstacle to unusual securitisations. To make them work, issuers may have to pay a big price by securitising only a small fraction of the forecast cash flow, by paying a higher interest rate or by providing other safeguards. Last year, pop's Mr Bowie had to persuade his record company to guarantee investors' money in case his music fails to sell as expected before he could complete the $55m securitisation of his future royalties.

Most of this strange paper ends up on the portfolios of pension funds and insurance companies which are willing to bear the risk in exchange for some extra return. When Punch Taverns, a British firm, issued £535m ($889m) of securities in March tied to beer sales and publicans' rental payments at 1,428 pubs, the main buyers were non-British banks. In general, such securities must be held to maturity. Unlike mortgage-backed securities, the price of which changes constantly in response to interest-rate movements, there is no easy way to reckon whether the revenues from future beer sales are worth more today than yesterday. This makes the securities difficult to value and therefore hard to trade.

The possibilities are limited only by investment bankers' imaginations—and the gullibility of the bond-rating agencies. The raters, whose imprimatur is often essential for a security's success, say they are currently refusing favourable ratings to far more proposed issues than they endorse. Despite all the hype about exotic securities, that means that the thriving securitisations are likely to be the duller ones.

backing that makes it equivalent to a government-sponsored agency.[1] Indeed, supporting this view is the fact that FNMA has a secured line of credit available from the U.S. Treasury should it need funds in an emergency. FNMA is a more active agency than GNMA in creating pass-through securities. While GNMA merely sponsors such programs, FNMA actually helps create pass-throughs by buying and holding mortgages on its balance sheet; it also issues bonds directly to finance those purchases.

Specifically, FNMA creates mortgage-backed securities (MBSs) by purchasing packages of mortgage loans from banks and thrifts; it finances such purchases by selling MBSs to outside investors such as life insurers and pensions funds. In addition, it engages in swap transactions whereby FNMA swaps MBSs with an FI for original mortgages. Since FNMA securities carry FNMA guarantees as to the full and timely payment of interest and principal, the FI receiving the MBSs can then resell them on the capital market or hold them in its portfolio. Unlike GNMA, the FNMA securitizes conventional mortgage loans as well as FHA/VA insured loans as long as the conventional loans have acceptable loan to value or collateral ratios normally not exceeding 80 percent. Conventional loans with high loan to value ratios usually require additional private sector credit insurance before they are accepted into FNMA securitization pools.

FHLMC

The Federal Home Loan Mortgage Corporation, or "Freddie Mac," performs a function similar to that of FNMA except that its major securitization role has historically involved savings banks. Like FNMA, it is a stockholder-owned corporation with a line of credit from the Treasury. Further, like FNMA, it buys mortgage loan pools from FIs and swaps MBSs for loans. The FHLMC also sponsors conventional loan pools as well as FHA/VA mortgage pools and guarantees timely payment of interest and ultimate payment of principal on the securities it issues.

The Incentives and Mechanics of Pass-Through Security Creation

In order to analyze the securitization process, we trace through the mechanics of a mortgage pool securitization. In so doing, we gain insights into the return-risk benefits of this process to the mortgage-originating FI as well as the attractiveness of these securities to investors. Given that more than $2 trillion of mortgage-backed securities are outstanding—a large proportion sponsored by the GNMA—we analyze an example of the creation of a GNMA pass-through security next.[2]

Suppose a bank has just originated 1,000 new residential mortgages in its local area. The average size of each mortgage is $100,000; thus, the total size of the new mortgage pool is

$$1,000 \times \$100,000 = \$100 \text{ million}$$

Each mortgage, because of its small size, will receive credit risk insurance protection from the FHA. This insurance costs a small fee to the originating bank. In

[1]See R. W. Spahr and M. A. Sunderman, "The Effect of Prepayment Modeling in Pricing Mortgage-Backed Securities," *Journal of Housing Research* 3, (1992), pp. 381–400.

[2]In mid-1997, outstanding mortgage pools were $2.13 trillion, with GNMA pools amounting to $521 billion; FNMA, $674 billion; and FHLMC, $567 billion.

addition, each of these new mortgages has an initial stated maturity of 30 years and a mortgage rate—often called the mortgage coupon—of 12 percent per annum. Suppose the bank originating these loans relies mostly on liabilities such as demand deposits as well as its own capital or equity to finance its assets. Under current capital adequacy requirements, each $1 of new residential mortgage loans has to be backed by some capital. Since the risk-adjusted value of residential mortgages is 50 percent of face value and the risk-based capital requirement is 8 percent, the bank capital needed to back the $100 million mortgage portfolio would be

$$\text{Capital requirement} = \$100 \text{ million} \times .5 \times .08 = \$4 \text{ million}$$

Even though the difference between $100 million and $4 million is $96 million, the bank must issue more than $96 million in liabilities (here, demand deposits) due to a 10 percent noninterest-bearing reserve requirement imposed on these liabilities by the Federal Reserve. Note that since there is currently a 0 percent reserve requirement on CDs and time deposits, the FI would need no extra funds to pay reserve requirements if it used CDs to fund the mortgage portfolio. The reserve requirement on demand deposits is an additional tax over and above the capital requirement on funding the bank's residential mortgage portfolio.[3]

Given these considerations, the bank's initial postmortgage balance sheet may look like that in Table 28–1. This balance sheet reflects the $4 million capital requirement that has to be held against mortgage assets and the 10 percent reserve requirement on demand deposits ($106.6 \times .1 = 10.66$). This leaves $96 million out of the $106.66 million in demand deposits raised to fund the mortgage portfolio of $100 million.

In addition to the capital and reserve requirement taxes, the bank has to pay an annual insurance premium to the FDIC based on the risk of the bank. Assuming a deposit insurance premium of 27 basis points (for the lowest-quality banks), the fee would be[4]

$$\$106.66 \text{ million} \times .0027 = \$287,982$$

Although the bank is earning a 12 percent mortgage coupon on its mortgage portfolio, it is facing three levels of regulatory taxes:

1. Capital requirements.
2. Reserve requirements.
3. FDIC insurance premiums.

TABLE 28–1   Bank Balance Sheet
(in millions of dollars)

Assets		Liabilities	
Cash reserves	$ 10.66	Demand deposits	$106.66
Long-term mortgages	100.00	Capital	4.00
	$110.66		$110.66

---

[3]Implicitly viewing the capital requirement as a tax assumes that regulators set the minimum level above the level that would be privately optimal.

[4]In 1998 the deposit insurance premium was zero for the highest-quality banks (see Chapter 19).

Thus, one incentive to securitize is to reduce the regulatory tax burden on the FI to increase its after-tax return.[5] In addition to facing regulatory taxes on its residential mortgage portfolio earnings, the bank in Table 28–1 has two risk exposure problems:

Gap Exposure or $D_A > kD_L$.   The FI funds the 30-year mortgage portfolio out of short-term deposits; thus, it has a duration mismatch.[6] This would be true even if the mortgage assets have been funded with short-term CDs, time deposits, or other purchased funds.

Illiquidity Exposure.   The bank is holding a very illiquid asset portfolio of long-term mortgages and no excess reserves; it is exposed to the potential liquidity shortages discussed in Chapter 17, including the risk of having to conduct mortgage asset fire sales to meet large unexpected demand deposit withdrawals.

One possible solution to this duration mismatch and illiquidity risk problem is to lengthen the bank's on-balance-sheet liabilities by issuing longer-term deposits or other liability claims, such as medium-term notes. Another solution is to engage in interest rate swaps to transform the bank's liabilities into those of a long-term, fixed-rate nature (see Chapter 26). These techniques do not resolve the problem of regulatory taxes and the burden they impose on the FI's returns.

By contrast, creating GNMA pass-through securities can largely resolve the duration and illiquidity risk problems on the one hand and reduce the burden of regulatory taxes on the other. This requires the bank to securitize the $100 million in residential mortgages by issuing GNMA pass-through securities. In our example, the bank can do this since the 1,000 underlying mortgages each have FHA/VA mortgage insurance, the same stated mortgage maturity of 30 years, and coupons of 12 percent. Therefore, they are eligible for securitization under the GNMA program if the bank is an approved lender (which we assume it is).

The bank begins the securitization process by packaging the $100 million in mortgage loans and removing them from the balance sheet by placing them with a third-party trustee, in a special-purpose vehicle (SPV) off the balance sheet. This third-party trustee may be another bank of high creditworthiness or a legal trustee. Next, the bank determines that (1) GNMA will guarantee, for a fee, the timing of interest and principal payments on the bonds issued to back the mortgage pool and (2) the bank itself will continue to service the pool of mortgages for a fee, even after they are placed in trust. Then an issue of GNMA pass-through securities is made backed by the underlying $100 million pool of mortgages. These GNMA securities or pass-through bonds are sold to outside investors in the capital market. Large purchasers of these securities include insurance companies and pension funds.

Now we consider the attractiveness of these bonds to investors. In particular, investors in these bonds are protected against two levels or types of default risk.

Default Risk by the Mortgagees.   Suppose that because of rapidly falling house prices—such as happened in Phoenix, Arizona in the 1980s—a homeowner walked

---

[5]Other reasons for securitization include greater geographic diversification of the loan portfolio. Specifically, many FIs originate mortgages from the local community; the ability to securitize facilitates replacing them with MBSs based on mortgages from other cities and regions.

[6]As we discuss in Chapters 8 and 9, core demand deposits usually have a duration of less than three years. Depending on prepayment assumptions, mortgages normally have durations of at least 4.5 years.

away from a mortgage, leaving behind a low-valued house to be foreclosed at a price below the outstanding mortgage. This might expose the mortgage bondholders to losses unless there are external guarantors. Through FHA/VA housing insurance, government agencies bear the risk of default, thereby protecting bondholders against such losses.

Default Risk by Bank/Trustee.   Suppose the bank that had originated the mortgages went bankrupt or the trustee absconded with the mortgage interest and principal due to bondholders. Because it guaranteed the prompt timing of interest and principal payments on GNMA securities, GNMA would bear the cost of making the promised payments in full and on time to GNMA bondholders.

Given this default protection, the GNMA bondholders' (or investors') returns from holding these bonds would be the monthly repayments of interest and principal on the 1,000 mortgages in the pool, after the deduction of a mortgage-servicing fee by the mortgage-originating bank and a monthly timing insurance fee to be paid to GNMA. The total sum of these fees is around 50 basis points, or $\frac{1}{2}$ percent, with approximately 6 basis points going as a fee to GNMA for timing insurance and the remaining 44 basis points going to the mortgage originator as a servicing fee. As a result, the stated coupons on the GNMA bonds would be set at approximately $\frac{1}{2}$ percent below the coupon rate on the underlying mortgages. In our example:

Mortgage coupon rate	=	12.00%
minus		
Servicing fee	=	0.44
minus		
GNMA insurance fee	=	0.06
GNMA pass-through bond coupon	=	11.50%

Suppose that GNMA issues $100 million face value bonds at par to back the pool of mortgage loans. The minimum size of a single bond is $25,000; each bondholder gets a pro rata monthly share of all the interest and principal received by the bank minus servicing costs and insurance fees. Thus, if a life insurance company bought 25 percent of the GNMA bond issue (or 1,000 bonds × $25,000 each = $25 million), it would get a 25 percent share of the 360 promised monthly payments from the mortgages comprising the mortgage pool.

Every month, each mortgagee makes a payment to the bank. The bank aggregates these payments and passes the funds through to GNMA bond investors via the trustee net of servicing fee and insurance fee deductions. To make things easy, most fixed-rate mortgages are **fully amortized** over the mortgage's life. This means that as long as the mortgagee does not seek to prepay the mortgage early within the 30-year period, due to either moving house or a refinancing if mortgage rates fall, bondholders can expect to get a constant stream of payments each month analogous to the stream of income on other fixed-coupon, fixed-income bonds.

The problem is that mortgagees do not act in such a mechanistic fashion. For a variety of reasons, they relocate or refinance their mortgages (especially when current mortgage rates are below mortgage coupon rates). This propensity to **prepay** means that *realized* coupons/cash flows on pass-through securities can often deviate substantially from the stated or expected coupon flows in a no-prepayment

Fully Amortized
An equal periodic repayment on a loan that reflects part interest and part principal over the life of the loan.

Prepay
A borrower pays back a loan before maturity to the FI that originated the loan.

world. This unique prepayment risk provides the attraction of pass-throughs to some investors but leads other, more risk-averse, investors to avoid these instruments. Before we analyze in greater detail the unique nature of prepayment risk, we summarize the steps followed in the creation of a pass-through in Figure 28–1. Then we analyze how this securitization has helped solve the duration, illiquidity, and regulatory tax problems of the FI manager.

In the previous discussion we traced the GNMA securitization process, the origination of mortgages on the balance sheet (Figure 28–1, Box 1) through to the sale of GNMA bonds to outside investors (Box 4). To close the securitization process, the cash proceeds of the sale of GNMA bonds (Box 5) net of any underwriting fees go to the originating bank. As a result, the bank has substituted long-term mortgages for cash by using the GNMA securitization mechanism. Abstracting from the various fees and underwriting costs in the securitization process, the balance sheet of the bank might look like the one in Table 28–2 immediately after the securitization has taken place.

FIGURE 28–1

Summary of a GNMA Pass-Through

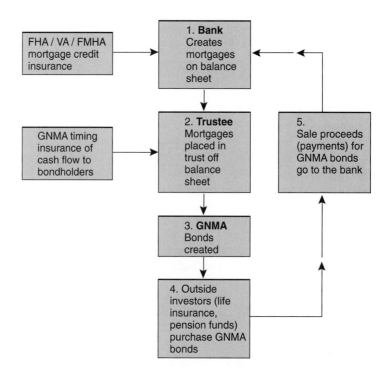

TABLE 28–2   The Bank's Balance Sheet after Securitization
(in millions of dollars)

Assets		Liabilities	
Cash reserves	$ 10.66	Demand deposits	$106.66
Cash proceeds from mortgage securitization	100.00	Capital	4.00
	$110.66		$110.66

There has been a dramatic change in the balance sheet exposure of the bank. First, $100 million illiquid mortgage loans have been replaced by $100 million cash. Second, the duration mismatch has been reduced since both D_A and D_L are now low. Third, the bank has an enhanced ability to deal with and reduce its regulatory taxes. Specifically, capital requirements can be reduced since the risk-adjusted asset value of cash is zero compared to a risk-adjusted asset value of 50 percent for residential mortgages. Reserve requirement and deposit insurance premiums are also reduced if the bank uses part of the cash proceeds from the GNMA sale to pay off or retire demand deposits and downsize its balance sheet.

Of course, keeping an all or highly liquid asset portfolio and/or downsizing is a way to reduce regulatory taxes, but these strategies are hardly likely to enhance an FI's profits. The real logic of securitization is that the cash proceeds from the mortgage/GNMA sale can be reused to create or originate new mortgages, which in turn can be securitized. In so doing, the bank is acting more like an asset (mortgage) broker than a traditional asset transformer, as we discussed in Chapter 6. The advantage of being an asset broker is that the bank profits from mortgage pool servicing fees plus up-front points and fees from mortgage origination. At the same time, the bank no longer has to bear the illiquidity and duration mismatch risks and regulatory taxes that arise when it acts as an asset transformer and holds mortgages to maturity on its balance sheet. Put more simply, the bank's profitability becomes more fee dependent than interest rate spread dependent.

The limits of this securitization process clearly depend on the supply of mortgages (and other assets) that can be securitized and the demand by investors for pass-through securities. As was noted earlier, the unique feature of pass-through securities from the demand-side perspective of investors is prepayment risk. To understand the unique nature of this risk and why it might deter or limit investments by other FIs and investors, we next analyze the characteristics of pass-through securities more formally.

Prepayment Risk on Pass-Through Securities

To understand the effects of prepayments on pass-through security returns, you have to understand the nature of the cash flows received by investors from the underlying portfolio of mortgages. In the United States, most conventional mortgages are fully amortized. This means that the mortgagee pays back to the mortgage lender (mortgagor) a constant amount each month that contains some principal and some interest. While the total monthly promised payment remains unchanged, the interest component declines throughout the life of the mortgage contract and the principal component increases.

The problem for the bank is to figure a constant monthly payment that exactly pays off the mortgage loan at maturity. This constant payment is formally equivalent to a monthly "annuity" paid by the mortgagee. Consider our example of 1,000 mortgages comprising a $100 million mortgage pool that is to be paid off monthly over 360 months at an annual mortgage coupon rate of 12 percent:

$$\text{Size of pool} = 100{,}000{,}000$$
$$\text{Maturity} = 30 \text{ years } (n = 30)$$
$$\text{Number of monthly payments} = 12 \ (m = 12)$$
$$r = \text{Annual mortgage coupon rate} = 12 \text{ percent}$$
$$R = \text{Constant monthly payment to pay off the mortgage over its life}$$

Thus, we wish to solve for R from the following equation:

$$100,000,000 = \left[R\left(1 + \frac{r}{m}\right)^{-1} + R\left(1 + \frac{r}{m}\right)^{-2} + \ldots + R\left(1 + \frac{r}{m}\right)^{-360} \right]$$

$$= R\left[\left(1 + \frac{r}{m}\right)^{-1} + \left(1 + \frac{r}{m}\right)^{-2} + \ldots + \left(1 + \frac{r}{m}\right)^{-360} \right]$$

The term in square brackets is a geometric expansion that in the limit equals

$$100,000,000 = \left[\frac{1 - \dfrac{1}{\left(1 + \frac{r}{m}\right)^{mn}}}{\frac{r}{m}} \right] \times R$$

The new term in square brackets is the present value of the annuity factor, *PVAF*, or $100,000,000 = R[PVAF]$. Rearranging to solve for R, the required equal monthly payment on the mortgages, we have

$$R = \frac{100,000,000}{PVAF}$$

$$R = \frac{100,000,000}{\left[\dfrac{1 - \dfrac{1}{\left(1 + \frac{r}{m}\right)^{mn}}}{\frac{r}{m}} \right]}$$

$$R = \frac{100,000,000}{\left[\dfrac{1 - \dfrac{1}{\left(1 + \frac{.12}{12}\right)^{360}}}{\frac{.12}{.12}} \right]} = \$1,028,613$$

As a result, $R = \$1,028,613$, or, given 1,000 individual mortgages, $\$1,028.61$ per mortgage rounding to the nearest cent. Thus, payments by the 1,000 mortgagees of an average monthly mortgage payment of $\$1,028.61$ will pay off the mortgages outstanding over 30 years, assuming no prepayments.

The aggregate monthly payments of $\$1,028,610$ comprise different amounts of principal and interest each month.[7] In Table 28–3 we break down the aggregate monthly amortized mortgage payments of $R = \$1,028,610$ into their interest and principal components. In month 1, the interest component is 12 percent divided by 12 (or 1 percent) times the outstanding balance on the mortgage pool ($\$100$ million). This comes to $\$1,000,000$, meaning that the remainder of the aggregate monthly payment, or $\$28,610$, can be used to pay off outstanding principal on the pool. At the end of month 1, the outstanding principal balance on the mortgages has

---

[7]Because of the rounding of each monthly payment to the nearest cent, we assume that aggregate monthly cash flows are $1,000 \times \$1,028.61$ cents $= \$1,028,610$.

been reduced by $28,610 to $99,971,390. In month 2 and thereafter, the interest component declines and the principal component increases, but the two still sum to $1,028,610. Thus, in month 2, the interest component has declined to $999,714 (or 1 percent of the outstanding principal at the beginning of month 2) and the principal component of the payment has increased to $28,896. We show graphically the changing nature of these payments in Figure 28–2.

While 12 percent is the coupon or interest rate the housebuyers pay on the mortgages, the rate passed through to GNMA investors is $11\frac{1}{2}$ percent, reflecting an average 6-basis-point insurance fee paid to GNMA and a 44-basis-point servicing fee paid to the originating bank. The servicing fees are normally paid monthly rather than as lump-sum single payments up front to create the appropriate collection/servicing incentives over the life of the mortgage for the originating bank. For example, the bank's incentive to act as an efficient collection/servicing agent over 360 months would probably decline if it received a single large up-front fee in month 1 and nothing thereafter.

The effect of the $\frac{1}{2}$ percent fee is to reduce the cash flows passed through to the bondholders. As can be checked, using a *PVAF* that reflects an 11.5 percent annual rate rather than a 12 percent annual rate, GNMA bondholders would collectively receive $990,291 per month over the 30 years instead of $1,028,610 under conditions of no prepayments.

As we have shown so far, the cash flows on the pass-through directly reflect the interest and principal cash flows on the underlying mortgages minus service and insurance fees. However, over time, mortgage rates change. Let Y be the current annual mortgage coupon rate, which could be higher or lower than 12 percent, and let y be the yield on newly issued par value GNMA pass-through bonds. With no

TABLE 28–3   Fully Amortized Mortgages

Month	Outstanding Balance Payment	Fixed Monthly (R)	Interest Component	Principal Component	Principal Remaining
1	$100,000,000	$1,028,610	$1,000,000	$28,610	$99,971,390
2	99,971,390	1,028,610	999,714	28,896	99,942,494
.	.	.	.	.	.
.	.	.	.	.	.
.	.	.	.	.	.
360	.	.	.	.	.

FIGURE 28–2

Interest and Principal Components of the Fully Amortized Mortgage

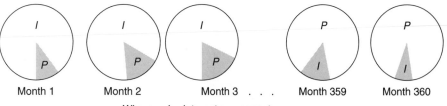

Month 1   Month 2   Month 3 . . .   Month 359   Month 360

Where   *I* = Interest component
         P = Principal component

prepayments, the market value of the 12 percent mortgage coupon pool (11½) percent actual coupons) could be calculated as

$$V = \frac{\$990,291}{\left(1 + \dfrac{y}{12}\right)^1} + \frac{\$990,291}{\left(1 + \dfrac{y}{12}\right)^2} + \ldots + \frac{\$990,291}{\left(1 + \dfrac{y}{12}\right)^{360}}$$

If y is less than 11½ percent, the market value of the pool will be greater than its original value; if y is greater than 11½ percent, the pool will decrease in value. However, valuation is more complex than this since we have ignored the prepayment behavior of the 1,000 mortgages. In effect, prepayment risk has two principal sources: refinancing and housing turnover.

Refinancing.   As the coupon rates on new mortgages fall, there is an increased incentive for individuals in the pool to pay off old high-cost mortgages and refinance at lower rates. However, refinancing involves transaction costs and recontracting costs. Many banks and thrifts have sought to charge prepayment penalty fees on the outstanding mortgage balance prepaid.[8] In addition, there are often origination costs or points for new mortgages to consider along with the cost of appraisals and credit checks. As a result, mortgage rates may have to fall by some amount below the current coupon rate before there is a significant increase in prepayments in the pool.[9] The Contemporary Perspectives box on p. 678 discusses the wave of refinancings that occurred in 1998 as interest rates on new mortgages fell.

Housing Turnover.   The other factor that affects prepayments is the propensity of the mortgagees in the pool to move before their mortgages reach maturity. The decision to move or turn over a house may be due to a complex set of factors, such as the level of house prices, the size of the underlying mortgage, the general health of the economy, and even the season (e.g., spring is a good time to move). In addition,

Assumable Mortgage
The mortgage contract is transferred from the seller to the buyer of a house.

if the existing mortgage is an **assumable mortgage,** the buyer of the house takes over the outstanding mortgage's payments. Thus, the sale of a house in a pool does not necessarily imply that the mortgage has to be prepaid. By contrast, nonassumability means a one-to-one correspondence between sale of a house and mortgage prepayment. Most GNMA pools allow mortgages to be assumable; the reverse holds true for pass-throughs sponsored by FNMA and FHLMC.

In Figure 28–3 we plot the prepayment frequency of a pool of mortgages in relation to the spread between the current mortgage coupon rate (Y) and the mortgage coupon rate (r) in the existing pool (12 percent in our example). As you can see, when the current mortgage rate (Y) is above the rate in the pool ($Y > r$), mortgage prepayments are small, reflecting monthly forced turnover as people have to relocate because of jobs, divorces, marriages, and other considerations. Even when the current mortgage rate falls below r, those remaining in the mortgage pool do not rush to prepay because up-front refinancing, contracting, and penalty costs are likely to outweigh any present value savings from lower mortgage rates. However, as current mortgage rates continue to fall, the propensity for mortgage holders to

---

[8]However, federal regulations typically forbid prepayment penalties on residential first mortgages.

[9]Follian and Tzany found that only when the mortgage rate fell below the coupon rate by 60 basis points was there an incentive to refinance a mortgage with an average of 10 years left to maturity. As might be expected, this required differential declined as the holding period increased.

prepay increases significantly. Conceptually, mortgage holders have a very valuable call option on the mortgage when this option is in the money.[10] That is, when current mortgage rates fall sufficiently low so that the present value savings of refinancing outweigh the exercise price (the cost of prepayment penalties and other fees and costs), the mortgage will be called.

Since the bank has sold the mortgage cash flows to GNMA investors and must by law pass through all payments received (minus servicing and guaranty fees), investors' cash flows directly reflect the rate of prepayment. As a result, instead of receiving an equal monthly cash flow, R, as is done under a no-prepayment scenario, the actual cash flows (CF) received on these securities by investors fluctuate monthly with the rate of prepayments (see Figure 28–4).

In a no-prepayment world, each month's cash flows are the same: $R_1 = R_2 = \ldots = R_{360}$. However, in a world with prepayments each month's realized cash flows from the mortgage pool can differ. In Figure 28–4 we show a rising level of cash flows from month 3 onward peaking in month 60, reflecting the effects of early prepayments by some of the 1,000 mortgagees in the pool. This leaves less outstanding principal and interest to be paid in later years. For example, if 300 mortgagees fully prepay by month 60, only 700 mortgagees will remain in the pool at that date. The effect of prepayments is to lower dramatically the principal and interest cash flows received in the later months of the pool's life. For instance, in Figure 28–4, the cash flow received by GNMA bondholders in month 360 is very small relative to month 60 and even months 1 and 2. This reflects the decline in the pool's outstanding principal.

FIGURE 28–3

The Prepayment Relationship

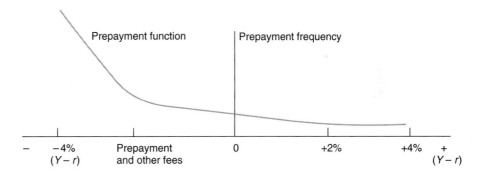

FIGURE 28–4

The Effects of Prepayments on Pass-Through Bondholders' Cash Flows

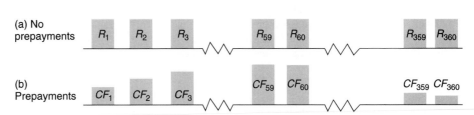

---

[10]The option is a call option on the value of the mortgage since falling rates increase the value of calling the old mortgage and refinancing a new mortgage at lower rates for the owner of the call option, who is the mortgagee. See M. J. Brennan and E. S. Schwartz, "Savings Bonds, Retractable Bonds, and Callable Bonds," *Journal of Financial Economics* 5 (1977), pp. 67–88. This option can also be viewed as a put option on interest rates.

Contemporary Perspectives

LOW RATES SPUR SURGE IN HOME BUYING AND REFINANCING

Nick Ravo

Interest rates have fallen to a four-year low in recent weeks, causing a surge of home buying and mortgage refinancings that has created a windfall for consumers, lenders and real estate agents in the New York metropolitan region.

"I am probably getting 50 percent more phone calls than a year ago," said Ellen Bitton, president of the Park Avenue Mortgage Group in Manhattan.

As of Wednesday, the average rate on a 30-year fixed-rate mortgage was 7.1 percent, with 1.31 points, according to HSH Associates, a mortgage analyst in Butler, N. J.—slightly above the 6.83 percent of Oct. 15, 1993. A point is a fee paid at closing that is equal to 1 percent of the loan. The average adjustable rate was 5.59 percent, with 1.35 points, up from a low of 4.15 percent on Oct. 29, 1993.

"Our phone volume has increased by 500 to 600 percent, and this is the third time something like this has happened in the 90's," said Bruce R. Lublin, president of the Homerica Mortgage Corporation in Harrison, N.Y.

The lower interest rates have made buying a home more attractive and fueled business at real estate brokerages.

"It has led more people to put their homes on the market and make the move to a more desirable neighborhood," said John Dibs, the owner of RE/MAX Liberty, a real estate broker in Ozone Park, Queens. "At the same time, more purchasers have entered the home buying market to take advantage of the low interest rates. Over all, I'm currently experiencing an increase in purchasing activity and inventory.

In 1992 and 1993, 30-year fixed-rate mortgages dipped below 7 percent for the first time in more than a quarter-century and some adjustable-rate mortgages had initial rates as low as 3 percent. Then, like now, more than 70 percent of all new mortgages were refinancings.

Christopher Ryan, a Danbury, Conn., firefighter, and his wife, Donna, who operates a day-care center at their home in nearby Sherman, Conn., recently refinanced their mortgage after watching their one-year adjustable-rate mortgage jump to 8.5 percent, swelling their monthly payment by $400 above what it was in 1995. So in January, they refinanced to a mortgage that is fixed at seven years and adjusts annually so that; it has a lower rate, 7 percent, than their old loan and saves them $125 a month.

"We could have gotten down to 6.5 percent," Mr. Ryan said. "But I jumped the gun and locked in about two days before the big rate drop."

On Wednesday, People's Bank in Bridgeport, Conn., received 75 refinancing applications; the norm is 30.

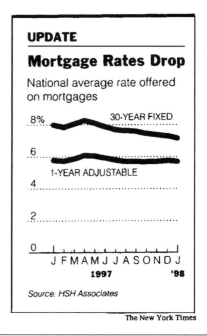

UPDATE

Mortgage Rates Drop

National average rate offered on mortgages

Source: HSH Associates

The New York Times

The lowering of current mortgage interest rates and faster prepayments have some good news and bad news effects on the current market valuation of the 12 percent mortgage pool, that is, the $11\frac{1}{2}$ percent GNMA bond.

Good News Effects.   First, lower market yields reduce the discount rate on any mortgage cash flow and increase the present value of any given stream of cash flows. This would also happen for any fixed-income security.

Contemporary Perspectives

"Volume has risen dramatically during the first six weeks of 1998 compared to the first six weeks of 1997, more than tripled, and the weather has been about the same, so the increase is not weather-driven," said Dorothea Brennan, a bank spokeswoman.

Mortgage brokers' business has jumped so much that they are writing about as many loans as are banks. It has not always been that way. Before the early 90's, few people used mortgage brokers, intermediaries who find loans for borrowers and help them with the applications but do not make loans themselves. The industry was small and, to some degree, had a slightly shady reputation. Instead, borrowers usually, almost reflexively, shopped for rates at local lenders.

The National Association of Mortgage Brokers, a trade organization, said that the percentage of home mortgage applications written by brokers increased to 52 percent last year, from 20 percent in 1987. Most of them are refinancing loans.

"Seventy-five percent of my business is currently devoted to mortgage refinancing," said Neil Bader, chief executive of the Skyscraper Mortgage Company in Manhattan. "It is double what it was at this time last year."

Most of the recent refinancing activity has been into 30-year fixed-rate loans. Rates on one-year adjustable mortgages have not fallen so sharply. Indeed, many homeowners who took them out in recent years have found that they are paying higher rates than they would for a 30-year fixed-rate loan.

The savings on mortgages can be substantial when rates decline. Circumstances have outdated the old formula for practical refinancing of "2-2-2," meaning borrowers had been in a home at least two years, intended to stay at least two more years and refinanced at a rate at least two percentage points lower than their current mortgage rate.

When is the rate difference wide enough? Many mortgage brokers believe that a drop in rates of even half a percentage point can justify refinancing, if the fees of the loan are wrapped into the loan or are paid by the broker. Such loans are sometimes called "zero-cost" refinancings; in exchange for about three-eighths of a percentage point in the rate, all other fees are paid.

The savings can be substantial, however, even when rates drop just a little. Consider a homeowner with an existing mortgage of $200,000, and a mortgage rate of 7.25 percent. The monthly payment is $1,364. At a refinanced rate of 7 percent, just a quarter-percent lower, the monthly payment would be $1,330, a savings of $34 per month.

Robert Gold, a lawyer and real estate developer who lives in Greenwich Village in Manhattan, recently refinanced the mortgage on his one-bedroom co-op apartment using a mortgage broker.

By refinancing from a 7.25 percent one-year adjustable-rate mortgage into a 7.125 percent mortgage that has a fixed rate for 10 years, Mr. Gold could take out $35,000 in equity from his home and only bump up his payments by about $100 a month.

"It's wonderful to be able to get the appreciation out of an apartment after eight years," he said," and be able to lock in a very comfortable rate for a 10-year period."

_____

Second, lower yields lead to faster prepayment of the mortgage pool's principal. As a result, instead of principal payments being skewed toward the end of the pool's life, the principal is received (paid) back much faster.

Bad News Effects. First, with early prepayment come fewer interest payments in absolute terms. Thus, instead of receiving scheduled interest payments over 360 months, some of these payments are irrevocably lost as principal outstanding is paid early; that is, mortgage holders are not going to pay interest on mortgage loans they no longer have outstanding.

Second, faster cash flow due to prepayments induced by interest rate falls can only be reinvested at lower interest rates when they are received. That is, instead of reinvesting monthly cash flows at 12 percent, investors may reinvest only at lower rates such as 8 percent.

Prepayment Models

Clearly, managers running FI investment portfolios need to factor in assumptions about the prepayment behavior of mortgages before they can assess the fair value and risk of their GNMA and FNMA/FHLMC bond portfolios. Next, we consider three alternative ways to model prepayment effects using the Public Securities Association (PSA) prepayment model, other empirical models, and option valuation models.

To begin, we look carefully at the results of one prepayment model. Look at the reported prices and yields on pass-through securities in Figure 28–5. The first column in the figure shows the sponsor of the issue (GNMA/FNMA/FMAC), the stated maturity of the issue (30 years or 15 years), the mortgage coupons on the mortgages in each pool (e.g., 7 percent), and information about the maximum delay between the receipt of interest by the servicer/sponsor and the actual payment of interest to bondholders. The Gold next to FMAC indicates a maximum stated delay of 55 days; this is the same as FNMA and FHLMC and 10 days more than GNMA.[11] The current market price is shown in column (2), with the daily price change in column (3) (in 32nds).

FIGURE 28–5

*Pass-Through Securities,
June 4, 1998*

MORTGAGE-BACKED SECURITIES							
For indicative purposes, from Bear Stearns Cos./Street Pricing Service							
		PRICE (Jul) (Pts-32ds)	PRICE CHANGE (32ds)	AVG LIFE (years)	SPRD TO AVG LIFE (8ps)	SPREAD CHANGE	PSA (Prepay Speed)	YIELD TO MAT.*
30-YEAR								
FMAC GOLD	6.5%	99-13	– 01	9	108	unch	150	6.64%
FMAC GOLD	7.0%	101-12	– 01	7.8	122	unch	190	6.79
FMAC GOLD	7.5%	102-21	– 01	5.8	135	unch	265	6.91
FNMA	6.5%	99-09	– 01	9	107	unch	150	6.64
FNMA	7.0%	101-09	– 01	7.7	120	unch	190	6.77
FNMA	7.5%	102-22	– 01	5.8	129	– 1	265	6.86
GNMA	6.5%	99-13	– 01	9.5	107	– 1	130	6.64
GNMA	7.0%	101-13	– 01	8.9	124	– 1	150	6.81
GNMA	7.5%	102-28	– 01	7.4	141	– 1	195	6.98
15-YEAR								
FMAC GOLD	6.0%	98-28	– 01	5.5	71	– 1	160	6.28%
FNMA	6.0%	98-24	– 01	5.5	70	– 1	160	6.27
GNMA	6.0%	99-06	– 01	5.6	64	– 1	150	6.21

*Extrapolated from benchmarks based on projections from Bear Stearns prepayment model, assuming interest rates remain unchanged. †-Price.

COLLATERALIZED MORTGAGE OBLIGATIONS

Spread of CMO yields above U.S. Treasury securities of comparable maturity, in basis points (100 basis points = 1 percentage point of interest)

MAT	SPREAD	CHG FROM PREV DAY
SEQUENTIALS		
2-year	66	unch
5-year	90	unch
10-year	114	unch
20-year	90	unch
PACS		
2-year	47	unch
5-year	70	unch
10-year	92	unch
20-year	76	unch
VNMA 953	1-E†	102-8
VNMA 961	1-E	100-4
VNMA 962	1-E	101-25

Source: *The Wall Street Journal,* June 4, 1998. Reprinted by permission of The Wall Street Journal, © 1995 Dow Jones & Company, Inc. All Rights Reserved Worldwide.

---

[11]FMAC (or Farmer MAC) stands for the Federal Agricultural Mortgage Corporation. FMAC is smaller than the three main mortgage sponsoring agencies (GNMA, FNMA, and FHLMC) and specializes in agricultural mortgages.

Professional Perspectives

THE MORTGAGE PREPAYMENT OPTION

Prafulla G. Nabar, Ph.D.
Lehman Brothers

The pricing of the prepayment option distinguishes the process of valuation for mortgage-backed securities (MBSs) from that for other fixed income securities such as Treasuries. The prepayment option allows the mortgagee to prepay the mortgage, either partly or fully, at any time during its life. The investor in the MBS thus holds a short position in the prepayment option and a long position in the fixed income security whose cash flows consist of the monthly payments on the underlying mortgages.

At Lehman Brothers, the valuation of the prepayment option begins with the estimation of prepayment probabilities, using our prepayment model, for each of the future months through the life of the MBS. In our prepayment model, prepayments are considered to be caused by either housing turnover or mortgage refinancing. Housing turnover, which results from the sale of the house or default on the mortgage, is modeled as a function of a seasoning curve, seasonality and activity in the housing market. The seasoning curve is based on the premise that up to a certain mortgage age, the newer a mortgage the lesser the propensity to prepay it. Seasonality accounts for the fact that

people tend to change houses more during certain months of the year. Housing market activity captures the effect of the economic conditions and the supply of new housing. Refinancing takes into account the mortgagee's incentive to refinance the mortgage. This incentive depends on the mortgage rate prevailing in the market at each point in time. In addition, it depends on the slope of the yield curve since mortgage holders have an incentive to refinance into mortgages of lesser maturities at lower rates that depend on the slope of the yield curve. Refinancing also accounts for the burnout of a pool of mortgages are measured by the reluctance shown by mortgagees in that pool to refinance their mortgages in the past. The prepayment probabilities are then used to compute the expected cash flows from the MBS to be used in the valuation of the security.

Biographical Summary

Prafulla G. Nabar is a Senior Analyst with Lehman Brothers. Before joining Lehman Brothers, he taught at New York University and Southern Methodist University.

Column (4) shows the weighted-average life of the bond reflecting an assumed prepayment schedule. This weighted-average life is not the same as duration, which measures the weighted-average time to maturity based on the relative present values of cash flows as weights. Instead, it is a significant simplification of the duration measure seeking to concentrate on the expected timing of payments of principal. Technically, **weighted-average life (WAL)** is measured by

Weighted-Average Life (WAL)
The product of the time when principal payments are received and the amount of principal received divided by total principal outstanding.

$$WAL = \frac{\Sigma \text{ Time} \times \text{Expected principal received}}{\text{Total principal outstanding}}$$

For example, consider a loan with two years to maturity and $100 million in principal. Investors expect $40 million of the principal to be repaid at the end of year 1 and the remaining $60 million to be repaid at maturity.

Time	Expected Principal Payments	Time × Principal
1	$ 40	$ 40
2	60	120
	$100	$160

$$WAL = \frac{160}{100} = 1.6 \text{ years}$$

As you can see from Figure 28–5, the *WALs* of these pools are all 9.5 years or less. The fifth and sixth columns show the yield spread of mortgage-backed securities over Treasuries and its daily change. The yield spread shown here is the spread to average life, while the more complicated (and most used) is the option-adjusted spread (OAS), which is explained in detail later.

The OAS can be calculated by using the yield to maturity in the final column [column (8)] and deducting from this the yield on a matched maturity Treasury bond. The yield to maturity in the final column is calculated according to prepayment behavior estimated and valued by Bear Stearns, the investment bank. As will be discussed later, allowing for prepayment behavior, the bond is valued and its yield calculated using an explicit prepayment "option" model. This is only one way to calculate the prepayment behavior of mortgagees and the effects of their behavior on yields. Two alternative ways of modeling prepayment behavior are (1) the Public Securities Association (PSA) model approach and (2) the empirical model approach. These two approaches are discussed in the next section, along with the option-based approach.

PSA Model.   The prepayment model developed by the Public Securities Association is an empirically based model that reflects an average rate of prepayment based on the past experience of pools of FHA-insured mortgages.

Essentially, the PSA model assumes that the prepayment rate starts at 0.2 percent (per annum) in the first month, increasing by 0.2 percent per month for the first 30 months, until the annualized prepayment rate reaches 6 percent. This model assumes that the prepayment rate then levels off at a 6 percent annualized rate for the remaining life of the pool[12] (see Figure 28–6). Issuers or investors who assume that their mortgage pool prepayments exactly match this pattern are said to assume 100 percent PSA behavior. Realistically, the actual prepayment rate on any specific mortgage pool backing a specific pass-through security may differ from PSA's assumed pattern for general and economic reasons, including:

1. The level of the pool's coupon relative to the current mortgage coupon rate (the weighted-average coupon).
2. The age of the mortgage pool.
3. Whether the payments are fully amortized.
4. Assumability of mortgages in the pool.
5. Size of the pool.
6. Conventional or nonconventional mortgages (FHA/VA).
7. Geographic location.
8. Age and job status of mortgagees in the pool.

One approach would be to approximately control for these factors by assuming some fixed deviation of any specific pool from PSA's assumed average or benchmark pattern. For example, one pool may be assumed to be 75 percent PSA, and another 125 percent PSA. The former has a slower prepayment rate than historically experienced; the latter, a faster rate. Note these values in Figure 28–7 relative to 100 percent PSA. In column (7) of Figure 28–5 it can be seen that FMAC gold, 6.5 percent 30-year bonds have a PSA of 150. That is, they are expected to prepay at a rate

---

[12]Or, after month 30, prepayments are made at approximately ½ percent per *month*.

FIGURE 28–6

PSA Prepayment Model

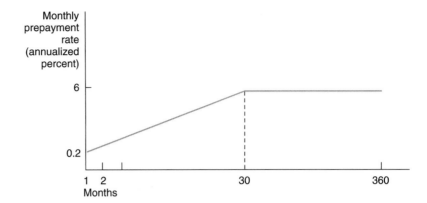

FIGURE 28–7

*Deviations from
100 Percent PSA*

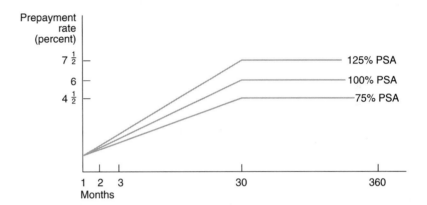

of 50 percent faster than that normally experienced for 30-year mortgage-backed securities. This is because interest rates on new mortgages in June 1998 were well below historic levels.

Other Empirical Models.   FIs that are trading, dealing, and issuing pass-throughs have also developed their own proprietary empirical models of prepayment behavior to get a pricing edge on other issuers/investors. Clearly, the FI that can develop the best, most accurate, prepayment model stands to make large profits either in originating and issuing such bonds or in trading such instruments in the secondary market. As a wide variety of empirical models have been developed, we briefly look at the types of methodology followed.

Specifically, most empirical models are proprietary versions of the PSA model in which FIs make their own estimates of the pattern of monthly prepayments. From this modeling exercise, an FI can estimate either the fair price or the fair yield on the pass-through. Of course, those FIs that make the most profits from buying and selling pass-throughs over time are the ones that have most accurately predicted actual prepayment behavior.

In constructing an empirical valuation model, FIs begin by estimating a prepayment function from observing the experience of mortgage holders prepaying during any particular period on mortgage pools similar to the one to be valued. This is conditional, of course, on the mortgages not having been prepaid prior to that period. These conditional prepayment rates in month $i(p_i)$ for similar pools would be modeled as functions of the important economic variables driving prepayment—for

FIGURE 28–8

*Estimated Prepayment
Function for a Given Pool*

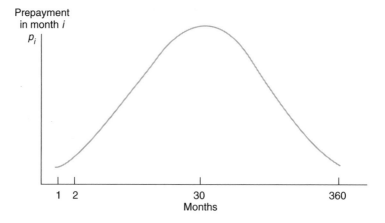

Burn-Out Factor
The aggregate percent
of the mortgage pool
that has been prepaid
prior to the month
under consideration.

example, $p_i = f$ (mortgage rate spread, age, collateral, geographic factors, **burn-out factor**). This modeling should take into account the idiosyncratic factors affecting this specific pool, such as its age and burn-out factor, as well as market factors affecting prepayments in general, such as the mortgage rate spread.[13]

Once the frequency distribution of the p_i's is estimated, as shown in Figure 28–8, the bank can calculate the expected cash flows on the mortgage pool under consideration and estimate its fair yield given the current market price of the pool.[14]

The next subsection is starred (*) and is left as reading for those interested in the finer points of theoretically modeling prepayment behavior.

Option Models.*   The third class of models uses option pricing theory to figure the fair yield on pass-throughs [see column (8) in Figure 28–5] and, in particular, the fair yield spread of pass-throughs over Treasuries. These so-called option-adjusted spread (OAS) models focus on the prepayment risk of pass-throughs as the essential determinant of the required yield spread of pass-through bonds over Treasuries. As such, they are open to the criticism that they fail to properly include nonrefinancing incentives to prepay and the variety of transaction costs and recontracting cost involved in refinancing. Recent research has tried to integrate the option model approach with the empirical model approach.[15]

Stripped to its basics, the option model views the fair price on a pass-through such as a GNMA as being decomposable into two parts:[16]

$$P_{GNMA} = P_{TBOND} - P_{PREPAYMENT\ OPTION}$$

---

[13]A burn-out factor is a summary measure of a pool's prepayments in total prior to month *i*. As such, it is meant to capture heterogeneity of prepayment behavior within any given pool rather than between pools. See E. S. Schwartz and W. N. Tourous, "Prepayment and the Valuation of Mortgage-Backed Securities," *Journal of Finance* 44 (1989), pp. 375–92.

[14]A commonly used empirical model is the proportional hazards model. This model produces a prepayment function similar to that in Figure 28–8 where, other things being equal, conditional prepayment rates are typically low in the early years of a mortgage, increase as the age of the mortgage increases, and then diminish with further seasoning (see Schwartz and Tourous, "Prepayment").

[15]See J. P. Kau et al., "A Generalized Valuation Model for Fixed-Rate Residential Mortgages," *Journal of Money, Credit and Banking* 24 (1992); and W. Archer and D. C. Ling, "Pricing Mortgage-Backed Securities: Should Contingent-Claim Models Be Abandoned for Empirical Models of Prepayments?" paper presented at the AFA Conference, Anaheim, California, January 1993.

[16]For an excellent review of these option models, see Spahr and Sunderman, "The Effect of Prepayment Modeling," ibid.

That is, the value of a GNMA bond to an investor (P_{GNMA}) is equal to the value of a standard noncallable Treasury bond of the same duration (P_{TBOND}) minus the value of the mortgage holder's prepayment call option ($P_{PREPAYMENT\ OPTION}$). Specifically, the ability of the mortgage holder to prepay is equivalent to the bond investor writing a call option on the bond and the mortgagee owning or buying the option. If interest rates fall, the option becomes more valuable as it moves into the money and more mortgages are prepaid early by having the bond called or the prepayment option exercised. This relationship can also be thought of in the yield dimension:

$$Y_{GNMA} = Y_{TBOND} + Y_{OPTION}$$

The investors' required yield on a GNMA should equal the yield on a similar duration T-bond plus an additional yield for writing the valuable call option. That is, the fair yield spread or **option-adjusted spread (OAS)** between GNMAs and T-bonds should reflect the value of this option.

Option-Adjusted Spread (OAS)
The required interest spread of a pass-through security over a Treasury when prepayment risk is taken into account.

To gain further insights into the option model approach and the OAS, we can develop an example along the lines of S. D. Smith showing how to calculate the value of the option-adjusted spread on GNMAs.[17] To do this, we make a number of simplifying assumptions indicative of the restrictive nature of many of these models:

1. The only reasons for prepayment are due to refinancing mortgages at lower rates; there is no prepayment for turnover reasons.

2. The current discount (zero-coupon) yield curve for T-bonds is flat (this could be relaxed).

3. The mortgage coupon rate is 10 percent on an outstanding pool of mortgages with an outstanding principal balance of $1,000,000.

4. The mortgages have a three-year maturity and pay principal and interest only once at the end of each year. Of course, real-world models would have 15- or 30-year maturities and pay interest and principal monthly. These assumptions are made for simplification purposes only.

5. Mortgage loans are fully amortized, and there is no servicing fee: again, this could be relaxed.

Thus, the annual fully amortized payment under no prepayment conditions is

$$R = \frac{1,000,000}{\left[\dfrac{1 - \dfrac{1}{(1 + .10)^3}}{.1}\right]} = \frac{1,000,000}{2.48685} = \$402,114$$

In a world without prepayments, no default risk, and current mortgage rates (y) of 9 percent, we would have the GNMA bond selling at a premium over par:

$$P_{GNMA} = \frac{R}{(1 + y)} + \frac{R}{(1 + y)^2} + \frac{R}{(1 + y)^3}$$

$$P_{GNMA} = \frac{\$402,114}{(1.09)} + \frac{\$402,114}{(1.09)^2} + \frac{\$402,114}{(1.09)^3}$$

$$P_{GNMA} = 1,017,869$$

---

[17]S. D. Smith, Analyzing Risk and Return for Mortgage-Backed Securities," Federal Reserve Bank of Atlanta, *Economic Review,* January–February 1991, pp. 2–11.

6. Because of prepayment penalties and other refinancing costs, mortgagees do not begin to prepay until mortgage rates, in any year, fall 3 percent or more below the mortgage coupon rate for the pool (10 percent in this example).

7. Interest rate movements over time change a maximum of 1 percent up or down each year. The time path of interest rates follows a binomial process.

8. With prepayments present, cash flows in any year can be the promised payment $R = \$402,114$, the promised payment ($R$) plus repayment of any outstanding principal, or zero if all mortgages have been prepaid or paid off in the previous year.

In Figure 28–9 we show the assumed time path of interest rates over the three years with associated probabilities (p).

End of Year 1.   Since rates can change up or down by only 1 percent per annum, the farthest they can be expected to fall in the first year is to 8 percent. At this level, no mortgage holder would prepay since any mortgage rate savings would be offset by the penalty costs of prepayment, that is, by the assumption it is worth prepaying only when the mortgage rate falls at least 3 percent below its coupon rate.

As a result, the GNMA pass-through investor could expect to receive $R = \$402,114$ with certainty. Thus, $CF_1 = \$402,114$.

End of Year 2.   In year 2, there are three possible mortgage interest rate scenarios. However, the only one that triggers prepayment is when mortgage rates fall to 7 percent (3 percent below the 10 percent mortgage coupon rate of the pool). According to Figure 28–9, this occurs with only a 25 percent probability. If prepayment does not occur with 75 percent probability, the investor receives $R = \$402,114$. If prepayment occurs with 25 percent probability, the investor receives:

$$R + \text{Principal balance remaining at end of year 2}$$

FIGURE 28–9

*Mortgage Rate Changes:
Assumed Time Path*

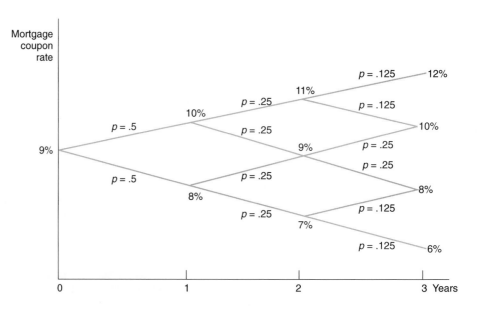

We can calculate the principal balance remaining at the end of year 2 as follows. At the end of the first year, we divide the amortized payment, $R = \$402,114$, into a payment of interest and a payment of principal. With a 10 percent mortgage coupon rate, the payment of interest component would be $.10 \times \$1,000,000 = \$100,000$, and the repayment of principal component $= \$402,114 - \$100,000 = \$302,114$. Thus, at the beginning of the second year, there would be $\$1,000,000 - \$302,114 = \$697,886$ principal outstanding. At the end of the second year, the promised amortized payment of $R = \$402,114$ can be broken down to an interest component 10 percent $\times \$697,886 = \$69,788.6$ and a principal component amount of $\$402,114 - \$69,788.6 = \$332,325.4$, leaving a principal balance at the end of year 2 of $\$1,000,000 - \$302,114 - \$332,325.4 = \$365,560.6$.

Consequently, if yields fall to 7 percent, the cash flow received by the investor in year 2 would be

$$R + \text{Principal balance outstanding at end of year 2} =$$
$$\$402,114 + \$365,560.6 = \$767,674.6$$

Thus, expected cash flows at the end of year 2 would be

$$CF_2 = .25(\$767,674.6) + .75(\$402,114)$$
$$= \$191,918.64 + \$301,585.5$$
$$= \$493,504.15$$

End of Year 3.   Since there is a 25 percent probability that mortgages will be prepaid in year 2, there must be a 25 percent probability that the investor will receive no cash flows at the end of year 3 since mortgage holders owe nothing in this year if all mortgages have already been paid off early in year 2. However, there is also a 75 percent probability that mortgages will not be prepaid at the end of year 2. Thus, at the end of year 3 (maturity), the investor has a 75 percent probability of receiving the promised amortized payment $R = \$402,114$. The expected cash flow in year 3 is

$$CF_3 = .25(0) + .75(\$402,114) = \$301,585.5$$

Derivation of the Option-Adjusted Spread.   As just discussed, we conceptually divide the required yield on a GNMA, or other pass-throughs, with prepayment risk, into the required yield on T-bonds plus a required spread for the prepayment call option given to the mortgage holders:

$$P = \frac{E(CF_1)}{(1 + d_1 + O_S)} + \frac{E(CF_2)}{(1 + d_2 + O_S)^2} + \frac{E(CF_3)}{(1 + d_3 + O_S)^3}$$

where

P = Price of GNMA
d_1 = Discount rate on one-year, zero-coupon Treasury bonds
d_2 = Discount rate on two-year, zero-coupon Treasury bonds
d_3 = Discount rate on three-year, zero-coupon Treasury bonds
O_S = Option-adjusted spread on GNMA

Assume that the T-bond yield curve is flat, so that

$$d_1 = d_2 = d_3 = 8\%$$

We can now solve for O_S:

$$1{,}017{,}869 = \frac{\$402{,}114}{(1 + .08 + O_S)} + \frac{\$493{,}504}{(1 + .08 + O_S)^2} + \frac{\$301{,}585.5}{(1 + .08 + O_S)^3}$$

Solving for O_S, we find that

$$O_S = 0.96\% \text{ (to two decimal places)}$$
$$Y_{GNMA} = Y_{TBOND} + O_S$$
$$= 8\% + 0.96\%$$
$$= 8.96\%$$

You can see that when prepayment risk is present, the expected cash flow yield at 8.96 percent is 4 basis points less than the required 9 percent yield on the GNMA when no prepayment occurs. The slightly lower yield results because the positive effects of early prepayment (such as earlier payment of principal) dominate the negative effects (such as loss of interest payments). Note, however, that this result might well be reversed if we altered our assumptions by allowing a wider dispersion of possible interest rate changes and having heavier penalties for prepayment.

Nevertheless, the option-adjusted spread approach is useful for FI managers in that they can place lower bounds on the yields they are willing to accept on GNMA and other pass-through securities before they place them in their portfolios. Realistically, some account has to be taken of nonrefinancing prepayment behavior and patterns; otherwise significant mispricing may occur.

Concept Questions

1. Should an FI with $D_A < kD_L$ seek to securitize its assets? Why or why not?
2. In general terms, discuss the three approaches developed by analysts to model prepayment behavior.
3. In the context of the option model approach, list three ways in which transaction and other contracting costs are likely to interfere with the accuracy of its predictions regarding the fair price or interest spread on a pass-through security.

The Collateralized Mortgage Obligation (CMO)

While pass-throughs are still the primary mechanism for securitization, the CMO is a second and growing vehicle for securitizing bank assets. Innovated in 1983 by the FHLMC and First Boston, the CMO is a device for making mortgage-backed securities more attractive to investors. The CMO does this by repackaging the cash flows from mortgages and pass-through securities in a different fashion to attract different types of investors. While a pass-through security gives each investor a pro rata share of any promised and prepaid cash flows on a mortgage pool, the CMO is a multiclass pass-through with a number of different bondholder classes or tranches. Unlike a pass-through, each bondholder class has a different guaranteed coupon just like a regular T-bond; more important, the allocation of early cash flows due to mortgage prepayments is such that at any one time, all prepayments go to retiring the principal outstanding of only one class of bondholders, leaving the other classes' prepayment protected for a period of time.

CMO
Collateralized mortgage obligation is a mortgage-backed bond issued in multiple classes or tranches.

Creation of CMOs

CMOs can be created either by packaging and securitizing whole mortgage loans or, more usually, by placing existing pass-throughs in a trust off the balance sheet.

The trust or third-party bank holds the GNMA pass-through as collateral and issues new CMO securities. The trust issues these CMOs in 3 to 17 different classes. We show a three-class or tranche CMO in Figure 28–10.

As you can see, issuing CMOs is often equivalent to double securitization. Mortgages are packaged, and a GNMA pass-through is issued. An investment bank such as Goldman Sachs or another CMO issuer such as FHLMC, a commercial bank, or a savings bank may buy this whole issue or a large part of the issue. Goldman Sachs would then place these GNMA securities as collateral with a trust and issue three new classes of bonds backed by the GNMA securities as collateral.[18] As a result, the investors in each CMO class have a sole claim to the GNMA collateral if the issuer fails. The investment bank or other issuer creates the CMO to make a profit, by repackaging the cash flows from the single-class GNMA pass-through into cash flows more attractive to different groups of investors. The sum of the prices at which the three CMO bond classes can be sold normally exceeds that of the original pass-through:

$$\sum_{i=1}^{3} P_{i,CMO} > P_{GNMA}$$

To understand the gains from repackaging, you must understand how CMOs restructure prepayment risk to make it more attractive to different classes of investors. We explain this in the following simple example.

The Value Additivity of CMOs

Suppose an investment bank buys a $150 million issue of GNMAs and places them in trust as collateral. It then issues a CMO with these three classes, which we also depict in Figure 28–11:

> Class A: Annual fixed coupon 7 percent, class size $50 million
> Class B: Annual fixed coupon 8 percent, class size $50 million
> Class C: Annual fixed coupon 9 percent, class size $50 million

FIGURE 28–10

The Creation of a CMO

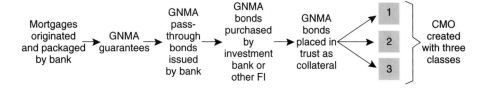

FIGURE 28–11

The Creation of a CMO

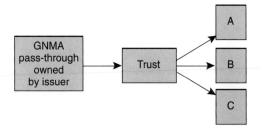

---

[18]These trusts are sometimes called REMICs, or real estate mortgage investment conduits.

Under a CMO, each class has a guaranteed or fixed coupon.[19] By restructuring the GNMA as a CMO, the bank can offer investors who buy bond class C a higher degree of mortgage prepayment protection compared to a pass-through. Those who buy class B receive an average degree of prepayment protection, and those who take class A receive virtually no prepayment protection.

Each month, mortgagees in the GNMA pool pay principal and interest on their mortgages; each payment includes the promised amortized amount (R) plus any additional payments as some of the mortgage holders prepay principal to refinance their mortgages or because they have sold their houses and are relocating. These cash flows are passed through to the owner of the GNMA bonds, in our example Goldman Sachs. The CMO issuer uses the cash flows to pay promised coupon interest to the three classes of CMO bondholders. Suppose that in month 1 the promised amortized cash flows (R) on the mortgages underlying the GNMA pass-through collateral are $1 million but there is an additional $1.5 million cash flow as a result of early mortgage prepayments. Thus, the cash flows in the first month available to pay promised coupons to the three classes of bondholders would be

$$R + \text{Prepayments} = \$1 \text{ million} + \$1.5 \text{ million} = \$2.5 \text{ million}$$

This cash flow is available to the trustee, who uses it in the following fashion:

1. *Coupon payments.* Each month (or more commonly, each quarter or half year), the trustee pays out the guaranteed coupons to the three classes of bondholders at annualized coupon rates of 7 percent, 8 percent, and 9 percent, respectively. Given the stated principal of $50 million for each class, the class A (7 percent coupon) bondholders receive approximately $291,667 in coupon payments in month 1, the class B (8 percent coupon) receive approximately $333,333 in month 1, and the class C (9 percent coupon) receive approximately $375,000 in month 1. Thus, the total promised coupon payments to the three classes amount to $1,000,000 (equal to R, the no-prepayment cash flows in the GNMA pool).

2. *Principal payments.* The trustee has $2.5 million available to pay out as a result of promised mortgage payments plus early prepayments, but the total payment of coupon interest amounts to $1 million. For legal and tax reasons, the remaining $1.5 million has to be paid out to the CMO bondholders. The unique feature of the CMO is that the trustee would pay this remaining $1.5 million only to class A bondholders to retire these bondholders' principal. At the end of month 1, only $50 million − $1.5 = $48.5 million class A bonds would remain outstanding, compared to $50 million class B and $50 million class C. These payment flows are shown graphically in Figure 28–12.

Let's suppose that in month 2 the same thing happens. The cash flows from the mortgage/GNMA pool exceed the promised coupon payments to the three classes of bondholders. Again, the trustee uses any excess cash flows to pay off or retire the principal of class A bondholders. If the excess cash flows again amount to $1.5 million, at the end of month 2 there will be only $48.5 − $1.5 = $47 million of class A bonds outstanding.

Given any positive flow of prepayments, it is clear that within a few years the class A bonds will be fully retired. In practice, this often occurs between 1.5 and 3 years after issue. After the trustee retires class A, only classes B and C remain.

---

[19]In some cases, coupons are paid monthly, in others quarterly, and in still others semiannually.

FIGURE 28–12

Allocation of Cash Flows to Owners of CMO Tranches

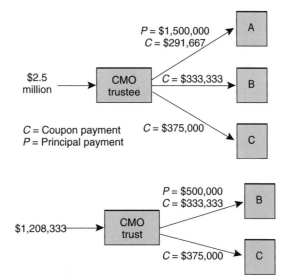

FIGURE 28–13

Allocation of Cash Flows to Remaining Tranches of CMO Bonds

As before, out of any cash flows received from the mortgage/GNMA pool, the trustee pays the bondholders their guaranteed coupons, C_B = \$333,333 and C_C = \$375,000 for a total of \$708,333. Suppose that total cash flows received by the trustee are \$1,208,333 in the first month after the total retirement of class A bonds, reflecting amortized mortgage payments by the remaining mortgagees in the pool plus any new prepayments. The excess cash flows of \$1,208,333 − \$708,333 = \$500,000 then go to retire the principal outstanding of CMO bond class B. At the end of that month, there are only \$49.5 million class B bonds outstanding. This is shown graphically in Figure 28–13.

As the months pass, the trustee will use any excess cash flows over and above the promised coupons to class B and C bondholders to retire bond class B's principal. Eventually, all of the \$50 million principal on class B bonds will be retired—in practice, five to seven years after CMO issue. After class B bonds are retired, all remaining cash flows will be dedicated to paying the promised coupon of class C bondholders and retiring the \$50 million principal on class C bonds. In practice, class C bonds can have an average life as long as 20 years.

Class A, B, and C Bond Buyers

Class A. These bonds have the shortest average life with a minimum of prepayment protection. They are, therefore, of great interest to investors seeking short-duration mortgage-backed assets to reduce the duration length of their mortgage-related asset portfolios. In recent years savings banks and commercial banks have been large buyers of CMO class A securities.

Class B. These bonds have some prepayment protection and expected durations of five to seven years depending on the level of interest rates. Mostly pension funds and life insurance companies purchase these bonds, although some banks and thrifts buy this bond class as well.

Class C. Because of their long expected duration, they are highly attractive to insurance companies and pension funds seeking long-term duration assets to match their long-term duration liabilities. Indeed, because of their failures to offer prepayment protection, regular GNMA pass-throughs may not be very attractive to these institutions. Class C CMOs, with their high but imperfect degree of prepayment protection, may be of greater interest to the FI managers of these institutions.

In summary, by splitting bondholders into different classes and by restructuring cash flows into forms more valued by different investor clienteles, the CMO issuer stands to make a profit.

Other CMO Classes

CMOs can always have more than the three classes described in the previous example. Indeed, issues of up to 17 different classes have been made. Clearly, the 17th-class bondholders would have an enormous degree of prepayment protection since the first 16 classes would have had their bonds retired before the principal outstanding on this bond class would be affected by early prepayments. In addition, trustees have created other special types of classes as products to attract investor interest; we discuss these classes next.

Z Class
An accrual class of a CMO that makes a payment to bondholders only when preceding CMO classes have been retired.

Class Z.   Frequently, CMO issues contain a **Z class** as the last regular class. The Z implicitly stands for zero, but these are not really zero-coupon bonds. This class has a stated coupon such as 10 percent and accrues interest for the bondholder on a monthly basis at this rate. The trustee does not pay this interest, however, until all other classes of bonds are fully retired. When the other classes have been retired, the Z-class bondholder receives the promised coupon and principal payments plus accrued interest payments. Thus, the Z class has characteristics of both a zero-coupon bond (no coupon payments for a long period) and a regular bond.

R Class
The residual class of a CMO giving the owner the right to any remaining collateral in the trust after all other bond classes have been retired plus any reinvestment income earned by the trust.

Class R.   In placing the GNMA collateral with the trustee, the CMO issuer normally uses very conservative prepayment assumptions. If prepayments are slower than expected, there is often excess collateral left over in the pool when all regular classes have been retired. Further, trustees often reinvest funds or cash flows received from the underlying instrument (GNMA) in the period prior to paying interest on the CMOs. In general, the size of any excess collateral and interest on interest gets bigger when rates are high and the timing of coupon intervals is semiannual rather than monthly. This residual **R class** or "garbage class" is a high-risk investment class that gives the investor the rights to the overcollateralization and reinvestment income on the cash flows in the CMO trust. Because the value of the returns in this bond class increases when interest rates increase, while normal bond values fall with interest rate increases, class R often has a negative duration. Thus, it is potentially attractive to banks and thrifts seeking to hedge their regular bond and fixed-income portfolios.[20]

Consider the example of a CMO with classes A, B, C, Z, and R in Table 28–4. From Table 28–4, you can see that the underlying pass-through bond held as collateral is a FNMA 9.99 percent coupon bond with an original maturity of 30 years, an issue size of $500 million, and a prepayment rate assumed to be twice the size assumed by the PSA model (200 percent PSA). The five CMO bond classes are issued in different amounts, with the largest class being B. Note that the principal amounts of the five classes sum to $500 million.

---

[20]Negative duration implies that bond prices increase with interest rates; that is, the price–yield curve is positively sloped.

TABLE 28–4   CMO with Five Bond Classes
(in millions of dollars)

Fannie Mac REMIC Trust 1987-1

Collateral

Type	Coupon	Amount	Original Term	Average Remaining Term	Assumed Prepayment Rate
FNMA	9.99%	$500	360 months	349 months	200% PSA

Bonds

Class	A	B	C	Z	R
Amount	$150.9	$238.6	$85.5	$24.0	$1.0
Bond type	Fixed	Fixed	Fixed	Accrual	Residual
Coupon (percent)	7.95	9.35	9.60	9.99	503.88
Price	99.8099	99.3083	N/A	89.4978	1445.1121
Yield (bond equivalent)	7.85	9.55	N/A	10.86	10.30
Weighted-average life (years)	1.6	5.9	11.2	18.4	3.6
Benchmark Treasury (years)	2	5	N/A	20	N/A
Spread over Treasury (basis points)	15	125	N/A	180	N/A

Note: All data in this table are as of the pricing date (FNMA has retained Class C).
Pricing date: 8/18/87.
Accrual date: 9/01/87.
First payment: 10/25/87.
Payment frequency/Delay: Monthly pay, 25-day delay.
Source: GAO/GGD-88-111 (1988).

Concept Questions

1. Would thrifts or insurance companies prefer Z-class CMOs? Explain your answer.
2. Are Z-class CMOs exactly the same as T-bond strips? If not, why not?
3. In our example, the coupon on the class C bonds was assumed to be higher than that on the class B bonds and the coupon on class B bonds was assumed to be higher than that on class A bonds. Under what term structure conditions might this not be the case?

The Mortgage-Backed Bond (MBB)

Mortgage (Asset)-Backed Bonds
Bonds collateralized by a pool of assets.

Mortgage (asset)-backed bonds are the third asset-securitization vehicle. These bonds differ from pass-throughs and CMOs in two key dimensions. First, while pass-throughs and CMOs help banks and thrifts remove mortgages from their balance sheets as forms of off-balance-sheet securitization, mortgage-backed bonds (MBBs) normally remain on the balance sheet. Second, while pass-throughs and CMOs have a direct link between the cash flows on the underlying mortgages and the cash flows on the bond vehicles, with MBBs the relationship is one of collateralization—there is no direct link between the cash flow on the mortgages backing the bond and the interest and principal payments on the bond.

Essentially, an FI issues a MBB so that if the FI fails, the MBB bondholders have a first claim to a segment of the FI's mortgage assets. Practically speaking, the

TABLE 28–5   Balance Sheet of Potential MBB Issuer
(in millions of dollars)

Assets		Liabilities	
Long-term mortgages	$20	Insured deposits	$10
		Uninsured deposits	10
	$20		$20

FI segregates a group of mortgage assets on its balance sheet and pledges this group as collateral backing the bond issue. A trustee normally monitors the segregation of assets and makes sure that the market value of the collateral exceeds the principal owed to bondholders. That is, FIs back most MBB issues by excess collateral. This excess collateral backing of the bond, plus the priority rights of the bondholders, generally ensures that these bonds can be sold with a high credit rating such as AAA. In contrast, the FI when evaluated as a whole, could be rated BBB or even lower. A high credit rating results in lower coupon interest than is paid if default risk is significant (see Chapter 11). To explain the potential benefits to an FI from issuing MBBs and the sources of any gains, we examine the following simple example.

Consider a bank with $20 million in long-term mortgages as assets. It is financing these mortgages with $10 million in short-term uninsured deposits (wholesale deposits over $100,000) and $10 million in insured deposits (under $100,000 retail deposits). Here we ignore the issues of capital and reserve requirements. Look at the balance sheet structure in Table 28–5.

This balance sheet poses problems for the FI manager. First, the bank has a positive duration gap ($D_A > kD_L$). Second, because of this interest rate risk and the potential default risk on the bank's mortgage assets, uninsured depositors are likely to require a positive and potentially significant risk premium paid on their deposits. By contrast, the insured depositors may require approximately the risk-free rate on their deposits as they are fully insured by the FDIC (see Chapter 19).

To reduce its duration gap exposure and lower its funding costs, the bank might segregate $12 million of the mortgages on the asset side of its balance sheet and pledge them as collateral backing a $10 million long-term MBB issue. Because of this overcollateralization, the mortgage-backed bond issued by the bank may cost less to issue, in terms of required yield, than uninsured deposits; that is, it may well be rated AAA while uninsured deposits might be rated BBB. The FI can therefore use the proceeds of the $10 million bond issue to retire the $10 million of uninsured deposits.

Consider the bank's balance sheet after the issue of the MBBs in Table 28–6. It might seem that the bank has miraculously engineered a restructuring of its balance sheet that has resulted in a better matching of D_A to D_L and a lowering of funding costs. The bond issue has lengthened the average duration of liabilities by replacing short-term deposits and lowered funding costs as bond coupon rates are below uninsured deposit rates. However, this outcome occurs only because the $10 million insured depositors do not worry about risk exposure since they are 100 percent insured by the FDIC. The result of the MBB issue and the segregation of $12 million of assets as collateral backing the $10 million bond issue is that the $10 million insured deposits are now backed only by $8 million in free or unpledged assets. If smaller depositors weren't insured by the FDIC, they would surely demand very

TABLE 28–6   Bank's Balance Sheet after MBB Issue
(in millions of dollars)

Assets		Liabilities	
Collateral = (market value of segregated mortgages)	$12	MBB	$10
Other mortgages	8	Insured deposits	10
	$20		$20

high risk premiums to hold these risky deposits. The implication of this is that the bank gains only because the FDIC is willing to bear enhanced credit risk through its insurance guarantees to depositors.[21] As a result, the bank is really gaining at the expense of the FDIC. Consequently, it is not surprising that the FDIC is concerned about the growing use of this form of securitization by risky banks and thrifts.

Other than regulatory discouragement and the risk of regulatory intervention, there are private return reasons why a bank might prefer the pass-through/CMO forms of securitization to issuing MBBs. The first is that MBBs tie up mortgages on the bank's balance sheet for a long time. This increases the illiquidity of the asset portfolio. Second, the amount of mortgages tied up is enhanced by the need to overcollateralize to ensure a high-quality credit risk rating for the bond issue; in our example, the overcollateralization was $2 million. Third, by keeping the mortgages on the balance sheet, the bank continues to be liable for capital adequacy and reserve requirement taxes. Because of these problems, MBBs are the least used of the three basic vehicles of securitization.

Concept Question

1. Would a AAA FI ever issue mortgage-backed bonds? Explain your answer.

Innovations in Securitization

We now turn our attention to the growing innovations in FIs' asset securitization. We discuss two major innovations and their use in return-risk management by FIs: mortgage pass-through strips and the extension of the securitization concept to other assets.

Mortgage Pass-Through Strips

The mortgage pass-through strip is a special type of a CMO with only two classes. The fully amortized nature of mortgages means that any given monthly payment, *R,* contains an interest component and a principal component. Beginning in 1987, investment banks and other FI issuers stripped out the interest component from the principal component and sold each payment stream separately to different bond class investors. They sold an interest only (IO) class and a principal only (PO) class;

---

[21] And does not make the risk-based deposit insurance premium to banks and thrifts sufficiently large to reflect this risk.

FIGURE 28–14

IO/PO Strips

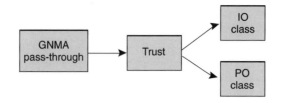

these two bond classes have very special cash flow characteristics, especially regarding the interest rate sensitivity of these bonds.

We show this stripping of the cash flows in Figure 28–14. We next consider the effects of interest rate changes on the value of each of these stripped instruments.

IO Strip
A bond sold to investors whose cash flows reflect the monthly interest payments received from a pool of mortgages.

IO Strips.   The owner of an **IO strip** has a claim to the present value of interest payments by the mortgagees in the GNMA pool, that is, to the IO segments of each month's cash flow received from the underlying mortgage pool:

$$P_{IO} = \frac{IO_1}{\left(1 + \dfrac{y}{12}\right)} + \frac{IO_2}{\left(1 + \dfrac{y}{12}\right)^2} + \frac{IO_3}{\left(1 + \dfrac{y}{12}\right)^3} + \ldots + \frac{IO_{360}}{\left(1 + \dfrac{y}{12}\right)^{360}}$$

When interest rates change, they affect the cash flows received on mortgages. We concentrate on two effects: the discount effect and the prepayment effect on the price or value of IOs, denoted by P_{IO}.

Discount Effect.   As interest rates (*y*) fall, the present value of any cash flows received on the strip—the IO payments—rises, increasing the value (P_{IO}) of the bond.

Prepayment Effect.   As interest rates fall, mortgagees prepay their mortgages. In absolute terms, the number of IO payments the investor receives is likely to shrink. For example, the investor might receive only 100 monthly IO payments instead of the expected 360 in a no-prepayment world. The shrinkage in the size and value of IO payments reduces the value (P_{IO}) of the bond.

Specifically, one can expect that as interest rates continue to fall below the mortgage coupon rate of the bonds in the pool, the prepayment effect gradually dominates the discount effect, so that over some range the price or value of the IO bond falls as interest rates fall. Note the price-yield curve in Figure 28–15 for an IO strip on a pass-through bond with 10 percent mortgage coupon rates.

Negative Duration
When the price of a bond increases or decreases as yields increase or decrease.

The price-yield curve slopes upward in the interest rate range below 10 percent. This means that as current interest rates rise or fall, IO values or prices rise or fall. As a result, the IO is a rare example of a **negative duration** asset that is very valuable as a portfolio-hedging device for an FI manager when included with regular bonds whose price-yield curves show the normal inverse relationship. That is, while as interest rates rise the value of the regular bond portfolio falls, the value of an IO portfolio may rise. Note in Figure 28–15 that at rates above the pool's mortgage coupon of 10 percent, the price-yield curve changes shape and tends to perform like any regular bond. In recent years, thrifts have been major purchasers of IOs to hedge the interest rate risk on the mortgages and other bonds held as assets in their portfolios. We depict the hedging power of IOs in Figure 28–16.

PO Strip
A bond sold to investors whose cash flows reflect the monthly principal payments received from a pool of mortgages.

PO Strips.   We consider next the **PO strip,** whose value (P_{PO}) is defined by

FIGURE 28–15

*Price-Yield Curve of a
10 Percent Strip*

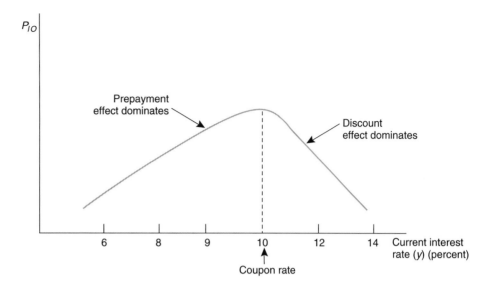

FIGURE 28–16

Hedging with 10s

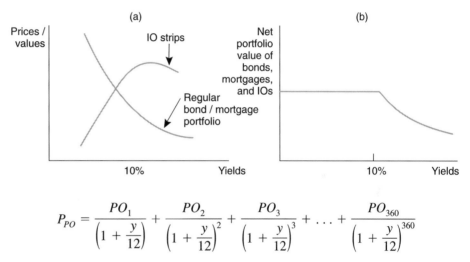

$$P_{PO} = \frac{PO_1}{\left(1 + \dfrac{y}{12}\right)} + \frac{PO_2}{\left(1 + \dfrac{y}{12}\right)^2} + \frac{PO_3}{\left(1 + \dfrac{y}{12}\right)^3} + \dots + \frac{PO_{360}}{\left(1 + \dfrac{y}{12}\right)^{360}}$$

where the PO_i represents the mortgage principal components of each monthly payment by the mortgage holders. This includes both the monthly amortized payment component of R that is principal, and any early prepayments of principal by the mortgagees. Again, we consider the effects on a PO's value (P_{PO}) of a change in interest rates.

Discount Effect.   As yields (y) fall, the present value of any principal payments must increase and the value of the PO strip rises.

Prepayment Effect.   As yields fall, the mortgage holders pay off principal early. Consequently, the PO bondholder receives the fixed principal balance outstanding on the pool of mortgages earlier than stated. Thus, this prepayment effect must also work to increase the value of the PO strip.

   As interest rates fall, both the discount and prepayment effects point to a rise in the value of the PO strip. The price-yield curve reflects an inverse relationship, but with a steeper slope than for normal bonds; that is, PO strip bond values are very

FIGURE 28–17

*Price-Yield Curve of a
PO Strip*

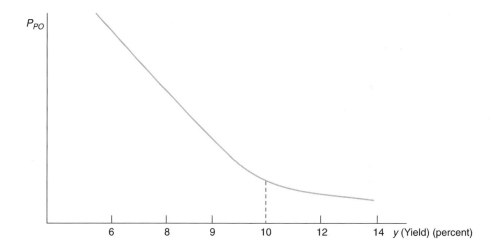

interest rate sensitive, especially for yields below the stated mortgage coupon rate. We show this in Figure 28–17 for a 10 percent PO strip. (Note that a regular coupon bond is affected only by the discount effect.) As you can see, when yields fall below 10 percent, the market value or price of the PO strip can increase very fast. At rates above 10 percent, it tends to behave like a regular bond (as the incentive to prepay disappears).

The IO–PO strip is a classic example of financial engineering. From a given GNMA pass-through bond, two new bonds have been created: the first with an upward-sloping price-yield curve over some range and the second with a steeply downward-sloping price-yield curve over some range. Each class is attractive to different investors and investor segments. The IO is attractive to thrifts and banks as on-balance-sheet hedging vehicles. The PO is attractive to financial institutions that wish to increase the interest rate sensitivity of their portfolios and to investors or traders who wish to take a naked or speculative position regarding the future course of interest rates. This high and complex interest sensitivity has resulted in major traders such as J. P. Morgan and Merrill Lynch, as well as many investors such as hedge funds, to suffer considerable losses on their investments in these instruments when interest rates have moved unexpectedly against them.

Securitization of Other Assets

While the major use of the three securitization vehicles—pass-throughs, CMOs, and mortgage-backed bonds—has been in packaging fixed-rate mortgage assets, these techniques can and have been used for other assets, including:

> Automobile loans.
> Credit card receivables (certificates of amortizing revolving debts).
> Small business loans guaranteed by the Small Business Administration.
> Junk bonds.
> Adjustable rate mortgages.
> Commercial and industrial loans (collateralized loan obligations (CLOs)).

Certificates of amortizing revolving debts are examples of securitizing assets other than mortgages. This securitization process is discussed in more detail next.

FIGURE 28–18

The Structure of a Credit Card Securitization

CARDs

Asset-backed securities backed by credit card receivables.

Certificates of Amortizing Revolving Debts (CARDs).   A good example is Chase which is a major sponsor of credit cards. Rather than holding all credit card receivables until they pay off, the bank segregates a set of receivables and sells them to an off-balance-sheet trust. (Chase retains the role of servicing the credit card pool, including collection, administration, and bookkeeping of the underlying credit card accounts.) As an example, it recently sold $280 million receivables to a trust. The trust in turn issued asset-backed securities (**CARDs**) in which investors had a pro rata claim on the cash flows from the credit card receivables. As the trust received payments on the credit card receivables each month, they were passed through to the bondholders. In practice, bonds of a lesser principal amount than the $280 million credit card pool are issued. In this example, $250 million in bonds were issued, with the difference—$30 million—being a claim retained by Chase. The reason for this is that credit card holders can either increase or repay their credit card balances at any time. The risk of variations in principal outstanding and thus collateral for the bonds is borne solely by the bank (i.e., the $30 million component), while the investors' collateral claim remains at $250 million until maturity unless a truly exceptional rate of debt repayment occurs. Indeed, Chase's segment is structured to bear even the most extreme cases of early repayment of credit card debts.

We show this credit card example in Figure 28–18. It is clear from the figure that this securitization of credit card assets is very similar in technology to the pass-through mortgage bond.

Concept Questions

1. Would an FI with $D_A < kD_L$ be interested in buying an IO strip for hedging purposes?
2. To which investors or investor segments is the IO attractive? To which investors or investor segments is the PO attractive? Explain your answer.

Can All Assets Be Securitized?

The extension of securitization technology to other assets raises questions about the limits of securitization and whether all assets and loans can be securitized. Conceptually the answer is that they can, as long as it is profitable to do so or the benefits to the FI from securitization outweigh the costs of securitization.[22] In Table 28–7, we summarize the benefits versus the costs of securitization.

From Table 28–7, given any set of benefits, the more costly and difficult it is to find asset packages of sufficient size and homogeneity, the more difficult and expensive it is to securitize. For example, commercial and industrial (C&I) loans have maturities running from a few months up to eight years; further, they have varying interest rate terms (fixed, LIBOR floating, federal funds–rate floating) and fees. In addition, they contain differing covenants and are made to firms in a wide variety of

---

[22]See C. Pavel, "Securitization," Federal Reserve Bank of Chicago, *Economic Perspectives*, 1985, pp. 16–31.

TABLE 28–7   Benefits versus Costs of Securitization

Benefits	Costs
1. New funding source (bonds versus deposits)	1. Cost of public/private credit risk insurance and guarantees
2. Increased liquidity of bank loans	2. Cost of overcollateralization
3. Enhanced ability to manage the duration gap $(D_A - kD_L)$	3. Valuation and packaging costs (the cost of asset heterogeneity)
4. If off balance sheet, the issuer saves on reserve requirements, deposit insurance premiums, and capital adequacy requirements	

industries. Despite this, banks and FIs have still been able to issue securitization packages called CLOs (collateralized loan obligations) containing high-quality low–default risk loans. Indeed, the volume of CLO issues has grown from $5 billion in 1996 to over $50 billion in 1998.[23] By contrast, it has been much harder to securitize low-quality loans. The Contemporary Perspectives box on p. 701 explains how and why National Westminster Bank securitized over $5 billion in high-quality commercial loans. Specifically, the harder it is to value a loan or asset pool, the greater the costs of securitization due to the need for overcollateralization or credit risk insurance. Thus, the potential boundary to securitization may well be defined by the relative degree of heterogeneity and credit quality of an asset type or group. It is not surprising that 30-year fixed-rate residential mortgages were the first assets to be securitized since they are the most homogeneous of all assets in bank balance sheets. For example, the existence of secondary markets for houses provides price information that allows for reasonably accurate market valuations of the underlying asset to be made, and extensive data are available on mortgage default rates by locality.

Concept Question

1. Can all assets and loans be securitized? Explain your answer.

Summary

In Chapter 6 we distinguished between FIs that are asset transformers and those that are asset brokers. By becoming increasingly reliant on securitization, banks and thrifts are moving away from being asset transformers that originate and hold assets to maturity; they are becoming asset brokers more reliant on servicing and other fees. This makes banks and thrifts look more similar to securities firms. Thus, over time, we can expect the traditional financial technology differences between commercial (and savings) banking and investment banking to diminish as more loans and assets are securitized. Three major forms of securitization—pass-through securities, collateralized mortgage obligations (CMOs), and mortgage-backed bonds—were discussed. Also, the impact of prepayment behavior on MBS valuation was discussed. Finally, recent innovations in securitization were described.

---

[23]See, for example, L. R. Quinn, "Slicing Up Bank Loans," *Investment Dealers Digest,* December 22, 1997, pp. 12–17.

Contemporary Perspectives

NATWEST TURNS $5BN CORPORATE LOANS INTO SECURITIES

John Gapper and Samer Iskandar

National Westminster Bank, the UK's largest bank, will to-day announce that it intends to remove $5bn of corporate loans from its balance sheet by transforming them into se-curities that will be sold to international investors.

The deal, involving loans to 300 large companies in the US and Europe, is the first of its kind in Europe. It could lead to other banks passing their earnings from corporate loans to investors in this way, rather than tying up their capital to back the loans.

Competition has forced down the rate of interest that banks earn on loans to large companies to low levels. However, banks do not want to half such lending, because it helps them gain other types of earnings from companies.

Banks have been reluctant to transform loans into bonds and other securities—a technique called "securitisa-tion"—until now, for fear of upsetting companies. How-ever, NatWest argues its customers will accept its decision.

Mr. Martin Owen, the chief executive of NatWest Mar-kets, the investment banking arm of NatWest, described the offering as a "golden scenario." He said that it would free the bank's capital, and offer investors valuable securities. "The conundrum we have solved is to transfer a loan with-out jeopardising a relationship," he said. NatWest would re-main in charge of administering the loans, and its customers would not notice any difference in how they were handled. By transforming $5bn of loans—which is about a third of NatWest's general loans to large companies—the bank will be able to free up about $390m of capital.

Source: *Financial Times,* September 25, 1996. Reprinted with per-mission from the September 25, 1996 issue of Financial Times.

Questions and Problems

1. What has been the effect of securitization on the asset portfolios of financial institutions?

2. What are the primary functions of GNMA? What is tim-ing insurance?

3. How does FNMA differ from GNMA?

4. How does FHLMC differ from FNMA? How are they the same?

5. What three levels of regulatory taxes do FIs face when making loans? How does securitization reduce the levels of taxation?

6. An FI is planning to issue $100 million in commercial loans. The FI will finance the loans by issuing demand deposits.

   a. What is the minimum amount of capital required by the Basle accord?

   b. What is the minimum amount of demand deposits needed to fund this loan assuming there is a 10 percent average reserve requirement on demand deposits?

   c. Show a simple balance sheet with total assets, total lia-bilities, and equity if this is the only project funded by the bank.

   d. How does this balance sheet differ from Table 28–1? Why?

7. Consider the FI in problem (6).

   a. What additional risk exposure problems does the FI face?

   b. What is the duration of a 30-year, 12 percent annual $100,000 monthly amortizing mortgage loan if the yield to maturity is 12 percent? *Hint:* Use a spread-sheet for calculations.

   c. What are some possible solutions to the duration mis-match and the illiquidity problems?

   d. What advantages does securitization have in dealing with the FI's risk exposure problems?

8. How are investors in pass-through bonds protected against default risk emanating from the mortgagees and the bank/trustee?

9. What specific changes occur on the balance sheet at the completion of the securitization process? What adjust-ments occur to the risk profile of the FI?

10. Consider the mortgage pass-through example presented in Table 28–3 and Figure 28–2. The total monthly pay-ment by the borrowers reflecting a 12 percent mortgage rate is $1,028,612.60. The payment passed through to the ultimate investors reflecting an 11.5 percent return is $990,291.43. Who receives the difference between these two payments? How are the shares determined?

11. Consider a GNMA mortgage pool with principal of $20 million. The maturity is 30 years with a monthly mortgage payment of 10 percent per annum. Assume no prepayments.

    a. What is the monthly mortgage payment (100 percent amortizing) on the pool of mortgages?

    b. If the GNMA insurance fee is 6 basis points and the servicing fee is 44 basis points, what is the yield on the GNMA pass-through?

    c. What is the monthly payment on the GNMA in part (b)?

    d. Calculate the first monthly servicing fee paid to the originating banks.

    e. Calculate the first monthly insurance fee paid to GNMA.

12. Calculate the value of (a) the mortgage pool and (b) the GNMA pass-through in question (11) if market interest rates increase 50 basis points. Assume no prepayments.

13. What would be the impact on GNMA pricing if the pass-through was not fully amortized? What is the present value of a $10 million pool of 15-year mortgages with an 8.5 percent per annum monthly mortgage coupon if market rates are 5 percent? The GNMA guarantee fee is assumed to be 6 basis points, and the bank servicing fee is 44 basis points.

    a. Assume that the GNMA is fully amortized.

    b. Assume that the GNMA is only half amortized. There is a lump-sum payment at the maturity of the GNMA that equals 50 percent of the mortgage pool's face value.

14. What is prepayment risk? How does prepayment risk affect the cash flow stream on a fully amortized mortgage loan? What are the two primary factors that cause early payment?

15. Under what conditions do mortgage holders have a call option on their mortgages? When is the call option in the money?

16. What are the benefits of market yields that are less than the average rate in the GNMA mortgage pool? What are the disadvantages of this rate inversion? To whom does the good news and the bad news accrue?

17. What is the weighted-average life (WAL) of a mortgage pool supporting pass-through securities? How does WAL differ from duration?

18. If 150 $200,000 mortgages are expected to be prepaid in three years and the remaining 150 $200,000 mortgages in a $60 million 15-year mortgage pool are to be prepaid in four years, what is the weighted-average life of the mortgage pool? Mortgages are fully amortized, with mortgage coupon rates set at 10 percent to be paid annually.

19. A bank originates a pool of 500 30-year mortgages, each averaging $150,000 with an annual mortgage coupon rate of 8 percent. Assume that the GNMA credit risk

insurance fee is 6 basis points and that the bank's servicing fee is 19 basis points.

    a. What is the present value of the mortgage pool?

    b. What is the monthly mortgage payment?

    c. For the first two payments, what portion is interest and what portion is principal repayment?

    d. What are the expected monthly cash flows to GNMA bondholders?

    e. What is the present value of the GNMA pass-through bonds? Assume that the risk-adjusted market annual rate of return is 8 percent compounded monthly.

    f. Would actual cash flows to GNMA bondholders deviate from expected cash flows as in part (d)? Why or why not?

    g. What are the expected monthly cash flows for the bank and GNMA?

    h. If all the mortgages in the pool are completely prepaid at the end of the second month, what is the pool's weighted-average life? *Hint:* Use your answer to part (c).

    i. What is the price of the GNMA pass-through security if its weighted-average life is equal to your solution for part (h)? Assume no change in market interest rates.

    j. What is the price of the GNMA pass-through with a weighted-average life equal to your solution for part (h) if market yields decline 50 basis points?

20. What is the difference between the yield spread to average life and the option-adjusted spread on mortgage-backed securities?

21. Explain precisely the prepayment assumptions of the Public Securities Association prepayment model.

22. What does an FI mean when it states that its mortgage pool prepayments are assumed to be 100 percent PSA equivalent?

23. What factors may cause the actual prepayment pattern to differ from the assumed PSA pattern? How would an FI adjust for the presumed occurrence of some of these factors?

24. What is the burnout factor? How is it used in modeling prepayment behavior? What other factors may be helpful in modeling the prepayment behavior of a given mortgage pool?

25. What is the goal of prepayment models which use option pricing theory? How do these models differ from the PSA or empirical models? What criticisms often are directed toward these models?

26. How does the price on a GNMA option relate to the yield on a GNMA option from the perspective of the investor? What is the option-adjusted spread (OAS)?

27. Use the options prepayment model to calculate the yield on a $12 million five-year fully amortized mortgage pass-through where the mortgage coupon rate is

7 percent paid annually. Market yields are 8 percent paid annually. Assume that there is no servicing or GNMA guarantee fee.

a. What is the annual payment on the GNMA pass-through?

b. What is the present value of the GNMA pass-through?

c. Interest rates movements over time are assumed to change a maximum of 1 percent per year. Both an increase of 1 percent and a decrease of 1 percent in interest rates are equally probable. If interest rates fall 3 percent below current mortgage rates, all mortgages in the pool will be completely prepaid. Diagram the interest rate tree and indicate the probabilities of each node in the tree.

d. What are expected annual cash flows for each possible situation over the five-year period?

e. The Treasury bond yield curve is flat at a discount yield of 6 percent. What is the option-adjusted spread on the GNMA pass-through?

28. What conditions would cause the yield on pass-through securities with prepayment risk to be less than the yield on pass-through securities without prepayment risk?

29. What is a collateralized mortgage obligation (CMO)? How is it similar to a pass-through security? How does it differ? In what way does the creation of a CMO use market segmentation to redistribute prepayment risk?

30. Consider $200 million of 30-year mortgages with a coupon of 10 percent per annum paid quarterly.

a. What is the quarterly mortgage payment?

b. What are the interest repayments over the first year of life of the mortgages? What are the principal repayments?

c. Construct a 30-year CMO using this mortgage pool as collateral. The pool has three tranches, where tranche A offers the least protection against prepayment and tranche C offers the most protection against prepayment. Tranche A of $50 million receives quarterly payments at 9 percent per annum, tranche B of $100 million receives quarterly payments at 10 percent per annum, and tranche C of $50 million receives quarterly payments at 11 percent per annum. Diagram the CMO structure.

d. Assume nonamortization of principal and no prepayments. What are the total promised coupon payments to the three classes? What are the principal payments to each of the three classes for the first year?

e. If, over the first year, the trustee receives quarterly prepayments of $10 million on the mortgage pool, how are these funds distributed?

f. How are the cash flows distributed if prepayments in the first half of the second year are $20 million quarterly?

g. How can the CMO issuer earn a positive spread on the CMO?

31. How does a class Z tranche of a CMO differ from a class R tranche? What causes a Z class to have characteristics of both a zero-coupon bond and a regular bond? What factors can cause an R class to have a negative duration?

32. Why would buyers of class C tranches of collateralized mortgage obligations (CMOs) be willing to accept a lower return than purchasers of Class A tranches?

33. What are mortgage-backed bonds (MBBs)? How do MBBs differ from pass-through securities and CMOs?

34. From the perspective of risk management, how does the use of MBBs by a bank assist the bank in managing credit and interest rate risk?

35. What are four reasons why a bank may prefer the use of either pass-through securities or CMOs to the use of MBBs?

36. What is an interest-only (IO) strip? How do the discount effect and the prepayment effect of an IO create a negative duration asset? What macroeconomic effect is required for this negative duration effect to be possible?

37. What is a principal-only (PO) strip? What causes the price-yield profile of a PO strip to have a steeper slope than does a normal bond?

38. An FI originates a pool of short-term real estate loans worth $20 million with maturities of five years and paying interest rates of 9 percent per annum.

a. What is the average payment received by the FI, including both principal and interest, if no prepayment is expected over the life of the loan?

b. If the loans are converted into pass-through certificates and the FI charges a servicing fee of 50 basis points, including insurance, what is the payment amount expected by the holders of the pass-through securities if no prepayment is expected?

c. Assume that the payments are separated into interest-only (IO) and principal-only (PO) payments, that prepayments of 5 percent occur at the end of years 3 and 4, and that the payment of the remaining principal occurs at the end of year 5. What are the expected annual payments for each instrument? Assume discount rates of 9 percent.

d. What is the market value of IOs and POs if the market interest rates for instruments of similar risk decline to 8 percent?

39. What are the factors which, in general, allow assets to be securitized? What are the costs involved in the securitization process?

40. How does an FI use loan sales and securitization to manage interest rate, credit, and liquidity risks? Summarize how each of the possible methods of securitization products affects the balance sheet and profitability of an FI in the management of these risks.

APPENDIXES

Interest Rate

Period	1%	2%	3%	4%	5%	6%	7%	8%	9%
1	1.0100	1.0200	1.0300	1.0400	1.0500	1.0600	1.0700	1.0800	1.0900
2	1.0201	1.0404	1.0609	1.0816	1.1025	1.1236	1.1449	1.1664	1.1881
3	1.0303	1.0612	1.0927	1.1249	1.1576	1.1910	1.2250	1.2597	1.2950
4	1.0406	1.0824	1.1255	1.1699	1.2155	1.2625	1.3108	1.3605	1.4116
5	1.0510	1.1041	1.1593	1.2167	1.2763.	1.3382	1.4026	1.4693	1.5386
6	1.0615	1.1262	1.1941	1.2653	1.3401	1.4185	1.5007	1.5869	1.6771
7	1.0721	1.1487	1.2299	1.3159	1.4071	1.5036	1.6058	1.7138	1.8280
8	1.0829	1.1717	1.2668	1.3686	1.4775	1.5938	1.7182	1.8509	1.9926
9	1.0937	1.1951	1.3048	1.4233	1.5513	1.6895	1.8385	1.9990	2.1719
10	1.1046	1.2190	1.3439	1.4802	1.6289	1.7908	1.9672	2.1589	2.3674
11	1.1157	1.2434	1.3842	1.5395	1.7103	1.8983	2.1049	2.3316	2.5804
12	1.1268	1.2682	1.4258	1.6010	1.7959	2.0122	2.2522	2.5182	2.8127
13	1.1381	1.2936	1.4685	1.6651	1.8856	2.1329	2.4098	2.7196	3.0658
14	1.1495	1.3195	1.5126	1.7317	1.9799	2.2609	2.5785	2.9372	3.3417
15	1.1610	1.3459	1.5580	1.8009	2.0789	2.3966	2.7590	3.1722	3.6425
16	1.1726	1.3728	1.6047	1.8730	2.1829	2.5404	2.9522	3.4259	3.9703
17	1.1843	1.4002	1.6528	1.9479	2.2920	2.6928	3.1588	3.7000	4.3276
18	1.1961	1.4282	1.7024	2.0258	2.4066	2.8543	3.3799	3.9960	4.7171
19	1.2081	1.4568	1.7535	2.1068	2.5270	3.0256	3.6165	4.3157	5.1417
20	1.2202	1.4859	1.8061	2.1911	2.6533	3.2071	3.8697	4.6610	5.6044
21	1.2324	1.5157	1.8603	2.2788	2.7860	3.3996	4.1406	5.0338	6.1088
22	1.2447	1.5460	1.9161	2.3699	2.9253	3.6035	4.4304	5.4365	6.6586
23	1.2572	1.5769	1.9736	2.4647	3.0715	3.8197	4.7405	5.8715	7.2579
24	1.2697	1.6084	2.0328	2.5633	3.2251	4.0489	5.0724	6.3412	7.9111
25	1.2824	1.6406	2.0938	2.6658	3.3854	4.2919	5.4274	6.8485	8.6231
30	1.3478	1.8114	2.4273	3.2434	4.3219	5.7435	7.6123	10.063	13.268
40	1.4889	2.2080	3.2620	4.8010	7.0400	10.286	14.974	21.725	31.409
50	1.6446	2.6916	4.3839	7.1067	11.467	18.420	29.457	46.902	74.358
60	1.8167	3.2810	5.8916	10.520	18.679	32.988	57.946	101.26	176.03

TABLE A–1 (*concluded*)

Interest Rate										
10%	12%	14%	15%	16%	18%	20%	24%	28%	32%	36%
1.1000	1.1200	1.1400	1.1500	1.1600	1.1800	1.2000	1.2400	1.2800	1.3200	1.3600
1.2100	1.2544	1.2996	1.3225	1.3456	1.3924	1.4400	1.5376	1.6384	1.7424	1.8496
1.3310	1.4049	1.4815	1.5209	1.5609	1.6430	1.7280	1.9066	2.0972	2.3000	2.5155
1.4641	1.5735	1.6890	1.7490	1.8106	1.9388	2.0736	2.3642	2.6844	3.0360	3.4210
1.6105	1.7623	1.9254	2.0114	2.1003	2.2878	2.4883	2.9316	3.4360	4.0075	4.6526
1.7716	1.9738	2.1950	2.3131	2.4364	2.6996	2.9860	3.6352	4.3980	5.2899	6.3275
1.9487	2.2107	2.5023	2.6600	2.8262	3.1855	3.5832	4.5077	5.6295	6.9826	8.6054
2.1436	2.4760	2.8526	3.0590	3.2784	3.7589	4.2998	5.5895	7.2058	9.2170	11.703
2.3579	2.7731	3.2519	3.5179	3.8030	4.4355	5.1598	6.9310	9.2234	12.166	15.917
2.5937	3.1058	3.7072	4.0456	4.4114	5.2338	6.1917	8.5944	11.806	16.060	21.647
2.8531	3.4785	4.2262	4.6524	5.1173	6.1759	7.4301	10.657	15.112	21.199	29.439
3.1384	3.8960	4.8179	5.3503	5.9360	7.2876	8.9161	13.215	19.343	27.983	40.037
3.4523	4.3635	5.4924	6.1528	6.8858	8.5994	10.699	16.386	24.759	36.937	54.451
3.7975	4.8871	6.2613	7.0757	7.9875	10.147	12.839	20.319	31.691	48.757	74.053
4.1772	5.4736	7.1379	8.1371	9.2655	11.974	15.407	25.196	40.565	64.359	100.71
4.5950	6.1304	8.1372	9.3576	10.748	14.129	18.488	31.243	51.923	84.954	136.97
5.0545	6.8660	9.2765	10.761	12.468	16.672	22.186	38.741	66.461	112.14	186.28
5.5599	7.6900	10.575	12.375	14.463	19.673	26.623	48.039	85.071	148.02	253.34
6.1159	8.6128	12.056	14.232	16.777	23.214	31.948	59.568	108.89	195.39	344.54
6.7275	9.6463	13.743	16.367	19.461	27.393	38.338	73.864	139.38	257.92	468.57
7.4002	10.804	15.668	18.822	22.574	32.324	46.005	91.592	178.41	340.45	637.26
8.1403	12.100	17.861	21.645	26.186	38.142	55.206	113.57	228.36	449.39	866.67
8.9543	13.552	20.362	24.891	30.376	45.008	66.247	140.83	292.30	593.20	1178.7
9.8497	15.179	23.212	28.625	35.236	53.109	79.497	174.63	374.14	783.02	1603.0
10.835	17.000	26.462	32.919	40.874	62.669	95.396	216.54	478.90	1033.6	2180.1
17.449	29.960	50.950	66.212	85.850	143.37	237.38	634.82	1645.5	4142.1	10143.
45.259	93.051	188.88	267.86	378.72	750.38	1469.8	5455.9	19427.	66521.	*
117.39	289.00	700.23	1083.7	1670.7	3927.4	9100.4	46890.	*	*	*
304.48	897.60	2595.9	4384.0	7370.2	20555.	56348.	*	*	*	*

*The factor is greater than 99,999.

TABLE A–2   Present Value of $1 to Be Received after *t* Periods $= 1/(1 + r)^t$

Interest Rate

Period	1%	2%	3%	4%	5%	6%	7%	8%	9%
1	0.9901	0.9804	0.9709	0.9615	0.9524	0.9434	0.9346	0.9259	0.9174
2	0.9803	0.9612	0.9426	0.9246	0.9070	0.8900	0.8737	0.8573	0.8417
3	0.9706	0.9423	0.9151	0.8890	0.8638	0.8396	0.8163	0.7938	0.7722
4	0.9610	0.9238	0.8885	0.8548	0.8227	0.7921	0.7629	0.7350	0.7084
5	0.9515	0.9057	0.8626	0.8219	0.7835	0.7473	0.7130	0.6806	0.6499
6	0.9420	0.8880	0.8375	0.7903	0.7462	0.7050	0.6663	0.6302	0.5963
7	0.9327	0.8706	0.8131	0.7599	0.7107	0.6651	0.6227	0.5835	0.5470
8	0.9235	0.8535	0.7894	0.7307	0.6768	0.6274	0.5820	0.5403	0.5019
9	0.9143	0.8368	0.7664	0.7026	0.6446	0.5919	0.5439	0.5002	0.4604
10	0.9053	0.8203	0.7441	0.6756	0.6139	0.5584	0.5083	0.4632	0.4224
11	0.8963	0.8043	0.7224	0.6496	0.5847	0.5268	0.4751	0.4289	0.3875
12	0.8874	0.7885	0.7014	0.6246	0.5568	0.4970	0.4440	0.3971	0.3555
13	0.8787	0.7730	0.6810	0.6006	0.5303	0.4688	0.4150	0.3677	0.3262
14	0.8700	0.7579	0.6611	0.5775	0.5051	0.4423	0.3878	0.3405	0.2992
15	0..8613	0.7430	0.6419	0.5553	0.4810	0.4173	0.3624	0.3152	0.2745
16	0.8528	0.7284	0.6232	0.5339	0.4581	0.3936	0.3387	0.2919	0.2519
17	0.8444	0.7142	0.6050	0.5134	0.4363	0.3714	0.3166	0.2703	0.2311
18	0.8360	0.7002	0.5874	0.4936	0.4155	0.3503	0.2959	0.2502	0.2120
19	0.8277	0.6864	0.5703	0.4846	0.3957	0.3305	0.2765	0.2317	0.1945
20	0.8195	0.6730	0.5537	0.4564	0.3769	0.3118	0.2584	0.2145	0.1784
21	0.8114	0.6598	0.5375	0.4388	0.3589	0.2942	0.2415	0.1987	0.1637
22	0.8034	0.6468	0.5219	0.4220	0.3418	0.2775	0.2257	0.1839	0.1502
23	0.7954	0.6342	0.5067	0.4057	0.3256	0.2618	0.2109	0.1703	0.1378
24	0.7876	0.6217	0.4919	0.3901	0.3101	0.2470	0.1971	0.1577	0.1264
25	0.7798	0.6095	0.4776	0.3751	0.2953	0.2330	0.1842	0.1460	0.1160
30	0.7419	0.5521	0.4120	0.3083	0.2314	0.1741	0.1314	0.0994	0.0754
40	0.6717	0.4529	0.3066	0.2083	0.1420	0.0972	0.0668	0.0460	0.0318
50	0.6080	0.3715	0.2281	0.1407	0.0872	0.0543	0.0339	0.0213	0.0134

TABLE A–2   (concluded)

| Interest Rate | | | | | | | | | | |
10%	12%	14%	15%	16%	18%	20%	24%	28%	32%	36%
0.9091	0.8929	0.8772	0.8696	0.8621	0.8475	0.8333	0.8065	0.7813	0.7576	0.7363
0.8264	0.7972	0.7695	0.7561	0.7432	0.7182	0.6944	0.6504	0.6104	0.5739	0.5407
0.7513	0.7118	0.6750	0.6575	0.6407	0.6086	0.5787	0.5245	0.4768	0.4348	0.3975
0.6830	0.6355	0.5921	0.5718	0.5523	0.5158	0.4823	0.4230	0.3725	0.3294	0.2923
0.6209	0.5674	0.5194	0.4972	0.4761	0.4371	0.4019	0.3411	0.2910	0.2495	0.2149
0.5645	0.5066	0.4556	0.4323	0.4104	0.3704	0.3349	0.2751	0.2274	0.1890	0.1580
0.5132	0.4523	0.3996	0.3759	0.3538	0.3139	0.2791	0.2218	0.1776	0.1432	0.1162
0.4665	0.4039	0.3506	0.3269	0.3050	0.2660	0.2326	0.1789	0.1388	0.1085	0.0854
0.4241	0.3606	0.3075	0.2843	0.2630	0.2255	0.1938	0.1443	0.1084	0.0822	0.0628
0.3855	0.3220	0.2697	0.2472	0.2267	0.1911	0.1615	0.1164	0.0847	0.0623	0.0462
0.3505	0.2875	0.2366	0.2149	0.1954	0.1619	0.1346	0.0938	0.0662	0.0472	0.0340
0.3186	0.2567	0.2076	0.1869	0.1685	0.1372	0.1122	0.0757	0.0517	0.0357	0.0250
0.2897	0.2292	0.1821	0.1625	0.1452	0.1163	0.0935	0.0610	0.0404	0.0271	0.0184
0.2633	0.2046	0.1597	0.1413	0.1252	0.0985	0.0779	0.0492	0.0316	0.0205	0.0135
0.2394	0.1827	0.1401	0.1229	0.1079	0.0835	0.0649	0.0397	0.0247	0.0155	0.0099
0.2176	0.1631	0.1229	0.1069	0.0930	0.0708	0.0541	0.0320	0.0193	0.0118	0.0073
0.1978	0.1456	0.1078	0.0929	0.0802	0.0600	0.0451	0.0258	0.0150	0.0089	0.0054
0.1799	0.1300	0.0946	0.0808	0.0691	0.0508	0.0376	0.0208	0.0118	0.0068	0.0039
0.1635	0.1161	0.0829	0.0703	0.0596	0.0431	0.0313	0.0168	0.0092	0.0051	0.0029
0.1486	0.1037	0.0728	0.0611	0.0514	0.0365	0.0261	0.0135	0.0072	0.0039	0.0021
0.1351	0.0926	0.0638	0.0531	0.0443	0.0309	0.0217	0.0109	0.0056	0.0029	0.0016
0.1228	0.0826	0.0560	0.0462	0.0382	0.0262	0.0181	0.0088	0.0044	0.0022	0.0012
0.1117	0.0738	0.0491	0.0402	0.0329	0.0222	0.0151	0.0071	0.0034	0.0017	0.0008
0.1015	0.0659	0.0431	0.0349	0.0284	0.0188	0.0126	0.0057	0.0027	0.0013	0.0006
0.0923	0.0588	0.0378	0.0304	0.0245	0.0160	0.0105	0.0046	0.0021	0.0010	0.0005
0.0573	0.0334	0.0196	0.0151	0.0116	0.0070	0.0042	0.0016	0.0006	0.0002	0.0001
0.0221	0.0107	0.0053	0.0037	0.0026	0.0013	0.0007	0.0002	0.0001	*	*
0.0085	0.0035	0.0014	0.0009	0.0006	0.0003	0.0001	*	*	*	*

*The factor is zero to four decimal places.

TABLE A–3   Present Value of an Annuity of $1 per Period for *t* Periods = $[1 - 1/(1 + r)^t]/r$

Interest Rate

Period	1%	2%	3%	4%	5%	6%	7%	8%	9%
1	0.9901	0.9804	0.9709	0.9615	0.9524	0.9434	0.9346	0.9259	0.9174
2	1.9704	1.9416	1.9135	1.8861	1.8594	1.8334	1.8080	1.7833	1.7591
3	2.9410	2.8839	2.8286	2.7751	2.7232	2.6730	2.6243	2.5771	2.5313
4	3.9020	3.8077	3.7171	3.6299	3.5460	3.4561	3.3872	3.3121	3.2397
5	4.8534	4.7135	4.5797	4.4518	4.3295	4.2124	4.1002	3.9927	3.8897
6	5.7955	5.6014	5.4172	5.2421	5.0757	4.9173	4.7665	4.6229	4.4859
7	6.7282	6.4720	6.2303	6.0021	5.7864	5.5824	5.3893	5.2064	5.0330
8	7.6517	7.3255	7.0197	6.7327	6.4632	6.2098	5.9713	5.7466	5.5348
9	8.5660	8.1622	7.7861	7.4353	7.1078	6.8017	6.5152	6.2469	5.9952
10	9.4713	8.9826	8.5302	8.1109	7.7217	7.3601	7.0236	6.7101	6.4177
11	10.3676	9.7868	9.2526	8.7605	8.3064	7.8869	7.4987	7.1390	6.8052
12	11.2551	10.5753	9.9540	9.3851	8.8633	8.3838	7.9427	7.5361	7.1607
13	12.1337	11.3484	10.6350	9.9856	9.3936	8.8527	8.3577	7.9038	7.4869
14	13.0037	12.1062	11.2961	10.5631	9.8986	9.2950	8.7455	8.2442	7.7862
15	13.8651	12.8493	11.9379	11.1184	10.3797	9.7122	9.1079	8.5595	8.0607
16	14.7179	13.5777	12.5611	11.6523	10.8378	10.1059	9.4466	8.8514	8.3126
17	15.5623	14.2919	13.1661	12.1657	11.2741	10.4773	9.7632	9.1216	8.5436
18	16.3983	14.9920	13.7535	12.6593	11.6896	10.8276	10.0591	9.3719	8.7556
19	17.2260	15.6785	14.3238	13.1339	12.0853	11.1581	10.3356	9.6036	8.9501
20	18.0456	16.3514	14.8776	13.5903	12.4622	11.4699	10.5940	9.8181	9.1285
21	18.8570	17.0112	15.4150	14.0292	12.8212	11.7641	10.8355	10.0168	9.2922
22	19.6604	17.6580	15.9369	14.4511	13.1630	12.0416	11.0612	10.2007	9.4424
23	20.4558	18.2922	16.4436	14.8568	13.4886	12.3034	11.2722	10.3741	9.5802
24	21.2434	18.9139	16.9355	15.2470	13.7986	12.5504	11.4593	10.5288	9.7066
25	22.0232	19.5235	17.4131	15.6221	14.0939	12.7834	11.6536	10.6748	9.8226
30	25.8077	22.3965	19.6004	17.2920	15.3725	13.7648	12.4090	11.2578	10.2737
40	32.8347	27.3555	23.1148	19.7928	17.1591	15.0463	13.3317	11.9246	10.7574
50	39.1961	31.4236	25.7298	21.4822	18.2559	15.7619	13.8007	12.2335	10.9617

TABLE A–3   *(concluded)*

| Interest Rate | | | | | | | | | |
10%	12%	14%	15%	16%	18%	20%	24%	28%	32%
0.9091	0.8929	0.8772	0.8696	0.8621	0.8475	0.8333	0.8065	0.7813	0.7576
1.7355	1.6901	1.6467	1.6257	1.6052	1.5656	1.5278	1.4568	1.3916	1.3315
2.4869	2.4018	2.3216	2.2832	2.2459	2.1743	2.1065	1.9813	1.8684	1.7663
3.1699	3.0373	2.9137	2.8550	2.7982	2.6901	2.5887	2.4043	2.2410	2.0957
3.7908	3.6048	3.4331	3.3522	3.2743	3.1272	2.9906	2.7454	2.5320	2.3452
4.3553	4.1114	3.8887	3.7845	3.6847	3.4976	3.3255	3.0205	2.7594	2.5342
4.8684	4.5638	4.2883	4.1604	4.0386	3.8115	3.6046	3.2423	2.9370	2.6775
5.3349	4.9676	4.6389	4.4873	4.3436	4.0776	3.8372	3.4212	3.0758	2.7860
5.7590	5.3282	4.9464	4.7716	4.6065	4.3030	4.0310	3.5655	3.1842	2.8681
6.1446	5.6502	5.2161	5.0188	4.8332	4.4941	4.1925	3.6819	3.2689	2.9304
6.4951	5.9377	5.4527	5.2337	5.0286	4.6560	4.3271	3.7757	3.3351	2.9776
6.8137	6.1944	5.6603	5.4206	5.1971	4.7932	4.4392	3.8514	3.3868	3.0133
7.1034	6.4235	5.8424	5.5831	5.3423	4.9095	4.5327	3.9124	3.4272	3.0404
7.3667	6.6282	6.0021	5.7245	5.4675	5.0081	4.6106	3.9616	3.4587	3.0609
7.6061	6.8109	6.1422	5.8474	5.5755	5.0916	4.6755	4.0013	3.4834	3.0764
7.8237	6.9740	6.2651	5.9542	5.6685	5.1624	4.7296	4.0333	3.5026	3.0882
8.0216	7.1196	6.3729	6.0472	5.7487	5.2223	4.7746	4.0591	3.5177	3.0971
8.2014	7.2497	6.4674	6.1280	5.8178	5.2732	4.8122	4.0799	3.5294	3.1039
8.3649	7.3658	6.5504	6.1982	5.8775	5.3162	4.8435	4.0967	3.5386	3.1090
8.5136	7.4694	6.6231	6.2593	5.9288	5.3527	4.8696	4.1103	3.5458	3.1129
8.6487	7.5620	6.6870	6.3125	5.9731	5.3837	4.8913	4.1212	3.5514	3.1158
8.7715	7.6446	6.7429	6.3587	6.0113	5.4099	4.9094	4.1300	3.5558	3.1180
8.8832	7.7184	6.7921	6.3988	6.0442	5.4321	4.9245	4.1371	3.5592	3.1197
8.9847	7.7843	6.8351	6.4338	6.0726	5.4509	4.9371	4.1428	3.5619	3.1210
9.0770	7.8431	6.8729	6.4641	6.0971	5.4669	4.9476	4.1474	3.5640	3.1220
9.4269	8.0552	7.0027	6.5660	6.1772	5.5168	4.9789	4.1601	3.5693	3.1242
9.7791	8.2438	7.1050	6.6418	6.2335	5.5482	4.9966	4.1659	3.5712	3.1250
9.9148	8.3045	7.1327	6.6605	6.2463	5.5541	4.9995	4.1666	3.5714	3.1250

TABLE A–4   Future Value of an Annuity of $1 per Period for *t* Periods $= [(1 + r)^t - 1]/r$

Interest Rate Period	1%	2%	3%	4%	5%	6%	7%	8%	9%
1	1.0000	1.0000	1.0000	1.0000	1.0000	1.0000	1.0000	1.0000	1.0000
2	2.0100	2.0200	2.0300	2.0400	2.0500	2.0600	2.0700	2.0800	2.0900
3	3.0301	3.0604	3.0909	3.1216	3.1525	3.1836	3.2149	3.2464	3.2781
4	4.0604	4.1216	4.1836	4.2465	4.3101	4.3746	4.4399	4.5061	4.5731
5	5.1010	5.2040	5.3091	5.4163	5.5256	5.6371	5.7507	5.8666	5.9847
6	6.1520	6.3081	6.4684	6.6330	6.8019	6.9753	7.1533	7.3359	7.5233
7	7.2135	7.4343	7.6625	7.8983	8.1420	8.3938	8.6540	8.9228	9.2004
8	8.2857	8.5830	8.8932	9.2142	9.5491	9.8975	10.260	10.637	11.028
9	9.3685	9.7546	10.159	10.583	11.027	11.491	11.978	12.488	13.021
10	10.462	10.950	11.464	12.006	12.578	13.181	13.816	14.487	15.193
11	11.567	12.169	12.808	13.486	14.207	14.972	15.784	16.645	17.560
12	12.683	13.412	14.192	15.026	15.917	16.870	17.888	18.977	20.141
13	13.809	14.680	15.618	16.627	17.713	18.882	20.141	21.495	22.953
14	14.947	15.974	17.086	18.292	19.599	21.015	22.550	24.215	26.019
15	16.097	17.293	18.599	20.024	21.579	23.276	25.159	27.152	29.361
16	17.258	18.639	20.157	21.825	23.657	25.673	27.888	30.324	33.003
17	18.430	20.012	21.762	23.698	25.840	28.213	30.840	33.750	36.974
18	19.615	21.412	23.414	25.645	28.132	30.906	33.999	37.450	41.301
19	20.811	22.841	25.117	27.671	30.539	33.760	37.379	41.446	48.018
20	22.019	24.297	26.870	29.778	33.066	36.786	40.995	45.762	51.160
21	23.239	25.783	28.676	31.969	35.719	39.993	44.865	50.423	56.765
22	24.472	27.299	30.537	34.248	38.505	43.392	49.006	55.457	62.873
23	25.716	28.845	32.453	36.618	41.430	46.996	53.436	60.893	69.532
24	26.973	30.442	34.426	39.083	44.502	50.816	58.177	66.765	76.790
25	28.243	32.030	36.459	41.646	47.727	54.865	63.249	73.106	84.701
30	34.785	40.568	47.575	56.085	66.439	79.058	97.461	113.28	136.31
40	48.886	60.402	75.401	95.026	120.80	154.76	199.64	259.06	337.88
50	64.463	84.579	112.80	152.67	209.35	290.34	406.53	573.77	815.08
60	81.670	114.05	163.05	237.99	353.58	533.13	813.52	1253.2	1944.8

TABLE A–4 (*concluded*)

Interest Rate

10%	12%	14%	15%	16%	18%	20%	24%	28%	32%	36%
1.0000	1.0000	1.0000	1.0000	1.0000	1.0000	1.0000	1.0000	1.0000	1.0000	1.0000
2.1000	2.1200	2.1400	2.1500	2.1600	2.1800	2.2000	2.2400	2.2800	2.3200	2.3600
3.3100	3.3744	3.4396	3.4725	3.5056	3.5724	3.6400	3.7776	3.9184	4.0624	4.2096
4.6410	4.7793	4.9211	4.9934	5.0665	5.2154	5.3680	5.6842	6.0156	6.3624	6.7251
6.1051	6.3528	6.6101	6.7424	6.8771	7.1542	7.4416	8.0484	8.6999	9.3983	10.146
7.7156	8.1152	8.5355	8.7537	8.9775	9.4420	9.9299	10.980	12.136	13.406	14.779
9.4872	10.089	10.730	11.067	11.414	12.142	12.916	14.615	16.534	18.696	21.126
11.436	12.300	13.233	13.727	14.240	15.327	16.499	19.123	22.163	25.678	29.732
13.579	14.776	16.085	16.786	17.519	19.086	20.799	24.712	29.369	34.895	41.435
15.937	17.549	19.337	20.304	21.321	23.521	25.959	31.643	38.593	47.062	57.352
18.531	20.655	23.045	24.349	25.733	28.755	32.150	40.238	50.398	63.122	78.998
21.384	24.133	27.271	29.002	30.850	34.931	39.581	50.895	65.510	84.320	108.44
24.523	28.029	32.089	34.352	36.786	42.219	48.497	64.110	84.853	112.30	148.47
37.975	32.393	37.581	40.505	43.672	50.818	59.196	80.493	109.61	149.24	202.93
31.772	37.280	43.842	47.580	51.660	60.965	72.035	100.82	141.30	198.00	276.98
35.950	42.753	50.980	55.717	60.925	72.939	87.442	126.01	181.87	262.36	377.69
40.545	48.884	59.118	65.075	71.673	87.068	105.93	157.25	233.79	347.31	514.66
45.599	55.750	68.394	75.836	84.141	103.74	128.12	195.99	300.25	459.45	700.94
51.159	63.440	78.969	88.212	98.603	123.41	154.74	244.03	385.32	607.47	954.28
57.275	72.052	91.025	102.44	115.38	146.63	186.69	303.60	494.21	802.86	1298.8
64.002	81.699	104.77	118.81	134.84	174.02	225.03	377.46	633.59	1060.8	1767.4
71.403	92.503	120.44	137.63	157.41	206.34	271.03	469.06	812.00	1401.2	2404.7
79.543	104.60	138.30	159.28	183.60	244.49	326.24	582.63	1040.4	1850.6	3271.3
88.497	118.16	158.66	184.17	213.98	289.49	392.48	723.46	1332.7	2443.8	4450.0
98.347	133.33	181.87	212.79	249.21	342.60	471.98	898.09	1706.8	3226.8	6053.0
164.69	241.33	356.79	434.75	530.31	790.95	1181.9	2640.9	5873.2	12941.	28172.3
442.59	767.09	1342.0	1779.1	2360.8	4163.2	7343.9	22729.	69377.	*	*
1163.9	2400.0	4994.5	7217.7	10436.	21813.	45497.	*	*	*	*
3034.8	7471.6	18535.	29220.	46058.	*	*	*	*	*	*

*The factor is greater than 99,999.

REFERENCES

Abbott, S. "Franklin Case Points Out Thrift Account Difficulties." *Futures,* July 1990, pp. 58–60.

Abken, P. A. "Beyond Plain Vanilla: A Taxonomy of Swaps." Federal Reserve Bank of Atlanta, *Economic Review,* March–April 1991, pp. 21–29.

Acharya, S., and I. Diwan. "Debt Conversion Schemes of Debtor Countries as a Signal of Creditworthiness: Theory and Evidence." Working Paper, Stern School of Business, New York University, June 1987.

Acharya, S., and J. F. Dreyfus. "Optimal Bank Reorganization Policies and the Pricing of Federal Deposit Insurance." *Journal of Finance* 44 (December 1988), pp. 1313–14.

Aguais, S. D., et al. "Creating Value from Both Loan Structure and Price." *Commercial Lending Review,* 1998, pp. 1–10.

Aharony, J., A. Saunders, and I. Swary. "The Effects of a Shift in Monetary Policy Regime on the Profitability and Risk of Commercial Banks." *Journal of Monetary Economics* 17 (1996), pp. 493–506.

Allen, L., J. Jagtiani, and A. Saunders, "The Role of Financial Advisors in Mergers and Acquisitions," Unpublished Working Paper, New York University, November 1998.

Allen, L., and A. Rai, "Operational Efficiency in Banking: An International Perspective," *Journal of Banking and Finance* 20 (1996), pp. 655–72.

Allen, L., and A. Saunders. "Bank Window Dressing: Theory and Evidence. *Journal of Banking and Finance* 16 (1992), pp. 585–624.

Allen, L., and A. Saunders. "Forbearance and Valuation of Deposit Insurance as a Callable Put." *Journal of Banking and Finance* 17 (1993), pp. 629–43.

Altman, E. I., and V. M. Kishore, "Defaults and Returns on High-Yield Bonds: Analysis Through 1997," Working Paper, New York University Salomon Center, January 1998.

Altman, E. I., and B. E. Simon. "The Investment Performance of Defaulted Bonds for 1987–1994." Stern School of Business, New York University, February 1995.

Altman, E. I., and H. J. Suggitt. "Default Rates in the Syndicated Loan Market: A Mortality Analysis." Working Paper S-97-39, New York University Salomon Center, December 1997.

Altman, E. I. "Default Risk, Mortality Rates, and the Performance of Corporate Bonds." *The Research Foundation of the Institute of Chartered Financial Analysts,* 1989.

_____. "How 1989 Changed the Hierarchy of Fixed Income Security Performance." In *Recent Developments in Finance,* ed. A. Saunders, Burr Ridge, IL: Irwin Professional Publishing, 1990, pp. 19–30.

_____. "Managing the Commercial Lending Process." In *Handbook of Banking Strategy,* ed. R. C. Aspinwall and R. A. Eisenbeis. New York: John Wiley & Sons, 1985, pp. 473–510.

_____. "Measuring Corporate Bond Mortality and Performance." *Journal of Finance* 44 (1989), pp. 909–22.

_____. "Valuation, Loss Reserves, and Pricing of Commercial Loans." *Journal of Commercial Bank Lending,* August 1993, pp. 9–25.

Amemiya, T. "Qualitative Response Models: A Survey." *Journal of Economic Literature* 19 (1991), pp. 483–536.

Angbazo, L. "Commercial Bank Net Interest Margins, Default Risk, Interest Rate Risk and Off-Balance Sheet Banking," *Journal of Banking and Finance* 21 (1997), pp. 55–81.

Angbazo, L., J. P. Mei, and A. Saunders, "Credit Spreads in the Market for Highly Leveraged Transaction Loans,"

Journal of Banking and Finance 22, nos. 10–11 (October 1998), pp. 1249–82.

Angelini, P., G. Maresca, and D. Russo. "An Assessment of Systematic Risk in the Italian Clearing System." Bank of Italy, Discussion Paper No. 207, 1993.

Archer, W., and D. C. Ling. "Pricing Mortgage-Backed Securities: Should Contingent-Claim Models Be Abandoned for Empirical Models of Prepayments?" Paper presented at the AFA Conference, Anaheim, CA, January 1993.

Asarnow, E., and J. Marker, "Historical Performance of the U.S. Corporate Loan Market 1968–1993," *Journal of Commercial Lending,* Spring 1995, pp. 13–22.

Avery, R. B., and A. Berger. "Loan Commitments and Bank Risk Exposure." *Journal of Banking and Finance* 15 (1991), pp. 173–92.

———. "Risk-Based Capital and Deposit Insurance Reform." *Journal of Banking Finance* 15 (1991), pp. 847–74.

Babbel, D. F. "Insuring Banks against Systematic Credit Risk." *Journal of Futures Markets* 9 (1989), pp. 487–506.

Ball, C., and W. N. Tourous. "Bond Price Dynamics and Options." *Journal of Financial and Quantitative Analysis* 18 (1983), pp. 517–31.

Bank for International Settlements, "Standardized Model for Market Risk," Basel, Switzerland, 1996.

Beatty, R., and J. Ritter. "Investment Banking, Reputation, and the Underpricing of Initial Public Offerings." *Journal of Financial Economics* 15 (1986), pp. 213–32.

Bellanger, S. "Stormy Weather: The FBSEA's Impact on Foreign Banks." *Bankers Magazine,* November–December 1992, pp. 25–31.

Benston, G. J. *The Separation of Commercial and Investment Banking: The Glass-Steagall Act Revisited and Reconsidered.* New York: St. Martin's Press, 1989.

———. "Universal Banking." *Journal of Economic Perspectives* 8, no. 3 (1994), pp. 121–43.

Benston, G. J., G. A. Hanweck, and D. Humphrey. "Scale Economies in Banking." *Journal of Money, Credit and Banking* 14 (1982), pp. 436–55.

Benston, G. J., and G. G. Kaufman. "Risk and Solvency Regulation of Depository Institutions: Past Policies and Current Options." Monograph Series in Finance and Economics, 1988–1, Salomon Center, New York University, 1988.

Benveniste, L., M. Singh, and W. J. Wilhelm. "The Failure of Drexel Burnham Lambert: Evidence on the Implications for Commercial Banks." Paper presented at the AFA Conference, Anaheim, CA, 1993.

Berger, A., D. Hancock, and D. Humphrey. "Bank Efficiency Derived from the Profit Function." *Journal of Banking and Finance* 17 (1993), pp. 317–47.

Berger, A., and D. Humphrey. "The Dominance of Inefficiencies over Scale and Product Mix in Banking." *Journal of Monetary Economics* 28 (1991).

———. "Megamergers in Banking and the Use of Cost Efficiency as an AntiTrust Defense." *The AntiTrust Bulletin* 37 (1992), pp. 541–600.

Berger, A., D. Humphrey, and L. B. Pulley. "Do Consumers Pay for One-Stop Banking? Evidence from an Alternative Revenue Function." *Journal of Banking and Finance* 20 (1996), pp. 1601–21.

Berger, A., W. C. Hunter, and S. G. Timme. "The Efficiency of Financial Institutions: A Review and Preview of Research Past, Present and Future." *Journal of Banking and Finance* 17 (1993), pp. 221–49.

Berger, A., and L. J. Mester. "Inside the Black-Box: What Explains Differences in the Efficiencies of Financial Institutions." *Journal of Banking and Finance* 21 (1997), pp. 895–947.

Berger, A., and G. Udell. "Does Risk-Based Capital Allocate Bank Credit?" *Journal of Money, Credit and Banking* 26 (August 1994, Part 2).

———. "Lines of Credit, Collateral, and Relationship Lending in Small Firm Finance." *Journal of Business* 68 (1995), pp. 351–82.

Bierwag, G. O., G. G. Kaufman, and A. Toevs. "Duration: Its Development and Use in Bond Portfolio Management." *Financial Analysts Journal* 39 (1983), pp. 15–35.

Billett, M. T., M. J. Flannery, and J. A. Garfinkel. "The Effect of Lender Identity on a Borrowing Firm's Equity Return." *Journal of Finance* 50 (1995), pp. 699–718.

Black, F., and M. Scholes. "The Pricing of Options and Corporate Liabilities." *Journal of Political Economy* 81 (1973), pp. 637–59.

Blumenthal, W. J. "Loan Trading: A New Business Opportunity for Your Bank." *Commercial Lending Review,* Winter 1997–1998, pp. 26–31.

Boehmer, E., and W. L. Megginson. "Determinants of Secondary Market Prices for Developing Country Syndicated Loans." *Journal of Finance* 45 (1990), pp. 1517–40.

Boeschoten, W. "Currency Use and Payment Patterns." *Financial and Monetary Studies* 23 (1992), pp. 73–74.

Boot, A. W. A., and A. V. Thakor. "Off-Balance-Sheet Liabilities, Deposit Insurance, and Capital Regulations." *Journal of Banking and Finance* 15 (1991), pp. 825–46.

Bouyoucos, P. J., M. H. Siegel, and E. B. Raisel. "Risk-Based Capital for Insurers: A Strategic Opportunity to Enhance Franchise Value." Goldman Sachs, Industry Resource Group, September 1992.

Boyd., J. D., and S. L. Graham. "Consolidation in U.S. Banking: Implications for Efficiency and Competition Risk," In *Bank Mergers and Acquisitions,* ed. Y. Amihud and G. Miller, Amsterdam: Kluwer, 1998, pp. 113–36.

Boyd, J. H., and E. C. Prescott. "Financial Intermediary Coalitions." *Journal of Economic Theory* 38 (1986), pp. 211–32.

Brennan, M. J., and E. S. Schwartz. "Savings Bonds, Retractable Bonds, and Callable Bonds." *Journal of Financial Economics* 5 (1977), pp. 67–88.

Brewer, E. "Bank Gap Management and the Use of Financial Futures." Federal Reserve Bank of Chicago, *Economic Perspectives,* March–April 1985.

Brewer, E., D. Fortier, and C. Pavel. "Bank Risk from Nonbank Activities." Federal Reserve Bank of Chicago, *Economic Perspectives,* July–August 1988, pp. 14–26.

Brown, K. C., and D. J. Smith. "Recent Innovations in Interest Rate Risk Management and the Reintermediation of Commercial Banking." *Financial Management* 17 (1988), pp. 45–58.

Bulow, J., and K. Rogoff. "A Constant Recontracting Model of Sovereign Debt." *Journal of Political Economy* 97 (1989), pp. 155–78.

Buser, S. A., A. H Chen, and E. J. Kane. "Federal Deposit Insurance, Regulatory Policy, and Optimal Bank Capital." *Journal of Finance* 36 (1981), pp. 51–60.

Canina, L., and S. Figlewski. "The Informational Content of Implied Volatility." *Review of Financial Studies* 6 (1993), pp. 659–81.

Carey, M. "Credit Risk in Private Debt Portfolios." *Journal of Finance* 53 (August 1998), pp. 1363–87.

Carey, M., et al. "Does Corporate Lending by Banks and Finance Companies Differ? Evidence on Specialization in Private Debt Contracting." *Journal of Finance* 53 (June 1998), pp. 845–78.

Carey, M., et al. "The Economics of Private Placements: A New Look." *Financial Markets, Institutions and Instruments* 2, no. 3 (1993), pp. 1–67.

Carnell, R. S. "A Partial Antidote to Perverse Incentives: The FDIC Improvement Act of 1991." Paper presented at the Conference on Rebuilding Public Confidence through Financial Reform, Ohio State University, Columbus, June 25, 1992.

Cebenoyan, S., et al. "Interstate Savings and Loans in the 1990s: A Performance and Risk Appraisal." University of Baltimore, Working Paper, 1998.

Chan, Y. S., S. I. Greenbaum, and A. V. Thakor. "Is Fairly Priced Deposit Insurance Possible?" *Journal of Finance* 47 (1992), pp. 227–46.

Chidambaran, N. K., T. A. Pugel, and A. Saunders. "An Investigation of the Performance of the US Property-Casualty Insurance Industry." *Journal of Risk and Insurance* 64 (June 1997), pp. 371–82.

Chirinko, R. S., G. Guill, and P. Hebert. "Developing a Systematic Approach to Credit Risk Management." *Journal of Retail Banking* 13 (1991), pp. 29–37.

Choudhury, S. P. "Choosing the Right Box of Credit Tricks." *Risk Magazine,* November 1997.

Christie, W. G., and P. H. Schultz. "Dealer Markets under Stress: The Performance of NASDAQ Market Makers during the November 15, 1991, Market Break." *Journal of Financial Services Research* 13 (June 1995), pp. 205–30.

Clark. J. A. "Economies of Scale and Scope at Depository Financial Institutions: A Review of the Literature." Federal Reserve Bank of Kansas City, *Economic Review,* September–October 1988, pp. 16–33.

Clark, M., and A. Saunders. "Glass-Steagall Revised: The Impact on Banks, Capital Markets, and the Small Investor." *The Banking Law Journal* 97 (1980), pp. 811–40.

_____. "Judicial Interpretation of Glass-Steagall: The Need for Legislative Action." *The Banking Law Journal* 97 (1990), pp. 721–40.

Coats, P. K., and L. F. Fant. "Recognizing Financial Distress Patterns: Using a Neural Network Tool." Working Paper, Department of Finance, Florida State University, September 1992.

Cook, T. Q. "Treasury Bills." In *Instruments of the Money Market.* Richmond, VA: Federal Reserve Bank of Richmond, 1986, pp. 81–93.

Credit Suisse Financial Products. Credit Risk$^+$. Technical Document, London/New York, October 1997.

CSC. "Sustaining Stable Financial Markets throughout the Millennium." Waltham, MA, 1998.

Cummins, J. D., and H. Geman. "Pricing Catastrophe Insurance Futures and Call Spreads: An Arbitrage Model." *The Journal of Fixed Income,* March 1995, pp. 46–57.

Cummins, J. D., S. E. Harrington, and R. Klein. "Insolvency Exercise, Risk-Based Capital and Prompt Corrective Action in Property-Liability Insurance." *Journal of Banking and Finance* 19 (1995), pp. 511–26.

Cummins, J. D., S. Tennyson, and M. A. Weiss. "Efficiency, Scale Economies and Consolidation in the U.S. Life Insurance Industry." *Journal of Banking and Finance* 23 (1999), pp. 325–57.

Cummins, J. D., and J. Vanderhei. "A Note on the Relative Efficiency of the Property-Liability Insurance Distribution Systems." *Bell Journal of Economics* 10 (Autumn 1979), pp. 709–19.

Cybo-Ottone, A., and M. Murgia. "Mergers and Acquisitions in the European Banking Markets." *Journal of Banking and Finance,* 1999 (forthcoming).

Davis, E. P. "Bank Credit Risk." Bank of England, Working Paper Series No. 8, April 1993.

Desai, A., and R. Stover. "Bank Holding Company Acquisitions, Stockholder Returns, and Regulatory Uncertainty." *Journal of Financial Research* 8 (1985), pp. 145–56.

DeYoung, R. "Could Publication of Bank Camel Ratings Improve Market Discipline?" OCC, working paper, 1998.

Diamond, D. W. "Financial Intermediaries and Delegated Monitoring." *Review of Economic Studies* 51 (1984), pp. 393–414.

Diamond, D. W., and P. H. Dybvig. "Bank Runs, Deposit Insurance and Liquidity." *Journal of Political Economy* 91 (1983), pp. 401–19.

Dreyfus, J. F., A. Saunders, and L. Allen. "Deposit Insurance and Regulatory Forbearance: Are Caps on Insured Deposits Optimal?" *Journal of Money, Credit and Banking* 26 (August 1994, Part 1), pp. 412–38.

Dufey, G., and I. Giddy. "Eurocurrency Deposit Risk." *Journal of Banking and Finance* 8 (1984), pp. 557–68.

Ederington, L. H. "The Hedging Performance of the New Futures Markets." *Journal of Finance* 34 (1979), pp. 157–70.

Edwards, F. R. "Derivatives Can Be Hazardous to Your Health." London School of Economics, Working Paper, December 1994.

Eichengreen, B., and R. Portes. "The Anatomy of Financial Crises." In *Threats to International Financial Stability,* ed. R. Portes and A. K. Swoboda. Cambridge: Cambridge University Press, 1987, pp. 10–51.

Eisenbeis, R. "Bank and Insurance Activities." New York University Conference on Universal Banking, February 1995.

Elton, E. J., and M. J. Gruber. *Modern Portfolio Theory and Investment Analysis,* 6th ed. New York: John Wiley & Sons, 1998.

Ely, D. P., and N. P. Varaiya. "Opportunity Costs Incurred by the RTC in Clearing Up S and L Insolvencies." *Quarterly Review of Economics and Finance* 36, no. 3 (1996), pp. 291–310.

Emmons, W. R. "Recent Developments in Wholesale Payment Systems." *Federal Reserve Bank of St. Louis Review,* November–December 1997, pp. 23–43.

Esty, B., et al. "Interest Rate Exposure and Bank Mergers." *Journal of Banking and Finance* 23 (1999), pp. 255–85.

Fama, E. "What's Different about Banks?" *Journal of Monetary Economics* 15 (1985), pp. 29–39.

Federal Reserve Bank of Minneapolis, Annual Report, 1997 (*Fixing FDICIA: A Plan to Address the Too-Big-To-Fail Problem*).

Federal Reserve Board of Governors "Revisions to Risk-Based Capital Standards to Account for Concentration of Credit Risk and Risks on Nontraditional Activities." *Memoranda,* Washington, D.C., March 26, 1993.

Felgren, S. D. "Banks as Insurance Agencies: Legal Constraints and Competitive Advances." Federal Reserve Bank of Boston, *New England Economic Review,* September–October 1995, pp. 34–49.

Fields, J. "Expense Preference Behavior in Mutual Life Insurers." *Journal of Financial Services Research* 1 (1989), pp. 113–30.

Fields, J., and N. B. Murphy. "An Analysis of Efficiency in the Delivery of Financial Services: The Case of Life Insurance Agencies." *Journal of Financial Services Research* 2 (1989), pp. 343–56.

Fields, J. A., C. Ghosh, and L. S. Klein. "From Competition to Regulation: The Six Year Battle to Regulate California's Insurance Markets." Working Paper, University of Connecticut, March 1996.

Figlewski, S. *Hedging with Financial Futures for Institutional Investors: From Theory to Practice.* Cambridge, MA: Ballinger, 1986.

——. "The Use of Futures and Options by Life Insurance Companies." *Best's Review,* 1989.

Flannery, M., and S. M. Sorescu. "Evidence of Bank Market Discipline in Subordinated Debenture Yields: 1983–1991." *Journal of Finance* 51, no. 4 (1996), pp. 1347–77.

——. "Risk-Based Capital and Interest Rate Risk." Press Release, Washington, D.C., July 30, 1992.

Flannery, M. J., and J. Houston. "Market Response to Federal Examinations of U.S. Bank Holding Companies." GSBA, University of Florida, October 1993. Mimeograph.

Flannery, M. J., and C. M. James. "The Effect of Interest Rate Changes on the Common Stock Returns of Financial Institutions." *Journal of Finance* 39 (1984), pp. 1141–53.

Fons, S. I. "Using Default Rates to Model the Term Structure of Credit Risk." *Financial Analysts Journal,* September–October 1994, pp. 25–32.

Furfine, C. "Declining Required Reserves and the Volatility of the Federal Funds Rate." Paper presented at the AEA Annual Meeting, Chicago, January 1998.

Gande, A., M. Puri, and A. Saunders. "Bank Entry, Competition and the Market for Corporate Securities Underwriting." *Journal of Financial Economics,* forthcoming, 1999.

Gande, A., M. Puri, A. Saunders, and I. Walter. "Bank Underwriting of Debt Securities: Modern Evidence." *Review of Financial Studies* 10 (1997), pp. 1175–1202.

Gendrau, B. C. "The Regulation of Bank Trading in Futures and Forwards Markets." In *Below the Bottom Line: The Use of Contingencies and Commitments by Commercial Banks.* Washington, D.C.: Federal Reserve Board of Governors, 1982.

General Accounting Office. "Bank Oversight Structure." GAO/GGD 97–23, November 1997, Washington, D.C.

——. *Bank Powers: Issues Relating to Banks Selling Insurance.* GAO/GGD 90–113, Washington, D.C.: U.S. Government Printing Office, September 1990.

——. "Bank and Thrift Regulation: Implementation of FDICIA: Prompt Regulatory Action Provisions." GAO/GGD 97–18, November 1997, Washington, D.C.

_____. "Electronic Banking: Experiences Reported by Banks in Implementing On-Line Banking." GAO/GGD 98–34, 1998, Washington, D.C.

_____. "Foreign Banks: Implementation of the Foreign Bank Supervision and Enhancement Act of 1991." GAO/GGD 96–187, September 1996, Washington, D.C.

Giddy, I., A. Saunders, and I. Walter. "Alternative Models for Clearance and Settlement: The Case of the Single European Capital Market." *Journal of Money, Credit and Banking,* 1996 November, Part 2, pp. 986–1000.

Gilligan, T., and M. L. Smirlock. "An Empirical Study of Joint Production and Scale Economies in Commercial Banking." *Journal of Banking and Finance* 8 (1984), pp. 67–79.

Gilligan, T., M. L. Smirlock, and W. Marshall. "Scale and Scope Economies in the Multiproduct Banking Firm." *Journal of Monetary Economics* 13 (May 1984), pp. 393–405.

Gilson, S. C., K. John, and L. Lang. "An Empirical Study of Private Reorganization of Firms in Default." *Journal of Financial Economics,* 1990, pp. 315–53.

Ginzberg, A., K. J. Maloney, and R. Wilner. "Risk Rating Migration and Valuation of Floating Rate Debt." Citicorp, Working Paper, March 1994.

Goldberg, L., G. Hanweck, M. Keenan, and A. Young. "Economies of Scale and Scope in the Securities Industry." *Journal of Banking and Finance* 15 (1991), pp. 91–108.

Goldberg, L., and A. Saunders. "The Causes of U.S. Bank Expansion Overseas: The Case of Great Britain." *Journal of Money, Credit and Banking* 12 (1980), pp. 630–44.

_____. "The Determinants of Foreign Banking Activity in the United States." *Journal of Banking and Finance* 5 (1981), pp. 17–32.

_____. "The Growth of Organizational Forms of Foreign Banks in the U.S." *Journal of Money, Credit and Banking* 13 (1981), pp. 365–74.

Goldberg, M. "Commercial Letters of Credit and Bankers Acceptances." In *Below the Bottom Line: The Use of Contingencies and Commitments by Commercial Banks.* Washington, D.C.: Federal Reserve Board of Governors, 1982.

Gollinger, T. L., and J. B. Morgan. "Calculation of an Efficient Frontier for a Commercial Loan Portfolio." *Journal of Portfolio Management,* Winter 1993, pp. 39–46.

Good, B. A. "Electronic Money." *Federal Reserve Bank of Cleveland,* Working Paper 97–16.

Goodman, L. S. "Diversifiable Risks in LDC Lending: A 20/20 Hindsight View." *Studies in Banking and Finance* 3 (1986), pp. 249–62.

Goodman, L. S., P. Fisher, and C. Anderson. "The Impact of Risk-Based Capital Requirements on Asset Allocation for Life Insurance Companies." Merrill Lynch, *Insurance Executive Review,* Fall 1992, pp. 14–21.

Gorton, G., and G. Pennacchi. "Are Loan Sales Really Off Balance Sheet?" In *Off-Balance-Sheet Activities,* ed. J. Ronen, A. Saunders, and A. C. Sondhi. New York: Quorum Books, 1989, pp. 19–40.

Gorton, G., and R. Rosen. "Banks and Derivatives." Working Paper, Wharton School, University of Pennsylvania, February 1995.

Grammatikos, T., and A. Saunders. "Addition to Bank Loan Loss Reserves: Good News or Bad News?" *Journal of Monetary Economics* 25 (1990), pp. 289–304.

Grammatikos, T., A. Saunders, and I. Swary. "Returns and Risks of U.S. Bank Foreign Currency Activities." *Journal of Finance* 41 (1986), pp. 670–81.

Greenbaum, S. I., H. Hong, and A. Thakor. "Bank Loan Commitments and Interest Rate Volatility." *Journal of Banking and Finance* 5 (1991), pp. 497–510.

Greenspan, A. "Remarks." Boston College Conference on Financial Markets and the Economy, Boston, September 19, 1994.

Griffiths, M. D., and D. B. Winters. "Day of the Week Effects in Federal Fund Rates: Further Empirical Findings." *Journal of Banking and Finance* 19 (1995), pp. 1265–84.

Grosse, T. "The Debt/Equity Swap in Latin America— In Whose Interest?" *Journal of International Financial Management and Accounting* 4 (Spring 1992), pp. 13–39.

Grossman, S. J., and O. D. Hart. "Corporate Financial Structure and Managerial Incentives." In *The Economics of Information and Uncertainty,* ed. J. McCall. Chicago: Chicago University Press, 1982.

Gruson, M. "Are Foreign Banks Still Welcome in the United States?" *Bankers Magazine,* September–October 1992, pp. 16–21.

_____. "Non-Banking Investments and Activities of Foreign Banks in the United States." Paper presented at the Salomon Center, New York University Conference on Universal Banking, 1995.

Hancock, D., and D. B. Humphrey. "Payment Transactions, Instruments and Systems: A Survey." *Journal of Banking and Finance* 21 (December 1997), pp. 1573–624.

Haraf, W. S. "The Collapse of Drexel Burnham Lambert: Lessons for Bank Regulators." *Regulation,* Winter 1991, pp. 22–25.

Harrington, S. E. "Prices and Profits in the Liability Insurance Market." In *Liability: Perspectives and Policy,* ed. R. E. Litan and C. Winston. Washington, D.C.: The Brookings Institution, 1988, pp. 45–54.

Hassen, M. K. "The Market Perception of Riskiness of Large U.S. Bank Commercial Letters of Credit." *Journal of Financial Services Research* 6 (1992), pp. 207–21.

Hassan, M. K., and L. Renteria-Guerrero. "The Experience of the Grameen Bank of Bangladesh in Community Development." *International Journal of Social Economics* 24, no. 12 (1997), pp. 1488–523.

Hassan, M. K., and W. H. Sackley. "Determinants of Thrift Institutions' Off-Balance-Sheet Activities: An Empirical Investigation." Working Paper, Department of Finance, University of New Orleans, 1995.

———. "A Methodological Investigation of Risk Exposure of Bank Off-Balance-Sheet Loan Commitment Activities." *Quarterly Review of Economics and Finance* (forthcoming).

Haubrich, J., and P. Wachtel. "Capital Requirements and Shifting Commercial Banking Portfolios." Federal Reserve Bank of Cleveland, *Economic Review* 24 (3rd quarter 1994), pp. 2–15.

Hawawini, G. "Controlling the Interest Rate Risk of Bonds: An Introduction to Duration Analysis and Immunization Strategies." *Finanzmarket and Portfolio Management* 1 (1986–1987), pp. 8–18.

Hendricks, D. "Netting Agreements and the Credit Exposures of OTC Derivatives Portfolios." Federal Reserve Bank of New York, *Quarterly Review,* Spring 1994.

Herring, R. J. "Innovations to Enhance Liquidity: The Implications for Systemic Risk." Wharton School, University of Pennsylvania, October 1992. Mimeograph.

Hirtle, B. "Derivatives, Portfolio Composition and Bank Holding Company Interest Rate Risk Exposure." *Journal of Financial Services Research,* 1997, pp. 234–266.

Ho, T., and A. Saunders. "A Catastrophe Model of Bank Failure." *Journal of Finance* 35 (1980), pp. 1189–1207.

———. "The Determinants of Bank Interest Rate Margins: Theory and Evidence." *Journal of Financial and Quantitative Analysis* 16 (1981), pp. 581–600.

———. "Fixed-Rate Loan Commitments, Takedown Risk, and the Dynamics of Hedging with Futures." *Journal of Financial and Quantitative Analysis* 18 (1983), pp. 499–516.

———. "A Micro Model of the Federal Funds Market." *Journal of Finance* 40 (1985), pp. 977–88.

Hoffman, D., and M. Johnson. "Operating Procedures." *Risk Magazine,* October 1996, pp. 60–63.

Holifield, S., M. Madaris, and W H. Sackley. "Correlation and Hedge Accounting Standards: The Case of Franklin Savings." Working Paper, Ohio State University, Columbus, 1993.

———. "Regulatory Risk and Hedge Accounting Standards in Financial Institutions." Working Paper, University of Southern Mississippi, April 1994.

Hoshi, T. "Back to the Future: Universal Banking in Japan." Paper presented at the Salomon Center, New York University Conference on Universal Banking, February 1995.

Houston, J. "Corporate Separateness and Organizational Structure of Bank Holding Companies." Working Paper, Department of Finance, University of Florida–Gainesville, April 1993.

Huertas, T F. "Redesigning Regulation: The Future of Finance in the United States." Federal Reserve–Central Bankers Symposium, Jackson Hole, WY, August 22, 1987. Mimeograph.

Hultman, C. W., and R. I. McGee. "Factors Affecting Foreign Bank Presence in the U.S." *Journal of Banking and Finance* 13 (1989), pp. 383–96.

Humphrey, D. "Payment Systems." World Bank Technical Paper No. 260, February 1995.

———. "Payments Finality and Risk of Settlement Failure." In *Technology and the Regulation of Financial Markets: Securities, Futures, and Banking,* ed. A. Saunders and L. J. White. Lexington, MA: Lexington Books, 1986, pp. 97–120.

Hunter, W. C., S. Timme, and W. K. Yang. "An Examination of Cost Subadditivity and Multproduct Production in Large U.S. Commercial Banks." *Journal of Money, Credit and Banking* 22 (1990), pp. 504–25.

Jacklin, C. S. "Bank Capital Requirements and Incentives for Lending." Working Paper, Stanford University, February 1993.

———. "Demand Deposits, Trading Restrictions, and Risk Sharing." In *Contractual Arrangements for Intertemporal Trade,* ed. E. Prescott and N. Wallace. Duluth: University of Minnesota Press, 1987.

Jagtiani, J., and A. Khanthavit. "Scale and Scope Economies at Large Banks: Including Off-Balance-Sheet Products and Regulatory Effects (1984–1991), *Journal of Banking and Finance,* 1996, pp. 1271–88.

James, C. "Losses Realized in Bank Failures." *Journal of Finance* 46 (1991), pp. 123–42.

———. "Some Evidence on the Uniqueness of Bank Loans." *Journal of Financial Economics* 19 (1987), pp. 217–35.

James, C., and C. Smith. "The Use of Index Amortizing Swaps by Banc One." *Journal of Applied Corporate Finance* 7, no. 5 (Fall 1994), pp. 54–59.

James, C., and P. Weir. "Borrowing Relationships, Intermediation, and the Costs of Issuing Public Securities." *Journal of Financial Economics* 28 (1990), pp. 149–71.

———. "Returns to Acquirers and Competition in the Acquisition Market: The Case of Banking." *Journal of Political Economy* 95 (1993), pp. 355–70.

Jayanthe, J., and P. E. Strahan. "The Benefits of Branching Deregulation." Federal Reserve Bank of New York, *Economic Policy Review,* December 1997, pp. 13–29.

John, K., T. John, and L. W. Senbet. "Risk Shifting Incentives of Depository Institutions: A New Perspective on Federal Deposit Insurance Reform." *Journal of Banking and Finance* 15 (1991), pp. 895–915.

Kambhu, J., F. Keane, and C. Benadon. "Price Risks Intermediation in the Over-the-Counter Derivatives Markets: Interpretation of a Global Survey." Federal Reserve Bank of New York, *Economic Policy Review,* April 1996, pp. 1–15.

Kanatas, G., and J. Qi. "Underwriting by Commercial Banks: Conflicts of Interest vs. Scope Economies." *Journal of Money, Credit and Banking* 30, no. 1, (February 1998), pp. 119–33.

Kane, E. "Accelerating Inflation, Technological Innovation and the Decreasing Effectiveness of Banking Regulation." *Journal of Finance* 36 (1981), pp. 335–67.

_____. "What Is the Value Added Large U.S. Banks Find in Offering Mutual Funds?" Boston College, Working Paper, November 1994.

Kane, E. J. "Three Paradigms for the Role of Capitalization Requirements in Insured Financial Institutions." *Journal of Banking and Finance* 19 (June 1995), pp. 431–460.

Kau, J. P., D. C. Keenan, W. J. Muller III, and J. F. Epperson. "A Generalized Valuation Model for Fixed-Rate Residential Mortgages." *Journal of Money, Credit and Banking* 24 (1992).

Kaufman, G. G. "Bank Contagion: Theory and Evidence." *Journal of Financial Services Research* 8 (1994), pp. 123–50.

_____. "Measuring and Managing Interest Rate Risk: A Primer." Federal Reserve Bank of Chicago, *Economic Perspectives,* 1984, pp. 16–29.

Keeton, W. R., and A. D. McKibben. "Changes in the Depository Industry in Tenth District States." Kansas City, *Economic Review,* 3rd Quarter 1997, pp. 55–76.

Kelly, E. J. "Conflicts of Interest: A Legal View." In *Deregulating Wall Street,* ed. I. Walter. New York: John Wiley & Sons, 1985, pp. 231–54.

KMV. "Portfolio Manager Model." *KMV Corporation,* San Francisco (undated).

Kolari, J., and A. Zardkoohi. *Banks' Costs, Structure, and Performance.* Lexington, MA: D.C. Heath, 1987.

Koppenhaver, G. O. "Standby Letters of Credit." Federal Reserve Bank of Chicago, *Economic Perspectives,* 1987, pp. 28–38.

Kracaw, W. A., and M. Zenner. "The Wealth Effects of Bank Financing Announcements in Highly Leveraged Transactions." *Journal of Finance* (1996), pp. 1931–46.

Kroszner, R. S., and R. G. Rajan. "Is the Glass-Steagall Act Justified? A Study of U.S. Experience with Universal Banking before 1933." Paper presented at the Western Finance Association, Vancouver, B.C., June 1993.

Laderman, E., and W. Passmore. "Is Mortgage Lending By Savings Associations Special?" Finance and Economics Discussion Series, 1998–25, Federal Reserve Board of Governors, Washington, D.C., 1998.

Lawrence, C. "Banking Costs, Generalized Functional Forms, and Estimation of Economies of Scale and Scope." *Journal of Money, Credit and Banking* 21 (1989), pp. 368–79.

_____. "How Safe is RiskMetrics?" *Risk Magazine,* January 1995.

Lawrence, C., and R. Shay. "Technology and Financial Intermediation in the Multiproduct Banking Firm: An Econometric Study of U.S. Banks." In *Technological Innovation Regulation and the Monetary Economy.* Cambridge, MA: Ballinger, 1996.

LeCompte, R. L. B., and S. D. Smith. "Changes in the Cost of Intermediation: The Case of Savings and Loans." *Journal of Finance* 45 (1990), pp. 1337–46.

Lee, S. H., H. M. Sung, and J. L. Urrutia. "The Behavior of Secondary Market Prices of LDC Syndicated Loans." *Journal of Banking and Finance* 20 (1996), pp. 537–54.

Lee, S-J, D. Mayers, and C. W. Smith Jr. "Guaranty Funds and Risk-Taking Behavior: Evidence from the Insurance Industry." *Journal of Financial Economics* 44 (1997), pp. 3–24.

Lee, W. "The Value of Risk Reduction to Investors." Research Paper No. 9312, Federal Reserve Bank of New York, 1993.

Levonian, M. C. "Interstate Banking and Risk." Federal Reserve Bank of San Francisco, *Weekly Letter,* No. 94–126, 1994.

_____. "Reduced Deposit Insurance Risk." Federal Reserve Bank of San Francisco, *Weekly Letter,* No. 95–108, February 24, 1995.

Litterman, R., and T. Iben. "Corporate Bond Valuation and the Term Structure of Credit Spreads." *Journal of Portfolio Management,* 1989, pp. 52–64.

Loderer, C. F., D. P. Sheehan, and G. B. Kadler. "The Pricing of Equity Offerings." *Journal of Financial Economics,* 1991, pp. 35–57.

Macey, J. R., and G. P. Miller. "Double Liability of Bank Shareholders: History and Implications." *Wake Forest Law Review* 27 (1992), pp. 31–62.

Madalla, A. S. *Limited-Dependent and Qualitative Variables in Econometrics.* Cambridge: Cambridge University Press, 1983.

Madura, J., and E. Zarruk. "Impact of the Debt Reduction Plan on the Value of LDC Debt." *International Review of Economics and Finance* 1 (1992), pp. 177–87.

McAllister, P. H., and J. J. Mingo. "Commercial Loan Risk Management, Credit Scoring and Pricing: The Need for a New Shared Data Base." *Journal of Commercial Lending,* May 1994, pp. 6–20.

McKillop, D. G., J. C. Glass, and Y. Morikawa. "The Composite Cost Function and Efficiency in Giant Japanese Banks." *Journal of Banking and Finance* 20 (1996), pp. 1651–71.

Mei, J. P., and A. Saunders. "Bank Risk and Too Big to Fail Guarantees: An Asset Pricing Perspective." *Journal of*

Real Estate Finance and Economics 10 (1995), pp. 199–224.

Meier, K. J. *The Political Economy of Regulation: The Case of Insurance.* Albany: State University of New York Press, 1988.

Melnik, A., and S. Plaut. "Loan Commitment Contracts, Terms of Lending and Credit Allocation." *Journal of Finance* 41 (1986), pp. 425–36.

Merton, R. C. "An Analytic Derivation of the Cost of Deposit Insurance and Loan Guarantees: An Application of Modern Option Pricing Theory." *Journal of Banking and Finance* 1 (1977), pp. 3–11.

_____. "A Functional Perspective of Financial Intermediation." *Financial Management* 24 (1995), pp. 23–41.

_____. "On the Cost of Deposit Insurance When There Are Surveillance Costs." *Journal of Business* 51 (1978), pp. 439–52.

_____. "On the Pricing of Corporate Debt: The Risk Structure of Interest Rates." *Journal of Finance* 29 (1974), pp. 449–70.

Mester, L. "Efficient Production of Financial Services: Scale and Scope Economies." Federal Reserve Bank of Philadelphia, *Economic Review,* January–February 1987, pp. 15–25.

_____. "Traditional and Nontraditional Banking: An Information Theoretic Approach." *Journal of Banking and Finance* 16 (1992), pp. 534–66.

Mester, L., and A. Saunders. "When Does the Prime Rate Change?" *Journal of Banking and Finance* 19 (1995), pp. 743–64.

Millon-Cornett, M., and S. De. "Common Stock Returns in Corporate Takeover Bids: Evidence of Interstate Bank Mergers." *Journal of Banking and Finance* 15 (1991), pp. 273–95.

Millon-Cornett, M., and H. Tehranian. "Changes in Corporate Performance Associated with Bank Acquisitions." *Journal of Financial Economics* 31 (1992), pp. 211–34.

Morgan, D. P. "The Credit Effects of Monetary Policy: Evidence Using Loan Commitments." *Journal of Money, Credit and Banking* 30 (February 1998), pp. 102–18.

Morgan, J. B. "Managing a Loan Portfolio Like an Equity Fund." *Bankers Magazine,* January–February 1989, pp. 228–35.

Morgan, J. P. CreditMetrics, Technical Document, New York, April 2, 1997.

Mun, K. C., and G. E. Morgan. "Should Interest Rate and Foreign Exchange Risk Management Be Integrated in International Banking?" Working Paper, VPI, 1994.

Munter, P. H., D. K. Clancy, and C. T. Moores. "Accounting for Financial Futures: A Question of Risk Reduction." *Advances in Accounting* 3 (1986), pp. 51–70.

Muscerella, C., and M. R. Vetsuypens. "A Simple Test of Baron's Model of IPO Underpricing." *Journal of Financial Economics* 24 (1989), pp. 125–36.

Nabar, P., S. Park, and A. Saunders. "Prime Rate Changes: Is There an Advantage in Being First?" *Journal of Business* 66 (1993), pp. 69–92.

Nance, D. R., C. W. Smith, and C. W. Smithson. "On the Determinants of Corporate Hedging." *Journal of Finance,* 1993, pp. 267–84.

Neuberger, J. "Conditional Risk and Return in Bank Holding Company Stocks: A Factor-GARCH Approach." Federal Reserve Bank of San Francisco, Working Paper, May 1994.

Noulas, A., S. C. Ray, and S. M. Miller. "Returns to Scale and Input Substitution for Large U.S. Banks." *Journal of Money, Credit and Banking* 22 (1990), pp. 94–108.

Office of Technology Assessment. *U.S. Banks and International Telecommunications Background Paper.* OTA–BP–TCT–100. Washington, D.C.: U.S. Government Printing Office, September 1992.

O'Hara, M., and W. Shaw. "Deposit Insurance and Wealth Effects: The Value of Being Too Big To Fail." *Journal of Finance* 45 (1990), pp. 1587–1600.

Palia, D. "Recent Evidence on Bank Mergers." *Financial Markets, Instruments and Institutions* 3, no. 5 (1994), pp. 36–59.

Palmer, M., and T. B. Sanders. "A Model for Diversifying International Loan Portfolios." *Journal of Financial Services Research,* 1996, pp. 359–371.

Pavel, C. "Loan Sales Have Little Effect on Bank Risk." Federal Reserve Bank of Chicago, *Economic Perspectives,* May–June 1988, pp. 23–31.

_____. "Securitization." Federal Reserve Bank of Chicago, *Economics Perspectives,* 1985, pp. 16–31.

Pennacchi, G. G. "Loan Sales and the Cost of Bank Capital." *Journal of Finance* 43 (1988), pp. 375–96.

Poole, W. "Commercial Bank Reserve Management in a Stochastic Model: Implications for Monetary Policy." *Journal of Finance* 23 (1968), pp. 769–91.

Puri, M. "Commercial Banks in Investment Banking: Conflict of Interest or Certification Role." *Journal of Financial Economics* 40 (1996), pp. 373–401.

_____. "Conflicts of Interest, Intermediation and Pricing of Underwritten Securities." *Journal of Financial Economics,* forthcoming..

Pyle, D. "Pricing Deposit Insurance: The Effects of Mismeasurement." Working Paper, University of California, Berkeley, 1983.

Reilly, F. K. *Investment Analysis and Portfolio Management,* 3rd ed. Chicago: Dryden Press, 1989.

Rhoades, S. A. "The Efficiency Effects of Bank Mergers: An Overview of Case Studies of Nine Mergers." *Journal of Banking and Finance* 22, no. 3 (March 1998), pp. 273–92.

Richards, H. W. "Daylight Overdraft and the Federal Reserves Payment System Risk Policy." *Federal Reserve Bulletin,* December 1995, pp. 1065–77.

Rock, K. "Why New Issues Are Underpriced." *Journal of Financial Economics* 15 (1986), pp. 187–212.

Ronn, E., and A. K. Verma. "Pricing Risk-Adjusted Deposit Insurance: An Option-Based Model." *Journal of Finance* 41 (1986), pp. 871–96.

Rose, P. S. "The Diversification and Cost Effects of Interstate Banking." *Financial Review* 3 (May 1996), pp. 431–51.

Ross, S., and R. Westerfield. *Corporate Finance.* St. Louis: Times Mirror–Mosby College Publishing, 1988.

Ross, S. A. "Institutional Markets, Financial Marketing and Financial Innovation." *Journal of Finance,* 1989, pp. 541–56.

Salomon Brothers. "Transaction Processing: Raising the Technological Hurdle." U.S. Equity Research (Commercial Banks), January 6, 1997.

Saunders, A. "Bank Safety and Soundness and the Risks of Corporate Securities Activities." In *Deregulating Wall Street,* ed. I. Walter. New York: John Wiley & Sons, 1995, pp. 171–206.

———. "Conflicts of Interest: An Economic View." In *Deregulating Wall Street,* ed. I. Walter. New York: John Wiley & Sons, 1985, pp. 207–30.

———. "Why Are So Many New Stock Issues Underpriced?" Federal Reserve Bank of Philadelphia, *Business Review,* March–April 1990, pp. 3–12.

Saunders, A. *Credit Risk Measurement: New Approaches to Value at Risk and Other Paradigms, Wiley Fronties in Finance.* New York: John Wiley and Sons, 1999.

Saunders, A., E. Strock, and N. G. Travlos. "Ownership Structure, Deregulation, and Bank Risk Taking." *Journal of Finance* 45 (1990), pp. 643–54.

Saunders, A., and T Urich. "The Effects of Shifts in Monetary Policy and Reserve Accounting Regimes on Bank Reserve Management Behavior in the Federal Funds Market." *Journal of Banking and Finance* 12 (1988), pp. 523–35.

Saunders, A., and I. Walter, eds. *Financial System Design: Universal Banking Considered.* Burr Ridge, IL: Irwin Professional Publishing, 1996.

———. *Universal Banking in the U.S.?* New York: Oxford University Press, 1994.

Saunders, A., and B. Wilson. "If History Could Be Rerun: The Provision and Pricing of Deposit Insurance in 1993." *Journal of Financial Intermediation* 4 (October 1995), pp. 396–413.

———. "Informed and Uninformed Depositor Runs and Panics: Evidence from the 1929–33 Period." *Journal of Financial Intermediation* 5 (1996), pp. 409–23.

Schaefer, S., and E. S. Schwartz. "Time Dependent Variance and the Pricing of Bond Options." *Journal of Finance* 42 (1987), pp. 1113–28.

Schaffer, S., and E. David. "Economies of Superscale in Commercial Banking." *Applied Economics* 23 (1991), pp. 283–93.

Schwartz, E. S., and W. N. Tourous. "Prepayment and the Valuation of Mortgage-Backed Securities." *Journal of Finance* 44 (1989), pp. 375–92.

Seth, R., et al. "Do Banks Follow Their Customers Abroad?" *Financial Markets, Instruments and Institutions,* no. 4, 1998.

Sezudio, R. S. "NAFTA: Opportunities Abound for U.S. and Canadian Financial Institutions." *Bankers Magazine,* July–August 1993, pp. 28–32.

Shockley, R. L., and A. V. Thakor. "Bank Loan Contracts: Data, Theory and Tests." *Journal of Money, Credit and Banking* 29 (November 1997, Part 1), pp. 517–34.

Silber, W. L. *Municipal Revenue Bond Costs and Bank Underwriting: A Survey of the Evidence.* Monograph Series in Finance and Economics. New York: Salomon Center for the Study of Financial Institutions, 1979.

Sinkey, J. F. *Commercial Bank Financial Management in the Financial Services Industry,* 4th ed. New York: Macmillan, 1992.

Sinkey, J. F., and D. Carter. "The Determinants of Hedging and Derivative Activities by U.S. Banks." Paper presented at the AFA, January 1995.

Smirlock, M., and J. Yawitz. "Asset Returns, Discount Rate Changes, and Market Efficiency." *Journal of Finance* 40 (1985), pp. 1141–58.

Smith, C. W., C. W. Smithson, and L. M. Wakeman. "The Market for Interest Rate Swaps." *Financial Management* 17 (1988), pp. 34–44.

Smith, C. W., C. W. Smithson, and D. S. Wilford. *Managing Financial Risk.* Cambridge, MA: Ballinger, 1990.

Smith, C. W., and R. M. Stutz. "The Determinants of Firms' Hedging Policies." *Journal of Financial and Quantitative Analysis* 20 (1985), pp. 391–406.

Smith, R., and I. Walter. *Street Smarts: Leadership, Conduct and Shareholder Value in the Securities Industry.* Boston: Harvard Business School Press, 1997.

Smith, S. D. "Analyzing Risk and Return for Mortgage-Backed Securities." Federal Reserve Bank of Atlanta, *Economic Review,* January–February 1991, pp. 2–11.

Society of Actuaries. "1986–1992 Credit Loss Experience Study: Private Placement Bonds." Schaumburg, IL, 1996.

Sorensen, E. F., and T. F. Bollier. "Pricing Swap Default Risk." *Financial Analysts Journal,* May–June 1994, pp. 23–33.

Spahr, R. W., and M. A. Sunderman. "The Effect of Prepayment Modeling in Pricing Mortgage-Backed Securities." *Journal of Housing Research* 3 (1992), pp. 381–400.

Spindt, P. A., and J. R. Hoffmeister. "The Micromechanics of the Federal Funds Market: Implications for Day of the Week Effects on Fund Rate Variability." *Journal of Financial and Quantitative Analysis* 23 (1988), pp. 401–16.

Spong, K., and J. D. Shoenhair. "Performance of Banks Acquired on an Interstate Basis." Federal Reserve Bank of Kansas City, *Financial Industry Perspectives,* December 1992, pp. 15–23.

Stapleton, R. C., and M. Subrahamanyam. "Interest Rate Caps and Floors." In *Financial Options: From Theory to Practice,* ed. S. Figlewski. Burr Ridge, IL: Irwin Professional Publishing, 1991, pp. 220–80.

Stiglitz, J., and A. Weiss. "Credit Rationing in Markets with Imperfect Information." *American Economic Review* 71 (1981), pp. 393–410.

Stigum, M. *The Money Market,* 3rd ed. Burr Ridge, IL: Irwin Professional Publishing, 1990.

Stoebe, R. "Macro Hedging Bank Investment Portfolios." *Bankers Magazine,* November–December 1994, pp. 45–48.

Swarmy, P. V. A. B., J. R. Barth, R. Y Chou, and J. S. Jahera. "Determinants of U.S. Commercial Bank Performance: Regulatory and Econometric Issues." Federal Reserve Board of Governors Working Paper, April 1995.

Swary, I. "Stock Market Reaction to Regulatory Action in the Continental Illinois Crisis." *Journal of Business* 59 (1986), pp. 451–73.

Taddei, A. J. "Banking Regulators Publish Recourse Capital Proposals." *The Financier* 4, no. 5 (December 1997).

Taylor, J. D. "Cross-Industry Differences in Business Failure Rates: Implications for Portfolio Management." *Commercial Lending Review,* 1998, pp. 36–46.

Thakor, A. V. "Toward a Theory of Bank Loan Commitments." *Journal of Banking and Finance* 6 (1982), pp. 55–84.

Thakor, A. V., and G. Udell. "An Economic Rationale for the Pricing Structure of Bank Loan Commitments." *Journal of Banking and Finance* 11 (1987), pp. 271–90.

Travlos, N. "Corporate Takeover Bids, Methods of Payment, and Bidding Firm Stock Returns." *Journal of Finance* 42 (1987), pp. 943–63.

Turvey, C. G. "Credit Scoring for Agricultural Loans: A Review with Applications." *Agricultural Finance Review* 51 (1991), pp. 43–54.

Wall, L., and D. R. Peterson. "The Effect of Continental Illinois Failure on the Financial Performance of Other Banks." *Journal of Monetary Economics,* 1990, pp. 77–99.

Wall, L. D., A. K. Reichert, and S. Mohanty. "Deregulation and the Opportunities for Commercial Bank Diversification." Federal Reserve Bank of Atlanta, *Economic Review,* September–October 1993, pp. 1–25.

Walter, I. *Secret Money: The World of International Financial Secrecy.* London: Allen Unwin, 1985.

Walter, I., and A. Saunders, *Global Competitiveness of New York City as a Financial Center.* Occasional Papers in Business, and Finance. New York: Stern Business School, 1992.

Whalen, G. "The Securities Activities of the Foreign Subsidiaries of US Banks: Evidence of Risk and Returns." Working Paper 98–2, OCC, Washington, D.C., February 1998.

White, L. H. "Scottish Banking and the Legal Restrictions Theory: A Closer Look." *Journal of Money, Credit and Banking* 22 (1990), pp. 526–36.

White, L. J. *The S and L Debacle.* New York: Oxford University Press, 1991.

Yawtiz, J. B. "Risk Premia on Municipal Bonds." *Journal of Financial and Quantitative Analysis* 13 (1978), pp. 475–85.

Yoshioka, K., and T. Nakajima. "Economies of Scale in Japan's Banking Industry." Bank of Japan, *Monetary and Economic Studies,* September 1987.

Zaik, E., et al. "RAROC at Bank of America: From Theory to Practice." *Journal of Applied Corporate Finance,* Summer 1996, pp. 83–93.

Solutions to Selected End-of-Chapter Problems

Chapter 1

2. d.
Year	< 1 Billion	> 10 Billion
1990	7.84%	5.69%
1991	7.90%	5.99%
1992	8.33%	6.64%
1993	8.74%	7.38%
1994	9.04%	7.44%
1995	9.27%	7.05%
1996	9.46%	7.37%
1997	9.59%	7.70%

8. Total assets = $41,554.

Chapter 2

8. a. $117,459.62
   b. $171,962.64
   c. $1,702,712.74
9. a. $156,454.87
   b. $14,754.88
   c. 7%: $147,835.99
      7%: $13,041.75
      9%: $14,857.72
      9%: $165,602.93
      7%: $14,609.11
      9%: $16,643.32
10. a. $194,244.98
    b. $229,398.42
    c. $205,899.68; $243,162.33

24.
Year	Minimum Investment Yield
1981	6.0%
1982	9.6
1983	12.0
1984	18.0
1985	16.3
1986	8.0
1987	4.6
1988	5.4
1989	9.2
1990	9.6
1991	8.8
1992	15.7
1993	6.9
1994	8.4
1995	6.4
1996	7.0
Arithmetic Average	9.5%
Minimum	4.6%
Maximum	18.0%

25. 6.4%
26. a. 103.5%
    b. 95.5%
27. $1,529,200

Chapter 3

12. Rising rates; $1,695,036.32 loss; $1,702,557.67 gain.
13. $94,000,000; $6,000,000; $25 per share.
14. $221,130,000; $5,670,000; $27 per share.

Chapter 4

10. 8.00%
12. a. NAV = $308.00
    b. E(NAV) = $256.00
    c. Maximum decrease = $2.00.
14. a. $NAV_{open-end}$ = $125.00
       $NAV_{closed-end}$ = $125.00
    b. $NAV_{open-end}$ = $127.50 or a 2.0% increase.
       $NAV_{closed-end}$ = $123.75 or a 1.0% decrease.
    c. $NAV_{open-end}$ = $225.00

Chapter 7

6. a. $400
   b. $300; Financing risk

c. $446
d. Higher; Bond value is $10,600.
11. Net interest income for year 1 is $ 1.0 million.
 Net interest income for year 2 is $0.5 million.
26. a. Appreciate
 b. Decrease NII by $1 million, or 33.3%.
 c. Asset value decreases from $100 million to $75 million. Liabilities decrease from $66.67 million to $50 million.
 Therefore net worth decreases by $8.33 million.
27. a. DM173,820,000; $125,005,394
 b. DM104,292,000; $75,003,236
 c. DM55,620,000; $40,000,000
 d. FX loss of DM13,908,000; $10,002,158
28. a. −3.51% from interest rate risk
 b. +7.20%; −3.51% from interest rate risk; +10.71% due to foreign exchange risk.

Chapter 8

3. GAP = +$100 million; ΔNII = +$1 million
 GAP = −$50 million; ΔNII = −$0.50 million
 GAP = +$10 million; ΔNII = +$0.10 million
 a. ΔNII = −$1 million;
 ΔNII = +$0.50 million;
 ΔNII = −$0.10 million
7. a. NII = $3.1 million
 b. NII = $2.7 million
 c. ΔNII = −$0.4 million
9. a. −$95 million; −$20 million; +$55 million
 b. ΔNII = −$0.475 million;
 ΔNII = $0.7125 million
 c. +$35 million
 d. ΔNII = $0.175 million; ΔNII = −$0.2625 million
12. Prices = $1,055.35; $1,059.95; $1,064.18; $1,000.00; $941.11; $937.93; $935.08
13. a. $1,136.27
 b. $1,064.92
 c. −6.28 percent
 d. $1,156.47; $1,073.79; −7.15 percent
14. a. $1,108.14
 b. $1,070.34
 c. −3.41 percent
 d. $1,147.84; 3.58 percent
16. MGAP = 19.16 years; Increase in rates.
17. a. MGAP = 15.73 years
 b. MGAP = 15.86 years
 c. Decrease to $32.46 million
 d. Yes, equity = $17.73
20. a. MGAP = 0
21. a. Average maturity = 4.0 years
 b. 25 percent in Acme, 75 percent in Beta.
 c. Average maturity = 3.25 years
22. a. Asset maturity = 10.55 years.
 b. Asset maturity = 10.68 years
 c. Asset maturity = 10.42 years
23. a. −$7.00

b. 9.537 percent
c. 2.1141 years
24. a. Asset maturity = 8.31 years.
 b. Liability maturity = 3.17 years
 c. MGAP = 5.14 years
 e. ΔAssets = −$30,057.93; −8.84 percent
 ΔLiabilities = −$14,665.73; −4.97 percent
 f. ΔEquity = −$15,392.20;
 %ΔEquity = −34.20 percent
 g. Equity = $29,899.20;
 ΔEquity = $15,100.80
25. a. MGAP = 0.0 years
 b. E(NII) = $3,400
 c. NII = $8,700; NII = −$1,900
26. a. MGAP = 0.0 years
 b. NII = $5,000; NII = $5,000
 c. NII = $5,000; NII = $5,000
27. 5.50 percent
28. 7.41 percent; 7.86 percent; 7.25 percent

Chapter 9

2. a. 1.9106; 1.9091; 1.9076
 c. 2 years; 2 years; 2 years
3. a. D = .73585 years
 b. $CF_{1/2}$ = $56,000; CF_1 = $53,000.
 c. $PV_{1/2}$ = $52,830.1887; PV_1 = $47,169.8113; $100,000.00
 d. $Proportion_{1/2}$ = .5283; $Proportion_1$ = .4717
 e. WAL = .73585
4. 4.0539 years; 4.0113 years; 3.9676 years
5. a. 3.3932 years; 2.5243 years; 1.7303 years
6. 5.2124 years; 5.1263 years
7. 13.50 years; 11.00 years; 9.33 years
8. 4.3588 years; 4.2397 years; 4.1378 years
9. a. 4.2814 years; 4.1699 years; 4.0740 years
10. a. D = 2.0 years for P&I at end of 2 years
 D = 1.9091 for I at t=1 and P&I at t=2
 D = 1.4762 for amortized payments of $57,619.05
12. D = 4.5026
13. D = 1.9061; $7.8094
14. a. MD = 6.5714 years
 b. −$6.5714; +$13.1429
 c. $993.4484; $1,013.2838; −$.0198; −$.1409
15. a. D = 4.0002
 b. FV = $1,673.02
 c. FV = $1,673.02
17. a. Bank A: −$54,262.43; −$58,892.32; +$4,629.89
 Bank B: −$53,932.12; −$54,487.79; −$555.67
19. a. DGAP = 8.2323 years
 b. $16,464.54
 e. 1.7077 years
20. a. 4.037 years
 b. 1.397 years
 c. 1.926 years
 d. 0.5535 years
 e. 0.8938 years
 f. −$1,966,360
 g. $983,180

21. a. $97,448,169.08; $88,767,123.29
    b. −$1,318,954.21
    c. D loan = 1.9091 years
       D liability = 1.0 years
    d. E(ΔLoan) = −$2,603,318.18
       E(ΔLiability) = −$1,250,000.00
    e. DGAP = 1.0091
    f. ΔEquity = −$1,353,318.18
22. a. 4.393 years
    b. 6.55 years
    c. 0.90 years
    d. DGAP = 5.86 years
    e. −$89,220
    f. +$44,610
26. a. D = 2.78 years
    c. 15 percent
27. a. 8.1%: $98,884,761
       7.9%: $101,136,484
       8.2%: $97,790,273
       7.8%: $102,294,718
    b. 8.1%: $98,874,000; −$10,761
       7.9%: $101,126,000; −$10,484
       8.2%: $97,748,000; −$42,273
       7.8%: $102,252,000; −$42,718
    c. 8.1%: $98,884,615; −$146
       7.9%: $101,136,625; $141
       8.2%: $97,790,482; $209
       7.8%: $102,294,478; −$240
28. 48; 34; 57
29. MD = 6.4759

Chapter 10

4. a. MD = 4.67 years
   b. 0.00198
   c. 0.925 percent
   d. $9,246.60
5. $29,240.32
6. $26,879.36; $38,013.16
7. a. 24.75 bp; 29.40 bp
9. a. 13.6986 years
   b. −3.425 percent
   c. −$3,511,630.23
   d. 15.15 bp
10. DEAR = $1,900,000; VAR = $6,008,327.55
11. $436,394.32; $751,357.17
12. VAR = $781,505.76
13. $533,219
14. $559,404; $750,000
16. a. $2,675,465.98; $7,072,135.78
    c. −$26,489.77; −$70,021.14
    d. Yen: −0.629%, 0.624%, −2.529%, −1.117%, 0.026%
       SF: −0.247%, 0.297%, −0.591%, 0.424%, 0.241%
    e.

Day	Yen	Swiss franc	Total Risk
2/4	$16,662.06	$17,295.22	$33,957.28
2/3	−$16,529.62	−$20,796.28	−$37,325.90
2/2	$66,992.63	$41,382.49	$108,375.12
2/1	$29,589.07	−$29,688.96	−$99.89
1/29	−$688.73	−$16,875.09	$17,563.82

20. a. $1.20 million
    b. $1.2875 million

c. $1.00 million
d. $3.4875 million
21. Unsystematic: $6,880,000
    Systematic: $7,840,000
    Total charge: $14,720,000

Chapter 11

9. 10.00%; 10.59%; 11.25%
10. a. 11.50 percent
    b. 12.97 percent
18. a. 98.95 percent
    b. 12.97 percent
20. a. 3,104
    b. Yes
    c. −$100; Z = 0.0434; No
22. 96.80 percent; 93.39 percent
    3.50 percent; 7.50 percent
23. 7.25 percent
24. a. 94.47 percent; 5.53 percent
    b. 0.50 percent; 0.50 percent
26. T-bond: 6.00 percent; 10.06 percent
    BBB: 9.21 percent; 11.74 percent
    1.87 percent; 2.94 percent; 1.50 percent
    4.76 percent; 6.18 percent
27. a. 8.1554 percent; 8.9328 percent
    b. 0.3228 percent; 0.5062 percent
    c. 0.7188 percent
29. a. Commercial: 0.10 percent; 0.20 percent
       Cumulative: 0.00 percent; 0.60 percent; 1.10 percent
       Mortgage: 0.70 percent
       Cumulative: 0.10 percent; 0.35 percent; 0.95 percent; 2.43 percent
30. A-Rated: 0.0%; 0.0%; 0.0011%; 0.0023%
    A-Rated: 0.0%; 0.0%; 0.0%; 0.0011%; 0.0034%
    B-Rated: 0.0%; 0.00106%; 0.00217%; 0.00337%; 0.00471%
    B-Rated: 0.0%; 0.00106%; 0.00323%; 0.00659%; 0.01127%
    C-Rated: 0.00100%; 0.00309%; 0.00556%; 0.00588%; 0.00750%
    C-Rated: 0.00100%; 0.00409%; 0.00962%; 0.01545%; 0.02283%
32. a. 8.89 percent
    b. 6.6667 years
    c. $15,625
    d. 3.73 percent
33. a. $177,148
    b. 0.07 percent
34. 1.0 percent
35. a. $4,851,478.10
    b. 6.031 percent
36. 6.00 percent; 6.59 percent
37. a. $113.27
    b. $108.06
    c. $4.19
    d. $6.91; $9.76
    e. $9.63; $21.24
39. a. 14.65 percent
       19.54 percent

19.54 percent
15.63 percent
2.98 percent
b. $1,600,000
$3,200,000
c. $1,600,000; 1.6 percent

Chapter 12

4. a. 62.50 percent
   b. 33.3 percent
5. 48.0 percent
7. a. 11.0 percent; 14.14 percent
   b. 11.0 percent; 7.07 percent
16. a. 8.20 percent; 18.30 percent
19. 13; 50; 25; 15

Chapter 13

1. a. iii
   b. v
   c. ii
   d. iii
   e. ii
   f. None of the above
   g. iii
   h. iii
   i. iv
   j. iv
   k. i
   l. iii
   m. iv
   n. ii
   o. ii
3. $40 million
5. a. $125,000,000
   b. $120,000,000
   c. $5,000,000
9. a. $15,625
   b. $16,375
10. a. 10.84 percent
    b. 10.86 percent
    c. 10.90 percent
    d. 10.59 percent
11. a. 10.95 percent; 12.01 percent
    b. APR = 12.01%; EAY = 12.38%
17. a. $1,000
    b. $98,767.12
19. a. $737.73
    b. $739.73

Chapter 14

5. a. NVP = $333,333
   b. AT Savings = $730,393
6. $484,975
11. Diseconomies of scale
13. Economies of scope.
15. a. 25.45 percent
    b. 20.91 percent

Chapter 15

3. −DM31 million
   Appreciation of the mark
5. a. $70,000
   b. $23,000
   c. −$31,000
   d. $700
   e. −$230
   f. −$620
7. a. 1 percent
   b. −8.00 percent
   c. 14.50 percent
8. a. NII = $26,838.24
   b. $1.1671/£
   c. Depreciate
9. a. $63,291.14
   b. 0.63 percent
   c. DM1.5709/$
12. a. 0.53 percent; 9.49 percent
    b. 1.26 percent
    c. 8.74 percent
13. a. 1.08 percent
    b. $0.180867/SK

Chapter 16

7. Yes. Z = 0.4865
13. a. Singapore
    b. Holland
17. a. $2.4 million
    b. $1.2 million
    c. Saves 0.017 pesos per dollar
    d. 5,400,000 pesos
18. a. $19.20 million
    b. Yes. P416.67/$
    c. P393.6/$
22. a. $51.3884 million
    b. $50.50 million
    c. $0.8884 million
23. a. $20,524,863.21
    b. $18,695,283.69
    c. $1,829,579.52
    d. $1,929,579.52 or 9.65 percent
24. a. $24,329,476.67
    b. $21,544,346.99
    c. $1,785,129.68
    e. $2,785,129.68 or 13.93 percent
25. a. $3,225.81
    b. $1,935.48
    c. More value.

Chapter 17

10. a. −$40,000; TA = $8,000
    b. −$30,000
    c. $10,000
12. a. $20 million
    b. $8 million
    c. $10,000
13. 0.948

14. 0.9267
15. a. $15 million
     b. $25 million
18. a. $45,026,296; $47,422,903
     b. $47,026,296; $49,422,903
22. $9,216; $9,408
23. a. $10.00
     b. 100,000 shares
     c. $9.95; $1,350,000

Chapter 18

8.   a. $19,013,000
     b. $1,013,000
     c. $18,155,857
9.   a. May 20 to June 2   Note: See change to
                               question. Change date on
                               question 9.a. from
     b. $24,078,000   1998 to 1984.
10. a. $19,013,000
     b. Yes.
     c. 4 percent = $39,480
     d. $2,180.59
11. a. $23,013,000
     b. $2,987,000
     c. $119,480
     d. $8,798.97
16. a. 5.93 percent
     b. 6.45 percent
     c. $0.10 per check
17. a. 5.55 percent
     b. 6.88 percent
     c. 4.75 percent
     d. $0.0257 per check

Chapter 19

21. a. $0.00
     b. $5 million
22. a. $0.0; $11.25; $13.75
     b. $0.0; $0.0; $25.00
     c. $0.0; $0.0; $5.00
     d. $0.0; $0.0; $0.0
     e. $0.0; $25.0; $0.0
23. a. $0.0; $2.0; $25.0; $3.0
     b. $0.0; $0.0; $25.0; $5.0
     c. $0.0; $0.0; $20.0; $0.0
     d. $0.0; $5.0; $25.0; $0.0

Chapter 20

4.   a. $46.44
     b. 12.9x
     c. 32.7x; 17.2x; 21.5x
     d. Undefined
6.   a. −$100,770
20. a. 6.422 percent
     b. 9.589 percent
     c. 15.0685 percent
21. a. 0.04; 0.08
     b. 0.0455; 0.0818
     c. 0.05; 0.08

d. 0.1204; 0.1574
e. 0.0490; 0.186
f. 0.0417; 0.0750
33. a. $110 million
     b. $10.340 million
     c. No. $5.17 million, $10.34 million
34. a. $95 million
     b. $9.32 million
     c. Yes. Excess $0.68 million
36. Yes.
39. a. $10.211 million
     b. No.
     c. $1.211 million
41. a. $8.8557 million
     b. $1.8557

Chapter 21

12. a. $32,500
     b. $500,000
     c. -$500,000
13. $1.134 million; $1.8 million; $0.0;
     −$149.4 million
14. a. $50,000
     b. Price of $95.00

Chapter 22

16. a. $4,400
     b. $6,800
     c. 6.8338 percent
17. a. 5,545.5
     b. 5,581.0
     c. 5,846.6

Chapter 24

5.   Forward contract to sell bonds at $104.
     Sale price of bonds in 2 months is $777,570.
7.   a. Obligated to receive $100,00 of bonds at $95,000.
     b. Long hedge.
     c. Lose $1,000
     d. Gain $2,000
9.   a. Sell
     b. Buy
     c. Sell
     d. Sell
     e. Buy
10. a. 9.896 years
     b. −$4,948.08
     c. −$4,700.67
     d. −$247.41
13. a. 2.4
     b. $3.273 million
     c. −$3.273 million
     d. −$3.088 million
17. a. Short
     b. 377 contracts
     d. 1,470 contracts
21. a. Long
     b. 6.88 (7) contracts
     c. 6.14 (6) contracts

22. a. 8.19 years
    b. Rate increases
    c. Short hedge
    d. −$77,805
    e. −$8,640 per contract
    f. 9.005 contracts
25. 272.75 contracts   Note: At the end of question # 25, after the question mark, add: "Assume Df = 9."
26. a. 1,293.57 contracts
    b. 0.0900
27. a. $252.78
    b. −$252.78
29. a. Depreciating
    b. Sell DM futures.
33. a. $25 million
    b. Appreciation
    c. Sell pound sterling futures
    d. 400 contracts
    e. −$2.5 million
    f. +$2.5 million
34. a. +$3.0 million
    b. Basis risk
    c. Use 333 contracts
35. a. Depreciating
    b. Sell DM futures
    c. 2,240 contracts
36. a. Depreciating
    b. $6.4 dollars
    c. buy DM futures
    d. $6.1 million
37. a. −DM50 million
    b. Depreciation
    c. −$1,150,000
    d. 800 contracts
    e. +$1,150,000
39. $700,000
41. $15,000

Chapter 25

7. a. Rising rates; Put
   b. Falling rates; Call
   c. Rising rates; Put
   d. Appreciating dollar; Put
   e. Depreciating DM; Put
   f. Rising rates; Call
11. a. 7.37 percent
    b. 7.74 percent
    c. $928,160
    e. $1.2885
    f. $1.2042
12. a. Rate decrease
    b. But call options
    c. $907.9921; $1,106.7754; $828.4091; $1,000.00; $1,231.1477
    e. 0.0; $9,677.54; 0.0; 0.0; $22,114.77
    f. $9,220.31
14. a. $2,765.56 per $100,000 contract.
    b. $875.00 per $100,000 contract.

c. $200 per $1,000,000 contract.
15. a. Decreases
    b. Increases
    c. Increases
    d. Increases
19. a Purchase call options   Note: Add the following words to the end of problem 19, part c after the question mark: "R = 8 percent."
    b. 14,746 contracts
    c. −$23,333,333
    d. $23,429,551
    e. $12,902.75
20. a. 6.3636 years
    b. 3,165 contracts
    c. −$2,636,364
    d. −$2,900,291
    e. $3,956,250
21. a. Purchase call options
    b. 237 contracts
    c. $329,578.13
    d. +/− $464,625.00
    e. +/− $550,580.00
22. a. Depreciating
    b. Call options
    c. Buy futures
    d. −$395,000; −$420,000; −$420,000
    e. −$400,000; −$400,000; −$400,000
    f. Futures
23. a. -$10 million
    b. Appreciation of DM
    c. Buy DM futures; Buy DM call options
    d. 0.0; $2,687.50
    e. $400, $13,375
    f. Put is in-the-money.
24. a. Dollar depreciating.
    b. Buy futures
    c. $6.4 million
    d. $6.1 million
    e. Purchase call options
    f. $6.3 million
34. Cap price = $16,298.56
    Floor price = $2,160.37
    Collar cost = $14,138.19
35. Cap price = $2,099.80
    Floor price = $18,853.70
    Collar cost = −$16,753.90
37. a. $2,000,000; $700,000
    b. $1,380,000; -$680,000
    c. $4,080,000; -$1,920,000
    d. $188,405,795

Chapter 26

4. a. Falling rates
   b. Rising rates
   c. Insurance: VR liability
      Finance: FR liability
   d. Finance co. is buyer;
      Insurance co. is seller
7. a. Yes.

b. Bank 1 is fixed rate, Bank 2 is variable rate.
c. 1.0 percent
8. a. FB: Finance = P + 1; Receive P + 1/2; Pay 11%
   SB: Finance = 11%; Receive 11%; Pay P + 1/2
   b. FB: Finance = P + 1; Receive P + 1; Pay 12.5%
   SB: Finance = 11%; Receive 12.5%; Pay P + 1
9. a. A in FR; B in VR
   b. A in VR; B in FR
   c. Net = .4
   d. For gains to A: A: Finance = L + 1/2; Receive L; Pay 10%
   B: Finance = 10%; Receive 10% Pay L
      For gains to B: A: Finance = L + 1/2; Receive L + 1/2; Pay 11%
   B: Finance = 10%; Receive 11% Pay L + 1/2
   e. Net = $400,000
   f. Net before cash market: A = $1,400,000; B; −$1,500,000
12. $787.5 million
13. a. Interest rate increases.
    b. −$0.45 million; $0.57 million; $0.86 million
    c. $0.45 million; $0.50 million; $0.65 million
14. a. Yes, since spread is 2 percent.
    b. DM3 million each year.
    c. Depreciation of DM.
    d. Short currency hedge by German bank.
    e. DM1.95 million; DM0.795 million; −DM50.5 million
    f. DM1.05 million; DM2.205 million; DM53.5 million
    DM3.00 million per year
    g. DM0.35 million; −DM0.21 million; −DM2.14 million
    DM3.00 million per year
    h. Exchange rate and interest risk.
    i. Short currency hedge and short interest rate hedge.
    j. CD: DM10.5 million; DM12.0 million; DM163.5 million
    Loan: DM13.5 million; DM13.5 million; DM163.5 million
    Spread: DM3 million; DM1.5 million; DM0.0 million
    k. CD: DM10.85 million; DM11.76 million; DM161.32 million
    Loan: DM10.85 million; DM11.76 million; DM161.32 million
    Spread: DM2.65 million; DM1.74 million; DM2.18 million
    l. Swap: −DM0.775 million; DM0.135 million; −DM0.305 million
    Total: DM1.875 million each year
15. a. $4,9375 million; $4.5625 million
    b. −$25 million; Change NII = −$0.375 million
    c. Short hedge
16. a. Rate decreases
    b. Swap asset cash flows.
    c. 25 basis points
17. a. DM1.5 million
    b. $50,000 = DM75,000; No swap flows
    c. Swap = DM50,000 = −$100,000
    d. Swap = −DM37,500 = $16,667

18. a. Swap = $10,000 = −DM15,000
    b. Swap = $10,988 = −DM16,900
    c. Swap = DM13,100 = −$8,518

Chapter 27

2. a. $9,872,298.88
   b. $9,809,303.83
   c. With recourse
8. a. $1,773,991.08
   b. $1,760,000–$1,780,000
   c. Nondistressed
16. a. DA = 5.2 years
    b. D = 6 years

Chapter 28

6. a. $8 million
   b. $102,222,222.22
11. a. $175,514.31
    b. 9.5 percent
    c. $168,170.84
    d. $6,462.25
    e. $881.22
12. a. $19,187,358.74
    b. $19,163,205.11
18. 3.35 years
19. a. $75,000,000.00
    b. $550,323.43
    c. $50,323.43 and $500,000.00
    $50,658.92 and $499,664.51
    d. $537,309.18
    e. $73,226,373.05
    g. $9,890.83; $3,123.42
    h. 1.9993 months
    i. $74,974,229.44
    j. $75,036,111.70
27. a. $2,926,688.33
    b. $11,685,417.88
    d. $2,926,688.33; $2,926,688.33; $2,926,688.33; $3.097875 million; $2.744 million
    e. 2.01 percent
30. a. $5,272,358.60
    b. $5.0 million; $4.993 million; $4.986 million; $4.979 million; $0.272 million; $0.279 million; $0.286 million; $0.293 million
    d. $1,125,000 quarterly; $2,500,000; $1,375,000 Quarterly principal $0.272 million; $0.278 million; $0.284 million; $0.291 million
    e. Quarterly principal $10.812 million; $11.055 million; $11.304 million; $11.558 million
38. a. $3,116,401.80
    b. $3,048,154.10
    c. $18,683,598.20; $17,248,720.24; $15,684,703.27; $13,125,108.43; $10,474,647.98
    d. MVIO = $6,090,089.72; MVPO = $14,586,586.92.

INDEX

First Republic Bancorp, 424
First Union Bank, 82
Fischer, P., 469n
Fisher equation, 324n
Fixed costs and geographic expansion, 553
Fixed-fixed currency swaps, 637–39
Fixed-floating currency swaps, 639
Fixed income, 194–96
Fixed-income
 market risk of securities, 184–86
Flannery, M. J., 88n, 427n, 428n
Flat term structure, 174–76
Fleming, John, 547
Float, 284
Floating-rate loans and bonds, 177–78
Floors, 608, 612
 caps, 616
 and credit risk, 616
Foot, Michael, 547
Ford Motor Credit, 75
Foreign bank loans, purchase and sale of,
 661–62
Foreign banks, 654, 655
 expansion of, in Unites States, 545–51
 regulation of, in Unites States, 547–48
Foreign Bank Supervision Enhancement Act
 (FBSEA) (1991), 547–48, 549–51
Foreign currency trading, 314–16
 profitability of, 315–16
Foreign deposits, 70
Foreign exchange, 186–87, 196
Foreign exchange risk, 111–13, 311–25
 asset and liability positions, 316–25
 currency trading, 313–16, 314–16
 hedging, 571–79
 rate volatility and exposure, 313–14
 return and risk of foreign investments,
 318–19
 sources of, 311–14
 using options to hedge, 603–5
Foreign investments
 multicurrency asset-liability positions,
 324–25
 return and risk of, 318–19
 risk and hedging, 319–24
Forward contracts, 272, 558
 hedging credit risk with, 579–83
 and hedging interest rate risk, 559–61
Forward exchange rate, 322
Forward market for foreign exchange (FX),
 312
Forward purchases and sales of when issued
 securities, 273–74
Forward rate, 228
Forwards
 and hedging foreign exchange risks, 572
 hedging with, 321–24
 regulator policies, 583
Fraudulent conveyance proceedings, 660
Frequency of loss, 41

Friedman, Milton, 428n, 480n
Fully amortized mortgages, 671
Funding source, cost of equity capital as,
 443–44
Funds
 closed-end bank loan mutual, 654
 concentration, 284
 source and geographic diversification,
 552
Furash, Edward F., 24
Furlong, F., 415n
Future contracts, hedging credit risk with,
 579–83
Futures
 and hedging foreign exchange risks,
 572–76
 macrohedging with, 563–70
 regulator policies, 583
Futures contracts, 272, 558–59
 and catastrophe risk, 582
Futures option, definition of, 598–99
Futures prices
 imperfect correlation between spot
 prices and, 574–76
 perfect correlation between spot prices
 and, 573
Future value of $1 at end of t periods, 704–5
Future Value of an Annuity Factor (FVAF),
 158n
 of $1 per period for t periods, 710–11

G-10 countries
 deposit insurance in, 428, 437–41
 permissible banking activities and bank
 ownership in, 508–15
Gande, A., 504n
Gap exposure, 670
Garfinkel, J. A., 88n
Garn-St. Germain Depository Institutions
 Act (1982), 12, 14, 381n, 393, 487,
 518, 522
Geman, H., 582n
Genan, H., 607n
Gendreau, B. C., 583n
General Electric Capital Corporation
 (GECC), 74, 80, 654
Generally Accepted Accounting Principles
 (GAAP), 448, 553
General Motors, 308
General Motors Acceptance Corp. (GMAC),
 75
General obligation (GO) bonds, 460
Geographic diversification, 537–53
 domestic, 516–35
 cost and revenue synergies impacting,
 523–29
 expansions, 517
 market- and firm-specific factors
 impacting, 530–32

Geographic diversification (*cont.*)
 regulatory factors impacting, 518–23
 success of, 532–34
 international
 advantages and disadvantages of
 expansion, 551–53
 expansions, 537–51
Germany, deposit insurance system in, 429
Gertler, M., 97n
Gibbs, Brian, 547
Giddy, I., 553n
Gilson, S. C., 224n, 371n
Gingrich, Newt, 23–24
Ginsburg, Ruth Bader, 23
Ginzburg, A., 226n
Glass-Steagall Act (1933), 11, 56, 480, 482,
 485, 487, 500, 548, 660
 and securities law interpretations as
 reason for loan sales, 659
Glossman, Diane, 288–89
GMAC Commercial Mortgage Corp.
 (GMACCM), 75–76
Gold, Robert, 679
Goldberg, Lawrence G., 551n, 657n
Goldman Sachs, 49, 50, 56, 480–81, 495,
 652, 653, 661–62
Good, Barbara A., 286n
Good bank, 655
Goodman, L. S., 341n, 469n
Gorton, G., 273n, 274n
Government loan sales and future, 661
Government National Mortgage Association
 (GNMA), 451n, 456, 665
 pass-through securities, 670
 and pass-through security, 665
 securitization process, 672–73
Graham, S., 534
Grammatikos, T., 321n, 332n, 356n
Grandfathered affiliate, 486
Grandfathered subsidiary, 519
Greenbaum, S. I., 263n, 414n
Greenspan, Alan, 307n, 560
Green Tree Financial Company, 81, 666
Grosse, R., 351n
Grossman, S. J., 219n
Group life insurance, 31
Gruber, M. J., 89n
Gruson, M., 549n, 550n
Guaranteed investment contracts (GICs), 98,
 370n, 469

Hains, Monique E., 23
Hancock, D., 309
Haraf, W. S., 401n
Harrington, S. E., 470n
Hart, O. D., 219n
Hassan, H. K., 21n, 265n, 271n
Haubich, J., 466n
Hawawini, G., 532